ARCHITECTURAL
GRAPHIC
STANDARDS

STUDENT EDITION

THE AMERICAN INSTITUTE OF ARCHITECTS

RAMSEY/SLEEPER

ARCHITECTURAL GRAPHIC STANDARDS

STUDENT EDITION
ABRIDGED FROM THE SEVENTH EDITION

ROBERT T. PACKARD, AIA
SEVENTH EDITION EDITOR

STEPHEN A. KLIMENT, FAIA
STUDENT EDITION EDITOR

JOHN WILEY & SONS
NEW YORK   CHICHESTER   BRISBANE   TORONTO   SINGAPORE

WILEY

This Student Edition was abridged from the Seventh Edition of Architectural Graphic Standards.

The drawings, tables, data, and other information in this book have been obtained from many sources, including government organizations, trade associations, suppliers of building materials, and professional architects or architectural firms. The American Institute of Architects (AIA), the Architectural Graphic Standards Committee of the AIA, and the publisher have made every reasonable effort to make this reference work accurate and authoritative, but do not warrant, and assume no liability for, the accuracy or completeness of the text or its fitness for any particular purpose. It is the responsibility of users to apply their professional knowledge in the use of information contained in this book, to consult the original sources for additional information when appropriate, and, if they themselves are not professional architects, to consult an architect when appropriate.

Library of Congress Cataloging in Publication Data:

Ramsey, Charles George, 1884–1963.
  [Architectural graphic standards]
  Ramsey/Sleeper architectural graphic standards / Robert T. Packard, 7th edition editor.—Student ed. abridged from the 7th ed. / Stephen A. Kliment, student edition editor.
    p. cm.
  At head of title: The American Institute of Architects.
  Bibliography: p.
  Includes index.
  ISBN 0–471–62060–2 (pbk.)
  1. Building—Details—Drawings. I. Sleeper, Harold Reeve, 1893–1960. II. Packard, Robert T. III. Kliment, Stephen A. IV. American Institute of Architects. V. Title.
TH2301.R36 1989   88–26053
721'.022'2—dc19   CIP

Printed in the United States of America

10 9 8 7 6 5 4 3 2

CONTENTS

PUBLISHER'S NOTE

In the fall of 1932, the lowest point of the Great Depression, I joined the House of Wiley and soon learned that there had been published in May a promising new book. Martin Matheson, then Manager of Marketing, had persuaded Charles George Ramsey, AIA, author of an earlier Wiley textbook, and his younger colleague, Harold Reeve Sleeper, FAIA, to develop their ideas and prepare the plates for what became *Architectural Graphic Standards*. Subsequently, Matheson directed the design and layout of the book and personally oversaw its production and manufacture.

The immediate acceptance and success of *Architectural Graphic Standards* extended far beyond its anticipated audience of architects, builders, draftsmen, engineers, and students. Interior designers, real estate agents and brokers, homeowners, insurance underwriters, and lovers of fine books are all among its known users and admirers.

Soon after the publication of *Architectural Graphic Standards* suggestions and requests came from many enthusiastic readers, which called for changes and additions. Inevitably, the decision was made to publish a second edition which was almost 25 percent larger. It appeared in 1936, a short time after the first. Recovery from the Great Depression had begun when the second edition came out, and the demand for *Architectural Graphic Standards* increased. To serve its users' growing needs work soon began on a third edition which, when published in 1941, was almost twice as large as the original edition.

Further editions were released, reflecting new materials, new design approaches, and new construction methods. All this led to dramatic increases in the bulk of the book. But as bulk grew, so did price—to the point that most students could no longer afford to have their own copy until after graduation.

John Wiley & Sons recognized this, and realizing that the full professional edition had much in it that was not essential to the typical studio, drafting, and related courses, decided to produce a special edition for students, one which would provide vital information, at a price students could afford.

Here is the result of that effort. I am confident it will meet students' demands and greatly increase the already large family of friends and users of Ramsey & Sleeper's great work.

W. BRADFORD WILEY
Chairman
John Wiley & Sons, Inc.

PREFACE

Architectural Graphic Standards stands today at the pinnacle of the architect's reference world. Harnessed by the American Institute of Architects, hundreds of architectural and consulting firms have contributed their wealth of experience—sharing plans, sections, details, knowledge of new and traditional materials, and how they come together in a building—by means of painstakingly prepared drawings that are reproduced in this book.

When *Architectural Graphic Standards* first appeared in 1932, it comprised a slim 233 pages. It was the work of a single architectural office. Four years later, a second edition was published, with 25 percent more material. Following the end of World War II, the suppressed demand for building exploded, and along with it came a great surge of new materials, new products, new methods for designing buildings, and new techniques for erecting them.

Architectural Graphic Standards became part of this surge. In 1951, by then in its fourth edition, the book had 614 pages, emerging as an inseparable companion to architects in the United States and throughout the world.

Although *Architectural Graphic Standards* was designed principally as a tool for practicing architects, it also gained wide acceptance in schools of architecture over the course of its first six editions.

By the time, however, that the 785-page seventh edition was published in 1981, cost pressures had pushed the price out of the range of most students. Knowing that there was no substitute, students made do as best they could—lining up for the few copies on library reserve; finding dog-eared, cannibalized copies handed down through generations of students; or investing in their own copy at the expense of three square meals or that important structures text.

John Wiley & Sons and the American Institute of Architects have always viewed their purpose as filling the needs of students as well as professionals and became concerned about the growing difficulty students had in gaining access to this important work. Wiley and the AIA therefore decided to publish an abridged, less expensive edition uniquely for students, while preserving as much of the most relevant content as possible.

We needed to determine what material must remain and what could go. To identify what material should be retained, we set guidelines for selecting it and chose who should apply those guidelines.

This process took three stages. The first stage was at the 1987 "Grassroots" convocation of chapter leaders of the American Institute of Architecture Students (AIAS)—a forum at which we listened to students' concerns and ideas about *Graphic Standards.*

Stage two was a broad-based, highly structured, written survey of architecture school faculty. A total of 277 professors responded to a detailed eight-page questionnaire which sought answers to such questions as the current use, classroom assignment and ownership of *Graphic Standards,* and the ranking of contents by degree of importance to each surveyed professor's course. The survey revealed a definite scale of usefulness of the full edition in the schools. General planning/design and sitework ranked first, followed closely by the major materials—wood, masonry, concrete, and metals. At the lower end of the scale were such items as equipment, electrical, special construction, and conveying systems.

In stage three, we invited a select Editorial Advisory Board to make specific page-by-page recommendations. The board was chosen to reflect a wide range of interests—large schools and small ones; two-year technical colleges and four-year (and more) professional schools; teachers and students; design versus technical emphasis; west, east, north, and south. Many of the board's members were chosen from the group which had taken part in the earlier survey. Each member identified those pages he or she felt should be retained, and those which could be omitted without jeopardizing the book's value to the student. The guidelines we offered the board were these:

1. Is the material required for design studio drawing of site plans, buildings, and interiors?

2. Is the material required for drafting construction details and for learning drafting conventions and symbols?

3. Is the material easily accessible in library reference books or course texts?

4. All else being equal, preserve graphic material over text and tables.

John Ray Hoke, Jr., AIA, publisher of the American Institute of Architects Press, and I chaired the Editorial Advisory Board. As we tabulated board members' individual preferences, we found to our satisfaction a remarkable degree of consensus.

Moreover, many on the board—which took its assignment very seriously—volunteered comments, and I want to share some of these with you:

—To meet students' need for in-depth materials, steer them to supplementary sources found in any school library. For example: *Mechanical and Electrical Equipment for Buildings,* by Stein, Reynolds, and McGuiness; the materials design handbooks published by the American Institute of Steel Construction, the American Institute of Timber Construction, the American Concrete Institute, the Brick Institute of America, and others; the general edition of *Architectural Graphic Standards;* key building codes; and the Parker/Ambrose series, especially *Simplified Engineering for Architects and Builders*.

—Create a ready reference, not a comprehensive encyclopedic one.

—Focus on the visual elements.

All of us at John Wiley and at the American Institute of Architects hope students will prize this unique edition. It is designed to provide that *factual* basis for solving design problems which is the essential stock-in-trade of a good professional.

Numerous people contributed to this Student Edition. On the Wiley side, Carol Beasley, publisher, championed the idea early, conceived and organized the broad-based survey of faculty members, encouraged input from student leaders, and successfully enlisted the support of John Wiley's top management to invest in the project; Robert J. Fletcher, general manager of production, took this book on as a special, personal project; Lisa Culhane

and Julie Harrington understood that without good marketing there are no customers. Many others provided valuable support.

At the AIA, John Hoke contributed his enthusiasm to all aspects of the project, especially in his role as co-chairman of the Editorial Advisory Board. Louis Marines, executive vice president and chief executive officer; Steve Etkin, vice president; and the other AIA officers continue to support the role of *Architectural Graphic Standards* in the architectural profession.

Above all, thanks to the hundreds of contributors of individual pages—architects, planners, consulting engineers, interior and industrial designers, owners, manufacturers, trade associations, fabricators, and special consultants. They are the unsung heroes of this work.

STEPHEN A. KLIMENT, FAIA
Editor
John Wiley & Sons, Inc.

ARCHITECTURAL GRAPHIC STANDARDS

STUDENT EDITION

CHAPTER 1   GENERAL PLANNING AND DESIGN DATA

INTRODUCTION TO ANTHROPOMETRIC DATA

The following anthropometric drawings show three values for each measurement: the top figure is for the large person or 97.5 percentile; the middle figure, the average person or 50 percentile; and the lower figure, the small person or 2.5 percentile. The chosen extreme percentiles thus include 95%. The remaining 5% include some who learn to adapt and others, not adequately represented, who are excluded to keep designs for the majority from becoming too complex and expensive. Space and access charts are designed to accept the 97.5 percentile large man and will cover all adults except a few giants. Therefore, use the 97.5 percentile to determine space envelopes, the 2.5 percentile to determine the maximum "kinetospheres" or reach areas by hand or foot, and the 50 percentile to establish control and display heights. To accommodate both men and women, it is useful at times to add a dimension of the large man to the corresponding dimension of the small woman and divide by 2 to obtain data for the average adult. This is the way height standards evolve. Youth data are for combined sex. Although girls and boys do not grow at the same rate, differences are small when compared with size variations.

Pivot point and link systems make it easy to construct articulating templates and manikins. Links are simplified bones. The spine is shown as a single link; since it can flex, pivot points may be added. All human joints are not simple pivots, though it is convenient to assume so. Some move in complicated patterns like the roving shoulder. Reaches shown are easy and comfortable; additional reach is possible by bending and rotating the trunk and by extending the shoulder. Stooping to reach low is better than stretching to reach high. The dynamic body may need 10% more space than the static posture allows. Shoes have been included in all measurements; allowance may need to be made for heavy clothing. Sight lines and angles of vision given in one place or another apply to all persons.

The metric system of measurement has been included, since it is used in scientific work everywhere and is the most practical system of measurement ever devised. Millimeters have been chosen to avoid use of decimals. Rounding to 5 mm aids mental retention while being within the tolerance of most human measurements.

Disabilities are to be reckoned as follows: 3.5% of men and 0.2% of women are color blind; 4.5% of adults are hard of hearing; over 30% wear glasses; 15 to 20% are handicapped, and 1% are illiterate. Left-handed people have increased in number to more than 10%.

SAFETY INFORMATION

Maximum safe temperature of metal handles is 50°C (122°F) and of nonmetallic handles, 62°C (144°F); maximum air temperature for warm air hand dryers is 60°C (140°F); water temperatures over 46.1°C (115°F) are destructive to human tissue. Environmental temperature range is 17.2 to 23.9°C (63 to 75°F). Weights lifted without discomfort or excessive strain are 22.7 kg (50 lb) for 90% of men and 15.9 kg (35 lb) for women; limit weight to 9.07 kg (20 lb) if carried by one hand for long distances. Push and pull forces, like moving carts, are 258 N (58 lbf) and 236 N (53 lbf) initially, but 129 N (29.1 lbf) and 142 N (32 lbf) if sustained. Noise above the following values can cause permanent deafness: 90 dB for 8 hr, 95 dB for 4 hr, 100 dB for 2 hr, 105 dB for 1 hr, and 110 dB for 0.5 hr.

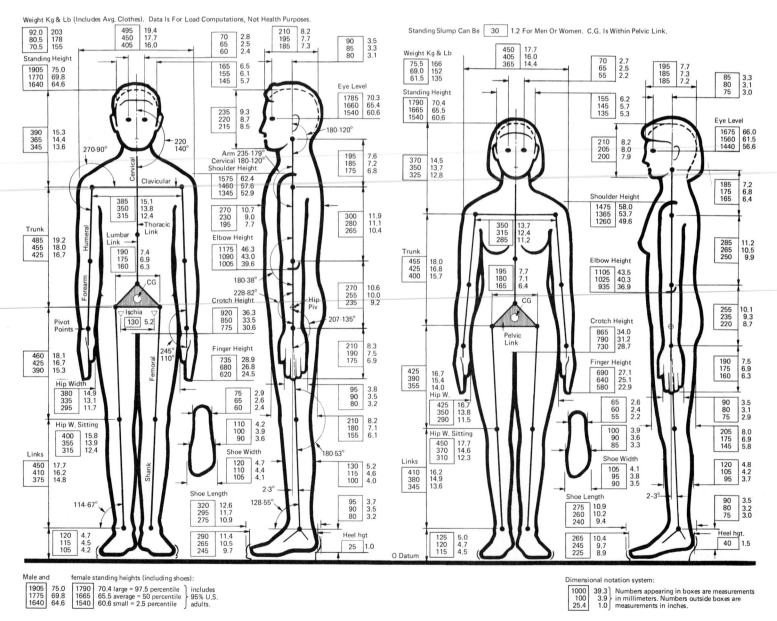

Weight Kg & Lb (Includes Avg. Clothes). Data Is For Load Computations, Not Health Purposes.

Standing Slump Can Be 30 1.2 For Men Or Women. C.G. Is Within Pelvic Link.

Niels Diffrient, Alvin R. Tilley; Henry Dreyfuss Associates; New York, New York

Male and female standing heights (including shoes):

1905	75.0	1790	70.4 large = 97.5 percentile	includes
1775	69.8	1665	65.5 average = 50 percentile	95% U.S.
1640	64.6	1540	60.6 small = 2.5 percentile	adults.

Dimensional notation system:

1000	39.3	Numbers appearing in boxes are measurements
100	3.9	in millimeters. Numbers outside boxes are
25.4	1.0	measurements in inches.

1 DESIGN ELEMENTS

Combined Sex Data

Ages Years	Standing Height A		Shoulder Width B		Head Width C		Head Length D		Head Height E		Shoulder Height F		Crotch Height G		Arm Length H		Foot Length J		Eye Level K		Weight Kg	Lb
15 (Large/Avg/Small)	1800	70.8	465	18.2	155	6.2	200	7.9	225	8.8	1460	57.5	860	33.9	790	31.1	270	10.6	1685	66.4	76.5	169
	1675	65.9	420	16.5	145	5.8	190	7.4	220	8.6	1370	54.0	790	31.1	790	31.1	250	9.9	1565	61.7	69.0	152
	1545	60.8	375	14.8	140	5.5	185	7.2	215	8.4	1260	49.6	730	28.7	685	26.9	230	9.1	1445	56.8	62.0	137
12	1625	63.9	395	15.6	155	6.1	200	7.9	215	8.5	1325	52.2	810	31.9	710	28.0	240	9.5	1520	59.9	51.5	114
	1485	58.5	350	13.7	145	5.7	185	7.3	215	8.4	1205	47.5	730	28.7	660	25.9	220	8.6	1385	54.5	37.0	82
	1350	53.2	300	11.9	135	5.3	170	6.8	210	8.2	1080	42.5	645	25.4	600	23.7	195	7.6	1250	49.2	23.5	52
9	1440	56.6	350	13.8	150	6.0	200	7.9	210	8.3	1165	45.8	705	27.7	640	25.1	220	8.6	1335	52.6	36.5	81
	1320	52.0	310	12.1	140	5.6	185	7.3	205	8.1	1065	42.0	630	24.9	585	23.1	200	7.8	1220	48.0	27.0	59
	1200	47.3	265	10.5	130	5.2	170	6.7	205	8.0	960	37.7	560	22.0	515	20.3	175	6.9	1100	43.3	17.0	38
7	1315	51.8	320	12.6	150	5.9	195	7.7	205	8.1	1060	41.8	630	24.7	585	23.1	200	7.9	1215	47.8	28.0	62
	1220	48.0	285	11.3	140	5.5	180	7.1	205	8.0	970	38.2	565	22.3	525	20.7	180	7.1	1120	44.0	22.0	49
	1125	44.2	250	9.9	130	5.1	165	6.5	200	7.8	890	35.1	505	19.8	470	18.6	160	6.3	1025	40.3	16.5	36
5	1185	46.7	290	11.5	145	5.8	195	7.6	200	7.9	945	37.3	545	21.5	515	20.3	181	7.1	1085	42.8	22.0	49
	1090	42.9	260	10.3	135	5.4	180	7.1	195	7.7	865	34.1	490	19.3	460	18.2	161	6.3	995	39.1	18.0	39
	995	39.1	230	9.1	125	5.0	165	6.5	190	7.5	780	30.7	430	17.0	415	16.3	141	5.6	890	35.0	13.5	29.5
3	930	36.7	240	9.5	135	5.2	175	6.9	195	7.7	735	28.9	375	14.7	415	16.4	141	5.6	835	32.8	13.0	29
1	725	28.6	205	8.0	125	4.9	160	6.3	175	6.9	565	22.2	245	9.6	305	12.0	110	4.3	640	25.1	9.0	20
Birth	505	19.9	150	6.0	95	3.7	100	4.0	125	4.9	375	14.9	170	6.6	195	7.6	80	3.1	440	17.4	3.5	7.5

(15–5 "With Shoes"; 3, 1, Birth "Without")

Ages	L		M		N		O		P		Q		R		S		T		U		V	
15	370	14.6	465	18.3	430	17.0	420	16.6	115	4.4	355	14.0	190	7.4	185	7.3	285	11.3	255	10.1	195	7.6
	350	13.8	430	17.0	400	15.7	390	15.3	105	4.1	325	12.7	175	6.9	175	6.9	270	10.6	240	9.4	180	7.0
	330	13.0	405	15.9	360	14.2	350	13.8	100	3.9	290	11.5	160	6.2	165	6.5	250	9.9	220	8.7	165	6.5
12	345	13.5	420	16.7	385	15.1	375	14.7	100	3.9	320	12.5	170	6.7	170	6.8	260	10.3	230	9.1	175	6.8
	320	12.6	390	15.3	345	13.6	335	13.2	95	3.8	280	11.1	160	6.0	160	6.3	245	9.6	215	8.5	160	6.2
	295	11.7	360	14.1	305	12.1	300	11.8	90	3.5	250	9.8	130	5.2	150	5.9	225	8.9	195	7.6	145	5.8
9	310	12.3	375	14.8	335	13.0	325	12.8	95	3.7	270	10.6	145	5.7	160	6.2	240	9.4	210	8.2	150	6.0
	290	11.4	350	13.8	300	11.9	290	11.4	90	3.5	245	9.6	130	5.1	145	5.8	220	8.6	190	7.4	140	5.7
	275	10.8	320	12.7	265	10.4	255	10.1	85	3.3	220	8.6	110	4.4	135	5.4	195	7.7	160	6.3	130	5.1
7	290	11.4	345	13.7	300	11.8	290	11.4	90	3.5	245	9.6	130	5.1	145	5.8	220	8.6	190	7.4	140	5.7
	280	11.0	325	12.8	270	10.6	260	10.3	85	3.3	220	8.7	115	4.5	140	5.5	200	7.8	165	6.5	130	5.2
	260	10.2	305	12.0	245	9.6	235	9.3	80	3.1	210	8.2	100	3.9	130	5.1	175	6.9	150	5.8	120	4.8
5	270	10.7	315	12.4	260	10.3	255	10.0	85	3.3	215	8.4	105	4.2	135	5.3	190	7.6	160	6.3	130	5.1
	255	10.0	300	11.8	235	9.3	220	8.8	80	3.1	200	7.8	90	3.6	125	4.9	170	6.7	145	5.7	120	4.7
	240	9.4	280	11.0	210	8.2	195	7.7	70	2.8	185	7.2	80	3.1	120	4.7	145	5.7	130	5.1	115	4.5

Avg Heel Hgt 20 .8

	Ages	High Reach A		Low Reach B		Reach Distance C		High Reach D		Reach Radius E		Eye Level F	
HS	15	2085	82.0	815	32.0	735	29.0	1440	56.7	660	25.9	1215	47.8
		1915	75.3	730	28.7	685	27.0	1375	54.1	610	24.1	1160	45.6
		1765	69.4	665	26.2	635	25.1	1315	51.7	570	22.4	1100	43.3
Jr. HS	12	1860	73.2	705	27.6	665	26.2	1320	52.0	600	23.6	1100	43.3
		1705	67.1	630	24.7	620	24.3	1250	49.2	555	21.9	1040	41.0
		1545	60.9	560	22.1	565	22.3	1185	46.6	510	20.1	990	38.9
4th.	9	1645	64.8	605	23.8	600	23.6	1175	46.3	540	21.2	975	38.4
		1510	59.4	555	21.8	550	21.7	1120	44.0	495	19.5	925	36.5
		1345	53.0	510	20.0	485	19.1	1040	40.9	435	17.1	880	34.6
2nd.	7	1505	59.3	545	21.5	550	21.7	1080	42.6	500	19.6	890	35.0
		1370	53.9	510	20.1	495	19.5	1015	40.0	445	17.5	850	33.5
		1245	49.0	485	19.0	445	17.5	960	37.7	395	15.6	815	32.0
KDG	5	1330	52.3	500	19.7	480	19.0	970	38.1	430	16.9	815	32.1
		1210	47.7	465	18.3	435	17.1	915	36.1	385	15.2	770	30.4
		1085	42.7	425	16.7	390	15.3	865	34.1	345	13.6	720	28.4

↑ Starting School Grades

Up To Ages	Hat Shelf Height G		Lavatory Height H		Work Top J		Work Depth K		Table Height L		Seat Length M	
15	1675	66.0	760	30.0	915	36.0	460	18.0	650	25.5	370	14.6
12	1485	58.5	685	27.0	795	31.3	420	16.5	590	23.3	340	13.3
9	1320	52.0	635	25.0	695	27.3	380	15.0	525	20.7	300	11.8
7	1220	48.0	585	23.0	635	25.0	355	14.0	480	18.9	275	10.8
5	1090	43.0	485	19.0	570	22.5	330	13.0	445	17.5	250	9.9

Ages	Seat Height N		Seat To Backrest O		Min Backrest Height P		Armrest Spacing Q		Seat Width R		Basic Table Width S	
15	405	15.9	150	6.0	175	6.8	445	17.5	380	15.0	760	30.0
12	370	14.6	145	5.7	160	6.2	420	16.5	370	14.5	710	28.0
9	325	12.8	135	5.4	140	5.6	355	14.0	330	13.0	610	24.0
7	290	11.4	130	5.1	130	5.1	330	13.0	305	12.0	610	24.0
5	265	10.4	120	4.8	125	5.0	305	12.0	280	11.0	535	21.0

Chalk Board Height — Comfortable High Reach — Hat Shelves At Head Height Rule Also Applies To Adults — 15° — 100 4 — Clothes Pole Or Hook Strip — Reach Distance C — Work Counter — Lav Rim — Chalk Rail — 15°

High Shelf 50 2 — 40° — 205 8 — Eye Level — Functional Grips — 0-20° — WC Hgt Ages 14+ 355 14, 9-14 305 12, 2-9 255 10

Min Armrest 150 6 — 50 2 — Min 280 11 — Greater For Storage

Standing heights (including shoes)—typical example:
1800 70.8 large 15 year youth = 97.5 percentile } combined
1675 65.9 average 15 year youth = 50 percentile } sex data
1545 60.8 small 15 year youth = 2.5 percentile } U.S. youths

Dimensional notation system:
1000 / 39.3 — Numbers appearing in boxes are measurements
100 / 3.9 — in millimeters. Numbers outside boxes are
25.4 / 1.0 — measurements in inches.

Niels Diffrient, Alvin R. Tilley; Henry Dreyfuss Associates; New York, New York

DESIGN ELEMENTS   1

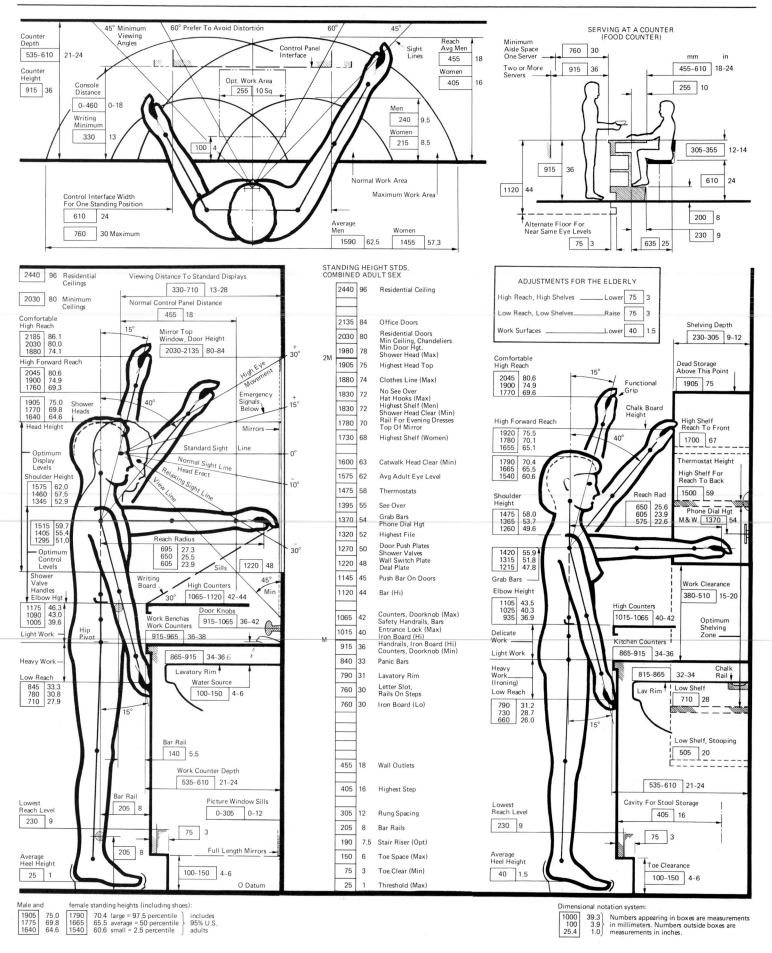

STANDING HEIGHT STDS.
COMBINED ADULT SEX

mm	in	
2440	96	Residential Ceiling
2135	84	Office Doors
2030	80	Residential Doors Min Ceiling, Chandeliers Min Door Hgt.
1980	78	Shower Head (Max)
1905	75	Highest Head Top
1880	74	Clothes Line (Max)
1830	72	No See Over Hat Hooks (Max)
1830	72	Highest Shelf (Men) Shower Head Clear (Min)
1780	70	Rail For Evening Dresses Top Of Mirror
1730	68	Highest Shelf (Women)
1600	63	Catwalk Head Clear (Min)
1575	62	Avg Adult Eye Level
1475	58	Thermostats
1395	55	See Over
1370	54	Grab Bars Phone Dial Hgt
1320	52	Highest File
1270	50	Door Push Plates Shower Valves
1220	48	Wall Switch Plate Deal Plate
1145	45	Push Bar On Doors
1120	44	Bar (Hi)
1065	42	Counters, Doorknob (Max) Safety Handrails, Bars
1015	40	Entrance Lock (Max) Iron Board (Hi)
915	36	Handrails, Iron Board (Hi) Counters, Doorknob (Min)
840	33	Panic Bars
790	31	Lavatory Rim
760	30	Letter Slot, Rails On Steps
760	30	Iron Board (Lo)
455	18	Wall Outlets
405	16	Highest Step
305	12	Rung Spacing
205	8	Bar Rails
190	7.5	Stair Riser (Opt)
150	6	Toe Space (Max)
75	3	Toe. Clear (Min)
25	1	Threshold (Max)

Male and female standing heights (including shoes):

1905	75.0	1790	70.4	large = 97.5 percentile	includes
1775	69.8	1665	65.5	average = 50 percentile	95% U.S.
1640	64.6	1540	60.6	small = 2.5 percentile	adults

ADJUSTMENTS FOR THE ELDERLY

		mm	in
High Reach, High Shelves	Lower	75	3
Low Reach, Low Shelves	Raise	75	3
Work Surfaces	Lower	40	1.5

Dimensional notation system:

1000	39.3	Numbers appearing in boxes are measurements
100	3.9	in millimeters. Numbers outside boxes are
25.4	1.0	measurements in inches.

Niels Diffrient, Alvin R. Tilley; Henry Dreyfuss Associates; New York, New York

1 **DESIGN ELEMENTS**

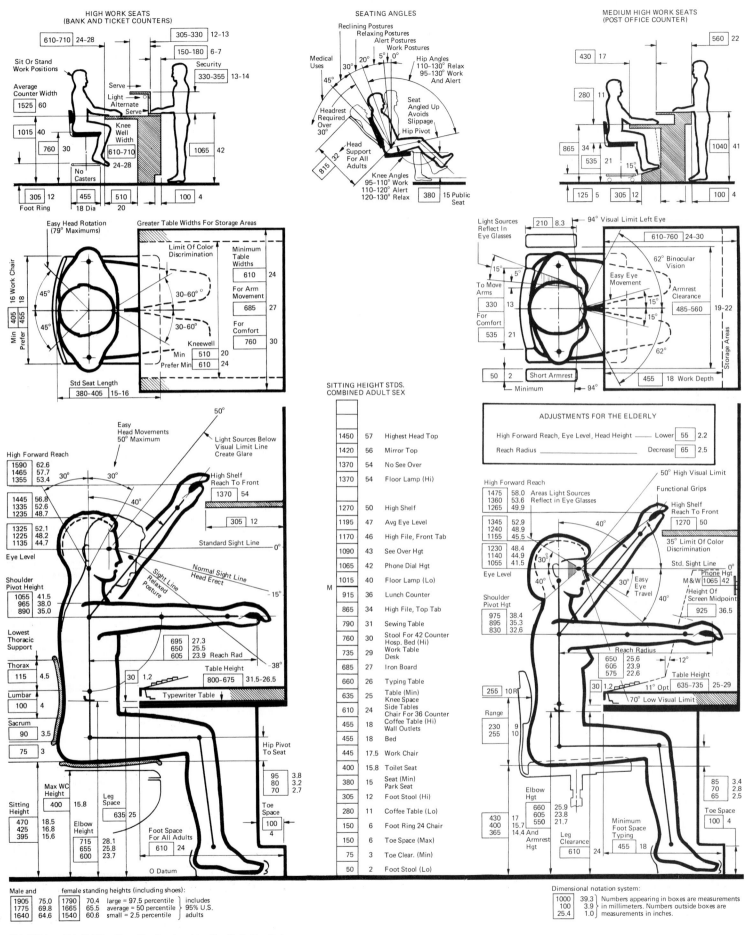

Niels Diffrient, Alvin R. Tilley; Henry Dreyfuss Associates; New York, New York

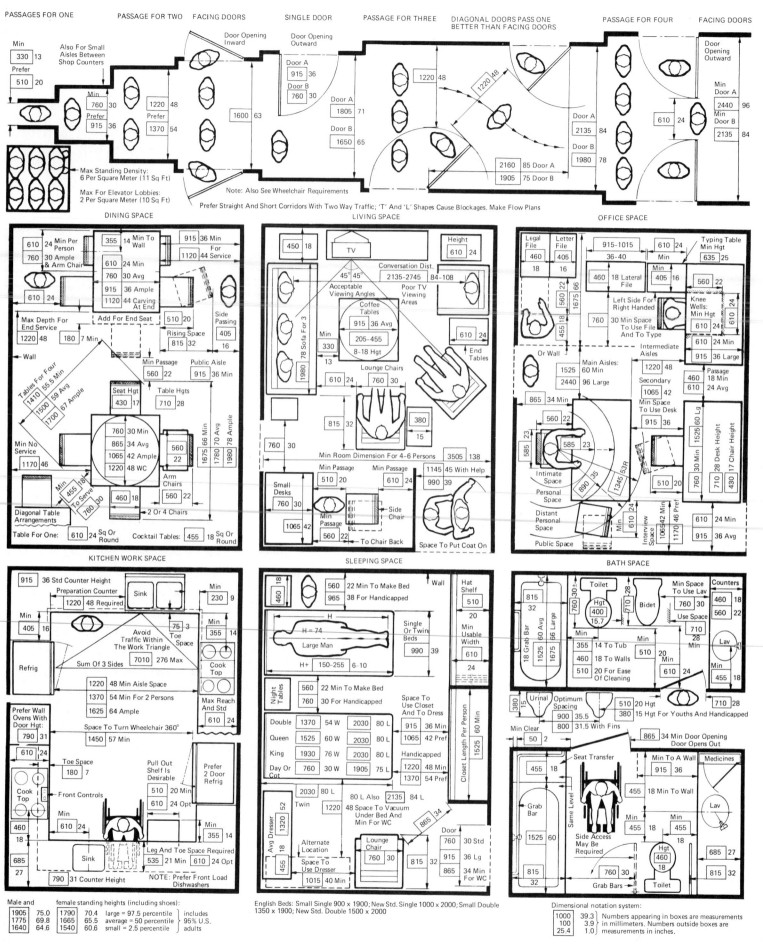

Niels Diffrient, Alvin R. Tilley; Henry Dreyfuss Associates; New York, New York

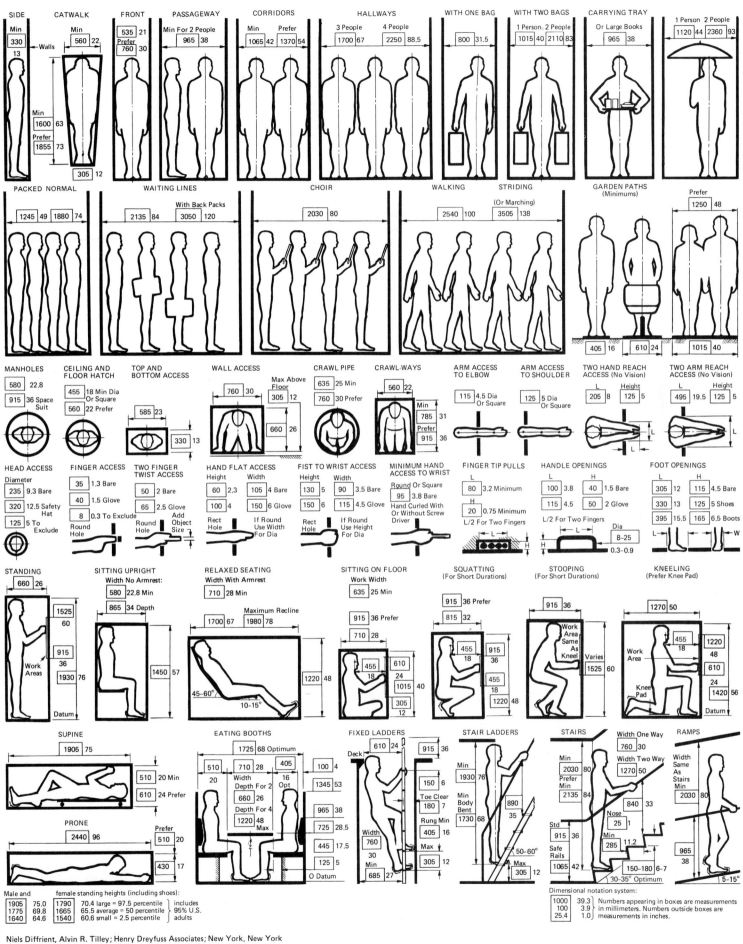

Niels Diffrient, Alvin R. Tilley; Henry Dreyfuss Associates; New York, New York

Dimensional notation system:

1000	39.3	Numbers appearing in boxes are measurements
100	3.9	in millimeters. Numbers outside boxes are
25.4	1.0	measurements in inches.

Male and female standing heights (including shoes):

1905	75.0	1790	70.4	large = 97.5 percentile	includes
1775	69.8	1665	65.5	average = 50 percentile	95% U.S.
1640	64.6	1540	60.6	small = 2.5 percentile	adults

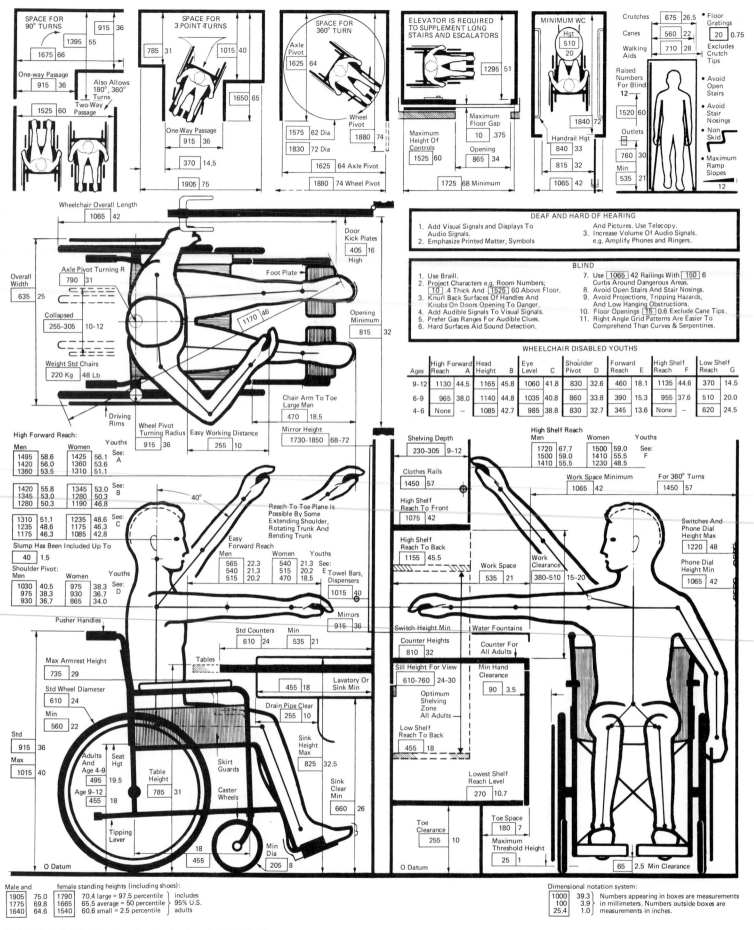

SPACE FOR 90° TURNS — 915 | 36, 1395 | 55, 1675 | 66

SPACE FOR 3 POINT TURNS — 785 | 31, 1015 | 40, 1650 | 65

One-way Passage 915 | 36 — Also Allows 180°, 360° Turns — Two-Way Passage 1525 | 60

SPACE FOR 360° TURN — Axle Pivot 1625 | 64, Wheel Pivot 1880 | 74

One-Way Passage 915 | 36, 370 | 14.5, 1575 | 62 Dia, 1830 | 72 Dia, 1625 | 64 Axle Pivot, 1905 | 75, 1880 | 74 Wheel Pivot

ELEVATOR IS REQUIRED TO SUPPLEMENT LONG STAIRS AND ESCALATORS — 1295 | 51, Maximum Floor Gap 10 | .375, Maximum Height Of Controls 1525 | 60, Opening 865 | 34, 1725 | 68 Minimum

MINIMUM WC — Hgt 510 | 20, 1840 | 72, Handrail Hgt 840 | 33, 815 | 32, 1065 | 42

Crutches 675 | 26.5, Canes 560 | 22, Walking Aids 710 | 28

Floor Gratings 20 | 0.75, Excludes Crutch Tips

Raised Numbers For Blind 12, 1520 | 60, Outlets 760 | 30, Min 535 | 21

• Avoid Open Stairs • Avoid Stair Nosings • Non Skid • Maximum Ramp Slopes 12

Wheelchair Overall Length 1065 | 42

Door Kick Plates 405 | 16 High

Foot Plate

Overall Width 635 | 25

Axle Pivot Turning R 790 | 31

Collapsed 255-305 | 10-12

1170 | 46

Opening Minimum 815 | 32

Weight Std Chairs 220 Kg | 48 Lb

Driving Rims

Wheel Pivot Turning Radius 915 | 36

Easy Working Distance 255 | 10

Chair Arm To Toe Large Man 470 | 18.5

Mirror Height 1730-1850 | 68-72

DEAF AND HARD OF HEARING
1. Add Visual Signals and Displays To Audio Signals.
2. Emphasize Printed Matter, Symbols And Pictures. Use Telecopy.
3. Increase Volume Of Audio Signals. e.g. Amplify Phones and Ringers.

BLIND
1. Use Braille.
2. Project Characters e.g. Room Numbers; 10 | .4 Thick And 1525 | 60 Above Floor.
3. Knurl Back Surfaces Of Handles And Knobs On Doors Opening To Danger.
4. Add Audible Signals To Visual Signals.
5. Prefer Gas Ranges For Audible Clues.
6. Hard Surfaces Aid Sound Detection.
7. Use 1065 | 42 Railings With 150 | 6 Curbs Around Dangerous Areas.
8. Avoid Open Stairs And Stair Nosings.
9. Avoid Projections, Tripping Hazards, And Low Hanging Obstructions.
10. Floor Openings 15 | 0.6 Exclude Cane Tips.
11. Right Angle Grid Patterns Are Easier To Comprehend Than Curves & Serpentines.

WHEELCHAIR DISABLED YOUTHS

Ages	High Forward Reach A		Head Height B		Eye Level C		Shoulder Pivot D		Forward Reach E		High Shelf Reach F		Low Shelf Reach G	
9-12	1130	44.5	1165	45.8	1060	41.8	830	32.6	460	18.1	1135	44.6	370	14.5
6-9	965	38.0	1140	44.8	1035	40.8	860	33.8	390	15.3	955	37.6	510	20.0
4-6	None	—	1085	42.7	985	38.8	830	32.7	345	13.6	None	—	620	24.5

High Forward Reach:

Men		Women		Youths
1495	58.6	1425	56.1	See: A
1420	56.0	1360	53.6	
1360	53.5	1310	51.1	
1420	55.8	1345	53.0	See: B
1345	53.0	1280	50.3	
1280	50.3	1190	46.8	
1310	51.1	1235	48.6	See: C
1235	48.6	1175	46.3	
1175	46.3	1085	42.8	

Slump Has Been Included Up To 40 | 1.5

Shoulder Pivot:

Men		Women		Youths
1030	40.5	975	38.3	See: D
975	38.3	930	36.7	
930	36.7	865	34.0	

Pusher Handles

Max Armrest Height 735 | 29

Std Wheel Diameter 610 | 24 — Min 560 | 22

Std 915 | 36 — Max 1015 | 40

Adults And Age 4-9 495 | 19.5 — Age 9-12 455 | 18

Seat Hgt

Tipping Lever

Table Height 785 | 31

Skirt Guards

Caster Wheels

455 | 18 — Min Dia 205 | 8

40°

Reach To Toe Plane Is Possible By Some Extending Shoulder, Rotating Trunk And Bending Trunk

Easy Forward Reach

Men		Women		Youths
565	22.3	540	21.3	See: E
540	21.3	515	20.2	
515	20.2	470	18.5	

Towel Bars, Dispensers 1015 | 40

Mirrors 915 | 36

Std Counters 610 | 24 — Min 535 | 21

Tables

Lavatory Or Sink Min 455 | 18

Drain Pipe Clear 255 | 10

Sink Height Max 825 | 32.5

Sink Clear Min 660 | 26

Shelving Depth 230-305 | 9-12

Clothes Rails 1450 | 57

High Shelf Reach To Front 1075 | 42

High Shelf Reach To Back 1155 | 45.5

Switch Height Min

Counter Heights 810 | 32

Sill Height For View 610-760 | 24-30

Optimum Shelving Zone All Adults

Low Shelf Reach To Back 455 | 18

Lowest Shelf Reach Level 270 | 10.7

Toe Clearance 255 | 10

High Shelf Reach

Men		Women		Youths
1720	67.7	1500	59.0	See: F
1500	59.0	1410	55.5	
1410	55.5	1230	48.5	

Work Space Minimum 1065 | 42 — For 360° Turns 1450 | 57

Work Space 535 | 21 — Work Clearance 380-510 | 15-20

Water Fountains — Counter For All Adults

Min Hand Clearance 90 | 3.5

Toe Space 180 | 7

Maximum Threshold Height 25 | 1

65 | 2.5 Min Clearance

Switches And Phone Dial Height Max 1220 | 48

Phone Dial Height Min 1065 | 42

O Datum

Male and female standing heights (including shoes):

1905	75.0	1790	70.4 large = 97.5 percentile	includes 95% U.S. adults
1775	69.8	1665	65.5 average = 50 percentile	
1640	64.6	1540	60.6 small = 2.5 percentile	

Dimensional notation system:

1000	39.3	Numbers appearing in boxes are measurements in millimeters. Numbers outside boxes are measurements in inches.
100	3.9	
25.4	1.0	

Niels Diffrient, Alvin R. Tilley; Henry Dreyfuss Associates; New York, New York

1 DESIGN ELEMENTS

NOTES

1. Codes and standards used on this page:
   ANSI = American National Standards Institute.
   BOCA = Building Officials and Code Administrators.
   NBC = National Building Code.
   SBCC = Southern Building Code Congress.
   UBC = Uniform Building Code.
2. T = tread; R = riser.
3. Maximum height between landings is 12 ft (most codes).

RULE-OF-THUMB FORMULAS

INTERIOR STAIRS

1. Riser + tread = 17 or 17 1/2 in.; 7 1/2 in. R + 10 in. T = 17 1/2 in.
2. Riser x tread = 70 or 75; thus 7.5 in. R x 10 in. T = 75 in.
3. 2(riser) + tread $\geq$ 24 in. $\leq$ 25 in.
4. Within any flight 3/16 in. max. variation in riser or tread height or width is permitted.

EXTERIOR STAIRS

Exterior stairs generally are not as steep as interior stairs, since space for wider treads and lower risers is usually available outdoors. Also, more dangerous conditions exist (ice, snow, rain). Wider treads and lower risers make exterior steps safer. The following formula has been devised by Thomas Church in "Gardens Are For People": 2(riser) + tread = 26 in.; thus for a 6 in. riser, 6 x 2 = 12 in., subtracted from 26 = 14 in. tread.

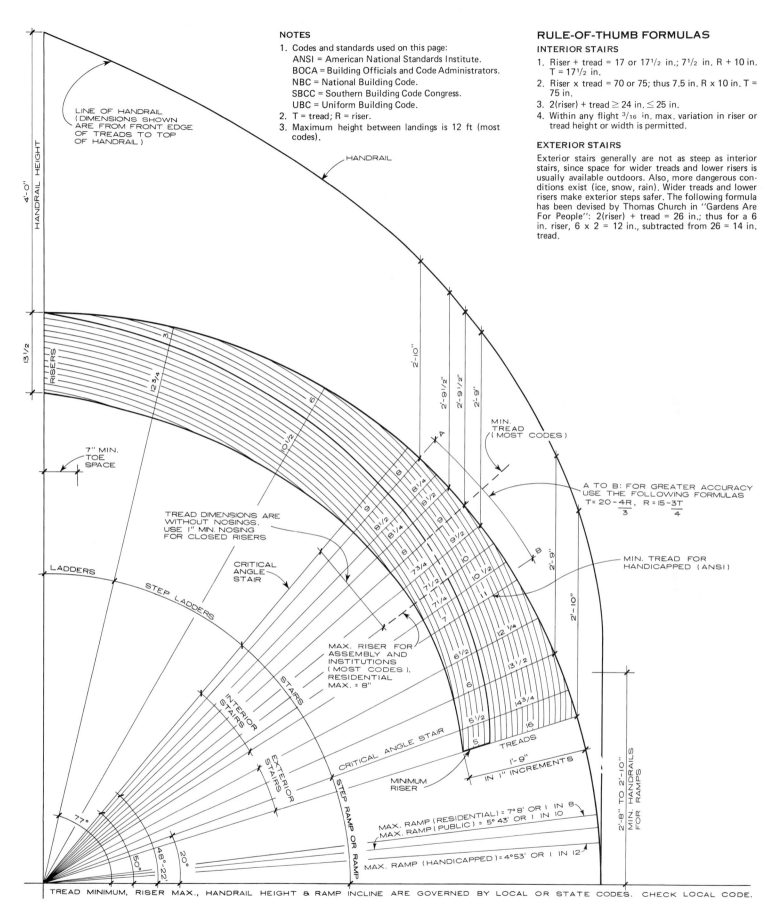

A TO B: FOR GREATER ACCURACY USE THE FOLLOWING FORMULAS
$$T = \frac{20 - 4R}{3}, \quad R = \frac{15 - 3T}{4}$$

TREAD MINIMUM, RISER MAX., HANDRAIL HEIGHT & RAMP INCLINE ARE GOVERNED BY LOCAL OR STATE CODES. CHECK LOCAL CODE.

TREADS AND RISERS

Paul Vaughan, AIA; Charleston, West Virginia

DESIGN ELEMENTS   **1**

BED SIZES

TYPES	W	L
Crib	30″	53″
Daybed	30″	75″
Single bed	39″	82″
Double bed	54″	82″
Queen size	60″	82″
King size	72″	84″

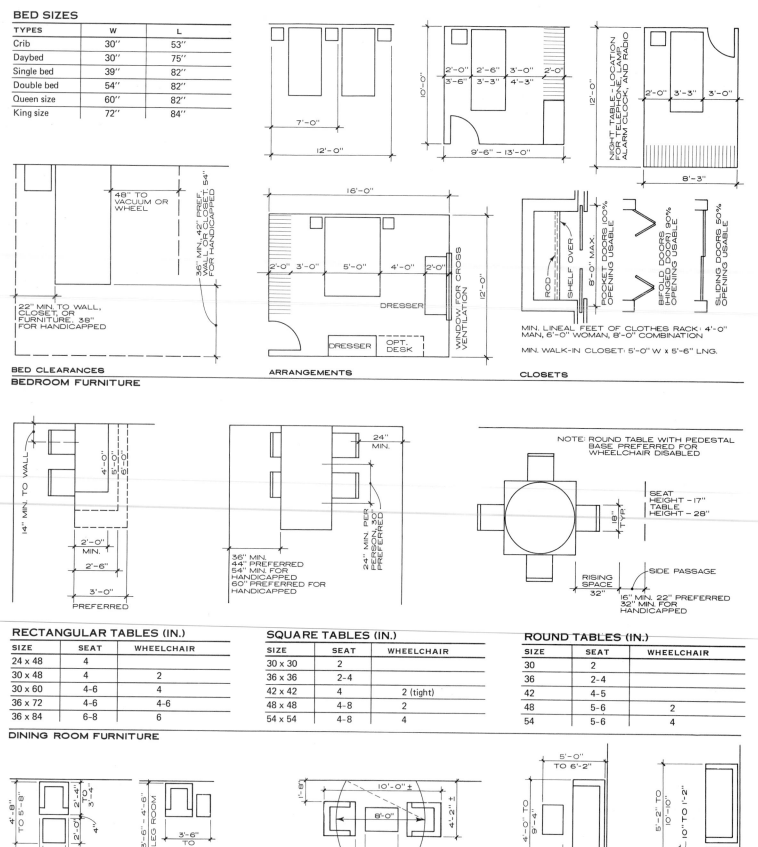

BED CLEARANCES   ARRANGEMENTS   CLOSETS

BEDROOM FURNITURE

RECTANGULAR TABLES (IN.)

SIZE	SEAT	WHEELCHAIR
24 x 48	4	
30 x 48	4	2
30 x 60	4-6	4
36 x 72	4-6	4-6
36 x 84	6-8	6

SQUARE TABLES (IN.)

SIZE	SEAT	WHEELCHAIR
30 x 30	2	
36 x 36	2-4	
42 x 42	4	2 (tight)
48 x 48	4-8	2
54 x 54	4-8	4

ROUND TABLES (IN.)

SIZE	SEAT	WHEELCHAIR
30	2	
36	2-4	
42	4-5	
48	5-6	2
54	5-6	4

DINING ROOM FURNITURE

ARMCHAIR WITH OTTOMAN   ARMCHAIR WITH END TABLE   TWO ARMCHAIRS AND COFFEE TABLE, SHOWING ARC OF CONVERSATION   SOFA WITH COFFEE TABLE   SOFA WITH END TABLE

LIVING ROOM FURNITURE

Arthur J. Pettorino, AIA; Hicksville, New York

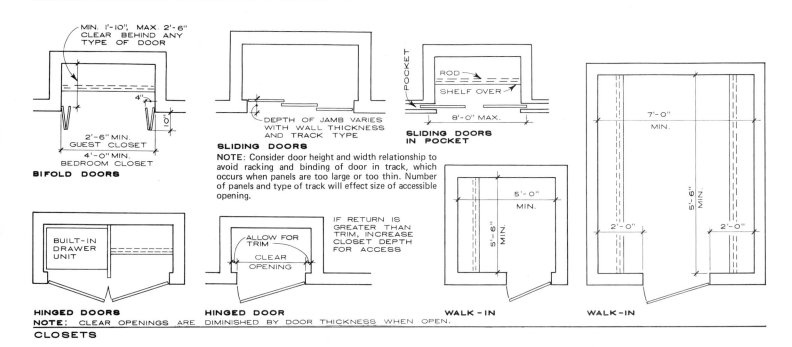

BIFOLD DOORS

MIN. 1'-10", MAX. 2'-6" CLEAR BEHIND ANY TYPE OF DOOR

2'-6" MIN. GUEST CLOSET
4'-0" MIN. BEDROOM CLOSET

4"

SLIDING DOORS

DEPTH OF JAMB VARIES WITH WALL THICKNESS AND TRACK TYPE

NOTE: Consider door height and width relationship to avoid racking and binding of door in track, which occurs when panels are too large or too thin. Number of panels and type of track will effect size of accessible opening.

SLIDING DOORS IN POCKET

POCKET
ROD
SHELF OVER
8'-0" MAX.

WALK-IN

5'-0" MIN.
5'-6" MIN.

WALK-IN

7'-0" MIN.
5'-6" MIN.
2'-0"   2'-0"

HINGED DOORS

BUILT-IN DRAWER UNIT

HINGED DOOR

ALLOW FOR TRIM
CLEAR OPENING

IF RETURN IS GREATER THAN TRIM, INCREASE CLOSET DEPTH FOR ACCESS

CLOSETS

NOTE: CLEAR OPENINGS ARE DIMINISHED BY DOOR THICKNESS WHEN OPEN.

NOTES

1. No closet bifold door should exceed 2 ft panel. Largest door stock in pocket and sliding door is 4 ft.
2. All closet doors should allow easy access to top shelves.
3. Doors for children's closets can be used as tackboards, chalkboards, or mirrors.
4. Consider use of hinged doors for storage fittings and mirrors.
5. Walk-in closets should be properly ventilated and lit.
6. Pole and shelf height for wheelchair-handicapped persons is 54 in. maximum.
7. Accessibility of closets varies with door types used. Figure bifold doors allow 66⅔% minimum of closet to be opened at once, pocket slides 100%, sliding doors 50% or more, and hinged doors 90%, allowing for trim.

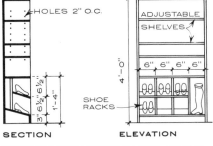

HOLES 2" O.C.

ADJUSTABLE SHELVES

6" 6" 6" 6"

4'-0"

SHOE RACKS

6½" 6½"
1'-4"
3"

SECTION   **ELEVATION**

SHELVES WITH SHOE RACKS UNDER

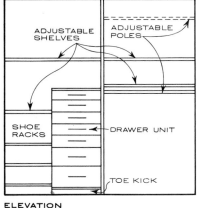

ADJUSTABLE SHELVES
ADJUSTABLE POLES
SHOE RACKS
DRAWER UNIT
TOE KICK

ELEVATION

ADJUSTABLE SHELF

48" MAX.

SECTION A-A

1'-0"
1'-1"
SHELVES AND POLES

SECTION B-B

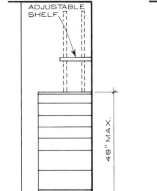

SHOE RACKS
A   B
DRAWER UNIT
A   B
6" PER PR.
CHILD'S SHOES

ALLOW 6" TO 8" BIFOLD DOORS TO STACK

CHILDREN'S CLOSETS

R. L. Speas, Jr.; Hugh N. Jacobsen, FAIA; Washington, D.C.

RESIDENTIAL STORAGE

SHELVING Standard shelving sizes are 6, 8, 10, and 12 in., although shelving up to 18 in. deep is desirable for closet shelving. Shelving may be either fixed or adjustable.

DRAWERS Typical drawers are from 16 to 24 in. deep, 12 to 36 in. wide, and 2 to 8 in. deep or deeper. Often built into casework, drawers may be of wood, metal, or molded plastic.

CABINETS AND CUPBOARDS Cabinets may be built in, as in kitchen and bathroom vanities, or freestanding. Base cabinets are typically 18 to 24 in. deep and from 24 to 42 in. wide or wider, and may be fitted with drawers, shelving, and special storage features. Doors are typically hinged. Wall hung cabinets usually are 12 in. deep.

CLOSETS Standard closet depth is 24 to 30 in. for clothing and 16 to 20 in. for linens.

BOXES Closet storage fittings such as boxes and garment bags can be used for supplemental or seasonal storage.

STORAGE REQUIREMENTS

BEDROOM Allow 4 to 6 ft of hanging space per person. Allow 12 in. of hanging space for 6 suits, 12 shirts, 8 dresses, or 6 pairs of pants.

LINEN STORAGE Place near bedrooms and bathrooms in a closet with 12 to 18 in. deep shelves. Supplemental storage in bins or baskets may be needed.

BATHROOMS A mirrored wall cabinet 4 to 6 in. deep is typical bathroom storage, supplemented by space for supplies of soap, toothpaste, and other toiletries.

GARDEN AND AUTOMOTIVE SUPPLIES Typically, a garage or storage shed is used for garden, automotive supplies, and outdoor furniture. Sheds should be located for convenient use.

COATS A closet near an entry door for coats and rainwear is desirable in most areas of the country.

CLEANING EQUIPMENT A closet at least 24 in. wide for storage of vacuum cleaners and household cleaning supplies is helpful.

KITCHEN/DINING See pages on kitchen planning for recommendations.

OTHER STORAGE Most families have additional storage needs. For custom design work, these needs must be analyzed and storage planned. Storage rooms and attic and basement areas are possible supplemental storage locations.

KITCHEN SPACE PLANNING

The layouts shown here, together with their general area requirements, are based on studies of furniture appliances, storage, and clearances for the average residential kitchen. They have been developed to accommodate storage, work, and required floor areas for various functions, but the location of appliances and their order should be determined by individual preferences, check clearances, traffic flow, and appliance functions rather than total square footage in determining kitchen size during early planning stages.

To simplify comparison of the various room types, basic sizes of furniture, appliances, and clearances have been standardized. However, the appliances shown in the kitchenettes are the more compact units available from some manufacturers (see Equip. pgs.). In all cases, the depth of the counter is assumed as 24″, the depth of base storage units as 20″, and the depth of wall storage units as 12″. Their widths vary in relation to their location.

A useful rule-of-thumb to determine storage area requirements for residential kitchens is: Provide a minimum of 18 square feet of space for basic storage with an additional 6 square feet for each person usually served.

The letters A, B, and C shown below refer to the "work centers" described on another page.

A—Refrigerator center
B—Sink center
C—Range center

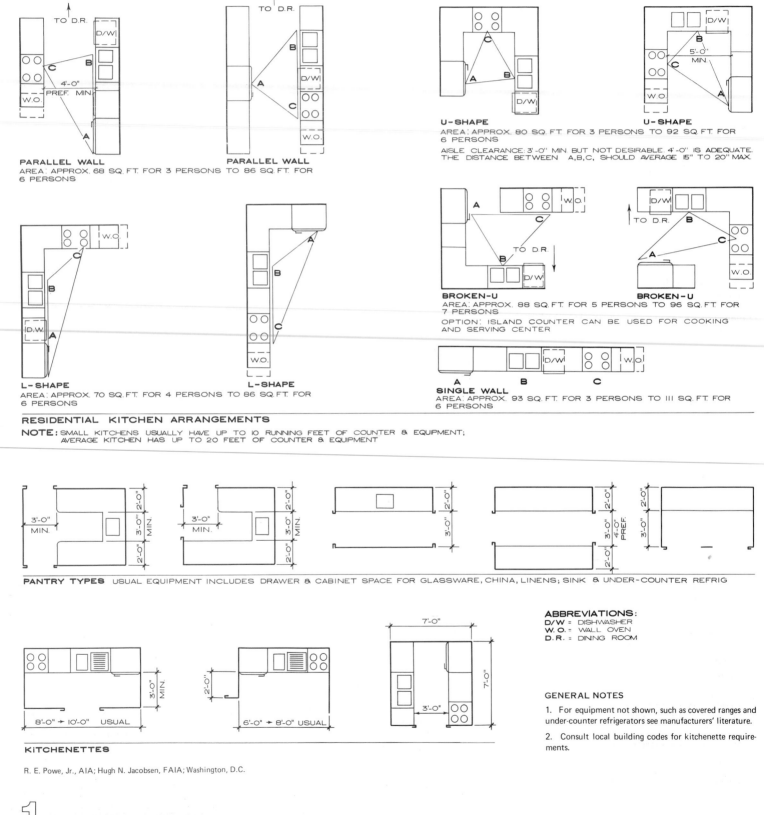

PARALLEL WALL
AREA: APPROX. 68 SQ. FT. FOR 3 PERSONS TO 86 SQ. FT. FOR 6 PERSONS

PARALLEL WALL

U-SHAPE
AREA: APPROX. 80 SQ. FT. FOR 3 PERSONS TO 92 SQ. FT. FOR 6 PERSONS
AISLE CLEARANCE: 3'-0" MIN. BUT NOT DESIRABLE. 4'-0" IS ADEQUATE. THE DISTANCE BETWEEN A,B,C, SHOULD AVERAGE 15" TO 20" MAX.

U-SHAPE

L-SHAPE
AREA: APPROX. 70 SQ. FT. FOR 4 PERSONS TO 86 SQ. FT. FOR 6 PERSONS

L-SHAPE

BROKEN-U
AREA: APPROX. 88 SQ. FT. FOR 5 PERSONS TO 96 SQ. FT. FOR 7 PERSONS
OPTION: ISLAND COUNTER CAN BE USED FOR COOKING AND SERVING CENTER

BROKEN-U

SINGLE WALL
AREA: APPROX. 93 SQ. FT. FOR 3 PERSONS TO 111 SQ. FT. FOR 6 PERSONS

RESIDENTIAL KITCHEN ARRANGEMENTS

NOTE: SMALL KITCHENS USUALLY HAVE UP TO 10 RUNNING FEET OF COUNTER & EQUIPMENT; AVERAGE KITCHEN HAS UP TO 20 FEET OF COUNTER & EQUIPMENT

PANTRY TYPES USUAL EQUIPMENT INCLUDES DRAWER & CABINET SPACE FOR GLASSWARE, CHINA, LINENS; SINK & UNDER-COUNTER REFRIG

ABBREVIATIONS:
D/W = DISHWASHER
W. O. = WALL OVEN
D. R. = DINING ROOM

KITCHENETTES

GENERAL NOTES

1. For equipment not shown, such as covered ranges and under-counter refrigerators see manufacturers' literature.

2. Consult local building codes for kitchenette requirements.

R. E. Powe, Jr., AIA; Hugh N. Jacobsen, FAIA; Washington, D.C.

KITCHEN WORK CENTERS

A residential kitchen may be considered in terms of three interconnected work centers, A, B and C, as shown below. Each encompasses a distinct phase of kitchen activity, and storage should be provided for the items that are most used in connection with each center.

The functions of the sink center are most common to the other two centers. It is recommended, therefore, that the sink center's location be convenient to each of the others (usually between them). The refrigerator center is best located near the entry and the range center near the dining area.

CABINETS SHOULD PROJECT FLUSH OVER REFRIGERATOR

FASCIA TO CLOSE OFF TOP OF CABINETS MAY BE PROVIDED

FASCIA (OR BULKHEAD) SPACE MAY BE USED FOR EXTRA CABINETS FOR RARELY USED ITEMS

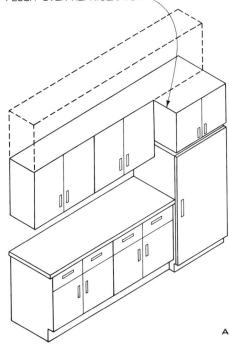

A

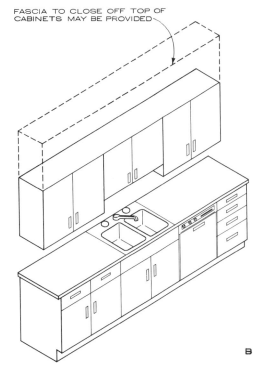

B

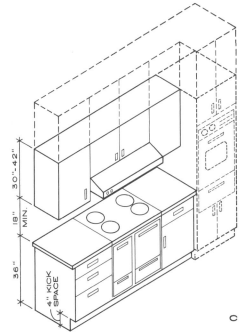

C

REFRIGERATOR CENTER
(RECEIVING AND FOOD PREPARATION)

Provide storage for mixer and mixing bowls; other utensils: sifter, grater, salad molds, cake and pie tins, occasional dishes, condiments, staples, canned goods, brooms, and miscellaneous items.

SINK CENTER
(FOOD PREPARATION, CLEANING, AND CLEANUP)

Provide storage for everyday dishes, glassware, pots and pans, cutlery, silver, pitchers and shakers, vegetable bins, linen, towel rack, wastebasket, cleaning materials and utensils, garbage can or disposal, and dishdrain. Some codes require louvres or other venting provision in the doors under enclosed sinks.

RANGE CENTER
(COOKING AND SERVING)

Provide storage for pots, potholders, frying pans, roaster, cooking utensils, grease container, seasoning, canned goods, bread bin, bread board, toaster, plate warmer, platters, serving dishes, and trays.

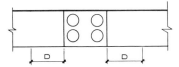

D = 18" to 24"
D = counter distance on either side of a cooking facility.

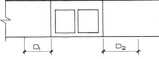

D_1 = 18" to 36"
D_2 = 24" to 36"
Provide work space on both sides of sink. If dishwasher is used allow at least 24" to the right or left.

D = 36" to 42"
D = counter space between range and nearest piece of equipment.

D = 15" minimum
Provide room at latch side of refrigerator for loading and unloading.

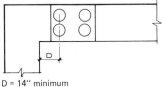

D = 14" minimum
D = clearance between the center of the front unit (or burner) and the turn of the counter.

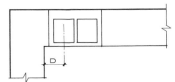

D = 14" minimum
D = clearance between the center of the sink bowl and the turn of the counter.

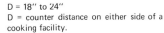

D = 16" minimum
D = clearance between latch side of refrigerator door and turn of the counter.

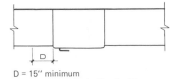

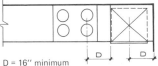

D = 16" minimum
D = clearance between center of front burner and nearest piece of high equipment or nearest wall; or between the center of a wall oven and an adjoining wall.

CLEARANCES AND COUNTER WIDTHS

KITCHENS FOR THE HANDICAPPED

The preferred cooktop and counter height is 30 to 33 in., but may be standard 36 in. if a pullout worksheet is provided at 30 to 33 in. Open floor space is necessary for wheelchair maneuverability; observe a 5 ft minimum turning radius. Smooth, nonskid flooring is required. Indoor-outdoor carpet is preferred, but difficult to maintain in a kitchen. Linoleum or vinyl asbestos tile is acceptable. Knee space is necessary under sink counter. Insulate pipes to avoid scalding. Provide cooktop controls at front to avoid reaching across hot surfaces. Wall ovens should preferably be set so that top of open oven door is 2 ft 7 in. above floor. Side-by-side refrigerator-freezer is preferred, although units with freezer on bottom are acceptable. Dishwashers should be front loading.

Round tables with pedestal base are preferred. A 4 ft diameter will accommodate two wheelchair users; a 4 ft 6 in. diameter will accommodate four wheelchair users.

Storage considerations for the wheelchair disabled include use of pegboard for pots, pans, and utensils. Vertical drawers in base cabinets allow for storage of food that would otherwise be out of reach of wheelchair users. Narrow shelving mounted to the backs of doors in cabinets or closets provides accessible storage for food and utensils.

Arthur J. Pettorino, AIA; Hicksville, New York

R. E. Powe, Jr., AIA; Hugh N. Jacobsen, FAIA; Washington, D.C.

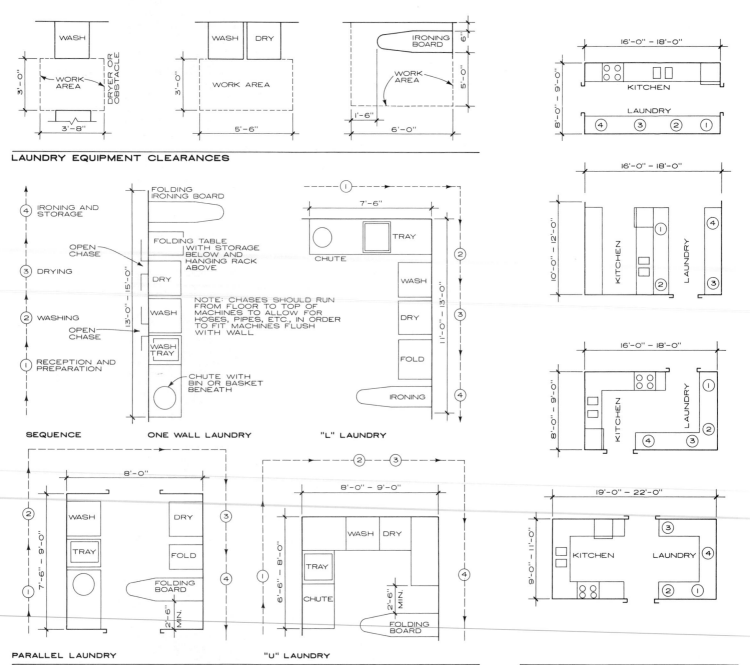

LAUNDRY EQUIPMENT CLEARANCES

SEQUENCE   ONE WALL LAUNDRY   "L" LAUNDRY

PARALLEL LAUNDRY   "U" LAUNDRY

TYPICAL LAUNDRIES

LAUNDRIES WITH KITCHEN

LAUNDRIES FOR THE HANDICAPPED

For the chairborne homemaker, having laundry facilities close to the kitchen is a practical way of coordinating several time consuming activities with a minimum of movement from place to place.

The basic necessities are an efficient automatic washer, a dryer, storage space for supplies, a good lightweight steam iron, and an adjustable ironing board that can be set at a comfortable seated-work height of about 29 in.

Look for a front loading drum type of washer. It is more accessible than the usual top loader, which is too high and has a tub that is too deep for the average wheelchair homemaker.

Most automatic dryers are designed as front loaders. Select a model with controls up front and within reach.

Arthur J. Pettorino, AIA; Hicksville, New York

R. E. Powe, Jr., AIA; Hugh N. Jacobsen, FAIA; Washington, D.C.

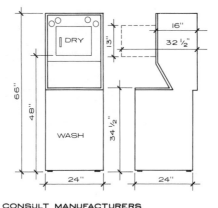

CONSULT MANUFACTURERS FOR VARIOUS MODELS

COMPACT LAUNDRY

APARTMENT HOUSE LAUNDRIES

In apartment house complexes, laundry rooms are usually located in the basement or on the ground floor of the building. This is a logical choice, as it is close to mechanical equipment, piping, and venting, which are necessary to laundry room operations. In addition, these areas, resting on grade, form an excellent surface for washer and dryer placement, for vibrations on this level do not affect apartment dwellers. Easy access is also provided. Folding tables and vending machines for soaps should also be incorporated into the laundry room design. Laundry rooms should be open to visual inspection to ensure the safety of the users. It is important to note that laundry rooms in large apartment buildings tend to become social gathering areas and should be designed to accommodate this function.

1 DESIGN ELEMENTS

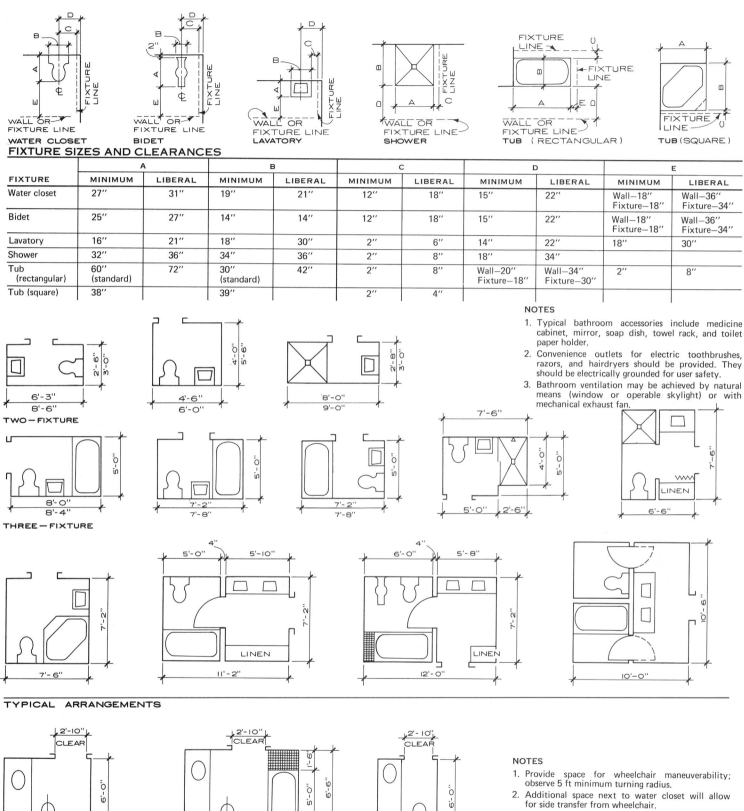

FIXTURE SIZES AND CLEARANCES

FIXTURE	A		B		C		D		E	
	MINIMUM	LIBERAL	MINIMUM	LIBERAL	MINIMUM	LIBERAL	MINIMUM	LIBERAL	MINIMUM	LIBERAL
Water closet	27″	31″	19″	21″	12″	18″	15″	22″	Wall—18″ Fixture—18″	Wall—36″ Fixture—34″
Bidet	25″	27″	14″	14″	12″	18″	15″	22″	Wall—18″ Fixture—18″	Wall—36″ Fixture—34″
Lavatory	16″	21″	18″	30″	2″	6″	14″	22″	18″	30″
Shower	32″	36″	34″	36″	2″	8″	18″	34″		
Tub (rectangular)	60″ (standard)	72″	30″ (standard)	42″	2″	8″	Wall—20″ Fixture—18″	Wall—34″ Fixture—30″	2″	8″
Tub (square)	38″		39″		2″	4″				

NOTES

1. Typical bathroom accessories include medicine cabinet, mirror, soap dish, towel rack, and toilet paper holder.
2. Convenience outlets for electric toothbrushes, razors, and hairdryers should be provided. They should be electrically grounded for user safety.
3. Bathroom ventilation may be achieved by natural means (window or operable skylight) or with mechanical exhaust fan.

TWO—FIXTURE

THREE—FIXTURE

TYPICAL ARRANGEMENTS

NOTES

1. Provide space for wheelchair maneuverability; observe 5 ft minimum turning radius.
2. Additional space next to water closet will allow for side transfer from wheelchair.
3. Provide knee space under sink. Insulate pipes to avoid scalding.
4. Use grab bars around water closet and tub.
5. Roll-in shower may replace tub, and is more convenient for many wheelchair disabled.
6. Bathroom door to be minimum 32 in. clear opening and to swing outward. Use lever hardware on both sides.

RECOMMENDED

MINIMUM (DIFFICULT)

ARRANGEMENTS FOR THE WHEELCHAIR DISABLED

Arthur J. Pettorino, AIA; Hicksville, New York

DESIGN ELEMENTS **1**

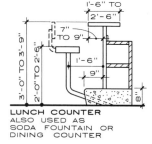

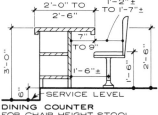

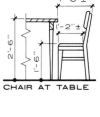

LUNCH COUNTER
ALSO USED AS
SODA FOUNTAIN OR
DINING COUNTER

DINING COUNTER
FOR CHAIR HEIGHT STOOL.
IF ABOVE 1'-6" AND COUNTER
HEIGHT ABOVE 2'-6", USE STEP
OR FOOT RAIL

CHAIR AT TABLE

SECTIONS THROUGH COUNTERS, TABLES, AND SEATS

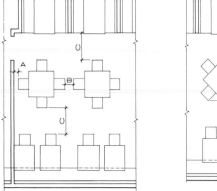

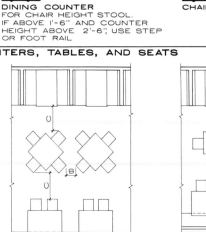

CLEARANCES
A = 6" MINIMUM (NO PASSAGE)
B = 1'-6" LIMITED PASSAGE
C = 2'-6" TO 3'-0" SERVICE AISLE

TYPICAL SEATING ARRANGEMENTS

AVERAGE CAPACITIES PER PERSON

TYPE OF ROOM	SQUARE FEET
Banquet	10-12
Cafeteria	12-15
Tearoom	10-14
Lunchroom/coffee shop	12-16
Dining room/restaurant	13-16
Specialty/formal dining	17-22

NOTE

Figures are general and represent minimum average dimensions. No maximum exists. Seating allowances and requirements may vary to suit individual operations.

GENERAL DESIGN CRITERIA

Service aisles: 30-42 in.

1. Square seating, 66 in. minimum between tables, 30 in. aisle plus two chairs back to back.
2. Diagonal seating, 36 in. minimum between corners of tables.
3. Wall seating, 30 in. minimum between wall and seat back.
4. Minimum of 30 in. for bus carts and flaming service carts.

Customer aisles:

1. Refer to local codes for restrictions on requirements.
2. Wheelchair requirements, 35-44 in. aisle.
3. Wall seating, 30 in. minimum between walls and table.

Tables:

1. Average 29 in. high.
2. Allow space around doors and food service areas.

SQUARE

PERSONS	A OR B	X
2	2'-0" to 2'-6"	2'-10" to 3'-6"
4	2'-6" to 3'-0"	3'-6" to 4'-3"

RECTANGLE

PERSONS	A	B
2	2'-6" to 3'-0"	2'-0" to 2'-6"
2 (on one side)	3'-4" to 4'-0"	
6	5'-10" to 6'-0"	2'-6" to 3'-0"
8	6'-10" to 7'-0"	

Tables wider than 2'-6" will seat one at each end.

CIRCLE

PERSONS	A
4-5	3'-6" to 4'-0"
6-7	4'-6" to 5'-0"
7-8	5'-6" to 6'-4"
8-10	6'-0" to 7'-2"

Round tables are usually recommended only for seating 5 persons or more.

"A" dim. depends on the perimeter (1'-10"-1'-2" per person), necessary to seat required number. For cocktails, 1'-6" is sufficient.

NOTE

Minimum sizes are satisfactory for drink service; larger sizes for food. Tables with widespread bases are more practical than four legged tables.

Tables and arrangements are affected by the type of operations and the style of service. The use of flaming trays, busing carts, high chairs for children, and handicapped access must be considered.

TABLES

NOTE

All dimensions are minimum clearances. Seating layouts show general configurations and are not intended to depict any specific type of operation. Tables may be converted from square to round to enlarge seating capacity. Booth seating makes effective use of corner space.

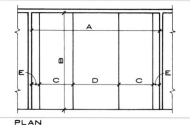

PLAN

A Seat back to seat back: 5'-0" to 6'-2".
B One person per side: 2'-0" to 2'-6".
   Two persons per side: 3'-6" to 4'-6".
   Recommended max. for serving and cleaning 4'-0".
C 1'-6" ±
D 2'-0" to 2'-6".
E 0" to 4"

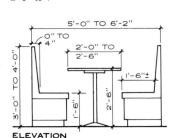

ELEVATION

NOTE

Local regulations determine actual booth sizes. Tables are often 2 in. shorter than seats, and may have rounded ends. Circular booths have overall diameter of 6 ft 4 in. +.

BOOTHS

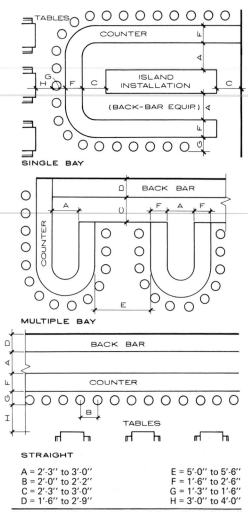

SINGLE BAY

MULTIPLE BAY

STRAIGHT

A = 2'-3" to 3'-0"	E = 5'-0" to 5'-6"
B = 2'-0" to 2'-2"	F = 1'-6" to 2'-6"
C = 2'-3" to 3'-0"	G = 1'-3" to 1'-6"
D = 1'-6" to 2'-9"	H = 3'-0" to 4'-0"

TYPICAL COUNTER ARRANGEMENTS

Cini-Grissom Associates, Inc.; Food Service Consultants; Washington, D.C.

1 DESIGN ELEMENTS

THEATER DESIGN CRITERIA

The planning of seating areas in places of assembly should involve the following considerations:

1. EFFICIENCY: The floor area efficiency in square feet per seat is a function of the row spacing, the average chair width, and the space allocation per seat for aisles. See following pages for further discussion of these factors.

Efficiency (F) = seat factor + aisle factor

$$F \ (sq \ ft/seat) = \frac{W_s T}{144} + \frac{IT}{144} \times \frac{1}{S_{avg}}$$

where W_s = average seat width (in.)
      T = row to row spacing (tread) (in.)
      I = average aisle width (in.) (42 in. width is typical)
      S_{avg} = average number of seats in a row per single aisle: 8 or fewer—inefficient layout; 14 to 16—maximum efficiency (multiple aisle seating); 18 to 50 and more—continental seating.

2. CAPACITY AND AUDIENCE AREA: Audience area = capacity x efficiency.

35-75	Classroom
75-150	Lecture room, experimental theater
150-300	Large lecture room, small theater
300-750	Average drama theater in educational setting
750-1500	Small commercial theater, repertory theater, recital hall
1500-2000	Medium large theater, large commercial theater
2000-3000	Average civic theater, concert hall, multiple use hall
3000-6000	Very large auditorium
Over 6000	Special assembly facilities

3. PERFORMING AREA (not including adjacent support area) (sq ft):

	MINIMUM	AVERAGE	MAXIMUM
Lectures (single speaker)	150	240	500
Revue, nightclub	350	450	700
Legitimate drama	250	550	1000
Dance	700	950	1200
Musicals, folk opera	800	1200	1800
Symphonic concerts	1500	2000	2500
Opera	1000	2500	4000
Pageant	2000	3500	5000

4. ORIENTATION OR SEATED SPECTATOR: Head strain is minimized by orienting chairs or rows of chairs so that spectators face the center of action of the performing area.

5. ANGLE OF VISION OF SPECTATOR: The human eye has a peripheral spread of vision of about 130°. This angle of view from chairs in the front rows will define the outer limits of the maximum sized performing area.

6. ANGLE OF ENCOUNTER: The angle of encounter is defined by the 130° peripheral spread of vision of a single performer standing at the "point of command." Patrons seated outside the spread of this angle will not have simultaneous eye contact with performer. Natural sound communication will also deteriorate for these patrons.

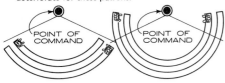

7. DISTANCE BETWEEN PERFORMANCE AND LAST ROW OF SPECTATORS: Achievement of visual and sound communication is enhanced by minimizing this distance while satisfying the preceding parameters.

Peter H. Frink; Frink and Beuchat: Architects; Philadelphia, Pennsylvania

SCREEN PROJECTION

- The minimum distance between the first row and the screen (D_F) is determined by the maximum allowable angle between the sightline from the first row to the top of the screen and the perpendicular to the screen at that point. A maximum angle of 30 to 35° is recommended.
- The maximum distance between the screen and the most distant viewer (MDV) should not exceed eight times the height of the screen image. An MDV two to three times the screen width is preferred.
- Screen width (W) is determined by the use of the appropriate aspect ratio between the screen image width and height.
- Curvature of screens may reduce the amount of apparent distortion for a larger audience area. Curvature of larger screens may help to keep the whole of the image in focus and may provide a more uniform distribution of luminance.

ZERO ENCIRCLEMENT (PROSCENIUM STAGE, PICTURE FRAME STAGE, END STAGE)

- The angle of audience spread in front of a masking frame is determined by the maximum size of the corner cutoff from a rectangularly shaped performing area that can be tolerated by seats at the side.
- Audience may not fill angle of encounter from point of command.
- Audience farthest from performing area.
- Large range in choice of size of performing area.
- Provisions for a large amount of scenic wall surfaces without masking sightlines.
- Horizontal movement of scenery typically made in both perpendicularly and parallel to centerline.
- Possibility of short differences in arrival time between direct and reflected sound at the spectator. This may be beneficial to music performances.

90° TO 130° ENCIRCLEMENT (PICTORIAL OPEN STAGE, WIDE FAN, HYBRID, THRUST STAGE)

- Audience spread defined and limited by angle of encounter from point of command.
- Performing area shape trapezoidal, rhombic, or circular.
- Audience closer to performing area than with zero encirclement.
- Picture frame less dominant.
- Range in choice of size of performing area.
- Provision for an amount of scenic wall surfaces possible without obscuring the performing area.
- Horizontal movement of scenery is possible in directions at 45° to and parallel to centerline.
- Shape of seating area places maximum number of seats within the directional limits of the sound of the unaided voice, beneficial for speech performance.

180° TO 270° ENCIRCLEMENT (GREEK THEATER, PENINSULAR, THREE-SIDED, THRUST STAGE, 3/4 ARENA STAGE, ELIZABETHAN STAGE)

- Audience spread well beyond angle of encounter from point of command in order to bring audience closer to performing area.
- Simultaneous eye contact between performer and all spectators not possible.
- Minimum range of choice in size of performing area.
- Provision of a small amount of scenic wall surfaces possible without masking sightlines.
- Horizontal movement of scenery is possible only parallel to centerline.
- Large encirclement by audience usually demands actor vomitory entrance through or under audience.

360° ENCIRCLEMENT (ARENA STAGE, THEATER IN THE ROUND, ISLAND STAGE, CENTER STAGE)

- Performer always seen from rear by some spectators.
- Simultaneous eye contact between performer and all spectators not possible.
- Audience closest to performance.
- No range of choice in size of performing area.
- No scenic wall surfaces possible without obscuring the view of the performing area.
- Horizontal movement of scenery not readily possible.
- Encirclement by audience demands actor vomitory entrance through audience area.

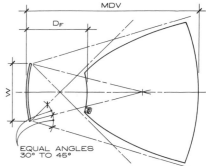

SCREEN PROJECTION

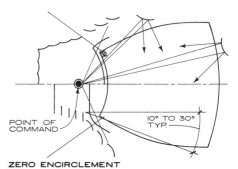

ZERO ENCIRCLEMENT

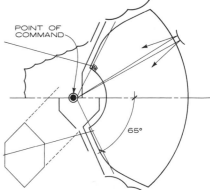

90° TO 130° ENCIRCLEMENT

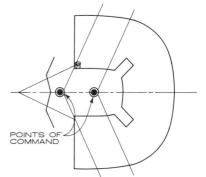

180° TO 270° ENCIRCLEMENT

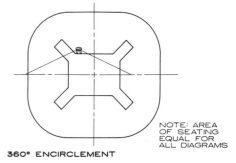

360° ENCIRCLEMENT

NOTE: AREA OF SEATING EQUAL FOR ALL DIAGRAMS

DESIGN ELEMENTS   1

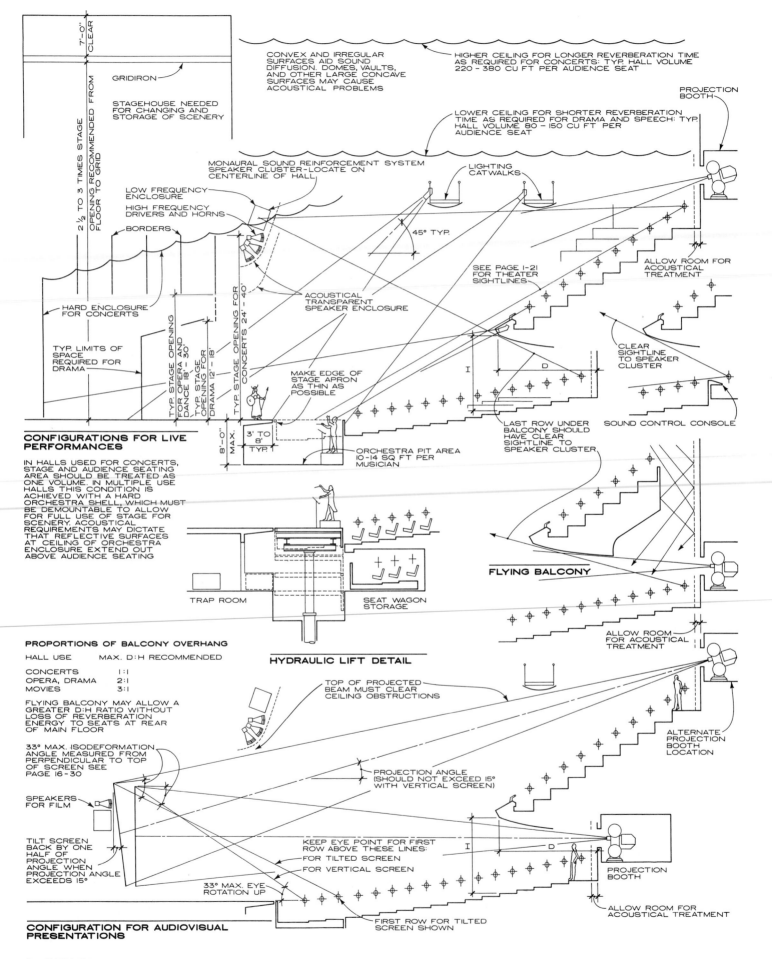

7'-0" CLEAR

2½ TO 3 TIMES STAGE OPENING RECOMMENDED FROM FLOOR TO GRID

GRIDIRON

STAGEHOUSE NEEDED FOR CHANGING AND STORAGE OF SCENERY

CONVEX AND IRREGULAR SURFACES AID SOUND DIFFUSION. DOMES, VAULTS, AND OTHER LARGE CONCAVE SURFACES MAY CAUSE ACOUSTICAL PROBLEMS

HIGHER CEILING FOR LONGER REVERBERATION TIME AS REQUIRED FOR CONCERTS: TYP. HALL VOLUME 220 - 380 CU FT PER AUDIENCE SEAT

PROJECTION BOOTH

LOWER CEILING FOR SHORTER REVERBERATION TIME AS REQUIRED FOR DRAMA AND SPEECH: TYP. HALL VOLUME 80 - 150 CU FT PER AUDIENCE SEAT

MONAURAL SOUND REINFORCEMENT SYSTEM SPEAKER CLUSTER-LOCATE ON CENTERLINE OF HALL

LIGHTING CATWALKS

LOW FREQUENCY ENCLOSURE

HIGH FREQUENCY DRIVERS AND HORNS

BORDERS

45° TYP.

SEE PAGE 1-21 FOR THEATER SIGHTLINES

ALLOW ROOM FOR ACOUSTICAL TREATMENT

HARD ENCLOSURE FOR CONCERTS

ACOUSTICAL TRANSPARENT SPEAKER ENCLOSURE

TYP. LIMITS OF SPACE REQUIRED FOR DRAMA

TYP. STAGE OPENING FOR OPERA AND DANCE 18'- 30'

TYP. STAGE OPENING FOR DRAMA 12'- 18'

TYP. STAGE OPENING FOR CONCERTS 24'- 40'

MAKE EDGE OF STAGE APRON AS THIN AS POSSIBLE

CLEAR SIGHTLINE TO SPEAKER CLUSTER

LAST ROW UNDER BALCONY SHOULD HAVE CLEAR SIGHTLINE TO SPEAKER CLUSTER

SOUND CONTROL CONSOLE

8'-0" MAX.

3' TO 8' TYP.

ORCHESTRA PIT AREA 10-14 SQ FT PER MUSICIAN

CONFIGURATIONS FOR LIVE PERFORMANCES

IN HALLS USED FOR CONCERTS, STAGE AND AUDIENCE SEATING AREA SHOULD BE TREATED AS ONE VOLUME. IN MULTIPLE USE HALLS THIS CONDITION IS ACHIEVED WITH A HARD ORCHESTRA SHELL, WHICH MUST BE DEMOUNTABLE TO ALLOW FOR FULL USE OF STAGE FOR SCENERY. ACOUSTICAL REQUIREMENTS MAY DICTATE THAT REFLECTIVE SURFACES AT CEILING OF ORCHESTRA ENCLOSURE EXTEND OUT ABOVE AUDIENCE SEATING

TRAP ROOM

SEAT WAGON STORAGE

FLYING BALCONY

ALLOW ROOM FOR ACOUSTICAL TREATMENT

PROPORTIONS OF BALCONY OVERHANG

HALL USE	MAX. D:H RECOMMENDED
CONCERTS	1:1
OPERA, DRAMA	2:1
MOVIES	3:1

FLYING BALCONY MAY ALLOW A GREATER D:H RATIO WITHOUT LOSS OF REVERBERATION ENERGY TO SEATS AT REAR OF MAIN FLOOR

33° MAX. ISODEFORMATION ANGLE MEASURED FROM PERPENDICULAR TO TOP OF SCREEN SEE PAGE 16-30

HYDRAULIC LIFT DETAIL

TOP OF PROJECTED BEAM MUST CLEAR CEILING OBSTRUCTIONS

PROJECTION ANGLE (SHOULD NOT EXCEED 15° WITH VERTICAL SCREEN)

ALTERNATE PROJECTION BOOTH LOCATION

SPEAKERS FOR FILM

TILT SCREEN BACK BY ONE HALF OF PROJECTION ANGLE WHEN PROJECTION ANGLE EXCEEDS 15°

KEEP EYE POINT FOR FIRST ROW ABOVE THESE LINES: FOR TILTED SCREEN FOR VERTICAL SCREEN

PROJECTION BOOTH

33° MAX. EYE ROTATION UP

ALLOW ROOM FOR ACOUSTICAL TREATMENT

CONFIGURATION FOR AUDIOVISUAL PRESENTATIONS

FIRST ROW FOR TILTED SCREEN SHOWN

Peter H. Frink; Frink and Beuchat: Architects; Philadelphia, Pennsylvania

1   DESIGN ELEMENTS

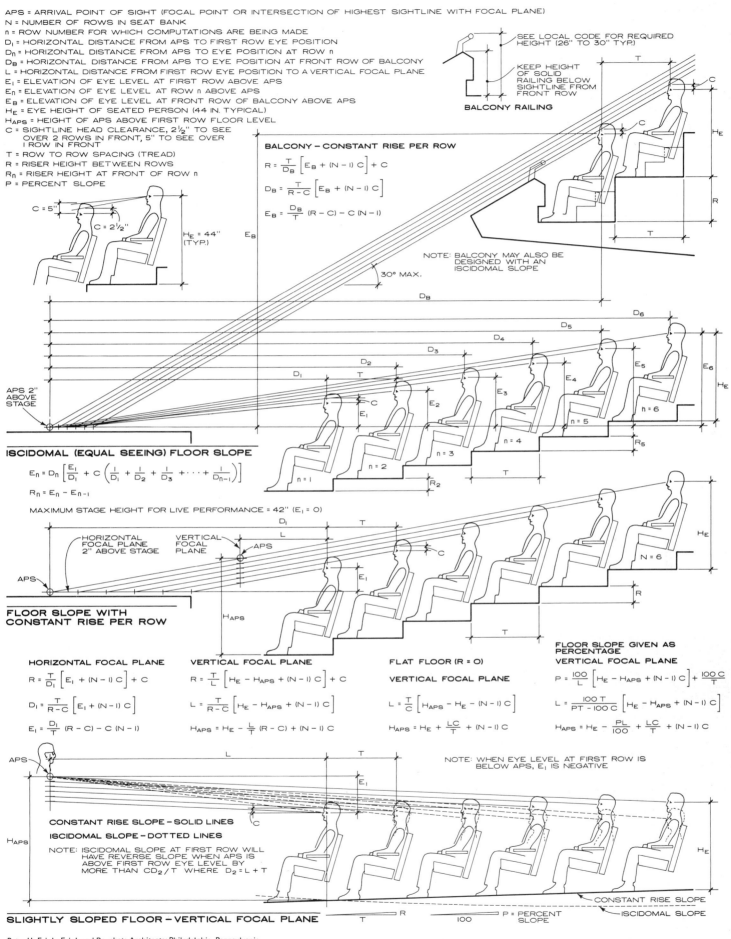

APS = ARRIVAL POINT OF SIGHT (FOCAL POINT OR INTERSECTION OF HIGHEST SIGHTLINE WITH FOCAL PLANE)
N = NUMBER OF ROWS IN SEAT BANK
n = ROW NUMBER FOR WHICH COMPUTATIONS ARE BEING MADE
D_1 = HORIZONTAL DISTANCE FROM APS TO FIRST ROW EYE POSITION
D_n = HORIZONTAL DISTANCE FROM APS TO EYE POSITION AT ROW n
D_B = HORIZONTAL DISTANCE FROM APS TO EYE POSITION AT FRONT ROW OF BALCONY
L = HORIZONTAL DISTANCE FROM FIRST ROW EYE POSITION TO A VERTICAL FOCAL PLANE
E_1 = ELEVATION OF EYE LEVEL AT FIRST ROW ABOVE APS
E_n = ELEVATION OF EYE LEVEL AT ROW n ABOVE APS
E_B = ELEVATION OF EYE LEVEL AT FRONT ROW OF BALCONY ABOVE APS
H_E = EYE HEIGHT OF SEATED PERSON (44 IN. TYPICAL)
H_{APS} = HEIGHT OF APS ABOVE FIRST ROW FLOOR LEVEL
C = SIGHTLINE HEAD CLEARANCE, 2½" TO SEE OVER 2 ROWS IN FRONT, 5" TO SEE OVER 1 ROW IN FRONT
T = ROW TO ROW SPACING (TREAD)
R = RISER HEIGHT BETWEEN ROWS
R_n = RISER HEIGHT AT FRONT OF ROW n
P = PERCENT SLOPE

SEE LOCAL CODE FOR REQUIRED HEIGHT (26" TO 30" TYP.)
KEEP HEIGHT OF SOLID RAILING BELOW SIGHTLINE FROM FRONT ROW

BALCONY RAILING

C = 5"
C = 2½"
H_E = 44" (TYP.)

BALCONY – CONSTANT RISE PER ROW

$$R = \frac{T}{D_B}\left[E_B + (N-1)\,C\right] + C$$

$$D_B = \frac{T}{R-C}\left[E_B + (N-1)\,C\right]$$

$$E_B = \frac{D_B}{T}(R-C) - C\,(N-1)$$

NOTE: BALCONY MAY ALSO BE DESIGNED WITH AN ISCIDOMAL SLOPE

30° MAX.

D_B

APS 2" ABOVE STAGE

ISCIDOMAL (EQUAL SEEING) FLOOR SLOPE

$$E_n = D_n\left[\frac{E_1}{D_1} + C\left(\frac{1}{D_1} + \frac{1}{D_2} + \frac{1}{D_3} + \cdots + \frac{1}{D_{n-1}}\right)\right]$$

$$R_n = E_n - E_{n-1}$$

MAXIMUM STAGE HEIGHT FOR LIVE PERFORMANCE = 42" (E_1 = 0)

HORIZONTAL FOCAL PLANE 2" ABOVE STAGE
VERTICAL FOCAL PLANE
APS

FLOOR SLOPE WITH CONSTANT RISE PER ROW

HORIZONTAL FOCAL PLANE

$$R = \frac{T}{D_1}\left[E_1 + (N-1)\,C\right] + C$$

$$D_1 = \frac{T}{R-C}\left[E_1 + (N-1)\,C\right]$$

$$E_1 = \frac{D_1}{T}(R-C) - C\,(N-1)$$

VERTICAL FOCAL PLANE

$$R = \frac{T}{L}\left[H_E - H_{APS} + (N-1)\,C\right] + C$$

$$L = \frac{T}{R-C}\left[H_E - H_{APS} + (N-1)\,C\right]$$

$$H_{APS} = H_E - \frac{L}{T}(R-C) + (N-1)\,C$$

FLAT FLOOR (R = 0)

VERTICAL FOCAL PLANE

$$L = \frac{T}{C}\left[H_{APS} - H_E - (N-1)\,C\right]$$

$$H_{APS} = H_E + \frac{LC}{T} + (N-1)\,C$$

FLOOR SLOPE GIVEN AS PERCENTAGE

VERTICAL FOCAL PLANE

$$P = \frac{100}{L}\left[H_E - H_{APS} + (N-1)\,C\right] + \frac{100\,C}{T}$$

$$L = \frac{100\,T}{PT - 100\,C}\left[H_E - H_{APS} + (N-1)\,C\right]$$

$$H_{APS} = H_E - \frac{PL}{100} + \frac{LC}{T} + (N-1)\,C$$

APS
H_{APS}

CONSTANT RISE SLOPE – SOLID LINES

ISCIDOMAL SLOPE – DOTTED LINES

NOTE: ISCIDOMAL SLOPE AT FIRST ROW WILL HAVE REVERSE SLOPE WHEN APS IS ABOVE FIRST ROW EYE LEVEL BY MORE THAN CD_2/T WHERE $D_2 = L + T$

NOTE: WHEN EYE LEVEL AT FIRST ROW IS BELOW APS, E_1 IS NEGATIVE

CONSTANT RISE SLOPE
ISCIDOMAL SLOPE

SLIGHTLY SLOPED FLOOR – VERTICAL FOCAL PLANE

$$\frac{R}{100} = P = \text{PERCENT SLOPE}$$

Peter H. Frink; Frink and Beuchat: Architects; Philadelphia, Pennsylvania

DESIGN ELEMENTS   **1**

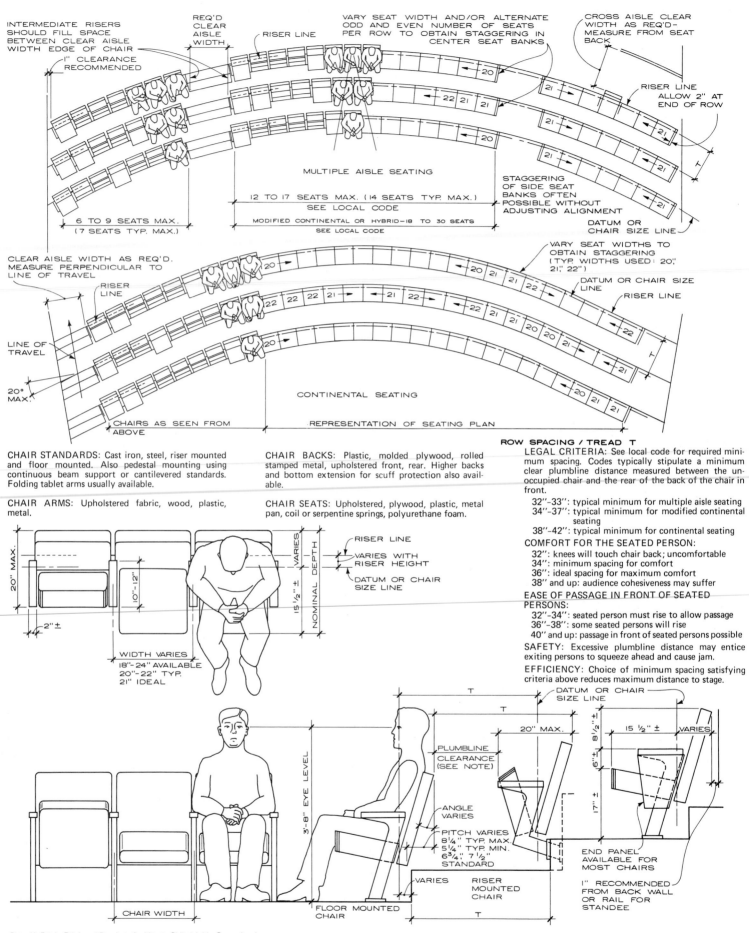

INTERMEDIATE RISERS SHOULD FILL SPACE BETWEEN CLEAR AISLE WIDTH EDGE OF CHAIR

REQ'D CLEAR AISLE WIDTH

RISER LINE

VARY SEAT WIDTH AND/OR ALTERNATE ODD AND EVEN NUMBER OF SEATS PER ROW TO OBTAIN STAGGERING IN CENTER SEAT BANKS

CROSS AISLE CLEAR WIDTH AS REQ'D- MEASURE FROM SEAT BACK

1" CLEARANCE RECOMMENDED

RISER LINE ALLOW 2" AT END OF ROW

MULTIPLE AISLE SEATING

12 TO 17 SEATS MAX. (14 SEATS TYP. MAX.) SEE LOCAL CODE

MODIFIED CONTINENTAL OR HYBRID—18 TO 30 SEATS SEE LOCAL CODE

STAGGERING OF SIDE SEAT BANKS OFTEN POSSIBLE WITHOUT ADJUSTING ALIGNMENT

6 TO 9 SEATS MAX. (7 SEATS TYP. MAX.)

DATUM OR CHAIR SIZE LINE

CLEAR AISLE WIDTH AS REQ'D. MEASURE PERPENDICULAR TO LINE OF TRAVEL

RISER LINE

VARY SEAT WIDTHS TO OBTAIN STAGGERING (TYP. WIDTHS USED: 20", 21", 22")

DATUM OR CHAIR SIZE LINE

RISER LINE

LINE OF TRAVEL

20° MAX.

CHAIRS AS SEEN FROM ABOVE

CONTINENTAL SEATING

REPRESENTATION OF SEATING PLAN

CHAIR STANDARDS: Cast iron, steel, riser mounted and floor mounted. Also pedestal mounting using continuous beam support or cantilevered standards. Folding tablet arms usually available.

CHAIR ARMS: Upholstered fabric, wood, plastic, metal.

CHAIR BACKS: Plastic, molded plywood, rolled stamped metal, upholstered front, rear. Higher backs and bottom extension for scuff protection also available.

CHAIR SEATS: Upholstered, plywood, plastic, metal pan, coil or serpentine springs, polyurethane foam.

ROW SPACING / TREAD T

LEGAL CRITERIA: See local code for required minimum spacing. Codes typically stipulate a minimum clear plumbline distance measured between the unoccupied chair and the rear of the back of the chair in front.

32"-33": typical minimum for multiple aisle seating
34"-37": typical minimum for modified continental seating
38"-42": typical minimum for continental seating

COMFORT FOR THE SEATED PERSON:

32": knees will touch chair back; uncomfortable
34": minimum spacing for comfort
36": ideal spacing for maximum comfort
38" and up: audience cohesiveness may suffer

EASE OF PASSAGE IN FRONT OF SEATED PERSONS:

32"-34": seated person must rise to allow passage
36"-38": some seated persons will rise
40" and up: passage in front of seated persons possible

SAFETY: Excessive plumbline distance may entice exiting persons to squeeze ahead and cause jam.

EFFICIENCY: Choice of minimum spacing satisfying criteria above reduces maximum distance to stage.

20" MAX.

10"-12"

2" ±

RISER LINE

VARIES WITH RISER HEIGHT

DATUM OR CHAIR SIZE LINE

VARIES / NOMINAL DEPTH

15 1/2" ±

WIDTH VARIES
18"-24" AVAILABLE
20"-22" TYP.
21" IDEAL

3'-8" EYE LEVEL

PLUMBLINE CLEARANCE (SEE NOTE)

DATUM OR CHAIR SIZE LINE

20" MAX.

15 1/2" ± VARIES

8 1/2" ±

6" ±

17" ±

ANGLE VARIES

PITCH VARIES
8 1/4" TYP. MAX.
5 1/4" TYP. MIN.
6 3/4" 7 1/2" STANDARD

CHAIR WIDTH

FLOOR MOUNTED CHAIR

VARIES RISER MOUNTED CHAIR

END PANEL AVAILABLE FOR MOST CHAIRS

1" RECOMMENDED FROM BACK WALL OR RAIL FOR STANDEE

Peter H. Frink; Frink and Beuchat: Architects; Philadelphia, Pennsylvania

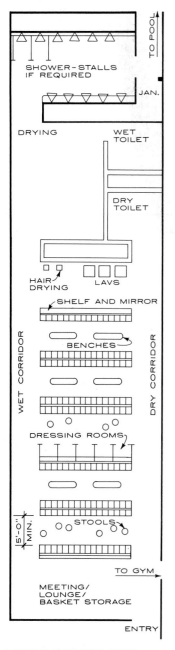

LOCKER/SHOWER UNIT

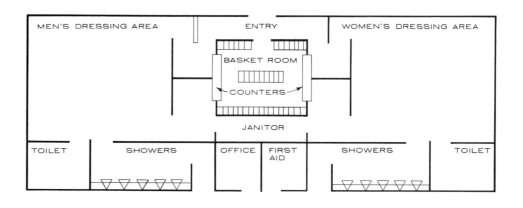

DRESSING UNIT FOR POOL

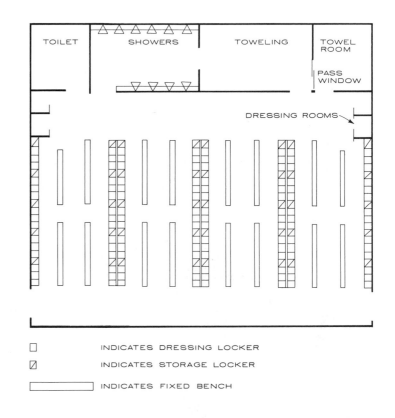

☐   INDICATES DRESSING LOCKER

▨   INDICATES STORAGE LOCKER

▭   INDICATES FIXED BENCH

TO SERVE GYMNASIUM AND POOL

NOTES

The best arrangement of lockers is the bay system, with a minimum 4 ft circulation aisle at each end of the bays. Ordinarily, the maximum number of lockers in a bay is 16. Locate dry (shoe) traffic at one end of the bays and wet (barefoot) traffic at the other end. For long bays with a single bench, make 3 ft breaks at 15 ft intervals.

Supervision of school lockers is the easiest if they are located in single banks along the two long walls, providing one or more bays that run the length of the room.

The number of lockers in a locker room depends on the anticipated number of members and/or size of classes. Separate locker areas should be encouraged. In small buildings interconnecting doors provide flexibility and allow for the handling of peak loads.

Individual dressing and shower compartments may be required for women's and girls' locker and shower rooms and for men's clubs. A shower stall for the handicapped may also be required.

YMCA Building and Furnishings Service; New York, New York

GYMNASIUM LOCKER ROOM

Basket storage, if included, is self-service. Maximum height is 8 tiers. A dehumidifying system should be provided to dry out basket contents overnight. Separate auxiliary locker rooms may be required. These may serve teams, part time instructors, the faculty, or volunteer leaders. A small room for the coach's use may be desirable.

The shower rooms should be directly accessible to the toweling room and the locker room that it serves. When a shower room is designed to serve a swimming pool, the room should be located so that all must pass through the showers prior to reaching the pool deck.

Separate wet and dry toilet areas are recommended. Wet toilets should be easily accessible from the shower room. When designed for use with a swimming pool, wet toilets should be located so that users must pass through the shower room after use of toilets.

Locker room entrance and exit doors should have vision barriers.

All facilities should be barrier free.

Floors should be of impervious material such as ceramic or quarry tile, with a Carborundum impregnated surface, and should slope toward the drains. Concrete floors (nonslip surface), if used, should be treated with a hardener to avoid the penetration of odors and moisture.

Walls should be of materials resistant to moisture and should have surfaces that are easily cleaned. All exterior corners in the locker rooms should be rounded.

Heavy duty, moisture resistant doors at locker room entrances and exits should be of sufficient size to handle the traffic flow and form natural vision barriers. Entrance/exit doors for the lockers should be equipped with corrosion resistant hardware.

Ceilings in shower areas should be of ceramic tile or other material impervious to moisture. Locker room ceilings should be acoustically treated with a material impervious to moisture and breakage. Floor drains should be kept out of the line of traffic where possible.

RECREATION   **1**

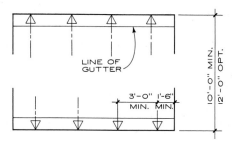

PLAN

GROUP SHOWERS

There must be a sufficient number of shower heads. Educational facilities with time constraints should have 10 shower heads for the first 30 persons and 1 shower head for every 4 additional persons. In recreational facilities 1 shower head for each 10 dressing lockers is a minimum. Temperature controls are necessary to keep water from exceeding 110°F. Both individual and master controls are needed for group showers.

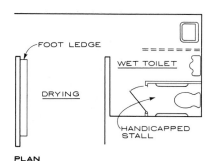

PLAN

DRYING ROOM AND WET TOILET

The drying room should have about the same area as the shower room. Provision for drainage should be made. Heavy duty towel rails, approximately 4 ft from the floor, are recommended. A foot drying ledge, 18 in. high and 8 in. wide as shown in the drawing, is desirable. An adjacent wet toilet is suggested. Avoid curbs between drying room and adjacent space. Towel service is desirable in a school. Size of area varies with material to be stored (can be used for distributing uniforms), with 200 sq ft usually being sufficient.

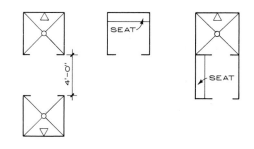

PLAN

INDIVIDUAL SHOWERS AND DRESSING ROOMS

INDIVIDUAL ROOMS	MINIMUM	OPTIMUM
Showers	3'-0" x 3'-6"	3'-6" x 3'-6"
Dressing Rooms	3'-0" x 3'-6"	3'-6" x 4'-0"

Individual dressing rooms and showers can be combined in a variety of configurations to obtain 1:1, 2:1, 3:1, and 4:1 ratios, respectively.

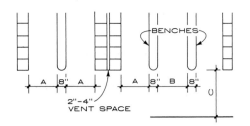

PLAN

AISLE SPACE FOR DRESSING ROOM
AISLE SPACE

	A	B	C
Recreation	2'-2"	1'-8"	3'-6"
School	2'-6"	2'-6"	4'-0"

Bench should be minimum 8 in. in width and 16 in. from the floor. Traffic breaks 3 ft minimum wide should occur at maximum intervals of 12 ft. Main traffic aisle to be wider for large number of locker bays. Avoid lockers that meet at 90° corner.

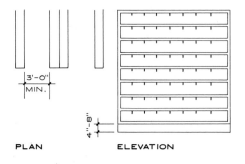

PLAN   ELEVATION

BASKET ROOM AND BASKET RACK

Basket racks vary from 7 to 10 tiers in height. Wide baskets require 1 ft shelf space, small baskets 10 in. shelf space, both fit 1 to 1½ ft deep shelf. Back-to-back shelving is 2 ft 3 in. wide. Height shelf-to-shelf is 9¼ in.

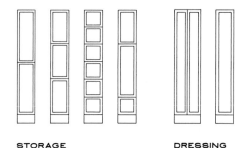

STORAGE   DRESSING

LOCKERS
STANDARD SIZES

Width	9", 12", 15", 18"
Depth	12", 15", 18"
Height	60", 72" (overall)

For schools, standard storage locker is 9 in. or 12 in. x 12 in. x 12 in. to 24 in. One storage locker per student enrolled plus 10% for expansion. Standard dressing lockers are 12 in. x 12 in. x 60 in. or 72 in. Number of dressing lockers should be equal to the peak period load plus 10 to 15% for variation.

LOCKER ROOM FACILITIES

ITEMS TO BE PROVIDED

1. Fixed benches 16 in. high.
2. Lockers on raised base.
3. Locker numbering system.
4. Hair dryers—one per 20 lockers.
5. Mirrors at lavatory.
6. Makeup mirror and shelf.
7. Drinking fountain (height as required).
8. Bulletin board.
9. Dressing booths if required.
10. Full length mirror.
11. Clock.
12. Door signs.
13. Sound system speaker if required.
14. Lighting at mirrors for grooming.
15. Lighting located over aisles and passages.
16. Adequate ventilation for storage lockers.
17. Windows located with regard to height and arrangement of lockers.
18. Visual supervision from adjacent office.

YMCA Building and Furnishings Service; New York, New York

RECOMMENDED MOUNTING HEIGHTS

Shower valve	4'-0"
Shower head	
Men	6'-6"
Women	6'-0"
Children	5'-0"
Hand dryer outlet	
Men	3'-8"
Women	3'-6"
Teenagers	3'-1"
Preteens	2'-8"
Hair dryer outlet	
Men	6'-0"
Women	5'-5"
Teenagers	5'-0"
Preteens	5'-0"
Clock	6'-6" min.
Robe hook	6'-3"
Towel bar	4'-0"

CABANAS

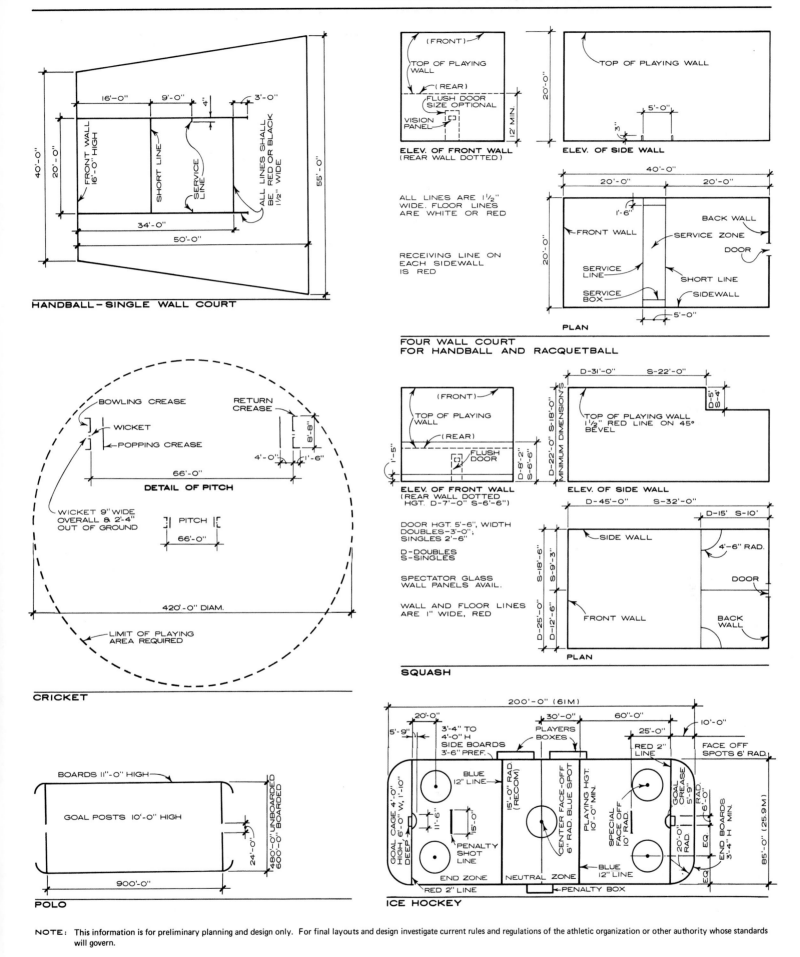

HANDBALL—SINGLE WALL COURT

FRONT WALL 16'-0" HIGH
SHORT LINE
SERVICE LINE
ALL LINES SHALL BE RED OR BLACK 1½" WIDE
16'-0" 9'-0" 4" 3'-0"
40'-0" 20'-0"
34'-0"
50'-0"
55'-0"

ELEV. OF FRONT WALL (REAR WALL DOTTED)
(FRONT)
TOP OF PLAYING WALL
(REAR)
FLUSH DOOR SIZE OPTIONAL
VISION PANEL
12' MIN.

ELEV. OF SIDE WALL
TOP OF PLAYING WALL
20'-0"
5'-0"
3"

ALL LINES ARE 1½" WIDE. FLOOR LINES ARE WHITE OR RED

RECEIVING LINE ON EACH SIDEWALL IS RED

PLAN
40'-0"
20'-0" 20'-0"
1'-6"
20'-0"
FRONT WALL
SERVICE LINE
SERVICE BOX
BACK WALL
SERVICE ZONE
DOOR
SHORT LINE
SIDEWALL
5'-0"

FOUR WALL COURT FOR HANDBALL AND RACQUETBALL

CRICKET

BOWLING CREASE
WICKET
POPPING CREASE
RETURN CREASE
8'-8"
4'-0" 1'-6"
66'-0"

DETAIL OF PITCH

WICKET 9" WIDE OVERALL & 2'-4" OUT OF GROUND
PITCH
66'-0"

420'-0" DIAM.
LIMIT OF PLAYING AREA REQUIRED

ELEV. OF FRONT WALL (REAR WALL DOTTED HGT. D-7'-0" S-6'-6")
(FRONT)
TOP OF PLAYING WALL
(REAR)
FLUSH DOOR
1'-5"
D-8'-2" S-5'-6"
D-22'-0" S-18'-0" MINIMUM DIMENSIONS

ELEV. OF SIDE WALL
D-31'-0" S-22'-0"
TOP OF PLAYING WALL 1½" RED LINE ON 45° BEVEL
D-5'-4"

DOOR HGT. 5'-6", WIDTH DOUBLES—3'-0", SINGLES 2'-6"

D—DOUBLES
S—SINGLES

SPECTATOR GLASS WALL PANELS AVAIL.

WALL AND FLOOR LINES ARE 1" WIDE, RED

PLAN
D-45'-0" S-32'-0"
D-15' S-10'
SIDE WALL
4'-6" RAD.
DOOR
S-18'-6"
S-9'-3"
D-25'-0"
D-12'-6"
FRONT WALL
BACK WALL

SQUASH

POLO
BOARDS 11"-0" HIGH
GOAL POSTS 10'-0" HIGH
480'-0" UNBOARDED 600'-0" BOARDED
24'-0"
900'-0"

ICE HOCKEY
200'-0" (61M)
20'-0"
5'-9"
3'-4" TO 4'-0" H SIDE BOARDS 3'-6" PREF.
PLAYERS BOXES
30'-0" 60'-0" 10'-0"
25'-0"
RED 2" LINE
FACE OFF SPOTS 6' RAD.
GOAL CAGE 4'-0" HIGH 6'-0" W, 1'-10" DEEP
BLUE 12" LINE
1'-6"
15'-0"
PENALTY SHOT LINE
15'-0" RAD (RECOM)
CENTER FACE-OFF 6" RAD. BLUE SPOT
PLAYING HGT. 10'-0" MIN.
SPECIAL FACE OFF 10' RAD.
GOAL CREASE 5'-9"
20'-0" RAD.
EQ 6'-0" RAD.
EQ
END BOARDS 3'-4" H MIN.
85'-0" (25.9M)
END ZONE
NEUTRAL ZONE
BLUE 12" LINE
RED 2" LINE
PENALTY BOX

NOTE: This information is for preliminary planning and design only. For final layouts and design investigate current rules and regulations of the athletic organization or other authority whose standards will govern.

Charles F. D. Egbert, AIA, Architect; Washington, D.C.

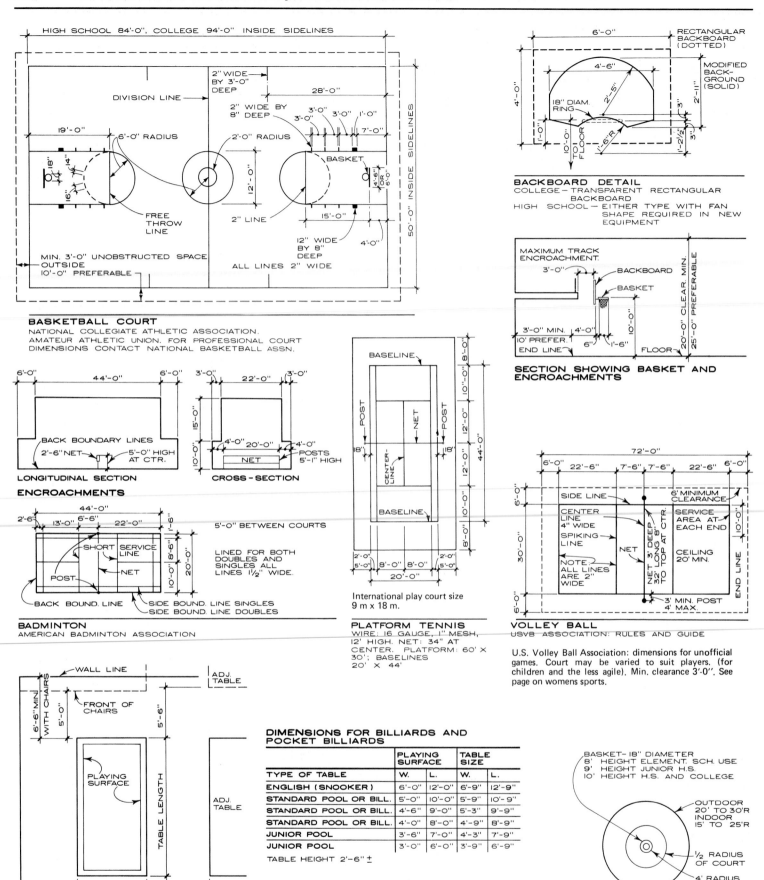

BASKETBALL COURT
NATIONAL COLLEGIATE ATHLETIC ASSOCIATION.
AMATEUR ATHLETIC UNION. FOR PROFESSIONAL COURT
DIMENSIONS CONTACT NATIONAL BASKETBALL ASSN.

BACKBOARD DETAIL
COLLEGE — TRANSPARENT RECTANGULAR
BACKBOARD
HIGH SCHOOL — EITHER TYPE WITH FAN
SHAPE REQUIRED IN NEW
EQUIPMENT

SECTION SHOWING BASKET AND ENCROACHMENTS

ENCROACHMENTS
LONGITUDINAL SECTION   CROSS-SECTION

BADMINTON
AMERICAN BADMINTON ASSOCIATION

5'-0" BETWEEN COURTS

LINED FOR BOTH
DOUBLES AND
SINGLES ALL
LINES 1½" WIDE.

PLATFORM TENNIS
WIRE: 16 GAUGE, 1" MESH,
12' HIGH. NET: 34" AT
CENTER. PLATFORM: 60' X
30'; BASELINES
20' X 44'

International play court size
9 m x 18 m.

VOLLEY BALL
USVB ASSOCIATION: RULES AND GUIDE

U.S. Volley Ball Association: dimensions for unofficial
games. Court may be varied to suit players. (for
children and the less agile). Min. clearance 3'-0". See
page on womens sports.

DIMENSIONS FOR BILLIARDS AND POCKET BILLIARDS

TYPE OF TABLE	PLAYING SURFACE		TABLE SIZE	
	W.	L.	W.	L.
ENGLISH (SNOOKER)	6'-0"	12'-0"	6'-9"	12'-9"
STANDARD POOL OR BILL.	5'-0"	10'-0"	5'-9"	10'-9"
STANDARD POOL OR BILL.	4'-6"	9'-0"	5'-3"	9'-9"
STANDARD POOL OR BILL.	4'-0"	8'-0"	4'-9"	8'-9"
JUNIOR POOL	3'-6"	7'-0"	4'-3"	7'-9"
JUNIOR POOL	3'-0"	6'-0"	3'-9"	6'-9"

TABLE HEIGHT 2'-6" ±

BILLIARDS AND POCKET BILLIARDS (POOL)
BILLIARD CONGRESS OF AMERICA

BASKET- 18" DIAMETER
8' HEIGHT ELEMENT. SCH. USE
9' HEIGHT JUNIOR H.S.
10' HEIGHT H.S. AND COLLEGE

OUTDOOR
20' TO 30'R
INDOOR
15' TO 25'R

½ RADIUS
OF COURT

4' RADIUS

GOAL-HI COURT

NOTE: This information is for preliminary planning and design only. For final layouts and design investigate current rules and regulations of the athletic organization or other authority whose standards will govern.

Charles F. D. Egbert, AIA, Architect; Washington, D.C.

1 RECREATION

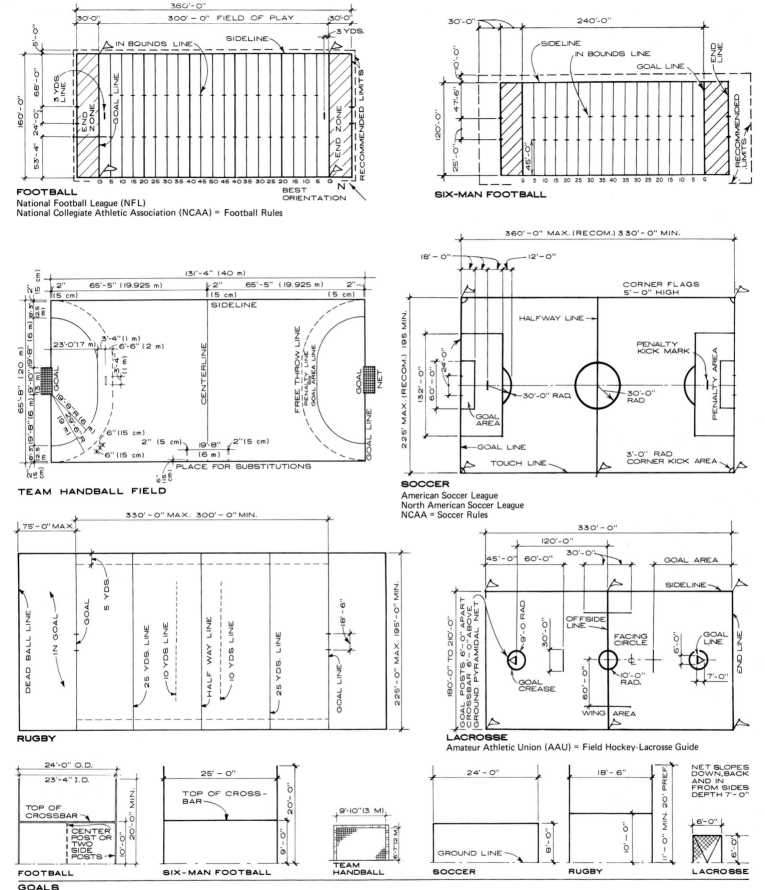

FOOTBALL
National Football League (NFL)
National Collegiate Athletic Association (NCAA) = Football Rules

SIX-MAN FOOTBALL

TEAM HANDBALL FIELD

SOCCER
American Soccer League
North American Soccer League
NCAA = Soccer Rules

RUGBY

LACROSSE
Amateur Athletic Union (AAU) = Field Hockey-Lacrosse Guide

FOOTBALL   SIX-MAN FOOTBALL   TEAM HANDBALL   SOCCER   RUGBY   LACROSSE

GOALS

NOTE

This information is for preliminary planning and design only. For final layouts and design investigate current rules and regulations of the athletic organization or other authority whose standards will govern.

Charles F. D. Egbert, AIA; Architect; Washington, D. C.

RECREATION **1**

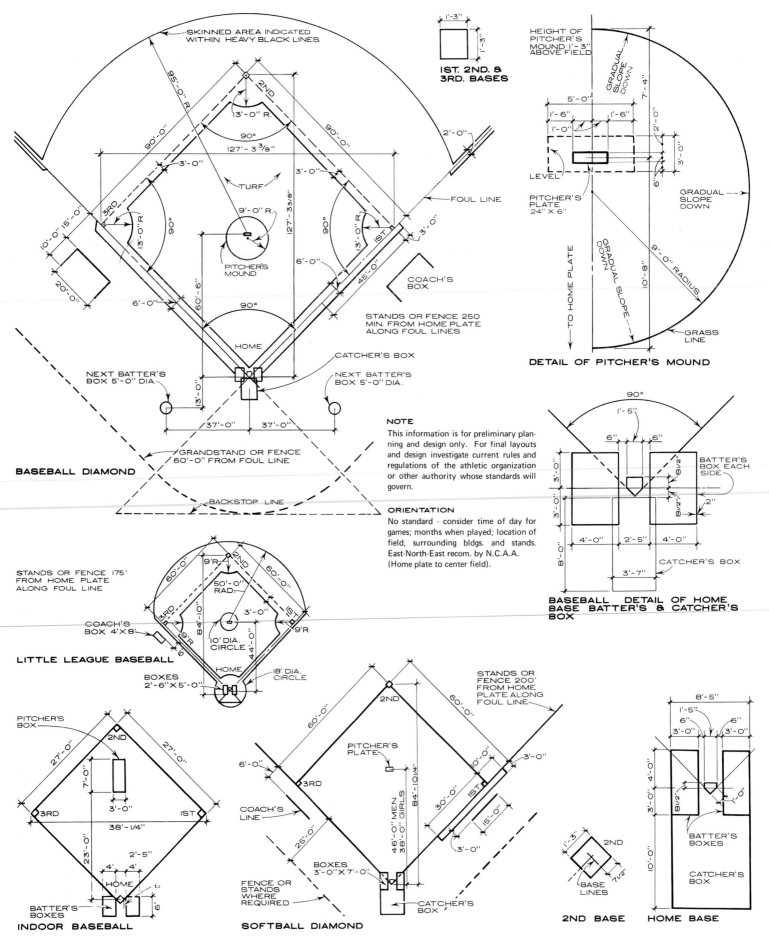

SKINNED AREA INDICATED WITHIN HEAVY BLACK LINES

IST. 2ND. & 3RD. BASES

HEIGHT OF PITCHER'S MOUND 1'-3" ABOVE FIELD

GRADUAL SLOPE DOWN

PITCHER'S PLATE 24" X 6"

LEVEL

TO HOME PLATE

GRADUAL SLOPE DOWN

GRADUAL SLOPE DOWN

9'-0" RADIUS

GRASS LINE

DETAIL OF PITCHER'S MOUND

95'-0" R

90'-0"

90'-0"

2ND

13'-0" R

90°

127'- 3³/₈"

3'-0"

TURF

2'-0"

FOUL LINE

3RD

13'-0" R

9'-0" R

9'-0" R

90°

1ST

3'-0"

3'-0"

127'- 3³/₈"

90°

10'-0" 15'-0"

90°

20'-0"

6'-0"

PITCHER'S MOUND

6'-0"

45'-0"

COACH'S BOX

60'-0"

90°

STANDS OR FENCE 250 MIN. FROM HOME PLATE ALONG FOUL LINES

HOME

CATCHER'S BOX

NEXT BATTER'S BOX 5'-0" DIA.

NEXT BATTER'S BOX 5'-0" DIA.

3'

37'-0"   37'-0"

GRANDSTAND OR FENCE 60'-0" FROM FOUL LINE

BASEBALL DIAMOND

BACKSTOP LINE

NOTE

This information is for preliminary planning and design only. For final layouts and design investigate current rules and regulations of the athletic organization or other authority whose standards will govern.

ORIENTATION

No standard - consider time of day for games; months when played; location of field, surrounding bldgs. and stands. East-North-East recom. by N.C.A.A. (Home plate to center field).

90°

1'- 5"

6"   6"

3'-0"

3'-0"

BATTER'S BOX EACH SIDE

8½"

4'-0"   2'-5"   4'-0"

8½"

2"

8'-0"

3'-7"

CATCHER'S BOX

BASEBALL DETAIL OF HOME BASE BATTER'S & CATCHER'S BOX

STANDS OR FENCE 175' FROM HOME PLATE ALONG FOUL LINE

60'-0"   60'-0"

2ND

9'R   9'R

50'-0" RAD.

3'-0"

3RD   1ST

9'R   9'R

84'-10"

10' DIA. CIRCLE

44'-0"

COACH'S BOX 4'X 8'

HOME

18' DIA. CIRCLE

LITTLE LEAGUE BASEBALL

BOXES 2'-6"X5'-0"

PITCHER'S BOX

27'-0"   27'-0"

2ND

7'-0"

3RD   1ST

3'-0"

38'-1/4"

23'-0"

2'-5"

4'   4'

HOME

BATTER'S BOXES

INDOOR BASEBALL

STANDS OR FENCE 200' FROM HOME PLATE ALONG FOUL LINE

60'-0"   60'-0"

2ND

6'-0"

PITCHER'S PLATE

3RD   1ST

3'-0"

0'-0"

84'-10¼"

46'-0" MEN 38'-0" GIRLS

30'-0"

15'-0"

COACH'S LINE

25'-0"

3'-0"

BOXES 3'-0"X7'-0"

FENCE OR STANDS WHERE REQUIRED

CATCHER'S BOX

SOFTBALL DIAMOND

8'-5"

1'-5"

6"   6"

3'-0"   3'-0"

4'-0"

8½"

1'-0"

3'-0"

BATTER'S BOXES

10'-0"

CATCHER'S BOX

HOME BASE

1'-3"

2ND

7½"

BASE LINES

2ND BASE

Charles F. D. Egbert, AIA; Architect; Washington, D. C.

1   **RECREATION**

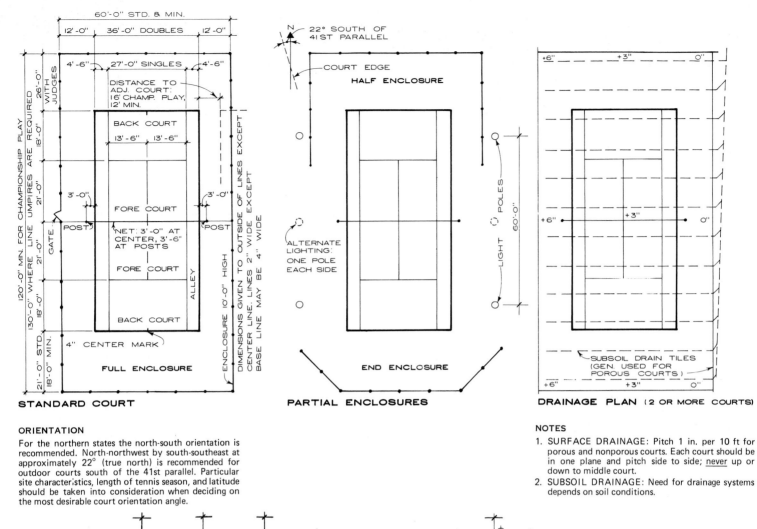

STANDARD COURT

PARTIAL ENCLOSURES

DRAINAGE PLAN (2 OR MORE COURTS)

ORIENTATION

For the northern states the north-south orientation is recommended. North-northwest by south-southeast at approximately 22° (true north) is recommended for outdoor courts south of the 41st parallel. Particular site characteristics, length of tennis season, and latitude should be taken into consideration when deciding on the most desirable court orientation angle.

NOTES

1. SURFACE DRAINAGE: Pitch 1 in. per 10 ft for porous and nonporous courts. Each court should be in one plane and pitch side to side; <u>never</u> up or down to middle court.
2. SUBSOIL DRAINAGE: Need for drainage systems depends on soil conditions.

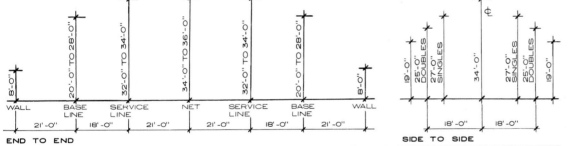

END TO END

SIDE TO SIDE

INDOOR TENNIS CEILING HEIGHT REQUIREMENTS

NOTE

This information is for preliminary planning and design only. For final layouts and design investigate current rules and regulations of the athletic organization or other authority whose standards will govern.

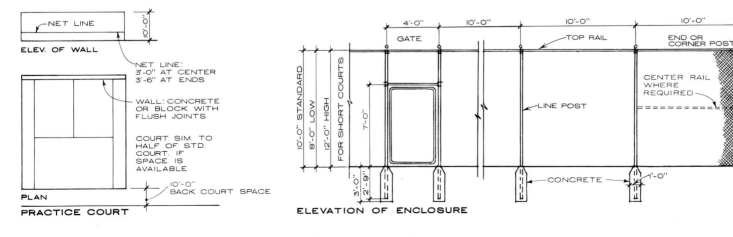

ELEV. OF WALL

PLAN

PRACTICE COURT

ELEVATION OF ENCLOSURE

NET LINE:
3'-0" AT CENTER
3'-6" AT ENDS

WALL: CONCRETE OR BLOCK WITH FLUSH JOINTS

COURT SIM. TO HALF OF STD. COURT. IF SPACE IS AVAILABLE

10'-0" BACK COURT SPACE

Pecsok, Jelliffe & Randall, AIA, Architects; Indianapolis, Indiana

RECREATION **1**

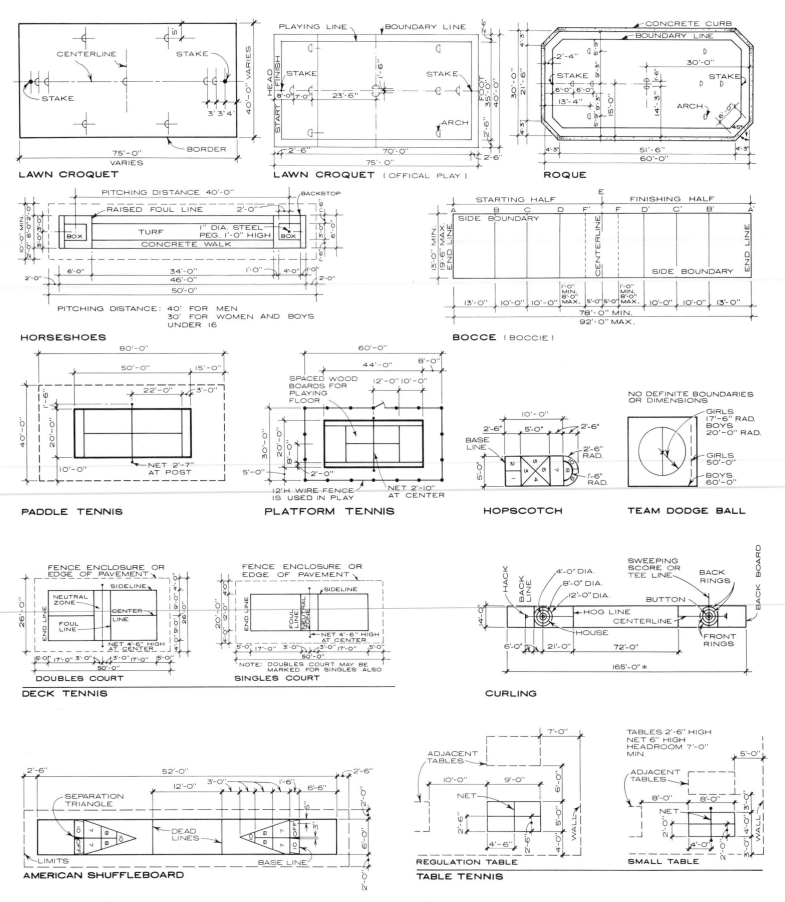

LAWN CROQUET

LAWN CROQUET (OFFICAL PLAY)

ROQUE

HORSESHOES

PITCHING DISTANCE: 40' FOR MEN
30' FOR WOMEN AND BOYS
UNDER 16

BOCCE (BOCCIE)

PADDLE TENNIS

PLATFORM TENNIS

HOPSCOTCH

TEAM DODGE BALL

DECK TENNIS

DOUBLES COURT

SINGLES COURT

CURLING

AMERICAN SHUFFLEBOARD

TABLE TENNIS

REGULATION TABLE

SMALL TABLE

NOTE: This information is for preliminary planning and design only. For final layouts and design investigate current rules and regulations of the athletic organization or other authority whose standards
will govern.

Charles F. D. Egbert, AIA, Architect; Washington, D.C.

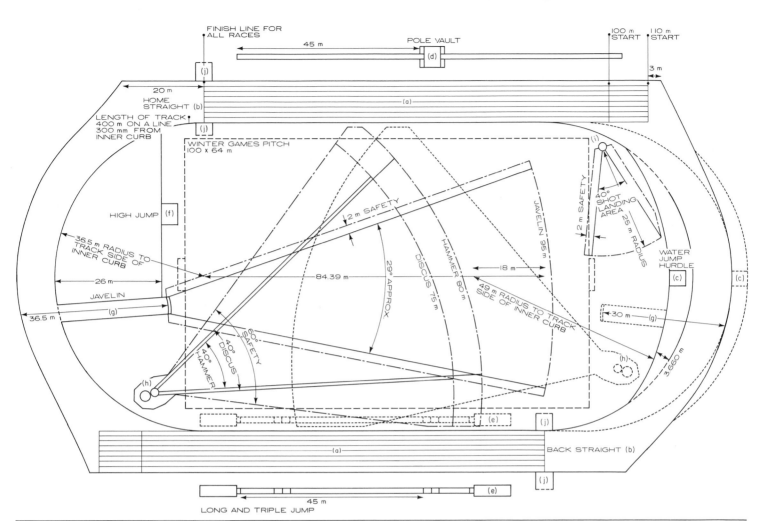

FINISH LINE FOR ALL RACES

POLE VAULT

100 m START   110 m START

45 m

(d)

3 m

20 m

HOME STRAIGHT (b)

(a)

(j)

LENGTH OF TRACK 400 m ON A LINE 300 mm FROM INNER CURB

(j)

WINTER GAMES PITCH 100 × 64 m

2 m SAFETY

2 m SAFETY

40° SHOT LANDING AREA

HIGH JUMP   (f)

36.5 m RADIUS TO TRACK SIDE OF INNER CURB

JAVELIN 95 m

25 m RADIUS

WATER JUMP HURDLE

(i)

29° APPROX

DISCUS 75 m

HAMMER 80 m

18 m

49 m RADIUS TO TRACK SIDE OF INNER CURB

(c)

(c)

26 m

84.39 m

JAVELIN

(g)

36.5 m

60° SAFETY

40° HAMMER

40° DISCUS

30 m

3.660 m

(h)

(h)

(e)

(j)

BACK STRAIGHT (b)

(a)

(j)

LONG AND TRIPLE JUMP

45 m

(e)

LAYOUT GUIDE FOR 400 m RUNNING TRACK AND FIELD EVENT LOCATIONS

NOTES

(a) Number of lanes
(b) Straights
(c) Steeplechase and water jump
(d) Pole vault
(e) Long and triple jumps

(f) High jump
(g) Javelin
(h) Hammer and discus in cage
(i) Putting and shot
(j) Paved areas

NATIONAL AND INTERNATIONAL COMPETITION

The diagram indicates how a 400 m track with a synthetic surface might be laid out for national and international competition. Different arrangements are possible to suit particular circumstances. For high level competition, however, alternatives for the siting of the throwing circles are of necessity limited if maximum distances are to be safely thrown. For Rules of Competition reference should be made to the Handbook of the International Amateur Athletic Federation.

TRACK AND LANES

The length of the running track should be not less than 400 m. The track should be not less than 7.32 m in width and should, if possible, be bordered on the inside with concrete or other suitable material, approximately 50 mm high, minimum 50 mm wide. The curb may be raised to permit surface water to drain away, in which case a maximum height of 65 mm must not be exceeded.

Where it is not possible for the inner edge of the running track to have a raised border, the inner edge shall be marked with lines 50 mm wide.

The measurement shall be taken 0.30 m outward from the inner border of the track or, where no border exists, 0.20 m from the line marking the inside of the track.

In all races up to and including 400 m, each competitor shall have a separate lane, with a minimum width

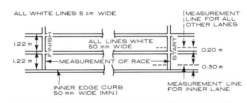

ALL WHITE LINES 5 cm WIDE

MEASUREMENT LINE FOR ALL OTHER LANES

1.22 m

ALL LINES WHITE 50 mm WIDE

1.22 m

MEASUREMENT OF RACE

0.20 m

0.30 m

INNER EDGE CURB 50 mm WIDE (MIN.)

MEASUREMENT LINE FOR INNER LANE

METHOD OF MARKING LANES

of 1.22 m and a maximum width of 1.25 m to be marked by lines 50 mm in width. The inner lane shall be measured as stated in the preceding text, but the remaining lanes shall be measured 0.20 m from the outer edges of the lines.

In international meetings the track should allow for at least six lanes and, where possible, for eight lanes, particularly for major international events.

The maximum allowance for lateral inclination of tracks shall not exceed 1 : 100, and the inclination in the running direction shall not exceed 1 : 1000.

The lateral inclination of the track should wherever possible be toward the inside lane.

SURFACE

Synthetic materials provide a consistently good surface capable of continuous and unlimited use in most weather conditions. Maintenance is minimal, consisting of periodic cleaning by hosing down or brushing, the repainting when necessary of the line markings, and an occasional repair.

Cinder surfaces require considerable maintenance by a skilled groundsman every time a track is used. They are not all-weather and seldom provide a consistently good running surface. They are, however, much cheaper to construct and are suitable for club use and training.

On cinder tracks an extra lane is necessary so that

sprint and hurdle events can be run on the six outer lanes to avoid the inner lane, which is subject to heavy use during long distance events.

ORIENTATION

It is often difficult to reconcile the requirements of wind directions and the need to avoid an approach into the setting sun. For these reasons it is now becoming common practice to provide, where possible, alternative directions for running, jumping, and throwing.

NUMBER OF LANES

Synthetic all-weather:

International competition:	8 lanes (9.76 m)
Area or regional competition:	6 lanes (7.32 m)

Cinder:

International competition:	8 lanes (9.76 m)
	9 lanes (straights)
Area or regional competition:	7 lanes (8.54 m)

THE FINISH

Two white posts shall denote the extremities of the finish line, and shall be placed at least 30 cm from the edge of the track.

The finish posts shall be of rigid construction about 1.4 m high, 80 mm wide, and 20 mm thick.

FORMULA FOR OTHER TRACK PROPORTIONS

Where a track of wider or narrower proportions or of different length is required, the appropriate dimensions can be calculated from the following formula:

$$L = 2P + 2\pi(R + 300\ mm)$$

where L = length of track (m)
P = length of parallels or distance apart of centers of curves (m)
R = radius to track side of inner curb (m)
π = 3.1416 (not $^{22}/_7$)

It is recommended that the radius of the semicircles should not normally be less than 32 m or more than 42 m for a 400 m circuit.

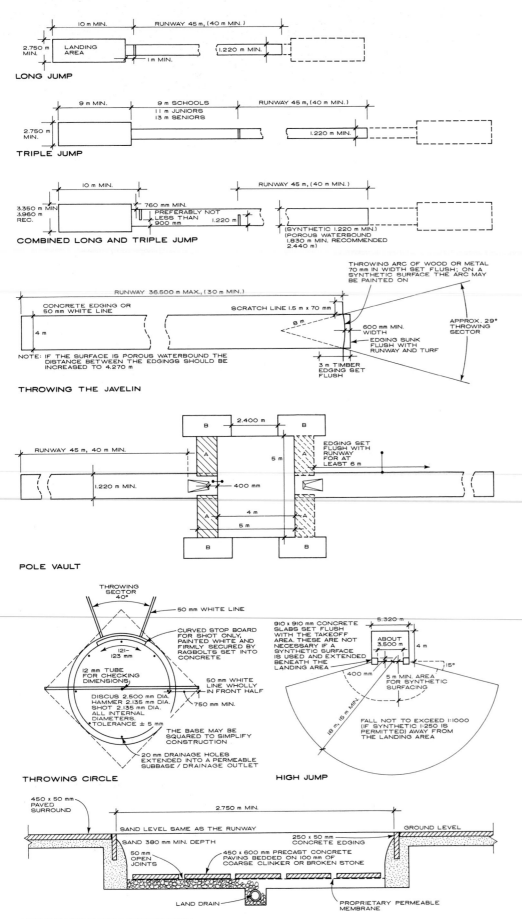

LONG JUMP

10 m MIN.
RUNWAY 45 m, (40 m MIN.)
2.750 m MIN.
LANDING AREA
1 m MIN.
1.220 m MIN.

TRIPLE JUMP

9 m MIN.
9 m SCHOOLS
11 m JUNIORS
13 m SENIORS
RUNWAY 45 m, (40 m MIN.)
2.750 m MIN.
1.220 m MIN.

COMBINED LONG AND TRIPLE JUMP

10 m MIN.
760 mm MIN.
PREFERABLY NOT LESS THAN 900 mm
1.220 m
RUNWAY 45 m, (40 m MIN.)
3.350 m MIN.
3.960 m REC.
(SYNTHETIC 1.220 m MIN.)
(POROUS WATERBOUND 1.830 m MIN. RECOMMENDED 2.440 m)

THROWING THE JAVELIN

RUNWAY 36.500 m MAX., (30 m MIN.)
CONCRETE EDGING OR 50 mm WHITE LINE
4 m
SCRATCH LINE 1.5 m x 70 mm
8 m
600 mm MIN. WIDTH
EDGING SUNK FLUSH WITH RUNWAY AND TURF
3 m TIMBER EDGING SET FLUSH
THROWING ARC OF WOOD OR METAL 70 mm IN WIDTH SET FLUSH; ON A SYNTHETIC SURFACE THE ARC MAY BE PAINTED ON
APPROX. 29° THROWING SECTOR
NOTE: IF THE SURFACE IS POROUS WATERBOUND THE DISTANCE BETWEEN THE EDGINGS SHOULD BE INCREASED TO 4.270 m

POLE VAULT

B
2.400 m
B
A
5 m
A
EDGING SET FLUSH WITH RUNWAY FOR AT LEAST 6 m
RUNWAY 45 m, 40 m MIN.
1.220 m MIN.
400 mm
A
4 m
A
5 m
B
B

THROWING CIRCLE

THROWING SECTOR 40°
50 mm WHITE LINE
CURVED STOP BOARD FOR SHOT ONLY, PAINTED WHITE AND FIRMLY SECURED BY RAGBOLTS SET INTO CONCRETE
121–123 mm
12 mm TUBE FOR CHECKING DIMENSIONS
DISCUS 2.500 mm DIA.
HAMMER 2.135 mm DIA.
SHOT 2.135 mm DIA.
ALL INTERNAL DIAMETERS.
TOLERANCE ± 5 mm
50 mm WHITE LINE WHOLLY IN FRONT HALF
750 mm MIN.
THE BASE MAY BE SQUARED TO SIMPLIFY CONSTRUCTION
20 mm DRAINAGE HOLES EXTENDED INTO A PERMEABLE SUBBASE / DRAINAGE OUTLET

HIGH JUMP

910 x 910 mm CONCRETE SLABS SET FLUSH WITH THE TAKEOFF AREA. THESE ARE NOT NECESSARY IF A SYNTHETIC SURFACE IS USED AND EXTENDED BENEATH THE LANDING AREA
5.320 m
ABOUT 3.500 m
4 m
15°
400 mm
5 m MIN. AREA FOR SYNTHETIC SURFACING
18 m, 15 m MIN.
FALL NOT TO EXCEED 1:1000 (IF SYNTHETIC 1:250 IS PERMITTED) AWAY FROM THE LANDING AREA

SECTION OF SAND LANDING AREA

450 x 50 mm PAVED SURROUND
2.750 m MIN.
SAND LEVEL SAME AS THE RUNWAY
GROUND LEVEL
SAND 380 mm MIN. DEPTH
250 x 50 mm CONCRETE EDGING
50 mm OPEN JOINTS
450 x 600 mm PRECAST CONCRETE PAVING BEDDED ON 100 mm OF COARSE CLINKER OR BROKEN STONE
LAND DRAIN
PROPRIETARY PERMEABLE MEMBRANE

400 m TRACK AND FIELD EVENTS—CONSTRUCTION DETAILS

These details are based on international standards. For additional information consult the IAAF, which is the International Amateur Athletic Federation. These details were provided by the National Playing Fields Association, London, England.

NOTE

To avoid adverse wind conditions during competition, landing areas for the long and triple jumps are desirable at both ends of the runway. A surround of paving slabs (450 x 600 mm) is an advantage. Takeoff board to be of wood or other suitable rigid material, set level with surface and painted white. See detail.

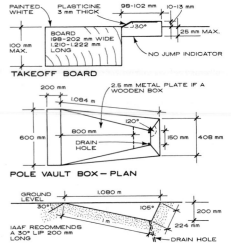

TAKEOFF BOARD

PAINTED WHITE
PLASTICINE 3 mm THICK
98–102 mm
10–13 mm
100 mm MAX.
BOARD 198–202 mm WIDE 1.210–1.222 mm LONG
30°
25 mm MAX.
NO JUMP INDICATOR

POLE VAULT BOX – PLAN

200 mm
1.084 m
2.5 mm METAL PLATE IF A WOODEN BOX
600 mm
800 mm
120°
DRAIN HOLE
150 mm
408 mm

POLE VAULT BOX – SECTION

GROUND LEVEL
1.080 m
30°
105°
200 mm
224 mm
DRAIN HOLE
IAAF RECOMMENDS A 30° LIP 200 mm LONG

POLE VAULT

A = Detachable soft landing units each 1 x 2 m.
B = Concrete platforms each 1 x 2.450 m x 75 mm thick minimum and set level with runway surface.

The soft landing area to be 5 x 5 m minimum. The distance between uprights or extension arms to be 3.660 m minimum/4.370 m maximum. A larger soft landing unit with a 1.300 m extension for the pole vault box cutout giving a total size of 5 x 6.300 m may be provided. The diagram shows a double runway with detachable A units and thus gives a choice of runways according to the wind direction.

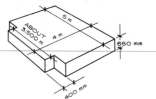

HIGH JUMP SOFT LANDING AREA

ABOUT 3.500 m
5 m
4 m
650 mm
400 mm

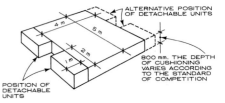

POLE VAULT SOFT LANDING AREA

4 m
5 m
2 m
ALTERNATIVE POSITION OF DETACHABLE UNITS
800 mm. THE DEPTH OF CUSHIONING VARIES ACCORDING TO THE STANDARD OF COMPETITION
POSITION OF DETACHABLE UNITS

For outdoor use soft landing units should be laid on duckboards on an ash base or other suitable materials (e.g., precast concrete paving on a porous base with 50 mm open joints).

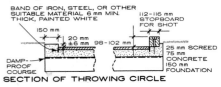

SECTION OF THROWING CIRCLE

BAND OF IRON, STEEL, OR OTHER SUITABLE MATERIAL 6 mm MIN. THICK, PAINTED WHITE
112–116 mm
STOPBOARD FOR SHOT
150 mm
20 mm ±6 mm
98–102 mm
25 mm SCREED
75 mm CONCRETE
150 mm FOUNDATION
DAMP-PROOF COURSE

GENERAL

Public pools are generally considered to be those that belong to municipalities, schools, country clubs, hotels, motels, apartments, and resorts. Permits for their construction are required in most areas from local and state boards of health as well as the departments of building, plumbing, and electricity.

Community pools should be integrated with existing and projected recreational facilities, such as picnic areas and parks, for maximum usage. Transportation access should be good, and there should be ample parking space. In a hot climate, enough shade should be provided, particularly in the lounging areas, and be so located that it can be easily converted to spectator space by erecting bleachers.

POOL DESIGN

Formerly most public pools were designed to meet competitive swimming requirements. The trend today is to provide for all-around use. The following should be considered:

1. Ratio of shallow water to deep water. Formerly 60% of pool area 5 ft deep and less was considered to be adequate. Now 80% is considered more realistic.
2. Ratio of loungers to bathers. Generally, no more than one-third of people attending a public pool are in the water at one time. Consequently the 6 to 8 ft walks formerly surrounding pools and used for lounging have been enlarged so that lounging area now approximates pool size.
3. For capacity formula see "Public Swimming Pool Capacity" diagram on another page.

RECOMMENDED DIMENSIONS

RELATED DIVING EQUIPMENT		MINIMUM DIMENSIONS								MINIMUM WIDTH OF POOL AT:		
MAX. BOARD LENGTH	MAX. HEIGHT OVER WATER	D_1	D_2	R	L_1	L_2	L_3	L_4	L_5	PT.A	PT.B	PT.C
10'	2/3 m 26"	2.13 m 7'-0"	2.59 m 8'-6"	1.68 m 5'-6"	0.76 m 2'-6"	2.44 m 8'-0"	3.20 m 10'-6"	2.13 m 7'-0"	8.53 m 28'-0"	4.88 m 16'-0"	5.49 m 18'-0"	5.49 m 18'-0"
12'	3/4 m 30"	2.29 m 7'-6"	2.74 m 9'-0"	1.83 m 6'-0"	0.91 m 3'-0"	2.74 m 9'-0"	3.66 m 12'-0"	1.22 m 4'-0"	8.53 m 28'-0"	5.49 m 18'-0"	6.10 m 20'-0"	6.10 m 20'-0"
16'	1 m	2.59 m 8'-6"	3.05 m 10'-0"	2.13 m 7'-0"	1.22 m 4'-0"	3.05 m 10'-0"	4.57 m 15'-0"	0.61 m 2'-0"	9.45 m 31'-0"	6.10 m 20'-0"	6.71 m 22'-0"	6.71 m 22'-0"
16'	3 m	3.35 m 11'-0"	3.66 m 12'-0"	2.59 m 8'-6"	1.83 m 6'-0"	3.20 m 10'-6"	6.40 m 21'-0"	0	11.43 m 37'-6"	6.70 m 22'-0"	7.32 m 24'-0"	7.32 m 24'-0"

Data source: National Swimming Pool Institute.

L_2, L_3, and L_4 combined represent the minimum distance from the tip of board to pool wall opposite diving equipment.

For board heights exceeding 3 m in height or platform diving shall comply with dimensional requirements of FINA, AAU, NCAA, N.F., etc.

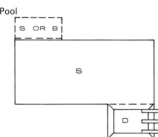

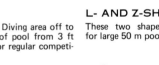

NOTE: Placement of boards shall observe the following minimum dimensions. With multiple board installations minimum pool widths must be increased accordingly.

1 m or deck level board to pool side	9' (2.74 m)
3 m board to pool side	11' (3.35 m)
1 m or deck level board to 3 m board	10' (3.05 m)
1 m or deck level to another 1 m or deck level board	8' (2.44 m)
3 m to another 3 m board	10' (3.05 m)

T-SHAPED POOL

Provides large shallow area(s). Diving area off to one side. Water in large part of pool from 3 ft 6 in. to 5 ft deep, adequate for regular competitive events.

L- AND Z-SHAPED POOL

These two shapes generally desired for large 50 m pools.

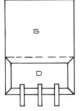

RECTANGULAR POOL

Standard design. Good for competitive swimming and indoor pool design. Shallow area often inadequate.

FAN SHAPED POOL

Successful where there is a high percentage of children. Largest area for shallow depth. Deep area can be roped off or separated by bulkhead.

BULKHEAD ALLOWS FOR COMPETITIVE MEETS

FREE FORM POOL

Kidney and oval shapes are the most common free forms. Use only where competitive meets are not a consideration.

MODIFIED L POOL

Provides for separate diving area. Shallow area with 4 ft min. depth may be roped off for competitive meets.

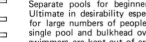

MULTIPLE POOLS

Separate pools for beginners, divers and swimmers. Ultimate in desirability especially if pool is intended for large numbers of people. Variation at left shows single pool and bulkhead over it with advantage that swimmers are kept out of area reserved for beginners. Both designs may use common filtration system.

WADING POOLS

Generally provided in connection with community and family club pools. Placed away from swimming area to avoid congestion. If near swimming pool, wading area should be fenced off for children's protection. To add play appeal provide spray fittings and small fountains in pool. Also provide seats and benches for adults who accompany children to pool.

PUBLIC POOL SHAPES

NOTE: S = swimming pool, D = diving pool, B = beginner's pool.

R. Jackson Smith, AIA; Designed Environments, Inc.; Stamford, Connecticut

National Swimming Pool Institute; Washington, D.C.

NOTES

1. The drawings below illustrate the use of a 7-point dimension grid that expresses the minimum desirable dimensions to be used when either specifying or designing a rectangular shaped pool for residential use.
2. Width, length, and depth dimensions may apply to residential pools of any shape.
3. The minimum length with diving board and wading area is 30 ft. The average length of a residential pool is 30 to 40 ft.
4. Standards for residential swimming pools have been published by the National Swimming Pool Institute (1972). The Fédération Internationale de Natation Amateur has published a new handbook, which is available from the AAU in Indianapolis, Indiana.

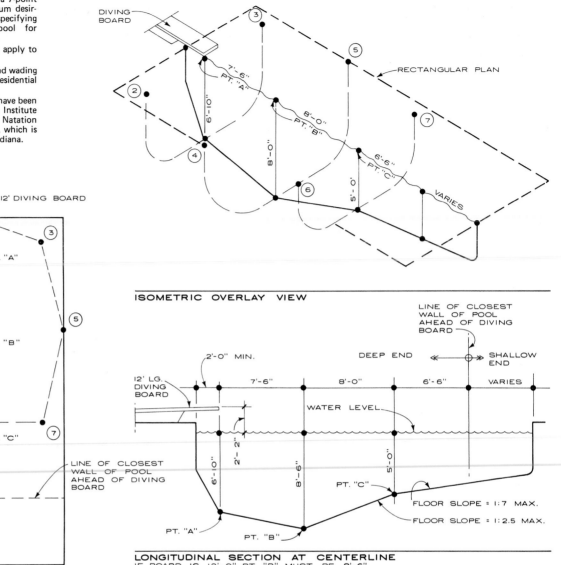

ISOMETRIC OVERLAY VIEW

LONGITUDINAL SECTION AT CENTERLINE
IF BOARD IS 12'-0" PT. "B" MUST BE 8'-6"
IF BOARD IS 10'-0" PT. "B" MUST BE 8'-0"

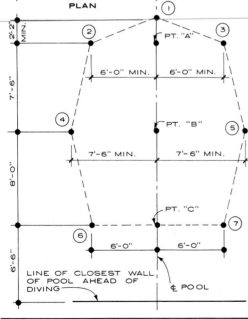

7-POINT GRID DIMENSION PLAN

Haver, Nunn and Collamer; Phoenix, Arizona

PERMITS AND RESTRICTIONS

Required in most areas from building, health, plumbing, and electrical departments and zoning boards. Check for setback restrictions and easements covering power and telephone lines, sewers, and storm drains.

SITE CONSIDERATIONS

Check the site for the following conditions, each of which will considerably increase the cost.

1. Fill that is more than 3 ft below pool deck.
2. Hard rock that requires drilling and blasting.
3. Underground water or springs that necessitate pumping or drains.
4. Accessibility of the site for mechanical equipment, minimum entry 8 ft wide by 7 ft 8 in. high, with a grade easy enough for a truck to reach the site.
5. Place the pool where it will get the most sun during swimming season. If possible, place deep end so a diver dives away from, not into, the afternoon sun. Avoid overhanging tree branches near the pool.
6. The slope of the site should be as level as possible; a steep slope requires retaining walls for the pool.

CONSTRUCTION AND SHAPES

Pools may be made of reinforced concrete (poured on the job, precast, or gunite sprayed), concrete block, steel, aluminum, or plastic with or without block backup. Concrete, aluminum, fiberglass, and steel pools are available in any shape—rectangular, square, kidney, oval or free form. Complete plastic installations and plastic pool liners with various backups are available only in manufacturers' standard shapes and sizes.

A rectangular pool is the most practical if site permits, since it gives the longest swimming distance.

POOL CAPACITY

Rule of thumb: 36 sq ft for each swimmer, 100 sq ft for each diver. A pool of 20 x 40 ft accommodates 14 persons at a time, but since not everyone is in the pool at once, pool and surroundings are adequate for 30 to 40 people.

FILTER REQUIREMENTS

Filter, motor, and electrical equipment shall be sheltered and waterproofed.

1 RECREATION

LENGTH OF POOLS

25 yards is the minimum length for American records, and meets interscholastic and intercollegiate requirements. (Pool should be 75'-1½'' long to allow for electronic timing panels at one end.)

Standards for International Competition are shown on 50 meter pool page.

WIDTH OF POOLS

Drawing below shows 7' lanes, with pool width of 45' (6 lanes). Strictly competitive pools should have 8' lanes, with pool width of 83' (10 lanes). Minimum widths include additional 18'' width outside lanes on both sides of pool.

NOTES

Gutters at sides of pool are desirable to reduce wave action in swimming meets or water polo. See lighting standards and diving board standards on other pages of this series for additional requirements for competitive pools.

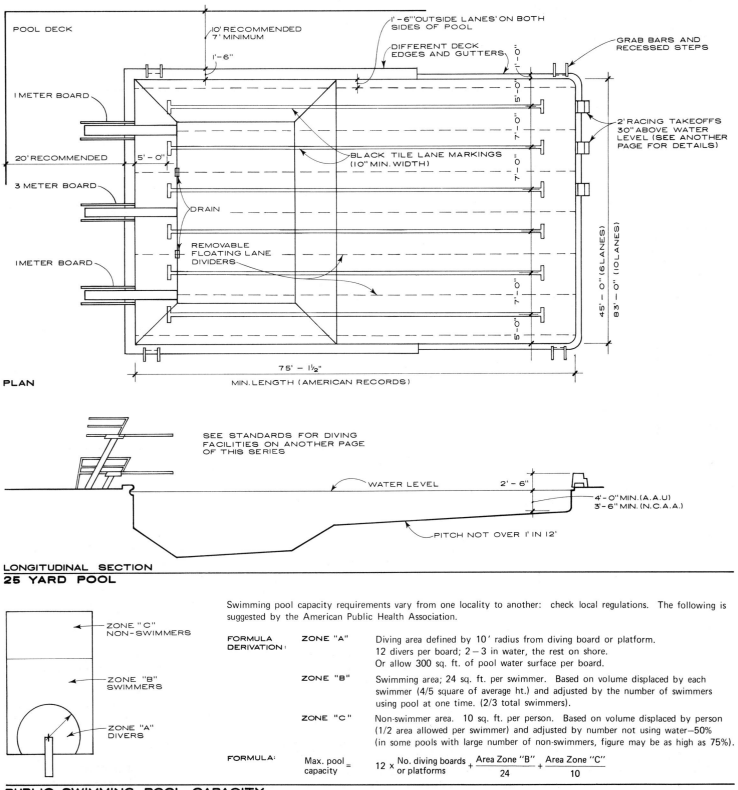

PLAN

**LONGITUDINAL SECTION
25 YARD POOL**

Swimming pool capacity requirements vary from one locality to another: check local regulations. The following is suggested by the American Public Health Association.

FORMULA DERIVATION:	ZONE "A"	Diving area defined by 10' radius from diving board or platform. 12 divers per board; 2 – 3 in water, the rest on shore. Or allow 300 sq. ft. of pool water surface per board.
	ZONE "B"	Swimming area; 24 sq. ft. per swimmer. Based on volume displaced by each swimmer (4/5 square of average ht.) and adjusted by the number of swimmers using pool at one time. (2/3 total swimmers).
	ZONE "C"	Non-swimmer area. 10 sq. ft. per person. Based on volume displaced by person (1/2 area allowed per swimmer) and adjusted by number not using water—50% (in some pools with large number of non-swimmers, figure may be as high as 75%).
FORMULA:	Max. pool capacity =	$12 \times$ No. diving boards or platforms $+ \dfrac{\text{Area Zone "B"}}{24} + \dfrac{\text{Area Zone "C"}}{10}$

PUBLIC SWIMMING POOL CAPACITY

R. Jackson Smith, AIA; Designed Environment, Inc.; Stamford, Connecticut

GENERAL NOTES

For judging competitive meets, F.I.N.A. officials recommend the springboard and diving platform arrangement indicated below in plan. Diving dimensions meet minimum F.I.N.A. standards. Fifty meters is minimum length for world records.

NOTE

*Length should be 50.03 m allowing an extra .03 m to compensate for possible future tile facing, structural defects and electrical timing panels.

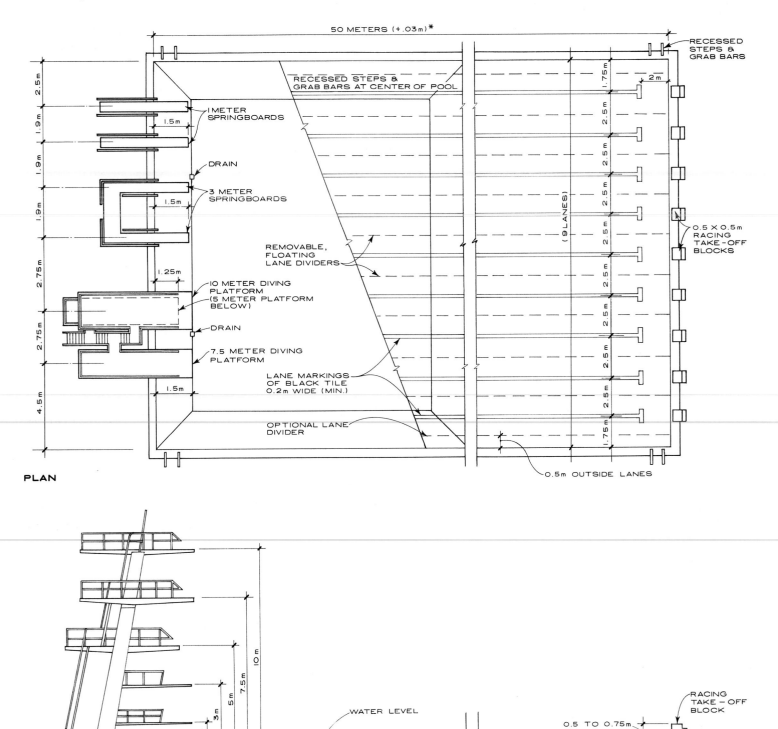

PLAN

LONGITUDINAL SECTION

R. Jackson Smith, AIA; Designed Environment, Inc.; Stamford, Connecticut

GENERAL NOTE

Each **DESIGN VEHICLE** in Groups I, II, and III represents a composite of the critical dimensions of the real vehicles within each group below. Parking lot dimensions on a following page are based on these groups and dimensions. For parking purposes, both compact and standard size vehicles are in Group II. Turning dimensions R, R1, and C are shown on page 52.

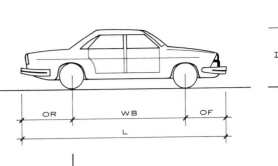

DESIGN VEHICLE

GROUP I		SMALL CARS
L	Length	15'-5''
W	Width	5'-10''
H	Height	4'-10''
WB	Wheelbase	9'-2''
OF	Overhang front	2'-6''
OR	Overhang rear	3'-9''
OS	Overhang sides	0'-7''
T	Track	4'-9''

GROUP II		COMPACTS
L	Length	16'-11''
W	Width	6'-3''
H	Height	5'-0''
WB	Wheelbase	10'-0''
OF	Overhang front	2'-8''
OR	Overhang rear	4'-3''
OS	Overhang sides	0'-8''
T	Track	4'-10''

GROUP III		STANDARD
L	Length	17'-9''
W	Width	6'-8''
H	Height	5'-2''
WB	Wheelbase	10'-7''
OF	Overhang front	2'-10''
OR	Overhang rear	4'-4''
OS	Overhang side	0'-9''
T	Track	5'-2''

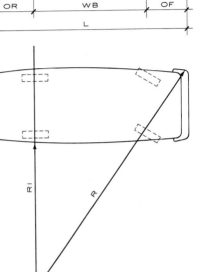

GROUP IV		LARGE CARS
L	Length	18'-0''
W	Width	6'-8''
H	Height	5'-4''
WB	Wheelbase	10'-8''
OF	Overhang front	2'-11''
OR	Overhang rear	4'-5''
OS	Overhang side	0'-9''
T	Track	5'-2''

LARGE VEHICLE DIMENSIONS*

VEHICLE	(L) LENGTH	(W) WIDTH	(OR) OVERHANG REAR
Intercity bus	45'-0''	9'-0''	10'-1''
City bus	40'-0''	8'-6''	6'-6''
School bus	39'-6''	8'-0''	12'-8''
Ambulance	20'-10 1/4''	6'-11''	5'-4''
Paramedic van	18'-0''	6'-7''	5'-2''
Hearse	20'-10 1/4''	6'-11''	5'-4''
Airport limousine	22'-5 3/4''	6'-4''	3'-11''
Trash truck	28'-2''	8'-0''	6'-0''
U.P.S. truck	23'-2''	7'-7''	8'-2''
Fire truck	31'-4''	8'-1''	10'-0''

*Exact sizes of large vehicles may vary.

NOTE
ANGLES SHOWN BELOW MAY VARY DEPENDING ON SPEED LOAD, TIRE PRESSURE, AND CONDITION OF SHOCK ABSORBERS

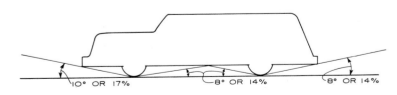

COMPOSITE VEHICLE WITH MAXIMUM WB, OF, AND OR

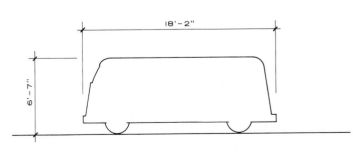

LARGE VAN

William T. Mahan, AIA; Santa Barbara, California

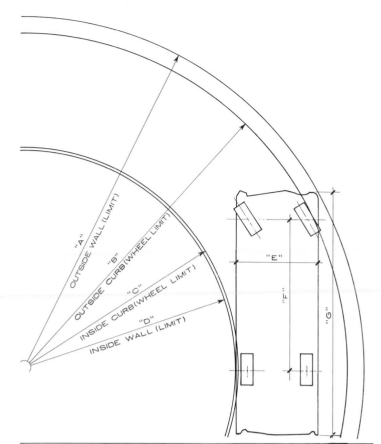

GOLF CARTS GASOLINE OR ELECTRIC POWER

3 WHEELS		4 WHEELS
46 3/4''	Overall Height	47 1/8''
10 3/4''	Floorboard Height	11 1/4''
27 3/4''	Seat Height	28 1/4''
102''	Length	102''
47''	Width	47''
68''	Wheel Base	68 3/4''
—	Front Wheel Tread	34''
34 5/8''	Rear Wheel Tread	34 5/8''
4 5/8''	Ground Clearance	4 5/8''
19'–6''	Clearance Circle	24'–0''

WIDTH AT HANDLEBAR 2'-7'' TO 3'-3''

When parked on stand motorcycle leans about 10°. Large vehicle requires about 3'–8'' of space.

HEAVYWEIGHTS WEIGH FROM ABOUT 400LB TO 661 LB

Consult manufacturers' information for width of motorcycle and sidecar.

POLICE TRICYCLE WIDTH AT BOX 4"-0"±

HEAVYWEIGHT MOTORCYCLES

AMBULANCES AND HEARSES
DIMENSIONS AND TURNING RADII

MAKE OF CAR	"A"	"B"	"C"	"D"	"E"	"F"	"G"
Cadillac	30'–0''	28'–6''	18'–11 1/2''	18'–9''	6'–11''	13'–0''	20'–10 1/4''
Dodge	23'–4''	21'–9''	13'–4 1/2''	12'–10 3/4''	6'–8''		18'–4''

AIRPORT LIMOUSINE

Checker	28'–3''				6'–4''	15'–9''	22'–5 3/4''

Folds flat. Converts to stroller. Body makes car bed.
BABY CARRIAGE

Handlebar width 23'' and up.
Weight about 230 lb to about 300 lb

LIGHTWEIGHT MOTORCYCLE

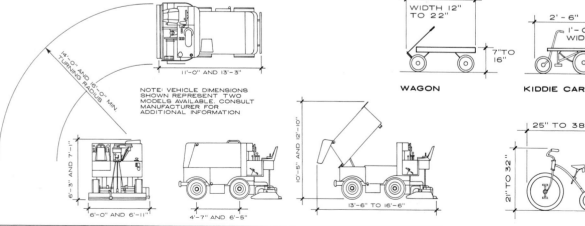

NOTE: VEHICLE DIMENSIONS SHOWN REPRESENT TWO MODELS AVAILABLE. CONSULT MANUFACTURER FOR ADDITIONAL INFORMATION

ZAMBONI ICE RESURFACER

WAGON

KIDDIE CAR

IRISH MAIL

TRICYCLE

SCOOTER

Foster C. Parriott; James M. Hunter & Associates; Boulder, Colorado

1   **TRANSPORTATION**

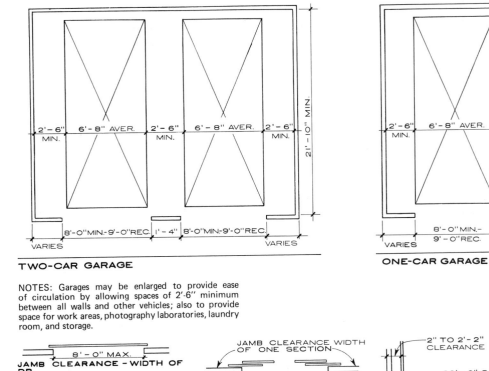

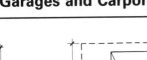

TWO-CAR GARAGE

ONE-CAR GARAGE

COMPACT CAR GARAGE

NOTES: Garages may be enlarged to provide ease of circulation by allowing spaces of 2'-6" minimum between all walls and other vehicles; also to provide space for work areas, photography laboratories, laundry room, and storage.

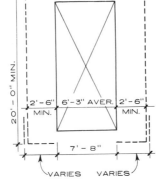

LOCATE SUPPORTS TO ALLOW FOR CAR DOOR SWING

8'-0" MAX.

JAMB CLEARANCE – WIDTH OF DR. SINGLE DOOR

JAMB CLEARANCE WIDTH OF ONE SECTION

ANY OPENING

MULTIPLE DOORS – TWO OR MORE CARS

2" TO 2'-2" CLEARANCE

20'-0" OPENING MAXIMUM

HINGED SECTIONS

STOR.   STOR.

NOTE
6 1/2" to 9" necessary from top of opening to ceiling (all sliding doors).

SLIDING DOORS

8'-0" MAX.

DOUBLE OR TRIPLE HINGED

ANY OPENING

MULTIPLE HINGED DOOR FOR TWO OR MORE CARS

ANY OPENING

90°   180°

OFFSET HINGE – MULTI-LEAVE

NOTE: For multiple and offset hinged doors, swinging to one or both sides, hinged in or out and used for 2 or more cars: 6 1/2" to 11" necessary from top of opening to ceiling.

HINGED DOORS

BACKOUT TYPE CARPORT

WIDTHS OF GARAGE HINGED DOORS

OPENING	TWO-DOOR	THREE-DOOR	FOUR-DOOR
8'-0"	4'-0"	2'-8"	2'-0"
8'-6"	4'-3"	2'-10"	2'-1 1/2"
9'-0"	4'-6"	3'-0"	2'-3"

DOOR HEIGHT + 1'-6"

7'-2" MIN.   6'-6" MIN.

TRACK

SECTIONAL DOORS

DOOR HEIGHT + 1'-6"

7'-2" MIN.   6'-6" MIN.

TRACK

ONE PIECE DOOR

5 1/2"

JAMB CONSIDERATIONS

STOR.
STOR.
STOR.
STOR.

LIFT DOORS – MOST WIDELY USED – AUTOMATIC OPTIONAL

NOTE
Heights: 6'–6", 6'–10", 7'–0", 7'–6" and 8'–0".
Lift doors generally 4'–0" sections high, sometimes 2'–0" or 3'–0".

PASS THRU TYPE CARPORT

CARPORTS

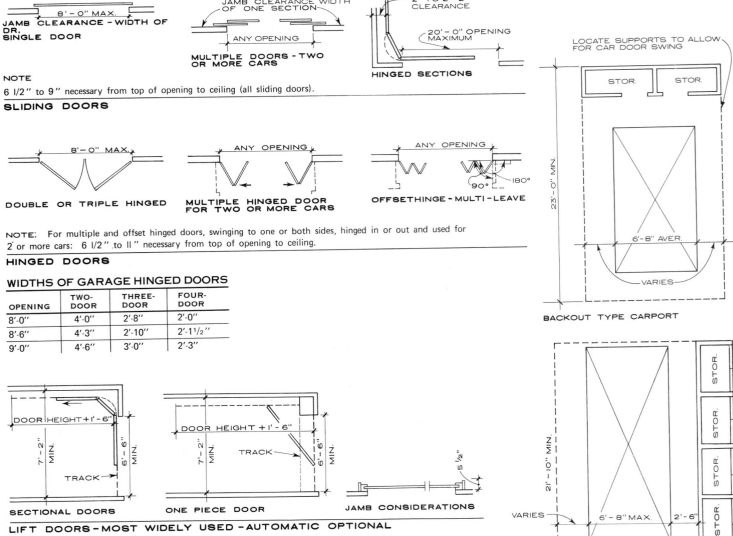

R. E. Powe, Jr., AIA; Hugh N. Jacobsen, FAIA; Washington, D.C.

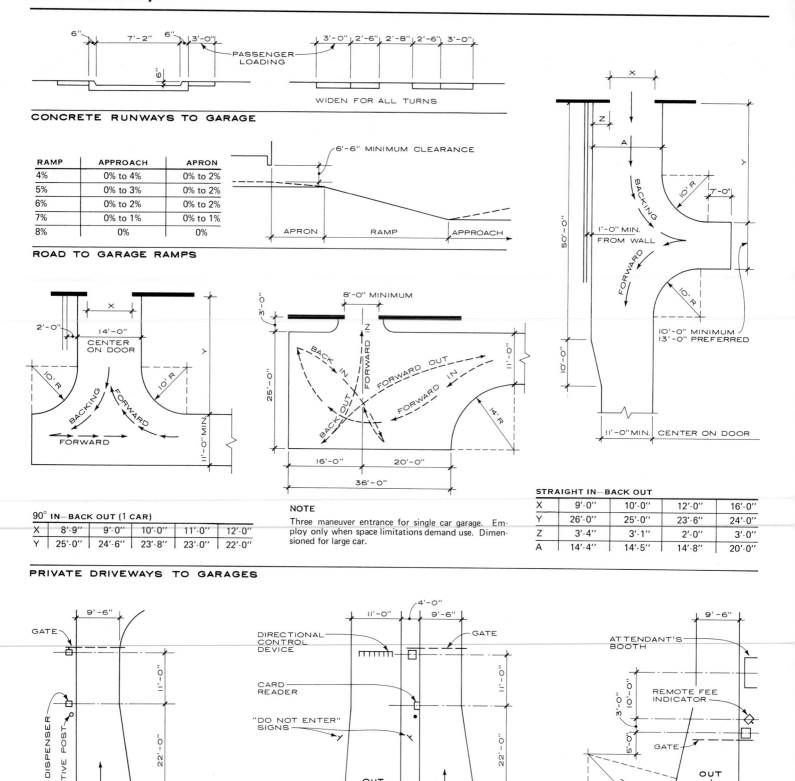

CONCRETE RUNWAYS TO GARAGE

RAMP	APPROACH	APRON
4%	0% to 4%	0% to 2%
5%	0% to 3%	0% to 2%
6%	0% to 2%	0% to 2%
7%	0% to 1%	0% to 1%
8%	0%	0%

ROAD TO GARAGE RAMPS

90° IN—BACK OUT (1 CAR)

X	8'-9"	9'-0"	10'-0"	11'-0"	12'-0"
Y	25'-0"	24'-6"	23'-8"	23'-0"	22'-0"

NOTE

Three maneuver entrance for single car garage. Employ only when space limitations demand use. Dimensioned for large car.

STRAIGHT IN—BACK OUT

X	9'-0"	10'-0"	12'-0"	16'-0"
Y	26'-0"	25'-0"	23'-6"	24'-0"
Z	3'-4"	3'-1"	2'-0"	3'-0"
A	14'-4"	14'-5"	14'-8"	20'-0"

PRIVATE DRIVEWAYS TO GARAGES

CONTROLLED ENTRANCE

CONTROLLED ENTRANCE-EXIT

ATTENDED EXIT

DRIVEWAYS FOR PARKING FACILITIES

William T. Mahan, AIA; Santa Barbara, California

GENERAL NOTES

Examples shown are for easy driving at moderate speed. See the preceding page for vehicle dimensions (L, W, and OR). The "U" drive shown below illustrates a procedure for designating any drive configuration, given the vehicle's dimensions and turning radii. The T (tangent) dimensions given here are approximate minimums only and may vary with the driver's ability and speed.

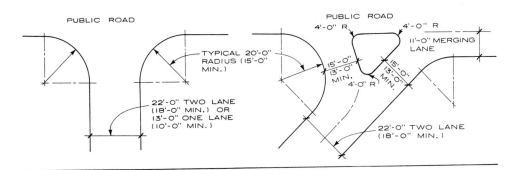

PRIVATE ROADS INTERSECTING PUBLIC ROADS

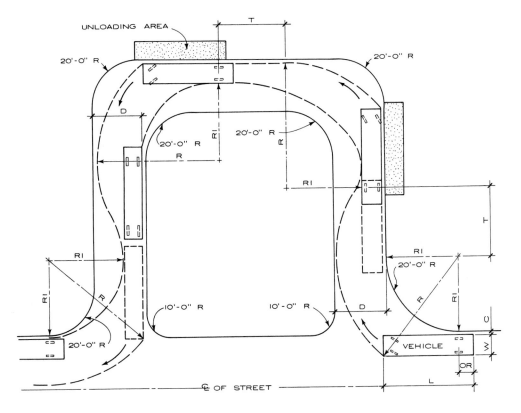

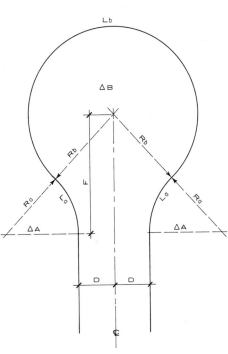

"U" DRIVE AND VEHICLE TURNING DIMENSIONS

VEHICLE	R	RI	T	D	C
Small car	19'-10"	10'-9"	12'-0"	10'-0'	6"
Compact car	21'-6"	11'-10"	15'-0"	10'-10"	7"
Standard car	22'-5"	12'-7"	15'-0"	11'-2"	8"
Large car	23'-0"	12'-7"	15'-0"	12'-0"	9"
Intercity bus*	55'-0"	33'-0"	30'-0"	22'-6"	1'-0"
City bus	53'-6"	33'-0"	30'-0"	22'-6"	1'-0"
School bus	43'-6"	26'-0"	30'-0"	19'-5"	1'-0"
Ambulance	30'-0"	18'-9"	25'-0"	13'-3"	1'-0"
Paramedic van	25'-0"	14'-0"	25'-0"	13'-0"	1'-0"
Hearse	30'-0"	18'-9"	20'-0"	13'-3"	1'-0"
Airport limousine	28'-3"	15'-1½"	20'-0"	15'-1½"	1'-0"
Trash truck†	32'-0"	18'-0"	20'-0"	16'-0"	1'-0"
U.P.S. truck	28'-0"	16'-0"	20'-0"	14'-0"	1'-0"
Fire truck	48'-0"	34'-4'	30'-0"	15'-8"	1'-0"

*Headroom = 14'.
†Headroom = 15'.

William T. Mahan, AIA; Santa Barbara, California

CUL-DE-SAC

	SMALL	LARGE
O	16'-0"	22'-0"
F	50'-11"	87'-3"
A	46.71°	35.58°
B	273.42°	251.15°
Ra	32'-0"	100'-0"
Rb	38'-0"	50'-0"
La	26'-1"	61'-8"
Lb	181'-4"	219'-2"

NOTE: R values for vehicles intended to use these culs-de-sac should not exceed Rb.

NOTE: Small car dimensions should be used only in lots designated for small cars or with entrance controls that admit only small cars. Placing small car stalls into a standard car layout is not recommended. Standard car parking dimensions will accommodate all normal passenger vehicles. Large car parking dimensions make parking easier and faster and are recommended for luxury, a high turnover, and use by the elderly. When the parking angle is 60° or less, it may be necessary to add 3 to 6 ft to the bay width to provide aisle space for pedestrians walking to and from their parked cars. Local zoning laws should be reviewed before proceeding.

RECOMMENDED RANGE OF STALL WIDTHS (SW)

WIDTH (ft)	8	9	10	11	12
Small car use					
All day parker use					
Standard car use					
Luxury and elderly use					
Supermarket and camper use					
Handicapped use*					

*Minimum requirements = 1 or 2 per 100 stalls or as specified by local, state, or federal law; place convenient to destination.

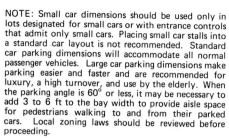

$PW = SW/\text{sine } \theta$

SINGLE LOADED WALL TO WALL (WITH BUMPERS)

SINGLE 4" LINE — DOUBLE LOADED WALL TO WALL (WITH CONTINUOUS CONCRETE CURB)

DOUBLE 4" LINE — DOUBLE LOADED WALL TO ℄ (WITH SAWTOOTH CONCRETE CURB)

DOUBLE LOADED ℄ TO ℄ (OR ℄ TO WALK EDGE)

WALK 10'-0" PREF. 7'-0" MIN. — ℄ OF BAY OR EDGE OF WALK

DETAIL "T" MARKER

PARALLEL PARKING STALLS AND "T" MARKER DETAIL

PARKING DIMENSIONS IN FEET AND INCHES

	SW	W	45°	50°	55°	60°	65°	70°	75°	80°	85°	90°
Group I: small cars	8'-0"	1	25'-9"	26'-6"	27'-2"	29'-4"	31'-9"	34'-0"	36'-2"	38'-2"	40'-0"	41'-9"
		2	40'-10"	42'-0"	43'-1"	45'-8"	48'-2"	50'-6"	52'-7"	54'-4"	55'-11"	57'-2"
		3	38'-9"	40'-2"	41'-5"	44'-2"	47'-0"	49'-6"	51'-10"	53'-10"	55'-8"	57'-2"
		4	36'-8"	38'-3"	39'-9"	42'-9"	45'-9"	48'-6"	51'-1"	53'-4"	55'-5"	57'-2"
Group II: standard cars	8'-6"	1	32'-0"	32'-11"	34'-2"	36'-2"	38'-5"	41'-0"	43'-6"	45'-6"	46'-11"	48'-0"
		2	49'-10"	51'-9"	53'-10"	56'-0"	58'-4"	60'-2"	62'-0"	63'-6"	64'-9"	66'-0"
		3	47'-8"	49'-4"	51'-6"	54'-0"	56'-6"	59'-0"	61'-2"	63'-0"	64'-6"	66'-0"
		4	45'-2"	46'-10"	49'-0"	51'-8"	54'-6"	57'-10"	60'-0"	62'-6"	64'-3"	66'-0"
	9'-0"	1	32'-0"	32'-9"	34'-0"	35'-4"	37'-6"	39'-8"	42'-0"	44'-4"	46'-2"	48'-0"
		2	49'-4"	51'-0"	53'-2"	55'-6"	57'-10"	60'-0"	61'-10"	63'-4"	64'-9"	66'-0"
		3	46'-4"	48'-10"	51'-4"	53'-10"	56'-0"	58'-8"	61'-0"	63'-0"	64'-6"	66'-0"
		4	44'-8"	46'-6"	49'-0"	51'-6"	54'-0"	57'-0"	59'-8"	62'-0"	64'-2"	66'-0"
	9'-6"	1	32'-0"	32'-8"	34'-0"	35'-0"	36'-10"	38'-10"	41'-6"	43'-8"	46'-0"	48'-0"
		2	49'-2"	50'-6"	51'-10"	53'-6"	55'-4"	58'-0"	60'-6"	62'-8"	64'-6"	65'-11"
		3	47'-0"	48'-2"	49'-10"	51'-6"	53'-11"	57'-0"	59'-8"	62'-0"	64'-3"	65'-11"
		4	44'-8"	45'-10"	47'-6"	49'-10"	52'-6"	55'-9"	58'-9"	61'-6"	63'-10"	65'-11"
Group III: large cars	9'-0"	1	32'-7"	33'-0"	34'-0"	35'-11"	38'-3"	40'-11"	43'-6"	45'-5"	46'-9"	48'-0"
		2	50'-2"	51'-2"	53'-3"	55'-4"	58'-0"	60'-4"	62'-9"	64'-3"	65'-5"	66'-0"
		3	47'-9"	49'-1"	52'-3"	53'-8"	56'-2"	59'-2"	61'-11"	63'-9"	65'-2"	66'-0"
		4	45'-5"	46'-11"	49'-0"	51'-8"	54'-9"	58'-0"	61'-0"	63'-2"	65'-2"	66'-0"
	9'-6"	1	32'-4"	32'-8"	33'-10"	34'-11"	37'-2"	39'-11"	42'-5"	45'-0"	46'-6"	48'-0"
		2	49'-11"	50'-11"	52'-2"	54'-0"	56'-6"	59'-3"	61'-9"	63'-4"	64'-8"	66'-0"
		3	47'-7"	48'-9"	50'-2"	52'-4"	55'-1"	58'-4"	60'-11"	63'-4"	64'-6"	66'-0"
		4	45'-3"	46'-8"	48'-5"	50'-8"	53'-8"	57'-0"	59'-10"	62'-2"	64'-6"	66'-0"
	10'-0"	1	32'-4"	32'-8"	33'-10"	34'-11"	37'-2"	39'-11"	42'-5"	45'-0"	46'-6"	48'-0"
		2	49'-11"	50'-11"	52'-2"	54'-0"	56'-6"	59'-3"	61'-9"	63'-4"	64'-8"	66'-0"
		3	47'-7"	48'-9"	50'-2"	52'-4"	55'-1"	58'-4"	60'-11"	62'-10"	64'-6"	66'-0"
		4	45'-3"	46'-8"	48'-5"	50'-8"	53'-8"	57'-0"	59'-10"	62'-2"	64'-1"	66'-0"

θ ANGLE OF PARK

NOTE: θ angles greater than 70° have aisle widths wide enough for two-way travel.

William T. Mahan, AIA; Santa Barbara, California

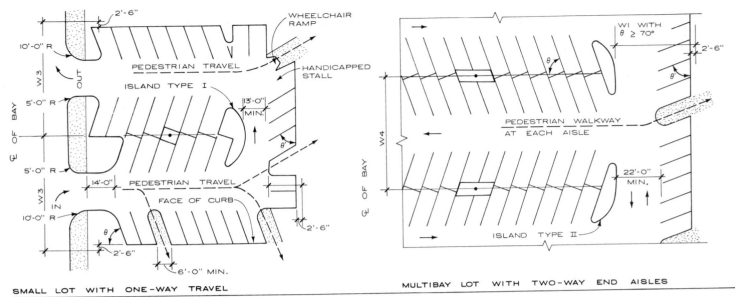

SMALL LOT WITH ONE-WAY TRAVEL

MULTIBAY LOT WITH TWO-WAY END AISLES

TYPICAL PARKING LAYOUTS

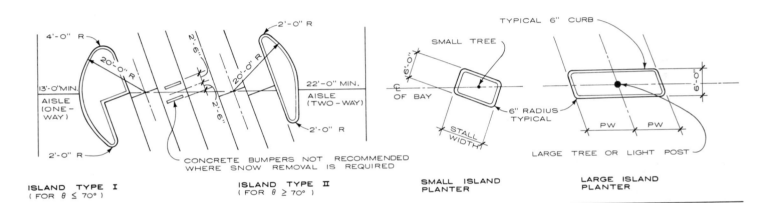

ISLAND TYPE I
(FOR θ ≤ 70°)

ISLAND TYPE II
(FOR θ ≥ 70°)

SMALL ISLAND
PLANTER

LARGE ISLAND
PLANTER

TYPICAL PLANTER ISLANDS

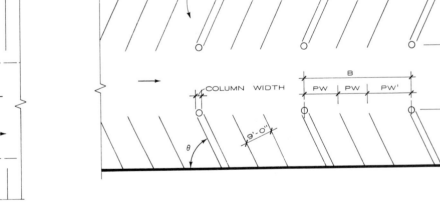

**TWO STALL 90° APARTMENT
CARPORTS**

X	9'-0"	10'-0"	11'-0"	12'-0"
Y	35'-0"	34'-0"	33'-0"	32'-0"

ANGLE PARKING WITH 3 STALLS PER COLUMN

θ	PW	PW'	W2	E	A	B	AREA/STALL
60°	10'-5"	13'-0"	55'-0"	18'-0"	19'-0"	33'-10"	310 sq ft
70°	9'-7"	11'-1"	59'-10"	18'-0"	23'-10"	30'-3"	302 sq ft
80°	9'-1"	10'-2"	63'-4"	18'-0"	27'-4"	28'-4"	300 sq ft

PARKING LAYOUTS WITH COLUMNS

William T. Mahan, AIA; Santa Barbara, California

TRANSPORTATION 1

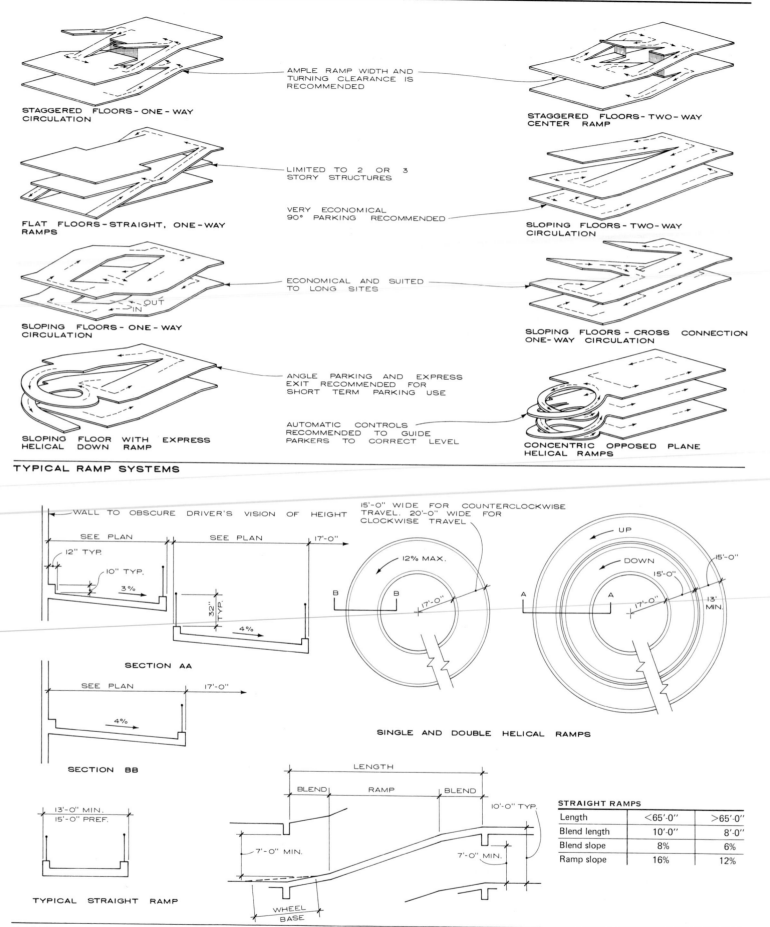

STAGGERED FLOORS – ONE – WAY CIRCULATION

STAGGERED FLOORS – TWO – WAY CENTER RAMP

AMPLE RAMP WIDTH AND TURNING CLEARANCE IS RECOMMENDED

FLAT FLOORS – STRAIGHT, ONE – WAY RAMPS

SLOPING FLOORS – TWO – WAY CIRCULATION

LIMITED TO 2 OR 3 STORY STRUCTURES

VERY ECONOMICAL 90° PARKING RECOMMENDED

SLOPING FLOORS – ONE – WAY CIRCULATION

SLOPING FLOORS – CROSS CONNECTION ONE – WAY CIRCULATION

ECONOMICAL AND SUITED TO LONG SITES

SLOPING FLOOR WITH EXPRESS HELICAL DOWN RAMP

CONCENTRIC OPPOSED PLANE HELICAL RAMPS

ANGLE PARKING AND EXPRESS EXIT RECOMMENDED FOR SHORT TERM PARKING USE

AUTOMATIC CONTROLS RECOMMENDED TO GUIDE PARKERS TO CORRECT LEVEL

TYPICAL RAMP SYSTEMS

WALL TO OBSCURE DRIVER'S VISION OF HEIGHT

15'-0" WIDE FOR COUNTERCLOCKWISE TRAVEL. 20'-0" WIDE FOR CLOCKWISE TRAVEL

SEE PLAN   SEE PLAN   17'-0"

12" TYP.

10" TYP.

3 %

32" TYP.

4 %

12% MAX.

17'-0"

UP

DOWN

15'-0"

15'-0"

17'-0"

13' MIN.

SECTION AA

SEE PLAN   17'-0"

4 %

SINGLE AND DOUBLE HELICAL RAMPS

SECTION BB

LENGTH

BLEND   RAMP   BLEND

10'-0" TYP.

13'-0" MIN.
15'-0" PREF.

7'-0" MIN.

7'-0" MIN.

TYPICAL STRAIGHT RAMP

WHEEL BASE

STRAIGHT RAMPS

	<65'-0"	>65'-0"
Length		
Blend length	10'-0"	8'-0"
Blend slope	8%	6%
Ramp slope	16%	12%

TYPICAL RAMP DETAILS

William T. Mahan, AIA; Santa Barbara, California

1   TRANSPORTATION

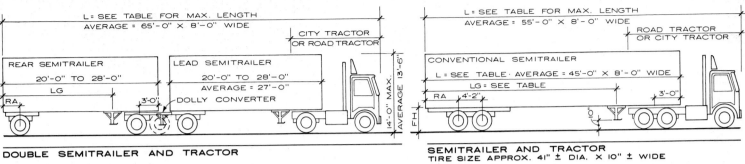

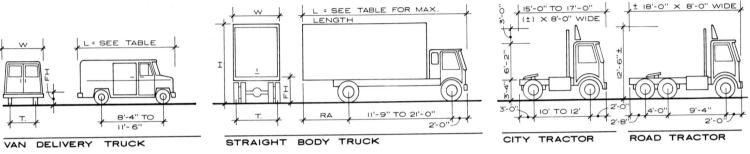

DOUBLE SEMITRAILER AND TRACTOR

SEMITRAILER AND TRACTOR
TIRE SIZE APPROX. 41" ± DIA. × 10" ± WIDE

VAN DELIVERY TRUCK

STRAIGHT BODY TRUCK

CITY TRACTOR   **ROAD TRACTOR**

DOUBLE SEMITRAILER AND TRACTOR–MAX. ALLOWABLE LENGTH

65'-0"	In all states except those below
55'-0"	Ga., Miss., N.J., N.Y.
60'-0"	Iowa, Minn., Mont.
70'-0"	Alaska, Nev., S.D.
75'-0"	Idaho, Ore.
85'-0"	Wyo.

NOT PERMITTED in Ala., Conn., Fla., Me., Mass., N.H., N.C., Pa., R.I., S.C., Tenn., Vt., Va., W.Va., Wis., Washington, D.C.

SEMITRAILER AND TRACTOR–
MAX. ALLOWABLE LENGTH

55'-0"	In all states except those below
56'-0"	Va., Me.
57'-0"	Ind., Ky.
59'-0"	Wis.
60'-0"	Ark., Calif., Del., Mass., Minn., Mont., Neb., Ohio, Ore., Vt.
65'-0"	Alaska, Ariz., Colo., Idaho, Kans., La., N.M., N.D., Okla., Texas, Utah, Wash.
70'-0"	Nev., S.D.
85'-0"	Wyo.

STRAIGHT BODY TRUCKS–
MAX. ALLOWABLE LENGTH

40'-0"	In all states except those below
35'-0"	Colo., Ky., Mass., Miss., N.H., N.J., N.Y., N.D., Wash., Wis.
36'-0"	Ind.
42'-0"	Ill., Kans.
45'-0"	Me., Texas, Utah
55'-0"	Conn., Ga.
60'-0"	Vt., Wyo.

AVERAGE DIMENSIONS OF VEHICLES

	TYPE OF VEHICLES			
	DOUBLE SEMITRAILER	CONVENTIONAL SEMITRAILER	STRAIGHT BODY TRUCK	VAN DELIVERY
Length (L)	65'-0"	55'-0"	17'-0" to 35'-0"	15'-0" to 20'-0"
Width (W)	8'-0"	8'-0"	8'-0"	7'-0"
Height (H)	13'-6"	13'-6"	13'-6"	7'-0"
Floor Height (FH)	4'-0" to 4'-6"	4'-0" to 4'-4"	3'-0" to 4'-0"	2'-0" to 2'-8"
Track (T)	6'-6"	6'-6"	5'-10"	5'-0" to 5'4"
Rear Axle (RA)	3'-0" to 4'-0"	4'-0" to 12'-0"	2'-3" to 12'-0"	—

VEHICLE HEIGHT–MAX. ALLOWABLE

13'-6"	In all states except those below
12'-6"	Ky., W.Va.
13'-0"	Colo.
14'-0"	Idaho, Nev., Wash., Wyo.
14'-6"	Neb.

LENGTH OF SEMITRAILER (ONLY)–
MAX. ALLOWABLE LENGTH

Unrestricted in all states except those below

35'-0"	Ore.
40'-0"	Calif.
45'-0"	Alaska, Ill., Me., Mass., Minn., Ohio, Utah, Wash., Wis.

AVERAGE SEMITRAILER DIMENSIONS

	LENGTH (L)			
	27'-0"	40'-0"	45'-0"	REFRIG. 40'-0"
Floor height (FH)	4'-2"	4'-2"	4'-2"	4'-9"
Rear axle (RA)	3'-0"	5'-2"	5'-10"	4'-5"
Landing gear (LG)	19'-0"	30'-0"	34'-6"	29'-5"
Cubic feet (CU)	1564±	2327±	2620±	2113±

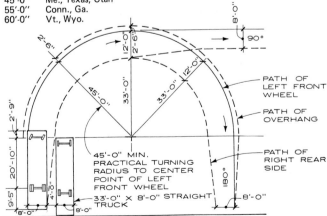

33'-0" STRAIGHT BODY TRUCK MIN. PRACTICAL TURNING RADIUS OF 45'-0"

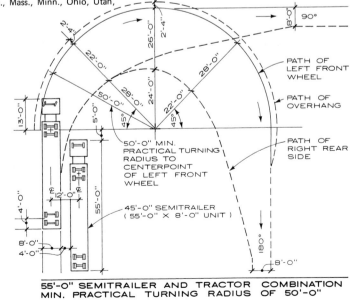

55'-0" SEMITRAILER AND TRACTOR COMBINATION MIN. PRACTICAL TURNING RADIUS OF 50'-0"

Robert H. Lorenz, AIA; Preston Trucking Company, Inc.; Preston, Maryland
The Operations Council, American Trucking Association; Washington, D.C.

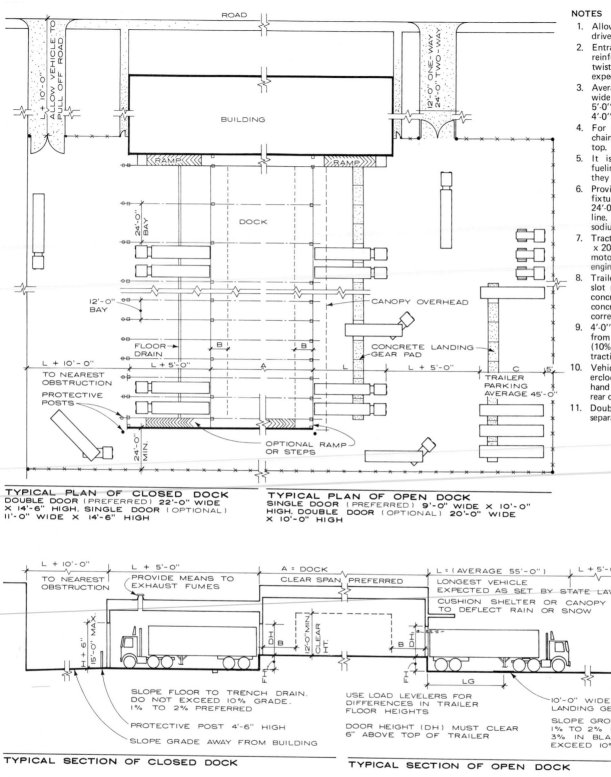

NOTES

1. Allow for off-street employee and/or driver parking.
2. Entrances and exits should be of reinforced concrete when excessive twisting and turning of vehicles are expected.
3. Average gate (swing or slide) 30'-0" wide for two-way traffic. People gate 5'-0" wide with concrete walkway 4'-0" to 6'-0" wide.
4. For yard security use a 6'-0" high chain link fence with barbed wire on top.
5. It is desirable to provide on-site fueling facilities for road units as they leave the yard.
6. Provide general yard lighting from fixtures mounted on building or on 24'-0" high minimum poles at fence line. Mercury vapor or high pressure sodium preferred.
7. Tractor parking requires 12'-0" wide x 20'-0" long slot minimum. Provide motor heater outlets for diesel engines in cold climates.
8. Trailer parking requires 12'-0" wide slot minimum. Provide 10'-0" wide concrete pad for landing gear. Score concrete at 12'-0" o.c. to aid in correct spotting of trailer.
9. 4'-0" wide minimum concrete ramp from dock to grade. 3 to 15% slope (10% average) score surface for traction.
10. Vehicles should circulate in a counterclockwise direction, making left hand turns, permitting driver to see rear of unit when backing into dock.
11. Double trailers are backed into dock separately.

TYPICAL PLAN OF CLOSED DOCK
DOUBLE DOOR (PREFERRED) 22'-0" WIDE X 14'-6" HIGH. SINGLE DOOR (OPTIONAL) 11'-0" WIDE X 14'-6" HIGH

TYPICAL PLAN OF OPEN DOCK
SINGLE DOOR (PREFERRED) 9'-0" WIDE X 10'-0" HIGH. DOUBLE DOOR (OPTIONAL) 20'-0" WIDE X 10'-0" HIGH

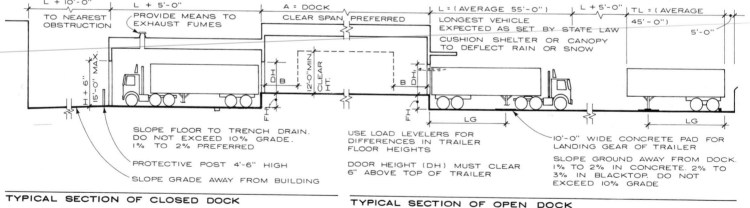

TYPICAL SECTION OF CLOSED DOCK

TYPICAL SECTION OF OPEN DOCK

AVERAGE VEHICLE DIMENSIONS

LENGTH OF VEHICLE (L)	FLOOR HEIGHT (FH)	VEHICLE HEIGHT (H)
55'-0" semitrailer	4'-0" to 4'-6"	14'-0"
37'-0" semitrailer	4'-0" to 4'-2"	13'-6"
25'-0" straight body	3'-8" to 4'-2"	13'-6"
18'-0" van	2'-0" to 2'-8"	7'-0"

NOTE: Refer to other pages for truck and trailer sizes.

AVERAGE WIDTHS OF DOCKS

TYPE OF OPERATION	TWO-WHEEL HAND TRUCK	FOUR-WHEEL HAND TRUCK	FORKLIFT TRUCK	DRAGLINE	AUTO SPUR DRAGLINE
Dock width (A)	50'-0"	60'-0"	60'-0" to 70'-0"	80'-0"	120'-0" to 140'-0"
Work aisle (B)	6'-0"	10'-0"	15'-0"	10'-0" to 15'-0"	10'-0" to 15'-0"

Robert H. Lorenz, AIA; Preston Trucking Company, Inc.; Preston, Maryland

The Operations Council, American Trucking Association; Washington, D. C.

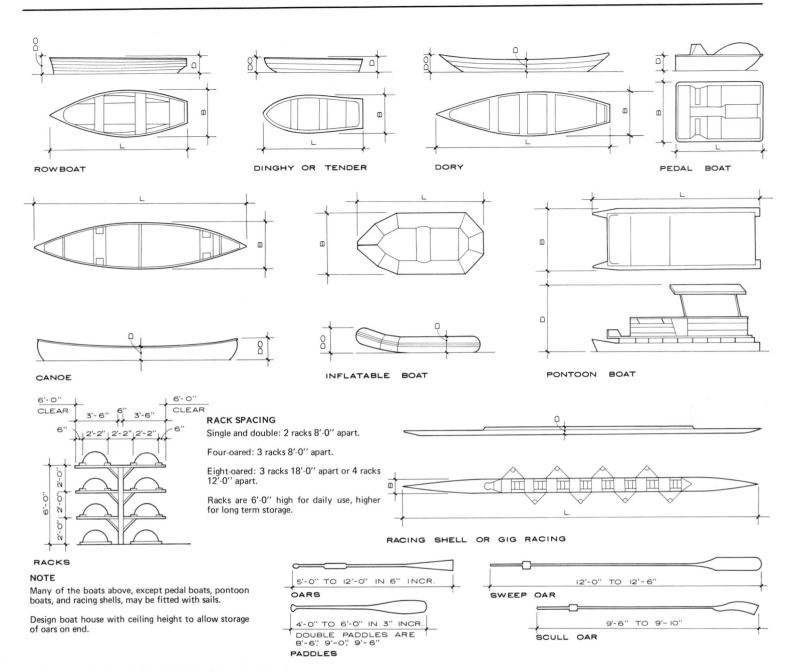

ROW BOAT

DINGHY OR TENDER

DORY

PEDAL BOAT

CANOE

INFLATABLE BOAT

PONTOON BOAT

RACK SPACING

Single and double: 2 racks 8'-0'' apart.

Four-oared: 3 racks 8'-0'' apart.

Eight-oared: 3 racks 18'-0'' apart or 4 racks 12'-0'' apart.

Racks are 6'-0'' high for daily use, higher for long term storage.

RACKS

RACING SHELL OR GIG RACING

NOTE

Many of the boats above, except pedal boats, pontoon boats, and racing shells, may be fitted with sails.

Design boat house with ceiling height to allow storage of oars on end.

5'-0'' TO 12'-0'' IN 6'' INCR.
OARS

4'-0'' TO 6'-0'' IN 3'' INCR.
DOUBLE PADDLES ARE 8'-6'', 9'-0'', 9'-6''
PADDLES

12'-0'' TO 12'-6''
SWEEP OAR

9'-6'' TO 9'-10''
SCULL OAR

TYPES AND SIZES OF TYPICAL SMALL BOATS

LO = LENGTH OVERALL, B = BEAM, D = DEPTH, DO = DEPTH OVERALL

CLASSIFICATION AND TYPE		LENGTH OVERALL	BEAM	DEPTH	DEPTH OVERALL	WEIGHT (LB)
Rowboats (many types and designs)		6'-5'' to 18'-0''	3'-11'' to 5'-5''	1'-2'' to 1'-8''	2'-0'' ±	50 to 270
DINGHY OR TENDER		6'-1'' to 14'-0''	2'-10'' to 5'-5''	1'-6'' to 1'-8''	1'-6'' to 1'-8''	40 to 155
DORY	Lifesaving	18'-0'' ±	4'-6'' ±	1'-8'' ±	1'-11'' ±	275
	Fisherman	12'-0'' to 16'-0''	3'-6'' to 5'-8''	1'-6'' to 1'-8''	1'-6'' to 1'-10''	64 to 320
PEDAL BOAT		7'-2'' to 10'-4''	5'-1'' to 5'-4''	1'-11''		115 to 140
INFLAT-ABLE	One-man	9'-0'' to 15'-0''	2'-10'' to 3'-0''	1'-0'' ±	2'-0'' to 2'-4''	44 to 85
	Standard	12'-0'' to 17'-0''	3'0'' to 3'-8''	1'-2''	1'-4''	55 to 79
	Fisherman	16'-0'' to 18'-0''	3'-5'' to 3'-7''	1'-0'' to 1'-1''	2'-0'' to 2'-4''	70 ±
CANOE	War	23'-0'' to 35'-0''	3'-8''	1'-3''	2'-3''	225
	Dinghy	8'-2'' to 12'-8''	4'-0'' to 5'-6''	1'-0'' to 1'-4''	1'-6'' to 1'-10''	56 to 119
	Riverboat	13'-9'' to 18'-0''	6'-10'' to 8'-0''	1'-6'' to 1'-9''	2'-0'' to 2'-8''	99 to 154
PONTOON BOAT		20'-0'' to 28'-0''	8'-0''	7'-8''		1015 to 1155
SHELL OR GIG	Single racing	25'-0'' to 28'-0''	1'-2''	6½''	10½''	30
	Double racing	29'-0'' to 33'-0''	1'-4''	7''	11''	60
	Four-oared	40'-0'' to 42'-0''	1'-9''	8½''	1'-0½''	120
	Eight-oared	56'-0'' to 62'-0''	2'-0'' to 2'-4''	1'-4''	1'-2'' to 1'-8''	270

David B. Richards; Rossetti Associates/Architects Planners; Detroit, Michigan

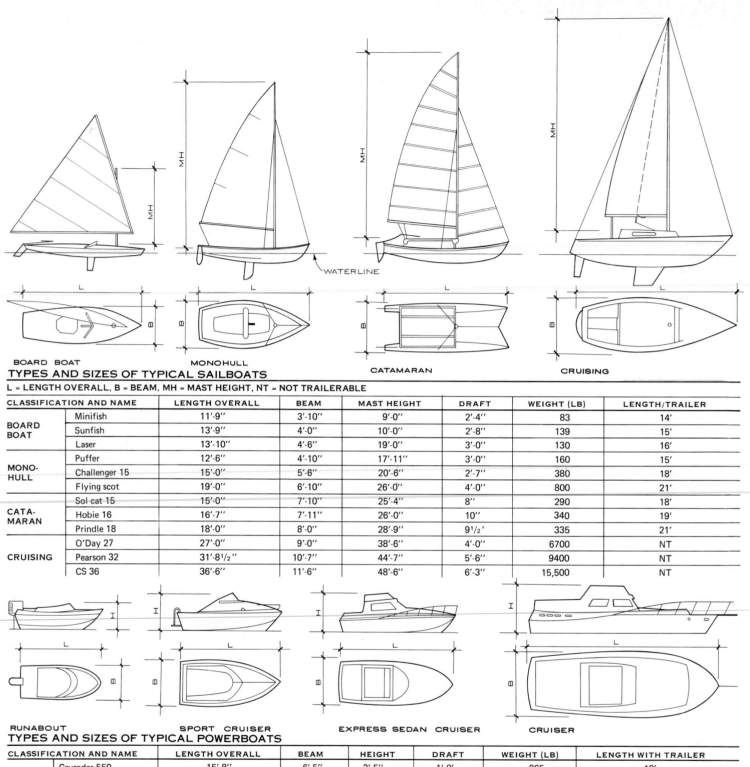

BOARD BOAT   MONOHULL   CATAMARAN   CRUISING

WATERLINE

TYPES AND SIZES OF TYPICAL SAILBOATS
L = LENGTH OVERALL, B = BEAM, MH = MAST HEIGHT, NT = NOT TRAILERABLE

CLASSIFICATION AND NAME		LENGTH OVERALL	BEAM	MAST HEIGHT	DRAFT	WEIGHT (LB)	LENGTH/TRAILER
BOARD BOAT	Minifish	11'-9''	3'-10''	9'-0''	2'-4''	83	14'
	Sunfish	13'-9''	4'-0''	10'-0''	2'-8''	139	15'
	Laser	13'-10''	4'-6''	19'-0''	3'-0''	130	16'
MONO-HULL	Puffer	12'-6''	4'-10''	17'-11''	3'-0''	160	15'
	Challenger 15	15'-0''	5'-6''	20'-6''	2'-7''	380	18'
	Flying scot	19'-0''	6'-10''	26'-0''	4'-0''	800	21'
CATA-MARAN	Sol cat 15	15'-0''	7'-10''	25'-4''	8''	290	18'
	Hobie 16	16'-7''	7'-11''	26'-0''	10''	340	19'
	Prindle 18	18'-0''	8'-0''	28'-9''	9½'	335	21'
CRUISING	O'Day 27	27'-0''	9'-0''	38'-6''	4'-0''	6700	NT
	Pearson 32	31'-8½''	10'-7''	44'-7''	5'-6''	9400	NT
	CS 36	36'-6''	11'-6''	48'-6''	6'-3''	15,500	NT

RUNABOUT   SPORT CRUISER   EXPRESS SEDAN CRUISER   CRUISER

TYPES AND SIZES OF TYPICAL POWERBOATS

CLASSIFICATION AND NAME		LENGTH OVERALL	BEAM	HEIGHT	DRAFT	WEIGHT (LB)	LENGTH WITH TRAILER
RUN-ABOUT	Crusader 550	15'-8''	6'-5''	3'-5''	1'-0'	865	19'
	Formula 18	18'-2''	7'-8''	3'-9½''	2'-4''	2618	21'
	Nordic 22	21'-8''	7'-10''	5'-2''	2'-3''	2800	25'
SPORT CRUISER	V-214	20'-6½''	8'-0''	6'-0''	2'-8''	6095	25'
	Crusader II	23'-6''	8'-0''	6'-3''	2'-6''	4375	28'
	Formula 255	25'-5''	8'-0''	7'-4''	2'-6''	6095	28'
SEDAN EXPRESS	F-25 Express	25'-0''	9'-4''	8'-4''	2'-2''	4800	NT
	Formula 26 sedan	26'-2''	9'-6''	9'-6''	2'-10''	7200	NT
	F-36 sedan	36'-0''	13'-0''	9'-6''	2'-11''	16,000	NT
CRUISER	F-36	36'-0''	13'-0''	12'-3''	2'-11''	17,000	NT
	F-40	40'-8''	14'-2½''	13'-1''	3'-7''	26,500	NT
	Viking 43	42'-8''	14'-9''	12'-0''	3'-9''	34,000	NT

David B. Richards; Rossetti Associates/Architects Planners; Detroit, Michigan

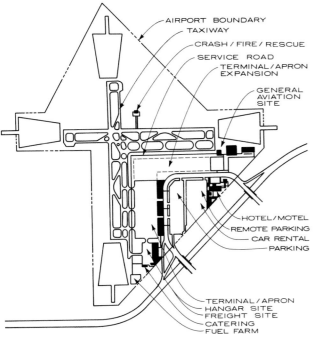

INTERSECTING RUNWAY LAYOUT

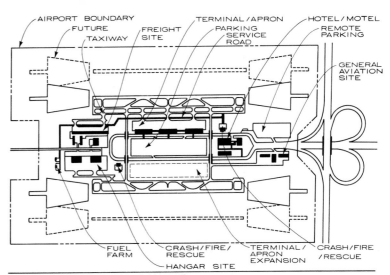

PARALLEL RUNWAY LAYOUT

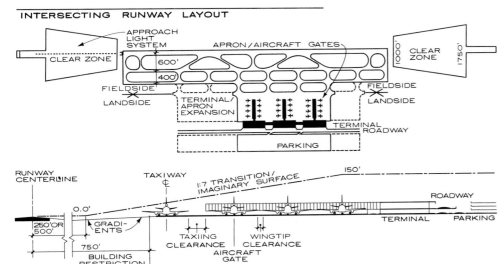

AIRPORT FIELDSIDE - LANDSIDE

Runway-taxiway configurations and apron terminal concepts appear in many variations, generally caused by climatic conditions, traffic characteristics, operational requirements, traffic volumes, and historical growth patterns.

Two airport plans are shown: (1) an intersecting runway configuration, total land area small to medium, the landside facilities are arranged within one quadrant, expansion capability is limited; (2) a parallel runway configuration, total land area medium to large, the landside facilities are arranged within the area between the runways, expansion capability is significant.

The airport fieldside consists of the runway-taxiway system, areas for clearances, and areas for navigational aides.

The airport landside consists of the passenger terminal with aircraft apron; airport ground transportation systems, roads, vehicular parking; support facilities, hangars, freight terminals, U.S. mail, catering, car rental, hotels, motels. The fieldside influences the location, plan development, and expansion capabilities of the landside facilities.

Example shows in plan and section the relationship between the runway-taxiway system and the apron terminal system. It is assumed that the runway is equipped with an instrument landing system in both directions.

Requirements, recommendations, minimum criteria for runway-taxiway systems are documented in the United States by the Department of Transportation/Federal Aviation Administration (DOT/FAA): FAR Part 77 "Objects Affecting the Airspace" and in series of Advisory Circulars. For airports outside the United States the requirements are documented by the International Civil Aviation Organization (ICAO): Aerodromes, Annex 14, 6th ed., September 1971, and Supplement, March 1974.

The following documents will provide more general information on airport master plan development:

1. FAA/AC 150/5070-6 Airport Master Plans.
2. FAA/AC 150/5335-1A Airport Design Standards.
3. Air Transport Association of America (ATA), Runway Capacity Criteria, Air Navigational Control Report No. 118, 5th ed.

Outside the United States:

1. ICAO/Aerodrome Manual, Part 2, Aerodrome Physical Characteristics.
2. ICAO/Airport Planning Manual (Doc. 9184-AN/902), Part 1, Master Planning, 1st ed.

OFFICIAL DOCUMENTS FOR PLANNING AIRPORT TERMINALS

1. FAA, Analysis of Concepts for Evaluation of Terminal Buildings, Report No. FAA-RD-73-82.
2. FAA, The Apron & Terminal Planning Report, No. FAA-RD-75-191. Includes aircraft dimensions, turn radii, aircraft jet blast contours for taxiing and breakaway thrust, and aircraft parking arrangements with staging of ground service equipment.
3. FAA, Advisory Circular No: AC 150/5360-7.
4. ATA, Airline Aircraft Gates and Passenger Terminal Space Approximations, AD/SC Report No. 4.

For airports outside the United States: ICAO, Annex 9, Facilitation; IATA, Airport Terminals Reference Manual, 6th ed.

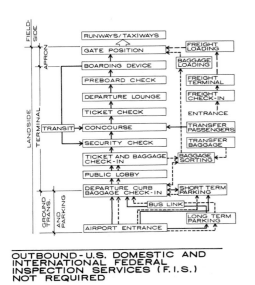

OUTBOUND - U.S. DOMESTIC AND INTERNATIONAL FEDERAL INSPECTION SERVICES (F.I.S.) NOT REQUIRED

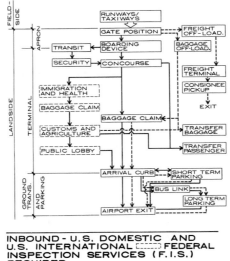

INBOUND - U.S. DOMESTIC AND U.S. INTERNATIONAL FEDERAL INSPECTION SERVICES (F.I.S.) REQUIRED

Walter Hart, AIA; Associates, Frank Gersbach, R.A., Benito Lao, AIA; North White Plains, New York

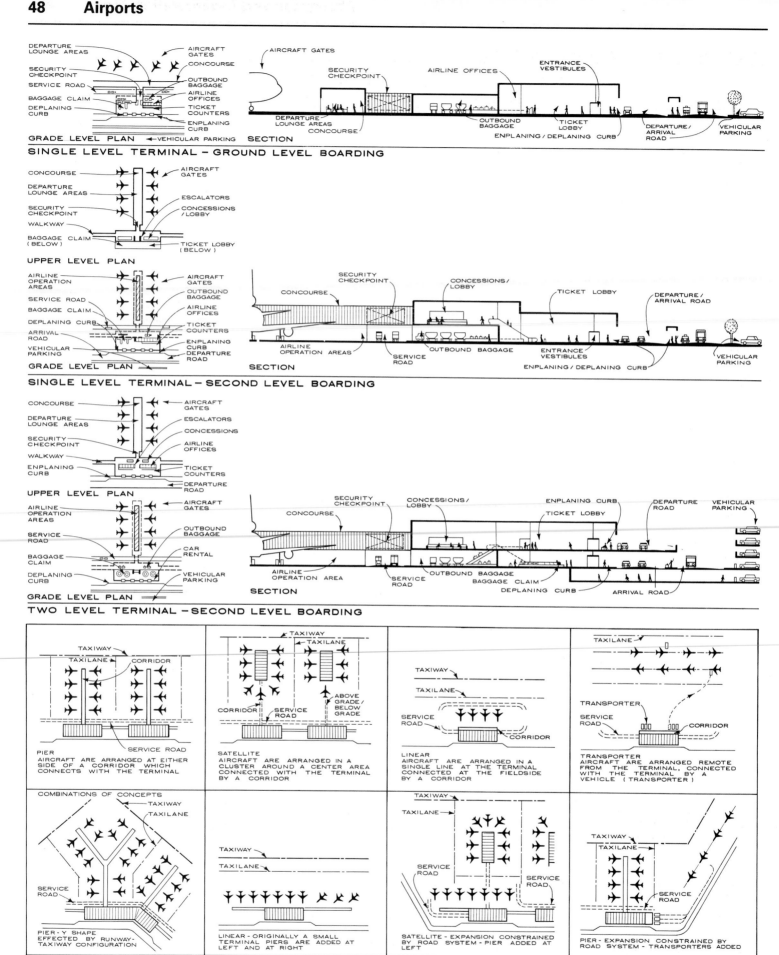

GRADE LEVEL PLAN ←VEHICULAR PARKING   **SECTION**

SINGLE LEVEL TERMINAL – GROUND LEVEL BOARDING

UPPER LEVEL PLAN

GRADE LEVEL PLAN   **SECTION**

SINGLE LEVEL TERMINAL – SECOND LEVEL BOARDING

UPPER LEVEL PLAN

GRADE LEVEL PLAN   **SECTION**

TWO LEVEL TERMINAL –SECOND LEVEL BOARDING

PIER
AIRCRAFT ARE ARRANGED AT EITHER SIDE OF A CORRIDOR WHICH CONNECTS WITH THE TERMINAL

SATELLITE
AIRCRAFT ARE ARRANGED IN A CLUSTER AROUND A CENTER AREA CONNECTED WITH THE TERMINAL BY A CORRIDOR

LINEAR
AIRCRAFT ARE ARRANGED IN A SINGLE LINE AT THE TERMINAL CONNECTED AT THE FIELDSIDE BY A CORRIDOR

TRANSPORTER
AIRCRAFT ARE ARRANGED REMOTE FROM THE TERMINAL, CONNECTED WITH THE TERMINAL BY A VEHICLE (TRANSPORTER)

COMBINATIONS OF CONCEPTS

PIER-Y SHAPE
EFFECTED BY RUNWAY-TAXIWAY CONFIGURATION

LINEAR - ORIGINALLY A SMALL TERMINAL PIERS ARE ADDED AT LEFT AND AT RIGHT

SATELLITE - EXPANSION CONSTRAINED BY ROAD SYSTEM - PIER ADDED AT LEFT

PIER - EXPANSION CONSTRAINED BY ROAD SYSTEM - TRANSPORTERS ADDED

CONCEPTS

Walter Hart, AIA; Associates, Frank Gersbach, R.A., Benito Lao, AIA; North White Plains, New York

1 TRANSPORTATION

USE OF ABSORPTION IN COMMON OCCUPANCIES (1)

ROOM OCCUPANCY	CEILING FULL	CEILING PARTIAL (2)	NRC RANGE (3) 0.60-0.75	NRC RANGE (3) OVER 0.75	WALL TREATMENT (4)	SPECIAL (5)
Auditoriums, churches, theaters, concert halls, lecture halls, radio, recording and T.V. studios, speech and music rooms						●
Classrooms, elementary	●		●			
Classrooms, college		●	●		●	
Commercial kitchens	●			●		
Computer and business machine rooms	●			●	●	
Corridors and lobbies	●		●		●	
Gymnasiums, arenas, and recreational spaces	●			●		●
Health care patient rooms	●		●			
Laboratories	●		●			
Libraries	●			●		
Mechanical equipment rooms						●
Meeting and conference rooms	● Small	● Large	●		●	
Open office plan	●			●	●	●
Private offices	●		●			
Restaurants	●		●		●	
Schools and industrial shops, factories	●			●	●	●
Stores and commercial shops	●		●			

NOTES

1. This table lists conservative "rule of thumb" recommendations for the use of absorption in common occupancies.

2. The remainder of the ceiling should be treated with a hard, sound reflecting finish, such as dense (not "acoustical") plaster, solid wood, or gypsum board.

It should be assumed in the use of this table that whenever sound absorbing treatment is not recommended, a hard, sound reflecting finish should be used.

3. NOISE REDUCTION COEFFICIENT: An arithmetic average of sound absorption coefficients of the four middle frequencies (250, 500, 1000, and 2000 Hz) is called the Noise Reduction Coefficient

(NRC). The NRC is a good means of comparing the performance characteristics of similar products.

4. Wall treatment is advisable in addition to ceiling treatment for the reduction of reflections, flutter, or echo. This treatment will further reduce noise and control reverberation.

5. For highly complex applications, consult an acoustical engineer.

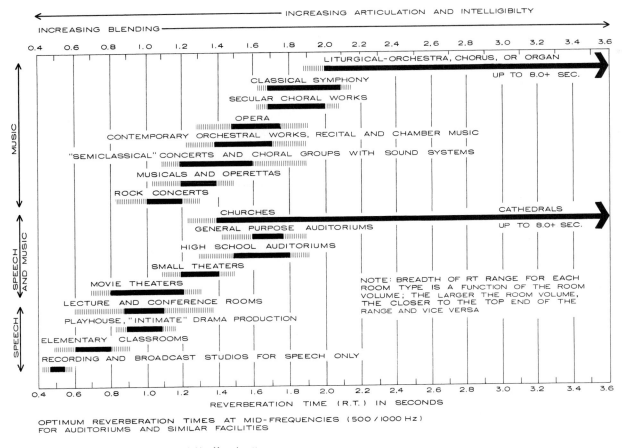

OPTIMUM REVERBERATION TIMES AT MID-FREQUENCIES (500/1000 Hz) FOR AUDITORIUMS AND SIMILAR FACILITIES

Don Klabin, AIA; Bolt, Beranek and Newman; Cambridge, Massachusetts

ENVIRONMENTAL FACTORS 1

OPEN PLAN OFFICES

Open plan offices utilize partial height screens or space dividers to separate work stations. Since there are no full height partitions or doors to block sound transmission, lack of acoustical privacy is often a serious problem. Speech transmitted between work stations can cause annoyance and distraction to office personnel and can interfere with confidential conversations. Noise from typewriters and business machines, although usually secondary to intruding speech, can also be a source of annoyance to office workers.

Proper acoustical design of open plan offices requires an understanding of the three main factors that are discussed in the three columns below. Specific design elements and guidelines are presented on the bottom half of the page. A thorough study of all of the material is encouraged, since successful acoustical design requires consideration of all elements.

CHARACTERISTICS OF SPEECH

A person talking may use various voice levels ranging from a lowered voice to a shout. In typical open plan office situations we are concerned mainly with normal conversational voice levels. Raised voice levels create serious privacy problems. The intelligibility of speech is contained in the 5 octave frequency bands from 250 to 4000 Hz, with the most important frequency region being around 2000 Hz. Another important characteristic of speech is its directionality. Speech is louder in front of a talker than it is in back of or beside him or her.

SOUND TRANSMISSION PATHS

Sound is transmitted between work stations in open plan offices by a number of different paths: (1) direct or transmitted through screens; (2) diffracted over and around screens; (3) reflected from the ceiling or luminaire; and (4) reflected from walls, windows, and other vertical surfaces. Factors that help reduce the sound transmitted between work stations are distance, the STC rating of the screen, the size and location of the screen, the height and sound absorbing properties of the ceiling, and the location and sound absorbing properties of the vertical surfaces.

SPEECH PRIVACY

Speech privacy and freedom from the distraction of intruding speech depend on how much the intruding speech is masked by the steady background noise in the space. In rare cases, adequate masking is provided by the building ventilation system, but usually an electronic sound masking system is required. The degree of speech privacy can be defined by the articulation index (AI), which is a measure of speech intelligibility. AI can range between 0 and 1. Zero represents no intelligibility and complete privacy; 1 represents complete intelligibility and no privacy.

NORMAL PRIVACY is the degree of privacy required by most office workers. It is achieved if the office occupant is not annoyed or distracted by an intruding conversation, even though hearing and understanding some of the conversation. Normal privacy usually requires an AI of 0.20 or less. This can be achieved without difficulty in well designed open plan offices.

CONFIDENTIAL PRIVACY is required if it is important that a person's conversations not be overheard and understood in adjacent work spaces. This is achieved if the AI is 0.05 or less. Confidential privacy is difficult, though not impossible, to achieve in open plan offices. An acoustic consultant should be retained.

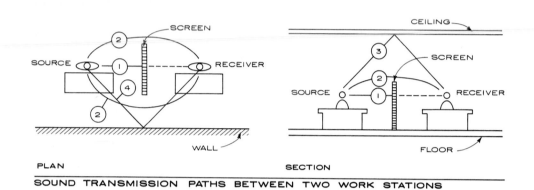

PLAN   SECTION

SOUND TRANSMISSION PATHS BETWEEN TWO WORK STATIONS

OPEN PLAN GUIDELINES FOR NORMAL PRIVACY

DISTANCE	Noise reduction increases with distance from the source. Locate personnel as far apart as possible commensurate with density requirements. A minimum distance of 8 ft between personnel is desirable.
ORIENTATION	Privacy can be improved by locating occupants back to back wherever possible in order to take advantage of directionality of the human voice.
CEILING	Make ceilings as high as possible. Desirable minimum height is 9 ft. Ceiling material should have an NRC of at least 0.70 and a sound absorption coefficient at 2000 Hz of at least 0.90.
LUMINAIRES	Ceiling mounted luminaires with flat lenses wider than 12 in. should be avoided. 6 in. wide units or units with parabolic louvers reflect less sound energy and are preferable.
SCREENS	Screens should break the line of sight between office occupants by 1 ft or more. Minimum screen height should be about 5 ft. All screens should have impervious septums and STC ratings of at least 24. Sound absorbing treatment providing an NRC of at least 0.70 is desirable on all screens.
FLOORS	Floors should be carpeted to reduce the noise of heel clicks, chair scraping, and other annoying noises originating at the floor. This is the major acoustical benefit of carpeting in open plan offices, and the NRC is not critical.
SOUND MASKING	Adequate sound masking is an essential part of good open plan design. In most open plan offices an electronic sound masking system is required. The sound level, tonal characteristics, and spatial uniformity of sound masking are critical in order to provide maximum speech masking and minimum annoyance. Loudspeakers usually are located above the acoustical ceiling and produce a sound similar to a well designed ventilating system.
VERTICAL SURFACES	Provide sound absorbing wall panels on vertical surfaces wherever possible, particularly around copy machines and other noisy equipment. The NRC of these panels should be at least 0.70. Windows can be treated with vertical acoustical blinds, or splayed to reflect sound up to the sound absorbing ceiling. Draperies are acoustically ineffective and should not be used to reduce reflected sound.

Parker W. Hirtle, AIA; Bolt, Beranek and Newman, Inc.; Cambridge, Massachusetts

1 ENVIRONMENTAL FACTORS

TERMS COMMONLY USED IN LIGHTING DESIGN

ENGLISH	SI	MEASURE OF
Candlepower	Candlepower	Intensity
Lumen	Lumen	Light flux
Footcandle (ft-c)	Lux	Density- lumen/ft² (lux/m²)
Reflectance (R)	Reflectance	$R = \dfrac{\text{ft-c (reflected)}}{\text{ft-c (incident)}}$
Transmission (T)		$T = \dfrac{\text{ft-c (transmitted)}}{\text{ft-c (incident)}}$
Footlambert (ft-L)	Candlepower/m²	Luminance ft-L = ft-c × R

SUBJECTIVE IMPRESSION APPEARS TO BE AFFECTED BY:

Visual clarity	Peripheral wall brightness Luminance in the center of the room Cool color light source and continuous spectrum output
Spaciousness	Peripheral lighting (not affected by color)
Relaxation	Nonuniform, peripheral (wall) lighting
Attention	Intensity of light and contrast Recommended contrast ratios: 2/1: subliminal differences 10/1: minimum for significant focal contrast 100/1: dominating contrast
Privacy, intimacy	Lighting of background and/or inanimate objects (centerpieces)
Gaiety, playfulness	Visual noise and "clutter" such as sparkle, random patterns
Somberness	Dimness and diffusion of light

SEEING

Although many of the characteristics of quality seeing conditions are known, it is a difficult area to define precisely. Research continues in an effort to uncover knowledge of how people see and what kind of lighting conditions are most desirable for every situation.

RECOGNITION OF TASKS

The human ability to recognize detail generally varies with respect to (1) contrast between the details of a task and its immediate surround, (2) luminance (or brightness) of the task, (3) size of the task, and (4) time of viewing.

Maximum visibility is attained when the luminance contrast of details against their background is greatest (e.g., black ink on white paper). Significant savings of electric energy can occur when the task contrast is maximized because the level of illumination needed is reduced. The same opportunity occurs with task size (e.g., large size type on a typewriter saves on the need for illumination). The luminance of the task depends on the amount of incident illumination and the reflectivity of the task. A small amount of light on white paper may be as effective for seeing as a large amount of illumination on dark cloth. With increased time available for viewing, illumination levels can be reduced (e.g., when speed is not critical).

VEILING REFLECTIONS

Substantial losses in contrast, hence in visibility and visual performance, can result when light is reflected from specular visual tasks (the task is "veiled"). This is perhaps the most significant factor in poor seeing conditions. Three factors govern these veiling reflections: (1) the nature of the task, (2) the observer's

Benjamin H. Evans, AIA; Blacksburg, Virginia

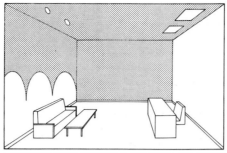

LIGHTING CAN DEFINE A CHANGE OF MOOD BETWEEN DESK AND MORE RELAXED SEATING AREA

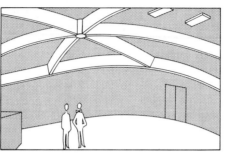

LUMINAIRE PATTERNS THAT CONFLICT WITH STRUCTURE CAN DESTROY HARMONY OF SPACE

ILLUMINATION

Proper illumination depends on the establishment of design goals that define the desired environment, rather than on the equipment needed. Lighting is the most expressive tool available for setting the tone for perception of the environment. It should be thought of as a design tool and not as an "add on" to provide light, and its consideration should be fundamental to any design effort.

Light should be considered to be what we "see by" and not that which we actually see. We do not see footcandles (the measure of quantity). We see luminance as a result of reflected or direct light. (When perceived rather than measured, it is called brightness.) The footlambert is the unit of measurement of brightness.

Of course, there must be enough light. (The unit of measure is the footcandle.) The quantities of illumination necessary for various visual tasks have been

orientation and viewing angle, and (3) the lighting system.

THE TASK

The luminance of the task (e.g., writing or printing on paper) depends on both the amount of light being reflected from it and the bright object or surface (e.g., luminaire) that may be reflected in it. Diffusing or matte papers and inks tend to reduce veiling reflections.

THE OBSERVER

If the eye is in such a position that the rays of light from the "offending zone" are reflected toward it, veiling reflections will occur. This situation can usually be observed in a space by placing a sheet of clear acetate or some other glossy surface over the task

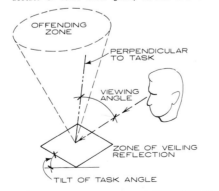

TASK LIGHTING

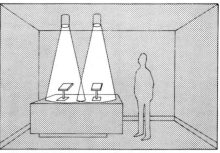

DOWNLIGHTS FOCUS ATTENTION ON OBJECT

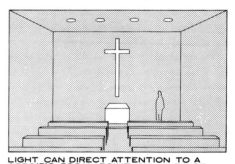

LIGHT CAN DIRECT ATTENTION TO A SPECIFIC FOCAL POINT BY A SHARP CONTRAST OF LIGHT AND DARK SURFACES

recommended by the Illuminating Engineering Society (IES) based on research. But the quantity of illumination needed on walls, floors, ceilings, and so on, for the creation of a beautiful and functional environment is very much left to the designer's logic, experience, and intuition. The proper lighting of all tasks, whether functional or esthetic, is vital to a total design, and recommended footcandle levels should be considered only as targets.

PURPOSE

Lighting can define the intended use of a space by focusing on points of attention and subduing less important areas. It can be used to express structural concepts by silhouetting beams, arches, and columns or to emphasize unusual contours. Mechanical equipment can be made to visually recede with dark paint and the absence of light. Light can help to define space use changes through brightened ceiling areas or changes of light patterns on walls.

(such as a book or paper with writing or printing) and observing the reflections (if any). Sources of light in this offending zone should be minimized for best seeing conditions.

LIGHTING SYSTEMS

The worst condition is a highly concentrated, bright source, above and forward, directed at the task. Paradoxically, it is also the condition under which the worker can most easily escape veiling reflections by tilting or reorienting the task so that the reflected rays do not reach the eye (e.g., as in turning the back so the light comes over the shoulder). Placement of lighting equipment and fenestrations in the general area above and forward of the task (or desk) should be avoided. When the nature of the tasks and their location are known, luminaires can be located to avoid the offending zone. When task locations are not known and flexibility is necessary, as for speculative office space, general low level ambient lighting, which tends to negate the effects of veiling reflections, and task lighting can be provided by plug-in units at the discretion of the tenant.

EQUIVALENT SPHERE ILLUMINATION (ESI)

ESI is a unit adopted by the IES for measuring the visibility potential of a particular task at a particular location and with a specific lighting system. It is a unit of measurement just as is the meterstick. It is not a standard of quality, but a way of taking into consideration those elements by which quality is judged. ESI cannot be measured over the area of a room as simply as raw footcandles, because ESI depends on a task, a location, an orientation, and a lighting system. A task has 50 ESI when it is as visible as it would be when illuminated by 50 ft-c of illuminance produced by a photometric sphere.

TASK AMBIENT LIGHTING

Task ambient (T/A) lighting systems have become popular because they provide higher intensity illumination on the task only and lower levels of ambient light for general circulation, thereby reducing electric energy usage. T/A systems are designed to give localized desk (or task) lighting and, usually, to project some percentage of illumination toward the ceiling for ambient (general purpose) lighting. A T/A lighting system generally requires fewer watts per square foot of floor space (as little as 1.5 W/sq ft) than does the conventional ceiling lighting system (up to 4 or 5 W/sq ft) and thus can be a significant energy saver. However, the principles of good lighting still apply, and not all T/A lighting systems provide sufficient task illumination without producing excessive ceiling reflections. Luminaires should be glarefree; the light source should not be visible from the working position. Direct glare from the normal passing position should be avoided. The downlight should illuminate the back panel of the work station as evenly as possible. A T/A system should not produce excessively bright spots of light on low ceilings and adjacent walls. Poor distribution of illumination on room surfaces can be visually disturbing to occupants.

LUMINAIRE SELECTION PARAMETERS

In selecting a luminaire that will create good seeing conditions several factors should be considered:

1. DIRECT GLARE is produced by excessive luminances in the visual field that affect the visual systems as the individual looks around the environment. It is usually associated with the luminaire zone from 45° to 90°. To minimize direct glare, the luminous intensity should be kept out of the 45° to 90° zone.

2. VISUAL COMFORT PROBABILITY (VCP) is the indicator used to evaluate the direct glare zone area of luminance. Luminaries are given a VCP rating, which indicates the percent of people who, if seated in the most undesirable location, will be expected to find the luminaire acceptable from the standpoint of direct glare (excessive luminances in the visual field).

3. Direct glare may not be a problem if all three of the following conditions are satisfied: (a) The VCP is 70 or more; (b) the ratio of maximum-to-average luminaire luminance does not exceed 5 to 1 at 45°, 55°, 65°, 75°, and 85° from nadir crosswise and lengthwise; (c) maximum luminaire luminances do not exceed:

> 2250 ft-L at 45°
> 1620 ft-L at 55°
> 1125 ft-L at 65°
> 750 ft-L at 75°
> 495 ft-L at 85°

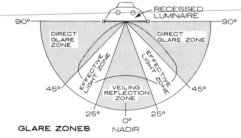

GLARE ZONES

ASHRAE STANDARD 90-75

The American Society for Heating, Refrigeration, and Air Conditioning Engineers has established a procedure for determining a "Lighting Power Budget," which has been adopted in some areas as a mechanism for determining how much electrical energy will be allowed for lighting purposes in new buildings. The lighting power budget is intended only as a mechanism for encouraging energy conservation in lighting and is not a design tool. Once the budget has been established, the designer is free to design the lighting system to achieve the best quality lighting within the budget and for the circumstances. Much can be done to conserve energy while staying within the lighting budget.

MAINTENANCE AND DEPRECIATION

All elements of the building that affect light need to be kept clean. Luminaires, diffusers, lenses, window glass, louvers, blinds, wall surfaces, and so on, tend to collect dust, which reduces their light-controlling efficiency. In the lighting formulas below a Luminaire Dirt Depreciation (LDD) factor is used to account for collected dust and dirt. The LDD figure used will depend on the type of atmosphere in the room and the frequency of cleaning. Also, lamps depreciate with time, with their effective lumen output reduced, which is accounted for in the calculations with the application of the Lamp Lumen Depreciation (LLD) factor.

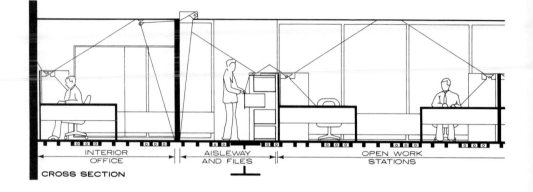

CROSS SECTION

SOME USEFUL FORMULAS FOR GENERAL LIGHTING DESIGN

$$\text{NUMBER OF LUMINAIRES} = \frac{\text{footcandles desired} \times \text{room area}}{\text{CU} \times \text{LLD} \times \text{LDD} \times \text{lamps/luminaire} \times \text{lumens/lamps}}$$

$$\text{AVERAGE FOOTCANDLES} = \frac{\text{lumens/lamp} \times \text{lamps/luminaire} \times \text{CU} \times \text{LLD} \times \text{LDD}}{\text{area of room (sq ft)}}$$

$$\text{TOTAL ILLUMINATION (W/sq ft)} = \frac{\text{footcandles desired}}{\text{overall lumens/watt} \times \text{CU} \times \text{LLD} \times \text{LDD}}$$

where   CU = Coefficient of Utilization
       LLD = Lamp Lumen Depreciation
       LDD = Luminaire Dirt Depreciation

NOTE

See manufacturer's photometric tables or the Lighting Handbook of the Illuminating Engineering Society for tables giving values of CU, LLD, LDD, lumens/lamps, and so on.

TYPICAL EXAMPLES

Room size 25 x 40 ft; ceiling height 9 ft; office area 70 ft-c; 2 x 4 ft recessed troffers with 4-40 W T12 lamps (3100 lm) each. From IES tables, Room Index = E and CU = 0.67 (plastic lens):

$$\text{NUMBER OF FIXTURES} = \frac{70 \times 25 \times 40}{0.67 \times 0.7 \times 4 \times 3100} = 8.4 \text{ (use 8 luminaires)}$$

$$\text{TOTAL ILLUMINATION (W/sq ft)} = \frac{8 \times 200 \text{ W/luminaire}}{25 \times 40} = 1.6 \text{ W/sq ft}$$

IES RECOMMENDED ILLUMINATION LEVELS (ESI AT THE TASK)

5 FT-C	10 FT-C	20 FT-C	30 FT-C	50 FT-C	70 FT-C	100 FT-C	150 FT-C	200 FT-C
Exits, at floor	Restaurant	Cleaning	Classrooms	Inspection	Commercial kitchen	Garage repair	Rough drafting	Fine drafting
TV viewing	Parking garages	Hospital room	Waiting rooms	Rough factory assembly	General writing and reading	Office reading	Accounting	Engraving
Theater foyer	Hotel bath	Stairways	Restrooms	Bank lobby	Dormitory desk	Sewing	Office fine work	Color printing inspection
	General residential	Hotel bedroom	Entrance foyers	Church pulpit	Handicraft	Merchandising areas	Proofreading	Critical seeing tasks
			Laundry	Checking and sorting				
			Reading printed material					

Benjamin H. Evans, AIA; Blacksburg, Virginia

DAYLIGHTING

Ample daylight is available throughout North America for lighting interior spaces during a large portion of the working day. This light is thought by many to be psychologically desirable, and there is some evidence that it has biological benefits. Its variability through the day provides some beneficial visual exercise. Its use in place of, or in conjunction with, other light sources can conserve energy. Daylight carries with it significant quantities of heat which, in properly designed buildings, may be used to conserve energy. Daylight produces less interior heat per unit of illumination, however, than do most forms of electric light.

The principles of good lighting apply equally to daylight and electric light. The difference is in the location of the light source, its color spectrum, and its variability.

SOURCE

Daylight comes directly from the sun, from the diffuse sky and clouds, and is reflected from the ground and other surrounding objects. Direct sun penetrating into interior workspaces may cause excessive luminance contrasts. Direct sun should be controlled by proper orientation of the building, or by louvers, overhangs, shades, blinds, or other devices. Diffuse light from the sky may cause excessive luminance contrasts when viewed by eyes concentrating on an interior task. In such cases, the sky should be filtered or shielded from view or the view of the task should be oriented away from the windows. As much as half the light entering a space can be reflected from the ground.

DESIGN GUIDELINES

ROOM DEPTH

The level of illumination will be shallower in the interior than near the window. A rule of thumb is that daylighting can be effective for task illumination up to about 20 to 24 ft away from the windows, but this depends on the size and location of the windows. A window high in the fenestration wall will deliver light deeper into the interior than a low window of the same size. Venetian blinds may be used to reflect daylight against the ceiling and into more remote areas of the space while preventing the penetration of direct sunlight and view of excessively luminous areas on the exterior. The cross-sectional diagrams below show how the depth of the room affects daylight.

FINISHES

Finishes of interior surfaces are important in the control of light and luminous ratios. Light colored surfaces, diffusely reflecting, will aid in the distribution of light and reduce luminance ratios. The diagrams below show how room surfaces affect daylight from a window. The ceiling is the most effective surface for reflecting light and should be very light in color (preferably white). The floor is one of the least significant, and it is here that the designer has the greatest opportunity for use of darker colors, such as those found in carpets, although very dark colors may cause excessive luminance differences.

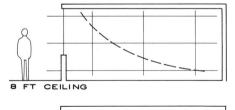

8 FT CEILING

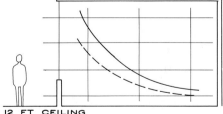

12 FT CEILING

The higher and larger the window, the more light there will be in the interior. The dashed illumination curve for the 8 ft ceiling can be compared with the solid curve for the 12 ft ceiling. Window areas below the level of the work surface are not effective in providing light on the task.

WINDOW HEIGHT

Benjamin H. Evans, AIA; Blacksburg, Virginia

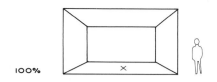

100%

All room surfaces are white, and the illumination level at point x is 100%.

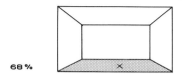

68%

With the floor painted black the illumination level is 68% of the all-white room.

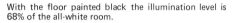

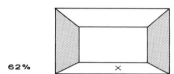

62%

With the sidewalls painted black.

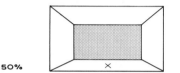

50%

The back wall has been painted black, and the illumination level at point x is only 50% of that in the all-white room.

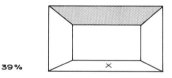

39%

With the ceiling painted black.

SURFACE FINISHES

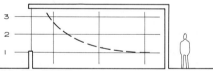

24 FT DEEP

The dashed curve indicates the illumination distribution for a typical 24 ft deep room.

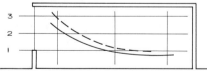

28 FT DEEP

The solid curve indicates the illumination level for a 28 ft deep room and can be compared with the dashed curve from the top diagram.

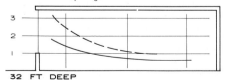

32 FT DEEP

The solid curve indicates the illumination level for a 32 ft deep room and can be compared with the dashed curve from the top diagram.

ROOM DEPTH

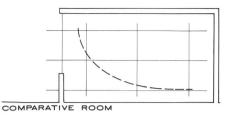

COMPARATIVE ROOM

A particular room produces a distribution of daylight as indicated by the dashed curve (repeated below).

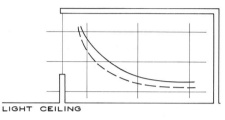

LIGHT CEILING

When the reflectivity of the ceiling is increased (painted white) the illumination level increases as indicated by the solid curve. The distribution curve flattens somewhat, since the increased ceiling reflectance increases illumination most toward the back wall.

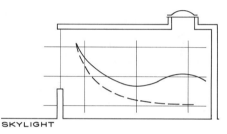

SKYLIGHT

The introduction of a skylight near the back wall increases the illumination in that area. (A clerestory, or a high window in the back wall, would produce similar results.)

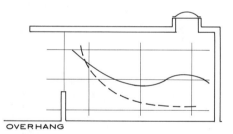

OVERHANG

An overhang can be used to reduce the illumination near the windows to a greater degree than in the back of the room. Another way to do this is with horizontal louvers on the exterior of the window wall or with interior venetian blinds.

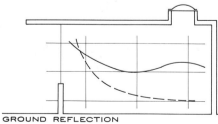

GROUND REFLECTION

Increasing the ground reflectivity (e.g., with a concrete walk) outside the window will increase the general level of interior illumination.

DAYLIGHTING METHODS

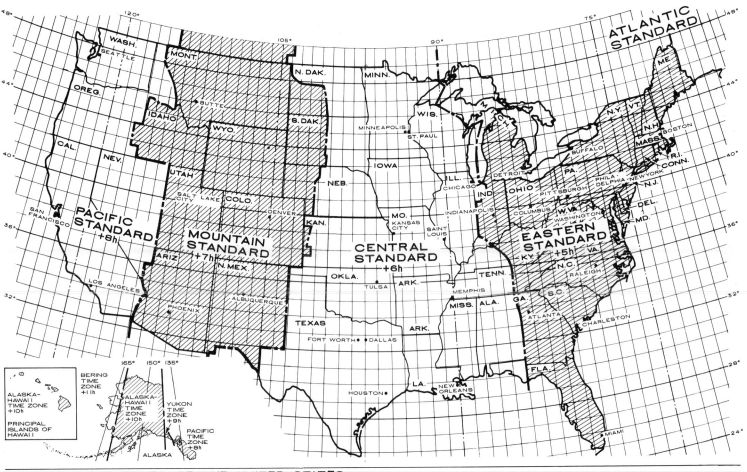

STANDARD TIME ZONES OF THE UNITED STATES
NOTE: Greenwich Standard Time is 0 h.

SOLAR TIME

Solar time generally differs from local standard or daylight saving time, and the difference can be significant, particularly when DST is in effect.

Because the sun appears to move at the rate of 360°/24 hr, its apparent motion is 4 min/1° of longitude. The procedure for finding AST (apparent solar time), explained in detail in the references cited previously, is

$$AST = LST + ET + 4(LSM - LON)$$

where ET = equation of time (min)
LSM = local standard time meridian (degrees of arc)
LON = local longitude, degrees of arc
4 = minutes of time required for 1.0° rotation of earth

The longitudes of the six standard time meridians that affect the United States are: eastern ST, 75°; central ST, 90°; mountain ST, 105°; Pacific ST, 120°; Yukon ST, 135°; Alaska-Hawaii ST, 150°.

The equation of time is the measure, in minutes, of the extent by which solar time, as told by a sundial, runs faster or slower than civil or mean time, as determined by a clock running at a uniform rate. The table below gives values of the declination and the equation of time for the 21st day of each month of a typical year (other than a leap year). This date is chosen because of its significance on four particular days: (a) the winter solstice, December 21, the year's shortest day, δ = -23° 27 min; (b) the vernal and autumnal equinoxes, March 21 and September 21, when the declination is zero and the day and night are equal in length; and (c) the summer solstice, June 21, the year's longest day, δ = +23° 27 min.

EXAMPLES

Find AST at noon, local summer time, on July 21 for Washington, D.C., longitude = 77°; and for Chicago, longitude = 87.6°.

SOLUTIONS

In summer, both Washington and Chicago use daylight saving time, and noon, local summer time, is actually 11:00 a.m., local standard time. For Washington, in the eastern time zone, the local standard time meridian is 75° east of Greenwich, and for July 21, the equation of time is -6.2 min. Thus noon, Washington summer time, is actually

$$11:00 - 6.2 \text{ min} + 4 \times (75 - 77) = 10:46 \text{ a.m.}$$

For Chicago, in the central time zone, the local standard time meridian is 90°. Chicago lies 2.4° east of that line, and noon, Chicago summer time, is

$$11:00 - 6.2 \text{ min} + 4 \times 2.4 = 11:03 \text{ a.m.}$$

The hour angle, H, for these two examples would be

for Washington: H = 0.25 x (12:00 - 10:46)
$$= 0.25 \times 74 = 18.8° \text{ east}$$

for Chicago: H = 0.25 x (12:00 - 11:03)
$$= 14.25° \text{ east}$$

YEAR DATE, DECLINATION, AND EQUATION OF TIME FOR THE 21st DAY OF EACH MONTH; WITH DATA* (A, B, C) USED TO CALCULATE DIRECT NORMAL RADIATION INTENSITY AT THE EARTH'S SURFACE

MONTH	JAN.	FEB.	MAR.	APR.	MAY	JUNE	JULY	AUG.	SEPT.	OCT.	NOV.	DEC.
Day of the year†	21	52	80	111	141	173	202	233	265	294	325	355
Declination, (δ) degrees	-19.9	-10.6	0.0	+11.9	+20.3	+23.45	+20.5	+12.1	0.0	-10.7	-19.9	-23.45
Equation of time (min)	-11.2	-13.9	-7.5	+1.1	+3.3	-1.4	-6.2	-2.4	+7.5	+15.4	+13.8	+1.6
Solar noon	Late			Early			Late			Early		
A: Btuh/sq ft	390	385	376	360	350	345	344	351	365	378	387	391
B: 1/m	0.142	0.144	0.156	0.180	0.196	0.205	0.207	0.201	0.177	0.160	0.149	0.142
C: dimensionless	0.058	0.060	0.071	0.097	0.121	0.134	0.136	0.122	0.092	0.073	0.063	0.057

*A is the apparent solar irradiation at air mass zero for each month; B is the atmospheric extinction coefficient; C is the ratio of the diffuse radiation on a horizontal surface to the direct normal irradiation.
†Declinations are for the year 1964.

John I. Yellott, P.E.; College of Architecture; Arizona State University; Tempe, Arizona

DIAGRAM		A EXCLUDES DIRECT SUN RAYS	B RE-RADIATES HEAT	C CONTROLS SKY GLARE	D CONTROLS GROUND GLARE & HEAT	E EFFECTIVE ORIENTATION	F RESTRICTS VIEW	G HINDERS FREE AIR MOVEMENT	H CONTROLS WINTER RAYS	I MAINTENANCE (NOT CLEANING)
1. OVERHANG	Length of overhang calculated to eliminate summer sun.	Seasonal	No	No	No	South	No	Yes	Yes	Minimum unless otherwise noted
2. VERTICAL SCREEN (WITH OVERHANG)	Length of louver calculated to eliminate summer sun. Length of louver for sky glare dependent on amount of control desired on exterior conditions and occupants normal eye level.	Optional: Completely or seasonal.	Minimal	Yes	Some—amount varies with design.	Any direction. depends on design.	Yes—If opaque blade in louver. No—if tinted glass blade.	Slight	Depends on design	High for louver.
3. VERTICAL SCREEN (WITHOUT OVERHANG)	Length of louver or glass panel calculated to eliminate summer sun. Length of louver for sky glare dependent on amount of control desired on exterior conditions and occupants normal eye level.	Optional: Completely or seasonal.	Minimal	Yes	Some—amount varies with design.	Any direction. depends on design.	Yes—If opaque blade in louver. No—if tinted glass blade.	No—if louvers. Yes—if glass panel unless vent slats are provided.	Depends on design	Low for glazing
4. ADJUSTABLE EXTERIOR HORIZONTAL LOUVERS	Louvers can be adjusted to control direct rays of sun.	Optional	Minimal	No	Yes	Any direction. South is least restrictive to view.	Yes	No	Depends on design	Varies—depending on scale and materials used.
5A. OVERHANG VERTICALLY LOUVERED	Length of overhang calculated to eliminate summer sun.	Seasonal	No	Yes	No	South	No	No	Yes	Varies—depends on material used.
5B. OVERHANG ANGLE LOUVERED	Length of overhang and pitch of louvers calculated to eliminate summer sun and permit winter rays full penetration.	Seasonal	No	No	No	No	No	No	Yes—with louvers as shown, can permit maximum winter sun if desired.	Varies—depends on material used.
6. EXTERIOR VERTICAL LOUVERED	If fixed louvers can be set so as to eliminate low angle sun rays for predetermined orientation. If operable, maximum control any orientation but with various amount of view interference.	Optional: Completely or seasonal depending on orientation or other factors.	Minimal	Some	Some	East or west, south with adequate overhang.	Yes	No	Depends on design	Moderate
		As desired.	Minimal	Can be good see J	Some	Any	Yes	No	Yes	High
7. SPEC. GLAZING (GLASS, PLASTIC, COATED GLASS)	Heat absorbing glazing controls solar heat gain. Heat absorbing and low transmission glazing controls heat gain and sky glare. Sandwich of glass and fixed louvers can control direct sun rays and sky glare and admits greater amounts of useful daylight.	No—reduces—depending on glazing material.	Can be substantial unless double glazing used.	Yes—ideal if darker sheets used in upper portion of window.	Yes	Any	No	See K	Yes—more than others	Low
		Seasonal	Low to minimal.	Yes	Same	Any	Yes	See K	Less than 7A	Low

J. Stanley Sharp, AIA; Handren, Sharp and Associates; New York, New York

ENVIRONMENTAL FACTORS 1

J	K	L
EFFECT ON INTERIOR LIGHTING	**CAUTIONS**	**VARIATIONS**
Harsh without ideal exterior conditions, or with no glare control in glass or interior control devices.	Tends to trap warm air. High sash if open may let heat into building.	Overhang with light & heat transmission glass. Overhang with open framing with removable material (fabric, fiber glass). Trellis with plant material—permits entry of winter sun. Fixed awning—similar characteristics, except maintenance is high. Operable awning—also similar, plus lower sun angle control (west), restricts view when down.
Good	Check clearance for operating sash and window cleaning.	Addition of vertical member may be used to cut off low angle oblique rays. Adjustable vertical blinds or awnings afford good control for low sun, or glare from beach or water, without permanent restriction of view. Maintenance is high.
Good	Check clearance for operating sash and window cleaning.	Addition of vertical member may be used to cut off low angle oblique rays. Adjustable vertical blinds or awnings afford good control for low sun, or glare from beach or water, without permanent restriction of view. Maintenance is high.
Good—could be used for darkening device.		Exterior operating shutters have similar characteristics, and can be opened when not required but with loss of sky glare control.
Diffused reflected light from louvers improves quality of daylighting by reducing contrast between interior ceiling and bright sky.		Egg crate overhang instead of louvers to control oblique sun rays. Adjustable louvered awnings (questionable in cold climates) require high maintenance.
Diffused reflected light from louvers improves quality of daylighting by reducing contrast between interior ceiling and bright sky.		Egg crate overhang instead of louvers to control oblique sun rays. Adjustable louvered awnings (questionable in cold climates) require high maintenance.
Varies depending on position in room.	Check clearance for operating sash and window cleaning.	Narrow windows with adequate side reveals or projecting blades have similar sun and glare control.
Good—if a limited view is acceptable.		When used with adequate overhang on south will eliminate all sun in summer months.
Good (see C) w/high levels of artificial light, interior visual comfort is improved as reduces contrast between work surfaces and window area. Good—combine w/7A for ideal sky glare control w/a restricting eye level view.	Open sash may defeat sun & glare control, but is appropriate for a/c buildings. Replacement delay is probable. / Open sash may defeat sun & glare control, but is appropriate for a/c buildings.	Allow only storm sash to be tinted to eliminate problem noted under B. / Louvered screen placed in front of glazing would control sun but restricts view, maintenance factor if movable, and sky glare control is lost.

J. Stanley Sharp, AIA; Handren, Sharp and Associates; New York, New York

GENERAL NOTES

Uncontrolled glare, generated by the sun's rays, can become uncomfortable in winter; in summer, this glare plus solar heat can be intolerable. Glare can be effectively controlled by either interior or exterior devices, but solar heat gain is best controlled by interception outside the building. Tinted glass and/or interior devices such as shades, horizontal blinds, vertical blinds, as well as various screening methods may be used to control sky glare and glare from the direct rays of the sun. However, they do little to reduce interior air temperature because the sun rays have been allowed to enter the room. Do not use any form of translucent glass where sun will fall directly on it because this will produce glare similar to the dirty windshield of a car. Objectionable glare (i.e., a brightness ratio in excess of 10:1 between peripheral vision and the immediate area of vision) can occur at any orientation, including north, through indirect sources, by reflection from various surfaces. For example, light from a slightly overcast sky or from patches of white clouds can be 30 to 300 times greater than the light reflected from a well-lighted work surface. Provisions for shielding these secondary sources are particularly important to good vision when occupants of a space must remain in relatively fixed positions.

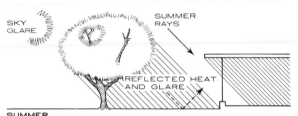

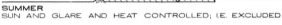

SUMMER
SUN AND GLARE AND HEAT CONTROLLED; I.E. EXCLUDED

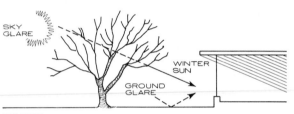

WINTER
SUN ACCEPTED- GLARE CAN BE A PROBLEM (SNOW IN PARTICULAR). CLOSELY SPACED LIMBS CAN CONTROL SKY GLARE.
SOUTH EXPOSURE

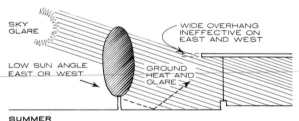

SUMMER
SUN GLARE AND HEAT CONTROLLED

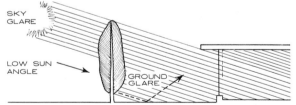

WINTER
LOW SUN ANGLE NOW ACCEPTED ; GLARE CONTROLLED BY DENSE BRANCH STRUCTURE ; HEAT CAN BE REASONABLY CONTROLLED AS DESIRED BY INSIDE DEVICES (SHADES, BLINDS, OR DRAPES).
EAST AND WEST EXPOSURE

APPLICATIONS IN CONJUNCTION WITH PLANTING
EXAMPLES OF HOW BASIC CONTROL DEVICES CAN BE USED IN CONJUNCTION WITH NATURAL FEATURES TO ACHIEVE GOOD SEASONAL RESULTS

NOTE
For more positive sky glare control in winter and summer, coniferous trees should be used.

SOLAR ANGLES

The position of the sun in relation to specific geographic locations, seasons, and times of day can be determined by several methods. Model measurements, by means of solar machines or shade dials, have the advantage of direct visual observations. Tabulative and calculative methods have the advantage of exactness. However, graphic projection methods are usually preferred by architects, as they are easily understood and can be correlated to both radiant energy and shading calculations.

SOLAR PATH DIAGRAMS

A practical graphic projection is the solar path diagram method. Such diagrams depict the path of the sun within the sky vault as projected onto a horizontal plane. The horizon is represented as a circle with the observation point in the center. The sun's position at any date and hour can be determined from the diagram in terms of its altitude (β) and azimuth (ϕ). (See figure on right.) The graphs are constructed in equidistant projection. The altitude angles are represented at 10° intervals by equally spaced concentric circles; they range from 0° at the outer circle (horizon) to 90° at the center point. These intervals are graduated along the south meridian. Azimuth is represented at 10° intervals by equally spaced radii; they range from 0° at the south meridian to 180° at the north meridian. These intervals are graduated along the periphery. The solar bearing will be to the east during morning hours, and to the west during afternoon hours.

(CONTINUED NEXT PAGE)

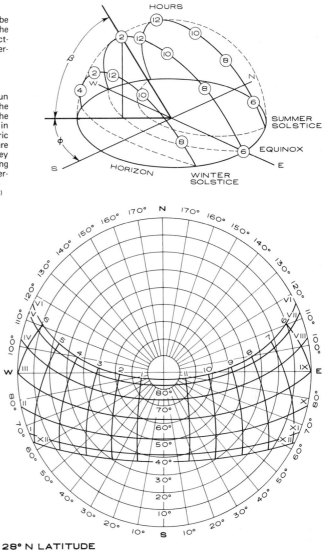

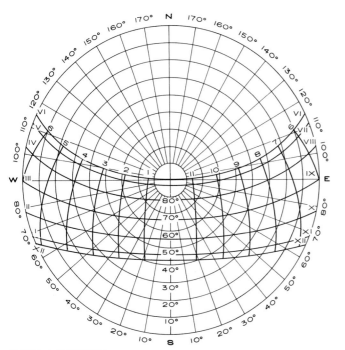

24°N LATITUDE

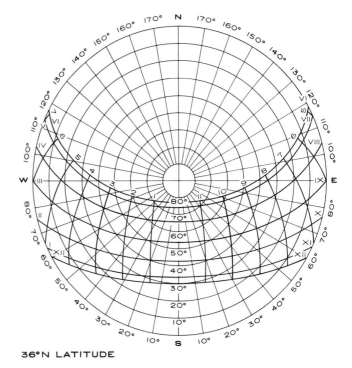

28° N LATITUDE

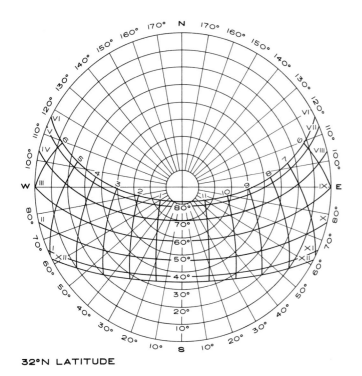

32°N LATITUDE

36°N LATITUDE

Victor Olgyay, AIA; Associate Professor; School of Architecture, Princeton University; Princeton, New Jersey

ENVIRONMENTAL FACTORS 1

SOLAR PATH DIAGRAMS (CONTINUED)

The earth's axis is inclined 23°27' to its orbit around the sun and rotates 15° hourly. Thus, from all points on the earth, the sun appears to move across the sky vault on various parallel circular paths with maximum declinations of ±23°27'. The declination of the sun's path changes in a cycle between the extremes of the summer solstice and winter solstice. Thus the sun follows the same path on two corresponding dates each year. Due to irregularities between the calendar year and the astronomical data, here a unified calibration is adapted. The differences, as they do not exceed 41', are negligible for architectural purposes.

The elliptical curves in the diagrams represent the horizontal projections of the sun's path. They are given on the 21st day of each month. Roman numerals designate the months. A cross grid of curves graduate the hours indicated in arabic numerals. Eight solar path diagrams are shown at 4° intervals from 24°N to 52°N latitude.

EXAMPLE

Find the sun's position in Columbus, Ohio, on February 21, 2 P.M.:

STEP 1. Locate Columbus on the map. The latitude is 40°N.

STEP 2. In the 40° sun path diagram select the February path (marked with II), and locate the 2 hr line. Where the two lines cross is the position of the sun.

STEP 3. Read the altitude on the concentric circles (32°) and the azimuth along the outer circle (35°30'W).

DECLINATION OF THE SUN

DATE	DECLINATION	CORRESP. DATE	DECLINATION	UNIFIED CALIBR.
June 21	+23°27'			+23°27'
May 21	+20°09'	July 21	+20°31'	+20°20'
Apr. 21	+11°48'	Aug. 21	+12°12'	+12°00'
Mar. 21	+0°10'	Sep. 21	+0°47'	+0°28'
Feb. 21	-10°37'	Oct. 21	-10°38'	-10°38'
Jan. 21	-19°57'	Nov. 21	-19°53'	-19°55'
Dec. 21	-23°27'			-23°27'

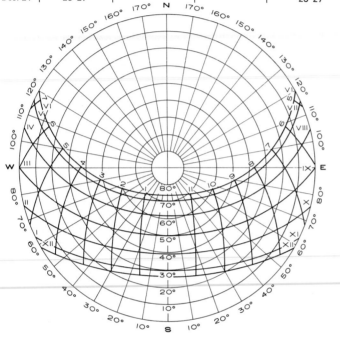

40°N LATITUDE

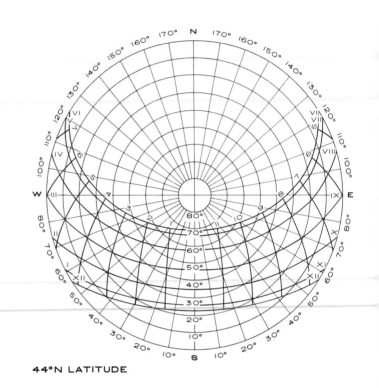

44°N LATITUDE

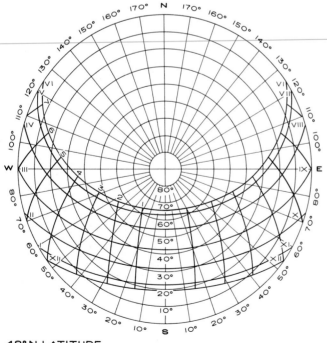

48°N LATITUDE

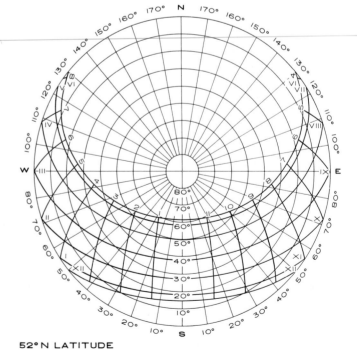

52°N LATITUDE

Victor Olgyay, AIA; Associate Professor; School of Architecture, Princeton University; Princeton, New Jersey

1 ENVIRONMENTAL FACTORS

SHADING DEVICES

The effect of shading devices can be plotted in the same manner as the solar path was projected. The diagrams show which part of the sky vault will be obstructed by the devices and are projections of the surface covered on the sky vault as seen from an observation point at the center of the diagram. These projections also represent those parts of the sky vault from which no sunlight will reach the observation point; if the sun passes through such an area the observation point will be shaded.

SHADING MASKS

Any building element will define a characteristic form in these projection diagrams, known as "shading masks." Masks of horizontal devices (overhangs) will create a segmental pattern; vertical intercepting elements (fins) produce a radial pattern; shading devices with horizontal and vertical members (eggcrate type) will make a combinative pattern. A shading mask can be drawn for any shading device, even for very complex ones, by geometric plotting. As the shading masks are geometric projections they are independent of latitude and exposed directions, therefore they can be used in any location and at any orientation. By overlaying a shading mask in the proper orientation on the sun-path diagram, one can read off the times when the sun rays will be intercepted. Masks can be drawn for full shade (100% mask) when the observation point is at the lowest point of the surface needing shading; or for 50% shading when the observation point is placed at the halfway mark on the surface. It is customary to design a shading device in such a way that as soon as shading is needed on a surface the masking angle should exceed 50%. Solar calculations should be used to check the specific loads. Basic shading devices are shown below, with their obstruction effect on the sky vault and with their projected shading masks.

SHADING MASK PROTRACTOR

The half of the protractor showing segmental lines is used to plot lines parallel and normal to the observed vertical surface. The half showing bearing and altitude lines is used to plot shading masks of vertical fins or any other obstruction objects. The protractor is in the same projection and scale as the sun-path diagrams (see pages on solar angles); therefore it is useful to transfer the protractor to a transparent overlay to read the obstruction effect.

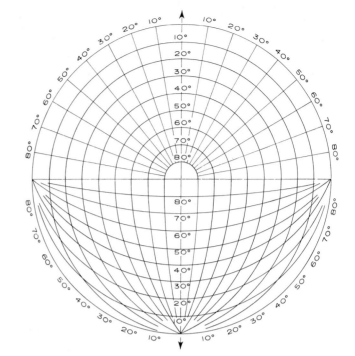

SHADING MASK PROTRACTOR

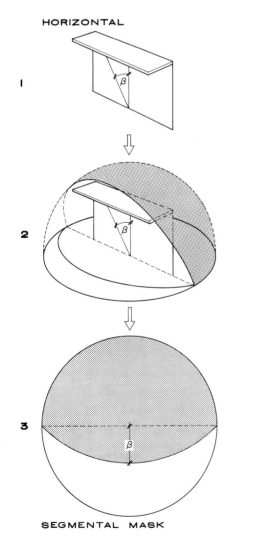

HORIZONTAL

VERTICAL

EGGCRATE

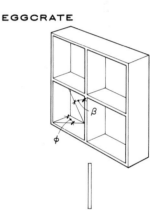

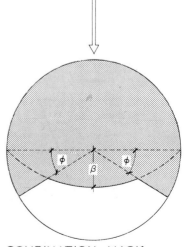

Horizontal devices produce segmental obstruction patterns, vertical fins produce radial patterns, and eggcrate devices produce combination patterns.

SEGMENTAL MASK

RADIAL MASK

COMBINATION MASK

Victor Olgyay, AIA; Associate Professor; School of Architecture, Princeton University; Princeton, New Jersey

ENVIRONMENTAL FACTORS   1

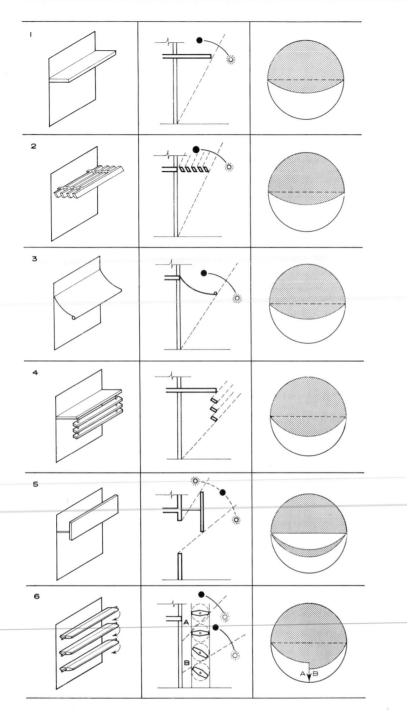

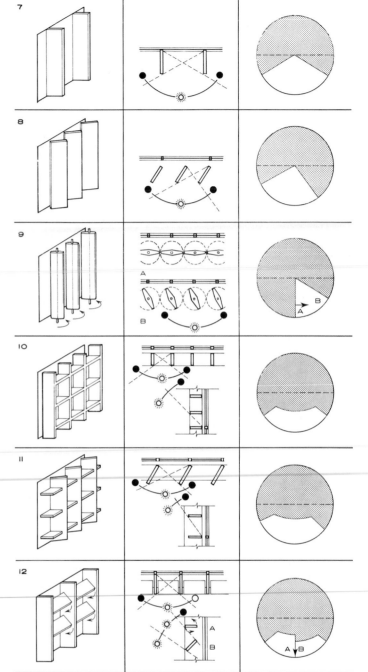

EXAMPLES OF VARIOUS TYPES OF SHADING DEVICES

The illustrations show a number of basic types of devices, classified as horizontal, vertical, and eggcrate types. The dash lines shown in the section diagram in each case indicate the sun angle at the time of 100% shading. The shading mask for each device is also shown, the extent of 100% shading being indicated by the gray area.

General rules can be deduced for the types of shading devices to be used for different orientations. Southerly orientations call for shading devices with segmental mask characteristics, and horizontal devices work in these directions efficiently. For easterly and westerly orientations vertical devices serve well, having radial shading masks. If slanted, they should incline toward the north, to give more protection from the southern positions of the sun. The eggcrate type of shading device works well on walls facing southeast, and is particularly effective for southwest orientations. Because of this type's high shading ratio and low winter head admission; its best use is in hot climate regions. For north walls, fixed vertical devices are recommended; however, their use is needed only for large glass surfaces, or in hot regions. At low latitudes on both south and north exposures eggcrate devices work efficiently.

Whether the shading devices be fixed or movable, the same recommendations apply in respect to the different orientations. The movable types can be most efficiently utilized where the sun's altitude and bearing angles change rapidly: on the east, southeast, and especially, because of the afternoon heat, on the southwest and west.

Victor Olgyay, AIA; Associate Professor; School of Architecture, Princeton University; Princeton, New Jersey

HORIZONTAL TYPES 1. Horizontal overhangs are most efficient toward south, or around southern orientations. Their mask characteristics are segmental. 2. Louvers parallel to wall have the advantage of permitting air circulation near the elevation. Slanted louvers will have the same characteristics as solid overhangs, and can be made retractable. 4. When protection is needed for low sun angles, louvers hung from solid horizontal overhangs are efficient. 5. A solid, or perforated screen strip parallel to wall cuts out the lower rays of the sun. 6. Movable horizontal louvers change their segmental mask characteristics according to their positioning.

VERTICAL TYPES 7. Vertical fins serve well toward the near east and near west orientations. Their mask characteristics are radial. 8. Vertical fins oblique to wall will result in asymmetrical mask. Separation from wall will prevent heat transmission. 9. Movable fins can shade the whole wall, or open up in different directions according to the sun's position.

EGGCRATE TYPES 10. Eggcrate types are combinations of horizontal and vertical types, and their masks are superimposed diagrams of the two masks. 11. Solid eggcrate with slanting vertical fins results in asymmetrical mask. 12. Eggcrate device with movable horizontal elements shows flexible mask characteristics. Because of their high shading ratio, eggcrates are efficient in hot climates.

1   ENVIRONMENTAL FACTORS

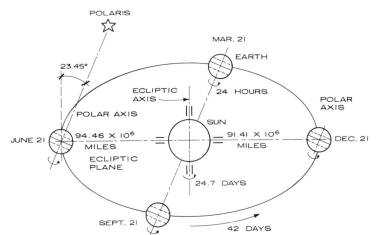

NOTE: THE TILT OF THE EARTH'S AXIS WITH RESPECT TO THE ECLIPTIC AXIS CAUSES THE CHANGING SEASONS AND THE ANNUAL VARIATIONS IN NUMBER OF HOURS OF DAYLIGHT AND DARKNESS.

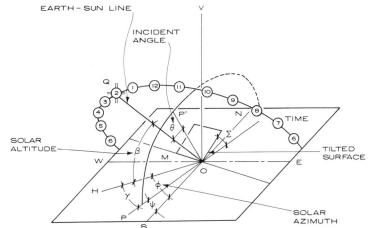
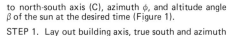

NOTE: Q DESIGNATES THE SUN'S POSITION SO OQ IS THE EARTH–SUN LINE WHILE OP' IS THE NORMAL TO THE TILTED SURFACE AND OP IS PERPENDICULAR TO THE INTERSECTION, OM, BETWEEN THE TILTED SURFACE AND THE HORIZONTAL PLANE.

ANNUAL MOTION OF THE EARTH ABOUT THE SUN

SOLAR CONSTANT

The sun is located at one focus of the earth's orbit, and we are only 147.2 million km (91.4 million miles) away from the sun in late December and early January, while the earth-sun distance on July 1 is about 152.0 million km (94.4 million miles).

Solar energy approaches the earth as electromagnetic radiation at wavelengths between 0.25 and 5.0 μm. The intensity of the incoming solar irradiance on a surface normal to the sun's rays beyond the earth's atmosphere, at the average earth-sun distance, is designated as the solar constant, I_{sc}. Although the value of I_{sc} has not yet been precisely determined by verified measurements made in outer space, the most widely used value is 429.2 Btu/sq ft · hr (1353 W/sq m) and the current ASHRAE values are based on this estimate. More recent measurements made at extremely high altitudes indicate that I_{sc} is probably close to 436.6 Btu/sq ft · hr (1377 W/sq m). The unit of radiation that is widely used by meteorologists is the langley, equivalent to one kilogram calorie/square centimeter. To convert from langleys/day to Btu/sq ft · day, multiply Ly/day by 369. To convert from W/sq m to Btu/sq ft · hr, multiply the electrical unit by 0.3172.

SOLAR ANGLES

At the earth's surface the amount of solar radiation received and the resulting atmospheric temperature vary widely, primarily because of the daily rotation of the earth and the fact that the rotational axis is tilted at an angle of 23.45° with respect to the orbital plane. This tilt causes the changing seasons with their varying lengths of daylight and darkness. The angle between the earth-sun line and the orbital plane, called the solar declination, d, varies throughout the year, as shown in the following table for the 21st day of each month.

JAN -19.9° APR +11.9° JUL +20.5° OCT -10.7°
FEB -10.6° MAY +20.3° AUG +12.1° NOV -19.9°
MAR   0.0°   JUN +23.5° SEP   0.0° DEC -23.5°

Very minor changes in the declination occur from year to year, and when more precise values are needed the almanac for the year in question should be consulted.

The earth's annual orbit about the sun is slightly elliptical, and so the earth-sun distance is slightly greater in summer than in winter. The time required for each annual orbit is actually 365.242 days rather than the 365 days shown by the calendar, and this is corrected by adding a 29th day to February for each year (except century years) that is evenly divisible by 4.

To an observer standing on a particular spot on the earth's surface, with a specified longitude, LON, and latitude, L, it is the sun that appears to move around the earth in a regular daily pattern. Actually it is the earth's rotation that causes the sun's apparent motion. The position of the sun can be defined in terms of its altitude β above the horizon (angle HOQ) and its azimuth ϕ, measured as angle HOS in the horizontal plane.

John I. Yellot, P.E.; College of Architecture; Arizona State University; Tempe, Arizona

At solar noon, the sun is, by definition, exactly on the meridian that contains the south-north line, and consequently the solar azimuth ϕ is 0.0°. The noon altitude β is:

$$= 90° - L + \delta$$

Because the earth's daily rotation and its annual orbit around the sun are regular and predictable, the solar altitude and azimuth may be readily calculated for any desired time of day as soon as the latitude, longitude, and date (declination) are specified.

SHADOW CONSTRUCTION WITH TRUE SUN ANGLES

Required information: angle of orientation in relation to north-south axis (C), azimuth ϕ, and altitude angle β of the sun at the desired time (Figure 1).

STEP 1. Lay out building axis, true south and azimuth ϕ of sun in plan (Figure 2).

STEP 2. Lay out altitude β upon azimuth ϕ. Construct any perpendicular to ϕ. From the intersection of this perpendicular and ϕ project a line perpendicular to elevation plane (building orientation). Measure distance x along this line from elevation plane. Connect the point at distance x from elevation plane to center to construct sun elevation β (Figure 2).

STEP 3. Use sun plan $\phi + C$ and sun elevation β to construct shadows in plan and elevation in conventional way (Figure 3).

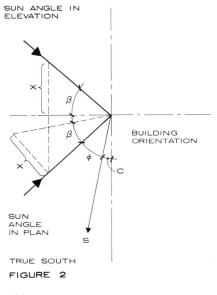

FIGURE 1

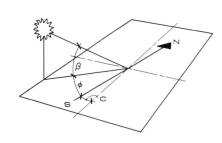

SUN ANGLE IN ELEVATION

BUILDING ORIENTATION

SUN ANGLE IN PLAN

TRUE SOUTH

FIGURE 2

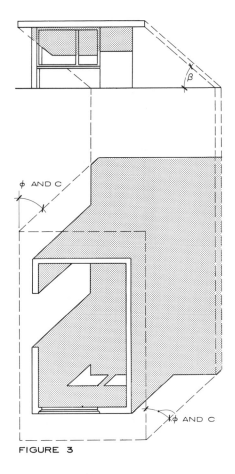

FIGURE 3

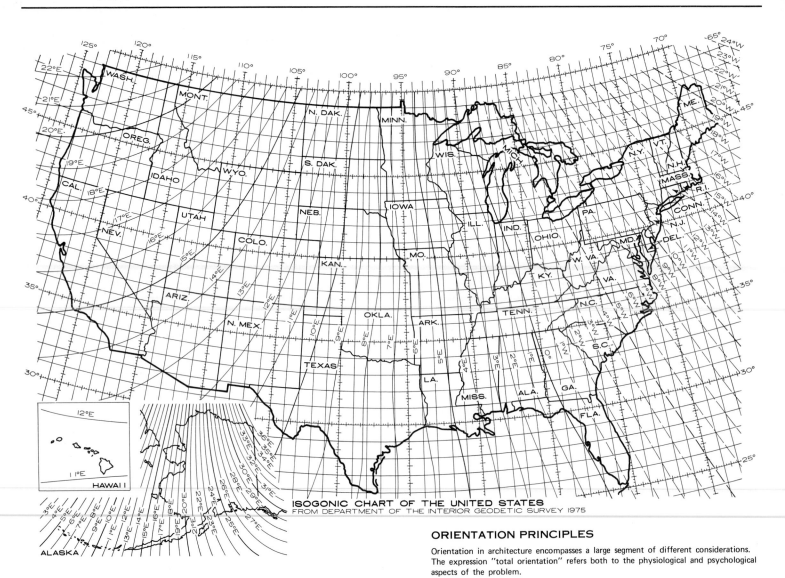

ISOGONIC CHART OF THE UNITED STATES
FROM DEPARTMENT OF THE INTERIOR GEODETIC SURVEY 1975

COMPASS ORIENTATION

The above map is the isogonic chart of the United States. The wavy lines from top to bottom show the compass variations from the true north. At the lines marked E the compass will point east of true north; at those marked W the compass will point west of true north. According to the location, correction should be done from the compass north to find the true north.

EXAMPLE: On a site in Wichita, Kansas, find the true north.

STEP 1.   Find the compass orientation on the site.

STEP 2.   Locate Wichita on the map. The nearest compass variation is the 10°E line.

STEP 3.   Adjust the orientation correction to true north.
The graphical example illustrates a building which lies 25° east with its axis from the compass orientation.

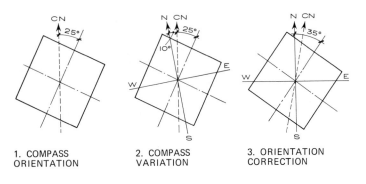

1. COMPASS
ORIENTATION

2. COMPASS
VARIATION

3. ORIENTATION
CORRECTION

Victor Olgyay, AIA; Associate Professor; School of Architecture, Princeton University; Princeton, New Jersey

ORIENTATION PRINCIPLES

Orientation in architecture encompasses a large segment of different considerations. The expression "total orientation" refers both to the physiological and psychological aspects of the problem.

At the physiological side the factors which affect our senses and have to be taken into consideration are: the thermal impacts—the sun, wind, and temperature effects acting through our skin envelope; the visible impacts—the different illumination and brightness levels affecting our visual senses; the sonic aspects—the noise impacts and noise levels of the surroundings influencing our hearing organs. In addition, our respiratory organs are affected by the smoke, smell, and dust of the environs.

On the psychological side, the view and the privacy are aspects in orientation which quite often override the physical considerations.

Above all, as a building is only a mosaic unit in the pattern of a town organization, the spatial effects, the social intimacy, and its relation to the urban representative directions—aesthetic, political, or social—all play a part in positioning a building.

THERMAL FORCES INFLUENCING ORIENTATION

The climatic factors such as wind, solar radiation, and air temperature play the most eminent role in orientation. The position of a structure in northern latitudes, where the air temperature is generally cool, should be oriented to receive the maximum amount of sunshine without wind exposure. In southerly latitudes, however, the opposite will be desirable; the building should be turned on its axis to avoid the sun's unwanted radiation and to face the cooling breezes instead.

At right the figure shows these regional requirements diagrammatically.

Adaptation for wind orientation is not of great importance in low buildings, where the use of windbreaks and the arrangement of openings in the high and low pressure areas can help to ameliorate the airflow situation. However, for high buildings, where the surrounding terrain has little effect on the upper stories, careful consideration has to be given to wind orientation.

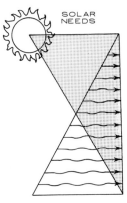

SOLAR
NEEDS

WIND NEEDS

NOTES

To visualize the thermal impacts on differently exposed surfaces four locations are shown approximately at the 24°, 32°, 40° and 44° latitudes. The forces are indicated on average clear winter and summer days. The air temperature variation is indicated by the outside concentric circles. Each additional line represents a 2°F difference from the lowest daily temperature. The direction of the impact is indicated according to the sun's direction as temperatures occur. (Note the low temperatures at the east side, and the high ones in westerly directions.)

The total (direct and diffuse) radiation impact on the various sides of the building is indicated with arrows. Each arrow represents 250 Btu/sq ft · day radiation. At the bottom of the page the radiations are expressed in numerical values.

The values show that in the upper latitudes the south side of a building receives nearly twice as much radiation in winter as in summer. This effect is even more pronounced at the lower latitudes, where the ratio is about one to four. Also, in the upper latitudes, the east and west sides receive about 2½ times more radiation in summer than in winter. This ratio is not as large in the lower latitudes; but it is noteworthy that in summer these sides receive two to three times as much radiation as the south elevation. In the summer the west exposure is more disadvantageous than the east exposure, as the afternoon high temperatures combine with the radiation effects. In all latitudes the north side receives only a small amount of radiation, and this comes mainly in the summer. In the low latitudes, in the summer, the north side receives nearly twice the impact of the south side. The amount of radiation received on a horizontal roof surface exceeds all other sides.

Experimental observations were conducted on the thermal behavior of building orientation at Princeton University's Architectural Laboratory. Below are shown the summer results of structures exposed to the cardinal directions. Note the unequal heat distribution and high heat impact of the west exposure compared to the east orientation. The southern direction gives a pleasantly low heat volume, slightly higher, however, than the north exposure.

JANUARY

N
W ← → E

JULY

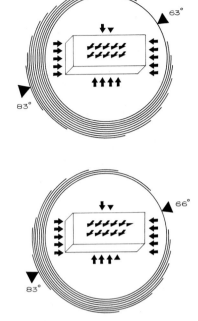

MINNEAPOLIS, MINN.

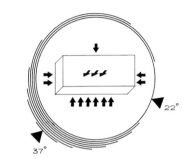

NEW YORK AREA

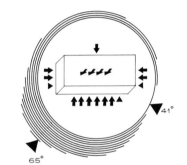

PHOENIX, ARIZ.

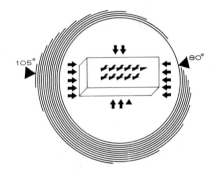

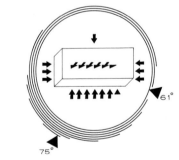

MIAMI, FLA.

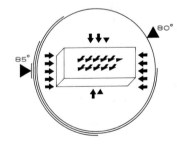

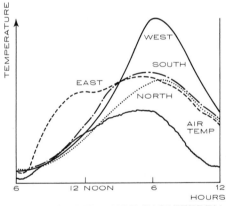

ROOM TEMPERATURE IN DIFFERENTLY ORIENTED HOUSES

ORIENTATION: CONCLUSIONS

1. The optimum orientation will lie near the south; however, will differ in the various regions, and will depend on the daily temperature distribution.
2. In all regions an orientation eastward from south gives a better yearly performance and a more equal daily heat distribution. Westerly directions perform more poorly with unbalanced heat impacts.
3. The thermal orientation exposure has to be correlated with the local wind directions.

TOTAL DIRECT AND DIFFUSED RADIATION (BTU/SQ FT · DAY)

LATITUDE	SEASON	EAST	SOUTH	WEST	NORTH	HORIZONTAL
44° LATITUDE	WINTER	416	1374	416	83	654
	SUMMER	1314	979	1314	432	2536
40° LATITUDE	WINTER	517	1489	517	119	787
	SUMMER	1277	839	1277	430	2619
32° LATITUDE	WINTER	620	1606	620	140	954
	SUMMER	1207	563	1207	452	2596
24° LATITUDE	WINTER	734	1620	734	152	1414
	SUMMER	1193	344	1193	616	2568

Victor Olgyay, AIA; Associate Professor; School of Architecture, Princeton University; Princeton, New Jersey

THERMAL COMFORT

Human thermal comfort is determined by the body's ability to dissipate the heat and moisture that are produced continuously by metabolic action. The rate of heat production varies with the size, age, sex, and degree of activity of the individuals whose comfort is under consideration. For men of average size, seated and doing light work, the metabolic rate is about 450 Btu/hr; for women under similar circumstances the comparable rate is about 385 Btu/hr. For a 155 lb man seated and doing moderate to heavy work, the rate ranges from 650 to 800 Btu/hr; standing and walking about while doing moderately heavy work will raise the rate to 1000 Btu/hr while the hardest sustained work will result in a metabolic rate of 2000 to 2400 Btu/hr. For an office with the usual complement of men and women, an average metabolic rate will range from 400 to 450 Btu/hr per person.

Thermal comfort is attained when the environment surrounding the individual can remove the bodily heat and moisture at the rate at which they are being produced. The removal, accomplished by convection, evaporation, and radiation, is regulated by the dry bulb temperature, the vapor pressure, and rate of movement of the air and the mean radiant temperature (MRT) of the surrounding surfaces. MRT is defined by ASHRAE as the temperature of an imaginary black enclosure in which the individual experiences the same rate of radiant heat exchange as in the actual environment. (See 1977 ASHRAE Handbook of Fundamentals, Chapter 8, for more information on MRT and human comfort.)

Heat and moisture removal are also strongly affected by the nature and amount of clothing being worn and by its insulating value. This quality can be evaluated in terms of a thermal resistance unit designated by clo, where 1 clo = 0.88°F/(Btu/hr · sq ft). Typical masculine office attire, complete with warm jacket and light trousers, has an insulating value of 1.12 clo while a woman's office dress is rated at 0.73 clo. Values for other combinations are given in the ASHRAE reference cited above, page 8.7, Tables 1-C and 1-D. Uncomfortably low ambient air temperatures can be made tolerable by putting on more and heavier clothing, thus increasing the clo value; the converse, unfortunately, is not true.

The properties of atmospheric air-water vapor mixtures in the temperature range normally experienced by the human body can be shown effectively on psychrometric charts, which can take many different forms. The most familiar is that put forth by Willis H. Carrier, who is generally regarded as the originator of the air-conditioning industry in the U.S.A. On the Carrier-type chart, shown in modified form in Fig. 1, the humidity ratio of moist air, in pounds or grains (1 lb = 7000 grains) of water vapor per pound of dry air, is plotted against the dry bulb temperature of the air. Significant psychrometric data are given in the table at temperature intervals of 5°F from 50 to 90°F.

The relative humidity of moist air is the ratio, expressed as a percentage, of the amount of water vapor actually present in a given quantity of that air to the amount that the same quantity of air could contain if it were completely saturated at the same temperature and pressure. The uppermost curved line on the chart, called the saturation line, denotes 100% relative humidity. The wet bulb temperature, measured by a thermometer with a water wetted sensor over which the air-vapor

mixture is flowing rapidly (800 to 900 fpm) is used in combination with the dry bulb temperature to find the % RH at conditions other than saturation. For example, at 75°F dry bulb and 60°F wet bulb the relative humidity is seen to be 40%.

The humidity ratio at this condition is 53 grains/lb of dry air while the dew point temperature, found by following the horizontal line of constant humidity ratio to its intersection with the saturation line, is 50°F.

The relatively restricted range of conditions within which most lightly clothed sedentary adults in the U.S.A. will experience thermal comfort is shown by the cross-hatched area on Fig. 1. Known as the ASHRAE comfort zone (also called "comfort envelope"), this area on the psychrometric chart represents the combinations of dry bulb temperature and relative humidity, which, when combined with an air movement of 45 fpm or less, will meet the thermal needs of most adults. For this chart, MRT = dry bulb temperature.

The effective temperature lines shown on Fig. 1 represent combinations of dry bulb temperature and relative humidity that will produce the same rate of heat and moisture dissipation by radiation, convection, and evaporation as an individual would experience in a black enclosure at the specified temperature and 50% relative humidity. As the % RH rises, the dry bulb temperature must be slightly reduced to produce the same feeling of comfort; as the % RH falls toward the 10 to 20% level experienced in desert climates, the dry bulb temperature may rise slightly without inducing discomfort.

The 65°F indoor temperature mandated by federal regulations for winter operation of public buildings is seen to be well below the normal comfort zone. Addition of clothing (higher clo values) may help to offset the discomfort that most occupants will experience at 65°F, regardless of the % RH, but extremities (fingers and toes) will be uncomfortably cold.

The upper range of the comfort zone is close to the 78°F effective temperature line, and so the 78°F dry bulb temperature that is mandated for summer operation of public buildings will be tolerable for most lightly clothed adults until the relative humidity rises above 60 to 65%. At that condition, discomfort will be experienced by many building occupants because of their inability to dissipate metabolic moisture. Increases in air velocity are beneficial under these conditions, but velocities above about 70 fpm will generally result in unpleasant working conditions because of drafts, blowing papers, and so on.

Figure 2 shows another version of the psychrometric chart in which wet bulb temperatures are plotted against dry bulb temperatures, with straight lines of constant % RH running upward from lower left to upper right. The effect of air velocity and clothing thermal resistance (expressed as clo units) is shown by the curved lines near the center of each diagram.

////// ASHRAE COMFORT ZONE

For these conditions, in which the mean radiant temperature equals the dry bulb temperature, relative humidity has only a small effect. As the activity level of the room occupants is lowered, reducing the metabolic rate, the comfortable air temperature range moves upward; as the activity level is increased, cooler air is required.

The effects of radiant energy transfer between individuals and the surfaces surrounding them can have significant influence on sensations of comfort or discomfort. An increase of 1°F in MRT is approximately equivalent to a 1.5°F increase in ambient air temperature. The use of radiant heating from moderately warm surfaces can help to offset the discomfort caused by air temperatures that are significantly below the ASHRAE comfort zone. Conversely, discomfort can be caused by large heated areas, such as sun warmed windows. An excessively high MRT can require a significant reduction in air temperature to create comfort. For an individual exposed to direct sunshine entering through an unshaded window, discomfort is almost certain to result.

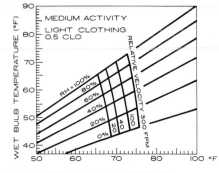

AIR TEMPERATURE = MEAN RADIANT TEMPERATURE

FIGURE 2

NOTE: Modified comfort chart for men, medium activity = 750 Btu/hr, thermal resistance of "light-clothing" = 0.5 clo.

MODIFIED COMFORT CHART

PROPERTIES OF WATER VAPOR AND SATURATED AIR

TEM-PERA-TURE (°F)	VAPOR PRES-SURE (IN. HG)	HUMID-ITY RATIO (GRAINS/LB)	ENTHALPY (BTU/LB)	SPE-CIFIC VOL-UME (CU FT/LB)
50	0.362	53.6	20.30	13.00
55	0.436	64.6	23.32	13.16
60	0.522	80.4	26.46	13.33
65	0.622	92.8	30.06	13.50
70	0.739	110.7	34.09	13.69
75	0.875	131.7	38.61	13.88
80	1.032	156.31	43.69	14.09
85	1.214	184.9	49.43	14.31
90	1.422	218.3	55.93	14.55

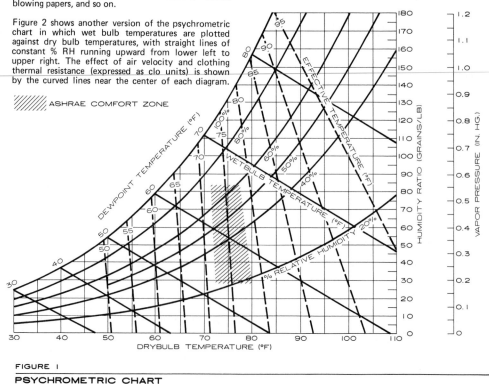

FIGURE 1

PSYCHROMETRIC CHART

John I. Yellott, P. E., Professor Emeritus, College of Architecture, Arizona State University; Tempe, Arizona

1   ENVIRONMENTAL FACTORS

DEFINITIONS AND SYMBOLS

BRITISH THERMAL UNIT (Btu): The quantity of heat required to raise the temperature of one pound of water one degree Fahrenheit (specifically, from 59°F to 60°F).

DEGREE DAYS (DD): A temperature-time unit used in estimating building heating requirements. For any given day, the number of DD equals the difference between the reference temperature, usually 65°F, and the mean temperature of the outdoor air for that day. DD per month or per year are the sum of the daily DD for that period.

DEWPOINT TEMPERATURE: The temperature corresponding to 100% relative humidity for an air-vapor mixture at constant pressure.

EMITTANCE (e): The ratio of the radiant energy emitted by a surface to that emitted by a perfect radiator (a black body) at the same temperature.

HUMIDITY, ABSOLUTE: The weight of water vapor contained in a unit volume of an air-vapor mixture.

HUMIDITY RATIO: The ratio of the mass of water vapor to the mass of dry air in a given air-vapor mixture.

HUMIDITY, RELATIVE (RH): The ratio of the partial pressure of the water vapor in a given air-vapor mixture to the saturation pressure of water at the existing temperature.

ISOTHERM: A line on a graph or map joining points of equal temperature.

OVERALL HEAT TRANSFER COEFFICIENT (U or $1/R_T$): The rate of heat transfer under steady state conditions through a unit area of a building component caused by a difference of one degree between the air temperatures on the two sides of the component. In U.S. practice, the units are Btu/sq ft · hr · °F.

PERM: Unit of water vapor transmission through a material, expressed in grains of vapor per hour per inch of mercury pressure difference (7000 grains = 1 lb).

REFLECTANCE: The ratio of the radiant energy reflected by a surface to the energy incident upon the surface.

SURFACE HEAT TRANSFER COEFFICIENT (h): The rate of heat transfer from a unit area of a surface to the adjacent air and environment caused by a temperature difference of one degree between the surface and the air. In U.S. practice, the units are Btu/sq ft · hr · °F.

THERM: A unit of thermal energy equal to 100,000 Btu.

THERMAL CONDUCTANCE (C or 1/R): Time rate of heat flow through unit area of a material when a temperature difference of one degree is maintained across a specified thickness of the material. In U.S. practice, the units are Btu/hr · sq ft · °F.

THERMAL CONDUCTIVITY (k): Time rate of heat flow through unit area and unit thickness of a homogeneous material when a temperature of gradient of one degree is maintained in the direction of heat flow. In U.S. practice, the units are: Btu/hr · sq ft · (F/in.) or, when thickness is measured in feet, Btu/hr · ft · °F.

THERMAL RESISTANCE (R): Unit of resistance to heat flow, expressed as temperature difference required to cause heat to flow through a unit area of a building component or material at the rate of one heat unit per hour. In U.S. practice, the units are F/Btu/hr · ft^2).

TOTAL THERMAL RESISTANCE (R_t): The total resistance to heat flow through a complete building section or construction assembly, generally expressed as the temperature difference in °F needed to cause heat to flow at the rate of 1 Btu per hour per sq ft of area.

VAPOR BARRIER: A moisture impervious layer applied to surfaces enclosing a humid space to prevent moisture migration to a point where it may condense because of reduced temperature.

VAPOR PERMEABILITY: The property of a material that permits migration of water vapor under the influence of a difference in vapor pressure across the material.

VAPOR PERMEANCE: The ratio of the water vapor flow rate, in grains per hour, through a material of any specified thickness to the vapor pressure difference between the two surfaces of the material, expressed in inches of mercury. The unit is the perm.

VAPOR PRESSURE (P_v): The partial pressure of the water vapor in an air-vapor mixture. It is determined by the dewpoint temperature or by the drybulb temperature and the relative humidity of the mixture. The units are psi or inches of mercury.

VAPOR RESISTANCE: The resistance of a material or an assembly to the passage of water vapor when a vapor pressure difference exists between the two surfaces of the material or assembly. The unit is the rep, which is the reciprocal of the perm.

THERMAL TRANSMISSION

Problems in the performance of building construction materials and assemblies are frequently associated with undesirable flow of heat, moisture, or both. The heat transfer characteristics of most building materials are published in standard references such as the ASHRAE Handbook of Fundamentals. While the published data are subject to manufacturing and testing tolerances and judgment must be used in applying them, they may generally be used with confidence for design purposes.

Heat transmission coefficients are generally expressed as conductivities, k, for which the thickness unit is 1 in., or in conductances, C, for a specified thickness. The resistance to heat flow through a material, R, is the reciprocal of the conductance. For a homogeneous material of thickness L in., the thermal resistance R = L/k.

For a surface or an airspace, where the heat flows by both radiation and convection, combined coefficients are used, symbolized by h with a subscript to designate which particular surface or airspace is being considered. Thermal resistances at surfaces and across airspaces are again designated by R with an appropriate subscript, where R = 1/h. Such R values are strongly influenced by the nature and orientation of the surfaces.

To estimate the rate of heat flow through a building section, the total resistance (R_t) of that section is found by reference to published standard value or by adding the resistances of the individual components of the section. The overall coefficient U is then found as the reciprocal of the total resistance: $U = 1/R_t$. The rate of heat flow Q (Btu/hr) through a wall section of exposed area A sq ft is the product of the overall coefficient U, the area A and the temperature difference ($t_i - t_o$): $Q = U \times A \times (t_i - t_o)$. This heat flow may be inward or outward, depending on t_i and t_o. The general procedure for finding the total thermal resistance and the U value for a given building section on which the sun is not shining is as follows:

1. Select the design outdoor conditions of air temperature (dry bulb), wind speed, and wind direction from local Weather Service records or ASHRAE recommendations. From this information select an outer surface coefficient h_o which will generally be 4.0 Btu/sq ft · hr · °F for summer and 6.0 for winter. Determine the indoor surface coefficient h_i which will be 1.46 Btu/sq ft · hr · °F under most conditions unless forced airflow exists along the wall of the window. Convert these to resistances with $R_o = 1/h_o$ and $R_i = 1/h_i$.
2. List all of the component elements of the section and determine the thermal resistance of each element by dividing the actual (not the nominal) thickness by its thermal conductivity k, except for airspaces. For airspaces, the thickness is taken into account in the conductance h_{as} and the thermal resistance R_{as} is the reciprocal of the conductance.
3. The total resistance of the building section is simply the sum of the individual resistances (make sure that every component is included properly). The U value of the section is then found from: $U = 1/R_t$. The U x A product is often needed to simplify the calculation of the total heat flow into or out of the building's envelope, as well as for the computations used to determine compliance with building energy performance standards.
4. For such building components as windows, skylights, and doors, U values may be found in standard references, for example, the ASHRAE Handbook of Fundamentals. Thermal resistances for a wide variety of common building materials are given in the table presented later in this section.

GENERAL NOTES

The foregoing does not include consideration of heat losses or gains due to ventilation air in large buildings or to infiltration of outdoor air through openings, cracks around windows and doors, construction imperfections, and so on. The energy required to heat this air in winter or to cool and dehumidify it in summer must be carefully estimated by methods given in the ASHRAE Handbook of Fundamentals. During both summer and winter, effects of the sun on both walls and windows must be taken into account.

The solution to the basic problem of attaining acceptable heat flow rates involves the selection of materials that are appropriate for the intended service and the incorporation of enough insulation within the building section to reduce the inward or outward heat flow to the desired rate. Since the indoor-outdoor temperature difference is one of the essential factors in the heat flow equation, the indoor temperature must be selected to comply with the pertinent code or other restriction. Temperatures from 65 to 72°F are generally used in winter while 75 to 78°F are typical summer values.

Selection of the outdoor design values involves careful consideration of the number of hours per year during which exceptionally low or high temperatures are encountered. National Weather Service temperature data are available for most locations in the United States and similar data exist for principal cities throughout the world. For winter design purposes, dry bulb temperatures are usually listed, which are exceeded by 99 and 97.5% of the total hours (2160) in December, January, and February. The 97.5% value is generally used for designing. Since the 54 hr (approximately) during which the outdoor air temperature will be lower than the stated value are experienced at intervals throughout the winter months. These temperatures are usually encountered in the early morning hours before sunrise, so that winter design heating loads tend to ignore solar effects. In summer, solar loads tend to dominate the air-conditioning picture.

Thermal conductances for walls, roofs, doors, and windows are combined in many of the energy conservation building standards to give a weighted average U value, designated as U_o. Allowable values for U_o depend on the building type and size and the number of heating degree days experienced at the building's location.

$$U_o = \frac{U_{xw} \times A_w + U_f \times A_f + U_d \times A_d}{A_w + A_f + A_d}$$

where the subscripts w, f, and d designate walls, fenestration, and door, respectively.

Allowable U_o values are specified in the ASHRAE Standard 90-75, which has been adopted by many states or other jurisdictions. For commercial buildings higher than three stories, U_o may range from 0.47 to 0.28 as the number of degree days per year increases from 500 to 8000. For commercial and institutional buildings of three stories or less, U_o ranges downward from 0.38 to 0.20 as degree days increase from 500 to 10,000. Estimation of summer cooling loads is also accomplished by using the U x A products as determined above, to which solar loads from fenestration must be added. Thermal resistances may be slightly higher in summer than in winter for the same building section because of variations in surface and airspace coefficients. By far the largest factor in most building heat gains is the load imposed by solar radiation entering through fenestration. Cooling load is also increased by internal heat sources within the structure including lighting, miscellaneous electrical loads, and the people in the building. Latent heat loads from moisture removal must also be considered. Properly qualified consultants should be called in to give advice in this field even before the orientation and fenestration of a proposed new building are fixed.

The energy conservation standards mentioned above also include provisions dealing with summer cooling requirements, which are set primarily by the latitude of the city in which the structure will be erected. The mass of the proposed building in terms of weight per square foot of wall area is also introduced to compensate in part for time lags caused by the thermal capacity of building components. It should be noted that cooling, a year-round requirement in many large buildings with high internal loads, is more costly in terms of energy consumption and cost than is heating. The internal heat gains that are helpful in winter are harmful in summer, since they can add greatly to the building's cooling load.

John I. Yellott, P. E.; College of Architecture; Arizona State University; Tempe, Arizona

SOLAR GAINS THROUGH SUNLIT FENESTRATION

Heat gains through sunlit fenestration constitute major sources of cooling load in summer. In winter, discomfort is often caused by excessive amounts of solar radiation entering through south facing windows. By contrast, passive solar design depends largely on admission and storage of the radiant energy falling on south facing and horizontal surfaces. Admission takes place both by transmission through glazing and by inward flow of absorbed energy. With or without the sun, heat flows through glazing, either inwardly or outwardly, whenever there is a temperature difference between the indoor and outdoor air. These heat flows may be calculated in the following manner.

The solar heat gain is estimated by a two-step process. The first step is to find, either from tabulated data or by calculation, the rate at which solar heat would be admitted under the designated conditions through a single square foot of double strength ($1/8$ in.) clear sheet glass. This quantity, called the solar heat gain factor (SHGF), is set by (a) the local latitude; (b) the date, hence the declination; (c) the time of day (solar time should be used); (d) the orientation of the window.

Tabulated values of SHGF are given in the 1977 ASHRAE Handbook of Fundamentals, Chapter 26, for latitudes from 0° (the equator) to 64° N by 8° increments and for orientations around the compass from N to NNW, by 22.5° increments. Selected values from the 40° table are given in an adjacent column.

Each individual fenestration system, consisting of glazing and shading devices, has a unique ability to admit solar heat. This property is evaluated in terms of its shading coefficient (SC), which is the ratio of the amount of solar heat admitted by the system under consideration to the solar heat gain factor for the same conditions. In equation form, this becomes:

$$\text{solar heat gain (Btu/sq ft} \cdot \text{hr)} = SC \times SHGF$$

Values of the shading coefficient are given in Chapter 26 of the 1977 ASHRAE Handbook of Fundamentals for the most widely used glazing materials alone and in combination with internal and external shading devices. Selected values for single and double glazing are given below:

SHADING COEFFICIENT FOR SELECTED GLAZING SYSTEMS

TYPE OF GLASS	SOLAR TRANS-MISSION	SHADING COEFFICIENT, SC
Clear		
$1/8$ in.	0.86	1.00
$1/4$ in.	0.78	0.94
Heat absorbing		
$1/8$ in.	0.64	0.83
$1/4$ in.	0.46	0.69
Insulating glass, clear both lights		
$1/8 + 1/8$ in.	0.71	0.88
$1/4 + 1/4$ in.	0.61	0.81
Heat absorbing out Clear in, $1/4$ in.	0.36	0.55

For combinations of glazing and shading devices, see the ASHRAE chapter cited above.

The heat flow due to temperature difference is found by multiplying the U-value for the specified fenestration system by the area involved and by the applicable temperature difference:

$$Q = A \times [SC \times SHGF + U \times (t_o - t_i)]$$

The same equation is used for both summer and winter, with appropriate U-values, but in winter the conduction heat flow is usually outward because the outdoor air is colder than the indoor air.

Example: find the total heat gain, in Btu/sq ft · hr, for 1000 sq ft of unshaded $1/4$ in. heat absorbing single glass, facing west, in Denver (40°N latitude) at 4:00 P.M. solar time on October 21. Indoor air temperature is 70°F; outdoor air temperature is 40°F.

Solution: from the accompanying table, for 4:00 P.M. on October 21 find the SHGF for west facing fenestration on October 21 to be 173 Btu/sq ft · hr. For $1/4$ in. heat absorbing glass, SC = 0.69 and U for winter conditions is 1.10 Btu/sq ft · hr · °F.

$$Q = 1000 \times [0.69 \times 173 + 1.10 \times (40 - 70)]$$
$$= 1000 \times (119.4 - 33.0) = 86,400 \text{ Btu/hr}$$

Even though the outdoor air is 30° cooler than the indoor air, the net heat gain through the window in question would be equivalent to 7.2 tons of refrigeration.

For the same window area in summer, on August 21 at 4:00 P.M. solar time, SHGF = 216, and the air temperatures may be taken as 95°F outdoors and 78°F indoors. The total heat gain will be:

$$Q = 1000 \times [0.69 \times 216 + 1.04 \times (95 - 78)]$$
$$= 1000 \times (149.0 + 17.7) = 166,700 \text{ Btu/hr}$$
$$= 13.9 \text{ tons of refrigeration}$$

The cooling load can be reduced by selecting a fenestration system with lower shading coefficient and U-value. Under the same conditions, a double glazed window with two lights of $1/4$ in. clear glass and a highly reflective translucent inner shading device would have U = 0.52 and SC = 0.37. The cooling load would then be reduced to 88,760 Btu/hr or 7.4 tons of refrigeration.

SOL-AIR TEMPERATURE

When the opaque surfaces of a structure are struck by solar radiation, much of the energy is absorbed by the irradiated surface, raising its temperature and increasing the rate of heat flow into the roof or wall. The time lag between the onset of irradiation and the resulting rise in the indoor surface temperature depends on the thickness and mass per unit area of the building element and on the thermal conductivity, specific heat, and density of the materials. The time lag is negligible for an uninsulated metal roof, but it can be a matter of hours for a massive concrete or masonry wall.

Heat flow through sunlit opaque building elements is estimated by using the sol-air temperature, t_{sa}, defined as an imaginary outdoor temperature that, in the absence of sunshine, would give the same rate of heat flow as actually exists at the specified time under the combined influence of the incident solar radiation and the ambient air temperature.

$$t_{sa} = I \times Abs./h_o$$

where I = solar irradiance (Btu/sq ft · hr)

Abs. = surface absorptance, dimensionless

h_o = outer surface coefficient (Btu/sq ft · hr · °F)

Surface absorptances range from as low as 0.30 for a white surface to 0.95 for a black built-up roof. Values of h_o range from the conventional 4.0 for summer with an assumed wind speed of 7.5 mph to a still air value of 3.0.

Example: find the rate of heat flow through a 1000 sq ft uninsulated black built-up roof, U = 0.3, under strong summer sunshine, I = 300 Btu/sq ft · hr, still air with 100°F outdoors, 78°F indoors.

Solution: the sol-air temperature is found from

$$t_{sa} = 300 \times \frac{0.95}{3.0} + 100 = 195°F$$

The rate of heat flow, neglecting the time lag, is

$$Q = 1000 \times 0.3 \times (195 - 78) = 35,100 \text{ Btu/hr}$$

With no sunshine on the roof, the heat flow is

$$\text{heat flow} = 1000 \times 0.3 \times (100 - 78) = 6600 \text{ Btu/hr}$$

The effect of the solar radiation is thus to increase the heat flow rate by 88%. A more massive roof with a lower U-value would show considerably less effect of the incoming solar radiation.

SOLAR INTENSITY AND SOLAR HEAT GAIN FACTORS FOR 40°N LATITUDE

DATE	SOLAR TIME (A.M.)	DIRECT NORMAL (BTUH/SQ FT)	N	E	S	W	HOR	SOLAR TIME (P.M.)
Jan 21	8	142	5	111	75	5	14	4
	10	274	16	124	213	16	96	2
	12	294	20	21	254	21	133	12
Feb 21	8	219	10	183	94	10	43	4
	10	294	21	143	203	21	143	2
	12	307	24	25	241	25	180	12
Mar 21	8	250	16	218	74	16	85	4
	10	297	25	153	171	25	186	2
	12	307	29	31	206	31	223	12
Apr 21	6	89	11	88	5	5	11	6
	8	252	22	224	41	21	123	4
	10	286	31	152	121	31	217	2
	12	293	34	36	154	36	252	12
May 21	6	144	36	141	10	10	31	6
	8	250	27	220	29	25	146	4
	10	277	34	148	83	34	234	2
	12	284	37	40	113	40	265	12
June 21	6	155	48	151	13	13	40	6
	8	246	30	216	29	27	153	4
	10	272	35	145	69	35	238	2
	12	279	38	41	95	41	267	12
Jul 21	6	138	37	137	11	11	32	6
	8	241	28	216	30	26	145	4
	10	269	35	146	81	35	231	2
	12	276	38	41	109	41	262	12
Aug 21	6	81	12	82	6	5	12	6
	8	237	24	216	41	23	122	4
	10	272	32	150	116	32	214	2
	12	280	35	38	149	38	247	12
Sep 21	8	230	17	205	71	17	82	4
	10	280	27	148	165	27	180	2
	12	290	30	32	200	32	215	12
Oct 21	8	204	11	173	89	11	43	4
	10	280	21	139	196	21	140	2
	12	294	25	27	234	27	177	12
Nov 21	8	136	5	108	72	5	14	4
	10	268	16	122	209	16	96	2
	12	288	20	21	250	21	132	12
Dec 21	8	89	3	67	50	3	6	4
	10	261	14	113	146	14	77	2
	12	285	18	19	253	19	113	12
			N	W	S	E	HOR	PM

John I. Yellott, P.E., Professor Emeritus; College of Architecture, Arizona State University; Tempe, Arizona

1 ENVIRONMENTAL FACTORS

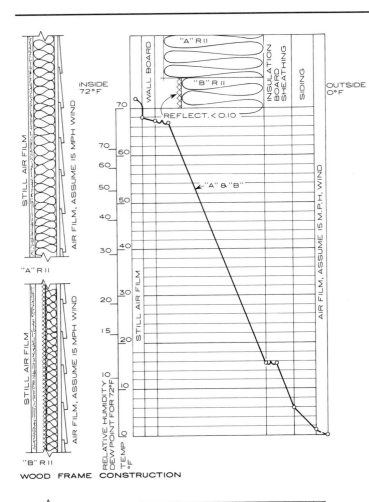

WOOD FRAME CONSTRUCTION

	WALL "A"			WALL "B"		
	R F/Btu*	°F Diff. Due to R*	Temp °F*	R F/Btu*	°F Diff Due to R*	Temp °F*
Indoor room air			72.0			72.0
Still air film (indoor)	0.68	3.2		0.68	3.2	
Indoor face of wall board			68.8			68.8
Gypsum or plaster board (1/2 in.)	0.45	2.1		0.45	2.1	
Back face of wall board			66.7			66.7
Stud air space remaining	negl.	—				
Inner face of insulation			66.7			66.7
Thermal insulation, R11-wo/refl.	11.00	51.37				
-w/refl.				11.00	51.37	
Outer face of insulation			15.3			15.3
Inner face of sheathing			15.3			15.3
Sheathing, 25/32 in., 20 lb.	2.06	9.6		2.06	9.6	
Outer face of sheathing			5.7			5.7
Inner face of siding			5.7			5.7
Siding, wood, 3/4 x 10, lapped	1.05	4.9		1.05	4.95	
Outer face of siding			0.8			0.8
Outdoor air film (15 mph wind)	0.17	0.80		0.17	0.80	
Outdoor air			0			0
TOTALS	15.41	72.0		15.41	72.0	

$$\text{Heat Loss/sf} = \frac{\text{Temp. Diff., Room to Outdoors}}{\text{Total Resistance, R}} = \frac{72-0}{15.41} = 4.7 \text{ Btu/hr. applies to insulated areas}$$

only; studs and other materials are heat paths which increase heat loss.

Wall "A"—Full thick fibrous insulation R11, non-reflective faces, air spaces insufficient to provide any significant resistance.

Wall "B"—Reflective faced fibrous insulation, R11 with the facing; air space 3/4 in. or more in width required with the facing to provide R11; that space must not be counted a second time.

Insulation thicknesses are not specified but only the R value of the material as manufactured; proper installation is implied.

*
Decimals are used to check calculations only — fractional Btu's are usually of no consequence.

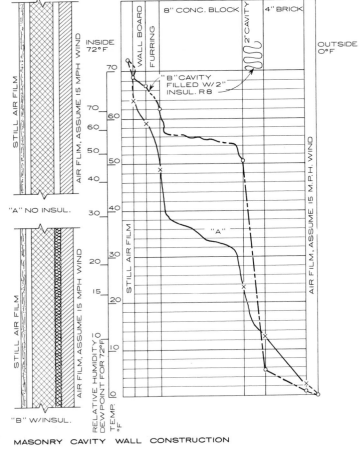

MASONRY CAVITY WALL CONSTRUCTION

	WALL "A"			WALL "B"		
	R F/Btu*	°F Diff. Due to R*	Temp °F*	R F/Btu*	°F Diff Due to R*	Temp °F*
Indoor room air			72.0			72.0
Still air film (indoor)	0.68	10.55		0.68	4.16	
Indoor face of wall board			61.45			67.84
Gypsum or plaster board (1/2 in.)	0.45	6.98		0.45	2.76	
Back face of wall board			54.47			65.08
Furring air space (3/4 in.)	0.90	13.95		0.90	5.52	
Inner face of concrete block			40.52			59.56
Concrete block, 8 in., 3 oval core sand & gravel	1.11	17.10		1.11	6.80	
Outer face of concrete block			23.42			52.76
"A" cavity, 2 in. air space	0.90	13.95		—	—	
"B" cavity, filled w/insulation R8	—	—		8.0	49.04	
Inner face of face brick			9.47			3.72
Face brick, nom. 4 in.	0.44	6.83		0.44	2.70	
Outer face of face brick			2.64			1.02
Outdoor air film (15 mph wind)	0.17	2.63		0.17	1.04	
Outdoor air			0			0
TOTALS	4.65	72.01		11.75	72.02	

$$\text{Heat Loss/sf} = \frac{\text{Temp. Diff., Room to Outdoors}}{\text{Total Resistance, R}} = \frac{72-0}{4.65} = 15.5 \text{ Btu/hr.} \quad \frac{72-0}{11.75} = 6.13 \text{ Btu/hr.}$$

Wall "A"—2 in. open cavity

Wall "B"—2 in. cavity filled with insulation R8. (Verify if water-repellent type is required) R value is for material as manufactured; proper installation is implied.

*Decimals are used to check calculations only—fractional Btu's are usually of no consequence.

NOTE: In tabulation the considerable difference between the temperatures of inside surfaces of the two walls. Occupants of conventional rooms with Wall "A" will be less comfortable than with Wall "B" because of colder inside surface temperature; 61°F vs. 68°F.

Owen L. Delevante, AIA; Glen Rock, New Jersey
E. C. Shuman, P. E.; Consulting Engineer; State College, Pennsylvania

ENVIRONMENTAL FACTORS 1

WINTER WEATHER DATA AND DESIGN CONDITIONS FOR THE UNITED STATES AND CANADA

STATE OR PROVINCE	CITY	LATITUDE (° ')	LONGITUDE (° ')	ELEVATION (FT)	WINTER DESIGN TEMP.*	AVE. WINTER TEMP.†	AVERAGE MONTHLY HEATING DEGREE DAYS‡									
							SEPT	OCT	NOV	DEC	JAN	FEB	MAR	APR	MAY	TOTAL
Ala.	Birmingham	33 3	86 5	61	21	54.2	6	93	363	555	592	462	363	108	9	2551
	Mobile	30 4	88 1	119	29	59.9	0	22	213	357	415	300	211	42	0	1560
Alaska	Fairbanks	64 5	147 5	436	−47	6.7	642	1203	1833	2254	2359	1901	1739	1068	555	14,279
	Juneau	58 2	134 4	17	1	32.1	483	725	921	1135	1237	1070	1073	810	601	9075
Ariz.	Flagstaff	35 1	111 4	6973	4	35.6	201	558	867	1073	1169	991	911	651	437	7152
	Tucson	32 1	111 0	2584	32	58.1	0	25	231	406	471	344	242	75	6	1800
Ark.	Little Rock	34 4	92 1	257	20	50.5	9	127	465	716	756	577	434	126	9	3219
Calif.	Bakersfield	35 2	119 0	495	32	55.4	0	37	282	502	546	364	267	105	19	2122
	Sacramento	38 3	121 3	17	32	54.4	0	62	312	533	561	392	310	173	76	2419
	San Diego	32 4	117 1	19	44	59.5	21	43	135	236	298	253	214	135	90	1458
	San Francisco	37 5	122 3	52	40	55.1	102	118	231	388	443	336	319	279	239	3001
Colo.	Alamosa	37 3	105 5	7536	−6	29.7	279	639	1065	1420	1476	1162	1020	696	440	8529
	Denver	39 5	104 5	5283	1	37.6	117	428	819	1035	1132	938	887	558	288	6283
Conn.	Hartford	41 1	73 1	7	9	37.3	117	394	714	1101	1190	1042	908	519	205	6235
Del.	Wilmington	39 4	75 3	78	14	42.5	51	270	588	927	980	874	735	387	112	4930
D.C.	Washington	38 5	77 0	14	17	45.7	33	217	519	834	871	762	626	288	74	4224
Fla.	Miami	25 5	80 2	7	47	71.1	0	0	0	65	74	56	19	0	0	214
	Tallahassee	30 2	84 2	58	30	60.1	0	28	198	360	375	286	202	36	0	1485
Ga.	Atlanta	33 4	84 3	1005	22	51.7	18	124	417	648	636	518	428	147	25	2961
	Savannah	32 1	81 1	52	27	57.8	0	47	246	437	437	353	254	45	0	1819
Hawaii	Honolulu	21 2	158 0	7	63	74.2	0	0	0	0	0	0	0	0	0	0
Idaho	Boise	43 3	116 1	2842	10	39.7	132	415	792	1017	1113	854	722	438	245	5809
Ill.	Chicago	42 0	87 5	658	−4	35.8	117	381	807	1166	1265	1086	939	534	260	6639
	Springfield	39 5	89 4	587	2	40.6	72	291	696	1023	1135	935	769	354	136	5429
Ind.	Indianapolis	39 4	86 2	793	2	39.6	90	316	723	1051	1113	949	809	432	177	5699
Iowa	Des Moines	41 3	93 4	948	−5	35.5	96	363	828	1225	1370	1187	915	438	180	6588
Kan.	Goodland	39 2	101 4	3645	0	37.8	81	381	810	1073	1166	955	884	507	236	6141
	Topeka	39 0	95 4	877	4	41.7	57	270	672	980	1122	893	722	330	124	5182
Ky.	Lexington	38 0	84 4	979	8	43.8	54	239	609	902	946	818	685	325	105	4683
La.	New Orleans	30 0	90 2	3	33	61.8	0	12	165	291	344	241	177	24	0	1254
	Shreveport	32 3	93 5	252	25	56.2	0	47	297	477	552	426	304	81	0	2184
Me.	Portland	43 4	70 2	61	−1	33.0	195	508	807	1215	1339	1182	1042	675	372	7511
Md.	Baltimore	39 1	76 4	146	13	43.7	48	264	585	905	936	820	679	327	90	4654
Mass.	Boston	42 2	71 0	15	9	40.0	60	316	603	983	1088	972	846	513	208	5634
Mich.	Detroit	42 2	83 0	633	6	37.2	87	360	738	1088	1181	1058	936	522	220	6232
	Escanaba	45 4	87 0	594	−7	29.6	243	539	924	1293	1445	1296	1203	777	456	8481
Minn.	Duluth	46 5	92 1	1426	−16	23.4	330	632	1131	1581	1745	1518	1355	840	490	10,000
	Minneapolis	44 5	93 1	822	−12	28.3	189	505	1014	1454	1631	1380	1166	621	288	8322
Miss.	Jackson	32 2	90 1	330	25	55.7	0	65	315	502	546	414	310	87	0	2239
Mo.	Columbia	39 0	92 2	778	4	42.3	54	251	651	967	1076	871	716	324	121	5046
Mont.	Billings	45 5	108 3	3367	−10	34.5	186	487	897	1135	1296	1100	970	570	285	7049
	Missoula	46 5	114 1	3200	−6	31.5	303	651	1035	1287	1420	1120	970	621	391	8125
Neb.	North Platte	41 1	100 4	2779	−4	35.5	123	440	885	1166	1271	1039	930	519	248	6684
	Omaha	41 2	95 5	978	−3	35.6	105	357	828	1175	1355	1126	939	465	208	6612
Nev.	Las Vegas	36 1	115 1	2162	28	53.5	0	78	387	617	688	487	335	111	6	2709
	Reno	39 3	119 5	4404	10	39.3	204	490	801	1026	1073	823	729	510	357	6332
N.H.	Concord	43 1	71 3	339	−3	33.0	177	505	822	1240	1358	1184	1032	636	298	7383
N.J.	Trenton	40 1	74 5	144	14	42.4	57	264	576	924	989	885	753	399	121	4980
N.M.	Albuquerque	35 0	106 4	5310	16	12.0	12	229	642	868	930	703	595	288	81	4348
N.Y.	Buffalo	43 0	78 4	705	6	34.5	141	440	777	1156	1256	1145	1039	645	329	7062
	New York	40 5	74 0	132	15	42.8	30	233	540	902	986	885	760	408	118	4871
N.C.	Charlotte	35 0	81 0	735	22	50.4	6	124	438	691	691	582	481	156	22	3191
	Wilmington	34 2	78 0	30	26	54.6	0	74	291	521	546	462	357	96	0	2347
N.D.	Bismarck	46 5	100 5	1647	−19	26.6	222	577	1088	1463	1708	1442	1203	645	329	8851
Ohio	Cleveland	41 2	81 5	777	5	37.2	105	384	738	1088	1159	1047	918	552	260	6351
	Columbus	40 0	82 5	812	5	39.7	84	347	714	1039	1088	949	809	426	171	5660
Okla.	Oklahoma City	35 2	97 4	1280	13	48.3	15	164	498	766	868	664	527	189	34	3725
	Tulsa	36 1	95 5	650	13	47.7	18	158	522	787	893	683	539	213	47	3860
Ore.	Salem	45 0	123 0	195	23	45.4	111	338	594	729	822	647	611	417	273	4754
Pa.	Pittsburgh	40 3	80 1	1137	5	38.4	105	375	726	1063	1119	1002	874	480	195	5987
	Williamsport	41 1	77 0	527	7	38.5	111	375	717	1073	1122	1002	856	468	177	5934
R.I.	Providence	41 4	71 3	55	9	38.8	96	372	660	1023	1110	988	868	534	236	5954
S.C.	Columbia	34 0	81 1	217	24	54.0	0	84	345	577	570	470	357	81	0	2484
S.D.	Rapid City	44 0	103 0	3165	−7	33.4	165	481	897	1172	1333	1145	1051	615	326	7345
Tenn.	Nashville	36 1	86 4	577	14	48.9	30	158	495	732	778	644	512	189	40	3578
Texas	Brownsville	25 5	97 3	16	39	67.6	0	0	66	149	205	106	74	0	0	600
	Dallas	32 5	96 5	481	22	55.3	0	62	321	524	601	440	319	90	6	2363
	El Paso	31 5	106 2	3918	24	52.9	0	84	414	648	685	445	319	105	0	2700
	Houston	29 4	95 2	50	32	61.0	0	6	183	307	384	288	192	36	0	1396
Utah	Salt Lake City	40 5	112 0	4220	8	38.4	81	419	849	1082	1172	910	763	459	233	6052
Vt.	Burlington	44 3	73 1	331	7	29.4	207	539	891	1349	1513	1333	1187	714	353	8269
Va.	Lynchburg	37 2	79 1	947	16	46.0	51	223	540	822	849	731	605	267	78	4166
Wash.	Seattle	47 4	122 2	14	27	46.9	129	329	543	657	738	599	577	396	242	4424
W. Va.	Charleston	38 2	81 4	939	11	44.8	63	254	591	865	880	770	648	300	96	4476
Wisc.	Green Bay	44 3	88 1	683	−9	30.3	174	484	924	1333	1494	1313	1141	654	305	8029
Wyo.	Casper	42 5	106 3	5319	−5	33.4	192	524	942	1169	1290	1084	1020	651	381	7410
CANADA																
Alta.	Edmonton	53 34	113 31	2219	−25	—	411	738	1215	1603	1810	1520	1330	765	400	10,268
B.C.	Vancouver	49 11	123 10	16	19	—	219	456	657	787	862	723	676	501	310	5515
Man.	Winnipeg	49 54	97 14	786	−27	—	322	683	1251	1757	2008	1719	1465	813	405	10,679
N.S.	Halifax	44 39	63 34	83	5	—	180	457	710	1074	1213	1122	1030	742	487	7361
Ont.	Toronto	43 41	79 38	578	−1	—	151	439	760	1111	1233	1119	1013	616	298	6827
Que.	Montreal	45 28	73 45	98	−10	—	165	521	882	1392	1566	1381	1175	684	316	8203

*Based on 97.5% Design Dry-Bulb values found in ASHRAE Handbook of Fundamentals, 1977.
†October–April, inclusive. ASHRAE Systems Handbook, 1976.
‡Based on the period 1931–1960, inclusive. ASHRAE Systems Handbook, 1976.

1   ENVIRONMENTAL FACTORS

PASSIVE SOLAR HEATING

Passive solar heating relies on the natural flow of energy through and around a building to provide comfort. Collection, storage, and distribution of energy are achieved by the three basic heat transfer processes: conduction, convection, and radiation. Efficient operation of passive systems can involve some user control to alter or override energy flows within a building or at its weatherskin.

As part of the development of any passive system, the designer should take into account the elements of energy conserving design. With passive solar heating, prevention and minimization of heat loss from the structure is fundamental in ensuring that the heating system will be effective. This includes proper insulation, orientation, and surface-to-volume ratios, as well as material, texture, and finish choices.

There are three generic categories for passive solar heating: direct gain, indirect gain (thermal storage wall, roof pond), and isolated gain (sunspace, thermosiphon). The primary elements to be considered with each generic category are collection, storage, distribution, and control.

1. SOLAR COLLECTION surfaces are generally of transparent or translucent plastics or fiberglass or are glass oriented in a southerly direction. When considering materials, attention should be paid to material degradation by solar exposure and other weather elements.
2. THERMAL STORAGE materials include concrete, brick, sand, tile, and stone, as well as water or other liquids. Phase change materials such as eutectic salts and paraffins are also feasible. Storage should be well placed to receive maximum solar exposure, either directly or indirectly. Total effective thermal storage capacity should be a minimum of 30 to 45 Btu/°F per sq ft of aperture. Adequate thermal storage capacity will absorb and retain the sun's heat until it is needed, minimizing daily internal temperature fluctuations.
3. HEAT DISTRIBUTION occurs through natural means by conduction, convection, and radiation. Fans or other mechanical equipment to distribute energy are generally avoided, yet sometimes required.
4. CONTROL mechanisms such as vents, dampers, movable insulation, and shading devices are helpful in ensuring a balanced heat distribution.

PASSIVE SOLAR COOLING

Passive solar cooling is simply the tempering of interior spaces by optimizing the use of natural thermal phenomena. A structure designed for natural cooling should incorporate features that minimize heat gain. Adequate insulation, proper overhangs, shading, orientation, and similar factors should be considered. When possible, external heat gain should be controlled before it reaches or penetrates the weatherskin.

When cooling is necessary for internal comfort, dissipation of heat is accomplished by cooling the interior mass, the air, or both. Conduction, convection, radiation, evaporation, and dehumidification are the thermal transfer processes used.

Many passive cooling methods exist: natural cross-ventilation, deep space radiation, day/night closing/opening, induction of precooled air, night cooling of interior air mass, earth mass heat sink, evaporative wicks, dessicant mass, and others. This science integrates traditional architectural solutions, modern developing materials, and a refined knowledge of thermal dynamics, as well as nature's patterns.

The identification and definitions of the three generic cooling categories are as follows:

1. DIRECT LOSS: Heat is lost or dissipated directly from the space.
2. INDIRECT LOSS: The heat loss occurs at the weatherskin.
3. ISOLATED LOSS: Heat loss occurs away from the weatherskin. For example, induced air can be precooled in the earth's mass or cooling ponds.

Dennis A. Andrejko, Architect, David Wright, AIA; SEAgroup; Nevada City, California

TYPES	HEATING	COOLING

DIRECT GAIN/LOSS

Direct gain is the most common passive solar building approach and most structures utilize it to some degree. Collection and storage are integral with the space. Southerly oriented glazing (collector) admits winter solar radiation to the space beyond. Within the space are adequate amounts of thermal storage incorporated as part of the building structure, which absorbs the solar energy. During the cooling season windows, walls, and roofs can be operable or openable for natural or induced ventilation, cooling both the mass and space.

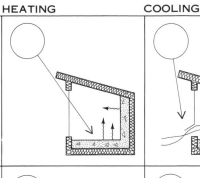

THERMAL STORAGE WALL— MASS WALL

Thermal storage walls are a "sun to mass to space" concept. Collection and storage are separated from the space, but linked thermally, transferring energy through the wall by conduction, then to the space by radiation. A mass wall can be vented to the interior if a convective heat flow is warranted during the day. In the mass wall system, storage is generally in masonry or concrete directly behind the south glazing. Mass walls should be vented to the exterior or shaded during summer months.

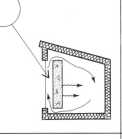

THERMAL STORAGE WALL— WATER WALL

In a water wall system a liquid, often held in barrels or tubes directly behind south facing glass, acts as the thermal storage medium. During the winter, solar radiation is absorbed by the contained water. As needed, this energy is gradually released to the interior. Water walls should be shaded or vented to the exterior during cooling periods. Additional cooling can be provided by venting the water wall at night where low nighttime temperatures prevail.

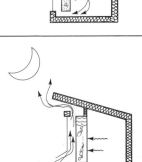

ROOF POND

The roof pond system places the liquid storage mass in the ceiling. During the heating season, operable insulation panels are moved during the day to expose the storage mass to the sun. Energy is absorbed by the roof pond, and at night the panels are replaced over the storage, allowing the stored energy to radiate to the building's interior. During summer, this process is reversed. During the day, internal heat is absorbed by the roof pond, which is insulated from the high summer sun. At night, the insulation is opened to allow the storage mass to radiate to deep space.

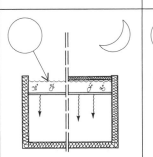

SUNSPACE

In sunspace designs, solar collection and primary thermal storage are isolated from all living spaces, although variations are possible. This allows the solar system to function independently of the building interior, although heat can be drawn from the sunspace as the thermal requirements dictate. When cooling is required, the sunspace can be used to induce a convective flow from the exterior, and should be shaded to prevent overheating of the space and storage mass.

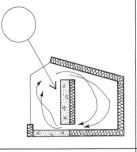
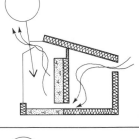

THERMOSIPHON

Thermosiphon, or natural convection, systems rely on the natural rise and fall of a fluid as it is heated and cooled. As the sun warms a collector surface the air rises, simultaneously pulling cooler air from the bottom of the storage and causing a natural convection loop. Heat is convected into the space or stored in the thermal mass until necessary for use. During a cooling season, the collector may be used as a "thermal chimney" to induce precooled air through the storage mass to cool it.

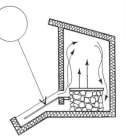
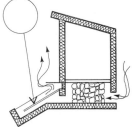

PASSIVE SOLAR HEATING—DESIGN PROCEDURE

Passive solar heating systems are integral to building design. The concepts relating to system operation must be applied at the earliest stages of design decision making.

Passive systems demand a skillful and total integration of all the architectural elements within each space—glazing, walls, floor, roof, and in some cases even interior surface colors. The way in which the glazing and thermal mass (heat storage materials, i.e., masonry, water) are designed generally determines the efficiency and level of thermal comfort provided by the system. Two concepts are critical to understanding the thermal performance of passively heated space. They are:

1. That the quantity of south glazing, insulating properties of the space, and the outdoor climatic conditions will determine the number of degrees the average indoor temperature in a space is above the average outdoor temperatures on any given day (Δt).
2. That the size, distribution, material, and in some cases (direct gain systems) surface color of thermal mass in the space will determine the daily fluctuation above and below the average indoor temperature (see Figure 1).

Calculating heat gain and loss is a relatively straightforward procedure. The storage and control of heat in a passively heated space, however, is the major problem confronting most designers. In the process of storing and releasing heat, thermal mass in a space will fluctuate in temperature, yet the object of the heating system is to maintain a relatively constant interior temperature. For each system, the integration of thermal mass in a space will determine the fluctuation of indoor temperature over the day.

EXAMPLE

In a direct gain system, with masonry thermal mass, the major determinant of fluctuations of indoor air temperature is both the amount of exposed surface area of masonry in the space and the distribution of sunlight over the masonry surface; in a thermal storage wall system, it is the thickness of the material used to construct the wall. The following is a procedure for sizing both direct gain and indirect gain thermal storage wall systems (masonry or water) for buildings with skin dominated heating loads.

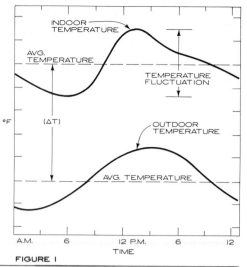

FIGURE I

DAILY TEMPERATURE FLUCTUATION

DIRECT GAIN

The major glass areas (collector) of each space must be oriented to the south (30°±) for maximum solar heat gain in winter. However, these windows can serve other functions as well, such as openings for light and views.

Each space must also contain enough mass for the storage of solar heat gain. This implies a heavy masonry building, but the masonry can be as thin as 4 in. If an interior water wall is used for heat storage, the lightweight construction (wood frame) can be used.

SOUTH GLAZING: One criterion for a well-designed space using this method is that it gains enough solar energy, on an average sunny day in winter, to maintain an average space temperature of 68°F± over the 24-hr period. By establishing this criterion, it is possible to develop ratios for the preliminary sizing of south glazing. Table 1 (see next page) lists ratios for various climates and locations that apply to a well-insulated residence.

EXAMPLE

In Denver, Colorado, at 40°N latitude, with an average January temperature of 30°F, a well-insulated space would need approximately 0.20 sq ft of south glazing for each square foot of space floor area (e.g., a 200 sq ft space needs 40 sq ft of south glazing).

In a direct gain system, sunlight can also be admitted into a space through clerestories and skylights, as well as vertical south facing windows. This approach may be taken (1) for privacy; (2) because of shading on the south facades; (3) because spaces are located along facades other than south; and (4) to avoid direct sunlight on people and furniture. Use the following guidelines when designing clerestories and skylights.

1. CLERESTORY: Locate the clerestory at a distance in front of interior thermal storage wall of roughly 1 to 1.5 times the height of the clerestory above the finished floor. Make the ceiling of the clerestory a light color to reflect and diffuse sunlight down into the space. In regions with heavy snowfall, locate the sill of the clerestory glazing 18 in. or more above the roof surface. (See Figure 2, next page.)
2. SAWTOOTH CLERESTORIES: Make angle α (as measured from horizontal) equal to or smaller than the altitude of the sun at noon on December 21, the winter solstice. Make the underside of the clerestories a light color. (See Figure 3, next page.)
3. SKYLIGHT: Use a south facing or horizontal skylight with a reflector to increase solar gain in winter, and shade both horizontal and south facing skylights in summer to prevent excessive solar gain. (See Figure 4, next page.)

THERMAL STORAGE MASS: The two most common materials used for storing heat are masonry and water. Masonry materials transfer heat from their surface to the interior at a slow rate. If direct sunlight is applied to the surface of a dark masonry material for an extended period of time, it will become uncomfortably hot, thereby giving much of its heat to the air in the space rather than conducting it away from the surface for storage. This results in daytime overheating and large daily temperature fluctuations in the space. To reduce fluctuations, direct sunlight should be spread over a large surface area of masonry. To accomplish this:

1. Construct interior walls and floors of masonry at least 4 in. in thickness.
2. Diffuse direct sunlight over the surface area of the masonry either by using a translucent glazing material—placing a number of small windows so that they admit sunlight in patches—or by reflecting direct sunlight off a light colored interior surface first. (See Figure 5, next page.)
3. Use the following guidelines for selecting interior surface colors and finishes:
   a. Masonry floors of a dark color.
   b. Masonry walls of any color.
   c. Lightweight construction (little thermal mass) of a light color to reflect sunlight onto masonry surfaces.
   d. Avoidance of direct sunlight on dark masonry surfaces for long periods of time.
   e. No wall-to-wall carpeting over masonry floors.

By following these recommendations, one can control temperature fluctuations in the space on clear winter days to approximately 10 to 15°F. These temperature fluctuations are for clear winter days and for at least 6 sq ft of exposed masonry surface area (either horizontal or vertical) in direct sunlight for each square foot of south glazing.

For an interior water wall, the volume of water in direct sunlight and the surface color of the container (thin metal or plastic) will determine the temperature fluctuation in a space over the day (see Table 2, next page). When using a water wall for heat storage:

1. Locate the wall so it receives direct sunlight between 10 A.M. and 2 P.M.
2. Make the surface of the container that is exposed to direct sunlight of a dark color (at least 75% solar absorption).
3. Use roughly 1 cu ft (7.48 gal) of water for each square foot of south glazing. (Adjust the volume of water in the space to the temperature fluctuation desired in the space.)

NOTE

With an interior water wall there are few restrictions regarding other wall and floor materials and surface colors in the space. The water can be stored within an interior wall or in freestanding containers, as long as the surface of the water wall is a thin material exposed to direct sunlight.

INDIRECT GAIN—THERMAL STORAGE WALLS

The predominant architectural expression of a thermal storage wall building is south facing glass. The glass functions as a collecting surface only, and admits no natural light into the space. However, windows can be included in the wall to admit natural light and direct heat and to permit a view.

Either water or masonry can be used for a thermal storage wall (a masonry thermal storage wall with thermocirculation vents is often referred to as a Trombe wall). Since the mass is concentrated along the south face of the building, there is no limit to the choice of construction materials and interior finishes in the remainder of the space.

SOUTH GLAZING: The criterion for a double glazed thermal storage wall is the same as for a direct gain system—that it transmit enough heat on an average sunny winter day to supply a space with all its heating needs for that day. Tables 3 and 4 (see next page) list guidelines for sizing the glazing of masonry or water walls, respectively.

EXAMPLE

In Boston, Massachusetts, at 42°N latitude, with an average January temperature of 31.4°F, a well-insulated space will need approximately 0.41 sq ft of double glazed water wall for each square foot of building floor area (e.g., a 200 sq ft space will need about 32 sq ft of glazing).

WALL DETAILS: While the procedure above gives guidelines for the overall size (surface area) of a thermal storage wall, the efficiency of the wall as a heating system depends mainly on its thickness, material, and surface color. (See Table 5, next page.) If the wall is too thin, the space will overheat during the day and be too cool in the evening; if it is too thick, it becomes inefficient as a heating source, since little energy is transmitted through it.

The choice of wall thickness, within the range given for each material in Table 5 (see next page), will determine the air temperature fluctuation in the space over the day. As a general rule, the greater the wall thickness the smaller the indoor temperature fluctuation. Table 6 (see next page) can be used to select a wall thickness.

The greater the absorption of solar energy at the exterior face of a thermal wall, the greater the quantity of incident energy transferred through the wall into the building. Therefore, make the outside face of the wall dark (preferably black) with a solar absorption of at least 85%.

In cold climates, the addition of thermocirculation vents in a masonry wall will significantly increase the performance of the wall. In mild climates, however, the vents are unnecessary, since winter daytime temperatures are comfortable and heating is usually not needed at that time. To size the vents:

1. Make the total area of each row of vents equal to approximately 1 sq ft for each 100 sq ft of exterior wall surface area.
2. Prevent reverse airflow at night by placing an operable damper over the vents at night.

Edward Mazria, AIA, Architect; Edward Mazria & Associates; Albuquerque, New Mexico

1

ENVIRONMENTAL FACTORS

TABLE 1. SIZING SOLAR WINDOWS FOR DIFFERENT CLIMATIC CONDITIONS

AVERAGE WINTER TEMP. (CLEAR DAY)[1]	SQUARE FEET OF GLAZING NEEDED FOR EACH SQUARE FOOT OF FLOOR AREA[2]			
	36°NL	40°NL	44°NL	48°NL
Cold climates				
20°F	0.24	0.25	0.29	0.31 (with night insul.)
25°F	0.22	0.23	0.25	0.28 (with night insul.)
30°F	0.19	0.20	0.22	0.24
Temperate climates				
35°F	0.16	0.17	0.19	0.21
40°F	0.13	0.14	0.16	0.17
45°F	0.10	0.11	0.12	0.13

NOTES

1. Temperatures listed are for December and January (usually the coldest months) and are monthly averages.
2. These ratios apply to a well insulated space with a heat load coefficient (HLC) of 8 Btu/day · sq ft floor · °F. If the rate of space heat loss is higher or lower, adjust the ratios according to the following formula:

$$\text{glazing/floor area} = \frac{HLC(t_i - t_{int}) - t_o}{I_t}$$

where HLC = space heating load coefficient (Btu/day · sq ft floor · °F)

t_i = daily average indoor temperature (normally 68°F for residential applications)

t_{int} = temperature increment due to internal heat generation from people, light, appliances, etc.—normally about 5° for residential applications

t_o = daily average outdoor temperature (clear day)

I_t = daily heat gain (clear day) (Btu/day · sq ft floor)

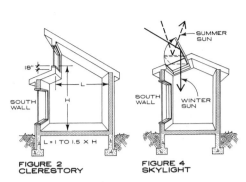

FIGURE 2 CLERESTORY

FIGURE 4 SKYLIGHT

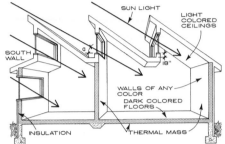

FIGURE 3 SAWTOOTH CLERESTORIES

TABLE 2. DAILY SPACE AIR TEMPERATURE FLUCTUATIONS[1] FOR DIRECT GAIN WATER STORAGE WALL SYSTEMS[2]

SOLAR ABSORPTION (SURFACE COLOR)	VOLUME[3] OF WATER WALL FOR EACH SQUARE FOOT OF SOUTH FACING GLASS			
	1 CU FT	1.5 CU FT	2 CU FT	3 CU FT
75% (dark color)	~17°F	15°F	13°F	12°F
90% (black)	15°F	12°F	10°F	9°F

NOTES

1. Temperature fluctuations are for a clear winter day with approximately 3 sq ft of exposed wall area for each square foot of south glass. If less wall area is exposed in the space, temperature fluctuations will be slightly higher. If additional mass is located in the space (such as masonry walls and/or floor) then fluctuations will be less than those listed and therefore less water can be used.
2. Assumes that 75% of the sunlight entering the space strikes the mass wall.
3. 1 cu ft of water = 62.4 lb or 7.48 gal.

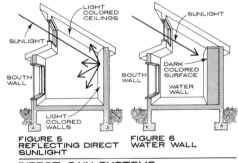

FIGURE 5 REFLECTING DIRECT SUNLIGHT

FIGURE 6 WATER WALL

DIRECT GAIN SYSTEMS

TABLE 3. SIZING AN INDIRECT GAIN MASONRY THERMAL STORAGE WALL (TROMBE WALL) FOR DIFFERENT CLIMATIC CONDITIONS

AVERAGE WINTER TEMP. (CLEAR DAY)	SQUARE FEET OF MASONRY WALL NEEDED FOR EACH SQUARE FOOT OF FLOOR AREA			
	36°NL	40°NL	44°NL	48°NL
Cold climates				
20°F	0.71	0.75	0.85	0.95
25°F	0.59	0.63	0.75	0.84
30°F	0.50	0.53	0.60	0.70
Temperate climates				
35°F	0.40	0.43	0.50	0.55
40°F	0.32	0.35	0.40	0.44
45°F	0.25	0.26	0.30	0.33

NOTE: These tables apply to a well insulated space with a heat load coefficient (HLC) of 8 Btu/day · sq ft floor · °F. If the rate of space heat loss is higher or lower, adjust the ratios accordingly. The surface area of the wall is assumed to be the same size as the glazing. For a thermal wall with a horizontal specular reflector equal to the height of the wall in length or one that utilizes night insulation (R-9), use 60% of the recommended ratios. Since the ratios are very large in cold climates, night insulation is recommended.

TABLE 5. SUGGESTED MATERIAL THICKNESS FOR INDIRECT GAIN THERMAL STORAGE WALLS

MATERIAL	RECOMMENDED THICKNESS
Adobe	8 to 12 in.
Brick (common)	10 to 14 in.
Concrete (dense)	12 to 18 in.
Water	6 in. or more

NOTE: When using water in tubes, cylinders, or other types of circular containers, have a container of at least a 9½ in. diameter or holding ½ cu ft (31 lb, 3.7 gal) of water for each one square foot of glazing.

TABLE 4. SIZING AN INDIRECT GAIN WATER FILLED THERMAL STORAGE WALL FOR DIFFERENT CLIMATIC CONDITIONS

AVERAGE WINTER TEMP. (CLEAR DAY)	SQUARE FEET OF WATER WALL NEEDED FOR EACH SQUARE FOOT OF FLOOR AREA			
	36°NL	40°NL	44°NL	48°NL
Cold climates				
20°F	0.52	0.55	0.65	0.80
25°F	0.45	0.47	0.55	0.64
30°F	0.36	0.39	0.45	0.55
Temperate climates				
35°F	0.28	0.31	0.35	0.40
40°F	0.23	0.25	0.29	0.32
45°F	0.17	0.18	0.20	0.24

NOTE: See note to Table 3.

TABLE 6. APPROXIMATE SPACE TEMPERATURE FLUCTUATIONS AS A FUNCTION OF INDIRECT GAIN THERMAL STORAGE WALL MATERIAL AND THICKNESS

MATERIALS	THICKNESS (IN.)					
	4	8	12	16	20	24
Adobe	—	18°	7°	7°	8°	—
Brick (common)	—	24°	11°	7°	—	—
Concrete (dense)	—	28°	16°	10°	6°	5°
Water (31°F)	—	18°	13°	11°	10°	9°

NOTE: Assumes a double glazed thermal wall. If additional mass is located in the space, such as masonry walls and/or floors, then temperature fluctuations will be less than those listed. Values are given for clear winter days.

Edward Mazria, AIA, Architect; Edward Mazria & Associates; Albuquerque, New Mexico

ENVIRONMENTAL FACTORS   **1**

PASSIVE SOLAR HEATING— CALCULATION PROCEDURE

The rules of thumb given in the design procedure make it possible to integrate passive solar systems in the schematic design of a building. They give enough detailed information to size a system that will function effectively. After schematic design for the building is complete, it is possible to calculate the thermal performance of each space and make adjustments to the system, if necessary.

The rules of thumb for sizing a system are based on clear day solar radiation and average clear day outdoor temperatures for the winter months. Essentially, this sizing procedure balances the heat lost from a space (kept at 68°F±) over the day with the energy collected from the sun (when shining) that same day. This condition is referred to as the design-day. Because design-day data have been used, it can be expected that the system will not perform as effectively under more severe conditions, although the massive nature of passive buildings tends to moderate the effects of weather extremes. It is reasonable to expect that a sizing procedure for the worst possible winter weather conditions is usually not practical. This would result in spaces that are uncomfortably warm during normal sunny weather and would lead to a design that is oversized and most likely uneconomical to build. For this reason, some form of backup heating system is desirable in most passive solar heated buildings.

Five steps are involved in calculating a system's performance:

1. Calculating the space heat load coefficient.
2. Calculating the monthly space heating requirements.
3. Calculating the monthly solar heating contribution.
4. Determining the average daily indoor temperature.
5. Determining the daily indoor temperature fluctuation.

HEATING LOAD COEFFICIENT

Heat is lost from a space through the skin of a building by two methods: heat loss through the walls, floor, roof, and windows (conduction losses) and heat loss through the exchange of warmed indoor air with cold outdoor air (infiltration losses). The space heat load coefficient is then the sum of the rate of the conduction losses plus the infiltration losses in Btu/day · °F.

The building heat load coefficient is computed by using standard ASHRAE space heat loss calculations:

heat load coefficient (Btu/day · °F)

$$= \frac{24 \times (\text{space heat loss})}{\text{inside temperature} - \text{outdoor design temperature}}$$

where space heat loss = calculated heat required to maintain the building at a fixed temperature if the outside temperature is equal to the design temperature, in Btu/hr.

MONTHLY SPACE HEATING REQUIREMENT

Compute the monthly space heating requirement ($Q_{r\ month}$) in Btu's by the number of degree-days for the month (DD_{month}).

$$Q_{r\ month} = HLC \times DD_{month}$$

Degree-days for major cities in the United States are given on a page titled WINTER WEATHER DATA AND DESIGN CONDITIONS.

MONTHLY SOLAR HEATING CONTRIBUTION

Three computations are necessary to determine the monthly solar heating contribution ($Q_{c\ month}$) for passive systems.

1. Computing the monthly solar load ratio (SLR) for each space.
2. Determining the fraction of the total space monthly heating requirement supplied by solar energy (SHF).
3. Computing the monthly solar heating contribution in Btu's.

MONTHLY SOLAR LOAD RATIO: The solar load ratio (SLR) is calculated for each month using the formula:

$$SLR = \frac{\text{monthly solar energy absorbed}}{Q_{r\ month}}$$

The monthly solar energy absorbed by a space is calculated by multiplying the total building collector area (A_{gl}) by the solar energy transmitted through the glazing (I_t) for that month and the percentage of energy absorbed within the building (space absorptance):

monthly solar energy absorbed

$$= A_{gl} \times I_t \times \text{space absorptance} \times \text{days per month}$$

where A_{gl} = unshaded surface area of collector glazing (sq ft)

I_t = average daily solar heat gain through on square foot of collector glazing (Btu/day)

space absorptance = the percentage of solar absorbed within the space. For a masonry or water thermal storage wall, the actual absorptance of the surface can be used. For a direct gain system, use 0.95 for a dark interior or deep space and 0.90 for a light interior or shallow space

FRACTION OF THE TOTAL MONTHLY HEATING REQUIREMENT SUPPLIED BY SOLAR EQUIPMENT

The following graphs present a simple method for determining the fraction of the total monthly space heating requirement supplied by a passive system (SHF). Simply follow a vertical line from the SLR (computed for a particular month in the previous step) on the horizontal scale until it intersects the curve that most closely represents the passive system being used. From this intersection draw a straight line to the scale on the left and read the solar heating fraction for that month. (See Figure 7, next page.)

MONTHLY SOLAR HEATING CONTRIBUTION

To compute the monthly solar heating contribution ($Q_{c\ month}$) in Btu's multiply the monthly space heating requirement ($Q_{r\ month}$) by the solar heating fraction (SHF) for that month, or

$$Q_{c\ month} = Q_{r\ month} \times SHF$$

The percentage of the annual building heating requirement supplied by solar energy is estimated, using the totaled space monthly values (yearly total) for Q_c and Q_r, by the formula:

$$\% \text{ solar year} = 100 \times \frac{\Sigma Q_{c\ month}}{\Sigma Q_{r\ year}}$$

AVERAGE DAILY INDOOR TEMPERATURE

After 1 to 3 days of similar weather conditions (clear or cloudy days in a row) a space will stabilize as a thermal system. This means that temperatures in the space remain roughly the same from day to day. Finding the daily average space temperature for this condition is relatively straightforward.

First, find the total daily solar heat gain for each space. An average sunny January day is a reasonable condition to illustrate a system's performance. For a direct gain system, using clear day January values for solar heat gain transmitted through glazing (I_t) from Mazria, calculate the heat gain through each unshaded skylight, clerestory, and window opening:

$$HG_{sol} = I_t \times A_{gl}$$

where I_t = solar heat gain through 1 sq ft of glazing (Btu/day)

A_{gl} = surface area of the unshaded portion of the glazing (sq ft)

The heat gain into a space from a thermal storage wall (HG_{tm}) can be calculated using the formula:

$$HG_{tm} = A_{gl} \times I_t \times F_r$$

where A_{gl} = surface area of the unshaded portion of the glazing (sq ft)

I_t = solar heat gain through 1 sq ft of glazing (Btu/day)

F_r = the fraction of incident energy on the face of the wall that is transferred to the space

Values of F_r for double glazed thermal storage walls (black exterior wall surface color) are plotted on graphs in Figures 8a and 8b (see next page). To find the value of F_r, first determine the overall U-value of the space (U_{sp}) by dividing the space HLC by the floor area, or

$$U_{sp} = \frac{HLC}{\text{space floor area}}$$

Next find the ratio of thermal wall area to space floor area. For example a 200 sq ft space with a 100 sq ft concrete thermal wall has a ratio of 100/200 or 0.50. Then from 0.50 on the horizontal scale of the graph, follow a vertical line until it intersects the curve for the overall U-value of space. From this intersection move horizontally to the left and read the fraction of energy transmitted through the wall on the vertical

scale. If, for example, the 200 sq ft space had an overall U-value of 6 Btu/day · sq ft$_{floor}$ · °F, then F will equal 0.35.

When more than one system provides heat to a space, add the heat gains from each system to arrive at the total space heat gain:

$$HG_{sp} = HG_{sol} + HG_{tm}$$

where HG_{sp} = total space heat gain.

Using the heat load coefficient (HLC) and daily heat gain (HG_{sp}), we find the average daily indoor temperature (t_i) by dividing HG_{sp} by HLC and adding the result to the average daily outdoor temperature (t_o) for the design-day:

$$t_i = \frac{HG_{sp}}{HLC} + t_o$$

In residential buildings to account for additional heat gains from lights, appliances, and people, add 5 to 7°F to the average daily indoor temperature. For other than residential applications, compute the temperature increment that is due to internal heat generation.

Because of the complicated nature of building design, there is no ideal average indoor temperature, but as the average temperature approaches 70°F, enough heat is admitted into a space to supply it with all its heating needs for that day. If the average indoor temperature is too low, it can be raised by reducing the rate of space heat loss (HLC), increasing the area of south glazing, or supplying heat to the space from an auxiliary heat source. If the average indoor temperature is above 70°F, then overheating can be expected during sunny winter days.

DAILY INDOOR TEMPERATURE FLUCTUATION

The effect of the thermal mass on indoor temperature fluctuations is explained on page titled, PASSIVE SOLAR HEATING—DESIGN PROCEDURE. However, since indoor temperature fluctuations are not always symmetrical about the daily average (an equal number of degrees above and below the average) a series of graphs plotting hourly temperatures for a variety of systems is included. To determine hourly indoor temperatures for a design-day, first select the graph that corresponds to your system. Next, using the average indoor temperature that you calculated in the previous step, plot the number of degrees the indoor air temperature is above or below the average for each hour.

DIRECT GAIN SYSTEMS: Masonry Heat Storage— Since the interior surface area of masonry exposed to direct sunlight greatly influences the indoor air temperature fluctuation over a 24 hr period, two cases are presented. The first case shows a ratio of surface area of exposed masonry to south glazing of 3 to 1 (see Figure 9a, next page). The second, a surface area of exposed masonry to south glazing of 9 to 1 (see Figure 9b, next page).

The following graphs plot hourly indoor temperatures above and below the daily average (t_i) for each case using various masonry materials:

1. DIRECT GAIN SYSTEM: Interior Waterwall. In this case the volume of water in direct sunlight is the major determinant of space temperature fluctuations over the day. The following graph plots indoor temperatures, above and below the daily average, for various quantities of water per square foot of south glazing. The surface of the water wall is assumed to be a dark color. (See Figure 10, next page.)
2. THERMAL STORAGE WALL SYSTEM: The material used to construct a thermal storage wall and the thickness of the wall are the major influences on indoor air temperature fluctuations. The following graphs plot indoor air temperatures for various thicknesses of a concrete masonry wall, brick wall, and a water wall.

REFERENCES

1. For a complete explanation of space heat loss calculations, see the Handbook of Fundamentals, American Society of Heating, Refrigerating, and Air Conditioning Engineers (ASHRAE, New York, 1977).
2. J. D. Balcomb and R. D. McFarland, "A Simple Empirical Method for Estimating the Performance of a Passive Solar Heated Building of the Thermal Storage Wall Type," Proceedings of the 2nd National Passive Solar Conference, Philadelphia, March 1978.
3. Edward Mazria, The Passive Solar Energy Book, Rodale Press, Emmaus, Pa., 1979.

Edward Mazria, AIA, Architect; Edward Mazria & Associates; Albuquerque, New Mexico

1

ENVIRONMENTAL FACTORS

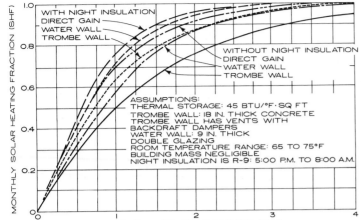

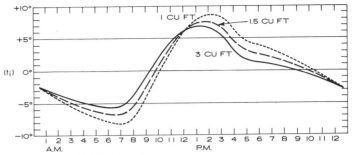

FIGURE 7 FRACTION OF MONTHLY SPACE HEATING REQUIREMENT SUPPLIED BY SOLAR ENERGY
SOURCE: W.O. WRAY, J.D. BALCOMB AND R.D. McFARLAND
LOS ALAMOS SCIENTIFIC LABORATORY, NEW MEXICO

(t$_i$) = AVERAGE INDOOR TEMPERATURE

FIGURE 10 HOURLY INDOOR TEMPERATURE FOR DIRECT GAIN SYSTEMS WITH VARIOUS VOLUMES OF WATER STORAGE PER SQUARE FOOT OF SOUTH FACING GLASS

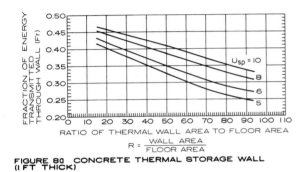

$$R = \frac{WALL\ AREA}{FLOOR\ AREA}$$

FIGURE 8a CONCRETE THERMAL STORAGE WALL (1 FT THICK)

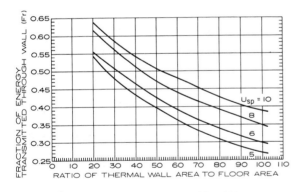

FIGURE 8b WATER THERMAL STORAGE WALL (ANY THICKNESS)

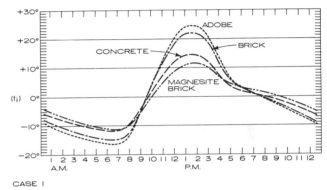

CASE 1
FIGURE 9a

CASE 2 (t$_i$) = AVERAGE INDOOR TEMPERATURE

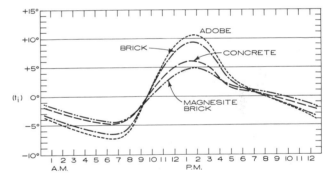

FIGURE 9b HOURLY INDOOR TEMPERATURE FOR DIRECT GAIN SYSTEMS WITH MASONRY HEAT STORAGE

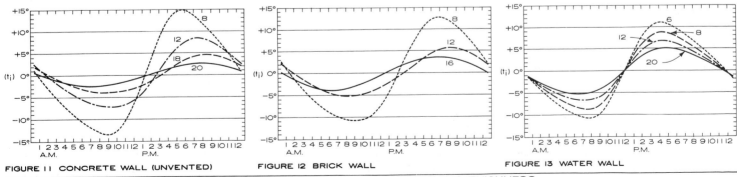

FIGURE 11 CONCRETE WALL (UNVENTED)

FIGURE 12 BRICK WALL

FIGURE 13 WATER WALL

HOURLY INDOOR TEMPERATURE FOR A THERMAL STORAGE WALL OF VARYING THICKNESS

Edward Mazria, AIA, Architect; Edward Mazria & Associates; Albuquerque, New Mexico

ENVIRONMENTAL FACTORS 1

GENERAL

This three step process evaluates energy conserving alternatives in terms of expected annual savings.

1. Step 1 quantifies peak heating and cooling savings (Btuh).
2. Step 2 converts peak savings to annual savings (Btu).
3. Step 3 establishes a dollar value for annual savings.

Cost benefit analysis involving annual savings and initial cost is a relatively simple matter when the process has been completed.

The following tables provide approximate values for outdoor design temperatures, R values, and ETD. For more detailed and precise information the 1977 ASHRAE Handbook of Fundamentals should be consulted.

TABLE A.   OUTDOOR DESIGN TEMPERATURES

CITY	WINTER	SUMMER
Phoenix, AR	34	107
Los Angeles, CA	43	80
San Francisco, CA	40	71
Denver, CO	1	91
Miami, FL	47	90
Chicago, IL	2	91
Bangor, MA	-6	81
Jackson, MS	25	95
Lincoln, NE	-2	95
New York, NY	15	89
Bismarck, ND	-19	91
Muskogee, OK	15	98
Philadelphia, PA	14	90
Dallas, TX	22	100
Seattle, WA	26	81

SOURCE: 1977 ASHRAE Fundamentals, Chapter 23, Table 1.

TABLE B.   SELECTED R VALUES (APPROXIMATE)

Glass, single	0.9
Glass, double or storm	1.5
Glass, triple	2.5
Brick (4″ thick nominal)	0.1
Concrete brick (4″ thick nominal)	0.7
Concrete 1″ thick	0.1
Wood 1″ thick	1.2
Insulation 1″ thick (most materials)	3.5
Insulation polyurethane 1″ thick (2 pcf)	5.5
Aluminum foil plus airspace, ceiling	3.0
Aluminum foil plus airspace, wall	2.0

NOTE: For increased thickness, increase R value as appropriate [i.e., 2″ wood R = 2.5 (1.25 x 2)].

TABLE C.   EQUIVALENT TEMPERATURE DIFFERENCE

DESIGN TEMPERATURE (°F)	90°	95°	100°
Walls—frame or veneer	19	24	29
8″ masonry	11	16	21
Ceilings and roof			
Dark color	39	44	49
Light color	31	36	41

For more accurate information consult ASHRAE Fundamentals, 1977, Chapter 25, Table 35.

TABLE D.   ENERGY UNITS FOR 1,000,000 BTU

HEATING	UNITS	COOLING	UNITS (kwh)
Coal	100 lb	EER 6	167
Oil	10 gal	EER 7	143
Natural gas	14 therms	EER 8	125
Propane	16 gal	EER 9	111
Electric resistance heat	293 kWh	EER 10	100
Electric heat pump COP 2	147 kWh	EER 11	91

NOTE: Assumes 70% combustion efficiency for heating fuels. If 60%, multiply by 0.86; if 80%, multiply by 1.14. For heat pump C.O.P. above 2, (divide) by COP/2.

F. J. Trost; Texas A & M University; College Station, Texas

EXAMPLE OF INSULATION APPLICATION

A building in Muskogee, OK, is to be reroofed, and the owner is considering adding R-19 insulation. Conditions are as follows: roof area = 1000 sq ft; roof R = 7; roof color = dark;   design temperatures = 70°F indoors, 15°F outdoors in winter; 80°F indoors, 98°F outdoors in summer.

STEP 1

Quantify winter peak heat loss in Btuh using the formula:

$$\frac{(area) \times (TD)}{R} = Btuh$$

where area = roof area (sq ft)

TD = temperature difference indoors to outdoors (°F)

R = total resistance value for the roof construction (including all components and air films)

Quantify summer peak heat gain in Btuh using the formula:

$$\frac{(area) \times (ETD)}{R} = Btuh$$

where ETD = equivalent temperature difference (use nearest value; from Table C)

The existing roof has an R value of 7; the new roof will have an R value of 26 (7 plus 19).

Winter heat loss (old)

$$\frac{(1000) \times (55)}{7} = 7857$$

Summer heat gain (old)

$$\frac{1000 \times (49)}{7} = 7000$$

Winter heat loss (new)

$$\frac{(1000) \times (55)}{26} = 2115$$

Summer heat gain (new)

$$\frac{1000 \times (49)}{26} = 1885$$

By subtracting the new values from the old values the peak energy savings are quantified:

Winter savings   Summer savings
5742 Btuh   5115 Btuh

STEP 2

To convert peak savings into annual savings refer to the heating and cooling maps E and F. Multiply the equipment hours by the peak savings in Btuh to obtain the annual Btu savings. For Muskogee, OK, the maps indicate 1200 heating hours and 1500 cooling hours. (Note: local full load hour information will provide more accuracy.)

Annual savings winter:

(1200) x (5742) = 6,890,400, say 6.9 million Btu

Annual savings summer:

(1500) x (5115) = 7,672,500, say 7.7 million Btu

STEP 3

Refer to Table D to determine the units of energy saved and use local utility rates to calculate the annual dollar savings. In this example we use natural gas for heating at X$ per therm and electricity for cooling at Y$ per kWh. Furthermore, we assume an EER of 6 for the air conditioner.

From Table D, 14 therms of gas are required per million Btu heating and 167 kWh per million Btu of cooling.

Annual savings:

(million Btu) (energy units) ($ per unit)

Heating savings:

(6.9) x (14) x (X) = $96.6 (X)

Cooling savings:

(7.7) x (167) x (Y) = $1287 (Y)

sum = total savings/present year

EXAMPLE OF GLAZING APPLICATION

A designer wishes to evaluate double glass for windows in a college dormitory to be constructed in New York City. The dormitory will have 2000 sq ft of window area. Design conditions are 15°F outdoors, 70°F indoors in winter; and 89°F outdoors, 80°F indoors in summer. All windows have external shading so the benefits of double glazing are limited to conducted heat gain and loss only.

STEP 1

Quantify peak heat loss and gain.

Winter heat loss (single)

$$\frac{(2000) \times 55}{0.9} = 122,222$$

Summer heat gain (single)

$$\frac{(2000) \times 9}{0.9} = 20,000$$

Winter heat loss (double)

$$\frac{(2000) \times 55}{1.5} = 73,333$$

Summer heat gain (double)

$$\frac{(2000) \times 9}{1.5} = 12,000$$

By subtracting double values from single values, peak energy savings are quantified.

Winter savings   Summer savings
48,889 Btuh   8000 Btuh

NOTE: Cooling savings are for conducted heat gain only; so the design TD is used as the ETD.

STEP 2

Convert the peak savings to annual savings. Maps indicate 2000 heating hours and 750 cooling hours.

Annual savings, winter

(2000) x (48,889) = 97,778,000, say 98 million Btu

Annual savings, summer

(750) x (8000) = 6,000,000

STEP 3

Calculate the annual utility savings if heating fuel is oil at Z$/gal and cooling is electric, EER = 7, and cost is Y$/kWh.

Heating savings

(98) x (10) x (Y) = $980 (Z)

Cooling savings

(6) x (143) x (Z) = $858 (Y)

sum = total savings/present year

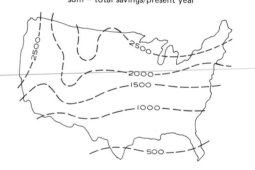

E. HEATING HOURS / YEAR

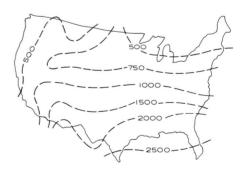

F. COOLING HOURS / YEAR

EQUIVALENT FULL LOAD EQUIPMENT, HOURS / YEAR

1   ENVIRONMENTAL FACTORS

THERMAL STORAGE WALLS

Thermal storage wall designs are passive solar heating approaches that include massive, south facing concrete or masonry walls painted a dark color and covered with glass or some other glazing material. These are known as Trombe walls. Opaque water filled tubes painted a dark color or of clear fiber reinforced plastic (FRP) are often used in lieu of masonry. As solar radiation is transmitted through the glazing material, the thermal storage wall absorbs heat directly, conducts it (and convects it in the case of water containers), and radiates heat to the interior space at night. Vents may be located at the top and bottom of Trombe wall designs to allow for heated air to rise into the living space. Dampers should be included in such vented designs to prevent reverse airflow at night.

Thermal storage walls should either be vented to outside and/or shaded to prevent them from overheating the interior in the summer. However, an unshaded Trombe wall that is vented to the outdoors can effectively induce natural ventilation by the "chimney effect."

Thermal storage walls do not necessarily require insulation but their performance is improved by its application. Exterior hinged insulating panels (which also reflect additional solar radiation onto the wall) or insulating roll shades or curtains may be deployed.

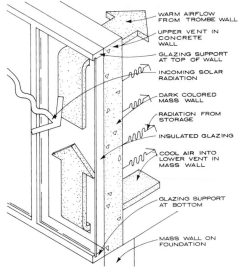

MASONRY WALL TYPE

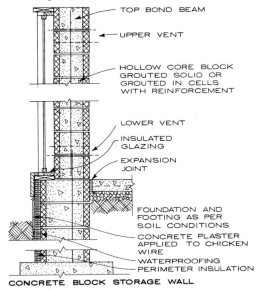

CONCRETE BLOCK STORAGE WALL

The interior finish on the wall must not prevent the wall's heat from radiating to the interior space. A thin plaster coat may be applied, but sheet materials or materials requiring adhesives should not be used.

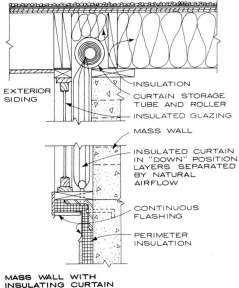

MASS WALL WITH INSULATING CURTAIN

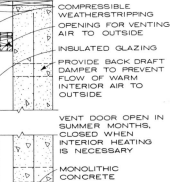

CONCRETE STORAGE WALL WITH OUTSIDE VENT

The exterior glazing component should be mounted 3 to 6 in. out from the wall if natural venting is used or 2 to 4 in. if the system is fan augmented. The use of insulation between the wall and glazing will govern this dimension.

Masonry storage wall designs will vary in thickness (to allow for different time delays of heat movement) depending on the thermal characteristics of the building and the climate in which the building is located.

FRAMING PLAN

FRAME WIDTH TO MATCH GLAZING MULLION SIZES—NOT LARGER THAN 4 × 8. LARGER MEMBERS—NOT LARGER THAN 8 × 8

SUPPORT AND HOLDDOWN FOR DAYTIME USE

REFLECTOR / SHUTTER

WATER WALL TYPE

STEEL CULVERT WATER CONTAINERS

WATER WALL

Thermal storage walls of the water container type may be designed as an integral part of the heated space or may be separated from the living space by a vented wall for added comfort control. Corrugated, galvanized steel culverts, FRP, and 55 gal steel drums are the most common containers.

Airspaces in water containers should be provided for the expansion of water. Water in steel containers should also contain a rust inhibitor, while water in FRP tubes should contain algicide to prevent algae growth.

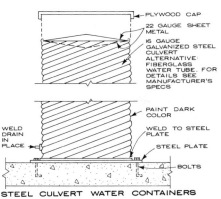

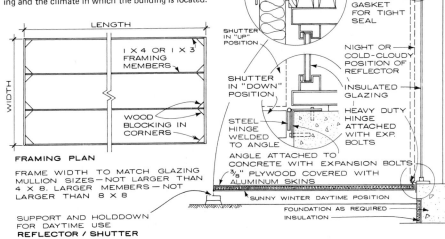

Professor Kenneth Haggard and Phillip Niles; California Polytechnic State University; San Luis Obispo, California

Lawrence Atkinson and Paul Karius; Atkinson/Karius/Architects; Denver, Colorado

ENVIRONMENTAL FACTORS   1

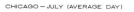

CHICAGO — JULY (AVERAGE DAY)

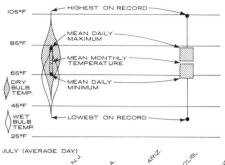

JULY (AVERAGE DAY)

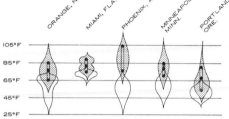

TEMPERATURE

A record of local daily and monthly temperatures will be a clear indication of the expected monthly heating and cooling loads as well as of the potential for diurnal "time lag" conditioning.

Dry bulb temperature is the sensible air temperature read from a standard thermometer; mean monthly temperatures, mean maximum and minimums, and record highs and lows should be recorded. The diurnal temperature swing is the range between day and night, or minimum and maximum mean temperatures. For load calculations, heating degree days and cooling hours provide a more accurate, cumulative calculation of mean monthly temperatures, measured daily as the number of degrees of difference between outdoor mean temperatures and a design base, usually 65°F.

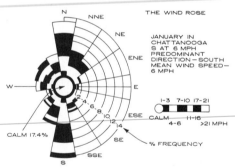

THE WIND ROSE

JANUARY IN CHATTANOOGA S AT 6 MPH PREDOMINANT DIRECTION — SOUTH MEAN WIND SPEED — 6 MPH

CALM 17.4%

% FREQUENCY

1-3 7-10 17-21
CALM   11-16
4-6   >21 MPH

MINNEAPOLIS — SEPT.

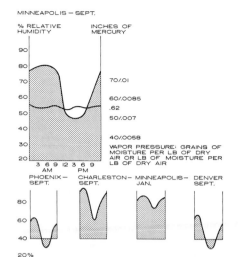

RELATIVE HUMIDITY

A record of monthly day and night moisture conditions, coincident with dry bulb temperatures, will indicate the severity of the summer cooling load, as well as the potential for evaporative cooling or the need for dehumidification.

Wet bulb temperature is the measure of the heat held latent in water vapor in the air. The more closely wet bulb temperature matches dry bulb temperatures, the more humid and latently heated is the air. Relative humidity is the amount of moisture in the air expressed as a percentage of the total amount of moisture the air can hold at a given temperature, while vapor pressure represents the amount of moisture actually in the air regardless of temperature. Any two of these factors—wet bulb, dry bulb, relative humidity, and vapor pressure—will give the other two factors on a psychrometric chart.

WIND

A record of monthly wind speeds and direction will indicate the severity of infiltration loads in winter, as well as the potential for natural ventilation in summer.

Wind direction at different times of day and night, in different seasons, will suggest the means to both deflect winter winds and accept summer breezes in building design. Wind speed states the seriousness and the usefulness of these winds, ranging from calm or 0 mph to greater than 20 mph, while wind frequency will reinforce the occurrence of each wind direction and speed.

GROUND TEMPERATURES AND SKY TEMPERATURES

Two additional monthly data points worthy of collection are effective sky temperatures to indicate the potential for radiant cooling and ground temperatures at various depths to indicate the potential for modifying the severity of winter and summer temperatures in harsh climates.

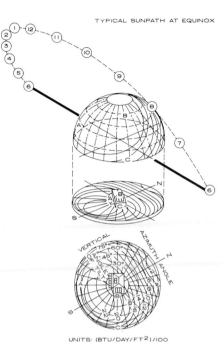

TYPICAL SUNPATH AT EQUINOX

UNITS: (BTU/DAY/FT²)/100

© The Architects Taos

SUN

A record of solar intensity and availability, called irradiation or insolation, will anticipate the cooling loads caused by sun conditions in summer, as well as the potential for solar heating in winter.

Solar intensity is the sun's heat measured in Btu/sq ft · hr, or per day or month, in a given location on horizontal and vertical surfaces.

Solar availability is the time the sun spends in a clear sky, measured in clear sky and cloudiness factors. Degree of altitude represents the sun's height on a vertical axis, higher in summer, and azimuth represents its location on the horizontal, compass directions, a wider range in summer. A north window generally receives bounced diffuse light while a window that sees the sun receives direct and diffuse light.

REFERENCES

National Bureau of Standards, Gaithersburg, Md. Horizontal and Vertical Radiation Data for 48 Cities and SOLMET (Tapes) Solar Radiation Data for 130 Cities.

AIA/House Beautiful's Regional Climate Study 1952, Twelve Regions, Michigan University Press, Ann Arbor, Mich.

ASHRAE's Handbook of Fundamentals, 1977.

National Climatic Center's Asheville N.C., National Climate Summary, 1978, NTIS.

DATA COLLECTION

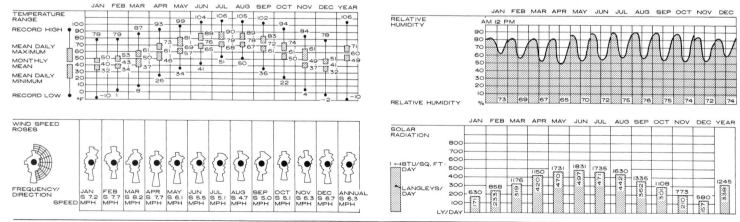

DATA DISPLAY

Vivian Loftness, Kevin Green and Fred Greenberg; AIA Research Corporation; under contract with National Oceanographic and Atmospheric Administration and U.S. Department of Energy

1

ENVIRONMENTAL FACTORS

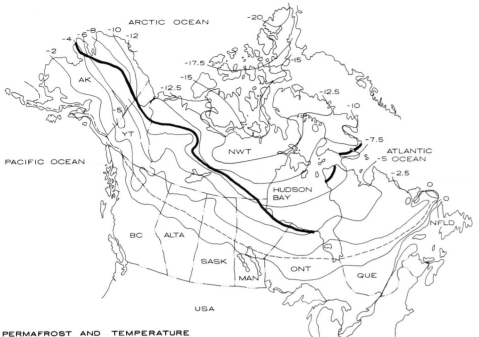

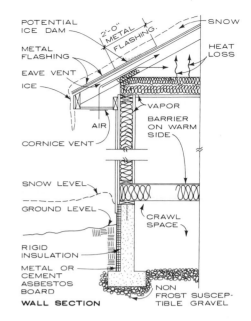

PERMAFROST AND TEMPERATURE ZONES — ALASKA AND CANADA

KEY: ———— MEAN ANNUAL AIR TEMPERATURE, C°
————— PROVINCE BOUNDARY
————— SOUTHERN LIMIT-DISCONTINUOUS PERMAFROST
━━━━ SOUTHERN LIMIT CONTINENTAL PERMAFROST
————— COUNTRY BOUNDARY

PERMAFROST, ICE WEDGES AND LENSES, AND FROST HEAVE

DEFINITION OF PERMAFROST: Ground of any kind that stays colder than the freezing temperature of water throughout several years.

TERMS

ACTIVE LAYER: Top layer of ground subject to annual freezing and thawing.

FROST HEAVING: Lifting or heaving of soil surface created by the freezing of subsurface frost susceptible material.

FROST SUSCEPTIBLE SOIL: Soil that has enough permeability and capillary action (wickability) to expand upon freezing.

ICE LENSE (TABER ICE): Pocket of ice.

ICE WEDGE: Wedge shaped mass of ice within the soil. Wedges range up to 3 or 4 wide and 10 deep.

PERELETOK: Frozen layer at the base of the active layer that remains unthawed during cold summers.

RESIDUAL THAW ZONE: Layer of unfrozen ground between the permafrost and active layer. This layer does not exist when annual frost extends to the permafrost, but is present during warm winters.

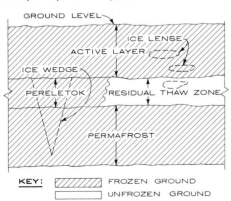

KEY: ▨ FROZEN GROUND
▢ UNFROZEN GROUND

CCC/HOK; Anchorage, Alaska

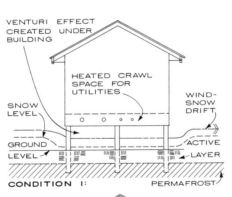

CONDITION 1:

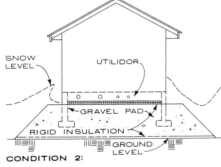

CONDITION 2:

CONDITIONS OF BUILDING ON PERMAFROST

CONDITION 1: Building elevated on piles allows for the dissipation of building heat to help prevent the ground from thawing. Added benefits include winter refreezing of ground by cold winter air and prevention of snowdrift buildup.

CONDITION 2: Building elevated on nonfrost susceptible gravel pad. Benefits include lessening of snowdrift problems and retardation of permafrost thaw. Existing ground cover can remain as insulation. Rigid insulation can also be used.

WALL SECTION

EAVE AND FOUNDATION DETAILING IN COLD CLIMATES

Snow buildup on the roof is warmed by heat loss from the building. The melting snow flows down the roof and is refrozen at the eave because of the eave's cold condition. The use of a cornice vent and insulation to create a "cold roof" helps to reduce the problem of ice damming. When an ice dam is created, the water backs up, leaking under roofing materials. The placement of metal flashing on the roof at least 2 ft 0 in. up from the wall line causes the snow and ice to slide off and also prevents moisture penetration.

All vapor barriers in cold and arctic conditions must be on the warm side to avoid condensation in the insulation. Use of rigid insulation on the exterior of the foundation wall (with a metal or cement asbestos board cover for protection) creates a heat bank and keeps the utility space from freezing.

PILES

In the arctic, piles are popular because they are a simple way of providing thermal isolation of heated structures, minimize disturbance of existing thermal regime, permit flow of flood waters, and prevent the buildup of drifting snow. However, frost heaving can force the piles upward during the freeze season without allowing the piles to return to the original level when the soil thaws.

Solutions to the problem of pile heaving:

1. Anchor the pile against uplift by placing anchors or notches on the pile within the permafrost zone.
2. Break the bond in the active layer. (Use bond breaking plastic wrap or grease pile in the active layer.)
3. To aviod thaw of the surrounding soil, use one of the three main one-way heat extractors: (a) The gaseous flow system or, (b) the liquid system, containing tubes with "Venturi" funnels to allow warm liquid to rise and cold liquid to sink, and (c) a mechanical refrigeration system. The designer must be careful not to allow heat to be transferred from the building to the pile (thus avoiding thawing the permafrost).

UTILITIES IN COLD CLIMATE AND ARCTIC CONDITIONS

Utilidors or utiliducts are the most common way to provide protection, easy access, and insulation of utility lines to avoid disturbance to the permafrost.

Human waste at isolated facilities may be handled by compost privies (waterless toilets) and chemical toilets, which are commonly referred to as "honey buckets." Disposal systems include incineration and sewage lagoons.

LOCATION

Generally the hot-dry regions of North America are in the SW corner of the United States and the NW corner of Mexico, below the snow line. They consist of valleys and deserts below 3000 ft in elevation with an annual temperature above 65°F.

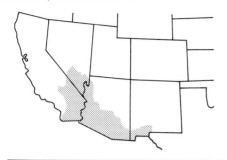

HOT—DRY REGION OF THE U.S.

CLIMATE SUMMARY

Some part of every day or night throughout the year is totally comfortable and pleasant; the balance of the time the climate is usually excessively hot or cold. The 3 to 5 months of summer are the most demanding and establish the critical design parameters; preventing heat gain is the objective. Winter nights are cold but winter days are comfortable. Lack of cloud cover means maximum solar radiation (above 80% annual possible sunshine), little rainfall (average less than 10 in./yr), and high evaporation rate (over 100 in./yr). Summer cooling loads are larger than winter heating loads for all building types.

CLIMATE CHARACTERISTICS

EXCESSIVE RADIATION

Solar radiation and thermal reradiation of heat stored in materials are the prime sources of discomfort. Daily temperature highs average over 100°F from mid-May into September. Clear night skys absorb summer heat but cause heavy frosts every winter.

LOW HUMIDITY

Precipitation averages under 10 in./yr. Infrequent rains are often heavy; resulting runoff produces flash floods. Evaporation rates average over 100 in./yr, resulting in very low relative humidities. Occasional dust storms are encountered.

HIGH DIURNAL TEMPERATURE VARIATION

Range between daily maxima and minima may exceed 50°F. However, in late summer, night temperatures may not drop below 80°F.

HIGH SEASONAL TEMPERATURE VARIATION

Winter lows and summer highs may vary as much as 100°F.

SIGNIFICANT MICROCLIMATES

Both natural and manmade microclimatic variations can occur in a relatively short distance: elevation and landscaping are the major influences.

PLANNING AND SITING

PLANNING

Encourage high density and compact planning; use party or common walls, concentrate development for mutual shading and insulation. Mixed land uses reduce travel time and the need for frequent travel.

PEDESTRIANS

Provide tight, protected circulation; encourage short pedestrian paths. Shading is necessary for pedestrians—use arcades, narrow alleyways, awnings, tree canopies, trellises.

LANDSCAPING

Vegetation is desirable for psychological and evaptranspiration cooling. Prefer native types: riparian near buildings, desert varieties in open areas. Cluster nonnative materials for maximum effect from engineered watering systems; use oasis concepts. Deciduous plants provide a sense of seasons and also winter sun penetration. Vegetative ground cover can reduce ground reflectance, shade the earth, and reduce air temperatures. Include rain holding and percolation areas in site shaping.

BUILDING FORM

ORIENTATION

Minimize exposure to W. Ideal orientation for openings is S. However, orientations from S to 25°E of S can provide appropriate shading control. Northerly orientations for openings are also desirable. Avoid swimming pools on W or N of building.

SHAPE

Compact building forms elongated on an E-W axis are preferable. Design forms to maximize self-shading. Generally keep volume-to-surface ratio high. Avoid courtyard and patio schemes except where building volume/surface ratio is large, or perimeter walls have maximum thermal resistance. Earth contact designs and underground approaches desirable.

MICROCLIMATE

Respond to existing microclimate conditions. Design adjacent microclimates on all sides. Landscape shields on E and W can temper sun and heat impact on buildings. Major elements can direct prevailing cooling breezes. Walled-in gardens and yards can hold cool air pools. Consider water features and heavy vegetation for cooling effect, but watch the costs of water.

FUNCTIONAL ZONING

Use varying construction strategies in a single building. High mass construction is recommended for day use or 24 hr use functions; light, highly insulated low mass construction preferred for occasional use or night use functions; use screened porches, exposed decks, and sheltered terraces for controlled outdoor uses, occupied on time-of-day or season basis.

THERMAL ZONING

Place noninhabited spaces on the W to buffer heat. Isolate heat producing activities. Use vestibules or lobbies in public spaces to provide thermal transitions.

NATURAL LIGHTING

Day lighting (diffuse solar radiation) of work spaces is recommended especially from N. All daylight sources (windows and skylights) should be self-shaded on the exterior. Since smaller window openings are preferred, natural lighting requires special design attention. Use light colored interiors to distribute daylight.

COLOR/TEXTURE

Use light reflective colors on roof and E, S, and W walls to reject summer heat. A greater range of choice is possible on N elevations. Avoid specular reflective surfaces (mirror finishes) because of their focusing nature. Use medium or darker colors adjacent to openings to avoid reflections into interiors. Bright colors are preferable for visual contrast in the bright sunshine of the region; colors in the shadows, such as eaves and soffits, are especially effective.

DESIGN STRATEGIES

Design for cooling by evaporation by considering vegetation, pools, fountains, roof ponds, sprays, landscape watering systems, and so on. Mechanical evaporation cooling systems are effective.

Provide heavy interior thermal mass protected by insulation from exterior temperatures for thermal conservation, combine high mass and low mass in a single structure for different times of use.

Use transitional zones both in construction (i.e., thick wall assemblies) and in planning (i.e., intermediate or transitional areas and seasonal spaces).

Design microclimates using both architectural and landscape materials and forms to modify climate and temper the natural extremes.

BUILDING ELEMENTS

FOUNDATIONS

Use masonry or concrete in earth contact; slab on grade, basement, or earth-bermed structures. Insulation necessary above grade.

EXTERIOR WALLS

Walls should be seasonally shaded whenever possible. In hot climates shading strategies are critical.

ROOFS

The roof is the most effective location for both shading and insulation. Roof surfaces should be reflective. Overhead insulation values should be approximately 1.5 times thermal resistance of walls. Vented attics are the common method of reducing overhead radiant heat gain. Double roofs, roof ponds, or sprayed roofs are also effective. Roof sprays are more effective than ponds and can bring down surface temperatures approximately 50°F; however, the process is very hard on materials.

THERMAL CAPACITY

Both capacity insulation and resistance insulation materials are important. Heat capacity construction is recommended in excess of 70 lb of heat absorbing building materials per cu ft of space. An ideal strategy is a minimum of a 10 hr heat lag.

THERMAL RESISTANCE

Minimum recommended thermal resistance in roofs is R30 and in walls, R19. Together with caulking, vapor barriers are recommended also to reduce infiltration.

WEATHERING

Masonry, concrete, and ceramic clay products can last indefinitely. Masonry construction requires frequent wetting during setting and curing. Adobe requires maintenance but can have an extended life. Generally, exposed metals show little weathering. Excessive heat and ultraviolet radiation are destructive of many materials such as wood and plastics.

OPENINGS

Doors, windows, and other openings should be selectively shaded according to season. Closures should be tightly fitted and should include weather stripping. Double glazing is cost effective for all elevations. Generally, ratio of opening to floor space should be small (12% or less). Provide for seasonal natural cross-ventilation. Partially movable shading may provide seasonal control. Shading devices should be self-venting by free convection to avoid heat buildup.

EQUIPMENT

EQUIPMENT CHOICES

Select equipment that minimizes heat production.

EVAPORATIVE COOLING

Above 1500 ft elevation conventional evaporative coolers can provide complete comfort more than 90% of the time. Below 1500 ft they can be effective more than 50% of the time. Systems require complete air changes every 2 to 3 min. They provide total comfort if the wet bulb temperature is below 70°F; reasonable comfort when wet bulb temperature is between 70 and 74°F. For wet-bulb temperature above 74°F evaporation coolers only produce relief. Duct sizes must allow air at 1600 ft/min, preferably 1200 ft/min for silence and efficiency.

AIR CONDITIONERS

Heat pumps are a good choice although the cooling load determines sizing. In these climates equipment must operate consistently at higher outdoor air temperatures (115°F and above). Conventional refrigerated air conditioners and heat pumps are normally rated at operating temperatures of 82 and 95°F. Equipment sizing should accommodate load operating conditions.

HEAT SINKS

Generally stable earth temperatures range from 68 to 75°F, thus the earth offers poor cooling sources. Clear night skies can offer 25% conductive/convective, 25% radiative, 50% evaporative cooling potential. Evaporative sprays are the most effective heat sinks; mechanical evaporation systems probably have the most potential.

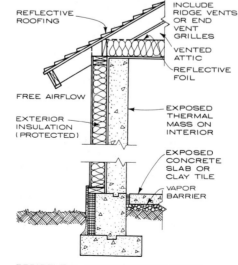

REFLECTIVE ROOFING

INCLUDE RIDGE VENTS OR END VENT GRILLES

VENTED ATTIC

REFLECTIVE FOIL

FREE AIRFLOW

EXTERIOR INSULATION (PROTECTED)

EXPOSED THERMAL MASS ON INTERIOR

EXPOSED CONCRETE SLAB OR CLAY TILE

VAPOR BARRIER

RESIDENTIAL CONSTRUCTION DETAIL

Professor Jeffrey Cook; College of Architecture; Arizona State University; Tempe, Arizona

1

ENVIRONMENTAL FACTORS

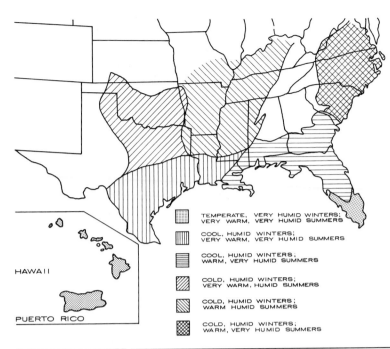

TEMPERATE, VERY HUMID WINTERS; VERY WARM, VERY HUMID SUMMERS

COOL, HUMID WINTERS; VERY WARM, VERY HUMID SUMMERS

COOL, HUMID WINTERS; WARM, VERY HUMID SUMMERS

COLD, HUMID WINTERS; VERY WARM, HUMID SUMMERS

COLD, HUMID WINTERS; WARM HUMID SUMMERS

COLD, HUMID WINTERS; WARM, VERY HUMID SUMMERS

HAWAII

PUERTO RICO

WARM – HUMID REGIONS OF THE UNITED STATES

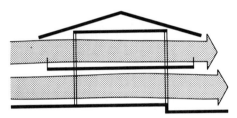

Suburban or rural, single family, where land is plentiful.

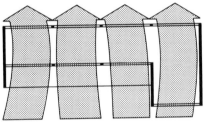

L-shaped plan allows a narrower frontage, screens and doors need perforation and careful attention to detail.

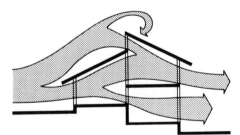

Double banked split level buildings generally stifle air motion, but can allow adequate cross ventilation through careful design.

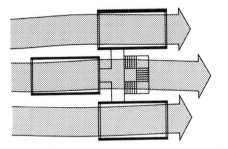

High density, tall apartment buildings must provide maximum external walls for two generous openings per habitable room.

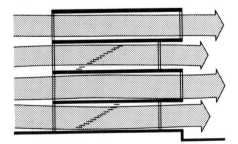

Maisonettes and split-levels can be economical solutions with access balconies, terraces, and corridors assisting in air movement and shading.

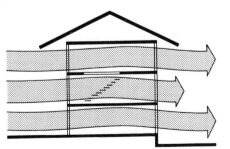

Multistory row development in medium density areas permits cross ventilation when deep room single banked plans are employed.

BUILDING FORM UNDER NATURAL CONDITIONS

Arthur Bowen, RIBA; Professor of Architecture & Planning; University of Miami; Coral Gables, Florida

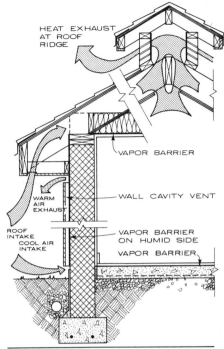

HEAT EXHAUST AT ROOF RIDGE

VAPOR BARRIER

WALL CAVITY VENT

WARM AIR EXHAUST

ROOF INTAKE
COOL AIR INTAKE

VAPOR BARRIER ON HUMID SIDE

VAPOR BARRIER

TYPICAL VENTILATION PATTERNS IN WALL SECTION

WARM-HUMID CONSTRUCTION

Characteristics of warm-humid climates are moist air, above average rainfall, variable air movement, damp ground, and air temperatures seldom exceeding skin temperature. Hot humid areas do not exist in the United States.

ORIENTATION

Under all conditions in overheated areas, the building structure must be vented for cooling. Human comfort may be achieved, when natural conditions prevail, by convective cooling of interior space and human skin. Building orientation must accomplish these needs; solar radiation response is of secondary concern as several methods are available to overcome this. When mechanical comfort conditions are employed, solar radiation considerations dominate orientation. Generally, all habitable rooms must have at least two external openings; bathrooms, stores, and kitchens should be placed in the leeward areas of buildings. Stack vents should be used to release heat from kitchens. Corridors, balconies, and terraces assist lateral air movement, while stairwells and elevators encourage vertical motion. Roofs should be pitched because of rainfall, unless needed for activities.

MATERIALS AND CONSTRUCTION METHODS

Diurnal temperatures vary by 10–15°F, so that thermal mass with a long time lag is unnecessary and may be undesirable under certain conditions. Appropriate materials should be poor conductors—wood, plastics, aluminum. Well ventilated structures are essential to prevent mildew or rotting of materials. Regular cleaning of fly screens will allow continuous airflow and control vermin that can be abundant in these regions. Exterior finishes should be of a light color.

SITE AND LANDSCAPE PLANNING

Airflow in and around buildings and urban areas is essential in warm-humid regions. Under natural conditions, single banked buildings should be staggered to achieve this. When mechanically controlled, cooling of the building envelope, only, need be assured. Generous employment of landscaped areas in and around buildings promotes cooling.

BUILDING FORM UNDER MECHANICALLY CONTROLLED CONDITIONS

Envelope must be ventilated with a pitched roof unless it is used for another purpose. Interior volume must be minimal with a low surface/volume ratio. Airflow through the building's interior must be prohibited.

ENVIRONMENTAL FACTORS   1

NATURAL VENTILATION IN AND AROUND BUILDINGS

Airflow may be gainfully employed in and around buildings for the following tasks:

1. To provide essential air exchange for hygienic purposes—for health and for odor removal.
2. To cool human skin by accelerating conductive and evaporative loss when this is needed.
3. To cool interior space when this is desirable.
4. To cool building fabric in overheated conditions.
5. To remove undesirable moisture from the building's fabric, surfaces, and interior spaces.

GLOBAL AND LOCAL WIND SYSTEMS

Global air movement is governed by three forces: pressure gradient, coriolis, and friction. Local conditions of topography, continentality, and urbanization modify or even supersede prevailing regional systems. Seasonal and diurnal changes are recorded throughout the United States, and this information may be obtained from the National Climate Center, Asheville, North Carolina, and the "Climatic Atlas of the United States" published by the United States Government Printing Office. A wind rose, wedge or matrix, should be compiled for each site, establishing the velocity, frequency, direction, and temperatures that affect it. (Figure 1.)

AIRFLOW PATTERNS

Air will flow from higher (+ve) to a lower (−ve) pressure zone. These pressures exist at a building's boundary and between exterior and interior air. (Figure 2.) Pressures may be manipulated in and around buildings by location and size of openings. Where air velocity is low, it will be accelerated when inlets are smaller than outlets. Where steady, desirable, prevailing winds occur in warm-humid conditions, restricted openings hinder comfort and both inlets and outlets should be large.

Wind flowing against a building causes a high pressure area on the windward side and a low pressure area or wind shadow on the leeward side.

Incoming airstreams may change direction several times, resulting in a decrease in velocities, but promoting turbulence that will improve air movement in areas where stagnation may otherwise occur. Velocities decrease when partitions are located close to the inlet but improve when located nearer the outlet.

CROSS VENTILATION PATTERNS

Partition perpendicular to initial flow alters pattern; back room supplied at cooling speed. (Figure 3.)

Flow is intercepted by partitions; blocking slows flow effect to considerable extent. Cooling effect becomes meager. (Figure 4.)

Partitions parallel to initial flow splits pattern but result remains at adequate high speeds. (Figure 5.)

High inlet and outlet produces poor air movement at body level. (Figure 6.)

Low inlet and outlet produces desirable low level airflow across human body. (Figure 7.)

Poor patterns result when low and high inlets alternate on opposite walls. (Figure 8.)

Louvers can direct airflow upward or downward. (Figure 9.)

Canopies produce an upward airstream that can be corrected by separating the projection from the wall or piercing the canopy. (Figures 10 and 11.)

External barriers reduce air movement through building. (Figure 12.)

Inlet and outlet size and locations radically affect airflow patterns in partitioned rooms. (Figures 13 and 14.)

EFFECTS OF SITE AND LANDSCAPE PLANNING

The building can be exposed or protected from air motion as determined by regional and local conditions. Orientation, shape, and the prudent selection and setting of landscape materials can provide optimum conditions at the building's boundary. Building materials and live plantings may be used individually and in various combinations to create wind barriers or wind scoops in harmony with building needs. Arbors of large canopy trees may reduce ambient temperatures 4–6°F and encourage cool, dense air to flow toward buildings. (Figure 15.)

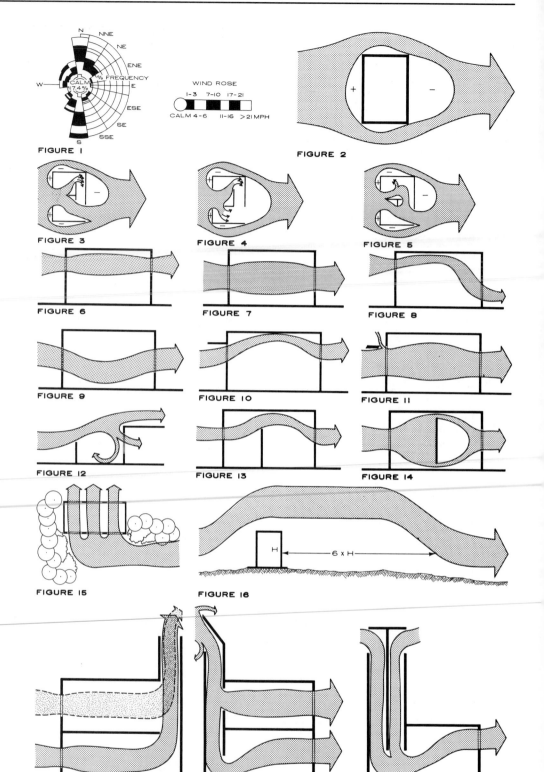

FIGURE 1
WIND ROSE
1-3 7-10 17-21
CALM 4-6 11-16 >21MPH

FIGURE 2

FIGURE 3

FIGURE 4

FIGURE 5

FIGURE 6

FIGURE 7

FIGURE 8

FIGURE 9

FIGURE 10

FIGURE 11

FIGURE 12

FIGURE 13

FIGURE 14

FIGURE 15

FIGURE 16

FIGURE 17

FIGURE 18

FIGURE 19

For winds up to 5 mph, a wind shadow is created on the leeward side of buildings, in depth approximately six times the height or width, whichever is the lesser dimension. The depth of the shadow increases with increasing wind velocity. (Figure 16.)

SOLAR INDUCED VENTILATION

Three categories of thermal chimneys can generate airflow: (1) anabatic or "stack effect," which is a conventional method of hot air release from interior space (Figure 17); (2) pressure or "down draft" chimney, which functions efficiently when predictable direction and velocity prevailing winds occur (Figure 18); and (3) "katabatic" or "cold draft" chimneys, which will only function efficiently when large diurnal temperature differences occur (Figure 19).

WALL OPENINGS

Wall openings traditionally are windows and doors. Pivoted and awning windows provide good ventilation. Sliding glass doors and windows provide only 50% of available opening unless rolled back completely. Adjustable louvered doors and windows provide privacy and good ventilation. A louvered "Caribbean" hood provides good rain protection and ventilation at the same time.

Arthur Bowen, RIBA; Professor of Architecture & Planning; University of Miami; Coral Gables, Florida

1   ENVIRONMENTAL FACTORS

GENERAL NOTES

Building attics, crawl spaces, and basements must be ventilated to remove moisture and water vapor resulting from human activity within the building. Moisture in basements and crawl spaces can occur, in addition, from water in the surrounding soil. The quantity of water vapor depends on building type (e.g., residence, school, hospital), activity (e.g., kitchen, bathroom, laundry), and air temperature and relative humidity. Proper ventilation and insulation must be combined so that the temperature of the ventilated space does not fall below the dew point; this is especially critical with low outdoor temperatures and high inside humidity. Inadequate ventilation will cause condensation and eventual deterioration of framing, insulation, and interior finishes.

The vent types shown allow natural ventilation of roofs and crawl spaces. Mechanical methods (e.g., power attic ventilators, whole house fans) can combine living space and attic ventilation, but openings for natural roof ventilation must still be provided. Protect all vents against insects and vermin with metal or fiberglass screen cloth. Increase net vent areas as noted in table.

VENTILATION REQUIREMENTS TO PREVENT CONDENSATION

SPACE	ROOF TYPE	TOTAL NET AREA OF VENTILATION	REMARKS
Joist (ceiling on underside of joists)	Flat	1/300. Uniformly distributed at eaves	Vent each joist space at both ends. Provide at least 1½" free space above insulation for ventilation
	Sloped	Ditto	Ditto. On gable roofs, drill 1" diameter holes through ridge beam in each joist space to provide through-ventilation to both sides of roof
Attic (unheated)	Gable	1/300. At least two louvers on opposite sides near ridge	
	Hip	1/300. Uniformly distributed at eaves. Provide additional 1/600 at ridge, with all vents interconnected	Ridge vents create stack effect from eaves; both are recommended over eaves vents alone

Total net vent area = 1/300 of building area at eaves line. With screens increase net area by: 1/4" screen, 1.0; #8 screen, 1.25; #16 screen, 2.00.

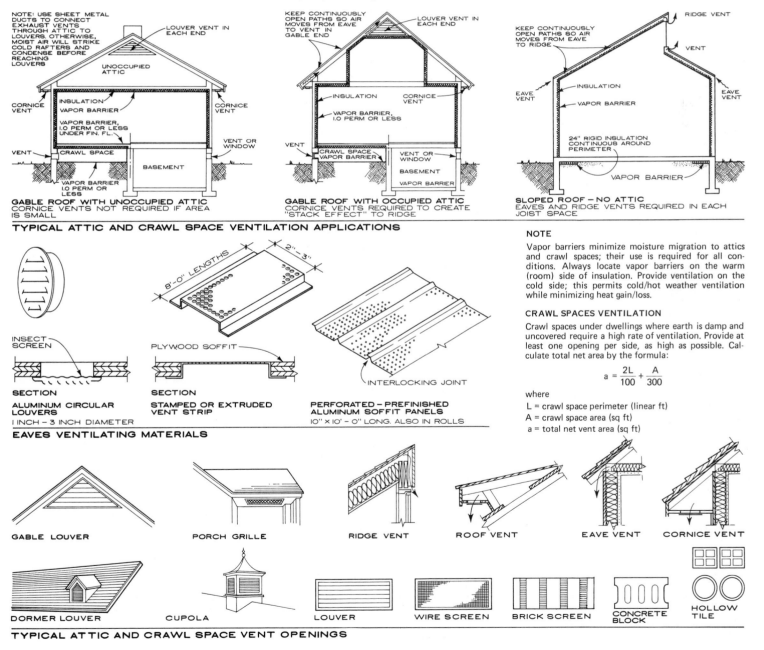

NOTE: USE SHEET METAL DUCTS TO CONNECT EXHAUST VENTS THROUGH ATTIC TO LOUVERS. OTHERWISE, MOIST AIR WILL STRIKE COLD RAFTERS AND CONDENSE BEFORE REACHING LOUVERS

LOUVER VENT IN EACH END

UNOCCUPIED ATTIC

CORNICE VENT

INSULATION

VAPOR BARRIER

VAPOR BARRIER, 1.0 PERM OR LESS UNDER FIN. FL.

CORNICE VENT

VENT

CRAWL SPACE

BASEMENT

VENT OR WINDOW

VAPOR BARRIER 1.0 PERM OR LESS

GABLE ROOF WITH UNOCCUPIED ATTIC
CORNICE VENTS NOT REQUIRED IF AREA IS SMALL

KEEP CONTINUOUSLY OPEN PATHS SO AIR MOVES FROM EAVE TO VENT IN GABLE END

LOUVER VENT IN EACH END

INSULATION

CORNICE VENT

VAPOR BARRIER, 1.0 PERM OR LESS

VENT

CRAWL SPACE VAPOR BARRIER

VENT OR WINDOW

BASEMENT

VAPOR BARRIER

GABLE ROOF WITH OCCUPIED ATTIC
CORNICE VENTS REQUIRED TO CREATE "STACK EFFECT" TO RIDGE

RIDGE VENT

KEEP CONTINUOUSLY OPEN PATHS SO AIR MOVES FROM EAVE TO RIDGE

VENT

INSULATION

EAVE VENT

VAPOR BARRIER

EAVE VENT

24" RIGID INSULATION CONTINUOUS AROUND PERIMETER

VAPOR BARRIER

SLOPED ROOF – NO ATTIC
EAVES AND RIDGE VENTS REQUIRED IN EACH JOIST SPACE

TYPICAL ATTIC AND CRAWL SPACE VENTILATION APPLICATIONS

INSECT SCREEN

SECTION

ALUMINUM CIRCULAR LOUVERS
1 INCH – 3 INCH DIAMETER

8'-0" LENGTHS

2"–3"

PLYWOOD SOFFIT

SECTION

STAMPED OR EXTRUDED VENT STRIP

INTERLOCKING JOINT

PERFORATED – PREFINISHED ALUMINUM SOFFIT PANELS
10" X 10'-0" LONG. ALSO IN ROLLS

EAVES VENTILATING MATERIALS

NOTE

Vapor barriers minimize moisture migration to attics and crawl spaces; their use is required for all conditions. Always locate vapor barriers on the warm (room) side of insulation. Provide ventilation on the cold side; this permits cold/hot weather ventilation while minimizing heat gain/loss.

CRAWL SPACES VENTILATION

Crawl spaces under dwellings where earth is damp and uncovered require a high rate of ventilation. Provide at least one opening per side, as high as possible. Calculate total net area by the formula:

$$a = \frac{2L}{100} + \frac{A}{300}$$

where

L = crawl space perimeter (linear ft)
A = crawl space area (sq ft)
a = total net vent area (sq ft)

GABLE LOUVER

PORCH GRILLE

RIDGE VENT

ROOF VENT

EAVE VENT

CORNICE VENT

DORMER LOUVER

CUPOLA

LOUVER

WIRE SCREEN

BRICK SCREEN

CONCRETE BLOCK

HOLLOW TILE

TYPICAL ATTIC AND CRAWL SPACE VENT OPENINGS

David Metzger, Architect, CSI; Wilkes and Faulkner Associates; Washington, D.C.

ENVIRONMENTAL FACTORS 1

WATER VAPOR MIGRATION

Water is present as vapor in indoor and outdoor air and as absorbed moisture in many building materials. Within the range of temperatures encountered in buildings water may exist in the liquid, vapor, or solid states. Moisture related problems may arise from changes in moisture content, from the presence of excessive moisture, or from the effects of changes of state such as freezing within wall insulation.

In the design and construction of buildings the behavior of moisture must be considered, including particularly the change from vapor to liquid (condensation). Such problems generally arise when moisture in relatively humid indoor air comes in contact with a cold surface such as a window or when the moisture migrates through walls to enter a region of relatively low temperature where condensation can occur.

Moisture problems in residences generally occur in winter when the outdoor temperature and vapor pressure are low and there are many indoor vapor sources. These may include cooking, laundering, bathing, breathing, and perspiration from the occupants, as well as automatic washers and driers, dishwashers and humidifiers. All of these sources combine to cause vapor pressure indoors to be much higher than outdoors, so that the vapor tends to migrate outward through the building envelope. Vapor cannot permeate glazed windows or metal doors, but most other building materials are permeable to some extent. Walls are particularly susceptible to this phenomenon, and such migration must be prevented or at least minimized by the use of low permeability membranes known as vapor barriers, which should be installed as close as possible to the indoor surface of the building.

Water vapor migration is relatively independent of air motion within the building, since such migration depends primarily on vapor pressure differences. Migration always takes place from regions of higher vapor pressure toward spaces such as wall cavities where the vapor pressure will be lower. When surfaces below the local dewpoint temperature are encountered, condensation will occur and moisture droplets will form. If the local drybulb temperature is at or below 32°F, freezing will occur, which may lead to permanent structural damage.

Moisture in building materials usually increases their thermal conductance to a significant and unpredictable extent. Porous materials that become saturated with moisture lose most of their insulating capability and may not regain it when they dry out. Dust, which usually settles in airspaces, may become permanently affixed to originally reflective surfaces. Moisture migration by evaporation, vapor flow, and condensation can transport significant quantities of latent heat, particularly through fibrous insulating materials.

Positive steps should be taken to prevent migration of moisture in the form of vapor and accumulation in the form of water or ice within building components. Vapor barriers, correctly located near the source of the moisture, are the most effective means of preventing such migration. Venting of moisture laden air from bathrooms, laundry rooms, and kitchens will reduce indoor vapor pressure, as will the introduction of outdoor air with low moisture content.

PERMEANCE AND PERMEABILITY OF MATERIALS TO WATER VAPOR

MATERIAL	PERMEANCE (PERM)	MATERIAL	PERMEANCE (PERM)
MATERIALS USED IN CONSTRUCTION		**BUILDING PAPERS, FELTS, ROOFING PAPERS**[3]	
Concrete (1:2:4 mix)	3.2[5]	Duplex sheet, asphalt laminated, aluminum foil one side (43)[4]	0.176
Brick-masonry (4 in. thick)	0.8–1.1		
Concrete masonry (8 in. cored, limestone aggregate)	2.4	Saturated and coated roll roofing (326)[4]	0.24
Asbestos-cement board (0.2 in. thick)	0.54	Kraft paper and asphalt laminated, reinforced 30-120-30 (34)[4]	1.8
Plaster on metal lath (3/4 in.)	15		
Plaster on plain gypsum lath (with studs)	20	Asphalt-saturated, coated vapor-barrier paper (43)[4]	0.6
Gypsum wallboard (3/8 in. plain)	50	Asphalt-saturated, not coated sheathing paper (22)[4]	20.2
Structural insulating board (sheathing quality)	20–50[5]	15-lb asphalt felt (70)[4]	5.6
Structural insulating board (interior, uncoated, 1/2 in.)	50–90	15-lb tar felt (70)[4]	18.2
Hardboard (1/8 in. standard)	11	Single kraft, double infused (16)[4]	42
Hardboard (1/8 in. tempered)	5		
Built-up roofing (hot mopped)	0.0	**LIQUID APPLIED COATING MATERIALS**	
Wood, fir sheathing, 3/4 in.	2.9		
Plywood (Douglas fir, exterior glue, 1/4 in.)	0.7	Paint—two coats	
Plywood (Douglas fir, interior, glue, 1/4 in.)	1.9	Aluminum varnish on wood	0.3–0.5
		Enamels on smooth plaster	0.5–1.5
Acrylic, glass fiber reinforced sheet, 56 mil	0.12	Primers and sealers on interior insulation board	0.9–2.1
Polyester, glass fiber reinforced sheet, 48 mil	0.05	Miscellaneous primers plus one coat flat oil paint on plastic	1.6–3.0
THERMAL INSULATIONS		Flat paint on interior insulation board	4
Cellular glass	0.0[5]	Water emulsion on interior insulation board	30–85
Mineral wool, unprotected	29.0	Paint—three coats	
Expanded polyurethane (R-11 blown)	0.4–1.6[5]	Exterior paint, white lead and oil on wood siding	0.3–1.0
Expanded polystyrene—extruded	1.2[5]	Exterior paint, white lead-zinc oxide and oil on wood	0.9
Expanded polystyrene—bead	2.0–5.8[5]	Styrene-butadiene latex coating, 2 oz/sq ft	11
PLASTIC AND METAL FOILS AND FILMS[2]		Polyvinyl acetate latex coating, 4 oz/sq ft	5.5
Aluminum foil (1 mil)	0.0	Asphalt cutback bastic	
Polyethylene (4 mil)	0.08	1/16 in. dry	0.14
Polyethylene (6 mil)	0.06	3/16 in. dry	0.0
Polyethylene (8 mil)	0.04	Hot melt asphalt	
Polyester (1 mil)	0.7	2 oz/sq ft	0.5
Polyvinylchloride, unplasticized (2 mil)	0.68	3.5 oz/sq ft	0.1
Polyvinylchloride, plasticized (4 mil)	0.8–1.4		

	ESTIMATED PERMEANCE
GWB (3/8″)	50.0
Vapor barrier	0.6 (lowest)
Insulation	29.0
Wood sheathing	2.9
4″ brick veneer	1.1 (next)

EXAMPLE

In this example the vapor barrier transmits 1 grain of moisture per square foot per hour for each unit of vapor pressure difference, and nothing else transmits less. However, since the cold brick veneer is nearly as low in permeance it is advisable to make certain that the vapor barrier is expertly installed, with all openings at pipes and with outlet boxes or joints carefully fitted or sealed. Alternatively, the brick veneer may have open mortar joints near the top and bottom to serve both as weep holes and as vapor release openings. They will also ventilate the wall and help to reduce heat gain in summer.

	ESTIMATED PERMEANCE
GWB (3/8″)	50.0
Furred space	—
8″ CMU	2.4
4″ brick veneer	1.1 (lowest)

EXAMPLE

Vapor (under pressure) would easily pass through the interior finish, be slowed up by the concrete masonry unit, and be nearly stopped by the cold brick veneer. Unless this design is radically improved, the masonry will become saturated and may cause serious water stains or apparent "leaks" in cold weather. In addition, alternating freezing and thawing of condensation within the masonry wall can physically damage the construction.

- List the materials, without surface films or airspaces, in the order of their appearance in the building section, beginning with the inside surface material and working to the outside.
- Against each material list the permeance (or permeability) value from the table or a more accurate value if available from tests or manufacturers' data. Where a range is given, select an average value or use judgment in assigning a value based on the character and potential installation method of the material proposed for use.
- Start at the top of the list and note any material that has less permeance than the materials above it on the list. At that point the possibility exists that vapor leaking through the first material may condense on the second, provided the dew point (condensation point) is reached and the movement is considerable. In that case, provide ventilation through the cold side material or modify the design to eliminate or change the material to one of greater permeance.

NOTES

1. The vapor transmission rates listed will permit comparisons of materials, but selection of vapor barrier materials should be based on rates obtained from the manufacturer or from laboratory tests. The range of values shown indicates variation among mean values for materials that are similar but of different density. Values are intended for design guidance only.
2. Usually installed as vapor barriers. If used as exterior finish and elsewhere near cold side, special considerations are required.
3. Low permeance sheets used as vapor barriers. High permeance use elsewhere in construction.
4. Bases (weight in lb/500 sq ft).
5. Permeability (PERM-in.).

Based on data from "ASHRAE Handbook of Fundamentals," 1977, Chapter 20.

Owen J. Delevante, AIA; Glen Rock, New Jersey

E. C. Shuman, P.E.; Consulting Engineer; State College, Pennsylvania

BUILDING SECTION ANALYSIS FOR POTENTIAL CONDENSATION

Any building section may be analyzed by simple calculations to determine where condensation might occur and what might be done in selecting materials or their method of assembly to eliminate that possibility. The section may or may not contain a vapor barrier or it may contain a relatively imperfect barrier; the building section may include cold side materials of comparatively high resistance to the passage of vapor (which is highly undesirable and is to be avoided). With few exceptions, the vapor resistance at or near the warm surface should be five times that of any components. The table above gives permeances and permeability of building and vapor barrier materials. These values can be used in analyzing building sections by the following simple method:

1 ENVIRONMENTAL FACTORS

CHAPTER 2 SITEWORK

INTRODUCTION

Site planning for any significant development project should be a sequential process, beginning with broad information-gathering and ending with specific, detailed design drawings. The process involves three basic stages—analysis, design, and implementation. The following chart indicates a planning process; however, specifics of the site—such as physical site characteristics, location, and community criteria—may modify the process. Certain steps in the process may be taken simultaneously, rather than on a precise step-by-step basis.

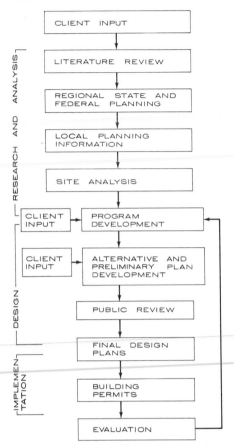

CLIENT CONTACT AND INPUT

The first step is the contact between client and site planner. Although the land planner should be involved as early as possible in the decision making process, the client may already have some broad objectives based on financial capabilities and market feasibility. In many cases, it may be advisable for the client to retain the site planner for assistance in selecting a site that meets the client's basic aims. It is important that the land planner obtain all client data relative to the site planning for the site.

LITERATURE REVIEW

In cases where the site planner has not had extensive exposure to all aspects of site planning, a review of the relevant literature on the subject may be in order. Energy conscious design, for example, is an area where substantial research is now under way and specific literature search may be advisable.

REGIONAL, STATE, AND FEDERAL PLANNING

The site planning process usually begins at the regional level. In some areas of the country, regional planning agencies have been established for the purpose of research and planning of intercommunity regional issues such as water management, transportation, population studies, pollution control, and other regional environmental concerns. Many communities have adopted

Gary Greenan, AIP, ASLA; Miami, Florida

plans that establish regional planning guidelines relative to land use planning. The site planner should discern those regional issues that are pertinent to the design of the site.

Some projects may also come under state and/or national criteria, although this is not a common occurrence. Adopted state plans may address broad issues applicable to large sites or impose constraints on sites involving issues of statewide concern. Additionally, some states require environmental impact statements for large scale projects. At the national level, the National Environmental Policy Act may require impact review particularly if dredge and fill permits are required from the Army Corps of Engineers. Another federal regulation that will affect many coastline projects is the Federal Flood Insurance program, which establishes minimum elevations for potential flood areas.

LOCAL PLANNING INFORMATION

At this stage the site planner becomes involved in collecting local planning information that will influence decisions made in the site planning process. Personal contact with local planning and zoning agencies is important in order to clearly comprehend local criteria. Following is a list of information that should be reviewed.

PLANNING DOCUMENTS

Many communities have adopted comprehensive plans that will indicate in general terms, and in some instances in specific terms, the particular land use and intensity of the site. Also, valuable information on the availability and/or phasing of public services and utilities, environmental criteria, traffic planning information, and population trends can be found in most comprehensive plans. Some communities may require that rezoning meet the criteria provided in their comprehensive plan.

In addition to the comprehensive plan, some communities adopt neighborhood or area studies that refine the comprehensive plan as it relates to subareas. Many of these studies stipulate specific zoning categories for individual parcels of land.

ZONING

The zoning on a tract of land determines specifically the intensity and type of land use that can occur. If the existing zoning does not permit the type of land use and intensity planned for the project, a zoning change will be required.

PUBLIC SERVICES AND UTILITIES

Although some of this information may be provided in the comprehensive plan or neighborhood study, the critical nature of the availability of these public facilities may require additional research, specifically in terms of the following:

1. Availability of public sewer service, access to trunk lines, capacity of the trunk lines, and available increases in the flow. (If sewerage is not immediately available, the projected phasing of these services must be determined, as well as other possible alternatives to sewage collection and treatment.)

2. Availability of potable water, with the same basic research approach as indicated for sewer service determination.

3. Local and state regulations on freshwater wells and septic tanks.

4. Access to public roads, existing and projected carrying capacity, and levels of service of the roads. (State and local road departments can provide this information.)

5. Availability and capacity of schools and other public facilities such as parks and libraries.

SITE ANALYSIS (SITE INVENTORY)

Site analysis is one of the site planner's major responsibilities. All of the on- and off-site environmental design determinants must be evaluated and synthesized during the site analysis process. The site analysis processes follow later in this section.

PROGRAM DEVELOPMENT

At the program development stage, the background research and the site analysis are combined with client input and synthesized into a set of site development concepts and strategies. Elements that form the basis for program development include market and financial criteria, federal, state, regional, and local planning information, development costs, and the client's basic objectives, combined with site opportunities and constraints as developed in the synthesis of environmental site determinants. Trade-offs and a balancing of the various determinants may need to be made in order to develop an appropriate approach to site development. Consideration of dwelling unit type, density, marketing, time phasing, and other similar criteria, as well as graphic studies of the site, constitute the program. Graphic representations depicting design concepts should be clearly developed for presentation to the client and others who may have input to the process. If the program cannot be accomplished under the existing zoning, the decision to request a zone change becomes a part of the program.

If the architect is other than the site planner, he or she should be retained at or before the program development stage. A close working relationship between the architect and site planner is important in the design phase of the site development process to develop architectural solutions that respond to site characteristics. If an impact statement is required, it should be initiated at the beginning of this stage.

ALTERNATIVE AND PRELIMINARY PLAN PREPARATION

Once the program is established and accepted by the client, alternative design solutions that meet the program objectives, including basic zoning criteria, are developed. The accepted alternative is further developed into the preliminary plan. This plan should be a relatively detailed plan showing all spatial relationships, landscaping, and similar information.

PUBLIC REVIEW

If a zone change is required to implement the plan, some form of public review will be required. Some communities will require substantial data, such as impact statements and other narrative and graphic exhibits, while others may only require an application for the zone change. Local requirements for zone changes can be complex, and it is imperative for the site planner or the client's attorney to be familiar with local criteria.

FINAL DESIGN PLANS

At this stage, the preliminary plan is further refined to include any modifications that may have been agreed upon at a public hearing. Final design plans including landscape plans and all required dimensioning must be provided in the final design. In addition, all drawings that are usually prepared by the surveyor or engineer, such as plats, utilities, street, and drainage plans, must be prepared. Upon approval, final design plans are recorded in the public records in the form of plats. Additionally, homeowner association agreements, deed restrictions, and other similar legal documents must be recorded and become binding on all owners and successive owners unless changed by legal processes. Bonding may be required for public facilities.

BUILDING PERMITS

Building permits may be issued when all final documents are recorded and architectural drawings have been reviewed and approved in accordance with local building codes. Depending on the agreement between site planner and client, the planner may continue his or her services into the supervision of the site development.

EVALUATION

This stage may come years later after the community has become a reality. The purpose is to review the process and the resulting program and assess it in the context of the community as it exists. This is an important aspect usually overlooked. It provides the site planner with valuable data for future planning programs.

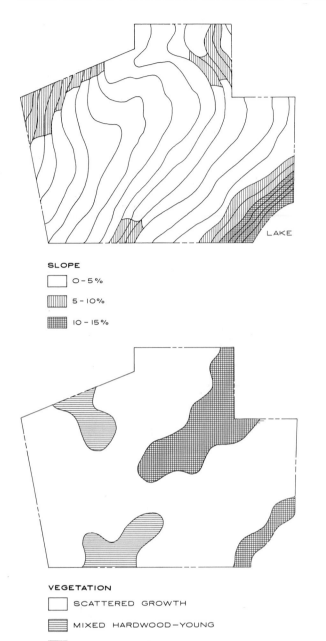

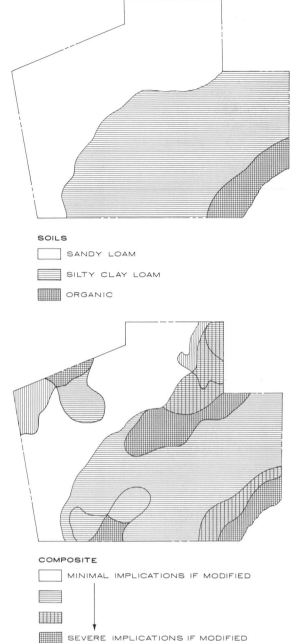

SLOPE

☐	0 – 5 %
▥	5 – 10 %
▦	10 – 15 %

SOILS

☐	SANDY LOAM
▤	SILTY CLAY LOAM
▦	ORGANIC

VEGETATION

☐	SCATTERED GROWTH
▤	MIXED HARDWOOD—YOUNG
▦	MATURE MIXED HARDWOOD AND COASTAL MARSH (ALONG LAKE EDGE)

COMPOSITE

☐	MINIMAL IMPLICATIONS IF MODIFIED
▤	
▥	
▦	SEVERE IMPLICATIONS IF MODIFIED

ENVIRONMENTAL SITE ANALYSIS PROCESS

If a site has numerous environmental design determinants, the site planner may need to analyze each environmental system individually in order to comprehend more clearly the environmental character of the site.

By preparing each analysis on transparencies, the site planner can use the overlay approach to site analysis. Each sheet is assigned values based on impact, ranging from areas of the site where change would have minimal effect to areas where change would result in severe disruption of the site. In essence, the separate sheets become abstractions with values assigned by the site planner and associated professionals. As each sheet is superimposed, a composite develops which, when completed, constitutes the synthesis of the environmental design determinants. Lighter tones indicate areas where modification would have minimal influence, darker tones indicate areas more sensitive to change. The sketches shown simulate the overlay process. The site planner may give greater or lesser weight

Gary Greenan, AIP, ASLA; Miami, Florida

Rafael Diaz, Graphics Coordinator; Miami, Florida

to certain parameters depending on the particular situation. In assigning values, the site planner should consider such factors as the value of maintaining the functioning of the individual site systems, the uniqueness of the specific site features, and the cost of modifying the site elements. The composite map is used by the site planner as an input in the site design process.

Following is a list of the environmental design determinants that may, depending on the particular site, need to be considered and included in an overlay format:

1. SLOPE: The slope analysis is developed on the contour map; consideration should include the percentage of slope and orientation of slope relative to the infrastructure and land uses.

2. SOIL PATTERNS: Consideration may include the analysis of soils in terms of erosion potential, compressibility and plasticity, capability of supporting plant growth, drainage capabilities, septic tank location (if relevant), and the proposed land uses and their infrastructure.

3. VEGETATION: Consideration should include indigenous and exotic species (values of each in terms of the environmental system), size and condition, the succession of growth toward climax conditions, uniqueness, the ability of certain species to tolerate construction activities, aesthetic values, and density of undergrowth.

4. WILDLIFE: Consideration of indigenous species, their movement patterns, the degree of changes that each species can tolerate, and feeding and breeding areas.

5. GEOLOGY: Consideration of underlying rock masses, the depth of different rock layers, and the suitability of different geological formations in terms of potential infrastructure and building.

6. SURFACE AND SUBSURFACE WATER: Consideration of natural drainage and patterns, aquifer recharge areas, erosion potential, and flood plains.

7. CLIMATE: Consideration of microclimatic conditions including prevailing breezes (at different times of the year), wind shadows, frost pockets, and air drainage patterns.

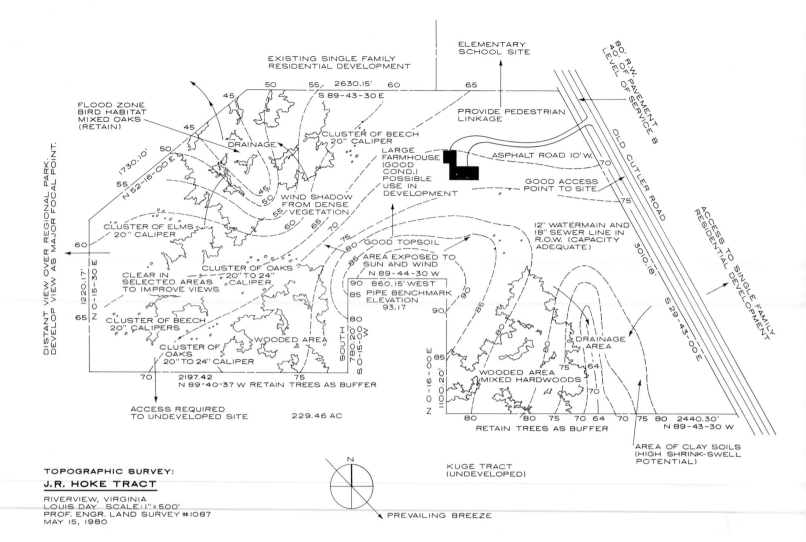

TOPOGRAPHIC SURVEY:

J.R. HOKE TRACT

RIVERVIEW, VIRGINIA
LOUIS DAY SCALE: 1"=500'
PROF. ENGR. LAND SURVEY #1087
MAY 15, 1980

SURVEY DATA

The first step in any site analysis is the gathering of physical site data. An aerial photograph and an accurate survey showing the following information are basic to any site analysis process:

1. Scale, north arrow, benchmark and date of survey.
2. Tract boundary lines.
3. Easements: location, width and purpose.
4. Names and locations of existing road rights-of-way on or adjacent to the tract including bridges, curbs, gutters, and culverts.
5. Position of buildings and other structures such as foundations, walls, fences, steps, and paved areas.
6. Utilities on or adjacent to the tract, including:
   a. Location of gas lines, fire hydrants, electric and telephone poles, and street lights.
   b. Direction, distance to and size of nearest water mains and sewers and invert elevation of sewers.
7. Location of swamps, springs, streams, bodies of water, drainage ditches, water shed areas, flood plains, and other physical features.
8. Outline of wooded areas with names and condition of plant material.
9. Contour intervals of 2 to 5 ft, depending on the slope gradients, and spot elevations at breaks in grade, along all drainage channels or swales and selected points as needed.

Gary Greenan, AIP, ASLA; Miami, Florida

Rafael Diaz, Graphics Coordinator; Miami, Florida

ADDITIONAL INFORMATION

Considerable additional information may be needed, depending on design consideration and site complexities such as soil information and studies on the geological structure of the site.

SITE ANALYSIS

As indicated in the previous site planning process, the site analysis is a major responsibility of the site planner. Two interrelated approaches are offered in the text. The first is the physical analysis of the site developed primarily from field inspections.

Using the survey, the aerial photograph, and, where warranted, infrared aerial photographs, the site designer, working in the field and in the office, verifies the survey and notes site design determinants. Site design determinants should include but not be limited to the following:

1. Areas of steep and moderate slopes.
2. Macro- and microclimatic conditions, including:
   a. Sun angles during different seasons.
   b. Prevailing breezes.
   c. Wind shadows.
   d. Frost pockets.
   e. Sectors where high or low points give protection from sun and wind.
   f. Solar energy considerations; if solar energy appears to be feasible, a detailed climatic anal-

ysis must be undertaken considering such factors as:
   Detailed sun charts.
   Daily averages of sunlight and cloud cover.
   Daily rain averages.
   Areas exposed to the sun at different seasons.
   Solar radiation patterns.
   Temperature patterns.
3. Areas of potential flood zones and routes of surface water runoff.
4. Possible road access to the site, including considerations of points of potential conflict with the existing road system and carrying capacities of adjacent roadways. (This information can usually be obtained from local or state road departments.)
5. Natural areas that from an ecological and aesthetic standpoint should be saved; all tree masses with names and condition of tree species and understory.
6. Significant wildlife habitats that would be affected by site modification.
7. Soil conditions relative to supporting plant material, areas suitable for construction, erosion potential, and septic tanks, if relevant.
8. Geological considerations relative to supporting structures.
9. Exceptional views; objectionable views (use on site photographs).
10. Adjacent existing and proposed land uses with notations on compatibility and incompatibility.

INTRODUCTION

These standards should be used only as a basic reference or beginning point in the determination of the spatial site functions. The final determination of intensity and dwelling type of a particular site should evolve as the end of a thorough planning process.

CLUSTER

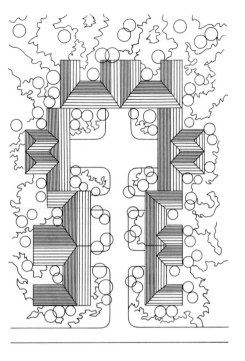

ATRIUM

O – LOT LINE

INTENSITY STANDARDS FOR RESIDENTIAL DEVELOPMENT

DWELLING UNIT TYPE	DWELLING UNITS PER ACRE	COMMON OPEN SPACE AS PERCENTAGE OF TOTAL SITE	PARKING PER UNIT (1)	TREES PER ACRE OF TOTAL SITE AREA (2)	PRIVATE OPEN SPACE (3)
Single family estate		Usually not provided	3+	15+	Depends on lot size
Single family	3 to 5 depending on lot size	Usually not provided	2.5+	15+	Depends on lot size
Duplex	5 to 10 depending on lot size	Usually not provided	2+ (4+ for each structure)	15+	Depends on lot size
0-lot line (4)	4 to 7 units per acre	Usually not provided	2.25+	15+	Depends on lot size
Single family cluster (5)	4 to 7	25 to 50%	2.25+	15 to 20± for first 3 acres, 10+ for remaining acreage	Depends on lot size
Atrium (6)	4 to 8 units per acre	Usually not provided	2.25+	15+	25% of total square footage
Suburban townhouse (7)	6 to 9	25% to 40%	2.25+	15 to 20± for first 3 acres, 10± for remaining acreage	500 to 700 sq ft
Urban townhouse (8)	8 to 16	15% to 25% if provided	2.0+	15 to 20± for first 3 acres, 10± for remaining acreage	400 to 600 sq ft
Walk-up apartments	10 to 25	25% to 40%	2.0± depending on number of bedrooms	15 to 20± for first 3 acres, 10± for remaining acreage	Usually not provided except on ground floor apartments
Midrise apartment up to 6 stories	15 to 35	30% 40%	2.0± depending on number of bedrooms	15 to 20± for first 3 acres, 10± for remaining acreage	Usually not provided except on ground floor apartments
Highrise apartments	30 to 75	35% to 60%	2.0± depending on number of bedrooms	15 to 20± for first 3 acres, 10± for remaining acreage	Usually not provided except on ground floor apartments
Planned unit development (9)	10 to 25 depending on type of planned unit development	25% 60%	2.0± depending on unit type	15 to 20± for first 3 acres, 10± for remaining acreage	Depends on individual unit type

NOTES

1. PARKING PER UNIT: In determining the parking per unit, the site design should consider the influence of public transportation and location of the development in relation to employment centers and supporting facilities. An excessive amount of parking spaces to accommodate infrequent special activities could result in excess pavement; depending on soil conditions, it is sometimes better to accommodate infrequent overflow parking on grassed areas or, where conditions permit, on commercial parking areas when not in use or at community centers.

2. TREES: Trees provide one of the major unifying design elements and act as climate modifiers; where a substantial number of trees do not already exist, extensive tree planting should be undertaken as part

of most planning programs. The determination of the number of trees per acre should be based more on the particular locale than on a uniform standard.

3. PRIVATE OPEN SPACE: Private open space should be private to the unit concerned and may be provided in the form of courtyards, entrance courts, and rear, side, and front yards. Both visual and aural privacy is important in the design of these spaces.

4. O-LOT LINE: A single family unit located directly on one side property line and possibly on the rear property line; the emphasis is on eliminating small side yards for larger, more usable open spaces.

5. SINGLE FAMILY CLUSTER: Single family units grouped in clusters in order to maximize open space; units may or may not be attached.

6. ATRIUM: A single family unit related to the early Greek and Roman prototypes which incorporate interior living spaces fronting on an interior court.

7. SUBURBAN TOWNHOUSE: A single family unit attached to other single family units with a common party wall; open space is usually a major element in the suburban townhouse development.

8. URBAN TOWNHOUSE: Early prototypes appear in the urban areas of many older cities; similar to suburban townhouse, although densities are usually higher and common open space is usually provided in the form of public open space.

9. PLANNED UNIT DEVELOPMENT: A mixture of housing types with emphasis on total community design; all the housing types included in the chart, plus associated retail support facilities and community amenities, may be found in a PUD development.

Gary Greenan, AIP, ASLA; Miami, Florida

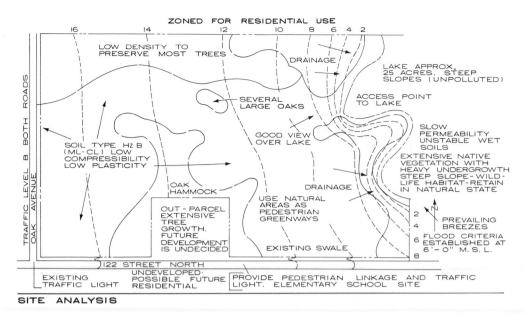

SITE ANALYSIS

INTRODUCTION

The illustrations indicate a design process, including the following:

1. SITE ANALYSIS: A synthesis of the physical environmental design determinants and offsite influences.
2. CONCEPT PLAN: A synthesis of the site analysis, research, and client input into design concepts—several concept plans may be prepared.
3. PRELIMINARY PLAN: A further sophistication and detailing of the concept plan.

DESIGN SCALE

In the design of the site, the site planner should be aware of four interdependent levels of design scale.

COMMUNITY

At the community scale (a neighborhood scale) the site planner should be aware of those elements that create design unity and give identity to the development as a whole. Major natural features, circulation systems, greenway systems, and public use spaces such as schools, shopping, and parks act as focal points and/or linkages in the total design of the project.

SUBCOMMUNITY

The first level down from the community scale is the subcommunity space. These are the spaces created by the grouping or clustering of housing units, associated parking, paths, and landscape into a form that responds to the environmental characteristics of the site and gives identity to the individual clusters.

TRANSITION

Transition spaces, in the form of entrance courts, patios, and yards, are those spaces that provide a transition from the totally private interior spaces to the public spaces. Consideration should be given to privacy for the individual unit and the environmental characteristics of the site such as breezes, sun angles, and landscape.

INTERIOR

This is the smallest scale that the site planner will be involved with. Emphasis should be placed on the interior design of the unit in terms of privacy and its relationship to the exterior microenvironment. A close working relationship between architect and site planner is essential.

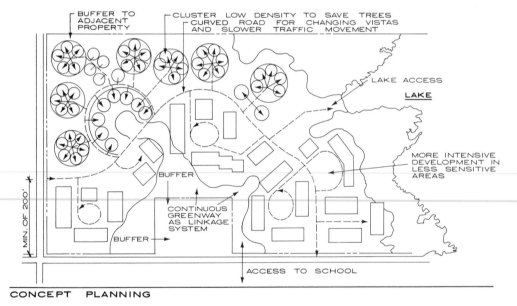

CONCEPT PLANNING

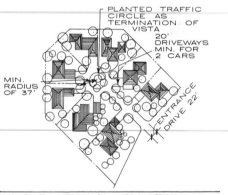

SINGLE FAMILY CLUSTER

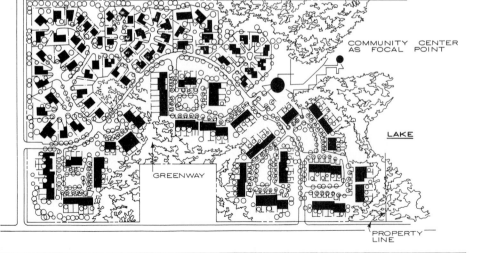

PRELIMINARY PLAN

Gary Greenan, AIP, ASLA; Miami, Florida

Rafael Diaz, Graphics Coordinator; Miami, Florida

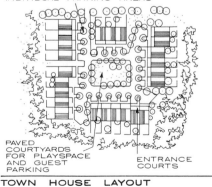

TOWN HOUSE LAYOUT

2   LAND PLANNING AND SITE DEVELOPMENT

FINAL DEVELOPMENT PLANS

After all necessary approvals under the zoning process have been granted, final site development plans are initiated. Unlike the design plans, which are prepared by the architect and landscape architect, the final site development plans are usually prepared by a registered surveyor and/or engineer. The professional preparing these plans should obtain a copy of the local subdivision code and, if available, a copy of the public works manual for specific local requirements. All drawings should show the name and location of the development, the date of preparation and any revisions, the scale, north point, datum, and approvals of local authorities. The following list of exhibits are typical requirements for most communities.

TENTATIVE OR PRELIMINARY PLAT

Platting is the process whereby a piece of land, referred to as the parent tract, is subdivided into two or more parcels. A plat specifically and legally describes the layout of the development. A tentative plat is the first step in the preparation of the final drawings and indicates the layout of the development in terms of lots and sizes of lots, lot frontages, road right-of-ways, setbacks, sidewalks, street offsets, and other graphic information relative to the design of the project. After approval of the tentative plat, the engineer can begin the utility plans and the street paving and drainage plans. Even if the local law does not require a tentative plat, it is advised that the professional prepare a sketch of the plat and meet with local authorities in order to avoid problems later in the final site development plan process.

STREET PAVING AND DRAINAGE PLANS

Street paving and drainage plans are final construction drawings prepared by an engineer indicating the following:

1. Plan for all streets and parking areas with starting points and radii.

2. Typical cross sections (some communities may also require road profiles).

3. Details and specifications of pavement base, surfacing and curbs.

4. Indication of methods to retain storm water runoff within the right-of-way (soil tests for percolation may be required). Also details and specifications for inlets, manholes, catch basins, and surface drainage channels.

5. Indication that roads will meet local, state, and federal flood criteria.

UTILITY PLANS

Utility plans are final drawings prepared by an engineer that indicate the location of water supply lines, sewage disposal lines, fire hydrants, and other utility functions usually located in the road right-of-way. In addition to approval by local public works departments, some communities require review of utility plans by the board of public health, fire department, and departments involved in pollution control.

FINAL PLAT

The final plat is usually the last stage of the final site development process prior to the issuance of building permits. A subdivision plat, when accepted and recorded in the public land records, establishes a legal description of the streets, residential lots and other sites in the development. If roads and other improvements are not constructed at the time of final platting, a bond, usually in excess of the estimated costs of the improvements, will be required. Following is a typical list of information that should be shown on the final plat:

1. Right-of-way lines of streets, easements, and other rights-of-way, and property lines of residential lots and other sites with accurate dimensions, bearings, and curve data.

2. Name and right-of-way width of each street or other right-of-way.

3. Location, dimensions, and purpose of any easements.

4. Identifying number for each lot or site.

5. Purpose for which sites, other than residential lots, are dedicated or reserved.

6. Minimum building setback line on all lots and other sites.

7. Location and description of monuments.

8. Reference to recorded subdivision plats of adjoining platted land by record name, date, and number.

9. Certification by surveyor or engineer.

10. Statement by owner(s) dedicating streets, rights-of-way and any sites for public use.

11. Approval by local authorities.

12. Title, scale, north arrow, and date.

BY RAFAEL DIAZ

SITE PLAN

Gary Greenan, AIP, ASLA; Miami, Florida

Rafael Diaz, Graphics Coordinator; Miami, Florida

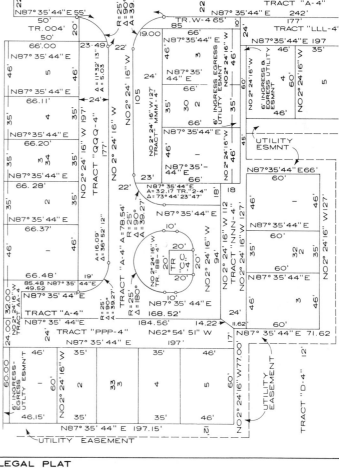

LEGAL PLAT
(SINCE STREETS ARE PRIVATE, THEY ARE INDICATED AS TRACTS)

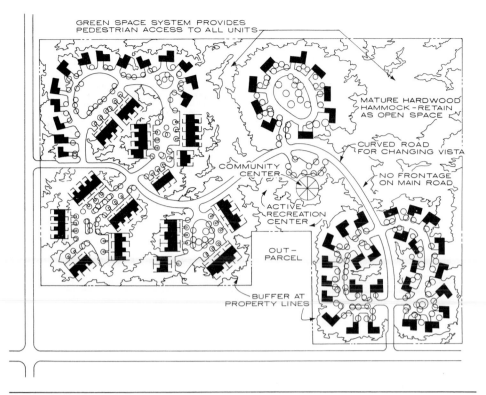

PLANNED UNIT DEVELOPMENT
(SAME NUMBER OF UNITS AS ON CONVENTIONAL PLAN)

The planned unit development ordinance usually incorporates standards for dwelling unit density, open space, and other spatial requirements. PUD ordinances usually place emphasis on total community design, with review of plans by local agencies and public hearing bodies as a primary requirement.

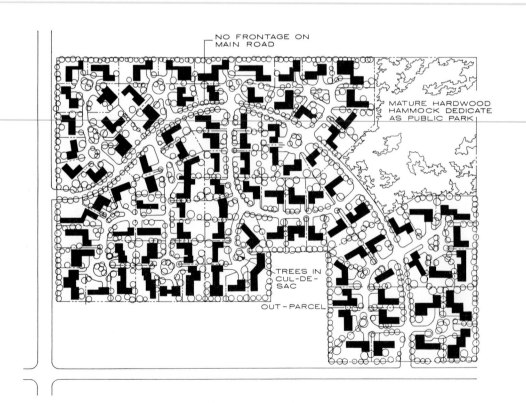

CONVENTIONAL SINGLE FAMILY

Gary Greenan, ASLA, AIP; Miami, Florida

Rafael Diaz, Graphics Coordinator; Miami, Florida

ADVANTAGES OF PLANNED UNIT DEVELOPMENT AND CLUSTER ZONING CONCEPTS

Although the lot-by-lot type of subdivision is still the prevalent development type in many suburban areas, the amenities that can be realized by the planned unit development and cluster zoning concepts are such that these approaches should be seriously considered.

In some communities the terms planned unit development (PUD) and cluster may be synonymous. Usually, however, the PUD is a more comprehensive approach than the cluster, with provisions for both single family and multifamily development and, in some instances, commercial and industrial activities. The term cluster refers to the grouping of single family residences in clusters on lots smaller than permitted by the single family zoning district, and compensating for the smaller lots with common open space areas of substantial and usable configurations.

Both methods offer the designer not only the flexibility of locating structures in a manner that responds to site features, but also the opportunity for developing imaginative architectural forms. A key element of these approaches is the common green space that gives design cohesiveness to the total project.

The responsibility for the maintenance of common space and associated common facilities is a major concern that must be resolved in PUD and cluster developments. The homeowners association is the most commonly accepted approach. The association should be established by recorded agreement before the sale of the first unit by the developer. Each homeowner is automatically a member and is assessed a proportionate share of the cost in maintaining the common facilities. The developer or his attorney should evaluate the best methods of developing a homeowners' association before the initiation of site development. Many jurisdictions require a legal instrument for the association prior to final approval of the project.

The use of common open space usually allows more flexibility in effectively fitting the development to the land than does the more typical lot-by-lot approach. Following are some of the obvious advantages gained by the proper use of the planned unit development concept:

1. With smaller individual lots, excess land can be massed together to provide larger and more useful community recreational space.
2. With the use of connecting community open spaces and fewer through traffic streets, children are better protected from vehicular traffic.
3. With larger amounts of open space, the natural character of the site can be preserved.
4. With the shorter networks of streets and utilities, construction costs can be reduced.

It should be emphasized that the standard subdivision approach still retains a major part of the housing market. Where the program suggests a more typical subdivision layout, the site planner has a responsibility to respond to the same environmental design determinants of the site as for a project being developed under more flexible zoning criteria. Creative planning can be accomplished using either approach.

CONVENTIONAL SINGLE FAMILY RESIDENTIAL ZONED DEVELOPMENT

The density determination for conventional single family residential zoning is based on minimum lot size requirements as provided by local ordinances. For planning purposes, the site planner can translate lot size to a net density figure which represents the total number of dwellings per acre within the site, after deducting for roads, parks, school sites, and other public facilities.

INTRODUCTION

The site designer should have a basic understanding of roadway layout in order to design circulation systems that function on the site and are compatible with systems off the site. Specific minimum standards that must be met are in effect for most municipalities.

HIERARCHY OF ROAD SYSTEMS

The site designer should be cognizant of the hierarchy of road systems and the purposes each system serves. At the upper end is the limited access freeway, which carries up to 1000 or 1300 vehicles per lane per hour at high rates of speed and up to 2000 per hour at slower speeds. Freeways are important to the site designer in terms of site selection for accessibility to freeway systems. Major or principal arterials and minor arterials are the intercommunity connectors that can carry, respectively, 600 to 800 cars per lane per hour and 400 to 500 per lane per hour, depending on traffic signals, parking along the street, intersections, and other physical impediments or friction to traffic flow. Arterials are important to the site planner, since these streets usually provide the direct access to a proposed overall development. Collectors that efficiently carry 100 to 250 trips per lane per hour are the street systems laid out by the site planner within the development to collect the traffic from neighborhood or local streets and load this traffic onto the arterials.

ESTIMATING TRAFFIC FLOWS

In larger developments, where traffic may be a major issue, the site designer must make some approximations of trip generations in order to design the appropriate internal collector system(s) and to determine potential impacts on the immediately adjacent roadways.

Many factors influence the number of trips generated by a development during the peak hours (usually 7:00 to 9:00 A.M. and 4:00 to 6:00 P.M.). Type of development (resort, retirement, young married, etc.), the amount of commercial activity, the type of units (single family, apartments, etc.), the availability of mass transit and other forms of public transportation, and the location of the development (rural vs. urban) are some of the factors that influence trip generation.

The figures used for preliminary estimations of peak direction traffic generation, based on middle income subcommunity without major public transportation facilities, are: 0.8± trips per single family residence and 0.6± per multifamily unit during peak hour traffic periods.

For purposes of estimating traffic (see sketch), the site planner counts the number and type of units to determine total estimated trips during peak hours and progressively adds the number of trips along the collector. From this information, the number of lanes for the internal collector can be determined based on vehicles per lane per peak hour, as well as the number of ingress and egress points that may be needed from the site, the type and number of traffic signals, and need for turning bays.

To determine the impact on immediately adjacent roadways, the anticipated direction of travel must be determined. For example, the direction toward the employment center is more significant (usually 70 to 80% of the traffic during morning peak hours) than that toward other areas. The traffic from the development is then added to the existing and/or projected arterial volume to determine existing and/or future carrying volume on the arterial.

ENVIRONMENTAL CONSIDERATIONS

The environmental characteristics of a site affect the location and development of a road system. It is the responsibility of the site designer to develop systems that recognize the ecological constraints of the particular site. Following is a checklist of environmental considerations for road alignment:

1. Minimize the disruption of existing topography by reducing cut and fill requirements and erosion and sedimentation problems.
2. Minimize the disruption of natural overland and subsurface water flows.
3. Minimize disruption of existing vegetation and animal life.
4. Avoid positive drainage along roadways (storm sewer systems) where such systems directly outfall into water bodies and cause pollution. Systems of swales along the roadway to filter nutrients from the roadway surface before entering natural water bodies, thereby minimizing water pollution.

Gary Greenan, ASLA, AIP; Miami, Florida

Rafael Diaz, Graphic Coordinator; Miami, Florida

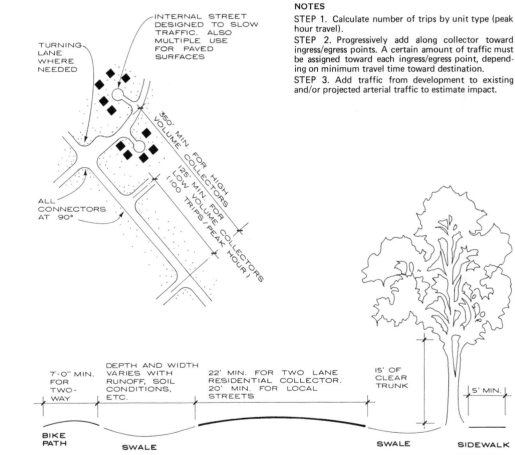

ROAD TYPES

TRAFFIC PROJECTION

NOTES

STEP 1. Calculate number of trips by unit type (peak hour travel).

STEP 2. Progressively add along collector toward ingress/egress points. A certain amount of traffic must be assigned toward each ingress/egress point, depending on minimum travel time toward destination.

STEP 3. Add traffic from development to existing and/or projected arterial traffic to estimate impact.

GENERAL DESIGN CONSIDERATION

NOTES

1. BIKE PATH. Grades should not exceed 5 to 6% for short distances (200 to 400 ft) or 2% for long distances. Separate bikepath from roadway with swale, plantings; where possible, bikepaths can be integrated into greenway systems rather than along roadway.

2. TREES. Species should be selected that tolerate smog and dust and whose root systems do not damage underground utilities or pavements. Where snow removal and/or icy conditions occur, trees should be placed far enough from the edge of the roadway to prevent damage from automobiles or chemicals applied to the roadway. Tree spacing should relate to species and desired effect; for example, as a general rule shade trees should be 35 to 50 ft apart.

3. STREET LIGHTING. Spacing should relate to amount of illumination desired, based on type of street, pedestrian use, crime prevention, and similar criteria. An approximate spacing for vehicular street use is 100 to 150 ft between light standards.

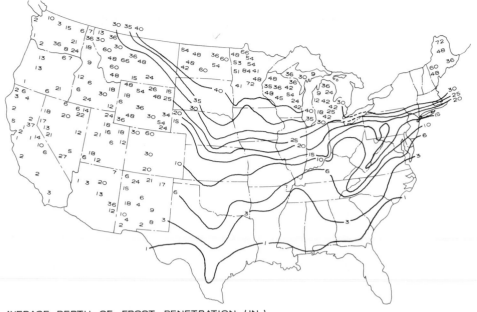

AVERAGE DEPTH OF FROST PENETRATION (IN.)
SOURCE: U.S. DEPT. OF COMMERCE WEATHER BUREAU

PRELIMINARY SUBSURFACE INFORMATION

A. Collect available information for soil, rock and water conditions, including the following:
   1. Topographic and aerial mapping.
   2. Geological survey maps and publications.
   3. Local, knowledge (history of site development, experience of nearby structures, flooding, subsidence, etc.).
   4. Existing subsurface data (boreholes, well records, water soundings).
   5. Reconnaissance site survey.
   6. Previous studies.
B. Evaluate available information for site acceptability. If available data are insufficient, consult a geotechnical engineer to perform a limited subsurface investigation to gather basic information.
C. Consult geotechnical engineer for potential foundation performance at each site as part of the selection process.

DETAILED SUBSURFACE INFORMATION

After selection of a potential site a subsurface and laboratory test investigation should be carried out by a qualified geotechnical engineer before design is undertaken.

The investigation should provide an adequate understanding of the subsurface conditions and the information should be assessed to determine potential foundation behavior.

The engineer should evaluate alternative foundation methods and techniques in conjunction with the architect.

The engineer or architect should provide inspection during construction to ensure that material and construction procedures are as specified and to evaluate unexpected soil, rock, or groundwater conditions that may be exposed by excavations.

SOIL TYPES AND THEIR PROPERTIES

| DIVISION | SYMBOLS | | | SOIL DESCRIPTION | VALUE AS A FOUNDATION MATERIAL | FROST ACTION | DRAINAGE |
	LETTER	HATCH-ING	COLOR				
Gravel and gravelly soils	GW		Red	Well graded gravel, or gravel-sand mixture, little or no fines	Excellent	None	Excellent
	GP		Red	Poorly graded gravel, or gravel-sand mixtures, little or no fines	Good	None	Excellent
	GM		Yellow	Silty gravels, gravel-sand-silt mixtures	Good	Slight	Poor
	GC		Yellow	Clayey-gravels, gravel-clay-sand mixtures	Good	Slight	Poor
Sand and sandy soils	SW		Red	Well-graded sands, or gravelly sands, little or no fines	Good	None	Excellent
	SP		Red	Poorly graded sands, or gravelly sands, little or no fines	Fair	None	Excellent
	SM		Yellow	Silty sands, sand-silt mixtures	Fair	Slight	Fair
	SC		Yellow	Clayey sands, sand-clay mixtures	Fair	Medium	Poor
Silts and clays LL < 50	ML		Green	Inorganic silts, rock flour, silty or clayey fine sands, or clayey silts with slight plasticity	Fair	Very high	Poor
	CL		Green	Inorganic clays of low to medium plasticity, gravelly clays, silty clays, lean clays	Fair	Medium	Impervious
	OL		Green	Organic silt-clays of low plasticity	Poor	High	Impervious
Silts and clays LL > 50	MH		Blue	Inorganic silts, micaceous or diatomaceous fine sandy or silty soils, elastic silts	Poor	Very high	Poor
	CH		Blue	Inorganic clays of high plasticity, fat clays	Very poor	Medium	Impervious
	OH		Blue	Organic clays of medium to high plasticity, organic silts	Very poor	Medium	Impervious
Highly organic soils	Pt		Orange	Peat and other highly organic soils	Not suitable	Slight	Poor

NOTES
1. Consult soil engineers and local building codes for allowable soil bearing capacities.
2. LL indicates liquid limit.

Mueser, Rutledge, Johnston & DeSimone; New York, New York

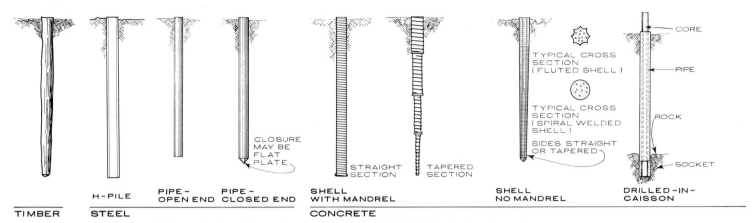

TIMBER   STEEL   CONCRETE

NOTE: A mandrel is a member inserted into a hollow pile to reinforce the pile shell while it is driven into the ground.

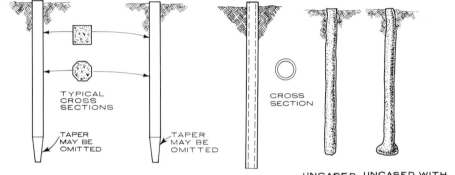

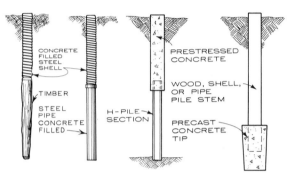

CONCRETE   COMPOSITE

GENERAL PILE DATA

PILE TYPE	MAXIMUM LENGTH (FT)	OPTIMUM LENGTH (FT)	SIZE (IN.)	MAXIMUM CAPACITY (TONS)	OPTIMUM LOAD RANGE (TONS)	USUAL SPACING
TIMBER	110	45–65	5–10 tip 12–20 butt	40	15–25	2'6'' to 3'0''
STEEL						
H-pile	250	40–150	8–14	200	50–200	2'6'' to 3'6''
Pipe—open end concrete filled	200	40–120	10–24	250	100–200	3'0'' to 4'0''
Pipe—closed end concrete filled	150	30–80	10–18	100	50–70	3'0'' to 4'0''
Shell—mandrel concrete filled straight or taper	100	40–80	8–18	75	40–60	3'0'' to 3'6''
Shell—no mandrel concrete filled	150	30–80	8–18	80	30–60	3'0'' to 3'6''
Drilled-in caisson concrete filled	250	60–120	24–48	3500	1000–2000	6'0'' to 8'0''
CONCRETE						
Precast	80	40–50	10–24	100	40–60	3'0''
Prestressed	200	60–80	10–24	200	100–150	3'0'' to 3'6''
Cylinder pile	150	60–80	36–54	500	250–400	6'0'' to 9'0''
Uncased or drilled	60	25–40	14–20	75	30–60	3'0'' to 3'6''
Uncased with enlarged base	60	25–40	14–20	150	40–100	6'0''
COMPOSITE						
Concrete—timber	150	60–100	5–10 tip 12–20 butt	40	15–25	3'0'' to 3'6''
Concrete—pipe	180	60–120	10–23	150	40–80	3'0'' to 4'0''
Prestressed concrete H-pile	200	100–150	20–24	200	120–150	3'6'' to 4'0''
Precast concrete tip	80	40	13–35	180	150	4'6''

NOTES

Timber piles must be treated with wood preservative when any portion is above permanent groundwater table.

Applicable material Specifications Concrete—ACL 318; Timber—ASTM D25: Structural Sections ASTM A36, A572 and A696.

For selection of type of pile consult foundation engineer.

Mueser, Rutledge, Johnston & DeSimone; New York, New York

GENERAL INFORMATION

Before an architectural design can proceed a plot or site plan must be drawn to scale, showing the relevant available information about the construction area. This plan should show the relationship of the new building to property lines (and monuments), street lines above and below ground, and other features. It usually will also show the new contour lines and needed elevation information, such as special bench marks.

In simple building layout, key corner marks are placed on pegs or hubs, using the transit and steel tapes to ensure right angles and correct distances. The initial layout on the ground should be established in correct relationship to baselines, property lines, buildings, and so on. Once the building is laid out, diagonals shoud be measured and compared to make certain that all the building angles are square.

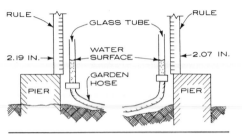

WATER TUBE LEVELING METHOD

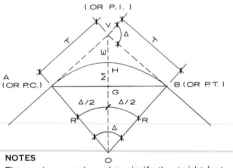

NOTES

The word tangent is used to signify the straight (not curved) portion of the building. From the plan some other relations that may be useful are also seen:

The long chord is c: $c = AB = AG + GB$
                        $= 2R \sin \tfrac{1}{2} \Delta$

The mid-ordinate is M: $M = HG = OH - OG$
                        $= R - R \cos \tfrac{1}{2} \Delta$

The external is E: $E = HV = OV - OH$
                        $= R/\cos \tfrac{1}{2} \Delta - R$

A frequently used relationship, however, is the tangent (or semitangent) of the curve, which is T:

$$T = AV = BV$$
$$= R \tan \tfrac{1}{2} \Delta$$

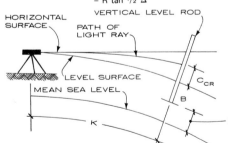

NOTES

Because of the curvature of the earth and the refraction or bending of light rays, the path of the ray of light departs both from the horizontal plane and from the level surface. In any situation employing fairly long sighting, a correction to the rod reading may be needed. The formula for the correction for curvature and refraction is

$$C_{CR} \text{ (ft)} = 0.572k^2$$

$$k = \text{sighted distance (miles)}$$

CURVATURE AND REFRACTION

Walter H. Sobel, FAIA and Associates; Chicago, Illinois

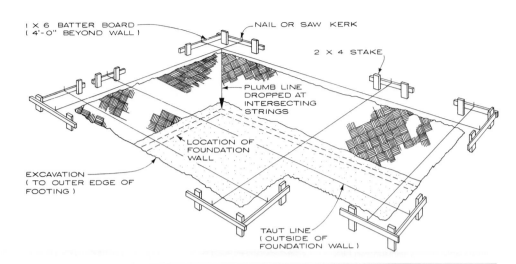

STAKING AND EXCAVATION (RESIDENTIAL)

NOTES

A transit or theodolite is basically an angle measuring instrument (it can also measure distances and elevations). It measures horizontal angles in the horizontal plane about an azimuth (vertical) axis, as well as vertical angles in a vertical plane about an elevation (horizontal) axis. To provide very great accuracy in setting a baseline at any angle to some existing reference line a technique is employed that involves repeated measuring of an angle. Essentially it consists of first laying out the angle, then measuring it carefully, and finally moving the newly set point as needed to achieve the proper angle. An engineer's level is used for surveying work of ordinary accuracy.

A   = ANGLE OF INTERSECTION
R   = RADIUS OF CURVE
P.I. = POINT OF INTERSECTION (V)
P.C. = POINT OF CURVATURE (A)
P.T. = POINT OF TANGENCY (B)

NOTES

On a construction site for a structure, it is important to place the project and its several components at the proper elevation. Control leveling will first be made to establish bench marks (BM) nearby to ensure this. Temporary bench marks for construction should be within 100 ft, at most 200 ft, of the location where they will be needed. Their location should be foreseen carefully enough to forstall any need to use a turning point between them and the constructed item (framework, pile, cap, etc.) that needs an elevation check.

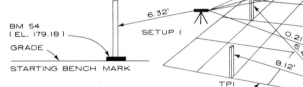

GRID SYSTEM

NOTES

A grid system is used for conveniently identifying the points whose elevation is required periodically. The level is set where both the bench mark and the desired points on the grid iron can be observed. Sighting on a known point (BM 54) gives the elevation of the instrument (H.1 = 185.50), from which elevations of grid points can be found by sighting each point in turn. This method may very well be used to take readings on a concrete floor slab or grade to detect local settlements or to determine that it has been finished to specification.

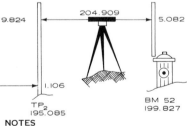

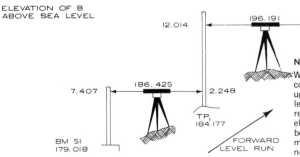

NOTES

When differential leveling is done, to set vertical control points one starts at a known elevation, sets up a transit or leveling device, reads a backsight on a level rod held on the known bench mark, and then reads a foresight on the rod held on a point whose elevation is needed. Temporarily, this new point becomes the known elevation. The instrument is then moved forward, and the process is begun anew to set a new point.

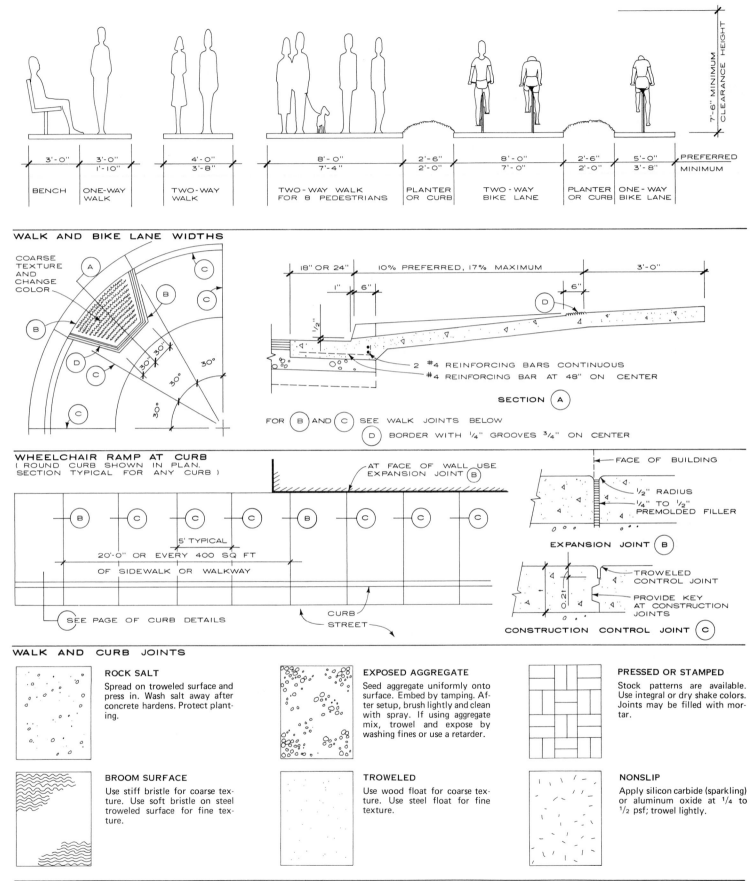

WALK AND BIKE LANE WIDTHS

3'-0"	3'-0" / 1'-10"	4'-0" / 3'-8"	8'-0" / 7'-4"	2'-6" / 2'-0"	8'-0" / 7'-0"	2'-6" / 2'-0"	5'-0" / 3'-8"
BENCH	ONE-WAY WALK	TWO-WAY WALK	TWO-WAY WALK FOR 8 PEDESTRIANS	PLANTER OR CURB	TWO-WAY BIKE LANE	PLANTER OR CURB	ONE-WAY BIKE LANE

7'-6" MINIMUM CLEARANCE HEIGHT

PREFERRED MINIMUM

COARSE TEXTURE AND CHANGE COLOR

18" OR 24" 10% PREFERRED, 17% MAXIMUM 3'-0"

2 #4 REINFORCING BARS CONTINUOUS
#4 REINFORCING BAR AT 48" ON CENTER

SECTION (A)

FOR (B) AND (C) SEE WALK JOINTS BELOW
(D) BORDER WITH 1/4" GROOVES 3/4" ON CENTER

WHEELCHAIR RAMP AT CURB
(ROUND CURB SHOWN IN PLAN. SECTION TYPICAL FOR ANY CURB)

AT FACE OF WALL USE EXPANSION JOINT (B)

5' TYPICAL
20'-0" OR EVERY 400 SQ FT
OF SIDEWALK OR WALKWAY

(SEE PAGE OF CURB DETAILS

CURB
STREET

FACE OF BUILDING

1/2" RADIUS
1/4" TO 1/2" PREMOLDED FILLER

EXPANSION JOINT (B)

TROWELED CONTROL JOINT
PROVIDE KEY AT CONSTRUCTION JOINTS

CONSTRUCTION CONTROL JOINT (C)

WALK AND CURB JOINTS

ROCK SALT
Spread on troweled surface and press in. Wash salt away after concrete hardens. Protect planting.

EXPOSED AGGREGATE
Seed aggregate uniformly onto surface. Embed by tamping. After setup, brush lightly and clean with spray. If using aggregate mix, trowel and expose by washing fines or use a retarder.

PRESSED OR STAMPED
Stock patterns are available. Use integral or dry shake colors. Joints may be filled with mortar.

BROOM SURFACE
Use stiff bristle for coarse texture. Use soft bristle on steel troweled surface for fine texture.

TROWELED
Use wood float for coarse texture. Use steel float for fine texture.

NONSLIP
Apply silicon carbide (sparkling) or aluminum oxide at 1/4 to 1/2 psf; trowel lightly.

WALK SURFACES AND TEXTURES

William T. Mahan, AIA; Santa Barbara, California

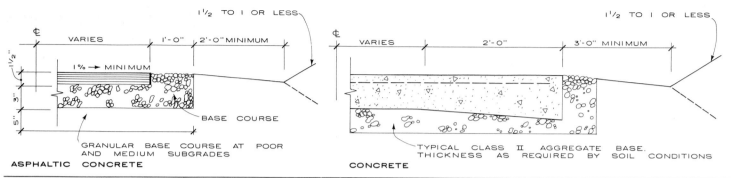

PAVING EDGES

1½ TO 1 OR LESS

VARIES   1'-0"   2'-0"MINIMUM

1% → MINIMUM

BASE COURSE

GRANULAR BASE COURSE AT POOR
AND MEDIUM SUBGRADES

ASPHALTIC CONCRETE

1½ TO 1 OR LESS

VARIES   2'-0"   3'-0" MINIMUM

TYPICAL CLASS II AGGREGATE BASE.
THICKNESS AS REQUIRED BY SOIL CONDITIONS

CONCRETE

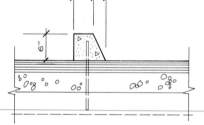

6"   1'-5" TO 1'-11"

6"   ← 4%

TYPICAL CLASS II
AGGREGATE BASE UNDER
ASPHALTIC CONCRETE

CURB AND GUTTER

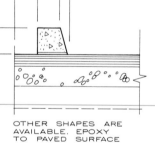

1'-5½"   1-5½"   ← 1%

TYPICAL NATIVE
MATERIAL COMPACTED
TO 90%

MOUNTABLE CURB

6"   1½"

14" TO 24"   6"

½" PREMOLDED FILLER
WITH BITUMINOUS
SEAL AT TOP

SEPARATE CURB

3"   9"

← 1% TO 2%

USE WHERE EROSION
REQUIRES CONTROL

IOWA CURB

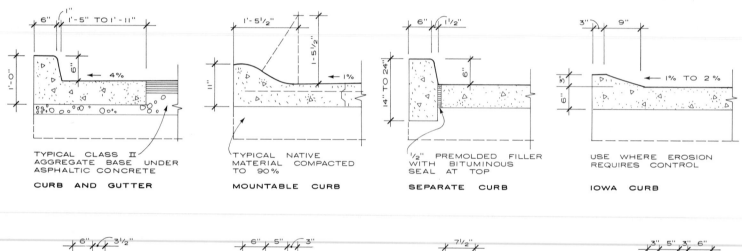

6"   3½"

6"

FORM ON PAVING SURFACE
REINFORCE WITH #4 BARS
VERTICAL DOWELS AT 4'-0"

DOWELED CURB

6"   5"   3"

6"

OTHER SHAPES ARE
AVAILABLE. EPOXY
TO PAVED SURFACE

EXTRUDED CURB

7½"

5"

AVAILABLE IN 4'-0" TO
8'-0" LENGTHS

PRECAST BUMPER

3" 5" 3" 6"

6"

USE ALONG DRIVE EDGE.
NOT RECOMMENDED AS
WHEEL STOP

ASPHALTIC BERM

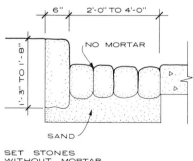

6"   2'-0" TO 4'-0"

NO MORTAR

1'-3" TO 1'-8"

SAND

SET STONES
WITHOUT MORTAR
IN 6" OF SAND

**STONE CURB AND
GUTTER**

6"

1'-3" TO 1'-8"

GRANITE OR LIMESTONE
CURB. IF PAVING IS
CONCRETE USE ½"
PREMOLDED JOINT FILLER

STONE CURB

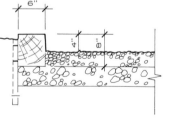

6"

4"   8"

USE REDWOOD OR
TREATED WOOD. PROVIDE
1" TIMES 2" STAKES, 4'-0"
ON CENTER

TIMBER CURB

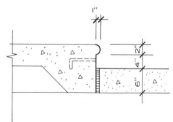

1"

2"

4"   6"

CURBS ARE AVAILABLE
IN DIFFERENT DEPTHS AND
A VARIETY OF RADII

STEEL CURB

CURBS AND GUTTERS

William T. Mahan, AIA; Santa Barbara, California

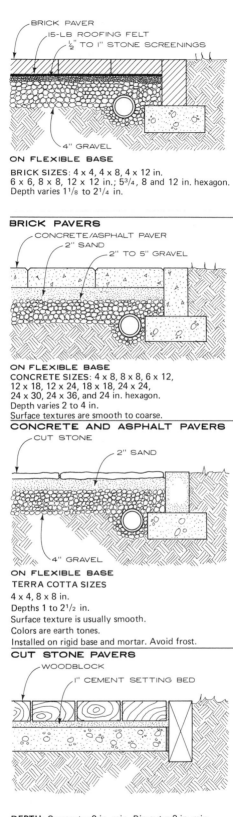

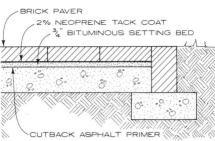

ON FLEXIBLE BASE

BRICK SIZES: 4 x 4, 4 x 8, 4 x 12 in.
6 x 6, 8 x 8, 12 x 12 in.; 5³/₄, 8 and 12 in. hexagon.
Depth varies 1¹/₈ to 2¹/₄ in.

Surface textures vary from moderately abrasive to smooth. Colors are from light to dark earth tones. Special flashed surfaces are also available. Brick pavers are recommended for residential and light commercial uses.

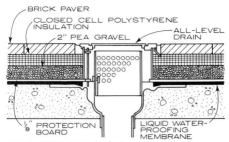

ON SUSPENDED BASE

Installed over waterproofing, roofing, slab, asphalt binder course or crushed stone base on bituminous setting.

BRICK PAVERS

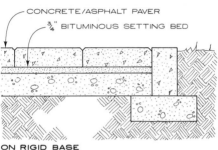

ON FLEXIBLE BASE

CONCRETE SIZES: 4 x 8, 8 x 8, 6 x 12,
12 x 18, 12 x 24, 18 x 18, 24 x 24,
24 x 30, 24 x 36, and 24 in. hexagon.
Depth varies 2 to 4 in.
Surface textures are smooth to coarse.

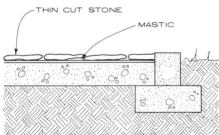

ON RIGID BASE

Colors are usually gray or white but are available with colored aggregates or colored cement matrix.
ASPHALT SIZES
5 x 12, 6 x 12, 8 x 8, and 8 in. hexagon.
Depth varies 1¹/₄ to 3 in.

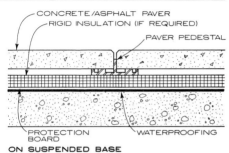

ON SUSPENDED BASE

Surface textures are abrasive but not coarse. Colors are natural black or exposed aggregate finish. Installed over waterproofing, roofing, slab, asphalt binder course, or crushed stone base on bituminous setting bed.

CONCRETE AND ASPHALT PAVERS

ON FLEXIBLE BASE

TERRA COTTA SIZES
4 x 4, 8 x 8 in.
Depths 1 to 2¹/₂ in.
Surface texture is usually smooth.
Colors are earth tones.
Installed on rigid base and mortar. Avoid frost.

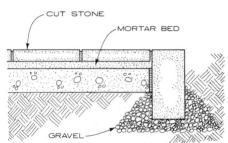

ON RIGID BASE

SLATE SIZES
4 in. min. x random.
Depths ³/₄ to 2¹/₂ in.
Surface texture is smooth.
Colors are grays and reds.
Installed on flexible base, no mortar. Keep well drained.

ON RIGID BASE

GRANITE SIZES: 4 x 4, 4 x 8, 5 x 8 in.
8 x 8, 12 x 12, Depth 2, 3, 4, and 10 in.

Surface texture is smooth. Colors are light and dark shades of red, gray and brown. Installed on rigid base and mortar for stability and heavy duty use; on flexible base for light duty use.

CUT STONE PAVERS

DEPTH: Crosscut = 2 in. min. Rip cut = 3 in. min.
Surface texture is smooth to slippery.
Colors are natural wood or color of preservatives.
Installed on flexible base that is well drained.
Wood should be pressure treated.

WOODBLOCK PAVERS

GENERAL NOTES

Paved areas should slope at a minimum of 0.5%, preferably 1.0%, in any direction. Main traffic areas should be kept dry.

Dan Mock and John M. Weed, ASLA; Houston, Texas

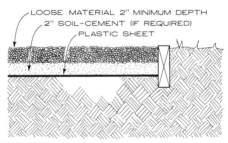

MATERIAL SIZES

Wood chips 1 in. nominal
Shredded bark mulch
¹/₄ in. stone chips
³/₄ in. pea gravel
¹/₂ in. decomposed granite
³/₄ in. crushed stone
1–2 in. washed stone

Installed on subgrade, plastic or soil-cement base.
Natural materials will decompose.

LOOSE MATERIALS

Pavers in mortar on rigid and suspended bases must have full expansion joint 20 ft on center. Rigid base on expansion soils is to be reinforced and doweled at joints. Porous base or subbase required in cold

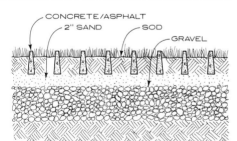

Size: 24 x 24 x 4 in. deep.
Surface texture is moderately abrasive.
Color is standard gray or white.
Installed without slab, mortar, or grout.
A preformed lattice unit used for embankment and storm run-off control, recreation areas, pathways, parking areas, and soil conservation.

GRID PAVING BLOCKS

regions with adequate subsurface drainage.

All pavers require edging members to contain horizontal movement at perimeter.

BIKE PATH CLASSIFICATIONS

Three bike path classifications have been generally accepted in the United States:

1. CLASS I: Completely separated right-of-way designated exclusively for bicycles. Through traffic, whether by motor vehicles or pedestrians, is not allowed. Cross flows by vehicles and pedestrians are allowed but minimized.
2. CLASS II: Restricted right-of-way designated exclusively or semiexclusively for bicycles. Through traffic by motor vehicles or pedestrians is not allowed. Cross flows by vehicles and pedestrians are allowed but minimized.
3. CLASS III: Shared right-of-way designated by signs or stencils. Any pathway that shares its through traffic right-of-way with either moving (but not parked) motor vehicles or pedestrians.

CLASS I: TOTAL SEPARATION / DIVIDING STRIP BETWEEN RIGHTS-OF-WAY ON SEPARATE SURFACES

CLASS II: TOTAL OR PARTIAL SEPARATION / ADJACENT, BUT SEPARATED RIGHTS-OF-WAY ON SAME SURFACE

CLASS III: NO SEPARATION / SHARED RIGHT-OF-WAY ON SAME SURFACE

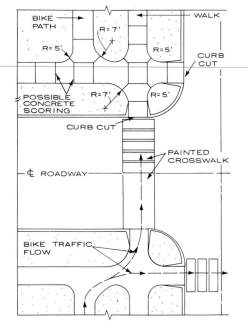

CLASS I: BIKE PATH, ON-GRADE INTERSECTION CONSIDERATIONS

Johnson, Johnson & Roy; Ann Arbor, Michigan

VERTICAL AND HORIZONTAL LAYOUT

The gradients of a bike path are directly related to the amount of use it will get. Extremes of steepness and flatness should be avoided if possible. The following gradients are recommended:

GRADIENT	LENGTH	
	NORM	MAXIMUM
1.5%	1000 ft	—
3%	400 ft	800 ft
4.5%	150 ft	300 ft
10%	30 ft	60 ft

The following formula can be used to determine horizontal radii used on bike paths:

$$R = 1.528V + 2.2*$$

where R = the unbraked radius of curvature (ft) negotiated by a bicycle on a flat, dry, bituminous concrete surface and V = the velocity of bicycle (mph).

*Formula applicable to a maximum design speed of 18 mph. Using this formula, the minimum radius acceptable for a 10 mph design speed would be 17.5 ft. The radii used at the base of gradients in excess of 4.5% and running longer than 100 ft should be longer to accept higher design speeds (20-30 mph). Shorter radii can be used along approaches to on-grade intersections to slow cyclists down as they merge with pedestrians.

BIKE PATH INTERSECTIONS

One of the most dangerous elements of a bike path system is the on-grade intersection that brings bicycles, pedestrians, and automobiles together. If possible, Class I bike paths should include complete grade separations. Often this is not economically feasible; therefore, the following recommendations should be considered:

1. If possible, merge bicycles and pedestrians a minimum of 100 ft from the intersection using warning signs for both cyclists and pedestrians.
2. Provide warning signs for motorists indicating special caution at intersections.
3. Maintain adequate lighting (see Chapter 1 on illumination).
4. Install walk-don't walk, electronic crosswalk signals at busy intersections.
5. Control placement and maintenance of plant materials so as to maintain adequate site distance and visibility.

Confusion at intersections tends to increase at Class II and III bike paths. Warning signs are therefore recommended along approaches to intersections for all three types of users (distance from intersections for signs varies with speed of vehicular traffic).

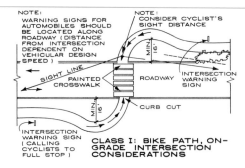

CLASS I: BIKE PATH, ON-GRADE INTERSECTION CONSIDERATIONS

BICYCLE SIZES

FRAME SIZE "W"	FRAME SIZE "F"
16"	12"
20"	13"
24"	16" boys 15" girls
26"	18", 19", 21", 23"
27"	19", 21", 23"

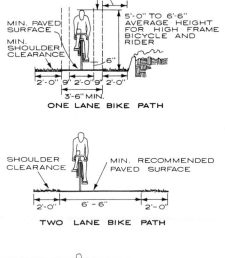

ONE LANE BIKE PATH

TWO LANE BIKE PATH

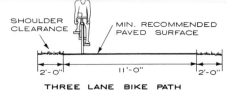

THREE LANE BIKE PATH

UPRIGHT, METAL BICYCLE RACK

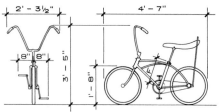

PRECAST CONCRETE / STEEL RING BICYCLE RACK

HOOP BICYCLE RACK

STEEL CABLE, SUPPLIED BY CYCLIST, SECURES FRONT WHEEL ALSO

BICYCLE PARKING

YOUTH'S SPORT W/"HIGHRISE" HANDLEBARS
FRAME SIZE (F) 13½", 14½"

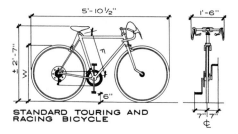

STANDARD TOURING AND RACING BICYCLE

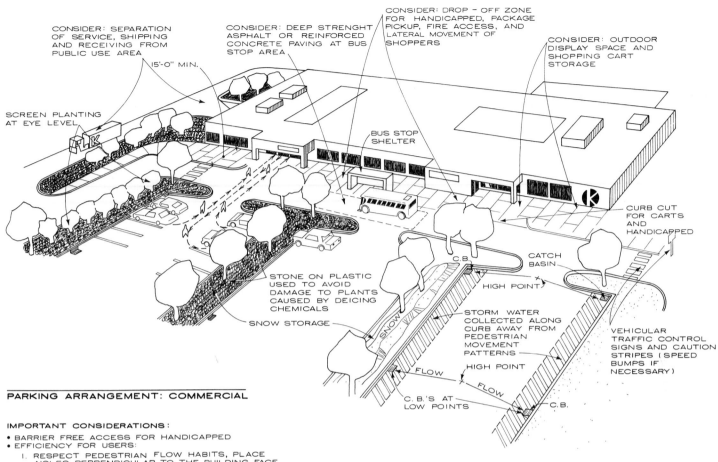

CONSIDER: SEPARATION OF SERVICE, SHIPPING AND RECEIVING FROM PUBLIC USE AREA

15'-0" MIN.

CONSIDER: DEEP STRENGTH ASPHALT OR REINFORCED CONCRETE PAVING AT BUS STOP AREA

CONSIDER: DROP - OFF ZONE FOR HANDICAPPED, PACKAGE PICKUP, FIRE ACCESS, AND LATERAL MOVEMENT OF SHOPPERS

CONSIDER: OUTDOOR DISPLAY SPACE AND SHOPPING CART STORAGE

SCREEN PLANTING AT EYE LEVEL

BUS STOP SHELTER

CURB CUT FOR CARTS AND HANDICAPPED

C.B.

CATCH BASIN

HIGH POINT

STONE ON PLASTIC USED TO AVOID DAMAGE TO PLANTS CAUSED BY DEICING CHEMICALS

STORM WATER COLLECTED ALONG CURB AWAY FROM PEDESTRIAN MOVEMENT PATTERNS

SNOW STORAGE

SNOW

FLOW

HIGH POINT

FLOW

VEHICULAR TRAFFIC CONTROL SIGNS AND CAUTION STRIPES (SPEED BUMPS IF NECESSARY)

C. B.'S AT LOW POINTS

C.B.

PARKING ARRANGEMENT: COMMERCIAL

IMPORTANT CONSIDERATIONS:

- BARRIER FREE ACCESS FOR HANDICAPPED
- EFFICIENCY FOR USERS:
  1. RESPECT PEDESTRIAN FLOW HABITS, PLACE AISLES PERPENDICULAR TO THE BUILDING FACE
  2. KEEP PEDESTRIAN WALKING AREAS IN PARKING LOT DRY AND FREE OF STANDING WATER
- PROVIDE SPACE FOR SNOW STORAGE
- PROVIDE FOR MASS TRANSIT ACCESS AT LARGER COMMERCIAL CENTERS

PLANTING CONSIDERATIONS

The distribution and placement of plants in parking areas can help to relieve the visually overwhelming scale of large parking lots. To maximize the impact of landscape materials, the screening capabilities of the plants must be considered. High branching canopy trees do not create a visual screen at eye level. When the landscaped area is concentrated in islands large enough to accommodate a diversified mixture of canopy and flowering trees, evergreen trees, and shrubs, visual screening via plants is much more effective. Planting low branching, densely foliated trees and shrubs can soften the visual impact of large parking areas. Consider the use of evergreens and avoid plants that drop fruit or sap.

DESIGN CONSIDERATIONS

While efficiency (number of spaces per gross acres) is the major practical consideration in the development of parking areas, several other important design questions exist. Barrier free design is mandatory in most communities. Parking spaces for the handicapped should be designated near building entrances. Curb cuts for wheelchairs should be provided at entrances. The lots should not only be efficient in terms of parking spaces provided, but should also allow maximum efficiency for pedestrians once they leave their vehicles.

Pedestrians habitually walk in the aisles behind parked vehicles. This should be recognized in the orientation of the aisles to building entrances. When aisles are perpendicular to the building face, pedestrians can walk to and from the building without squeezing between parked cars with carts and packages. Pedestrian movement areas should be graded to avoid creating standing water in the paths of pedestrians. Space should be provided for snow storage within parking areas, if required.

Johnson, Johnson & Roy, Inc.; Ann Arbor, Michigan

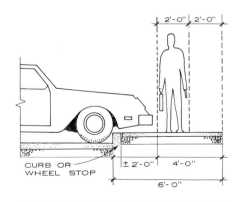

2'-0" 2'-0"

CURB OR WHEEL STOP

±2'-0"

4'-0"

6'-0"

AUTOMOBILE OVERHANG REQUIREMENT

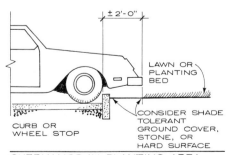

±2'-0"

LAWN OR PLANTING BED

CURB OR WHEEL STOP

CONSIDER SHADE TOLERANT GROUND COVER, STONE, OR HARD SURFACE

OVERHANGS IN PLANTING AREA

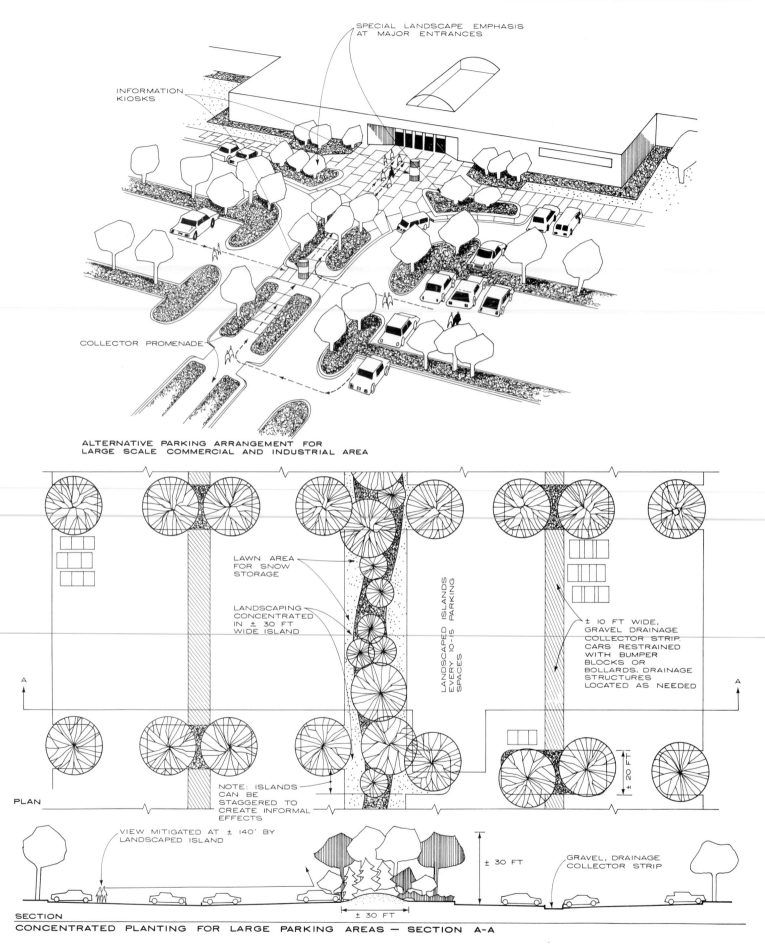

SPECIAL LANDSCAPE EMPHASIS
AT MAJOR ENTRANCES

INFORMATION
KIOSKS

COLLECTOR PROMENADE

ALTERNATIVE PARKING ARRANGEMENT FOR
LARGE SCALE COMMERCIAL AND INDUSTRIAL AREA

LAWN AREA
FOR SNOW
STORAGE

LANDSCAPING
CONCENTRATED
IN ± 30 FT
WIDE ISLAND

LANDSCAPED ISLANDS
EVERY 10-15 PARKING
SPACES

± 10 FT WIDE,
GRAVEL DRAINAGE
COLLECTOR STRIP.
CARS RESTRAINED
WITH BUMPER
BLOCKS OR
BOLLARDS. DRAINAGE
STRUCTURES
LOCATED AS NEEDED

A   A

PLAN

NOTE: ISLANDS
CAN BE
STAGGERED TO
CREATE INFORMAL
EFFECTS

± 20 FT

VIEW MITIGATED AT ± 140' BY
LANDSCAPED ISLAND

± 30 FT

GRAVEL, DRAINAGE
COLLECTOR STRIP

SECTION

± 30 FT

CONCENTRATED PLANTING FOR LARGE PARKING AREAS — SECTION A-A

Johnson, Johnson & Roy, Inc.; Ann Arbor, Michigan

2 SITE IMPROVEMENTS

CONSIDERATIONS

The following factors must be considered when installing or renovating outdoor lighting systems:

1. In general, overhead lighting is more efficient and economical than low level lighting.
2. Fixtures should provide an overlapping pattern of light at a height of about 7 ft.
3. Lighting levels should respond to site hazards such as steps, ramps, and steep embankments.
4. Posts and standards should be placed so that they do not create hazards for pedestrians or vehicles.

NOTE

All exterior installations must be provided with ground fault interruption circuit.

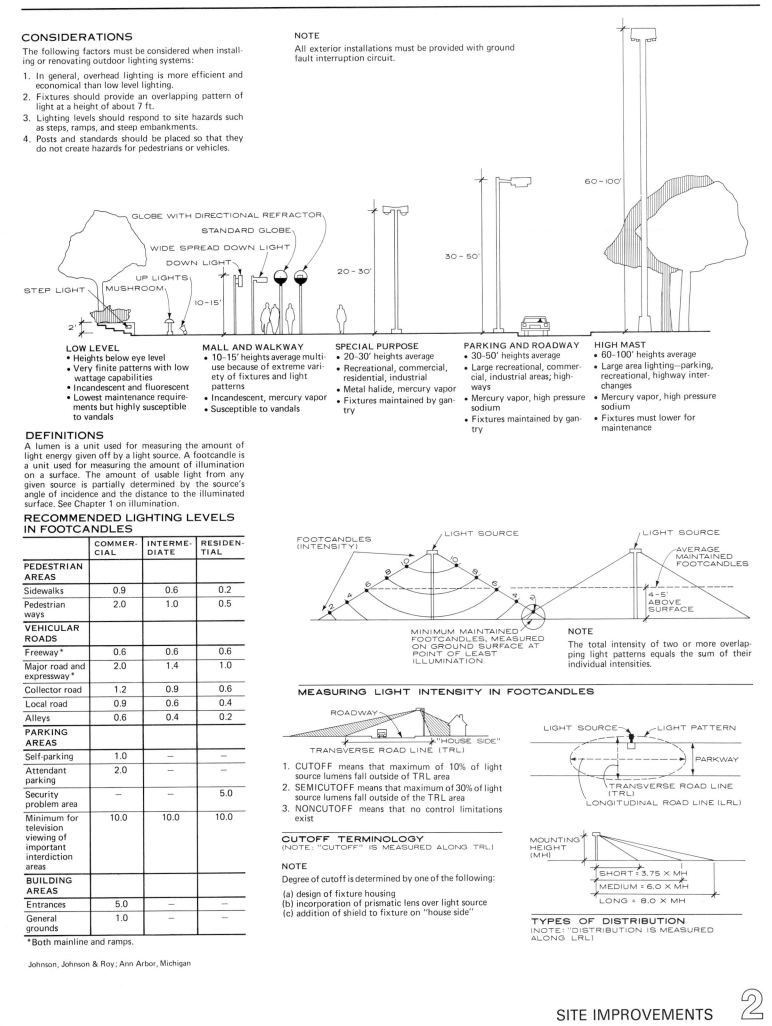

LOW LEVEL
- Heights below eye level
- Very finite patterns with low wattage capabilities
- Incandescent and fluorescent
- Lowest maintenance requirements but highly susceptible to vandals

MALL AND WALKWAY
- 10-15' heights average multi-use because of extreme variety of fixtures and light patterns
- Incandescent, mercury vapor
- Susceptible to vandals

SPECIAL PURPOSE
- 20-30' heights average
- Recreational, commercial, residential, industrial
- Metal halide, mercury vapor
- Fixtures maintained by gantry

PARKING AND ROADWAY
- 30-50' heights average
- Large recreational, commercial, industrial areas; highways
- Mercury vapor, high pressure sodium
- Fixtures maintained by gantry

HIGH MAST
- 60-100' heights average
- Large area lighting—parking, recreational, highway interchanges
- Mercury vapor, high pressure sodium
- Fixtures must lower for maintenance

DEFINITIONS

A lumen is a unit used for measuring the amount of light energy given off by a light source. A footcandle is a unit used for measuring the amount of illumination on a surface. The amount of usable light from any given source is partially determined by the source's angle of incidence and the distance to the illuminated surface. See Chapter 1 on illumination.

RECOMMENDED LIGHTING LEVELS IN FOOTCANDLES

	COMMER-CIAL	INTERME-DIATE	RESIDEN-TIAL
PEDESTRIAN AREAS			
Sidewalks	0.9	0.6	0.2
Pedestrian ways	2.0	1.0	0.5
VEHICULAR ROADS			
Freeway*	0.6	0.6	0.6
Major road and expressway*	2.0	1.4	1.0
Collector road	1.2	0.9	0.6
Local road	0.9	0.6	0.4
Alleys	0.6	0.4	0.2
PARKING AREAS			
Self-parking	1.0	—	—
Attendant parking	2.0	—	—
Security problem area	—	—	5.0
Minimum for television viewing of important interdiction areas	10.0	10.0	10.0
BUILDING AREAS			
Entrances	5.0	—	—
General grounds	1.0	—	—

*Both mainline and ramps.

Johnson, Johnson & Roy; Ann Arbor, Michigan

NOTE

The total intensity of two or more overlapping light patterns equals the sum of their individual intensities.

MEASURING LIGHT INTENSITY IN FOOTCANDLES

1. CUTOFF means that maximum of 10% of light source lumens fall outside of TRL area
2. SEMICUTOFF means that maximum of 30% of light source lumens fall outside of the TRL area
3. NONCUTOFF means that no control limitations exist

CUTOFF TERMINOLOGY
(NOTE: "CUTOFF" IS MEASURED ALONG TRL.)

NOTE

Degree of cutoff is determined by one of the following:

(a) design of fixture housing
(b) incorporation of prismatic lens over light source
(c) addition of shield to fixture on "house side"

TYPES OF DISTRIBUTION
(NOTE: "DISTRIBUTION IS MEASURED ALONG LRL)

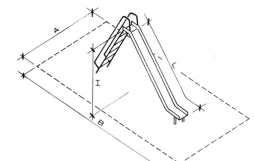

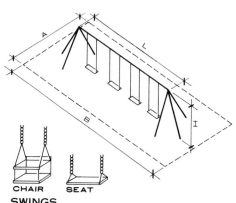

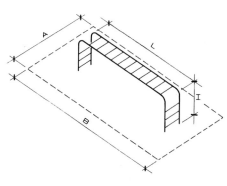

ADJACENT SLIDES: 7'- 6"
(CHUTES C. TO C.) OTHERS 10' O.C.

SLIDES

H	L	NURSERY		STRAIGHT		RACER	
		A	B	A	B	A	B
5	10	8	20				
6	12	8	22				
7	14	8	24				
8	16			12	30	20	30
10	20			12	35	20	35
12	24			15	40	25	40
13½	30			15	45	25	45

CHAIR   SEAT

SWINGS

NO SWINGS	CHAIR TYPE			SEAT TYPE						
	L	A	B	L	A	B	A	B	A	B
2	8	17	24	9	17	25	21	25	25	25
3	10	17	26	15	17	31	21	31	25	31
4	16	17	32	18	17	34	21	34	25	34
6	20,24	17	38	27,30	17	46	21	46	25	46
8				36	17	52	21	52	25	52
9				45	17	61	21	61	25	61
Height	8'			8',10',12'	8'		10'		12'	

HORIZONTAL LADDER

HEIGHT	LENGTH	A	B
6	12	8	25
7½	16	8	30

GENERAL PLANNING INFORMATION

EQUIPMENT	AREA (SQ FT)	CAPACITY (NUMBER OF CHILDREN)
Slide	450	4–6
Low swing	150	1
High swing	250	1
Horizontal ladder	375	6–8
Seesaw	100	2
Junior climbing gym	180	8–10
General climbing gym	500	15–20

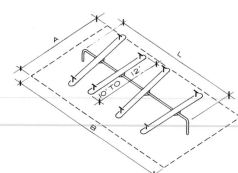

HEIGHT OF CENTER PIPE
1'-0" TO 3'-0" ABOVE GROUND

SEESAWS

BOARDS	1	2	3	4	6
L	3	6	9	12	18
A	20	20	20	20	20
B	5	10	15	20	25

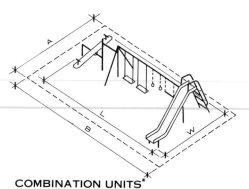

COMBINATION UNITS*

ENCLOSURE LIMITS
A = W + 12'-0"
B = L + 6'-0"

*Types and no. of units are variable.

LIMITS:
GEN. 18' x 18'
JR. 10' x 12'

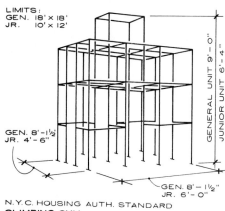

GEN. 8'-1½"
JR. 4'-6"

GEN. 8'-1½"
JR. 6'-0"

GENERAL UNIT 9'-0"
JUNIOR UNIT 6'-4"

N.Y.C. HOUSING AUTH. STANDARD
CLIMBING GYM

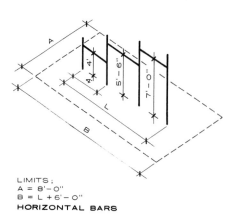

4'
5'-6"
7'-0"

LIMITS;
A = 8'-0"
B = L + 6'-0"
HORIZONTAL BARS

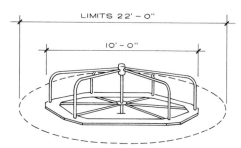

LIMITS 22'-0"

10'-0"

10 FT. DIAMETER IS CONSIDERED STAND-
ARD. OTHER DIAMETERS = 12',14'& 16'
LIMITS 24', 26' & 28' DIA.
MERRY – GO – ROUND

Vincent F. Nauseda; Sasaki, Dawson Associates, Inc.; Watertown, Massachusetts

NOTES

Several factors should be considered when designing with plants:

1. The physical environment of the site:
   - Soil conditions (acidity, porosity).
   - Available sunlight.
   - Available precipitation.
   - Seasonal temperature range.
   - Exposure of the site (wind).
2. The design needs of the project:
   - Directing movement.
   - Framing vistas.
   - Moderating the environment of the site.
   - Creating space by using plants to develop the base, vertical, and overhead planes.
3. The design character of the plants chosen:
   - Height.
   - Mass.
   - Silhouette (rounded, pyramidal, spreading).
   - Texture (fine, medium, coarse).
   - Color.
   - Seasonal interest (flowers, fruit, fall color).
   - Growth habits (fast or slow growing).

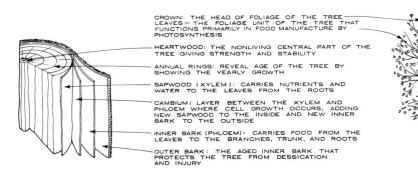

CROWN: THE HEAD OF FOLIAGE OF THE TREE
LEAVES — THE FOLIAGE UNIT OF THE TREE THAT FUNCTIONS PRIMARILY IN FOOD MANUFACTURE BY PHOTOSYNTHESIS

HEARTWOOD: THE NONLIVING CENTRAL PART OF THE TREE GIVING STRENGTH AND STABILITY

ANNUAL RINGS: REVEAL AGE OF THE TREE BY SHOWING THE YEARLY GROWTH

SAPWOOD (XYLEM): CARRIES NUTRIENTS AND WATER TO THE LEAVES FROM THE ROOTS

CAMBIUM: LAYER BETWEEN THE XYLEM AND PHLOEM WHERE CELL GROWTH OCCURS, ADDING NEW SAPWOOD TO THE INSIDE AND NEW INNER BARK TO THE OUTSIDE

INNER BARK (PHLOEM): CARRIES FOOD FROM THE LEAVES TO THE BRANCHES, TRUNK, AND ROOTS

OUTER BARK: THE AGED INNER BARK THAT PROTECTS THE TREE FROM DESSICATION AND INJURY

ROOTS: THE ROOTS ANCHOR THE TREE AND HELP HOLD THE SOIL AGAINST EROSION

ROOT HAIRS: THE TINY ROOT HAIRS ABSORB THE MINERALS FROM THE SOIL MOISTURE AND SEND THEM AS NUTRIENT SALTS IN THE SAPWOOD TO THE LEAVES

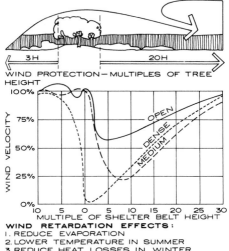

WIND PROTECTION — MULTIPLES OF TREE HEIGHT

WIND RETARDATION EFFECTS:
1. REDUCE EVAPORATION
2. LOWER TEMPERATURE IN SUMMER
3. REDUCE HEAT LOSSES IN WINTER
4. INCREASE RELATIVE HUMIDITY
5. REDUCE DUST AND SNOW BLOWING

DENSITY

The density of a planted wind buffer determines the area that is protected. Height and composition are also factors in wind protection.

PHYSICAL CHARACTERISTICS

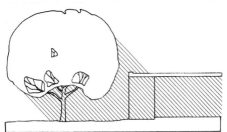

SUMMER

WINTER

RADIATION PROTECTION

In summer deciduous plants obstruct or filter the sun's strong radiation, thus cooling the area beneath them. In winter the sun penetrates through.

SOUND ATTENUATION

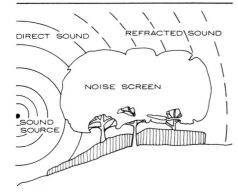

DIRECT SOUND   REFRACTED SOUND

NOISE SCREEN

SOUND SOURCE

Plantings of deciduous and evergreen materials reduce sound more effectively than deciduous plants alone. Planting on earth mounds increases the attenuating effects of the buffer.

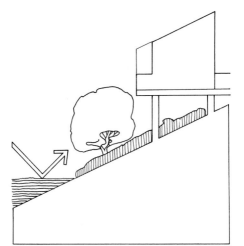

GLARE PROTECTION

The sun's vertical angle changes seasonally; therefore, the area subject to the glare of reflected sunlight varies. Plants of various heights screen glare from adjacent reflective surfaces (water, paving, glass, and building surfaces).

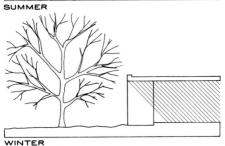
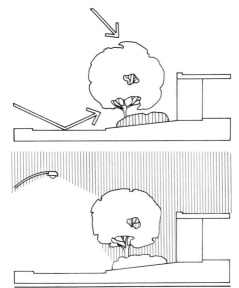

GLARE PROTECTION

Glare and reflection from sunlight and/or artificial sources can be screened or blocked by plants of various height and placement.

PARTICULATE MATTER TRAPPED ON THE LEAVES IS WASHED TO THE GROUND DURING A RAINFALL. GASEOUS AND OTHER POLLUTANTS ARE ASSIMILATED IN THE LEAVES

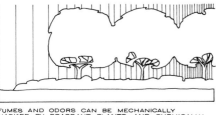

FUMES AND ODORS CAN BE MECHANICALLY MASKED BY FRAGRANT PLANTS AND CHEMICALLY METABOLIZED IN THE PHOTOSYNTHETIC PROCESS

AIR FILTRATION

Large masses of plants physically and chemically filter and deodorize the air to reduce air pollution.

A. E. Bye and Associates, Landscape Architects; Old Greenwich, Connecticut

Robin Roberts; Washington, D.C.

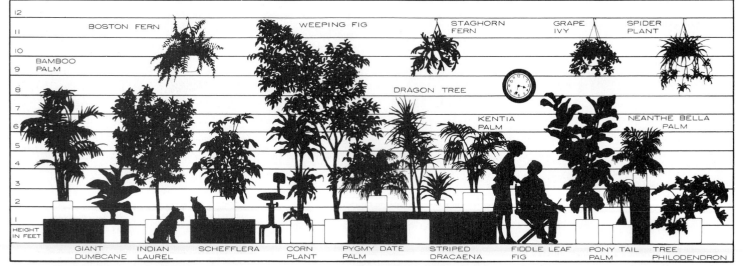

FORM, TEXTURE, AND SIZES OF SOME TYPICALLY USED INTERIOR PLANTS

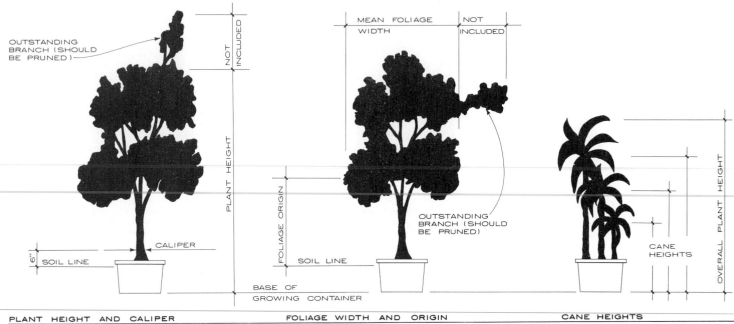

PLANT HEIGHT AND CALIPER   FOLIAGE WIDTH AND ORIGIN   CANE HEIGHTS

INTERIOR PLANT SPECIFICATIONS

NOTE

Plant height should be measured as overall height from the base of the growing container to mean foliage top. Isolated outstanding branches should not be included in height. (Since most plants are installed in movable planters, this overall height measurement should be utilized.)

NOTE

Foliage width should be measured across the nominal mean width dimension. Isolated outstanding branches should not be included in foliage width. Origin or start of foliage should be measured from the soil line.

NOTE

Many plant varieties are grown from rooted canes, with the plant being made up of one or more canes. The number of canes must be specified, if plant form is to be identified. Cane heights should always be measured from the base of the growing container.

OTHER PLANT SPECIFICATION FACTORS

1. Accurately describe plant form (e.g., multistem vs. standard tree form, clump form) and foliage spread desired. Indicate "clear trunk" measurements on trees, if desired. These measurements are from soil line to foliage origin point. Specify caliper, if significant.

2. Indicate lighting intensities designed or calculated for interior space where plants will be installed.

3. Indicate how plants will be used (i.e., in at-grade

planter or in movable decorative planter). If movable decorative planters are used, indicate interior diameter and height of planter for each plant specified, since growing container sizes vary considerably.

4. Specify both botanical and common plant names.

5. Indicate any special shipping instructions or limitations.

6. Specify in-plant height column, whether plant height is measured as overall height or above-the-

soil line height. Recommended height measurements:

Interior plants: overall plant height (i.e., from bottom of growing container to mean foliage top).
Exterior plants: above-the-soil line height.

7. Indicate whether plants are to be container grown or balled and burlapped (B & B) material.

8. Indicate location of all convenient water supply sources on all interior landscaping layouts.

Richard L. Gaines, AIA; Plantscape House; Apopka, Florida

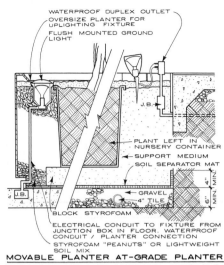

WATERPROOF DUPLEX OUTLET
OVERSIZE PLANTER FOR UPLIGHTING FIXTURE
FLUSH MOUNTED GROUND LIGHT

J.B.

PLANT LEFT IN NURSERY CONTAINER
SUPPORT MEDIUM
SOIL SEPARATOR MAT

J.B.

GRAVEL
4" TILE

6" MIN.

BLOCK STYROFOAM

ELECTRICAL CONDUIT TO FIXTURE FROM JUNCTION BOX IN FLOOR. WATERPROOF CONDUIT / PLANTER CONNECTION
STYROFOAM "PEANUTS" OR LIGHTWEIGHT SOIL MIX

MOVABLE PLANTER AT-GRADE PLANTER UPLIGHTING / PLANTING DETAILS

UPLIGHTING AND ELECTRICAL NEEDS

1. May be of some benefit to plants, but inefficient for plant photosynthesis because of plant physiological structure. Chlorophyll is usually in upper part of leaf.
2. Uplighting should never be utilized as sole lighting source for plants.
3. Waterproof duplex outlets above soil line with a waterproof junction box below soil line are usually adequate for "atmosphere" uplighting and water fountain pumps.

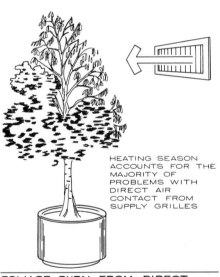

HEATING SEASON ACCOUNTS FOR THE MAJORITY OF PROBLEMS WITH DIRECT AIR CONTACT FROM SUPPLY GRILLES

FOLIAGE BURN FROM DIRECT HEAT CONTACT

HVAC EFFECT ON PLANTS

1. Air-conditioning (cooled air) is rarely detrimental to plants, even if it is "directed" at plants. The ventilation here is what counts! Good ventilation is a must with plants; otherwise oxygen and temperatures build up. Heat supply, on the other hand, when "directed" at plants, can truly be disastrous. Plan for supplies directed away from plants, but maintain adequate ventilation.
2. Extended heat or power failures of sufficient duration can damage plant health. The lower limit of temperature as a steady state is 65°F for plant survival. Brief drops to 55°F (less than 1 hr) are the lower limit before damage. Temperatures up to 85°F for only 2 days a week can usually be tolerated.
3. The relative humidity should not be allowed to fall below 30%, as plants prefer a relative humidity of 50-60%.

Richard L. Gaines, AIA; Plantscape House; Apopka, Florida

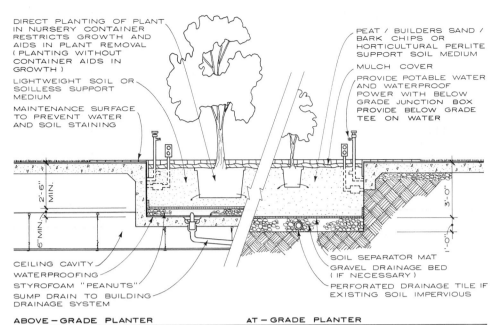

DIRECT PLANTING OF PLANT IN NURSERY CONTAINER RESTRICTS GROWTH AND AIDS IN PLANT REMOVAL (PLANTING WITHOUT CONTAINER AIDS IN GROWTH)
LIGHTWEIGHT SOIL OR SOILLESS SUPPORT MEDIUM
MAINTENANCE SURFACE TO PREVENT WATER AND SOIL STAINING

PEAT / BUILDERS SAND / BARK CHIPS OR HORTICULTURAL PERLITE SUPPORT SOIL MEDIUM
MULCH COVER
PROVIDE POTABLE WATER AND WATERPROOF POWER WITH BELOW GRADE JUNCTION BOX
PROVIDE BELOW GRADE TEE ON WATER

2'-6" MIN.

6" MIN.

3'-0"

1'-0"

CEILING CAVITY
WATERPROOFING
STYROFOAM "PEANUTS"
SUMP DRAIN TO BUILDING DRAINAGE SYSTEM

SOIL SEPARATOR MAT
GRAVEL DRAINAGE BED (IF NECESSARY)
PERFORATED DRAINAGE TILE IF EXISTING SOIL IMPERVIOUS

ABOVE-GRADE PLANTER   AT-GRADE PLANTER FLOOR PLANTER DETAILS

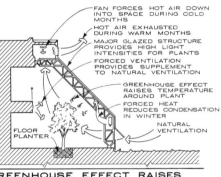

FAN FORCES HOT AIR DOWN INTO SPACE DURING COLD MONTHS
HOT AIR EXHAUSTED DURING WARM MONTHS
MAJOR GLAZED STRUCTURE PROVIDES HIGH LIGHT INTENSITIES FOR PLANTS
FORCED VENTILATION PROVIDES SUPPLEMENT TO NATURAL VENTILATION
GREENHOUSE EFFECT RAISES TEMPERATURE AROUND PLANT
FORCED HEAT REDUCES CONDENSATION IN WINTER
NATURAL VENTILATION
FLOOR PLANTER

GREENHOUSE EFFECT RAISES NEED FOR ADEQUATE VENTILATION

TEMPERATURE REQUIREMENTS

1. Most plants prefer human comfort range: 70-75°F daytime temperatures and 60-65°F nighttime temperatures.
2. An absolute minimum temperature of 50°F must be observed. Plant damage will result below this figure. Rapid temperature fluctuations of 30-40°F can also be detrimental to plants.
3. "Q-10" phenomenon of respiration: for every 10°C rise in temperature, plants' respiration rate and food consumption doubles.
4. Both photosynthesis and respiration decline and stop with time, as temperatures go beyond 80°F. Beware of the greenhouse effect!

WATER SUPPLY REQUIREMENTS

1. Movable and railing planters are often watered by watering can. Provide convenient access to hot and cold potable water by hose bibbs and/or service sinks (preferably in janitor's closet) during normal working hours, with long (min. 24 in.) faucet-to-sink or floor distances. Provide for maximum of 200 ft travel on all floors.
2. At-grade floor planters are usually watered by hose and extension wand. Provide hose bibbs above soil line (for maximum travel of 50 ft) with capped "tee" stub-outs beneath soil line. If soil temperature is apt to get abnormally low in winter, provide hot and cold water by mixer-faucet type hose bibbs.
3. High concentrations of fluoride and chlorine in water supply can cause damage to plants. Provide water with low concentrations of these elements and with a pH value of 5.0-6.0. Higher or lower pH levels can result in higher plant maintenance costs.

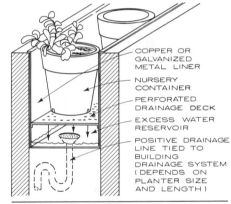

COPPER OR GALVANIZED METAL LINER
NURSERY CONTAINER
PERFORATED DRAINAGE DECK
EXCESS WATER RESERVOIR
POSITIVE DRAINAGE LINE TIED TO BUILDING DRAINAGE SYSTEM (DEPENDS ON PLANTER SIZE AND LENGTH)

RAILING PLANTER DETAIL

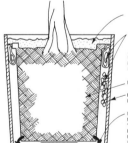

MULCH LAYER
CHICKEN WIRE SPACER / FILLER OR STYROFOAM "PEANUTS" AS FILLER KEEPS MULCH LAYER FROM FALLING BETWEEN PLANTER AND POT
NURSERY CONTAINER
MOVABLE DECORATIVE PLANTER
NOTE: ALWAYS SPECIFY MOVABLE PLANTERS WITH EXCESS WATER RESERVOIR SO THAT PLANT DOES NOT SIT IN WATER

MOVABLE DECORATIVE PLANTER DETAIL

STORAGE REQUIREMENTS

Provide a secured storage space of approximately 30 sq ft for watering equipment and other maintenance materials. It may be desirable to combine water supply and janitor needs in the same storage area.

AIR POLLUTION EFFECTS ON PLANTS

Problems result from inadequate ventilation. Excessive chlorine gas from swimming pool areas can be a damaging problem, as well as excessive fumes from toxic cleaning substances for floor finishes, etc. Ventilation a must here!

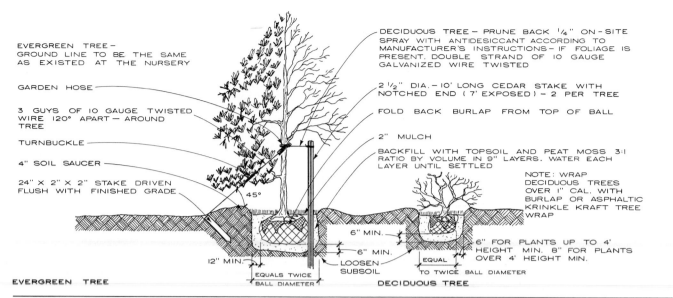

EVERGREEN TREE – GROUND LINE TO BE THE SAME AS EXISTED AT THE NURSERY

GARDEN HOSE

3 GUYS OF 10 GAUGE TWISTED WIRE 120° APART — AROUND TREE

TURNBUCKLE

4" SOIL SAUCER

24" X 2" X 2" STAKE DRIVEN FLUSH WITH FINISHED GRADE

DECIDUOUS TREE – PRUNE BACK ¼" ON-SITE SPRAY WITH ANTIDESICCANT ACCORDING TO MANUFACTURER'S INSTRUCTIONS – IF FOLIAGE IS PRESENT. DOUBLE STRAND OF 10 GAUGE GALVANIZED WIRE TWISTED

2 ½" DIA. – 10' LONG CEDAR STAKE WITH NOTCHED END (7' EXPOSED) – 2 PER TREE

FOLD BACK BURLAP FROM TOP OF BALL

2" MULCH

BACKFILL WITH TOPSOIL AND PEAT MOSS 3:1 RATIO BY VOLUME IN 9" LAYERS. WATER EACH LAYER UNTIL SETTLED

NOTE: WRAP DECIDUOUS TREES OVER 1" CAL. WITH BURLAP OR ASPHALTIC KRINKLE KRAFT TREE WRAP

45°

6" MIN.
6" MIN.
12" MIN.
LOOSEN SUBSOIL
EQUALS TWICE BALL DIAMETER

6" FOR PLANTS UP TO 4' HEIGHT MIN. 8" FOR PLANTS OVER 4' HEIGHT MIN.
EQUAL
TO TWICE BALL DIAMETER

EVERGREEN TREE

DECIDUOUS TREE

PLANTING DETAILS – TREES AND SHRUBS

SHRUBS AND MINOR TREES BALLED AND BURLAPPED

HEIGHT RANGE (FT)	MINIMUM BALL DIAMETER (IN.)	MINIMUM BALL DEPTH (IN.)
1½–2	10	8
2–3	12	9
3–4	13	10
4–5	15	11
5–6	16	12
6–7	18	13
7–8	20	14
8–9	22	15
9–10	24	16
10–12	26	17

NOTE: Ball sizes should always be of a diameter to encompass the fibrous and feeding root system necessary for the full recovery of the plant.

STANDARD SHADE TREES—BALLED AND BURLAPPED

CALIPER* (IN.)	HEIGHT RANGE (FT)	MAXIMUM HEIGHTS (FT)	MINIMUM BALL DIAMETER (IN.)	MINIMUM BALL DEPTH (IN.)
½–¾	5–6	8	12	9
¾–1	6–8	10	14	10
1–1¼	7–9	11	16	12
1¼–1½	8–10	12	18	13
1½–1¾	10–12	14	20	14
1¾–2	10–12	14	22	15
2–2½	12–14	16	24	16
2½–3	12–14	16	28	19
3–3½	14–16	18	32	20
3½–4	14–16	18	36	22
4–5	16–18	22	44	26
5–6	18 and up	26	48	29

*Caliper indicates the diameter of the trunk taken 6 in. above the ground level up to and including 4 in. caliper size and 12 in. above the ground level for larger sizes.

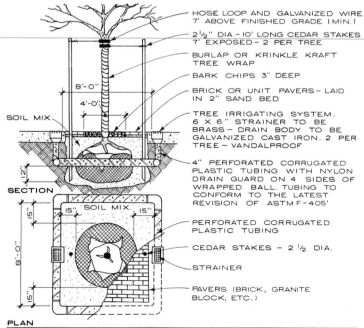

HOSE LOOP AND GALVANIZED WIRE 7' ABOVE FINISHED GRADE (MIN.)

2 ½" DIA. – 10' LONG CEDAR STAKES 7' EXPOSED – 2 PER TREE

BURLAP OR KRINKLE KRAFT TREE WRAP

BARK CHIPS 3" DEEP

BRICK OR UNIT PAVERS – LAID IN 2" SAND BED

TREE IRRIGATING SYSTEM. 6 X 6" STRAINER TO BE BRASS – DRAIN BODY TO BE GALVANIZED CAST IRON. 2 PER TREE – VANDALPROOF

4" PERFORATED CORRUGATED PLASTIC TUBING WITH NYLON DRAIN GUARD ON 4 SIDES OF WRAPPED BALL. TUBING TO CONFORM TO THE LATEST REVISION OF ASTM F-405'

PERFORATED CORRUGATED PLASTIC TUBING

CEDAR STAKES – 2 ½ DIA.

STRAINER

PAVERS (BRICK, GRANITE BLOCK, ETC.)

8'-0"
4'-0"
SOIL MIX
12"
SECTION

SOIL MIX
15" 15"
15"
8'-0"
15"
PLAN

PLANTING DETAIL – TREE IN PAVING

A. E. Bye & Associates, Landscape Architects; Old Greenwich, Connecticut

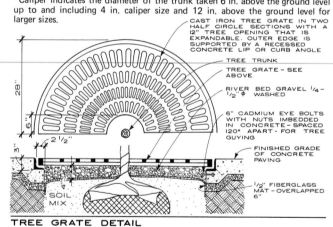

CAST IRON TREE GRATE IN TWO HALF CIRCLE SECTIONS WITH A 12" TREE OPENING THAT IS EXPANDABLE. OUTER EDGE IS SUPPORTED BY A RECESSED CONCRETE LIP OR CURB ANGLE

TREE TRUNK

TREE GRATE – SEE ABOVE

RIVER BED GRAVEL ¼–½" ⌀ WASHED

6" CADMIUM EYE BOLTS WITH NUTS IMBEDDED IN CONCRETE- SPACED 120° APART- FOR TREE GUYING

FINISHED GRADE OF CONCRETE PAVING

½" FIBERGLASS MAT – OVERLAPPED 6"

28"
6"
3"
2 ½"
SOIL MIX

TREE GRATE DETAIL

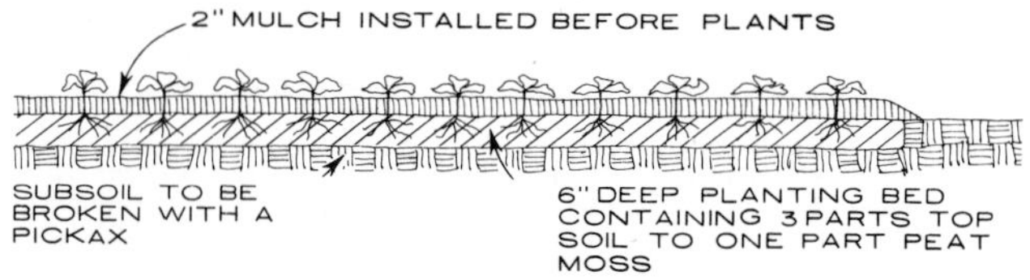

2" MULCH INSTALLED BEFORE PLANTS

SUBSOIL TO BE BROKEN WITH A PICKAX

6" DEEP PLANTING BED CONTAINING 3 PARTS TOP SOIL TO ONE PART PEAT MOSS

GROUND COVER PLANTING DETAIL
NOTE: GROUND COVERS SHOULD BE POT OR CONTAINER GROWN

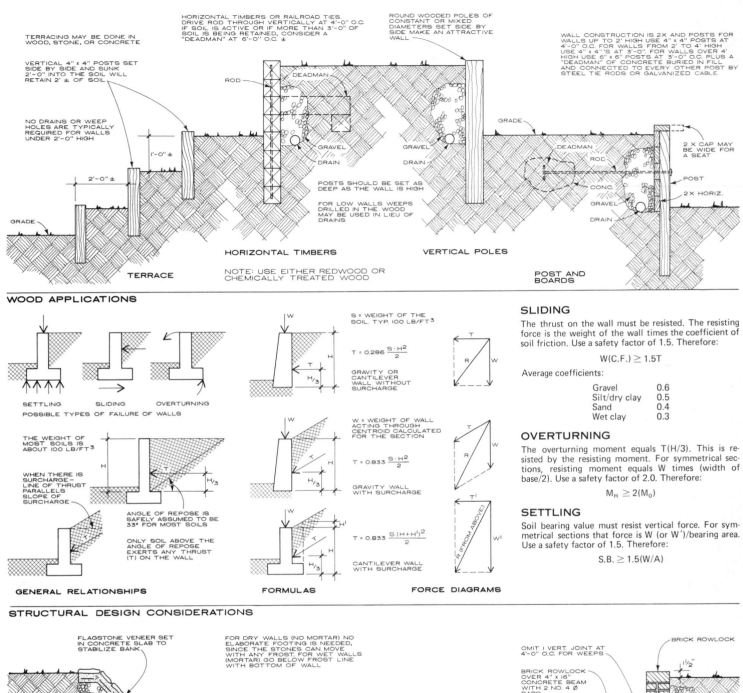

TERRACING MAY BE DONE IN WOOD, STONE, OR CONCRETE

VERTICAL 4" x 4" POSTS SET SIDE BY SIDE AND SUNK 2'-0" INTO THE SOIL WILL RETAIN 2' ± OF SOIL

NO DRAINS OR WEEP HOLES ARE TYPICALLY REQUIRED FOR WALLS UNDER 2'-0" HIGH

HORIZONTAL TIMBERS OR RAILROAD TIES. DRIVE ROD THROUGH VERTICALLY AT 4'-0" O.C. IF SOIL IS ACTIVE OR IF MORE THAN 3'-0" OF SOIL IS BEING RETAINED, CONSIDER A "DEADMAN" AT 6'-0" O.C. ±

ROUND WOODED POLES OF CONSTANT OR MIXED DIAMETERS SET SIDE BY SIDE MAKE AN ATTRACTIVE WALL

WALL CONSTRUCTION IS 2X AND POSTS FOR WALLS UP TO 2' HIGH USE 4" x 4" POSTS AT 4'-0" O.C. FOR WALLS FROM 2' TO 4' HIGH USE 4" x 4"'S AT 3'-0". FOR WALLS OVER 4' HIGH USE 6" x 6" POSTS AT 3'-0" O.C. PLUS A "DEADMAN" OF CONCRETE BURIED IN FILL AND CONNECTED TO EVERY OTHER POST BY STEEL TIE RODS OR GALVANIZED CABLE

ROD

DEADMAN

GRADE

2 X CAP MAY BE WIDE FOR A SEAT

GRADE

GRAVEL DRAIN

GRAVEL DRAIN

DEADMAN

ROD

CONC.

GRAVEL DRAIN

POST

2 X HORIZ.

POSTS SHOULD BE SET AS DEEP AS THE WALL IS HIGH

FOR LOW WALLS WEEPS DRILLED IN THE WOOD MAY BE USED IN LIEU OF DRAINS

1'-0" ±

2'-0" ±

GRADE

TERRACE

HORIZONTAL TIMBERS

NOTE: USE EITHER REDWOOD OR CHEMICALLY TREATED WOOD

VERTICAL POLES

POST AND BOARDS

WOOD APPLICATIONS

SETTLING   SLIDING   OVERTURNING

POSSIBLE TYPES OF FAILURE OF WALLS

THE WEIGHT OF MOST SOILS IS ABOUT 100 LB/FT³

WHEN THERE IS SURCHARGE — LINE OF THRUST PARALLELS SLOPE OF SURCHARGE

ANGLE OF REPOSE IS SAFELY ASSUMED TO BE 33° FOR MOST SOILS

ONLY SOIL ABOVE THE ANGLE OF REPOSE EXERTS ANY THRUST (T) ON THE WALL

GENERAL RELATIONSHIPS

S = WEIGHT OF THE SOIL. TYP. 100 LB/FT³

$$T = 0.286 \frac{S \cdot H^2}{2}$$

GRAVITY OR CANTILEVER WALL WITHOUT SURCHARGE

W = WEIGHT OF WALL ACTING THROUGH CENTROID CALCULATED FOR THE SECTION

$$T = 0.833 \frac{S \cdot H^2}{2}$$

GRAVITY WALL WITH SURCHARGE

$$T = 0.833 \frac{S(H+H^1)^2}{2}$$

CANTILEVER WALL WITH SURCHARGE

FORMULAS

T   R   W

T   R   W

T¹   R (FROM ABOVE)   W¹

FORCE DIAGRAMS

SLIDING

The thrust on the wall must be resisted. The resisting force is the weight of the wall times the coefficient of soil friction. Use a safety factor of 1.5. Therefore:

$$W(C.F.) \geq 1.5T$$

Average coefficients:

Gravel	0.6
Silt/dry clay	0.5
Sand	0.4
Wet clay	0.3

OVERTURNING

The overturning moment equals $T(H/3)$. This is resisted by the resisting moment. For symmetrical sections, resisting moment equals W times (width of base/2). Use a safety factor of 2.0. Therefore:

$$M_R \geq 2(M_0)$$

SETTLING

Soil bearing value must resist vertical force. For symmetrical sections that force is W (or W′)/bearing area. Use a safety factor of 1.5. Therefore:

$$S.B. \geq 1.5(W/A)$$

STRUCTURAL DESIGN CONSIDERATIONS

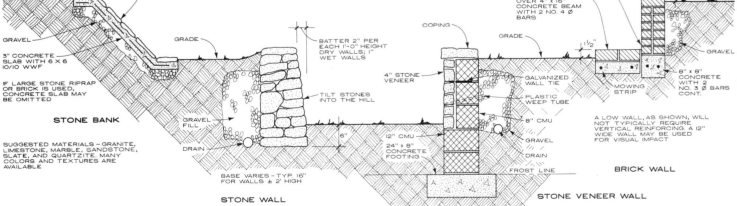

FLAGSTONE VENEER SET IN CONCRETE SLAB TO STABILIZE BANK

GRAVEL

3" CONCRETE SLAB WITH 6 X 6 10/10 WWF

IF LARGE STONE RIPRAP OR BRICK IS USED, CONCRETE SLAB MAY BE OMITTED

STONE BANK

SUGGESTED MATERIALS — GRANITE, LIMESTONE, MARBLE, SANDSTONE, SLATE, AND QUARTZITE. MANY COLORS AND TEXTURES ARE AVAILABLE

FOR DRY WALLS (NO MORTAR) NO ELABORATE FOOTING IS NEEDED, SINCE THE STONES CAN MOVE WITH ANY FROST. FOR WET WALLS (MORTAR) GO BELOW FROST LINE WITH BOTTOM OF WALL

GRADE

BATTER 2" PER EACH 1'-0" HEIGHT DRY WALLS; 1" WET WALLS

TILT STONES INTO THE HILL

GRAVEL FILL

DRAIN

6"

BASE VARIES — TYP. 16" FOR WALLS ± 2' HIGH

STONE WALL

COPING

4" STONE VENEER

12" CMU

24" x 8" CONCRETE FOOTING

8" CMU

GRAVEL DRAIN

GALVANIZED WALL TIE

PLASTIC WEEP TUBE

FROST LINE

STONE VENEER WALL

OMIT 1 VERT. JOINT AT 4'-0" O.C. FOR WEEPS

BRICK ROWLOCK OVER 4" x 16" CONCRETE BEAM WITH 2 NO. 4 Ø BARS

GRADE

1½"

1½"

MOWING STRIP

8" x 8" CONCRETE WITH 2 NO. 3 Ø BARS CONT.

BRICK ROWLOCK

GRAVEL

A LOW WALL, AS SHOWN, WILL NOT TYPICALLY REQUIRE VERTICAL REINFORCING. A 12" WIDE WALL MAY BE USED FOR VISUAL IMPACT

BRICK WALL

STONE AND MASONRY APPLICATIONS

Charles R. Heuer, AIA; Washington, D.C.

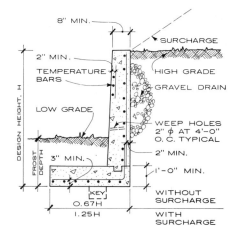

Place base below frost line. Dimensions are approximate.

CONCRETE OUTLINES FOR L TYPE RETAINING WALL

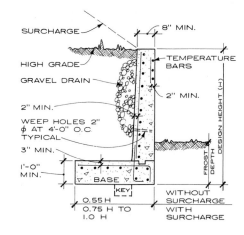

Soil pressure at toe equals 0.2 times the height in kips per square foot. Dimensions are preliminary.

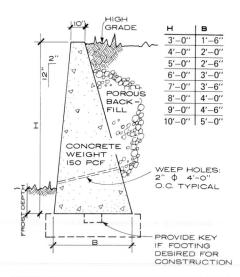

H	B
3'-0''	1'-6''
4'-0''	2'-0''
5'-0''	2'-6''
6'-0''	3'-0''
7'-0''	3'-6''
8'-0''	4'-0''
9'-0''	4'-6''
10'-0''	5'-0''

MASS CONCRETE RETAINING WALL WITHOUT SURCHARGE

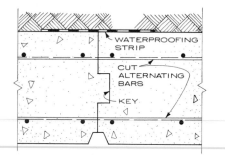

RETAINING WALL — VERTICAL CONTROL JOINT

RETAINING WALL — VERTICAL EXPANSION JOINT

NOTES

Provide control and/or construction joints in concrete retaining walls about every 25 ft and expansion joints about every fourth control and/or construction joint. Coated dowels should be used if average wall height on either side of a joint is different.

Consult with a structural engineer for final design of concrete retaining walls.

Use temperature bars if wall is more than 12 in. thick.

Keys shown dashed may be required to prevent sliding in high walls and those on moist clay.

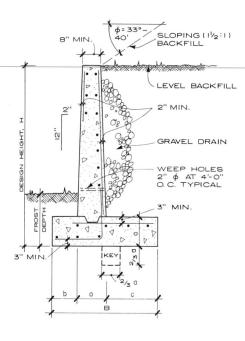

PRELIMINARY DIMENSIONS

BACKFILL SLOPING ϕ = 33° - 40' (1½:1)					BACKFILL LEVEL—NO SURCHARGE				
CONCRETE OUTLINES					CONCRETE OUTLINES				
HEIGHT OF WALL = H (FT)	B (FT)	a (FT)	b (FT)	c (FT)	HEIGHT OF WALL = H (FT)	B (FT)	a (FT)	b (FT)	c (FT)
3	2'-6''	0'-11''	0'-7''	1'-0''	3	1'-9''	0'-10½''	0'-4''	0'-6½''
4	3'-2''	1'-0''	0'-9''	1'-5''	4	2'-2''	0'-11''	0'-5''	0'-10''
5	3'-10''	1'-1''	1'-0''	1'-9''	5	2'-8''	0'-11''	0'-5''	1'-4''
6	4'-6''	1'-2''	1'-3''	2'-1''	6	3'-3''	1'-0''	0'-8''	1'-7''
7	5'-3''	1'-3''	1'-6''	2'-6''	7	3'-10''	1'-0''	1'-0''	1'-10''
8	5'-11''	1'-4''	1'-9''	2'-10''	8	4'-3''	1'-1''	1'-1''	2'-1''
9	6'-8''	1'-5''	2'-0''	3'-3''	9	4'-9''	1'-1''	1'-1''	2'-7''
10	7'-5''	1'-6''	2'-3''	3'-8''	10	5'-4''	1'-2''	1'-4''	2'-10''
11	8'-1''	1'-7''	2'-6''	4'-0''	11	5'-10''	1'-2''	1'-6''	3'-2''
12	8'-10''	1'-8''	2'-9''	4'-5''	12	6'-6''	1'-3''	1'-8''	3'-7''
13	9'-6''	1'-9''	3'-0''	4'-9''	13	7'-0''	1'-4''	1'-8''	4'-0''
14	10'-3''	1'-10''	3'-3''	5'-2''	14	7'-8''	1'-4''	2'-1''	4'-3''
15	11'-0''	1'-11''	3'-6''	5'-7''	15	8'-1''	1'-5''	2'-1''	4'-7''
16	11'-10''	2'-0''	3'-10''	6'-0''	16	8'-6''	1'-5''	2'-2''	4'-11''
17	12'-7''	2'-1''	4'-1''	6'-5''	17	9'-0''	1'-6''	2'-3''	5'-3''
18	13'-4''	2'-2''	4'-4''	6'-10''	18	9'-6''	1'-7''	2'-4''	5'-7''
19	14'-2''	2'-3''	4'-8''	7'-3''	19	10'-2''	1'-7''	2'-6''	6'-1''
20	15'-0''	2'-4''	5'-0''	7'-8''	20	10'-5''	1'-8''	2'-6''	6'-3''

Key shown dashed may be required to prevent sliding in high walls and those on moist clay.

CONCRETE OUTLINES FOR "T" TYPE RETAINING WALL WITH LEVEL AND SLOPING BACKFILL

Neubaur · Sohn, Engineers; Washington, D.C.

DIMENSIONS AND REINFORCEMENT

WALL	H	B	T	A	VERTICAL RODS IN THE WALL	HORIZONTAL RODS IN FOOTING
8 in. thickness	3'-4''	2'-4''	9''	8''	3/8'' @ 32''	3/8'' @ 27''
	4'-0''	2'-9''	9''	10''	1/2'' @ 32''	3/8'' @ 27''
	4'-8''	3'-3''	10''	12''	5/8'' @ 32''	3/8'' @ 27''
	5'-4''	3'-8''	10''	14''	1/2'' @ 16''	1/2'' @ 30''
	6'-0''	4'-2''	12''	15''	3/4'' @ 24''	1/2'' @ 25''

NOTE

These dimensions and reinforcement are for level backfill. Consult structural engineer for walls over 6 ft high, sloping fill, or vehicular loads.

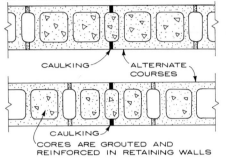

SHEAR - RESISTING CONTROL JOINT

NOTE

Long retaining walls should be broken into panels 20 to 30 ft in length by means of vertical control joints. Joints should be designed to resist shear and other lateral forces while permitting longitudinal movement.

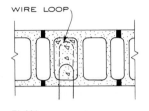

PLAN
VERTICAL ROD

NOTE

Place wire loop extending into core in mortar joints as wall is laid up. Loosen before mortar sets. After inserting bar, pull wire loop and bar to proper position and secure wire by tying free ends.

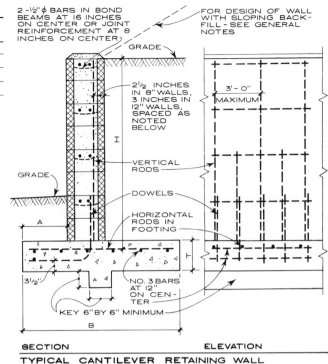

SECTION   **ELEVATION**
TYPICAL CANTILEVER RETAINING WALL

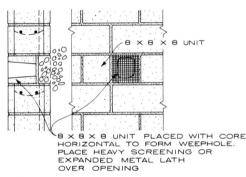

ALTERNATE WEEPHOLE DETAIL

NOTE

Four inch diameter weepholes located at 5 to 10 ft spacing along the base of the wall should be sufficient. Place about 1 cu ft of gravel or crushed stone around the intake of each weephole.

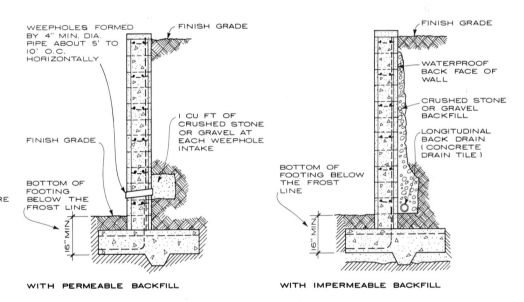

WITH PERMEABLE BACKFILL   **WITH IMPERMEABLE BACKFILL**

BACKFILLING PROCEDURES AND DRAINAGE

GENERAL NOTES

1. Concrete for footings should be mixed in the following approximate proportions: 1 part portland cement, 2 3/4 parts sand, and 4 parts gravel. Gravel should be well graded and not exceed 1 1/2 in. in size. Amount of water used for each bag of cement should not exceed 5 1/2 gal unless the sand is very dry.
2. Use fine grout where grout space is less than 3 in. in least dimension. Use coarse grout where the least dimension of the grout space is 3 in. or more.
3. Steel reinforcement should be clean, free from harmful rust, and in compliance with applicable ASTM standards for deformed bars and steel wire.
4. Alternate vertical bars may be stopped at the midheight of the wall. Vertical reinforcement is usually secured in place after the masonry work has been completed and before grouting.

5. Designs herein are based on an assumed soil weight (vertical pressure) of 100 pcf. Horizontal pressure is based on an equivalent fluid weight for the soil of 45 pcf.
6. Walls shown are designed with a safety factor against overturning of not less than 2 and a safety factor against horizontal sliding of not less than 1.5. Computations in the table for wall heights are based on level backfill. One method of providing for additional loads due to sloping backfill or surface loads is to consider them as an additional depth of soil, that is, an extra load of 300 psf can be treated as 3 ft of extra soil weighing 100 psf.
7. Top of masonry retaining walls should be capped or otherwise protected to prevent the entry of water into unfilled hollow cells and spaces. If bond beams are used, steel is placed in the beams as the wall is constructed. If desired, horizontal

joint reinforcement may be placed in each joint (8 in. o.c.) and the bond beams omitted.
8. Allow 24 hr for masonry to set before grouting. Pour grout in 4 ft layers, 1 hr between each pour. Break long walls into panels of 20 to 30 ft in length with vertical control joints. Allow 7 days for finished wall to set before backfilling. Prevent water from accumulating behind wall by means of 4 in. diameter weepholes at a 5 to 10 ft spacing (with screen and graded stone) or by a continuous drain with felt covered open joints in combination with waterproofing.
9. Where backfill exceeds 6 ft in height, provide a key under the base of the footing to resist the tendency of the wall to slide horizontally.
10. Heavy equipment used in backfilling should not approach closer to the top of the wall than a distance equal to the height of the wall.

Stephen J. Zipp, AIA; Wilkes and Faulkner Associates; Washington, D.C.

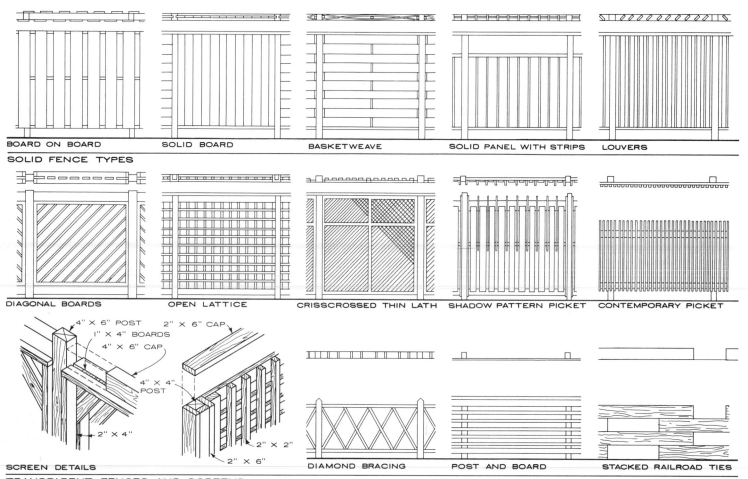

BOARD ON BOARD   SOLID BOARD   BASKETWEAVE   SOLID PANEL WITH STRIPS   LOUVERS

SOLID FENCE TYPES

DIAGONAL BOARDS   OPEN LATTICE   CRISSCROSSED THIN LATH   SHADOW PATTERN PICKET   CONTEMPORARY PICKET

SCREEN DETAILS   DIAMOND BRACING   POST AND BOARD   STACKED RAILROAD TIES

TRANSPARENT FENCES AND SCREENS

GENERAL NOTES

The following issues should be considered when selecting a wood fence pattern:

1. The topography of the site and the prevailing wind conditions.
2. The architectural style of surrounding buildings as well as the adjacent use of land.
3. The required height of the fence and the size of the property to be enclosed.

Wood fences can be constructed as solid walls and used near buildings for protection and privacy of outdoor spaces. A semitransparent wood screen is often used to enclose an outdoor room without totally obstructing views or restricting natural ventilation. Long open fence patterns are best used at the property line to define boundaries or limit access to a site.

MATERIALS

Wood posts and rails are usually made of red or white oak, western larch, many species of pine, eastern red cedar, or redwood. Wood or aluminum caps should be used wherever end grains are exposed to the weather.

Most heartwoods, especially cedar and redwood, have superior natural resistance to decay. Other exposed wood members should be treated with water soluble preservatives such as chromated copper arsenate (CCA) or pentachlorophenol dissolved in a volatile solvent. Creosote or pentachlorophenal in an oil solvent should be avoided, since they do not mix with stains or paints.

Uncoated wood rapidly weathers to a shade of gray. A broad range of colors are obtainable with standard paints, bleaches, and stains. Clear water repellents may be used with redwood and cedar. Natural finishes or penetrating stains allow more of the wood grain to show than paint and are preferable for severe weather exposures. Varnishes deteriorate rapidly in sunlight and water.

Fasteners should be of noncorrosive aluminum alloy or stainless steel. Top quality, hot dip galvanized steel is acceptable. Metal flanges, cleats, bolts, and screws are better than common nails.

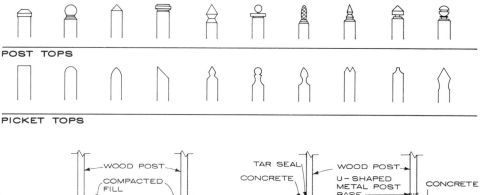

POST TOPS

PICKET TOPS

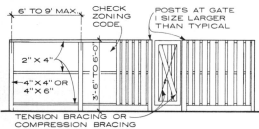

TYPICAL FENCE DIMENSIONS

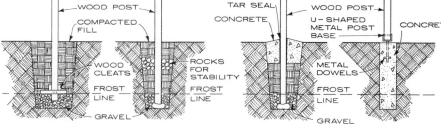

FOOTING DETAILS

Charles R. Heuer, AIA; Washington, D.C.

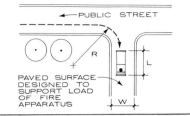

FIRE APPARATUS ACCESS

Fire apparatus (i.e., pumpers, ladder trucks, tankers) should have unobstructed access to buildings. Check with local fire department for apparatus turning radius (R), length (L), and other operating characteristics.

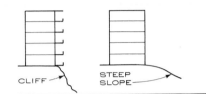

RESTRICTED ACCESS

Be sure that buildings constructed near cliffs or steep slopes do not restrict access by fire apparatus to only one side of building. Grades greater than 10% make operation of fire apparatus difficult and dangerous.

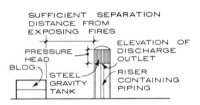

GRAVITY TANK

Gravity tanks can provide reliable source of pressure to building standpipe or sprinkler systems. Available pressure head increases by 0.434 psi/ft increase of water above tank discharge outlet. Tank capacity in gallons depends on fire hazard, water supply, and other factors. Tanks require periodic maintenance and protection against freezing during cold weather. Locations subject to seismic forces or high winds require special consideration. Gravity tanks also can be integrated within building design.

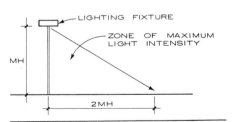

OUTDOOR LIGHTING

Streets that are properly lighted enable fire fighters to locate hydrants quickly and to position apparatus at night. Avoid layouts that place hydrants and standpipe connections in shadows. In some situations, lighting fixtures can be integrated into exterior of buildings. All buildings should have a street address number on or near the main entrance.

M. David Egan, P.E.; College of Architecture, Clemson University; Clemson, South Carolina

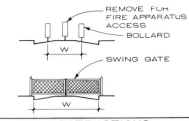

ACCESS OBSTRUCTIONS

Bollards used for traffic control and fences for security should allow sufficient open road width (W) for access by fire apparatus. Bollards and gates can be secured by standard fire department keyed locks (check with department having jurisdiction).

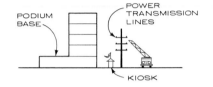

STREET FURNITURE AND ARCHITECTURAL OBSTRUCTIONS

Utility poles can obstruct use of aerial ladders for rescue and fire supression operations. Kiosks, outdoor sculpture, fountains, newspaper boxes, and the like can also seriously impede fire fighting operations. Wide podium bases can prevent ladder access to the upper stories of buildings. Canopies and other nonstructural building components can also prevent fire apparatus operations close to buildings.

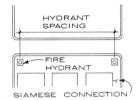

FIRE HYDRANT AND STANDPIPE CONNECTION LAYOUT

Locate fire hydrants at street intersections and at intermediate points along roads so that spacing between hydrants does not exceed about 300 ft. (Check with local authority having fire jurisdiction for specific requirements.) Hydrants should be placed 2 to 10 ft from curb lines. Siamese connections to standpipes should be visible, marked conspicuously, and be within 200 ft of hydrant to allow rapid connection by fire fighters.

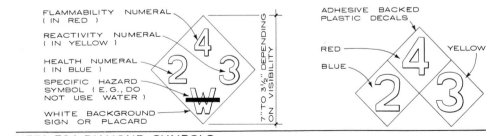

NFPA 704 DIAMOND SYMBOLS

Standard diamond symbols provide information fire fighters need to avoid injury from hazardous building contents. 0 numeral is the lowest degree of hazard, 4 is highest. Locate symbols near building entrances. Correct spatial arrangement for two kinds of diamond symbols are shown. Consider integrating symbols with overall graphics design of building. (Refer to "Identification of the Fire Hazards of Materials," NFPA No. 704, available from the National Fire Protection Association.)

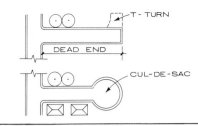

DRIVEWAY LAYOUTS

Long dead ends (greater than 150 ft) can cause time consuming, hazardous backup maneuvers. Use t-turns, culs-de-sacs, and curved driveway layouts to allow unimpeded access to buildings.

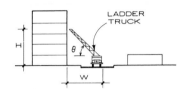

DRIVEWAY WIDTHS

For full extension of aerial ladders at a safe climbing angle (θ), sufficient driveway width (W) is required. Estimate the required width in feet by: $W = (H - 6) \cot \theta + 4$, where preferred climbing angles are 60 to 80°. Check with local fire department for aerial apparatus operating requirements.

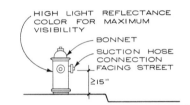

FIRE HYDRANT PLACEMENT

Fire hose connections should be at least 15″ above grade. Do not bury hydrants or locate them behind shrubs or other visual barriers. Avoid locations where runoff water and snow can accumulate. Bollards and fences used to protect hydrants from vehicular traffic must not obstruct fire fighters' access to hose connections. Suction hose connection should usually face the side of arriving fire apparatus.

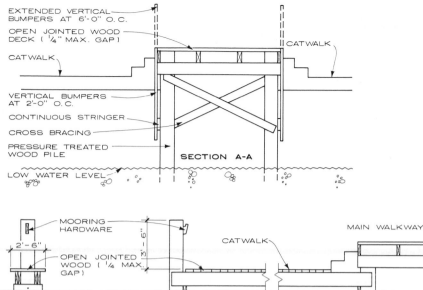

SECTION A-A

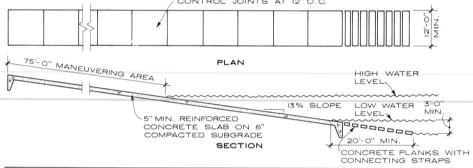

SLIP AND CATWALK CONSTRUCTION

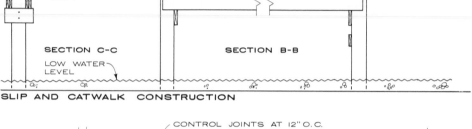

BOAT LAUNCHING RAMP

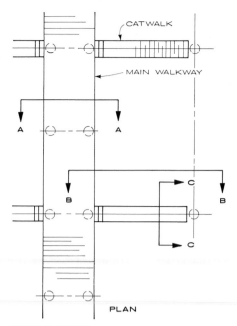

PLAN

GENERAL NOTES

1. Wood marine construction must be pressure treated with a preservative. Wood preservatives for use in marine applications fall into two general categories, creosote and waterborne. To select a specific preservative from within these categories, the decaying agents must be identified. A preservative may then be chosen based on the recommendations of the American Wood Preservers Institute.
2. Waterborne preservatives are recommended for decks because creosote stains shoes and bare feet.
3. The preservatives selected should be approved by the Environmental Protection Agency.
4. Dock height above water is determined by average deck level and probable water level. Maintain a 12 in. minimum dimension between water and deck. Floating docks may be required in tidal waters. Consult manufacturer for construction information.
5. Cross bracing should be minimized to avoid entanglement of swimmers.

LAUNCHING RAMPS

1. Launching ramps are for sheltered waters only.
2. A catwalk may be provided alongside the ramp.
3. Floating ramps may be required in tidal waters.

TABLE OF DIMENSIONS FOR SLIPS AND CATWALKS TO BE USED WITH DIAGRAM

LENGTH GROUP FOR BOAT	BEAM TO BE PROVIDED FOR	MIN. CLEAR WIDTH OF SLIP	GROSS SLIP WIDTH TYPE A	GROSS SLIP WIDTH TYPE B	GROSS SLIP WIDTH TYPE C	1ST CATWALK SPAN LENGTH D	2ND CATWALK SPAN LENGTH E	3RD CATWALK SPAN LENGTH F	DISTANCE G TO ANCHOR PILE
Up to 14'	6'–7"	8'–10"	10'–9"	10'–6"	11'–2"	12'–0"			17'–0"
Over 14' to 16'	7'–4"	9'–8"	11'–7"	11'–4"	12'–0"	12'–0"			19'–0"
Over 16' to 18'	8'–0"	10'–5"	12'–4"	12'–1"	12'–9"	14'–0"			21'–0"
Over 18' to 20'	8'–7"	11'–1"	13'–0"	12'–9"	13'–5"	8'–0"	8'–0"		23'–0"
Over 20' to 22'	9'–3"	11'–9"	13'–8"	13'–5"	14'–1"	10'–0"	8'–0"		25'–0"
Over 22' to 25'	10'–3"	13'–1"	15'–0"	14'–9"	15'–5"	10'–0"	8'–0"		28'–0"
Over 25' to 30'	11'–3"	14'–3"	16'–2"	15'–11"	16'–7"	10'–0"	10'–0"		33'–0"
Over 30' to 35'	12'–3"	15'–8"	17'–7"	17'–4"	18'–0"	12'–0"	10'–0"		38'–0"
Over 35' to 40'	13'–3"	16'–11"	18'–10"	18'–7"	19'–3"	12'–0"	12'–0"		43'–0"
Over 40' to 45'	14'–1"	17'–11"	19'–10"	19'–7"	20'–3"	14'–0"	12'–0"		48'–0"
Over 45' to 50'	14'–11"	19'–0"	20'–11"	20'–8"	21'–4"	9'–0"	9'–0"	10'–0"	53'–0"
Over 50' to 60'	16'–6"	21'–0"	22'–11"	22'–8"	23'–4"	11'–0"	11'–0"	12'–0"	63'–0"
Over 60' to 70'	18'–1"	23'–0"	26'–8"	24'–8"	25'–4"	11'–0"	11'–0"	12'–0"	73'–0"
Over 70' to 80'	19'–9"	24'–11"	28'–7"	26'–7"	26'–3"	11'–0"	11'–0"	12'–0"	83'–0"

David E. Rose; Rossen/Neumann Associates; Southfield, Michigan

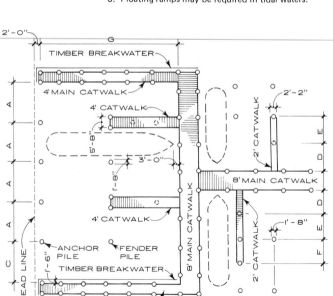

DIAGRAM

CHAPTER 3 CONCRETE

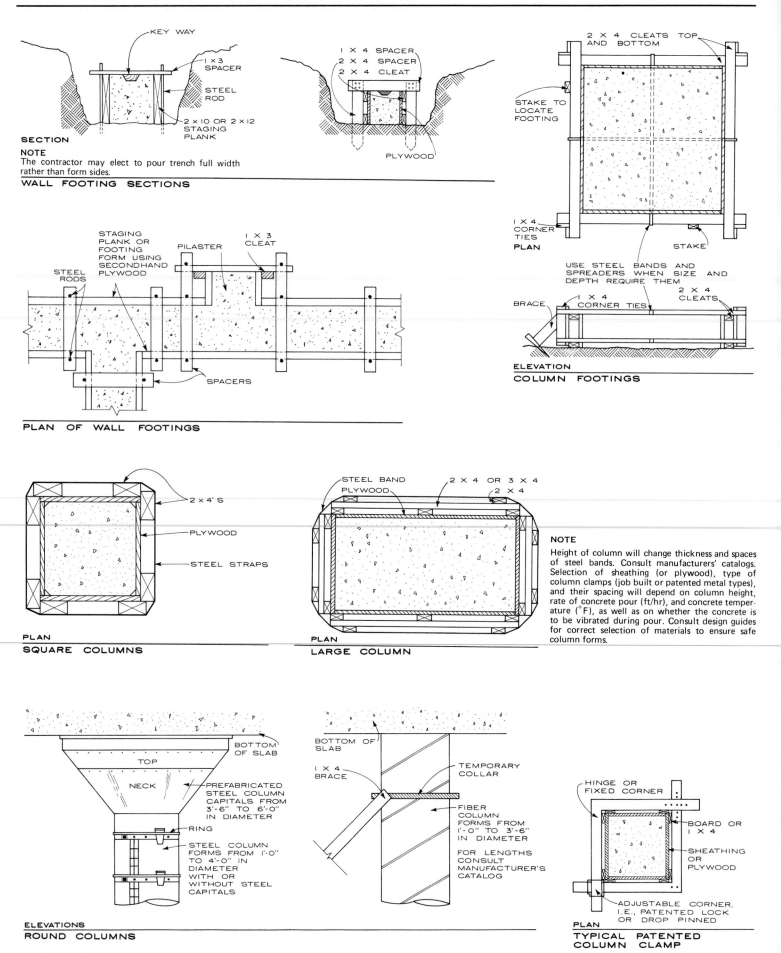

SECTION

NOTE

The contractor may elect to pour trench full width rather than form sides.

WALL FOOTING SECTIONS

PLAN OF WALL FOOTINGS

PLAN
SQUARE COLUMNS

PLAN
LARGE COLUMN

PLAN

ELEVATION
COLUMN FOOTINGS

NOTE

Height of column will change thickness and spaces of steel bands. Consult manufacturers' catalogs. Selection of sheathing (or plywood), type of column clamps (job built or patented metal types), and their spacing will depend on column height, rate of concrete pour (ft/hr), and concrete temperature (°F), as well as on whether the concrete is to be vibrated during pour. Consult design guides for correct selection of materials to ensure safe column forms.

ELEVATIONS
ROUND COLUMNS

PLAN
TYPICAL PATENTED COLUMN CLAMP

Tucker Concrete Form Co.; Malden, Massachusetts

3   CONCRETE FORMWORK

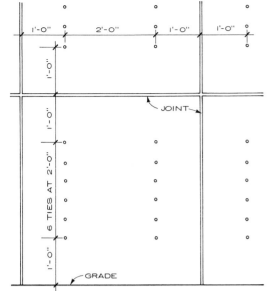

ELEVATION

EXPOSED CONCRETE WITH RUSTICATION STRIP (IF DESIRED)

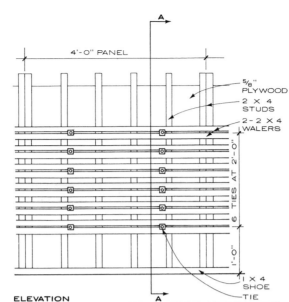

ELEVATION

SAMPLE WALL FORM

Mortar-tight forms are required for architectural exposed concrete. Consult manufacturers' literature on the proper use of metal forms or plywood forms with metal frames.

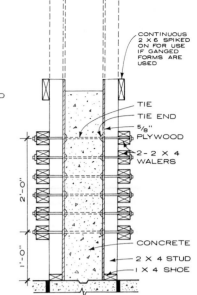

SECTION A-A

The section above will change if there are any variations in the thickness of plywood used, the type and strength of ties, or the size of studs and walers.

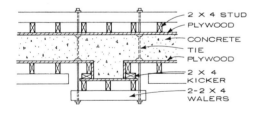

HORIZONTAL STRIP   **VERTICAL STRIP**

RUSTICATION STRIPS

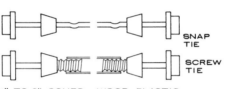

SNAP TIE

SCREW TIE

1" TO 2" CONES — WOOD, PLASTIC, STEEL ARE AVAILABLE

TYPICAL TIES

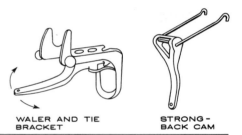

WALER AND TIE BRACKET   **STRONG-BACK CAM**

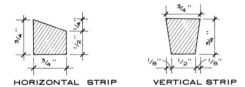

PLAN

SMALL PILASTER

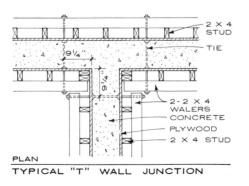

PLAN

TYPICAL CORNER

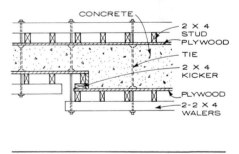

PLAN

TYPICAL WALL WITH OFFSET

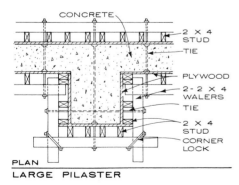

PLAN

LARGE PILASTER

PLAN

TYPICAL "T" WALL JUNCTION

FORM DESIGN NOTES

1. Pressure depends on rate of pour (ft/hr) and concrete temperature (°F). Vibration of concrete is also a factor in form pressure.
2. Provide cleanout doors at bottom of wall forms.
3. Various types of form ties are on the market. Some are not suitable for architectural concrete work, i.e., they cannot be withdrawn from the concrete.
4. Various plastic cones 1½ in. in diameter and ½ in. deep can be used and the holes are left ungrouted to form a type of architectural feature.
5. Consult manufacturers' catalogs for form design and tie strength information.

Tucker Concrete Form Company; Malden, Massachusetts

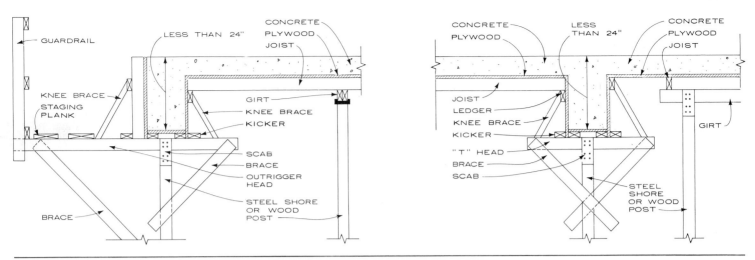

TYPICAL SLAB AND SHALLOW BEAM FORMING

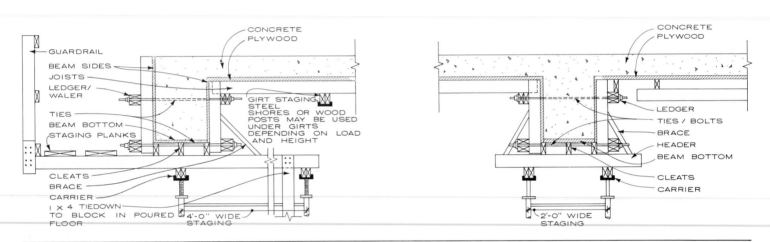

TYPICAL SLAB AND HEAVY BEAM FORMING

NOTES

1. Staging, steel shores, or wood posts may be used under girts depending on loads and height requirements.

2. For flat slabs of flat plate forming, metal "flying forms" are commonly used.

3. Patented steel forms or fillers are also available for nontypical conditions on special order. See manufacturer's catalogs. Fiber forms, too, are on the market in similar sizes. Plywood deck is required for forming.

4. $5/8$ in. exterior plywood is the thickness of stock used on all details.

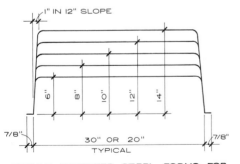

TYPICAL PATENTED STEEL FORMS FOR CONCRETE JOIST FLOOR SYSTEM

NOTE

Smaller filler sizes are available for nontypical conditions.

See manufacturer's catalogs.
Fiber forms also on market in similar size.
Plywood deck is required for forming.

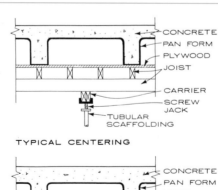

TYPICAL CENTERING

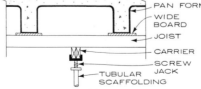

ALTERNATE SYSTEM

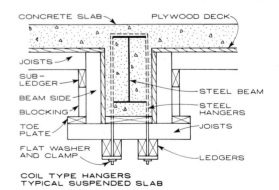

COIL TYPE HANGERS TYPICAL SUSPENDED SLAB

Tucker Concrete Form Co.; Malden, Massachusetts

3 **CONCRETE FORMWORK**

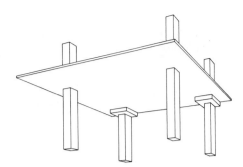

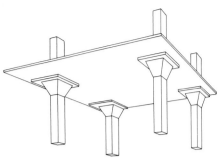

FLAT SLABS TO HAVE DROP
PANELS OR COLUMN CAPITALS.
FOR SUPERIMPOSED LOADS
OVER 100 PSF, USE BOTH DROP
PANELS AND COLUMN CAPITALS

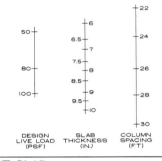

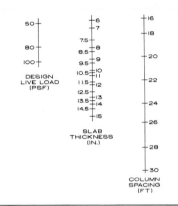

DESIGN
LIVE LOAD
(PSF)

SLAB
THICKNESS
(IN.)

COLUMN
SPACING
(FT)

FLAT PLATE

DESIGN
LIVE LOAD
(PSF)

SLAB
THICKNESS
(IN.)

COLUMN
SPACING
(FT)

FLAT SLAB

DESIGN
LIVE LOAD
(PSF)

SLAB
THICKNESS
(IN.)

COLUMN
SPACING
(FT)

TWO-WAY SOLID SLAB

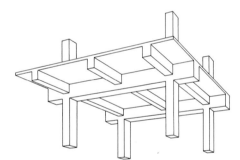

TAPERED PANS AT GIRDER TO
RESIST SHEAR FORCES

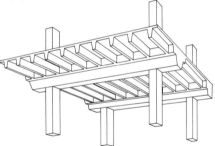

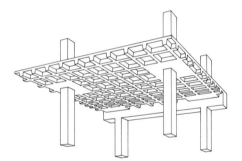

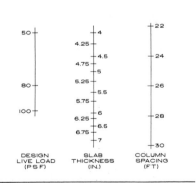

DESIGN
LIVE LOAD
(PSF)

SLAB
THICKNESS
(IN.)

COLUMN
SPACING
(FT)

ONE-WAY SOLID SLAB
(SPAN = ½ THE COLUMN SPACING)

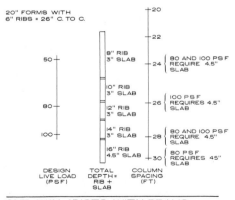

20" FORMS WITH
6" RIBS = 26" C. TO C.

8" RIB
3" SLAB

10" RIB
3" SLAB

12" RIB
3" SLAB

14" RIB
3" SLAB

16" RIB
4.5" SLAB

80 AND 100 PSF
REQUIRE 4.5"
SLAB

100 PSF
REQUIRES 4.5"
SLAB

80 AND 100 PSF
REQUIRE 4.5"
SLAB

80 PSF
REQUIRES 45"
SLAB

DESIGN
LIVE LOAD
(PSF)

TOTAL
DEPTH=
RIB +
SLAB

COLUMN
SPACING
(FT)

ONE-WAY JOISTS WITH BEAMS
(METAL PAN CONSTRUCTION)

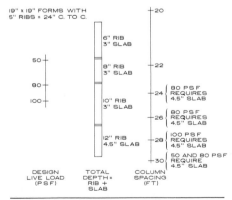

19" x 19" FORMS WITH
5" RIBS = 24" C. TO C.

6" RIB
3" SLAB

8" RIB
3" SLAB

10" RIB
3" SLAB

12" RIB
4.5" SLAB

80 PSF
REQUIRES
4.5" SLAB

80 PSF
REQUIRES
4.5" SLAB

100 PSF
REQUIRES
4.5" SLAB

50 AND 80 PSF
REQUIRE
4.5" SLAB

DESIGN
LIVE LOAD
(PSF)

TOTAL
DEPTH=
RIB +
SLAB

COLUMN
SPACING
(FT)

TWO-WAY JOISTS WITHOUT BEAMS
(WAFFLE FLAT PLATE
CONSTRUCTION)

To use bar graphs, lay straight edge across chart and line up with design live load required on left bar and with selected column spacing on right bar. Slab thickness required is indicated where straight edge intersects center bar.

The examples above are all calculated by the ultimate design strength method around the following parameters:

1. Concrete strength of 4000 psi at 28 days.
2. Steel reinforcing strength of 60,000 psi.
3. Steel to concrete ratio of minimum steel.

The information represented on this page is intended to be used as a preliminary design guide only and not to replace complete analysis and calculation of each project condition by a licensed professional engineer.

Killebrew/Rucker/Associates, Inc.; Architects/Planners/Engineers; Wichita Falls, Texas

CAST-IN-PLACE CONCRETE CONSTRUCTION: PRELIMINARY DATA

REINFORCED CONCRETE

Reinforced concrete consists of concrete and reinforcing steel; the concrete resists the compressive stresses and the reinforcing steel resists the tensile stresses.

Concrete is a mixture of hydraulic cement (usually portland cement), aggregate, admixtures, and water. The concrete strength develops by the hydration of the portland cement, which binds the aggregates together.

TYPES OF CEMENT

Five types of portland cement are manufactured to meet ASTM standards.

Type I is a general purpose cement for all uses when special properties, such as resistance to sulfate attack by water in the soil or the heat of hydration would be undesirable, are not required.

Type II cement provides moderate protection from sulfate attack for concrete in drainage structures and a lower heat of hydration for concrete use in heavy retaining walls, piers, and abutments.

Type III cement provides high strengths at an early age, a week or less. Type III is used when rapid removal of forms is desired and in cold weather to reduce time of controlled curing conditions.

Type IV cement has a low heat of hydration and is used for massive concrete structures such as gravity dams.

Type V cement is sulfate resisting cement for use where the soil and groundwater have a high sulfate content.

ADMIXTURES

Admixtures are various compounds, other than cement, water, and aggregates, added to a mixture to modify the fresh or hardened properties of concrete.

Air entraining admixtures disperse small air bubbles in the concrete, which improves the concrete's resistance to freezing and thawing and to scaling by deicing chemicals. Recommended total air contents are shown in Table 1 for different exposure conditions and for maximum size of aggregate.

Water reducing admixtures reduce the quantity of mixing water needed for a given consistency and may delay the set time and entrain air.

Other mixtures are used to retard or accelerate the set of concrete.

Some water reducing and accelerating admixtures may increase dry shrinkage.

Pozzolans can be used to reduce the amount of cement in a concrete mix.

Superplasticizers allow for much lower water-cement ratios to be used than with the usual water reducing admixtures.

AGGREGATES

The aggregate portion of a concrete mix is divided into fine and coarse aggregates. The fine aggregate generally is sand of particles less than $3/8$ in. large. The coarse aggregate is crushed stone or gravel greater than $3/8$ in. Sand, crushed rock, or gravel concrete weighs 135 to 165 pcf. Lightweight aggregate is manufactured from expanded shale, slate, clay, or slag, and the concrete weighs from 85 to 115 pcf.

Normal weight aggregates must meet ASTM Specification C33.

The aggregate represents 60 to 80% of the volume of the concrete, and the gradation (range of particle sizes) affects the amount of cement and water required in the mix, the physical properties during placing and finishing, and the compressive strength. Aggregates should be clean, hard, strong, and free of surface materials.

REINFORCING STEEL

Reinforcing steel, manufactured as round rods with raised deformations for adhesion and resistance to slip in the concrete, is available in several grades (yield strengths) and diameters manufactured to ASTM standards. Commonly used reinforcing rods have yield strengths of 40,000 and 60,000 psi available in sizes from #3 to #18, the size being the diameter in eighths of an inch. Welded wire mesh has yield strengths of 60,000 to 70,000 psi, and the wire is either plain or deformed.

Table 3 summarizes the various grades of reinforcing steel, and Figure 1 shows the system of reinforcing rod identification.

SLUMP TEST

The standard slump cone test is only to determine the consistency among batches of concrete of the same mix design; it should not be used to compare mixes of greatly different mix proportions. A slump test mold is a funnel shaped sheet metal form that is 12 in. high, 8 in. in diameter at the base, and 4 in. in diameter at the top. The slump mold is filled from the top in three levels, each level being tamped 25 times with a $5/8$ in. diameter rod. After the top is smoothed evenly, the mold is slowly removed, allowing the concrete to slump down from its original height. The metal mold is

placed next to the slumped concrete, and the difference from the tops of each is measured in inches. A "right" slump consistency does not exist for all concrete work. It can vary from 1 to 6 in., depending on the specific requirements of the job. Table 2 lists typical slumps for various types of construction. Workability is the ease or difficulty of placing, consolidating, and finishing the concrete. Concrete should be workable and should not segregate or bleed excessively before finishing.

CYLINDER TEST

A major problem with concrete tests is that the most important data, the compressive strength, cannot be determined until after curing has begun. This occasionally has caused the removal of deficient concrete several weeks after it was placed. A compression test is made by placing three layers of concrete in a cardboard cylinder 6 in. in diameter and 12 in. high. Each layer is rodded 25 times with a $5/8$ in. diameter steel rod. The cylinder should be protected from damage but placed in the same temperature and humidity environment as the concrete from which the sample was obtained. At the end of the test curing time, usually determined to be 7 or 28 days, the outer cylinder is removed and placed in a press. The point at which the cylinder fails in compression is registered on a gauge in pounds, and the strength of the concrete is calculated in pounds per square inch.

PLACING CONCRETE

Concrete should be placed as near its final position as possible and should not be moved horizontally in forms because segregation of the mortar from the coarser material may occur. Concrete should be placed in horizontal layers of uniform thickness, each layer being thoroughly consolidated before the next layer is positioned.

Consolidation of concrete can be achieved either by hand tamping or rodding and by mechanical internal or external vibration. The frequency and amplitude of an internal mechanical vibration should be appropriate for the plastic properties (stiffness or slump) and space in the forms to prevent segregation of the concrete during placing.

External vibration can be accomplished by surface vibration for thin sections (slabs) that cannot be practically consolidated by internal vibration. Surface vibrators may be used directly on the surface of slabs or with plates attached to the concrete form stiffeners. External vibration must be done for a longer time (1 to 2 min) than for internal vibration (5 to 15 sec) to achieve the same consolidation.

TABLE 1. RECOMMENDED AIR CONTENT PERCENTAGE

NOMINAL MAXIMUM SIZE OF COARSE AGGREGATE (IN.)	EXPOSURE	
	MILD	EXTREME
$3/8$ (10 mm)	4.5	7.5
$1/2$ (13 mm)	4.0	6.0
$3/4$ (19 mm)	3.5	6.0
1 (25 mm)	3.0	6.0
$1^1/_2$ (40 mm)	2.5	5.5
2 (50 mm)	2.0	5.0
3 (75 mm)	1.5	4.5

TABLE 2. RECOMMENDED SLUMPS FOR VARIOUS TYPES OF CONSTRUCTION

CONCRETE CONSTRUCTION	SLUMP (IN.)	
	MAXIMUM*	MINIMUM
Reinforced foundation walls and footings	3	1
Plain footings, caissons, and substructure walls	3	1
Beams and reinforced walls	4	1
Building columns	4	1
Pavements and slabs	3	1
Mass concrete	2	1

*May be increased 1 in. for consolidation by hand methods such as rodding and spading.

Quentin L. Reutershan, AIA, Architect; Potsdam, New York

Gordon B. Batson, P.E.; Potsdam, New York

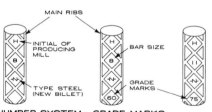

NUMBER SYSTEM — GRADE MARKS

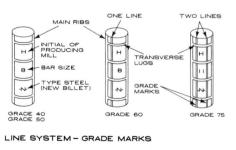

LINE SYSTEM — GRADE MARKS

FIGURE 1. REINFORCING BAR IDENTIFICATION

TABLE 3. REINFORCING STEEL GRADES AND STRENGTHS

DEFORMED BILLET	MINIMUM YIELD POINT OR YIELD STRENGTH (PSI)	ULTIMATE STRENGTH (PSI)
ASTM A-615		
Grade 40	40,000	70,000
Grade 50	50,000	90,000
Rail steel ASTM A-616		
Grade 50	50,000	80,000
Grade 60	60,000	90,000
Axly steel ASTM A-617		
Grade 40	40,000	70,000
Grade 60	50,000	90,000
Deformed wire ASTM A-496 Welded fabric	70,000	80,000
Cold drawn ASTM A-82 Welded fabric		
< W 1.2 Size	56,000	70,000
≥ W 1.2	65,000	75,000

CAST-IN-PLACE CONCRETE CONSTRUCTION: PRELIMINARY DATA

PROPERTIES OF CONCRETE

Minimum concrete compressive strength at 28 days of age is generally stated in contract specifications for the concrete in various structural elements, such as columns, beams, slabs, and foundations. The normal 28-day compressive strength for commercial-ready mix concrete is 3000 to 4000 psi; however, higher strengths of 5000 to 7000 psi are generally required for pre- or posttensioned concrete and higher strengths of 10,000 to 12,000 psi may be required for highrise concrete structures.

A design mix for 3000 psi concrete with a 20% safety factor would be 517 lb of cement (5½ sacks), 1300 lb of sand, 1800 lb of gravel, and 34 gal of water (6.2 gal per sack), which would yield a cu yd of concrete, the standard unit of measure.

The compressive strength depends primarily on the type of cement, water-cement ratio, and the quality of the aggregate; the most important strength determining parameter is the water-cement ratio. The lower the water-cement ratio, the greater the compressive strength for workable mixes.

Figure 2 shows the general relationship between compressive strength of Type I cements and the water-cement ratio expressed in terms of weight of water per 100 lb of cement cured for 1 and 28 days. Table 4 lists recommended water-cement ratios for different types of structures and exposures, and Table 5 lists maximum water-cement ratios.

When cement, aggregate, and water are mixed, a chemical reaction is started that is independent of drying. Concrete does not need air to cure. It can set under water. Water starts the reaction. Concrete sets or becomes firm within hours after it has been mixed, but curing, the process of attaining strength, takes considerably longer. Standard (Type 1) cement is assumed to achieve 100% of its designed compressive strength 28 days after mixing. The majority of the strength is achieved in the first days of curing. Approximately 50% of the total compressive strength is reached in 3 days; 70% is reached in 7 days. The remaining 30% occurs in the last 21 days at a much slower rate. The compressive strength of the concrete may continue to increase beyond the designed strength, as shown in Figure 3.

Normal unit weight concrete is 145 to 155 pcf, and lightweight concrete varies from 100 to 115 pcf. Lightweight concrete can be used to reduce the dead load of a structure.

CURING AND PROTECTION

Two physical properties have a very pronounced effect on the final compressive strength and curing attained by concrete—temperature and the rate at which the water used in mixing is allowed to leave the concrete. The optimum temperature for curing concrete is 73°F

(22.8°C). Any great variance from this mark reduces its compressive strength. Freezing concrete during curing not only affects the compressive strength but also greatly reduces the ability of the material to resist weathering.

Proper curing of concrete is essential if the design strength of concrete mix is to be obtained. This requires that moisture be available for the hydration of the cement at temperatures above 50°F and that the concrete be protected against temperatures below 40°F during the early stages of curing.

Hydration is a chemical reaction between the water and the lime in the cement when concrete is curing. The longer the water is presented in the concrete, the longer the reaction takes place, hence the stronger it becomes.

Moisture conditions can be maintained by sprinkling wet coverings of burlap or mats, waterproof paper, or plastic sheets over concrete, plastic sheets placed on ground before slab is poured, liquid curing compound sprayed on the surface of fresh concrete, and concrete left in forms for a longer period.

HOT AND COLD WEATHER CONSTRUCTION

Hot and cold weather construction requires that additional precautions be taken to ensure proper curing of the concrete. High temperatures accelerate the hardening of concrete and more water is needed to maintain the consistency of the mix and more cement is required to prevent a strength reduction due to the added water. Chilled water or ice may be used to reduce the temperature of the aggregates, and admixtures can be used to retard the initial set. Hot weather construction begins at temperatures ranging from 75°F to 100°F.

Generally in cold weather heat must be provided to keep the concrete above 40°F during placing and the early stages of curing for a period of 7 days. Protection against freezing may be necessary for up to 2 weeks. This is accomplished by covering the concrete with plastic sheets and heating the interior space with a portable heater called a salamander. Type III and IIIA cement, low water-cement ratio, accelerator type admixtures, and steam curing can be employed to reduce the time the concrete must be protected. Concrete should never be placed directly on frozen ground. Fresh concrete that has frozen during curing should be removed and replaced because frozen concrete containing ice crystals has very little strength.

PROPORTION OF STRUCTURAL ELEMENTS

Rules of thumb for approximating proportions of solid rectangular beams and slabs are one inch of depth for each foot of span, and the beam width is about two-thirds the depth. The area of steel will vary from 1 to 2% of cross-sectional area of the beam or slab. Columns will generally have higher steel percentages than beams. The maximum for columns is 8% of the cross-sectional area; however, the common range is 3 to 6%.

TABLE 4. MAXIMUM WATER-CEMENT RATIOS FOR VARIOUS EXPOSURE CONDITIONS

EXPOSURE CONDITION	NORMAL WEIGHT CONCRETE, ABSOLUTE WATER-CEMENT RATIO BY WEIGHT
Concrete protected from exposure to freezing and thawing or application of deicer chemicals	Select water-cement ratio on basis of strength, workability, and finishing needs
Watertight concrete* In fresh water In seawater	0.50 0.45
Frost resistant concrete* Thin sections; any section with less than 2-in. cover over reinforcement and any concrete exposed to deicing salts	0.45
All other structures	0.50
Exposure to sulfates* Moderate Severe	0.50 0.45
Placing concrete under water	Not less than 650 lb of cement per cubic yard (386 kg/m³)
Floors on grade	Select water-cement ratio for strength, plus minimum cement requirements

*Contain entrained air within the limits of Table 1.

TABLE 5. MAXIMUM PERMISSIBLE WATER-CEMENT RATIOS FOR CONCRETE WHEN STRENGTH DATA FROM TRIAL BATCHES OR FIELD EXPERIENCE ARE NOT AVAILABLE

SPECIFIED COMPRESSIVE STRENGTH F_c' (PSI*)	MAXIMUM ABSOLUTE PERMISSIBLE WATER-CEMENT RATIO, BY WEIGHT	
	NON AIR ENTRAINED CONCRETE	AIR ENTRAINED CONCRETE
2500	0.67	0.54
3000	0.58	0.46
3500	0.51	0.40
4000	0.44	0.35
4500	0.38	†
5000	†	†

NOTE: 1000 psi ≈ 7 MPa.
*28-day strength. With most materials, the water-cement ratios shown will provide average strengths greater than required.
†For strengths above 4500 psi (non air entrained concrete) and 4000 psi (air entrained concrete), proportions should be established by the trial batch method.

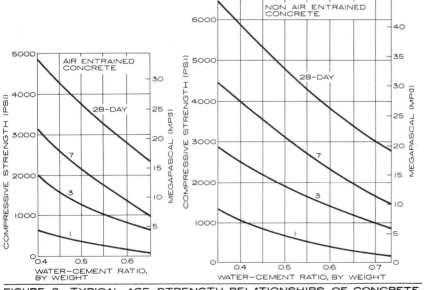

FIGURE 2. TYPICAL AGE-STRENGTH RELATIONSHIPS OF CONCRETE BASED ON COMPRESSION TESTS OF CYLINDERS, USING TYPE I CEMENT AND MOIST-CURING AT 70°F

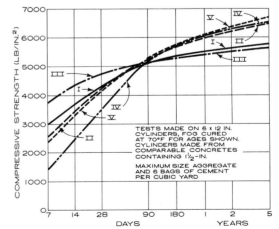

FIGURE 3. RATES OF STRENGTH DEVELOPMENT FOR CONCRETE MADE WITH VARIOUS TYPES OF CEMENT

Quentin L. Reutershan, AIA, Architect; Potsdam, New York

Gordon B. Batson, P.E.; Potsdam, New York

ASTM STANDARD REINFORCING BAR SIZES—NOMINAL DIAMETER

BAR SIZE DESIGNATION	WEIGHT PER FOOT		DIAMETER		CROSS-SECTIONAL AREA SQUARED	
	LB	KG	IN.	CM	IN.	CM
#3	0.376	0.171	0.375	0.953	0.11	0.71
#4	0.668	0.303	0.500	1.270	0.20	1.29
#5	1.043	0.473	0.625	1.588	0.31	2.00
#6	1.502	0.681	0.750	1.905	0.44	2.84
#7	2.044	0.927	0.875	2.223	0.60	3.87
#8	2.670	1.211	1.000	2.540	0.79	5.10
#9	3.400	1.542	1.128	2.865	1.00	6.45
#10	4.303	1.952	1.270	3.226	1.27	8.19
#11	5.313	2.410	1.410	3.581	1.56	10.07
#14	7.650	3.470	1.693	4.300	2.25	14.52
#18	13.600	6.169	2.257	5.733	4.00	25.81

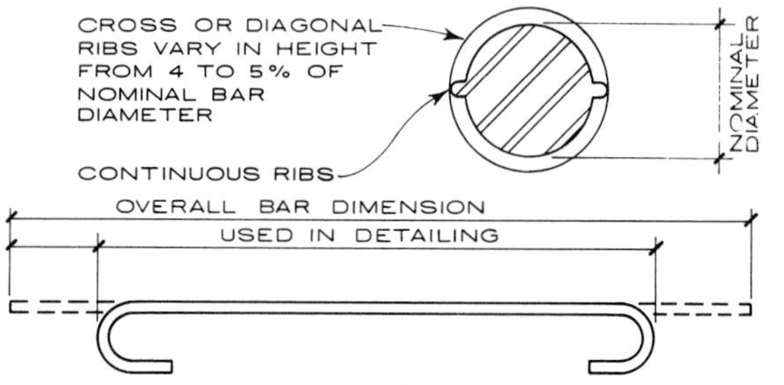

REINFORCING BAR DIMENSIONING

COMMON STOCK STYLES OF WELDED WIRE FABRIC

	NEW DESIGNATION	OLD DESIGNATION	STEEL AREA PER FOOT				APPROX-IMATE WEIGHT PER 100 SQ FT	
			LONGITU-DINAL		TRANS-VERSE			
	SPACING—CROSS SECTIONAL AREA (IN.)—(SQ IN./100)	SPACING—WIRE GAUGE (IN.)—(AS & W)	IN.	CM	IN.	CM	LB	KG
Rolls	6 x 6—W1.4 x W1.4	6 x 6—10 x 10	0.028	0.071	0.028	0.071	21	9.53
Rolls	6 x 6—W2.0 x W2.0	6 x 6—8 x 8 (1)	0.040	0.102	0.040	0.102	29	13.15
Rolls	6 x 6—W2.9 x W2.9	6 x 6—6 x 6	0.058	0.147	0.058	0.147	42	19.05
Rolls	6 x 6—W4.0 x W4.0	6 x 6—4 x 4	0.080	0.203	0.080	0.203	58	26.31
Rolls	4 x 4—W1.4 x W1.4	4 x 4—10 x 10	0.042	0.107	0.042	0.107	31	14.06
Rolls	4 x 4—W2.0 x W2.0	4 x 4—8 x 8 (1)	0.060	0.152	0.060	0.152	43	19.50
Rolls	4 x 4—W2.9 x W2.9	4 x 4—6 x 6	0.087	0.221	0.087	0.221	62	28.12
Rolls	4 x 4—W4.0 x W4.0	4 x 4—4 x 4	0.120	0.305	0.120	0.305	85	38.56
Sheets	6 x 6—W2.9 x W2.9	6 x 6—6 x 6	0.058	0.147	0.058	0.147	42	19.05
Sheets	6 x 6—W4.0 x W4.0	6 x 6—4 x 4	0.080	0.203	0.080	0.203	58	26.31
Sheets	6 x 6—W5.5 x W5.5	6 x 6—2 x 2 (2)	0.110	0.279	0.110	0.279	80	36.29
Sheets	4 x 4—W4.0 x W4.0	4 x 4—4 x 4	0.120	0.305	0.120	0.305	85	38.56

NOTES
1. Exact W-number size for 8 gauge is W2.1.
2. Exact W-number size for 2 gauge is W5.4.

STANDARD STEEL WIRE SIZES AND GAUGES

A.S.&W GAUGE	DIAMETER		AREA SQUARED		WEIGHT PER FOOT	
	IN.	CM	IN.	CM	LB	KG
00	0.3310	0.8407	0.0860	0.5549	0.2922	0.1325
0	0.3065	0.7785	0.0738	0.4762	0.2506	0.1137
1	0.2830	0.7188	0.0629	0.4058	0.2136	0.0969
2	0.2625	0.6668	0.0541	0.3491	0.1829	0.0830
— (1/4″)	0.2500	0.6350	0.0491	0.3168	0.1667	0.0756
3	0.2437	0.6190	0.0466	0.3007	0.1584	0.0718
4	0.2253	0.5723	0.0397	0.2561	0.1354	0.0614
5	0.2070	0.5258	0.0337	0.2174	0.1143	0.0518
6	0.1920	0.4877	0.0290	0.1871	0.0983	0.0446
7	0.1770	0.4496	0.0246	0.1587	0.0836	0.0379
8	0.1620	0.4115	0.0206	0.1329	0.0700	0.0318
9	0.1483	0.3767	0.0173	0.1116	0.0587	0.0266
10	0.1350	0.3429	0.0143	0.0922	0.0486	0.0220
11 (1/8″)	0.1250	0.3175	0.0114	0.0736	0.0387	0.0176
12	0.1055	0.2680	0.0087	0.0561	0.0297	0.0135
13	0.0915	0.2324	0.0066	0.0426	0.0223	0.0101
14	0.0800	0.2032	0.0050	0.0323	0.0171	0.0078
15	0.0720	0.1838	0.0041	0.0265	0.0138	0.0063
16 (1/16″)	0.0625	0.1588	0.0031	0.0200	0.0104	0.0047

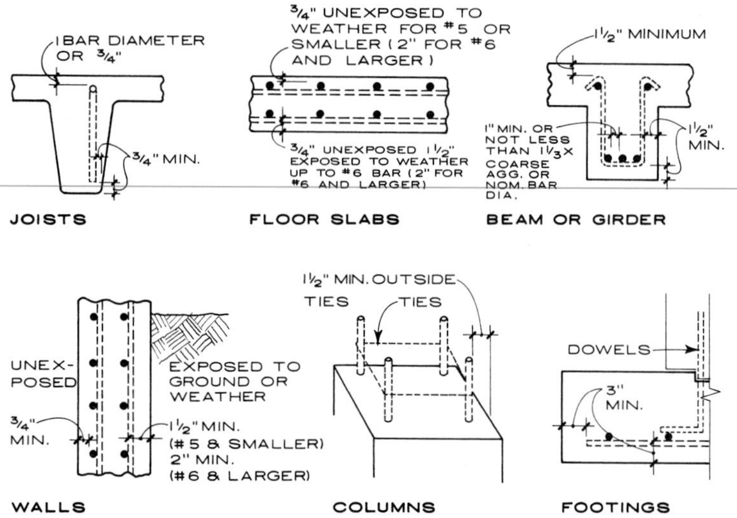

PROTECTION FOR REINFORCEMENT

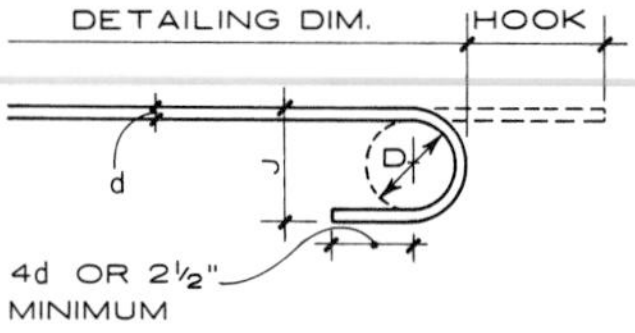

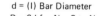

180° HOOK

d = (1) Bar Diameter
D = 6d for No. 3 to No. 8 Bars
D = 8d for No. 9 to No. 11 Bars
J = D + 2d
H = 5d + D/2 (or) 2 1/2″ + d + D/2 minimum

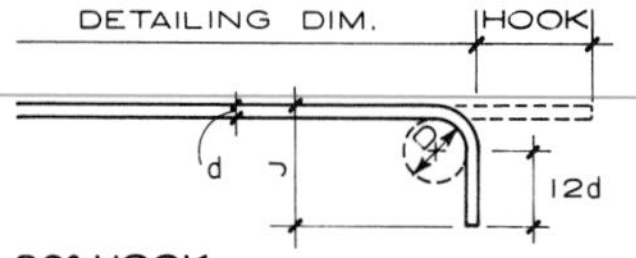

90° HOOK

d = (1) Bar Diameter
D = 6d for No. 3 to No. 8 bars
D = 8d for No. 9 to No. 11 bars
J = 13d + D/2

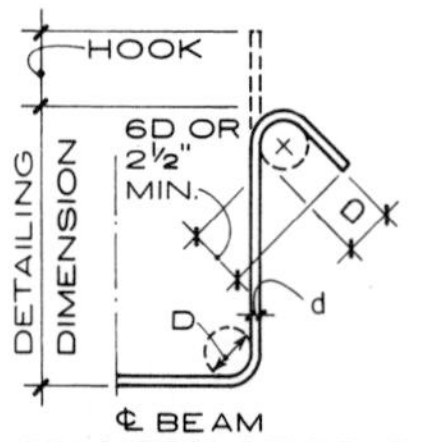

135° HOOK STIRRUP — TIES SIMILAR

d = (1) Bar Diameter
D = 1 1/2″ for No. 3
D = 2″ for No. 4
D = 2 1/2″ for No. 5
D = 6d for No. 6 to No. 8

STANDARD REINFORCING BAR HOOK DETAILS

LAP SPLICE REQUIREMENTS
1977 CODE IN BAR DIAMETERS

F_y (KSI)	SPIRAL COLUMN	TIED COLUMN	LOOSE
40	15.0	16.6	20
50	18.75	20.75	25
60	22.5	24.9	30
75	32.6	36.2	43.5
80	36.0	39.9	48.0

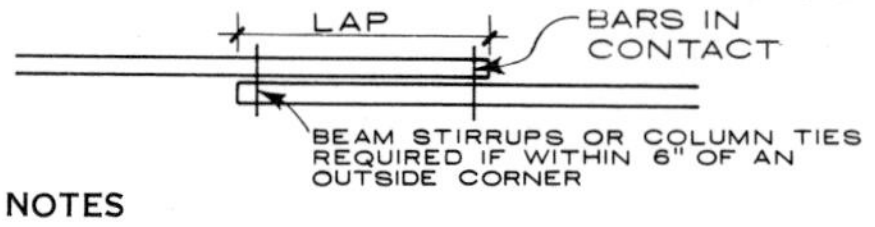

NOTES
1. These requirements are for compression lap splices only.
2. Lap splice lengths are minimum for Fc′ ≥ 3000 psi.
3. Minimum lap is 12 in.
4. Maximum reinforcing bar size permitted in lap splice is No. 11.

TEMPERATURE REINFORCEMENT FOR STRUCTURAL FLOOR AND ROOF SLAB (ONE WAY) (IN PERCENTAGE OF CROSS-SECTIONAL AREA OF CONCRETE)

REINFORCEMENT		CONCRETE SLABS	
GRADE	TYPE		
40/50	Deformed bars	0.20%	Max. spacing five times slab thickness
—	Welded wire fabric	0.18%	
60	Deformed bars	0.18%	

Dave Keppler; Haver, Nunn and Collamer; Phoenix, Arizona

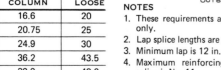

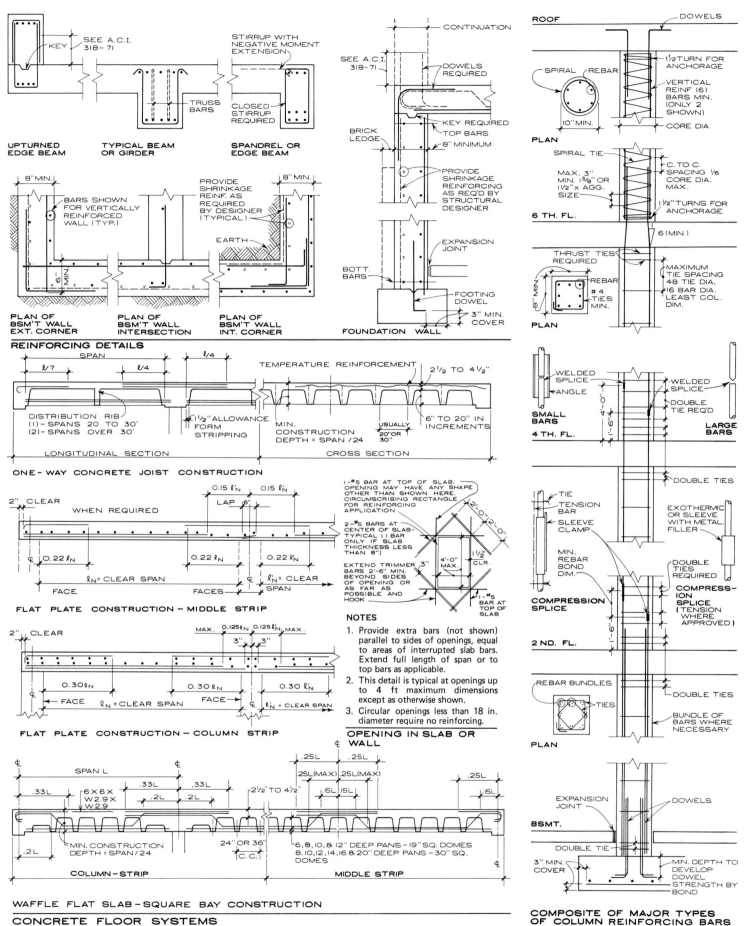

REINFORCING DETAILS

ONE-WAY CONCRETE JOIST CONSTRUCTION

FLAT PLATE CONSTRUCTION – MIDDLE STRIP

FLAT PLATE CONSTRUCTION – COLUMN STRIP

WAFFLE FLAT SLAB – SQUARE BAY CONSTRUCTION

CONCRETE FLOOR SYSTEMS

NOTES

1. Provide extra bars (not shown) parallel to sides of openings, equal to areas of interrupted slab bars. Extend full length of span or to top bars as applicable.

2. This detail is typical at openings up to 4 ft maximum dimensions except as otherwise shown.

3. Circular openings less than 18 in. diameter require no reinforcing.

OPENING IN SLAB OR WALL

COMPOSITE OF MAJOR TYPES OF COLUMN REINFORCING BARS

Thomas A. Lines; Haver, Nunn and Collamer; Phoenix, Arizona

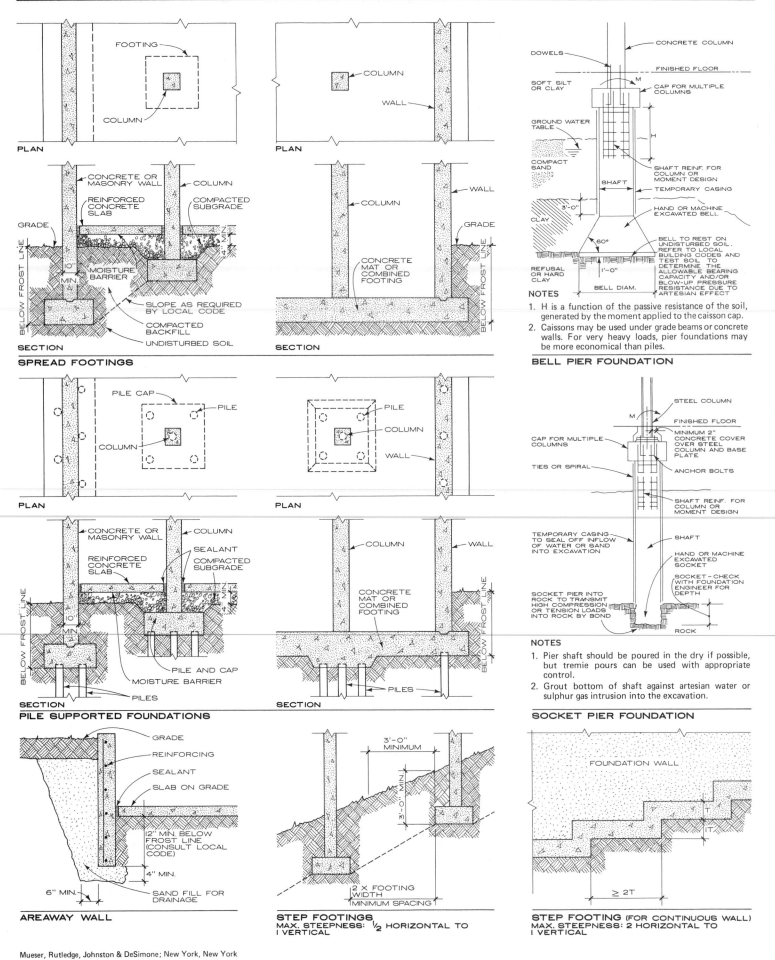

SPREAD FOOTINGS

PLAN

FOOTING

COLUMN

SECTION

CONCRETE OR MASONRY WALL
REINFORCED CONCRETE SLAB
GRADE
COLUMN
COMPACTED SUBGRADE
BELOW FROST LINE
10" MIN.
MOISTURE BARRIER
SLOPE AS REQUIRED BY LOCAL CODE
COMPACTED BACKFILL
UNDISTURBED SOIL

PLAN

COLUMN
WALL

SECTION

WALL
COLUMN
GRADE
BELOW FROST LINE
CONCRETE MAT OR COMBINED FOOTING

BELL PIER FOUNDATION

DOWELS
CONCRETE COLUMN
FINISHED FLOOR
SOFT SILT OR CLAY
M
CAP FOR MULTIPLE COLUMNS
GROUND WATER TABLE
COMPACT SAND
H
SHAFT REINF. FOR COLUMN OR MOMENT DESIGN
SHAFT
TEMPORARY CASING
3'-0"
CLAY
HAND OR MACHINE EXCAVATED BELL
60°
BELL TO REST ON UNDISTURBED SOIL. REFER TO LOCAL BUILDING CODES AND TEST SOIL TO DETERMINE THE ALLOWABLE BEARING CAPACITY AND/OR BLOW-UP PRESSURE RESISTANCE DUE TO ARTESIAN EFFECT
REFUSAL OR HARD CLAY
1'-0"
BELL DIAM.

NOTES

1. H is a function of the passive resistance of the soil, generated by the moment applied to the caisson cap.
2. Caissons may be used under grade beams or concrete walls. For very heavy loads, pier foundations may be more economical than piles.

PILE SUPPORTED FOUNDATIONS

PLAN

PILE CAP
PILE
COLUMN

SECTION

CONCRETE OR MASONRY WALL
REINFORCED CONCRETE SLAB
COLUMN
SEALANT
COMPACTED SUBGRADE
BELOW FROST LINE
10" MIN.
PILE AND CAP
MOISTURE BARRIER
PILES

PLAN

PILE
COLUMN
WALL

SECTION

COLUMN
WALL
CONCRETE MAT OR COMBINED FOOTING
BELOW FROST LINE
PILES

SOCKET PIER FOUNDATION

STEEL COLUMN
FINISHED FLOOR
M
CAP FOR MULTIPLE COLUMNS
MINIMUM 2" CONCRETE COVER OVER STEEL COLUMN AND BASE PLATE
TIES OR SPIRAL
ANCHOR BOLTS
SHAFT REINF. FOR COLUMN OR MOMENT DESIGN
TEMPORARY CASING TO SEAL OFF INFLOW OF WATER OR SAND INTO EXCAVATION
SHAFT
HAND OR MACHINE EXCAVATED SOCKET
SOCKET PIER INTO ROCK TO TRANSMIT HIGH COMPRESSION OR TENSION LOADS INTO ROCK BY BOND
SOCKET - CHECK WITH FOUNDATION ENGINEER FOR DEPTH
ROCK

NOTES

1. Pier shaft should be poured in the dry if possible, but tremie pours can be used with appropriate control.
2. Grout bottom of shaft against artesian water or sulphur gas intrusion into the excavation.

AREAWAY WALL

GRADE
REINFORCING
SEALANT
SLAB ON GRADE
12" MIN. BELOW FROST LINE (CONSULT LOCAL CODE)
4" MIN.
6" MIN.
SAND FILL FOR DRAINAGE

STEP FOOTINGS
MAX. STEEPNESS: 1/2 HORIZONTAL TO 1 VERTICAL

3'-0" MINIMUM
3'-0" MIN.
2 X FOOTING WIDTH MINIMUM SPACING

STEP FOOTING (FOR CONTINUOUS WALL)
MAX. STEEPNESS: 2 HORIZONTAL TO 1 VERTICAL

FOUNDATION WALL
T
T
≥ 2T

Mueser, Rutledge, Johnston & DeSimone; New York, New York

GENERAL NOTES

Factors to consider in construction of all concrete slabs on grade include assurance of uniform subgrade, quality of concrete, adequacy of structural capacity, type and spacing of joints, finishing, curing, and the application of special surfaces. It is vital to design and construct the subgrade as carefully as the floor slab itself. The subgrade support must be reasonably uniform, and the upper portion of the subgrade should be of uniform material and density. A subbase, a thin layer of granular material placed on the subgrade, should be used in most cases to cushion the slab.

Wear resistance is directly related to concrete strength. A low water-cement ratio improves the surface hardness and finishability as well as internal strength of concrete. Low water-cement ratio, low slump, and well graded aggregates with coarse aggregate size as large as placing and finishing requirements will permit and enhance the quality of concrete.

Exterior concrete subjected to freeze-thaw cycles should have 6 to 8% entrained air. Reinforcement is unnecessary where frequent joint spacing is used. Where less frequent joint spacing is necessary, reinforcement is put in the top one third depth to hold together any shrinkage cracks that form. Control joint spacing of 15 to 25 ft square is recommended. Checkerboard pouring patterns allow for some shrinkage between pours, but the process is more costly and is not recommended for large areas. The total shrinkage process takes up to one year. Strip pouring, allowing for a continuous pour with control joints cut after concrete has set, is a fast economical method, recommended for large areas.

Three types of joints are recommended:

1. ISOLATION JOINTS (also called expansion joints): Allow movement between slab and fixed parts of the building such as columns, walls, and machinery bases.
2. CONTROL JOINTS: Induce cracking at preselected locations.
3. CONSTRUCTION JOINTS: Provide stopping places during floor construction. Construction joints also function as control and isolation joints.

Sawcut control joints should be made as early as is practical after finishing the slab and should be filled in areas with wet conditions, hygienic and dust control requirements, or considerable traffic

by hard wheeled vehicles, such as forklift trucks. A semirigid filler with Shore Hardness "A" of at least 80 should be used.

Concrete floor slabs are monolithically finished by floating and troweling the concrete to a smooth dense finish. Depressions of more than 1/8 in. in 10 ft or variations of more than 1/4 in. from a level plane are undesirable. Special finishes are available to improve appearance. These include sprinkled (shake) finishes and high strength concrete toppings, either monolithic or separate (two-stage floor).

A vaporproof barrier should be placed under all slabs on grade where the passage of water vapor through the floor is undesirable. Permeance of vapor barrier should not exceed 0.20 perms.

Generally the controlling factor in determining the thickness of a floor on ground is the heaviest concentrated load it will carry, usually the wheel load plus impact of an industrial truck. Because of practical considerations, the minimum recommended thickness for an industrial floor is about 5 in. For Class 1, 2, and 3 floors, the minimum thickness should be 4 in.

The floor thickness required for wheel loads on relatively small areas may be obtained from the table for concrete; an allowable flexural tensile stress (psi) can be estimated from the approximate formula $f_t = 4.6\sqrt{f'_c}$ in which f'_c is the 28-day concrete compressive strength. If f_t is not 300 psi, the table can be used by multiplying the actual total load by the ratio of 300 to the stress used and entering the chart with that value.

Assume that a 5000 psi concrete slab is to be designed for an industrial plant floor over which there will be considerable traffic—trucks with loads of 10,000 lb/wheel, each of which has a contact area of about 30 sq in. Assume that operating conditions are such that impact will be equivalent to about 25% of the load. The equivalent static load will then be 12,500 lb. The allowable flexural tensile stress for 5000 psi concrete is

$$4.6\sqrt{5000} = 325 \text{ psi}$$

The allowable loads in the table are based on a stress of 300 psi, so that the design load must be corrected by the factor 300/325. Thus 11,500 lb on an area of 30 sq in. requires a slab about 7 1/2 in. thick.

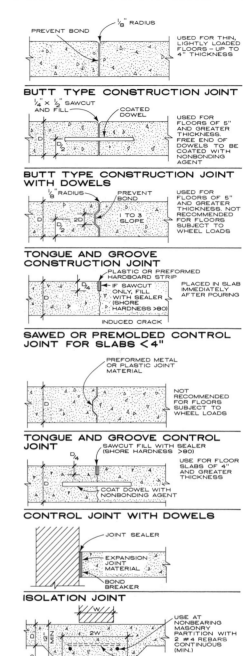

BUTT TYPE CONSTRUCTION JOINT

BUTT TYPE CONSTRUCTION JOINT WITH DOWELS

TONGUE AND GROOVE CONSTRUCTION JOINT

SAWED OR PREMOLDED CONTROL JOINT FOR SLABS < 4"

TONGUE AND GROOVE CONTROL JOINT

CONTROL JOINT WITH DOWELS

ISOLATION JOINT

THICKENED SLAB

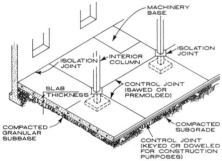

CONTROL JOINTS FOR A SLAB ON GRADE

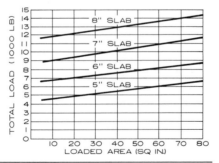

MAXIMUM WHEEL LOADS FOR INDUSTRIAL FLOORS (FLEXURAL TENSILE STRESS = 300 PSI)

CLASSIFICATION OF CONCRETE SLABS ON GRADE

CLASS	SLUMP RANGE (IN.)	MINIMUM COMPRESSIVE STRENGTH (PSI)	USUAL TRAFFIC	USE	SPECIAL CONSIDERATION	CONCRETE FINISHING TECHNIQUE
1	2–4	3500	Light foot	Residential or tile covered	Grade for drainage; plane smooth for tile	Medium steel trowel
2	2–4	3500	Foot	Offices, schools, hospitals, residential	Nonslip aggregate, mix in surface Color shake, special	Steel trowel; special finish for nonslip Steel trowel, color exposed aggregate
3	2–4	3500	Light foot and pneumatic wheels	Drives, garage floors, sidewalks for residences	Crown; pitch joints	Float, trowel, and broom
4	1–3	4000	Foot and pneumatic wheels	Light industrial, commercial	Careful curing	Hard steel trowel and brush for nonslip
5	1–3	4500	Foot and wheels—abrasive wear	Single course industrial, integral topping	Careful curing	Special hard aggregate, float and trowel
6	2–4	3500	Foot and steel tire vehicles—severe abrasion	Bonded two-course, heavy industrial	Base: textured surface and bond Top: special aggregate	Base: surface leveled by screeding Top: special power floats
7	1–3	4000	Same as Classes 3, 4, 5, 6	Unbonded topping	Mesh reinforcing; bond breaker on old concrete surface	—

Setter, Leach & Lindstrom, Inc.; Minneapolis, Minnesota

GENERAL CONSIDERATIONS

1. Concrete strength usually 5000 psi at 28 days and at least 3000 psi at time of prestressing. Hardrock aggregate or lightweight concrete used. Low slump controlled mix is required to reduce shrinkage. Shrinkage after prestressing increases prestress losses.

2. Post-tensioning systems can be divided into three categories depending on whether the tendon is wire, strand, or bar. Wire systems use 0.25 in. diameter wires that have a minimum strength of 240,000 psi and are usually cut to length in the shop. Strand systems use tendons composed of seven wires wrapped together that have a minimum strength of 270,000 psi and are cut in the field. Bar systems use bars ranging in diameter from $5/8$ to $1^3/8$ in. in diameter, with a minimum strength of 145,000 psi; they may be smooth or deformed. The system used will determine the type of anchorage used, which in turn will affect the size of blockout required in the edge of slab or beam for the anchorage to be recessed.

3. Tendons are greased and wrapped, or placed in conduits to reduce frictional losses during stressing operations. Length of continuous tendons limited to about 100 ft if stressed from one end. Long tendons require simultaneous stressing from both ends to reduce friction losses. Tendons may be grouted after stressing or left unbonded. Bonded tendons have structural advantages that are more important for beams and primary structural members.

4. Minimum average prestress (net prestress force/area of concrete) = 150 to 250 psi for flat plates, 200 to 500 psi for beams. Exceeding these values very much will cause excessive prestress losses because of creep.

5. Field inspection of post-tensioned concrete is critical to ensure proper size and location of tendons and to monitor the tendon stress. Tendon stress should be checked by measuring elongation of the tendon, and by gauge pressures on the stressing jack.

6. Provisions must be made for the shortening of post-tensioned beams and slabs caused by elastic compression, shrinkage, and creep. Shearwalls, curtain walls, or other stiff elements that adjoin post-tensioned members should be built after the post-tensioning has been done or should be isolated from these members with an expansion joint. Otherwise, additional post-tensioning force will be required to overcome the stiffness of the walls; cracking of the walls may also occur.

7. Fire tests have been conducted on prestressed beam and slab assemblies according to ASTM E119 test procedures; they compare favorably with conventionally reinforced concrete. There is little difference between beams using grouted tendons and those using ungrouted tendons.

8. References for further study:
   a. Post-Tensioning Institute, "Post-Tensioning Manual."
   b. Prestressed Concrete Institute, "Design Handbook for Precast and Prestressed Concrete."
   c. Lin, T.Y., "Design of Prestressed Concrete Structures."
   d. American Concrete Institute, "Building Code Requirements for Reinforced Concrete" (ACI-318-77).

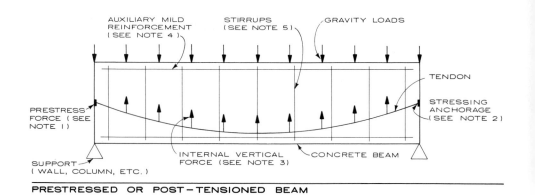

PRESTRESSED OR POST-TENSIONED BEAM

NOTES

1. Prestressing force puts entire beam cross-section into compression, thereby reducing unwanted tension cracks.

2. Permanent tension is introduced into tendon and "locked in" with the stressing anchorage in one of two ways. In prestressed concrete, the tendon is elongated in a stressing bed before the concrete is poured. In post-tensioned concrete, the tendon is elongated after concrete has been poured and allowed to cure by means of hydraulic jacks pushing against the beam itself. The principle in both cases is the same. Post-tensioned beams permit casting at the site for members too large or heavy for transporting from factory to site.

3. Vertical internal force on beam is caused by tendency of tendon to "straighten out" under tension.

It reduces downward beam deflection and allows shallower beams and longer spans than in conventionally reinforced beams.

4. Auxiliary mild reinforcement provides additional strength, controls cracking, and produces more ductile behavior.

5. Stirrups are used to provide additional shear strength in the beam and to support the tendons and longitudinal mild reinforcement. Stirrups should be open at the top to allow the reinforcing to be fabricated and placed before the tendon is placed.

6. Shoring must be left in place until the post-tensioning operation is performed. After stressing, reshoring may be required to prevent overloading during additional construction.

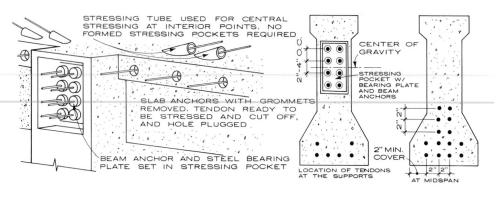

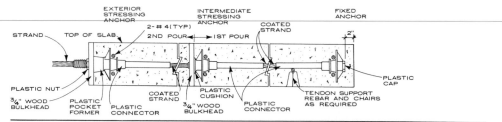

TYPICAL UNBONDED SINGLE STRAND TENDON INSTALLATION

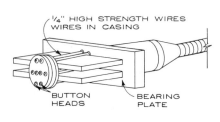

8 WIRE BBRV POST-TENSIONING ANCHOR (GROUTED)

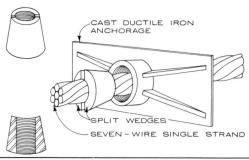

SINGLE STRAND TENDON ANCHORAGE (UNBONDED)

THREAD BAR ANCHORAGE (GROUTED)

Leo A. Daly, Architecture-Engineering-Planning; Omaha, Nebraska

3 PRECAST CONCRETE

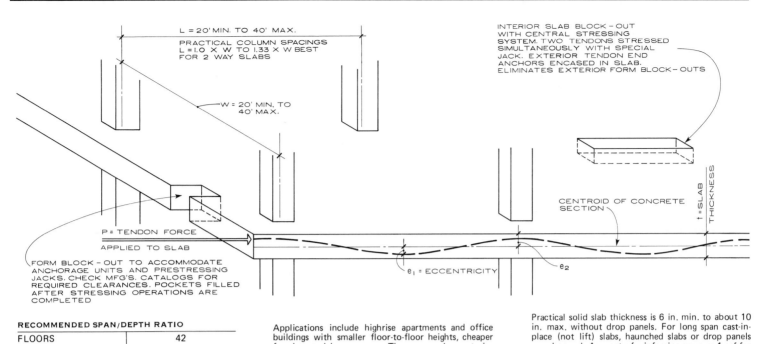

RECOMMENDED SPAN/DEPTH RATIO

FLOORS	42
ROOF	48

Check deflections and vibration

Applications include highrise apartments and office buildings with smaller floor-to-floor heights, cheaper forming, and longer spans. There are no beams to interfere with ducts and piping, and a sprayed-on ceiling may be applied directly to slab soffit.

Practical solid slab thickness is 6 in. min. to about 10 in. max. without drop panels. For long span cast-in-place (not lift) slabs, haunched slabs or drop panels may be used. Amount of reinforcing averages 1 psf for 24 to 28 ft bays, as compared to 2 to 3 psf for conventional concrete.

FLAT PLATE CONSTRUCTION

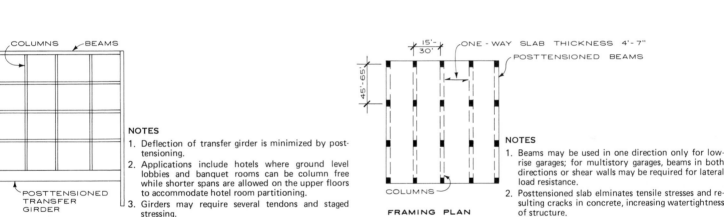

NOTES

1. Deflection of transfer girder is minimized by post-tensioning.
2. Applications include hotels where ground level lobbies and banquet rooms can be column free while shorter spans are allowed on the upper floors to accommodate hotel room partitioning.
3. Girders may require several tendons and staged stressing.

TRANSFER GIRDER IN MULTISTORY BUILDING

NOTES

1. Beams may be used in one direction only for low-rise garages; for multistory garages, beams in both directions or shear walls may be required for lateral load resistance.
2. Posttensioned slab eliminates tensile stresses and resulting cracks in concrete, increasing watertightness of structure.

PARKING GARAGE FLOORS

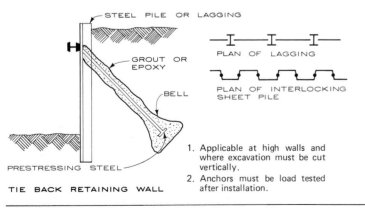

1. Applicable at high walls and where excavation must be cut vertically.
2. Anchors must be load tested after installation.

TIE BACK RETAINING WALL

MISCELLANEOUS APPLICATIONS

1. GRANDSTANDS: Cantilevered posttensioned roofs can eliminate columns that interrupt sight lines.
2. DOMED STRUCTURES: Posttensioned rings may be used to resist the thrust at the base of the dome.
3. MAT FOUNDATIONS: Posttensioned mat foundations distribute column loads over the entire area of the mat and may be more economical than pile foundations.
4. SLABS-ON-GROUND: Posttensioning is often used to eliminate cracking resulting from swelling soils which are a problem in many parts of the United States. Other types of construction where posttensioning may be used include waffle slabs, folded plates, and shell structures.

APPLICATIONS OF POSTTENSIONED CONCRETE

Leo A. Daly, Architecture-Engineering-Planning; Omaha, Nebraska

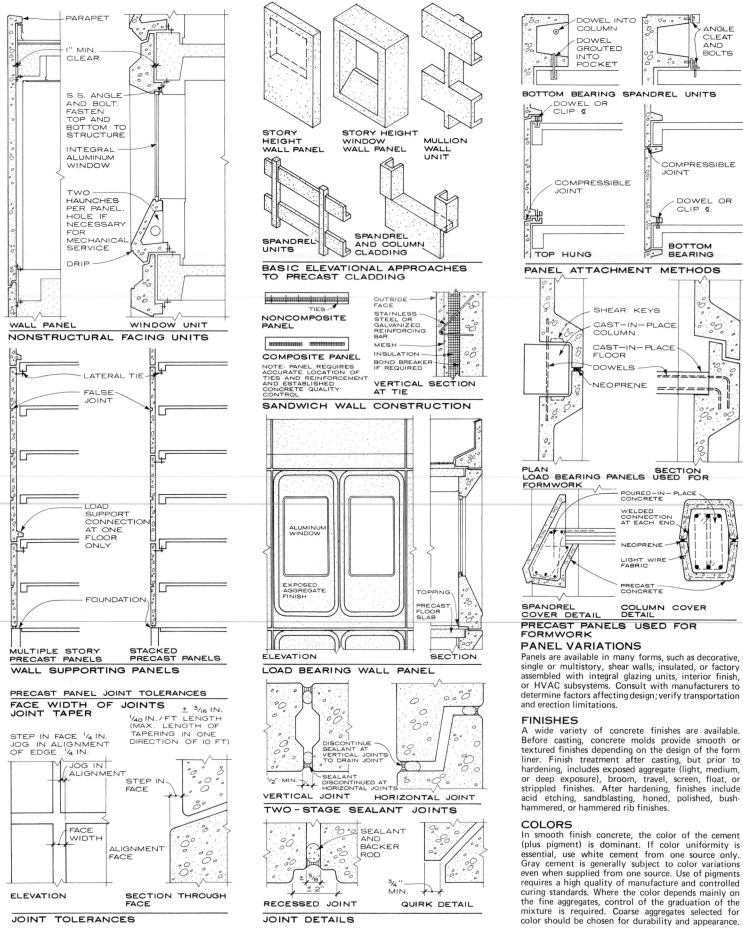

NONSTRUCTURAL FACING UNITS

PARAPET

1" MIN. CLEAR

S.S. ANGLE AND BOLT. FASTEN TOP AND BOTTOM TO STRUCTURE

INTEGRAL ALUMINUM WINDOW

TWO HAUNCHES PER PANEL. HOLE IF NECESSARY FOR MECHANICAL SERVICE

DRIP

WALL PANEL WINDOW UNIT

WALL SUPPORTING PANELS

LATERAL TIE

FALSE JOINT

LOAD SUPPORT CONNECTION AT ONE FLOOR ONLY

FOUNDATION

MULTIPLE STORY PRECAST PANELS STACKED PRECAST PANELS

PRECAST PANEL JOINT TOLERANCES

FACE WIDTH OF JOINTS

JOINT TAPER ± 3/16 IN.

STEP IN FACE 1/4 IN. 1/40 IN./FT LENGTH (MAX. LENGTH OF TAPERING IN ONE DIRECTION OF 10 FT)

JOG IN ALIGNMENT OF EDGE 1/4 IN.

JOG IN ALIGNMENT

STEP IN FACE

FACE WIDTH

ALIGNMENT FACE

ELEVATION SECTION THROUGH FACE

JOINT TOLERANCES

Bruce Lambert, Architect; Washington, D.C.

BASIC ELEVATIONAL APPROACHES TO PRECAST CLADDING

STORY HEIGHT WALL PANEL

STORY HEIGHT WINDOW WALL PANEL

MULLION WALL UNIT

SPANDREL UNITS

SPANDREL AND COLUMN CLADDING

SANDWICH WALL CONSTRUCTION

TIES

NONCOMPOSITE PANEL

COMPOSITE PANEL

NOTE: PANEL REQUIRES ACCURATE LOCATION OF TIES AND REINFORCEMENT AND ESTABLISHED CONCRETE QUALITY CONTROL

OUTSIDE FACE

STAINLESS STEEL OR GALVANIZED REINFORCING BAR

MESH

INSULATION

BOND BREAKER IF REQUIRED

VERTICAL SECTION AT TIE

LOAD BEARING WALL PANEL

ALUMINUM WINDOW

EXPOSED AGGREGATE FINISH

ELEVATION SECTION

TOPPING

PRECAST FLOOR SLAB

TWO-STAGE SEALANT JOINTS

DISCONTINUE SEALANT AT VERTICAL JOINTS TO DRAIN JOINT

SEALANT DISCONTINUED AT HORIZONTAL JOINTS

1/2" MIN.

VERTICAL JOINT HORIZONTAL JOINT

JOINT DETAILS

SEALANT AND BACKER ROD

± 5/8
± 2"

RECESSED JOINT

3/4" MIN.

QUIRK DETAIL

PANEL ATTACHMENT METHODS

DOWEL INTO COLUMN

DOWEL GROUTED INTO POCKET

ANGLE CLEAT AND BOLTS

BOTTOM BEARING SPANDREL UNITS

DOWEL OR CLIP ¢

COMPRESSIBLE JOINT

COMPRESSIBLE JOINT

DOWEL OR CLIP ¢

TOP HUNG BOTTOM BEARING

PRECAST PANELS USED FOR FORMWORK

SHEAR KEYS

CAST-IN-PLACE COLUMN

CAST-IN-PLACE FLOOR

DOWELS

NEOPRENE

PLAN
LOAD BEARING PANELS USED FOR FORMWORK

SECTION

POURED-IN-PLACE CONCRETE

WELDED CONNECTION AT EACH END

NEOPRENE

LIGHT WIRE FABRIC

PRECAST CONCRETE

SPANDREL COVER DETAIL COLUMN COVER DETAIL

PANEL VARIATIONS

Panels are available in many forms, such as decorative, single or multistory, shear walls, insulated, or factory assembled with integral glazing units, interior finish, or HVAC subsystems. Consult with manufacturers to determine factors affecting design; verify transportation and erection limitations.

FINISHES

A wide variety of concrete finishes are available. Before casting, concrete molds provide smooth or textured finishes depending on the design of the form liner. Finish treatment after casting, but prior to hardening, includes exposed aggregate (light, medium, or deep exposure), broom, travel, screen, float, or strippled finishes. After hardening, finishes include acid etching, sandblasting, honed, polished, bush-hammered, or hammered rib finishes.

COLORS

In smooth finish concrete, the color of the cement (plus pigment) is dominant. If color uniformity is essential, use white cement from one source only. Gray cement is generally subject to color variations even when supplied from one source. Use of pigments requires a high quality of manufacture and controlled curing standards. Where the color depends mainly on the fine aggregates, control of the graduation of the mixture is required. Coarse aggregates selected for color should be chosen for durability and appearance.

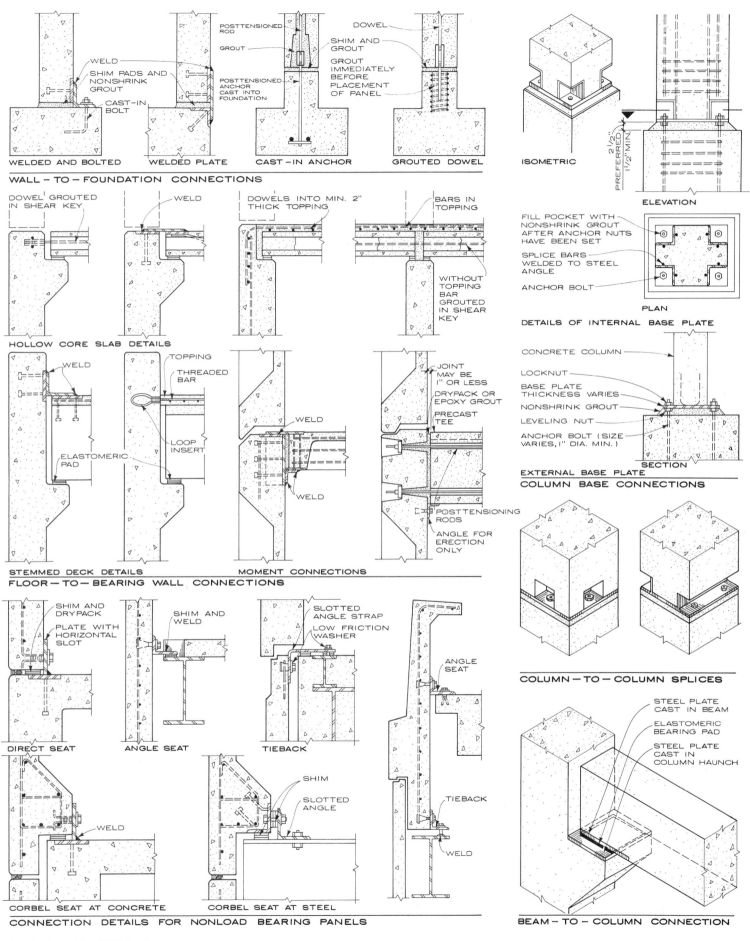

WELDED AND BOLTED

WELD

SHIM PADS AND NONSHRINK GROUT

CAST-IN BOLT

WELDED PLATE

POSTTENSIONED ROD

GROUT

POSTTENSIONED ANCHOR CAST INTO FOUNDATION

CAST-IN ANCHOR

DOWEL

SHIM AND GROUT

GROUT IMMEDIATELY BEFORE PLACEMENT OF PANEL

GROUTED DOWEL

WALL — TO — FOUNDATION CONNECTIONS

DOWEL GROUTED IN SHEAR KEY

WELD

DOWELS INTO MIN. 2" THICK TOPPING

BARS IN TOPPING

WITHOUT TOPPING BAR GROUTED IN SHEAR KEY

HOLLOW CORE SLAB DETAILS

WELD

ELASTOMERIC PAD

TOPPING

THREADED BAR

LOOP INSERT

WELD

WELD

JOINT MAY BE 1" OR LESS

DRYPACK OR EPOXY GROUT

PRECAST TEE

POSTTENSIONING RODS

ANGLE FOR ERECTION ONLY

STEMMED DECK DETAILS

MOMENT CONNECTIONS

FLOOR — TO — BEARING WALL CONNECTIONS

SHIM AND DRYPACK

PLATE WITH HORIZONTAL SLOT

DIRECT SEAT

SHIM AND WELD

ANGLE SEAT

SLOTTED ANGLE STRAP

LOW FRICTION WASHER

TIEBACK

ANGLE SEAT

SHIM

SLOTTED ANGLE

WELD

TIEBACK

WELD

WELD

CORBEL SEAT AT CONCRETE

CORBEL SEAT AT STEEL

CONNECTION DETAILS FOR NONLOAD BEARING PANELS

ISOMETRIC

2 1/2" PREFERRED 1 1/2" MIN.

ELEVATION

FILL POCKET WITH NONSHRINK GROUT AFTER ANCHOR NUTS HAVE BEEN SET

SPLICE BARS WELDED TO STEEL ANGLE

ANCHOR BOLT

PLAN

DETAILS OF INTERNAL BASE PLATE

CONCRETE COLUMN

LOCKNUT

BASE PLATE THICKNESS VARIES

NONSHRINK GROUT

LEVELING NUT

ANCHOR BOLT (SIZE VARIES, 1" DIA. MIN.)

SECTION

EXTERNAL BASE PLATE

COLUMN BASE CONNECTIONS

COLUMN — TO — COLUMN SPLICES

STEEL PLATE CAST IN BEAM

ELASTOMERIC BEARING PAD

STEEL PLATE CAST IN COLUMN HAUNCH

BEAM — TO — COLUMN CONNECTION

Bruce Lambert, Architect; Washington, D.C.

PRECAST CONCRETE 3

SLAB AND PANEL SYSTEM

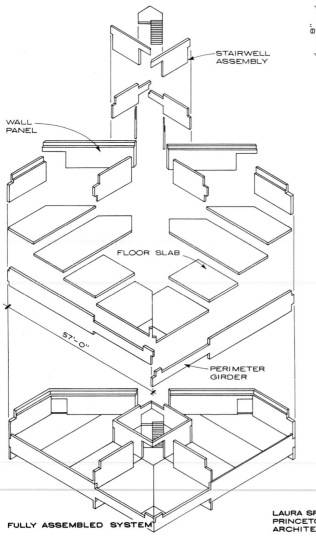

STAIRWELL ASSEMBLY

WALL PANEL

FLOOR SLAB

57'-0"

PERIMETER GIRDER

FULLY ASSEMBLED SYSTEM

NOTE
This precast wall system utilizes load bearing precast window panel units measuring 12 ft high, 10 ft wide, and 3 ft deep to support the precast concrete double tee floor. Units are attached to the floor and top and bottom with welded plates.

MECHANICAL SERVICES

PLAN

LOAD BEARING WINDOW PANEL

AIR CONDITIONING UNIT

ELEVATION   **SECTION**

DEPARTMENT OF HOUSING AND URBAN DEVELOPMENT WASHINGTON, D.C.
ARCHITECT: MARCEL BREUER AND HERBERT BECKHARD, NOLEN·SWINBURNE AND ASSOCIATES

WALL PANEL SYSTEM

Bruce Lambert, Architect; Washington, D.C.

8"

SLAB TO SLAB DETAIL

8"

WALL PANEL
BUTYL ROD
FLOOR SLAB

ELASTOMERIC PAD

SLAB TO WALL DETAIL

GIRDER
WELD
SLAB

ELASTOMERIC PAD

SLAB TO GIRDER DETAIL

NOTE
This precast prestressed floor, wall, and girder system is shop fabricated and field assembled to form a completed structure. Slab and wall panels are welded to posttensioned girders. All members are left exposed throughout and utilize 5000 psi concrete using buff gray cement.

LAURA SPELMAN ROCKEFELLER HALL
PRINCETON UNIVERSITY, PRINCETON, N.J.
ARCHITECT: I.M. PEI AND PARTNERS

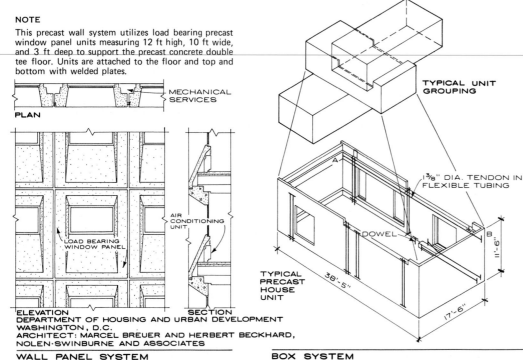

TYPICAL UNIT GROUPING

$1\frac{3}{8}$" DIA. TENDON IN FLEXIBLE TUBING

DOWEL

A

B

11'-6"

38'-5"

17'-6"

TYPICAL PRECAST HOUSE UNIT

BOX SYSTEM

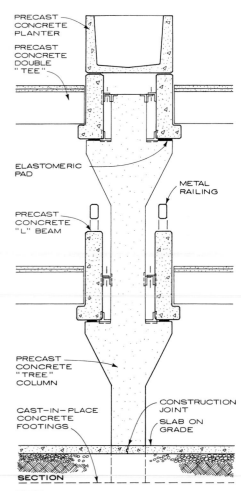

PRECAST CONCRETE PLANTER
PRECAST CONCRETE DOUBLE "TEE"

ELASTOMERIC PAD

PRECAST CONCRETE "L" BEAM

METAL RAILING

PRECAST CONCRETE "TREE" COLUMN

CAST-IN-PLACE CONCRETE FOOTINGS

CONSTRUCTION JOINT
SLAB ON GRADE

SECTION

NOTE
This precast prestressed column and beam system consists of precast double tees spanning 57.5 ft to precast leader beams. Ledger beams are bolted and welded to 18 x 24 in. full height haunched column to stiffen the structural frame.

PARKING STRUCTURE, FNMA HEADQUARTERS
WASHINGTON, D.C.
ARCHITECT: JOHN CARL WARNECKE, FAIA

COLUMN AND BEAM SYSTEM

GROUT TUBE
GROUT
REINFORCING BARS
$2\frac{1}{2}$" DIA. PIN

5" SLAB

SPONGE RUBBER
STEEL PLATE
$3\frac{1}{2}$" DIA. PIPE SLEEVE

DOWEL DETAIL

NOTE
This three dimensional precast posttensioned concrete system utilizes a five sided building envelope that is cast monolithically and then stacked and connected together in a variety of groupings. Walls are typically 5 in. thick. Services run vertically outside the units.

HABITAT '67, MONTREAL, CANADA
ASSOCIATED ARCHITECTS: MOSHE SAFDIE AND DAVID, BAROTT, BOULVA

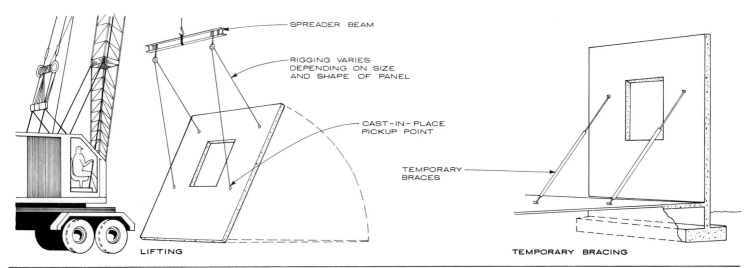

LIFTING

TEMPORARY BRACING

- SPREADER BEAM
- RIGGING VARIES DEPENDING ON SIZE AND SHAPE OF PANEL
- CAST-IN-PLACE PICKUP POINT
- TEMPORARY BRACES

CONSTRUCTION PROCEDURES

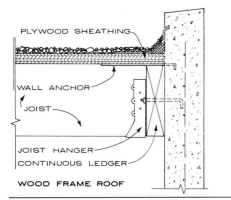

- PLYWOOD SHEATHING
- WALL ANCHOR
- JOIST
- JOIST HANGER
- CONTINUOUS LEDGER

WOOD FRAME ROOF

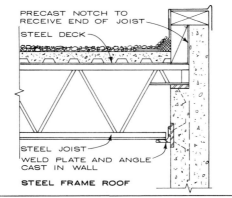

- PRECAST NOTCH TO RECEIVE END OF JOIST
- STEEL DECK
- STEEL JOIST
- WELD PLATE AND ANGLE CAST IN WALL

STEEL FRAME ROOF

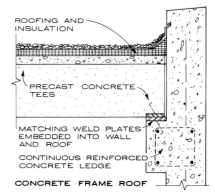

- ROOFING AND INSULATION
- PRECAST CONCRETE TEES
- MATCHING WELD PLATES EMBEDDED INTO WALL AND ROOF
- CONTINUOUS REINFORCED CONCRETE LEDGE

CONCRETE FRAME ROOF

PANEL CONNECTIONS AT ROOF

GENERAL NOTES

Tilt-up construction is a form of precast concrete construction. Walls are cast on the site in a horizontal position, tilted to the vertical position, set in place, and made an integral part of the completed structure. The designer should consult with possible contractors before the design and construction details are definitely established. Even small changes in design or construction procedure may result in an appreciable saving in time and money as well as providing a better structure.

APPLICATIONS

Tilt-up walls are very economical and are adaptable to a wide range of architectural uses. They have been used in many types of structures from private homes and garages to multistory office buildings, although by far the greatest use has been in one-story industrial and commercial buildings.

DESIGN

Wall panels must be designed for the conditions to which they will be subjected during erection and in the completed structure. The general design of the building determines whether the walls are load bearing or non-load bearing either with a continuous footing or supported on the column footings only. The panels are designed like walls of reinforced concrete built in the conventional manner, the only difference being in the details.

LIFTING STRESSES

Lifting a wall panel creates stresses not encountered in conventional cast-in-place construction, and with some pickup arrangements the exact determination of these stresses can be complicated. The method of attaching the lifting equipment must be known in order to determine the stresses. Rigging details will vary depending on the size and shape of the individual panel.

Harnish, Morgan, and Causey, Architects; Ontario, California

Taylor & Gaines, Structural Engineers; Pasadena, California

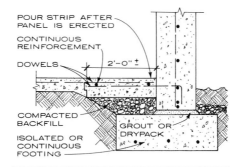

- POUR STRIP AFTER PANEL IS ERECTED
- CONTINUOUS REINFORCEMENT
- DOWELS
- 2'-0" ±
- COMPACTED BACKFILL
- ISOLATED OR CONTINUOUS FOOTING
- GROUT OR DRYPACK

SLAB AND FOOTING DETAIL

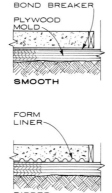

- BOND BREAKER
- PLYWOOD MOLD

SMOOTH

- SELECT STONES ON SAND BED

STONE

- FORM LINER

RIBBED

- PLASTIC SHEETING
- GRAVEL

DIMPLED

SURFACE TREATMENTS

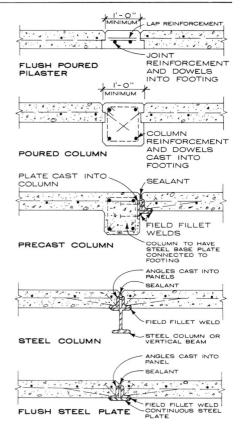

FLUSH POURED PILASTER

- 1'-0" MINIMUM
- LAP REINFORCEMENT
- JOINT REINFORCEMENT AND DOWELS INTO FOOTING

POURED COLUMN

- 1'-0" MINIMUM
- COLUMN REINFORCEMENT AND DOWELS CAST INTO FOOTING

PRECAST COLUMN

- PLATE CAST INTO COLUMN
- SEALANT
- FIELD FILLET WELDS
- COLUMN TO HAVE STEEL BASE PLATE CONNECTED TO FOOTING

STEEL COLUMN

- ANGLES CAST INTO PANELS
- SEALANT
- FIELD FILLET WELD
- STEEL COLUMN OR VERTICAL BEAM

FLUSH STEEL PLATE

- ANGLES CAST INTO PANEL
- SEALANT
- FIELD FILLET WELD
- CONTINUOUS STEEL PLATE

VERTICAL WALL JOINTS

PRECAST CONCRETE 3

FLAT DECK MEMBERS

TABLE 1 *
SAFE SUPERIMPOSED SERVICE LOADS (PSF) FOR SOLID FLAT SLABS

SLAB THICKNESS (IN.)	SLAB DESIGNATION	TOPPING THICKNESS (IN.)	SPAN (FT)													
			12	14	16	18	20	22	24	26	28	30	32	34	36	38	40
4"	FS4	NONE	160	105	68												
	FS4+2	2	284	167	91												
6"	FS6	NONE		261	182	128	90	61									
	FS6+2	2			262	172	108	60									
8"	FS8	NONE				227	165	119	84								
	FS8+2	2				298	206	139	87								

TABLE 2 *
SAFE SUPERIMPOSED SERVICE LOADS (PSF) FOR HOLLOW CORE SLABS (4 FT WIDTH)

SLAB THICKNESS (IN.)	SLAB DESIGNATION	TOPPING THICKNESS (IN.)	SPAN (FT)													
			12	14	16	18	20	22	24	26	28	30	32	34	36	38	40
6"	4HC6	NONE		291	225	168	126	96	73								
	4HC6+2	2					222	158	111	75	47						
8"	4HC8	NONE				269	213	169	135	107	85	66	52				
	4HC8+2	2						264	205	154	115	83	58				
10"	4HC10	NONE					274	232	186	150	122	100	81	66	52		
	4HC10+2	2							270	215	172	137	103	76	54		
12"	4HC12	NONE									166	138	115	95	79	66	54
	4HC12+2	2								234	209	182	149	122	97	74	55

LOAD TABLES FOR FLAT DECK MEMBERS

* NOTE: 1. NORMAL WEIGHT (150 PCF) CONCRETE SLAB AND TOPPING
2. SLABS f_c = 5000 PSI
3. STRAND DESIGNATION CODE = 50-S

4'-0"
TYPE "A"   6", 8", 12"

3'-4"
TYPE "E"   4", 6", 8", 10", 12"

4'-0"
TYPE "B"   4", 6", 8", 10"

4'-0"
TYPE "F"   8", 12"

8'-0"
TYPE "C"   6", 8", 10", 12"

8'-0"
TYPE "G"   8", 12"

1'-4", 1'-8", 2'-0"
TYPE "D"   6", 8", 10", 12"

4'-0"
TYPE "H"   4", 6", 8", 10", 12"

NOTES

1. Normal weight (150 pcf) or lightweight concrete (115 pcf) is used in standard slab construction. Topping concrete is usually normal weight concrete with a cylinder strength of 3000 psi. All units are prestressed with strand release when concrete strength is 3500 psi.

2. Strands are available in various sizes and strengths according to individual manufacturers. Strand placement may vary, which will change load capacity, camber values, and fire resistance. Contact the local supplier for strand placement and allowable loading.

3. Camber will vary substantially depending on slab design, span, and loading. Nonstructural components attached to members may be affected by camber variations. Calculations of topping quantities should recognize camber variations.

4. Safe superimposed service loads include a dead load of 10 psf for untopped concrete and 15 psf for topped concrete. The remainder is live load.

5. Smooth or textured soffits may be available in some types; check with the supplier.

HOLLOW CORE SLAB TYPES
ALL SECTIONS ARE NOT AVAILABLE FROM ALL PRODUCERS
CHECK AVAILABILITY WITH LOCAL MANUFACTURERS

Bruce Lambert, Architect; Washington D.C.

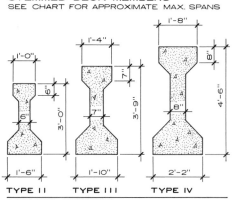

TYPE A 8'-0"
TYPE B 10'-0"
OPTIONAL TOPPING
7 3/4"
1/2"
D VARIES
4'-0"
5'-0"
4 3/4"

DOUBLE TEE (DT)

TYPE C 8'-0"
TYPE D 10'-0"
OPTIONAL TOPPING
1/2"
3"
D VARIES
8"

SINGLE TEE (ST)

STRAND PATTERN DESIGNATION
NO. OF STRANDS (20)
S=STRAIGHT D=DEPRESSED
208·D1
NO. OF DEPRESSION POINTS
DIAMETER OF STRAND IN 16THS

NORMAL WEIGHT CONCRETE
f'c = 5000 PSI

NOTES

1. Safe loads shown indicate dead load of 10 psf for untopped members and 15 psf for topped members. Remainder is live load.
2. Designers should contact the manufacturers in the geographic area of the proposed structure to determine availability, exact dimensions, and load tables for various sections.
3. Camber should be checked for its effect on non-structural members (i.e., partitions, folding doors, etc.), which should be placed with adequate allowance for error. Calculations of topping quantities should also recognize camber variations.
4. Normal weight concrete is assumed to be 150 lb/cu ft; lightweight concrete is assumed to be 115 lb/cu ft.

STEMMED DECK MEMBERS
SEE CHART FOR APPROXIMATE MAX. SPANS

1'-8"
1'-4"
1'-0"
8"
6"
7"
1'-8"
7"
3'-9"
8"
4'-6"
3'-0"
6"
7"
1'-6"
1'-10"
2'-2"

TYPE II   TYPE III   TYPE IV

AASHTO GIRDERS

TABLE OF SAFE SUPERIMPOSED SERVICE LOAD* (PLF) FOR AASHTO GIRDER

DESIG-NA-TION	NO. OF STRANDS	SPAN (FT)						
		36	40	44	48	52	56	60
Type II	14	3520	2785	2241	1826			
Type III	22	7231	5757	4667	3837	3192	2679	2266
Type IV	32		9848	7996	6588	5492	4622	3920

Bruce Lambert, Architect; Washington, D.C.

APPROXIMATE MAXIMUM SPAN FOR STEMMED DECK SECTIONS

DECK TYPE	DEPTH D (IN.)	CONCRETE WEIGHT	DESIGNATION	TOPPING DEPTH (IN.)	STRAND DESIGNATION	MAX. SPAN (FT)	SAFE LOAD (PSF)
A	12	Normal weight	8DT12	0	88·D1	40	40
			8DT12+2	2	68·D1	34	39
		Lightweight	8LDT12	0	68·D1	40	35
			8LDT12+2	2	68·D1	36	36
A	18	Normal weight	8DT18	0	108·D1	58	34
			8DT18+2	2	88·D1	46	48
		Lightweight	8LDT18	0	108·D1	60	37
			8LDT18+2	2	88·D1	50	39
A	24	Normal weight	8DT24	0	148·D1	74	38
			8DT24+2	2	128·D1	60	56
		Lightweight	8LDT24	0	148·D1	80	35
			8LDT24+2	2	108·D1	62	44
A	32	Normal weight	8DT32	0	228·D1	88	56
			8DT32+2	2	208·D1	76	76
		Lightweight	8LDT32	0	228·D1	100	41
			8LDT32+2	2	208·D1	82	67
B	32	Normal weight	10DT32	0	228·D1	86	49
			10DT32+2	2	208·D1	74	62
		Lightweight	10LDT32	0	228·D1	98	35
			10LDT32+2	2	208·D1	78	59
C	36	Normal weight	8ST36	0	228·D1	100	44
			8ST36+2	2	188·D1	82	61
		Lightweight	8LST36	0	228·D1	110	38
			8LST36+2	2	168·D1	86	50
D	48	Normal weight	10ST48	0	248·D1	112	42
		Lightweight	10LST48	0	248·D1	120	41

TABLE OF SAFE SUPERIMPOSED SERVICE LOAD* (PLF) FOR PRECAST BEAM SECTIONS

TYPE	DESIG-NA-TION	NO. STRAND	H (IN.)	H1/H2 (IN.)	SPAN (FT)								
					18	22	26	30	34	38	42	46	50
RECTANGULAR BEAM	12RB24	10	24		6726	4413	3083	2248	1684	1288	1000		
	12RB32	13	32			7858	5524	4059	3080	2394	1894	1519	1230
	16RB24	13	24		8847	5803	4052	2954	2220	1705	1330		
	16RB32	18	32			7434	5464	4147	3224	2549	2036	1642	
B = 12" OR 16"	16RB40	22	40				8647	6599	5163	4117	3332	2728	
L-SHAPED BEAM	18LB20	9	20	12/8	5068	3303	2288	1650	1218				
	18LB28	12	28	16/12		6578	4600	3360	2531	1949	1524	1200	
	18LB36	16	36	24/12			7903	5807	4405	3422	2706	2168	1755
	18LB44	19	44	28/16				8729	6666	5219	4166	3370	2754
	18LB52	23	52	36/16					9538	7486	5992	4871	4007
	18LB60	27	60	44/16							8116	6630	5481
INVERTED TEE BEAM	24IT20	9	20	12/8	5376	3494	2412	1726	1266				
	24IT28	13	28	16/12		6951	4848	3529	2648	2030			
	24IT36	16	36	24/12			8337	6127	4644	3598	2836	2265	1825
	24IT44	20	44	28/16				9300	7075	5514	4378	3525	2868
	24IT52	24	52	36/16					7916	6326	5132	4213	
	24IT60	28	60	44/16							8616	7025	5800

*Safe loads shown indicate 50% dead load and 50% live load; 800 psi top tension has been allowed, therefore additional top reinforcement is required.

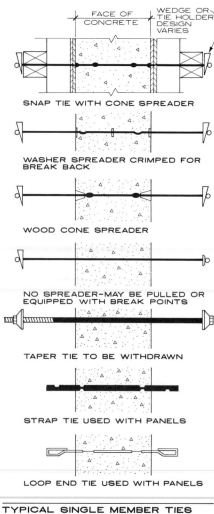

SNAP TIE WITH CONE SPREADER

WASHER SPREADER CRIMPED FOR BREAK BACK

WOOD CONE SPREADER

NO SPREADER—MAY BE PULLED OR EQUIPPED WITH BREAK POINTS

TAPER TIE TO BE WITHDRAWN

STRAP TIE USED WITH PANELS

LOOP END TIE USED WITH PANELS

TYPICAL SINGLE MEMBER TIES

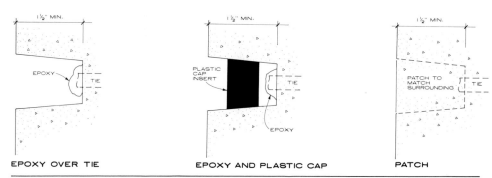

EPOXY OVER TIE   EPOXY AND PLASTIC CAP   PATCH

TIE HOLE TREATMENT OPTIONS

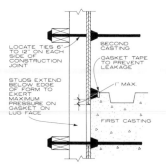

TYPICAL CONSTRUCTION JOINT

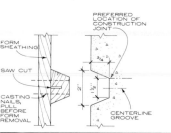

RUSTICATION AT CONSTRUCTION JOINT

CONCRETE SURFACES—GENERAL

The variety of architectural finishes is as extensive as the cost and effort expended to achieve them. There are three basic ways to improve or change the appearance of concrete:

1. Changing materials, that is, using a colored matrix and exposed aggregates.
2. Changing the mold or form by such means as a form liner.
3. By treating or tooling the concrete surface in the final stages of hardening.

The aim is to obtain maximum benefit from one of three features—color, texture, and pattern—all of which are interrelated. Color is the easiest method of changing the appearance of concrete. It should not be used on a plain concrete surface with a series of panels, since color matches are difficult to achieve. The exception is possible when white cement is used, usually as a base for the pigment to help reduce changes of color variation. Since white cement is expensive, many effects are tried with gray cement to avoid an entire plain surface. Colored concrete is most effective when it is used with an exposed aggregate finish.

FORM LINERS

1. Sandblasted Douglas fir or long leaf yellow pine dressed one side away from the concrete surface.
2. Flexible steel strip formwork adapted to curbed surfaces (Schwellmer System).
3. Resin coated, striated, or sandblasted plywood.
4. Rubber mats.
5. Thermoplastic sheets with high glass or texture laid over stone, for example.
6. Formed plastics.
7. Plaster of Paris molds for sculptured work.
8. Clay (sculpturing and staining concrete).
9. Hardboard (screen side).

D. Neil Rankins; SHWC, Inc.; Dallas, Texas

10. Standard steel forms.
11. Wood boarding and reversed battens.
12. Square edged lumber dressed one side.
13. Resawn wood boards.

RELEASE AGENTS

1. Oils, petroleum based, used on wood, concrete, and steel forms.
2. Soft soaps.
3. Talcum.
4. Whitewash used on wood with tannin in conjunction with oils.
5. Calcium stearate powder.
6. Silicones used on steel forms.
7. Plastics used on wood forms.
8. Lacquers used on plywood and plaster forms.
9. Resins used on plywood forms.
10. Sodium silicate.
11. Membrane used over any form.
12. Grease used on plaster forms.
13. Epoxy resin plastic used on plywood.

CATEGORIES OF COMMON AGGREGATE

1. QUARTZ: Clear, white, rose.
2. MARBLE: Green, yellow, red, pink, blue, gray, white, black.
3. GRANITE: Pink, gray, black, white.
4. CERAMIC: Full range.
5. VITREOUS/GLASS: Full range.

CRITICAL FACTORS AFFECTING SURFACES

DESIGN DRAWINGS should show form details, including openings, control joints, construction joints, expansion joints, and other important specifics.

1. CEMENT: Types and brands.
2. AGGREGATES: Sources of coarse and fine aggregates.
3. TECHNIQUES: Uniformity in mixing and placing.
4. FORMS: Closure techniques or concealing joints in formwork materials.
5. SLUMP CONTROL: Ensure compliance with design.
6. CURING METHODS: Ensure compliance with design.

TIES

A concrete tie is a tensile unit adapted to hold concrete forms secure against the lateral pressure of unhardened concrete. Two general types of concrete ties exist:

1. Continuous single member where the tensile unit is a single piece and the holding device engages the tensile unit against the exterior of the form. Standard types: working load = 2500 to 5000 lb.
2. Internal disconnecting where the tensile unit has an inner part with threaded connections to removable external members, which have suitable devices of securing them against the outside of the form. Working load = 6000 to 36,000 lb.

GUIDELINES FOR PATCHING

1. Design the patch mix to match the original, with small amount of white cement; may eliminate coarse aggregate or hand place it. Trial and error is the only reliable match method.
2. Saturate area with water and apply bonding agent to base of hole and to water of patch mix.
3. Pack patch mix to density of original.
4. Place exposed aggregate by hand.
5. Bristle brush after setup to match existing material.
6. Moist cure to prevent shrinking.
7. Use form or finish to match original.

CHECKLIST IN PLANNING FOR ARCHITECTURAL CONCRETE PLACING TECHNIQUES:

Pumping vs. bottom drop or other type of bucket.

1. FORMING SYSTEM: Evaluate whether architectural concrete forms can also be used for structural concrete.
2. SHOP DRAWINGS: Determine form quality and steel placement.
3. VIBRATORS: Verify that proper size, frequency, and power are used.
4. RELEASE AGENTS: Consider form material, color impact of agents, and possible use throughout job.
5. CURING COMPOUND: Determine how fast it wears off.
6. WORK CREW: Make certain that a good foreman is supervising the project.
7. SAMPLES: Require approval of forms and finishes.

ARCHITECTURAL CONCRETE

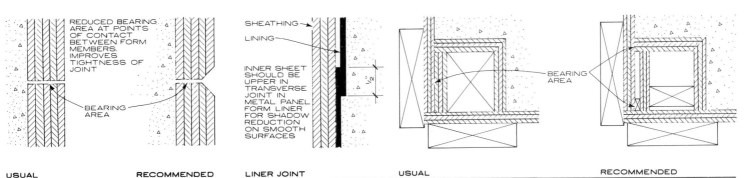

USUAL   RECOMMENDED   LINER JOINT   USUAL   RECOMMENDED

FORM JOINTS

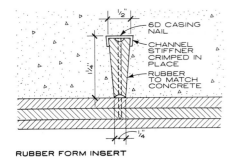

RUBBER FORM INSERT

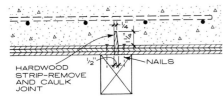

WOOD FORM INSERT

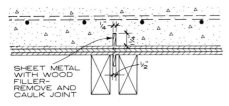

SHEET METAL FORM INSERT

CONTROL JOINTS

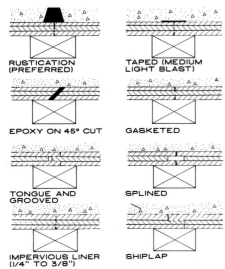

PLYWOOD BUTT JOINTS FOR
EXPOSED AGGREGATE FINISHES

D. Neil Rankins; SHWC, Inc.; Dallas, Texas

CATEGORIES OF ARCHITECTURAL CONCRETE SURFACES

CATEGORY	FINISH	COLOR	FORMS	CRITICAL DETAILS
1. As cast	Remains as is after form removal—usually board marks or wood grain	Cement first influence, fine aggregate second influence	Plastic best All others • Wire brushed plywood • Sandblasted plywood • Exposed grain plywood • Unfinished sheathing lumber • Ammonia sprayed wood • Tongue + groove bands spaced	Slump = $2\frac{1}{2}$-$3\frac{1}{2}$'' Joinery of forms Proper release agent Point form joints to avoid marks
2. Abrasive blasted surfaces A. Brush blast	Uniform scour cleaning	Cement + fine aggregate have = influence	All smooth	Scouring after 7 days Slump = $2\frac{1}{2}$-$3\frac{1}{2}$''
B. Light blast	Sandblast to expose fine and some coarse aggregate	Fine aggregate primary coarse aggregate + cement secondary	All smooth	10% more coarse aggregate Slump = $2\frac{1}{2}$-$3\frac{1}{2}$'' Blasting between 7 and 45 days
C. Medium exposed aggregate	Sandblasted to expose coarse aggregate	Coarse aggregate	All smooth	Higher than normal coarse aggregate Slump = 2-3'' Blast before 7 days
D. Heavy exposed aggregate	Sandblasted to expose coarse aggregate 80% viable	Coarse aggregate	All smooth	Special mix coarse aggregate Slump = 0-2'' Blast within 24 hr Use high frequency vibrator
3. Chemical retardation of surface set	Chemicals expose aggregate Aggregate can be adhered to surface	Coarse aggregate and cement	Glass fiber best and all smooth	Grade of chemical determines depth of etch Stripping scheduled to prevent long drying between stripping and washoff
4. Mechanically fractured surfaces, scaling, bush hammering, jackhammering tooling	Varied	Cement Fine and coarse Aggregate	Textured	Aggregate particles $\frac{3}{8}$'' for scaling and tooling Aggregate particles
5. Combination/fluted	Striated/abrasive blasted/irregular pattern Corrugated/abrasive Vertical rusticated/abrasive blasted Reeded and bush hammered Reeded and hammered Reeded and chiseled	The shallower the surface, the more influence aggregate fines and cement have	Wood or rubber strips, corrugated sheet metal, glass fiber, or asbestos cement	Depends on type of finish desired Wood flute kerfed and nailed loosely

ARCHITECTURAL CONCRETE   3

NOTES

1. See page on stair dimensions for code requirements for stairs.
2. Structural designer to determine reinforcement and verify structural assumptions.

* Denotes BOCA Code.
** Denotes ANSI A117.1.

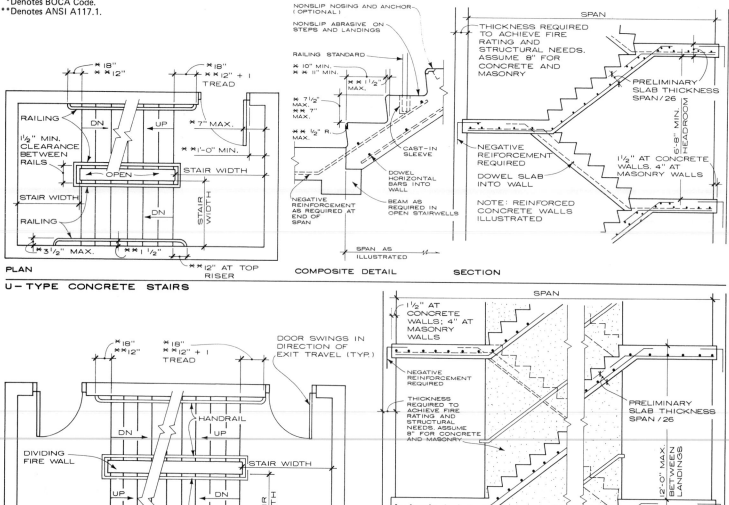

PLAN

U—TYPE CONCRETE STAIRS

COMPOSITE DETAIL   **SECTION**

PLAN

SCISSOR TYPE CONCRETE STAIRS

SECTION

NOTE REINFORCED CONCRETE TOWER ILLUSTRATED

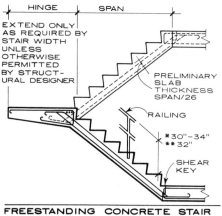

FREESTANDING CONCRETE STAIR

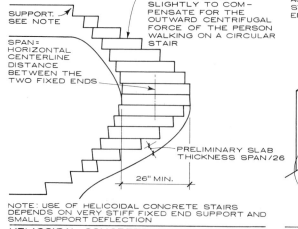

NOTE: USE OF HELICOIDAL CONCRETE STAIRS DEPENDS ON VERY STIFF FIXED END SUPPORT AND SMALL SUPPORT DEFLECTION

HELICOIDAL CONCRETE STAIR

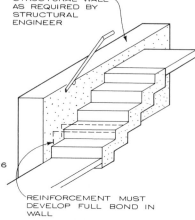

CANTILEVER CONCRETE STAIR

Karlsberger and Associates, Inc.; Columbus, Ohio

CHAPTER 4 MASONRY

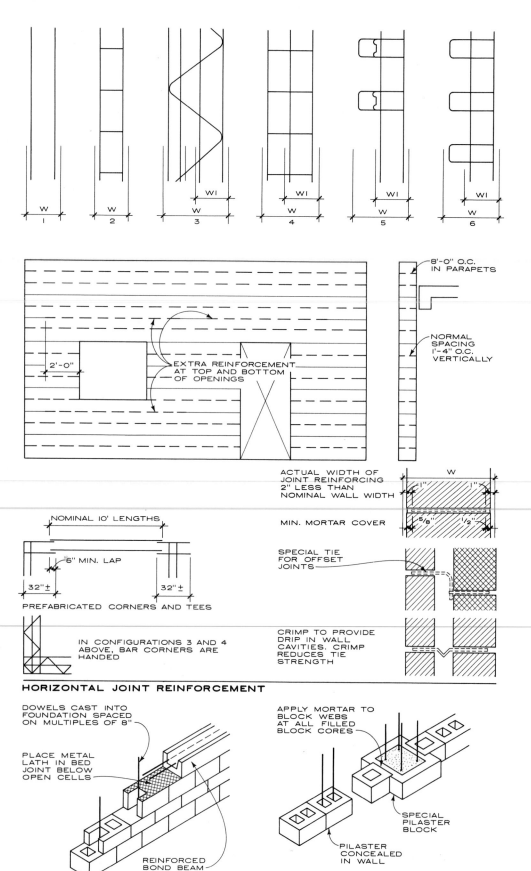

HORIZONTAL JOINT REINFORCEMENT

DOWELS CAST INTO FOUNDATION SPACED ON MULTIPLES OF 8"

PLACE METAL LATH IN BED JOINT BELOW OPEN CELLS

REINFORCED BOND BEAM

HORIZONTAL AND VERTICAL REINFORCEMENT

APPLY MORTAR TO BLOCK WEBS AT ALL FILLED BLOCK CORES

SPECIAL PILASTER BLOCK

PILASTER CONCEALED IN WALL

REINFORCED PILASTERS

STEEL BAR REINFORCEMENT

Metz Train Olson & Youngren; Chicago, Illinois

HORIZONTAL JOINT REINFORCEMENT

Horizontal joint reinforcement is used in masonry walls to control shrinkage cracks, to bond multiwythe (composite) walls, to anchor veneer and cavity wall facing to backup masonry, and to increase the structural strength of the wall.

Reinforcing is available in a great variety of sizes and configurations. Not all manufacturers make all combinations of constructions. Consult local suppliers.

Typical configurations shown are available in both truss and ladder designs. Truss designs provide greater flexural strength.

Refer to the reinforcing configurations shown at the left of this column.

1. Truss configuration with two longitudinal rods suitable for single wythe and lightly reinforced composite walls. Meets most code requirements for bonding multiwythe walls when spaced 16 in. on center vertically and collar joint is filled with mortar.
2. Ladder version of 1.
3. Combination reinforcement and tie for composite and cavity walls. Suitable for anchoring brick veneer or to tie brick cavity wall facing to masonry backup.
4. Similar to 3 but providing four longitudinal wires.
5. Ladder reinforcing with separate adjustable veneer anchor.
6. Ladder reinforcing with tab type tie for anchoring brick facing to backup.

NORMAL CONSTRUCTIONS

1. Metal:
   Plain steel wire.
   Plain steel wire with galvanized cross wire.
   Galvanized wire.
   Hot dip galvanized after fabrication.
   Stainless steel.
2. Width:
   Nominal wall thickness (W) minus 2 in.
   Available backup widths (W) in.: 3, 4, 6, 8, 10, 12, 13, 14, 16.
   Available backup widths (WI) in.: 3, 4, 6, 8, 10.
3. Size of wire (cross wires may be different from longitudinal wires):
   10 gauge: light interior.
   9 gauge: standard.
   8 gauge: heavy duty.
   $3/16$ gauge: extra heavy duty.

SELECTION

Corrosion resistance is required by most codes for reinforcing in exterior walls. Severity of exposure determines selection of metal finish and thickness.

Nine gauge wire develops strength adequate to control shrinkage in concrete masonry walls at normal spacing. Heavier weights increase corrosion resistance and provide greater flexural strength.

PRECAUTIONS

Sections of reinforcing must be lapped 6 in. to prevent a point of weakness.

Do not continue reinforcing through control joints.

Avoid placing flashings in the same joint as reinforcing.

Use prefabricated corners and tees to prevent excessive metal thickness where lapped sections cross.

STEEL BAR REINFORCEMENT

Concrete reinforcing bars may be used to reinforce masonry wall in lieu of horizontal joint reinforcement. Place steel and grout as described on page concerned with reinforced masonry.

Reinforced bond beams spaced 4 ft o.c. vertically may be substituted for horizontal joint reinforcing used to control shrinkage. Vertical reinforcing may be required for earthquake design and for walls without support at the top. Consult local codes.

4   MASONRY ACCESSORIES

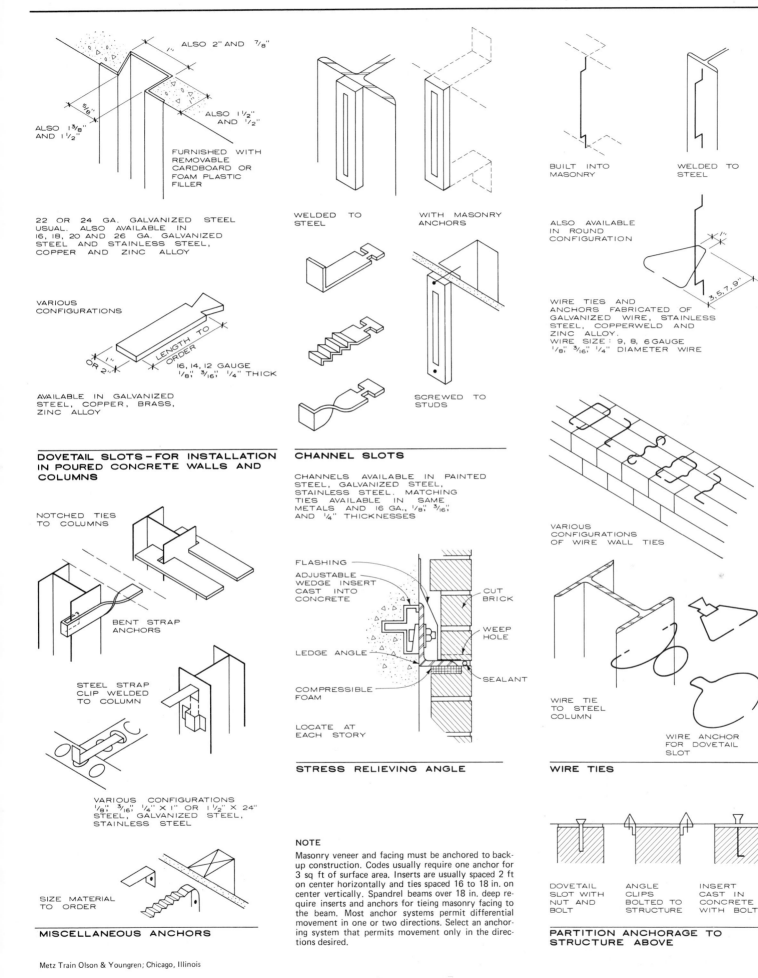

ALSO 2" AND 7/8"

ALSO 1 1/2" AND 1/2"

ALSO 1 3/8" AND 1 1/2"

FURNISHED WITH REMOVABLE CARDBOARD OR FOAM PLASTIC FILLER

22 OR 24 GA. GALVANIZED STEEL USUAL. ALSO AVAILABLE IN 16, 18, 20 AND 26 GA. GALVANIZED STEEL AND STAINLESS STEEL, COPPER AND ZINC ALLOY

VARIOUS CONFIGURATIONS

LENGTH TO ORDER

OR 2", 1"

16, 14, 12 GAUGE 1/8", 3/16", 1/4" THICK

AVAILABLE IN GALVANIZED STEEL, COPPER, BRASS, ZINC ALLOY

WELDED TO STEEL

WITH MASONRY ANCHORS

SCREWED TO STUDS

BUILT INTO MASONRY

WELDED TO STEEL

ALSO AVAILABLE IN ROUND CONFIGURATION

3, 5, 7, 9"

1"

WIRE TIES AND ANCHORS FABRICATED OF GALVANIZED WIRE, STAINLESS STEEL, COPPERWELD AND ZINC ALLOY. WIRE SIZE: 9, 8, 6 GAUGE 1/8", 3/16", 1/4" DIAMETER WIRE

DOVETAIL SLOTS — FOR INSTALLATION IN POURED CONCRETE WALLS AND COLUMNS

NOTCHED TIES TO COLUMNS

BENT STRAP ANCHORS

STEEL STRAP CLIP WELDED TO COLUMN

VARIOUS CONFIGURATIONS 1/8", 3/16", 1/4" X 1" OR 1 1/2" X 24" STEEL, GALVANIZED STEEL, STAINLESS STEEL

CHANNEL SLOTS

CHANNELS AVAILABLE IN PAINTED STEEL, GALVANIZED STEEL, STAINLESS STEEL. MATCHING TIES AVAILABLE IN SAME METALS AND 16 GA., 1/8", 3/16", AND 1/4" THICKNESSES

FLASHING

ADJUSTABLE WEDGE INSERT CAST INTO CONCRETE

CUT BRICK

WEEP HOLE

LEDGE ANGLE

SEALANT

COMPRESSIBLE FOAM

LOCATE AT EACH STORY

STRESS RELIEVING ANGLE

VARIOUS CONFIGURATIONS OF WIRE WALL TIES

WIRE TIE TO STEEL COLUMN

WIRE ANCHOR FOR DOVETAIL SLOT

WIRE TIES

SIZE MATERIAL TO ORDER

MISCELLANEOUS ANCHORS

Metz Train Olson & Youngren; Chicago, Illinois

NOTE

Masonry veneer and facing must be anchored to back-up construction. Codes usually require one anchor for 3 sq ft of surface area. Inserts are usually spaced 2 ft on center horizontally and ties spaced 16 to 18 in. on center vertically. Spandrel beams over 18 in. deep require inserts and anchors for tieing masonry facing to the beam. Most anchor systems permit differential movement in one or two directions. Select an anchoring system that permits movement only in the directions desired.

DOVETAIL SLOT WITH NUT AND BOLT

ANGLE CLIPS BOLTED TO STRUCTURE

INSERT CAST IN CONCRETE WITH BOLT

PARTITION ANCHORAGE TO STRUCTURE ABOVE

RUNNING

¹/₃ RUNNING

6TH COURSE HEADERS

COMMON

6TH COURSE FLEMISH HEADERS

COMMON

GARDEN WALL

ENGLISH CORNER — DUTCH CORNER

ENGLISH

STACK

ENGLISH CORNER — DUTCH CORNER

ENGLISH CROSS OR DUTCH

DUTCH CORNER — ENGLISH CORNER

FLEMISH

FLEMISH (DOUBLE STRETCHER)

FLEMISH (CROSS)

FLEMISH (DIAGONAL)

BRICK BONDS

COLLAR JOINT

HEAD JOINT

BED JOINT

TERMS APPLIED TO JOINTS

STRUCK (POOR)

CONCAVE OR RODDED (GOOD)

FLUSH OR PLAIN CUT (FAIR)

FLUSH & RODDED (FAIR)

SCINTLED (POOR)

WEATHERED (GOOD)

RULED (FAIR)

"V" SHAPED (GOOD)

BEADED (POOR)

RAKED (POOR)

TYPES OF JOINTS (WEATHERABILITY)

BRICK JOINTS

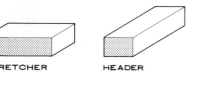

STRETCHER   HEADER   SOLDIER

SHINER   ROWLOCK   SAILOR

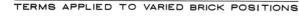

TERMS APPLIED TO VARIED BRICK POSITIONS

Brick Institute of America; McLean, Virginia

SIZES OF MODULAR BRICK

UNIT DESIGNATION	NOMINAL DIMENSIONS			MODULAR COURSING
	THICKNESS	HEIGHT	LENGTH	
MODULAR	4″	2²/₃″	8″	3C = 8″
ENGINEER	4″	3¹/₅″	8″	5C = 16″
ECONOMY	4″	4″	8″	1C = 4″
DOUBLE	4″	5¹/₃″	8″	3C = 16″
ROMAN	4″	2″	12″	2C = 4″
NORMAN	4″	2²/₃″	12″	3C = 8″
NORWEGIAN	4″	3¹/₅″	12″	5C = 16″
UTILITY[1]	4″	4″	12″	1C = 4″
TRIPLE	4″	5¹/₃″	12″	3C = 16″
SCR BRICK	6″	2²/₃″	12″	3C = 8″
6″ NORWEGIAN	6″	3¹/₅″	12″	5C = 16″
6″ JUMBO	6″	4″	12″	1C = 4″
8″ JUMBO	8″	4″	12″	1C = 4″
8″ SQUARE	4″	8″	8″	1C = 8″
12″ SQUARE	4″	12″	12″	1C = 12″

[1] Also called Norman Economy, General and King Norman.
*For special shapes contact local brick manufacturers.

STANDARD MODULAR
4" x 2 2/3" x 8" NOMINAL

BRICK SIZES:
* For 3/8" Joint   3 5/8" x 2 1/4" x 7 5/8"
** For 1/2" Joint   3 1/2" x 2 3/16" x 7 1/2"

NORMAN
4" x 2 2/3" x 12" NOMINAL

BRICK SIZES:
* For 3/8" Joint   3 5/8" x 2 1/4" x 11 5/8"
** For 1/2" Joint   3 1/2" x 2 3/16" x 11 1/2"

SCR BRICK
6" x 2 2/3" x 12" NOMINAL
For 1/2" Joint   5 1/2" x 2 1/8" x 11 1/2"

Joint selected determines brick size
3 courses = 2 modules (8")

ENGINEER
4" x 3 1/5" x 8" NOMINAL

BRICK SIZES:
* For 3/8" Joint   3 5/8" x 2 13/16" x 7 5/8"
For 1/2" Joint   3 1/2" x 2 11/16" x 7 1/2"

Joint selected determines brick size.
5 courses = 4 modules (16").

ECONOMY
4" x 4" x 8" NOMINAL

BRICK SIZES:
* For 3/8" Joint   3 5/8" x 3 5/8" x 7 5/8"
** For 1/2" Joint   3 1/2" x 3 1/2" x 7 1/2"

UTILITY
4" x 4" x 12" NOMINAL

BRICK SIZES:
For 3/8" Joint   3 5/8" x 3 5/8" x 11 5/8"
For 1/2" Joint   3 1/2" x 3 1/2" x 11 1/2"

Joint selected determines brick size.
1 course = 1 module (4")

NOMINAL HEIGHT OF 2 2/3" COURSES

Course	Height	Course	Height
31	6'-10 2/3"	61	13'-6 2/3"
30	6'-8"	60	13'-4"
29	6'-5 1/3"	59	13'-1 1/3"
28	6'-2 2/3"	58	12'-10 2/3"
27	6'-0"	57	12'-8"
26	5'-9 1/3"	56	12'-5 1/3"
25	5'-6 2/3"	55	12'-2 2/3"
24	5'-4"	54	12'-0"
23	5'-1 1/3"	53	11'-9 1/3"
22	4'-10 2/3"	52	11'-6 2/3"
21	4'-8"	51	11'-4"
20	4'-5 1/3"	50	11'-1 1/3"
19	4'-2 2/3"	49	10'-10 2/3"
18	4'-0"	48	10'-8"
17	3'-9 1/3"	47	10'-5 1/3"
16	3'-6 2/3"	46	10'-2 2/3"
15	3'-4"	45	10'-0"
14	3'-1 1/3"	44	9'-9 1/3"
13	2'-10 2/3"	43	9'-6 2/3"
12	2'-8"	42	9'-4"
11	2'-5 1/3"	41	9'-1 1/3"
10	2'-2 1/3"	40	8'-10 2/3"
9	2'-0"	39	8'-8"
8	1'-9 1/3"	38	8'-5 1/3"
7	1'-6 2/3"	37	8'-2 2/3"
6	1'-4"	36	8'-0"
5	1'-1 1/3"	35	7'-9 1/3"
4	10 2/3"	34	7'-6 2/3"
3	8"	33	7'-4"
2	5 1/3"	32	7'-1 1/3"
1	2 2/3"		

NOMINAL HEIGHTS OF 3 1/5" COURSES

Course	Height	Course	Height
29	7'-8 4/5"	59	15'-8 4/5"
28	7'-5 3/5"	58	15'-5 3/5"
27	7'-2 2/5"	57	15'-2 2/5"
26	6'-11 1/5"	56	14'-11 1/5"
25	6'-8"	55	14'-8"
24	6'-4 4/5"	54	14'-4 4/5"
23	6'-1 3/5"	53	14'-1 3/5"
22	5'-10 2/5"	52	13'-10 2/5"
21	5'-7 1/3"	51	13'-7 1/5"
20	5'-4"	50	13'-4"
19	5'-0 4/5"	49	13'-0 4/5"
18	4'-9 3/5"	48	12'-9 3/5"
17	4'-6 2/5"	47	12'-6 2/5"
16	4'-3 1/5"	46	12'-3 1/5"
15	4'-0"	45	12'-0"
14	3'-8 4/5"	44	11'-8 4/5"
13	3'-5 3/5"	43	11'-5 3/5"
12	3'-2 2/5"	42	11'-2 2/5"
11	2'-11 1/5"	41	10'-11 1/5"
10	2'-8"	40	10'-8"
9	2'-4 4/5"	39	10'-4 4/5"
8	2'-1 3/5"	38	10'-1 3/5"
7	1'-10 2/5"	37	9'-10 2/5"
6	1'-7 1/5"	36	9'-7 1/5"
5	1'-4"	35	9'-4"
4	1'-0 4/5"	34	9'-0 4/5"
3	9 3/5"	33	8'-9 3/5"
2	6 2/5"	32	8'-6 2/5"
1	3 1/5"	31	8'-3 1/5"
		30	8'-0"

NOMINAL HEIGHTS OF 4" COURSES

Course	Height	Course	Height
21	7'-0"	43	14'-4"
20	6'-8"	42	14'-0"
19	6'-4"	41	13'-8"
18	6'-0"	40	13'-4"
17	5'-8"	39	13'-0"
16	5'-4"	38	12'-8"
15	5'-0"	37	12'-4"
14	4'-8"	36	12'-0"
13	4'-4"	35	11'-8"
12	4'-0"	34	11'-4"
11	3'-8"	33	11'-0"
10	3'-4"	32	10'-8"
9	3'-0"	31	10'-4"
8	2'-8"	30	10'-0"
7	2'-4"	29	9'-8"
6	2'-0"	28	9'-4"
5	1'-8"	27	9'-0"
4	1'-4"	26	8'-8"
3	1'-0"	25	8'-4"
2	8"	24	8'-0"
1	4"	23	7'-8"
		22	7'-4"

NOTES
Not all sizes made in all sections of U.S.; check with local manufacturers for sizes available.

Brick Institute of America; McLean, Virginia

*3/8" Joint used for facing brick.
**1/2" Joint used for glazed and structural units and building brick.

Grid lines (—·—·—·—) are 4" modules. Vertical dimensions are from bottom of mortar joint to bottom of mortar joint.

VERTICAL BRICK COURSES

NUMBER OF BRICKS AND JOINTS	HEIGHT	
	3/8" JOINTS	1/2" JOINTS
1 brk. & 1 jt.	2 5/8"	2 3/4"
2 brks. & 2 jts.	5 1/4"	5 1/2"
3 brks. & 3 jts.	7 7/8"	8 1/4"
4 brks. & 4 jts.	10 1/2"	11"
5 brks. & 5 jts.	1'- 1 1/8"	1'- 1 3/4"
6 brks. & 6 jts.	1'- 3 3/4"	1'- 4 1/2"
7 brks. & 7 jts.	1'- 6 3/8"	1'- 7 1/4"
8 brks. & 8 jts.	1'- 9"	1'-10"
9 brks. & 9 jts.	1'-11 5/8"	2'- 0 3/4"
10 brks. & 10 jts.	2'- 2 1/4"	2'- 3 1/2"
11 brks. & 11 jts.	2'- 4 7/8"	2'- 6 1/4"
12 brks. & 12 jts.	2'- 7 1/2"	2'- 9"
13 brks. & 13 jts.	2'-10 1/8"	2'-11 3/4"
14 brks. & 14 jts.	3'- 0 3/4"	3'- 2 1/2"
15 brks. & 15 jts.	3'- 3 5/8"	3'- 5 1/4"
16 brks. & 16 jts.	3'- 6"	3'- 8"
17 brks. & 17 jts.	3'- 8 5/8"	3'-10 3/4"
18 brks. & 18 jts.	3'-11 1/4"	4'- 1 1/2"
19 brks. & 19 jts.	4'- 1 7/8"	4'- 4 1/4"
20 brks. & 20 jts.	4'- 4 1/2"	4'- 7"
21 brks. & 21 jts.	4'- 7 1/8"	4'- 9 3/4"
22 brks. & 22 jts.	4'- 9 3/4"	5'- 0 1/2"
23 brks. & 23 jts.	5'- 0 3/8"	5'- 3 1/4"
24 brks. & 24 jts.	5'- 3"	5'- 6"
25 brks. & 25 jts.	5'- 5 5/8"	5'- 8 3/4"
26 brks. & 26 jts.	5'- 8 1/4"	5'-11 1/2"
27 brks. & 27 jts.	5'-10 7/8"	6'- 2 1/4"
28 brks. & 28 jts.	6'- 1 1/2"	6'- 5"
29 brks. & 29 jts.	6'- 4 1/8"	6'- 7 3/4"
30 brks. & 30 jts.	6'- 6 3/4"	6'-10 1/2"
31 brks. & 31 jts.	6'- 9 3/8"	7'- 1 1/4"
32 brks. & 32 jts.	7'- 0"	7'- 4"
33 brks. & 33 jts.	7'- 2 5/8"	7'- 6 3/4"
34 brks. & 34 jts.	7'- 5 1/4"	7'- 9 1/2"
35 brks. & 35 jts.	7'- 7 7/8"	8'- 0 1/4"
36 brks. & 36 jts.	7'-10 1/2"	8'- 3"
37 brks. & 37 jts.	8'- 1 1/8"	8'- 5 3/4"
38 brks. & 38 jts.	8'- 3 3/4"	8'- 8 1/2"
39 brks. & 39 jts.	8'- 6 3/8"	8'-11 1/4"
40 brks. & 40 jts.	8'- 9"	9'- 2"
41 brks. & 41 jts.	8'-11 5/8"	9'- 4 3/4"
42 brks. & 42 jts.	9'- 2 1/4"	9'- 7 1/2"
43 brks. & 43 jts.	9'- 4 7/8"	9'-10 1/4"
44 brks. & 44 jts.	9'- 7 1/2"	10'- 1"
45 brks. & 45 jts.	9'-10 1/8"	10'- 3 3/4"
46 brks. & 46 jts.	10'- 0 3/4"	10'- 6 1/2"
47 brks. & 47 jts.	10'- 3 3/8"	10'- 9 1/4"
48 brks. & 48 jts.	10'- 6"	11'- 0"
49 brks. & 49 jts.	10'- 8 5/8"	11'- 2 3/4"
50 brks. & 50 jts.	10'-11 1/4"	11'- 5 1/2"
51 brks. & 51 jts.	11'- 1 7/8"	11'- 8 1/4"
52 brks. & 52 jts.	11'- 4 1/2"	11'-11"
53 brks. & 53 jts.	11'- 7 1/8"	12'- 1 3/4"
54 brks. & 54 jts.	11'- 9 3/4"	12'- 4 1/2"
55 brks. & 55 jts.	12'- 0 3/8"	12'- 7 1/4"
56 brks. & 56 jts.	12'- 3"	12'-10"
57 brks. & 57 jts.	12'- 5 5/8"	13'- 0 3/4"
58 brks. & 58 jts.	12'- 8 1/4"	13'- 3 1/2"
59 brks. & 59 jts.	12'-10 7/8"	13'- 6 1/4"
60 brks. & 60 jts.	13'- 1 1/2"	13'- 9"
61 brks. & 61 jts.	13'- 4 1/8"	13'-11 3/4"
62 brks. & 62 jts.	13'- 6 3/4"	14'- 2 1/2"
63 brks. & 63 jts.	13'- 9 3/8"	14'- 5 1/4"
64 brks. & 64 jts.	14'- 0"	14'- 8"
65 brks. & 65 jts.	14'- 2 5/8"	14'-10 3/4"
66 brks. & 66 jts.	14'- 5 1/4"	15'- 1 1/2"
67 brks. & 67 jts.	14'- 7 7/8"	15'- 4 1/4"
68 brks. & 68 jts.	14'-10 1/2"	15'- 7"
69 brks. & 69 jts.	15'- 1 1/8"	15'- 9 3/4"
70 brks. & 70 jts.	15'- 3 3/4"	16'- 0 1/2"
71 brks. & 71 jts.	15'- 6 3/8"	16'- 3 1/4"
72 brks. & 72 jts.	15'- 9"	16'- 6"
73 brks. & 73 jts.	15'-11 5/8"	16'- 8 3/4"
74 brks. & 74 jts.	16'- 2 1/4"	16'-11 1/2"
75 brks. & 75 jts.	16'- 4 7/8"	17'- 2 1/4"
76 brks. & 76 jts.	16'- 7 1/2"	17'- 5"

HORIZONTAL BRICK COURSES

NUMBER OF BRICKS AND JOINTS	LENGTH OF COURSE	
	3/8" JOINTS	1/2" JOINTS
1 brk. & 0 jt.	0'- 8"	0'- 8"
1 1/2 brks. & 1 jt.	1'- 0 3/8"	1'- 0 1/2"
2 brks. & 1 jt.	1'- 4 3/8"	1'- 4 1/2"
2 1/2 brks. & 2 jts.	1'- 8 3/4"	1'- 9"
3 brks. & 2 jts.	2'- 0 3/4"	2'- 1"
3 1/2 brks. & 3 jts.	2'- 5 1/8"	2'- 5 1/2"
4 brks. & 3 jts.	2'- 9 1/8"	2'- 9 1/2"
4 1/2 brks. & 4 jts.	3'- 1 1/2"	3'- 2"
5 brks. & 4 jts.	3'- 5 1/2"	3'- 6"
5 1/2 brks. & 5 jts.	3'- 9 7/8"	3'-10 1/2"
6 brks. & 5 jts.	4'- 1 7/8"	4'- 2 1/2"
6 1/2 brks. & 6 jts.	4'- 6 1/4"	4'- 7"
7 brks. & 6 jts.	4'-10 1/4"	4'-11"
7 1/2 brks. & 7 jts.	5'- 2 5/8"	5'- 3 1/2"
8 brks. & 7 jts.	5'- 6 5/8"	5'- 7 1/2"
8 1/2 brks. & 8 jts.	5'-11"	6'- 0"
9 brks. & 8 jts.	6'- 3"	6'- 4"
9 1/2 brks. & 9 jts.	6'- 7 3/8"	6'- 8 1/2"
10 brks. & 9 jts.	6'-11 3/8"	7'- 0 1/2"
10 1/2 brks. & 10 jts.	7'- 3 3/4"	7'- 5"
11 brks. & 10 jts.	7'- 7 3/4"	7'- 9"
11 1/2 brks. & 11 jts.	8'- 0 1/8"	8'- 1 1/2"
12 brks. & 11 jts.	8'- 4 1/8"	8'- 5 1/2"
12 1/2 brks. & 12 jts.	8'- 8 1/2"	8'-10"
13 brks. & 12 jts.	9'- 0 1/2"	9'- 2"
13 1/2 brks. & 13 jts.	9'- 4 7/8"	9'- 6 1/2"
14 brks. & 13 jts.	9'- 8 7/8"	9'-10 1/2"
14 1/2 brks. & 14 jts.	10'- 1 1/4"	10'- 3"
15 brks. & 14 jts.	10'- 5 1/4"	10'- 7"
15 1/2 brks. & 15 jts.	10'- 9 5/8"	10'-11 1/2"
16 brks. & 15 jts.	11'- 1 5/8"	11'- 3 1/2"
16 1/2 brks. & 16 jts.	11'- 6"	11'- 8"
17 brks. & 16 jts.	11'-10"	12'- 0"
17 1/2 brks. & 17 jts.	12'- 2 3/8"	12'- 4 1/2"
18 brks. & 17 jts.	12'- 6 3/8"	12'- 8 1/2"
18 1/2 brks. & 18 jts.	12'-10 3/4"	13'- 1"
19 brks. & 18 jts.	13'- 2 3/4"	13'- 5"
19 1/2 brks. & 19 jts.	13'- 7 1/8"	13'- 9 1/2"
20 brks. & 19 jts.	13'-11 1/8"	14'- 1 1/2"
20 1/2 brks. & 20 jts.	14'- 3 1/2"	14'- 6"
21 brks. & 20 jts.	14'- 7 1/2"	14'-10"
21 1/2 brks. & 21 jts.	14'-11 7/8"	15'- 2 1/2"
22 brks. & 21 jts.	15'- 3 7/8"	15'- 6 1/2"
22 1/2 brks. & 22 jts.	15'- 8 1/4"	15'-11"
23 brks. & 22 jts.	16'- 0 1/4"	16'- 3"
23 1/2 brks. & 23 jts.	16'- 4 5/8"	16'- 7 1/2"
24 brks. & 23 jts.	16'- 8 5/8"	16'-11 1/2"
24 1/2 brks. & 24 jts.	17'- 1"	17'- 4"
25 brks. & 24 jts.	17'- 5"	17'- 8"
25 1/2 brks. & 25 jts.	17'- 9 3/8"	18'- 0 1/2"
26 brks. & 25 jts.	18'- 1 3/8"	18'- 4 1/2"
26 1/2 brks. & 26 jts.	18'- 5 3/4"	18'- 9"
27 brks. & 26 jts.	18'- 9 3/4"	19'- 1"
27 1/2 brks. & 27 jts.	19'- 2 1/8"	19'- 5 1/2"
28 brks. & 27 jts.	19'- 6 1/8"	19'- 9 1/2"
28 1/2 brks. & 28 jts.	19'-10 1/2"	20'- 2"
29 brks. & 28 jts.	20'- 2 1/2"	20'- 6"
29 1/2 brks. & 29 jts.	20'- 6 7/8"	20'-10 1/2"
30 brks. & 29 jts.	20'-10 7/8"	21'- 2 1/2"
30 1/2 brks. & 30 jts.	21'- 3 1/4"	21'- 7"
31 brks. & 30 jts.	21'- 7 1/4"	21'-11"
31 1/2 brks. & 31 jts.	21'-11 5/8"	22'- 3 1/2"
32 brks. & 31 jts.	22'- 3 5/8"	22'- 7 1/2"
32 1/2 brks. & 32 jts.	22'- 8"	23'- 0"
33 brks. & 32 jts.	23'- 0"	23'- 4"
33 1/2 brks. & 33 jts.	23'- 4 3/8"	23'- 8 1/2"
34 brks. & 33 jts.	23'- 8 3/8"	24'- 0 1/2"
34 1/2 brks. & 34 jts.	24'- 0 3/4"	24'- 5"
35 brks. & 34 jts.	24'- 4 3/4"	24'- 9"
35 1/2 brks. & 35 jts.	24'- 9 1/8"	25'- 1 1/2"
36 brks. & 35 jts.	25'- 1 1/8"	25'- 5 1/2"
36 1/2 brks. & 36 jts.	25'- 5 1/2"	25'-10"
37 brks. & 36 jts.	25'- 9 1/2"	26'- 2"
37 1/2 brks. & 37 jts.	26'- 1 7/8"	26'- 6 1/2"
38 brks. & 37 jts.	26'- 5 7/8"	26'-10 1/2"
38 1/2 brks. & 38 jts.	26'-10 1/4"	27'- 3"

NUMBER OF BRICKS AND JOINTS	LENGTH OF COURSE	
	3/8" JOINTS	1/2" JOINTS
39 brks. & 38 jts.	27'- 2 1/4"	27'- 7"
39 1/2 brks. & 39 jts.	27'- 6 5/8"	27'-11 1/2"
40 brks. & 39 jts.	27'-10 5/8"	28'- 3 1/2"
40 1/2 brks. & 40 jts.	28'- 3"	28'- 8"
41 brks. & 40 jts.	28'- 7"	29'- 0"
41 1/2 brks. & 41 jts.	28'-11 3/8"	29'- 4 1/2"
42 brks. & 41 jts.	29'- 3 3/8"	29'- 8 1/2"
42 1/2 brks. & 42 jts.	29'- 7 3/4"	30'- 1"
43 brks. & 42 jts.	29'-11 3/4"	30'- 5"
43 1/2 brks. & 43 jts.	30'- 4 1/8"	30'- 9 1/2"
44 brks. & 43 jts.	30'- 8 1/8"	31'- 1 1/2"
44 1/2 brks. & 44 jts.	31'- 0 1/2"	31'- 6"
45 brks. & 44 jts.	31'- 4 1/2"	31'-10"
45 1/2 brks. & 45 jts.	31'- 8 7/8"	32'- 2 1/2"
46 brks. & 45 jts.	32'- 0 7/8"	32'- 6 1/2"
46 1/2 brks. & 46 jts.	32'- 5 1/4"	32'-11"
47 brks. & 46 jts.	32'- 9 1/4"	33'- 3"
47 1/2 brks. & 47 jts.	33'- 1 5/8"	33'- 7 1/2"
48 brks. & 47 jts.	33'- 5 5/8"	33'-11 1/2"
48 1/2 brks. & 48 jts.	33'-10"	34'- 4"
49 brks. & 48 jts.	34'- 2"	34'- 8"
49 1/2 brks. & 49 jts.	34'- 6 3/8"	35'- 0 1/2"
50 brks. & 49 jts.	34'-10 3/8"	35'- 4 1/2"
50 1/2 brks. & 50 jts.	35'- 2 3/4"	35'- 9"
51 brks. & 50 jts.	35'- 6 3/4"	36'- 1"
51 1/2 brks. & 51 jts.	35'-11 1/8"	36'- 5 1/2"
52 brks. & 51 jts.	36'- 3 1/8"	36'- 9 1/2"
52 1/2 brks. & 52 jts.	36'- 7 1/2"	37'- 2"
53 brks. & 52 jts.	36'-11 1/2"	37'- 6"
53 1/2 brks. & 53 jts.	37'- 3 7/8"	37'-10 1/2"
54 brks. & 53 jts.	37'- 7 7/8"	38'- 2 1/2"
54 1/2 brks. & 54 jts.	38'- 0 1/4"	38'- 7"
55 brks. & 54 jts.	38'- 4 1/4"	38'-11"
55 1/2 brks. & 55 jts.	38'- 8 5/8"	39'- 3 1/2"
56 brks. & 55 jts.	39'- 0 5/8"	39'- 7 1/2"
56 1/2 brks. & 56 jts.	39'- 5"	40'- 0"
57 brks. & 56 jts.	39'- 9"	40'- 4"
57 1/2 brks. & 57 jts.	40'- 1 3/8"	40'- 8 1/2"
58 brks. & 57 jts.	40'- 5 3/8"	41'- 0 1/2"
58 1/2 brks. & 58 jts.	40'- 9 3/4"	41'- 5"
59 brks. & 58 jts.	41'- 1 3/4"	41'- 9"
59 brks. & 58 jts.	41'- 1"	41'- 9"
59 1/2 brks. & 59 jts.	41'- 6 1/8"	42'- 1 1/2"
60 brks. & 59 jts.	41'-10 1/8"	42'- 5 1/2"

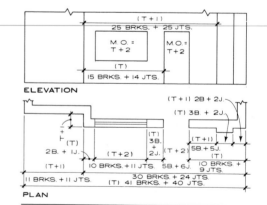

ELEVATION

PLAN

EXAMPLE SHOWING USE OF TABLE

T: Dimensions and number of joints as given in the table, that is, one joint less than the number of bricks.

T + 1: One brick joint added to figure given in the table, that is, the number of bricks is equal to the number of joints.

T + 2: Two brick joints added to figure given in the table, that is, one joint more than the number of bricks.

Brick Institute of America; McLean, Virginia

4   UNIT MASONRY

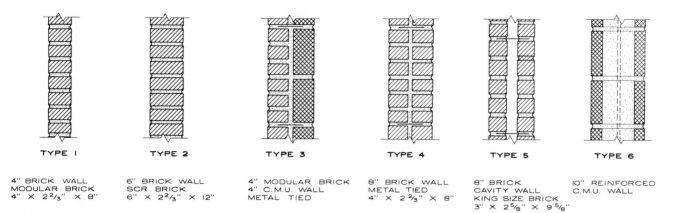

TYPE 1	TYPE 2	TYPE 3	TYPE 4	TYPE 5	TYPE 6	
4" BRICK WALL MODULAR BRICK 4" × 2²/₃" × 8"	6" BRICK WALL SCR BRICK 6" × 2²/₃" × 12"	4" MODULAR BRICK 4" C.M.U. WALL METAL TIED	8" BRICK WALL METAL TIED 4" × 2²/₃" × 8"	8" BRICK CAVITY WALL KING SIZE BRICK 3" × 2⁵/₈" × 9⁵/₈"	10" REINFORCED C.M.U. WALL	

PROPERTIES OF MASONRY WALLS

WALL TYPE NUMBER		1	2	3	4	5[1]	6
Allowable compressive load (lb/linear ft)	Type M mortar	9	27,000[2]	7778[2,3]	36,600[2,3]	9	9
	Type S mortar		23,625[2]	6863[2,3]	32,025[2,3]		
	Type N mortar		20,250[2]	6405[2,3]	27,450[2,3]		
Lateral support spacing (ft-in.)	Load bearing		9'-0"	12'-0"	13'-4"		
Material quantity (per 100 sq ft)[7]	Mortar (cu ft)	5.5	7.9	11	14.1	7.8	
	Brick/C.M.U.	675	450	675/113	1350	960	
U value (Btu/sq ft · hr · F°)	Uninsulated	0.78	0.66	0.30-0.49[8]	0.58	0.40	
U value with 1 in. rigid insulation	(Polystyrene)	0.15	0.15	0.11-0.13[8]	0.14	0.13	
Wall weight (lb/sq ft)	Unplastered	40	60	52-69[8]	80	60	
Average sound resistance (S.T.C.)	Unplastered	45	51	45-50[8]	52	49(est.)	
Fire resistance (hr)[10]	Unplastered	1	2	4	2-4[8]	3	

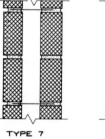
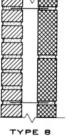
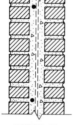

TYPE 7	TYPE 8	TYPE 9	TYPE 10	TYPE 11	TYPE 12	
10" CAVITY WALL SPLIT FACE C.M.U. 4" C.M.U.	10" CAVITY WALL—4" BRICK AND 4" C.M.U.	10" REINFORCED BRICK MASONRY WALL (R.B.M.)	12" CAVITY WALL—4" BRICK AND 6" C.M.U.	10" REINFORCED C.M.U. WALL	6" C.M.U. WALL	

PROPERTIES OF MASONRY WALLS

WALL TYPE NUMBER		7[1]	8[1]	9	10[1]	11	12
Allowable compressive load (lb/linear ft)	Type M mortar	6090	6090	9	7770	9	5738
	Type S mortar	5220	5220		6660		5063
	Type N mortar	4785	4785		6105		4725
Lateral support spacing (ft-in.)	Load bearing	12'-0"	12'-0"		15'-0"		9'-0"
Material quantity (per 100 sq ft)	Mortar (cu ft)	12	15	11/18.8	15		6
	Brick/C.M.U.	113/113	675/113	1350	675/113		113
U value (Btu/sq ft · hr · F°)	Uninsulated	0.23-0.33[8]	0.23-0.33[8]	0.44	0.22-0.32[8]		0.32-0.59[8]
U value with 1 in. rigid insulation	(Polystyrene)	0.11-0.12[8]	0.11-0.12[8]	0.13	0.11-0.12[8]		0.12-0.14[8]
Wall weight (lb/sq ft)	Unplastered	52-69[8]	52-69[8]	94.2	58-84[8]		20-46[8]
Average sound resistance (S.T.C.)	Unplastered	55	55	59	55		30-45[8]
Fire resistance (hr)[10]	Unplastered	4	4	4	4		1-2[8]

NOTES

1. Use straight metal wire ties—no drips.
2. Brick compressive strength: 8000 psi plus.
3. Collar joints filled with mortar (¹/₂").
4. If loads bear on only one wythe, allowable loads are reduced by 20%.
5. Masonry compressive strength (F'M) = 3000 psi h/t = 25.
6. Load bearing strengths are based on allowable compressive strengths, taken from the empirical ANSI A41.1, American Standard Building Code Requirements for masonry.

7. Waste is not included, as this will vary with the job. A waste factor of 2 to 5% is frequently applied for masonry units and 10 to 20% for mortar.
8. A range of values is shown for several categories because of aggregate type and density of units.
9. Rational design and engineered masonry should be used in order to handle all variables under load bearing conditions.
10. Verify Fire Resistance Rating in Building Code.

Robert Joseph Sangiamo, AIA; New York, New York

Davis, Brody & Associates; New York, New York

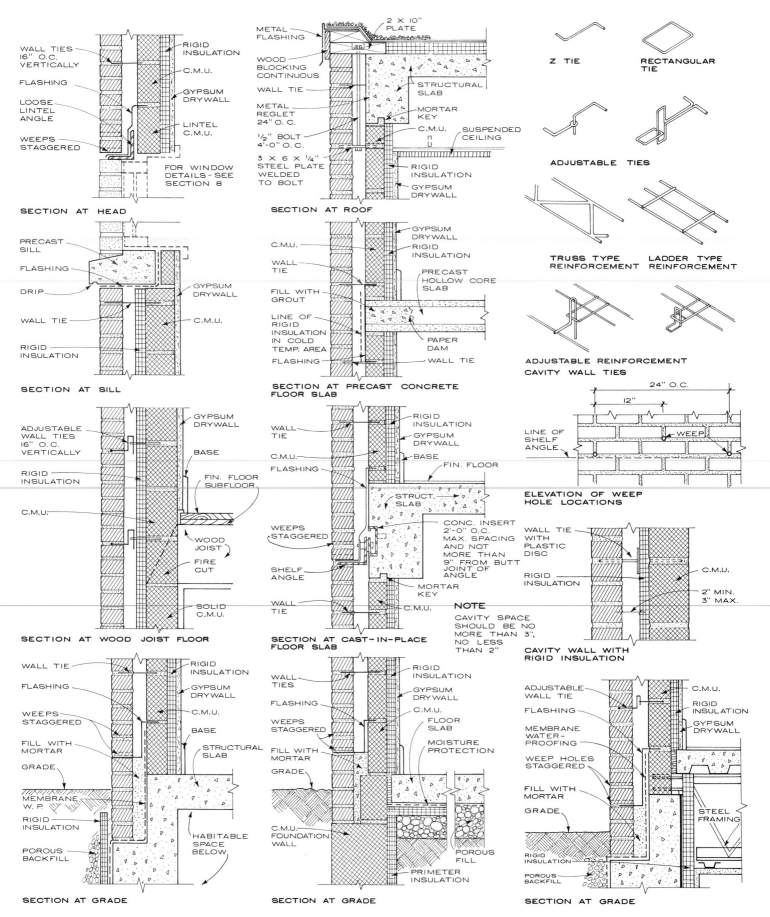

SECTION AT HEAD

- WALL TIES 16" O.C. VERTICALLY
- FLASHING
- LOOSE LINTEL ANGLE
- WEEPS STAGGERED
- RIGID INSULATION
- C.M.U.
- GYPSUM DRYWALL
- LINTEL C.M.U.
- FOR WINDOW DETAILS-SEE SECTION 8

SECTION AT SILL

- PRECAST SILL
- FLASHING
- DRIP
- WALL TIE
- RIGID INSULATION
- GYPSUM DRYWALL
- C.M.U.

SECTION AT WOOD JOIST FLOOR

- ADJUSTABLE WALL TIES 16" O.C. VERTICALLY
- RIGID INSULATION
- C.M.U.
- GYPSUM DRYWALL
- BASE
- FIN. FLOOR SUBFLOOR
- WOOD JOIST
- FIRE CUT
- SOLID C.M.U.

SECTION AT GRADE

- WALL TIE
- FLASHING
- WEEPS STAGGERED
- FILL WITH MORTAR
- GRADE
- MEMBRANE W.P.
- RIGID INSULATION
- POROUS BACKFILL
- RIGID INSULATION
- GYPSUM DRYWALL
- C.M.U.
- BASE
- STRUCTURAL SLAB
- HABITABLE SPACE BELOW

SECTION AT ROOF

- METAL FLASHING
- WOOD BLOCKING CONTINUOUS
- WALL TIE
- METAL REGLET 24" O.C.
- ½" BOLT 4'-0" O.C.
- 3 × 6 × ¼" STEEL PLATE WELDED TO BOLT
- 2 × 10" PLATE
- STRUCTURAL SLAB
- MORTAR KEY
- C.M.U.
- SUSPENDED CEILING
- RIGID INSULATION
- GYPSUM DRYWALL

SECTION AT PRECAST CONCRETE FLOOR SLAB

- GYPSUM DRYWALL
- RIGID INSULATION
- C.M.U.
- WALL TIE
- FILL WITH GROUT
- LINE OF RIGID INSULATION IN COLD TEMP. AREA
- FLASHING
- PRECAST HOLLOW CORE SLAB
- PAPER DAM
- WALL TIE

SECTION AT CAST-IN-PLACE FLOOR SLAB

- WALL TIE
- C.M.U.
- FLASHING
- WEEPS STAGGERED
- SHELF ANGLE
- WALL TIE
- RIGID INSULATION
- GYPSUM DRYWALL
- BASE
- FIN. FLOOR
- STRUCT. SLAB
- CONC. INSERT 2'-0" O.C. MAX. SPACING AND NOT MORE THAN 9" FROM BUTT JOINT OF ANGLE
- MORTAR KEY
- C.M.U.

NOTE
CAVITY SPACE SHOULD BE NO MORE THAN 3", NO LESS THAN 2"

SECTION AT GRADE

- WALL TIES
- FLASHING
- WEEPS STAGGERED
- FILL WITH MORTAR
- GRADE
- C.M.U. FOUNDATION WALL
- RIGID INSULATION
- GYPSUM DRYWALL
- C.M.U.
- FLOOR SLAB
- MOISTURE PROTECTION
- POROUS FILL
- PRIMETER INSULATION

Z TIE   RECTANGULAR TIE

ADJUSTABLE TIES

TRUSS TYPE REINFORCEMENT   LADDER TYPE REINFORCEMENT

ADJUSTABLE REINFORCEMENT CAVITY WALL TIES

ELEVATION OF WEEP HOLE LOCATIONS

- 24" O.C.
- 12"
- LINE OF SHELF ANGLE
- WEEP

CAVITY WALL WITH RIGID INSULATION

- WALL TIE WITH PLASTIC DISC
- RIGID INSULATION
- C.M.U.
- 2" MIN. 3" MAX.

SECTION AT GRADE

- ADJUSTABLE WALL TIE
- FLASHING
- MEMBRANE WATER-PROOFING
- WEEP HOLES STAGGERED
- FILL WITH MORTAR
- GRADE
- RIGID INSULATION
- POROUS BACKFILL
- C.M.U.
- RIGID INSULATION
- GYPSUM DRYWALL
- STEEL FRAMING

Robert J. Sangiamo, AIA; New York, New York
Davis, Brody & Associates; New York, New York

4 UNIT MASONRY

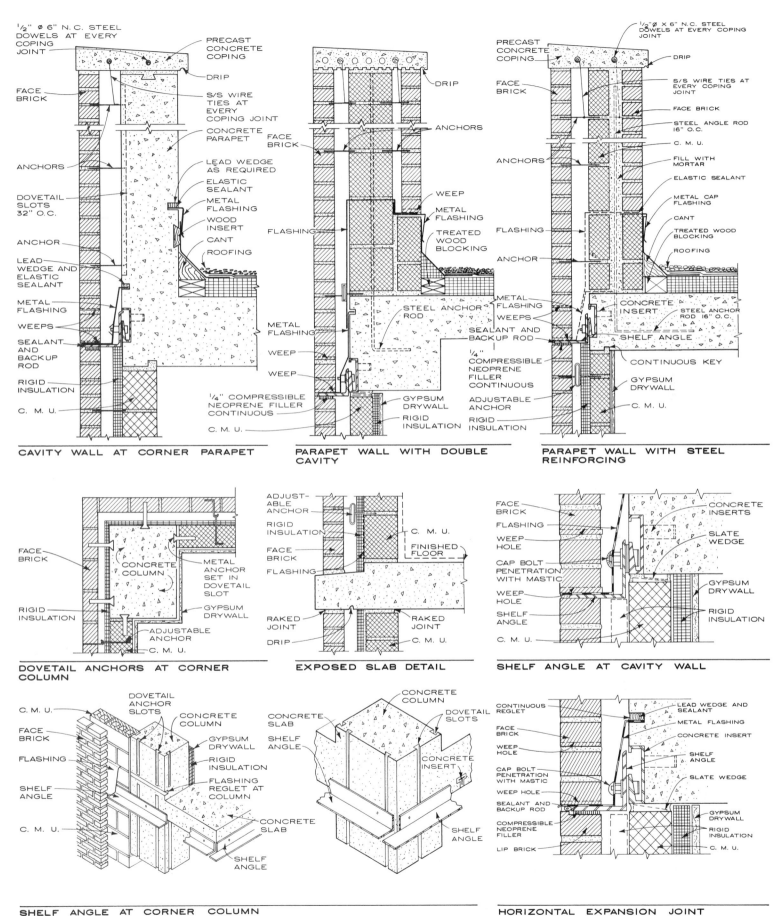

½" ⌀ 6" N.C. STEEL DOWELS AT EVERY COPING JOINT

FACE BRICK

ANCHORS

DOVETAIL SLOTS 32" O.C.

ANCHOR

LEAD WEDGE AND ELASTIC SEALANT

METAL FLASHING

WEEPS

SEALANT AND BACKUP ROD

RIGID INSULATION

C. M. U.

PRECAST CONCRETE COPING

DRIP

S/S WIRE TIES AT EVERY COPING JOINT

CONCRETE PARAPET

LEAD WEDGE AS REQUIRED

ELASTIC SEALANT

METAL FLASHING

WOOD INSERT

CANT

ROOFING

CAVITY WALL AT CORNER PARAPET

FACE BRICK

FLASHING

METAL FLASHING

WEEP

WEEP

¼" COMPRESSIBLE NEOPRENE FILLER CONTINUOUS

C. M. U.

DRIP

ANCHORS

WEEP

METAL FLASHING

TREATED WOOD BLOCKING

STEEL ANCHOR ROD

GYPSUM DRYWALL

RIGID INSULATION

ADJUSTABLE ANCHOR

RIGID INSULATION

PARAPET WALL WITH DOUBLE CAVITY

½"⌀ × 6" N.C. STEEL DOWELS AT EVERY COPING JOINT

PRECAST CONCRETE COPING

FACE BRICK

ANCHORS

FLASHING

ANCHOR

METAL FLASHING

WEEPS

SEALANT AND BACKUP ROD

¼" COMPRESSIBLE NEOPRENE FILLER CONTINUOUS

DRIP

S/S WIRE TIES AT EVERY COPING JOINT

FACE BRICK

STEEL ANGLE ROD 16" O.C.

C. M. U.

FILL WITH MORTAR

ELASTIC SEALANT

METAL CAP FLASHING

CANT

TREATED WOOD BLOCKING

ROOFING

CONCRETE INSERT

STEEL ANCHOR ROD 16" O.C.

SHELF ANGLE

CONTINUOUS KEY

GYPSUM DRYWALL

C. M. U.

PARAPET WALL WITH STEEL REINFORCING

FACE BRICK

RIGID INSULATION

CONCRETE COLUMN

METAL ANCHOR SET IN DOVETAIL SLOT

GYPSUM DRYWALL

ADJUSTABLE ANCHOR

C. M. U.

DOVETAIL ANCHORS AT CORNER COLUMN

ADJUSTABLE ANCHOR

RIGID INSULATION

FACE BRICK

FLASHING

RAKED JOINT

DRIP

C. M. U.

FINISHED FLOOR

RAKED JOINT

C. M. U.

EXPOSED SLAB DETAIL

FACE BRICK

FLASHING

WEEP HOLE

CAP BOLT PENETRATION WITH MASTIC

WEEP HOLE

SHELF ANGLE

C. M. U.

CONCRETE INSERTS

SLATE WEDGE

GYPSUM DRYWALL

RIGID INSULATION

SHELF ANGLE AT CAVITY WALL

C. M. U.

FACE BRICK

FLASHING

SHELF ANGLE

C. M. U.

DOVETAIL ANCHOR SLOTS

CONCRETE COLUMN

GYPSUM DRYWALL

RIGID INSULATION

FLASHING REGLET AT COLUMN

CONCRETE SLAB

SHELF ANGLE

SHELF ANGLE AT CORNER COLUMN

CONCRETE COLUMN

CONCRETE SLAB

SHELF ANGLE

CONCRETE INSERT

DOVETAIL SLOTS

CONCRETE INSERT

SHELF ANGLE

SHELF ANGLE

CONTINUOUS REGLET

FACE BRICK

WEEP HOLE

CAP BOLT PENETRATION WITH MASTIC

WEEP HOLE

SEALANT AND BACKUP ROD

COMPRESSIBLE NEOPRENE FILLER

LIP BRICK

LEAD WEDGE AND SEALANT

METAL FLASHING

CONCRETE INSERT

SHELF ANGLE

SLATE WEDGE

GYPSUM DRYWALL

RIGID INSULATION

C. M. U.

HORIZONTAL EXPANSION JOINT

Robert J. Sangiamo, AIA; New York, New York

Davis, Brody & Associates; New York, New York

UNIT MASONRY   4

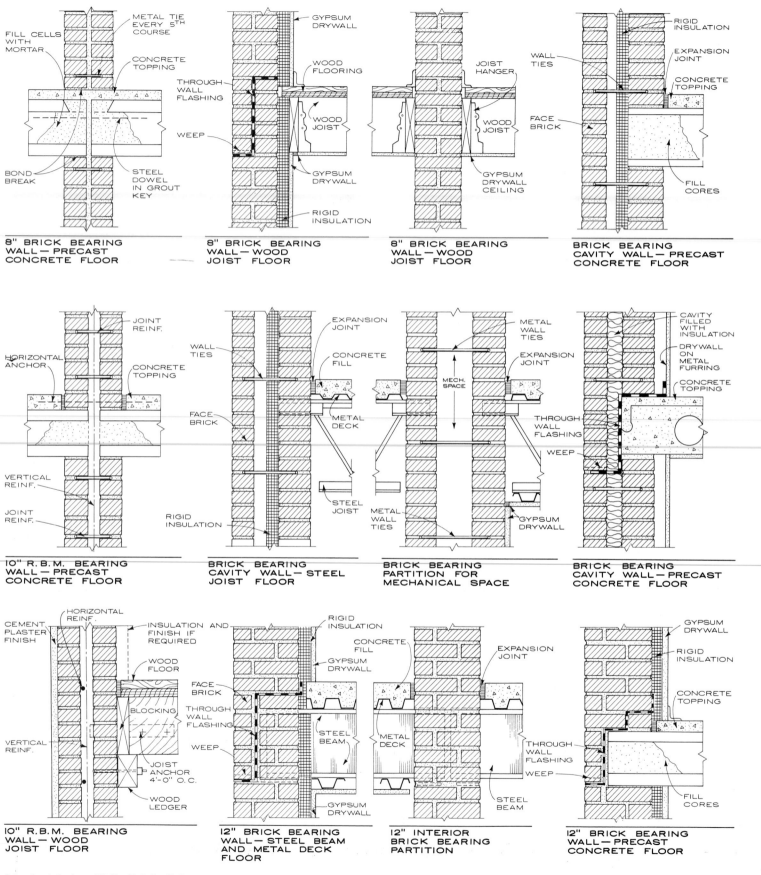

8" BRICK BEARING WALL—PRECAST CONCRETE FLOOR

FILL CELLS WITH MORTAR
METAL TIE EVERY 5TH COURSE
CONCRETE TOPPING
BOND BREAK
STEEL DOWEL IN GROUT KEY

8" BRICK BEARING WALL—WOOD JOIST FLOOR

GYPSUM DRYWALL
WOOD FLOORING
THROUGH WALL FLASHING
WEEP
WOOD JOIST
GYPSUM DRYWALL
RIGID INSULATION

8" BRICK BEARING WALL—WOOD JOIST FLOOR

JOIST HANGER
WOOD JOIST
GYPSUM DRYWALL CEILING

BRICK BEARING CAVITY WALL—PRECAST CONCRETE FLOOR

RIGID INSULATION
WALL TIES
EXPANSION JOINT
CONCRETE TOPPING
FACE BRICK
FILL CORES

10" R.B.M. BEARING WALL—PRECAST CONCRETE FLOOR

JOINT REINF.
HORIZONTAL ANCHOR
CONCRETE TOPPING
VERTICAL REINF.
JOINT REINF.

BRICK BEARING CAVITY WALL—STEEL JOIST FLOOR

WALL TIES
FACE BRICK
RIGID INSULATION
EXPANSION JOINT
CONCRETE FILL
METAL DECK
STEEL JOIST

BRICK BEARING PARTITION FOR MECHANICAL SPACE

METAL WALL TIES
EXPANSION JOINT
MECH. SPACE
METAL WALL TIES
GYPSUM DRYWALL

BRICK BEARING CAVITY WALL—PRECAST CONCRETE FLOOR

CAVITY FILLED WITH INSULATION
DRYWALL ON METAL FURRING
CONCRETE TOPPING
THROUGH WALL FLASHING
WEEP

10" R.B.M. BEARING WALL—WOOD JOIST FLOOR

HORIZONTAL REINF.
CEMENT PLASTER FINISH
INSULATION AND FINISH IF REQUIRED
WOOD FLOOR
BLOCKING
VERTICAL REINF.
JOIST ANCHOR 4'-0" O.C.
WOOD LEDGER

12" BRICK BEARING WALL—STEEL BEAM AND METAL DECK FLOOR

RIGID INSULATION
CONCRETE FILL
GYPSUM DRYWALL
FACE BRICK
THROUGH WALL FLASHING
WEEP
STEEL BEAM
GYPSUM DRYWALL

12" INTERIOR BRICK BEARING PARTITION

CONCRETE FILL
EXPANSION JOINT
METAL DECK
STEEL BEAM

12" BRICK BEARING WALL—PRECAST CONCRETE FLOOR

GYPSUM DRYWALL
RIGID INSULATION
CONCRETE TOPPING
THROUGH WALL FLASHING
WEEP
FILL CORES

Robert Joseph Sangiamo, AIA; New York, New York

Davis, Brody & Associates; New York, New York

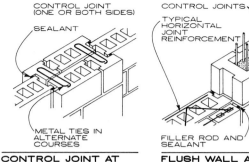

CONTROL JOINT AT PIER

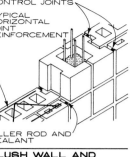

FLUSH WALL AND PLASTER CONTROL JOINTS

CONTROL JOINT BLOCK

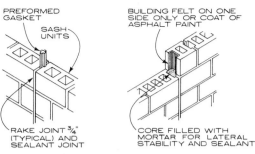

FLUSH WALL CONTROL JOINTS

PRINCIPLES

Masonry materials expand and contract in response to temperature changes. Dimensional changes also occur in masonry because of moisture variations. To compensate for these dimensional changes and thus control cracking in masonry, keep the following in mind:

1. Proper product specifications and construction procedures limit moisture related movements. For example, Type I moisture controlled concrete masonry units are manufactured to minimize moisture related movement.
2. Proper steel reinforcing, including horizontal joint reinforcing, increases the tensile resistance of masonry walls.
3. Properly placed expansion joints and control joints accommodate movement and provide for controlled crack locations.

EXPANSION JOINTS

The purpose of expansion joints is to relieve tension and compression between separate portions of a masonry wall resulting from temperature and/or moisture induced dimensional movements.

Exterior and interior masonry wythes of cavity walls should be connected with flexible metal ties. Horizontal expansion joints should be located below shelf angles or structural frames supporting masonry walls or panels. Shelf angles should contain sufficient interruptions to accommodate thermal movements. Horizontal expansion joints (soft joints, slip channel, etc.) should also be provided above exterior masonry walls or panels abutting structural frames and at interior non-load-bearing masonry walls abutting the underside of floor or roof structures above.

CONTROL JOINTS

The purpose of control joints is to provide tension relief between individual portions of a masonry wall that may change from their original dimensions. They must provide for lateral stability across the joint and contain a through wall seal.

Control joints should be located in long straight walls, at major changes in wall heights, at changes in wall thickness, above joints in foundations, at columns and pilasters, at one or both sides of wall openings, near wall intersections, and near junctions of walls in L, T, or U shaped buildings. Joints should continue through roof parapets.

SEALANTS

The type of sealant recommended varies depending on the surface to which it is applied. Some sealants require a primer but one part primerless sealants are available that are capable of withstanding compression and extension up to 50% in a single direction. A variety of colors are available to blend with masonry. Polyethylene foam rod backup material should be used so that, when compressed, it will fit tightly. Sealant depth should equal the joint width up to $1/2$ in. wide; for joints over $1/2$ in. wide, the caulking depth should be $1/2$ in. As a general rule, use one part silicones, urethanes, or thiokols for exterior caulking and acrylics for interior caulking. Joint width should be three times the expected movement for low modulus silicones and four times the expected movement for other elastomers (polysulfides and urethanes).

Setter, Leach & Lindstrom, Inc.; Minneapolis, Minnesota

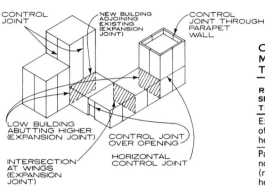

LOCATION OF CONTROL AND EXPANSION JOINTS

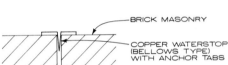

CONTROL JOINT SPACING FOR MOISTURE CONTROLLED ASTM C90 TYPE I BLOCK UNITS

RECOMMENDED SPACING OF CONTROL JOINTS	VERTICAL SPACING OF JOINT REINFORCEMENT			
	NONE	24"	16"	8"
Expressed as ratio of panel length to height (L/H)	2	$2^1/2$	3	4
Panel length (L) not to exceed (regardless of height (H))	40'	45'	50'	60'

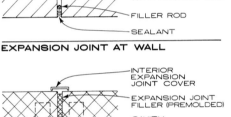

EXPANSION JOINT AT WALL

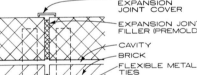

EXPANSION JOINT AT MASONRY CAVITY WALL

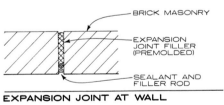

EXPANSION JOINT AT WALL

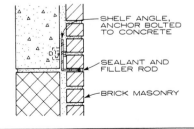

HORIZONTAL EXPANSION JOINT

CONTROL JOINT AT STRAIGHT WALL

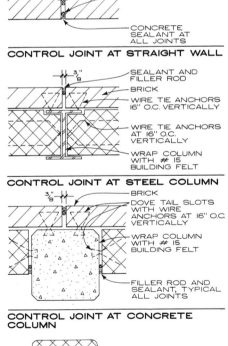

CONTROL JOINT AT STEEL COLUMN

CONTROL JOINT AT CONCRETE COLUMN

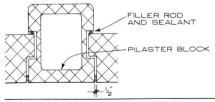

CONTROL JOINT AT PILASTER

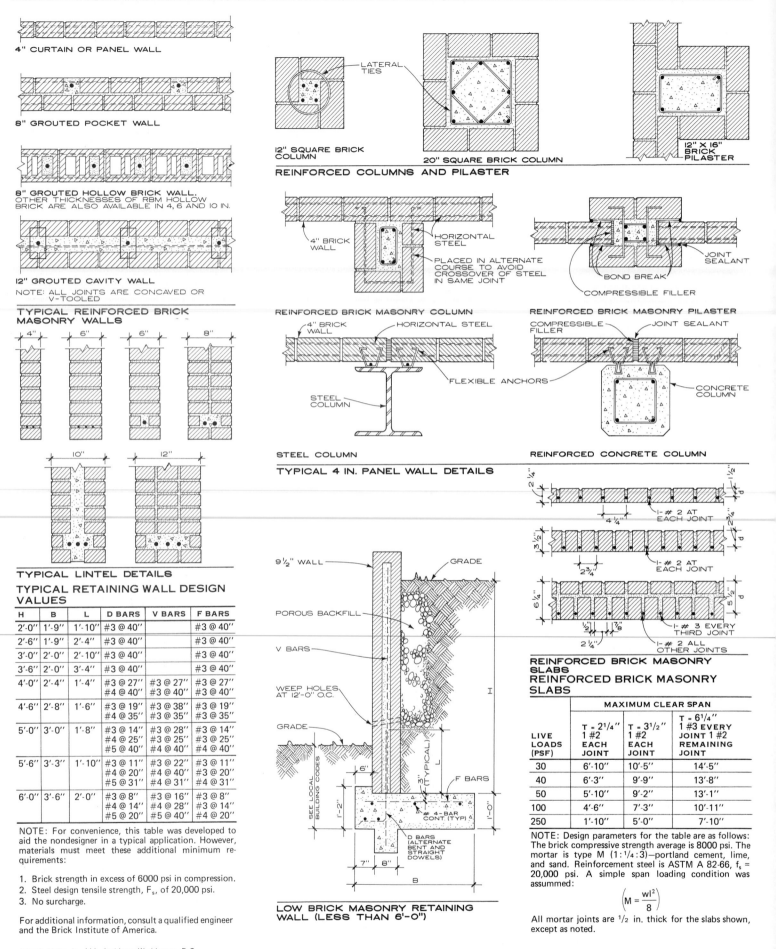

4" CURTAIN OR PANEL WALL

8" GROUTED POCKET WALL

8" GROUTED HOLLOW BRICK WALL.
OTHER THICKNESSES OF RBM HOLLOW BRICK ARE ALSO AVAILABLE IN 4, 6 AND 10 IN.

12" GROUTED CAVITY WALL
NOTE: ALL JOINTS ARE CONCAVED OR V-TOOLED

TYPICAL REINFORCED BRICK MASONRY WALLS

TYPICAL LINTEL DETAILS

TYPICAL RETAINING WALL DESIGN VALUES

H	B	L	D BARS	V BARS	F BARS
2'-0''	1'-9''	1'-10''	#3 @ 40''		#3 @ 40''
2'-6''	1'-9''	2'-4''	#3 @ 40''		#3 @ 40''
3'-0''	2'-0''	2'-10''	#3 @ 40''		#3 @ 40''
3'-6''	2'-0''	3'-4''	#3 @ 40''		#3 @ 40''
4'-0''	2'-4''	1'-4''	#3 @ 27'' #4 @ 40''	#3 @ 27'' #3 @ 40''	#3 @ 27'' #3 @ 40''
4'-6''	2'-8''	1'-6''	#3 @ 19'' #4 @ 35''	#3 @ 38'' #3 @ 35''	#3 @ 19'' #3 @ 35''
5'-0''	3'-0''	1'-8''	#3 @ 14'' #4 @ 25'' #5 @ 40''	#3 @ 28'' #3 @ 25'' #4 @ 40''	#3 @ 14'' #3 @ 25'' #4 @ 40''
5'-6''	3'-3''	1'-10''	#3 @ 11'' #4 @ 20'' #5 @ 31''	#3 @ 22'' #4 @ 40'' #4 @ 31''	#3 @ 11'' #3 @ 20'' #4 @ 31''
6'-0''	3'-6''	2'-0''	#3 @ 8'' #4 @ 14'' #5 @ 20''	#3 @ 16'' #4 @ 28'' #5 @ 40''	#3 @ 8'' #3 @ 14'' #4 @ 20''

NOTE: For convenience, this table was developed to aid the nondesigner in a typical application. However, materials must meet these additional minimum requirements:

1. Brick strength in excess of 6000 psi in compression.
2. Steel design tensile strength, F_s, of 20,000 psi.
3. No surcharge.

For additional information, consult a qualified engineer and the Brick Institute of America.

John R. Hoke, Jr., AIA, Architect; Washington, D.C.

12" SQUARE BRICK COLUMN — LATERAL TIES

20" SQUARE BRICK COLUMN

12" X 16" BRICK PILASTER

REINFORCED COLUMNS AND PILASTER

4" BRICK WALL — HORIZONTAL STEEL PLACED IN ALTERNATE COURSE TO AVOID CROSSOVER OF STEEL IN SAME JOINT

JOINT SEALANT — BOND BREAK — COMPRESSIBLE FILLER

REINFORCED BRICK MASONRY COLUMN

REINFORCED BRICK MASONRY PILASTER

4" BRICK WALL — HORIZONTAL STEEL

STEEL COLUMN — FLEXIBLE ANCHORS

COMPRESSIBLE FILLER — JOINT SEALANT — FLEXIBLE ANCHORS — CONCRETE COLUMN

STEEL COLUMN

REINFORCED CONCRETE COLUMN

TYPICAL 4 IN. PANEL WALL DETAILS

1-#2 AT EACH JOINT
1-#2 AT EACH JOINT
1-#3 EVERY THIRD JOINT
1-#2 ALL OTHER JOINTS

REINFORCED BRICK MASONRY SLABS

REINFORCED BRICK MASONRY SLABS

LIVE LOADS (PSF)	MAXIMUM CLEAR SPAN		
	$T = 2\frac{1}{4}''$ 1 #2 EACH JOINT	$T = 3\frac{1}{2}''$ 1 #2 EACH JOINT	$T = 6\frac{1}{4}''$ 1 #3 EVERY JOINT 1 #2 REMAINING JOINT
30	6'-10''	10'-5''	14'-5''
40	6'-3''	9'-9''	13'-8''
50	5'-10''	9'-2''	13'-1''
100	4'-6''	7'-3''	10'-11''
250	1'-10''	5'-0''	7'-10''

NOTE: Design parameters for the table are as follows: The brick compressive strength average is 8000 psi. The mortar is type M $(1:\frac{1}{4}:3)$—portland cement, lime, and sand. Reinforcement steel is ASTM A 82-66, f_s = 20,000 psi. A simple span loading condition was assumed:

$$\left(M = \frac{wl^2}{8} \right)$$

All mortar joints are $\frac{1}{2}$ in. thick for the slabs shown, except as noted.

9½" WALL — GRADE
POROUS BACKFILL
V BARS
WEEP HOLES AT 12'-0" O.C.
GRADE
SEE LOCAL BUILDING CODES
F BARS
#4-BAR CONT. (TYP)
D BARS (ALTERNATE BENT AND STRAIGHT DOWELS)

LOW BRICK MASONRY RETAINING WALL (LESS THAN 6'-0")

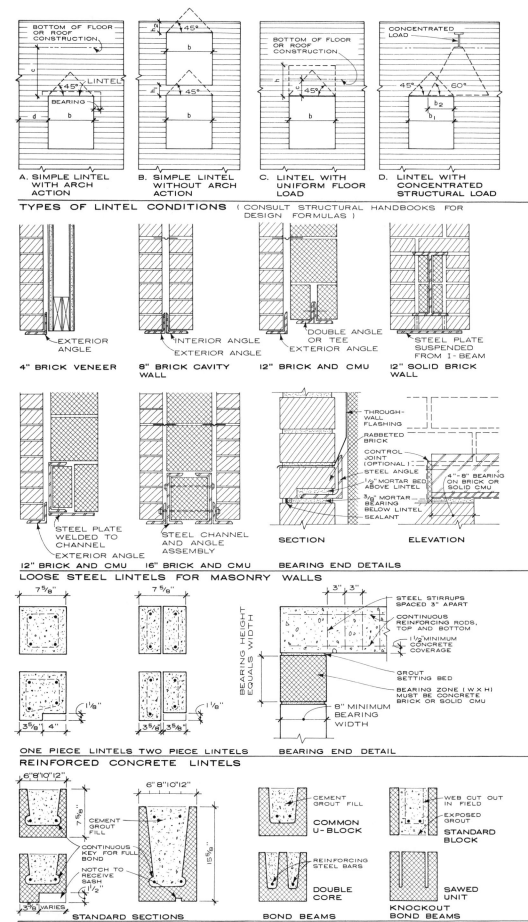

TYPES OF LINTEL CONDITIONS (CONSULT STRUCTURAL HANDBOOKS FOR DESIGN FORMULAS)

A. SIMPLE LINTEL WITH ARCH ACTION

B. SIMPLE LINTEL WITHOUT ARCH ACTION

C. LINTEL WITH UNIFORM FLOOR LOAD

D. LINTEL WITH CONCENTRATED STRUCTURAL LOAD

LOOSE STEEL LINTELS FOR MASONRY WALLS

4" BRICK VENEER

8" BRICK CAVITY WALL

12" BRICK AND CMU

12" SOLID BRICK WALL

12" BRICK AND CMU

16" BRICK AND CMU

BEARING END DETAILS

REINFORCED CONCRETE LINTELS

ONE PIECE LINTELS

TWO PIECE LINTELS

BEARING END DETAIL

PRECAST CONCRETE MASONRY LINTELS

STANDARD SECTIONS

BOND BEAMS

COMMON U-BLOCK

STANDARD BLOCK

DOUBLE CORE

SAWED UNIT

KNOCKOUT BOND BEAMS

Metz, Train, Olson and Youngren, Inc.; Chicago, Illinois

NOTES FOR LINTEL CONDITIONS

A. Simple lintel with arch action carries wall load only in triangle above opening:

$$c \geq b \quad \text{and} \quad d \geq b$$

B. Simple lintel without arch action carries less wall load than triangle above opening:

$$h_1 \text{ or } h_2 < 0.6b$$

C. Lintel with uniform floor load carries both wall and floor loads in rectangle above opening:

$$c < b$$

D. Lintel with concentrated load carries wall and portion of concentrated load distributed along length b_2.

NOTES ON STEEL LINTELS

1. Consult a structural engineer in the case of long span lintels, lintels in bearing walls, and any loading conditions not covered here.
2. Deflections greater than 1/700 result in local cracking at corners of opening.
3. Long lintels should be set with control joint at ends to provide space for thermal expansion.
4. Heavily loaded lintels bearing directly on masonry units may cause localized spalling of the masonry unit.

STEEL LINTELS FOR MASONRY
NUMBER AND SIZE OF ANGLES REQUIRED
No superimposed loads

CLEAR SPAN (MAX.)	EXTERIOR ANGLES	INTERIOR ANGLES
4'-0"	$\angle 3\frac{1}{2}" \times 3\frac{1}{2}" \times \frac{5}{16}"$	$2\angle s\ 3\frac{1}{2}" \times 3\frac{1}{2}" \times \frac{5}{16}"$
6'-0"	$\angle 4" \times 3\frac{1}{2}" \times \frac{5}{16}"$	$2\angle s\ 4" \times 3\frac{1}{2}" \times \frac{5}{16}"$
8'-0"	$\angle 5" \times 3\frac{1}{2}" \times \frac{5}{16}"$	$2\angle s\ 5" \times 3\frac{1}{2}" \times \frac{5}{16}"$

NOTES

1. Design based on 4 in. face brick with 8 in. CMU backup.
2. $F_y = 36,000$ psi.
3. Allow 6 in. bearing at each end.

PRECAST CONCRETE AND REINFORCED CMU LINTELS—
NUMBER AND SIZE OF REBARS REQUIRED
No superimposed loads

LINTEL TYPE	CLEAR SPAN (MAX.)	8" BRICK WALL (80 LB/SQ FT)	8" CMU WALL (50 LB/SQ FT)
Reinforced concrete ($7\frac{5}{8}"$ square)	4'-0"	4-#3	4-#3
	6'-0"	4-#4	4-#3
	8'-0"	4-#5	4-#4
Precast CMU ($7\frac{5}{8}"$ square)	4'-0"	2-#4	2-#4
	6'-0"	2-#5	2-#4
	8'-0"	2-#6	2-#5

NOTES

1. Weight of lintel included in all reinforcing calculations.
2. Reinforced CMU lintels designed without shear reinforcing stirrups.
3. Allow $7\frac{5}{8}$ in. bearing: both types of lintel.
4. $f_c' = 3000$ lb/sq in. for both precast concrete and CMU grout.
5. $f_y = 60,000$ lb/sq in.

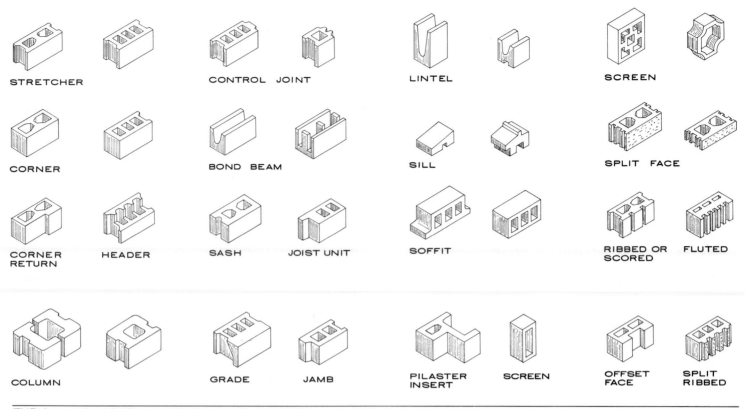

STRETCHER CONTROL JOINT LINTEL SCREEN

CORNER BOND BEAM SILL SPLIT FACE

CORNER RETURN HEADER SASH JOIST UNIT SOFFIT RIBBED OR SCORED FLUTED

COLUMN GRADE JAMB PILASTER INSERT SCREEN OFFSET FACE SPLIT RIBBED

TYPICAL CONCRETE MASONRY UNIT SHAPES

CONCRETE MASONRY UNIT SPECIFICATIONS AND FIRE RESISTANCE DATA

1. A solid (load bearing) concrete block is a unit whose cross-sectional area in every plane parallel to the bearing surface is not less than 75% of the gross cross-sectional area measured in the same plane. (ASTM C145—75.)
2. A hollow concrete block is a unit whose cross-sectional area in every plane parallel to the bearing surface is less than 75% of the gross cross-sectional area measured in the same plane. (ASTM C90—75.)
3. Actual dimension is 3/8 to 1/2 in. less than nominal shown.
4. All shapes shown are available in all dimensions given in chart except for width (W) which may be otherwise noted.
5. Because the number of shapes and sizes for concrete masonry screen units is virtually unlimited, it is advisable for the designer to check on availability of any specific shape during early planning.
6. Screen units should be of high quality, even though they seldom are employed in load bearing construction. When tested with their hollow cells parallel to the direction of the load, screen units should have a compressive strength exceeding 1000 psi of gross area; a quality of concrete unit comparable to "Specifications for Hollow Load-Bearing Concrete Masonry Units" ASTM C90—75.
7. Building codes are quite specific in the degree of fire protection required in various areas of buildings. Local building regulations will govern the concrete masonry wall section best suited for specific applications. Fire resistance ratings of concrete masonry walls are based on fire tests made at Underwriters' Laboratories, Inc., National Bureau of Standards, Portland Cement Association, and other recognized laboratories. Methods of test are described in ASTM E119 "Standard Method of Fire Tests of Building Construction and Materials."
8. The fire resistance ratings of most concrete masonry walls are determined by heat transmission measured by temperature rise on the cold side. Fire endurance can be calculated as a function of the aggregate type used in the block unit, and the solid thickness of the wall, or the equivalent solid thickness of the wall when working with hollow units.
9. Equivalent thickness of hollow units is calculated from actual thickness and the percentage of solid materials. Both needed items of information are normally reported by the testing laboratory using standard ASTM procedures, such as ASTM C140 "Methods of Sampling and Testing Concrete Masonry Units." When walls are plastered or otherwise faced with fire resistant materials, the thickness of these materials is included in calculating the equivalent thickness effective for fire resistance. Estimated fire resistance ratings shown in the table are for fully protected construction in which all structural members are of incombustible materials. Where combustible members are framed into walls, equivalent solid thickness protecting each such member should not be less than 93% of the thicknesses shown. Plaster is effective in increasing fire resistance when combustible members are framed into masonry walls, as is filling core spaces with various fire resistant materials.
10. The following are minimum equivalent thicknesses for rating of:

	1 HR	2 HR	3 HR	4 HR
Expanded slag	2.2	3.3	4.2	5.0
Expanded shale or clay	2.5	3.7	4.7	5.5
Limestone, scoria, cinders unexpanded slag	2.7	4.0	5.0	5.9
Calcareous gravel	2.8	4.2	5.3	6.2
Siliceous gravel	3.0	4.5	5.7	6.7

Equivalent thickness is the solid thickness that would be obtained if the same amount of concrete contained in a hollow unit were recast without core holes. Calculate fire resistance as follows: equivalent thickness equals the percentage of block solidity (based on aggregate type) times actual block thickness (in.). Refer to table for hour rating of wall.

NOMINAL DIMENSIONS OF TYPICAL CONCRETE MASONRY UNIT SHAPES

Height (H) = 4", 8"
Length (L) = 8", 12", 16", 18", 24"
Width (W) = 2", 3", 4", 6", 8", 10", 12"

R VALUE OF SINGLE WYTHE CONCRETE MASONRY UNITS

NOMINAL UNIT THICKNESS (IN.)	DENSITY OF CONCRETE IN CMU (PCF)				
	60	80	100	120	140
4	2.07	1.68	1.40	1.17	0.77
6	2.25	1.83	1.53	1.29	0.86
8	2.30	2.12	1.75	1.46	0.98
10	3.00	2.40	1.97	1.63	1.08
12	3.29	2.62	2.14	1.81	1.16

U VALUE OF SINGLE WYTHE CONCRETE MASONRY UNITS

NOMINAL UNIT THICKNESS (IN.)	DENSITY OF CONCRETE IN CMU (PCF)				
	60	80	100	120	140
4	0.34	0.40	0.44	0.50	0.62
6	0.32	0.37	0.42	0.47	0.59
8	0.32	0.34	0.38	0.43	0.55
10	0.26	0.31	0.35	0.40	0.52
12	0.24	0.29	0.34	0.38	0.50

Robert J. Sangiamo, AIA, and Davis, Brody & Associates; New York, New York

4 **UNIT MASONRY**

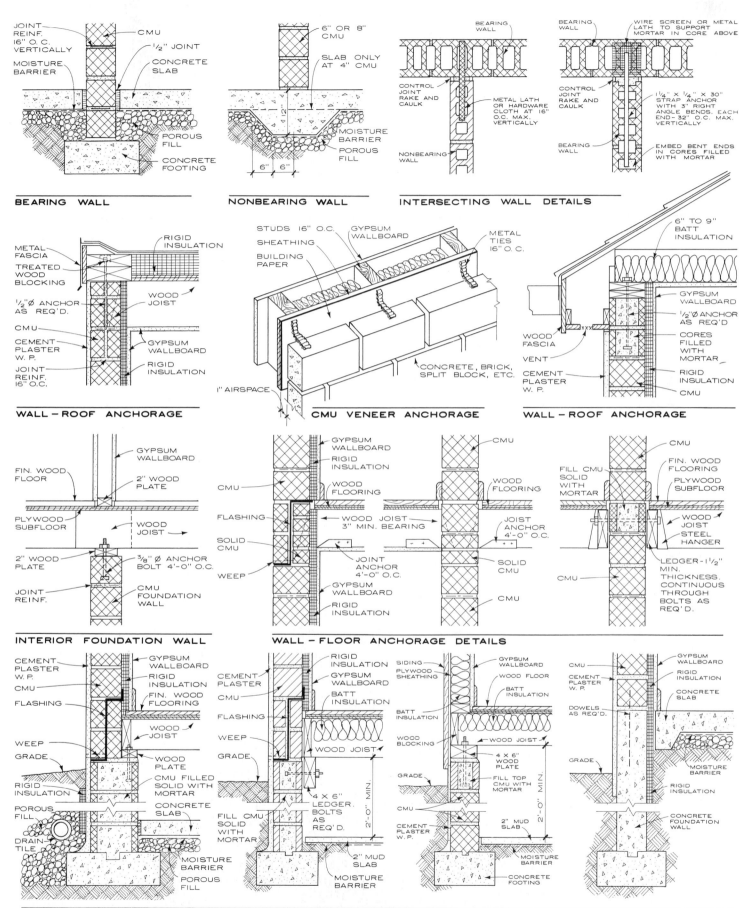

BEARING WALL

JOINT REINF. 16" O.C. VERTICALLY
CMU
1/2" JOINT
MOISTURE BARRIER
CONCRETE SLAB
Pop POROUS FILL
CONCRETE FOOTING

NONBEARING WALL

6" OR 8" CMU
SLAB ONLY AT 4" CMU
MOISTURE BARRIER
POROUS FILL
6" 6"

INTERSECTING WALL DETAILS

BEARING WALL
CONTROL JOINT RAKE AND CAULK
METAL LATH OR HARDWARE CLOTH AT 16" O.C. MAX. VERTICALLY
NONBEARING WALL

BEARING WALL
WIRE SCREEN OR METAL LATH TO SUPPORT MORTAR IN CORE ABOVE
CONTROL JOINT RAKE AND CAULK
1/4" X 1/4" X 30" STRAP ANCHOR WITH 3" RIGHT ANGLE BENDS. EACH END - 32" O.C. MAX. VERTICALLY
BEARING WALL
EMBED BENT ENDS IN CORES FILLED WITH MORTAR

WALL – ROOF ANCHORAGE

METAL FASCIA
TREATED WOOD BLOCKING
1/2"Ø ANCHOR AS REQ'D.
CMU
CEMENT PLASTER W.P.
JOINT REINF. 16" O.C.
RIGID INSULATION
WOOD JOIST
GYPSUM WALLBOARD
RIGID INSULATION

CMU VENEER ANCHORAGE

STUDS 16" O.C.
SHEATHING
BUILDING PAPER
GYPSUM WALLBOARD
METAL TIES 16" O.C.
CONCRETE, BRICK, SPLIT BLOCK, ETC.
1" AIRSPACE

WALL – ROOF ANCHORAGE

6" TO 9" BATT INSULATION
WOOD FASCIA
VENT
CEMENT PLASTER W.P.
GYPSUM WALLBOARD
1/2"Ø ANCHOR AS REQ'D
CORES FILLED WITH MORTAR
RIGID INSULATION
CMU

INTERIOR FOUNDATION WALL

GYPSUM WALLBOARD
FIN. WOOD FLOOR
2" WOOD PLATE
PLYWOOD SUBFLOOR
WOOD JOIST
2" WOOD PLATE
3/8"Ø ANCHOR BOLT 4'-0" O.C.
JOINT REINF.
CMU FOUNDATION WALL

WALL – FLOOR ANCHORAGE DETAILS

GYPSUM WALLBOARD
RIGID INSULATION
CMU
WOOD FLOORING
FLASHING
SOLID CMU
WEEP
WOOD JOIST 3" MIN. BEARING
JOINT ANCHOR 4'-0" O.C.
GYPSUM WALLBOARD
RIGID INSULATION

CMU
WOOD FLOORING
JOIST ANCHOR 4'-0" O.C.
SOLID CMU
CMU

CMU
FILL CMU SOLID WITH MORTAR
CMU
FIN. WOOD FLOORING
PLYWOOD SUBFLOOR
WOOD JOIST
STEEL HANGER
LEDGER - 1 1/2" MIN. THICKNESS. CONTINUOUS THROUGH BOLTS AS REQ'D.

FOUNDATION DETAILS – WOOD FRAME BUILDINGS

CEMENT PLASTER W.P.
CMU
FLASHING
WEEP
GRADE
RIGID INSULATION
POROUS FILL
DRAIN TILE
GYPSUM WALLBOARD
RIGID INSULATION
FIN. WOOD FLOORING
WOOD JOIST
WOOD PLATE
CMU FILLED SOLID WITH MORTAR
CONCRETE SLAB
MOISTURE BARRIER
POROUS FILL

CEMENT PLASTER
CMU
FLASHING
WEEP
GRADE
FILL CMU SOLID WITH MORTAR
RIGID INSULATION
GYPSUM WALLBOARD
BATT INSULATION
WOOD JOIST
WOOD PLATE
4 X 6" LEDGER. BOLTS AS REQ'D.
2" MUD SLAB
MOISTURE BARRIER
2'-0" MIN.

SIDING
PLYWOOD SHEATHING
BATT INSULATION
WOOD BLOCKING
GRADE
CMU
CEMENT PLASTER W.P.
GYPSUM WALLBOARD
WOOD FLOOR
BATT INSULATION
WOOD JOIST
4 X 6" WOOD PLATE
FILL TOP CMU WITH MORTAR
2" MUD SLAB
MOISTURE BARRIER
CONCRETE FOOTING
2'-0" MIN.

CMU
DOWELS AS REQ'D.
GRADE
GYPSUM WALLBOARD
RIGID INSULATION
CONCRETE SLAB
CEMENT PLASTER W.P.
MOISTURE BARRIER
RIGID INSULATION
CONCRETE FOUNDATION WALL

Robert J. Sangiamo, AIA; New York, New York

Davis, Brody & Associates; New York, New York

UNIT MASONRY 4

GENERAL NOTES

Natural stone has a wide variety of applications in building, as a facing, a veneer, or decoration. The major factors and dangers in the suitability and use of stone fall under two broad but overlapping headings: strength properties and aesthetic qualities. The three features of building stone that most affect their selection by architects for aesthetic reasons are color, pattern, and texture.

To obtain an accurate picture of stone colors, it is recommended that you use a color chart, such as the Rock Color Chart, published by the Geological Society of America (Boulder, Colorado 80302).

Patterns are highly varied and impart the special features that make building stones a unique material.

Texture also is varied and ranges from coarse fragments to fine grains and crystalline structures. It varies with the hardness of minerals composing the stone and the manner in which the stone is fabricated, such as cleavage and polishing.

The three classes of rock are igneous, sedimentary, and metamorphic. The common construction stones are marketed under the names given in the following table, although specialty stones such as soapstone or serpentine are sold under their names. Each type of stone listed has various commercial grades. Limestone, for example, is sold under three categories quarried in different locations, of two types (oolitic and dolomitic). Travertine is also classed as a limestone.

Factors in selecting stone include strength and aesthetic qualities. Color, pattern, and texture are important features of stone, affected by fabrication methods and finish. Granites and slates tend to hold their colors, while limestone may change under exposure.

Physical characteristics of stone must be suitable for its intended use. Moisture penetration, weatherability, and resistance to pollution may be decisive factors for exterior facing, as well as anchorage and joint design.

Consideration may be given to the following minimum list of selection factors:

1. Price.
2. Availability.
3. Finishes available.
4. Absorption, weatherability.
5. Color.
6. Thickness limitations.

Developments in the detailing of stone have helped to control cost, using new systems of installation. Factors involved in detailing include design of joints, selection of mortars, and the use of sealants. Proper attention to anchorage of each piece of stone is important, and the use of relieving angles may be required to prevent excessive compressive loads.

Since detailing varies with each installation, the designer should be aware of the technical aspects of designing with stone and should work closely with the stone suppliers and the stone setting specialty contractors.

STONE CLASSIFIED ACCORDING TO QUALITIES AFFECTING USE

CLASS	COLOR	TEXTURE	SPECIAL FEATURES	PARTINGS	HARDNESS	CHIEF USES
Sandstone	Very light buff to light chocolate brown or brick red; may tarnish to brown	Granular, showing sand grains, cemented together	Ripple marks; oblique color bands ("cross bedding")	Bedding planes; also fractures transverse to beds	Fairly hard if well cemented	General; walls; building; flagstone
Limestone	White, light gray to light buff	Fine to crystalline; may have fossils	May show fossils	Parallel to beds; also fractures across beds	Fairly soft; steel easily scratches	All building uses
Marble	Highly varied: snow white to black; also blue-gray and light to dark olive green; also pinkish	Finely granular to very coarsely crystalline showing flat-sided crystals	May show veins of different colors or angular rock pieces or fossils	Usually not along beds but may have irregular fractures	Slightly harder than limestone	May be used for building stone but usually in decorative panels
Granite (light igneous rock)	Almost white to pink-and-white or gray-and-white	Usually coarsely crystalline; crystals may be varicolored; may be fine grained	May be banded with pink, white or gray streaks and veins	Not necessarily any regular parting but fractures irregularly	Harder than limestone and marble; keeps cut shape well	Building stone, but also in paneling if attractively colored
Dark igneous rock	Gray, dark olive green to black; Laurvikite is beautifully crystalline	Usually coarsely crystalline if quarried but may be fine grained	May be banded with lighter and darker gray bands and veins	Not necessarily any regular parting but may facture irregularly	About like granite; retains cut shape well	Building stone but also used in panels if nicely banded or crystalline
Lavas	Varies: pink, purple, black; if usable, rarely almost white	Fine grained; may have pores locally	Note rare porosity	Not necessarily any regular parting, as a rule, but some have parallel fractures	About as strong as granite; if light colored, usually softer	Good foundation and building stone; not decorative
Quartzite	Variable: white, buff, red, brown	Dense, almost glassy ideally	Very resistant to weather and impact	Usually no special parting	Very hard if well cemented, as usually the case	Excellent for building but hard to "shape"
Slate	Grayish-green, brick red or dark brown, usually gray; may be banded	Finely crystalline; flat crystals give slaty fracture	Some slates have color-fading with age	Splits along slate surface, often crossing color bands	Softer than granite or quartzite; scratches easily	Roofing; blackboards; paving
Gneiss	Usually gray with some pink, white or light gray bands	Crystalline, like granite, often with glassy bands (veins)	Banding is decorative; some bands very weak, however	No special parting; tends to break along banding	About like granite	Used for buildings; also may be decorative if banded

STRUCTURAL PROPERTIES OF REPRESENTATIVE STONES

STRUCTURAL PROPERTY		IGNEOUS ROCK		SEDIMENTARY ROCK		METAMORPHIC ROCK	
		GRANITE	TRAPROCK	LIMESTONE	SANDSTONE	MARBLE	SLATE
Composition—ultimate strength	(psi)	15,000–30,000	20,000	4,000–20,000	3,000–20,000	10,000–23,000	10,000–15,000
Composition—allowable working stress	(psi)	800–1,500		500–1,000	400–700	500–900	1,000
Shear—ultimate strength	(psi)	1,800–2,700		1,000–2,000	1,200–2,500	900–1,700	
Shear—allowable working stress	(psi)	200		200	150	150	
Tension—allowable working stress	(psi)	150		125	75	125	
Weight	(psf)	156–170	180–185	147–170	135–155	165–178	170–180
Specific gravity		2.4–2.7	2.96	2.1–2.8	2.0–2.6	2.4–2.8	2.7–2.8
Absorption of water (parts by weight)		1/750		1/38	1/24	1/300	1/430
Modulus of elasticity	(psi)	6–10,000,000	12,000,000	4–14,000,000	1–7,500,000	4–13,500,000	12,000,000
Coefficient of expansion	(psf)	0.0000040		0.0000045	0.0000055	0.0000045	0.0000058

NOTE: Individual samples vary greatly.

The McGuire & Shook Corporation; Indianapolis, Indiana

4   STONE

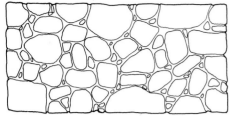

UNCOURSED FIELDSTONE PATTERN

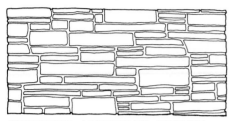

UNCOURSED LEDGEROCK PATTERN

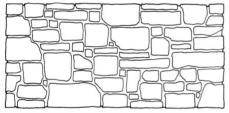

UNCOURSED WEB WALL OR MOSAIC PATTERN

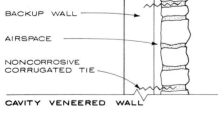

UNCOURSED ROUGHLY SQUARED PATTERN

RUBBLE STONE MASONRY PATTERNS—ELEVATIONS

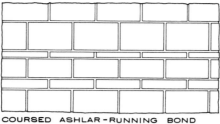

COURSED ASHLAR—RUNNING BOND

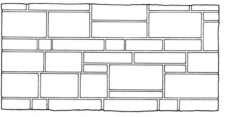

RANDOM COURSED ASHLAR

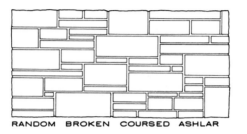

RANDOM BROKEN COURSED ASHLAR

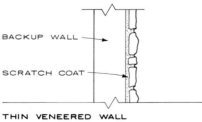

RANDOM ROUGH BEDDED ASHLAR

SPLIT STONE MASONRY PATTERNS—ELEVATIONS

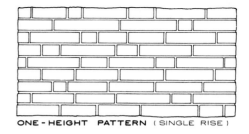

ONE-HEIGHT PATTERN (SINGLE RISE)

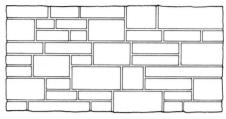

TWO-HEIGHT PATTERN (40% – 2¼"; 60% – 5")

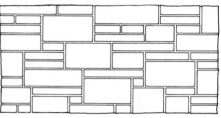

THREE-HEIGHT PATTERN (15% – 2¼"; 40% – 5"; 45% – 7¾")

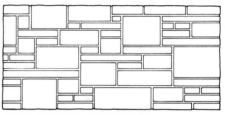

FOUR-HEIGHT PATTERN

SPLIT STONE MASONRY HEIGHT PATTERNS—ELEVATIONS

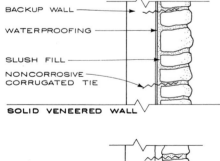

SOLID VENEERED WALL

- BACKUP WALL
- WATERPROOFING
- SLUSH FILL
- NONCORROSIVE CORRUGATED TIE

- BACKUP WALL
- AIRSPACE
- NONCORROSIVE CORRUGATED TIE

CAVITY VENEERED WALL

TYPICAL WALL SECTIONS

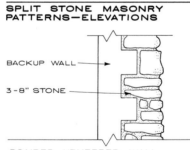

- BACKUP WALL
- 3-8" STONE

BONDED VENEERED WALL
(TIES RECOMMENDED IN SOME CASES, E.G., LIMESTONE)

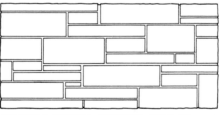

- BACKUP WALL
- SCRATCH COAT

THIN VENEERED WALL

GENERAL NOTES

1. A course is a horizontal row of stone. Bond pattern is described by the horizontal arrangement of vertical joints. (See also Brickwork.) Structural bond refers to the physical tying together of load bearing and veneer portions of a composite wall. Structural bond can be accomplished with metal ties or with stone units set as headers through veneer and into the backup.

2. Ashlar masonry is composed of squared-off building stone units of various sizes. Cut Ashlar is dressed to specific design dimensions at the mill. Ashlar is often used in random lengths and heights, with jointing worked out on the job.

3. All ties and anchors must be made of noncorrosive material. Chromium-nickel stainless steel types 302 and 304 and eraydo alloy zinc are the most resistant to corrosion and staining. Hot dipped galvanized is widely used, but is not as resistant, hence is prohibited by some building codes. Copper, brass, and bronze will stain under some conditions. Local building codes often govern the types of metal that may be used for stone anchors.

4. Nonstaining cement mortar should be used on porous and light colored stones. At all corners use extra ties and, when possible, larger stones. Joints are usually ½ to 1½ in. for rough work and ⅜ to ¾ in. for Ashlar.

Building Stone Institute; New York, New York

George M. Whiteside, III, AIA and James D. Lloyd; Kennett Square, Pennsylvania

Alexander Keyes; Darrel Rippeteau, Architect; Washington, D.C.

STONE

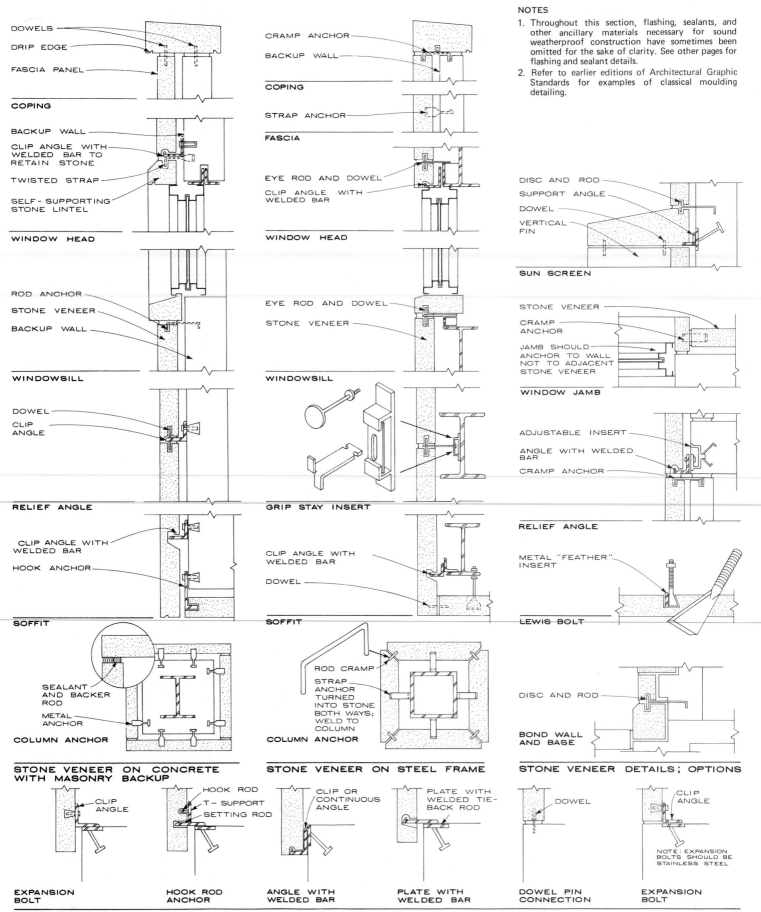

NOTES

1. Throughout this section, flashing, sealants, and other ancillary materials necessary for sound weatherproof construction have sometimes been omitted for the sake of clarity. See other pages for flashing and sealant details.
2. Refer to earlier editions of Architectural Graphic Standards for examples of classical moulding detailing.

DOWELS
DRIP EDGE
FASCIA PANEL

COPING

BACKUP WALL
CLIP ANGLE WITH WELDED BAR TO RETAIN STONE
TWISTED STRAP
SELF-SUPPORTING STONE LINTEL

WINDOW HEAD

ROD ANCHOR
STONE VENEER
BACKUP WALL

WINDOWSILL

DOWEL
CLIP ANGLE

RELIEF ANGLE

CLIP ANGLE WITH WELDED BAR
HOOK ANCHOR

SOFFIT

SEALANT AND BACKER ROD
METAL ANCHOR

COLUMN ANCHOR

STONE VENEER ON CONCRETE WITH MASONRY BACKUP

CRAMP ANCHOR
BACKUP WALL

COPING

STRAP ANCHOR

FASCIA

EYE ROD AND DOWEL
CLIP ANGLE WITH WELDED BAR

WINDOW HEAD

EYE ROD AND DOWEL
STONE VENEER

WINDOWSILL

GRIP STAY INSERT

CLIP ANGLE WITH WELDED BAR
DOWEL

SOFFIT

ROD CRAMP
STRAP ANCHOR TURNED INTO STONE BOTH WAYS; WELD TO COLUMN

COLUMN ANCHOR

STONE VENEER ON STEEL FRAME

DISC AND ROD
SUPPORT ANGLE
DOWEL
VERTICAL FIN

SUN SCREEN

STONE VENEER
CRAMP ANCHOR
JAMB SHOULD ANCHOR TO WALL NOT TO ADJACENT STONE VENEER

WINDOW JAMB

ADJUSTABLE INSERT
ANGLE WITH WELDED BAR
CRAMP ANCHOR

RELIEF ANGLE

METAL "FEATHER" INSERT

LEWIS BOLT

DISC AND ROD

BOND WALL AND BASE

STONE VENEER DETAILS; OPTIONS

CLIP ANGLE

HOOK ROD
T-SUPPORT
SETTING ROD

CLIP OR CONTINUOUS ANGLE

PLATE WITH WELDED TIE-BACK ROD

DOWEL

CLIP ANGLE

NOTE: EXPANSION BOLTS SHOULD BE STAINLESS STEEL

EXPANSION BOLT

HOOK ROD ANCHOR

ANGLE WITH WELDED BAR

PLATE WITH WELDED BAR

DOWEL PIN CONNECTION

EXPANSION BOLT

BASE DETAILS

Building Stone Institute; New York, New York
George M. Whiteside, III, AIA and James D. Lloyd; Kennett Square, Pennsylvania
Alexander Keyes; Darrel Rippeteau, Architect; Washington, D.C.

 STONE

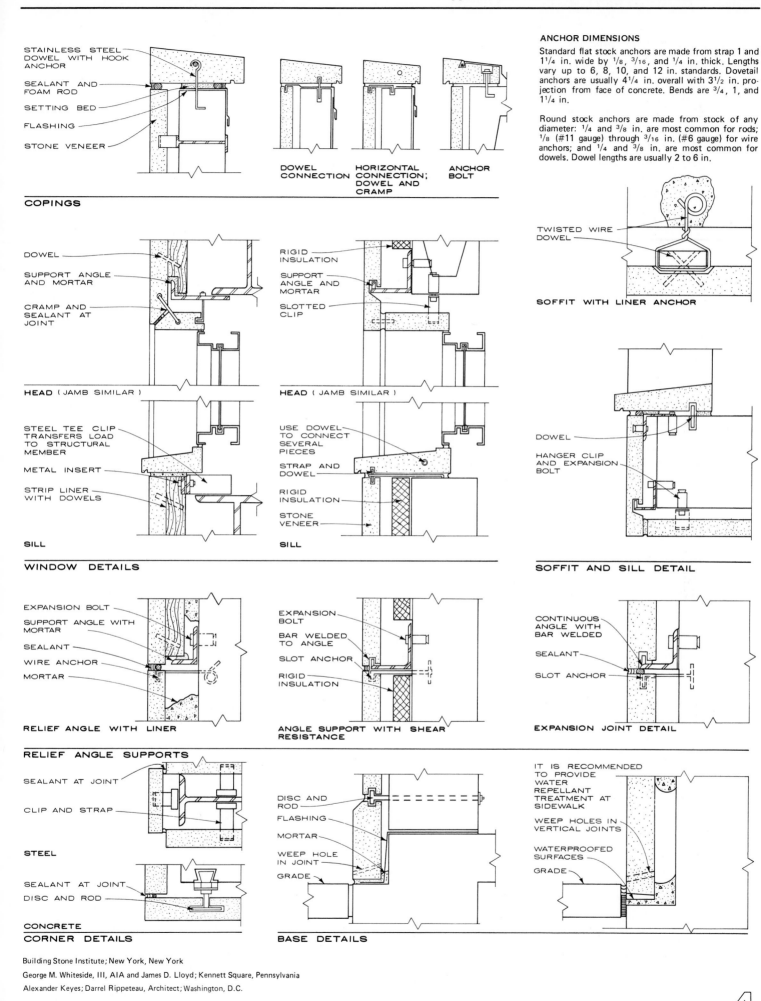

ANCHOR DIMENSIONS

Standard flat stock anchors are made from strap 1 and 1¼ in. wide by ⅛, 3/16, and ¼ in. thick. Lengths vary up to 6, 8, 10, and 12 in. standards. Dovetail anchors are usually 4¼ in. overall with 3½ in. projection from face of concrete. Bends are ¾, 1, and 1¼ in.

Round stock anchors are made from stock of any diameter: ¼ and ⅜ in. are most common for rods; ⅛ (#11 gauge) through 3/16 in. (#6 gauge) for wire anchors; and ¼ and ⅜ in. are most common for dowels. Dowel lengths are usually 2 to 6 in.

STAINLESS STEEL DOWEL WITH HOOK ANCHOR
SEALANT AND FOAM ROD
SETTING BED
FLASHING
STONE VENEER

DOWEL CONNECTION
HORIZONTAL CONNECTION; DOWEL AND CRAMP
ANCHOR BOLT

COPINGS

DOWEL
SUPPORT ANGLE AND MORTAR
CRAMP AND SEALANT AT JOINT

RIGID INSULATION
SUPPORT ANGLE AND MORTAR
SLOTTED CLIP

HEAD (JAMB SIMILAR)   HEAD (JAMB SIMILAR)

STEEL TEE CLIP TRANSFERS LOAD TO STRUCTURAL MEMBER
METAL INSERT
STRIP LINER WITH DOWELS

USE DOWEL TO CONNECT SEVERAL PIECES
STRAP AND DOWEL
RIGID INSULATION
STONE VENEER

SILL   SILL

WINDOW DETAILS

TWISTED WIRE DOWEL

SOFFIT WITH LINER ANCHOR

DOWEL
HANGER CLIP AND EXPANSION BOLT

SOFFIT AND SILL DETAIL

EXPANSION BOLT
SUPPORT ANGLE WITH MORTAR
SEALANT
WIRE ANCHOR
MORTAR

EXPANSION BOLT
BAR WELDED TO ANGLE
SLOT ANCHOR
RIGID INSULATION

CONTINUOUS ANGLE WITH BAR WELDED
SEALANT
SLOT ANCHOR

RELIEF ANGLE WITH LINER   **ANGLE SUPPORT WITH SHEAR RESISTANCE**   **EXPANSION JOINT DETAIL**

RELIEF ANGLE SUPPORTS

SEALANT AT JOINT
CLIP AND STRAP

STEEL

SEALANT AT JOINT
DISC AND ROD

CONCRETE

DISC AND ROD
FLASHING
MORTAR
WEEP HOLE IN JOINT
GRADE

IT IS RECOMMENDED TO PROVIDE WATER REPELLANT TREATMENT AT SIDEWALK
WEEP HOLES IN VERTICAL JOINTS
WATERPROOFED SURFACES
GRADE

CORNER DETAILS   **BASE DETAILS**

Building Stone Institute; New York, New York

George M. Whiteside, III, AIA and James D. Lloyd; Kennett Square, Pennsylvania

Alexander Keyes; Darrel Rippeteau, Architect; Washington, D.C.

STONE 4

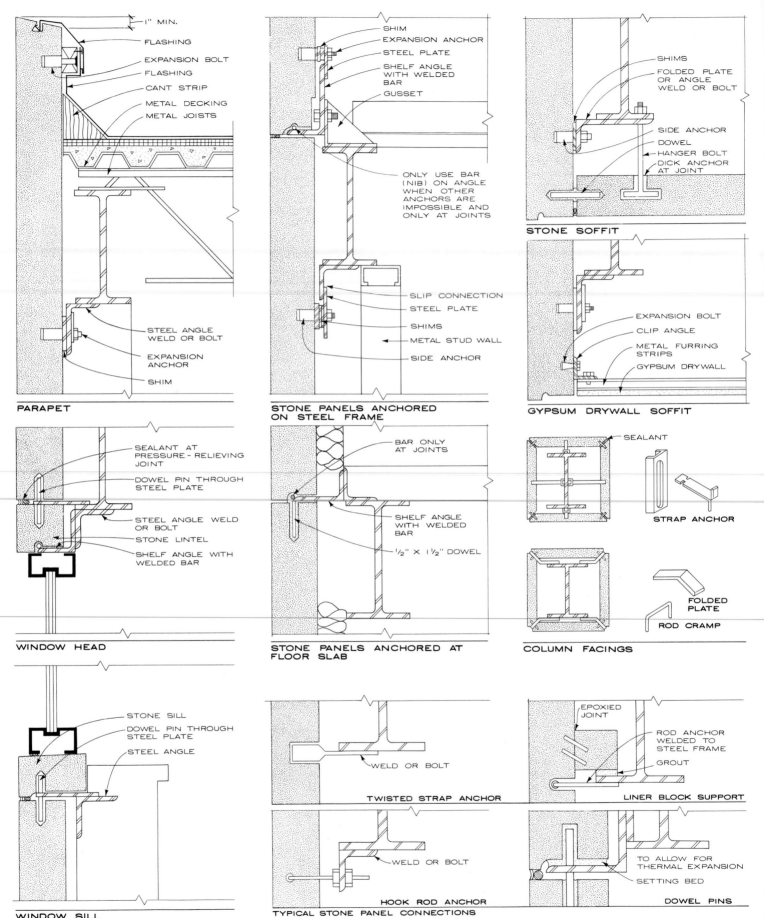

PARAPET

- 1" MIN.
- FLASHING
- EXPANSION BOLT
- FLASHING
- CANT STRIP
- METAL DECKING
- METAL JOISTS
- STEEL ANGLE WELD OR BOLT
- EXPANSION ANCHOR
- SHIM

STONE PANELS ANCHORED ON STEEL FRAME

- SHIM
- EXPANSION ANCHOR
- STEEL PLATE
- SHELF ANGLE WITH WELDED BAR
- GUSSET
- ONLY USE BAR (NIB) ON ANGLE WHEN OTHER ANCHORS ARE IMPOSSIBLE AND ONLY AT JOINTS
- SLIP CONNECTION
- STEEL PLATE
- SHIMS
- METAL STUD WALL
- SIDE ANCHOR

STONE SOFFIT

- SHIMS
- FOLDED PLATE OR ANGLE WELD OR BOLT
- SIDE ANCHOR
- DOWEL
- HANGER BOLT
- DICK ANCHOR AT JOINT

GYPSUM DRYWALL SOFFIT

- EXPANSION BOLT
- CLIP ANGLE
- METAL FURRING STRIPS
- GYPSUM DRYWALL

WINDOW HEAD

- SEALANT AT PRESSURE-RELIEVING JOINT
- DOWEL PIN THROUGH STEEL PLATE
- STEEL ANGLE WELD OR BOLT
- STONE LINTEL
- SHELF ANGLE WITH WELDED BAR

STONE PANELS ANCHORED AT FLOOR SLAB

- BAR ONLY AT JOINTS
- SHELF ANGLE WITH WELDED BAR
- 1/2" X 1 1/2" DOWEL

COLUMN FACINGS

- SEALANT
- STRAP ANCHOR
- FOLDED PLATE
- ROD CRAMP

WINDOW SILL

- STONE SILL
- DOWEL PIN THROUGH STEEL PLATE
- STEEL ANGLE

TYPICAL STONE PANEL CONNECTIONS

- WELD OR BOLT
- TWISTED STRAP ANCHOR
- WELD OR BOLT
- HOOK ROD ANCHOR
- EPOXIED JOINT
- ROD ANCHOR WELDED TO STEEL FRAME
- GROUT
- LINER BLOCK SUPPORT
- TO ALLOW FOR THERMAL EXPANSION
- SETTING BED
- DOWEL PINS

Building Stone Institute; New York, New York
George M. Whiteside, III, AIA, and James D. Lloyd; Kennett Square, Pennsylvania
Alexander Keyes; Darrel Rippeteau, Architect; Washington, D.C.

4 **STONE**

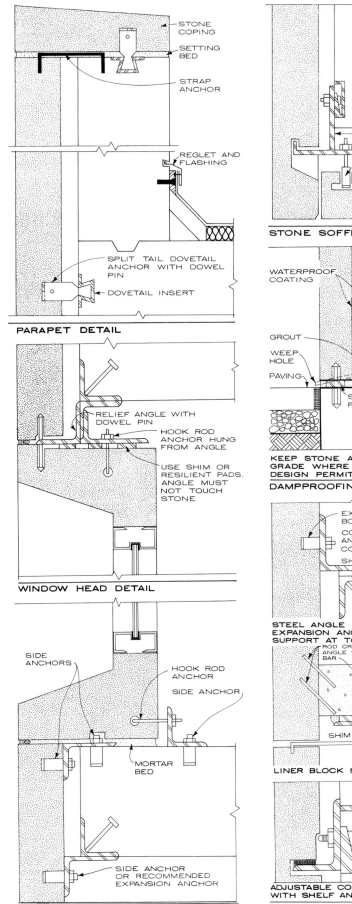

PARAPET DETAIL

- STONE COPING
- SETTING BED
- STRAP ANCHOR
- REGLET AND FLASHING
- SPLIT TAIL DOVETAIL ANCHOR WITH DOWEL PIN
- DOVETAIL INSERT

WINDOW HEAD DETAIL

- RELIEF ANGLE WITH DOWEL PIN
- HOOK ROD ANCHOR HUNG FROM ANGLE
- USE SHIM OR RESILIENT PADS. ANGLE MUST NOT TOUCH STONE

WINDOW SILL DETAIL

- SIDE ANCHORS
- HOOK ROD ANCHOR
- SIDE ANCHOR
- MORTAR BED
- SIDE ANCHOR OR RECOMMENDED EXPANSION ANCHOR

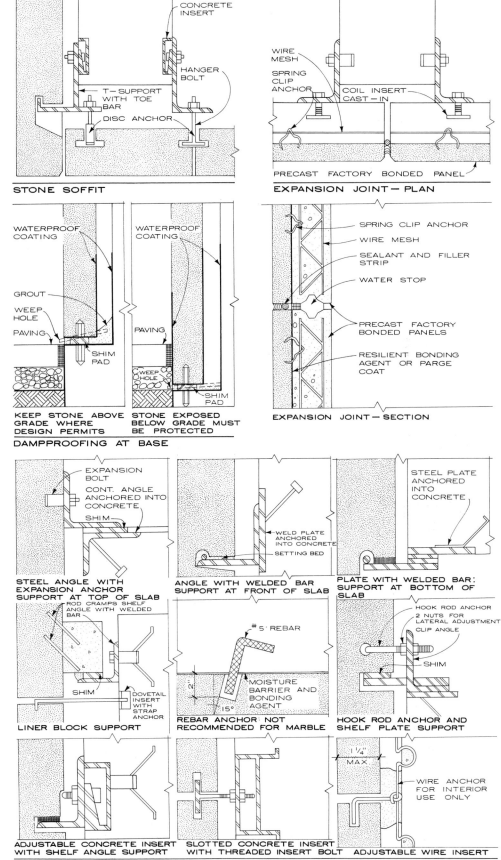

STONE SOFFIT

- CONCRETE INSERT
- HANGER BOLT
- T–SUPPORT WITH TOE BAR
- DISC ANCHOR

EXPANSION JOINT – PLAN

- WIRE MESH
- SPRING CLIP ANCHOR
- COIL INSERT CAST–IN
- PRECAST FACTORY BONDED PANEL

DAMPPROOFING AT BASE

KEEP STONE ABOVE GRADE WHERE DESIGN PERMITS
- WATERPROOF COATING
- GROUT
- WEEP HOLE
- PAVING
- SHIM PAD

STONE EXPOSED BELOW GRADE MUST BE PROTECTED
- WATERPROOF COATING
- PAVING
- WEEP HOLE
- SHIM PAD

EXPANSION JOINT – SECTION

- SPRING CLIP ANCHOR
- WIRE MESH
- SEALANT AND FILLER STRIP
- WATER STOP
- PRECAST FACTORY BONDED PANELS
- RESILIENT BONDING AGENT OR PARGE COAT

STEEL ANGLE WITH EXPANSION ANCHOR SUPPORT AT TOP OF SLAB
- EXPANSION BOLT
- CONT. ANGLE ANCHORED INTO CONCRETE
- SHIM

ANGLE WITH WELDED BAR SUPPORT AT FRONT OF SLAB
- WELD PLATE ANCHORED INTO CONCRETE
- SETTING BED

PLATE WITH WELDED BAR; SUPPORT AT BOTTOM OF SLAB
- STEEL PLATE ANCHORED INTO CONCRETE

LINER BLOCK SUPPORT
- ROD CRAMPS SHELF ANGLE WITH WELDED BAR
- SHIM
- DOVETAIL INSERT WITH STRAP ANCHOR

REBAR ANCHOR NOT RECOMMENDED FOR MARBLE
- #5 REBAR
- 2"
- 15°
- MOISTURE BARRIER AND BONDING AGENT

HOOK ROD ANCHOR AND SHELF PLATE SUPPORT
- HOOK ROD ANCHOR 2 NUTS FOR LATERAL ADJUSTMENT CLIP ANGLE
- SHIM

ADJUSTABLE CONCRETE INSERT WITH SHELF ANGLE SUPPORT

SLOTTED CONCRETE INSERT WITH THREADED INSERT BOLT

ADJUSTABLE WIRE INSERT
- 1 1/4" MAX
- WIRE ANCHOR FOR INTERIOR USE ONLY

TYPICAL CONNECTIONS OF STONE PANELS TO CONCRETE FRAME

Building Stone Institute; New York, New York

George M. Whiteside, III, AIA and James D. Lloyd; Kennett Square, Pennsylvania

Alexander Keyes; Darrel Rippeteau, Architect; Washington, D.C.

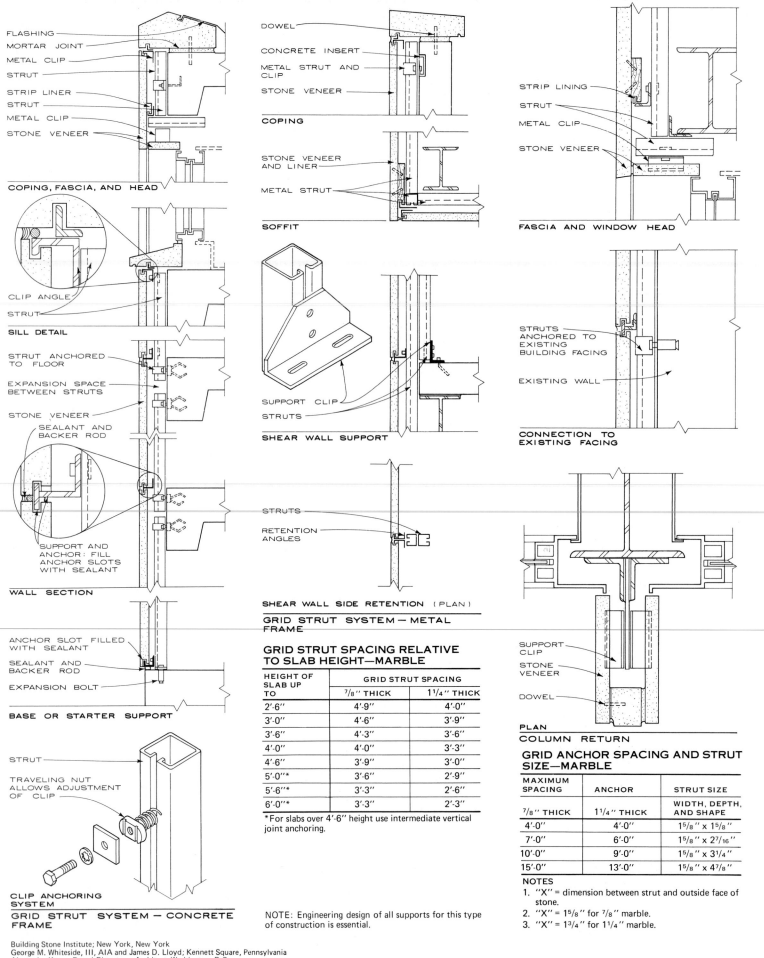

COPING, FASCIA, AND HEAD

- FLASHING
- MORTAR JOINT
- METAL CLIP
- STRUT
- STRIP LINER
- STRUT
- METAL CLIP
- STONE VENEER

SILL DETAIL

- CLIP ANGLE
- STRUT

WALL SECTION

- STRUT ANCHORED TO FLOOR
- EXPANSION SPACE BETWEEN STRUTS
- STONE VENEER
- SEALANT AND BACKER ROD
- SUPPORT AND ANCHOR: FILL ANCHOR SLOTS WITH SEALANT

BASE OR STARTER SUPPORT

- ANCHOR SLOT FILLED WITH SEALANT
- SEALANT AND BACKER ROD
- EXPANSION BOLT

CLIP ANCHORING SYSTEM

- STRUT
- TRAVELING NUT ALLOWS ADJUSTMENT OF CLIP

GRID STRUT SYSTEM — CONCRETE FRAME

COPING

- DOWEL
- CONCRETE INSERT
- METAL STRUT AND CLIP
- STONE VENEER

SOFFIT

- STONE VENEER AND LINER
- METAL STRUT

SHEAR WALL SUPPORT

- SUPPORT CLIP
- STRUTS

SHEAR WALL SIDE RETENTION (PLAN)

- STRUTS
- RETENTION ANGLES

GRID STRUT SYSTEM — METAL FRAME

GRID STRUT SPACING RELATIVE TO SLAB HEIGHT—MARBLE

HEIGHT OF SLAB UP TO	GRID STRUT SPACING	
	⅞″ THICK	1¼″ THICK
2′-6″	4′-9″	4′-0″
3′-0″	4′-6″	3′-9″
3′-6″	4′-3″	3′-6″
4′-0″	4′-0″	3′-3″
4′-6″	3′-9″	3′-0″
5′-0″*	3′-6″	2′-9″
5′-6″*	3′-3″	2′-6″
6′-0″*	3′-3″	2′-3″

*For slabs over 4′-6″ height use intermediate vertical joint anchoring.

FASCIA AND WINDOW HEAD

- STRIP LINING
- STRUT
- METAL CLIP
- STONE VENEER

CONNECTION TO EXISTING FACING

- STRUTS ANCHORED TO EXISTING BUILDING FACING
- EXISTING WALL

PLAN
COLUMN RETURN

- SUPPORT CLIP
- STONE VENEER
- DOWEL

GRID ANCHOR SPACING AND STRUT SIZE—MARBLE

MAXIMUM SPACING		ANCHOR	STRUT SIZE
⅞″ THICK	1¼″ THICK		WIDTH, DEPTH, AND SHAPE
4′-0″	4′-0″		1⅝″ x 1⅝″
7′-0″	6′-0″		1⅝″ x 2⁷⁄₁₆″
10′-0″	9′-0″		1⅝″ x 3¼″
15′-0″	13′-0″		1⅝″ x 4⅞″

NOTES

1. "X" = dimension between strut and outside face of stone.
2. "X" = 1⅝″ for ⅞″ marble.
3. "X" = 1¾″ for 1¼″ marble.

NOTE: Engineering design of all supports for this type of construction is essential.

Building Stone Institute; New York, New York
George M. Whiteside, III, AIA and James D. Lloyd; Kennett Square, Pennsylvania
Alexander Keyes; Darrel Rippeteau, Architect; Washington, D.C.

4   **STONE**

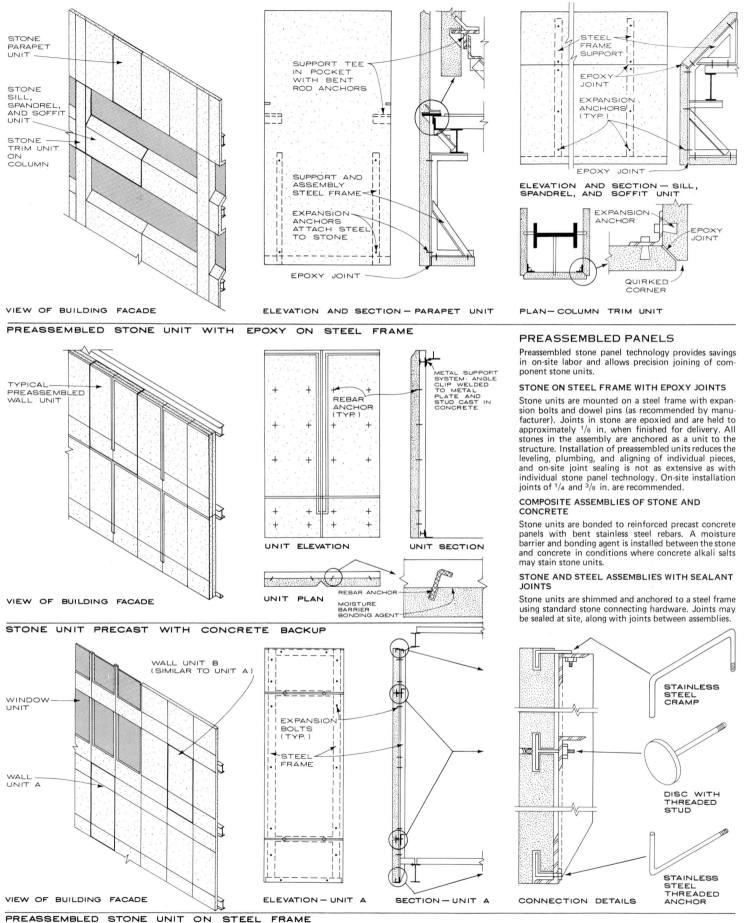

STONE PARAPET UNIT

STONE SILL, SPANDREL, AND SOFFIT UNIT

STONE TRIM UNIT ON COLUMN

VIEW OF BUILDING FACADE

SUPPORT TEE IN POCKET WITH BENT ROD ANCHORS

SUPPORT AND ASSEMBLY STEEL FRAME

EXPANSION ANCHORS ATTACH STEEL TO STONE

EPOXY JOINT

ELEVATION AND SECTION — PARAPET UNIT

STEEL FRAME SUPPORT

EPOXY JOINT

EXPANSION ANCHORS (TYP.)

EPOXY JOINT

ELEVATION AND SECTION — SILL, SPANDREL, AND SOFFIT UNIT

EXPANSION ANCHOR

EPOXY JOINT

QUIRKED CORNER

PLAN — COLUMN TRIM UNIT

PREASSEMBLED STONE UNIT WITH EPOXY ON STEEL FRAME

TYPICAL PREASSEMBLED WALL UNIT

VIEW OF BUILDING FACADE

REBAR ANCHOR (TYP.)

METAL SUPPORT SYSTEM: ANGLE CLIP WELDED TO METAL PLATE AND STUD CAST IN CONCRETE

UNIT ELEVATION

UNIT SECTION

UNIT PLAN

REBAR ANCHOR

MOISTURE BARRIER BONDING AGENT

STONE UNIT PRECAST WITH CONCRETE BACKUP

WINDOW UNIT

WALL UNIT B (SIMILAR TO UNIT A)

WALL UNIT A

VIEW OF BUILDING FACADE

EXPANSION BOLTS (TYP.)

STEEL FRAME

ELEVATION — UNIT A

SECTION — UNIT A

CONNECTION DETAILS

STAINLESS STEEL CRAMP

DISC WITH THREADED STUD

STAINLESS STEEL THREADED ANCHOR

PREASSEMBLED STONE UNIT ON STEEL FRAME

PREASSEMBLED PANELS

Preassembled stone panel technology provides savings in on-site labor and allows precision joining of component stone units.

STONE ON STEEL FRAME WITH EPOXY JOINTS

Stone units are mounted on a steel frame with expansion bolts and dowel pins (as recommended by manufacturer). Joints in stone are epoxied and are held to approximately $1/8$ in. when finished for delivery. All stones in the assembly are anchored as a unit to the structure. Installation of preassembled units reduces the leveling, plumbing, and aligning of individual pieces, and on-site joint sealing is not as extensive as with individual stone panel technology. On-site installation joints of $1/4$ and $3/8$ in. are recommended.

COMPOSITE ASSEMBLIES OF STONE AND CONCRETE

Stone units are bonded to reinforced precast concrete panels with bent stainless steel rebars. A moisture barrier and bonding agent is installed between the stone and concrete in conditions where concrete alkali salts may stain stone units.

STONE AND STEEL ASSEMBLIES WITH SEALANT JOINTS

Stone units are shimmed and anchored to a steel frame using standard stone connecting hardware. Joints may be sealed at site, along with joints between assemblies.

Building Stone Institute; New York, New York

George M. Whiteside, III, AIA, and James D. Lloyd; Kennett Square, Pennsylvania

Alexander Keyes; Darrel Rippeteau, Architect; Washington, D.C.

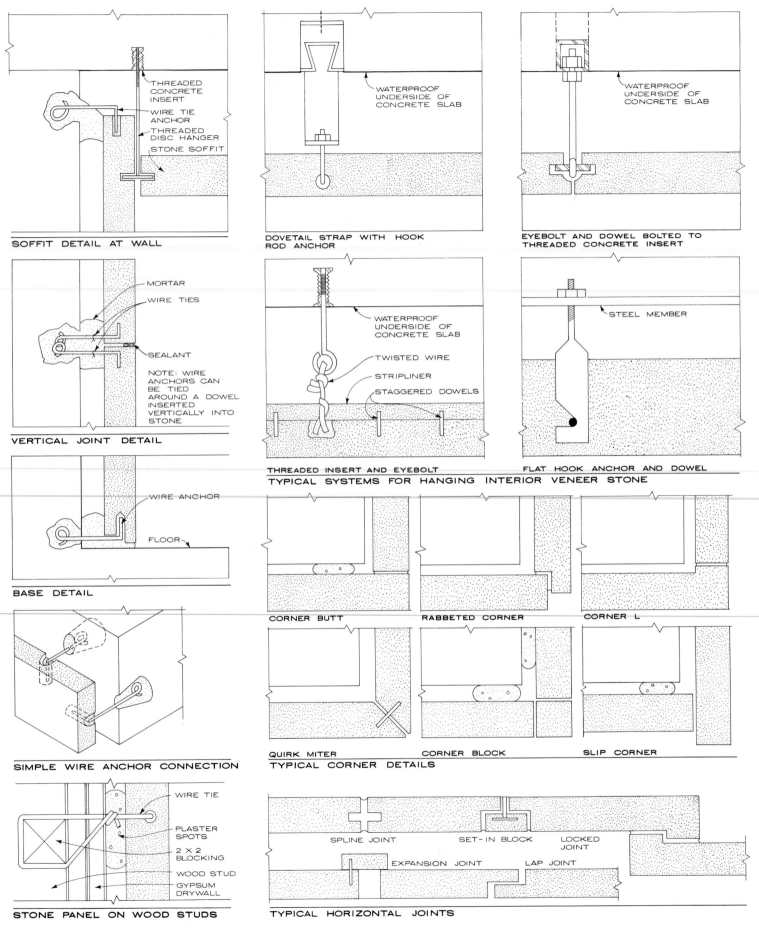

SOFFIT DETAIL AT WALL

THREADED CONCRETE INSERT
WIRE TIE ANCHOR
THREADED DISC HANGER
STONE SOFFIT

DOVETAIL STRAP WITH HOOK ROD ANCHOR

WATERPROOF UNDERSIDE OF CONCRETE SLAB

EYEBOLT AND DOWEL BOLTED TO THREADED CONCRETE INSERT

WATERPROOF UNDERSIDE OF CONCRETE SLAB

VERTICAL JOINT DETAIL

MORTAR
WIRE TIES
SEALANT

NOTE: WIRE ANCHORS CAN BE TIED AROUND A DOWEL INSERTED VERTICALLY INTO STONE

THREADED INSERT AND EYEBOLT

WATERPROOF UNDERSIDE OF CONCRETE SLAB
TWISTED WIRE
STRIPLINER
STAGGERED DOWELS

FLAT HOOK ANCHOR AND DOWEL

STEEL MEMBER

TYPICAL SYSTEMS FOR HANGING INTERIOR VENEER STONE

BASE DETAIL

WIRE ANCHOR
FLOOR

CORNER BUTT   RABBETED CORNER   CORNER L

SIMPLE WIRE ANCHOR CONNECTION

QUIRK MITER   CORNER BLOCK   SLIP CORNER

TYPICAL CORNER DETAILS

STONE PANEL ON WOOD STUDS

WIRE TIE
PLASTER SPOTS
2 X 2 BLOCKING
WOOD STUD
GYPSUM DRYWALL

SPLINE JOINT   SET-IN BLOCK   LOCKED JOINT
EXPANSION JOINT   LAP JOINT

TYPICAL HORIZONTAL JOINTS

Building Stone Institute; New York, New York
George M. Whiteside, III, AIA and James D. Lloyd; Kennett Square, Pennsylvania
Alexander Keyes; Darrel Rippeteau, Architect; Washington, D.C.

4   STONE

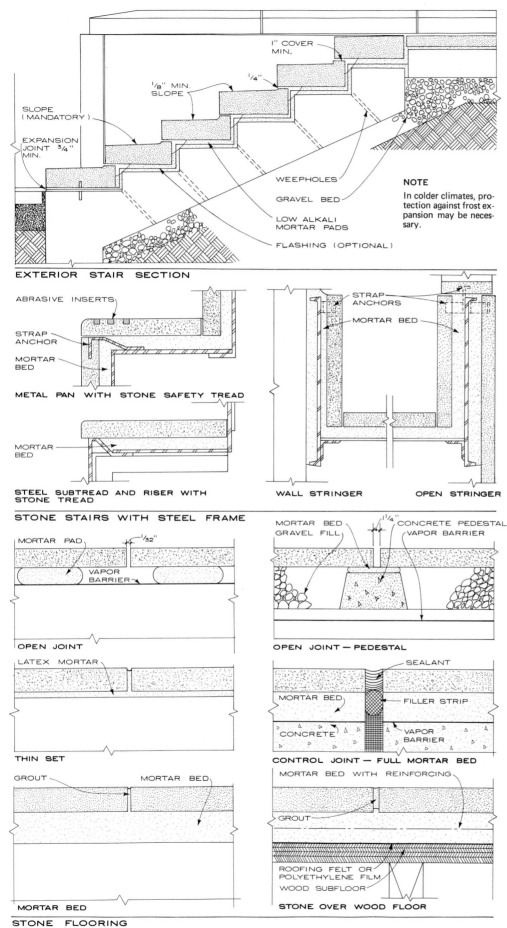

EXTERIOR STAIR SECTION

- SLOPE (MANDATORY)
- EXPANSION JOINT ¾" MIN.
- ⅛" MIN. SLOPE
- ¼"
- 1" COVER MIN.
- WEEPHOLES
- GRAVEL BED
- LOW ALKALI MORTAR PADS
- FLASHING (OPTIONAL)

NOTE

In colder climates, protection against frost expansion may be necessary.

METAL PAN WITH STONE SAFETY TREAD

- ABRASIVE INSERTS
- STRAP ANCHOR
- MORTAR BED

STEEL SUBTREAD AND RISER WITH STONE TREAD

- MORTAR BED

STONE STAIRS WITH STEEL FRAME

- STRAP ANCHORS
- MORTAR BED

WALL STRINGER **OPEN STRINGER**

STONE FLOORING

OPEN JOINT

- MORTAR PAD
- 1/32"
- VAPOR BARRIER

THIN SET

- LATEX MORTAR

MORTAR BED

- GROUT
- MORTAR BED

OPEN JOINT — PEDESTAL

- MORTAR BED GRAVEL FILL
- 1¼"
- CONCRETE PEDESTAL VAPOR BARRIER

CONTROL JOINT — FULL MORTAR BED

- SEALANT
- MORTAR BED
- FILLER STRIP
- CONCRETE
- VAPOR BARRIER

STONE OVER WOOD FLOOR

- MORTAR BED WITH REINFORCING
- GROUT
- ROOFING FELT OR POLYETHYLENE FILM
- WOOD SUBFLOOR

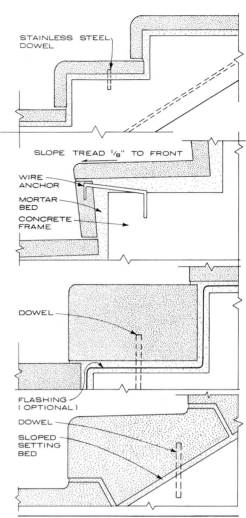

STONE STAIRS WITH CONCRETE FRAME

- STAINLESS STEEL DOWEL
- SLOPE TREAD ⅛" TO FRONT
- WIRE ANCHOR
- MORTAR BED
- CONCRETE FRAME
- DOWEL
- FLASHING (OPTIONAL)
- DOWEL
- SLOPED SETTING BED

DESIGN FACTORS FOR STONE STAIRS

Stone used for steps should have an abrasive resistance of 10 (measured on a scale from a minimum of 6 to a maximum of 17). When different varieties of stone are used, their abrasive hardness should be similar to prevent uneven wear.

Dowels and anchoring devices should be noncorrosive.

If a safety tread is not used on stairs, a light bush hammered soft finish or nonslip finish is recommended.

To prevent future staining, dampproof the face of all concrete or concrete block, specify low alkali mortar, and provide adequate drainage (slopes and weepholes).

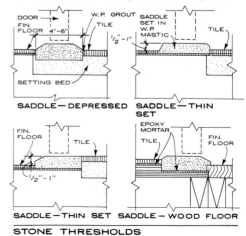

- DOOR
- FIN. FLOOR 4"–6"
- W.P. GROUT
- TILE
- SADDLE SET IN W.P. MASTIC
- ½"–1"
- TILE
- SETTING BED

SADDLE — DEPRESSED **SADDLE — THIN SET**

- FIN. FLOOR
- TILE
- ½"–1"
- EPOXY MORTAR
- TILE
- FIN. FLOOR

SADDLE — THIN SET **SADDLE — WOOD FLOOR**

STONE THRESHOLDS

Building Stone Institute; New York, New York

George M. Whiteside, III, AIA and James D. Lloyd; Kennett Square, Pennsylvania

Alexander Keyes; Darrel Rippeteau, Architect; Washington, D.C.

STONE **4**

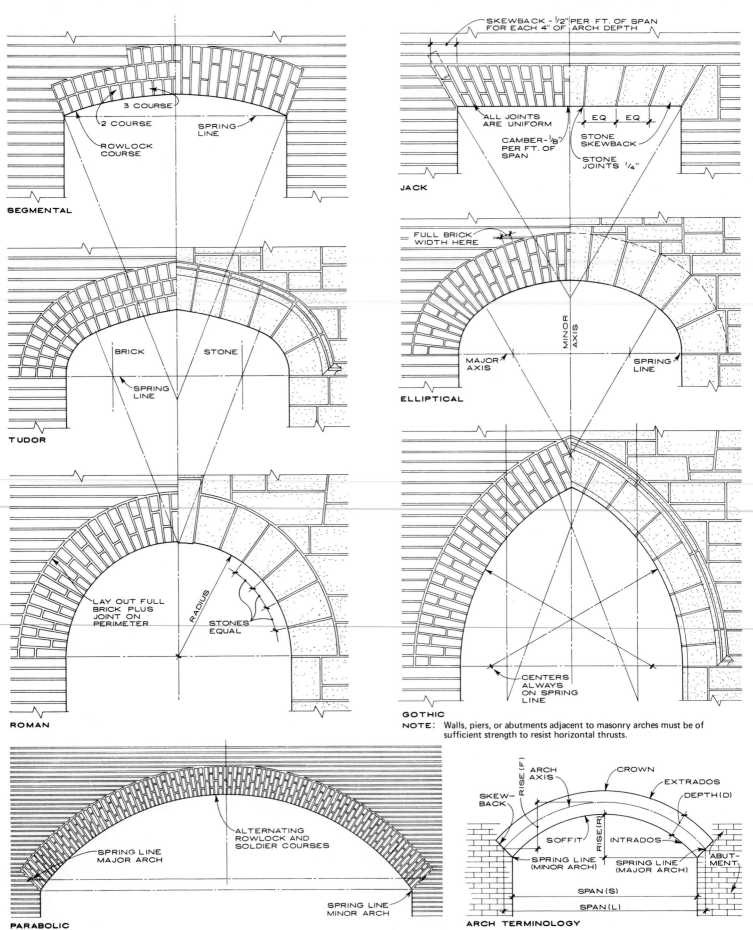

SEGMENTAL

3 COURSE
2 COURSE
ROWLOCK COURSE
SPRING LINE

JACK

SKEWBACK - 1/2" PER FT. OF SPAN FOR EACH 4" OF ARCH DEPTH
ALL JOINTS ARE UNIFORM
CAMBER-1/8" PER FT. OF SPAN
EQ EQ
STONE SKEWBACK
STONE JOINTS 1/4"

TUDOR

BRICK
STONE
SPRING LINE

ELLIPTICAL

FULL BRICK WIDTH HERE
MINOR AXIS
MAJOR AXIS
SPRING LINE

ROMAN

LAY OUT FULL BRICK PLUS JOINT ON PERIMETER
RADIUS
STONES EQUAL

GOTHIC

CENTERS ALWAYS ON SPRING LINE

NOTE: Walls, piers, or abutments adjacent to masonry arches must be of sufficient strength to resist horizontal thrusts.

PARABOLIC

SPRING LINE MAJOR ARCH
ALTERNATING ROWLOCK AND SOLDIER COURSES
SPRING LINE MINOR ARCH

ARCH TERMINOLOGY

SKEW-BACK
RISE (F)
ARCH AXIS
CROWN
EXTRADOS
DEPTH (D)
SOFFIT
RISE (R)
INTRADOS
SPRING LINE (MINOR ARCH)
SPRING LINE (MAJOR ARCH)
ABUT-MENT
SPAN (S)
SPAN (L)

Brick Institute of America; McLean, Virginia

4 ARCHES

INTRODUCTION

A traditional masonry fireplace with its foundation, hearth, and chimney is a special element in a building and requires special design consideration. The masonry chimney is usually the heaviest single part of a wood frame structure and therefore requires a special foundation. The same holds true for masonry buildings where walls are not thick enough to incorporate the chimney or where the chimney is not designed into a masonry wall. Beyond the structural requirements, a fireplace and chimney must be designed with the proper spaces and relationships between spaces to sustain combustion and to carry smoke away safely. In the latter area, fireplace design is bound by the physical laws of nature and by various building codes. The internal diagram of a working fireplace (right) shows the several required parts and their vertical organization. Each part is further illustrated on succeeding pages in details of practical designs.

An ordinary masonry fireplace is only about one-third as efficient for heating as is a good stove or circulating heater. Other pages describe more efficient prefabricated fireplace units which incorporate air heating and circulating devices. A fireplace should not be located near doors to the exterior.

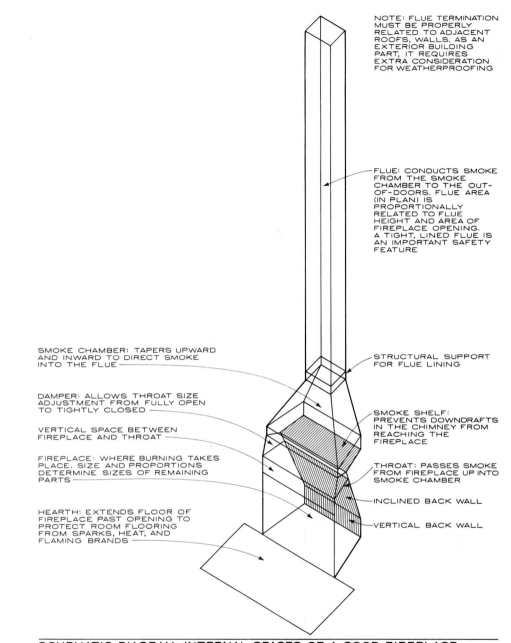

NOTE: FLUE TERMINATION MUST BE PROPERLY RELATED TO ADJACENT ROOFS, WALLS. AS AN EXTERIOR BUILDING PART, IT REQUIRES EXTRA CONSIDERATION FOR WEATHERPROOFING

FLUE: CONDUCTS SMOKE FROM THE SMOKE CHAMBER TO THE OUT-OF-DOORS. FLUE AREA (IN PLAN) IS PROPORTIONALLY RELATED TO FLUE HEIGHT AND AREA OF FIREPLACE OPENING. A TIGHT, LINED FLUE IS AN IMPORTANT SAFETY FEATURE

SMOKE CHAMBER: TAPERS UPWARD AND INWARD TO DIRECT SMOKE INTO THE FLUE

DAMPER: ALLOWS THROAT SIZE ADJUSTMENT FROM FULLY OPEN TO TIGHTLY CLOSED

VERTICAL SPACE BETWEEN FIREPLACE AND THROAT

FIREPLACE: WHERE BURNING TAKES PLACE. SIZE AND PROPORTIONS DETERMINE SIZES OF REMAINING PARTS

HEARTH: EXTENDS FLOOR OF FIREPLACE PAST OPENING TO PROTECT ROOM FLOORING FROM SPARKS, HEAT, AND FLAMING BRANDS

STRUCTURAL SUPPORT FOR FLUE LINING

SMOKE SHELF: PREVENTS DOWNDRAFTS IN THE CHIMNEY FROM REACHING THE FIREPLACE

THROAT: PASSES SMOKE FROM FIREPLACE UP INTO SMOKE CHAMBER

INCLINED BACK WALL

VERTICAL BACK WALL

FIREPLACE

FIRST FLOOR

ASH DUMP

AN AIR INTAKE MAY BE INSTALLED IN THE ASH PIT WALL TO INTRODUCE OUTSIDE AIR INTO THE FIREPLACE VIA THE ASH DUMP

ASH PIT

CLEAN-OUT DOOR

BASEMENT

OPTIONAL ACCESSORY SPACES FOR IMPROVED FIREPLACE OPERATION

SCHEMATIC DIAGRAM: INTERNAL SPACES OF A GOOD FIREPLACE AND CHIMNEY

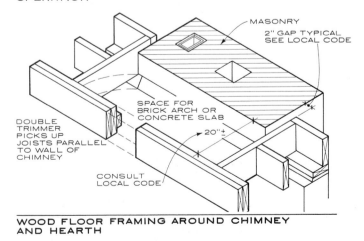

MASONRY

2" GAP TYPICAL SEE LOCAL CODE

SPACE FOR BRICK ARCH OR CONCRETE SLAB

DOUBLE TRIMMER PICKS UP JOISTS PARALLEL TO WALL OF CHIMNEY

20"+

CONSULT LOCAL CODE

WOOD FLOOR FRAMING AROUND CHIMNEY AND HEARTH

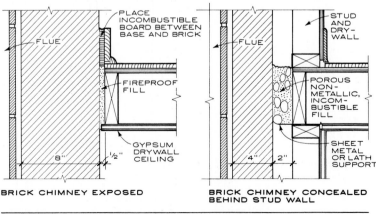
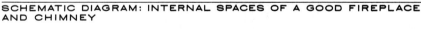

PLACE INCOMBUSTIBLE BOARD BETWEEN BASE AND BRICK

FLUE

FIREPROOF FILL

GYPSUM DRYWALL CEILING

8"   ½"

BRICK CHIMNEY EXPOSED

STUD AND DRY-WALL

FLUE

POROUS NON-METALLIC, INCOMBUSTIBLE FILL

SHEET METAL OR LATH SUPPORT

4"   2"

BRICK CHIMNEY CONCEALED BEHIND STUD WALL

INSULATION OF WOOD FRAMING MEMBERS AT A CHIMNEY

Darrel Rippeteau, Architect; Washington, D.C.

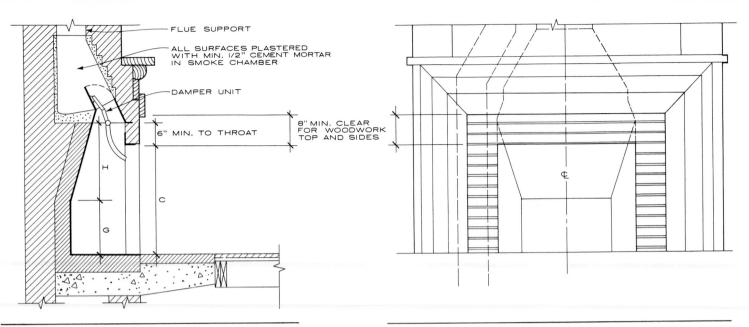

SECTION

ELEVATION

RECOMMENDED DIMENSIONS FOR WOOD BURNING FIREPLACES, HEARTH, AND FLUE (IN.)

FIREPLACE OPENING			BACK-WALL WIDTH (MIN.)	VERTICAL BACKWALL HEIGHT	INCLINED BACKWALL HEIGHT	FLUE LINING	
WIDTH B	HEIGHT C	DEPTH A	F	G	H	RECTANGULAR (OUTSIDE)	ROUND (INSIDE)
24	24	16–18	14	14	16	8½ x 13	10
28	24	16–18	14	14	16	8½ x 13	10
30	28–30	16–18	16	14	18	8½ x 13	10
36	28–30	16–18	22	14	18	8½ x 13	12
42	28–30	16–18	28	14	18	13 x 13	12
48	32	18–20	32	14	24	13 x 13	15
54	36	18–20	36	14	28	13 x 18	15
60	36	18–20	44	14	28	13 x 18	15
54	40	20–22	36	17	29	13 x 18	15
60	40	20–22	44	17	30	18 x 18	18
66	40	20–22	44	17	30	18 x 18	18
72	40	22–28	51	17	30	18 x 18	18

PLAN   DIMENSIONS D & E – SEE LOCAL CODES

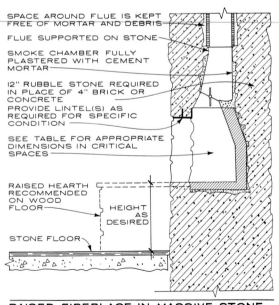

SECTION

CUTAWAY VIEW

TRADITIONAL MASONRY FIREPLACE WITH ENERGY CONSERVATION MODIFICATIONS

RAISED FIREPLACE IN MASSIVE STONE WALL – SECTION

Darrel Rippeteau, Architect; Washington, D.C.

4   FIREPLACES

HEAT CIRCULATING FIREPLACE FOR INSTALLATION IN MASONRY

These special fireplaces are constructed of steel and must be properly enclosed in masonry to obtain a complete wood burning unit. When placed on a firebrick hearth, the steel fireplace includes all of the essential combustion and smoke handling spaces described earlier in the chapter. In addition, the circulator provides a heat transfer chamber with inlets and outlets that draw in cool air, heat it, and expel warm air by natural convection. The air heating cycle can be augmented with electric fans in the intakes (not in the outlets). The steel shell provides a form for the masonry enclosure, but it is not a structural element. Enclosing masonry must be held at least 1/2 in. away from the shell to allow for expansion and contraction in the metal. The 1/2 in. space is taken up with fireproof insulation that covers the entire circulator.

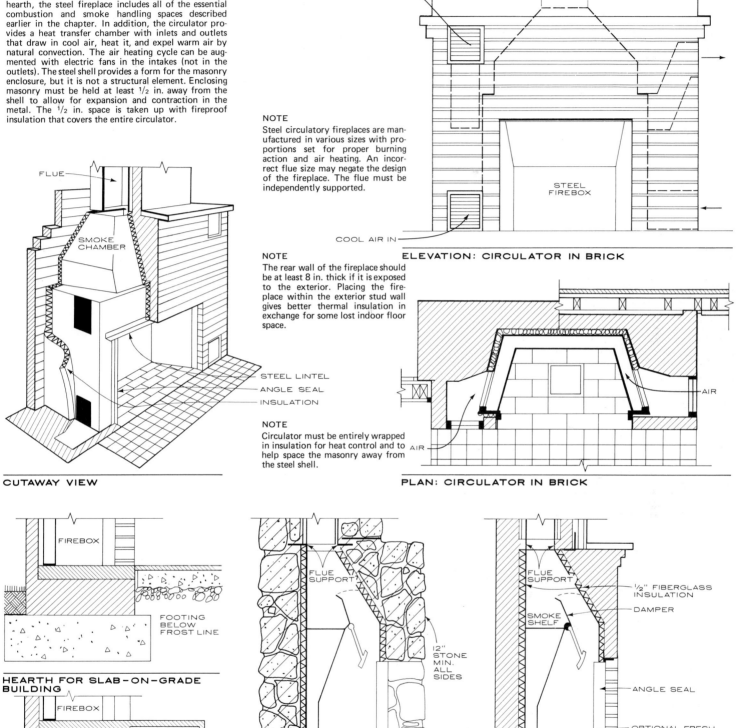

CUTAWAY VIEW

ELEVATION: CIRCULATOR IN BRICK

PLAN: CIRCULATOR IN BRICK

NOTE

Steel circulatory fireplaces are manufactured in various sizes with proportions set for proper burning action and air heating. An incorrect flue size may negate the design of the fireplace. The flue must be independently supported.

NOTE

The rear wall of the fireplace should be at least 8 in. thick if it is exposed to the exterior. Placing the fireplace within the exterior stud wall gives better thermal insulation in exchange for some lost indoor floor space.

NOTE

Circulator must be entirely wrapped in insulation for heat control and to help space the masonry away from the steel shell.

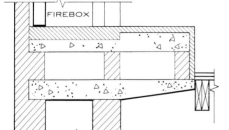

HEARTH FOR SLAB-ON-GRADE BUILDING

RAISED HEARTH

SECTION: CIRCULATOR IN STONE

SECTION: CIRCULATOR IN BRICK

Darrel Rippeteau, Architect; Washington, D.C.

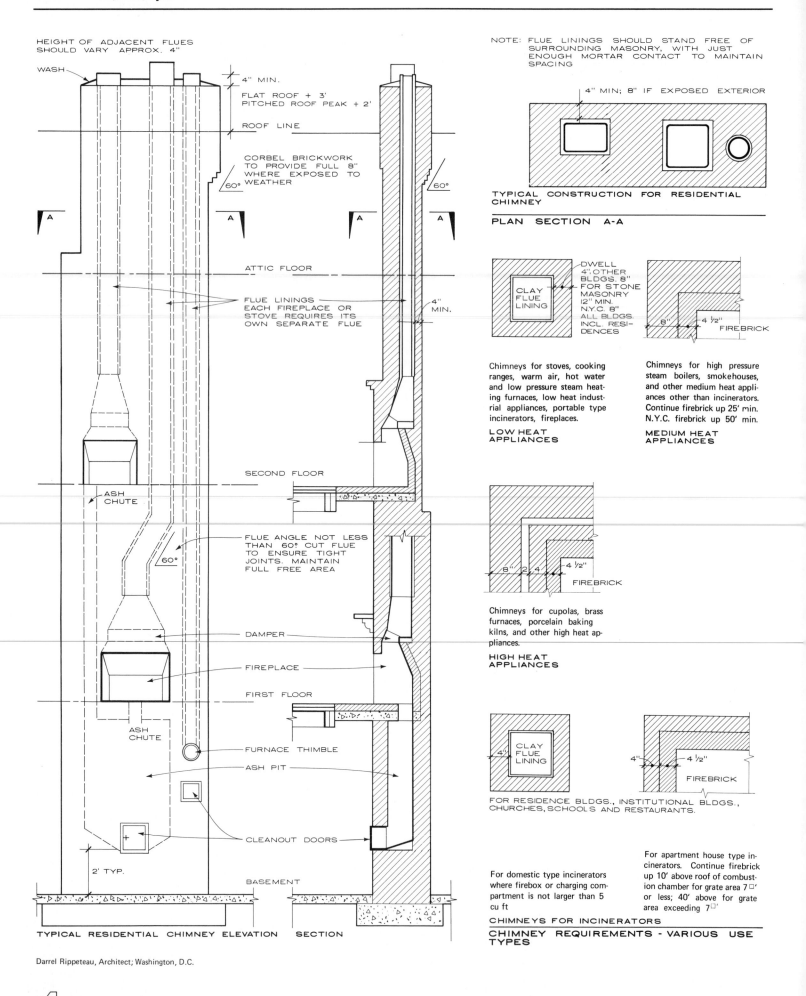

HEIGHT OF ADJACENT FLUES SHOULD VARY APPROX. 4"

WASH

4" MIN.

FLAT ROOF + 3'
PITCHED ROOF PEAK + 2'

ROOF LINE

CORBEL BRICKWORK TO PROVIDE FULL 8" WHERE EXPOSED TO WEATHER

60°   60°

A   A   A   A

ATTIC FLOOR

FLUE LININGS EACH FIREPLACE OR STOVE REQUIRES ITS OWN SEPARATE FLUE

4" MIN.

SECOND FLOOR

ASH CHUTE

FLUE ANGLE NOT LESS THAN 60°. CUT FLUE TO ENSURE TIGHT JOINTS. MAINTAIN FULL FREE AREA

60°

DAMPER

FIREPLACE

FIRST FLOOR

ASH CHUTE

FURNACE THIMBLE

ASH PIT

CLEANOUT DOORS

2' TYP.

BASEMENT

TYPICAL RESIDENTIAL CHIMNEY ELEVATION   SECTION

NOTE: FLUE LININGS SHOULD STAND FREE OF SURROUNDING MASONRY, WITH JUST ENOUGH MORTAR CONTACT TO MAINTAIN SPACING

4" MIN; 8" IF EXPOSED EXTERIOR

TYPICAL CONSTRUCTION FOR RESIDENTIAL CHIMNEY

PLAN SECTION A-A

CLAY FLUE LINING

DWELL 4". OTHER BLDGS. 8" FOR STONE MASONRY 12" MIN. N.Y.C. 8" ALL BLDGS. INCL. RESIDENCES

8"   4½"   FIREBRICK

Chimneys for stoves, cooking ranges, warm air, hot water and low pressure steam heating furnaces, low heat industrial appliances, portable type incinerators, fireplaces.

LOW HEAT APPLIANCES

Chimneys for high pressure steam boilers, smokehouses, and other medium heat appliances other than incinerators. Continue firebrick up 25' min. N.Y.C. firebrick up 50' min.

MEDIUM HEAT APPLIANCES

8"   2   4   4½"   FIREBRICK

Chimneys for cupolas, brass furnaces, porcelain baking kilns, and other high heat appliances.

HIGH HEAT APPLIANCES

CLAY FLUE LINING

4"   4½"   FIREBRICK

FOR RESIDENCE BLDGS., INSTITUTIONAL BLDGS., CHURCHES, SCHOOLS AND RESTAURANTS.

For domestic type incinerators where firebox or charging compartment is not larger than 5 cu ft

For apartment house type incinerators. Continue firebrick up 10' above roof of combustion chamber for grate area 7□' or less; 40' above for grate area exceeding 7□'

CHIMNEYS FOR INCINERATORS

CHIMNEY REQUIREMENTS - VARIOUS USE TYPES

Darrel Rippeteau, Architect; Washington, D.C.

CHAPTER 5 METALS

STRUCTURAL ECONOMY—STEEL FRAMING

The most commonly used strength grade of structural steel is 36,000 psi yield strength (ASTM A36). For heavily loaded members such as columns, girders, or trusses where buckling, lateral stability, deflection, or vibration does not control member selection, higher yield strength steels may be economically utilized. A 50,000 psi yield strength is most frequently used among high strength, low alloy steels.

The Manual of Steel Construction of the AISC contains column and beam load tables for both 36,000 and 50,000 psi yield strengths.

High strength, low alloy steels are available in several grades, and some possess superior corrosion resistance to such a degree that they are classified as "weathering steel." Table 1 contains data for several ASTM alloys used for structural members.

TABLE 1   STRUCTURAL STEEL DATA

ATSM DESIGNATION	STRENGTH GRADES (KSI)	ATMOSPHERIC CORROSION RESISTANCE	REMARKS
A572	42, 45, 50, 55, 60, 65	Same as carbon steel	Most commonly used of low alloy steels
A441	40, 42, 46, 50	Twice the resistance of carbon steel	Primarily for welded structures—not frequently used
A242	42, 46, 50*	5 to 8 times the resistance of carbon steel	Used exposed as "weathering steel" or painted
A588	42, 46, 50*	4 times the resistance of carbon steel	Used exposed as "weathering steel" or painted

*50 KSI normally provided, but reduced for thicker material.

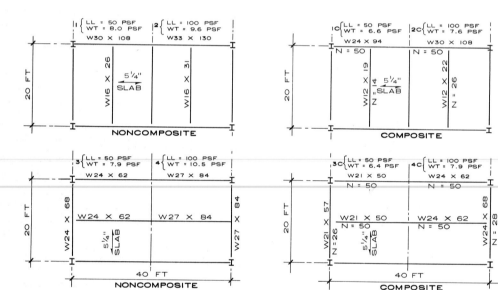

TABLE 2   ALTERNATE FRAMING

	SHORT BEAMS, LONG GIRDERS				LONG BEAMS, SHORT GIRDERS			
	LL = 50 PSF		LL = 100 PSF		LL = 50 PSF		LL = 100 PSF	
	1	1C	2	2C	3	3C	4	4C
Girder depth	30″	24″	33″	30″	24″	21″	27″	24″
Steel weight per bay (lb)	6400	5280	7680	6080	6320	5140	8400	6320
Weight ratio— Noncomposite : composite	1.21 : 1		1.26 : 1		1.23 : 1		1.33 : 1	
No. shear studs	0	106	0	154	0	126	0	128
Cost ratio (see Note 5)	1.16 : 1		1.19 : 1		1.16 : 1		1.27 : 1	

NOTES

1. Floor slab: 5¼ in. total thickness—3¼ in. lightweight concrete over 2 in. composite metal deck, all schemes. This provides a 2 hr fire rating without spraying the deck.
2. Additional dead load allowance for finishes, etc.: 30 psf, all schemes.
3. All steel ASTM A36.
4. Shear studs: ¾ in. dia. x 3½ in. long. N = 50 indicates total number of studs per beam.
5. The cost ratio between noncomposite and composite floor steel is approximately 95% of the weight ratio. The cost of studs accounts for the difference.
6. Vibration of floor beams should be analyzed.

Walter D. Shapiro, P.E.; Tor, Shapiro & Associates; New York, New York

Figure above shows approximate weight of noncomposite structural steel floor or roof framing versus bay size.

NOTES

1. Roof of 15 ft high one-story structure, H-series open web joists on continuous A36 girders (weight of A36 columns included). Joist span = 30 ft.
2. Same as (1) except that joist span = 45 ft.
3. Typical level of five-story garage, V-50 steel throughout (weight of columns included) bay width = 20 ft.
4. Same as (3) except that bay width = 30 ft.

NOTES

The weight of structural steel per square foot of floor area increases with bay size, as does the depth of the structure. Cost of structural steel may not rise as rapidly as weight if savings can be realized by reducing the number of pieces to be fabricated and erected. Improved space utilization afforded by larger bay sizes is offset by increases in wall area and building volume resulting from increased structure depth.

Steel frame economy can be improved by incorporating as many of these cost reducing factors into the structure layout and design as architectural requirements permit:

1. Keep columns in line in both directions and avoid offsets or omission of columns.
2. Design for maximum repetition of member sizes within each level and from floor to floor.
3. Reduce the number of beams and girders per level to reduce fabrication and erection time and cost.
4. Maximize the use of simple beam connections by bracing the structure at a limited number of moment resisting bents or by the most efficient method, cross-bracing.
5. Utilize high strength steels for columns and floor members where studies indicate that cost can be reduced while meeting other design parameters.
6. Use composite design, but consider effect of in-slab electric raceways or other discontinuities.
7. Consider open web steel joists, especially for large roofs of one-story structures, and for floor framing in many applications.

An analysis of alternate framing schemes for a 20 x 40 ft interior floor bay appears in Table 2.

One constant relationship that may be noted in the analysis is the decrease in girder depth when using long beams and short girders. The weight of steel for roofs or lightly loaded floors is generally least when long beams and short girders are used. For heavier loadings long girders and short filler beams should result in less steel weight. The most economical framing type (composite, noncomposite, continuous, simple spans, etc.) and arrangement must be determined for each structure, considering such factors as structure depth, building volume, wall area, mechanical system requirements, deflection or vibration limitations, wind or seismic load interaction between floor system and columns or shear walls.

Composite construction combines two different materials or two different grades of a material to form a structural member that utilizes the most desirable properties of each material. Examples of composite construction are all around us but may go unrecognized as such. Perhaps the earliest composite structural unit was the mud brick reinforced with straw. Other common examples are: nineteenth century trusses of wood and iron; modern trusses and open web joists of wood and steel; reinforced concrete, which combines the tensile strength of steel with the compressive strength of concrete; cable supported concrete roofs and bridges; fiberglass reinforced plastics; wire reinforced safety glass; plywood; glued laminated wood beams.

Composite systems currently used in building construction include:

1. Concrete topped composite steel decks.
2. Steel beams acting compositely with concrete slabs.
3. Steel columns encased by or filled with concrete.
4. Open web joists of wood and steel or joists with plywood webs and wood chords.
5. Trusses combining wood and steel.
6. Hybrid girders utilizing steels of different strengths.
7. Cast-in-place concrete slab on precast concrete joists or beams.

To make two different materials act compositely as one unit they must be joined at their interface by one or a combination of these means:

1. Chemical bonding (concrete).
2. Gluing (plywood, glulam).
3. Welding (steel, aluminum).
4. Screws (sheet metal, wood).
5. Bolts (steel, wood).
6. Shear studs (steel to concrete).
7. Keys or embossments (steel deck to concrete, concrete to concrete).
8. Dowels (concrete to concrete).
9. Friction (positive clamping force must be present).

Individual elements of the composite unit must be securely fastened to prevent slippage with respect to one another. This principle can be demonstrated by bending a telephone book at its free edges and then trying to bend the book at its binding—the binding makes all the pages resist bending in a combined effort, unlike the free edges where pages slip and slide, offering little resistance.

The illustrations of composite systems show points of potential slippage, which occur where load is transferred from one element of the composite member to another.

Comparative designs are shown below for a floor beam and a roof joist to demonstrate possible reductions in structure weight and cost savings through use of composite design. Additional information on structural economy is presented in this chapter.

FLOOR: DEAD LOAD = 80 PSF ROOF: D.L. = 20 PSF
LIVE LOAD = 100 PSF   L.L. = 30 PSF
TOTAL = 180 PSF   TOTAL = 50 PSF

L = 30 FT
(FLOOR BEAMS AND ROOF JOISTS)
FLOOR BEAMS SPACED 10 FT ON CENTER
ROOF JOISTS SPACED 5 FT ON CENTER

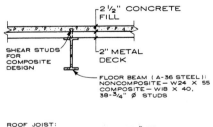

2 1/2" CONCRETE FILL
SHEAR STUDS FOR COMPOSITE DESIGN
2" METAL DECK
FLOOR BEAM (A-36 STEEL):
NONCOMPOSITE—W24 X 55
COMPOSITE—W18 X 40, 38-3/4" Ø STUDS

ROOF JOIST:
STEEL BEAM (A-36)—W14 X 22 #/FT
STEEL JOIST—24J6 (9.9 #/FT) OR 20H5 (8.4 #/FT)
WOOD-STEEL JOIST—26" DEEP(5 #/FT) DOUBLE 1.5" X 2.3"
(SEE DET. 4B ABOVE) MICRO-LAM CHORDS, STEEL TUBE
DIAGONALS—1 1/2" TO 1" DIA.

COMPARATIVE DESIGN EXAMPLE

Walter D. Shapiro, P. E.; Tor, Shapiro & Associates; New York, New York

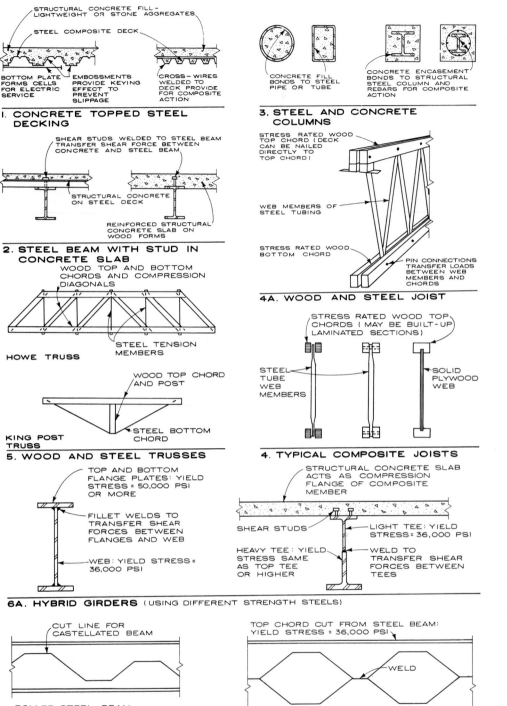

STRUCTURAL CONCRETE FILL-LIGHTWEIGHT OR STONE AGGREGATES
STEEL COMPOSITE DECK
BOTTOM PLATE FORMS CELLS FOR ELECTRIC SERVICE
EMBOSSMENTS PROVIDE KEYING EFFECT TO PREVENT SLIPPAGE
CROSS-WIRES WELDED TO DECK PROVIDE FOR COMPOSITE ACTION

1. CONCRETE TOPPED STEEL DECKING

SHEAR STUDS WELDED TO STEEL BEAM TRANSFER SHEAR FORCE BETWEEN CONCRETE AND STEEL BEAM
STRUCTURAL CONCRETE ON STEEL DECK
REINFORCED STRUCTURAL CONCRETE SLAB ON WOOD FORMS

2. STEEL BEAM WITH STUD IN CONCRETE SLAB

WOOD TOP AND BOTTOM CHORDS AND COMPRESSION DIAGONALS
STEEL TENSION MEMBERS

HOWE TRUSS

WOOD TOP CHORD AND POST
STEEL BOTTOM CHORD

KING POST TRUSS

5. WOOD AND STEEL TRUSSES

TOP AND BOTTOM FLANGE PLATES: YIELD STRESS = 50,000 PSI OR MORE
FILLET WELDS TO TRANSFER SHEAR FORCES BETWEEN FLANGES AND WEB
WEB: YIELD STRESS = 36,000 PSI

6A. HYBRID GIRDERS (USING DIFFERENT STRENGTH STEELS)

CUT LINE FOR CASTELLATED BEAM
ROLLED STEEL BEAM BEFORE CUTTING

TOP CHORD CUT FROM STEEL BEAM: YIELD STRESS = 36,000 PSI
WELD
FINISHED BEAM
BOTTOM CHORD CUT FROM DIFFERENT WEIGHT STEEL BEAM: YIELD STRESS SAME AS OR HIGHER THAN THAT FOR TOP CHORD

6 CASTELLATED BEAMS

CONCRETE FILL BONDS TO STEEL PIPE OR TUBE
CONCRETE ENCASEMENT BONDS TO STRUCTURAL STEEL COLUMN AND REBARS FOR COMPOSITE ACTION

3. STEEL AND CONCRETE COLUMNS

STRESS RATED WOOD TOP CHORD (DECK CAN BE NAILED DIRECTLY TO TOP CHORD)
WEB MEMBERS OF STEEL TUBING
STRESS RATED WOOD BOTTOM CHORD
PIN CONNECTIONS TRANSFER LOADS BETWEEN WEB MEMBERS AND CHORDS

4A. WOOD AND STEEL JOIST

STRESS RATED WOOD TOP CHORDS (MAY BE BUILT-UP LAMINATED SECTIONS)
STEEL TUBE WEB MEMBERS
SOLID PLYWOOD WEB

4. TYPICAL COMPOSITE JOISTS

STRUCTURAL CONCRETE SLAB ACTS AS COMPRESSION FLANGE OF COMPOSITE MEMBER
SHEAR STUDS
LIGHT TEE: YIELD STRESS = 36,000 PSI
HEAVY TEE: YIELD STRESS SAME AS TOP TEE OR HIGHER
WELD TO TRANSFER SHEAR FORCES BETWEEN TEES

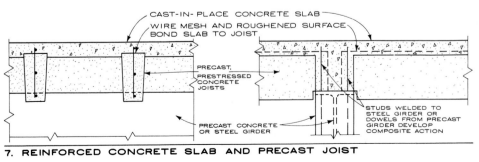

CAST-IN-PLACE CONCRETE SLAB
WIRE MESH AND ROUGHENED SURFACE BOND SLAB TO JOIST
PRECAST, PRESTRESSED CONCRETE JOISTS
PRECAST CONCRETE OR STEEL GIRDER
STUDS WELDED TO STEEL GIRDER OR DOWELS FROM PRECAST GIRDER DEVELOP COMPOSITE ACTION

7. REINFORCED CONCRETE SLAB AND PRECAST JOIST

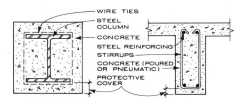
CONCRETE ENCASEMENT

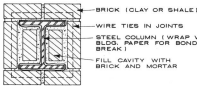
MASONRY ENCLOSURE

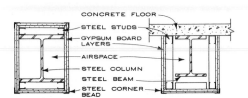
GYPSUM MEMBRANE ENCLOSURE

MINERAL FIBER MEMBRANE ENCLOSURE

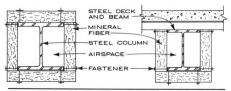
SPRAY-ON CONTOUR

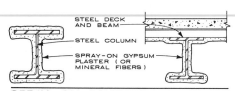
LIQUID FILLED COLUMN

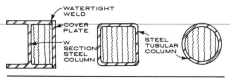
COATINGS

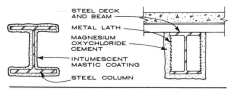
FLAME SHIELDS

UNPROTECTED STEEL

At temperatures greater than 1000°F, mild steel loses about one half of its ultimate room temperature strength. Consequently, fire tests on steel beams and columns are terminated when the steel's surface temperatures reach a predetermined limit or when the applied design loading can no longer be sustained (specific alternate test procedures are given by ASTM Standard Methods E 119). Fire resistance ratings are expressed in terms of duration in hours of fire exposure to standard temperature conditions in a test furnace (e.g., 3/4 hr, 1 hr, 2 hr, 3 hr). For further information on fire resistance tests and fire protection of steel, see American Iron and Steel Institute's handbook, "Fire-Resistant Steel-Frame Construction."

CONCRETE ENCASEMENT

Achieved fire resistance for steel members encased in concrete depends on thickness of protective concrete cover, concrete mixture, and structural restraint (i.e., method of support and method of confining thermal expansion). Lightweight aggregate concrete has better fire resistance than normal weight concrete because of its higher moisture content and higher thermal resistance to heat flow. Heavier members require less cover for equivalent fire resistance, since they have greater mass. For data on columns encased in concrete, see National Fire Protection Association's "Fire Protection Handbook." Gunite, a mixture of cement, sand, and water, can be spray-applied by air pressure, but requires steel reinforcing. For exterior applications, reinforcing steel with less than 2 in. of concrete cover usually requires corrosion resistant primers.

MASONRY ENCLOSURE

Masonry materials (brick, concrete block, gypsum block, hollow clay tile) can be used to encase steel columns. The cores (or cells), which provide openings for reinforcing, also can be filled with mortar or insulating materials such as vermiculite to increase thermal resistance to heat flow. For data on fire resistance of masonry constructions, see National Concrete Masonry Association's "Fire Safety with Concrete Masonry."

GYPSUM MEMBRANE ENCLOSURE

Gypsum board or troweled plaster (e.g., vermiculite-gypsum, perlite-gypsum) or lath can be used to protect steel at building locations not exposed to moisture. Gypsum retards heat flow to steel by releasing chemically combined water (called "calcination") at temperatures above 180°F. To protect steel columns, gypsum board layers can be attached to steel studs by means of self-tapping screws or installed behind a galvanized or stainless sheet steel cover. For data on fire resistance of gypsum constructions, see Gypsum Association's "Fire Resistance Design Data Manual."

MINERAL FIBER MEMBRANE ENCLOSURE

When exposed to fire, mineral fiber (made from molten rock or slag) retards heat flow to steel because of its low thermal conductivity (it can withstand temperatures above 2000°F without melting). Mineral fiber requires a protective covering when exposed to outdoor conditions or the possibility of damage from accidental impact or abrasion.

SPRAY-ON CONTOUR

Spray-on applied cementitious mixtures (lightweight aggregate plasters with insulating fibers or vermiculite) or mineral fibers mixed with inorganic binders provide thermal barrier to heat from fire. The steel surface must be clean and free of loose paint, rust, oil, and grease before spraying, and a protective primer may be required. In addition, spraying should not be scheduled during cold conditions. Lightweight spray-on contours can be easily damaged during installation of nearby gas and water pipes, air ducts, and the like, and they are subject to flaking during normal use. Pins, studs, and other mechanical fasteners can be used to secure moisture or abrasion resistant protective finish coatings. Applications more than 2 in. thick generally require wire mesh or lath reinforcement.

LIQUID FILLED COLUMNS

During a fire the liquid, circulating by convection from fire floor columns, removes heat. Storage tanks or city water mains can be used to replace water converted to steam (vented by pressure relief valves or rupture discs). Pumps also may be used to avoid stagnant areas within an interconnected water circulation system of columns and piping. To prevent corrosion, use a rust inhibitor such as potassium nitrate. To prevent freezing in cold climates, use an antifreeze such as potassium carbonate. During construction, strict quality control is essential to achieve a watertight system.

COATINGS

Intumescent mastic coatings can be spray-applied like paint. When exposed to fire, the coating absorbs heat above about 300°F by expanding into a thick, lightweight thermal barrier more than about 150 times its initial thickness. This gas filled multicellular layer retards heat flow by releasing cooling gases and blocks off oxygen supply. Coatings should only be applied to steel surfaces that are free of dirt, scale, and oil. A multilayer system, consisting of intumescent mastic layers with glass fiber reinforcing between, is needed to achieve fire resistance ratings greater than 1 hr.

When exposed to heat, magnesium oxychloride cement retards heat flow to steel by releasing water of hydration at temperatures above about 570°F. Corrosion resistant priming may be required to assure proper adhesion of magnesium oxychloride to steel surfaces. In high intensity fires (e.g., flammable liquid or gas fires), magnesium oxychloride does not spall and the magnesium oxide residue acts as an efficient heat reflector.

FLAME SHIELDS

Steel flame shields can deflect heat and flames from burning building away from exterior structural steel members. For example, girder top and bottom flanges avoid direct flame impingement during fire by having flame shield protection with thermal insulation behind girder.

NOTES

1. Check prevailing building code for required fire resistance ratings of building constructions. Begin planning steel fire protection during the early stages of a project so that it can be integrated into building design. Consult early with authority having jurisdiction and insurance underwriting groups such as Industrial Risk Insurers, American Insurance Association, or Factory Mutual System.

2. Refer to fire resistance data based on ASTM E 119 test procedures from Underwriters' Laboratories, Factory Mutual, and other nationally recognized testing laboratories.

3. In general, fire resistance of constructions with cavity airspace (e.g., walls, floor-ceilings) will be greater than similar identical weight constructions without airspace.

4. If possible, locate cavity airspace on side of construction opposite potential fire exposure.

5. For most situations, fire resistance of constructions with thermal insulating materials such as mineral fiber and glass fiber in cavity airspace (e.g., doors, walls) will be greater than identical constructions without cavity insulation. Be careful, however, since adding thermal insulation to suspended floor-ceiling assemblies may lower fire resistance by causing metal suspension grid system to buckle or warp from elevated surface temperatures.

6. When plenum spaces above suspended ceilings are used for mechanical system return airflow, fire resistance of floor-ceiling assemblies will be diminished. Conversely, plenums under positive pressure from supply airflow can achieve greater fire resistances than neutral pressure conditions (e.g., no air circulation in plenum).

7. For beams and columns, the higher the ratio of weight (e.g., pounds per unit length) to heated perimeter (i.e., surface area exposed to fire) the greater the fire resistance.

8. Beams and columns with membrane enclosure protection will have less surface area exposed to fire than identical members with spray-on applied contour protection. In addition, membrane enclosures (e.g., gypsum board, mineral fiber, magnesium oxychloride, or metal lath) form airspaces on both sides of W and S section webs.

M. David Egan, P.E.; College of Architecture, Clemson University, Clemson, South Carolina

5

GENERAL INFORMATION

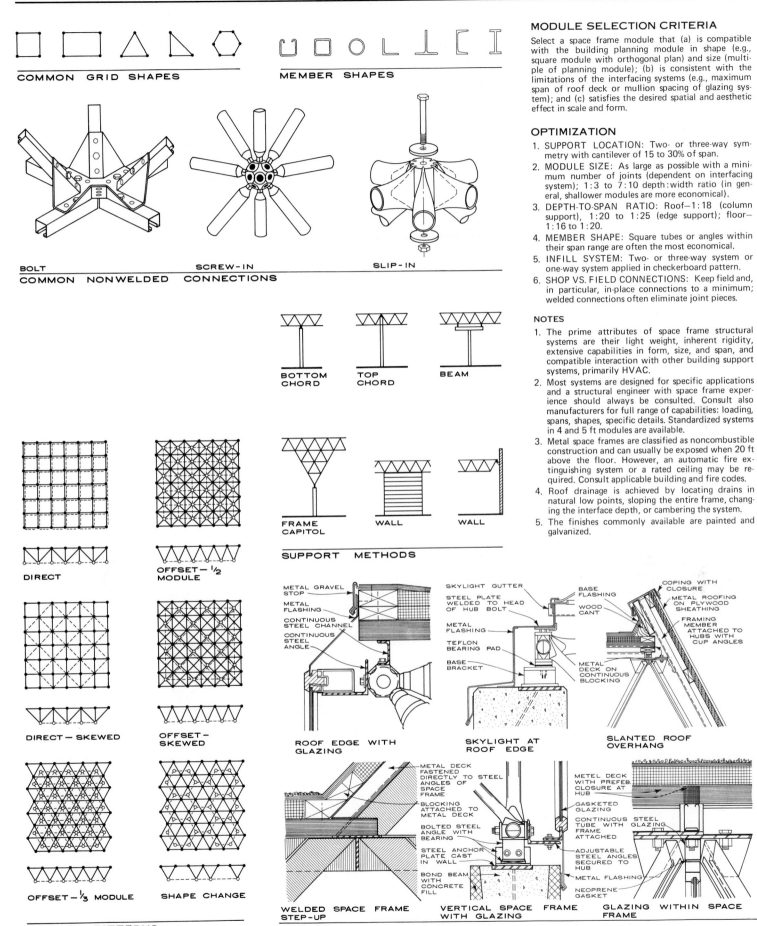

COMMON GRID SHAPES

MEMBER SHAPES

BOLT   SCREW-IN   SLIP-IN
COMMON NONWELDED CONNECTIONS

BOTTOM CHORD   TOP CHORD   BEAM

DIRECT   OFFSET—½ MODULE

DIRECT—SKEWED   OFFSET-SKEWED

OFFSET—⅓ MODULE   SHAPE CHANGE

COMMON PATTERNS

FRAME CAPITOL   WALL   WALL

SUPPORT METHODS

ROOF EDGE WITH GLAZING   SKYLIGHT AT ROOF EDGE   SLANTED ROOF OVERHANG

WELDED SPACE FRAME STEP-UP   VERTICAL SPACE FRAME WITH GLAZING   GLAZING WITHIN SPACE FRAME

DETAILS

MODULE SELECTION CRITERIA

Select a space frame module that (a) is compatible with the building planning module in shape (e.g., square module with orthogonal plan) and size (multiple of planning module); (b) is consistent with the limitations of the interfacing systems (e.g., maximum span of roof deck or mullion spacing of glazing system); and (c) satisfies the desired spatial and aesthetic effect in scale and form.

OPTIMIZATION

1. SUPPORT LOCATION: Two- or three-way symmetry with cantilever of 15 to 30% of span.
2. MODULE SIZE: As large as possible with a minimum number of joints (dependent on interfacing system); 1:3 to 7:10 depth:width ratio (in general, shallower modules are more economical).
3. DEPTH-TO-SPAN RATIO: Roof—1:18 (column support), 1:20 to 1:25 (edge support); floor—1:16 to 1:20.
4. MEMBER SHAPE: Square tubes or angles within their span range are often the most economical.
5. INFILL SYSTEM: Two- or three-way system or one-way system applied in checkerboard pattern.
6. SHOP VS. FIELD CONNECTIONS: Keep field and, in particular, in-place connections to a minimum; welded connections often eliminate joint pieces.

NOTES

1. The prime attributes of space frame structural systems are their light weight, inherent rigidity, extensive capabilities in form, size, and span, and compatible interaction with other building support systems, primarily HVAC.
2. Most systems are designed for specific applications and a structural engineer with space frame experience should always be consulted. Consult also manufacturers for full range of capabilities: loading, spans, shapes, specific details. Standardized systems in 4 and 5 ft modules are available.
3. Metal space frames are classified as noncombustible construction and can usually be exposed when 20 ft above the floor. However, an automatic fire extinguishing system or a rated ceiling may be required. Consult applicable building and fire codes.
4. Roof drainage is achieved by locating drains in natural low points, sloping the entire frame, changing the interface depth, or cambering the system.
5. The finishes commonly available are painted and galvanized.

Steven W. Henkelman, R.A.; Cope, Linder, Walmsley; Philadelphia, Pennsylvania

STRUCTURAL METAL FRAMING   5

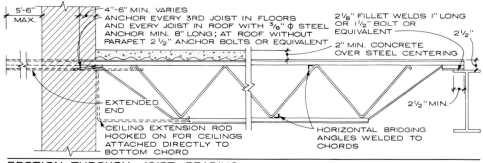

SECTION THROUGH JOIST BEARING

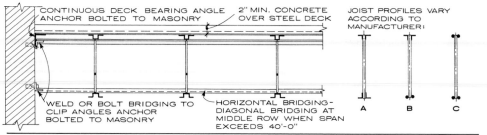

SECTION THROUGH JOISTS

NOTES

The following information applies to both open web and long span steel joists.

JOIST DESIGNATION:

25 LJ 10 ← Chord

- Type of steel: J—normal; H—high strength
- Longspan (DL—deep longspan)
- Nominal depth (in.)

Because of increased popularity of H-series joists, J-series joists have been eliminated from the load tables by the Steel Joist Institute.

1. ROOF CONSTRUCTION: Joists are usually covered by steel deck topped with either rigid insulation board or lightweight concrete fill and built-up felt and gravel roof. Plywood, poured gypsum, or structural wood fiber deck systems can also be used with built-up roof.

2. CEILINGS: Ceiling supports can be suspended from or mounted directly to bottom chords of joists, although suspended systems are recommended because of dimensional variations in actual joist depths.

3. FLOOR CONSTRUCTION: Joists usually covered by 2 to 2½ in. concrete on steel centering. Concrete thickness may be increased for electrical conduit or electrical/communications raceways. Precast concrete, gypsum planks, or plywood can also be used for the floor system.

4. VIBRATION: Objectionable vibrations can occur in open web joist and 2½ in. concrete slab designs for open floor areas at spans between 24 and 40 ft, especially at 28 ft. When a floor area cannot have partitions, objectionable vibrations can be prevented or reduced by increasing slab thickness, joist spacing, or floor slopes. Attention should also be given to support framing beams which can magnify a vibration problem.

5. OPENINGS IN FLOOR OR ROOF SYSTEMS: Small openings between joists are framed with angles of channel supported on the adjoining two joists. Larger openings necessitating interruption of joists are framed with steel angle or channel headers spanning the adjoining two joists. The interrupted joists bear on the headers.

6. ROOF DRAINAGE: Roof drainage should be carefully considered on level or near level roofs especially with parapet walls. Roof insulation can be sloped, joists can be sloped or obtained with sloping top chords in one or both directions, and overflow scuppers should be provided in parapet walls.

PRELIMINARY JOIST SELECTION: The tables below are not to be used for final joist design but are intended as an aid in speeding selection of steel joists for preliminary design and planning. The final design must be a separate and thorough process, involving a complete investigation of the pertinent conditions. This page is not for that purpose. Consult structural engineer.

EXAMPLE: Assume a particular clear span. By assuming a joist spacing and estimating the total load a joist can immediately be selected from the table. Then proceed with preliminary design studies.

NOTES

1. Total safe load = live load + dead load. Dead load includes weight of joist. For dead loads and recommended live loads, see pages on weights of materials. Local codes will govern.

2. Span not to exceed a depth 24 times that of a nominal joist.

3. For more detailed information refer to standard specifications and load tables adopted jointly by the Steel Joist Institute and the American Institute of Steel Construction.

NUMBER OF ROWS OF BRIDGING (FT)

DISTANCES ARE CLEAR SPAN DIMENSIONS

CHORD SIZE*	1 ROW	2 ROWS	3 ROWS	4 ROWS	5 ROWS†
#3	Up to 13	13–17	17–28	–	–
#4	Up to 16	16–21	21–32	–	–
#5	Up to 16	16–21	21–33	33–38	38–40
#6	Up to 18	18–22	22–36	36–40	40–48
#7	Up to 20	20–25	25–41	41–46	46–48
#8	Up to 21	21–27	27–43	43–48	48–60
#9	Up to 23	23–30	30–46	46–52	52–60
#10	Up to 24	24–30	30–47	47–53	53–60
#11	Up to 24	24–31	31–48	48–55	55–60

*Last digit(s) of joist designation shown on load table below.

†Where five rows of bridging are required and spans are over 40 ft, the middle row shall be diagonal with bolted connections at chords and intersections.

SELECTED LOAD TABLES: H SERIES— TOTAL SAFE UNIFORMLY DISTRIBUTED LOAD (LB/FT)

JOIST DESIGNATION		CLEAR SPAN (FT)												
		8	12	16	20	24	28	32	36	42	48	54	60
H Series f_s = 30,000 psi	8H3	600	400	232									
	10H3		417	302	193								
	12H4		533	400	300	208							
	14H5			475	380	300	220						
	16H6			575	460	383	293	224					
	18H7				520	433	371	303	240				
	20H7				540	450	386	325	257				
	22H8					483	414	363	322	247			
	24H8					500	429	375	333	271	207		
	26H9						514	450	400	343	268		
	28H9						514	450	400	343	289	229	
	30H10							506	450	386	338	276	224
	30H11							544	483	414	363	319	259

NOTE: Number preceding letter is joist depth; 14H5 is 14 in. deep.

Setter, Leach & Lindstrom, Inc.; Minneapolis, Minnesota

5   **METAL JOISTS**

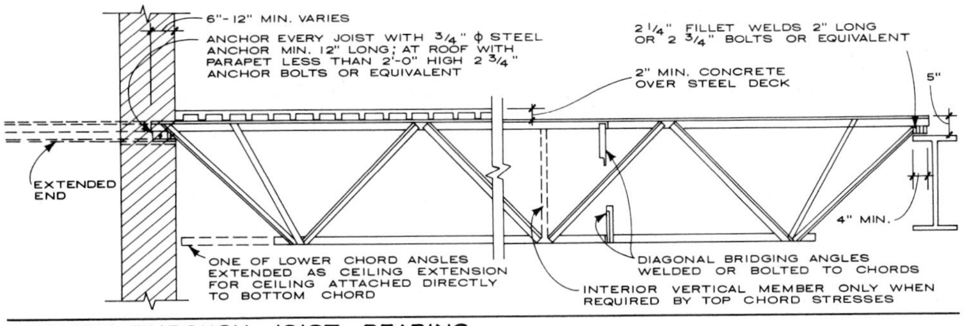

SECTION THROUGH JOIST BEARING

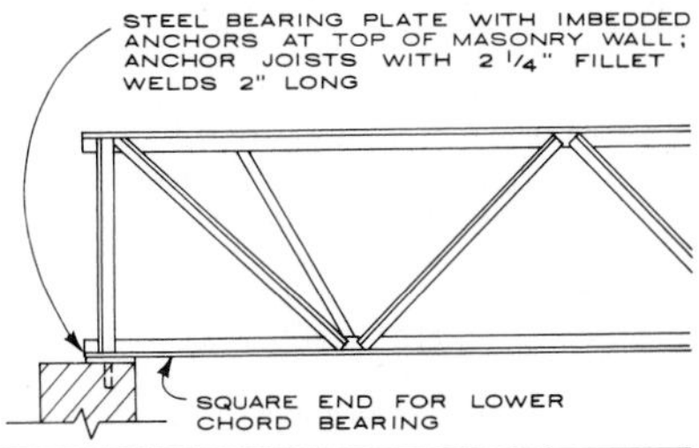

SQUARE END

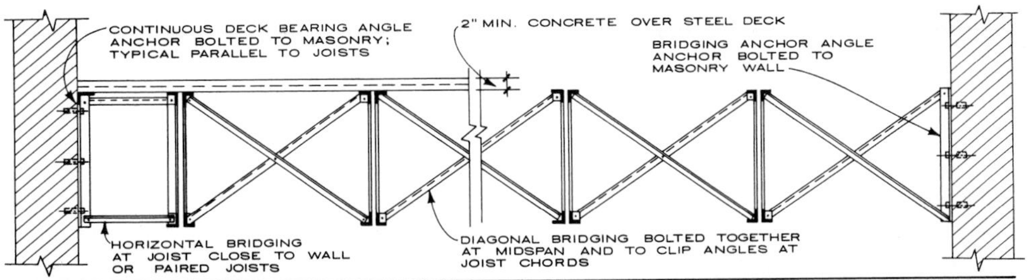

SECTION THROUGH JOISTS

BRIDGING SPACING (FT)*

LH CHORD SIZE†	MAXIMUM SPACING (FT)
02-09	11
10-14	16
15-17	21
DHL CHORD SIZE†	**MAXIMUM SPACING (FT)**
10	14
11-14	16
15-17	21
18-19	26

*Joist span not to exceed 24 x depth for roofs, 20 x depth for floors.
†Last two digits of joist designation shown in load tables.

PRELIMINARY JOIST SELECTION

The tables below are not to be used for final joist design but are intended as an aid in speeding selection of steel joists for preliminary design and planning.

The final design must be a separate thorough process, involving a complete investigation of the pertinent conditions. This page is not for that purpose. Consult a structural engineer.

EXAMPLE

Assume a particular clear span. By assuming a joist spacing and estimating the total load a joist can immediately be selected from the table. Then proceed with preliminary design studies.

NOTES

1. Total safe load = live load + dead load. Dead load includes weight of joist. For dead loads and recommended live loads, see pages on weights of materials. Local codes will govern.
2. Span not to exceed 24 times the depth of a nominal joist.
3. For more detailed information refer to standard specifications and load tables adopted jointly by the Steel Joist Institute and the American Institute of Steel Construction.

FIRE RESISTANCE RATINGS

TIME (HR)	FLOOR ASSEMBLIES	TIME (HR)	ROOF ASSEMBLIES
1 or 1½	2″ reinforced concrete, listed ½″ (⅝″ for 1½ hr) acoustical tile ceiling, concealed ceiling grid suspended from joists	1	Built-up roofing on 2″ structural wood fiber units, listed ¾″ acoustical ceiling tiles, concealed ceiling grid suspended from joists
	2″ reinforced concrete, listed ½″ acoustical board ceiling listed exposed ceiling grid suspended from joists		Built-up roofing and insulation on 26 gauge min. steel deck, listed ⅝″ acoustical ceiling boards, listed exposed ceiling grid suspended from joists
	2″ reinforced concrete, listed ½″ gypsum board ceiling fastened to joists		Built-up roofing over 2″ vermiculite on centering, listed ½″ acoustical ceiling boards, listed exposed ceiling grid suspended from joists
2	2½″ reinforced concrete, listed ⅝″ acoustical tile ceiling, listed concealed ceiling grid suspended from joists		
	2½″ reinforced concrete, listed ½″ acoustical board ceiling, listed exposed ceiling grid suspended from joists	2	Built-up roofing on 2″ listed gypsum building units, listed ⅝″ acoustical ceiling boards, listed exposed ceiling grid suspended from joists
	2″ reinforced concrete, listed ⅝″ gypsum board ceiling fastened to joists		Built-up roofing on 22 gauge min. steel deck, suspended ⅞″ metal lath and plaster ceiling
	2½″ reinforced concrete, listed ½″ gypsum board ceiling fastened to joists		

NOTE: Listed by Underwriters Laboratories or Factory Mutual approved, as appropriate. Ratings are the result of tests made in accordance with ASTM Standard E 119. A more complete list can be obtained from the SJI Technical Digest concerning the design of fire resistive assemblies with steel joists.

SELECTED LOAD TABLES: LH AND DLH SERIES—TOTAL SAFE UNIFORMLY DISTRIBUTED LOAD (LB/FT)

JOIST DESIGNATION		CLEAR SPAN (FT)												
		28	32	36	42	48	54	60	66	72	78	84	90	96
LH Series f_s = 30,000 psi	18LH05	581	448	355										
	20LH06	723	560	444										
	24LH07			588	446	343								
	28LH09				639	499	401							
	32LH10						478	389						
	36LH11							451	378	322				
	40LH12								472	402	346			
	44LH13										423	369		
	48LH14											444	390	346
		90	96	102	108	114	120	126	132	138	144			
DLH Series f_s = 30,000 psi	52DLH13	433	381	338										
	56DLH14			411	368									
	60DLH15				442	398	361							
	64DLH16					466	421	382						
	68DLH17							460	420					
	72DLH18								505	463	426			

NOTE: Number preceding letter is joist depth; 32LH10 is 32 in. deep.

Setter, Leach & Lindstrom, Inc.; Minneapolis, Minnesota

EXAMPLES OF THE MANY TYPES OF DECK AVAILABLE (SEE TABLES):

1. Roof deck.
2. Floor deck (noncomposite).
3. Composite floor deck interacting with concrete.
4. Permanent forms for self-supporting concrete slabs.
5. Cellular deck (composite or noncomposite).
6. Acoustical roof deck.
7. Acoustic cellular deck (composite or noncomposite).
8. Electric raceway cellular deck.
9. Prevented roof deck (used with lightweight insulating concrete fill).

All metal floor and roof decks must be secured to all supports, generally by means of "puddle welds" made through the deck to supporting steel. Steel sheet lighter than 22 gauge (0.0295 in. thick) should be secured by use of welding washers (see illustration).

Shear studs welded through floor deck also serve to secure the deck to supporting steel. Power actuated and pneumatically driven fasteners may also be used in certain applications.

Side laps between adjacent sheets of deck must be secured by button-punching standing seams, welding, or screws, in accordance with manufacturer's recommendations.

Decks used as lateral diaphragms must be welded to steel supports around their entire perimeter to ensure development of diaphragm action. More stringent requirements may govern the size and/or spacing of attachments to supports and side lap fasteners or welds.

Roof deck selection must take into consideration construction and maintenance loads as well as the capacity to support uniformly distributed live loads. Consult current Steel Deck Institute recommendations and Factory Mutual requirements.

Floor deck loadings are virtually unlimited in scope, ranging from light residential and institutional loads to heavy duty industrial floors utilizing composite deck with slabs up to 24 in. thick. The designer can select the deck type, depth, and gauge most suitable for the application.

Fire resistance ratings for roof deck assemblies are published by Underwriters Laboratories and Factory Mutual. Ratings of 1 to 2 hr are achieved with spray-on insulation: a 1 hr rating with suspended acoustical ceiling and a 2 hr rating with a metal lath and plaster ceiling.

Floor deck assembly fire resistive ratings are available both with and without spray-applied fireproofing, and with regular weight or lightweight concrete fill. From 1 to 3 hr ratings are possible using only concrete fill—consult Underwriters Laboratory Fire Resistance Index for assembly ratings.

Consult manufacturer's literature and technical representatives for additional information. Consult "Steel Deck Institute Design Manual for Floor Decks and Roof Decks" and "Tentative Recommendations for the Design of Steel Deck Diaphragms" by the Steel Deck Institute.

ADVANTAGES OF METAL ROOF DECKS:

1. High strength-to-weight ratio reduces roof dead load.
2. Can be erected in most weather conditions.
3. Variety of depths and rib patterns available.
4. Acoustical treatment is possible.
5. Serve as base for insulation and roofing.
6. Fire ratings can be obtained with standard assemblies.
7. Provide lateral diaphragm.
8. Can be erected quickly.
9. Can be erected economically.

The use of vapor barriers on metal deck roofs is not customary for normal building occupancies. For high relative humidity exposure a vapor barrier may be provided as part of the roofing system, but the user should be aware of the great difficulties encountered in installing a vapor barrier on metal deck. Punctures of the vapor barrier over valleys might reduce or negate entirely the effectiveness of the vapor barrier.

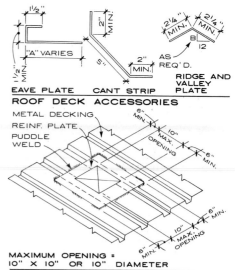

ROOF DECK ACCESSORIES

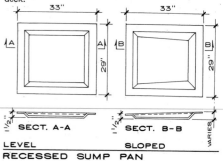

MAXIMUM OPENING = 10" X 10" OR 10" DIAMETER

REINFORCING PLATE

Small openings (up to 6 x 6 in. or 6 in. dia.) may usually be cut in roof or floor deck without reinforcing the deck. Openings up to 10 x 10 in. or 10 in. dia. require reinforcing of the deck by either welding a reinforcing plate to the deck all around the opening, or by providing channel shaped headers and/or supplementary reinforcing parallel to the deck span. Reinforcing plates should be 14 gauge sheets with a minimum projection of 6 in. beyond all sides of the opening, and they should be welded to each cell of the deck.

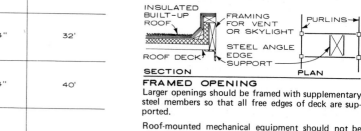

LEVEL   SLOPED

RECESSED SUMP PAN

Preformed recessed sump pans are available from deck manufacturers for use at roof drains.

FRAMED OPENING

Larger openings should be framed with supplementary steel members so that all free edges of deck are supported.

Roof-mounted mechanical equipment should not be placed directly on metal roof deck. Equipment on built-up or prefabricated curbs should be supported directly on main and supplementary structural members and the deck must also be supported along all free edges (see illustration). Heavy items such as cooling towers which must be elevated should be supported by posts extending through pitch pockets directly onto structural members below the deck. Openings through the deck may be handled as previously discussed.

ROOF DECK (ACOUSTICAL ROOF DECKS ARE AVAILABLE IN MANY OF THESE PROFILES—CONSULT MANUFACTURERS)

TYPICAL EXAMPLES	ECONOMICAL SPANS	USUAL WIDTH	MAX. LENGTH AVAILABLE
1½" NARROW RIB	4'-6'	24"-36"	36'-42'
1½" INTERMEDIATE RIB	5'-7'	24"-36"	40'-42'
1½" WIDE RIB	6'-9'	24"-30"	32'-42'
(3" profile)	8'-16'	24"	40'
(4½" profile)	15'-18'	12"	32'
(1½" profile)	7'-11'	24"	32'
(3 1/16" profile)	10'-20'	24"	40'
(7½" cellular profile)	12'-30'	12"	40'-42'
(7½" cellular profile)	13'-33'	24"	40'

Walter D. Shapiro, P.E.; Tor, Shapiro & Associates; New York, New York

FLOOR DECK – COMPOSITE WITH CONCRETE FILL

TYPICAL EXAMPLES	ECONOMICAL SPANS	USUAL WIDTH	MAX. LENGTH AVAILABLE
1½" profile	4'- 9'	30"	36'
2" profile	8'- 12'	30"	40'- 45'
3" profile	8'- 15'	24"	40'
7½" / 6" / 4½" / 3" profile	8'- 24'	12"	40'

FLOOR DECK – COMPOSITE CELLULAR (ACOUSTIC DECK AVAILABLE IN SOME PROFILES; CONSULT MANUFACTURERS)

	ECONOMICAL SPANS	USUAL WIDTH	MAX. LENGTH AVAILABLE
1½" profile, 6"	6'- 12'	24"	40'
⅝" profile	6'- 12'	24"	40'
2" profile	6'- 12'	30"	36'- 45'
3" profile	10'- 16'	24"	40'
7½" / 6" / 4½" / 3" profile	8'- 24'	24"	40'

CORRUGATED FORMS FOR CONCRETE SLABS – NONCOMPOSITE

	ECONOMICAL SPANS	USUAL WIDTH	MAX. LENGTH AVAILABLE
½" profile	1'- 2'	96"	2'- 6'
9/16" profile	1'- 6"- 3'	30"	40'
15/16" profile	3'- 5'	29"	40'
profile 4"	3'- 5'	28"	30'- 40'
15/16" profile 4½"	4'- 9'	27"	30'- 40'
2" profile 6"	7'- 12'	24"	30'- 40'

Walter D. Shapiro, P.E.; Tor, Shapiro & Associates; New York, New York

ADVANTAGES OF METAL FLOOR DECKS:

1. Provide a working platform, eliminating temporary wood planking in highrise use.
2. Composite decks provide positive reinforcement for concrete slabs.
3. Noncomposite and composite decks serve as forms for concrete, eliminate forming and stripping.
4. Fire ratings can be achieved without spray-on fireproofing or rated ceilings.
5. Acoustical treatment is possible.
6. Electric raceways may be built into floor slab.
7. Economical floor assemblies.

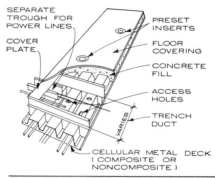

ELECTRICAL TRENCH DUCT

Electric raceways may be built into floor slabs by use of cellular deck or special units that are blended with plain deck. Two-way distribution is achieved by use of trench ducts that sit astride the cellular units at right angles. Use of trench ducts with composite floor deck may reduce or eliminate entirely the effectiveness of composite action at the trench duct. This is also true for composite action between steel floor beams and concrete fill. Trench duct locations must be taken into account in deciding whether composite action is possible.

Openings in composite deck may be blocked out on top of the deck and the deck can be burned out after the concrete has set and become self-supporting. Reinforcing bars can be added alongside openings to replace positive moment deck steel area lost at openings.

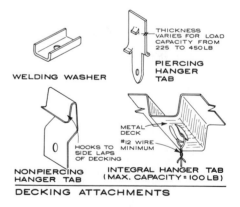

DECKING ATTACHMENTS

A convenient and economical means for supporting lightweight acoustical ceilings is by attaching suspension system to hanger tabs at side laps, piercing tabs driven through deck, or prepunched tabs in roof deck (see illustrations above). These tabs and metal decks must not be used to support plaster ceilings, piping, ductwork, electric equipment, or other heavy loads. Such elements must be supported directly from structural joists, beams, girders, and so on, or from supplementary subframing, and not from metal deck.

METAL DECKING   5

ALLOWABLE LOADS FOR SIMPLE SPAN STEEL "C" JOISTS (LB/LINEAR FOOT) MADE OF 40 KSI MATERIAL

SPAN	SECTION (DEPTH/ GAUGE)	SINGLE MEMBER TOTAL ALLOWABLE LOAD	SINGLE MEMBER ALLOWABLE LIVE LOAD	DOUBLE MEMBER TOTAL ALLOWABLE LOAD	DOUBLE MEMBER ALLOWABLE LIVE LOAD
8'	6"/18	201	189	402*	378
	6"/16	245	230	490	460
	6"/14	301	283	602	566
	8"/18	295	295	590*	590
	8"/16	359	359	718*	718
	8"/14	442	442	884*	884
	10"/16	506	506	1012*	1012
	10"/14	627	627	1254*	1254
10'	6"/18	129	97	258	194
	6"/16	157	118	314	236
	6"/14	193	144	386	288
	8"/18	188	186	376*	372
	8"/16	230	228	460*	456
	8"/14	283	280	566	560
	10"/16	326	326	652*	652
	10"/14	401	401	802*	802
12'	6"/18	89	56	178	112
	6"/16	109	68	218	136
	6"/14	134	83	268	166
	8"/18	131	108	262*	216
	8"/16	159	131	318	262
	8"/14	196	162	392	324
	10"/16	226	226	452*	452
	10"/14	278	278	556*	556
14'	6"/18	65	35	130	70
	6"/16	80	43	160	86
	6"/14	98	52	196	204
	8"/18	96	68	192	136
	8"/16	117	83	234	166
	8"/14	144	102	288	204
	10"/16	166	150	332*	300
	10"/14	204	184	408	368
16'	6"/18	50	23	100	46
	6"/16	61	28	122	56
	6"/14	75	35	150	70
	8"/18	73	45	146	90
	8"/16	89	55	178	110
	8"/14	110	68	220	136
	10"/16	127	100	254	200
	10"/14	156	123	312	246
18'	8"/18	58	32	116	64
	8"/16	71	39	142	78
	8"/14	87	48	174	96
	10"/16	100	70	200	140
	10"/14	123	86	246	172
20'	8"/18	47	23	94	46
	8"/16	57	28	114	56
	8"/14	70	35	140	70
	10"/16	81	51	162	102
	10"/14	100	63	200	126
22'	8"/18	39	17	78	34
	8"/16	47	21	94	42
	8"/14	58	26	116	52
	10"/16	67	38	134	76
	10"/14	82	47	164	94
24'	10"/16	56	29	112	58
	10"/14	69	36	138	72

NOTES

The tables on this page are not to be used for final design.
They are intended to serve only as aides in the preliminary selection of members.
Consult appropriate manufacturers' literature for final and/or additional information.
*Ends of members require additional reinforcing, such as by end clips.

Ed Hesner; Rasmussen & Hobbs Architects; Takoma, Washington

MEMBERS AVAILABLE IN 14, 16, 18, 20, & 22 GAUGE MATERIAL

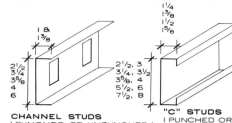

CHANNEL STUDS (PUNCHED OR UNPUNCHED) "C" STUDS (PUNCHED OR UNPUNCHED) "C" JOISTS

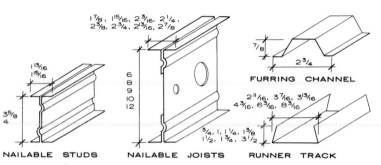

NAILABLE STUDS NAILABLE JOISTS RUNNER TRACK FURRING CHANNEL

LIGHT GAUGE FRAMING MEMBERS

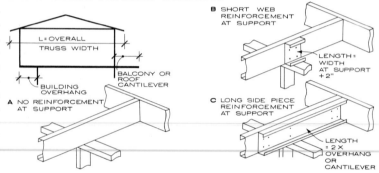

A NO REINFORCEMENT AT SUPPORT
B SHORT WEB REINFORCEMENT AT SUPPORT — LENGTH = WIDTH AT SUPPORT + 2"
C LONG SIDE PIECE REINFORCEMENT AT SUPPORT — LENGTH = 2 × OVERHANG OR CANTILEVER
L = OVERALL TRUSS WIDTH — BUILDING OVERHANG — BALCONY OR ROOF CANTILEVER

REQUIRED WEB REINFORCEMENT

SECTION (DEPTH/ GAUGE)	OVER-HANG DEPTH (FT)	L = 28'-0" 30 PSF 16"	L = 28'-0" 30 PSF 24"	L = 28'-0" 40 PSF 16"	L = 28'-0" 40 PSF 24"	L = 32'-0" 30 PSF 16"	L = 32'-0" 30 PSF 24"	L = 32'-0" 40 PSF 16"	L = 32'-0" 40 PSF 24"	L = 40'-0" 30 PSF 16"	L = 40'-0" 30 PSF 24"	L = 40'-0" 40 PSF 16"	L = 40'-0" 40 PSF 24"
6"/16	1	B	B	B	B	B	B	B	B	B	C	B	C
	1½	B	C	B	C	B	C	B	–	B	–	C	–
	2	B	–	C	–	B	–	C	–	C	–	–	–
6"/14	1	A	B	A	B	A	B	A	B	A	B	B	C
	1½	A	B	A	B	A	B	B	B	A	B	B	–
	2	A	C	B	–	A	C	B	–	C	–	C	–
8"/16	1	B	B	B	B	B	B	B	B	C	B	C	C
	1½	B	B	B	B	B	B	B	C	B	C	B	C
	2	B	B	B	C	B	C	B	C	B	C	B	–
8"/14	1	A	B	A	B	A	B	A	B	A	B	B	B
	1½	A	B	A	B	A	B	A	B	A	B	B	C
	2	A	B	A	B	A	B	B	B	B	B	B	C
10"/16	1	B	B	B	B	B	B	B	C	B	C	C	C
	1½	B	B	B	B	B	B	B	C	B	C	B	C
	2	B	B	B	B	B	B	B	C	B	C	B	C
10"/14	1	A	B	A	B	A	B	A	B	A	B	B	B
	1½	A	B	A	B	A	B	A	B	A	B	B	B
	2	A	B	A	B	A	B	B	B	B	B	B	B

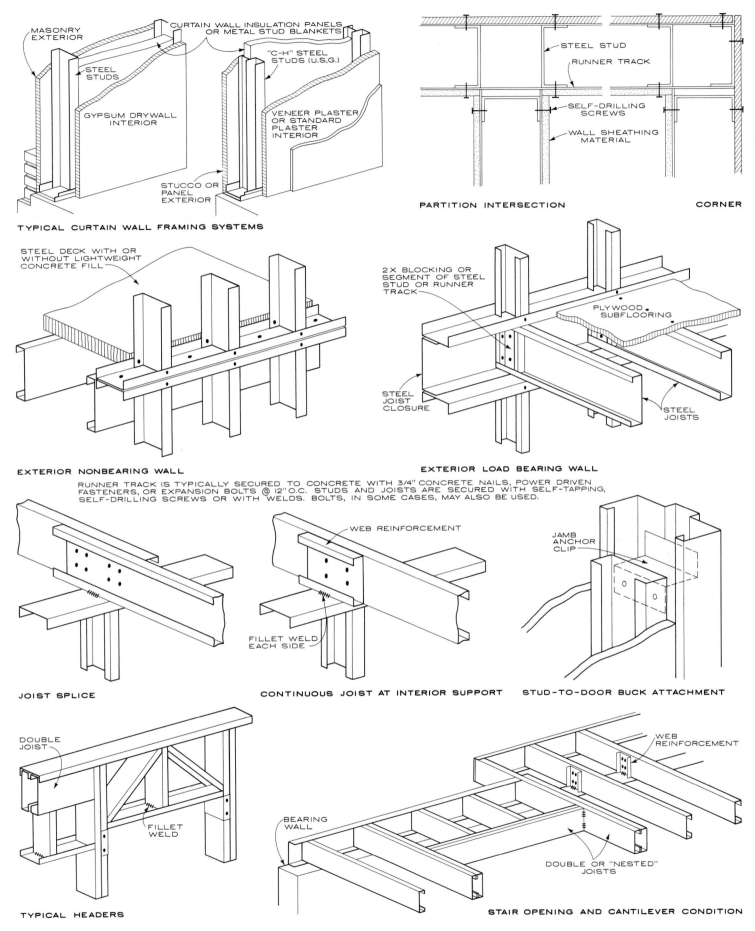

MASONRY EXTERIOR

STEEL STUDS

CURTAIN WALL INSULATION PANELS OR METAL STUD BLANKETS

"C-H" STEEL STUDS (U.S.G.)

GYPSUM DRYWALL INTERIOR

VENEER PLASTER OR STANDARD PLASTER INTERIOR

STUCCO OR PANEL EXTERIOR

TYPICAL CURTAIN WALL FRAMING SYSTEMS

STEEL STUD

RUNNER TRACK

SELF-DRILLING SCREWS

WALL SHEATHING MATERIAL

PARTITION INTERSECTION   **CORNER**

STEEL DECK WITH OR WITHOUT LIGHTWEIGHT CONCRETE FILL

2 X BLOCKING OR SEGMENT OF STEEL STUD OR RUNNER TRACK

PLYWOOD SUBFLOORING

STEEL JOIST CLOSURE

STEEL JOISTS

EXTERIOR NONBEARING WALL

EXTERIOR LOAD BEARING WALL

RUNNER TRACK IS TYPICALLY SECURED TO CONCRETE WITH 3/4" CONCRETE NAILS, POWER DRIVEN FASTENERS, OR EXPANSION BOLTS @ 12"O.C. STUDS AND JOISTS ARE SECURED WITH SELF-TAPPING, SELF-DRILLING SCREWS OR WITH WELDS. BOLTS, IN SOME CASES, MAY ALSO BE USED.

WEB REINFORCEMENT

JAMB ANCHOR CLIP

FILLET WELD EACH SIDE

JOIST SPLICE   **CONTINUOUS JOIST AT INTERIOR SUPPORT**   **STUD-TO-DOOR BUCK ATTACHMENT**

DOUBLE JOIST

FILLET WELD

BEARING WALL

WEB REINFORCEMENT

DOUBLE OR "NESTED" JOISTS

TYPICAL HEADERS

STAIR OPENING AND CANTILEVER CONDITION

Ed Hesner; Rasmussen & Hobbs Architects; Takoma, Washington

LIGHTGAUGE METAL FRAMING   5

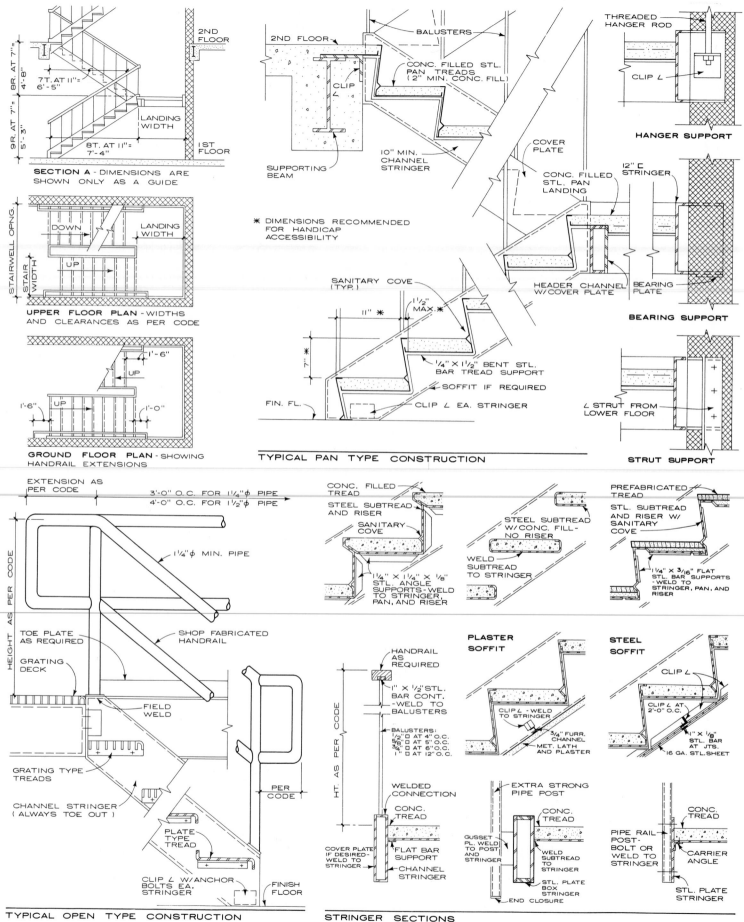

SECTION A - DIMENSIONS ARE SHOWN ONLY AS A GUIDE

UPPER FLOOR PLAN - WIDTHS AND CLEARANCES AS PER CODE

GROUND FLOOR PLAN - SHOWING HANDRAIL EXTENSIONS

* DIMENSIONS RECOMMENDED FOR HANDICAP ACCESSIBILITY

TYPICAL PAN TYPE CONSTRUCTION

HANGER SUPPORT

BEARING SUPPORT

STRUT SUPPORT

TYPICAL OPEN TYPE CONSTRUCTION

STRINGER SECTIONS

PLASTER SOFFIT

STEEL SOFFIT

John D. Harvey, AIA; Wheatley Associates; Charlotte, North Carolina

5   METAL FABRICATION

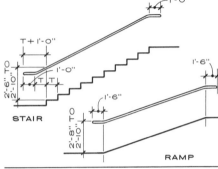

STANDARD RAILING

8'-0" O.C. MAX.

STANDARD STAIR RAILING

1 1/2" O.D. STEEL 2" O.D. WOOD HANDRAIL

STANDARD HANDRAILS

STAIR

RAMP

2'-6" TO 2'-10"

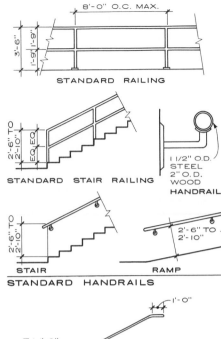

OSHA RAILING STANDARDS

NOTE: MANY BUILDING CODES CONTAIN MORE RESTRICTIVE REQUIREMENTS ESPECIALLY FOR POST AND RAIL SPACING AND STRUCTURAL LOAD CAPACITY

STAIR

RAMP

RAILING STANDARDS (OSHA)

1. All floor openings, including open sides of stair landings, must be protected by a standard railing or be covered.
2. Open sides of all stairs must be protected by a standard stair railing.
3. Handrails are required on all stairs as follows:
   a. Open sided stairs less than 44 in. wide, the stair railing will suffice.
   b. Closed sided stairs less than 44 in. wide, one standard handrail (preferably on right side descending).
   c. Stairs between 44 and 88 in. wide, one standard handrail each side or standard stair railing if open.
   d. Stairs more than 88 in. wide, one handrail or stair rail each side and one intermediate handrail in center.
4. All railings and handrails must be designed to support a load of 200 lb applied at any point in any direction.

HANDRAIL STANDARDS (ANSI)

Handrails are required on both sides of stairs or ramps at a height of 30 to 34 in. If children are the principal users, an additional rail is required at a height of 24 in. Extensions of 1 ft beyond the top riser at the top and bottom of ramps and an extension of 1 ft plus one tread width at the bottom of stairs are required. Continuity of rails is required along the entire length of the stair or ramp and on at least one side of landings. The inside rail on switchback stairs must be continuous.

Clearance between rail and wall shall be a maximum of 1 1/2 in. Projecting ends of handrails must be returned smoothly to wall, floor, or post.

John C. Lunsford, AIA; Varney, Sexton, Sydnor Associates-Architects; Phoenix, Arizona

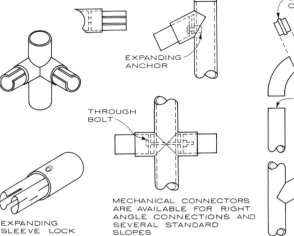

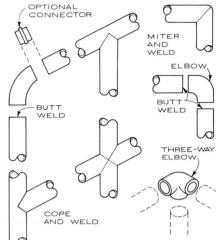

EXPANDING ANCHOR

THROUGH BOLT

EXPANDING SLEEVE LOCK

MECHANICAL CONNECTORS ARE AVAILABLE FOR RIGHT ANGLE CONNECTIONS AND SEVERAL STANDARD SLOPES

NONWELDED CONNECTIONS

OPTIONAL CONNECTOR

MITER AND WELD

ELBOW

BUTT WELD

BUTT WELD

COPE AND WELD

THREE-WAY ELBOW

WELDED CONNECTIONS

TYPICAL PIPE RAILING CONNECTIONS

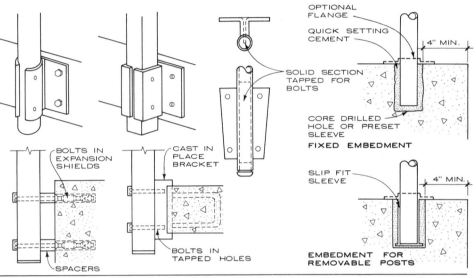

OPTIONAL FLANGE

QUICK SETTING CEMENT

SOLID SECTION TAPPED FOR BOLTS

CORE DRILLED HOLE OR PRESET SLEEVE

4" MIN.

FIXED EMBEDMENT

BOLTS IN EXPANSION SHIELDS

CAST IN PLACE BRACKET

BOLTS IN TAPPED HOLES

SPACERS

SLIP FIT SLEEVE

4" MIN.

EMBEDMENT FOR REMOVABLE POSTS

POST ANCHORS AND BRACKETS

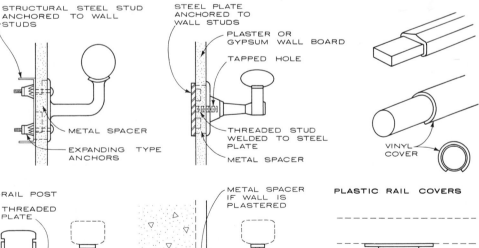

STRUCTURAL STEEL STUD ANCHORED TO WALL STUDS

METAL SPACER

EXPANDING TYPE ANCHORS

STEEL PLATE ANCHORED TO WALL STUDS

PLASTER OR GYPSUM WALL BOARD

TAPPED HOLE

THREADED STUD WELDED TO STEEL PLATE

METAL SPACER

VINYL COVER

PLASTIC RAIL COVERS

RAIL POST

THREADED PLATE

THREADED END OF BRACKET

METAL SPACER IF WALL IS PLASTERED

THREADED STUD IN EXPANSION SHIELD OR WEDGE TYPE BOLT

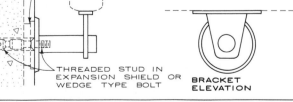

BRACKET ELEVATION

HANDRAIL BRACKETS AND ANCHORAGE

METAL FABRICATION   **5**

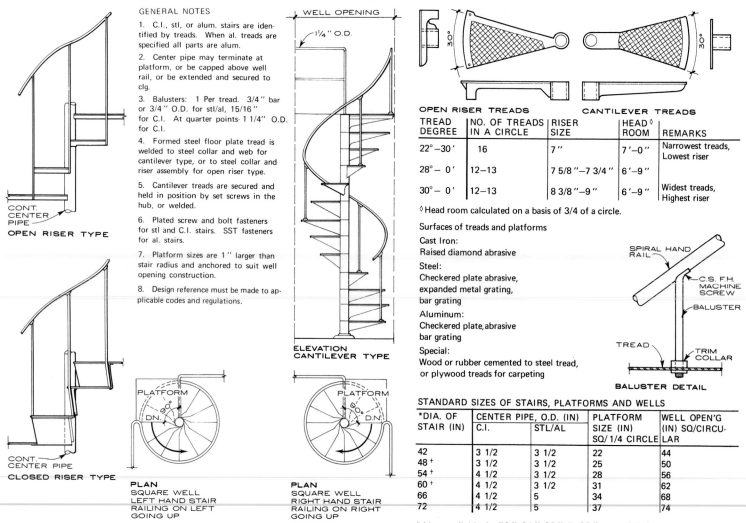

GENERAL NOTES

1. C.I., stl, or alum. stairs are identified by treads. When al. treads are specified all parts are alum.

2. Center pipe may terminate at platform, or be capped above well rail, or be extended and secured to clg.

3. Balusters: 1 Per tread. 3/4" bar or 3/4" O.D. for stl/al, 15/16" for C.I. At quarter points- 1 1/4" O.D. for C.I.

4. Formed steel floor plate tread is welded to steel collar and web for cantilever type, or to steel collar and riser assembly for open riser type.

5. Cantilever treads are secured and held in position by set screws in the hub, or welded.

6. Plated screw and bolt fasteners for stl and C.I. stairs. SST fasteners for al. stairs.

7. Platform sizes are 1" larger than stair radius and anchored to suit well opening construction.

8. Design reference must be made to applicable codes and regulations.

CONT. CENTER PIPE

OPEN RISER TYPE

CONT. CENTER PIPE

CLOSED RISER TYPE

WELL OPENING
1¼" O.D.

ELEVATION CANTILEVER TYPE

PLATFORM
DN.

PLAN
SQUARE WELL
LEFT HAND STAIR
RAILING ON LEFT
GOING UP

PLATFORM
DN.

PLAN
SQUARE WELL
RIGHT HAND STAIR
RAILING ON RIGHT
GOING UP

OPEN RISER TREADS **CANTILEVER TREADS**

TREAD DEGREE	NO. OF TREADS IN A CIRCLE	RISER SIZE	HEAD◊ ROOM	REMARKS
22°–30'	16	7"	7'-0"	Narrowest treads, Lowest riser
28°– 0'	12–13	7 5/8"–7 3/4"	6'-9"	
30°– 0'	12–13	8 3/8"–9"	6'-9"	Widest treads, Highest riser

◊ Head room calculated on a basis of 3/4 of a circle.

Surfaces of treads and platforms

Cast Iron:
Raised diamond abrasive

Steel:
Checkered plate abrasive,
expanded metal grating,
bar grating

Aluminum:
Checkered plate, abrasive
bar grating

Special:
Wood or rubber cemented to steel tread,
or plywood treads for carpeting

SPIRAL HAND RAIL
C.S. F.H. MACHINE SCREW
BALUSTER
TREAD
TRIM COLLAR

BALUSTER DETAIL

STANDARD SIZES OF STAIRS, PLATFORMS AND WELLS

*DIA. OF STAIR (IN)	CENTER PIPE, O.D. (IN) C.I.	STL/AL	PLATFORM SIZE (IN) SQ/ 1/4 CIRCLE	WELL OPEN'G (IN) SQ/CIRCULAR
42	3 1/2	3 1/2	22	44
48 +	3 1/2	3 1/2	25	50
54 +	4 1/2	3 1/2	28	56
60 +	4 1/2	3 1/2	31	62
66	4 1/2	5	34	68
72	4 1/2	5	37	74

*Also available in 78" 84" 90" & 98" - special sizes.
+Most residential stairs - with 28° treads, larger dia.
  Residential stairs usually 22°–30'

SPIRAL STAIRS OF CAST IRON, STEEL OR ALUMINUM

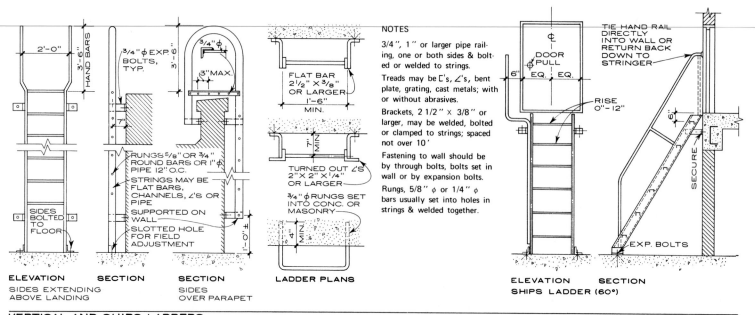

2'-0"
3'-6" HAND BARS
3/4"φ EXP. BOLTS, TYP.
3"MAX.
7"
3/4"φ
3'-6"

RUNGS 5/8" OR 3/4" ROUND BARS OR 1" φ PIPE 12" O.C.
STRINGS MAY BE FLAT BARS, CHANNELS, ∠'s OR PIPE
SUPPORTED ON WALL
SLOTTED HOLE FOR FIELD ADJUSTMENT

FLAT BAR 2½" X 3/8" OR LARGER
1'-6" MIN.
7" MIN.
TURNED OUT ∠'s 2" X 2" X 1/4" OR LARGER
3/4"φ RUNGS SET INTO CONC. OR MASONRY
4" MIN.
1'-0"

NOTES

3/4", 1" or larger pipe railing, one or both sides & bolted or welded to strings.

Treads may be ⌐'s, ∠'s, bent plate, grating, cast metals; with or without abrasives.

Brackets, 2 1/2" X 3/8" or larger, may be welded, bolted or clamped to strings; spaced not over 10'

Fastening to wall should be by through bolts, bolts set in wall or by expansion bolts.

Rungs, 5/8" φ or 1/4" φ bars usually set into holes in strings & welded together.

DOOR PULL
6" EQ. EQ.
RISE 0"-12"

TIE HAND RAIL DIRECTLY INTO WALL OR RETURN BACK DOWN TO STRINGER
SECURE
6"
EXP. BOLTS

ELEVATION   **SECTION**
SIDES EXTENDING   SIDES
ABOVE LANDING   OVER PARAPET

SIDES BOLTED TO FLOOR

LADDER PLANS

ELEVATION   **SECTION**
SHIPS LADDER (60°)

VERTICAL AND SHIPS LADDERS

Paul R. Schieve, Sr. and Joseph Hornyak; Tippetts, Abbett, McCarthy, Stratton; New York, New York

5 ## METAL FABRICATION

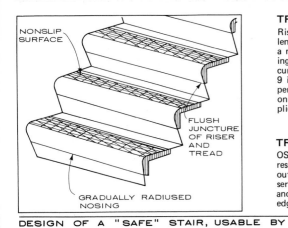

- NONSLIP SURFACE
- FLUSH JUNCTURE OF RISER AND TREAD
- GRADUALLY RADIUSED NOSING

TREAD SIZE

Riser and tread dimensions must be uniform for the length of the stair. ANSI specifications recommend a minimum tread dimension of 11 in., nosing to nosing, and a riser height of 5 to 7 in. for maximum secure footing. Stairs with tread dimensions of less than 9 in. must be open riser stairs. These are a hazard for persons with leg braces, however, and should be used only where another stair, elevator, or ramp that complies with the standards is available.

TREAD COVERING

OSHA standards require finishes to be "reasonably slip resistant" with nosings of nonslip finish. Treads without nosings are acceptable provided that the tread is serrated or is of definite nonslip design. Uniform color and texture are recommended for clear delineation of edges.

NOSING DESIGN

ANSI specifications recommend nosings without abrupt edges which project no more than 1 1/2 in. beyond the edge of the riser. A "safe stair" will use a slightly rounded, abrasive nosing, firmly anchored to the tread, with no overhangs and a clearly visible edge.

RAILINGS

Handrails should be mounted at height 32 to 34 in. above the nosings and should be graspable for their entire length. A 1 3/4 to 2 in. diameter rounded handrail is recommended. It should extend 1 ft to 1 ft 6 in. beyond the top and bottom of the stair.

LIGHTING

Illumination of the stair with directional lighting from the lower landing will increase the visibility of the tread edge.

DESIGN OF A "SAFE" STAIR, USABLE BY THE PHYSICALLY HANDICAPPED

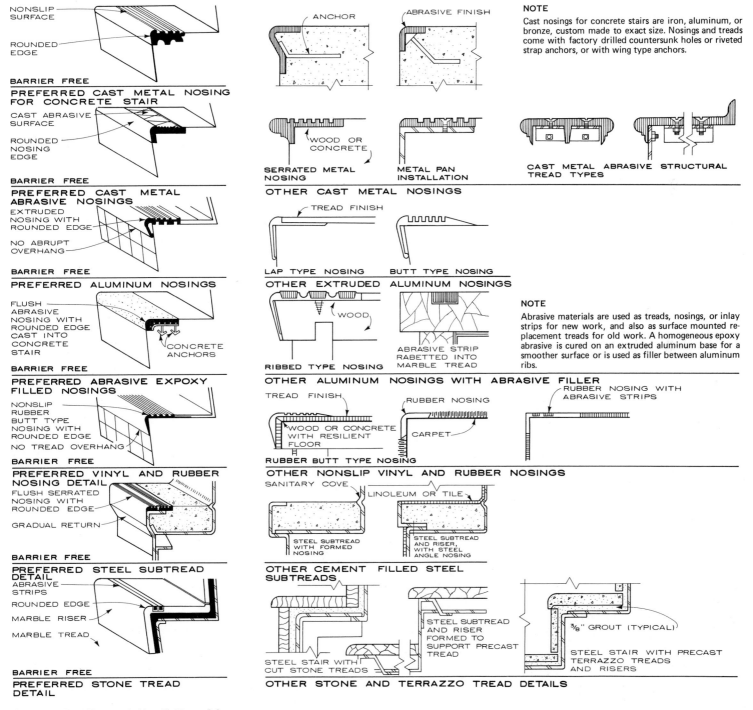

- NONSLIP SURFACE
- ROUNDED EDGE

BARRIER FREE
PREFERRED CAST METAL NOSING FOR CONCRETE STAIR

- CAST ABRASIVE SURFACE
- ROUNDED NOSING EDGE

BARRIER FREE
PREFERRED CAST METAL ABRASIVE NOSINGS

- EXTRUDED NOSING WITH ROUNDED EDGE
- NO ABRUPT OVERHANG

BARRIER FREE
PREFERRED ALUMINUM NOSINGS

- FLUSH ABRASIVE NOSING WITH ROUNDED EDGE CAST INTO CONCRETE STAIR
- CONCRETE ANCHORS

BARRIER FREE
PREFERRED ABRASIVE EXPOXY FILLED NOSINGS

- NONSLIP RUBBER BUTT TYPE NOSING WITH ROUNDED EDGE
- NO TREAD OVERHANG

BARRIER FREE
PREFERRED VINYL AND RUBBER NOSING DETAIL

- FLUSH SERRATED NOSING WITH ROUNDED EDGE
- GRADUAL RETURN

BARRIER FREE
PREFERRED STEEL SUBTREAD DETAIL

- ABRASIVE STRIPS
- ROUNDED EDGE
- MARBLE RISER
- MARBLE TREAD

BARRIER FREE
PREFERRED STONE TREAD DETAIL

- ANCHOR
- ABRASIVE FINISH

OTHER CAST METAL NOSINGS

- WOOD OR CONCRETE
- SERRATED METAL NOSING
- METAL PAN INSTALLATION
- CAST METAL ABRASIVE STRUCTURAL TREAD TYPES

- TREAD FINISH
- LAP TYPE NOSING
- BUTT TYPE NOSING

OTHER EXTRUDED ALUMINUM NOSINGS

- WOOD
- RIBBED TYPE NOSING
- ABRASIVE STRIP RABETTED INTO MARBLE TREAD

OTHER ALUMINUM NOSINGS WITH ABRASIVE FILLER

- TREAD FINISH
- RUBBER NOSING
- RUBBER NOSING WITH ABRASIVE STRIPS
- WOOD OR CONCRETE WITH RESILIENT FLOOR
- CARPET
- RUBBER BUTT TYPE NOSING

OTHER NONSLIP VINYL AND RUBBER NOSINGS

- SANITARY COVE
- LINOLEUM OR TILE
- STEEL SUBTREAD WITH FORMED NOSING
- STEEL SUBTREAD AND RISER, WITH STEEL ANGLE NOSING

OTHER CEMENT FILLED STEEL SUBTREADS

- STEEL SUBTREAD AND RISER FORMED TO SUPPORT PRECAST TREAD
- STEEL STAIR WITH CUT STONE TREADS
- 3/8" GROUT (TYPICAL)
- STEEL STAIR WITH PRECAST TERRAZZO TREADS AND RISERS

OTHER STONE AND TERRAZZO TREAD DETAILS

NOTE

Cast nosings for concrete stairs are iron, aluminum, or bronze, custom made to exact size. Nosings and treads come with factory drilled countersunk holes or riveted strap anchors, or with wing type anchors.

NOTE

Abrasive materials are used as treads, nosings, or inlay strips for new work, and also as surface mounted replacement treads for old work. A homogeneous epoxy abrasive is cured on an extruded aluminum base for a smoother surface or is used as filler between aluminum ribs.

Olga Barmine; Darrel Rippeteau, Architect; Washington, D.C.

METAL FABRICATION   5

CHAPTER 6 WOOD

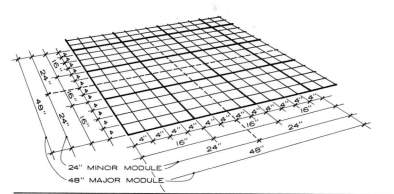

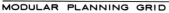

24" MINOR MODULE
48" MAJOR MODULE

MODULAR PLANNING GRID

THE MODULAR PLAN

The key to cost savings in frame construction is preplanning, using standard lumber and panel sizes. The major consideration is the 4 x 8 building unit panel dimension. Since most building components are based on this unit of measurement, a preplanned modular system can eliminate unnecessary waste of material and labor. The modular planning grid is divided into 4, 16, 24, 48 in. units, with 48 in. being the major module and 24 in. the minor module. These can be used as the planning guides for exterior overall dimensioning. Floor, ceiling, and roof construction can easily be coordinated with these dimensions.

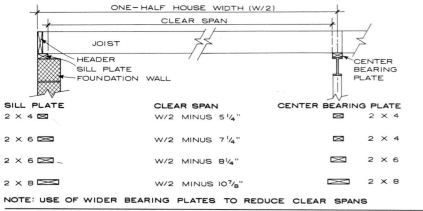

SILL PLATE	CLEAR SPAN	CENTER BEARING PLATE
2 x 4	W/2 MINUS 5¼"	2 x 4
2 x 6	W/2 MINUS 7¼"	2 x 4
2 x 6	W/2 MINUS 8¼"	2 x 6
2 x 8	W/2 MINUS 10⅞"	2 x 8

NOTE: USE OF WIDER BEARING PLATES TO REDUCE CLEAR SPANS

CLEAR SPAN OF JOIST

FLOOR PLANNING

Most common joist spacing is at 12, 16, 24 in. on center, depending on the design floor loads. Joists can also be spaced at 13.7, 19.2 in. on center, thus dividing the 8 ft length of plywood subfloor panels into seven and five equal parts, respectively. Use of the 48 in. module on house width permits greater use of full 4 x 8 plywood subflooring and minimizes cutting and waste. A maximum savings can be achieved with the 48 in. house width module if the largest of the subfloor panels are preplanned. Full 48 in. wide panels can be used without ripping for the 24, 28, and 32 ft house width when joists are either lapped or trimmed to meet correct dimension.

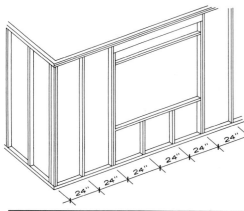

WALL FRAMING

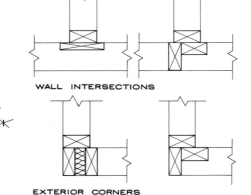

WALL INTERSECTIONS

EXTERIOR CORNERS

WALLS, DOORS, AND WINDOWS

Cost savings will be greatest when the overall size of the house plus the size and location of wall openings coincide with standard modular stud spacing. A simple practical approach to this kind of modular preplanning is to separate the exterior wall elements to the minor and major division points with stud spacing at the minor module dimension of 24 in. o.c.

Maximum flexibility in placing window and door openings is achieved by having the 16 in. module coincide with the 24 in. module. The precise location of wall openings on the 16 in. module eliminates extra wall framing frequently required in nonmodular residential construction. Test and structural analysis show that, for many installations, 24 in. on center 2 x 4 construction can be used for walls supporting the upper roof of two-story units.

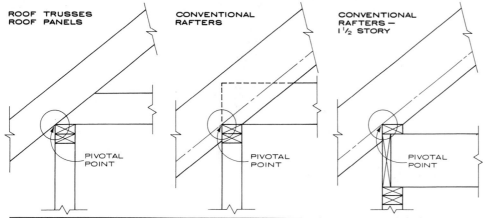

PIVOTAL POINT OF ROOF

ROOF FRAMING

Increments for house width are in 24 in. multiples. Six 48 in. module depths and five 24 in. module widths fulfill most roof span requirements. Standard roof slopes combined with modular house width provide all dimensions required for design of rafter, truss, and panel roofs. The pivotal point shown is the fixed point of reference in the module line of the exterior wall. Modular roof design and construction dimensions are determined from this point.

Haver, Nunn, Collamer; Phoenix, Arizona

Robin A. Roberts; Washington, D.C.

MODULAR PLANNING   6

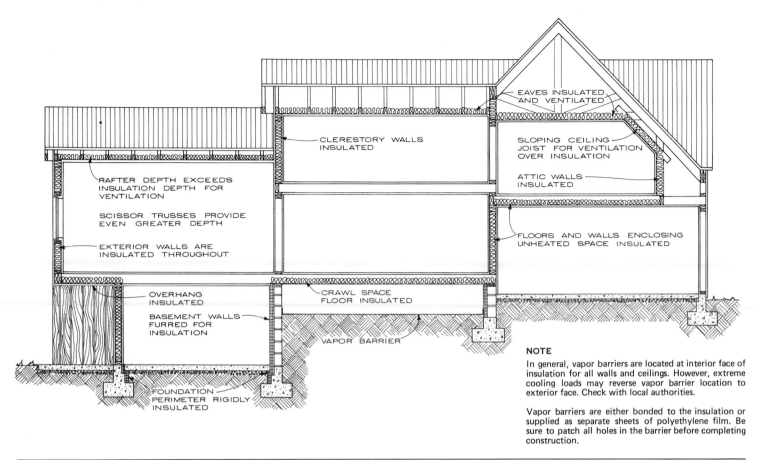

CLERESTORY WALLS INSULATED

RAFTER DEPTH EXCEEDS INSULATION DEPTH FOR VENTILATION

SCISSOR TRUSSES PROVIDE EVEN GREATER DEPTH

EXTERIOR WALLS ARE INSULATED THROUGHOUT

EAVES INSULATED AND VENTILATED

SLOPING CEILING JOIST FOR VENTILATION OVER INSULATION

ATTIC WALLS INSULATED

FLOORS AND WALLS ENCLOSING UNHEATED SPACE INSULATED

OVERHANG INSULATED

BASEMENT WALLS FURRED FOR INSULATION

CRAWL SPACE FLOOR INSULATED

VAPOR BARRIER

FOUNDATION PERIMETER RIGIDLY INSULATED

NOTE

In general, vapor barriers are located at interior face of insulation for all walls and ceilings. However, extreme cooling loads may reverse vapor barrier location to exterior face. Check with local authorities.

Vapor barriers are either bonded to the insulation or supplied as separate sheets of polyethylene film. Be sure to patch all holes in the barrier before completing construction.

INSULATED FRAME RESIDENCE

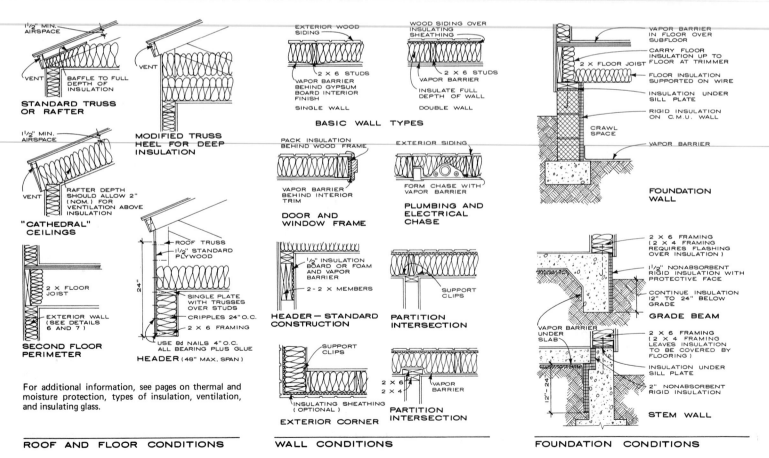

STANDARD TRUSS OR RAFTER

1½" MIN. AIRSPACE

VENT

BAFFLE TO FULL DEPTH OF INSULATION

MODIFIED TRUSS HEEL FOR DEEP INSULATION

VENT

"CATHEDRAL" CEILINGS

1½" MIN. AIRSPACE

VENT

RAFTER DEPTH SHOULD ALLOW 2" (NOM.) FOR VENTILATION ABOVE INSULATION

SECOND FLOOR PERIMETER

2 X FLOOR JOIST

EXTERIOR WALL (SEE DETAILS 6 AND 7)

ROOF TRUSS
1½" STANDARD PLYWOOD

24"

SINGLE PLATE WITH TRUSSES OVER STUDS

CRIPPLES 24" O.C.

2 X 6 FRAMING

USE 8d NAILS 4" O.C. ALL BEARING PLUS GLUE

HEADER (48" MAX. SPAN)

EXTERIOR WOOD SIDING

2 X 6 STUDS

VAPOR BARRIER BEHIND GYPSUM BOARD INTERIOR FINISH

SINGLE WALL

WOOD SIDING OVER INSULATING SHEATHING

2 X 6 STUDS

VAPOR BARRIER

INSULATE FULL DEPTH OF WALL

DOUBLE WALL

BASIC WALL TYPES

PACK INSULATION BEHIND WOOD FRAME

VAPOR BARRIER BEHIND INTERIOR TRIM

DOOR AND WINDOW FRAME

EXTERIOR SIDING

FORM CHASE WITH VAPOR BARRIER

PLUMBING AND ELECTRICAL CHASE

½" INSULATION BOARD OR FOAM AND VAPOR BARRIER

2-2 X MEMBERS

HEADER — STANDARD CONSTRUCTION

SUPPORT CLIPS

INSULATING SHEATHING (OPTIONAL)

EXTERIOR CORNER

SUPPORT CLIPS

PARTITION INTERSECTION

2 X 6
2 X 4

VAPOR BARRIER

PARTITION INTERSECTION

VAPOR BARRIER IN FLOOR OVER SUBFLOOR

CARRY FLOOR INSULATION UP TO FLOOR AT TRIMMER

2 X FLOOR JOIST

FLOOR INSULATION SUPPORTED ON WIRE

INSULATION UNDER SILL PLATE

RIGID INSULATION ON C.M.U. WALL

CRAWL SPACE

VAPOR BARRIER

FOUNDATION WALL

2 X 6 FRAMING (2 X 4 FRAMING REQUIRES FLASHING OVER INSULATION)

1½" NONABSORBENT RIGID INSULATION WITH PROTECTIVE FACE

CONTINUE INSULATION 12" TO 24" BELOW GRADE

GRADE BEAM

VAPOR BARRIER UNDER SLAB

2 X 6 FRAMING (2 X 4 FRAMING LEAVES INSULATION TO BE COVERED BY FLOORING)

INSULATION UNDER SILL PLATE

2" NONABSORBENT RIGID INSULATION

12"-24"

STEM WALL

For additional information, see pages on thermal and moisture protection, types of insulation, ventilation, and insulating glass.

ROOF AND FLOOR CONDITIONS

WALL CONDITIONS

FOUNDATION CONDITIONS

Ralph D. Provencal, AIA; Olympia, Washington

6 **INSULATION**

MONOPLANER WOOD TRUSSES,
LIGHT METAL PLATE CONNECTED
OR PLYWOOD

Monoplaner trusses usually of 2″ nominal lumber, spaced 2′– 0″ o.c. Camber as required. Dry wall ceiling may be attached directly to trusses. Plywood sheathing staggered joints.

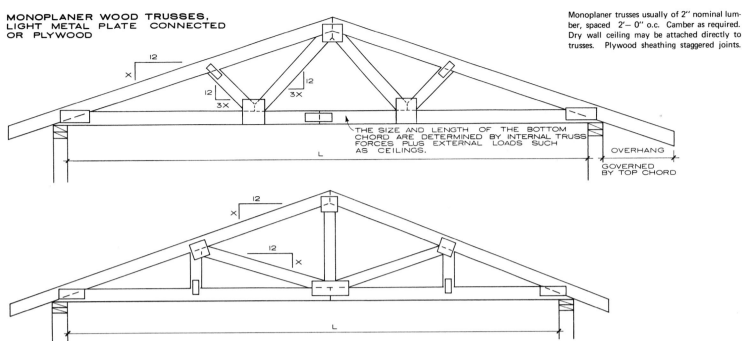

THE SIZE AND LENGTH OF THE BOTTOM CHORD ARE DETERMINED BY INTERNAL TRUSS FORCES PLUS EXTERNAL LOADS SUCH AS CEILINGS.

OVERHANG

GOVERNED BY TOP CHORD

APPROXIMATE MAXIMUM SPANS (FT)

	L FOR 2 x 4		L FOR 2 x 4	
X	40 psf	50 psf	40 psf	50 psf
2	22	19	33	28
3	25	21	38	32
4	26	22	41	35
5	27	23	42	36
6	27	24	42	37

FOUR PANEL TRUSSES

Approximate maximum spans for 2 x 4 and 2 x 6 top chords for trusses above (4 panel) using machine stress rated (MSR) lumber with f = 1200 psi and E = 1,200,000 psi. Trusses spaced 2 ft o.c. (Assume 15% of live load increase for snow load condition.) All web members 2 x 4. All bottom chords 2 x 4 except where ceiling or external loads required.

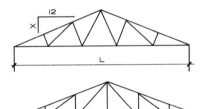

SIX PANEL TRUSSES

Six panel trusses allow spans up to approximately 60 ft. Truss design and allowable spans are based on tension values in bottom chord. Consult the Truss Plate Institute for full information on truss design and truss installation practice.

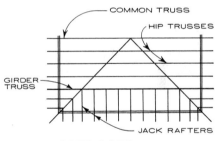

COMMON TRUSS

HIP TRUSSES

GIRDER TRUSS

JACK RAFTERS

HIPPED ROOF

Plates manufactured from zinc coated (hot dip process) sheet steel conforming to current ASTM A446 Grade A. Plates applied to both sides of joint. Where nails are required through connector plates they shall be $1^1/2$ in. long with $9/32$ in. head and a 0.12 in. (8d) deformed or annular ringed shank.

NAIL – ON
18-20 GAUGE

PRONGS
18-20 GAUGE

TEETH
14-20 GAUGE

SELF–CLINCHING NAILS
20 GAUGE

PLATE TYPES

GENERAL NOTES

1. Trusses designed in accordance with Truss Plate Institute Design Specifications and National Design Specifications for wood construction.
2. Plates sized for axial loads, eccentricity, net section of metal and fastener design value.

3. Truss members should be clamped in a mechanical or hydraulic jig with sufficient pressure to bring members into reasonable contact at all joints during application of connector plates.

4. Provide adequate anchorage and erection bracing as specified by plate manufacturer or as designed in accordance with NDS. Refer also to Bracing Wood Trusses, BWT-76.

Joseph A. Wilkes, FAIA; Wilkes and Faulkner; Washington, D.C.

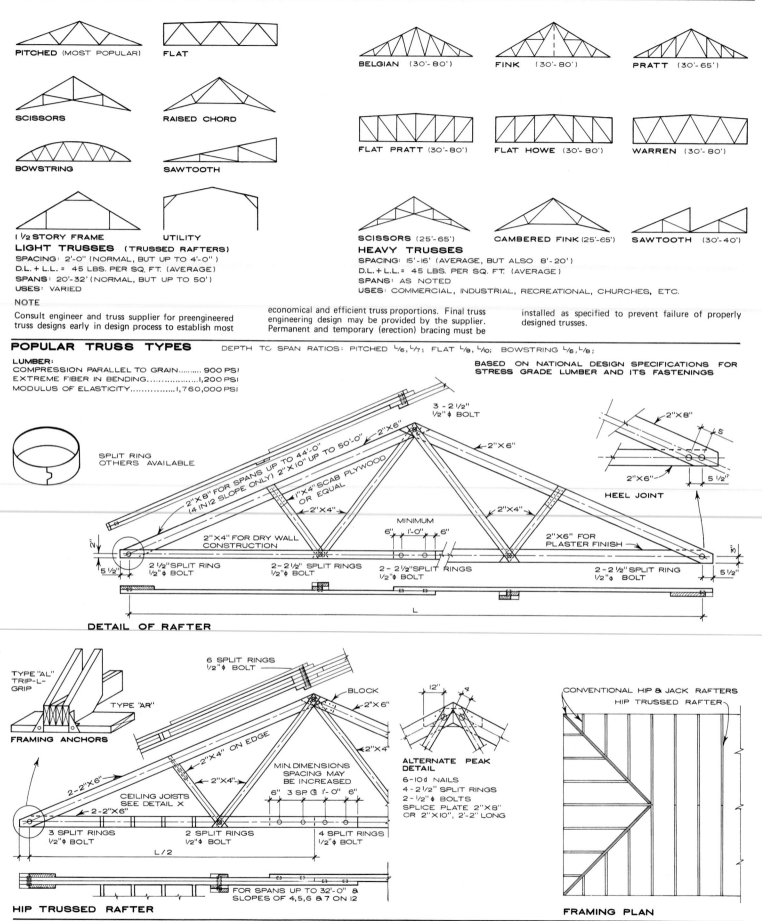

PITCHED (MOST POPULAR)   FLAT

SCISSORS   RAISED CHORD

BOWSTRING   SAWTOOTH

1 1/2 STORY FRAME   UTILITY

LIGHT TRUSSES (TRUSSED RAFTERS)
SPACING: 2'-0" (NORMAL, BUT UP TO 4'-0")
D.L.+ L.L. = 45 LBS. PER SQ. FT. (AVERAGE)
SPANS: 20'-32' (NORMAL, BUT UP TO 50')
USES: VARIED

NOTE

Consult engineer and truss supplier for preengineered truss designs early in design process to establish most economical and efficient truss proportions. Final truss engineering design may be provided by the supplier. Permanent and temporary (erection) bracing must be installed as specified to prevent failure of properly designed trusses.

BELGIAN (30'-80')   FINK (30'-80')   PRATT (30'-65')

FLAT PRATT (30'-80')   FLAT HOWE (30'-80')   WARREN (30'-80')

SCISSORS (25'-65')   CAMBERED FINK (25'-65')   SAWTOOTH (30'-40')

HEAVY TRUSSES
SPACING: 15'-16' (AVERAGE, BUT ALSO 8'-20')
D.L.+ L.L.= 45 LBS. PER SQ. FT. (AVERAGE)
SPANS: AS NOTED
USES: COMMERCIAL, INDUSTRIAL, RECREATIONAL, CHURCHES, ETC.

POPULAR TRUSS TYPES

DEPTH TO SPAN RATIOS: PITCHED 1/6, 1/7; FLAT 1/8, 1/10; BOWSTRING 1/6, 1/8;

LUMBER:
COMPRESSION PARALLEL TO GRAIN......... 900 PSI
EXTREME FIBER IN BENDING.................1,200 PSI
MODULUS OF ELASTICITY.................1,760,000 PSI

BASED ON NATIONAL DESIGN SPECIFICATIONS FOR STRESS GRADE LUMBER AND ITS FASTENINGS

SPLIT RING
OTHERS AVAILABLE

3 - 2 1/2" 1/2" φ BOLT

2"X 8" FOR SPANS UP TO 44'-0" (4 IN 12 SLOPE ONLY) 2"X 10" UP TO 50'-0"

2"X6"

2"X6"

1"X4" SCAB PLYWOOD OR EQUAL

2"X4"

MINIMUM
6" 1'-0" 6"

2"X4"

2"X4" FOR DRY WALL CONSTRUCTION

2"X6" FOR PLASTER FINISH

2'   5 1/2"

2 1/2" SPLIT RING 1/2" φ BOLT

2 - 2 1/2" SPLIT RINGS 1/2" φ BOLT

2 - 2 1/2" SPLIT RINGS 1/2" φ BOLT

2 - 2 1/2" SPLIT RING 1/2" φ BOLT

5 1/2"

L

2"X8"

S

2"X6"

5 1/2"

HEEL JOINT

DETAIL OF RAFTER

TYPE "AL" TRIP-L-GRIP

TYPE "AR"

FRAMING ANCHORS

6 SPLIT RINGS 1/2" φ BOLT

BLOCK

2"X6"

2"X4"

2-2"X6"

2"X4" ON EDGE

CEILING JOISTS SEE DETAIL X

2"X4"

MIN. DIMENSIONS SPACING MAY BE INCREASED
6" 3 SP @ 1'-0" 6"

2-2"X6"

3 SPLIT RINGS 1/2" φ BOLT

2 SPLIT RINGS 1/2" φ BOLT

4 SPLIT RINGS 1/2" φ BOLT

L/2

FOR SPANS UP TO 32'-0" & SLOPES OF 4,5,6 & 7 ON 12

HIP TRUSSED RAFTER

12"

ALTERNATE PEAK DETAIL
6-10d NAILS
4 - 2 1/2" SPLIT RINGS
2 - 1/2" φ BOLTS
SPLICE PLATE 2"X8" OR 2"X10", 2'-2" LONG

CONVENTIONAL HIP & JACK RAFTERS
HIP TRUSSED RAFTER

FRAMING PLAN

RING CONNECTOR TRUSSES

Joseph A. Wilkes; FAIA; Wilkes and Faulkner; Washington, D.C.

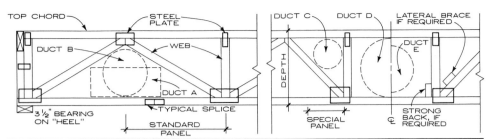

RESIDENTIAL TYPE TRUSSED FLOOR JOIST
STEEL PLATE CONNECTED
WOOD TRUSSED RAFTERS SPANS

	RESIDENTIAL LIVE LOADS								
	FLOORS 55 PSF (A)			ROOFS 40 PSF (B)		55 PSF (C)		(DOUBLE CHORDS) 55 PSF (C)	
	TRUSSED RAFTERS SPACING (C TO C)								
DEPTH	12″	16″	24″	16″	24″	16″	24″	16″	24″
12″	23-6	21-0	17-1	24-0	21-4	21-11	18-2		
13″	24-11	22-0	17-11						
14″	26-4	22-11	18-8	27-5	23-3	24-5	19-10		
15″	27-7	23-10	19-5						
16″	28-7	24-9	20-1	30-3	25-0	26-4	21-4	31-10	27-10
18″	30-6	26-4	21-5	32-11	26-9	28-1	22-9	35-1	30-7
20″	32-4	27-11	22-8	34-8	28-0	29-7	23-11	38-1	33-1
22″	34-0	26-9	23-11						
24″	35-8	30-10	25-0	38-3	30-11	32-7	26-4	43-10	36-7
28″				41-6	33-6	35-5	28-7	49-2	39-11
32″				44-3	35-7	37-8	30-4	52-9	42-9
36″				47-0	37-10	40-1	32-3	56-3	45-7
48″								60-0	53-3

	COMMERCIAL LIVE LOADS								
	FLOORS 80 PSF (D)			100 PSF (E)			120 PSF (F)		
	TRUSSED RAFTERS SPACING (C TO C)								
DEPTH	12″	16″	24″	12″	16″	24″	12″	16″	24″
12″	19-0	17-3	15-1	17-3	15-8	13-7	16-0	14-7	12-4
14″	21-4	19-4	16-6	19-4	17-7	14-9	18-0	16-4	13-6
16″	23-6	21-5	17-10	21-5	19-5	15-11	19-10	17-11	14-6
18″	25-8	23-4	19-0	23-4	21-0	17-0	21-8	19-2	15-6
20″	27-8	24-10	20-2	25-2	22-3	18-0	23-4	20-3	16-5
24″	31-6	27-5	22-2	28-5	24-6	19-10	25-11	22-4	18-1
16″*	27-7	25-1	21-11	25-1	22-9	19-11	23-2	21-2	18-5
24″*	38-0	34-6	30-1	34-6	31-4	27-4	32-0	29-1	25-1
32″*	47-1	42-9	36-1	42-9	38-10	32-3	39-8	36-1	29-5

Top chord live load	40 psf	20 psf	35 psf	60 psf	80 psf	100 psf
Top chord dead load	10 psf	10 psf	10 psf	10 psf	10 psf	10 psf
Bottom chord dead load	5 psf	10 psf	10 psf	10 psf	10 psf	10 psf
Total load	(A) 55 psf	(B) 40 psf	(C) 55 psf	(D) 80 psf	(E) 100 psf	(F) 120 psf

NOTES

1. Spans are clear, inside to inside, for bottom chord bearing. Values shown would vary very slightly for a truss with top chord loading.
2. Spans should not exceed 24 x depth of truss.
3. Designed deflection limit under total load is ℓ/240 for roofs, ℓ/360 for residential floors, and ℓ/480 for commercial floors.
4. Roof spans include a +15% short term stress.

5. Asterisk (*) indicates that truss has double chords, top and bottom.
6. Spans shown are for only one type of lumber; in this case—#2 Southern pine, with an f_b value of 1550. Charts are available for other grades and species. Lumber and grades may be mixed in the same truss, but chord size must be identical. Repetitive member bending stress is used in this chart.

DUCT SIZES

Ease of running electrical and mechanical services through framing is a major advantage of trussed joists. Most manufacturers provide a large rectangular open panel at midspan; this void will generally accommodate a trunk line.

Sizes given here are approximations. Because web size and angles vary with different brands, the designer is cautioned to verify individual sizes carefully. Note that shape E is the duct that will fit in a flat truss with double chords top and bottom.

Michael Bengis, AIA; Hopatcong, N.J.

DEPTH OF TRUSS AND SIZE OF DUCTWORK

DEPTH	12″	16″	20″	24″
SHAPE				
A	4 x 9	6 x 12	7 x 13	8 x 14
B	7″	10″	12″	14″
C	5″	7″	8″	9″
D	9″	13″	17″	21″
E	6″	10″	14″	18″

GENERAL

Monoplaner trusses are usually made up from 2 x 4 or 2 x 6 lumber. Spacing, normally 24 in. o.c., varies for special uses, especially in agriculture. Camber is designed for dead load only. Bottom chord furring generally is not required for drywall ceiling. Joints in plywood floor or roof should be staggered. Many trusses are approved by model codes, such as BOCA, ICBO, FHA, and SBC.

$$\frac{\text{CAMBER}}{\text{(USUAL)}} = \frac{L(FT)}{60}$$

BRACING

Adequate bracing of trusses is vital. Sufficient support at right angles to plane of truss must be provided to hold each truss member in its designated position. Consider bracing during design, fabrication, and erection. In addition, provide permanent bracing/anchorage as an integral part of the building. Strongbacks are often used.

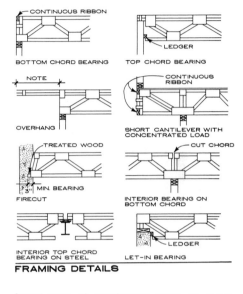

FRAMING DETAILS

Several types of manufactured trusses are shown below. Span limits are for a 55 psf total load, truss 24 in. o.c. Spans: small—20 to 40 ft, medium—40 to 60 ft, long—60 to 80 ft, very long—80 to 100 ft. This information is for initial design only.

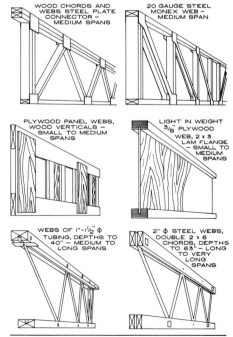

TYPES OF WOOD TRUSSED RAFTERS

WOOD TRUSSES ⑥

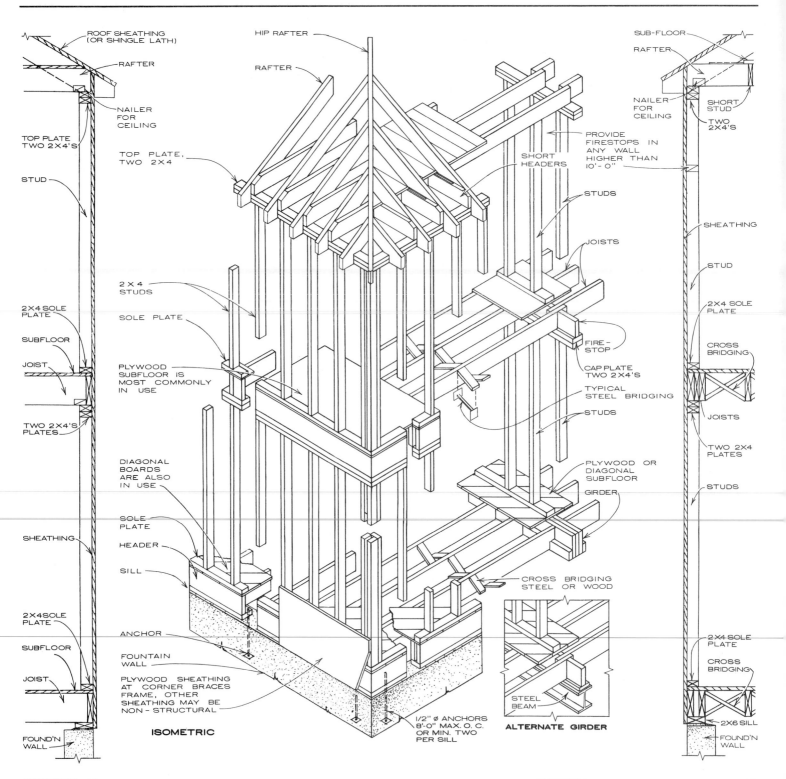

ISOMETRIC

ALTERNATE GIRDER

SECTION - CEILING JOISTS PARALLEL TO RAFTERS: FLOOR JOISTS PERPENDICULAR TO EXTERIOR WALLS   SCALE 3/8"=1'-0"

SECTION - CEILING JOISTS PERPENDICULAR TO RAFTERS: FLOOR JOISTS PARALLEL TO EXTERIOR WALLS.   SCALE:3/8"=1'-0"

NOTES

WESTERN OR PLATFORM FRAMING

Subfloor extends to outer edge of the frame and provides a flat, work surface at each floor. Common practice is to assemble walls on subfloor and tilt them into place. Arrangement of members in platform framing equilizes vertical shrinkage within the structure.

FIRESTOPPING

All concealed spaces in framing with 2" blocking, fitted to openings and arranged to prevent drafts between spaces.

Joseph A. Wilkes; FAIA; Wilkes and Faulkner; Washington, D.C.

EXTERIOR WALL FRAMING

One Story Buildings: 2x4's, 16'' or 24'' o.c.
Two & Three Stories: 2x4's, 16'' o.c.

BRACING EXTERIOR WALLS

Suitable sheathing acts as bracing. Where required for additional stiffness or bracing, 1x4's may be let into outer face of studs at 45° angle secured top, bottom and to studs.

BRIDGING FOR FLOOR JOISTS

May be omitted when flooring is properly nailed to joists. However, where nominal depth-to-thickness ratio of joists exceeds 6 bridging should be installed at 8' – 0" intervals. (F.H.A. also allows omission of bridging under certain conditions--see F.H.A. publication No. 300, 1963, revised 1965.)

Steel bridging is available. Some types do not require nails.

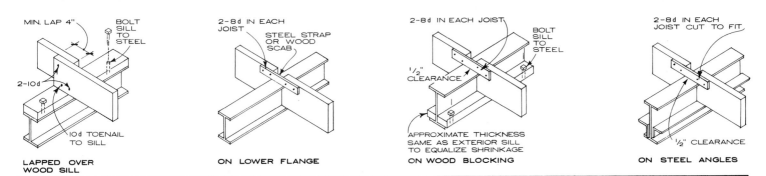

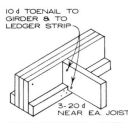

MIN. LAP 4"
BOLT SILL TO STEEL
2-10d
10d TOENAIL TO SILL

LAPPED OVER WOOD SILL

2-8d IN EACH JOIST
STEEL STRAP OR WOOD SCAB

ON LOWER FLANGE

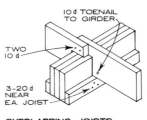

2-8d IN EACH JOIST
BOLT SILL TO STEEL
1/2" CLEARANCE
APPROXIMATE THICKNESS SAME AS EXTERIOR SILL TO EQUALIZE SHRINKAGE

ON WOOD BLOCKING

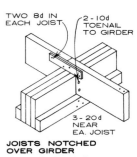

2-8d IN EACH JOIST CUT TO FIT
1/2" CLEARANCE

ON STEEL ANGLES

WOOD JOISTS SUPPORTED ON STEEL GIRDERS

10d TOENAIL TO GIRDER & TO LEDGER STRIP
3-20d NEAR EA. JOIST

JOIST NOTCHED OVER LEDGER STRIP
NOTCHING OVER BEARING NOT RECOMMENDED

GIRDER & JOIST NOTCHED FOR HANGER

JOIST IN JOIST HANGER IRON
ALSO CALLED STIRRUP OR BRIDLE IRON

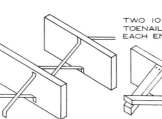

10d TOENAIL TO GIRDER
TWO 10d
3-20d NEAR EA. JOIST

OVERLAPPING JOISTS NOTCHED OVER GIRDER
BEARING ONLY ON LEDGER, NOT ON TOP OF GIRDER

TWO 8d IN EACH JOIST
2-10d TOENAIL TO GIRDER
3-20d NEAR EA. JOIST

JOISTS NOTCHED OVER GIRDER
BEARING ONLY ON LEDGER, NOT ON TOP OF GIRDER

WOOD JOISTS SUPPORTED ON WOOD GIRDERS

TWO 10d EACH END ON ONE SIDE, OTHERS STAG. 16" APART
10d TOENAIL TO POST EA. SIDE

TWO PIECE GIRDER
GIRDER JOINTS ONLY AT SUPPORTS STAGGER JOINTS

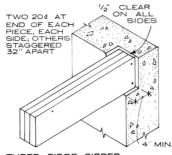

TWO 20d AT END OF EACH PIECE, EACH SIDE; OTHERS STAGGERED 32" APART
1/2" CLEAR ON ALL SIDES
4" MIN.

THREE PIECE GIRDER
FOR FOUR PIECE GIRDER: ADD NAILED WITH 20d TO THREE PC.

STEEL BRIDGING
SOME HAVE BUILT-IN TEETH, NEEDS NO NAILS

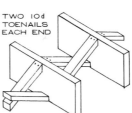

TWO 10d TOENAILS EACH END

1" X 3" CROSS BRIDGING
LOWER ENDS NOT NAILED, UNTIL FLOORING IS LAYED

2-10d TOENAILS EA. END

SOLID BRIDGING
USED UNDER PARTITIONS FOR HEAVY LOADING STAGGER BOARDS FOR EASE OF NAILING

10d TOENAILS
ANCHOR BOLT

2 X 6 SILL

ANCHOR BOLT
10d FOR 4 X 6
8d FOR 3 X 6

3 X 6, 4 X 6 SILL
HALVED AT CORNERS

ANCHOR BOLT
10d

4 X 6 DOUBLE SILL
NAILS STAGGERED ALONG SILL 24" ON CENTER

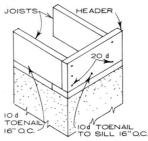

JOISTS   HEADER
20 d
10d TOENAIL 16" O.C.
10d TOENAIL TO SILL 16" O.C.

PLATFORM FRAMING
TOENAIL TO SILL NOT REQUIRED IF DIAGONAL SHEATHING USED

METAL WASHERS

TYPES OF SILL ANCHOR BOLTS

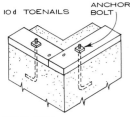

2 X 8 JOIST
"A"
SILL
GIRDER

SHRINKAGE
SELECT JOIST-GIRDER DETAIL WHICH HAS THE APPROXIMATE SAME SHRINKAGE "A" AS THE SILL DETAIL USED

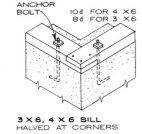
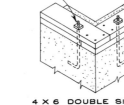

DU-AL-CLIP

METAL FRAMING DEVICES

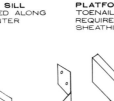

TY-DOWN ANCHOR

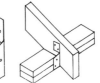

TRIP-L-GRIP

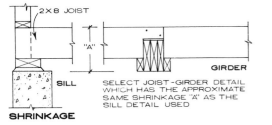

16 – 18 GAUGE ZINC COATED STEEL

Joseph A. Wilkes, FAIA; Wilkes and Faulkner; Washington, D.C.

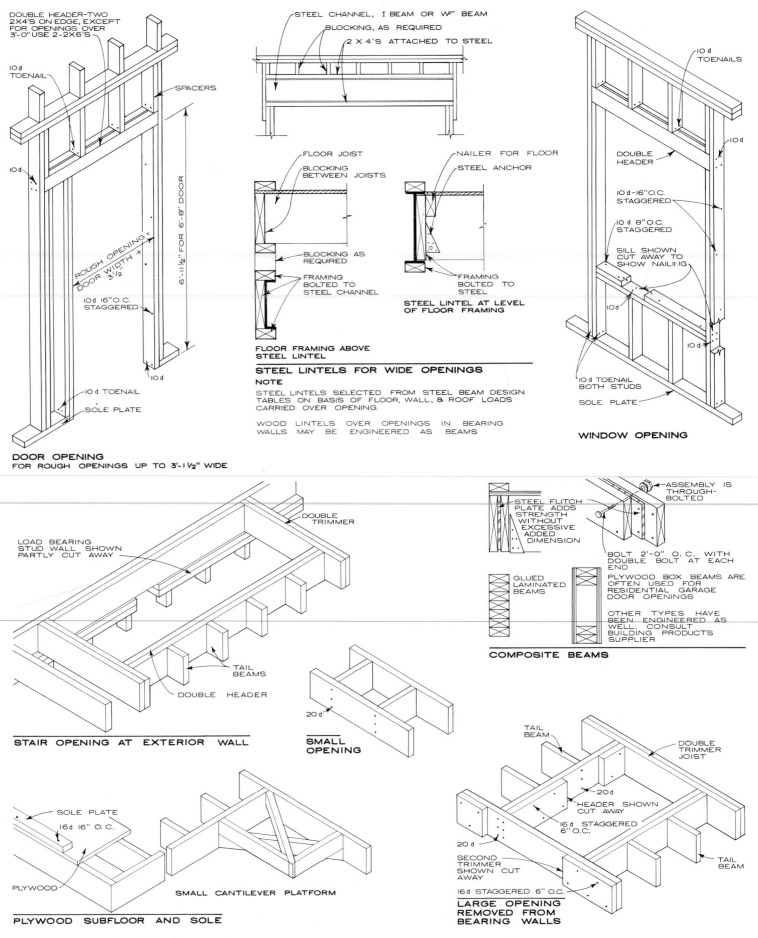

DOUBLE HEADER-TWO 2X4'S ON EDGE, EXCEPT FOR OPENINGS OVER 3'-0" USE 2-2X6'S

10 d TOENAIL

SPACERS

10 d

ROUGH OPENING = DOOR WIDTH + 3½"

6'-11½" FOR 6'-8" DOOR

10d 16" O.C. STAGGERED

10 d

10 d TOENAIL

SOLE PLATE

DOOR OPENING
FOR ROUGH OPENINGS UP TO 3'-1½" WIDE

STEEL CHANNEL, I BEAM OR WF BEAM

BLOCKING, AS REQUIRED

2 X 4'S ATTACHED TO STEEL

FLOOR JOIST

BLOCKING BETWEEN JOISTS

NAILER FOR FLOOR

STEEL ANCHOR

BLOCKING AS REQUIRED

FRAMING BOLTED TO STEEL CHANNEL

FRAMING BOLTED TO STEEL

STEEL LINTEL AT LEVEL OF FLOOR FRAMING

FLOOR FRAMING ABOVE STEEL LINTEL

STEEL LINTELS FOR WIDE OPENINGS
NOTE
STEEL LINTELS SELECTED FROM STEEL BEAM DESIGN TABLES ON BASIS OF FLOOR, WALL, & ROOF LOADS CARRIED OVER OPENING.

WOOD LINTELS OVER OPENINGS IN BEARING WALLS MAY BE ENGINEERED AS BEAMS

10 d TOENAILS

DOUBLE HEADER

10 d

10 d-16" O.C. STAGGERED

10 d 8" O.C. STAGGERED

SILL SHOWN CUT AWAY TO SHOW NAILING

10 d

10 d

10 d TOENAIL BOTH STUDS

SOLE PLATE

WINDOW OPENING

LOAD BEARING STUD WALL SHOWN PARTLY CUT AWAY

DOUBLE TRIMMER

TAIL BEAMS

DOUBLE HEADER

STAIR OPENING AT EXTERIOR WALL

20 d

SMALL OPENING

STEEL FLITCH PLATE ADDS STRENGTH WITHOUT EXCESSIVE ADDED DIMENSION

ASSEMBLY IS THROUGH-BOLTED

BOLT 2'-0" O.C. WITH DOUBLE BOLT AT EACH END

GLUED LAMINATED BEAMS

PLYWOOD BOX BEAMS ARE OFTEN USED FOR RESIDENTIAL GARAGE DOOR OPENINGS

OTHER TYPES HAVE BEEN ENGINEERED AS WELL, CONSULT BUILDING PRODUCTS SUPPLIER

COMPOSITE BEAMS

SOLE PLATE

16d 16" O.C.

PLYWOOD

SMALL CANTILEVER PLATFORM

PLYWOOD SUBFLOOR AND SOLE

TAIL BEAM

DOUBLE TRIMMER JOIST

20 d

HEADER SHOWN CUT AWAY

16 d STAGGERED 6" O.C.

20 d

SECOND TRIMMER SHOWN CUT AWAY

TAIL BEAM

16d STAGGERED 6" O.C.

LARGE OPENING REMOVED FROM BEARING WALLS

Joseph A. Wilkes, FAIA; Wilkes and Faulkner; Washington, D.C.

⑥   **LIGHT WOOD FRAMING**

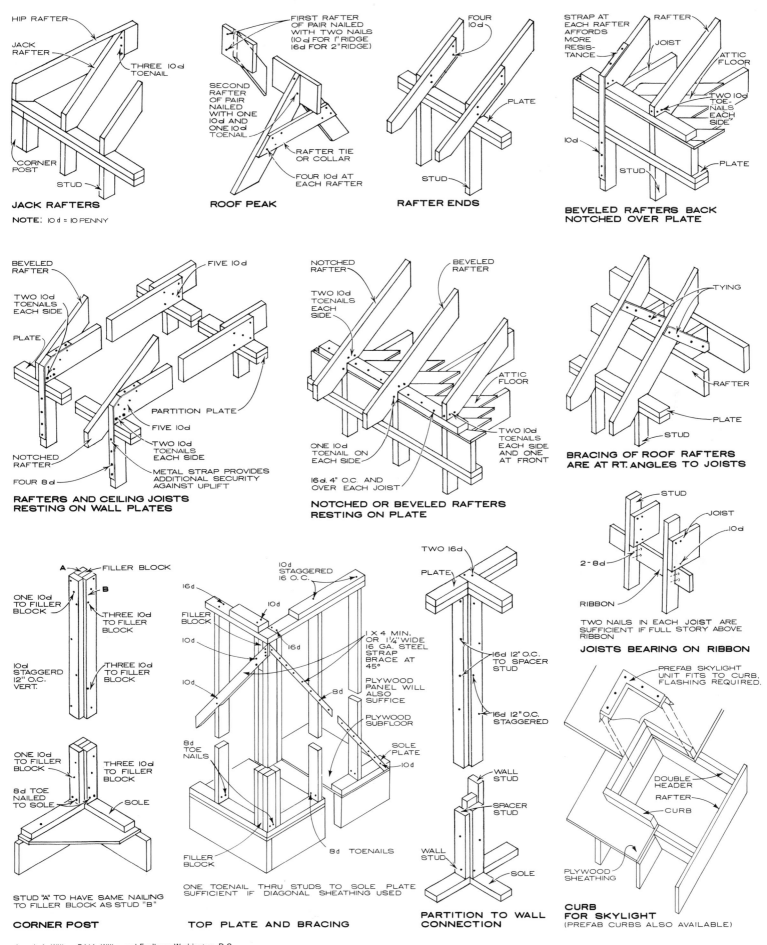

HIP RAFTER
JACK RAFTER
THREE 10d TOENAIL
CORNER POST
STUD

JACK RAFTERS

NOTE: 10d = 10 PENNY

FIRST RAFTER OF PAIR NAILED WITH TWO NAILS (10d FOR 1" RIDGE 16d FOR 2" RIDGE)
SECOND RAFTER OF PAIR NAILED WITH ONE 10d AND ONE 10d TOENAIL
RAFTER TIE OR COLLAR
FOUR 10d AT EACH RAFTER

ROOF PEAK

FOUR 10d
PLATE
STUD

RAFTER ENDS

STRAP AT EACH RAFTER AFFORDS MORE RESISTANCE
RAFTER
JOIST
ATTIC FLOOR
TWO 10d TOE-NAILS EACH SIDE
10d
STUD
PLATE

BEVELED RAFTERS BACK NOTCHED OVER PLATE

BEVELED RAFTER
FIVE 10d
TWO 10d TOENAILS EACH SIDE
PLATE
PARTITION PLATE
FIVE 10d
NOTCHED RAFTER
TWO 10d TOENAILS EACH SIDE
FOUR 8d
METAL STRAP PROVIDES ADDITIONAL SECURITY AGAINST UPLIFT

RAFTERS AND CEILING JOISTS RESTING ON WALL PLATES

NOTCHED RAFTER
BEVELED RAFTER
TWO 10d TOENAILS EACH SIDE
ATTIC FLOOR
ONE 10d TOENAIL ON EACH SIDE
TWO 10d TOENAILS EACH SIDE AND ONE AT FRONT
16d. 4" O.C. AND OVER EACH JOIST

NOTCHED OR BEVELED RAFTERS RESTING ON PLATE

TYING
RAFTER
PLATE
STUD

BRACING OF ROOF RAFTERS ARE AT RT. ANGLES TO JOISTS

STUD
JOIST
10d
2-8d
RIBBON

TWO NAILS IN EACH JOIST ARE SUFFICIENT IF FULL STORY ABOVE RIBBON

JOISTS BEARING ON RIBBON

A
FILLER BLOCK
B
ONE 10d TO FILLER BLOCK
THREE 10d TO FILLER BLOCK
10d STAGGERD 12" O.C. VERT.
THREE 10d TO FILLER BLOCK
ONE 10d TO FILLER BLOCK
THREE 10d TO FILLER BLOCK
8d TOE NAILED TO SOLE
SOLE

STUD "A" TO HAVE SAME NAILING TO FILLER BLOCK AS STUD "B"

CORNER POST

10d STAGGERED 16 O.C.
16d
FILLER BLOCK
10d
16d
10d
8d TOE NAILS
1 X 4 MIN. OR 1¼" WIDE 16 GA. STEEL STRAP BRACE AT 45°
PLYWOOD PANEL WILL ALSO SUFFICE
PLYWOOD SUBFLOOR
8d
SOLE PLATE
10d
FILLER BLOCK
8d TOENAILS

ONE TOENAIL THRU STUDS TO SOLE PLATE SUFFICIENT IF DIAGONAL SHEATHING USED

TOP PLATE AND BRACING

TWO 16d
PLATE
16d 12" O.C. TO SPACER STUD
16d 12" O.C. STAGGERED
WALL STUD
SPACER STUD
WALL STUD
SOLE

PARTITION TO WALL CONNECTION

PREFAB SKYLIGHT UNIT FITS TO CURB. FLASHING REQUIRED.
DOUBLE HEADER
RAFTER
CURB
PLYWOOD SHEATHING

CURB FOR SKYLIGHT (PREFAB CURBS ALSO AVAILABLE)

Joseph A. Wilkes; FAIA; Wilkes and Faulkner; Washington, D.C.

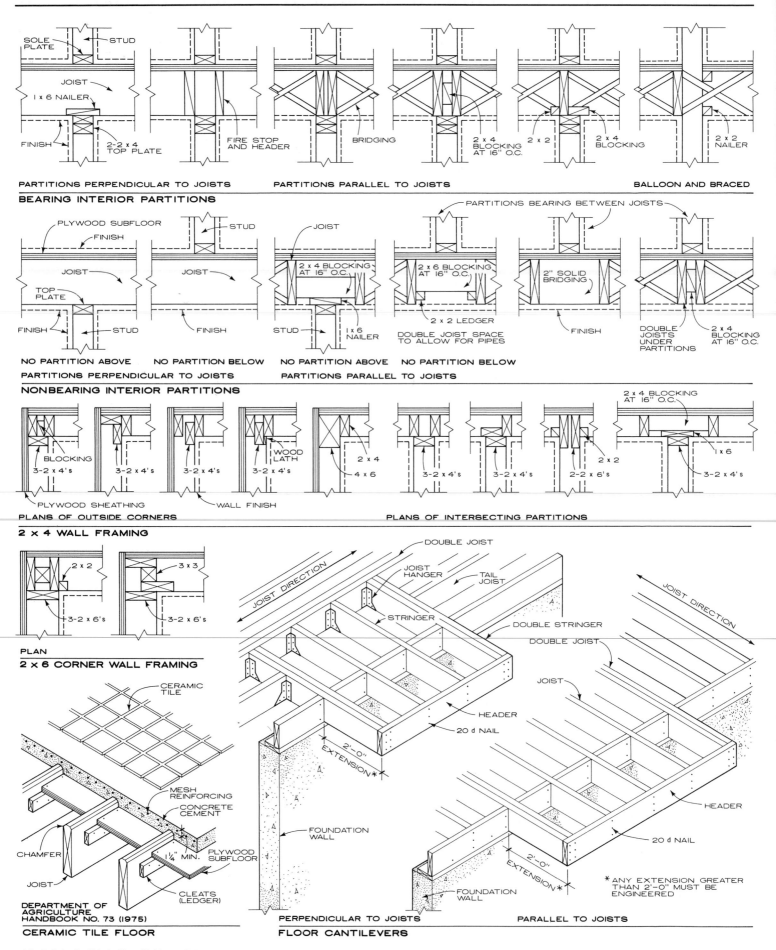

PARTITIONS PERPENDICULAR TO JOISTS   PARTITIONS PARALLEL TO JOISTS   BALLOON AND BRACED

BEARING INTERIOR PARTITIONS

NO PARTITION ABOVE   NO PARTITION BELOW   NO PARTITION ABOVE   NO PARTITION BELOW

PARTITIONS PERPENDICULAR TO JOISTS   PARTITIONS PARALLEL TO JOISTS

NONBEARING INTERIOR PARTITIONS

PLANS OF OUTSIDE CORNERS   PLANS OF INTERSECTING PARTITIONS

2 x 4 WALL FRAMING

PLAN

2 x 6 CORNER WALL FRAMING

DEPARTMENT OF
AGRICULTURE
HANDBOOK NO. 73 (1975)

CERAMIC TILE FLOOR   **FLOOR CANTILEVERS**

PERPENDICULAR TO JOISTS   PARALLEL TO JOISTS

John R. Hoke, Jr., AIA, Architect; Washington, D.C.

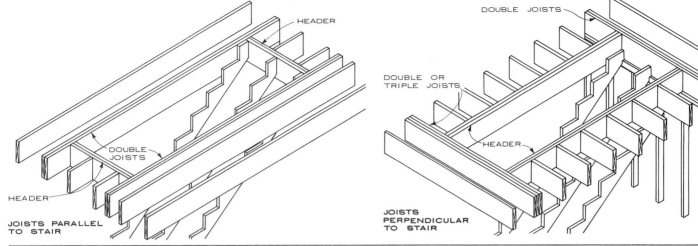

DOUBLE JOISTS

DOUBLE OR TRIPLE JOISTS

HEADER

HEADER

DOUBLE JOISTS

HEADER

JOISTS PARALLEL TO STAIR

JOISTS PERPENDICULAR TO STAIR

FLOOR OPENINGS

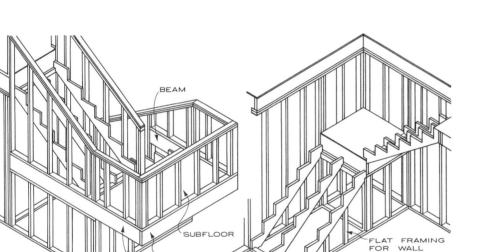

BEAM

SUBFLOOR

RIM JOIST

BEAM

CANTILEVERED

FLAT FRAMING FOR WALL FINISH

PLATFORM

LANDINGS

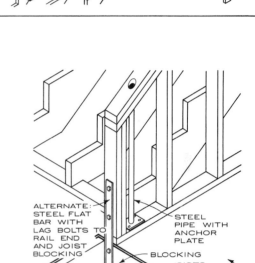

ALTERNATE: STEEL FLAT BAR WITH LAG BOLTS TO RAIL END AND JOIST BLOCKING

STEEL PIPE WITH ANCHOR PLATE

BLOCKING

JOISTS

SUBFLOOR

ANCHORS AT END OF SOLID RAIL

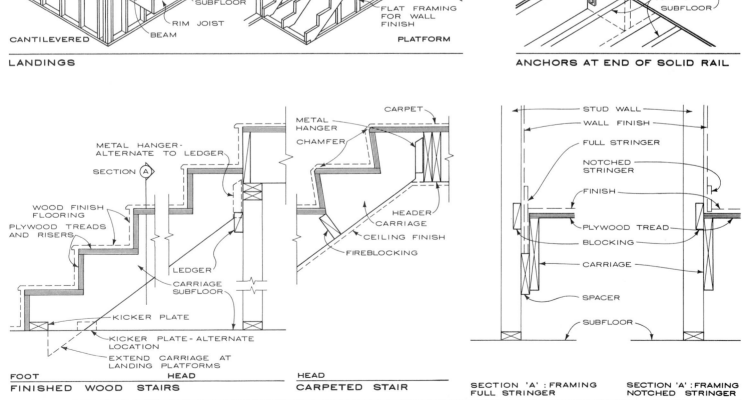

METAL HANGER - ALTERNATE TO LEDGER

SECTION (A)

WOOD FINISH FLOORING

PLYWOOD TREADS AND RISERS

LEDGER

CARRIAGE

SUBFLOOR

KICKER PLATE

KICKER PLATE - ALTERNATE LOCATION

EXTEND CARRIAGE AT LANDING PLATFORMS

CARPET

METAL HANGER

CHAMFER

HEADER

CARRIAGE

CEILING FINISH

FIREBLOCKING

FOOT   HEAD   HEAD

FINISHED WOOD STAIRS   **CARPETED STAIR**

STUD WALL

WALL FINISH

FULL STRINGER

NOTCHED STRINGER

FINISH

PLYWOOD TREAD

BLOCKING

CARRIAGE

SPACER

SUBFLOOR

SECTION 'A': FRAMING FULL STRINGER   SECTION 'A': FRAMING NOTCHED STRINGER

CARRIAGE DETAILS FOR CARPENTER BUILT STAIRS

The Bumgardner Partnership/Architects; Seattle, Washington

LIGHT WOOD FRAMING 6

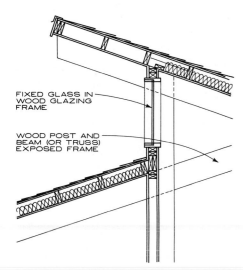

FIXED GLASS IN WOOD GLAZING FRAME

WOOD POST AND BEAM (OR TRUSS) EXPOSED FRAME

A fixed glass light is shown in wood glazing frame, with wood mullions coincident with structural beam or truss framing members. Intermediate mullions may be used, if desired, to divide clerestory glazing into smaller panels. Continuous strip glazing is possible between roof curb and soffit finish using minimum mullions (i.e., small structural gaskets or the like) with supporting structure located behind. Care should be taken to avoid solar glare; because of height above floor, interior shading from drapes or similar devices is difficult to accomplish.

CLERESTORY WINDOW (FIXED)

LUMBER WITH FINISH CASING

SOLID BEAM

SPACED BUILT-UP BEAM OR TRUSS

EXPOSED WOOD BEAM DETAILS

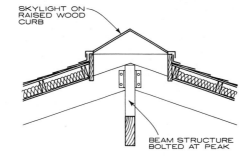

SKYLIGHT ON RAISED WOOD CURB

BEAM STRUCTURE BOLTED AT PEAK

PYRAMID SKYLIGHT AT ROOF PEAK

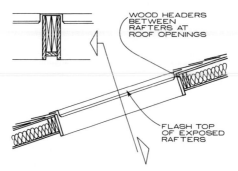

WOOD HEADERS BETWEEN RAFTERS AT ROOF OPENINGS

FLASH TOP OF EXPOSED RAFTERS

OPENINGS IN ROOFS

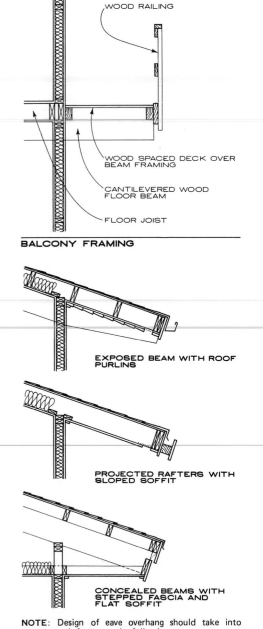

CEILING JOIST

ROOF BEAMS

BEAM FACING WITH FLASHING ABOVE

STUD FRAMING

WOOD RAILING

WOOD SPACED DECK OVER BEAM FRAMING

CANTILEVERED WOOD FLOOR BEAM

FLOOR JOIST

BALCONY FRAMING

EXPOSED BEAM WITH ROOF PURLINS

PROJECTED RAFTERS WITH SLOPED SOFFIT

CONCEALED BEAMS WITH STEPPED FASCIA AND FLAT SOFFIT

NOTE: Design of eave overhang should take into account such factors as the following:

1. Whether overhang protection is required.
2. The need for gutters or downspouts.
3. Economy of soffit materials.
4. Maximum cantilever distance for projected rafters or beams (structural).
5. Eave ventilation of attic spaces.
6. Decay resistance of exposed beam ends, fascia boards, and other materials exposed to the weather.

EAVE OVERHANG DETAILS

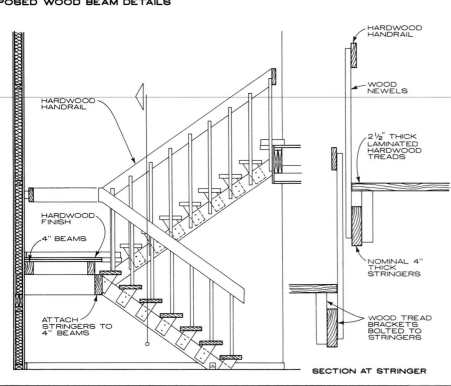

HARDWOOD HANDRAIL

HARDWOOD HANDRAIL

HARDWOOD FINISH

4" BEAMS

ATTACH STRINGERS TO 4" BEAMS

HARDWOOD HANDRAIL

WOOD NEWELS

2½" THICK LAMINATED HARDWOOD TREADS

NOMINAL 4" THICK STRINGERS

WOOD TREAD BRACKETS BOLTED TO STRINGERS

SECTION AT STRINGER

OPEN STAIRWELL AND BEAM FRAMED STAIR

Knight and Koonce and Associates; Bogalusa, Louisiana

⑥ **LIGHT WOOD FRAMING**

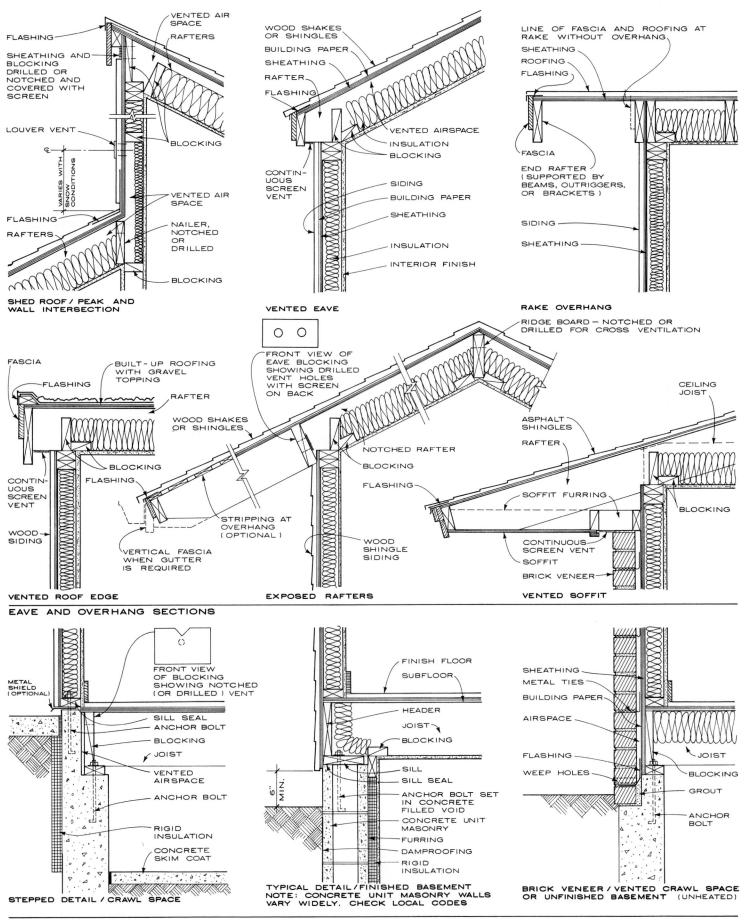

FLASHING

SHEATHING AND BLOCKING DRILLED OR NOTCHED AND COVERED WITH SCREEN

VENTED AIR SPACE

RAFTERS

LOUVER VENT

VARIES WITH SNOW CONDITIONS

BLOCKING

VENTED AIR SPACE

FLASHING

RAFTERS

NAILER, NOTCHED OR DRILLED

BLOCKING

SHED ROOF / PEAK AND WALL INTERSECTION

WOOD SHAKES OR SHINGLES

BUILDING PAPER

SHEATHING

RAFTER

FLASHING

CONTINUOUS SCREEN VENT

VENTED AIRSPACE

INSULATION

BLOCKING

SIDING

BUILDING PAPER

SHEATHING

INSULATION

INTERIOR FINISH

VENTED EAVE

LINE OF FASCIA AND ROOFING AT RAKE WITHOUT OVERHANG

SHEATHING

ROOFING

FLASHING

FASCIA

END RAFTER (SUPPORTED BY BEAMS, OUTRIGGERS, OR BRACKETS)

SIDING

SHEATHING

RAKE OVERHANG

FASCIA

FLASHING

BUILT-UP ROOFING WITH GRAVEL TOPPING

RAFTER

BLOCKING

FLASHING

CONTINUOUS SCREEN VENT

WOOD SIDING

VERTICAL FASCIA WHEN GUTTER IS REQUIRED

VENTED ROOF EDGE

FRONT VIEW OF EAVE BLOCKING SHOWING DRILLED VENT HOLES WITH SCREEN ON BACK

WOOD SHAKES OR SHINGLES

STRIPPING AT OVERHANG (OPTIONAL)

NOTCHED RAFTER

BLOCKING

FLASHING

WOOD SHINGLE SIDING

EXPOSED RAFTERS

RIDGE BOARD – NOTCHED OR DRILLED FOR CROSS VENTILATION

CEILING JOIST

ASPHALT SHINGLES

RAFTER

SOFFIT FURRING

BLOCKING

CONTINUOUS SCREEN VENT

SOFFIT

BRICK VENEER

VENTED SOFFIT

EAVE AND OVERHANG SECTIONS

METAL SHIELD (OPTIONAL)

FRONT VIEW OF BLOCKING SHOWING NOTCHED (OR DRILLED) VENT

SILL SEAL

ANCHOR BOLT

BLOCKING

JOIST

VENTED AIRSPACE

ANCHOR BOLT

RIGID INSULATION

CONCRETE SKIM COAT

STEPPED DETAIL / CRAWL SPACE

FINISH FLOOR

SUBFLOOR

HEADER

JOIST

BLOCKING

SILL

SILL SEAL

6" MIN.

ANCHOR BOLT SET IN CONCRETE FILLED VOID

CONCRETE UNIT MASONRY

FURRING

DAMPROOFING

RIGID INSULATION

TYPICAL DETAIL / FINISHED BASEMENT
NOTE: CONCRETE UNIT MASONRY WALLS VARY WIDELY. CHECK LOCAL CODES

SHEATHING

METAL TIES

BUILDING PAPER

AIRSPACE

FLASHING

WEEP HOLES

JOIST

BLOCKING

GROUT

ANCHOR BOLT

BRICK VENEER / VENTED CRAWL SPACE OR UNFINISHED BASEMENT (UNHEATED)

FOUNDATION WALL SECTIONS

The Bumgardner Partnership/Architects; Seattle, Washington

LIGHT WOOD FRAMING 6

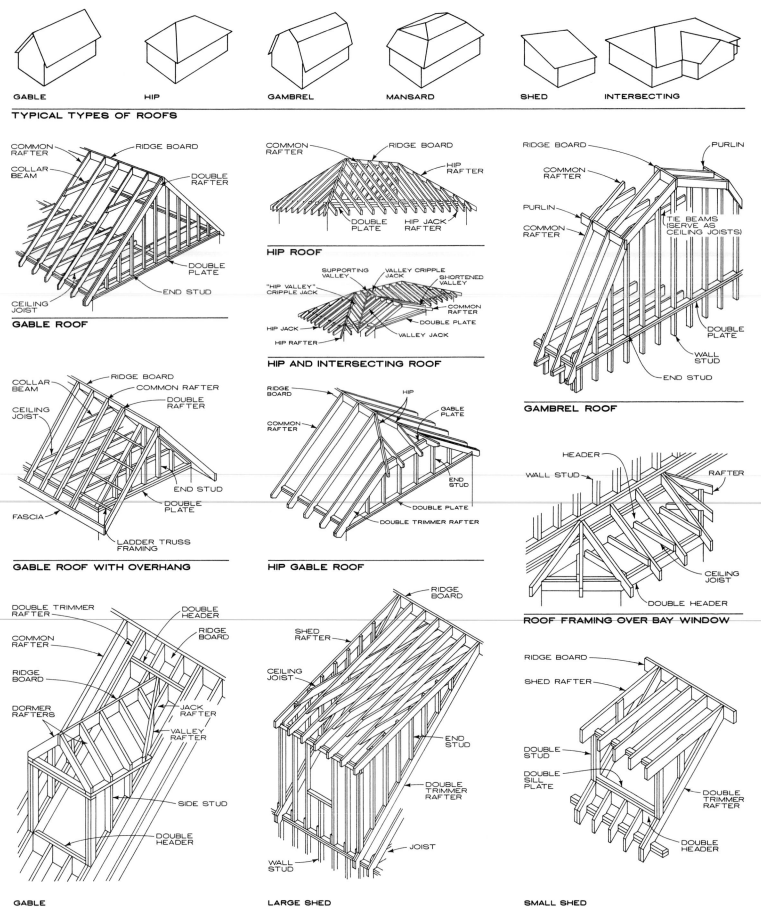

TYPICAL TYPES OF ROOFS

GABLE   HIP   GAMBREL   MANSARD   SHED   INTERSECTING

GABLE ROOF

HIP ROOF

HIP AND INTERSECTING ROOF

GAMBREL ROOF

GABLE ROOF WITH OVERHANG

HIP GABLE ROOF

ROOF FRAMING OVER BAY WINDOW

GABLE   LARGE SHED   SMALL SHED

DORMERS

John R. Hoke, Jr., AIA, Architect; Washington, D.C.

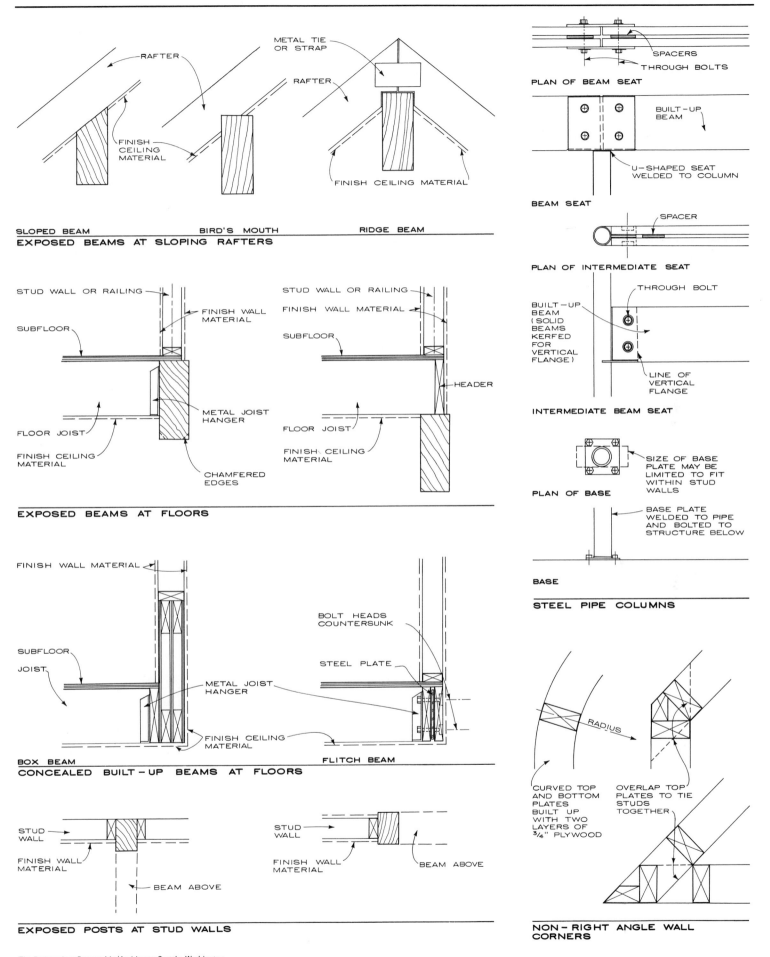

EXPOSED BEAMS AT SLOPING RAFTERS

SLOPED BEAM   BIRD'S MOUTH   RIDGE BEAM

EXPOSED BEAMS AT FLOORS

CONCEALED BUILT-UP BEAMS AT FLOORS

BOX BEAM   FLITCH BEAM

EXPOSED POSTS AT STUD WALLS

PLAN OF BEAM SEAT

BEAM SEAT

PLAN OF INTERMEDIATE SEAT

INTERMEDIATE BEAM SEAT

PLAN OF BASE

BASE

STEEL PIPE COLUMNS

NON-RIGHT ANGLE WALL CORNERS

The Bumgardner Partnership/Architects; Seattle, Washington

LIGHT WOOD FRAMING   6

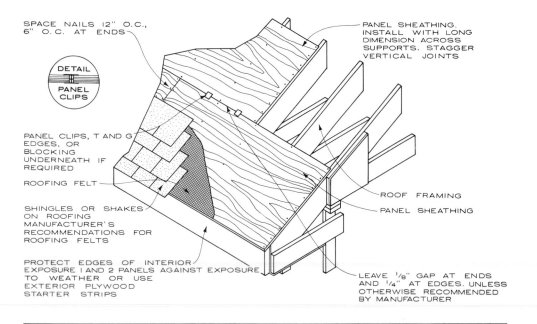

SPACE NAILS 12" O.C.,
6" O.C. AT ENDS

DETAIL
PANEL
CLIPS

PANEL CLIPS, T AND G
EDGES, OR
BLOCKING
UNDERNEATH IF
REQUIRED

ROOFING FELT

SHINGLES OR SHAKES
ON ROOFING
MANUFACTURER'S
RECOMMENDATIONS FOR
ROOFING FELTS

PROTECT EDGES OF INTERIOR
EXPOSURE 1 AND 2 PANELS AGAINST EXPOSURE
TO WEATHER OR USE
EXTERIOR PLYWOOD
STARTER STRIPS

PANEL SHEATHING.
INSTALL WITH LONG
DIMENSION ACROSS
SUPPORTS. STAGGER
VERTICAL JOINTS

ROOF FRAMING
PANEL SHEATHING

LEAVE 1/8" GAP AT ENDS
AND 1/4" AT EDGES. UNLESS
OTHERWISE RECOMMENDED
BY MANUFACTURER

STRUCTURAL-USE PANEL ROOF SHEATHING

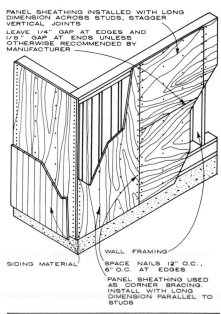

PANEL SHEATHING INSTALLED WITH LONG
DIMENSION ACROSS STUDS, STAGGER
VERTICAL JOINTS

LEAVE 1/4" GAP AT EDGES AND
1/8" GAP AT ENDS UNLESS
OTHERWISE RECOMMENDED BY
MANUFACTURER

WALL FRAMING

SIDING MATERIAL

SPACE NAILS 12" O.C.,
6" O.C. AT EDGES

PANEL SHEATHING USED
AS CORNER BRACING.
INSTALL WITH LONG
DIMENSION PARALLEL TO
STUDS

**STRUCTURAL-USE PANEL WALL
SHEATHING**

STRUCTURAL-USE PANEL ROOF SHEATHING

Panel grades commonly used for roof (and wall) sheathing are APA rated sheathing exposure 1, 2, and exterior, and Structural I and II, rated sheathing exposure 1 and exterior. Refer to American Plywood Association recommendations for unsupported edges.

STRUCTURAL-USE PANEL WALL SHEATHING

Common grade is same as used in roof sheathing. Use panel clips, tongue and groove panels, or blocking between studs to support edges. Refer to American Plywood Association recommendations for unsupported edges.

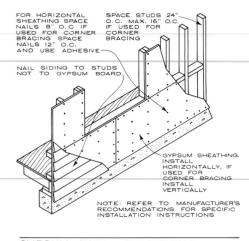

FOR HORIZONTAL
SHEATHING SPACE
NAILS 8" O.C. IF
USED FOR CORNER
BRACING SPACE
NAILS 12" O.C.
AND USE ADHESIVE

SPACE STUDS 24"
O.C. MAX. 16" O.C.
IF USED FOR
CORNER
BRACING

NAIL SIDING TO STUDS
NOT TO GYPSUM BOARD

GYPSUM SHEATHING.
INSTALL
HORIZONTALLY. IF
USED FOR
CORNER BRACING
INSTALL
VERTICALLY

NOTE: REFER TO MANUFACTURER'S
RECOMMENDATIONS FOR SPECIFIC
INSTALLATION INSTRUCTIONS

GYPSUM WALL SHEATHING

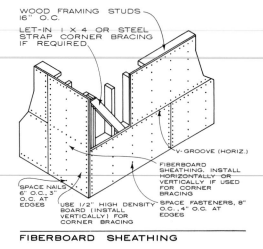

WOOD FRAMING STUDS
16" O.C.

LET-IN 1 X 4 OR STEEL
STRAP CORNER BRACING
IF REQUIRED

V-GROOVE (HORIZ.)

FIBERBOARD
SHEATHING. INSTALL
HORIZONTALLY OR
VERTICALLY IF USED
FOR CORNER
BRACING

SPACE NAILS
6" O.C., 3"
O.C. AT
EDGES

USE 1/2" HIGH DENSITY
BOARD (INSTALL
VERTICALLY) FOR
CORNER BRACING

SPACE FASTENERS, 8"
O.C., 4" O.C. AT
EDGES

FIBERBOARD SHEATHING

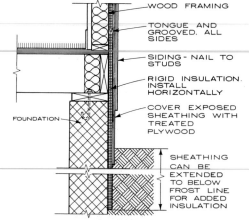

WOOD FRAMING

TONGUE AND
GROOVED. ALL
SIDES

SIDING - NAIL TO
STUDS

RIGID INSULATION.
INSTALL
HORIZONTALLY

COVER EXPOSED
SHEATHING WITH
TREATED
PLYWOOD

FOUNDATION

SHEATHING
CAN BE
EXTENDED
TO BELOW
FROST LINE
FOR ADDED
INSULATION

PLASTIC SHEATHING

GYPSUM WALL SHEATHING

Fire rated panels are available in 1/2 and 5/8 in. thicknesses. Gypsum board is not an effective vapor barrier.

FIBERBOARD SHEATHING

Also called insulation board. Can be treated or impregnated with asphalt. Available in regular or 1/2 in. high density panels.

PLASTIC SHEATHING

Usually made of polyurethane or polystyrene. Can be considered an effective vapor barrier, hence wall must be effectively vented. All edges are usually tongue and groove.

SHEATHING MATERIALS

CHARACTERISTICS	STRUCTURAL-USE PANEL	GYPSUM	FIBERBOARD	PLASTIC
Available base	Yes	No	Only high density	No
Vapor barrier	No	No	If asphalt treated	Yes
Insulation value "R" (1/2 in. thickness)	.62	0.7	2.6	6.25
Corner bracing	Yes	Yes (see manufacturer's recommendation)	Only high density	No
Panel sizes (ft)	4 x 8, 4 x 9, 4 x 10	4 x 8, 4 x 10, 4 x 12, 4 x 14	4 x 8, 4 x 9, 4 x 10, 4 x 12	16 x 96, 24 x 48, 24 x 96
Panel thickness (in.)	5/16, 3/8, 7/16, 1/2, 5/8, 3/4	1/4, 3/8, 1/2, 5/8	1/2, 25/32	3/4–6 (for roof)

John D. Bloodgood, Architects, P.C.; Des Moines, Iowa

American Plywood Association

 ROUGH CARPENTRY

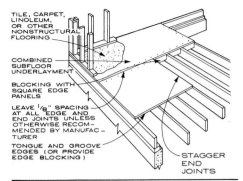

STRUCTURAL-USE PANEL SUBFLOOR/ UNDERLAYMENT

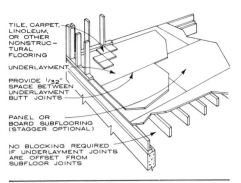

PLYWOOD UNDERLAYMENT

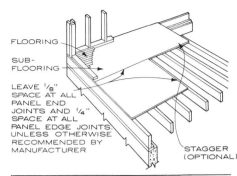

STRUCTURAL-USE PANEL SUBFLOOR

COMBINED SUBFLOOR/ UNDERLAYMENT (1)

PANEL GRADE	PANEL SPAN RATING	PANEL THICKNESS (IN.)	MAXIMUM SPACING (2, 3) (IN.)
APA rated STURD-I-FLOOR Exposure 1, 2, or Exterior	16 o.c.	$19/32$, $5/8$	16
	20 o.c.	$19/32$, $5/8$, $23/32$, $3/4$	20
	24 o.c.	$23/32$, $3/4$, $7/8$	24
	48 o.c.	$1 1/8$	32 (2X joists) 48 (4X joists)

1. For direct application of tile, carpeting, linoleum, or other nonstructural flooring.
2. Panel is assumed continuous over two or more spans, with long dimension across supports.
3. In some nonresidential buildings special conditions require construction in excess of thicknesses given.

NAILING SCHEDULE

To minimize the effects of framing shrinkage, ring shank or spiral thread nails should be used. Use 6d deformed shank nails for thicknesses through $3/4$ in. Use 8d for panels $7/8$ in. and thicker. Space nails at 6 in. along panel edges and at 10 in. along intermediate supports except 6 in. for 48-in. span. Nails should be driven flush or preferably slightly set below surface of the underlayment. Do not fill nail holes. If thin resilient flooring is to be applied, fill and thoroughly sand joints. (Separate underlayment recommended over nonveneer faced panels.)

ALLOWABLE CLEAR SPANS FOR APA (1): GLUED FLOOR SYSTEM (PARTIAL LIST)

		APA GLUED FLOOR SPANS			
JOIST SPECIES-GRADE	JOIST SIZE	RATED SHEATHING 16 o.c.	RATED STURD-I-FLOOR		
			16 o.c.	20 o.c.	24 o.c.
Douglas fir Larch-No. 2	2 x 6	10'-6''	10'-6''	4'-7''	8'-7''
	2 x 8	13'-10''	13'-10''	12'-7''	11'-3''
	2 x 10	17'-6''	17'-7''	16'-1''	14'-5''
	2 x 12	21'-1''	21'-3''	19'-7''	17'-6''
Douglas fir South-No. 1	2 x 6	10'-2''	10'-4''	9'-11''	9'-1''
	2 x 8	13'-2''	13'-4''	12'-8''	12'-0''
	2 x 10	16'-6''	16'-8''	15'-11''	15'-4''
	2 x 12	19'-11''	20'-1''	19'-1''	18'-4''
Hem-fir No. 1	2 x 6	10'-3''	10'-3''	9'-5''	8'-5''
	2 x 8	13'-5''	13'-7''	12'-5''	11'-1''
	2 x 10	16'-10''	17'-0''	15'-10''	14'-2''
	2 x 12	20'-4''	20'-6''	19'-3''	17'-2''
Mountain hemlock No. 2	2 x 6	9'-6''	9'-6''	8'-8''	7'-9''
	2 x 8	12'-3''	12'-6''	11'-6''	10'-3''
	2 x 10	15'-5''	15'-8''	14'-8''	13'-1''
	2 x 12	18'-7''	18'-9''	17'-9''	15'-11''
Southern pine KD No. 2	2 x 6	10'-6''	10'-8''	9'-9''	8'-8''
	2 x 8	13'-8''	13'-10''	12'-10''	11'-6''
	2 x 10	17'-2''	17'-4''	16'-4''	14'-8''
	2 x 12	20'-9''	20'-11''	19'-10''	17'-9''

John D. Bloodgood, Architects, P.C.; Des Moines, Iowa
American Plywood Association

PLYWOOD UNDERLAYMENT (1)

PLYWOOD GRADES AND SPECIES GROUP	APPLICATION (2)	MINIMUM PLYWOOD THICKNESS (IN.)
Groups 1, 2, 3, 4, 5 UNDERLAYMENT INT-APA (with interior or exterior glue), or UNDERLAYMENT EXT-APA (C-C plugged)	Over plywood sub-floor	$1/4$
	Over lumber sub-floor or other uneven surfaces	$3/8$
Same grades as above, but Group 1 only.	Over lumber floor up to 4 in. wide. Face grain must be perpendicular to boards	$1/4$

1. For floors to receive tile, carpeting, linoleum, or other nonstructural flooring.
2. Where floors may be subject to unusual moisture conditions, use panels with exterior glue or UNDERLAYMENT C-C Plugged, EXT-APA. C-D. Plugged is not an adequate substitute for underlayment grade, since it does not ensure equivalent dent resistance.
3. Recommended grades have a solid surface backed with a special inner ply construction that resists punch-through, dents, and concentrated loads.

NAILING SCHEDULE

Use 3d ring shank nails for underlayment up to $1/2$ in. thickness, 4d for $5/8$ in. and thicker. Use 16 gauge staples, except that 18 gauge may be used with $1/4$ in. thick underlayment. Crown width should be $3/8$ in. for 16 gauge staples, $3/16$ in. for 18 gauge. Length should be sufficient to penetrate subflooring at least $5/8$ in. or extend completely through. Space fasteners at 3 in. along panel edges and at 6 in. each way in the panel interior, except for $3/8$ in. or thicker underlayment applied with ring shank nails. In this case, use 6 in. spacing along edges and 8 in. spacing each way in the panel interior. Unless subfloor and joists are of thoroughly seasoned material and have remained dry during construction, countersink nail heads below surface of the underlayment just prior to laying finish floors to avoid nail popping.

NOTES

1. For complete information on glued floors, including joist span tables (based on building code criteria and lumber sizes), application sequence, and list of recommended adhesives and adhesive dispensing equipment, contact the American Plywood Association.
2. Place APA STURD-I-FLOOR T&G panels across the joists with end joints staggered. Leave $1/8$ in. space at all end and edge joints.
3. Although T&G is used most often, square edge may be used if 2 x 4 blocking is placed under panel edge joints between joists.

NAILING SCHEDULE

The panels should be secured with power driven fasteners or nailed with 6d deformed shank nails, spaced 12 in. at all supports. (8d common smooth nails may be substituted.)

STRUCTURAL-USE PANEL SUBFLOORING (1)

PANEL SPAN RATING	PANEL THICKNESS (IN.)	MAXIMUM SPACING (2, 3, 6) (IN.)
30/12	$5/8$	12 (4)
24/16	$7/16$	16
32/16	$1/2$, $5/8$	16 (5)
36/16	$3/4$	16 (5)
42/20	$5/8$, $3/4$, $7/8$	20 (5)
48/24	$3/4$, $7/8$	24
$1 1/8$'' groups (1, 2)	$1 1/8$	32 (2X joists)
$1 1/4$'' groups (3, 4)	$1 1/4$	48 (4X joists)

1. Applies to APA rated sheathing grades only.
2. The spans assume panel continuous over two or more spans with long dimension across supports.
3. In some nonresidential buildings special conditions may require construction in excess of minimums given.
4. May be 16 in. if $25/32$ in. wood strip flooring is installed at right angles to joists.
5. May be 24 in. if $25/32$ in. wood strip flooring is installed at right angles to joists.
6. Spans are limited to the values shown because of the possible effect of concentrated loads.

NAILING SCHEDULE

Use 6d common nails for $1/2$ in. panels, 8d for thicknesses from $5/8$ to $7/8$ in., and 10d for $1 1/8$ and $1 1/4$ in. thicknesses. Space nails at 6 in. along panel edges for all thicknesses. Along intermediate supports, space nails at 10 in.; when panel spans 48 in., however, space nails at 6 in. Nail at 6 in. on center along panel edges. Along intermediate supports space nails 6 in. apart for 48 in. span and 10 in. apart for 32 in. spans.

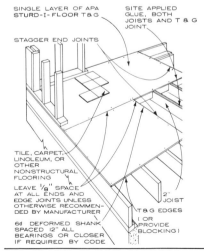

APA GLUED FLOOR SYSTEM

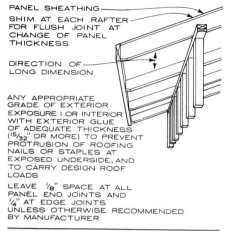

PANEL SHEATHING

SHIM AT EACH RAFTER FOR FLUSH JOINT AT CHANGE OF PANEL THICKNESS

DIRECTION OF LONG DIMENSION

ANY APPROPRIATE GRADE OF EXTERIOR EXPOSURE I OR INTERIOR WITH EXTERIOR GLUE OF ADEQUATE THICKNESS ($^{15}/_{32}$" OR MORE) TO PREVENT PROTRUSION OF ROOFING NAILS OR STAPLES AT EXPOSED UNDERSIDE, AND TO CARRY DESIGN ROOF LOADS

LEAVE $^1/_8$" SPACE AT ALL PANEL END JOINTS AND $^1/_4$" AT EDGE JOINTS UNLESS OTHERWISE RECOMMENDED BY MANUFACTURER

OPEN SOFFIT

PANEL SHEATHING

PROTECT EDGES OF EXPOSURE I AND 2 SHEATHING AGAINST EXPOSURE TO WEATHER

DIRECTION OF FACE GRAIN

CONTINUOUS SCREENED VENT OR EQUALLY SPACED LOUVERED VENTS

ANY APPROPRIATE GRADE OF EXTERIOR APA PLYWOOD FOR SOFFIT

CLOSED SOFFIT

LEAVE $^1/_8$" SPACE AT ALL PANEL END JOINTS AND $^1/_4$" SPACE AT ALL PANEL EDGE JOINTS UNLESS OTHERWISE RECOMMENDED BY MANUFACTURER

ASPHALT, ASBESTOS, OR WOOD SHINGLES. FOLLOW MANUFACTURER'S RECOMMENDATIONS FOR ROOFING FELT

PANEL SHEATHING

PROTECT EDGES OF EXPOSURE I AND 2 PANELS AGAINST EXPOSURE TO WEATHER, OR USE EXTERIOR PLYWOOD STARTER STRIP

EXTERIOR PLYWOOD SOFFIT

PANEL CLIP

GABLE ROOF

EXTERIOR EXPOSURE I OR INTERIOR WITH EXTERIOR GLUE PANELS AT OPEN SOFFIT

BUILT-UP ROOFING

PANEL EDGES SHOULD HAVE BLOCKING PANEL CLIPS OR TONGUE AND GROOVED

LEAVE $^1/_8$" SPACE AT ALL PANEL END JOINTS AND $^1/_4$" SPACE AT ALL PANEL EDGE JOINTS UNLESS OTHERWISE RECOMMENDED BY MANUFACTURER

PANEL SHEATHING

FLAT — LOW PITCHED ROOF

EXTERIOR OPEN SOFFITS/ COMBINED CEILING DECKING (1)

PANEL DESCRIPTIONS, MINIMUM RECOMMENDATIONS	GROUP	MAXIMUM SPAN (IN.)
$^{15}/_{32}$" APA 303 siding	1, 2, 3, 4	16
$^1/_2$" APA sanded	1, 2, 3, 4	
$^1/_2$" APA sanded	1, 2, 3	24
$^{19}/_{32}$" APA 303 siding	1, 2, 3, 4	
$^5/_8$" APA sanded	1, 2, 3, 4	
$^5/_8$" APA sanded	1	
$^{23}/_{32}$" APA 303 siding	1, 2, 3, 4	32 (2)
$^3/_4$" APA sanded	1, 2, 3, 4	
$1^1/_8$" APA textured	1, 2, 3, 4	48 (2)

NOTES

1. Plywood is assumed to be continuous across two or more spans with face grain across supports.
2. For spans of 32 or 48 in. in open soffit construction, provide adequate blocking, tongue-and-groove edges, or other support such as panel clips. Minimum loads are at least 40 psf live load, plus 5 psf dead load, except for $1^1/_8$ in. panels of Group 2, 3, or 4 species, which support 35 psf live load.

NAILING SCHEDULE: For open soffits, use 6d common smooth, ring shank, or spiral thread nails for $^1/_2$ in. or smaller thicknesses; use 8d nails for plywood $^5/_8$ to 1 in. thick. Use 8d ring shank or spiral thread or 10d common smooth shank nails for $1^1/_8$ in. textured panels. Space nails 6 in. at panel edges, 12 in. at intermediate supports, except for 48 in. spans where nails should be spaced 6 in. at all supports.

EXTERIOR CLOSED PLYWOOD SOFFITS

NOMINAL PLYWOOD THICKNESS	GROUP	MAXIMUM SPAN (IN.) ALL EDGES SUPPORTED
$^{11}/_{32}$" APA 303 siding or APA sanded		24
$^{15}/_{32}$" APA 303 siding or APA sanded	1, 2, 3, 4	32
$^{19}/_{32}$" APA 303 siding or APA sanded		48

NOTE: Plywood is assumed to be continuous across two or more spans with face grain across supports.

NAILING SCHEDULE: For closed soffits, use non-staining box or casing nails, 6d for $^5/_{16}$ and $^7/_{16}$ in. panels and 8d for $^5/_8$ in. panels. Space nails 6 in. at panel edges and 12 in. along intermediate supports.

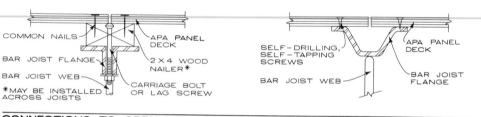

COMMON NAILS

APA PANEL DECK

BAR JOIST FLANGE

2 × 4 WOOD NAILER *

BAR JOIST WEB

*MAY BE INSTALLED ACROSS JOISTS

CARRIAGE BOLT OR LAG SCREW

SELF-DRILLING, SELF-TAPPING SCREWS

APA PANEL DECK

BAR JOIST WEB

BAR JOIST FLANGE

CONNECTIONS TO OPEN WEB STEEL JOISTS

APA PANEL ROOF DECKING (1)

PANEL SPAN RATING	PANEL THICKNESS (IN.)	MAXIMUM SPAN (IN.)		NAIL SIZE AND TYPE	NAIL SPACING (IN.)	
		WITH EDGE SUPPORT	WITHOUT EDGE SUPPORT		PANEL EDGES	INTERMEDIATE
12/0	$^5/_{16}$	12	12			
16/0	$^5/_{16}$ $^3/_8$	16	16			
20/0	$^5/_{16}$ $^3/_8$	20	20	6d common		
24/0	$^3/_8$ $^7/_{16}$ $^1/_2$	24	20			
24/16	$^7/_{16}$ $^1/_2$	24	24			
32/16	$^1/_2$	32	28		6	12
32/16	$^5/_8$	32	28			
42/20 (5)	$^5/_8$ $^3/_4$ $^7/_8$	42	32	8d common		
48/24 (5)	$^3/_4$ $^7/_8$	48	36		6	6

NOTES

1. Apply to APA rated panel sheathing.
2. All panels will support at least 40 psf live load plus 5 psf dead load at maximum span, except as noted. Uniform load deflection limit is $^1/_{180}$ span under live load plus dead load, or $^1/_{240}$ under live load only.
3. Special conditions may require construction in excess of the given minimums.
4. Panel is assumed to be continuous across two or more spans with long dimension across supports.
5. PS1 plywood panels with span ratings of 42/20 and 48/24 will support 35 psf live load plus 5 psf dead load at maximum span. For 40 psf live load, specify Structural 1.

NAILING SCHEDULE: Use 6d common smooth, ring shank, or spiral thread nails for plywood $^1/_2$ in. thick or thinner and 8d for plywood to 1 in. thick. Use 8d ring shank or spiral thread or 10d common smooth for 2-4-1, $1^1/_8$ and $1^1/_4$ in. panels. Space nails 6 in. at panel edges and 12 in. at intermediate supports, except for 48 in. or longer spans where nails should be spaced 6 in. at all supports.

John D. Bloodgood, Architects, P.C.; Des Moines, Iowa
American Plywood Association

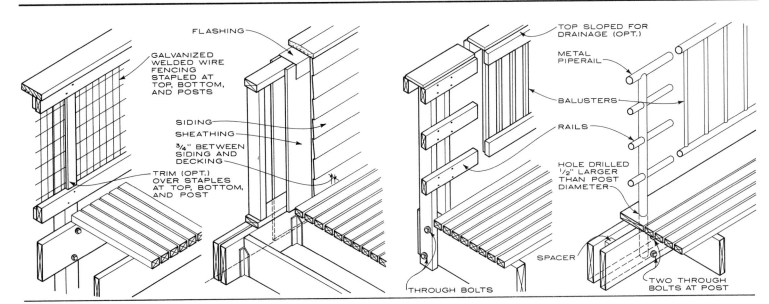

FLASHING
GALVANIZED WELDED WIRE FENCING STAPLED AT TOP, BOTTOM, AND POSTS
SIDING
SHEATHING
3/4" BETWEEN SIDING AND DECKING
TRIM (OPT.) OVER STAPLES AT TOP, BOTTOM, AND POST

TOP SLOPED FOR DRAINAGE (OPT.)
METAL PIPERAIL
BALUSTERS
RAILS
HOLE DRILLED 1/2" LARGER THAN POST DIAMETER
SPACER
TWO THROUGH BOLTS AT POST
THROUGH BOLTS

RAILINGS

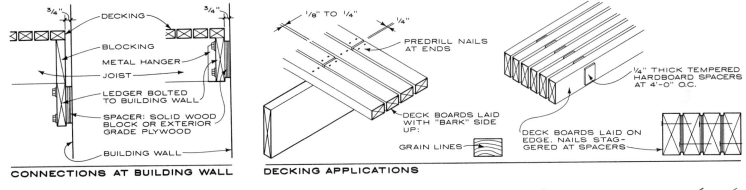

3/4"   DECKING   3/4"
BLOCKING
METAL HANGER
JOIST
LEDGER BOLTED TO BUILDING WALL
SPACER: SOLID WOOD BLOCK OR EXTERIOR GRADE PLYWOOD
BUILDING WALL

1/8" TO 1/4"   1/4"
PREDRILL NAILS AT ENDS
DECK BOARDS LAID WITH "BARK" SIDE UP:
GRAIN LINES
1/4" THICK TEMPERED HARDBOARD SPACERS AT 4'-0" O.C.
DECK BOARDS LAID ON EDGE, NAILS STAGGERED AT SPACERS

CONNECTIONS AT BUILDING WALL   **DECKING APPLICATIONS**

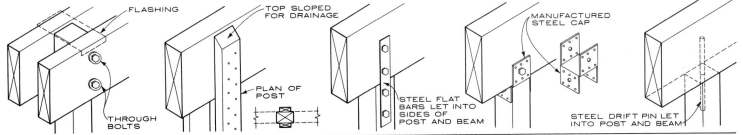

FLASHING
THROUGH BOLTS

TOP SLOPED FOR DRAINAGE
PLAN OF POST

STEEL FLAT BARS LET INTO SIDES OF POST AND BEAM

MANUFACTURED STEEL CAP

STEEL DRIFT PIN LET INTO POST AND BEAM

POST AND BEAM CONNECTIONS

RELATIVE COMPARISON OF VARIOUS QUALITIES OF WOOD USED IN DECK CONSTRUCTION

	DOUGLAS FIR—LARCH	SOUTHERN PINE	HEMLOCK FIR*	SOFT PINES†	WESTERN RED CEDAR	REDWOOD	SPRUCE	CYPRESS
Hardness	Fair	Fair	Poor	Poor	Poor	Fair	Poor	Fair
Warp resistance	Fair	Fair	Fair	Good	Good	Good	Fair	Fair
Ease of working	Poor	Fair	Fair	Good	Good	Fair	Fair	Fair
Paint holding	Poor	Poor	Poor	Good	Good	Good	Fair	Good
Stain acceptance†	Fair	Fair	Fair	Fair	Good	Good	Fair	Fair
Nail holding	Good	Good	Poor	Poor	Poor	Fair	Fair	Fair
Heartwood decay resistance	Fair	Fair	Poor	Poor	Good	Good	Poor	Good
Proportion of heartwood	Good	Poor	Poor	Fair	Good	Good	Poor	Good
Bending strength	Good	Good	Fair	Poor	Poor	Fair	Fair	Fair
Stiffness	Good	Good	Good	Poor	Poor	Fair	Fair	Fair
Strength as a post	Good	Good	Fair	Poor	Fair	Good	Fair	Fair
Freedom from pitch	Fair	Poor	Good	Fair	Good	Good	Good	Good

*Includes West Coast and eastern hemlocks.
†Includes western and northeastern pines.
‡Categories refer to semitransparent oil base stain.

The Bumgardner Partnership/Architects; Seattle, Washington

MAXIMUM SPAN OF DECK BOARDS

	FLAT		ON EDGE	
	1 x 4	2 x 2 (x3)(x4)	2 x 3	2 x 4
Douglas fir, larch, and southern pine	1'-4''	5'-0''	7'-6''	12'-0''
Hemlock-fir, Douglas-fir, southern	1'-2''	4'-0''	6'-6''	10'-0''
Western pines and cedars, redwoods, spruce	1'-0''	3'-6''	5'-6''	9'-0''

NOTE

Size and spacing of joists, posts, and beams may be selected according to other pages in chapter.

ROUGH CARPENTRY   6

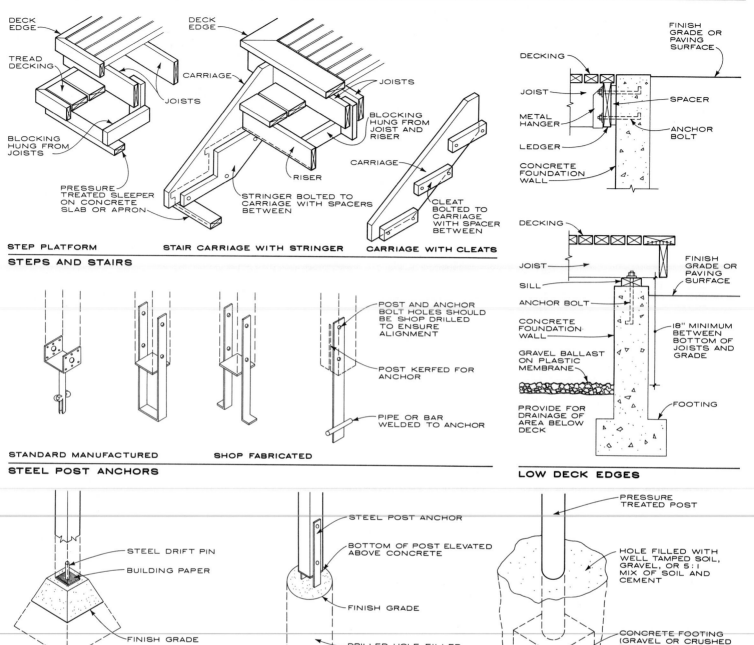

STEPS AND STAIRS

STEP PLATFORM   STAIR CARRIAGE WITH STRINGER   CARRIAGE WITH CLEATS

STEEL POST ANCHORS

STANDARD MANUFACTURED   SHOP FABRICATED

LOW DECK EDGES

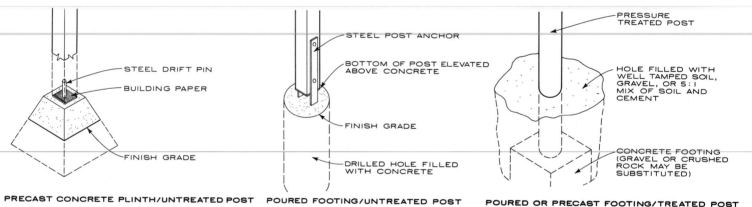

POSTS AND FOOTINGS

PRECAST CONCRETE PLINTH/UNTREATED POST   POURED FOOTING/UNTREATED POST   POURED OR PRECAST FOOTING/TREATED POST

FASTENERS

1. Smooth shank nails lose holding strength after repeated wet/dry cycles. Ring or spiral grooved shank nails are preferable.
2. Use galvanized or plated fasteners to avoid corrosion and staining.
3. To reduce board splitting by nailing: blunt nail points; predrill (3/4 of nail diameter); stagger nailing; place nails no closer to edge than one half of board thickness.
4. Avoid end grain nailing and toe nailing if possible.
5. Use flat washers under heads of lag screws and bolts, and under nuts.

MOISTURE PROTECTION

1. All wood members should be protected from weather by pressure treatment or field application of preservatives, stains, or paints.
2. All wood in direct contact with soil must be pressure treated.
3. Bottoms of posts on piers should be 6 in. above grade.
4. Sterilize or cover soil with membrane to keep plant growth away from wood members so as to minimize moisture exchange.
5. Treat all ends, cuts, holes, and so on with preservative prior to placement.
6. Decking and flat trim boards, 2 x 6 and wider, should be kerfed on the underside with 3/4 in. deep saw cuts at 1 in. on center to prevent cupping.
7. Avoid horizontal exposure of endgrain or provide adequate protection by flashing or sealing. Avoid or minimize joint situations where moisture may be trapped by using spacers and/or flashing, caulking, sealant, plastic roofing cement.

CONSTRUCTION

1. WOOD SELECTION: Usual requirements are good decay resistance, nonsplintering, fair stiffness, strength, hardness, and warp resistance. Selection varies according to local climate and exposure.
2. BRACING: On large decks, or decks where post heights exceed 5 ft, lateral stability should be achieved with horizontal bracing (metal or wood diagonal ties on top or bottom of joists, or diagonal application of decking) in combination with vertical bracing (rigid bolted or gusseted connections at top of posts, knee bracing, or "X" bracing between posts), and/or connection to a braced building wall. Lateral stability should be checked by a structural engineer.

The Bumgardner Partnership/Architects; Seattle, Washington

⑥   **ROUGH CARPENTRY**

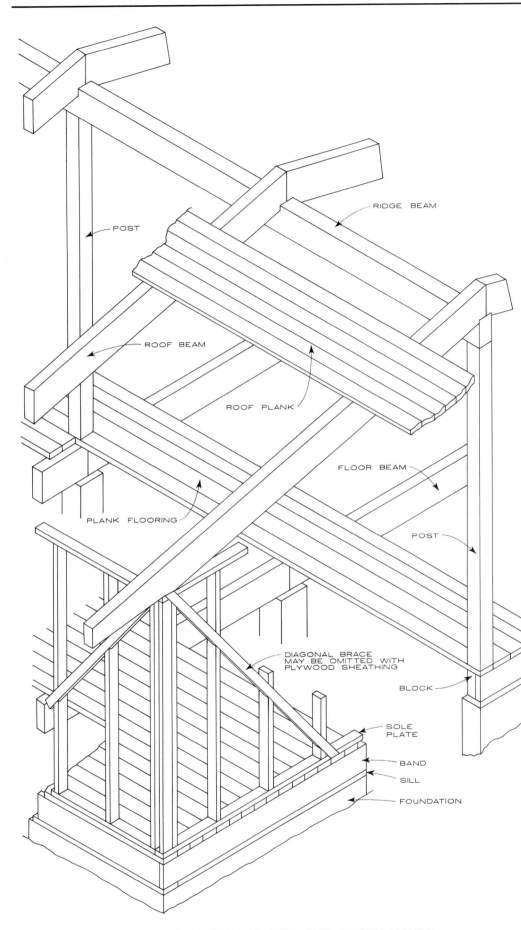

DESCRIPTION

Use of two inch nominal thickness plank for subfloors or roofs supported on beams spaced 6 to 8 feet apart.

PRINCIPLES OF DESIGN

Two inch plank used more efficiently when continuous over more than one span.

Uses standard lumber lengths such as 12, 14 and 16 feet with beams 6, 7 or 8 feet apart.

Design permitting, end joints between supports allows use of random lengths.

ADVANTAGES OF SYSTEM

Architectural effect provided by exposed plank and beam ceiling. Added effective height of ceiling at no increase in wall height.

Fewer members permits savings in labor.

Cross-bridging not required.

LIMITATIONS OF SYSTEM

Bearing partitions and heavy loads such as bathtubs, refrigerators etc., may require additional framing. Concealment must be provided for wiring, piping and duct work.

Insulation value of two inch deck may be adequate, but where additional insulation is required it may be attached below deck or as rigid insulation above deck under roofing.

CONSTRUCTION DETAILS AND FASTENING

Members of built-up beams should be securely spiked together from both outside faces. Spaced beams should be blocked at frequent intervals, and each member should be securely nailed to blocking. Where planks butt over a single member, a nominal beam width of three or more inches is necessary to provide a suitable bearing and nailing surface for the planks. Planks should be both blind and face-nailed to the beam. In this construction posts (rather than studs) carry the loads, which are concentrated and must be designed for conditions, but not smaller than 4 x 4 inches. Built-up posts should be spiked together.

When solid beams butt at a column, a nominal column dimension of 6 or more inches parallel to direction of beam is recommended to provide suitable bearing. Spike bearing blocks to column where necessary to increase bearing surface.

TYPICAL PLANK AND BEAM FRAMING FOR ONE STORY HOUSE

Joseph A. Wilkes, FAIA; Wilkes and Faulkner; Washington, D.C.

HEAVY TIMBER 6

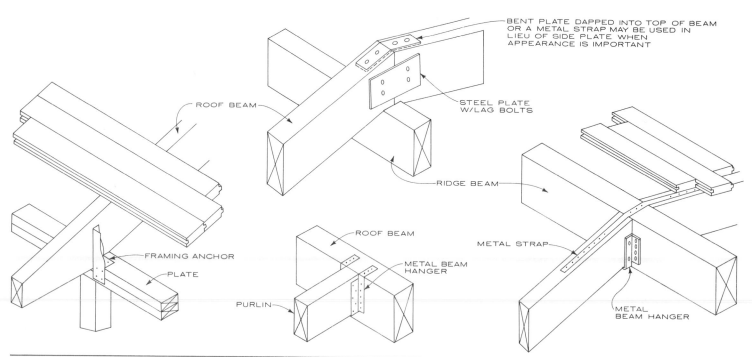

BENT PLATE DAPPED INTO TOP OF BEAM OR A METAL STRAP MAY BE USED IN LIEU OF SIDE PLATE WHEN APPEARANCE IS IMPORTANT

STEEL PLATE W/LAG BOLTS

ROOF BEAM

RIDGE BEAM

FRAMING ANCHOR

PLATE

ROOF BEAM

METAL BEAM HANGER

PURLIN

METAL STRAP

METAL BEAM HANGER

ROOF BEAM ANCHORAGE DETAILS

DESIGN TABLE FOR NOMINAL 2 IN. PLANK

REQUIRED VALUES FOR FIBER STRESS IN BENDING (f) AND MODULUS OF ELASTICITY (E) TO SUPPORT SAFELY A LIVE LOAD OF 20, 30, OR 40 LB/SQ FT WITHIN A DEFLECTION LIMITATION OF $\ell/240$, $\ell/300$, OR $\ell/360$.

SPAN (FT)	LIVE LOAD (PSF)	DEFLECTION LIMIT	TYPE A — SINGLE SPAN f (PSI)	E (PSI)	TYPE B — DOUBLE SPAN f (PSI)	E (PSI)	TYPE C — THREE SPAN f (PSI)	E (PSI)	TYPE D — COMBINATION SINGLE AND DOUBLE SPAN f (PSI)	E (PSI)	TYPE E — RANDOM LAYUP f (PSI)	E (PSI)
	20	$\ell/240$	360	576,000	360	239,000	288	305,000	360	408,000	360	442,000
		$\ell/300$	360	720,000	360	299,000	288	381,000	360	509,000	360	553,000
		$\ell/360$	360	864,000	360	359,000	288	457,000	360	611,000	360	664,000
6	30	$\ell/240$	480	864,000	480	359,000	384	457,000	480	611,000	480	664,000
		$\ell/300$	480	1,080,000	480	448,000	384	571,000	480	764,000	480	829,000
		$\ell/360$	480	1,296,000	480	538,000	384	685,000	480	917,000	480	995,000
	40	$\ell/240$	600	1,152,000	600	478,000	480	609,000	600	815,000	600	885,000
		$\ell/300$	600	1,440,000	600	598,000	480	762,000	600	1,019,000	600	1,106,000
		$\ell/360$	600	1,728,000	600	717,000	480	914,000	600	1,223,000	600	1,327,000
	20	$\ell/240$	490	915,000	490	380,000	392	484,000	490	647,000	490	702,000
		$\ell/300$	490	1,143,000	490	475,000	392	605,000	490	809,000	490	878,000
		$\ell/360$	490	1,372,000	490	570,000	392	726,000	490	971,000	490	1,054,000
7	30	$\ell/240$	653	1,372,000	653	570,000	522	726,000	653	971,000	653	1,054,000
		$\ell/300$	653	1,715,000	653	712,000	522	907,000	653	1,213,000	653	1,317,000
		$\ell/360$	653	2,058,000	653	854,000	522	1,088,000	653	1,456,000	653	1,581,000
	40	$\ell/240$	817	1,829,000	817	759,000	653	968,000	817	1,294,000	817	1,405,000
		$\ell/300$	817	1,187,000	817	949,000	653	1,209,000	817	1,618,000	817	1,756,000
		$\ell/360$	817	2,744,000	817	1,139,000	653	1,451,000	817	1,941,000	817	2,107,000
	20	$\ell/240$	640	1,365,000	640	567,000	512	722,000	640	966,000	640	1,049,000
		$\ell/300$	640	1,707,000	640	708,000	512	903,000	640	1,208,000	640	1,311,000
		$\ell/360$	640	2,048,000	640	850,000	512	1,083,000	640	1,449,000	640	1,573,000
8	30	$\ell/240$	853	2,048,000	853	850,000	682	1,083,000	853	1,449,000	853	1,573,000
		$\ell/300$	853	2,560,000	853	1,063,000	682	1,345,000	853	1,811,000	853	1,966,000
		$\ell/360$	853	3,072,000	853	1,275,000	682	1,625,000	853	2,174,000	853	2,359,000
	40	$\ell/240$	1,067	2,731,000	1,067	1,134,000	853	1,144,000	1,067	1,932,000	1,067	2,097,000
		$\ell/300$	1,067	3,413,000	1,067	1,417,000	853	1,805,000	1,067	2,145,000	1,067	2,621,000
		$\ell/360$	1,067	4,096,000	1,067	1,700,000	853	2,166,000	1,067	2,898,000	1,067	3,146,000

Ed Hesner; Rasmussen & Hobbs Architects, AIA; Takoma, Washington

6 **HEAVY TIMBER**

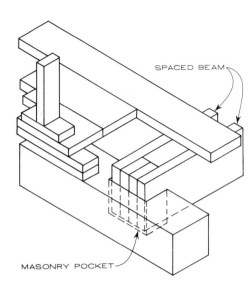

FIRST FLOOR FRAMING AT
EXTERIOR WALL BEAM SET IN
FOUNDATION

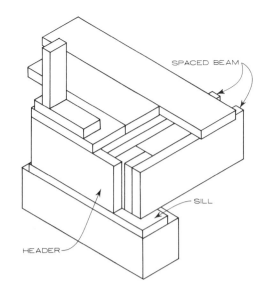

FIRST FLOOR FRAMING AT
EXTERIOR WALL BEAM BEARING
ON SILL

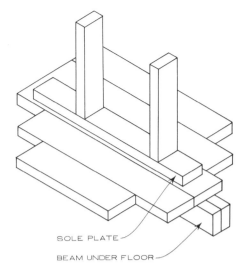

NON-BEARING PARTITION PAR-
ALLEL TO PLANK SUPPORTED BY
BEAM UNDER FLOOR

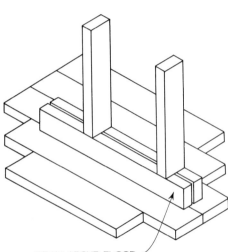

NON-BEARING PARTITION PARALLEL
TO PLANK SUPPORTED BY BEAM
ABOVE FLOOR

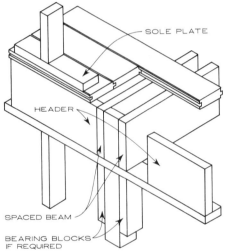

SPACED BEAM BEARING AT
EXTERIOR WALL

The details in this column are preferable from the
standpoint of equalizing shrinkage of horizontal
lumber partition supports.

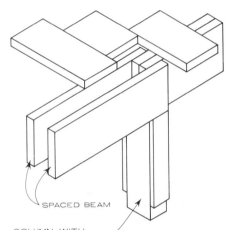

SPACED BEAM BEARING OVER
BASEMENT SUPPORT

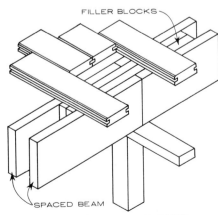

SPACED BEAM BEARING OVER
INTERIOR POST

Joseph A. Wilkes, FAIA; Wilkes and Faulkner, Washington, D.C.

SQUARE EDGE

TONGUE & GROOVE

GROOVED PLANK
WITH SPLINE

GROOVED PLANK
WITH EXPOSED
SPLINE

GROOVED PLANK
MOULDED SPLINE

RABBETED PLANK
BATTEN INSERT

JOINT TYPES IN EXPOSED PLANK
CEILINGS

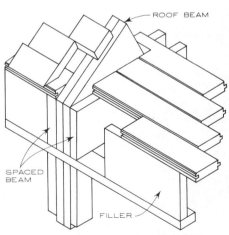

SOLID ROOF BEAM AND SPACED
FLOOR BEAM BEARING ON
EXTERIOR WALL

HEAVY TIMBER 6

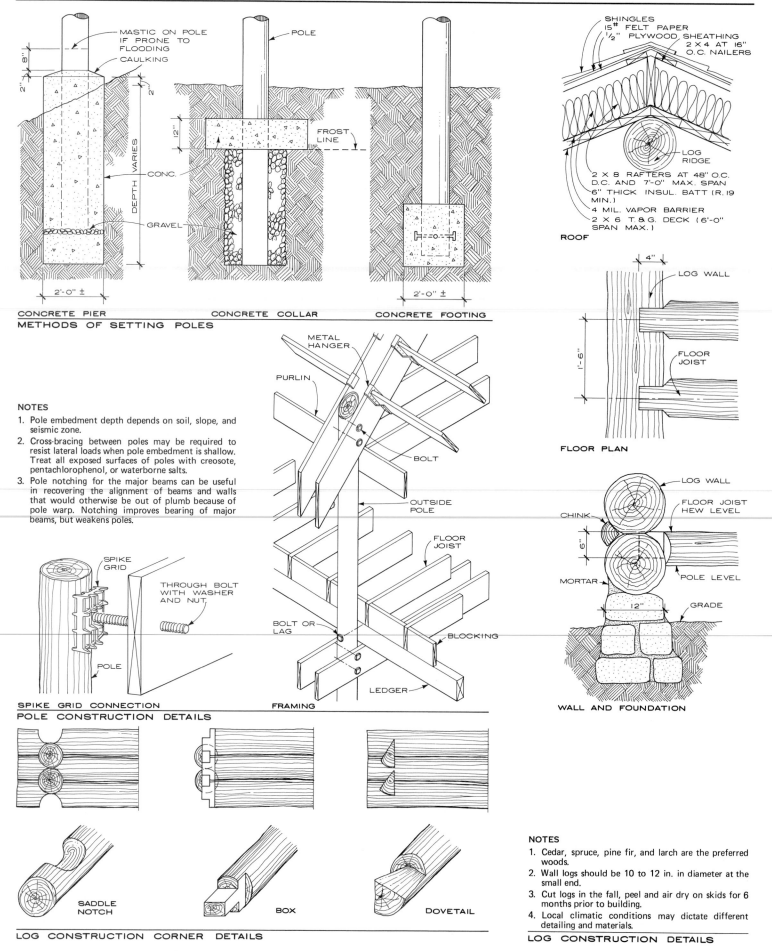

MASTIC ON POLE IF PRONE TO FLOODING

CAULKING

8"

2"

DEPTH VARIES

CONC.

GRAVEL

2'-0" ±

CONCRETE PIER

POLE

2"

12"

FROST LINE

CONC.

GRAVEL

CONCRETE COLLAR

POLE

2'-0" ±

CONCRETE FOOTING

METHODS OF SETTING POLES

SHINGLES
15# FELT PAPER
1/2" PLYWOOD SHEATHING
2 X 4 AT 16" O.C. NAILERS

LOG RIDGE

2 X 8 RAFTERS AT 48" O.C. D.C. AND 7'-0" MAX. SPAN
6" THICK INSUL. BATT (R.19 MIN.)
4 MIL. VAPOR BARRIER
2 X 6 T. & G. DECK (6'-0" SPAN MAX.)

ROOF

4"

LOG WALL

FLOOR JOIST

1'-6"

FLOOR PLAN

NOTES

1. Pole embedment depth depends on soil, slope, and seismic zone.
2. Cross-bracing between poles may be required to resist lateral loads when pole embedment is shallow. Treat all exposed surfaces of poles with creosote, pentachlorophenol, or waterborne salts.
3. Pole notching for the major beams can be useful in recovering the alignment of beams and walls that would otherwise be out of plumb because of pole warp. Notching improves bearing of major beams, but weakens poles.

METAL HANGER

PURLIN

BOLT

OUTSIDE POLE

FLOOR JOIST

BOLT OR LAG

BLOCKING

LEDGER

FRAMING

LOG WALL

FLOOR JOIST HEW LEVEL

CHINK

6"

POLE LEVEL

MORTAR

12"

GRADE

WALL AND FOUNDATION

SPIKE GRID

THROUGH BOLT WITH WASHER AND NUT.

POLE

SPIKE GRID CONNECTION

POLE CONSTRUCTION DETAILS

SADDLE NOTCH

BOX

DOVETAIL

LOG CONSTRUCTION CORNER DETAILS

NOTES

1. Cedar, spruce, pine fir, and larch are the preferred woods.
2. Wall logs should be 10 to 12 in. in diameter at the small end.
3. Cut logs in the fall, peel and air dry on skids for 6 months prior to building.
4. Local climatic conditions may dictate different detailing and materials.

LOG CONSTRUCTION DETAILS

Robert T. Gordon, Architect, and Dan Williams, Architect; Bruce Hawtin, AIA; Jackson, Wyoming

6 **HEAVY TIMBER**

BEAM HANGER

When supported members are seasoned material, the top of the supported member may be set flush with the top of the hanger strap.

When supported members are of unseasoned material, the hangers should be so dimensioned that the top edge of the supported member is raised above the top of the supporting member, or top of hanger strap to allow for shrinkage as the members season in place. For supported members with moisture content at or above fiber saturation when installed, the distance raised should be about 5% of the members depth above its bearing point.

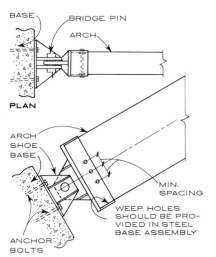

TRUE HINGE ANCHORAGE FOR ARCHES

Recommended for arches where true hinge action is desired

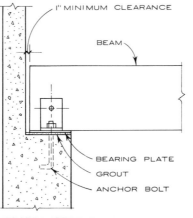

BEAM ANCHORAGE

This detail is intended for anchorages which are required to resist both uplift and horizontal forces. It may have one or more anchor bolts in masonry and one or more bolts with or without shear plates through the beam.

Provide minimum of one inch clearance or impervious moisture barrier on all wall contact surfaces, ends, sides and tops (if masonry exists above beam end).

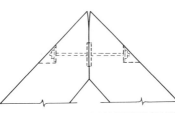

ARCH PEAK CONNECTIONS

This connection is intended for arches with a slope of 4:12 and greater, and will transfer both vertical forces (shear) and horizontal forces (tension and compression). It consists of two shear plates back to back and a through bolt or threaded rod with washers counterbored into the arch. To avoid local crushing of the peak tips of the arch due to dead load deflection, the tips are often beveled off as shown.

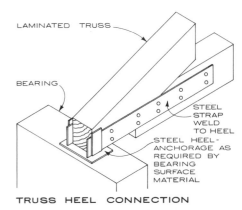

TRUSS HEEL CONNECTION

If substantial cross grain shrinkage is anticipated, double steel straps may be used in place of a single strap.

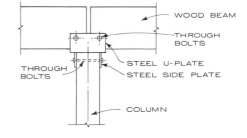

BEAM TO COLUMN CONNECTION

Steel U-plate passes under abutting beams and is welded to steel plates bolted to column. U-plate may also be welded directly to steel pipe column support where applicable.

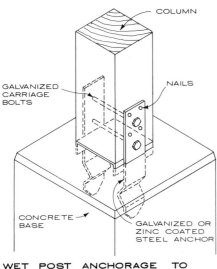

WET POST ANCHORAGE TO CONCRETE BASE

This detail is recommended for heavy duty use where moisture protection is desired. Anchor is set and leveled in wet concrete after screeding.

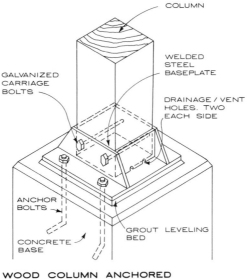

WOOD COLUMN ANCHORED WITH STEEL BASEPLATE

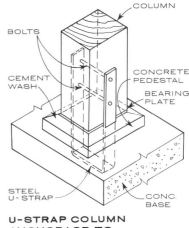

U-STRAP COLUMN ANCHORAGE TO CONCRETE BASE

This detail is recommended for industrial buildings and warehouses to resist both horizontal forces and uplift. Moisture barrier is recommended. It may be used with shear plates.

Douglas W. Brewer, AIA; Brown and Page Architects; Alexandria, Virginia

HEAVY TIMBER 6

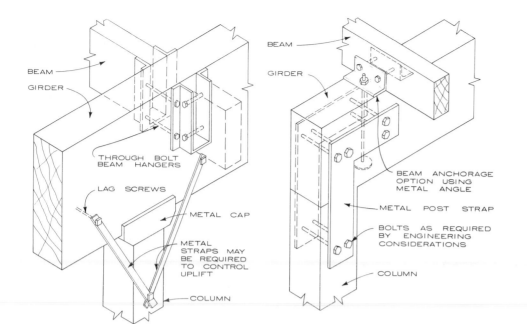

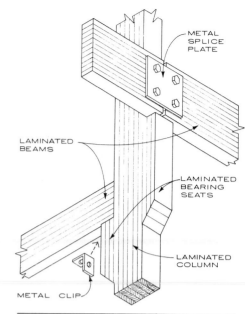

WOOD COLUMN, GIRDER, AND BEAM

GIRDER TO COLUMN CONNECTION

LAMINATED COLUMN WITH INTEGRALLY LAMINATED BEARING SEATS

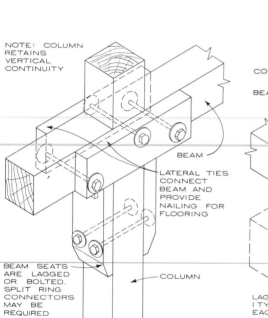

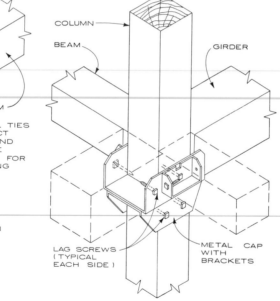

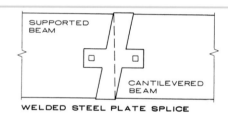

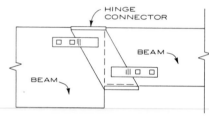

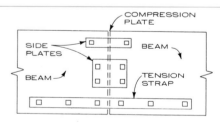

FLOOR BEAM FRAMING AT COLUMN

METAL COLUMN CAP WITH BEAM SEATS

HINGE CONNECTOR

WELDED STEEL PLATE SPLICE

MOMENT SPLICING

BEAM SPLICING

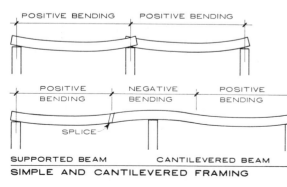

SIMPLE AND CANTILEVERED FRAMING

SIMPLE FRAMING: This illustration shows the "positive" or downward bending that occurs in conventional framing with simple spans.

CANTILEVERED FRAMING: This illustration shows the combination of "positive" (downward) and "negative" (upward) bending that occurs with beams spliced at quarterpoint producing supported beam and cantilevered beam. The two types of bending counterbalance each other, which produces more uniform stresses and uses material more efficiently. In-line joists simplify plywood subflooring.

MOMENT SPLICE: Compression stress is taken in bearing on the wood through a steel compression plate. Tension is taken across the splice by means of steel straps and sheer plates. Side plates and straps are used to hold sides and tops of members in position. Shear is taken by shear plates in end grain. Bolts and shear plates are used as design and construction considerations require.

Joseph A. Wilkes, FAIA; Wilkes and Faulkner; Washington, D.C.

STRUCTURAL GLUED LAMINATED TIMBER

The term "structural glued laminated timber" refers to an engineered, stress rated product of a timber laminating plant, comprising assemblies of suitably selected and prepared wood laminations securely bonded together with adhesives. The grain of all laminations is approximately parallel longitudinally. Laminations may be comprised of pieces end joined to form any length, of pieces placed or glued edge to edge to make wider ones, or of pieces bent to curved form during gluing.

STANDARD DEPTHS

Dimension lumber, surfaced to 1¹/₂ in. (38 mm), is normally used to laminate straight members and those curved members that have radii of curvature within the bending radius limitations for the species. Boards, surfaced to ³/₄ in. (19 mm), are recommended for laminating curved members when the bending radius is too short to permit the use of dimension lumber, provided that the bending radius limitations for the species are observed. Other lamination thicknesses may be used to meet special requirements.

STANDARD WIDTHS

Nominal width	in.	3	4	6	8	10	12	14	16
Net finished width	in.	2¹/₄	3¹/₈	5¹/₈	6³/₄	8³/₄	10³/₄	12¹/₄	14¹/₄
	mm	57	79	130	171	222	273	311	362

CAMBER

Camber is curvature (circular or parabolic) fabricated into structural glued laminated beams opposite to the anticipated deflection movement. The recommended minimum camber is on the order of one and one half times dead load deflection which, after plastic deformation has taken place, will usually produce a near level floor or roof beam under dead load conditions. Additional camber or slope should be provided to ensure proper drainage at roof beams. On level roof beams of long span and floor beams of multistory buildings it may be desirable to provide additional camber to counter the optical illusion that the beam sags.

FIRE SAFETY

The self-insulating qualities of heavy timber sizes create a slow burning characteristic. Good structural details, elimination of concealed spaces, and use of fire stops to interfere with passage of flames up or across a structure contribute to the fire performance of heavy timber construction in fire. While timber will burn, it retains its strength under fire longer than unprotected metals, which lose their strength quickly under extreme heat.

Building codes generally exempt heavy timber framing from interior finish requirements for preventing flame spread.

Fire retardant treatments may be applied to glued laminated timber but they do not substantially increase the fire resistance of heavy timber construction. When fire retardant treatments are used, the reduction of strength as related to type and penetration of treatment, the compatibility of treatment and adhesive, the use of special gluing procedures, difficulty of application, and the effect on wood color as well as on fabricating procedures should be investigated.

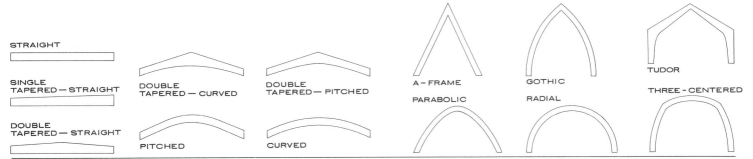

STRUCTURAL GLUED LAMINATED TIMBER SHAPES

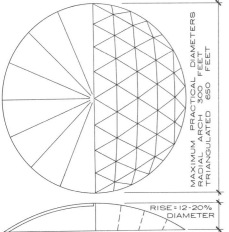

NOTES ON SHAPES

1. Beam names describe top and bottom surfaces of the beam. "S" designates a sawn or "tapered" surface. Sloped or "pitched" surfaces should be used on the tension side of the beam.
2. More complex shapes may be fabricated. Contact the American Institute of Timber Construction (AITC).

LAMINATED DOME SYSTEMS

The triangulated and the radial arch are the two basic types of structural glued laminated wood dome systems available. Both systems require a tension ring at the dome spring line to convert axial thrusts to vertical loads. Consideration must be given to the perimeter bond beam design since wind forces will produce loads in this member. The length of main members of the radial arch system, which must span a distance greater than half the dome diameter, limit the maximum practical dome diameter. The far smaller members of the triangulated dome result in the greater diameters. The triangulated system can be designed for five or more segments with an equal number of peripheral supports at each segment.

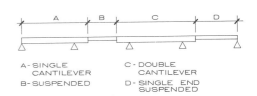

CANTILEVERED AND CONTINUOUS SPAN SYSTEMS

Cantilever beam systems may be comprised of any of the various types and combinations of beams shown above. Cantilever systems generally permit longer spans or larger loads per a given size member than do simple span systems. Substantial design economies can be effected by decreasing the depths of the members in the suspended portions of a cantilever system. For economy the negative bending moment at the support of a cantilevered beam should be equal in magnitude to the positive moment.

Continuous span beams are commonly used in both building and bridge construction to reduce maximum moments, thus reducing section size required.

ALLOWABLE UNIT STRESS RANGES FOR STRUCTURAL GLUED LAMINATED TIMBER—NORMAL DURATION OF LOADING

SPECIES	EXTREME FIBER IN BENDING, F_b (PSI)	TENSION PARALLEL TO GRAIN, F_t (PSI)	COMPRESSION PARALLEL TO GRAIN, F_c (PSI)	HORIZONTAL SHEAR F_v (PSI)	COMPRESSION PERPENDICULAR TO GRAIN, $F_{c\perp}$ (PSI)	MODULUS OF ELASTICITY, E (MILLION PSI)
DRY CONDITIONS OF USE = MOISTURE CONTENT IN SERVICE LESS THAN 16%						
Douglas fir and larch	1600 to 2600	900 to 1100	1500	165	385 to 450	1.6 to 1.8
Hem-fir	1800 to 2400	900	1250	155	245	1.6 to 1.7
Southern pine	1600 to 2600	800 to 1100	700 to 1500	140 to 200	385 to 450	1.5 to 1.8
California redwood	1600 to 2200	1100 to 1200	1600 to 2000	125	325	1.4
WET CONDITIONS OF USE = MOISTURE CONTENT IN SERVICE 16% OR MORE (REQUIRES WET USE ADHESIVES)						
Douglas fir and larch	1280 to 2080	720 to 880	1100	145	260 to 300	1.3 to 1.5
Hem-fir	1440 to 1920	720	910	135	165	1.3 to 1.4
Southern pine	1280 to 2080	640 to 880	510 to 1100	125 to 175	260 to 300	1.25 to 1.5
California redwood	1280 to 1760	880 to 960	1170 to 1460	110	220	1.2

The Hodne/Stageberg Partners, Inc.; Minneapolis, Minnesota

APPEARANCE GRADES

Structural glued laminated timber is produced in three appearance grades:

1. INDUSTRIAL: For use where appearance is not a primary concern.
2. ARCHITECTURAL: For use where appearance is a factor.
3. PREMIUM: For uses that demand the finest appearance.

These appearance grades do not modify design stresses, fabrication controls, grades of lumber used, or other provisions of the applicable standards. Descriptions of the three grades follow. A textured ("rough sawn") surface may be called for instead of the surfacing described. In all grades laminations will possess the natural growth characteristics of the lumber grade.

INDUSTRIAL APPEARANCE GRADE

Void filling is not required. The wide face of laminations exposed to view will be free of loose knots and open knot holes. Edge joints will not be filled. Members will be surfaced two sides only, an occasional miss being permitted along individual laminations.

ARCHITECTURAL APPEARANCE GRADE

In exposed surfaces, knot holes and other voids measuring over ¾ in. (19 mm) will be replaced with clear wood inserts or a neutral colored filler. Inserts will be selected with reasonable care for similarity of the grain and color to the adjacent wood in the lamination. The wide face of laminations exposed to view will be free of loose knots and open knot holes. The material will be selected with reasonable care for similarity of the grain and color of laminations at end and edge joints. Voids greater than ¹⁄₁₆ in. (2 mm) wide in edge joints appearing on the wide face of laminations exposed to view will be filled. When an opaque finish is specified, requirements for similarity of grain and color will be disregarded, exposed faces will be surfaced smooth. Misses are not permitted. The corners on the wide face of laminations exposed to view will be eased. Current practice for eased edges is for a radius between ⅛ in. (3 mm) and ½ in. (13 mm).

PREMIUM APPEARANCE GRADE

Similar to Architectural Grade except that in exposed surfaces, all knot holes and other voids will be replaced with wood inserts or a neutral colored filler as described for Architectural Grade. In addition, knots will be limited in size to 20% of the net face width of the lamination, with not over two maximum size knots occurring in a 6 ft (1.8 m) length of the exposed wide face of the laminations.

FINISHES

Available finishes for glued laminated timber include sealers, stains and paints.

End sealers retard moisture transmission and minimize checking and are normally applied to the ends of all members.

Surface sealers increase resistance to soiling, control grain raising, minimize checking, and serve as a moisture retardant. They fall within two classifications. Penetrating sealers provide limited protection and are suitable for use when final finish requires staining or a natural finish. Primer and sealer coats provide maximum protection by sealing the surface of the wood, but should not be specified when the final finish requires a natural or stained finish. Wood color is modified by any sealer application. Wood sealers followed by staining will look different from stained untreated wood.

GLUED LAMINATED COLUMNS

Structural glued laminated timber columns offer higher allowable stresses, controlled appearance, and the ability to fabricate variable sections.

For simple rectangular columns, the "slenderness ratio," or the ratio of the unsupported length between points of lateral support to the least column dimension, may not exceed 50.

The least dimension for tapered columns is taken as the sum of the smaller dimension and one-third the difference between the smaller and greater dimensions.

Spaced columns consist of two or more members with their longitudinal axes parallel, separated at the ends and at the midpoint by blocking, and joined at the ends by shear fastenings. The members are considered to act together to carry the total column load, and because of the end fixity developed, a greater slenderness ratio than that allowed for solid columns is permitted.

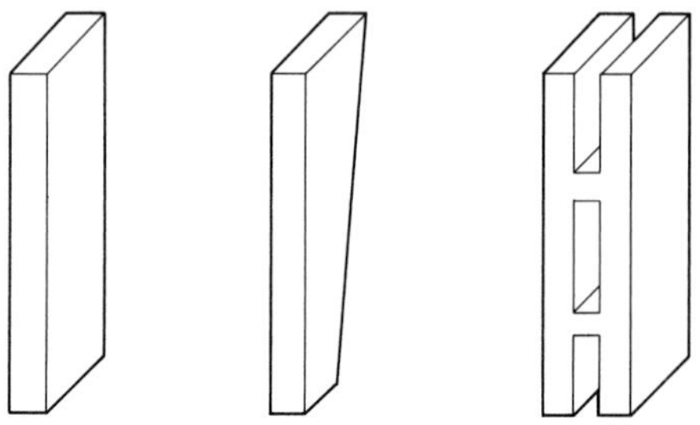

NOTES ON BEAM DESIGN CHART

1. Total load carrying capacity includes beam weight. Floor beams are designed for uniform loads of 40 psf live load and 10 psf dead load.
2. Allowable stresses: F_b = 2400 psi (reduced by size factor), F_v = 165 psi, E = 1,800,000 psi.
3. Deflection limits = roof = ¹⁄₁₈₀, floor = ¹⁄₃₆₀.
4. Values are for preliminary design purposes only. For more complete information see the AITC "Timber Construction Manual."

RECTANGULAR   TAPERED   SPACED

LAMINATED FLOOR, ROOF BEAM, AND PURLIN DESIGN CHART—
TYPICAL SINGLE SPAN SIMPLY SUPPORTED GLUED LAMINATED BEAMS (MEMBER SIZES IN INCHES)

SPAN (FT)	SPACING (FT)	TOTAL LOAD CARRYING CAPACITY (PSF)						FLOOR BEAMS 50 PSF
		30 PSF	35 PSF	40 PSF	45 PSF	50 PSF	55 PSF	
12	6	3⅛ x 6	3⅛ x 6	3⅛ x 7½	3⅛ x 7½	3⅛ x 7½	3⅛ x 7½	3⅛ x 9
	8	3⅛ x 6	3⅛ x 7½	3⅛ x 9	3⅛ x 9	3⅛ x 9	3⅛ x 9	3⅛ x 10½
	10	3⅛ x 7½	3⅛ x 7½	3⅛ x 9	3⅛ x 9	3⅛ x 9	3⅛ x 10½	3⅛ x 10½
	12	3⅛ x 7½	3⅛ x 9	3⅛ x 9	3⅛ x 9	3⅛ x 10½	3⅛ x 10½	3⅛ x 12
16	8	3⅛ x 9	3⅛ x 9	3⅛ x 10½	3⅛ x 10½	3⅛ x 12	3⅛ x 12	3⅛ x 13½
	12	3⅛ x 10½	3⅛ x 12	3⅛ x 12	3⅛ x 12	3⅛ x 13½	3⅛ x 13½	3⅛ x 15
	14	3⅛ x 12	3⅛ x 12	3⅛ x 13½	3⅛ x 13½	3⅛ x 15	3⅛ x 15	3⅛ x 15
	16	3⅛ x 12	3⅛ x 13½	3⅛ x 13½	3⅛ x 15	3⅛ x 15	3⅛ x 16½	3⅛ x 15
20	8	3⅛ x 12	3⅛ x 12	3⅛ x 13½	3⅛ x 13½	3⅛ x 13½	3⅛ x 15	3⅛ x 16½
	12	3⅛ x 13½	3⅛ x 13½	3⅛ x 15	3⅛ x 16½	3⅛ x 16½	5⅛ x 13½	5⅛ x 15
	16	3⅛ x 15	3⅛ x 16½	3⅛ x 18	3⅛ x 18	5⅛ x 15	5⅛ x 16½	5⅛ x 18
	20	3⅛ x 16	3⅛ x 18	5⅛ x 15	5⅛ x 16½	5⅛ x 16½	5⅛ x 18	5⅛ x 18
24	8	3⅛ x 13½	3⅛ x 15	3⅛ x 15	3⅛ x 16½	5⅛ x 16½	3⅛ x 18	5⅛ x 19½
	12	3⅛ x 16½	3⅛ x 16½	3⅛ x 18	5⅛ x 15	5⅛ x 16½	5⅛ x 16½	5⅛ x 21
	16	3⅛ x 18	5⅛ x 16½	5⅛ x 16½	5⅛ x 18	5⅛ x 18	5⅛ x 19½	5⅛ x 24
	20	5⅛ x 16½	5⅛ x 16½	5⅛ x 18	5⅛ x 19½	5⅛ x 19½	5⅛ x 21	5⅛ x 25½
28	8	3⅛ x 16½	3⅛ x 16½	3⅛ x 18	3⅛ x 18	5⅛ x 16½	5⅛ x 16½	5⅛ x 19½
	12	3⅛ x 18	5⅛ x 16½	5⅛ x 18	5⅛ x 18	5⅛ x 18	5⅛ x 19½	5⅛ x 21
	16	5⅛ x 18	5⅛ x 18	5⅛ x 19½	5⅛ x 19½	5⅛ x 21	5⅛ x 22½	5⅛ x 24
	20	5⅛ x 18	5⅛ x 19½	5⅛ x 21	5⅛ x 22½	5⅛ x 24	5⅛ x 25½	5⅛ x 25½
32	8	3⅛ x 18	5⅛ x 16½	5⅛ x 18	5⅛ x 18	5⅛ x 18	5⅛ x 19½	5⅛ x 21
	12	5⅛ x 18	5⅛ x 19½	5⅛ x 19½	5⅛ x 21	5⅛ x 21	5⅛ x 22½	5⅛ x 24
	16	5⅛ x 19½	5⅛ x 21	5⅛ x 22½	5⅛ x 22½	5⅛ x 24	5⅛ x 25½	5⅛ x 24
	20	5⅛ x 21	5⅛ x 22½	5⅛ x 24	5⅛ x 25½	5⅛ x 27	5⅛ x 28½	6¾ x 27
40	12	5⅛ x 22½	5⅛ x 24	5⅛ x 24	5⅛ x 25½	5⅛ x 27	6¾ x 25½	6¾ x 28½
	16	5⅛ x 24	5⅛ x 25½	5⅛ x 27	5⅛ x 28½	6¾ x 27	6¾ x 28½	6¾ x 31½
	20	5⅛ x 27	5⅛ x 28½	6¾ x 27	6¾ x 28½	6¾ x 30	6¾ x 31½	6¾ x 33
	24	5⅛ x 28½	6¾ x 27	6¾ x 28½	6¾ x 31½	6¾ x 33	6¾ x 34½	6¾ x 36
48	12	5⅛ x 27	5⅛ x 28½	5⅛ x 30	5⅛ x 30	6¾ x 28½	6¾ x 30	6¾ x 33
	16	5⅛ x 30	6¾ x 28½	6¾ x 30	6¾ x 30	6¾ x 31½	6¾ x 34½	6¾ x 37½
	20	6¾ x 28½	6¾ x 30	6¾ x 31½	6¾ x 34½	6¾ x 36	6¾ x 37½	8¾ x 36
	24	6¾ x 30	6¾ x 33	6¾ x 34½	6¾ x 37½	6¾ x 39	8¾ x 36	8¾ x 39
60	12	6¾ x 30	6¾ x 31½	6¾ x 33	6¾ x 34½	6¾ x 36	6¾ x 37½	8¾ x 39
	16	6¾ x 33	6¾ x 34½	6¾ x 36	6¾ x 39	8¾ x 36	8¾ x 37½	8¾ x 42
	20	6¾ x 36	6¾ x 37½	8¾ x 36	8¾ x 37½	8¾ x 40½	8¾ x 42	8¾ x 45
	24	6¾ x 39	8¾ x 36	8¾ x 39	8¾ x 42	8¾ x 43½	8¾ x 45	8¾ x 48

The Hodne/Stageberg Partners, Inc.; Minneapolis, Minnesota

PATTERNED

EXTRA THICK

DOUBLE T & G

GLUE LAMINATED

SINGLE T & G

SPLINE

PATTERNED

MACHINE SHAPED

GLUE LAMINATED SIZES

THICKNESS		WIDTH	
NOMINAL	ACTUAL	NOMINAL	ACTUAL
3″	2 3/16″, 2 1/4″	6″ and 8″ are standard	5 3/8″, 7 1/8″
3″ super	2 7/8″		
5″	2 21/32″		
	1 7/8″	6″, 8″	5 3/8″, 7 1/8″
	2 1/4″	8″	7 1/8″
	3″		
	3 3/4″	6″, 8″	5 3/8″, 7 1/8″
	4 1/4″	6″	5 3/8″

NOTE: Verify sizes with manufacturers.

MACHINE SHAPED SIZES

THICKNESS		WIDTH	
NOMINAL	ACTUAL	NOMINAL	ACTUAL
2″	1 1/2″	6″ std (others available)	5 1/4″
3″	2 1/2″		
4″	3 1/2″		

NOTES

General availability is decreasing. Check source for the sizes and quantities available in desired species.

WEIGHT AND INSULATION FACTORS (U FACTOR IN BTU/HR · SQ FT · °F)

SPECIES	NOMINAL THICKNESS	WEIGHT (PSF)	U VALUE
Inland red cedar	3″	4.5	0.24
	3″ thick	5.8	0.20
	5″	7.5	0.15
White fir Idaho white pine	3″	5.0	0.27
	3″ thick	7.3	0.22
	5″	9.5	0.17
Southern yellow pine Douglas fir Larch	3″	6.5	0.30
	3″ thick	8.1	0.25
	5″	10.5	0.20

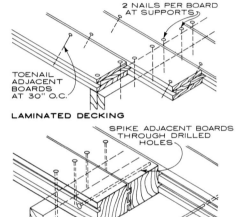

2 NAILS PER BOARD AT SUPPORTS

TOENAIL ADJACENT BOARDS AT 30″ O.C.

LAMINATED DECKING

SPIKE ADJACENT BOARDS THROUGH DRILLED HOLES

SOLID DECKING

FASTENING

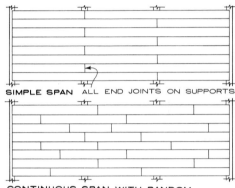

SIMPLE SPAN — ALL END JOINTS ON SUPPORTS

CONTINUOUS SPAN WITH RANDOM LENGTHS

NOTES

Use of random lengths reduces waste. The deck must be continuous over at least three spans (four supports). End joint requirements are critical; consult deck manufacturers.

LAMINATED DECK—ALLOWABLE UNIFORMLY DISTRIBUTED TOTAL LOADS GOVERNED BY DEFLECTION

DECK THICKNESS NOMINAL	ACTUAL	SPAN (FT)	INLAND RED CEDAR E=1.2 (INLAND RED CEDAR FACE AND BACK) F=1590 SIMPLE SPAN 1/180	1/240	1/360	CONTINUOUS SPAN WITH RANDOM LENGTHS 1/180	1/240	1/360	INLAND RED CEDAR E=1.3 (IDAHO WHITE PINE OR WHITE FIR BACK) F=1590 SIMPLE SPAN 1/180	1/240	1/360	CONTINUOUS SPAN WITH RANDOM LENGTHS 1/180	1/240	1/360	IDAHO WHITE PINE E=1.2 INLAND WHITE FIR E=1.2 F=1850 SIMPLE SPAN 1/180	1/240	1/360	CONTINUOUS SPAN WITH RANDOM LENGTHS 1/180	1/240	1/360	DOUGLAS FIR/LARCH E=1.8 SOUTHERN PINE E=1.8 F=2640 SIMPLE SPAN 1/180	1/240	1/360	CONTINUOUS SPAN WITH RANDOM LENGTHS 1/180	1/240	1/360
			PSF	PSF	PSF	PSF	PSF	PSF	PSF	PSF	PSF	PSF	PSF	PSF	PSF	PSF	PSF	PSF	PSF	PSF	PSF	PSF	PSF	PSF
3″ 2 3/16″	2 1/4″	8	71	53	35	121	91	60	76	57	38	129	98	64	89	67	44	150	113	75	115	86	57	195	146	97
		9	50	38	25	85	64	42	54	41	27	92	69	46	63	47	31	106	79	53	81	61	40	137	103	68
		10	37	27	18	62	46	31	40	29	20	67	49	33	46	34	23	77	58	38	59	44	29	100	75	50
		11	27	21	13	46	35	23	29	22	14	49	37	24	34	26	17	58	44	29	44	33	22	75	56	37
		12	21	16	10	36	27	18	22	17	11	39	29	19	26	20	13	45	34	22	34	26	17	58	43	29
		13	17	12	8	28	21	14	18	13	9	30	22	15	21	16	10	35	26	17	27	20	13	45	34	22
3″ 2 7/8″	2 7/8″	13	39	29	19	65	49	32	43	33	21	73	54	36	48	36	24	82	61	41	58	43	29	98	73	49
		14	31	23	15	52	39	26	34	26	17	58	44	29	39	29	19	65	49	32	47	34	23	78	59	39
		15	25	18	12	42	32	21	28	20	14	48	35	24	32	24	16	53	40	26	38	28	19	63	48	31
		16	20	16	10	35	26	17	23	18	11	39	29	19	26	19	13	44	33	22	31	23	15	53	40	26
		17	17	13	8	29	22	14	20	14	10	33	24	16	21	16	10	37	28	18	26	19	13	44	33	22
5″ 3 21/32″	3 21/32″	16	42	32	21	71	53	35	46	34	23	77	58	38	53	39	26	89	67	44	63	47	31	107	80	53
		17	35	26	17	59	45	29	38	29	19	64	48	32	44	33	22	74	56	37	53	40	26	89	67	44
		18	30	22	15	50	38	25	32	24	16	54	41	27	37	28	18	63	47	31	44	33	22	75	56	37
		19	25	19	12	43	32	21	27	20	13	46	35	23	31	24	15	53	40	26	38	28	19	64	48	32
		20	22	16	11	37	27	18	23	18	11	40	30	20	27	20	13	46	34	23	32	24	16	55	41	27
		21	19	14	9	32	24	16	20	15	10	34	26	17	23	17	11	39	30	19	28	21	14	47	35	23

NOTES

1. Tabulated loads derived from data provided by the Potlatch Corporation.

2. Numerous other deck thicknesses and wood species are available.

3. Actual deck design should be based on manufacturers' specifications for each deck board type.

Darrel Rippeteau, Architect; Washington, D.C.

FINISH CARPENTRY 6

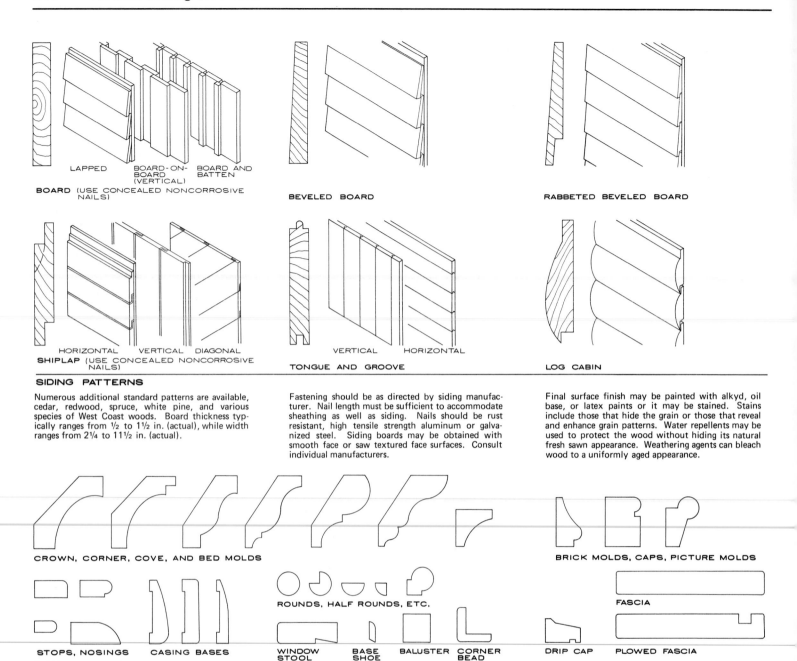

LAPPED   BOARD-ON-BOARD (VERTICAL)   BOARD AND BATTEN

BOARD (USE CONCEALED NONCORROSIVE NAILS)

BEVELED BOARD

RABBETED BEVELED BOARD

HORIZONTAL   VERTICAL   DIAGONAL

SHIPLAP (USE CONCEALED NONCORROSIVE NAILS)

VERTICAL   HORIZONTAL

TONGUE AND GROOVE

LOG CABIN

SIDING PATTERNS

Numerous additional standard patterns are available, cedar, redwood, spruce, white pine, and various species of West Coast woods. Board thickness typically ranges from 1/2 to 1 1/2 in. (actual), while width ranges from 2 1/4 to 11 1/2 in. (actual).

Fastening should be as directed by siding manufacturer. Nail length must be sufficient to accommodate sheathing as well as siding. Nails should be rust resistant, high tensile strength aluminum or galvanized steel. Siding boards may be obtained with smooth face or saw textured face surfaces. Consult individual manufacturers.

Final surface finish may be painted with alkyd, oil base, or latex paints or it may be stained. Stains include those that hide the grain or those that reveal and enhance grain patterns. Water repellents may be used to protect the wood without hiding its natural fresh sawn appearance. Weathering agents can bleach wood to a uniformly aged appearance.

CROWN, CORNER, COVE, AND BED MOLDS

BRICK MOLDS, CAPS, PICTURE MOLDS

ROUNDS, HALF ROUNDS, ETC.

FASCIA

STOPS, NOSINGS   CASING BASES

WINDOW STOOL   BASE SHOE   BALUSTER   CORNER BEAD

DRIP CAP   PLOWED FASCIA

MOLDING AND TRIM

Numerous patterns and dimensions of trim are produced in a variety of hard and soft woods for interior and exterior use. For a complete line of patterns, sizes, and wood species available, contact lumber associations active in area of use.

Material thickness and panel patterns are major cost factors. Patterns shown here represent only a few of the many shapes available. One pattern is often available in a choice of dimensions.

Custom designs can be economically manufactured if designed with thought to minimum handling, simple cutting, and use of standard finish sizes.

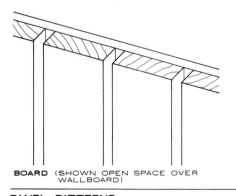

BOARD (SHOWN OPEN SPACE OVER WALLBOARD)

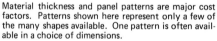

V-JOINTED TONGUE AND GROOVE

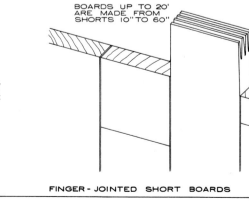

BOARDS UP TO 20' ARE MADE FROM SHORTS 10" TO 60"

FINGER-JOINTED SHORT BOARDS

PANEL PATTERNS

Darrel Rippeteau, Architect; Washington, D.C.

6   **FINISH CARPENTRY**

GENERAL NOTES

1. Height of handrail 2 ft 6 in. to 2 ft 10 in. Height of railing at landings 3 ft to 3 ft 6 in.
2. Extensions of handrails at top and bottom of stairs may effect total length of required run. Verify with local code.
3. Stringer (10 to 12 in. wide, $^5/_4$ to $^6/_4$ in. thick) to be accurately cut to receive risers, treads, and wedges. Wedges to be glued and driven up tight.
4. Block riser and tread between stringers as shown. Blocks to be glued and screwed in place. Omit blocks when center carriage is used.
5. Stair width: 36 in. minimum. (See local code requirements.)
6. No more than 9 ft vertical between landings.
7. Rise not to exceed 7½ in. and run not to be less than 10 in.
8. See other pages for handicapped requirements.
9. Construction details on this page are for a shop built stair reflecting Architectural Woodwork Institute Premium Grade standards.

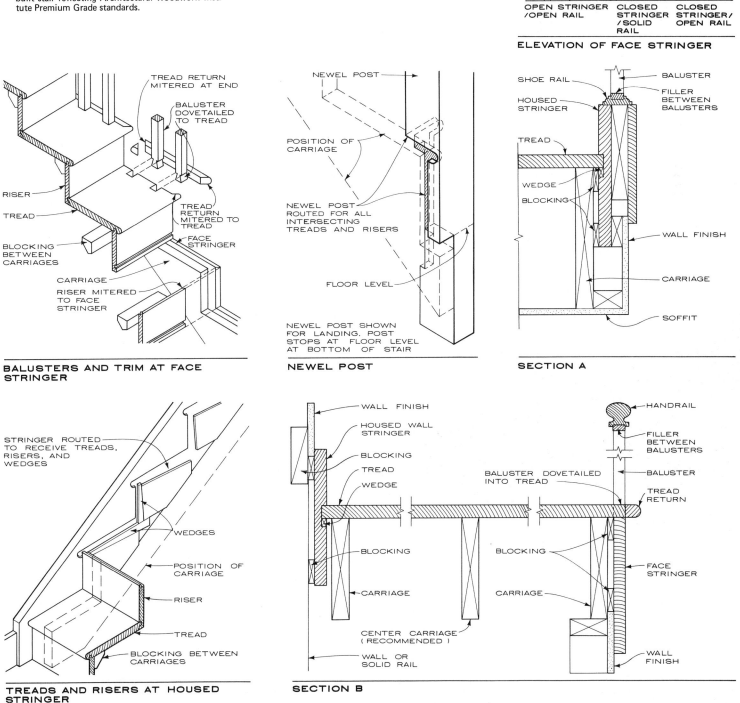

ELEVATION OF FACE STRINGER

BALUSTERS AND TRIM AT FACE STRINGER

NEWEL POST

SECTION A

TREADS AND RISERS AT HOUSED STRINGER

SECTION B

The Bumgardner Partnership/Architects; Seattle, Washington

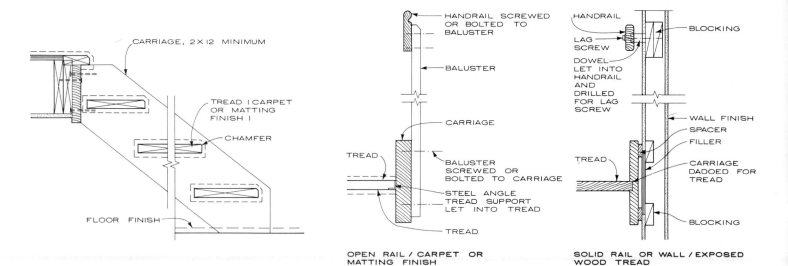

CARRIAGE, 2×12 MINIMUM

TREAD (CARPET OR MATTING FINISH)

CHAMFER

FLOOR FINISH

OPEN RISER STAIR

HANDRAIL SCREWED OR BOLTED TO BALUSTER

BALUSTER

CARRIAGE

BALUSTER SCREWED OR BOLTED TO CARRIAGE

TREAD

STEEL ANGLE TREAD SUPPORT LET INTO TREAD

TREAD

OPEN RAIL / CARPET OR MATTING FINISH

HANDRAIL

LAG SCREW

DOWEL LET INTO HANDRAIL AND DRILLED FOR LAG SCREW

BLOCKING

WALL FINISH

SPACER

FILLER

CARRIAGE DADOED FOR TREAD

TREAD

BLOCKING

SOLID RAIL OR WALL / EXPOSED WOOD TREAD

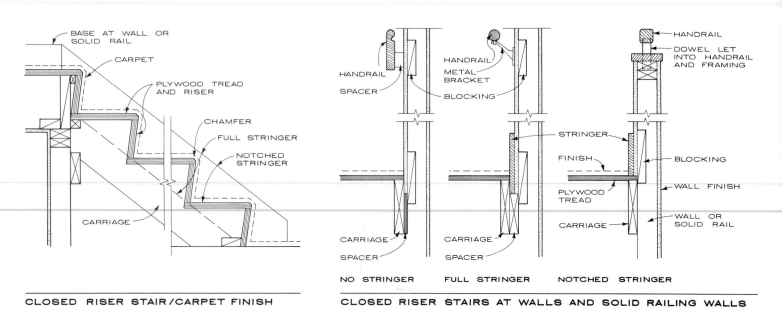

BASE AT WALL OR SOLID RAIL

CARPET

PLYWOOD TREAD AND RISER

CHAMFER

FULL STRINGER

NOTCHED STRINGER

CARRIAGE

CLOSED RISER STAIR / CARPET FINISH

HANDRAIL SPACER

HANDRAIL METAL BRACKET

BLOCKING

HANDRAIL

DOWEL LET INTO HANDRAIL AND FRAMING

STRINGER

FINISH

PLYWOOD TREAD

CARRIAGE

BLOCKING

WALL FINISH

WALL OR SOLID RAIL

CARRIAGE

SPACER

CARRIAGE

SPACER

NO STRINGER   FULL STRINGER   NOTCHED STRINGER

CLOSED RISER STAIRS AT WALLS AND SOLID RAILING WALLS

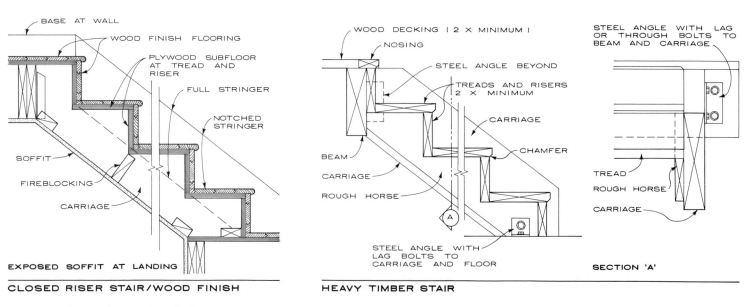

BASE AT WALL

WOOD FINISH FLOORING

PLYWOOD SUBFLOOR AT TREAD AND RISER

FULL STRINGER

NOTCHED STRINGER

SOFFIT

FIREBLOCKING

CARRIAGE

EXPOSED SOFFIT AT LANDING

CLOSED RISER STAIR / WOOD FINISH

WOOD DECKING (2 × MINIMUM)

NOSING

STEEL ANGLE BEYOND

TREADS AND RISERS 2 × MINIMUM

CARRIAGE

CHAMFER

BEAM

CARRIAGE

ROUGH HORSE

STEEL ANGLE WITH LAG BOLTS TO CARRIAGE AND FLOOR

HEAVY TIMBER STAIR

STEEL ANGLE WITH LAG OR THROUGH BOLTS TO BEAM AND CARRIAGE

TREAD

ROUGH HORSE

CARRIAGE

SECTION 'A'

The Bumgardner Partnership/Architects; Seattle, Washington

6 **FINISH CARPENTRY**

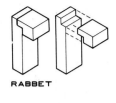
RABBET

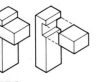
DADO

DADO & RABBET

DADO, TONGUE & RABBET

STOPPED DADO

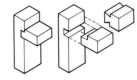
DOVETAIL DADO

RABBET & DADO

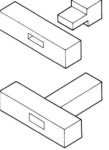
FULL (OR THROUGH)

BLIND AND STUB

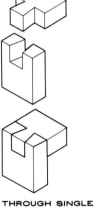
THROUGH SINGLE

THROUGH MULTIPLE

STOPPED LAP

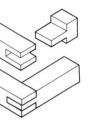
SHIP (OR OPEN)

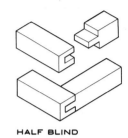
HALF BLIND

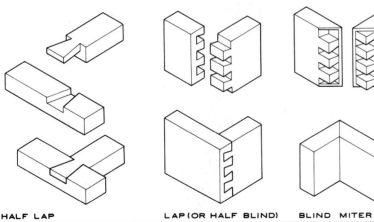
HALF LAP

LAP (OR HALF BLIND)

BLIND MITER

DOVETAIL

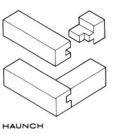
HAUNCH

HAUNCH — BLIND

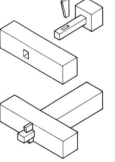
KEYED

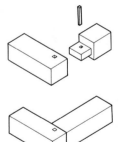
PINNED BLIND

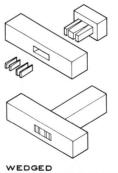
WEDGED

MORTISE & TENON

NOTES

1. Wood joints may be grouped into three classes: (1) right angle joints, (2) end joints, and (3) edge joints.

2. End joints are used to increase the length of a wood member. By proper utilization of end joints short lengths can be used which might otherwise have been wasted.

3. Edge joints are used to increase the width of a wood member. By giving narrow widths greater use of narrow stock may result.

4. A rabbet (rebate) is a right angle cut made along a corner edge of a wood member. A dado is a rectangular groove cut across the grain of a wood member. If this groove extends along the edge or face of a wood member (being cut parallel to the grain) it is known as a plough (plow).

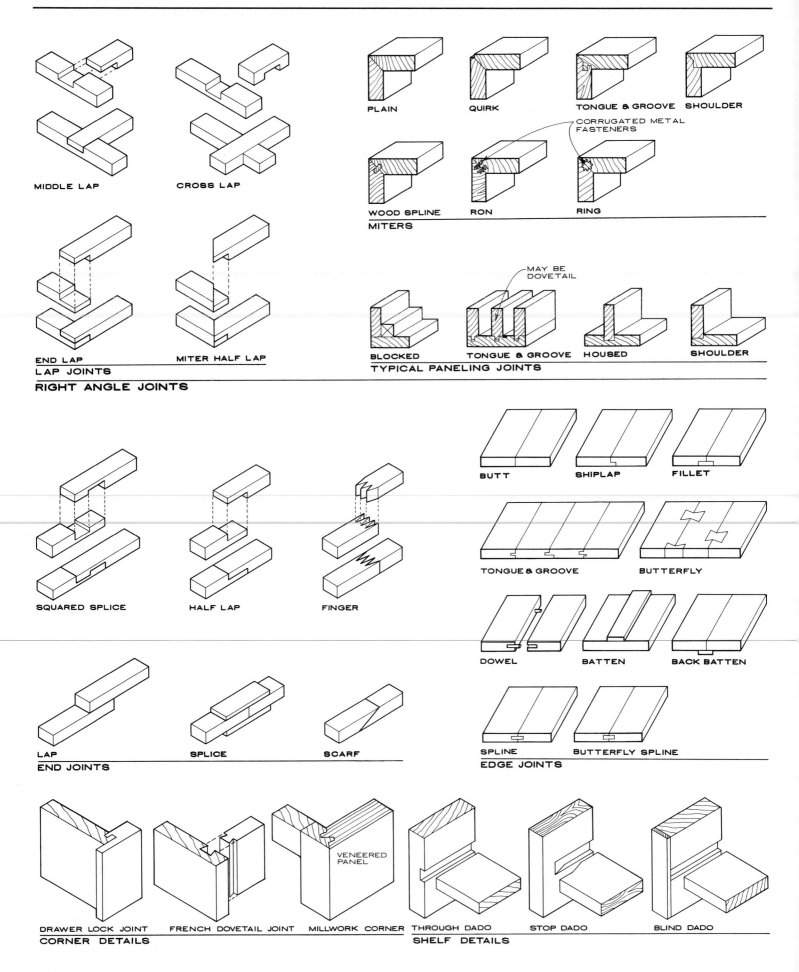

MIDDLE LAP

CROSS LAP

PLAIN

QUIRK

TONGUE & GROOVE

SHOULDER

CORRUGATED METAL FASTENERS

WOOD SPLINE

RON

RING

MITERS

END LAP

MITER HALF LAP

LAP JOINTS

MAY BE DOVETAIL

BLOCKED

TONGUE & GROOVE

HOUSED

SHOULDER

TYPICAL PANELING JOINTS

RIGHT ANGLE JOINTS

SQUARED SPLICE

HALF LAP

FINGER

BUTT

SHIPLAP

FILLET

TONGUE & GROOVE

BUTTERFLY

DOWEL

BATTEN

BACK BATTEN

LAP

SPLICE

SCARF

END JOINTS

SPLINE

BUTTERFLY SPLINE

EDGE JOINTS

DRAWER LOCK JOINT

FRENCH DOVETAIL JOINT

MILLWORK CORNER

VENEERED PANEL

THROUGH DADO

STOP DADO

BLIND DADO

CORNER DETAILS

SHELF DETAILS

CHAPTER 7 THERMAL AND MOISTURE PROTECTION

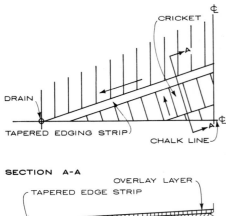

TAPERED INSULATION

NOTES

TAPERED INSULATION SYSTEMS: Consist of a series of factory prefabricated panels that are tapered to provide a positive slope on flat roof decks when used in conjunction with fill insulation of appropriate thickness. The tapered panels are produced from perlite, foam glass, urethane, and/or polystyrene. Standard available slopes vary from 1/8 to 1/2 in./ft. After installation of the fill layer and the tapered layers of insulation, an overlay layer is applied. As in the installation of any insulation system, joints of successive layers must be staggered in both dimensions. In the system, each block is identified for positions by a code number on the block. It is important that shop drawings, showing complete roof layout including drains, valleys, and cricket details, be provided.

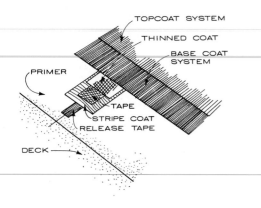

FLUID ROOFING

NOTES

NEOPRENE HYPALON: A single component, air curing, liquid coating designed to yield elastomeric films for high strength waterproof membranes for roof, deck, wall, floor, and subgrade applications over a wide variety of substrates such as concrete, plywood, insulation, metal, and built-up roofing. They are not recommended for continuous water emersion or for long term exposure to severe weathering. Coatings exposed to weather and some chemical environments require a hypalon topcoat.

Hypalon coatings are leadfree, air curing, liquid elastomeric coating. Used as weathering, ultraviolet protective, fire retardant coating.

Neoprene coating is applied in sufficient coats to secure a total minimum coverage of 3 gal/square (wet film thickness of 48 mils). Dry film 12 mils. Hypalon is applied in two coats with a wet film thickness of 16 mils/coat. Using not less than 1 gal/square per coat.

Robert E. Fehlberg, FAIA; CTA Architects Engineers; Billings, Montana

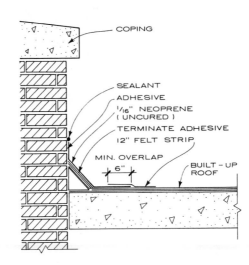

ELASTOMERIC FLASHING

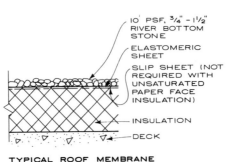

TYPICAL ROOF MEMBRANE APPLICATION

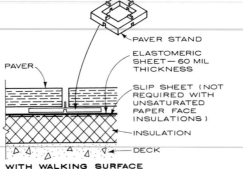

WITH WALKING SURFACE

SHEET ELASTOMERIC ROOF

NOTES

ELASTOMERIC SHEET ROOFING: This loosely laid roof consists of an elastomeric sheet that covers the entire roof continuously from edge to edge. The vapor barrier, insulation, and roof membrane are laid loosely. The polyvinyl sheet is seamed into a homogeneous skin, which is fastened to the deck only at roof edges and roof interruptions. This creates a one-piece loose membrane over the whole surface of the roof, which moves with the structure. Every seam and point where water could enter the roof are sealed with the same material as the roof itself and desolved in a solvent that cures to become an integral part of the roof.

The whole assembly is then ballasted with washed river bottom gravel—3/4 to 1 1/2 in. in its smallest dimension. This ballast protects the roof from casual traffic and aging and reduces peak temperatures of the roof during the summer by as much as 40°F.

Loosely laid membrane materials may be PVC (polyvinyl chloride), CPE (chlorinated polyethylene), or EPDM (ethylene propylene diene monomer). CPE and EPDM are recommended occasionally for certain applications; the most common material specified is PVC—unsupported or reinforced.

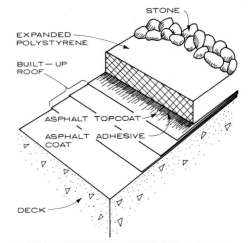

INSULATED ROOF MEMBRANE APPLICATION

NOTES

INSULATED ROOF MEMBRANE: Apply directly to the roof deck and with insulation on top of it. The membrane is on the warm side of the insulation and is practically invulnerable. It is not subject to roof traffic, ultraviolet degradation, thermocycling, and exposure that cause alligatoring, splitting, ridging, and other deterioration. These causes of roof failure are substantially reduced or totally eliminated. The heat gain or loss is just the same as if the insulation were installed under the membrane, because the expanded polystyrene does not absorb water. And, even in high humidity buildings, there is no need to install a vapor barrier because the membrane is the vapor barrier.

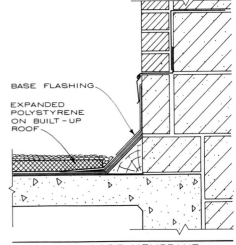

ROOF DRAIN DETAIL

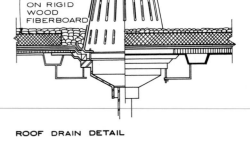

INSULATED ROOF MEMBRANE

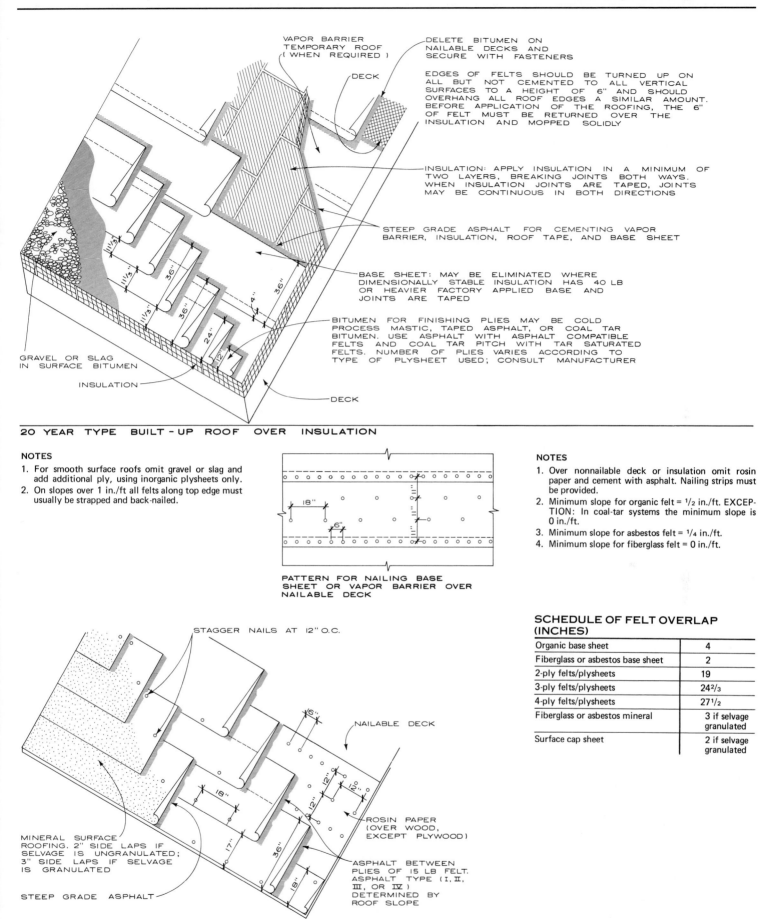

VAPOR BARRIER
TEMPORARY ROOF
(WHEN REQUIRED)

DECK

DELETE BITUMEN ON
NAILABLE DECKS AND
SECURE WITH FASTENERS

EDGES OF FELTS SHOULD BE TURNED UP ON
ALL BUT NOT CEMENTED TO ALL VERTICAL
SURFACES TO A HEIGHT OF 6" AND SHOULD
OVERHANG ALL ROOF EDGES A SIMILAR AMOUNT.
BEFORE APPLICATION OF THE ROOFING, THE 6"
OF FELT MUST BE RETURNED OVER THE
INSULATION AND MOPPED SOLIDLY

INSULATION: APPLY INSULATION IN A MINIMUM OF
TWO LAYERS, BREAKING JOINTS BOTH WAYS.
WHEN INSULATION JOINTS ARE TAPED, JOINTS
MAY BE CONTINUOUS IN BOTH DIRECTIONS

STEEP GRADE ASPHALT FOR CEMENTING VAPOR
BARRIER, INSULATION, ROOF TAPE, AND BASE SHEET

BASE SHEET: MAY BE ELIMINATED WHERE
DIMENSIONALLY STABLE INSULATION HAS 40 LB
OR HEAVIER FACTORY APPLIED BASE AND
JOINTS ARE TAPED

BITUMEN FOR FINISHING PLIES MAY BE COLD
PROCESS MASTIC, TAPED ASPHALT, OR COAL TAR
BITUMEN. USE ASPHALT WITH ASPHALT COMPATIBLE
FELTS AND COAL TAR PITCH WITH TAR SATURATED
FELTS. NUMBER OF PLIES VARIES ACCORDING TO
TYPE OF PLYSHEET USED; CONSULT MANUFACTURER

GRAVEL OR SLAG
IN SURFACE BITUMEN

INSULATION

DECK

20 YEAR TYPE BUILT-UP ROOF OVER INSULATION

NOTES

1. For smooth surface roofs omit gravel or slag and add additional ply, using inorganic plysheets only.
2. On slopes over 1 in./ft all felts along top edge must usually be strapped and back-nailed.

PATTERN FOR NAILING BASE
SHEET OR VAPOR BARRIER OVER
NAILABLE DECK

NOTES

1. Over nonnailable deck or insulation omit rosin paper and cement with asphalt. Nailing strips must be provided.
2. Minimum slope for organic felt = $1/2$ in./ft. EXCEPTION: In coal-tar systems the minimum slope is 0 in./ft.
3. Minimum slope for asbestos felt = $1/4$ in./ft.
4. Minimum slope for fiberglass felt = 0 in./ft.

SCHEDULE OF FELT OVERLAP (INCHES)

Organic base sheet	4
Fiberglass or asbestos base sheet	2
2-ply felts/plysheets	19
3-ply felts/plysheets	$24^{2}/_{3}$
4-ply felts/plysheets	$27^{1}/_{2}$
Fiberglass or asbestos mineral	3 if selvage granulated
Surface cap sheet	2 if selvage granulated

STAGGER NAILS AT 12" O.C.

NAILABLE DECK

ROSIN PAPER
(OVER WOOD,
EXCEPT PLYWOOD)

MINERAL SURFACE
ROOFING. 2" SIDE LAPS IF
SELVAGE IS UNGRANULATED;
3" SIDE LAPS IF SELVAGE
IS GRANULATED

ASPHALT BETWEEN
PLIES OF 15 LB FELT.
ASPHALT TYPE (I, II,
III, OR IV)
DETERMINED BY
ROOF SLOPE

STEEP GRADE ASPHALT

MINERAL SURFACE BUILT-UP ROOF

Kent Wong; Hewlett, Jamison, Atkinson & Luey; Portland, Oregon

Developed by Angelo J. Forlidas, AIA; Charlotte, North Carolina: from data furnished by Robert M. Stafford, P.E., Consulting Engineer; Charlotte, North Carolina

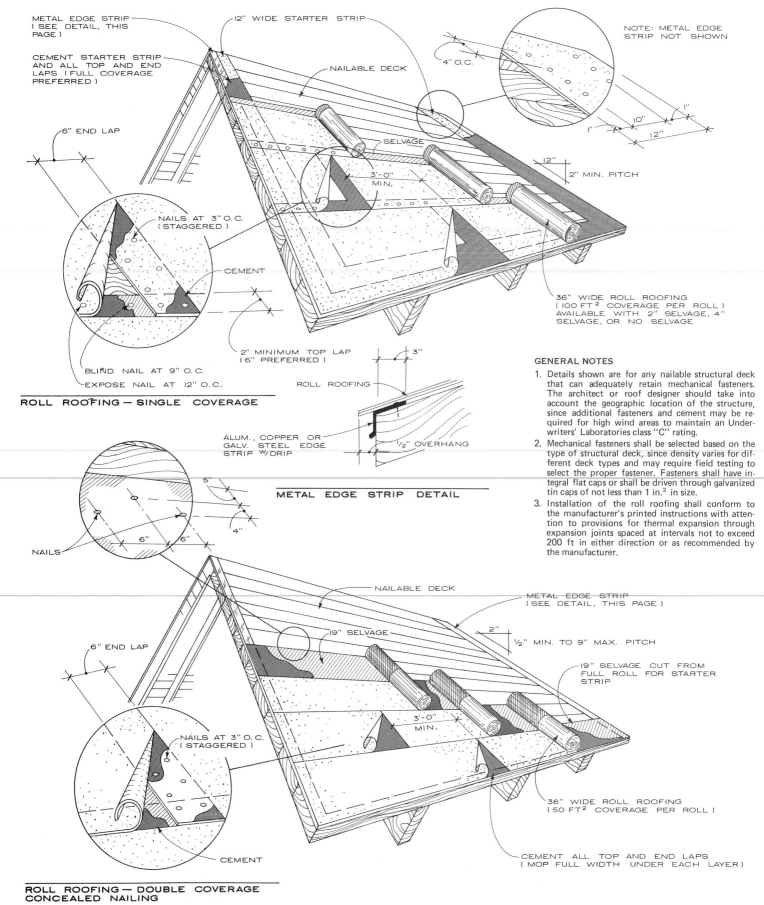

METAL EDGE STRIP
(SEE DETAIL, THIS
PAGE)

CEMENT STARTER STRIP
AND ALL TOP AND END
LAPS (FULL COVERAGE
PREFERRED)

12" WIDE STARTER STRIP

NAILABLE DECK

NOTE: METAL EDGE
STRIP NOT SHOWN

4" O.C.

1"

10"

1"

12"

SELVAGE

6" END LAP

3'-0"
MIN.

12"

2" MIN. PITCH

NAILS AT 3" O.C.
(STAGGERED)

CEMENT

36" WIDE ROLL ROOFING
(100 FT² COVERAGE PER ROLL)
AVAILABLE WITH 2" SELVAGE, 4"
SELVAGE, OR NO SELVAGE

2" MINIMUM TOP LAP
(6" PREFERRED)

BLIND NAIL AT 9" O.C.

EXPOSE NAIL AT 12" O.C.

ROLL ROOFING — SINGLE COVERAGE

3"

ROLL ROOFING

ALUM., COPPER OR
GALV. STEEL EDGE
STRIP w/DRIP

½" OVERHANG

METAL EDGE STRIP DETAIL

GENERAL NOTES

1. Details shown are for any nailable structural deck that can adequately retain mechanical fasteners. The architect or roof designer should take into account the geographic location of the structure, since additional fasteners and cement may be required for high wind areas to maintain an Underwriters' Laboratories class "C" rating.

2. Mechanical fasteners shall be selected based on the type of structural deck, since density varies for different deck types and may require field testing to select the proper fastener. Fasteners shall have integral flat caps or shall be driven through galvanized tin caps of not less than 1 in.² in size.

3. Installation of the roll roofing shall conform to the manufacturer's printed instructions with attention to provisions for thermal expansion through expansion joints spaced at intervals not to exceed 200 ft in either direction or as recommended by the manufacturer.

5"

4"

6"

6"

NAILS

NAILABLE DECK

METAL EDGE STRIP
(SEE DETAIL, THIS PAGE)

19" SELVAGE

2"

½" MIN. TO 9" MAX. PITCH

19" SELVAGE CUT FROM
FULL ROLL FOR STARTER
STRIP

6" END LAP

3'-0"
MIN.

NAILS AT 3" O.C.
(STAGGERED)

36" WIDE ROLL ROOFING
(50 FT² COVERAGE PER ROLL)

CEMENT

CEMENT ALL TOP AND END LAPS
(MOP FULL WIDTH UNDER EACH LAYER)

**ROLL ROOFING — DOUBLE COVERAGE
CONCEALED NAILING**

James E. Phillips, AIA, Liles/Associates/Architects; Greenville, South Carolina

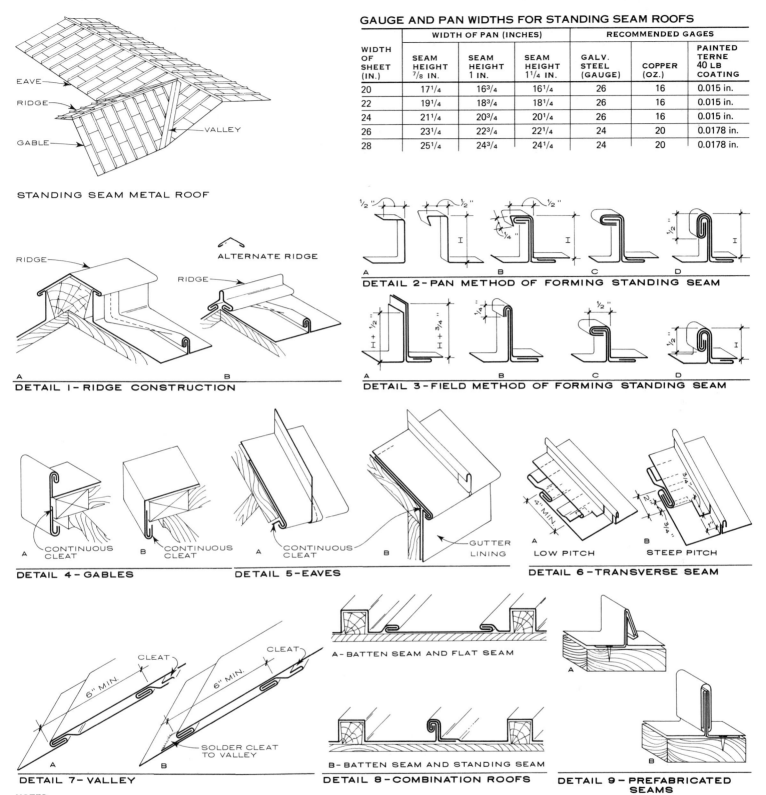

STANDING SEAM METAL ROOF

GAUGE AND PAN WIDTHS FOR STANDING SEAM ROOFS

WIDTH OF SHEET (IN.)	WIDTH OF PAN (INCHES)			RECOMMENDED GAGES		
	SEAM HEIGHT 7/8 IN.	SEAM HEIGHT 1 IN.	SEAM HEIGHT 1 1/4 IN.	GALV. STEEL (GAUGE)	COPPER (OZ.)	PAINTED TERNE 40 LB COATING
20	17 1/4	16 3/4	16 1/4	26	16	0.015 in.
22	19 1/4	18 3/4	18 1/4	26	16	0.015 in.
24	21 1/4	20 3/4	20 1/4	26	16	0.015 in.
26	23 1/4	22 3/4	22 1/4	24	20	0.0178 in.
28	25 1/4	24 3/4	24 1/4	24	20	0.0178 in.

DETAIL 1 – RIDGE CONSTRUCTION

DETAIL 2 – PAN METHOD OF FORMING STANDING SEAM

DETAIL 3 – FIELD METHOD OF FORMING STANDING SEAM

DETAIL 4 – GABLES

DETAIL 5 – EAVES

DETAIL 6 – TRANSVERSE SEAM

DETAIL 7 – VALLEY

DETAIL 8 – COMBINATION ROOFS

A – BATTEN SEAM AND FLAT SEAM

B – BATTEN SEAM AND STANDING SEAM

DETAIL 9 – PREFABRICATED SEAMS

NOTES

1. Standing seam roofing may be applied on slopes of 3 in./ft or greater. If the surface to receive the roofing is other than wood, nailing strips must be provided to receive the cleats. See general notes on metal roofs for recommended surface preparation.

2. The spacing of seams may vary between reasonable limits to suit the architectural style of a given building. The two methods of installing standing seam roofing are the pan and the roll method. In the pan method, the sides of the sheets are formed as shown in A of detail 2. Top and bottom edges of pans are formed as shown in A and B of detail 6. Pans are installed with cleats spaced not more than 12 inches on center. Each pan is locked to the one below as shown in A and B of detail 7. The adjacent row of pans is next installed and the standing seams completed as in C and D of detail 2.

3. The roll method consists of a series of long sheets joined together at their ends with double flat lock seams and sent to the job in rolls. The standing seam is field formed as shown in A of detail 3. The roofing is installed in lengths reaching from the eave to the ridge and attached with cleats spaced not more than 12 in. on center. After a second length is installed and cleated in place, the standing seam is formed as shown in detail 3.

4. A of detail 5 shows method of terminating metal roofing at the eave where roofing is locked over a continuous cleat. B of detail 5 shows method of terminating metal roofing at a built-in gutter. Roofing is loose locked to a continuous cleat and the flange on back edge of gutter. Seam terminations must be soldered.

5. A and B of detail 9 show two common prefabricated standing seams now in use. The use of newly developed electronic seaming machines is recommended for long runs of standing seams.

See also Metal Roofs for general notes.

Straub, VanDine, Dziurman/Architects; Troy, Michigan

Emory E. Hinkel, Jr.; A. G. Odell, Jr. and Associates; Charlotte, North Carolina

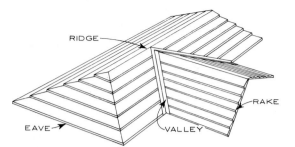

BERMUDA TYPE METAL ROOF

RECOMMENDED GAUGES OR WEIGHTS FOR PAN WIDTHS

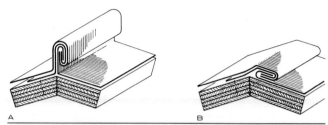

WIDTH OF SHEET (IN.)	WIDTH OF PAN "D" (IN.)	COPPER (OZ)	GALVANIZED STEEL (GAUGE)	STAINLESS STEEL (GAUGE)	PAINTED TERNE 40 LB COATING
20	16½	16	26	28	0.015 IN.
22	18½	16	26	28	0.015 IN.
24	20½	16	26	26	0.015 IN.
26	22½	20	24	26	0.0178 IN.
28	24½	20	24	26	0.0178 IN.

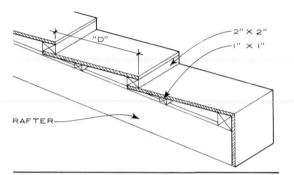

DETAIL 1-WOOD FRAMING

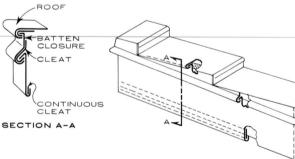

DETAIL 2-SEAM TYPES AT HIP OR RIDGE

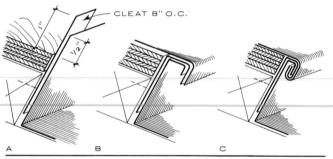

DETAIL 3-CONSTRUCTION AT BATTEN

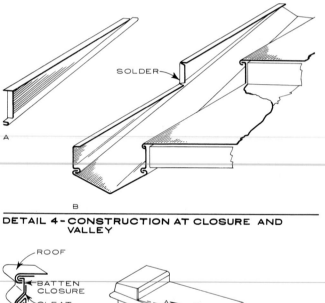

DETAIL 4-CONSTRUCTION AT CLOSURE AND VALLEY

DETAIL 5-EAVE

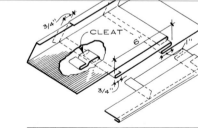

DETAIL 6-EXPANSION JOINT

SECTION A-A

DETAIL 7-CONSTRUCTION AT RAKE

NOTES

1. The Bermuda roof may be used for roofs having a slope greater than 2½ in./ft. Wood framing must be provided as shown in detail 1. Dimension "D" and gauge of metal will depend on the size of sheet used. See chart. Consult general notes on metal roofs for recommended surface preparation.

2. Bermuda roof is applied beginning at the eave. The first pan is hooked over a continuous cleat as shown in detail 5. The upper portion of the first and each succeeding pan is attached as shown in detail 3. Cleats spaced on 8 in. centers are nailed to batten as in A of detail 3. Joint is developed as shown in B of detail 3 and malleted against batten as shown in C of detail 3. All cross seams are single locked and soldered except at expansion joints. Cross seams should be staggered. Expansion joints should be used at least every 25 ft and formed as shown in detail 6. Roofing is joined at hip or ridge by use of a standing seam as shown in A of detail 2. Seam may be malleted down as shown in B of detail 2.

3. Detail 4 shows the method of forming valleys. Valley sections are lapped 8 in. in direction of flow.

Individual closures for sides of valley are formed as shown in A of detail 4 and must be soldered as indicated in B of detail 4. A method of terminating the roof at rake is shown in detail 7. The face plate (optional) is held in place by continuous cleats at both top and bottom. The batten closure is formed as a cleat to hold edge of roof pan as shown in section A-A of detail 7.

See also Metal Roofs for general notes.

Straub, VanDine, Dziurman/Architects; Troy, Michigan

Emory E. Hinkel, Jr.; A. G. Odell, Jr. and Associates; Charlotte, North Carolina

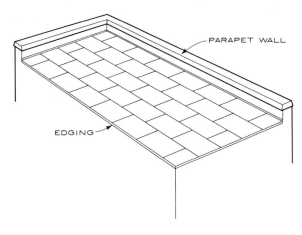

FLAT SEAM ROOF

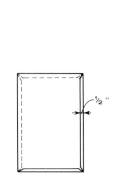

DETAIL 1- ROOFING
SHEET

DETAIL 2- FLAT SEAM ROOF

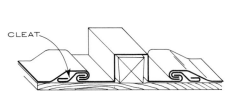

DETAIL 3- EXPANSION BATTEN

DETAIL 4- JUNCTION AT
PARAPET WALL

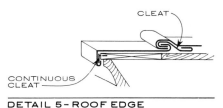

DETAIL 5- ROOF EDGE

NOTES

1. The flat seam method of roofing as illustrated is most commonly used on roofs of slight pitch or for the covering of curved surfaces such as towers or domes.

2. The joints connecting the sheets of roofs having a pitch greater than 1/2 in./ft may be sealed with caulking compound or white lead. The joints of roofs having a pitch of less than 1/2 in./ft must be malleted and thoroughly sweated full with solder.

3. Roofs of slight pitch should be divided by expansion batten as shown in detail 3, into sections not exceeding maximum total areas of 30 ft².

4. Consult general notes on metal roofs for recommended surface preparation.

5. The metal sheets may be pretinned if required, 1 1/2 in. back from all edges and on both sides of the sheet. Pans are formed by notching and folding the sheets as shown in detail 1.

6. The pans are held in place by cleating as shown. After pans are in place, all seams are malleted and soldered or sealed.

7. Detail 4 shows the junction of a roof and a parapet wall. Metal base flashing is cleated to deck on 2 ft centers and extended up wall; 8 in. pans are locked and soldered to base flashing. Metal counter flashing covers 4 in. of the base flashing. Detail 5 illustrates the installation of flashing at edge of roof. Flashing is formed as shown and attached to the face by a continuous cleat nailed on 1 ft centers and cleated to the roof deck. Pans are locked and soldered or sealed to the flashing. See also general notes below.

GENERAL NOTES

1. Detail drawings for metal roof types are diagrammatic only. The indication of adjoining construction is included merely to establish its relation to the sheet metal work and is not intended as a recommendation of architectural design. Any details that may suggest an architectural period do not limit the application of sheet metal to that or any other architectural style.

2. Weights of metals and roof slopes indicated on detail drawings are minimum as recommended by the Sheet Metal and Air Conditioning Contractors'
National Association and may vary from recommendations of some manufacturers.

3. Metals used must be of a thickness or gauge heavy enough and in correct proportion to the breadth and scale of the work. Provide expansion joints for freedom of movement.

4. Prevent direct contact of metal roofing with dissimilar metals that cause electrolysis.

5. A wide range of metals, alloys, and finishes are available for metal roofing. The durability as well as the maintenance requirements of each should be
taken into consideration when selecting roofing.

6. The surface to receive the metal roofing should be thoroughly dry and covered by a saturated roofing felt in case of leakage due to construction error or wind driven moisture. A rosin paper should be applied over the felt to avoid bonding between felt and metal.

7. Many of the prefabricated batten and standing seam devices are not as watertight as with conventional methods and are therefore more suitable for steeply pitched roofs such as mansards.

Straub, VanDine, Dziurman/Architects; Troy, Michigan

Emory E. Hinkel, Jr.; A. G. Odell, Jr. and Associates; Charlotte, North Carolina

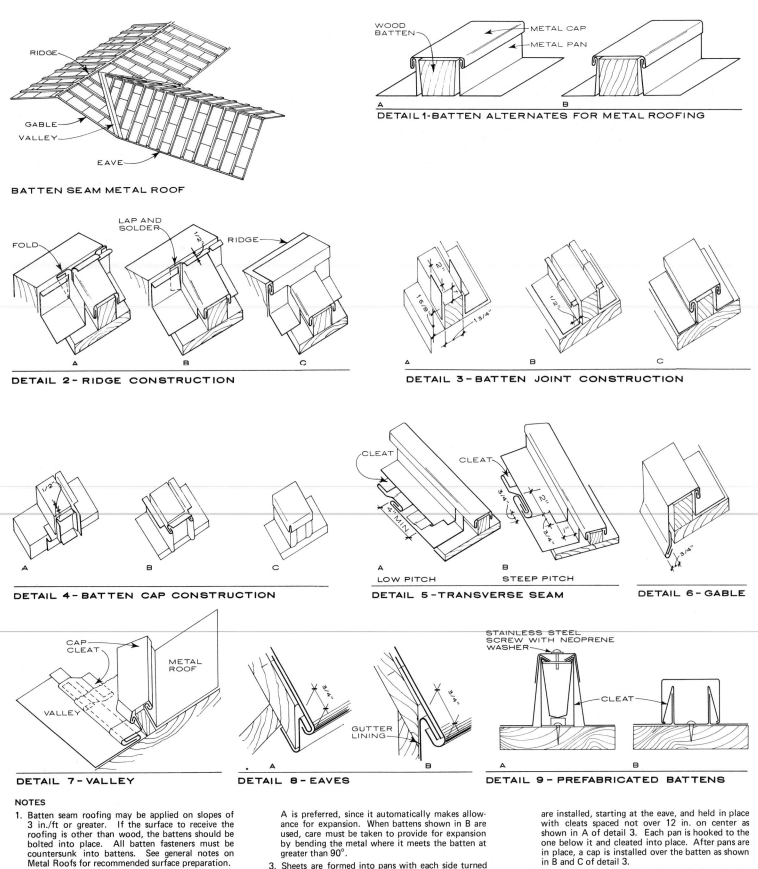

RIDGE
GABLE
VALLEY
EAVE

BATTEN SEAM METAL ROOF

WOOD BATTEN — METAL CAP — METAL PAN
A   B
DETAIL 1-BATTEN ALTERNATES FOR METAL ROOFING

LAP AND SOLDER
FOLD   RIDGE
A   B   C
DETAIL 2- RIDGE CONSTRUCTION

A   B   C
DETAIL 3-BATTEN JOINT CONSTRUCTION

A   B   C
DETAIL 4-BATTEN CAP CONSTRUCTION

CLEAT   CLEAT
A   B
LOW PITCH   STEEP PITCH
DETAIL 5-TRANSVERSE SEAM

DETAIL 6 - GABLE

CAP CLEAT   METAL ROOF
VALLEY
DETAIL 7-VALLEY

GUTTER LINING
A   B
DETAIL 8 - EAVES

STAINLESS STEEL SCREW WITH NEOPRENE WASHER
CLEAT
A   B
DETAIL 9 - PREFABRICATED BATTENS

NOTES

1. Batten seam roofing may be applied on slopes of 3 in./ft or greater. If the surface to receive the roofing is other than wood, the battens should be bolted into place. All batten fasteners must be countersunk into battens. See general notes on Metal Roofs for recommended surface preparation.

2. The spacing of the wood battens may vary within reasonable limits to suit the architectural style and scale of the building, but the recommended maximum distance is 20 in. between battens. Care should be taken to space the battens in such a manner that waste of metal is held to a minimum. Battens may be shaped as shown in A or B of detail 1.

A is preferred, since it automatically makes allowance for expansion. When battens shown in B are used, care must be taken to provide for expansion by bending the metal where it meets the batten at greater than 90°.

3. Sheets are formed into pans with each side turned up 2 1/8 in. A 1/2 in. flange is turned toward the center of the pan as shown in B of detail 3. At lower end of the pan, the sheet is notched and a hook edge is formed as in A or B of detail 5. For low pitched roofs the upper end of the sheet is formed as in A of detail 5. On steeper roofs the upper end is formed as shown in B of detail 5. Pans

are installed, starting at the eave, and held in place with cleats spaced not over 12 in. on center as shown in A of detail 3. Each pan is hooked to the one below it and cleated into place. After pans are in place, a cap is installed over the batten as shown in B and C of detail 3.

4. A number of manufacturers have developed metal roofing systems using several prefabricated devices. A and B of detail 9 show two common prefabricated battens in use.

5. See also Standing Seam Metal Roofing for details on combination batten and standing or flat seam roofing. See also Metal Roofs for general notes.

Straub, VanDine, Dziurman/Architects; Troy, Michigan

Emory E. Hinkel, Jr.; A. G. Odell, Jr. and Associates; Charlotte, North Carolina

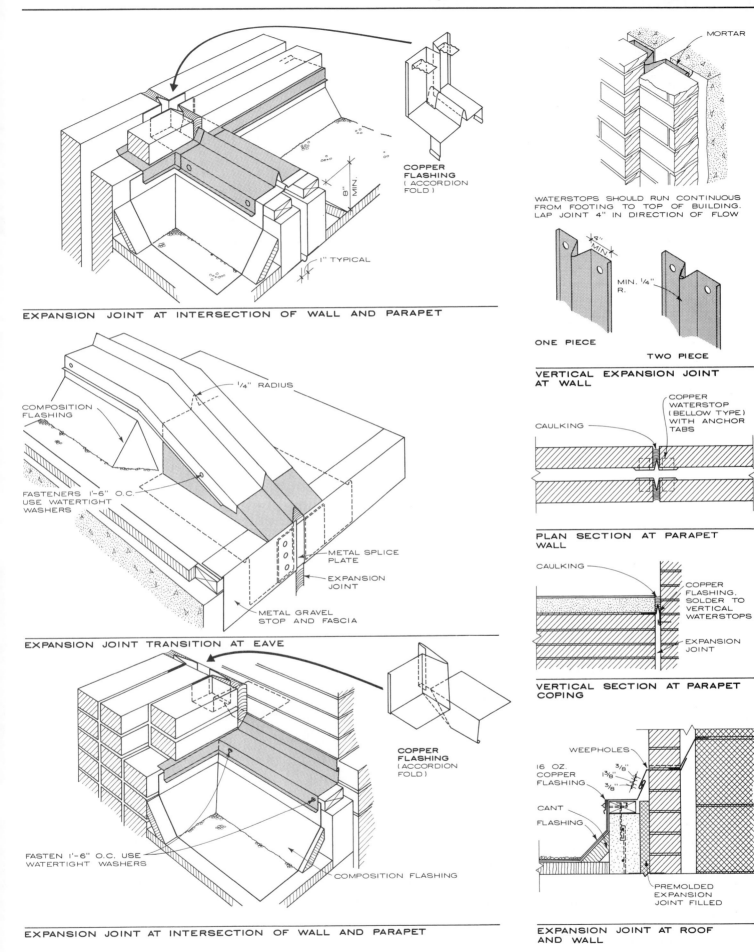

MORTAR

COPPER FLASHING (ACCORDION FOLD)

8" MIN.

1" TYPICAL

EXPANSION JOINT AT INTERSECTION OF WALL AND PARAPET

WATERSTOPS SHOULD RUN CONTINUOUS FROM FOOTING TO TOP OF BUILDING. LAP JOINT 4" IN DIRECTION OF FLOW

2" MIN

MIN. 1/4" R.

MIN. 1/4" R.

ONE PIECE

TWO PIECE

VERTICAL EXPANSION JOINT AT WALL

1/4" RADIUS

COMPOSITION FLASHING

FASTENERS 1'-6" O.C. USE WATERTIGHT WASHERS

METAL SPLICE PLATE

EXPANSION JOINT

METAL GRAVEL STOP AND FASCIA

COPPER WATERSTOP (BELLOW TYPE) WITH ANCHOR TABS

CAULKING

PLAN SECTION AT PARAPET WALL

CAULKING

COPPER FLASHING. SOLDER TO VERTICAL WATERSTOPS

EXPANSION JOINT

EXPANSION JOINT TRANSITION AT EAVE

COPPER FLASHING (ACCORDION FOLD)

VERTICAL SECTION AT PARAPET COPING

WEEPHOLES

16 OZ. COPPER FLASHING

3/8"

1 3/8"

3/8"

CANT

FLASHING

FASTEN 1'-6" O.C. USE WATERTIGHT WASHERS

COMPOSITION FLASHING

PREMOLDED EXPANSION JOINT FILLED

EXPANSION JOINT AT INTERSECTION OF WALL AND PARAPET

EXPANSION JOINT AT ROOF AND WALL

CTA Architects Engineers; Billings, Montana

ROOF SPECIALTIES

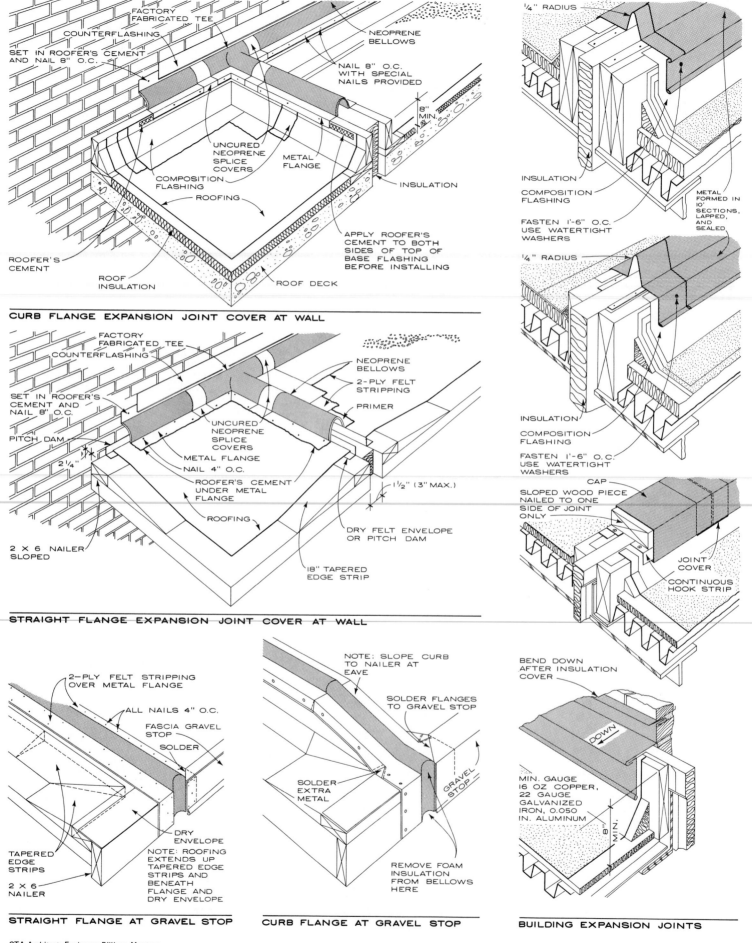

CURB FLANGE EXPANSION JOINT COVER AT WALL

FACTORY FABRICATED TEE
COUNTERFLASHING
SET IN ROOFER'S CEMENT AND NAIL 8" O.C.
ROOFER'S CEMENT
ROOF INSULATION
ROOF DECK
UNCURED NEOPRENE SPLICE COVERS
COMPOSITION FLASHING
ROOFING
METAL FLANGE
NEOPRENE BELLOWS
NAIL 8" O.C. WITH SPECIAL NAILS PROVIDED
8" MIN.
INSULATION
APPLY ROOFER'S CEMENT TO BOTH SIDES OF TOP OF BASE FLASHING BEFORE INSTALLING

STRAIGHT FLANGE EXPANSION JOINT COVER AT WALL

FACTORY FABRICATED TEE
COUNTERFLASHING
SET IN ROOFER'S CEMENT AND NAIL 8" O.C.
PITCH DAM
2 1/4"
UNCURED NEOPRENE SPLICE COVERS
METAL FLANGE
NAIL 4" O.C.
ROOFER'S CEMENT UNDER METAL FLANGE
ROOFING
2 X 6 NAILER SLOPED
NEOPRENE BELLOWS
2-PLY FELT STRIPPING
PRIMER
1 1/2" (3" MAX.)
DRY FELT ENVELOPE OR PITCH DAM
18" TAPERED EDGE STRIP

STRAIGHT FLANGE AT GRAVEL STOP

2-PLY FELT STRIPPING OVER METAL FLANGE
ALL NAILS 4" O.C.
FASCIA GRAVEL STOP
SOLDER
DRY ENVELOPE
TAPERED EDGE STRIPS
2 X 6 NAILER
NOTE: ROOFING EXTENDS UP TAPERED EDGE STRIPS AND BENEATH FLANGE AND DRY ENVELOPE

CURB FLANGE AT GRAVEL STOP

NOTE: SLOPE CURB TO NAILER AT EAVE
SOLDER FLANGES TO GRAVEL STOP
SOLDER EXTRA METAL
GRAVEL STOP
REMOVE FOAM INSULATION FROM BELLOWS HERE

1/4" RADIUS
INSULATION
COMPOSITION FLASHING
FASTEN 1'-6" O.C. USE WATERTIGHT WASHERS
METAL FORMED IN 10' SECTIONS, LAPPED, AND SEALED

1/4" RADIUS
INSULATION
COMPOSITION FLASHING
FASTEN 1'-6" O.C. USE WATERTIGHT WASHERS

CAP
SLOPED WOOD PIECE NAILED TO ONE SIDE OF JOINT ONLY
JOINT COVER
CONTINUOUS HOOK STRIP

BUILDING EXPANSION JOINTS

BEND DOWN AFTER INSULATION COVER
DOWN
MIN. GAUGE 16 OZ COPPER, 22 GAUGE GALVANIZED IRON, 0.050 IN. ALUMINUM
8" MIN.

CTA Architects Engineers; Billings, Montana

7 **ROOF SPECIALTIES**

WIDTH OF RECTANGULAR GUTTERS FOR GIVEN ROOF AREAS AND RAINFALL INTENSITIES

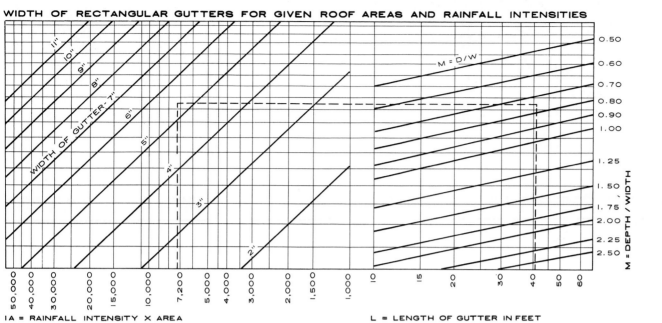

IA = RAINFALL INTENSITY X AREA

L = LENGTH OF GUTTER IN FEET

NOTE

The terms "leader," "conductor," and "downspout" all mean the same thing.

SAMPLE PROBLEM

To size rectangular gutter for a building 120 x 30 ft. located in New York City. This building has a flat roof with a raised roof edge on three sides. A gutter is to be located on one of the 120 ft. sides. So that each section of gutter will not exceed 50 ft., three downspouts will be used with 2 gutter expansion joints. The area to be drained by each section of gutter will be 1200 sq. ft., the rainfall intensity from map below is 6 in., the length of each gutter section is 40 ft., and the ratio of gutter depth to width is 0.75. On chart above find the vertical line representing L = 40. Proceed vertically along this line to its intersection with the oblique line representing M = 0.75. Pass horizontally to the left to intersect the vertical line representing IA = 7200. The point of intersection occurs between the oblique line representing gutter widths of 5 and 6 in. The required width of gutter is, therefore, 6 in. and its depth need be only 4 ½ in.

DESIGN AREAS FOR PITCHED ROOFS

PITCH	FACTOR
LEVEL TO 3 IN./FT.	1.00
4 TO 5 IN./FT.	1.05
6 TO 8 IN./FT.	1.10
9 TO 11 IN./FT.	1.20
12 IN./FT.	1.30

NOTE: When a roof is sloped neither the plan nor actual area should be used in sizing drainage. Multiply the plan area by the factor shown above to obtain design area.

INFLUENCE OF GUTTER SHAPE ON DESIGN

1. RECTANGULAR GUTTERS:

Use graph at top of page.

2. IRREGULAR SHAPES:

Determine equivalent rectangular size and use same method.

3. SEMICIRCULAR GUTTERS:

First size downspout from tables below. Then use gutter 1 inch larger in diameter.

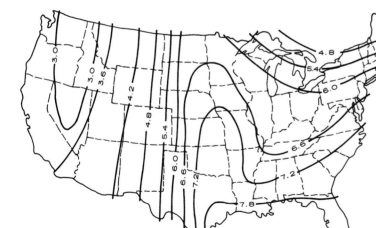

RAINFALL INTENSITY MAP
NOTE

Map shows hourly rainfall intensity in inches per hour for 5 minute periods to be expected once in 10 years. Normally this is adequate for design, but some storms have been twice as intense in some areas. See local records.

Lawrence W. Cobb; Columbia, South Carolina

DOWNSPOUT CAPACITY

INTENSITY IN IN./HR. LASTING 5 MIN.	SQ. FT. ROOF/ SQ. IN. DOWNSPOUT
2	600
3	400
4	300
5	240
6	200
7	175
8	150
9	130
10	120
11	110

GENERAL NOTES

Most gutters are run level for appearance. However, a slope of $1/16$ in. per foot is desirable for drainage.

For residential work allow 100 sq. ft. of roof area per 1 sq. in. of downspout.

DOWNSPOUT SIZES

TYPE	AREA SQ. IN.	NOM. SIZE IN.	ACT. SIZE IN.
PLAIN ROUND	7.07	3	3
	12.57	4	4
	19.63	5	5
	28.27	6	6
CORR. ROUND	5.94	3	3
	11.04	4	4
	17.72	5	5
	25.97	6	6
CORR. RECT.	3.80	2	$1^{3}/_4 \times 2^{1}/_4$
	7.73	3	$2^{3}/_8 \times 3^{1}/_4$
	11.70	4	$2^{3}/_4 \times 4^{1}/_4$
	18.75	5	$3^{1}/_4 \times 5$
PLAIN RECT.	3.94	2	$1^{1}/_4 \times 2^{1}/_4$
	6.00	3	2×3
	12.00	4	3×4
	20.00	5	$3^{1}/_4 \times 4^{3}/_4$
	24.00	6	4×6

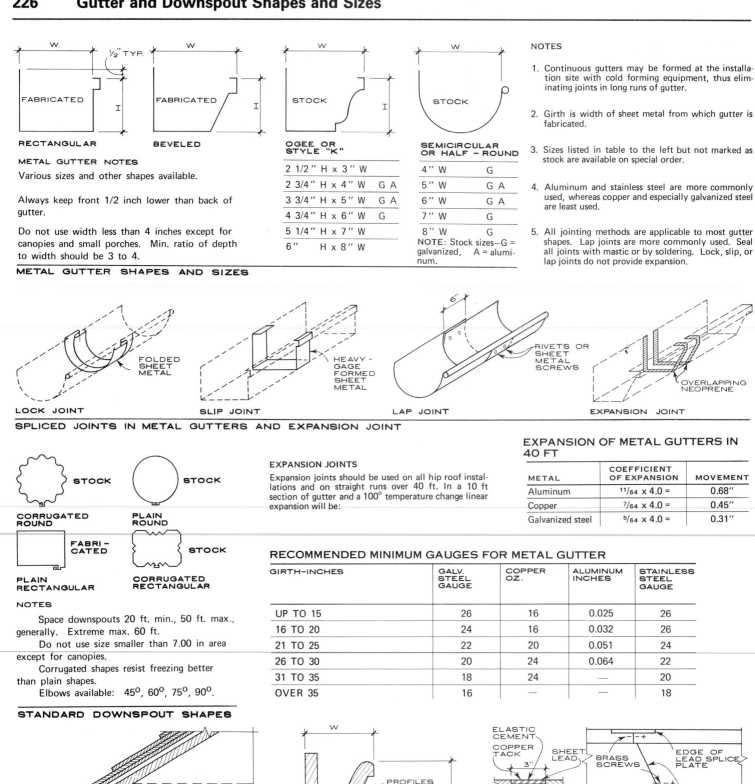

NOTES

1. Continuous gutters may be formed at the installation site with cold forming equipment, thus eliminating joints in long runs of gutter.

2. Girth is width of sheet metal from which gutter is fabricated.

3. Sizes listed in table to the left but not marked as stock are available on special order.

4. Aluminum and stainless steel are more commonly used, whereas copper and especially galvanized steel are least used.

5. All jointing methods are applicable to most gutter shapes. Lap joints are more commonly used. Seal all joints with mastic or by soldering. Lock, slip, or lap joints do not provide expansion.

RECTANGULAR   **BEVELED**   **OGEE OR STYLE "K"**   **SEMICIRCULAR OR HALF-ROUND**

METAL GUTTER NOTES

Various sizes and other shapes available.

Always keep front 1/2 inch lower than back of gutter.

Do not use width less than 4 inches except for canopies and small porches. Min. ratio of depth to width should be 3 to 4.

OGEE OR STYLE "K"		
2 1/2" H x 3" W		
2 3/4" H x 4" W	G	A
3 3/4" H x 5" W	G	A
4 3/4" H x 6" W	G	
5 1/4" H x 7" W		
6" H x 8" W		

SEMICIRCULAR OR HALF-ROUND	
4" W	G
5" W	G A
6" W	G A
7" W	G
8" W	G

NOTE: Stock sizes—G = galvanized, A = aluminum.

METAL GUTTER SHAPES AND SIZES

LOCK JOINT (FOLDED SHEET METAL)   **SLIP JOINT** (HEAVY-GAGE FORMED SHEET METAL)   **LAP JOINT** (RIVETS OR SHEET METAL SCREWS)   **EXPANSION JOINT** (OVERLAPPING NEOPRENE)

SPLICED JOINTS IN METAL GUTTERS AND EXPANSION JOINT

CORRUGATED ROUND STOCK   **PLAIN ROUND** STOCK

PLAIN RECTANGULAR FABRICATED   **CORRUGATED RECTANGULAR** STOCK

EXPANSION JOINTS

Expansion joints should be used on all hip roof installations and on straight runs over 40 ft. In a 10 ft section of gutter and a 100° temperature change linear expansion will be:

EXPANSION OF METAL GUTTERS IN 40 FT

METAL	COEFFICIENT OF EXPANSION	MOVEMENT
Aluminum	$11/64 \times 4.0 =$	0.68"
Copper	$7/64 \times 4.0 =$	0.45"
Galvanized steel	$5/64 \times 4.0 =$	0.31"

NOTES

    Space downspouts 20 ft. min., 50 ft. max., generally. Extreme max. 60 ft.

    Do not use size smaller than 7.00 in area except for canopies.

    Corrugated shapes resist freezing better than plain shapes.

    Elbows available: 45°, 60°, 75°, 90°.

STANDARD DOWNSPOUT SHAPES

RECOMMENDED MINIMUM GAUGES FOR METAL GUTTER

GIRTH-INCHES	GALV. STEEL GAUGE	COPPER OZ.	ALUMINUM INCHES	STAINLESS STEEL GAUGE
UP TO 15	26	16	0.025	26
16 TO 20	24	16	0.032	26
21 TO 25	22	20	0.051	24
26 TO 30	20	24	0.064	22
31 TO 35	18	24	—	20
OVER 35	16	—	—	18

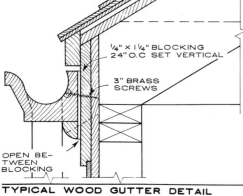

TYPICAL WOOD GUTTER DETAIL

1/4" x 1 1/4" BLOCKING 24" O.C SET VERTICAL
3" BRASS SCREWS
OPEN BETWEEN BLOCKING

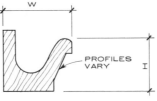

PROFILES VARY

REDWOOD	FIR
3" H x 4" W	3" H x 4" W
4" H x 4" W	4" H x 5" W
4" H x 6" W	4" H x 6" W
	5" H x 7" W

NOTE

Wood gutters are still in use in New York State and the New England States.

WOOD GUTTERS

ELASTIC CEMENT
COPPER TACK
SHEET LEAD
BRASS SCREWS
EDGE OF LEAD SPLICE PLATE

SECTION A-A   **ELEVATION**   SPLICE

BRASS JOINT FITTINGS AVAILABLE

3" & 3/4" BRASS SCREWS COARSE THREADED SECURING SPLICE. SCREWS CSK. & HOLES PUTTIED
COPPER TACKS 3/4" O.C.

SECTION   **PLAN**

SPLICED JOINT IN WOOD GUTTER

Lawrence W. Cobb; Columbia, South Carolina

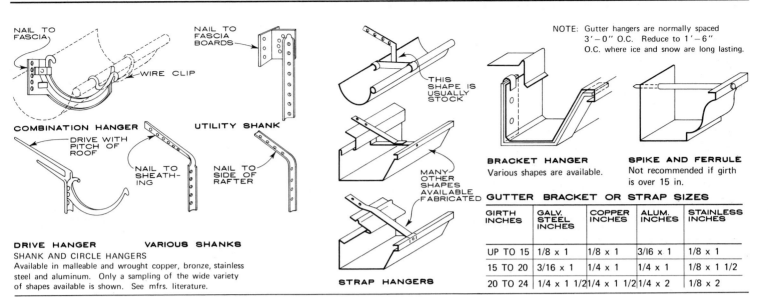

NOTE: Gutter hangers are normally spaced 3'-0" O.C. Reduce to 1'-6" O.C. where ice and snow are long lasting.

COMBINATION HANGER

NAIL TO FASCIA — WIRE CLIP

UTILITY SHANK

NAIL TO FASCIA BOARDS

DRIVE HANGER **VARIOUS SHANKS**

DRIVE WITH PITCH OF ROOF

NAIL TO SHEATHING

NAIL TO SIDE OF RAFTER

SHANK AND CIRCLE HANGERS
Available in malleable and wrought copper, bronze, stainless steel and aluminum. Only a sampling of the wide variety of shapes available is shown. See mfrs. literature.

THIS SHAPE IS USUALLY STOCK

MANY OTHER SHAPES AVAILABLE FABRICATED

STRAP HANGERS

BRACKET HANGER
Various shapes are available.

SPIKE AND FERRULE
Not recommended if girth is over 15 in.

GUTTER BRACKET OR STRAP SIZES

GIRTH INCHES	GALV. STEEL INCHES	COPPER INCHES	ALUM. INCHES	STAINLESS INCHES
UP TO 15	1/8 x 1	1/8 x 1	3/16 x 1	1/8 x 1
15 TO 20	3/16 x 1	1/4 x 1	1/4 x 1	1/8 x 1 1/2
20 TO 24	1/4 x 1 1/2	1/4 x 1 1/2	1/4 x 2	1/8 x 2

GUTTER HANGERS

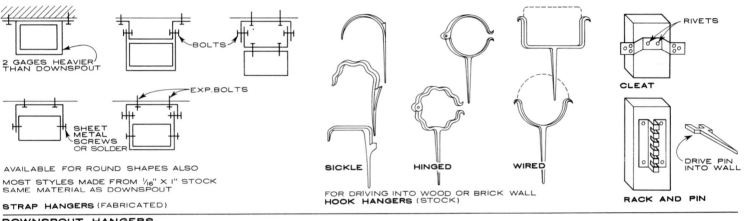

2 GAGES HEAVIER THAN DOWNSPOUT

BOLTS

EXP. BOLTS

SHEET METAL SCREWS OR SOLDER

AVAILABLE FOR ROUND SHAPES ALSO

MOST STYLES MADE FROM 1/16" X 1" STOCK SAME MATERIAL AS DOWNSPOUT

STRAP HANGERS (FABRICATED)

SICKLE **HINGED** **WIRED**

FOR DRIVING INTO WOOD OR BRICK WALL
HOOK HANGERS (STOCK)

RIVETS

CLEAT

DRIVE PIN INTO WALL

RACK AND PIN

DOWNSPOUT HANGERS

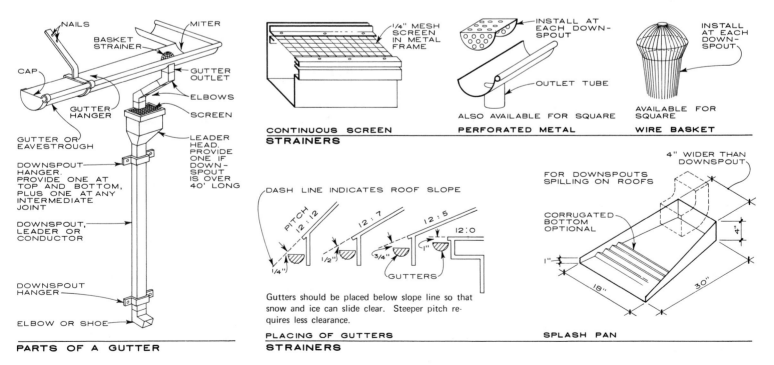

NAILS

BASKET STRAINER

CAP

GUTTER HANGER

GUTTER OR EAVESTROUGH

DOWNSPOUT HANGER. PROVIDE ONE AT TOP AND BOTTOM, PLUS ONE AT ANY INTERMEDIATE JOINT

DOWNSPOUT, LEADER OR CONDUCTOR

DOWNSPOUT HANGER

ELBOW OR SHOE

MITER

GUTTER OUTLET

ELBOWS

SCREEN

LEADER HEAD. PROVIDE ONE IF DOWNSPOUT IS OVER 40' LONG

PARTS OF A GUTTER

1/4" MESH SCREEN IN METAL FRAME

CONTINUOUS SCREEN

INSTALL AT EACH DOWNSPOUT

OUTLET TUBE

ALSO AVAILABLE FOR SQUARE

PERFORATED METAL

INSTALL AT EACH DOWNSPOUT

AVAILABLE FOR SQUARE

WIRE BASKET

STRAINERS

DASH LINE INDICATES ROOF SLOPE

PITCH 12:12 12:7 12:5 12:0

1/4" 1/2" 3/4" 1"

GUTTERS

Gutters should be placed below slope line so that snow and ice can slide clear. Steeper pitch requires less clearance.

PLACING OF GUTTERS
STRAINERS

4" WIDER THAN DOWNSPOUT

FOR DOWNSPOUTS SPILLING ON ROOFS

CORRUGATED BOTTOM OPTIONAL

4"

1" 18" 30"

SPLASH PAN

Lawrence W. Cobb; Columbia, South Carolina

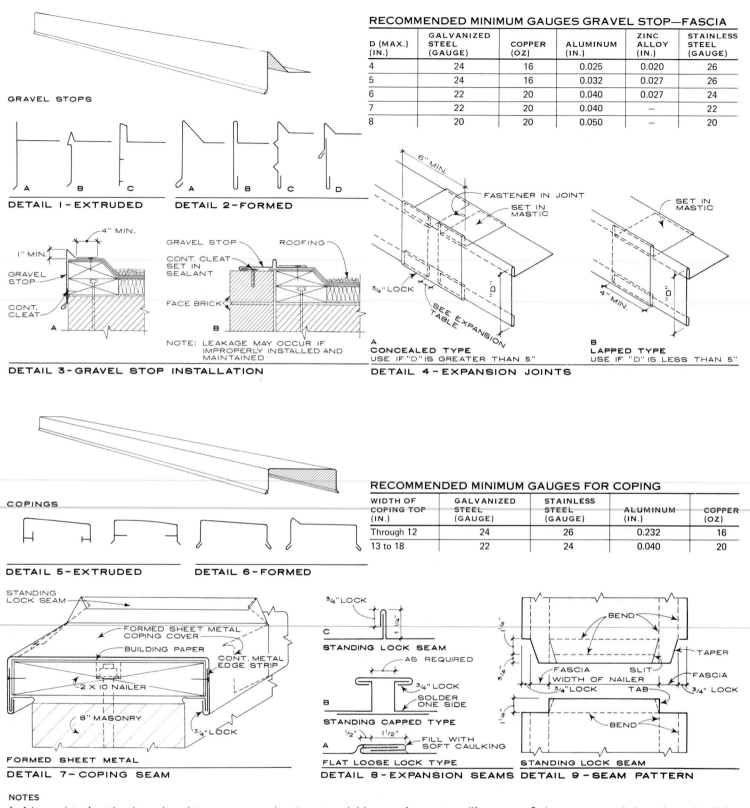

GRAVEL STOPS

DETAIL 1-EXTRUDED DETAIL 2-FORMED

DETAIL 3-GRAVEL STOP INSTALLATION

NOTE: LEAKAGE MAY OCCUR IF IMPROPERLY INSTALLED AND MAINTAINED

RECOMMENDED MINIMUM GAUGES GRAVEL STOP—FASCIA

D (MAX.) (IN.)	GALVANIZED STEEL (GAUGE)	COPPER (OZ)	ALUMINUM (IN.)	ZINC ALLOY (IN.)	STAINLESS STEEL (GAUGE)
4	24	16	0.025	0.020	26
5	24	16	0.032	0.027	26
6	22	20	0.040	0.027	24
7	22	20	0.040	—	22
8	20	20	0.050	—	20

DETAIL 4-EXPANSION JOINTS

A CONCEALED TYPE USE IF "D" IS GREATER THAN 5"

B LAPPED TYPE USE IF "D" IS LESS THAN 5"

COPINGS

DETAIL 5-EXTRUDED DETAIL 6-FORMED

RECOMMENDED MINIMUM GAUGES FOR COPING

WIDTH OF COPING TOP (IN.)	GALVANIZED STEEL (GAUGE)	STAINLESS STEEL (GAUGE)	ALUMINUM (IN.)	COPPER (OZ)
Through 12	24	26	0.232	16
13 to 18	22	24	0.040	20

DETAIL 7-COPING SEAM

DETAIL 8-EXPANSION SEAMS   DETAIL 9-SEAM PATTERN

NOTES

1. A large variety of metal copings and gravel stops are available in both extruded aluminum and formed metals. Illustrated here are only a few of those offered. A multitude of colors, textures and finishes are also available.

2. For additional strength, longitudinal breaks may be formed in wide fascia as shown in C of detail 2. Two piece construction as shown in D of detail 2 is also recommended for wide fascia.

3. Where the fascia exceeds 5 in., a continuous cleat should be used at the drip edge.

4. Nailing the gravel stop or coping directly to the wall is not recommended because of temperature differentials between the metal and the wall. The use of a watertight washer such as neoprene at all fasteners is recommended.

5. All gravel stops should be installed on a raised curb with a 1 in. lip formed as shown in detail 3. This places the junction between the gravel stop and roofing membrane above standing water.

6. B of detail 3 shows a concealed gravel stop. Extreme care must be exercised when installing this type of gravel stop because it is somewhat more vulnerable to weather and moisture. A of detail 3 shows a more typical gravel stop installation procedure.

7. Allowance for expansion and contraction at joints should be made as shown in A and B of detail 4. Soldered or welded joints are not recommended except at corners. All joints should be set in mastic. Expansion joints for metal copings similar to detail 4.

8. In areas of extreme temperature changes, galvanized steel may require more maintenance than other metals mentioned.

Straub, Van Dine, Dziurman/Architects; Troy, Michigan

Ferebee, Walters and Associates; Charlotte, North Carolina

7 **ROOF SPECIALTIES**

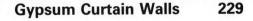

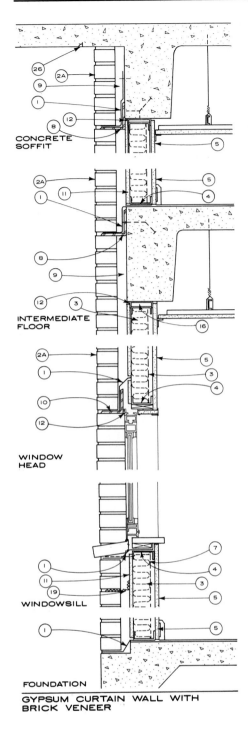

CONCRETE SOFFIT

INTERMEDIATE FLOOR

WINDOW HEAD

WINDOWSILL

FOUNDATION

GYPSUM CURTAIN WALL WITH BRICK VENEER

KEY

1 CONTINUOUS FLASHING: With weep holes at exterior face; up inside face of stud.

2 EXTERIOR FINISH:

  A Brick. or
  B Stucco: cement lime. Mixture applied to galvanized metal lath.

3 FIBERGLASS INSULATION:

  3½ in.   R-11
  3⅝ in.   R-13
  6 in.   R-19
  Fill cavity with insulation.

4 STUDS AND RUNNERS: 3⅝ to 7½ in. 20 gauge galvanized steel minimum. Check local codes for loading requirements. Optional double partition eliminates conduction through studs.

5 INTERIOR FINISH: Any system compatible with metal stud construction.

6 CONTROL JOINTS: Check manufacturer's recommendation for maximum spacing.

7 VAPOR BARRIER: Polyethylene film. Integral with insulation or foil back gypsum board.

8 RELIEVING ANGLES FOR BRICK VENEER: Check local building codes for maximum spacing.

9 AIRSPACE: 1 in. minimum.

10 LINTEL ANGLE REQUIRED AT OPENINGS: With brick exterior finish. Note that flashing and weepholes are required.

11 GYPSUM SHEATHING.

12 SEALANT BACKER AND SEALANT.

13 CORNER BEAD WITH DRIP.

14 CASING BEAD.

15 DRIP CAP.

16 FLEXIBLE JOINT: At top of studs and runners under structural frame members.

17 METAL FASCIA SYSTEM.

18 ROOFING.

19 NONCORROSIVE MASONRY TIE: Fasten to metal studs. Check local codes for spacing requirements.

20 PREFABRICATED SCREED AND DRIP.

21 CONTROL JOINT: Check manufacturer's recommendations for type and maximum spacing.

22 9 IN. MINIMUM WIDE FELT STRIPS: Stapled to sheathing.

23 THERMAL INSULATION.

24 SEALANT.

25 STRUCTURAL FRAME MEMBER.

26 DRIP.

27 STEEL CLIP ANGLE: Fastened to structural members.

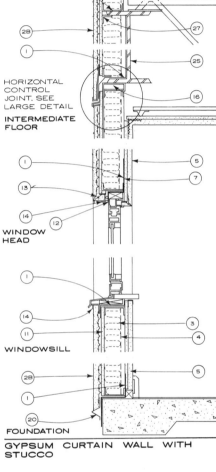

ROOF

INTERMEDIATE FLOOR

HORIZONTAL CONTROL JOINT. SEE LARGE DETAIL

WINDOW HEAD

WINDOWSILL

FOUNDATION

GYPSUM CURTAIN WALL WITH STUCCO

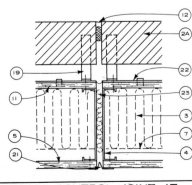

VERTICAL CONTROL JOINT AT BRICK VENEER

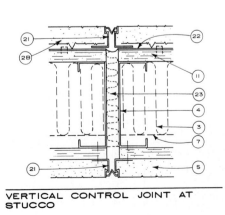

VERTICAL CONTROL JOINT AT STUCCO

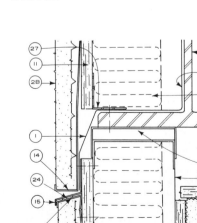

HORIZONTAL CONTROL JOINT AT STUCCO

Isaak and Isaak, Architects; Professional Association; Manchester, New Hampshire

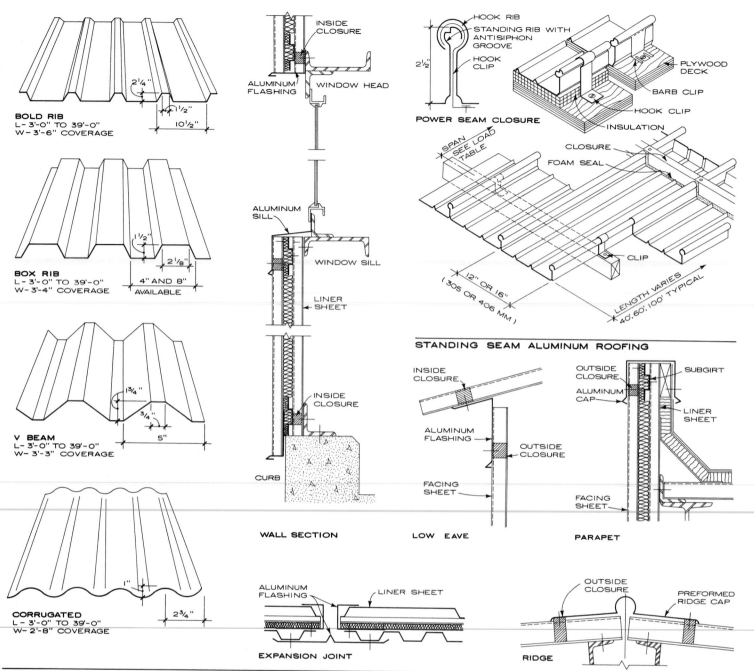

FORMED ALUMINUM ROOFING AND SIDING

NOTES

1. Endlaps for roofing and siding shall be at least 6 in. and fastened at every rib. Two fasteners may be required when designing for a negative (uplift) loading condition.

2. Minimum sidelaps shall be equal to one rib or corrugation and laid away from prevailing wind. Fasteners shall be spaced a maximum of 12 in. on center for all types of roofing and siding.

3. For roofing, fasteners shall pierce only the high corrugation. For siding, fasteners shall pierce either the high or low corrugation. Consult manufacturer for proper sheet metal fasteners and accessories.

4. Minimum slopes for sheet roofing are as follows:
   a. 1 in. depth corrugated—3 in 12.
   b. 1½ in. depth ribbed—2 in 12.
   c. 1¾ in. v-corrugated—2 in 12.

5. See page on Metal Walls for insulation details and fire rated wall assemblies.

John A. Schulte; Hellmuth, Obata & Kassabaum, Inc.; St. Louis, Missouri

MAXIMUM SPAN TABLE FOR FORMED ALUMINUM ROOFING AND SIDING (IN.)

DESIGN LOAD (PSF)	BOLD RIB		4" BOX RIB		V BEAM		CORRUGATED		STANDING SEAM	
	0.032 IN. THICK	0.040 IN. THICK	0.032 IN. THICK	0.040 IN. THICK	0.032 IN. THICK	0.040 IN. THICK	0.032 IN. THICK	0.040 IN. THICK	0.032 IN. THICK	0.040 IN. THICK
20	95	123	100	120	131	151	90	98	103	124
30	77	100	82	98	107	124	73	80	86	104
40	67	87	71	85	92	107	64	69	77	92
50	60	76	63	76	83	96	57	62	70	83

NOTE: Values are based on uniform positive (downward) and walking loads on single span only.

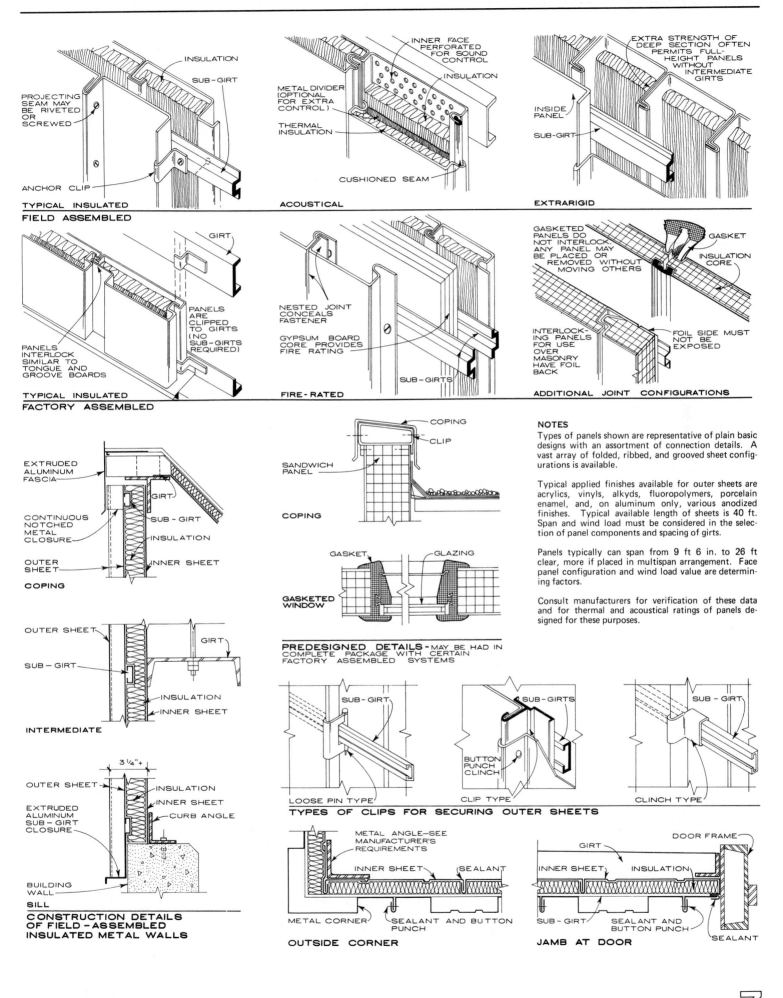

TYPICAL INSULATED FIELD ASSEMBLED

INSULATION

SUB-GIRT

PROJECTING SEAM MAY BE RIVETED OR SCREWED

ANCHOR CLIP

ACOUSTICAL

INNER FACE PERFORATED FOR SOUND CONTROL

INSULATION

METAL DIVIDER (OPTIONAL FOR EXTRA CONTROL)

THERMAL INSULATION

CUSHIONED SEAM

EXTRARIGID

EXTRA STRENGTH OF DEEP SECTION OFTEN PERMITS FULL-HEIGHT PANELS WITHOUT INTERMEDIATE GIRTS

INSIDE PANEL

SUB-GIRT

TYPICAL INSULATED FACTORY ASSEMBLED

GIRT

PANELS ARE CLIPPED TO GIRTS (NO SUB-GIRTS REQUIRED)

PANELS INTERLOCK SIMILAR TO TONGUE AND GROOVE BOARDS

FIRE-RATED

NESTED JOINT CONCEALS FASTENER

GYPSUM BOARD CORE PROVIDES FIRE RATING

SUB-GIRTS

ADDITIONAL JOINT CONFIGURATIONS

GASKETED PANELS DO NOT INTERLOCK. ANY PANEL MAY BE PLACED OR REMOVED WITHOUT MOVING OTHERS

GASKET

INSULATION CORE

INTERLOCK-ING PANELS FOR USE OVER MASONRY HAVE FOIL BACK

FOIL SIDE MUST NOT BE EXPOSED

COPING

EXTRUDED ALUMINUM FASCIA

GIRT

SUB-GIRT

INSULATION

INNER SHEET

CONTINUOUS NOTCHED METAL CLOSURE

OUTER SHEET

INTERMEDIATE

OUTER SHEET

GIRT

SUB-GIRT

INSULATION

INNER SHEET

SILL

3 1/4"+

OUTER SHEET

INSULATION

INNER SHEET

CURB ANGLE

EXTRUDED ALUMINUM SUB-GIRT CLOSURE

BUILDING WALL

CONSTRUCTION DETAILS OF FIELD-ASSEMBLED INSULATED METAL WALLS

COPING

COPING

CLIP

SANDWICH PANEL

GASKETED WINDOW

GASKET

GLAZING

PREDESIGNED DETAILS—MAY BE HAD IN COMPLETE PACKAGE WITH CERTAIN FACTORY ASSEMBLED SYSTEMS

NOTES

Types of panels shown are representative of plain basic designs with an assortment of connection details. A vast array of folded, ribbed, and grooved sheet configurations is available.

Typical applied finishes available for outer sheets are acrylics, vinyls, alkyds, fluoropolymers, porcelain enamel, and, on aluminum only, various anodized finishes. Typical available length of sheets is 40 ft. Span and wind load must be considered in the selection of panel components and spacing of girts.

Panels typically can span from 9 ft 6 in. to 26 ft clear, more if placed in multispan arrangement. Face panel configuration and wind load value are determining factors.

Consult manufacturers for verification of these data and for thermal and acoustical ratings of panels designed for these purposes.

TYPES OF CLIPS FOR SECURING OUTER SHEETS

SUB-GIRT

LOOSE PIN TYPE

SUB-GIRTS

BUTTON PUNCH CLINCH

CLIP TYPE

SUB-GIRT

CLINCH TYPE

OUTSIDE CORNER

METAL ANGLE—SEE MANUFACTURER'S REQUIREMENTS

INNER SHEET

SEALANT

METAL CORNER

SEALANT AND BUTTON PUNCH

JAMB AT DOOR

DOOR FRAME

GIRT

INNER SHEET

INSULATION

SUB-GIRT

SEALANT AND BUTTON PUNCH

SEALANT

FACING MATERIALS AVAILABLE

1. Aluminum.
2. Aluminized steel.
3. Galvanized steel.

FINISHES AVAILABLE

1. Anodized aluminum.
2. 50% silicone—modified polyester baked enamel paint.
3. Fluorocarbon baked enamel paint.
4. Porcelain enamel on aluminized steel.

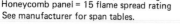

INSULATING VALUES	MAX. U FACTOR
2 in. urethane core	0.065
3 in. honeycomb core	0.41
2 in. honeycomb with fill	0.107

NOTE

Some codes restrict the use of the urethane core panel. The honeycomb panels are more acceptable.

Urethane panel = 25 flame spread rating
Honeycomb panel = 15 flame spread rating
See manufacturer for span tables.

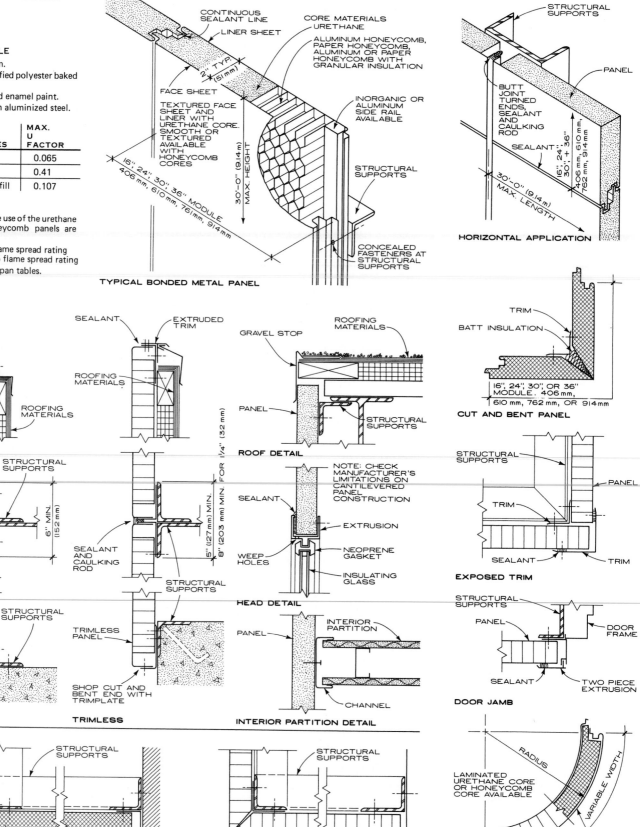

TYPICAL BONDED METAL PANEL

HORIZONTAL APPLICATION

CUT AND BENT PANEL

EXPOSED TRIM

DOOR JAMB

ROOF DETAIL

HEAD DETAIL

INTERIOR PARTITION DETAIL

EXPOSED TRIM   TRIMLESS

WALL DETAILS

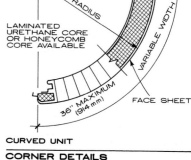

CURVED UNIT

CORNER DETAILS

EXPOSED TRIM   TRIMLESS

SOFFIT DETAILS

John A. Schutle; Hellmuth, Obata, & Kassabaum, Inc.; St. Louis, Missouri

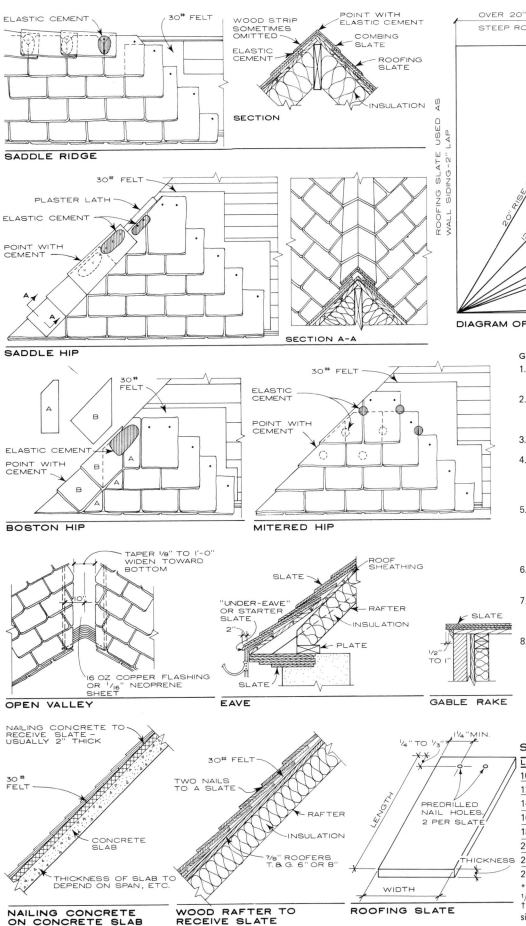

SADDLE RIDGE

SADDLE HIP

SECTION A-A

BOSTON HIP

MITERED HIP

OPEN VALLEY

EAVE

GABLE RAKE

NAILING CONCRETE ON CONCRETE SLAB

WOOD RAFTER TO RECEIVE SLATE

ROOFING SLATE

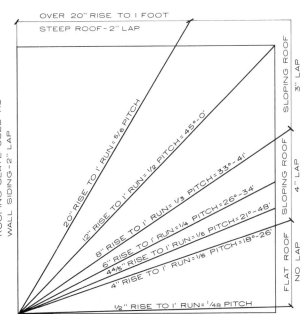

ROOFING SLATE USED AS WALL SIDING—2" LAP

OVER 20" RISE TO I FOOT
STEEP ROOF–2" LAP

20" RISE TO I' RUN= 5/6 PITCH

12" RISE TO I' RUN= 1/2 PITCH =45°-0'

8" RISE TO I' RUN= 1/3 PITCH=33°-41'

6" RISE TO I' RUN= 1/4 PITCH=26°-34'

4 4/5" RISE TO I' RUN= 1/5 PITCH=21°-48'

4" RISE TO I' RUN= 1/6 PITCH =18°-26'

1/2" RISE TO I' RUN= 1/48 PITCH

SLOPING ROOF — 3" LAP
SLOPING ROOF — 4" LAP
FLAT ROOF — NO LAP

DIAGRAM OF PROPER LAP FOR RISE / RUN

GENERAL NOTES

1. COMMERCIAL STANDARD: The quarry run of $3/16$ in. thickness; includes tolerable variations above and below $3/16$ in.
2. TEXTURAL: A rough textured slate roof with uneven butts; the slates vary in thickness and size, which is generally not true of slate more than $3/8$ in. thick.
3. GRADUATED: A textural roof of large slates; more variation in thickness, size, and color.
4. A SQUARE OF ROOFING SLATE: A number of slates of any size sufficient to cover 100 ft² with a 3 in. lap. Weight per square: $3/16$ in.—800 lb; $1/4$ in. —900 lb; $3/8$ in.—1100 lb; $1/2$ in.—1700 lb; $3/4$ in.— 2600 lb.
5. STANDARD NOMENCLATURE FOR SLATE COLOR: Black, blue black, mottled gray, purple, green, mottled purple and green, purple variegated, red; to be preceded by the word "Unfading" or "Weathering." Other colors and combinations are termed specials.
6. PROPER JOINTING FOR PITCHED ROOFS: Requires a 3 in. minimum vertical overlap. Overlap varies with pitch; see graph above.
7. FELT: With Commercial Standard Slate use 30# saturated felt. With graduated roofs use 30# for $1/4$ in. slate and 45#, 55#, or 65# prepared roll roofing for heavier slate.
8. NAIL FASTENING: Use large head, slaters' hard copper wire nails, cut copper, cut brass, or cut yellow metal slating nails. Each slate punched with two nail holes. Use nails that are 1 in. longer than thickness of slate. Cover all exposed heads with elastic cement. In dry climates hot dip galvanized nails may be used.

STANDARD SLATE DIMENSIONS*

LENGTH (IN.)	WIDTH (IN.)
10†	6, 7, 8
12†	6, 7, 8, 9, 10
14†	7, 8, 9, 10, 11, 12
16	8, 9, 10, 11, 12, 14
18	9, 10, 11, 12, 13, 14
20	9, 10, 11, 12, 13, 14
22	10, 11, 12, 13, 14
24	11, 12, 13, 14, 16

*The slates are split in these thicknesses: $3/16$, $1/4$, $1/8$, $1/2$, and $3/4$ in.
†$1/2$ in. and larger slates are not often used in these sizes. Random widths are usually used.

Domenic F. Valente, AIA, Architect & Planner; Medford, Massachusetts

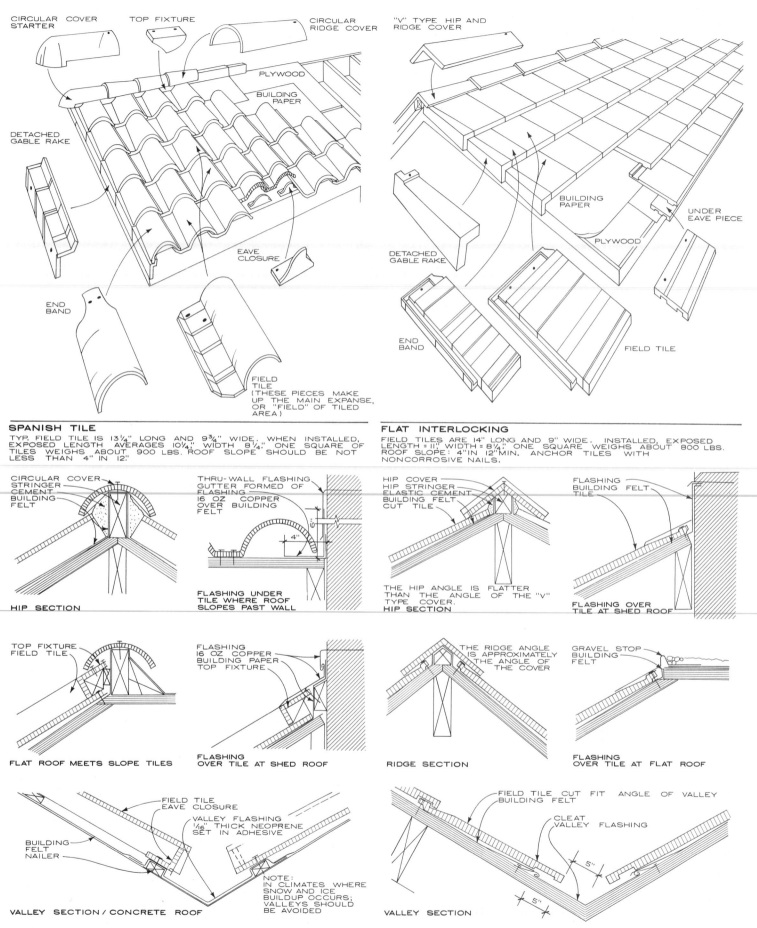

CIRCULAR COVER STARTER

TOP FIXTURE

CIRCULAR RIDGE COVER

"V" TYPE HIP AND RIDGE COVER

PLYWOOD

BUILDING PAPER

DETACHED GABLE RAKE

EAVE CLOSURE

END BAND

FIELD TILE (THESE PIECES MAKE UP THE MAIN EXPANSE, OR "FIELD" OF TILED AREA)

BUILDING PAPER

PLYWOOD

DETACHED GABLE RAKE

END BAND

UNDER EAVE PIECE

FIELD TILE

SPANISH TILE

TYP. FIELD TILE IS 13¼" LONG AND 9¾" WIDE. WHEN INSTALLED, EXPOSED LENGTH AVERAGES 10¼" WIDTH 8¼." ONE SQUARE OF TILES WEIGHS ABOUT 900 LBS. ROOF SLOPE SHOULD BE NOT LESS THAN 4" IN 12."

FLAT INTERLOCKING

FIELD TILES ARE 14" LONG AND 9" WIDE. INSTALLED, EXPOSED LENGTH = 11" WIDTH = 8¼." ONE SQUARE WEIGHS ABOUT 800 LBS. ROOF SLOPE: 4"IN 12"MIN. ANCHOR TILES WITH NONCORROSIVE NAILS.

CIRCULAR COVER STRINGER CEMENT BUILDING FELT

HIP SECTION

THRU-WALL FLASHING GUTTER FORMED OF FLASHING 16 OZ COPPER OVER BUILDING FELT

4"

FLASHING UNDER TILE WHERE ROOF SLOPES PAST WALL

HIP COVER HIP STRINGER ELASTIC CEMENT BUILDING FELT CUT TILE

THE HIP ANGLE IS FLATTER THAN THE ANGLE OF THE "V" TYPE COVER.

HIP SECTION

FLASHING BUILDING FELT TILE

FLASHING OVER TILE AT SHED ROOF

TOP FIXTURE FIELD TILE

FLAT ROOF MEETS SLOPE TILES

FLASHING 16 OZ COPPER BUILDING PAPER TOP FIXTURE

FLASHING OVER TILE AT SHED ROOF

THE RIDGE ANGLE IS APPROXIMATELY THE ANGLE OF THE COVER

RIDGE SECTION

GRAVEL STOP BUILDING FELT

FLASHING OVER TILE AT FLAT ROOF

FIELD TILE EAVE CLOSURE

VALLEY FLASHING 1/16" THICK NEOPRENE SET IN ADHESIVE

BUILDING FELT NAILER

NOTE: IN CLIMATES WHERE SNOW AND ICE BUILDUP OCCURS; VALLEYS SHOULD BE AVOIDED

VALLEY SECTION / CONCRETE ROOF

FIELD TILE CUT FIT ANGLE OF VALLEY BUILDING FELT

CLEAT VALLEY FLASHING

5"

5"

VALLEY SECTION

Darrel Rippeteau, Architect; Washington, D.C.

7 SHINGLES AND ROOFING TILES

RED CEDAR HANDSPLIT SHAKES

GRADE	LENGTH AND THICKNESS	DESCRIPTION
No. 1 handsplit and resawn	15″ starter-finish 18 x $\frac{1}{2}$″ medium 18 x $\frac{3}{4}$″ heavy 24 x $\frac{3}{8}$″ 24 x $\frac{1}{2}$″ medium 24 x $\frac{3}{4}$″ heavy	These shakes have split faces and sawn backs. Cedar logs are first cut into desired lengths. Blanks or boards of proper thickness are split and then run diagonally through a bandsaw to produce two tapered shakes from each blank
No. 1 tapersplit	24 x $\frac{1}{2}$″	Produced largely by hand, using a sharp bladed steel froe and a wooden mallet. The natural shinglelike taper is achieved by reversing the block, end-for-end, with each split
No. 1 straight	18 x $\frac{3}{8}$″ side wall 18 x $\frac{3}{8}$″ 24 x $\frac{3}{8}$″	Produced in the same manner as tapersplit shakes except that by splitting from the same end of the block, the shakes acquire the same thickness throughout

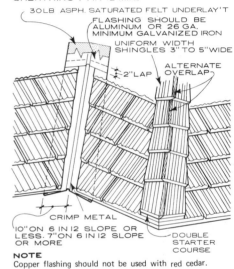

INSTALLATION OF SHAKES OVER SPACED SHEATHING (4 IN 12 MIN.)

RED CEDAR SHINGLES

ROOF PITCH	NO. 1 BLUE LABEL*			NO. 2 RED LABEL†			NO. 3 BLACK LABEL‡		
	MAXIMUM EXPOSURE RECOMMENDED FOR ROOFS								
	16″	18″	24″	16″	18″	24″	16″	18″	24″
3 in 12 to 4 in 12	$3\frac{3}{4}$″	$4\frac{1}{4}$″	$5\frac{3}{4}$″	$3\frac{1}{2}$″	4″	$5\frac{1}{2}$″	3″	$3\frac{1}{2}$″	5″
4 in 12 and steeper	5″	$5\frac{1}{2}$″	$7\frac{1}{2}$″	4″	$4\frac{1}{2}$″	$6\frac{1}{2}$″	$3\frac{1}{2}$″	4″	$5\frac{1}{2}$″

*Premium Grade: 100% heartwood, 100% clear, 100% edge grain, for highest quality.
†Intermediate Grade: not less then 10″ clear on 16″ shingles, 11″ clear on 18″ shingles, 16″ clear on 24″ shingles. Flat grain and limited sapwood permitted.
‡Utility Grade: 6″ clear on 16″ and 18″ shingles, 10″ clear on 24″ shingles. For economy applications.

UNDERLAYMENT AND SHEATHING

ROOFING TYPE	SHEATHING	UNDERLAYMENT	NORMAL SLOPE		LOW SLOPE	
Wood shakes and shingles	Solid or spaced	No. 30 asphalt saturated felt (interlayment)	4 in 12 and up	Underlayment starter course; interlayment over entire roof	3 in 12 to 4 in 12	Single layer underlayment over entire roof; interlayment over entire roof

NOTES
1. Shakes not recommended on slopes less than 4 in 12.
2. Breathing type building paper—such as deadening felt—may be applied over either type of sheating, although paper is not used in most applications.

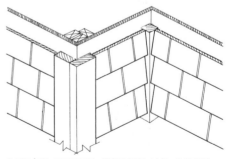

NOTE
Copper flashing should not be used with red cedar.

VALLEY HIP AND RIDGE APPLICATION OF SHAKES & SHINGLES

SHINGLES AND SHAKES USED FOR ROOFING

EXPOSURE FOR SHINGLES & SHAKES USED FOR SIDING

SHINGLE LENGTH	EXPOSURE OF SHINGLES	
	SGL. COURSE	DBL. COURSE
16″	6″ TO $7\frac{1}{2}$″	8″ TO 12″
18″	6″ TO $8\frac{1}{2}$″	9″ TO 14″
24″	8″ TO $11\frac{1}{2}$″	12″ TO 20″

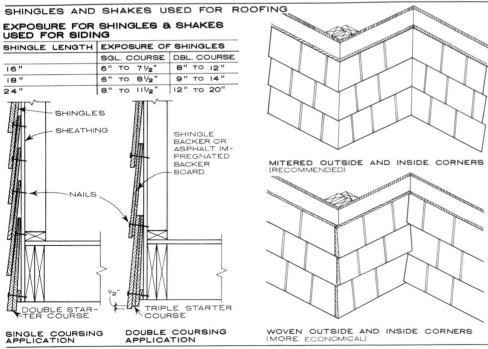

SINGLE COURSING APPLICATION

DOUBLE COURSING APPLICATION

MITERED OUTSIDE AND INSIDE CORNERS (RECOMMENDED)

WOVEN OUTSIDE AND INSIDE CORNERS (MORE ECONOMICAL)

CORNER BOARDS OUTSIDE AND INSIDE CORNERS

NAILING (DEFORMED SHANK NON-FERROUS)
THICKNESS AND NAILS

16″ long	5 butts = 2″	3d
18″ long	5 butts = $2\frac{1}{4}$″	3d
24″ long	4 butts = 2″	4d
25″ to 27″	1 butt = $\frac{1}{2}$″	5 or 6d
25″ to 27″	1 butt = $\frac{5}{8}$″ to $1\frac{1}{4}$″	7 or 8d

SHEATHING NOTES
Sheathing may be strip-type, solid 1″ x 6″ diagonal type, plywood, fiberboard or gypsum. Horizontal wood nailing strips, 1″ x 2″, should be used over fiberboard and gypsum sheathing. Space strips equal to shingle exposure.

WOOD SHINGLES AND SHAKES FOR SIDING

Developed by: Holroyd and Gray, Architects; Charlotte, North Carolina; from data furnished by: Robert M. Stafford, P. E.; Consulting Engineer; Charlotte, North Carolina

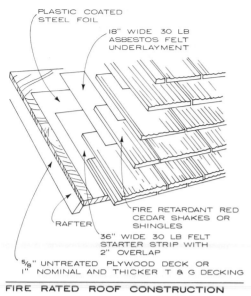

PLASTIC COATED STEEL FOIL

18" WIDE 30 LB ASBESTOS FELT UNDERLAYMENT

FIRE RETARDANT RED CEDAR SHAKES OR SHINGLES

RAFTER

36" WIDE 30 LB FELT STARTER STRIP WITH 2" OVERLAP

$5/8$" UNTREATED PLYWOOD DECK OR 1" NOMINAL AND THICKER T & G DECKING

FIRE RATED ROOF CONSTRUCTION

NOTES

In treating shakes, fire retardant chemicals are pressure impregnated into the wood cells, and chemicals are then fixed in the wood to prevent leaching. Treatment does not alter appearance. Fire retardant red cedar shakes are classified as Class C by U.L. With the addition of the deck constructed of $5/8$ in. plywood with exterior glue or 1 in. nominal T&G boards, overlaid with a layer of approved asbestos felt lapped 2 in. on all joints and between each shake is an 18 in. wide strip of approved asbestos felt not exposed to the weather, Class B classification by U.L. is used. Decorative stains may be applied.

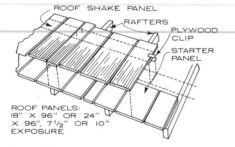

ROOF SHAKE PANEL

RAFTERS

PLYWOOD CLIP

STARTER PANEL

ROOF PANELS: 18" X 96" OR 24" X 96". $7 1/2$" OR 10" EXPOSURE

ROOF PANEL

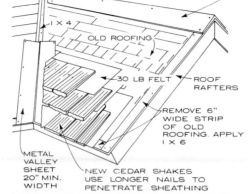

REMOVE OLD RIDGE COVERING. REPLACE WITH CEDAR BEVEL SIDING

1 X 4

OLD ROOFING

30 LB FELT

ROOF RAFTERS

REMOVE 6" WIDE STRIP OF OLD ROOFING. APPLY 1 X 6

METAL VALLEY SHEET 20" MIN. WIDTH

NEW CEDAR SHAKES USE LONGER NAILS TO PENETRATE SHEATHING

WOOD SHAKES APPLIED TO EXISTING ROOF

NOTES

Shakes can also be applied over any existing wall or roof. Brick or other masonry requires vertical frame-boards and horizontal nailing strips.

Over stucco, horizontal nailing strips are attached directly to wall. Nails should penetrate shading or studs. Over wood, apply shakes directly just as if on new sheathing.

NOTES

Shakes and shingles plus sheathing go up in one operation. 8 ft roof panels have 16 individual handsplit shakes bonded to 6 in. wide $1/2$ in. plywood strip, which form a solid deck when the panels are nailed. A 4 to 12 in. or steeper roof pitch is recommended.

After application of starter panels, attach panels directly to rafters. Although designed to center on 16 or 24 in. spacing, they may meet between rafters. Use two 6d nails at each rafter.

Robert E. Fehlberg, FAIA; CTA Architects—Engineers; Billings, Montana

NOMENCLATURE

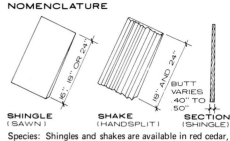

SHINGLE (SAWN)

SHAKE (HANDSPLIT)

SECTION (SHINGLE)

BUTT VARIES .40" TO .50"

Species: Shingles and shakes are available in red cedar, redwood, and tidewater red cypress.

GENERAL NOTES

1. Wood shingles and shakes are manufactured from wood species that are naturally resistant to water, sunlight, rot, and hail. They are typically installed in the natural state, although stains, primers, and paint may be applied.

2. Nails must be hot dipped in zinc or aluminum. Nail heads should be driven flush with the surface of the shingle or shake, but never into the wood.

3. Underlayment and sheathing should be designed to augment the protection provided by the shingles or shakes, depending on roof pitch and climate. For instance, a low pitched roof in an area subject to wind driven snow should have solid sheathing and an additional underlayment.

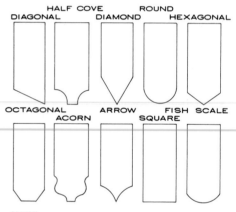

HALF COVE

DIAGONAL   DIAMOND   ROUND   HEXAGONAL

OCTAGONAL   ARROW   FISH SCALE
ACORN   SQUARE

NOTE

Fancy butt shingles are 5 in. wide and $7 1/2$ in. long. Custom produced to individual orders.

FANCY BUTT RED CEDAR SHINGLES

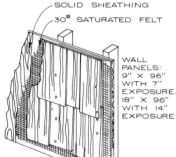

SOLID SHEATHING

30# SATURATED FELT

WALL PANELS: 9" X 96" WITH 7" EXPOSURE. 18" X 96" WITH 14" EXPOSURE.

APPLIED TO SHEATHING

NAILED DIRECTLY TO STUDS

NAILING STRIPS

NAIL ONE NAIL AT EACH STRIP

30# SATURATED FELT

APPLIED DIRECTLY TO STUD   APPLIED TO NAILING STRIPS

NOTES

8 ft sidewall panels are of three-ply construction.

1. Surface layer of individual #1 grade shingles or shakes.
2. Cross binder core of plywood veneer.

SIDEWALL PANELS

3. Undercourse layer of shingle backing panels.

Panels can be applied to nailing strips or directly to studs where Code permits. Use 30 lb saturated fill lapped 3 in. vertically and horizontally. Stagger joints between panels. Matching sidewall or mansard style corners are available.

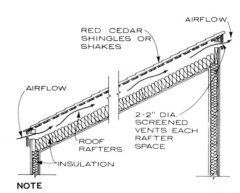

AIRFLOW

RED CEDAR SHINGLES OR SHAKES

AIRFLOW

2-2" DIA. SCREENED VENTS EACH RAFTER SPACE

ROOF RAFTERS

INSULATION

NOTE

A recommended ratio of total free area to adding area should not be less than 1:150 for adequate ventilation.

SECTION
VENTILATION OF ROOF

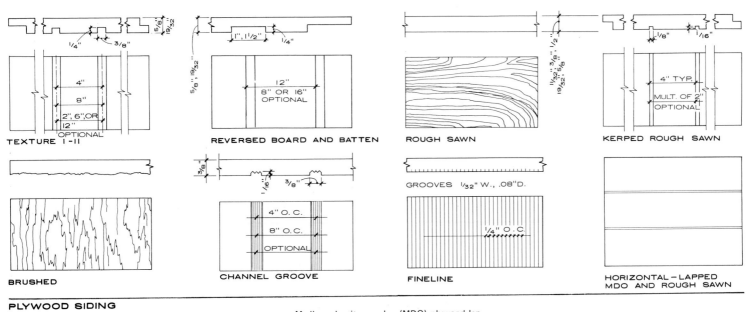

TEXTURE 1-11

REVERSED BOARD AND BATTEN

ROUGH SAWN

KERPED ROUGH SAWN

BRUSHED

CHANNEL GROOVE

GROOVES 1/32" W., .08"D.

FINELINE

HORIZONTAL – LAPPED
MDO AND ROUGH SAWN

PLYWOOD SIDING

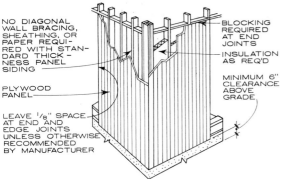

PANEL SIDING VERTICAL APPLICATION

NO DIAGONAL WALL BRACING, SHEATHING, OR PAPER REQUIRED WITH STANDARD THICKNESS PANEL SIDING

BLOCKING REQUIRED AT END JOINTS

INSULATION AS REQ'D

MINIMUM 6" CLEARANCE ABOVE GRADE

PLYWOOD PANEL

LEAVE 1/8" SPACE AT END AND EDGE JOINTS UNLESS OTHERWISE RECOMMENDED BY MANUFACTURER

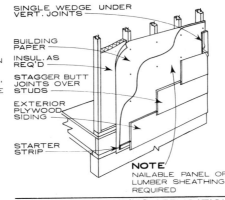

PLYWOOD LAP SIDING APPLICATION

Medium density overlay (MDO) plywood lap siding: standard thickness is 3/8 in. in lengths to 16 ft on order; standard widths are 12 or 16 in.

SINGLE WEDGE UNDER VERT. JOINTS

BUILDING PAPER

INSUL. AS REQ'D

STAGGER BUTT JOINTS OVER STUDS

EXTERIOR PLYWOOD SIDING

STARTER STRIP

NOTE
NAILABLE PANEL OR LUMBER SHEATHING REQUIRED

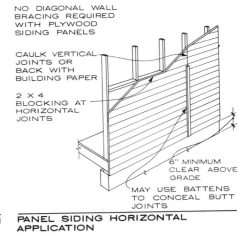

PANEL SIDING HORIZONTAL APPLICATION

NO DIAGONAL WALL BRACING REQUIRED WITH PLYWOOD SIDING PANELS

CAULK VERTICAL JOINTS OR BACK WITH BUILDING PAPER

2 X 4 BLOCKING AT HORIZONTAL JOINTS

6" MINIMUM CLEAR ABOVE GRADE

MAY USE BATTENS TO CONCEAL BUTT JOINTS

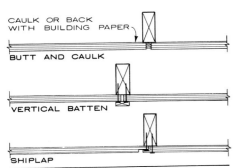

CAULK OR BACK WITH BUILDING PAPER

BUTT AND CAULK

VERTICAL BATTEN

SHIPLAP

VERTICAL JOINTS

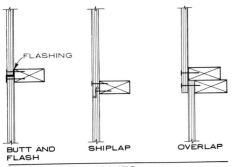

FLASHING

BUTT AND FLASH

SHIPLAP

OVERLAP

HORIZONTAL JOINTS

NAILING CHART FOR PLYWOOD SIDING

APPLICATION	PLYWOOD THICKNESS (IN.)	MAX. SPACING OF SUPPORTS (C.–C.)	NAIL SIZE AND TYPE (a)	NAIL SPACING (IN.)	
				PANEL EDGES	INTERMEDIATE
Panel siding	11/32"	16"	6d casing or siding	6"	12"
	15/32" (c)	24"	6d casing or siding	6"	12"
	19/32" or thicker (c)	24"	8d casing or siding	6"	12"
Lap siding (b)	11/32"	—	6d casing or siding	8" along bottom edge	4" at vert. joint 8" at studs (siding wider than 12")
	15/32"	—	8d casing or siding		

NOTES

(a) Use galvanized, aluminum, or other noncorrosive nails. Use same schedule for panel siding and siding over sheathing.

(b) Apply over separate nailable panel or lumber sheathing only.

(c) Only panels 15/32" and thicker which have certain groove depths and spacings qualify for 24" o.c. span rating.

MINIMUM BENDING RADII FOR PLYWOOD PANELS

The following are found to be appropriate minimum radii for mill run panels, thickness as shown, bent dry. Shorter radii can be developed by selection for bending of areas free of knots and short grain, and/or by wetting or steaming. Exterior type of plywood should be used for such wetting or steaming. Panels to be glued should be redried before gluing. The radii given are minimum; an occasional panel may develop localized fractures at these radii. Bending radii (ft) for panel bent in direction:

1. Panel thickness (in.): 1/4, 5/16, 3/8, 1/2, 5/8, and 3/4.
2. Across grain: 2, 2, 3, 6, 8, and 12.
3. Parallel to grain: 5, 6, 8, 12, 16, and 20.

NOTES

The types of plywood recommended for exterior siding are: A.P.A. grade trademarked medium density overlay (MDO), Type 303 siding or Texture 1-11 (T1-11 special 303 siding). T1-11 plywood siding is manufactured with 3/8 in. wide parallel grooves and shiplapped edges. MDO is recommended for paint finishes and is available in variety of surfaces. 303 plywood panels are also available in a wide variety of surfaces. The most common A.P.A. plywood siding panel dimensions are 4 x 8 ft but the panels are also available in 9 and 10 ft lengths, lap siding to 16 ft.

John D. Bloodgood, Architect, P.C.; Des Moines, Iowa
American Plywood Association

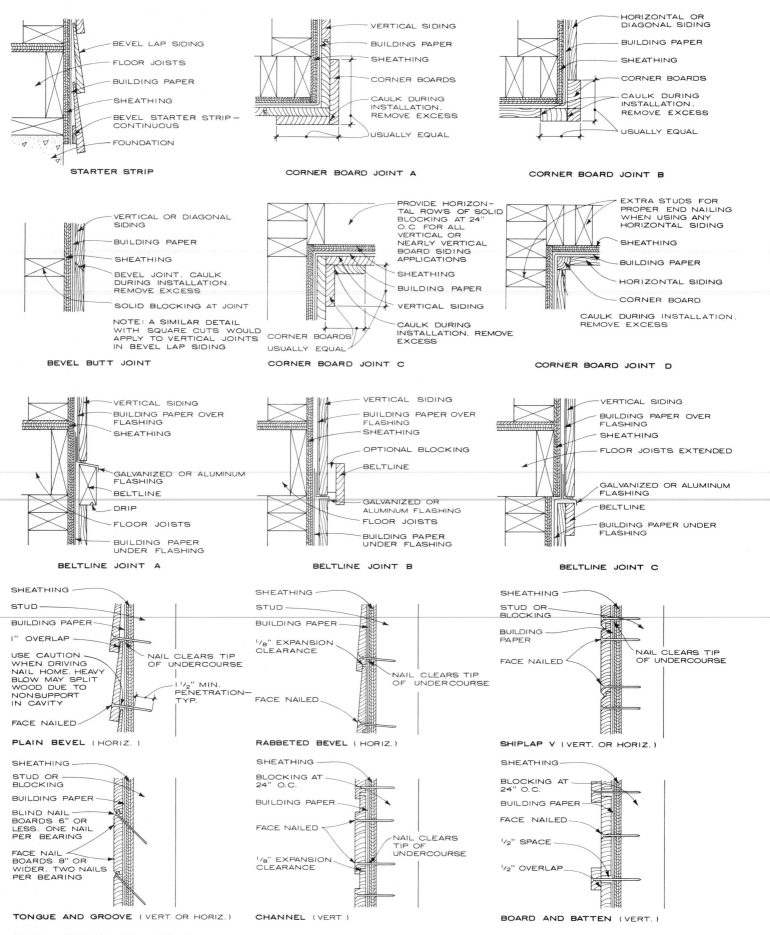

BEVEL LAP SIDING
FLOOR JOISTS
BUILDING PAPER
SHEATHING
BEVEL STARTER STRIP — CONTINUOUS
FOUNDATION

STARTER STRIP

VERTICAL SIDING
BUILDING PAPER
SHEATHING
CORNER BOARDS
CAULK DURING INSTALLATION. REMOVE EXCESS
USUALLY EQUAL

CORNER BOARD JOINT A

HORIZONTAL OR DIAGONAL SIDING
BUILDING PAPER
SHEATHING
CORNER BOARDS
CAULK DURING INSTALLATION. REMOVE EXCESS
USUALLY EQUAL

CORNER BOARD JOINT B

VERTICAL OR DIAGONAL SIDING
BUILDING PAPER
SHEATHING
BEVEL JOINT. CAULK DURING INSTALLATION. REMOVE EXCESS
SOLID BLOCKING AT JOINT

NOTE: A SIMILAR DETAIL WITH SQUARE CUTS WOULD APPLY TO VERTICAL JOINTS IN BEVEL LAP SIDING

BEVEL BUTT JOINT

PROVIDE HORIZONTAL ROWS OF SOLID BLOCKING AT 24" O.C. FOR ALL VERTICAL OR NEARLY VERTICAL BOARD SIDING APPLICATIONS
SHEATHING
BUILDING PAPER
VERTICAL SIDING
CAULK DURING INSTALLATION. REMOVE EXCESS
CORNER BOARDS USUALLY EQUAL

CORNER BOARD JOINT C

EXTRA STUDS FOR PROPER END NAILING WHEN USING ANY HORIZONTAL SIDING
SHEATHING
BUILDING PAPER
HORIZONTAL SIDING
CORNER BOARD
CAULK DURING INSTALLATION. REMOVE EXCESS

CORNER BOARD JOINT D

VERTICAL SIDING
BUILDING PAPER OVER FLASHING
SHEATHING
GALVANIZED OR ALUMINUM FLASHING
BELTLINE
DRIP
FLOOR JOISTS
BUILDING PAPER UNDER FLASHING

BELTLINE JOINT A

VERTICAL SIDING
BUILDING PAPER OVER FLASHING
SHEATHING
OPTIONAL BLOCKING
BELTLINE
GALVANIZED OR ALUMINUM FLASHING
FLOOR JOISTS
BUILDING PAPER UNDER FLASHING

BELTLINE JOINT B

VERTICAL SIDING
BUILDING PAPER OVER FLASHING
SHEATHING
FLOOR JOISTS EXTENDED
GALVANIZED OR ALUMINUM FLASHING
BELTLINE
BUILDING PAPER UNDER FLASHING

BELTLINE JOINT C

SHEATHING
STUD
BUILDING PAPER
1" OVERLAP
USE CAUTION WHEN DRIVING NAIL HOME. HEAVY BLOW MAY SPLIT WOOD DUE TO NONSUPPORT IN CAVITY
FACE NAILED
NAIL CLEARS TIP OF UNDERCOURSE
1 1/2" MIN. PENETRATION — TYP.

PLAIN BEVEL (HORIZ.)

SHEATHING
STUD
BUILDING PAPER
1/8" EXPANSION CLEARANCE
NAIL CLEARS TIP OF UNDERCOURSE
FACE NAILED

RABBETED BEVEL (HORIZ.)

SHEATHING
STUD OR BLOCKING
BUILDING PAPER
FACE NAILED
NAIL CLEARS TIP OF UNDERCOURSE

SHIPLAP V (VERT. OR HORIZ.)

SHEATHING
STUD OR BLOCKING
BUILDING PAPER
BLIND NAIL BOARDS 6" OR LESS. ONE NAIL PER BEARING
FACE NAIL BOARDS 8" OR WIDER. TWO NAILS PER BEARING

TONGUE AND GROOVE (VERT. OR HORIZ.)

SHEATHING
BLOCKING AT 24" O.C.
BUILDING PAPER
FACE NAILED
1/8" EXPANSION CLEARANCE
NAIL CLEARS TIP OF UNDERCOURSE

CHANNEL (VERT)

SHEATHING
BLOCKING AT 24" O.C.
BUILDING PAPER
FACE NAILED
1/2" SPACE
1/2" OVERLAP

BOARD AND BATTEN (VERT.)

Jerry Graham; CTA Architects Engineers; Billings, Montana

SCHEDULE OF UNDERLAYMENT

SLOPE	TYPE OF UNDERLAYMENT
Normal slope: 4 in 12 and up	Single layer of 15 lb asphalt saturated felt over entire roof
Low slope: 2 in 12 to 4 in 12	Two layers of 15 lb asphalt saturated felt over entire roof

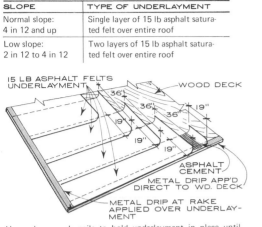

Use only enough nails to hold underlayment in place until shingles are laid.

APPLICATION OF UNDERLAYMENT ON LOW SLOPE ROOFS

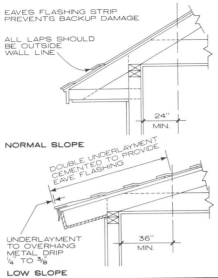

EAVE FLASHING

SCHEDULE OF SHINGLE TYPES

DESCRIPTION	DESIGN	MATERIAL	U.L. RATING	WEIGHT	SIZE
Three-tab square butt		Fiberglass Organic felts	A C	215–225 lb/sq 235–300 lb/sq	36" x 12"
Two-tab square butt		Fiberglass Organic felts	A C	260–325 lb/sq 300 lb/sq	36" x 12"
Laminated overlay		Fiberglass Organic felts	A C	300 lb/sq 330–380 lb/sq	36" x 14"
Random edge cut		Fiberglass Organic felts	A C	225–260 lb/sq 250 lb/sq	36" x 12"

NOTE: Exposure 5", edge lap 2".

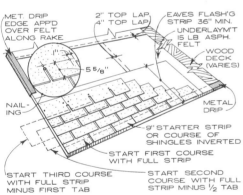

THREE TAB SQUARE BUTT STRIP SHINGLES

HIP AND RIDGE

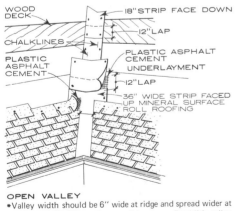

OPEN VALLEY

*Valley width should be 6" wide at ridge and spread wider at the rate of 1/8"/foot downward to eave. Establish valley width using chalkline from ridge to cove.

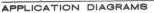

CLOSED VALLEY

APPLICATION DIAGRAMS

Robert E. Fehlberg, FAIA; CTA Architects Engineers; Billings, Montana

EAVE FLASHING

Eave flashing is required wherever the January daily average temperature is 25°F or less or where there is a possibility of ice forming along the eaves.

NORMAL SLOPE—4 IN./FT OR OVER

A course of 90 lb mineral surfaced roll roofing or a course of 50 lb smooth roll roofing is installed to overhang the underlay and metal edge from 1/4 to 3/8 in. Extend up the roof far enough to cover a point at least 24 in. inside the interior wall line of the building. When the overhang requires flashing wider than 36 in., the horizontal lap joint is cemented and located on the roof deck extending beyond the exterior line of the building.

LOW SLOPE—2 TO 4 IN./FT

Cover the deck with two layers of 15# asphalt saturated felt. Begin with a 19 in. starter course laid along the eaves, followed by a 36 in. wide sheet laid even with the eaves and completely overlapping the starter course. The starter course is covered with asphalt cement. Thereafter, 36 in. sheets are laid in asphalt cement, each to overlap the preceding course 19 in., exposing 17 in. of the underlying sheet.

The plies are placed in asphalt cement to a point at least 36 in. inside the interior wall line of the building.

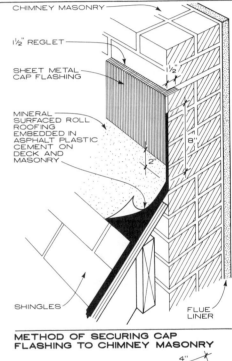

METHOD OF SECURING CAP FLASHING TO CHIMNEY MASONRY

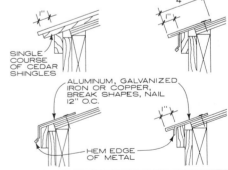

DRIP EDGE DETAILS

NAILING OF SHINGLES RECOMMENDATION	
DECK TYPE	NAIL LENGTH
1" Wood sheathing	1 1/4"
3/8" Plywood	7/8"
1/2" Plywood	1"
Reroofing over asphalt shingles	1 3/4"

NAIL TYPES: SMOOTH, ANNULAR THREADED, SCREW THREADED

MINIMUM THICKNESS (GAUGES OR WEIGHT) FOR COMMON FLASHING CONDITIONS

MATERIALS	BASE COURSE	WALL OPENINGS HEAD AND SILL	THROUGH WALL AND SPANDREL	CAP AND BASE FLASHING	VERTICAL AND HORIZONTAL SURFACES	ROOF EDGE RIDGES AND HIPS	CRICKETS VALLEY OR GUTTER	CHIMNEY PAN	LEDGE FLASHING	ROOF PENETRATIONS	COPING WIDTH UP TO 12"	COPING WIDTH ABOVE 12"	EDGE STRIPS	CLEATS	NOTE
Copper	10 oz	10 oz	10 oz	16 oz	16 oz	16 oz	16 oz	16 oz	16 oz	16 oz	16 oz	20 oz	20 oz	16 oz	
Aluminum	0.019"	0.019"	0.019"	0.019"	0.019"	0.019"	0.019"	0.019"	0.019"	0.040"	0.032"	0.040"	0.024"	✕	Note 6
Stainless steel	30 GA	30 GA	30 GA	26 GA	30 GA	26 GA	26 GA	30 GA	26 GA	26 GA	26 GA	24 GA	24 GA	✕	Note 5
Galvanized steel	26 GA	26 GA	26 GA	26 GA	26 GA	24 GA	24 GA	26 GA	24 GA	24 GA	24 GA	22 GA	26 GA	22 GA	Note 2
Zinc alloy	0.027"	0.027"	0.027"	0.027"	0.027"	0.027"	0.027"	0.027"	0.027"	0.027"	0.027"	0.032"	0.040"	0.027"	Note 4
Lead	3#	2½#	2½#	2½#	3#	3#	3#	3#	3#	3#	3#	3#	3#	3#	Note 3
Painted terne	40#	40#	40#	20#	40#	20#	40#	20#	40#	40#	✕	✕	20#	40#	Note 8
1/16" elastomeric sheet	See Note 7			✕	✕	✕	✕	✕		See Note 7			✕	✕	Note 7

GENERAL NOTES

1. All sizes and weights of material given in chart are minimum. Actual conditions may require greater strength.
2. All galvanized steel must be painted.
3. With lead flashing use 16 oz copper cleats. If any part is exposed, use 3# lead cleats.
4. Coat zinc with asphaltum paint when in contact with redwood or cedar. High acid content (in these woods only) develops stains.
5. Type 302 stainless steel is an all purpose flashing type. Cleats not needed.
6. Use only aluminum manufactured for the purpose of flashing. Cleats not needed.
7. See manufacturer's literature for use and types of elastic flashing.
8. In general cleats will be of the same material as flashing, but heavier weight or thicker gauge.
9. In selecting metal flashing precaution must be taken not to place flashing in direct contact with dissimilar metals that cause electrolysis.
10. Spaces marked ✕ in the table are uses not recommended for that material.

GALVANIC CORROSION (ELECTROLYSIS) POTENTIAL BETWEEN COMMON FLASHING MATERIALS AND SELECTED CONSTRUCTION MATERIALS

FLASHING MATERIALS \ CONSTRUCTION MATERIALS	COPPER	ALUMINUM	STAINLESS STEEL	GALVANIZED STEEL	ZINC	LEAD	BRASS	BRONZE	MONEL	UNCURED MORTAR OR CEMENT	WOODS WITH ACID (REDWOOD AND RED CEDAR)	IRON/STEEL
Copper		●	●	◖	●	◖	◖	◖	◖	○	○	●
Aluminum	○		○	○	○	◖	●	●	●	●	●	◖
Stainless steel	◖	●		◖	●	◖	●	●	○	○	○	◖
Galvanized steel	○	○	○		○	◖	◖	◖	◖	◖	◖	◖
Zinc alloy	○					◖	●	●	●	●	●	●
Lead							◖	◖	◖	●	○	○

● Galvanic action will occur, hence direct contact should be avoided.
◖ Galvanic action may occur under certain circumstances and/or over a period of time.
○ Galvanic action is insignificant, metals may come into direct contact under normal circumstances.

GENERAL NOTE: Galvanic corrosion is apt to occur when water runoff from one material comes in contact with a potentially reactive material.

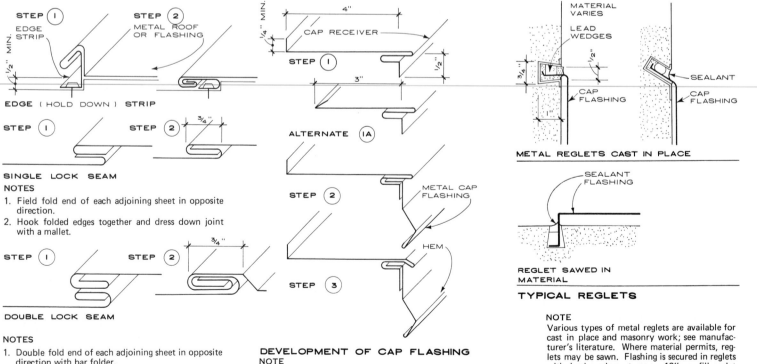

STEP 1 EDGE STRIP
STEP 2 METAL ROOF OR FLASHING
½" MIN.
EDGE (HOLD DOWN) STRIP

STEP 1 **STEP 2** ¾"
SINGLE LOCK SEAM

NOTES
1. Field fold end of each adjoining sheet in opposite direction.
2. Hook folded edges together and dress down joint with a mallet.

STEP 1 **STEP 2** ¾"
DOUBLE LOCK SEAM

NOTES
1. Double fold end of each adjoining sheet in opposite direction with a bar folder.
2. Slide edges together and dress down joint with a mallet.

¼" MIN. 4"
CAP RECEIVER ½"
STEP 1
3"
ALTERNATE 1A
STEP 2
METAL CAP FLASHING
HEM
STEP 3

DEVELOPMENT OF CAP FLASHING
NOTE
Hem in cap flashing recommended for stiffness; but may be omitted if heavier gauge material used.

MATERIAL VARIES
LEAD WEDGES
CAP FLASHING
SEALANT
CAP FLASHING
METAL REGLETS CAST IN PLACE

SEALANT
FLASHING
REGLET SAWED IN MATERIAL

TYPICAL REGLETS
NOTE
Various types of metal reglets are available for cast in place and masonry work; see manufacturer's literature. Where material permits, reglets may be sawn. Flashing is secured in reglets with lead wedges at max. 12" cc, fill reglet with nonhardening water proof compound.

Michael Scott Rudden, The Stephens Associates P.C.—Architects; Albany, New York

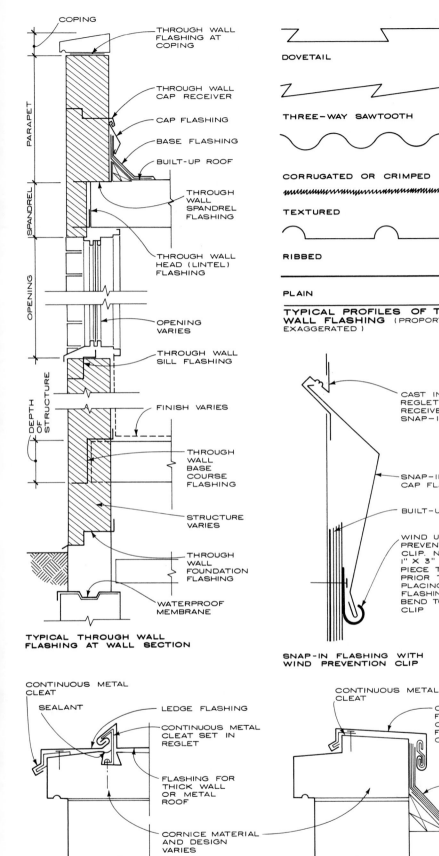

TYPICAL THROUGH WALL
FLASHING AT WALL SECTION

(labels within diagram:)
COPING
THROUGH WALL FLASHING AT COPING
THROUGH WALL CAP RECEIVER
CAP FLASHING
BASE FLASHING
BUILT-UP ROOF
THROUGH WALL SPANDREL FLASHING
THROUGH WALL HEAD (LINTEL) FLASHING
OPENING VARIES
THROUGH WALL SILL FLASHING
FINISH VARIES
THROUGH WALL BASE COURSE FLASHING
STRUCTURE VARIES
THROUGH WALL FOUNDATION FLASHING
WATERPROOF MEMBRANE
PARAPET
SPANDREL
OPENING
DEPTH OF STRUCTURE

(profiles, center top:)
DOVETAIL
THREE-WAY SAWTOOTH
CORRUGATED OR CRIMPED
TEXTURED
RIBBED
PLAIN

TYPICAL PROFILES OF THROUGH WALL FLASHING (PROPORTIONS EXAGGERATED)

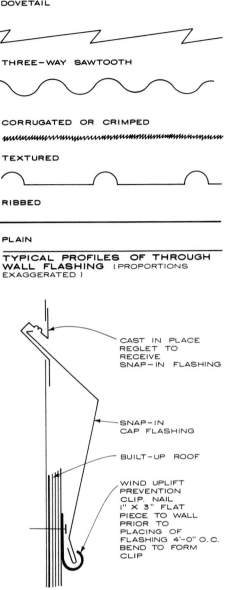

SNAP-IN FLASHING WITH
WIND PREVENTION CLIP

(labels:)
CAST IN PLACE REGLET TO RECEIVE SNAP-IN FLASHING
SNAP-IN CAP FLASHING
BUILT-UP ROOF
WIND UPLIFT PREVENTION CLIP. NAIL 1" X 3" FLAT PIECE TO WALL PRIOR TO PLACING OF FLASHING 4'-0" O.C. BEND TO FORM CLIP

DEFINITIONS

BASE FLASHINGS are essentially a continuation of the built-up roofing membrane at the upturned edges, applied in an operation separate from the application of the roof membrane itself.

CAP FLASHINGS (COUNTERFLASHINGS) are normally made of sheet metal and shield the exposed top of the base flashing. Some nonmetallic cap flashings are made of asbestos felts, and are waterproofed with highly fabrated asbestos flashing cement.

CONCEALED FLASHINGS are invisible from the exterior or interior of the building. Metal sheet or foil, fabric, plastic, or various combinations of these materials may be used, depending on climate and structural requirements.

EXPOSED FLASHINGS are exposed to view and affect the aesthetics of the building. Metals are almost entirely used. Attention must be paid to the corrosive potential between dissimilar metals.

NOTES

1. Select flashing that is flexible for molding to flashing supports and can withstand expected thermal, wind, and structural movement. Provide expansion joints in place of flashing as required by conditions.
2. Consult manufacturer's literature for choice of flashing materials and details.
3. Avoid sharp bends in bituminous base flashings. Use cant strips with 45° maximum bend.
4. Provision for differential movement between roof deck and wall is recommended.
5. Ribbed or embossed through wall flashing is not recommended for earthquake areas.
6. Base flashing should extend 8 to 12 in. above highest anticipated waterline. Metal counterflashings should lap base flashing at least 4 in. minimum. Lap all vertical joints.

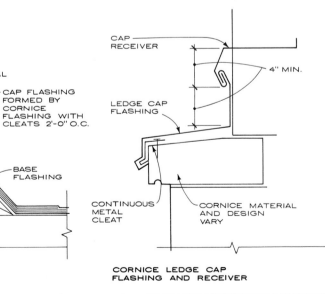

CORNICE FLASHING WITH
METAL ROOF

(labels:)
CONTINUOUS METAL CLEAT
SEALANT
LEDGE FLASHING
CONTINUOUS METAL CLEAT SET IN REGLET
FLASHING FOR THICK WALL OR METAL ROOF
CORNICE MATERIAL AND DESIGN VARIES

CORNICE FLASHING WITH
CAP FLASHING

(labels:)
CONTINUOUS METAL CLEAT
CAP FLASHING FORMED BY CORNICE FLASHING WITH CLEATS 2'-0" O.C.
BASE FLASHING

CORNICE LEDGE CAP
FLASHING AND RECEIVER

(labels:)
CAP RECEIVER
4" MIN.
LEDGE CAP FLASHING
CONTINUOUS METAL CLEAT
CORNICE MATERIAL AND DESIGN VARY

CORNICE FLASHING

Michael Scott Rudden, The Stephens Associates P.C.—Architects; Albany, New York

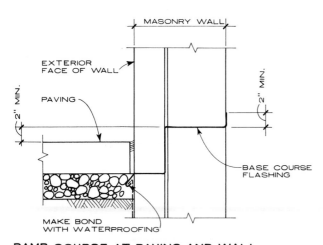

MASONRY WALL

EXTERIOR
FACE OF WALL

PAVING

2" MIN.

2" MIN.

BASE COURSE
FLASHING

MAKE BOND
WITH WATERPROOFING

DAMP COURSE AT PAVING AND WALL

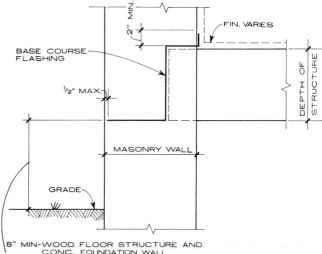

2" MIN.

FIN. VARIES

BASE COURSE
FLASHING

1/2" MAX.

MASONRY WALL

DEPTH OF STRUCTURE

GRADE

8" MIN-WOOD FLOOR STRUCTURE AND
CONC. FOUNDATION WALL
12" MIN-WOOD FLOOR STRUCTURE AND
MASONRY FOUNDATION WALL

DAMP COURSE AT FLOOR CONSTRUCTION

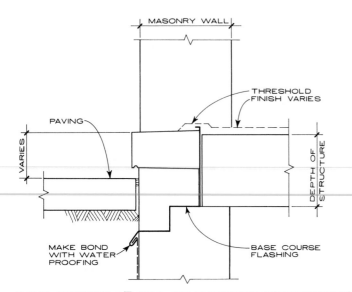

MASONRY WALL

THRESHOLD
FINISH VARIES

PAVING

VARIES

DEPTH OF STRUCTURE

MAKE BOND
WITH WATER
PROOFING

BASE COURSE
FLASHING

DAMP COURSE AT SILL OF MASONRY CONSTRUCTION

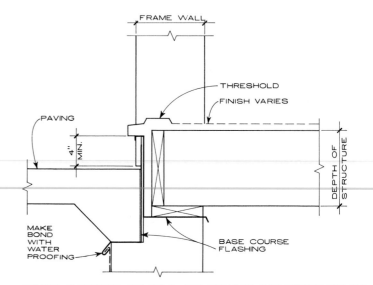

FRAME WALL

THRESHOLD
FINISH VARIES

PAVING

4" MIN.

DEPTH OF STRUCTURE

MAKE
BOND
WITH
WATER
PROOFING

BASE COURSE
FLASHING

DAMP COURSE AT SILL OF FRAME CONSTRUCTION

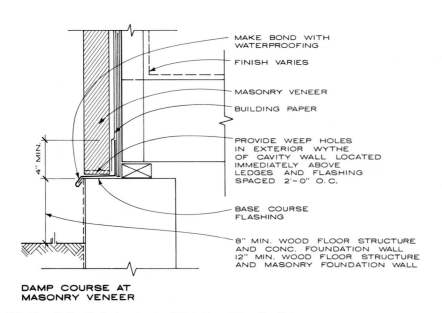

MAKE BOND WITH
WATERPROOFING

FINISH VARIES

MASONRY VENEER

BUILDING PAPER

PROVIDE WEEP HOLES
IN EXTERIOR WYTHE
OF CAVITY WALL LOCATED
IMMEDIATELY ABOVE
LEDGES AND FLASHING
SPACED 2'-0" O.C.

BASE COURSE
FLASHING

4" MIN.

8" MIN. WOOD FLOOR STRUCTURE
AND CONC. FOUNDATION WALL
12" MIN. WOOD FLOOR STRUCTURE
AND MASONRY FOUNDATION WALL

**DAMP COURSE AT
MASONRY VENEER**

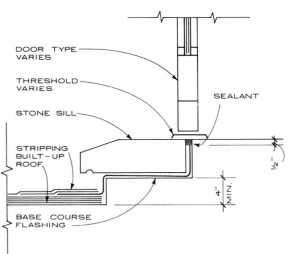

DOOR TYPE
VARIES

THRESHOLD
VARIES

STONE SILL

STRIPPING
BUILT-UP
ROOF

BASE COURSE
FLASHING

SEALANT

1/2"

4" MIN.

**DAMP COURSE AT SILL TO
BUILT-UP ROOF**

Michael Scott Rudden, The Stephens Associates P.C.—Architects; Albany, New York

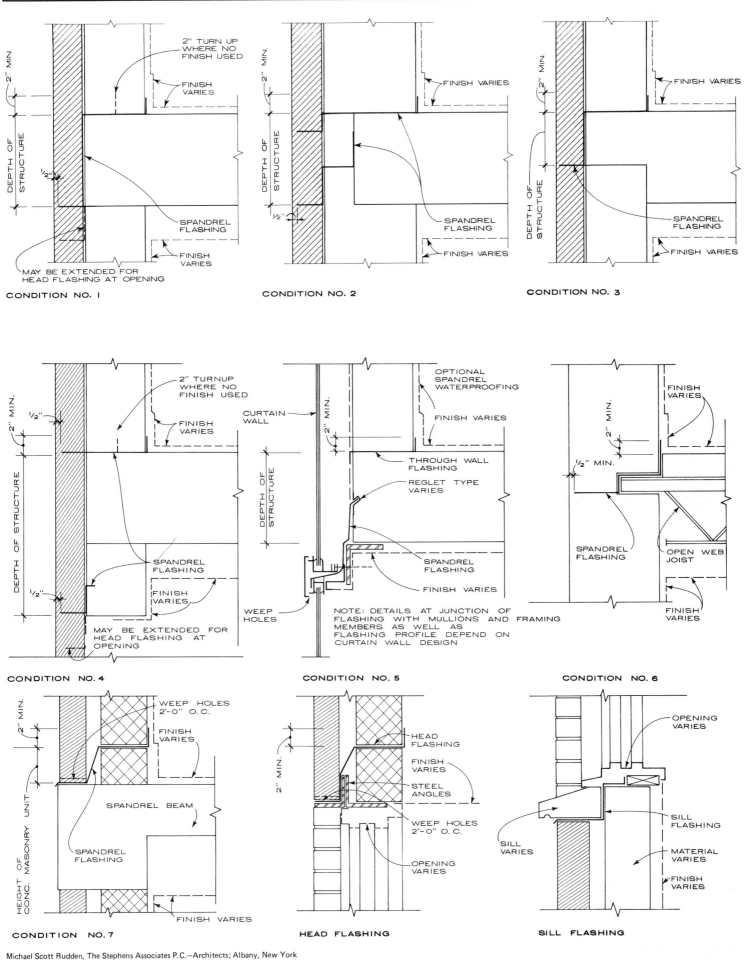

2" TURN UP WHERE NO FINISH USED

FINISH VARIES

2" MIN.

DEPTH OF STRUCTURE

1/2"

SPANDREL FLASHING

FINISH VARIES

MAY BE EXTENDED FOR HEAD FLASHING AT OPENING

CONDITION NO. 1

FINISH VARIES

2" MIN.

DEPTH OF STRUCTURE

1/2"

SPANDREL FLASHING

FINISH VARIES

CONDITION NO. 2

FINISH VARIES

2" MIN.

DEPTH OF STRUCTURE

SPANDREL FLASHING

FINISH VARIES

CONDITION NO. 3

2" TURNUP WHERE NO FINISH USED

FINISH VARIES

2" MIN.

1/2"

DEPTH OF STRUCTURE

SPANDREL FLASHING

FINISH VARIES

1/2"

MAY BE EXTENDED FOR HEAD FLASHING AT OPENING

CONDITION NO. 4

CURTAIN WALL

2" MIN.

DEPTH OF STRUCTURE

OPTIONAL SPANDREL WATERPROOFING

FINISH VARIES

THROUGH WALL FLASHING

REGLET TYPE VARIES

SPANDREL FLASHING

FINISH VARIES

WEEP HOLES

NOTE: DETAILS AT JUNCTION OF FLASHING WITH MULLIONS AND FRAMING MEMBERS AS WELL AS FLASHING PROFILE DEPEND ON CURTAIN WALL DESIGN

CONDITION NO. 5

FINISH VARIES

2" MIN.

1/2" MIN.

SPANDREL FLASHING

OPEN WEB JOIST

FINISH VARIES

CONDITION NO. 6

WEEP HOLES 2'-0" O.C.

FINISH VARIES

2" MIN.

SPANDREL BEAM

HEIGHT OF CONC. MASONRY UNIT

SPANDREL FLASHING

FINISH VARIES

CONDITION NO. 7

HEAD FLASHING

FINISH VARIES

STEEL ANGLES

2" MIN.

WEEP HOLES 2'-0" O.C.

OPENING VARIES

HEAD FLASHING

OPENING VARIES

SILL FLASHING

SILL VARIES

MATERIAL VARIES

FINISH VARIES

SILL FLASHING

Michael Scott Rudden, The Stephens Associates P.C.—Architects; Albany, New York

FLASHING **7**

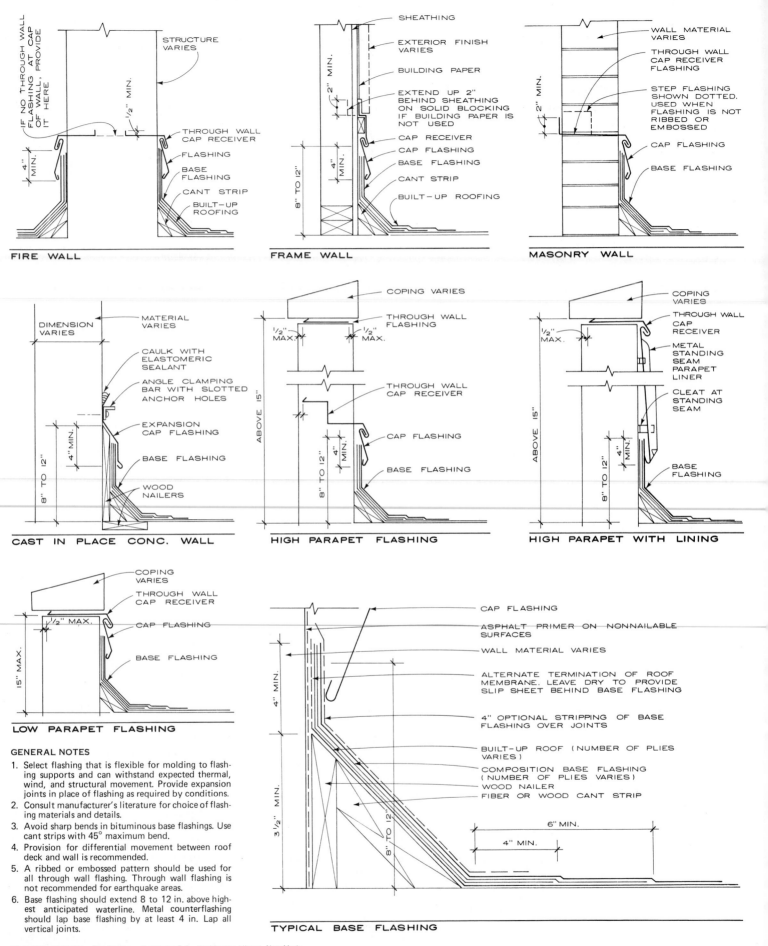

FIRE WALL

FRAME WALL

MASONRY WALL

CAST IN PLACE CONC. WALL

HIGH PARAPET FLASHING

HIGH PARAPET WITH LINING

LOW PARAPET FLASHING

TYPICAL BASE FLASHING

GENERAL NOTES

1. Select flashing that is flexible for molding to flashing supports and can withstand expected thermal, wind, and structural movement. Provide expansion joints in place of flashing as required by conditions.
2. Consult manufacturer's literature for choice of flashing materials and details.
3. Avoid sharp bends in bituminous base flashings. Use cant strips with 45° maximum bend.
4. Provision for differential movement between roof deck and wall is recommended.
5. A ribbed or embossed pattern should be used for all through wall flashing. Through wall flashing is not recommended for earthquake areas.
6. Base flashing should extend 8 to 12 in. above highest anticipated waterline. Metal counterflashing should lap base flashing by at least 4 in. Lap all vertical joints.

Michael Scott Rudden, The Stephens Associates P.C.—Architects; Albany, New York

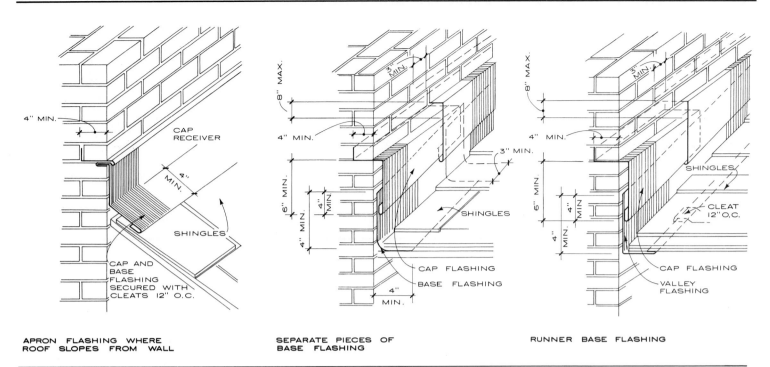

4" MIN.

CAP RECEIVER

4" MIN.

SHINGLES

CAP AND BASE FLASHING SECURED WITH CLEATS 12" O.C.

APRON FLASHING WHERE ROOF SLOPES FROM WALL

8" MAX.

3" MIN.

4" MIN.

6" MIN.

4" MIN.

4" MIN.

3" MIN.

SHINGLES

CAP FLASHING

BASE FLASHING

4" MIN.

SEPARATE PIECES OF BASE FLASHING

8" MAX.

3" MIN.

4" MIN.

6" MIN.

4" MIN.

4" MIN.

SHINGLES

CLEAT 12" O.C.

CAP FLASHING

VALLEY FLASHING

RUNNER BASE FLASHING

PITCHED ROOF WITH WALL FLASHING

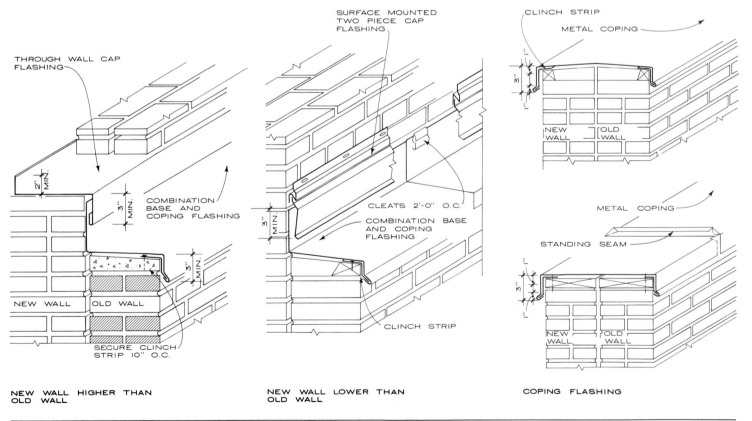

THROUGH WALL CAP FLASHING

2" MIN.

3" MIN.

COMBINATION BASE AND COPING FLASHING

3" MIN.

NEW WALL   OLD WALL

SECURE CLINCH STRIP 10" O.C.

NEW WALL HIGHER THAN OLD WALL

SURFACE MOUNTED TWO PIECE CAP FLASHING

3" MIN.

3" MIN.

CLEATS 2'-0" O.C.

COMBINATION BASE AND COPING FLASHING

CLINCH STRIP

NEW WALL LOWER THAN OLD WALL

CLINCH STRIP

METAL COPING

1"

3"

1"

NEW WALL   OLD WALL

METAL COPING

STANDING SEAM

1"

3"

1"

NEW WALL   OLD WALL

COPING FLASHING

NEW WALL TO OLD WALL FLASHING

NOTE

Through wall flashing not recommended in earthquake areas.

Michael Scott Rudden; The Stephens Associates P.C.—Architects; Albany, New York

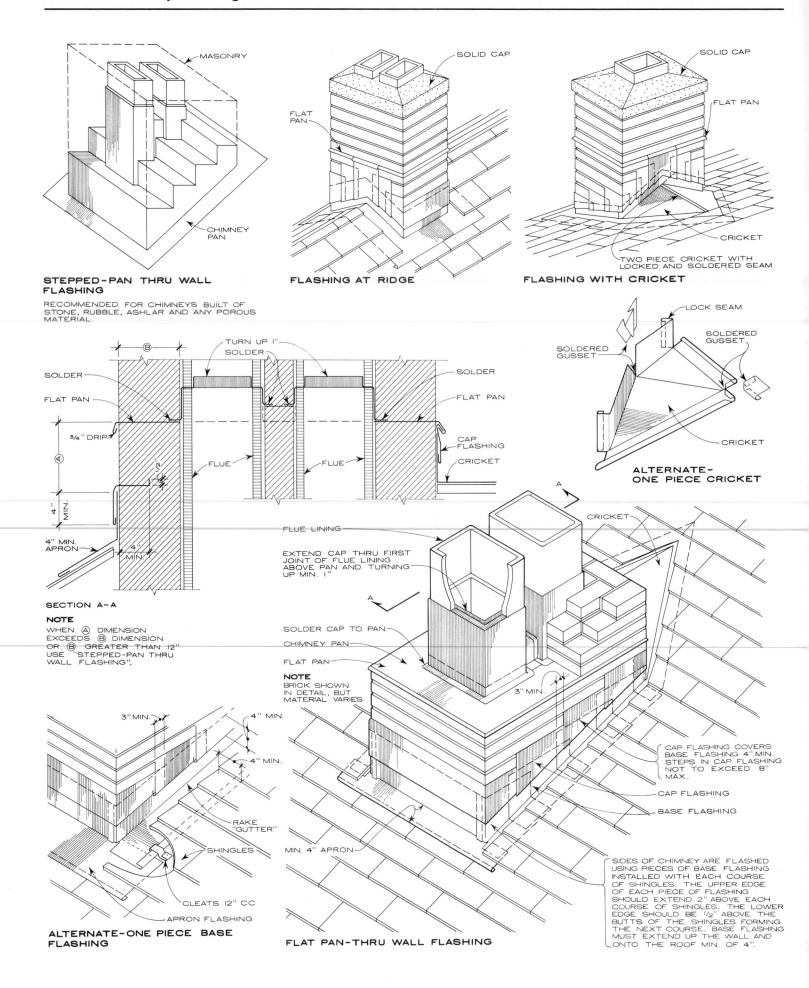

STEPPED-PAN THRU WALL
FLASHING

RECOMMENDED FOR CHIMNEYS BUILT OF
STONE, RUBBLE, ASHLAR AND ANY POROUS
MATERIAL.

MASONRY

CHIMNEY
PAN

FLASHING AT RIDGE

SOLID CAP

FLAT
PAN

FLASHING WITH CRICKET

SOLID CAP

FLAT PAN

CRICKET

TWO PIECE CRICKET WITH
LOCKED AND SOLDERED SEAM

LOCK SEAM

SOLDERED
GUSSET

SOLDERED
GUSSET

CRICKET

ALTERNATE-
ONE PIECE CRICKET

SECTION A-A

TURN UP 1"
SOLDER
SOLDER
FLAT PAN
3/4" DRIP
FLUE
FLUE
SOLDER
FLAT PAN
CAP
FLASHING
CRICKET
4" MIN.
APRON
4"
MIN.

NOTE
WHEN Ⓐ DIMENSION
EXCEEDS Ⓑ DIMENSION
OR Ⓑ GREATER THAN 12"
USE "STEPPED-PAN THRU
WALL FLASHING".

FLUE LINING

EXTEND CAP THRU FIRST
JOINT OF FLUE LINING
ABOVE PAN AND TURNING
UP MIN. 1"

SOLDER CAP TO PAN
CHIMNEY PAN
FLAT PAN

NOTE
BRICK SHOWN
IN DETAIL, BUT
MATERIAL VARIES

CRICKET

3" MIN.

CAP FLASHING COVERS
BASE FLASHING 4" MIN.
STEPS IN CAP FLASHING
NOT TO EXCEED 8"
MAX.

CAP FLASHING

BASE FLASHING

3" MIN.
4" MIN.
4" MIN.

RAKE
"GUTTER"

SHINGLES

CLEATS 12" CC
APRON FLASHING

ALTERNATE-ONE PIECE BASE
FLASHING

MIN. 4" APRON

FLAT PAN-THRU WALL FLASHING

SIDES OF CHIMNEY ARE FLASHED
USING PIECES OF BASE FLASHING
INSTALLED WITH EACH COURSE
OF SHINGLES. THE UPPER EDGE
OF EACH PIECE OF FLASHING
SHOULD EXTEND 2" ABOVE EACH
COURSE OF SHINGLES. THE LOWER
EDGE SHOULD BE 1/2" ABOVE THE
BUTTS OF THE SHINGLES FORMING
THE NEXT COURSE. BASE FLASHING
MUST EXTEND UP THE WALL AND
ONTO THE ROOF MIN. OF 4".

7   FLASHING

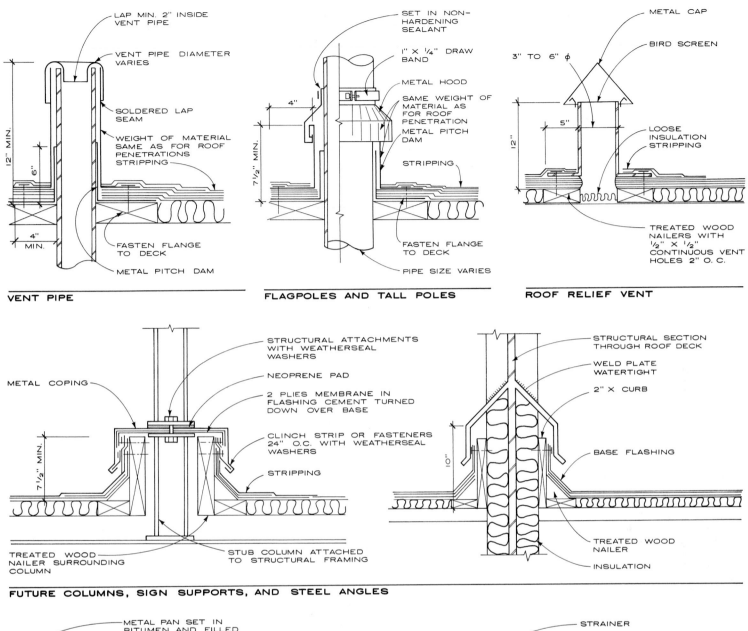

LAP MIN. 2" INSIDE VENT PIPE

VENT PIPE DIAMETER VARIES

SOLDERED LAP SEAM

WEIGHT OF MATERIAL SAME AS FOR ROOF PENETRATIONS STRIPPING

12" MIN.

6"

4" MIN.

FASTEN FLANGE TO DECK

METAL PITCH DAM

VENT PIPE

SET IN NON-HARDENING SEALANT

1" X 1/4" DRAW BAND

METAL HOOD

SAME WEIGHT OF MATERIAL AS FOR ROOF PENETRATION METAL PITCH DAM

STRIPPING

4"

7 1/2" MIN.

FASTEN FLANGE TO DECK

PIPE SIZE VARIES

FLAGPOLES AND TALL POLES

METAL CAP

BIRD SCREEN

3" TO 6" ∅

LOOSE INSULATION STRIPPING

12"

5"

TREATED WOOD NAILERS WITH 1/2" X 1/2" CONTINUOUS VENT HOLES 2" O. C.

ROOF RELIEF VENT

METAL COPING

STRUCTURAL ATTACHMENTS WITH WEATHERSEAL WASHERS

NEOPRENE PAD

2 PLIES MEMBRANE IN FLASHING CEMENT TURNED DOWN OVER BASE

CLINCH STRIP OR FASTENERS 24" O.C. WITH WEATHERSEAL WASHERS

STRIPPING

7 1/2" MIN.

TREATED WOOD NAILER SURROUNDING COLUMN

STUB COLUMN ATTACHED TO STRUCTURAL FRAMING

STRUCTURAL SECTION THROUGH ROOF DECK

WELD PLATE WATERTIGHT

2" X CURB

BASE FLASHING

10"

TREATED WOOD NAILER

INSULATION

FUTURE COLUMNS, SIGN SUPPORTS, AND STEEL ANGLES

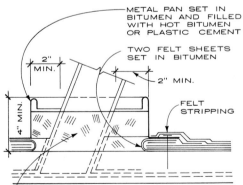

METAL PAN SET IN BITUMEN AND FILLED WITH HOT BITUMEN OR PLASTIC CEMENT

TWO FELT SHEETS SET IN BITUMEN

2" MIN.

2" MIN.

4" MIN.

FELT STRIPPING

FOR WOOD DECKS FILL 1" DEEP WITH CEMENT MORTAR BEFORE POURING BITUMEN

NOTE

Whenever possible avoid the use of pitch pockets in favor of curbs with base and cap flashing around the penetrating member.

PITCH POCKET

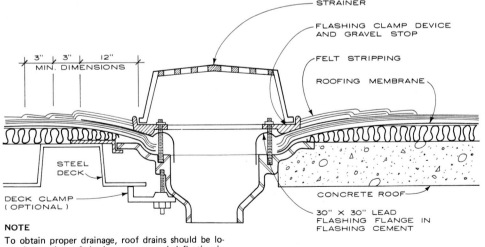

STRAINER

FLASHING CLAMP DEVICE AND GRAVEL STOP

FELT STRIPPING

ROOFING MEMBRANE

3" 3" 12"
MIN. DIMENSIONS

STEEL DECK

DECK CLAMP (OPTIONAL)

CONCRETE ROOF

30" X 30" LEAD FLASHING FLANGE IN FLASHING CEMENT

NOTE

To obtain proper drainage, roof drains should be located at points of the lowest expected deflection in roof deck.

ROOF DRAIN

Michael Scott Rudden, The Stephens Associates, P.C.—Architects; Albany, New York

FLASHING **7**

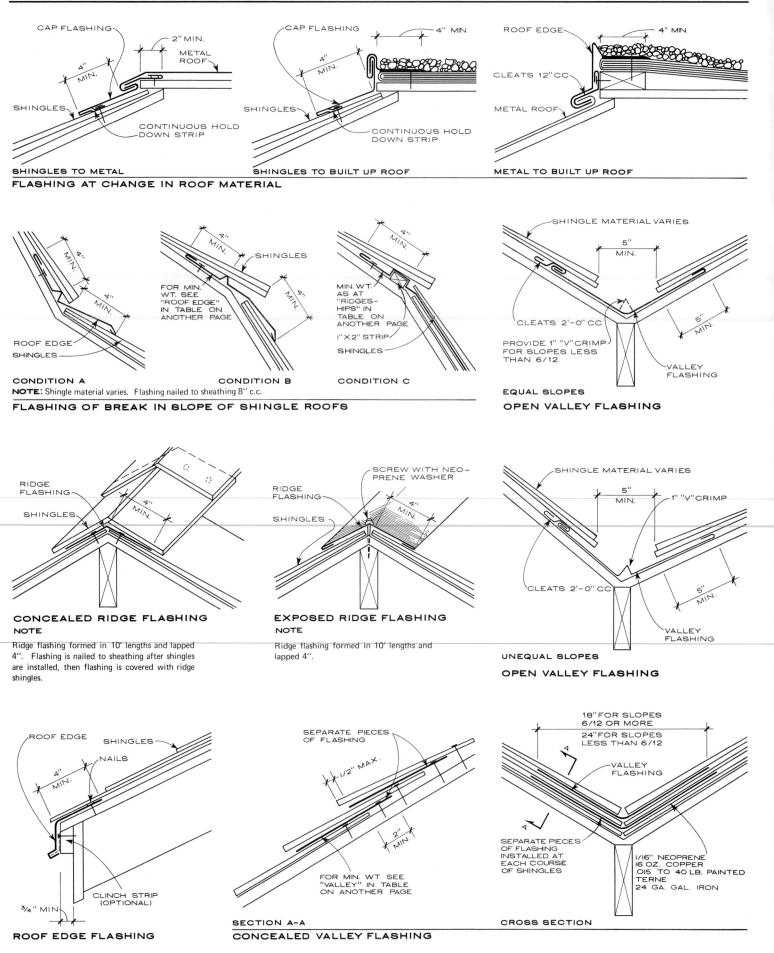

CAP FLASHING
2" MIN.
METAL ROOF
4" MIN.
SHINGLES
CONTINUOUS HOLD DOWN STRIP

SHINGLES TO METAL

CAP FLASHING
4" MIN.
4" MIN.
SHINGLES
CONTINUOUS HOLD DOWN STRIP

SHINGLES TO BUILT UP ROOF

ROOF EDGE
4" MIN.
CLEATS 12" CC
METAL ROOF

METAL TO BUILT UP ROOF

FLASHING AT CHANGE IN ROOF MATERIAL

4" MIN.
4" MIN.
ROOF EDGE
SHINGLES

CONDITION A

4" MIN.
SHINGLES
4" MIN.
FOR MIN. WT. SEE "ROOF EDGE" IN TABLE ON ANOTHER PAGE

CONDITION B

4" MIN.
MIN. WT. AS AT "RIDGES-HIPS" IN TABLE ON ANOTHER PAGE
1"X2" STRIP
SHINGLES

CONDITION C

NOTE: Shingle material varies. Flashing nailed to sheathing 8" c.c.

FLASHING OF BREAK IN SLOPE OF SHINGLE ROOFS

SHINGLE MATERIAL VARIES
5" MIN.
5" MIN.
CLEATS 2'-0" CC
PROVIDE 1" "V" CRIMP FOR SLOPES LESS THAN 6/12.
VALLEY FLASHING

EQUAL SLOPES
OPEN VALLEY FLASHING

RIDGE FLASHING
SHINGLES
4" MIN.

CONCEALED RIDGE FLASHING
NOTE.
Ridge flashing formed in 10' lengths and lapped 4". Flashing is nailed to sheathing after shingles are installed, then flashing is covered with ridge shingles.

SCREW WITH NEO-PRENE WASHER
RIDGE FLASHING
SHINGLES
4" MIN.

EXPOSED RIDGE FLASHING
NOTE.
Ridge flashing formed in 10' lengths and lapped 4".

SHINGLE MATERIAL VARIES
5" MIN.
1" "V" CRIMP
CLEATS 2'-0" CC
5" MIN.
VALLEY FLASHING

UNEQUAL SLOPES
OPEN VALLEY FLASHING

ROOF EDGE
SHINGLES
NAILS
4" MIN.
CLINCH STRIP (OPTIONAL)
3/4" MIN.

ROOF EDGE FLASHING

SEPARATE PIECES OF FLASHING
1/2" MAX.
2" MIN.
FOR MIN. WT. SEE "VALLEY" IN TABLE ON ANOTHER PAGE

SECTION A-A
CONCEALED VALLEY FLASHING

18" FOR SLOPES 6/12 OR MORE
24" FOR SLOPES LESS THAN 6/12
VALLEY FLASHING
SEPARATE PIECES OF FLASHING INSTALLED AT EACH COURSE OF SHINGLES
1/16" NEOPRENE
16 OZ. COPPER
.015 TO 40 LB. PAINTED TERNE
24 GA. GAL. IRON

CROSS SECTION

Michael Scott Rudden; The Stephens Associates, P.C.–Architects; Albany, New York

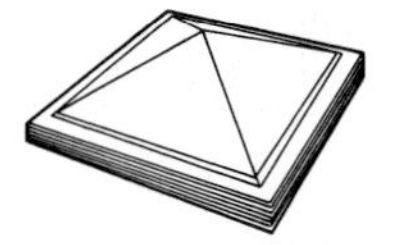

PYRAMID SKYLIGHT

SINGLE OR DOUBLE GLAZED
OUTSIDE CURB DIMENSIONS

33½" × 33½"	8" RISE
40¼" × 40¼"	10" RISE
49½" × 49½"	12" RISE
58¼" × 58¼"	14" RISE
78¼" × 78¼"	18" RISE

INSULATED CURB

SINGLE OR DOUBLE GLAZED
STANDARD CURB HEIGHT
4" OR 9"–12" IS AVAILABLE
SIZES AS FOR SQUARE AND
RECTANGULAR

CONTINUOUS ARCHED

SINGLE OR DOUBLE GLAZED

22¼"	RISE 6"
33¼"	RISE 7"
39¼"	RISE 8"
51¼"	RISE 10"
63¼"	RISE 12"
75¼"	RISE 14"

BUILT-UP CURB SQUARE

SINGLE OR DOUBLE GLAZED

22¼" × 22¼"	RISE 5"
25½" × 25½"	RISE 7"
33½" × 33½"	RISE 8"
40¼" × 40¼"	RISE 10"
49½" × 49½"	RISE 12"
58¼" × 58¼"	RISE 14"
78¼" × 78¼"	RISE 18"

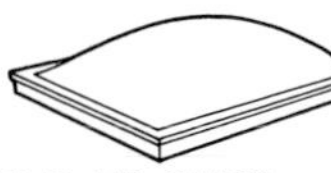

BUILT-UP CURB RECTANGULAR

SINGLE OR DOUBLE GLAZED

25½" × 49½"	RISE 7"
33½" × 49½"	RISE 10"
33½" × 72¾"	RISE 10"
40¼" × 78¼"	RISE 12"
49½" × 93¾"	RISE 13"
60¾" × 72¾"	RISE 16"
60¾" × 93¾"	RISE 16"

SINGLE OR DOUBLE GLAZED
INSIDE DIAMETER

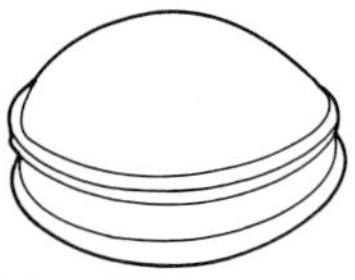

31"	DOME RISE 11"
43"	DOME RISE 13"
54"	DOME RISE 19"
67"	DOME RISE 22"
79"	DOME RISE 25"

STANDARD CURB HEIGHT
4" OR 9"–12" AVAILABLE

CIRCULAR

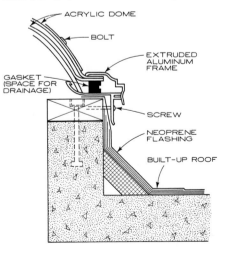

RIDGE LIGHT

SINGLE GLAZED
RAKE DIMENSION

24"–30"–36"–42"–48"

STANDARD SKYLIGHT TYPES

FRAMING SYSTEMS

In selecting the structural members, the designer should consider the thermal movement differential between the aluminum and the glazing materials.

Framing systems should provide complete control of both condensation and water infiltration.

Gutter systems should be as simple and functional as possible. Design must take into account compatibility of materials and provision of adequate slope for drainage.

The supporting structure, as well as the enclosure itself, must be engineered to carry the total resultant forces of the particular live load, wind load, and dead load in accordance with state and local codes.

The minimum rise to span on curved (vaulted or domed) structures should be 22%, the point at which maximum economy is achieved.

SKYLIGHTS WITH MOVABLE SECTIONS

Most skylights can be designed with movable sections. Consideration must be given to design and aesthetic acceptance of motors, tracks, and other operating parts.

FINISHES

Finishes for aluminum components are available in the following:

1. Mill finish.
2. Clear anodized.
3. Duranodic bronze or black.
4. Acrylic enamel.
5. Fluorocarbons.

GLAZING

The thickness and geometric profile of all glass and acrylic glazing materials should be carefully selected for compliance with building codes and manufacturer's recommendations.

The following glazing materials are listed in an approximate order of cost, from lowest to highest:

1. Textured, obscure wire glass.
2. Flat acrylic.
3. Clear polished wire glass.
4. Formed acrylic.
5. Tempered glass.
6. Polycarbonates.
7. Laminated glass.
8. Insulated units of tempered, reflective, and/or laminated glass.

ACRYLIC AND POLYCARBONATE GLAZING

Glazing with flat sheet plastics should usually be restricted to the arched enclosures. Its thickness should be selected based on cold formed radii, rabbet dimensions, and design loading. For other applications of plastic glazing, consult manufacturer's design data.

Domes or other thermoformed acrylic shapes should not exceed a maximum base dimension of 10 x 10 ft. The structural properties of formed acrylic units are determined by both geometry and thickness. Tinted acrylics, for economy, should be limited to the ¼ in. thickness.

Because of the thermal movement and moisture infiltration, hermetically sealed insulating units, incorporating acrylics or polycarbonates, should not be used.

Mar resistant coatings for plastics should be specified if frequent cleaning or heavy pedestrian contact is anticipated.

GLASS

The use of plate glass in skylights should be avoided. Most building codes permit or approve the use of wire or laminated safety glass. Note that wire glass is not available in tinted shades. The maximum available widths for the wire and laminated glasses are 60 and 48 in., respectively.

Careful consideration should be given to glazing overhead enclosures with tempered glass. The maximum width dimension for tempered should be no more than 72 in.

Glazing with high performance insulated glass units provides important energy savings and offers the architect numerous functional and aesthetic design choices.

The actual size of a glass unit is governed by total design loading and manufacturer's recommendations.

AVAILABLE LIGHT ZONES

PERCENTAGE OF ROOF AREA REQUIRED FOR SKYLIGHTING

LIGHT ZONE	LIGHT DESIGN LEVELS		
	30 FT-C	60 FT-C	120 FT-C
1	3.3	5.2	13.3
2	2.8	4.3	10.8
3	1.8	3.2	6.9
4	1.5	2.8	4.0

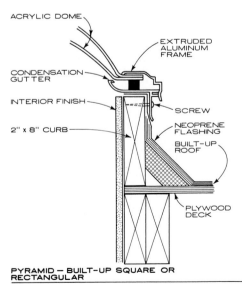

PYRAMID – BUILT-UP SQUARE OR RECTANGULAR

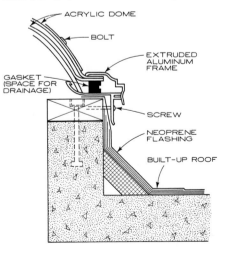

CONTINUOUS ARCH

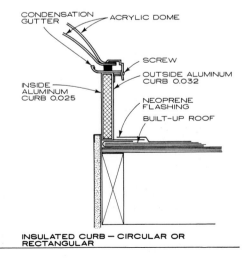

INSULATED CURB – CIRCULAR OR RECTANGULAR

CURB DETAILS

Jerry Graham; CTA Architects Engineers; Billings, Montana

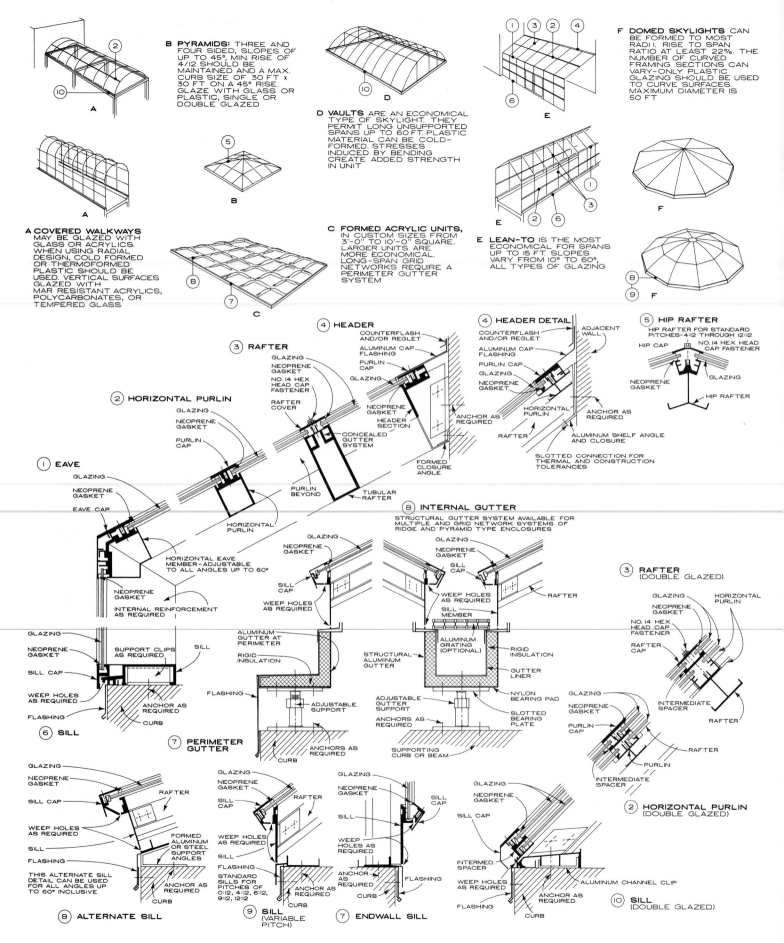

B PYRAMIDS: THREE AND FOUR SIDED, SLOPES OF UP TO 45°, MIN. RISE OF 4/12 SHOULD BE MAINTAINED AND A MAX. CURB SIZE OF 30 FT x 30 FT ON A 45° RISE. GLAZE WITH GLASS OR PLASTIC, SINGLE OR DOUBLE GLAZED

D VAULTS ARE AN ECONOMICAL TYPE OF SKYLIGHT. THEY PERMIT LONG UNSUPPORTED SPANS UP TO 60 FT. PLASTIC MATERIAL CAN BE COLD-FORMED. STRESSES INDUCED BY BENDING CREATE ADDED STRENGTH IN UNIT

F DOMED SKYLIGHTS CAN BE FORMED TO MOST RADII. RISE TO SPAN RATIO AT LEAST 22%. THE NUMBER OF CURVED FRAMING SECTIONS CAN VARY-ONLY PLASTIC GLAZING SHOULD BE USED TO CURVE SURFACES. MAXIMUM DIAMETER IS 50 FT

A COVERED WALKWAYS MAY BE GLAZED WITH GLASS OR ACRYLICS. WHEN USING RADIAL DESIGN, COLD FORMED OR THERMOFORMED PLASTIC SHOULD BE USED. VERTICAL SURFACES GLAZED WITH MAR RESISTANT ACRYLICS, POLYCARBONATES, OR TEMPERED GLASS

C FORMED ACRYLIC UNITS, IN CUSTOM SIZES FROM 3'-0" TO 10'-0" SQUARE. LARGER UNITS ARE MORE ECONOMICAL. LONG-SPAN GRID NETWORKS REQUIRE A PERIMETER GUTTER SYSTEM

E LEAN-TO IS THE MOST ECONOMICAL FOR SPANS UP TO 15 FT. SLOPES VARY FROM 10° TO 60°, ALL TYPES OF GLAZING

CTA Architects Engineers; Billings, Montana

7 ROOF ACCESSORIES

THERMAL INSULATION

Thermal insulation controls heat flow under temperatures ranging from absolute zero to 3000°F. This broad range can be subdivided into four general temperature regimes that classify applications for various types of insulation:

1. LOW TEMPERATURES: Insulation for vessels containing cryogenic materials, such as liquified natural gas.
2. AMBIENT TEMPERATURES: Insulation for building structures.
3. MEDIUM TEMPERATURES: Insulation for tanks, pipes, and equipment in industrial process heat applications.
4. HIGH TEMPERATURES: Refractory or other specialized insulation materials used in foundry work, nuclear power facilities, the aerospace industry, and so on.

Architects and builders are generally concerned with the design and material performance of building insulations that operate within ambient temperature limits. As temperatures range much above or below ambient conditions, design and performance requirements change and must be matched with insulation materials that withstand the stress introduced by extreme temperatures, large temperature differentials, and thermal cycling.

BUILDING INSULATION—THERMAL FUNCTIONS

The two major functions of building insulations are to (1) control temperatures of inside surfaces that affect the comfort of occupants and aid or deter condensation and (2) conserve energy by reducing heat transmission through building sections that determine the energy requirements for both heating and cooling. Economics in fuel consumption can be calculated with reasonable accuracy and balanced against initial costs of insulation for heating and cooling with equipment (see figure).

ADDITIONAL FUNCTIONS

Thermal insulations may also perform several other functions:

1. Add structural strength to a wall, ceiling, or floor section.
2. Provide support for a surface finish.
3. Impede water vapor transmission.
4. Prevent or reduce damage to equipment and structure from exposure to fire and freezing conditions.
5. Reduce noise and vibration.

BASIC MATERIALS

Thermal insulation is made from the following basic materials:

1. MINERAL FIBROUS: Material such as glass, rock, slag, or asbestos that is melted and spun into thin fibers.
2. MINERAL CELLULAR: Material such as foamed glass, calcium silicate, perlite, vermiculite, foamed concrete, or ceramic.
3. ORGANIC FIBROUS: Material such as wood, cane, cotton, hair, cellulose, or synthetic fibers.
4. ORGANIC CELLULAR: Material such as cork, foamed rubber, polystyrene, or polyurethane.
5. METALLIC: Aluminum or other foils, or metallized organic reflective membranes that must face air, gas filled, or evacuated spaces.

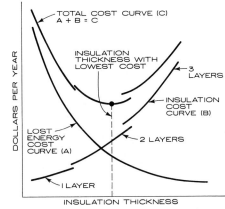

DETERMINATION OF ECONOMIC THICKNESS OF INSULATION

PHYSICAL STRUCTURE AND FORM

Thermal insulation is available in the following physical forms:

1. LOOSE FILL: Dry granules, nodules, or fibers poured or blown into place.
2. FLEXIBLE OR SEMIRIGID: Blankets and batts of woollike material.
3. RIGID: Boards and blocks.
4. MEMBRANE: Reflective insulation.
5. SPRAY APPLIED: Mineral fiber or insulating concrete.
6. POURED-IN-PLACE: Insulating concrete.
7. FOAMED-IN-PLACE: Polyurethane, urea formaldehyde.

MECHANISMS OF HEAT TRANSFER

Heat flows through materials and space by conduction, convection, and radiation. Convection and conduction are functions of the roughness of surfaces, air movement, and the temperature difference between the air and surface. Mass insulations, by their low densities, are designed to suppress conduction and convection across their sections by the entrapment of air molecules within their structure. Convective air currents are stilled by the surrounding matrix of fibers or cells, and the chances of heat transfer by the collision of air molecules is reduced. Radiant heat transfer between objects operates independently of air currents and is controlled by the character of the surfaces (emissivity) and the temperature difference between warm objects emitting radiation and cooler object absorbing radiation.

The resistance of these modes of heat transfer may be retarded by the elements of a building wall section.

1. OUTSIDE SURFACE FILMS: The outside surface traps a thin film of air, which resists heat flow. This film varies with wind velocity and surface roughness.
2. MATERIAL LAYERS: Each layer of material contributes to the resistance of heat flow, usually according to its density. A layer of suitable insulation is normally many times more effective in resisting heat transfer than the combination of all other materials in the section.
3. AIRSPACE: Each measureable airspace also adds to the overall resistance. Foil faced surfaces of low emissivities that form the boundaries of the airspace can further reduce the rate of radiant transfer across the space.
4. INSIDE SURFACE FILM: The inside surface of the building section also traps a thin film of air. The air film thus formed is usually thicker because of much lower air velocities.

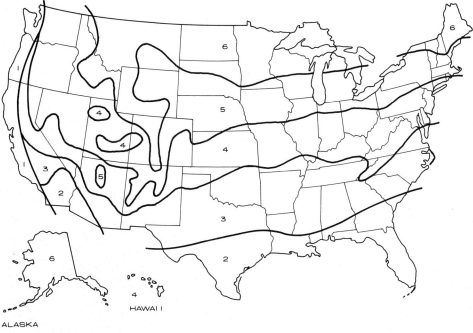

NOTE: RECOMMENDED INSULATION ZONES FOR HEATING AND COOLING

MAP OF INSULATION ZONES

David F. Hill; Burt Hill Kosar Rittelmann Associates; Butler, Pennsylvania

Donald Bosserman, AIA; Saunders, Cheng & Appleton; Alexandria, Virginia

RECOMMENDED MINIMUM THERMAL RESISTANCES (R) OF INSULATION

ZONE	CEILING	WALL	FLOOR
1	19	11	11
2	26	13	11
3	26	19	13
4	30	19	19
5	33	19	22
6	38	19	22

NOTE: The minimum insulation R values recommended for various parts of the United States as delineated on the zone map above.

INSULATION 7

COEFFICIENT OF HEAT TRANSMISSION

Calculations of heating and cooling loads are based on the rate of heat flow through building sections along with ventilation and moisture requirements. The symbol U designates the overall coefficient of heat transmission for any section of building shell. The units for U are Btu's per square foot of building section per hour per °F temperature difference between inside and outside air (Btu/sq ft · hr · °F).

U-values of composite building sections are calculated by first determining the individual conductivities (k) or conductances (C) of each material comprising the section. The conductivity of a homogeneous material is measured as Btu's per square foot per hour per °F temperature difference per inch thickness of the material. The reciprocal, R, is the thermal resistivity. The resistance of any thickness of a material is its resistivity per inch times its total thickness. Nonhomogeneous materials such as concrete masonry units are given conductance and resistance values for their standard thicknesses. In calculating the overall U-coefficients only the resistances are used. The sum is taken of the resistance values of all the materials in the section plus the resistance values of the inside and outside surface films to yield an overall R-value. The reciprocal, 1/R equals the U-coefficient.

FACTORS AFFECTING INSULATION PERFORMANCE

The most serious factor affecting the performance of building insulation is the presence of water. While the effect of moisture is not too serious when moisture exists in the vapor phase, the conductivity is greatly increased by the presence of condensed moisture. Water or ice in insulation will impair or destroy the insulating value; it may cause deterioration of the insulation or eventual structural damage by rot, corrosion, or the expansion action of freezing water. Whether or not moisture accumulates within the insulation depends on the operating temperatures, ambient conditions, and the effectiveness of water vapor barriers in relation to other vapor resistances within the composite structure.

The moisture resistance depends on the basic material of the insulation and the type of physical structure. Most insulations are hygroscopic and will gain or lose moisture in proportion to the relative humidity of the air in contact with the insulation. Fibrous and granular insulations permit transmission of water vapor to the colder side of the structure. A vapor barrier should, therefore, be used with the materials and installed on the warm side where moisture transmission is a factor. Certain insulations with a closed cellular structure are relatively impervious to water and water vapor. Often, these materials are marketed as rigid boards and installed on the outside of stud work as sheathing. To avoid moisture accumulation, in this application their vapor permeance should be at least five times that of the interior vapor barrier, or they should be modified by perforations or venting along their joints to allow water vapor to escape.

Conductivity also varies with density. A change in density due to the degree of compaction of fibrous or granular types of insulation increases conductivity. For fibrous types, minimum conductivity is ideally obtained when fibers are uniformly spaced and are perpendicular to the direction of heat flow. Other factors such as the diameter of the fiber or the amount of binder that influence the bond or contact of the fiber may also affect conductivity.

For cellular insulation a specific combination of cell size and density will produce an optimum thermal conductivity. The type of gas trapped in the cells also affects conductivity. Flourocarbon gas, having a lower conductivity than air, is used to expand rigid urethane to maximize its thermal resistance. Unless encased in a gas impermeable membrane, urethane conductivities usually increase over time as oxygen and nitrogen seep into the cell structure and the flourocarbon gas diffuses out.

THE IMPORTANCE OF PROPER DESIGN AND INSTALLATION

To perform at maximum efficiency, insulation systems must be properly designed and their installation closely supervised. Vapor barriers must be properly located in the wall section and carefully placed to fully cover all areas. Edges should be sealed and joints overlapped. Attachment by glueing instead of stapling should be practiced if possible because the effectiveness of vapor barriers may be greatly reduced if openings, even very small ones, exist in the barrier.

Low density fibrous and loose fill insulations, though widely used, are most susceptible to increased heat transfer by improper installation. If batts or granular materials are compacted, conductivities increase because of higher densities. These types of insulations should also completely fill the space between studs or rafters to prevent convective air currents and infiltration. The performance of fibrous batts installed vertically with airspaces on either side is seriously impaired because of the air interchange between the two voids. Special attention should also be given to the sources of greatest heat loss. Insulating and sealing window frames, wall plates at foundations, and electrical outlets along perimeter walls is crucial for reducing air infiltration. The perimeter of the floor joist system in frame construction, ordinarily overlooked, should be detailed to allow space for application of insulation along its length.

ECONOMIC THICKNESS

The cost of lost energy is directly related to the rate of heat transfer through the insulation and the dollar value of that energy. As shown in the figure, the cost of lost energy decreases as insulation thickness increases. Since the optimal economic thickness is the lowest total cost of lost energy plus the installed insulation over the life of the insulation, these two costs must be compared on similar terms. Either the cost of insulation must be annualized and compared to the average annual cost of the lost energy, or the cost of the energy lost each year must be expressed in present dollars and compared to the annual cost of the insulation investment.

The economic thickness will be affected by the length of time over which the insulation cost is annualized. With the life cycle–cost method the economic thickness is usually greatest because the fuel savings that would accrue over the many years the insulation is in service can be used to pay for the most insulation (i.e., the payback period = the life cycle). If a shorter payback is required for the insulation, this maximum life cycle economic thickness becomes thinner because there are fewer years of energy savings allotted to pay for the insulation.

The annualized cost of installed insulation must be adjusted for the cost of money that can be a discount rate including the desired rate of return on the insulation investment. Cost of maintenance should also be included in the annual costs.

The cost of fuel including efficiency conversion plus the expected yearly price escalation above the inflation rate or the average cost of fuel over the life cycle or payback period should be forecast as accurately as possible before calculating economic thickness.

MATERIAL PROPERTIES OF COMMON BUILDING INSULATION

BUILDING INSULATIONS	DENSITY (LB/CU FT)	RESISTANCE (R) (HR/SQ FT·°F·BTU PER 1 IN. THICKNESS)	WATER VAPOR PERMEABILITY (PERM-IN.)	WATER ABSORPTION (% BY WEIGHT)	FIRE RESISTANCE FLAME SPREAD	FIRE RESISTANCE FUEL CONTRIBUTED	FIRE RESISTANCE SMOKE DEVELOPED	TOXICITY	EFFECTS OF AGING DIMENSIONAL STABILITY	DEGRADATION DUE TO TEMPERATURE	DEGRADATION DUE TO MOISTURE	DEGRADATION DUE TO FUNGAL OR BACTERIAL GROWTH	DEGRADATION DUE TO WEATHERING	CORROSIVENESS
Fiberglass	0.6–1.0	3.16	100	1%	15–20	5–15	0–20	Some fumes if burned	None	OK below 180°F	None	None	None	None
Rock or slag wool	1.5–2.5	3.2–3.7	100	2%	15	0	0	None	None	None	Transient	None	None	None
Cellulose	2.2–3.0	3.2–3.7	High	5–20%	15–40	0–40	0–45	CO if burned	Settles 0–20%	None	Not severe	Maybe	?	Steel Aluminum Copper
Molded polystyrene	0.8–2.0	3.8–4.4	1.2–3.0	4%[1]	5–25	5–80	10–400	CO if burned	None	If above 165°F	None	None	UV degrades	
Extruded polystyrene	0.8–2.0	3.8–4.4	1.2–3.0	0.7%	5–25	5–80	10–400	CO if burned	None	If above 165°F	None	None	UV degrades	None
Polyurethane	2.0	5.8–6.2[2]	2–3	Negligible	30–50	10–25	155–200	CO if burned	0–12% change	If above 250°F	?	None	None	None
Polyisocyanurate	2.0	5.8–6.2[2]	2–3	Negligible	25	5	55–200	CO if burned	0–12% change	If above 250°F	?	None	None	None
Urea formaldehyde	0.6–0.9	4.2	4.5–100	18%[3]	0–25	0–30	0–10	Negligible	Shrinks 1–4% in 28 days	If above 415°F	?	None	?	?
Perlite (loose fill)	2–11	2.5–3.7	High	Low	0	0	0	None	None	If above 1200°F	None	None	None	None
Vermiculite (loose fill)	4–10	2.4–3.0	High	None	0	0	0	None	None	If above 1000°F	None	None	None	None
Insulating concrete	12–88	0.85[4]/1.2[5]	Varies with density	?	0	0	0	None	None	If above 1000°C	None	None	Below 30#/ft[3]	None

NOTES
1. By volume.
2. Aged unfaced or spray applied.
3. At 60% rh, 65°F.
4. At 40 lb/cu ft.
5. At 25 lb/cu ft.

David F. Hill; Burt Hill Kosar Rittelmann Associates; Butler, Pennsylvania

7 INSULATION

DEFINITIONS

Waterproofing is a system intended to prevent the passage of water through walls and floors.

Dampproofing is to prevent the passage of moisture or collection of water vapors. This system is not capable of withstanding hydrostatic pressures.

GENERAL NOTES

1. Membrane, hydrolithic and chemical admixtures in concrete are typical types of waterproofing and dampproofing systems. Choice of the appropriate system depends upon the prevailing hydrostatic conditions. Consult manufacturers for system properties and uses.
2. Specify installation to conform strictly to the recommendations of the manufacturer of the system selected.
3. The details on the following pages are typical conditions only.

TYPICAL SYSTEMS

TYPE	DESCRIPTION	GENERAL USES
MEMBRANES	Tar or asphalt bitumens on and between layer(s) of felt made of rag, asbestos and wood fiber or of fabric made of cotton and glass. Butyl rubber and polyvinyl chloride sheets with laps sealed with adhesives and cements.	Exterior, below grade on walls and under floors. Under walking surfaces of roofs.
HYDROLITHIC COATINGS	Sprayed, troweled or brushed on coatings of asphaltic bitumens and plastics.	Exterior, below grade on walls.
	Coatings of plaster or cement mixed with ferrous particles.	Interior, below grade on walls and floors.
CONCRETE ADMIXTURES	Liquid, paste or powder admixtures used integrally to render concrete impermeable.	Walls and floors above and below grade, concrete canopies and covered walks.
METAL WATERPROOFING	Plain metal sheets, and metal sheets coated with fabric and/or plastic sheets sealed by soldering, adhesives and cements. Generally the metal is lead or copper.	Shower stalls and pans, pools, around floor and roof drains. Under walking surfaces on roofs.

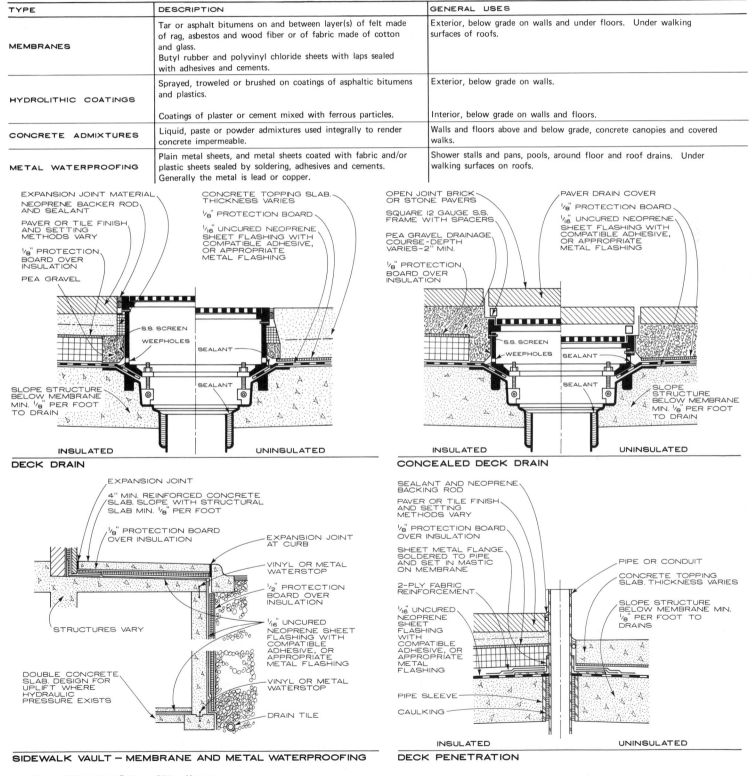

DECK DRAIN

CONCEALED DECK DRAIN

SIDEWALK VAULT — MEMBRANE AND METAL WATERPROOFING

DECK PENETRATION

Jerry Graham; CTA Architects-Engineers; Billings, Montana

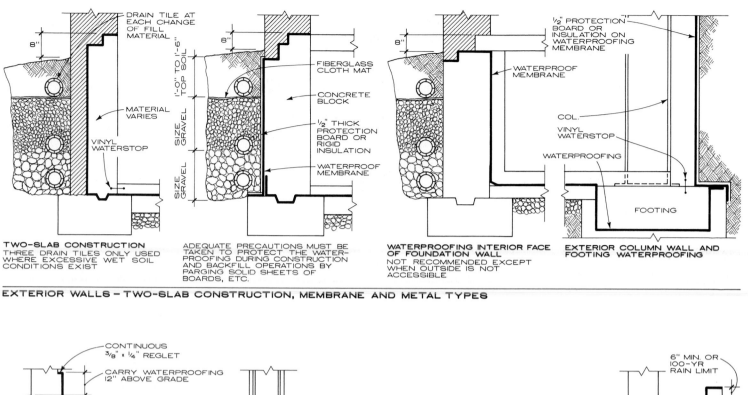

TWO-SLAB CONSTRUCTION
THREE DRAIN TILES ONLY USED WHERE EXCESSIVE WET SOIL CONDITIONS EXIST

ADEQUATE PRECAUTIONS MUST BE TAKEN TO PROTECT THE WATER-PROOFING DURING CONSTRUCTION AND BACKFILL OPERATIONS BY PARGING SOLID SHEETS OF BOARDS, ETC.

WATERPROOFING INTERIOR FACE OF FOUNDATION WALL
NOT RECOMMENDED EXCEPT WHEN OUTSIDE IS NOT ACCESSIBLE

EXTERIOR COLUMN WALL AND FOOTING WATERPROOFING

EXTERIOR WALLS – TWO-SLAB CONSTRUCTION, MEMBRANE AND METAL TYPES

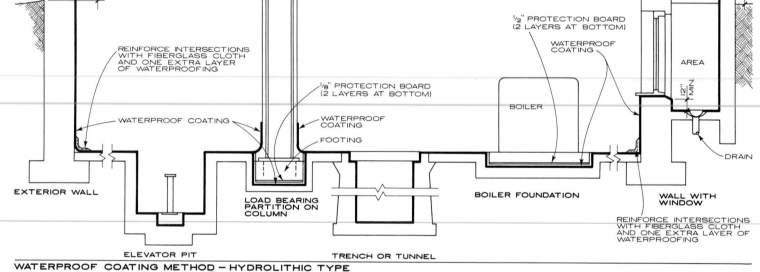

WATERPROOF COATING METHOD – HYDROLITHIC TYPE
RECOMMENDED ONLY WHEN OUTSIDE IS NOT ACCESSIBLE

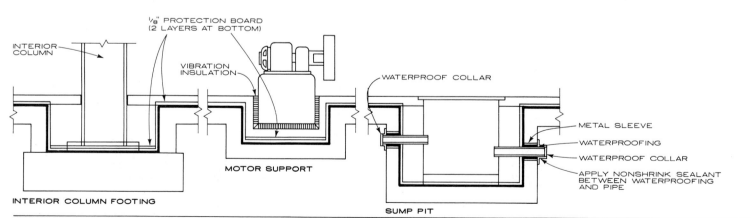

WATERPROOFING WITH PROTECTIVE SLAB – MEMBRANE TYPE

Larry O. Opseth, AIA; Meyers and Bennett Architects/BRW; Minneapolis, Minnesota

William C. Nichols, AIA; Atlanta, Georgia

7 WATERPROOFING SYSTEMS

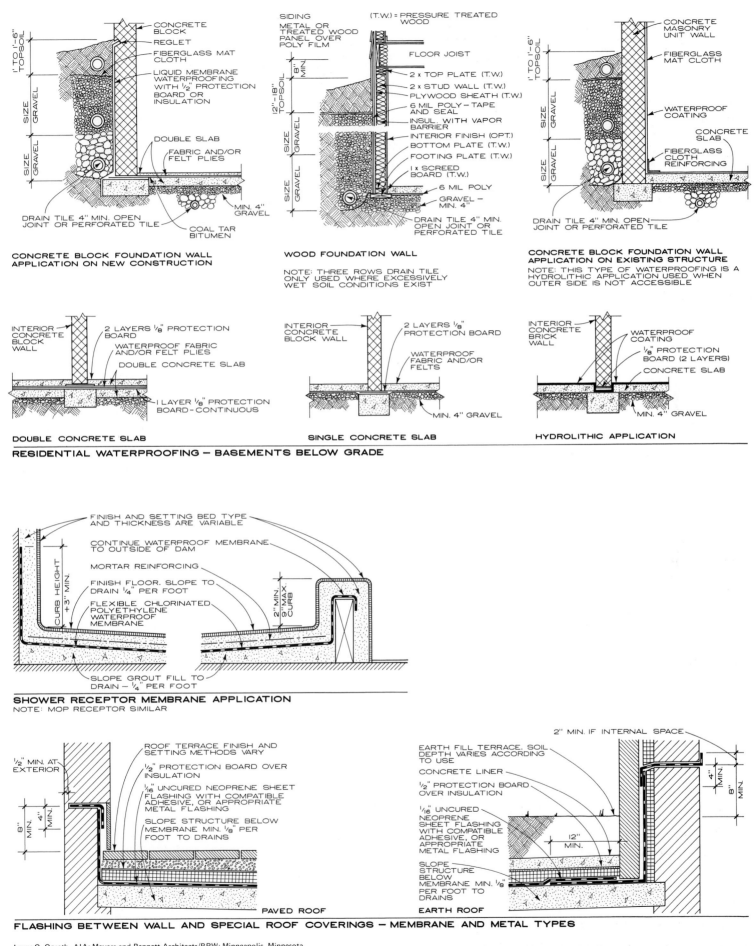

CONCRETE BLOCK FOUNDATION WALL
APPLICATION ON NEW CONSTRUCTION

WOOD FOUNDATION WALL

NOTE: THREE ROWS DRAIN TILE
ONLY USED WHERE EXCESSIVELY
WET SOIL CONDITIONS EXIST

CONCRETE BLOCK FOUNDATION WALL
APPLICATION ON EXISTING STRUCTURE
NOTE: THIS TYPE OF WATERPROOFING IS A
HYDROLITHIC APPLICATION USED WHEN
OUTER SIDE IS NOT ACCESSIBLE

DOUBLE CONCRETE SLAB

SINGLE CONCRETE SLAB

HYDROLITHIC APPLICATION

RESIDENTIAL WATERPROOFING – BASEMENTS BELOW GRADE

SHOWER RECEPTOR MEMBRANE APPLICATION
NOTE: MOP RECEPTOR SIMILAR

PAVED ROOF

EARTH ROOF

FLASHING BETWEEN WALL AND SPECIAL ROOF COVERINGS – MEMBRANE AND METAL TYPES

Larry O. Opseth, AIA; Meyers and Bennett Architects/BRW; Minneapolis, Minnesota

Jerry Graham; CTA Architects Engineers; Billings, Montana

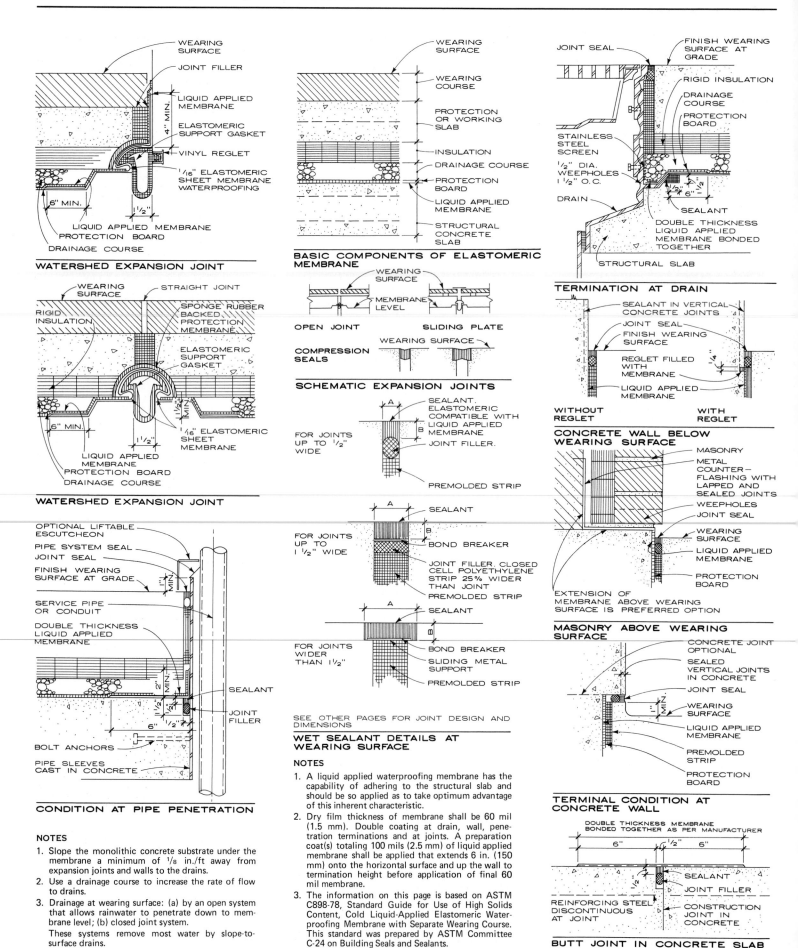

WATERSHED EXPANSION JOINT

Labels: WEARING SURFACE; JOINT FILLER; LIQUID APPLIED MEMBRANE; ELASTOMERIC SUPPORT GASKET; VINYL REGLET; ¹/₁₆" ELASTOMERIC SHEET MEMBRANE WATERPROOFING; 4" MIN.; 6" MIN.; 1½"; LIQUID APPLIED MEMBRANE; PROTECTION BOARD; DRAINAGE COURSE

WATERSHED EXPANSION JOINT

Labels: WEARING SURFACE; STRAIGHT JOINT; RIGID INSULATION; SPONGE RUBBER BACKED PROTECTION MEMBRANE; ELASTOMERIC SUPPORT GASKET; ¹/₁₆" ELASTOMERIC SHEET MEMBRANE; 6" MIN.; 1½"; LIQUID APPLIED MEMBRANE; PROTECTION BOARD; DRAINAGE COURSE

CONDITION AT PIPE PENETRATION

Labels: OPTIONAL LIFTABLE ESCUTCHEON; PIPE SYSTEM SEAL; JOINT SEAL; FINISH WEARING SURFACE AT GRADE; SERVICE PIPE OR CONDUIT; DOUBLE THICKNESS LIQUID APPLIED MEMBRANE; 2" MIN.; SEALANT; JOINT FILLER; 6"; ½"; BOLT ANCHORS; PIPE SLEEVES CAST IN CONCRETE

NOTES

1. Slope the monolithic concrete substrate under the membrane a minimum of ¹/₈ in./ft away from expansion joints and walls to the drains.
2. Use a drainage course to increase the rate of flow to drains.
3. Drainage at wearing surface: (a) by an open system that allows rainwater to penetrate down to membrane level; (b) closed joint system.
   These systems remove most water by slope-to-surface drains.

Robert E. Fehlberg, FAIA; CTA Architects-Engineers; Billings Montana

Charles J. Parise, FAIA, FASTM; Smith, Hinchman & Grylls; Detroit, Michigan

BASIC COMPONENTS OF ELASTOMERIC MEMBRANE

Labels: WEARING SURFACE; WEARING COURSE; PROTECTION OR WORKING SLAB; INSULATION; DRAINAGE COURSE; PROTECTION BOARD; LIQUID APPLIED MEMBRANE; STRUCTURAL CONCRETE SLAB

SCHEMATIC EXPANSION JOINTS

OPEN JOINT   SLIDING PLATE

COMPRESSION SEALS

Labels: WEARING SURFACE; MEMBRANE LEVEL; WEARING SURFACE

WET SEALANT DETAILS AT WEARING SURFACE

FOR JOINTS UP TO ½" WIDE — SEALANT, ELASTOMERIC COMPATIBLE WITH LIQUID APPLIED MEMBRANE; JOINT FILLER.; PREMOLDED STRIP

FOR JOINTS UP TO 1½" WIDE — SEALANT; BOND BREAKER; JOINT FILLER. CLOSED CELL POLYETHYLENE STRIP 25% WIDER THAN JOINT; PREMOLDED STRIP

FOR JOINTS WIDER THAN 1½" — SEALANT; BOND BREAKER; SLIDING METAL SUPPORT; PREMOLDED STRIP

SEE OTHER PAGES FOR JOINT DESIGN AND DIMENSIONS

NOTES

1. A liquid applied waterproofing membrane has the capability of adhering to the structural slab and should be so applied as to take optimum advantage of this inherent characteristic.
2. Dry film thickness of membrane shall be 60 mil (1.5 mm). Double coating at drain, wall, penetration terminations and at joints. A preparation coat(s) totaling 100 mils (2.5 mm) of liquid applied membrane shall be applied that extends 6 in. (150 mm) onto the horizontal surface and up the wall to termination height before application of final 60 mil membrane.
3. The information on this page is based on ASTM C898-78, Standard Guide for Use of High Solids Content, Cold Liquid-Applied Elastomeric Waterproofing Membrane with Separate Wearing Course. This standard was prepared by ASTM Committee C-24 on Building Seals and Sealants.

TERMINATION AT DRAIN

Labels: JOINT SEAL; FINISH WEARING SURFACE AT GRADE; RIGID INSULATION; DRAINAGE COURSE; PROTECTION BOARD; STAINLESS STEEL SCREEN; ½" DIA. WEEPHOLES 1½" O.C.; DRAIN; 6"; SEALANT; DOUBLE THICKNESS LIQUID APPLIED MEMBRANE BONDED TOGETHER; STRUCTURAL SLAB

CONCRETE WALL BELOW WEARING SURFACE

WITHOUT REGLET   WITH REGLET

Labels: SEALANT IN VERTICAL CONCRETE JOINTS; JOINT SEAL; FINISH WEARING SURFACE; REGLET FILLED WITH MEMBRANE; LIQUID APPLIED MEMBRANE

MASONRY ABOVE WEARING SURFACE

Labels: MASONRY; METAL COUNTER-FLASHING WITH LAPPED AND SEALED JOINTS; WEEPHOLES; JOINT SEAL; WEARING SURFACE; LIQUID APPLIED MEMBRANE; PROTECTION BOARD; EXTENSION OF MEMBRANE ABOVE WEARING SURFACE IS PREFERRED OPTION

TERMINAL CONDITION AT CONCRETE WALL

Labels: CONCRETE JOINT OPTIONAL; SEALED VERTICAL JOINTS IN CONCRETE; JOINT SEAL; WEARING SURFACE; LIQUID APPLIED MEMBRANE; PREMOLDED STRIP; PROTECTION BOARD

BUTT JOINT IN CONCRETE SLAB

Labels: DOUBLE THICKNESS MEMBRANE BONDED TOGETHER AS PER MANUFACTURER; 6"; ½"; 6"; ½"; SEALANT; JOINT FILLER; REINFORCING STEEL DISCONTINUOUS AT JOINT; CONSTRUCTION JOINT IN CONCRETE

MAJOR COMPONENTS

The major components of a good joint seal are the substrate, primer, joint-filler, bond breaker, and sealant.

SUBSTRATE

The more common substrates are masonry concrete, metal, and glass. These are generally classified as porous or nonporous.

Some substrates may not be suitable for achieving a joint unless treated mechanically, chemically, or both.

When the substrate has a coating, the coating must be compatible with the sealant and its bond to the substrate and sealant must be adequate.

Proprietary treatments or protective coatings on metal and waterproofing or water repellent treatments on concrete may inhibit bonding. Consult both substrate and sealant manufacturers for suitable joint preparation methods and the primers to be used before applying joint materials. Adhesion testing of trial applications in the field is recommended.

Surface laitance and incompatible or bond inhibiting, form release agents on concrete surfaces must be removed.

Substrates must be clean, dry, sound, and free of loose particles, contaminants, foreign matter, water soluble material, and frost.

Joints in masonry and concrete should be sealed before cleaning exposed surfaces and applying required protective barriers.

PRIMER

The purpose of a primer is to improve the adhesion of a sealant to a substrate. Many sealants require primers on all substrates, some on only certain substrates or on none at all. Most require a primer for maximum adhesion to concrete and masonry surfaces.

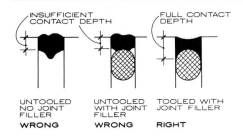

WRONG — UNTOOLED NO JOINT FILLER (INSUFFICIENT CONTACT DEPTH)
WRONG — UNTOOLED WITH JOINT FILLER
RIGHT — TOOLED WITH JOINT FILLER (FULL CONTACT DEPTH)

PURPOSE FOR JOINT-FILLER AND TOOLING

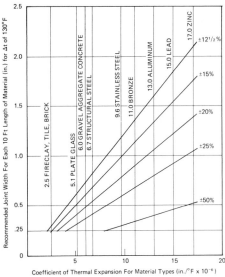

RECOMMENDED JOINT WIDTH FOR SEALANTS WITH VARIOUS MOVEMENT CAPABILITIES

JOINT DESIGN

The geometry of a joint seal is related to numerous factors including desired appearance, spacing of joints,

Charles J. Parise, FAIA; FASTM; Smith, Hinchman & Grylls; Detroit, Michigan

---

Normally the sealant manufacturer's standard published recommendations should be adhered to regarding the use of primers or surface conditioners for optimum adhesion. However, field tests may be required to determine the proper treatment and sealant/primer selection.

JOINT-FILLERS

A joint-filler is used to control the depth of sealant in the joint and permit full wetting of the intended interface when tooled. It can also serve as a temporary joint seal for weather protection when conditions are unsuitable for immediate sealant application, but normally should be replaced before sealant is applied with a new permanent joint-filler.

Some joint-fillers may be incompatible with the substrate and sealant, causing stains on either one of them or both. Some may be factory coated with a suitable material that provides a barrier to staining. To confirm its suitability, the barrier coating should be acceptable to both the sealant and joint-filler manufacturers.

Joint-fillers for vertical application may be flexible, compatible, closed cell plastic foam or sponge rubber rod stock and elastomeric tubing of such materials as neoprene, butyl, and EPDM. They should resist permanent deformation before and during sealant application, and be nonabsorbent to water or gas, and resist flowing upon mild heating, since this can cause bubbling of the sealant. Open cell sponge type materials such as urethane foam may be satisfactory, provided that their water absorption characteristics are recognized. The sealant should be applied immediately after joint-filler placement to prevent water absorption from rain. Elastomeric tubing of neoprene, butyl, or EPDM may be applied immediately as a temporary seal until the primary sealant is put in place, after which they serve to a limited degree as a secondary water barrier. When used as temporary seals, joint-fillers should be

movement in joint, movement capability of sealant to be used, required sealant width to accommodate anticipated movement, and tooling method.

SEALANT WIDTH

The required width of the sealant is determined by the application temperature range of the sealant, the temperature extremes anticipated at the site location, and the movement capability of the sealant to be used.

An application temperature from 40 to 100°F should be assumed in determining the anticipated amount of joint movement in the design of joints.

The minimum joint widths for various building materials in 10 ft sections and for sealants with the movement capability range indicated are shown in the accompanying table.

SEALANT DEPTH

The sealant depth, when applied, depends on the sealant width. The following guidelines are normally accepted practice.

1. For a recommended minimum width of 1/4 in., the depth should be 1/4 in.
2. For joints in concrete masonry or stone, the depth of the sealant may be equal to the sealant width in joints up to 1/2 in. For joints 1/2 to 1 in. wide, the sealant depth should be 1/2 in. For joints 1 to 2 in. wide, the sealant depth should not be greater than one half the sealant width. For widths exceeding 2 in., the depth should be determined by the sealant manufacturer.
3. For sealant widths over 1/4 in. in metal, glass, and other nonporous surface joints, the sealant depth should be a minimum of one half the sealant width and should in no case exceed the width.

When determining location of the joint-filler in the joint, consideration should be given to the reduction in sealant depth with concave and recessed tooled joints and the joint should be designed accordingly.

APPLICATION

Thoroughly clean all joints, removing all foreign matter such as dust, paint (unless it is a permanent protective coating), oil, grease, waterproofing or water repellent treatments, water, surface dirt, and frost.

Clean porous materials such as concrete, masonry, and unglazed surfaces of ceramic tile by brushing, grinding, blast cleaning, mechanical abrading, acid washing, or a combination of these methods to provide

---

able to remain resilient at temperatures down to –15°F and have low compression set.

Joint-fillers for horizontal application for floors, pavements, sidewalks, patios, and other light traffic areas may be compatible, extruded, closed cell, high density, flexible foams, cork board, resin impregnated fiberboard, or elastomeric tubing or rods. These joint-fillers should remain resilient down to –15°F, exhibit good recovery, not cause the sealant to bubble in the joint because of heat, and be capable of supporting the sealant in traffic areas. They should not exude liquids under compression, which could hydraulically cause sealant failure by forcing the sealant from the joint. Combinations of joint-filler materials can be used to satisfy the several requirements of a joint seal. A premolded joint-filler may be used to form a joint in concrete, and an additional joint-filler material may be installed under compression across the width and to the proper depth just before the sealant is applied to provide a clean, dry, compatible backup.

BOND BREAKER

A bond breaker may be necessary to prevent adhesion of the sealant to any surface or material where such adhesion would be detrimental to the performance of the sealant.

The use of a joint-filler to which the sealant will not adhere may preclude the need for a bond breaker.

The bond breaker may be a polyethylene tape with pressure sensitive adhesive on one side or various liquid applied compounds as recommended by the sealant manufacturer.

SEALANT

Sealants are classified as single component or multi-component, nonsag or self-leveling, and traffic or nontraffic use, as well as according to movement capability. Characteristics of some generic types are listed in the accompanying table.

a clean, sound substrate for optimum sealant adhesion. The surface of concrete may be cut back to remove contaminants and expose a clean surface when acceptable to the purchaser.

Remove laitance from concrete by acid washing, grinding, or mechanical abrading.

Remove form oils from concrete by blast cleaning.

Remove loose particles originally present or resulting from grinding, abrading, or blast cleaning by blowing out joints with oilfree compressed air (or vacuuming) prior to application of primer or sealant.

Clean nonporous surfaces, such as metal, glass, porcelain enamel, and glazed surfaces of ceramic tile chemically or by other means that are not harmful to the substrate and are acceptable to the substrate manufacturer.

Remove temporary protective coatings on metallic surfaces by a solvent that leaves no residue. Apply the solvent with clean oilfree cloths or lintless paper towels. Do not allow the solvent to air-dry without wiping. Wipe dry with a clean dry cloth or lintless paper towels. Permanent coatings that are to remain must not be removed or damaged.

Install masking tape at joint edges when necessary to avoid undesirable sealant smears on exposed visible surfaces. Use a nonstaining, nonabsorbent, compatible type.

Install primer when and as recommended by the sealant manufacturer for optimum adhesion.

Install compatible joint-filler uniformly to proper depth without twisting and braiding.

Install sealant in strict accordance with the manufacturer's recommendations and precautions. Completely fill the recess provided in the joint. Sealants are more safely applied at temperatures above 40°F. Joints must be dry.

Tool sealant so as to force it into the joint, eliminating air pockets and ensuring contact of the sealant with the sides of the joint. Use appropriate tool to provide a concave, flush, or recessed joint as required.

Immediately after tooling the joint remove masking tape carefully, if used, without disturbing the sealant.

Reference: ASTM Committee C-24 "Standard Guide For Use of Chemically Curing Elastomeric Sealants." Highlights of text, graph, and figures are reprinted with permission from the American Society for Testing and Materials.

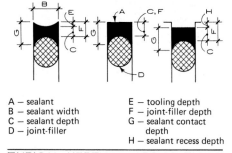

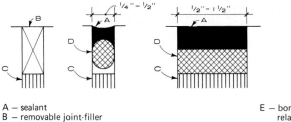
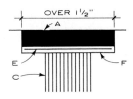

A – sealant
B – sealant width
C – sealant depth
D – joint-filler

E – tooling depth
F – joint-filler depth
G – sealant contact depth
H – sealant recess depth

TYPICAL VERTICAL APPLICATIONS, PROFILES AND TERMINOLOGY

A – sealant
B – removable joint-filler
C – premolded joint-filler cast in concrete
D – joint-filler installed under compression

E – bond breaker (use over sliding metal support in relatively wide joints)
F – concrete shoulder provides vertical support

USE OF MULTIPLE JOINT-FILLERS IN HORIZONTAL APPLICATIONS IN CAST-IN-PLACE CONCRETE

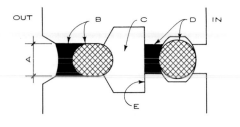

A – 1″ minimum for access to interior air seal
B – sealant and joint-filler preferred for rain screen; preformed compression seal also used
C – pressure equalization chamber; vent to outside, and chamber baffles at every second floor vertically and same distance horizontally
D – sealant and joint-filler installed from outside to facilitate continuity of air seal; building framework hinders application of continuous air seal from interior
E – concrete shoulders required for tooling screed

TWO-STAGE PRESSURE EQUALIZED JOINT SEAL

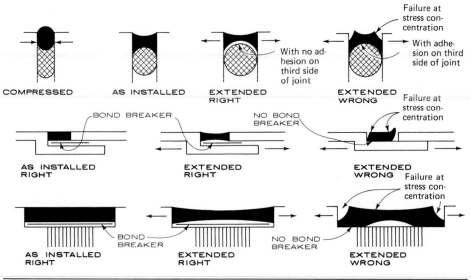

SEALANT CONFIGURATIONS WITH MOVEMENT AND EFFECT OF THREE-SIDED ADHESION

CHARACTERISTICS OF COMMON ELASTOMERIC SEALANTS

	ACRYLIC (SOLVENT RELEASES) (ONE-PART)	POLYSULFIDE		POLYURETHANE		SILICONE (ONE-PART)
		TWO-PART	ONE-PART	TWO-PART	ONE-PART	
Chief ingredients	Acrylic terpolymer, inert pigments, stabilizer, and selected fillers	Polysulfide polymers, activators, pigments, plasticizers, inert fillers, gelling, and curing agents		Polyurethane prepolymer, inert fillers, pigment, plasticizers, accelerators, activators, and extenders	Polyurethane prepolymer, inert fillers, pigment, and plasticizers	Siloxane polymer, pigment, and selected fillers
Percent solids	85–95	95–100	95–100	95–100	95–100	95–100
Curing process	Solvent release and very slow chemical cure	Chemical reaction with curing agent	Chemical reaction with moisture in the air	Chemical reaction with curing agent	Chemical reaction with moisture in air	Chemical reaction with moisture in the air
Curing characteristics	Skins on exposed surface; interior remains soft and tacky	Cures uniformly throughout; rate affected by temperature and humidity	Skins over, cures progressively inward; final cure uniform throughout	Cures uniformly throughout; rate affected by temperature and humidity	Skins over, cures progressively inward, final cure uniform throughout	Cures progressively inward; final cure uniform throughout
Primer	Generally not required	Manufacturer's approved primer required for porous surfaces, sometimes for other surfaces		Manufacturer's approved primer required for most surfaces		Manufacturer's approved primer required for most surfaces
Application temperature (°F)	40–120, must be heated	40–100	60–100	40–120	40–120	0–120
Tackfree time	1–7 days	6–24 hr	6–72 hr	1–24 hr	Slightly tacky until weathered	1 hr or less
Hardness, Shore A Cured 1 to 6 months, aged 5 years	0–25 45–55	15–45 30–60	25–35 40–50	20–40 35–55	25–45 30–50	20–40 35–55
Toxicity	Nontoxic	Curing agent is toxic	Contains toxic ingredients	Toxic; gloves recommended for handling		Nontoxic
Use characteristics	Excellent adhesion; poor low temperature flexibility; not usable in traffic areas; unpleasant odor 5–12 days	Wide range of appropriate applications; curing time depends on temperature and humidity	Unpleasant odor; broad range of cured hardnesses available	Sets very fast; broad range of cured hardnesses; excellent for concrete joints and traffic areas	Excellent for concrete joints and traffic areas, but substrate must be absolutely dry; short package stability	Requires contact with air for curing; low abrasion resistance; not tough enough for use in traffic areas

Charles J. Parise, FAIA; FASTM; Smith, Hinchman & Grylls; Detroit, Michigan

CHAPTER 8   DOORS AND WINDOWS

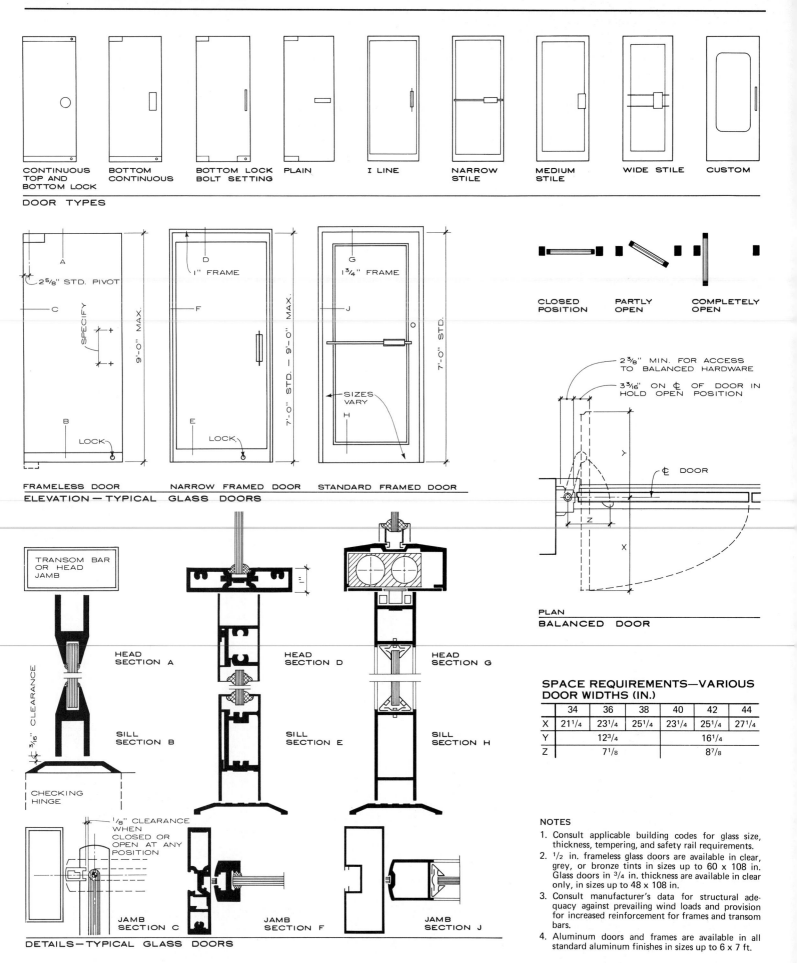

DOOR TYPES

CONTINUOUS TOP AND BOTTOM LOCK | BOTTOM CONTINUOUS | BOTTOM LOCK BOLT SETTING | PLAIN | I LINE | NARROW STILE | MEDIUM STILE | WIDE STILE | CUSTOM

ELEVATION — TYPICAL GLASS DOORS

FRAMELESS DOOR — 2⅝" STD. PIVOT — A — C — SPECIFY — B — LOCK — 9'-0" MAX.

NARROW FRAMED DOOR — 1" FRAME — D — F — E — LOCK — 7'-0" STD. - 9'-0" MAX.

STANDARD FRAMED DOOR — 1¾" FRAME — G — J — SIZES VARY — H — 7'-0" STD.

CLOSED POSITION | PARTLY OPEN | COMPLETELY OPEN

2⅜" MIN. FOR ACCESS TO BALANCED HARDWARE

3³⁄₁₆" ON ₵ OF DOOR IN HOLD OPEN POSITION

₵ DOOR

PLAN — BALANCED DOOR

DETAILS — TYPICAL GLASS DOORS

TRANSOM BAR OR HEAD JAMB

HEAD SECTION A | HEAD SECTION D | HEAD SECTION G

SILL SECTION B | SILL SECTION E | SILL SECTION H

³⁄₁₆" CLEARANCE

CHECKING HINGE

⅛" CLEARANCE WHEN CLOSED OR OPEN AT ANY POSITION

JAMB SECTION C | JAMB SECTION F | JAMB SECTION J

SPACE REQUIREMENTS—VARIOUS DOOR WIDTHS (IN.)

	34	36	38	40	42	44
X	21¼	23¼	25¼	23¼	25¼	27¼
Y		12¾			16¼	
Z		7⅛			8⅞	

NOTES

1. Consult applicable building codes for glass size, thickness, tempering, and safety rail requirements.
2. ½ in. frameless glass doors are available in clear, grey, or bronze tints in sizes up to 60 x 108 in. Glass doors in ¾ in. thickness are available in clear only, in sizes up to 48 x 108 in.
3. Consult manufacturer's data for structural adequacy against prevailing wind loads and provision for increased reinforcement for frames and transom bars.
4. Aluminum doors and frames are available in all standard aluminum finishes in sizes up to 6 x 7 ft.

G. Lawson Drinkard, III, AIA; The Vickery Partnership, Architects; Charlottesville, Virginia

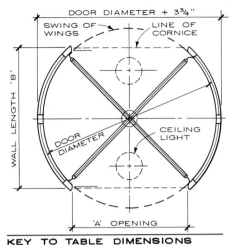

KEY TO TABLE DIMENSIONS

STANDARD DOOR DIMENSIONS

DIAMETER	A (OPENING)	B (WALL LENGTH)
6'-6''	4'-5¼''	4'-11⅝''
6'-8''	4'-6¹¹⁄₁₆''	5'-1¹⁄₁₆''
6'-10''	4'-8⅛''	5'-2½''
7'-0''	4'-9½''	5'-3⅞''
7'-2''	4'-10¹⁵⁄₁₆''	5'-5⁵⁄₁₆''
7'-4''	5'-0⅜''	5'-6¾''
7'-6''	5'-1¾''	5'-8⅛''

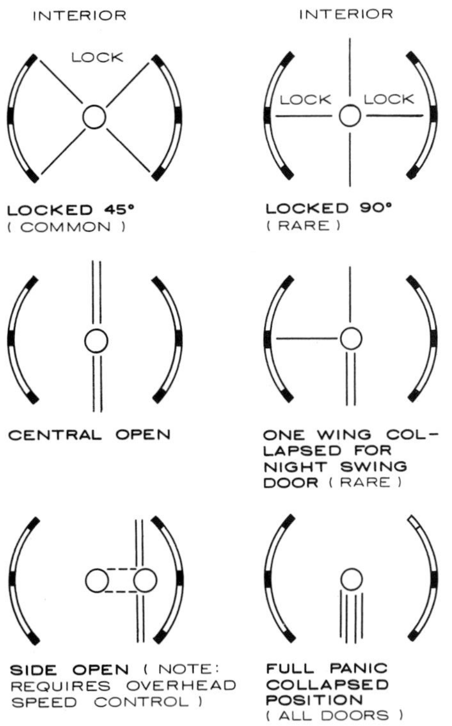

Curved sliding night door available for security if code permits. Enclosure walls and wings may be designed to roll aside.

PLANS SHOWING LOCKED AND FOLDED WING POSITIONS

LAYOUT TYPES

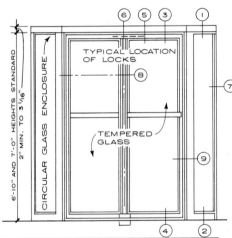

DOOR ELEVATION

NOTES

1. Circular glass enclosure walls may be simply annealed ¼ in. glass. However, this varies with different government bodies. Some jurisdictions require laminated or wire glass. Tempered glass is not available for this use. Refer to Consumer Products Safety Commission Standards for Glazing.

2. Theoretical capacity each way = 2880 per hour. Practical capacity = 2000 per hour.

3. Doors fabricated from stainless steel, aluminum, or bronze sections are available. Wall enclosure may be all metal, all glass, partial glass, or housed-in construction.

4. Provide heating and cooling source integral with or immediately adjacent to enclosure.

5. Motor drive recommended with constant low speed.

6. For general use, use 6 ft 6 in. diameter. For hotels, department stores, or other large traffic areas, use 7 ft or greater diameter.

7. Codes may allow 50% of legal exiting requirements by means of revolving doors. Some do not credit any and require hinged doors adjacent. Verify with local authorities.

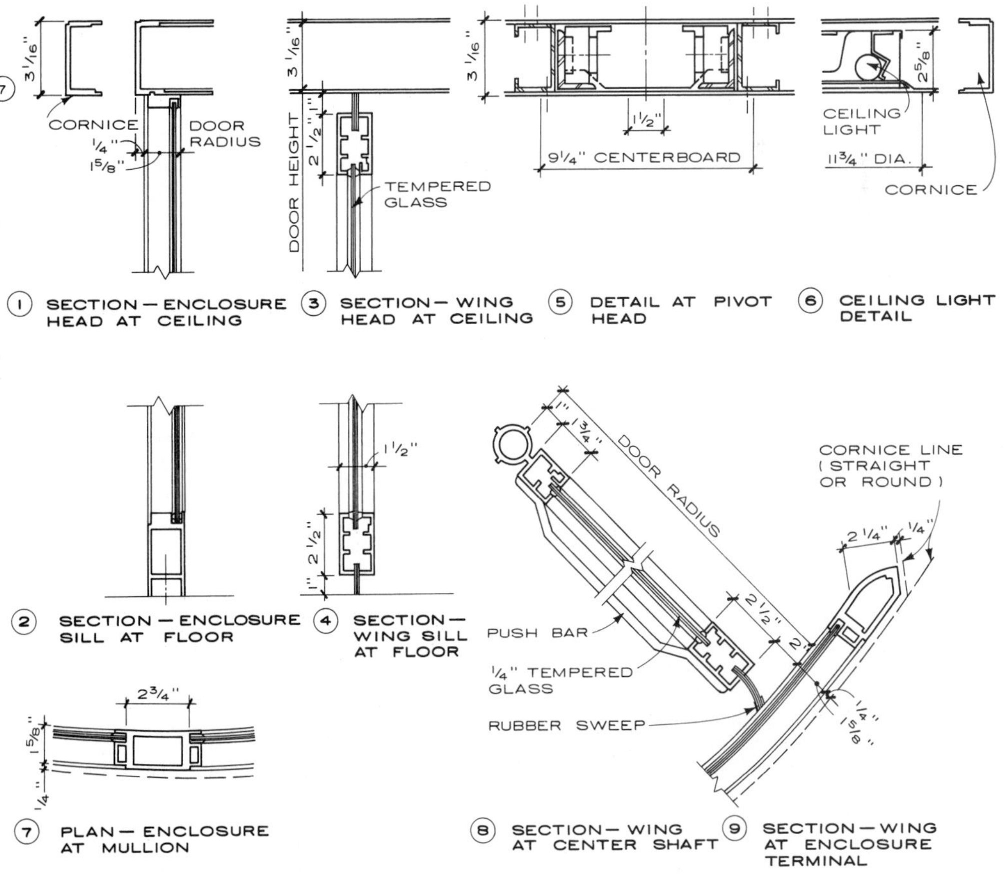

Skidmore, Owings & Merrill

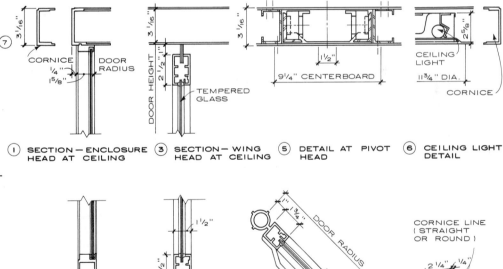

① SECTION—ENCLOSURE HEAD AT CEILING ③ SECTION—WING HEAD AT CEILING ⑤ DETAIL AT PIVOT HEAD ⑥ CEILING LIGHT DETAIL

② SECTION—ENCLOSURE SILL AT FLOOR ④ SECTION—WING SILL AT FLOOR ⑦ PLAN—ENCLOSURE AT MULLION ⑧ SECTION—WING AT CENTER SHAFT ⑨ SECTION—WING AT ENCLOSURE TERMINAL

TYPICAL DOOR DETAILS

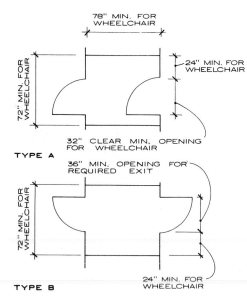

TYPE A

78" MIN. FOR WHEELCHAIR

72" MIN. FOR WHEELCHAIR

24" MIN. FOR WHEELCHAIR

32" CLEAR MIN. OPENING FOR WHEELCHAIR

36" MIN. OPENING FOR REQUIRED EXIT

72" MIN. FOR WHEELCHAIR

24" MIN. FOR WHEELCHAIR

TYPE B

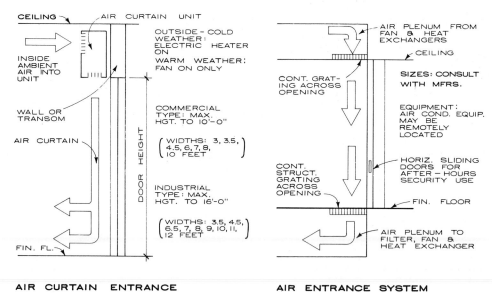

AIR CURTAIN ENTRANCE

CEILING / AIR CURTAIN UNIT

INSIDE AMBIENT AIR INTO UNIT

WALL OR TRANSOM

AIR CURTAIN

FIN. FL.

DOOR HEIGHT

OUTSIDE – COLD WEATHER: ELECTRIC HEATER ON
WARM WEATHER: FAN ON ONLY

COMMERCIAL TYPE: MAX. HGT. TO 10'-0"
(WIDTHS: 3, 3.5, 4.5, 6, 7, 8, 10 FEET)

INDUSTRIAL TYPE: MAX. HGT. TO 16'-0"
(WIDTHS: 3.5, 4.5, 6.5, 7, 8, 9, 10, 11, 12 FEET)

AIR ENTRANCE SYSTEM

AIR PLENUM FROM FAN & HEAT EXCHANGERS

CEILING

SIZES: CONSULT WITH MFRS.

CONT. GRATING ACROSS OPENING

EQUIPMENT: AIR COND. EQUIP. MAY BE REMOTELY LOCATED

CONT. STRUCT. GRATING ACROSS OPENING

HORIZ. SLIDING DOORS FOR AFTER – HOURS SECURITY USE

FIN. FLOOR

AIR PLENUM TO FILTER, FAN & HEAT EXCHANGER

1. Provide doors for handicapped to operate at less than 8 lb pressure.
2. Minimum turning radius of wheelchair is 36 in.; desirable space is 60 x 60 in.

VESTIBULES

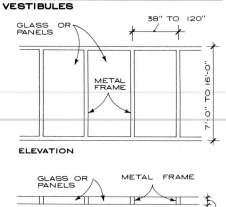

GLASS OR PANELS

38" TO 120"

METAL FRAME

7'-0" TO 16'-0"

ELEVATION

GLASS OR PANELS

METAL FRAME

DIMENSION VARIES WITH HGT. OF WALL

PLAN

METAL FRAME SYSTEM

Consult manufacturers' data regarding energy conservation, sound, installation details, and limitations of use.

SPECIAL ENTRANCES

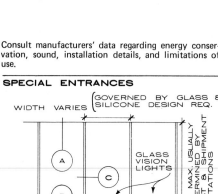
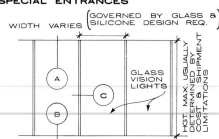

WIDTH VARIES (GOVERNED BY GLASS & SILICONE DESIGN REQ.)

HGT. MAX. USUALLY DETERMINED BY COST & SHIPMENT LIMITATIONS

GLASS VISION LIGHTS

A

C

B

ELEVATION

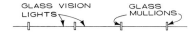

GLASS VISION LIGHTS

GLASS MULLIONS

PLAN

ALL GLASS SYSTEM

Consult manufacturers' data regarding energy conservation, soil, installation details, limitations, and first costs and maintenance costs early in the design phase.

Hand or floor mat activated and pneumatic, hydraulic, or electric powered automatic doors are available from various sources. This type of door is either horizontally sliding (both single and biparting) or pivotal (single or double). Both types usually have "break out" features from inside that allow them to be used as exit doors. "Power-off" safety features can be provided to ensure safe passage by the general public, including the handicapped. Minimum clear opening width for the handicapped is 32 in.

All glass used in doors, sidelights, and vestibule return lights, within 48 in. of a doorjamb, must be safety glazed. See Glass Doors: Entrances.

AUTOMATIC DOORS (POWER OPER.)

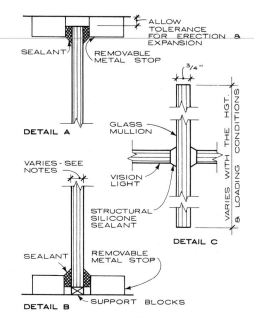

ALLOW TOLERANCE FOR ERECTION & EXPANSION

SEALANT

REMOVABLE METAL STOP

DETAIL A

3/4"

GLASS MULLION

VISION LIGHT

STRUCTURAL SILICONE SEALANT

VARIES – SEE NOTES

VARIES WITH THE HGT. & LOADING CONDITIONS

DETAIL C

SEALANT

REMOVABLE METAL STOP

SUPPORT BLOCKS

DETAIL B

ALL GLASS DETAILS

Design each component part (other than glass) so that deflections normal to wall plane at full locally required loading will not exceed $1/200$ of the clear span of the component part, but limit deflection of glass supporting members to $1/300$ of the distance over which such glass is supported. Do not permit deflections parallel to wall plane to exceed 75% of the glass edge clearances or other clearances provided between component parts. Base calculations for such deflections on the combination of maximum direct loading, building deflections, thermal stresses, and erection tolerances. Do not permit permanent deflections in this type of work.

Glass or panel thickness varies with width and height. Consult span charts in glass manufacturer's structural data sheets, then confirm data with the manufacturer.

Comply with the requirements of local and state laws or ordinances with respect to the use and application of safety glazing materials at all locations of both indoor and outdoor glass walls.

LARGE GLASS WALLS

Skidmore, Owings and Merrill

All glass wall systems are engineered, custom fabricated combinations of clear glass vertical mullion lights and silicone structural sealant at the mullion and vision interfaces.

Glass mullion systems replace the conventional masonry, wood, or metal supports for large glass walls and may be used inside or out. No opaque materials are used except for simple metal sections at the head and sill. Engineers usually rely on $3/4$ in. thick mullions as the principal supporting element. The thickness and width of the large vision lights for clear glass (or, under special conditions, tinted glass) are governed by glass and silicone design requirements at the design wind load. Reputable glass manufacturers with expertise in this type of construction should be consulted at the very beginning of a project where an all glass system is proposed.

8   ENTRANCES AND STOREFRONTS

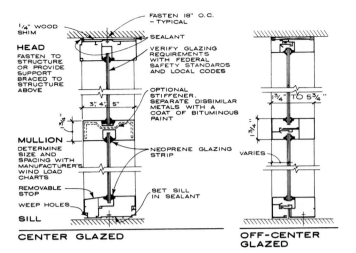

CENTER GLAZED

OFF-CENTER GLAZED

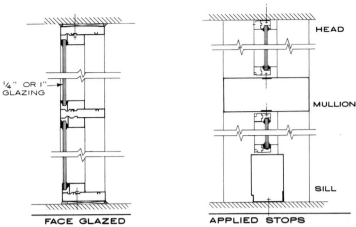

FACE GLAZED

APPLIED STOPS

Various anodized color finishes are available. Class I (0.7 mil) or Class II (0.4 mil) in black, bronze, or clear is standard with most manufacturers.

NOTES

1. Review tinted and coated glass applications and details to eliminate possibility of thermal breakage.
2. Weep holes are required at sill for double glazing.
3. For specific applications, refer to manufacturers' current recommendations.
4. Other materials such as hollow metal or wood can be used for custom work.

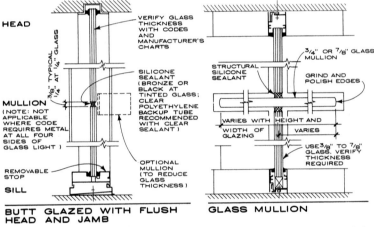

BUTT GLAZED WITH FLUSH HEAD AND JAMB

GLASS MULLION

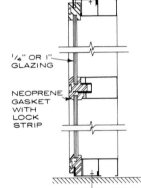

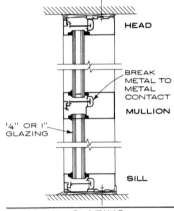

GASKET GLAZED

THERMAL GLAZING

Mitered glass edges at corners are not recommended. Maximum vertical span for butt glazing is 10 x 8 ft wide.

Mullions are clear glass. Tinted or coated glass lights may be considered for small areas. Maximum vertical span is 30 x 9 ft wide.

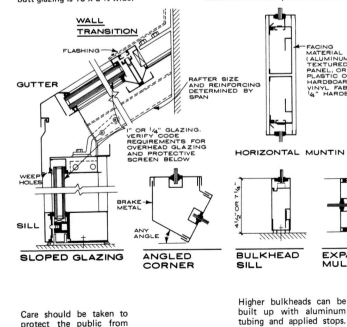

SLOPED GLAZING

ANGLED CORNER

BULKHEAD SILL

EXPANSION MULLION

HORIZONTAL MUNTIN

DOOR TRANSOM WITH CLOSER AND ILLUMINATED EXIT SIGN

HEAD WITH RECEPTOR

VARIABLE POCKET GLAZING

Care should be taken to protect the public from the possibility of overhead glass breakage.

Higher bulkheads can be built up with aluminum tubing and applied stops. Locate expansion mullions 20 ft o.c.

Use variable pocket glazing where deflection or dimensional tolerance problems exist.

O'Leary Terasawa & Takahashi, AIA Architects; Los Angeles, California

GLASS: DEFINITION

A hard and brittle amorphous substance, made by fusing silica (sometimes in combination with the oxides of boron or phosphorus) with certain basic oxides (notably those of sodium, potassium, calcium, magnesium, and lead) and cooling the product rapidly to prevent crystallization or devitrification. Most glasses melt between 800 and 950°C. Heat resisting glass generally contains a high proportion of boric oxide. The brittleness of glass is such that minute surface scratches during manufacture greatly reduce its strength.

INDUSTRY QUALITY STANDARDS

FEDERAL SPECIFICATION DD-G-451: Establishes the thickness and dimensional tolerances and the quality characteristics of flat glass products.

FEDERAL SPECIFICATION DD-G-1403: Establishes standards for tempered glass, heat strengthened glass, and spandrel glass.

AMERICAN NATIONAL STANDARD 2971: Establishes standards for testing safety glazing material.

NOTE: Because of the continuing revisions in available processes, qualities, finishes, colors, sizes, thicknesses, and limitations consult glass manufacturers for current information. The information that follows represents the guidelines of one or more manufacturers.

BASIC TYPES OF GLASS (CLEAR GLASS)

WINDOW AND SHEET GLASS

Manufactured by a horizontally flat or vertical draw process and then annealed slowly to produce natural flat fired, high gloss surfaces. Generally has residential and industrial applications. Inherent surface waves are noticeable in sizes larger than 4 sq ft. For minimum distortion, install the larger sizes with the wave running horizontally. When specifying, list the width first.

FLOAT GLASS

Generally accepted as the successor to polished plate glass, it has become the quality standard of the glass industry in architectural, mirror, and specialty applications. Manufactured by floating on a surface of molten tin and then annealed slowly to produce a transparent flat glass, thus eliminating grinding and polishing.

PLATE GLASS

Transparent flat glass ground and polished after rolling. Cylindrical and conic shapes may, within limits, be bent to desired curvature.

VARIATIONS OF BASIC TYPES OF GLASS

PATTERNED GLASS

Known also as rolled or figured glass, it is made by passing molten glass through rollers that are etched to produce the appropriate design. Most often only one side of the glass is imprinted with a pattern; it is possible to imprint both sides, however.

WIRE GLASS

Available as clear polished glass or in various patterns, most commonly with embedded welded square or diamond wire. Some distortion, wire discoloration, and misalignment are inherent. Some $1/4$ in. (6 mm) wired glass products are recognized as certified safety glazing materials for use in hazardous locations. For applicable fire and safety codes that govern their use, refer to ANSI Z97.1.

CATHEDRAL GLASS

Known also as art glass, stained glass, or opalescent glass. It is produced in many colors, textures, and patterns, is usually $1/8$ in. thick, and is used primarily in decorating leaded glass windows. Specialty firms usually contract this highly exacting art.

OBSCURE GLASS

For the purpose of obscurity or for the creation of a design, the entire surface on one or both sides of glass can be sandblasted, acid etched, or both. When a glass surface is altered by any of these methods, the glass is weakened and may become difficult to clean.

Skidmore, Owings and Merrill

HEAT ABSORBING OR TINTED GLASS

The glass absorbs much of the sun's energy because of admixture contents and then dissipates the heat to both the exterior and interior. The exterior glass surfaces reflect a portion of the energy depending on the sun's position. Heat absorbing glass has a higher temperature when exposed to the sun than does clear glass; thus the central area will expand more than the cooler shaded edges, causing edge tensile stress buildup.

DESIGN CONSIDERATIONS

1. It is advantageous to provide conditions that cause the glass edges to warm as rapidly as do the other lights, such as framing systems with low heat capacity and minimal glass grip or stops to avoid shading problems. Structural rubber gaskets have been used.
2. The thicker the glass the greater the solar energy absorbtion.
3. Indoor shading devices such as blinds and draperies reflect energy back through the glass, thus increasing temperature. The spaces between indoor shading and the glass, including ceiling pockets, should be properly vented. Heating elements should always be located on the interior side of shading devices, directing warm air away from the glass.

REFLECTIVE GLASS

Reflective glass coatings may be applied to float, plate, heat strengthened, tempered, laminated, or insulated spandrel glass. The vast number of combinations precludes listing them all.

Glass utilizing reflective coatings may be divided into three basic classifications:

1. Single glazing with a coating on one surface.
2. Laminated glass with the coating either between the glass plys or on the exterior surface.
3. Insulating glass units with the coating on the exterior surface or on either of the interior surfaces.

The application of the reflective coating on the exterior surface allows for the creation of a visually uniform surface composed of components of any or all of these glass classifications. Extreme care must be observed in handling, glazing, and cleaning this type of glass to avoid scratching the coating.

HEAT STRENGTHENED AND TEMPERED GLASS

Produced by reheating and rapidly cooling annealed glass, it has greatly increased mechanical strength and resistance to thermal stresses. Neither type can be altered after fabrication; hence the manufacturer, taking into account all limitations, must furnish the exact desired size and shape. Glazing problems may be encountered because of inherent warpage. Refer to Federal Specifications DD-G-1404 for allowable tolerances.

HEAT STRENGTHENED GLASS

Twice as strong as annealed glass. Does not pulverize into crystal-like form when broken, as does tempered glass.

TEMPERED GLASS

Four to five times the strength of annealed glass; breaks into innumerable small, cubelike fragments, but much safer than annealed glass. Shallow patterned glass may be tempered also. Visible tong marks are usually prevalent along the short side near the edge, since the glass is held in a vertical position during tempering. Some manufacturers can eliminate these marks. Strain patterns are inherent and may be observed under certain lighting conditions or by viewing with polarized eyeglasses.

SPANDREL GLASS

Heat strengthened through the process of firefusing an opaque ceramic color to the interior surface of sheet, plate, or float glass. May be fully tempered if GSA guide specification No. PBS-4-0885 is conformed with.

A variety of standard colors and special finishes are available. Supplied with a color frit only or with integral insulation and one of the following: (1) foil vapor barrier, (2) sheet metal backing, or (3) cement asbestos board backing. Pinholes and nonuniformity of color are apparent if used without solid opaque backup. If supplied without integral insulation, at least $1/2$ in. air space is required between glass back and backup material.

LAMINATED GLASS

SAFETY GLASS

(See also Wire Glass, Mirrors)

A tough, clear sheet of plastic film (sometimes known as the interlayer) 0.015 in. (0.636 mm) minimum thickness sandwiched under heat and pressure between piles of sheet, plate, float, wired, heat absorbing tinted, reflective, heat strengthened, full tempered glass, or a number of combinations of each.

When fractured, particles tend to adhere to the plastic film. Always weep the glazing cavity to the exterior.

ACOUSTICAL GLASS

Safety glass with a plastic film of 0.045 in. (1.143 mm) minimum thickness.

SECURITY GLASS

Safety glass with a plastic film of 0.060 in. (1.5 mm) minimum thickness for bullet resistant and burglar resistant glass. Bullet resisting glass consists of three to five plies from $3/4$ to 3 in. in overall thickness. Avoid sealants with organic solvents or oil which can react with the plastic film. (See Plastics in Glazing.)

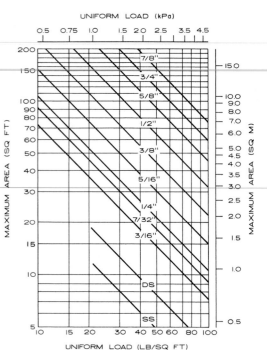

GRAPH A
Float and sheet glass supported four edges

Example: If it is determined from Graph A that a light of $1/4$" (6 mm) float should withstand 20 psf (0.96 kPa), $1/4$" (6 mm) Tuf-flex of the same size would be expected to withstand 80 psf (3.8 kPa) and $1/4$" (6 mm), wired glass 10 psf (0.48 kPa).

$$\text{Design load for use with graphs} = \frac{\text{chosen design factor}}{2.5} \times \text{actual design load}$$

INSULATING GLASS

The primary function is to reduce the air-to-air heat transfer. Insulating glass units are manufactured from two or more pieces of glass, separated by a hermetically sealed air space. Two types of units are available:

1. GLASS EDGE OR GLASS SEAL UNIT: Primarily for residential use, constructed by fusing edges of two lights of glass together with 3/16 in. (5 mm) space filled with a dry gas at atmospheric pressure. Use at high altitudes is not recommended. Do not glaze with lockstrip structural gaskets.

2. ORGANIC SEALED EDGE UNIT: Primarily for commercial and industrial use, as well as for some residential applications. Constructed with two sheets of glass separated by a metal or organic spacer (filled with a moisture absorbing material) around the edges and hermetically sealed. It is available either with or without metal edge banding. Units without banding allow for inspection of glass edges before installation.

Available with 1/4 and 1/2 in. air space in plate, float, patterned, heat absorbing, tinted, reflective, heat strengthened, tempered, and laminated glass. The thickness of the two glass panes, however, should not differ by more than 1/16 in. Performance characteristics, glass thickness, maximum fabricated sizes, and a multitude of various combinations may be found in the manufacturer's literature.

Heat absorbing units must have the heat absorbing glass to the exterior. In sloped insulated glazing, located over populated areas, heat strengthened laminated glass should be considered for use in the interior light; the glass manufacturer and governing codes and authorities on fire and safety should be consulted, however. Triple glazing units are available for special applications. Provide for the drainage of any moisture that might collect and destroy the organic seal. On metal edge units the sealant must extend above the metal edge.

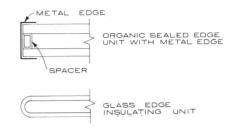

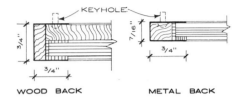

INSULATING GLASS UNITS

INSULATING GLASS

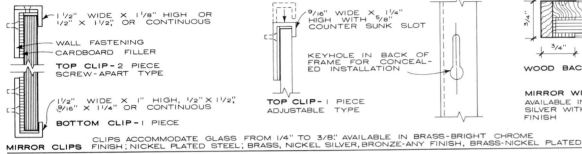

WOOD BACK   METAL BACK

MIRROR WITH METAL FRAME
AVAILABLE IN BRASS, BRONZE & NICKEL SILVER WITH ANY POLISHED OR PLATED FINISH

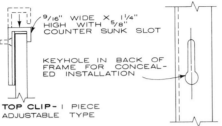

MIRROR CLIPS   CLIPS ACCOMMODATE GLASS FROM 1/4" TO 3/8". AVAILABLE IN BRASS-BRIGHT CHROME FINISH; NICKEL PLATED STEEL; BRASS, NICKEL SILVER, BRONZE-ANY FINISH, BRASS-NICKEL PLATED

MIRROR GLAZING DETAILS

MIRRORS

Most commonly manufactured from surfacing sheet, float, or plate glass, hermetically sealing a silver coating with a uniform film of electrolytic copper plating. A protective coating of paint is then applied to seal out moisture from the silver. When sheet glass is used, the quality should be A-silvering or B-silvering. Float or plate glass should be selected for mirror glazing quality. Incidental applications include safety, observation (two-way), and institutional uses.

For applications of mirrored acrylic plastics, see Glazing with Plastics.

CONVEX AND CONCAVE MIRRORS

Mirrors can be used to provide both security and safety for "blind spots" from visual vantage points. Twisted or bent mirrors are used to create distorted images.

SAFETY MIRRORS

Used for cladding full height, hinged, pivoted, or sliding doors. Commonly manufactured by one of the following methods:

1. Silvering fully tempered glass—visually inferior to regular glass mirrors because of inherent warpage of tempered glass.
2. Silvering the back of laminated glass—visually inferior.
3. Silvering a light of glass and laminating it to another glass light with the silvering inside the unit—visually the best of the three.

OBSERVATION (ONE-WAY OR TWO-WAY) MIRRORS

Commonly used for research and security in observation areas. Designed to provide vision through one side while reflecting images when viewed from the opposite side. To facilitate this function, the observers' area should have dull, subdued colors and low lighting levels with controlled dimming. The area to be observed should have light colors and a high illumination level, as suggested in the light ratio table.

Light ratio = observed area : viewing area.

LIGHT RATIO TABLE

BASE		LIGHT RATIO	
GLASS	DESCRIPTION	PREFERRED	ACCEPTABLE
Float	Clear	10:1	5:1
	Laminated	10:1	5:1
	Gray	4:1	2:1

Observation mirrors can be manufactured in the following forms (for comments, see Safety Mirrors):

1. Single glazed, for interior applications. Extreme care must be taken to avoid damaging the reflective coating through abrasion.
2. Safety tempered.
3. Safety laminated. The mirror coating is usually located between the two bonded plys of glass, thus protecting it against abrasion.
4. Security laminated. A single light of observation mirror glass that is laminated between two lights of clear glass with a plastic film interlayer.

INSTITUTIONAL MIRRORS

Used in detention or security areas and in areas involving high risk to personal safety. Often made of highly polished noncorrosive metal with reinforced rounded corners and edges. Commonly made for attachment to masonry walls with flat head spanner screws.

MOUNTING APPLICATIONS

Mirrors can be mounted by way of frames or they can be surface mounted frameless by any of the following methods:

1. MASTIC: Mastic specifically made for mirrors is not generally recommended for use without clips, channels, or other auxiliary supportive devices. Certain design considerations, mirror sizes, and weights may, however, make this type of installation desirable. Mounting surfaces should be clean, dry, smooth, and plumb. Avoid applying to papered surfaces. Paint the back of the mirror with an extra coat of water resistant paint. Spot apply mastic to dry mirror back; it should not cover more than approximately 25% of the mirror area or exceed 1/2 to 5/8 in. in thickness, so as to allow for trueing the mirror and adequate ventilation. Always provide support along the bottom edge and brace the mirror until the mastic sets.

2. DOUBLE FACED TAPE: The tape must be compatible with the mirror backing and supportive surface. Thicknesses and quantities depend on adhesive qualities of the tape. A tape with a capability of 1 lb for every 1/2 sq in. is recommended. To prevent moisture collection, install tape vertically, cutting the top edge to a point. Provide a bottom edge support that allows for drainage.

3. BOTTOM CHANNEL AND CLIPS.

4. WOOD FRAME BACK: Used to level a single mirror or multiple mirrors in a uniform plane. Paint the surface facing the mirror back to prevent wood resins from spoiling the silver. All mechanical fastening devices should be countersunk into the frame. Use clips at the bottom edge; provide paper padding to prevent metal contact.

5. ROSETTES OR SCREWS: Only experienced glaziers should undertake this type of work, since extreme care is needed. To prevent the glass from coming in contact with the metal screw anchor, make the hole in the mirror of adequate size to accommodate a rubber sleeve fitting around the screw. A felt cushion should be placed behind the rosette on the face of the glass. It is recommended that mirrors up to 10 sq ft in area be supported at each corner, 4 in. in from the edges; mirrors over 10 sq ft in area should have holes about 36 in. on centers.

Surface mounted, frameless mirrors should have all exposed edges ground and polished. If a continuous bottom channel is used, the bottom edge should be ground and painted to protect it from possible moisture intrusion. The paint must be water resistant and compatible with the coating on the mirror's back, as it must overlap the back to seal the edge. To avoid moisture penetration, mirrors should not be mounted directly against felt or felt paper and unpainted plaster, wood, or plywood.

When walls are entirely covered with mirrors, either in vertical panels or rectilinear stacked panels, the mirror edges must be flat polished with an appropriate thin 1/16 in. divider strip placed between all butt joints. In working with large areas, use a wood frame system, with members behind each vertical and horizontal joint, to allow for proper leveling.

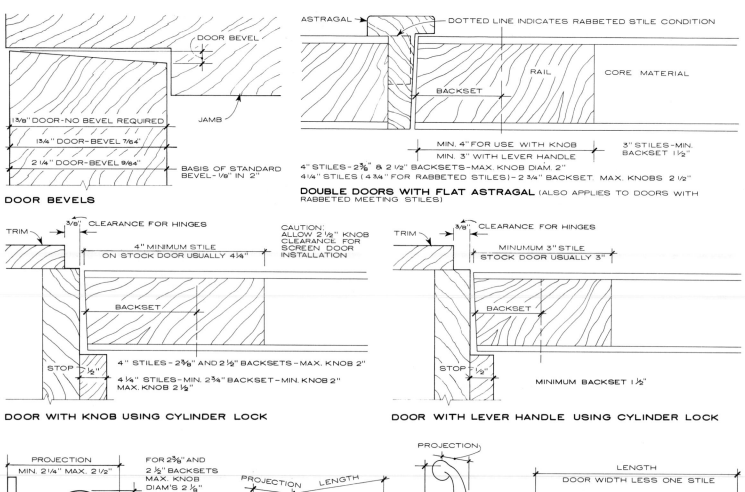

DOOR BEVELS

1 3/8" DOOR-NO BEVEL REQUIRED
1 3/4" DOOR-BEVEL 7/64"
2 1/4" DOOR-BEVEL 9/64"

DOOR BEVEL
JAMB
BASIS OF STANDARD BEVEL-1/8" IN 2"

ASTRAGAL
DOTTED LINE INDICATES RABBETED STILE CONDITION
RAIL
CORE MATERIAL
BACKSET
MIN. 4" FOR USE WITH KNOB
MIN. 3" WITH LEVER HANDLE
3" STILES-MIN. BACKSET 1 1/2"
4" STILES-2 3/8" & 2 1/2" BACKSETS-MAX. KNOB DIAM. 2"
4 1/4" STILES (4 3/4" FOR RABBETED STILES)-2 3/4" BACKSET. MAX. KNOBS 2 1/2"

DOUBLE DOORS WITH FLAT ASTRAGAL (ALSO APPLIES TO DOORS WITH RABBETED MEETING STILES)

TRIM
3/8" CLEARANCE FOR HINGES
4" MINIMUM STILE ON STOCK DOOR USUALLY 4 1/4"
CAUTION: ALLOW 2 1/2" KNOB CLEARANCE FOR SCREEN DOOR INSTALLATION
BACKSET
STOP 1/2"
4" STILES-2 3/8" AND 2 1/2" BACKSETS-MAX. KNOB 2"
4 1/4" STILES-MIN. 2 3/4" BACKSET-MIN. KNOB 2" MAX. KNOB 2 1/2"

DOOR WITH KNOB USING CYLINDER LOCK

TRIM
3/8" CLEARANCE FOR HINGES
MINUMUM 3" STILE STOCK DOOR USUALLY 3"
BACKSET
STOP 1/2"
MINIMUM BACKSET 1 1/2"

DOOR WITH LEVER HANDLE USING CYLINDER LOCK

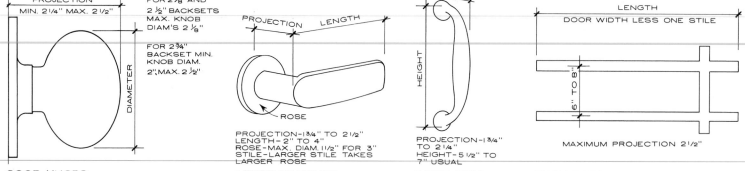

PROJECTION MIN. 2 1/4" MAX. 2 1/2"
FOR 2 3/8" AND 2 1/2" BACKSETS MAX. KNOB DIAM'S 2 1/8"
FOR 2 3/4" BACKSET MIN. KNOB DIAM. 2", MAX. 2 1/2"
DIAMETER

DOOR KNOBS

PROJECTION LENGTH
ROSE
PROJECTION-1 3/4" TO 2 1/2"
LENGTH-2" TO 4"
ROSE-MAX. DIAM. 1 1/2" FOR 3"
STILE-LARGER STILE TAKES
LARGER ROSE

LEVER HANDLES

PROJECTION
HEIGHT
PROJECTION-1 3/4" TO 2 1/4"
HEIGHT-5 1/2" TO 7" USUAL

DOOR PULL

LENGTH DOOR WIDTH LESS ONE STILE
6" TO 8"
MAXIMUM PROJECTION 2 1/2"

PUSH BARS

NOTE: FOR MOUNTING HEIGHTS SEE NEXT PAGE - REFER TO MANUFACTURER'S CATALOGS FOR EXACT HARDWARE SIZES AND DIMENSIONS

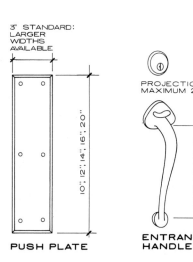

3" STANDARD: LARGER WIDTHS AVAILABLE
10", 12", 14", 16", 20"

PUSH PLATE

PROJECTION MAXIMUM 2 1/2"
5" TO 7" USUAL

ENTRANCE HANDLE

2 1/2" TO 6"
WALL TYPE
3 1/2"
3 1/2"
WALL TYPES

FLOOR TYPES

1/8"
1/2"
DOOR SILENCER
FLUSH BUMPER
1"
4 1/2" OR 6 1/2"
ROLLER BUMPER
4" TO 7"
DOOR HOLDER

FLOOR STOPS

STOPS AND HOLDERS

F. J. Trost, SMS Architects; New Caanan, Connecticut
Door and Hardware Institute; Arlington, Virginia

8 **HARDWARE**

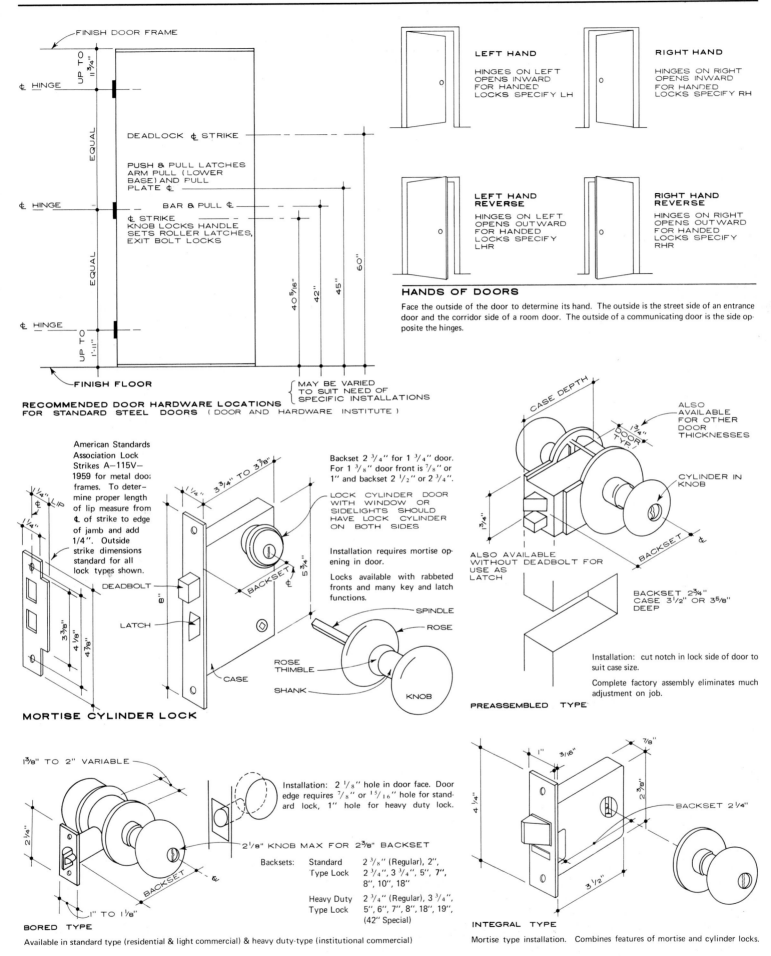

FINISH DOOR FRAME

UP TO 11¾"

℄ HINGE

EQUAL

DEADLOCK ℄ STRIKE

PUSH & PULL LATCHES
ARM PULL (LOWER
BASE) AND PULL
PLATE ℄

BAR & PULL ℄

℄ HINGE

℄ STRIKE
KNOB LOCKS HANDLE
SETS ROLLER LATCHES,
EXIT BOLT LOCKS

EQUAL

℄ HINGE

UP TO 1'-11"

FINISH FLOOR

40 5/16"
42"
45"
60"

MAY BE VARIED
TO SUIT NEED OF
SPECIFIC INSTALLATIONS

**RECOMMENDED DOOR HARDWARE LOCATIONS
FOR STANDARD STEEL DOORS** (DOOR AND HARDWARE INSTITUTE)

LEFT HAND

HINGES ON LEFT
OPENS INWARD
FOR HANDED
LOCKS SPECIFY LH

RIGHT HAND

HINGES ON RIGHT
OPENS INWARD
FOR HANDED
LOCKS SPECIFY RH

**LEFT HAND
REVERSE**

HINGES ON LEFT
OPENS OUTWARD
FOR HANDED
LOCKS SPECIFY
LHR

**RIGHT HAND
REVERSE**

HINGES ON RIGHT
OPENS OUTWARD
FOR HANDED
LOCKS SPECIFY
RHR

HANDS OF DOORS

Face the outside of the door to determine its hand. The outside is the street side of an entrance door and the corridor side of a room door. The outside of a communicating door is the side opposite the hinges.

American Standards Association Lock Strikes A–115V–1959 for metal door frames. To determine proper length of lip measure from ℄ of strike to edge of jamb and add 1/4". Outside strike dimensions standard for all lock types shown.

¼" LIP
¼"

DEADBOLT

LATCH

3⅜"
4⅛"
4⅞"

8"

BACKSET ℄

1¼"
3/4" TO 3⅞"

5¾"

CASE

Backset 2¾" for 1¾" door. For 1⅜" door front is ⅞" or 1" and backset 2½" or 2¾".

LOCK CYLINDER DOOR WITH WINDOW OR SIDELIGHTS SHOULD HAVE LOCK CYLINDER ON BOTH SIDES

Installation requires mortise opening in door.

Locks available with rabbeted fronts and many key and latch functions.

SPINDLE
ROSE
ROSE THIMBLE
SHANK
KNOB

MORTISE CYLINDER LOCK

CASE DEPTH

¾" TYP

ALSO AVAILABLE FOR OTHER DOOR THICKNESSES

CYLINDER IN KNOB

3¾"

BACKSET ℄

ALSO AVAILABLE WITHOUT DEADBOLT FOR USE AS LATCH

BACKSET 2¾"
CASE 3½" OR 3⅝" DEEP

Installation: cut notch in lock side of door to suit case size.

Complete factory assembly eliminates much adjustment on job.

PREASSEMBLED TYPE

1⅜" TO 2" VARIABLE

2¼"

BACKSET ℄

1" TO 1⅛"

Installation: 2⅛" hole in door face. Door edge requires ⅞" or 15/16" hole for standard lock, 1" hole for heavy duty lock.

2⅛" KNOB MAX FOR 2⅜" BACKSET

Backsets:	Standard Type Lock	2⅜" (Regular), 2", 2¾", 3¾", 5", 7", 8", 10", 18"
	Heavy Duty Type Lock	2¾" (Regular), 3¾", 5", 6", 7", 8", 18", 19", (42" Special)

BORED TYPE

Available in standard type (residential & light commercial) & heavy duty-type (institutional commercial)

1" 3/16" 7/8"

4¼"

2⅜"

BACKSET 2¼"

3½"

INTEGRAL TYPE

Mortise type installation. Combines features of mortise and cylinder locks.

F. J. Trost, SMS Architects; New Canaan, Connecticut

Door and Hardware Institute; Arlington, Virginia

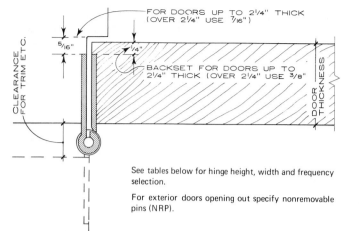

FOR DOORS UP TO 2 1/4" THICK (OVER 2 1/4" USE 7/16")

5/16"

1/4"

CLEARANCE FOR TRIM ETC.

BACKSET FOR DOORS UP TO 2 1/4" THICK (OVER 2 1/4" USE 3/8")

DOOR THICKNESS

See tables below for hinge height, width and frequency selection.

For exterior doors opening out specify nonremovable pins (NRP).

HINGE TYPES AND INSTALLATION DIMENSIONS

TEMPLATE

NON-TEMPLATE (FOR WOOD DOORS)

STANDARD FOR ALL HINGES

ROUNDED TO AVOID ATTACHING WEARING APPAREL ETC.

BUTTON TIP   HOSPITAL TIP

CONSULT MANUFACTURERS FOR OTHER AVAILABLE TIPS

NOTE

1. Use 2 hinges on doors less than 5'—0" high. Add 1 hinge for each additional 2'—6" of door height. Always specify 3 hinges per door.

2. Use ball bearing hinges on doors equipped with closers.

3. Use high frequency hinges on high frequency openings, average frequency hinges on average frequency openings, low frequency hinges on low frequency openings.

4. 2 or 4 ball or oilite bearings available on most hinge types (4 for extra heavy).

HINGE SELECTION TABLES

HINGE HEIGHT—DETERMINED BY DOOR WIDTH AND THICKNESS

DOOR THICKNESS	DOOR WTH.	HINGE HGT.
3/4" to 1 1/8" CABINET	to 24	2 1/2
7/8" & 1 1/8" SCREEN OR COMB.	to 36	3
1 3/8"	to 36	3 1/2
1 3/4"	to 36	4
	over 36-41	4 1/2
	42 to 48	4 1/2*
2", 2 1/4", 2 1/2"	to 42	5
	over 42	6
TRANSOMS		
1 1/4" & 1 3/8"		3
1 3/4"		3 1/2
2", 2 1/4", 2 1/2"		4

NOTE: Height of a hinge is always first dimension not including tips.

* Extra heavy hinges should be specified for heavy doors and doors where high frequency service is expected. Extra heavy hinges should be 4 1/2", 5", & 6" sizes.

HINGE WIDTH—DETERMINED BY DOOR THICKNESS AND CLEARANCE REQUIRED

DOOR THICKNESS	CLEARANCE REQUIRED *	HINGE WIDTH
1 3/8	1 1/4	3 1/2
	1 3/4	4
1 3/4	1	4
	1 1/2	4 1/2
	2	5
	3	6
2	1	4 1/2
	1 1/2	5
	2 1/2	6
2 1/4	1	5
	2	6
2 1/2	3/4	5
	1 3/4	6
3	3/4	6
	2 3/4	8
	4 3/4	10

* NOTE: Clearance is computed for door flush with casing.

FREQUENCY OF DOOR OPERATION

TYPE OF BUILDING AND DOOR	ESTIMATED FREQUENCY		
	DAILY	YEARLY	
LARGE DEPT. STORE ENTRANCE	5,000	1,500,000	HIGH FREQUENCY
LARGE OFFICE BUILDING ENTRANCE	4,000	1,200,000	
THEATER ENTRANCE PERFORMANCE	1,000	450,000	
SCHOOL ENTRANCE	1,250	225,000	
SCHOOL TOILET DOOR	1,250	225,000	
STORE OR BANK ENTRANCE	500	150,000	
OFFICE BUILDING TOILET DOOR	400	118,000	
SCHOOL CORRIDOR DOOR	80	15,000	AVERAGE FREQUENCY
OFFICE BUILDING CORRIDOR DOOR	75	22,000	
STORE TOILET DOOR	60	18,000	
DWELLING ENTRANCE	40	15,000	
DWELLING TOILET DOOR	25	9,000	LOW FREQ.
DWELLING CORRIDOR DOOR	10	3,600	
DWELLING CLOSET DOOR	6	2,200	

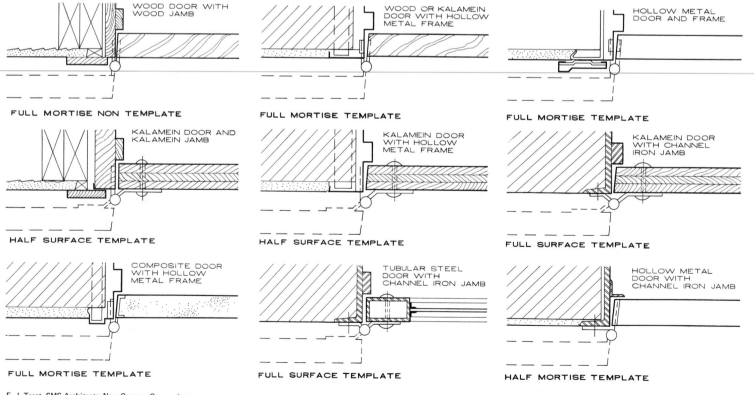

FULL MORTISE NON TEMPLATE — WOOD DOOR WITH WOOD JAMB

FULL MORTISE TEMPLATE — WOOD OR KALAMEIN DOOR WITH HOLLOW METAL FRAME

FULL MORTISE TEMPLATE — HOLLOW METAL DOOR AND FRAME

HALF SURFACE TEMPLATE — KALAMEIN DOOR AND KALAMEIN JAMB

HALF SURFACE TEMPLATE — KALAMEIN DOOR WITH HOLLOW METAL FRAME

FULL SURFACE TEMPLATE — KALAMEIN DOOR WITH CHANNEL IRON JAMB

FULL MORTISE TEMPLATE — COMPOSITE DOOR WITH HOLLOW METAL FRAME

FULL SURFACE TEMPLATE — TUBULAR STEEL DOOR WITH CHANNEL IRON JAMB

HALF MORTISE TEMPLATE — HOLLOW METAL DOOR WITH CHANNEL IRON JAMB

F. J. Trost, SMS Architects; New Caanan, Connecticut

Door and Hardware Institute; Arlington, Virginia

HARDWARE

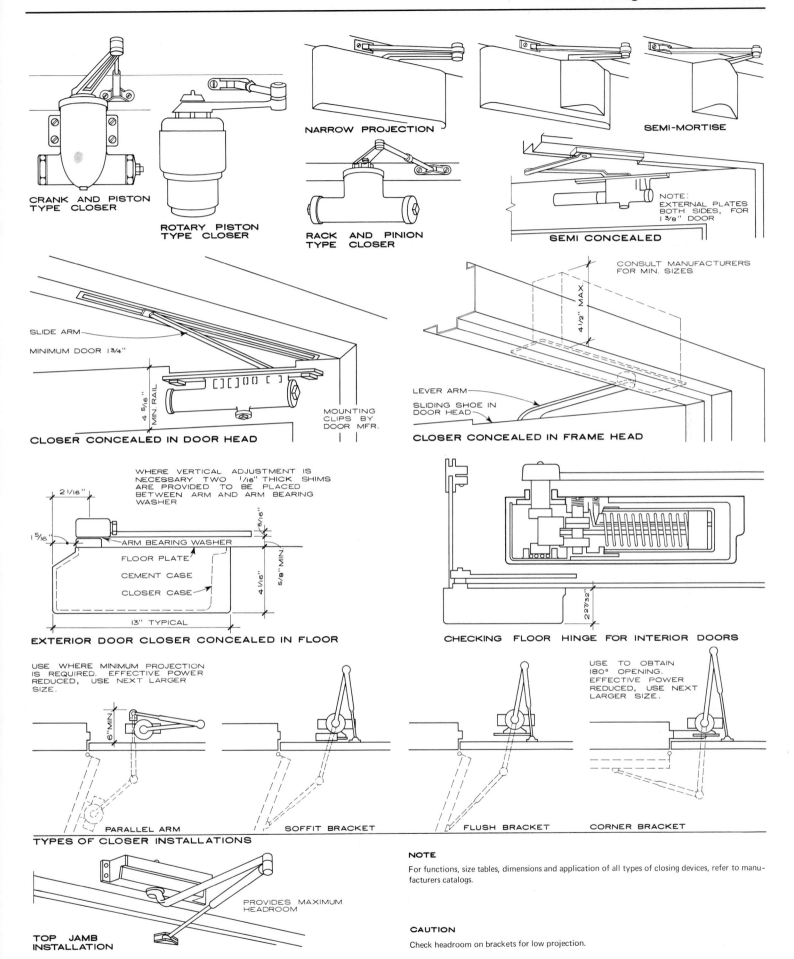

CRANK AND PISTON TYPE CLOSER

ROTARY PISTON TYPE CLOSER

RACK AND PINION TYPE CLOSER

NARROW PROJECTION

SEMI-MORTISE

NOTE: EXTERNAL PLATES BOTH SIDES, FOR 1 3/8" DOOR

SEMI CONCEALED

SLIDE ARM

MINIMUM DOOR 1 3/4"

4 5/16" MIN. RAIL

MOUNTING CLIPS BY DOOR MFR.

CLOSER CONCEALED IN DOOR HEAD

CONSULT MANUFACTURERS FOR MIN. SIZES

4 1/2" MAX.

LEVER ARM

SLIDING SHOE IN DOOR HEAD

CLOSER CONCEALED IN FRAME HEAD

WHERE VERTICAL ADJUSTMENT IS NECESSARY TWO 1/16" THICK SHIMS ARE PROVIDED TO BE PLACED BETWEEN ARM AND ARM BEARING WASHER

2 1/16"

1 5/16"

5/16"

ARM BEARING WASHER

FLOOR PLATE

CEMENT CASE

CLOSER CASE

5/8" MIN.

4 1/6"

13" TYPICAL

EXTERIOR DOOR CLOSER CONCEALED IN FLOOR

2 27/32"

CHECKING FLOOR HINGE FOR INTERIOR DOORS

USE WHERE MINIMUM PROJECTION IS REQUIRED. EFFECTIVE POWER REDUCED, USE NEXT LARGER SIZE.

6" MIN.

PARALLEL ARM

SOFFIT BRACKET

FLUSH BRACKET

USE TO OBTAIN 180° OPENING. EFFECTIVE POWER REDUCED, USE NEXT LARGER SIZE.

CORNER BRACKET

TYPES OF CLOSER INSTALLATIONS

PROVIDES MAXIMUM HEADROOM

TOP JAMB INSTALLATION

NOTE

For functions, size tables, dimensions and application of all types of closing devices, refer to manufacturers catalogs.

CAUTION

Check headroom on brackets for low projection.

F. J. Trost, SMS Architects; New Caanan, Connecticut
Door and Hardware Institute; Arlington, Virginia

HARDWARE 8

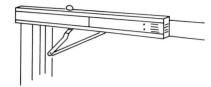

CLOSER, HOLDER, AND DETECTOR
PUSH–SIDE MOUNTED

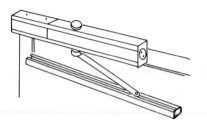

CLOSER AND HOLDER ONLY
PUSH–SIDE MOUNTED

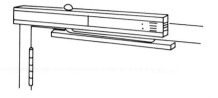

CLOSER, HOLDER, AND DETECTOR
PULL–SIDE MOUNTED

CLOSER AND HOLDER ONLY
PULL–SIDE MOUNTED

A COMBINATION CLOSER, HOLDER, AND DE-
TECTOR is available with either ionization, photoelectric, or heat sensing detectors for discovering
the presence of smoke or any of the products of
combustion and for closing the door for life safety.

A COMBINATION CLOSER AND HOLDER (only)
will hold door in open position when incorporated
with an independent detector or wired into any type
of fire detecting system.

All these units have unlimited hold-open from 0°
to approximately 170°, or limited hold-open from
85° to 170° for cross corridor doors.

SURFACE MOUNTED COMBINATION CLOSERS, HOLDERS, AND DETECTORS

FIRE AND SMOKE DETECTION SYSTEMS

1. Heat sensing detectors operate on the basis of fixed temperature or a rate of temperature rise. Door closers are activated upon release of a heat activated device such as a fusable link. Closing mechanisms may consist of gravity operated weights or wound steel springs.

2. Smoke sensing detectors detect both visible and invisible airborne particles. Various operating principles include ionization, photoelectric, resistance, sampling, and cloud chamber detection.

   a. Ionization detection closers contain a small quantity of radioactive material within the sensing chamber. The resulting ionized air permits an electric current flow between electrodes. When entrance of smoke particles reduces the flow to a preset level, the detection circuit responds. Closing mechanisms usually consist of a detector, electromechanical holding device, and a door closer.

   Ionization detectors will sense ordinary products of combustion from such sources as kitchens, motors, power tools, and automobile exhausts.

   b. Photoelectric detection closers consists of a light source and a photoelectric cell. Actuation occurs when smoke becomes dense enough to change the reflectance of light reaching the photoelectric device. Photoelectric detectors may be of spot or beam type. Closing mechanisms consist of a detector, electromechanical holding device, and a door closer.

   c. Other types of smoke detectors include electrical bridging, sampling, and cloud chambers. Each has operating characteristics similar to ionization and photoelectric detectors.

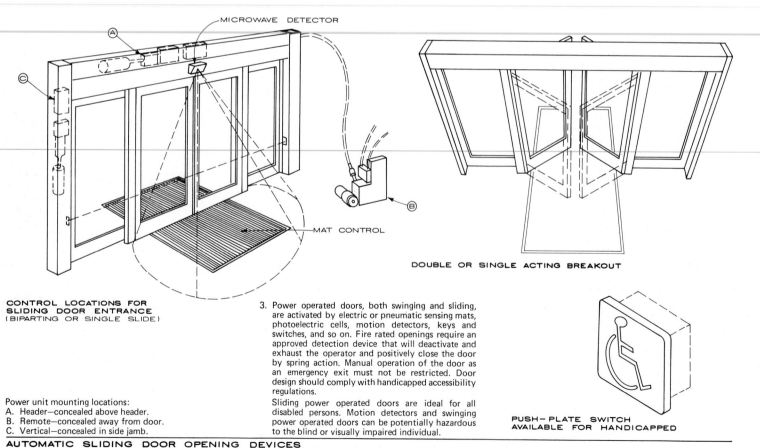

CONTROL LOCATIONS FOR
SLIDING DOOR ENTRANCE
(BIPARTING OR SINGLE SLIDE)

Power unit mounting locations:
A. Header—concealed above header.
B. Remote—concealed away from door.
C. Vertical—concealed in side jamb.

DOUBLE OR SINGLE ACTING BREAKOUT

3. Power operated doors, both swinging and sliding, are activated by electric or pneumatic sensing mats, photoelectric cells, motion detectors, keys and switches, and so on. Fire rated openings require an approved detection device that will deactivate and exhaust the operator and positively close the door by spring action. Manual operation of the door as an emergency exit must not be restricted. Door design should comply with handicapped accessibility regulations.

Sliding power operated doors are ideal for all disabled persons. Motion detectors and swinging power operated doors can be potentially hazardous to the blind or visually impaired individual.

PUSH–PLATE SWITCH
AVAILABLE FOR HANDICAPPED

AUTOMATIC SLIDING DOOR OPENING DEVICES

Lee A. Anderson; SRGF, Inc., Architects; Champaign, Illinois

Sam A. Buzbee, AIA; Mott, Mobley, Richter, McGowan & Griffin; Fort Smith, Arkansas

⑧ **HARDWARE**

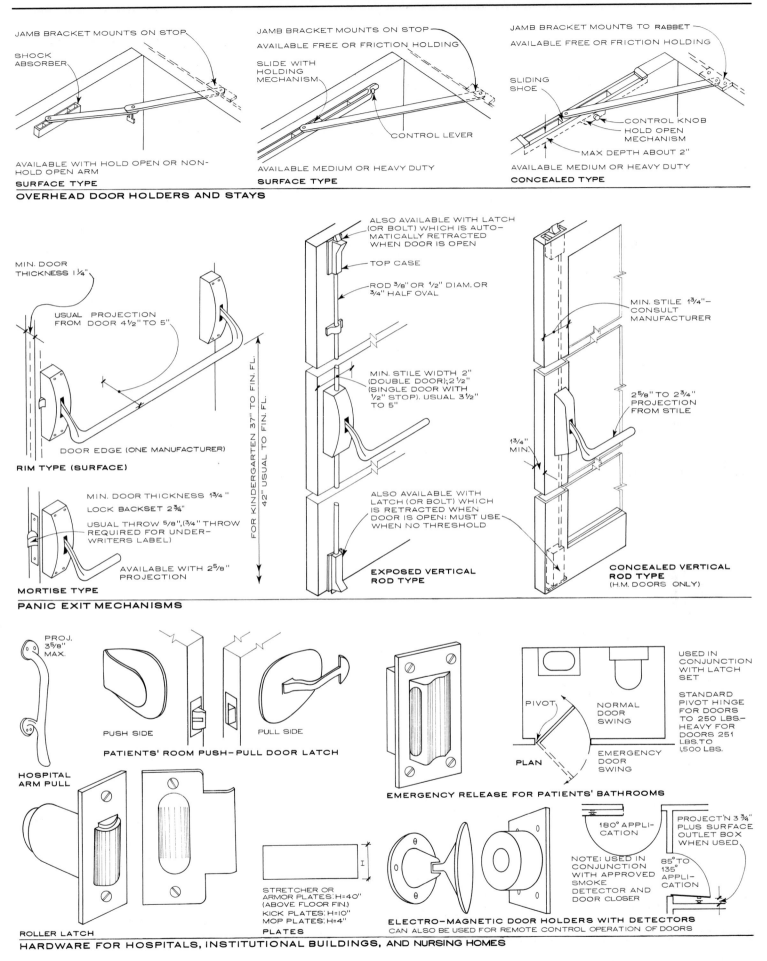

JAMB BRACKET MOUNTS ON STOP

SHOCK ABSORBER

AVAILABLE WITH HOLD OPEN OR NON-HOLD OPEN ARM

SURFACE TYPE

JAMB BRACKET MOUNTS ON STOP

AVAILABLE FREE OR FRICTION HOLDING

SLIDE WITH HOLDING MECHANISM

CONTROL LEVER

AVAILABLE MEDIUM OR HEAVY DUTY

SURFACE TYPE

JAMB BRACKET MOUNTS TO RABBET

AVAILABLE FREE OR FRICTION HOLDING

SLIDING SHOE

CONTROL KNOB HOLD OPEN MECHANISM

MAX DEPTH ABOUT 2"

AVAILABLE MEDIUM OR HEAVY DUTY

CONCEALED TYPE

OVERHEAD DOOR HOLDERS AND STAYS

MIN. DOOR THICKNESS 1¼"

USUAL PROJECTION FROM DOOR 4½" TO 5"

DOOR EDGE (ONE MANUFACTURER)

RIM TYPE (SURFACE)

MIN. DOOR THICKNESS 1¾"

LOCK BACKSET 2¾"

USUAL THROW ⅝", (¾" THROW REQUIRED FOR UNDERWRITERS LABEL)

AVAILABLE WITH 2⅝" PROJECTION

MORTISE TYPE

ALSO AVAILABLE WITH LATCH (OR BOLT) WHICH IS AUTOMATICALLY RETRACTED WHEN DOOR IS OPEN

TOP CASE

ROD ⅜" OR ½" DIAM. OR ¾" HALF OVAL

MIN. STILE WIDTH 2" (DOUBLE DOOR); 2½" (SINGLE DOOR WITH ½" STOP). USUAL 3½" TO 5"

FOR KINDERGARTEN 37" TO FIN. FL.
42" USUAL TO FIN. FL.

ALSO AVAILABLE WITH LATCH (OR BOLT) WHICH IS RETRACTED WHEN DOOR IS OPEN: MUST USE WHEN NO THRESHOLD

EXPOSED VERTICAL ROD TYPE

MIN. STILE 1¾"– CONSULT MANUFACTURER

2⅝" TO 2¾" PROJECTION FROM STILE

1¾" MIN.

CONCEALED VERTICAL ROD TYPE (H.M. DOORS ONLY)

PANIC EXIT MECHANISMS

PROJ. 3⅝" MAX.

PUSH SIDE

PULL SIDE

PATIENTS' ROOM PUSH-PULL DOOR LATCH

HOSPITAL ARM PULL

ROLLER LATCH

STRETCHER OR ARMOR PLATES: H=40" (ABOVE FLOOR FIN.) KICK PLATES: H=10" MOP PLATES: H=4"

PLATES

PIVOT

NORMAL DOOR SWING

PLAN

EMERGENCY DOOR SWING

EMERGENCY RELEASE FOR PATIENTS' BATHROOMS

USED IN CONJUNCTION WITH LATCH SET

STANDARD PIVOT HINGE FOR DOORS TO 250 LBS– HEAVY FOR DOORS 251 LBS. TO 1,500 LBS.

180° APPLICATION

NOTE: USED IN CONJUNCTION WITH APPROVED SMOKE DETECTOR AND DOOR CLOSER

PROJECT'N 3¾" PLUS SURFACE OUTLET BOX WHEN USED

85° TO 135° APPLICATION

ELECTRO-MAGNETIC DOOR HOLDERS WITH DETECTORS CAN ALSO BE USED FOR REMOTE CONTROL OPERATION OF DOORS

HARDWARE FOR HOSPITALS, INSTITUTIONAL BUILDINGS, AND NURSING HOMES

F. J. Trost, SMS Architects; New Canaan, Connecticut

Door and Hardware Institute; Arlington, Virginia

INTRODUCTION:

The following is a selection of hollow metal details from various manufacturers. They are in no way intended to favor a manufacturer or a product. Details vary. Consult manufacturers literature.

Hollow metal is divided into a frame section and a door section. The frame section can be used with wood doors. Both sections are complete in themselves.

NOMENCLATURE

Active Leaf	The door leaf of a pair in which the lock is normally installed.
Astragal (overlapping)	A vertical molding attached to the meeting edge of one leaf of a pair of doors for protection against weather conditions and to retard passage of smoke, flame and gasses.
Astragal (split)	A vertical molding attached to both leaves at a pair of doors at the meeting edge for protection against weather conditions.
Barrier Screen	See Smoke Screen.
Beveled Edge	The edge at a door that is not at a 90° angle to the face of the door (std. bevel is 1/8" in 2").
Blank Jamb	Vertical member of frame without hardware preparation. Used when doors are furnished with push and pull hardware or surface mounted strikes and single active floor hinges.
Borrowed Light	Four-sided frame prepared for glass installation in field.
Bullnose Trim	The face & jamb width joined by a radius rather than a 90° break.
Cabinet Jamb	Frame in three or more pieces applied as the finished frame over rough buck.
Cap	See Soffit.
Cased Opening	Frame section which does not have any stops.
Covemold Frame	Frame having contour faces (exposed) simulating contour of wood frame.
Cut-Out	A preparation for hardware and/or accessories.
Double Acting Door	Type of door prepared for pivot or spring type hinge permitting the door to swing 90° in either direction.
Double Egress Frame	Double rabbeted double frame prepared to receive two single-acting doors swinging in opposite directions.
Dutch Door	Door having two separate leaves, one hung above the other. Shelf on lower leaf, optional.

Face	Exposed part of frame parallel to face of wall.
Filler Plate	A blank plate used to fill mortised cutouts.
Flat Frame	Frame having flat faces exposed.
Floor Clearance	Distance between bottom of door and finished floor.
Glass Stop	Fixed trim on a glass tight door against which glass is set.
Glazing Bead	A removable trim at glazing opening to hold glass securely in place.
Hand	Term used to designate direction in which door swings.
Handing	The swinging of the door e.g., right hand or left hand. To determine the hand of a door, view the door from the outside. The side that the hinges are on is the hand of the door. If the door swings away from the viewer, the hand is a regular hand, i.e. right or left hand. If the door swings to the viewer, the door is reverse swing, i.e. right hand reverse swing or left hand reverse swing.
Head	Horizontal frame member at top of door opening or top member of transom frames.
Header	See Head.
Hinge Backset	Distance from edge to hinge to stop on frame.
Hinge Filler Plate	Plate installed for a hinge cut-out when no hinge is required.
Inactive Leaf	The door leaf in a pair of doors which is normally held closed by top and bottom bolts.
Jamb	Vertical frame member; between door and glass or wall; between glass and door or wall. See also Mullion.
Jamb Depth	Over-all width of frame section.
Knock Down (KD) Frame	Door frame furnished by manufacturer in three or more basic parts for assembly in field.
Lock Backset	Distance from edge of door to centerline of cylinder or knob.
Masonry Box	See Plaster Guard.
Mortise Preparation	Reinforcing drilling and tapping for hardware which is to be mortised into door or frame.
Mullion	Vertical or horizontal frame member; between glass and glass, or door and door.
Muntin	Non-structural member used to subdivide an open area in frame or door.

Opening Size	Size of frame opening measured between rabbets and finished floor.
Plaster Guard	Metal shield attached behind hinge and strike reinforcement to prevent mortar or plaster from entering mounting holes.
Return	See Backband.
Reveal	That part of the backband which extends beyond finished wall.
Reveal	Distance from face of frame to surface of finished wall.
Reversing Channel	See End Channel.
Reverse Bevel	Refers to hand of door or lock when doors swing to outside.
Rough Opening	Size of wall opening into which frame is installed.
Rubber Silencer	A part attached to the stop of a frame to cushion the closing of door.
Section Width	See Jamb Depth.
Single Acting Door	Type of door prepared for a pivot type or spring-type single-acting hinge permitting the door to swing 90° in one direction only.
Smoke Screen	A door frame combined with sidelights on either or both sides of door openings, including transom opening when and if required.
Soffit	Underside of stop on frame.
Split Jambs	Frames with jamb width in two pieces.
Stilts	See Floor Struts.
Stop	Part of frame against which door closes or glass rests.
Strike Stile	Vertical member of an inactive door leaf which receives the strike.
Strut Guide	Metal piece attached inside throat of frame which guides and holds ceiling strut to frame (usually incorporated in clip).
Sub Buck	See Rough Buck.
Surface Hardware Preparation	Reinforcing or machining or both, for hardware which is applied to surface of door or frame in field.
Top & Bottom Cap	Horizontal channel used in doors which do not have a flush top or bottom.
Transom Bar	The part of a transom frame which separates the top of the door from the transom.
Trim	(1) See face. (2) An applied face.
Trimmed Opening	See Cased Opening.

James W. G. Watson, AIA; Ronald A. Spahn and Associates; Cleveland Heights, Ohio

8 METAL DOORS

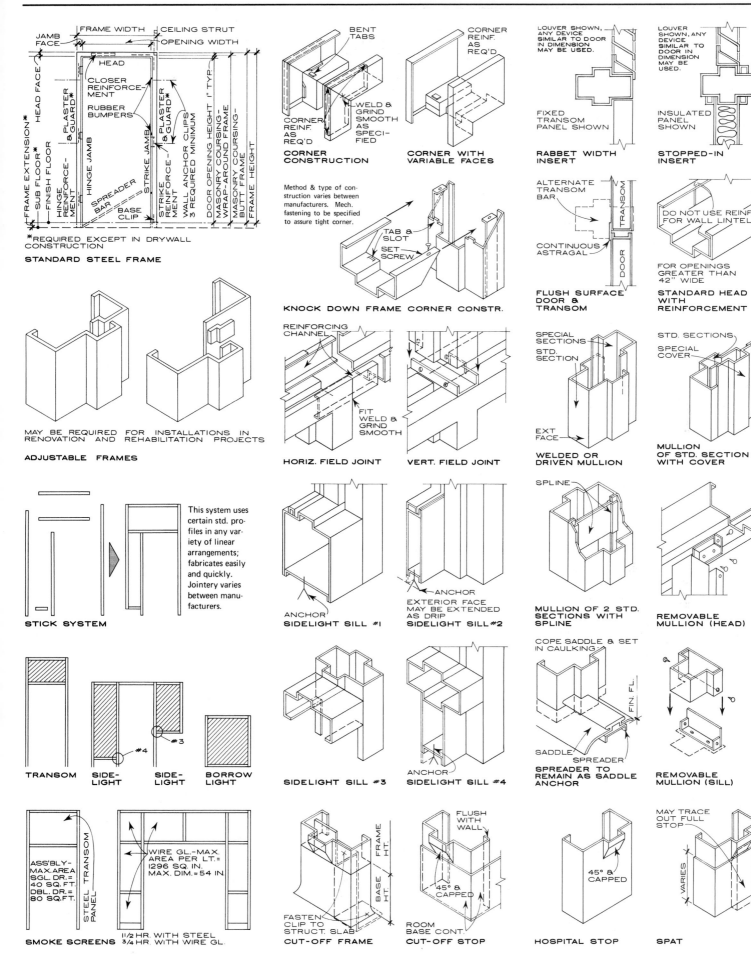

STANDARD STEEL FRAME

FRAME WIDTH / CEILING STRUT / OPENING WIDTH / JAMB FACE / HEAD FACE / FRAME EXTENSION* / SUB FLOOR* / FINISH FLOOR / HEAD / CLOSER REINFORCEMENT 1" TYP. / RUBBER BUMPERS / PLASTER & GUARD / HINGE JAMB / HINGE REINFORCEMENT / SPREADER BAR / BASE CLIP / STRIKE JAMB / STRIKE REINFORCEMENT / PLASTER & GUARD / WALL ANCHOR CLIPS 3 REQUIRED MINIMUM / DOOR OPENING HEIGHT 1" TYP. / MASONRY COURSING WRAP-AROUND FRAME / MASONRY COURSING BUTT FRAME / FRAME HEIGHT

*REQUIRED EXCEPT IN DRYWALL CONSTRUCTION

ADJUSTABLE FRAMES

MAY BE REQUIRED FOR INSTALLATIONS IN RENOVATION AND REHABILITATION PROJECTS

STICK SYSTEM

This system uses certain std. profiles in any variety of linear arrangements; fabricates easily and quickly. Jointery varies between manufacturers.

TRANSOM / SIDELIGHT #4 / SIDELIGHT #3 / BORROW LIGHT

SMOKE SCREENS

ASS'BLY-MAX.AREA SGL. DR.= 40 SQ.FT. DBL. DR.= 80 SQ.FT. / STEEL TRANSOM PANEL / WIRE GL.-MAX. AREA PER LT.= 1296 SQ. IN. MAX. DIM.= 54 IN. / 1 1/2 HR. WITH STEEL 3/4 HR. WITH WIRE GL.

CORNER CONSTRUCTION

BENT TABS / CORNER REINF. AS REQ'D / WELD & GRIND SMOOTH AS SPECIFIED

CORNER WITH VARIABLE FACES

CORNER REINF. AS REQ'D

Method & type of construction varies between manufacturers. Mech. fastening to be specified to assure tight corner.

TAB & SLOT / SET SCREW

KNOCK DOWN FRAME CORNER CONSTR.

HORIZ. FIELD JOINT

REINFORCING CHANNEL / FIT WELD & GRIND SMOOTH

VERT. FIELD JOINT

SIDELIGHT SILL #1

ANCHOR

SIDELIGHT SILL #2

ANCHOR / EXTERIOR FACE MAY BE EXTENDED AS DRIP

SIDELIGHT SILL #3

SIDELIGHT SILL #4

ANCHOR

CUT-OFF FRAME

FASTEN CLIP TO STRUCT. SLAB / FRAME HT. / BASE HT.

CUT-OFF STOP

FLUSH WITH WALL / 45° & CAPPED / ROOM BASE CONT.

RABBET WIDTH INSERT

LOUVER SHOWN, ANY DEVICE SIMILAR TO DOOR IN DIMENSION MAY BE USED. / FIXED TRANSOM PANEL SHOWN

STOPPED-IN INSERT

LOUVER SHOWN, ANY DEVICE SIMILAR TO DOOR IN DIMENSION MAY BE USED. / INSULATED PANEL SHOWN

FLUSH SURFACE DOOR & TRANSOM

ALTERNATE TRANSOM BAR / TRANSOM / CONTINUOUS ASTRAGAL / DOOR

STANDARD HEAD WITH REINFORCEMENT

DO NOT USE REINF. FOR WALL LINTEL. / FOR OPENINGS GREATER THAN 42" WIDE

WELDED OR DRIVEN MULLION

SPECIAL SECTIONS / STD. SECTION / EXT FACE

MULLION OF STD. SECTION WITH COVER

STD. SECTIONS / SPECIAL COVER

MULLION OF 2 STD. SECTIONS WITH SPLINE

SPLINE

REMOVABLE MULLION (HEAD)

SPREADER TO REMAIN AS SADDLE ANCHOR

COPE SADDLE & SET IN CAULKING / FIN. FL. / SADDLE / SPREADER

REMOVABLE MULLION (SILL)

HOSPITAL STOP

45° & CAPPED

SPAT

MAY TRACE OUT FULL STOP / VARIES

James W. G. Watson, AIA; Ronald A. Spahn and Associates; Cleveland Heights, Ohio

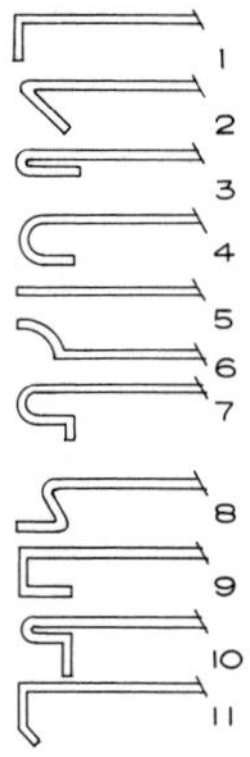

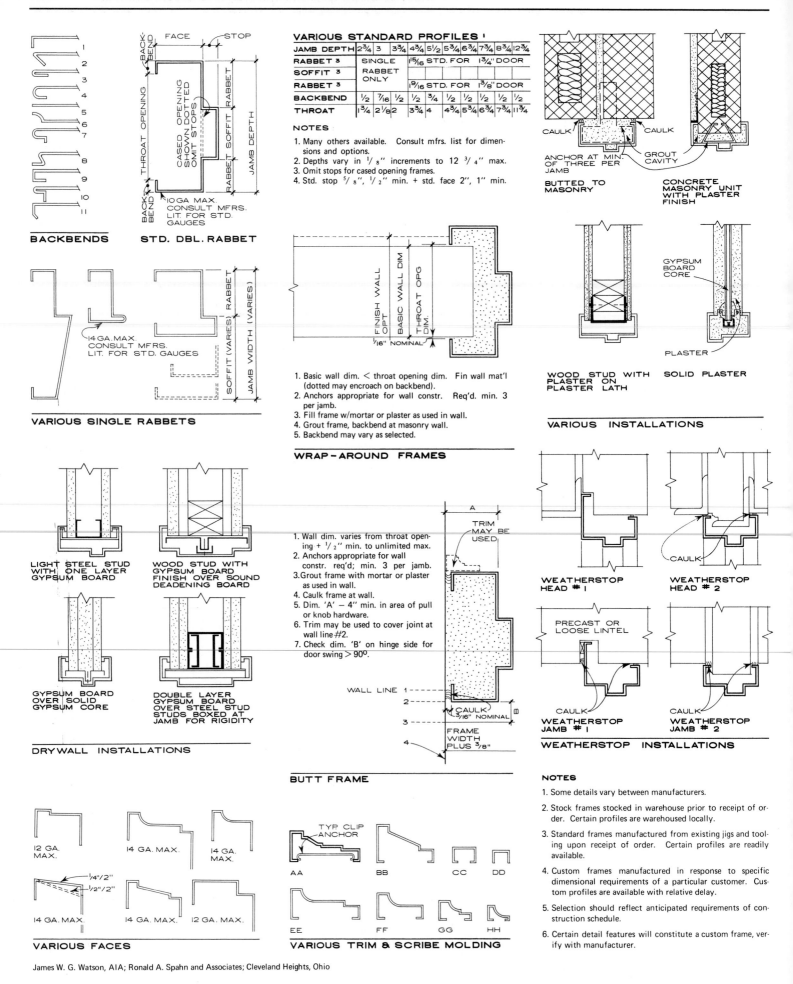

1
2
3
4
5
6
7
8
9
10
11

BACKBENDS

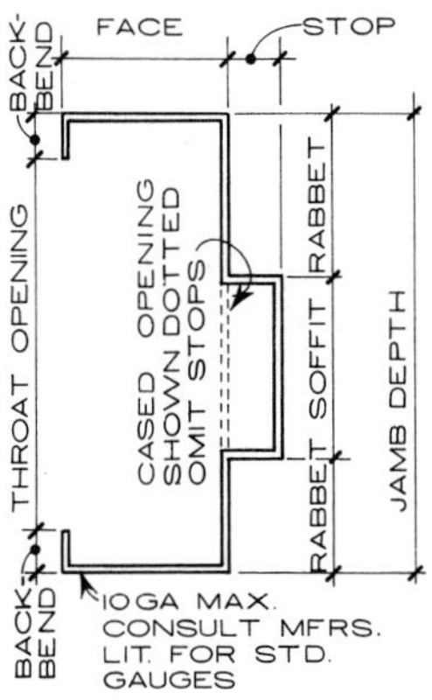

FACE
STOP
BACK-BEND
THROAT OPENING
CASED OPENING SHOWN DOTTED OMIT STOPS
RABBET
SOFFIT
RABBET
JAMB DEPTH
BACK-BEND
10 GA. MAX.
CONSULT MFRS.
LIT. FOR STD.
GAUGES

STD. DBL. RABBET

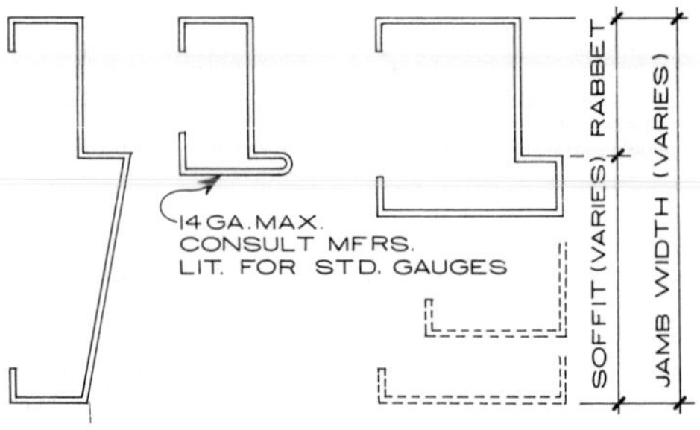

14 GA. MAX.
CONSULT MFRS.
LIT. FOR STD. GAUGES
RABBET
SOFFIT (VARIES)
JAMB WIDTH (VARIES)

VARIOUS SINGLE RABBETS

VARIOUS STANDARD PROFILES [1]

JAMB DEPTH	2¾	3	3¾	4¾	5½	5¾	6¾	7¾	8¾	12¾
RABBET [3]	SINGLE RABBET ONLY			1 15/16 STD. FOR 1¾" DOOR						
SOFFIT [3]										
RABBET [3]				1 9/16 STD. FOR 1⅜" DOOR						
BACKBEND	½	7/16	½	½	¾	½	½	½	½	½
THROAT	1¾	2⅛	2	3¾	4	4¾	5¾	6¾	7¾	11¾

NOTES

1. Many others available. Consult mfrs. list for dimensions and options.
2. Depths vary in 1/8" increments to 12 3/4" max.
3. Omit stops for cased opening frames.
4. Std. stop 5/8", 1/2" min. + std. face 2", 1" min.

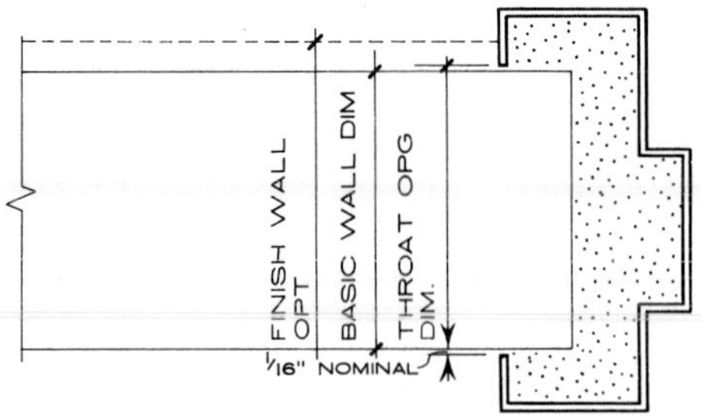

FINISH WALL OPT.
BASIC WALL DIM
THROAT OPG DIM.
1/16" NOMINAL

1. Basic wall dim. < throat opening dim. Fin wall mat'l (dotted may encroach on backbend).
2. Anchors appropriate for wall constr. Req'd. min. 3 per jamb.
3. Fill frame w/mortar or plaster as used in wall.
4. Grout frame, backbend at masonry wall.
5. Backbend may vary as selected.

WRAP-AROUND FRAMES

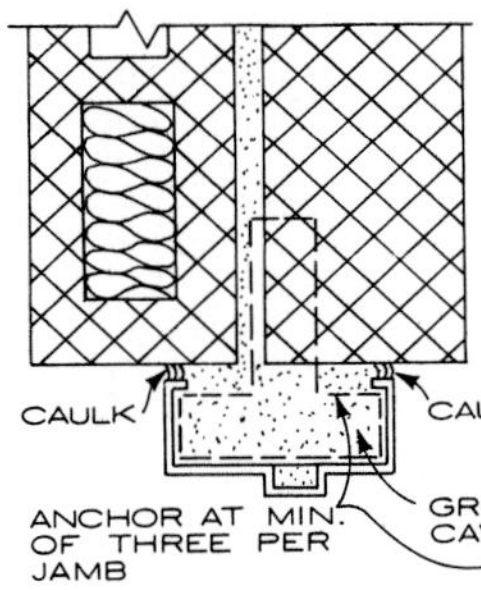

CAULK
CAULK
ANCHOR AT MIN. OF THREE PER JAMB
GROUT CAVITY

BUTTED TO MASONRY

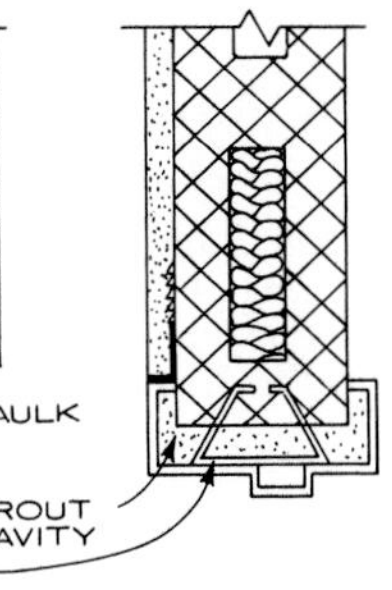

CONCRETE MASONRY UNIT WITH PLASTER FINISH

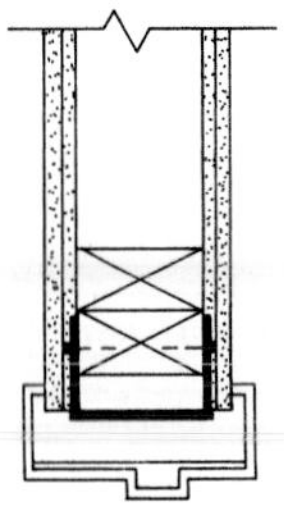

WOOD STUD WITH PLASTER ON PLASTER LATH

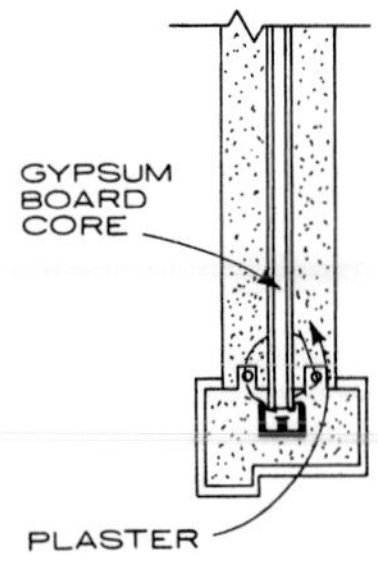

GYPSUM BOARD CORE
PLASTER

SOLID PLASTER

VARIOUS INSTALLATIONS

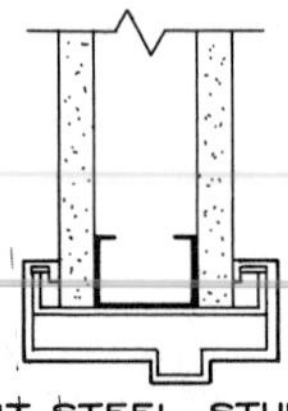

LIGHT STEEL STUD WITH ONE LAYER GYPSUM BOARD

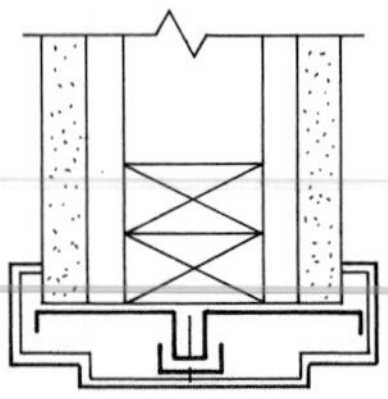

WOOD STUD WITH GYPSUM BOARD FINISH OVER SOUND DEADENING BOARD

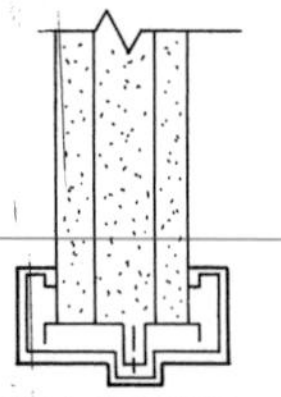

GYPSUM BOARD OVER SOLID GYPSUM CORE

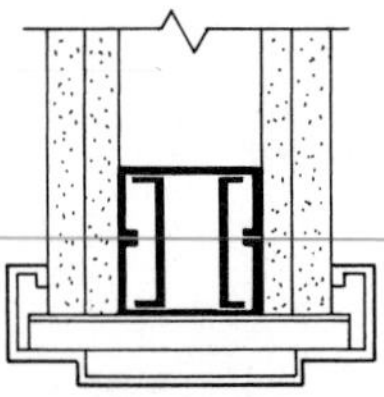

DOUBLE LAYER GYPSUM BOARD OVER STEEL STUD STUDS BOXED AT JAMB FOR RIGIDITY

DRYWALL INSTALLATIONS

1. Wall dim. varies from throat opening + 1/2" min. to unlimited max.
2. Anchors appropriate for wall constr. req'd; min. 3 per jamb.
3. Grout frame with mortar or plaster as used in wall.
4. Caulk frame at wall.
5. Dim. 'A' – 4" min. in area of pull or knob hardware.
6. Trim may be used to cover joint at wall line #2.
7. Check dim. 'B' on hinge side for door swing > 90°.

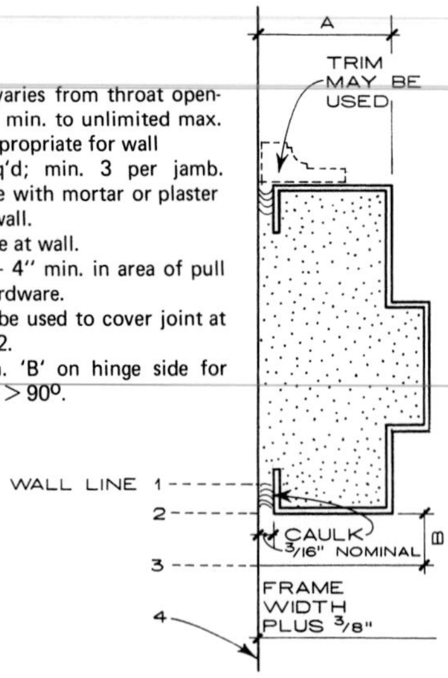

A
TRIM MAY BE USED
WALL LINE 1
2
CAULK
3/16" NOMINAL
B
3
FRAME WIDTH PLUS 3/8"
4

BUTT FRAME

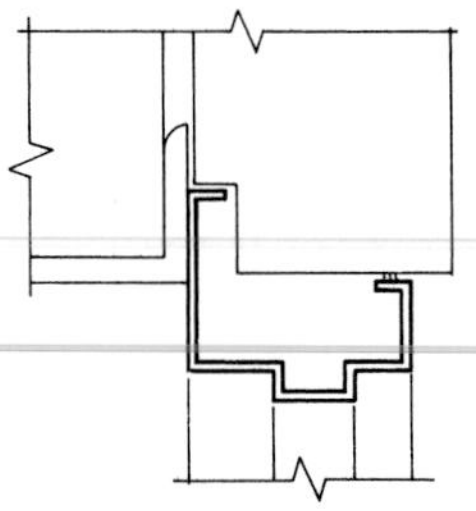

WEATHERSTOP HEAD # 1

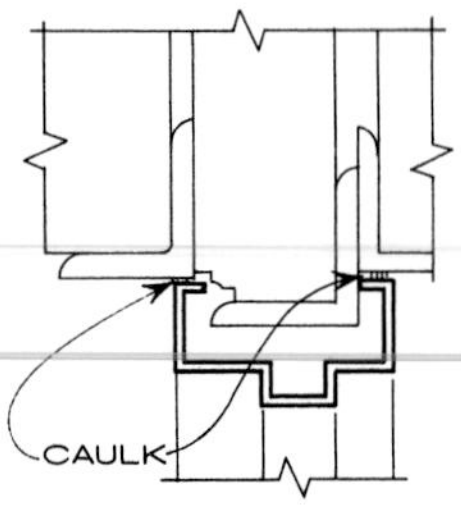

CAULK

WEATHERSTOP HEAD # 2

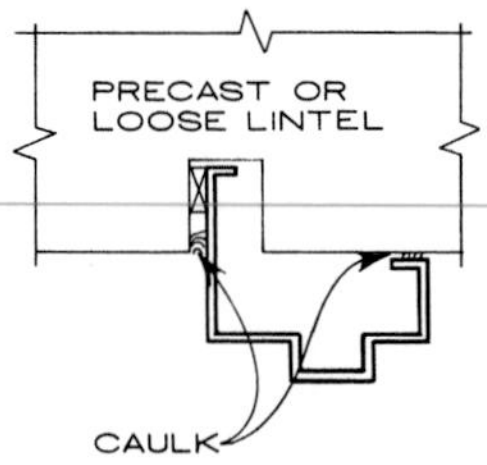

PRECAST OR LOOSE LINTEL
CAULK

WEATHERSTOP JAMB # 1

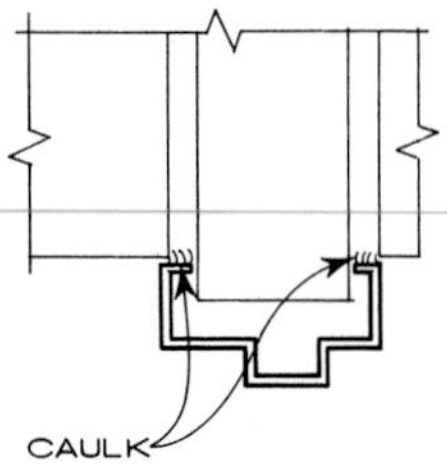

CAULK

WEATHERSTOP JAMB # 2

WEATHERSTOP INSTALLATIONS

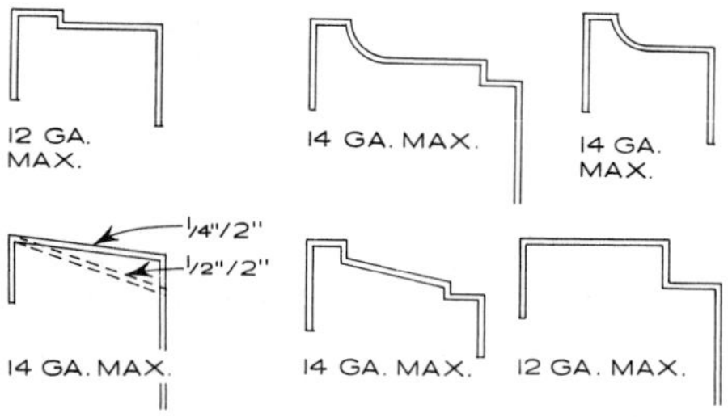

12 GA. MAX.
14 GA. MAX.
14 GA. MAX.
1/4"/2"
1/2"/2"
14 GA. MAX.
14 GA. MAX.
12 GA. MAX.

VARIOUS FACES

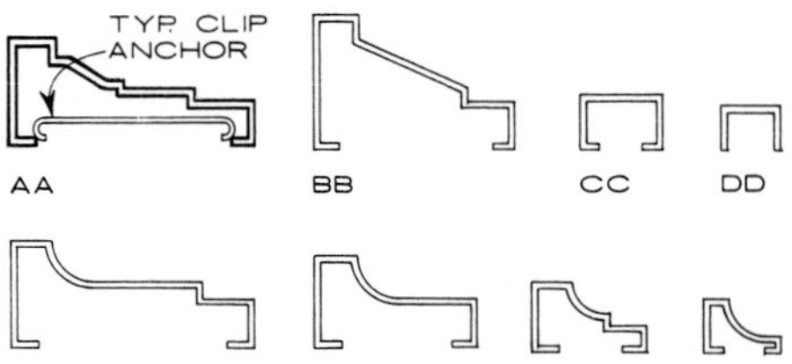

TYP. CLIP ANCHOR
AA
BB
CC
DD
EE
FF
GG
HH

VARIOUS TRIM & SCRIBE MOLDING

NOTES

1. Some details vary between manufacturers.
2. Stock frames stocked in warehouse prior to receipt of order. Certain profiles are warehoused locally.
3. Standard frames manufactured from existing jigs and tooling upon receipt of order. Certain profiles are readily available.
4. Custom frames manufactured in response to specific dimensional requirements of a particular customer. Custom profiles are available with relative delay.
5. Selection should reflect anticipated requirements of construction schedule.
6. Certain detail features will constitute a custom frame, verify with manufacturer.

James W. G. Watson, AIA; Ronald A. Spahn and Associates; Cleveland Heights, Ohio

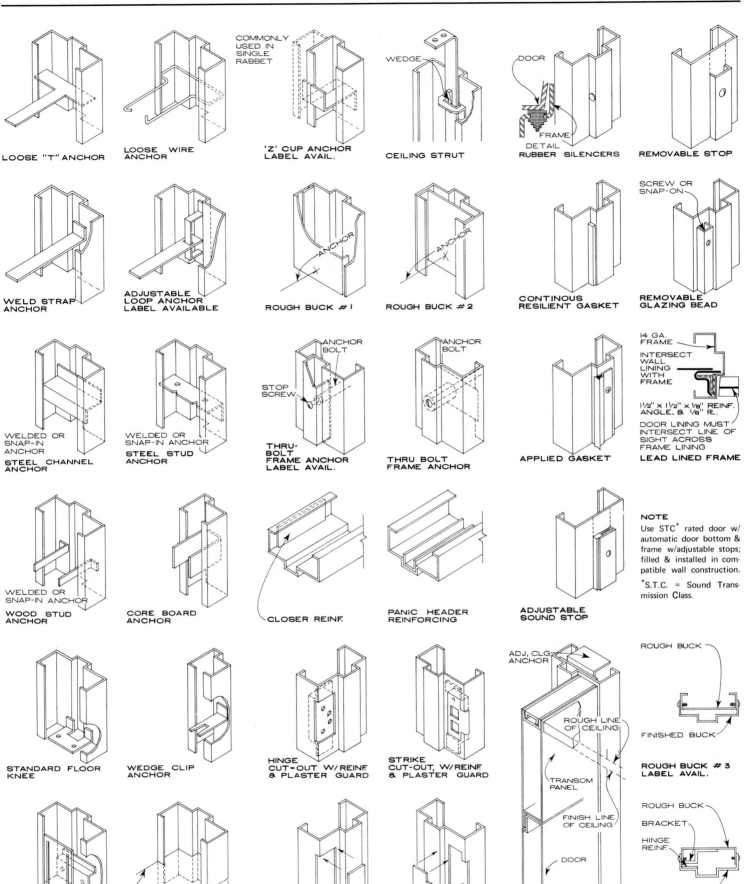

LOOSE "T" ANCHOR

LOOSE WIRE ANCHOR

COMMONLY USED IN SINGLE RABBET

'Z' CUP ANCHOR LABEL AVAIL.

WEDGE

CEILING STRUT

DOOR

FRAME DETAIL

RUBBER SILENCERS

REMOVABLE STOP

WELD STRAP ANCHOR

ADJUSTABLE LOOP ANCHOR LABEL AVAILABLE

ROUGH BUCK #1

ANCHOR

ROUGH BUCK #2

ANCHOR

CONTINOUS RESILIENT GASKET

SCREW OR SNAP-ON

REMOVABLE GLAZING BEAD

WELDED OR SNAP-IN ANCHOR
STEEL CHANNEL ANCHOR

WELDED OR SNAP-IN ANCHOR
STEEL STUD ANCHOR

ANCHOR BOLT

STOP SCREW

THRU-BOLT FRAME ANCHOR LABEL AVAIL.

ANCHOR BOLT

THRU BOLT FRAME ANCHOR

APPLIED GASKET

14 GA. FRAME

INTERSECT WALL LINING WITH FRAME

1½" × 1½" × ⅛" REINF. ANGLE, & ⅛" PL.

DOOR LINING MUST INTERSECT LINE OF SIGHT ACROSS FRAME LINING

LEAD LINED FRAME

WELDED OR SNAP-IN ANCHOR
WOOD STUD ANCHOR

CORE BOARD ANCHOR

CLOSER REINF.

PANIC HEADER REINFORCING

ADJUSTABLE SOUND STOP

NOTE
Use STC* rated door w/ automatic door bottom & frame w/adjustable stops; filled & installed in compatible wall construction.

*S.T.C. = Sound Transmission Class.

STANDARD FLOOR KNEE

WEDGE CLIP ANCHOR

HINGE CUT-OUT W/REINF. & PLASTER GUARD

STRIKE CUT-OUT, W/REINF. & PLASTER GUARD

ADJ. CLG. ANCHOR

ROUGH LINE OF CEILING

TRANSOM PANEL

FINISH LINE OF CEILING

DOOR

ROUGH BUCK

FINISHED BUCK

ROUGH BUCK #3 LABEL AVAIL.

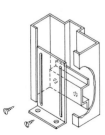

ADJUSTABLE FLOOR KNEE

FINISH FLOOR

EXTENDED FRAME W/BASE ANCHOR

HINGE CUT-OUT W/ BLANK COVER

STRIKE CUT OUT W/ BLANK COVER

HEADLESS DOOR FRAME LABEL AVAIL.

ROUGH BUCK

BRACKET

HINGE REINF.

FINISHED BUCK

ROUGH BUCK #4 LABEL AVAIL.

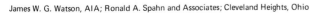

James W. G. Watson, AIA; Ronald A. Spahn and Associates; Cleveland Heights, Ohio

METAL DOORS 8

GENERAL

Fire doors are the most widely used and accepted means for the protection of both vertical and horizontal openings. Suitability of fire doors is determined by test by nationally recognized testing laboratories. The doors are tested as they are installed in the field; that is, with the frame, hardware, wired glass panels, and other accessories necessary to complete the installation.

NFPA 80, Standard for the Installation of Fire Doors and Windows, classifies the various types of openings commonly encountered.

TYPES OF OPENINGS

1. CLASS A OPENINGS: These are in walls separating buildings or dividing a single building into fire areas. Doors for the protection of these openings have a fire protection rating of 3 hr.
2. CLASS B OPENINGS: These are in enclosures of vertical communication through buildings (stairs, elevators, etc.). Doors for the protection of these openings have a fire protection rating of 1 or $1\frac{1}{2}$ hr.
3. CLASS C OPENINGS: These are in corridor and room partitions. Doors for the protection of these openings have a fire protection rating of $\frac{3}{4}$ hr.
4. CLASS D OPENINGS: These are in exterior walls, which are subject to severe fire exposure from outside of the building. Doors and shutters for the protection of these openings have a fire protection rating of $1\frac{1}{2}$ hr.
5. CLASS E OPENINGS: These are in exterior walls, which are subject to moderate or light fire exposure from outside of the building. Doors, shutters, or windows for the protection of these openings have a fire protection rating of $\frac{3}{4}$ hr.

TYPES OF DOORS

There are several types of construction for fire doors; a few are as follows:

1. COMPOSITE DOORS: These are of the flush design and consist of a manufactured core material with chemically impregnated wood edge banding and untreated wood face veneers, or laminated plastic faces, or surrounded by and encased in steel.
2. HOLLOW METAL DOORS: These are of formed steel of the flush and paneled designs of #20 gauge or heavier steel.
3. METAL CLAD (KALAMEIN) DOORS: These are of flush and paneled design consisting of metal covered wood cores or stiles and rails and insulated panels covered with steel of 20 gauge or lighter.
4. SHEET METAL DOORS: These are of formed #22 gauge or lighter steel and of the corrugated, flush, and paneled designs.
5. ROLLING STEEL DOORS: These are of the interlocking steel slat design or plate steel construction.
6. TIN CLAD DOORS: These are of two- or three-ply wood core construction, covered with #30 gauge galvanized steel or terneplate (maximum size 14 by 20 in.); or #24 gauge galvanized steel sheets not more than 48 in. wide.
7. CURTAIN TYPE DOORS: These consist of interlocking steel blades or a continuous formed spring steel curtain in a steel frame.

DOOR LABELS

FRAME LABEL

UNDERWRITERS   LABELS

Wm. G. Miner, AIA; Architect; Washington, D.C.

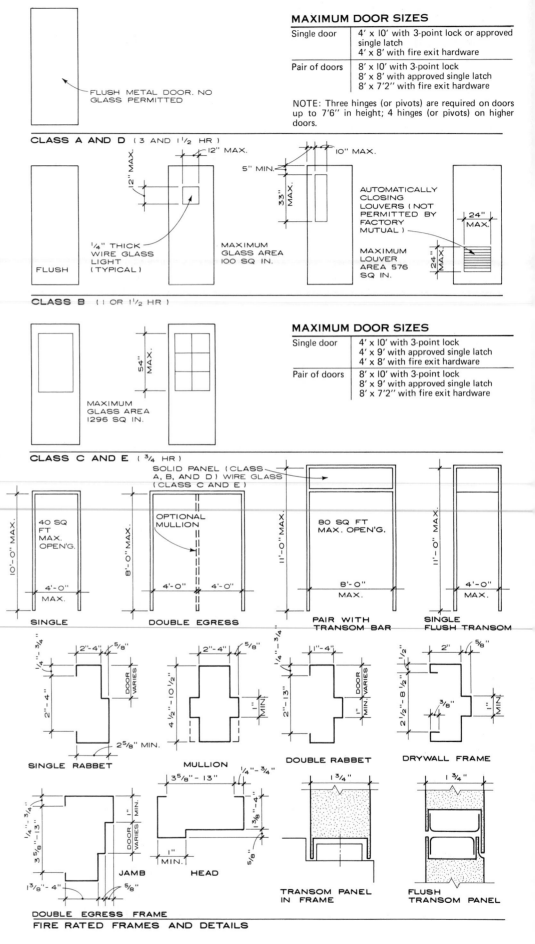

FLUSH METAL DOOR. NO GLASS PERMITTED

MAXIMUM DOOR SIZES

Single door	4' x 10' with 3-point lock or approved single latch
	4' x 8' with fire exit hardware
Pair of doors	8' x 10' with 3-point lock
	8' x 8' with approved single latch
	8' x 7'2'' with fire exit hardware

NOTE: Three hinges (or pivots) are required on doors up to 7'6'' in height; 4 hinges (or pivots) on higher doors.

CLASS A AND D (3 AND $1\frac{1}{2}$ HR)

FLUSH

$\frac{1}{4}$'' THICK WIRE GLASS LIGHT (TYPICAL)

MAXIMUM GLASS AREA 100 SQ IN.

AUTOMATICALLY CLOSING LOUVERS (NOT PERMITTED BY FACTORY MUTUAL)

MAXIMUM LOUVER AREA 576 SQ IN.

CLASS B (1 OR $1\frac{1}{2}$ HR)

MAXIMUM GLASS AREA 1296 SQ IN.

MAXIMUM DOOR SIZES

Single door	4' x 10' with 3-point lock
	4' x 9' with approved single latch
	4' x 8' with fire exit hardware
Pair of doors	8' x 10' with 3-point lock
	8' x 9' with approved single latch
	8' x 7'2'' with fire exit hardware

CLASS C AND E ($\frac{3}{4}$ HR)

SOLID PANEL (CLASS A, B, AND D) WIRE GLASS (CLASS C AND E)

40 SQ FT MAX. OPEN'G. — SINGLE

OPTIONAL MULLION — DOUBLE EGRESS

80 SQ FT MAX. OPEN'G. — PAIR WITH TRANSOM BAR

SINGLE FLUSH TRANSOM

SINGLE RABBET

MULLION

DOUBLE RABBET

DRYWALL FRAME

JAMB

HEAD

DOUBLE EGRESS FRAME

TRANSOM PANEL IN FRAME

FLUSH TRANSOM PANEL

FIRE RATED FRAMES AND DETAILS

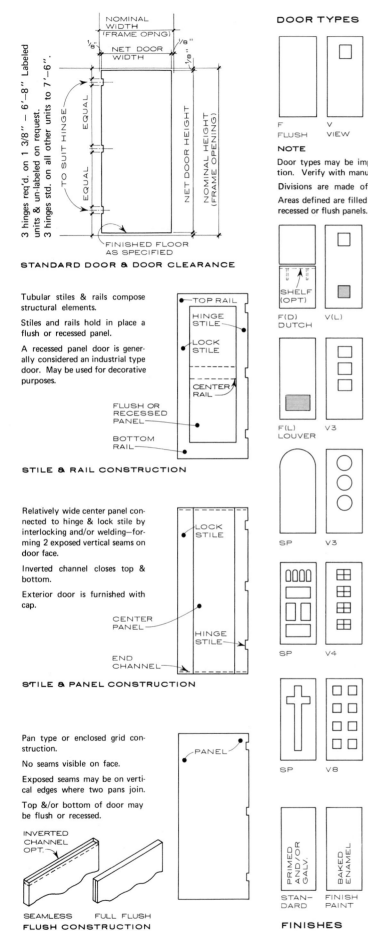

STANDARD DOOR & DOOR CLEARANCE

3 hinges req'd. on 1 3/8" – 6'–8" Labeled units & un-labeled on request.
3 hinges std. on all other units to 7'–6".

NOMINAL WIDTH (FRAME OPNG)
NET DOOR WIDTH
TO SUIT HINGE
EQUAL
EQUAL
EQUAL
NET DOOR HEIGHT
NOMINAL HEIGHT (FRAME OPENING)
FINISHED FLOOR AS SPECIFIED

Tubular stiles & rails compose structural elements.

Stiles and rails hold in place a flush or recessed panel.

A recessed panel door is generally considered an industrial type door. May be used for decorative purposes.

TOP RAIL
HINGE STILE
LOCK STILE
CENTER RAIL
FLUSH OR RECESSED PANEL
BOTTOM RAIL

STILE & RAIL CONSTRUCTION

Relatively wide center panel connected to hinge & lock stile by interlocking and/or welding—forming 2 exposed vertical seams on door face.

Inverted channel closes top & bottom.

Exterior door is furnished with cap.

LOCK STILE
CENTER PANEL
HINGE STILE
END CHANNEL

STILE & PANEL CONSTRUCTION

Pan type or enclosed grid construction.

No seams visible on face.

Exposed seams may be on vertical edges where two pans join.

Top &/or bottom of door may be flush or recessed.

PANEL
INVERTED CHANNEL OPT.

SEAMLESS   FULL FLUSH

FLUSH CONSTRUCTION

DOOR TYPES

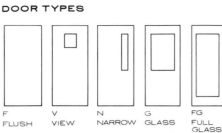

| F FLUSH | V VIEW | N NARROW | G GLASS | FG FULL GLASS |

NOTE

Door types may be imposed on any door construction. Verify with manufacturer.

Divisions are made of stiles and rails or muntins.

Areas defined are filled with glass, screening, louvers, recessed or flush panels.

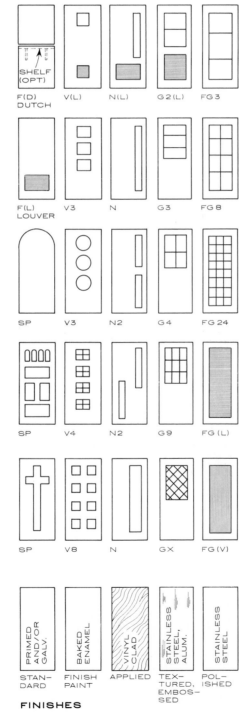

SHELF (OPT)
F(D) DUTCH | V(L) | N(L) | G2(L) | FG3

F(L) LOUVER | V3 | N | G3 | FG8

SP | V3 | N2 | G4 | FG24

SP | V4 | N2 | G9 | FG(L)

SP | V8 | N | GX | FG(V)

| PRIMED AND/OR GALV. STANDARD | BAKED ENAMEL FINISH PAINT | VINYL CLAD APPLIED | STAINLESS STEEL, ALUM. TEXTURED, EMBOSSED | STAINLESS STEEL POLISHED |

FINISHES

DOOR TOP WITH GLAZED OPENING

CAP TOP OPTIONAL

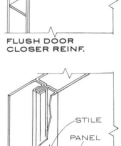

FLUSH DOOR CLOSER REINF.

INVERTED CHANNEL

STILE & PANEL DOOR TOP WITH GLAZED OPENING

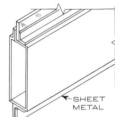

STILE
PANEL

STILE & PANEL JOINT

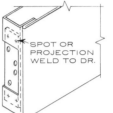

SPOT OR PROJECTION WELD TO DR.

HINGE REINFORCEMENT

SHEET METAL

STILE & RAIL DOOR

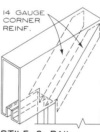

14 GAUGE CORNER REINF.

STILE & RAIL CORNER

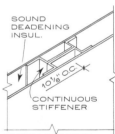

SOUND DEADENING INSUL.
10 1/2" O.C.
CONTINUOUS STIFFENER

FLUSH CONSTR.

KRAFT HONEYCOMB CORE

FLUSH DOOR CORE

VARIABLE AS REQUIRED

LOCK REINFORCEMENT

CONT. EDGE STIFFENER
CONT. WELD SEAM

FLUSH DOOR BOTTOM & EDGE CONSTR.

STILE & RAIL DOOR BOTTOM CONSTR.

James W. G. Watson, AIA; Ronald A. Spahn and Associates; Cleveland Heights, Ohio

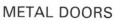

MINIMUM GAUGES FOR COMMERCIAL STEEL DOORS

ITEM	GAUGE NO.	EQUIVALENT THICKNESS (IN.)
Door frames	16	0.0598
Surface applied hardware reinforcement	16	0.0598
Doors—hollow steel construction		
Panels and stile	18	0.0478
Doors—composite construction		
Perimeter channel	18	0.0478
Surface sheets	22	0.0299
Reinforcement		
Surface applied hardware	16	0.0598
Lock and strike	16	0.0598
Hinge	10	0.1345
Flush bolt	16	0.0598
Glass molding	20	0.0359
Glass muntins	22	0.0299

NOTES

1. The steel door tables represent minimum standards published by the U.S. Department of Commerce for standard stock commercial, 1 3/4 in. thick steel doors and frames, and flush type interior steel doors and frames (doors not more than 3 ft in width).
2. Specifications for custom hollow metal doors and frames are published by the National Association of Architectural Metal Manufacturers. Standards may also vary according to location or the agency— always consult with the local authorities and/or agencies to determine what they require. Doors must be selected according to the project requirements such as frequency of usage, type of traffic, conditions required by the enclosed space, and environmental conditions.

MINIMUM GAUGES FOR INTERIOR STEEL DOORS

ITEM	GAUGE NO.	EQUIVALENT THICKNESS (IN.)
Door frames, 1 3/8 in. thick	18	0.0478
Door frames, 1 3/4 in. thick	16	0.0598
Stiles and panels	20	0.0359
Reinforcement		
Lock and strike	16	0.0598
Hinge	11	0.1196
Closer	14	0.0747

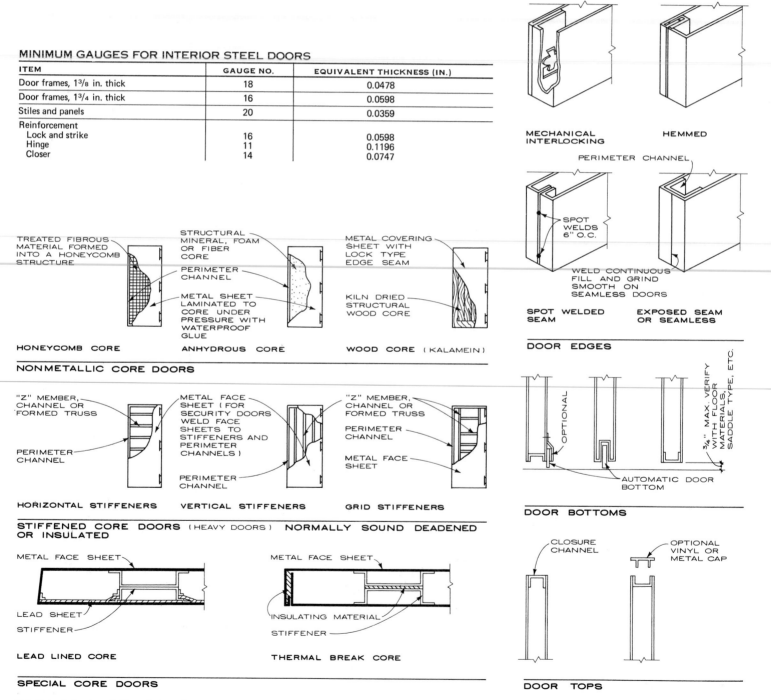

TREATED FIBROUS MATERIAL FORMED INTO A HONEYCOMB STRUCTURE

STRUCTURAL MINERAL, FOAM OR FIBER CORE

PERIMETER CHANNEL

METAL SHEET LAMINATED TO CORE UNDER PRESSURE WITH WATERPROOF GLUE

METAL COVERING SHEET WITH LOCK TYPE EDGE SEAM

KILN DRIED STRUCTURAL WOOD CORE

HONEYCOMB CORE   ANHYDROUS CORE   WOOD CORE (KALAMEIN)

NONMETALLIC CORE DOORS

"Z" MEMBER, CHANNEL OR FORMED TRUSS

METAL FACE SHEET (FOR SECURITY DOORS WELD FACE SHEETS TO STIFFENERS AND PERIMETER CHANNELS)

"Z" MEMBER, CHANNEL OR FORMED TRUSS

PERIMETER CHANNEL

METAL FACE SHEET

PERIMETER CHANNEL

PERIMETER CHANNEL

HORIZONTAL STIFFENERS   VERTICAL STIFFENERS   GRID STIFFENERS

STIFFENED CORE DOORS (HEAVY DOORS) **NORMALLY SOUND DEADENED OR INSULATED**

METAL FACE SHEET

LEAD SHEET
STIFFENER

METAL FACE SHEET

INSULATING MATERIAL
STIFFENER

LEAD LINED CORE   **THERMAL BREAK CORE**

SPECIAL CORE DOORS

MECHANICAL INTERLOCKING   HEMMED

PERIMETER CHANNEL

SPOT WELDS 6" O.C.

WELD CONTINUOUS FILL AND GRIND SMOOTH ON SEAMLESS DOORS

SPOT WELDED SEAM   EXPOSED SEAM OR SEAMLESS

DOOR EDGES

OPTIONAL

3/4" MAX. VERIFY WITH FLOOR MATERIALS, SADDLE TYPE, ETC.

AUTOMATIC DOOR BOTTOM

DOOR BOTTOMS

CLOSURE CHANNEL

OPTIONAL VINYL OR METAL CAP

DOOR TOPS

Kelly Sacher & Associates; Architects Engineers Planners; N. Babylon, New York

8   **METAL DOORS**

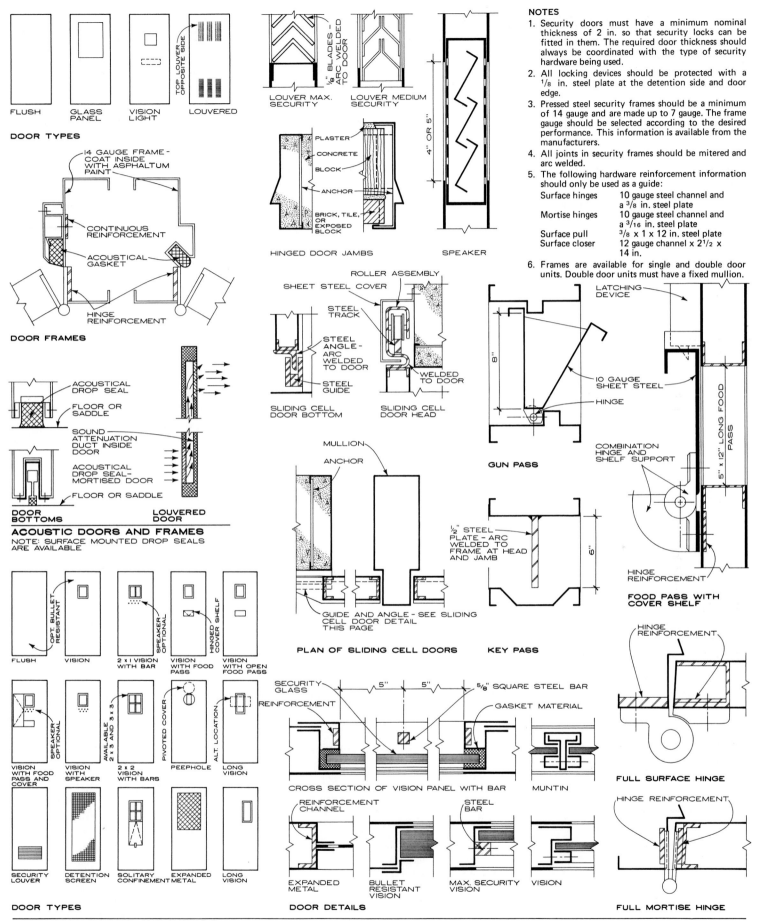

DOOR TYPES
FLUSH · GLASS PANEL · VISION LIGHT · LOUVERED
TOP LOUVER OPPOSITE SIDE

DOOR FRAMES
14 GAUGE FRAME - COAT INSIDE WITH ASPHALTUM PAINT
CONTINUOUS REINFORCEMENT
ACOUSTICAL GASKET
HINGE REINFORCEMENT

ACOUSTIC DOORS AND FRAMES
ACOUSTICAL DROP SEAL
FLOOR OR SADDLE
SOUND ATTENUATION DUCT INSIDE DOOR
ACOUSTICAL DROP SEAL - MORTISED DOOR
FLOOR OR SADDLE
DOOR BOTTOMS
LOUVERED DOOR
NOTE: SURFACE MOUNTED DROP SEALS ARE AVAILABLE

LOUVER MAX. SECURITY · LOUVER MEDIUM SECURITY
⅛ BLADES - ARC WELDED TO DOOR
PLASTER · CONCRETE · BLOCK · ANCHOR · BRICK, TILE, OR EXPOSED BLOCK
HINGED DOOR JAMBS
4" OR 5"
SPEAKER

ROLLER ASSEMBLY
SHEET STEEL COVER
STEEL TRACK
STEEL ANGLE - ARC WELDED TO DOOR
STEEL GUIDE
WELDED TO DOOR
SLIDING CELL DOOR BOTTOM · SLIDING CELL DOOR HEAD

MULLION · ANCHOR
GUIDE AND ANGLE - SEE SLIDING CELL DOOR DETAIL THIS PAGE
PLAN OF SLIDING CELL DOORS

½" STEEL PLATE - ARC WELDED TO FRAME AT HEAD AND JAMB
6"
KEY PASS

8"
10 GAUGE SHEET STEEL
HINGE
GUN PASS

LATCHING DEVICE
5" x 12" LONG FOOD PASS
COMBINATION HINGE AND SHELF SUPPORT
HINGE REINFORCEMENT
FOOD PASS WITH COVER SHELF

HINGE REINFORCEMENT
FULL SURFACE HINGE

HINGE REINFORCEMENT
FULL MORTISE HINGE

DOOR TYPES
FLUSH · VISION · OPT. BULLET RESISTANT · 2 x 1 VISION WITH BAR · SPEAKER OPTIONAL · VISION WITH FOOD PASS · HINGED COVER SHELF · VISION WITH OPEN FOOD PASS
VISION WITH FOOD PASS AND COVER · SPEAKER OPTIONAL · VISION WITH SPEAKER · 2 x 2 VISION WITH BARS · AVAILABLE 2 x 3 AND 3 x 3 · PEEPHOLE · PIVOTED COVER · LONG VISION · ALT. LOCATION
SECURITY LOUVER · DETENTION SCREEN · SOLITARY CONFINEMENT · EXPANDED METAL · LONG VISION

DOOR DETAILS
SECURITY GLASS · REINFORCEMENT
5" · 5" · ⅝" SQUARE STEEL BAR
GASKET MATERIAL
CROSS SECTION OF VISION PANEL WITH BAR · MUNTIN
REINFORCEMENT CHANNEL · STEEL BAR
EXPANDED METAL · BULLET RESISTANT VISION · MAX. SECURITY VISION · VISION

DETENTION DOORS AND DETAILS

NOTES

1. Security doors must have a minimum nominal thickness of 2 in. so that security locks can be fitted in them. The required door thickness should always be coordinated with the type of security hardware being used.
2. All locking devices should be protected with a ⅛ in. steel plate at the detention side and door edge.
3. Pressed steel security frames should be a minimum of 14 gauge and are made up to 7 gauge. The frame gauge should be selected according to the desired performance. This information is available from the manufacturers.
4. All joints in security frames should be mitered and arc welded.
5. The following hardware reinforcement information should only be used as a guide:

Surface hinges	10 gauge steel channel and a ⅜ in. steel plate
Mortise hinges	10 gauge steel channel and a 3/16 in. steel plate
Surface pull	⅜ x 1 x 12 in. steel plate
Surface closer	12 gauge channel x 2½ x 14 in.

6. Frames are available for single and double door units. Double door units must have a fixed mullion.

Kelly, Sacher & Associates; Architects, Engineers, Planners; N. Babylon, New York

METAL DOORS 8

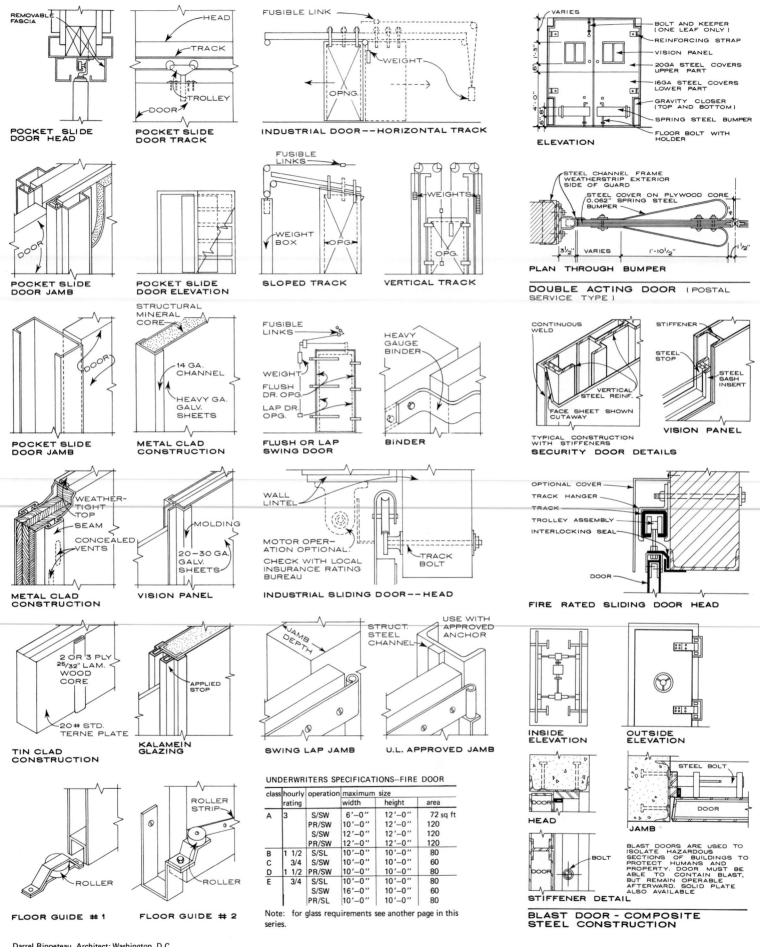

POCKET SLIDE
DOOR HEAD

POCKET SLIDE
DOOR TRACK

INDUSTRIAL DOOR--HORIZONTAL TRACK

ELEVATION

POCKET SLIDE
DOOR JAMB

POCKET SLIDE
DOOR ELEVATION

SLOPED TRACK

VERTICAL TRACK

PLAN THROUGH BUMPER

DOUBLE ACTING DOOR (POSTAL
SERVICE TYPE)

POCKET SLIDE
DOOR JAMB

METAL CLAD
CONSTRUCTION

FLUSH OR LAP
SWING DOOR

BINDER

SECURITY DOOR DETAILS

VISION PANEL

METAL CLAD
CONSTRUCTION

VISION PANEL

INDUSTRIAL SLIDING DOOR--HEAD

FIRE RATED SLIDING DOOR HEAD

TIN CLAD
CONSTRUCTION

KALAMEIN
GLAZING

SWING LAP JAMB

U.L. APPROVED JAMB

INSIDE
ELEVATION

OUTSIDE
ELEVATION

HEAD

JAMB

FLOOR GUIDE #1

FLOOR GUIDE #2

STIFFENER DETAIL

BLAST DOOR - COMPOSITE
STEEL CONSTRUCTION

UNDERWRITERS SPECIFICATIONS—FIRE DOOR

class	hourly rating	operation	maximum size		
			width	height	area
A	3	S/SW	6'-0"	12'-0"	72 sq ft
		PR/SW	10'-0"	12'-0"	120
		S/SW	12'-0"	12'-0"	120
		PR/SW	12'-0"	12'-0"	120
B	1 1/2	S/SL	10'-0"	10'-0"	80
C	3/4	S/SW	10'-0"	10'-0"	60
D	1 1/2	PR/SW	10'-0"	10'-0"	80
E	3/4	S/SL	10'-0"	10'-0"	80
		S/SW	16'-0"	10'-0"	60
		PR/SL	10'-0"	10'-0"	80

Note: for glass requirements see another page in this series.

Darrel Rippeteau, Architect; Washington, D.C.

James W. G. Watson, AIA; Ronald A. Spahn and Associates, Cleveland Heights, Ohio

8 METAL DOORS

PROJECTED

NOTE

This is the workhorse of metal windows, available in many combinations of fixed and operating sash. Usually the lowest light will project in and the upper vents project out for maximum comfort and convenience. However, the flexibility of substituting fixed lights for vents and omitting muntins permits a variety of configurations.

Available in various weights, these windows are frequently used in institutional, commercial, and industrial projects. They will receive single or double glazing, from inside or outside. A wide assortment of hardware has been developed to meet almost every need, including special accessories for manual or mechanical operation of sash above normal reach.

SECURITY

NOTE

Another variation of the projected sash, this window provides an integral grill permitting ventilation but restricting the size of an object that can pass through the window. Used in institutions requiring detention or tight security against outside entry, this sash minimizes the psychological, installation, and maintenance problems associated with a separate grill.

DOUBLE HUNG

NOTE

The traditional window of the United States wood window industry, metal double hung windows are finding wide application in projects where economy and flush window treatment are paramount. Single hung windows, which provide a fixed light in lieu of the top sash, are employed where economy is particularly critical. Triple hung windows are another variation, providing three operating sash for ease of operation in tall windows.

SLIDING

NOTE

Horizontally sliding or rolling sash provide flush interior and exterior wall surfaces without the need for counterbalancing hardware intrinsic in the double hung window. Initially they were popular as economical sash in residential applications; the sliding window industry has subsequently made substantial product improvements. Their inherent weatherproofing problems have been overcome with careful engineering and workmanship utilizing heavier members. Generally speaking, horizontally or squarely proportioned sash will operate more smoothly than tall, narrow sash. Most manufacturers apply full width insect screens on the exterior.

William A. Klene, AIA, Architect; Herndon, Virginia

COMBINATION

NOTE

An economical variation of the projected sash which is used where a larger amount of light than ventilation is desired. This sash was developed for suburban classroom use but has found wide application in other structures. Operating vents may be designed to project in or out. Insect screens pose different problems in both situations.

CASEMENT

NOTE

Consisting of vertically proportioned sash that swing outward, somewhat like a door, casement windows offer an aesthetic appeal not furnished by other window types. Insect screens are necessarily placed on the inside. Thus underscreen mechanical operators are usually provided. Otherwise the screen would have to be hinged or equipped with wickets for access to manual pulls.

AWNING

NOTE

A window that has grown in popularity from its Southern residential origins, an awning window offers 100% ventilation combined with a degree of rain protection not attainable with casement sash. Awning sash can be fully weatherstripped and will readily receive double glazing or storm sash. Since their inherent horizontal proportions are not currently in vogue, their use has diminished recently. Insect screens are mounted in the interior, and rotary operators are standard.

JALOUSIE

NOTE

When the individual sash depth of the awning window is reduced to the point where it becomes, in effect, an operating louver, horizontal sash members are unnecessary. This has a profound effect on appearance and the ability to provide weatherstripping. Most often found in residences and commercial work, particularly where ventilation is most desirable, jalousie windows are not as widely used as most other sash. Sash widths are limited to the free span capability of the blade materials (usually glass, wood, or metal). Storm sash are readily available and, in some instances, are an integral part of the jalousie. Insect screens are necessarily placed on the interior, with operating hardware usually placed at normal hand height.

PIVOTED

NOTE

Popular in multistory, air-conditioned commercial buildings, horizontally or vertically pivoting sash are used only for maintenance. Though they usually rotate 90°, some manufacturers produce a sash that rotates 180°. Effective weatherstripping is mandatory in both cases. Wind action on walls of highrise structures must be considered in sash design. Top or side hung sash are also produced by some manufacturers for occasional opening of fixed sash.

GENERAL NOTES

1. Most types are readily available in steel or aluminum. Steel sash tend to be more rigid and have thinner sight lines. They will be galvanized and/or bonderized and primed prior to finishing if so specified. While aluminum sash may be more economical and may offer greater inherent corrosion resistance, they have greater thermal expansion and conductance. Both are available in a variety of finishes.
2. All operating sash are regularly mulled to fixed sash, thus providing for economy, appearance, and a variety of functions.
3. Thoughtful selection of glazing material is as important as window type selection. Plastic glazing materials generally have greater coefficients of thermal expansion than glass, requiring deeper glazing legs and stops.
4. Effective thermal isolation requires double glazing (some manufacturers offer triple glazing or dual sash), continuous weatherstripping, and a "thermal break" in aluminum sash for colder climates.
5. Many manufacturers produce more than one quality window. SWI criteria for various weights of steel sash are useful in making comparisons. Current criteria for aluminum sash are based on performance of a tested specimen, hence require careful consideration unless the manufacturer has a well established reputation.
6. Many manufacturers have ceased using "stock sizes" and produce only custom work. Consequently, special shapes and configurations are easier to obtain, particularly in monumental or commercial grades. Some manufacturers also produce specialized windows that are sound resistant, contain venetian blinds, and so on. Since there is little correlation between the manufacturers' dimensioning systems, individual consultation is imperative where dimensions are critical.
7. Residential grades are somewhat more standardized, generally based on available dimensions of welded edge insulating glass.
8. Muntins, either simulating or forming small glass lights, are usually available for residential sash, if desired.
9. Installation details must take into account internal condensation in most climates. Hardware selection must consider insect screens as well as mounting heights, operating convenience, security, and so on.
10. Most codes have a minimum light and ventilation, minimum wind load resistance, and maximum thermal transmittance requirements, as well as minimum egress provisions from residential sleeping space. All these factors may affect window selection.
11. Prefinished window frames are generally installed after contiguous masonry rather than being built in.

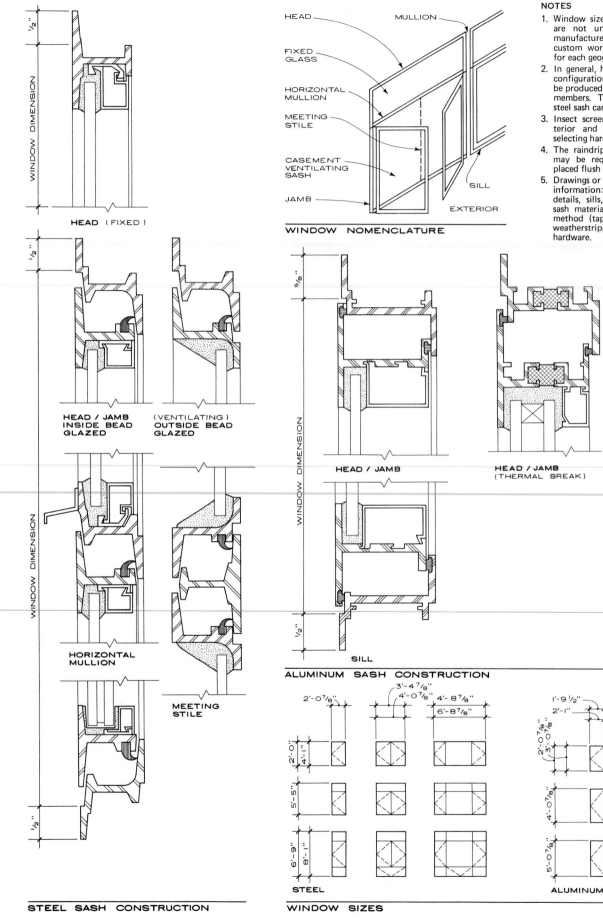

HEAD (FIXED)

HEAD / JAMB INSIDE BEAD GLAZED

(VENTILATING) OUTSIDE BEAD GLAZED

HORIZONTAL MULLION

MEETING STILE

STEEL SASH CONSTRUCTION

WINDOW NOMENCLATURE

HEAD

MULLION

FIXED GLASS

HORIZONTAL MULLION

MEETING STILE

CASEMENT VENTILATING SASH

JAMB

SILL

EXTERIOR

NOTES

1. Window sizes and dimensioning methods, as listed, are not uniform for all manufacturers. Some manufacturers have no stock sizes, producing only custom work. Check with those who supply sash for each geographical area.

2. In general, heavier grades of windows offer greater configuration flexibility. Larger operating sash can be produced with heavier members than with lighter members. Thus the fixed lights shown for taller steel sash can be avoided, if desired.

3. Insect screens are necessarily installed on the interior and must be taken into account when selecting hardware.

4. The raindrip indicated on the horizontal mullion may be required at ventilating heads if sash is placed flush with exterior face of wall.

5. Drawings or specification must contain the following information: window size and location, installation details, sills, stools, flashing, sealing, and anchors; sash material and finish; glazing material; glazing method (tape, putty, or bead, inside or outside); weatherstripping, insect screen material, and hardware.

HEAD / JAMB

HEAD / JAMB (THERMAL BREAK)

HEAD / JAMB (TUBULAR)

SILL

ALUMINUM SASH CONSTRUCTION

WINDOW SIZES

STEEL

ALUMINUM

William A. Klene, AIA, Architect; Herndon, Virginia

8 **METAL WINDOWS**

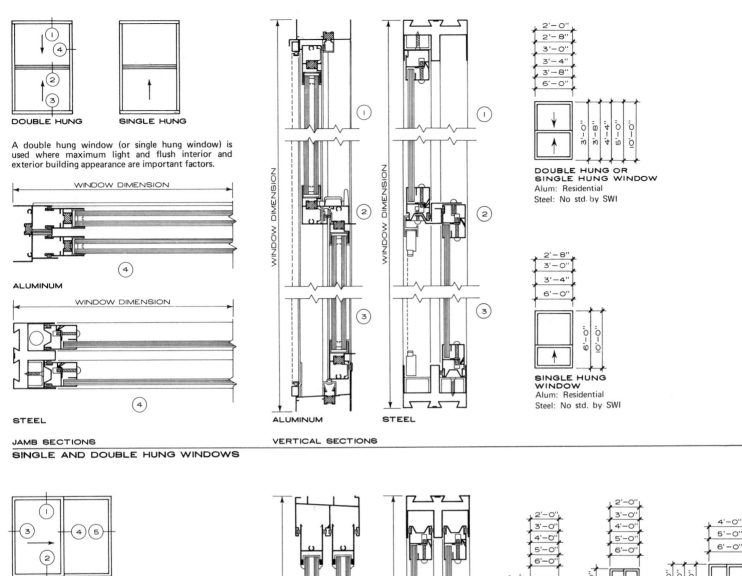

DOUBLE HUNG   **SINGLE HUNG**

A double hung window (or single hung window) is used where maximum light and flush interior and exterior building appearance are important factors.

WINDOW DIMENSION

ALUMINUM

WINDOW DIMENSION

STEEL

JAMB SECTIONS

SINGLE AND DOUBLE HUNG WINDOWS

WINDOW DIMENSION   WINDOW DIMENSION

ALUMINUM   **STEEL**

VERTICAL SECTIONS

2'-0"
2'-8"
3'-0"
3'-4"
3'-8"
6'-0"

3'-0" 3'-8" 4'-4" 5'-0" 10'-0"

DOUBLE HUNG OR SINGLE HUNG WINDOW
Alum: Residential
Steel: No std. by SWI

2'-8"
3'-0"
3'-4"
6'-0"

6'-0" 10'-0"

SINGLE HUNG WINDOW
Alum: Residential
Steel: No std. by SWI

SLIDING

A horizontal sliding glass window (single or double) is used where maximum light, flush interior and exterior building appearance, simple manual operation, and accessibility are important factors.

WINDOW DIMENSION

ALUMINUM

WINDOW DIMENSION

STEEL

JAMB SECTIONS

SLIDING WINDOWS

David W. Johnson; Washington, D.C.

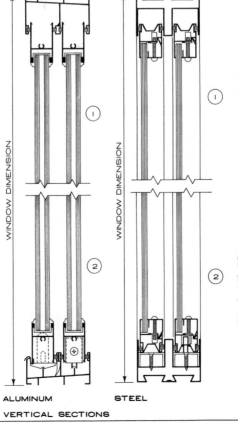

WINDOW DIMENSION   WINDOW DIMENSION

ALUMINUM   **STEEL**

VERTICAL SECTIONS

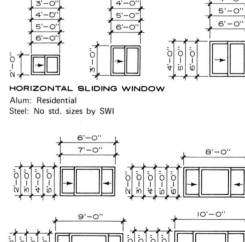

2'-0"
3'-0"
4'-0"
5'-0"
6'-0"

2'-0"
3'-0"
4'-0"
5'-0"
6'-0"

4'-0"
5'-0"
6'-0"

2'-0"   3'-0"   4'-0" 5'-0" 6'-0"

HORIZONTAL SLIDING WINDOW
Alum: Residential
Steel: No std. sizes by SWI

6'-0"
7'-0"

8'-0"

9'-0"

10'-0"

2'-0" 3'-0" 4'-0" 5'-0"

COMBINATION WINDOW (HOR. SLIDING—FIXED)
Alum: Residential
Steel: No std. sizes by SWI

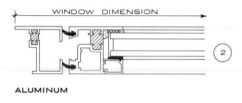

ELEVATION

NOTE

A reversible window is used mostly in multistory, air conditioned buildings where window washing from the interior is desired. It is normally opened for cleaning only; however, it may be combined with a hopper if ventilation is required.

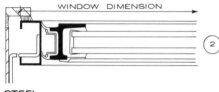

ALUMINUM

WINDOW DIMENSION

STEEL

JAMB SECTIONS
REVERSIBLE WINDOWS

ALUMINUM

STEEL

VERTICAL SECTIONS

CLOSED CELL SPONGE NEOPRENE WEATHER STRIPPING

PRESSURE EQUALIZATION SLOTS

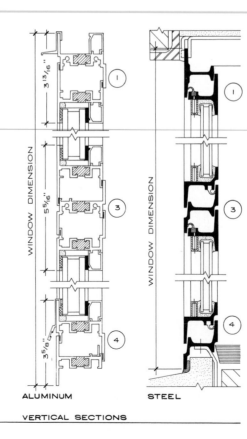

ELEVATIONS

ADDITIONAL BARS OPTIONAL

SCREW ATTACHED GLAZING BEAD TYPICAL

STEEL ANGLE CLIP AND STEEL CHANNEL VENT CONNECTING BAR

ALUMINUM   **STEEL**

VERTICAL SECTIONS

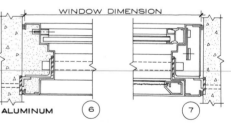

ALUMINUM   **STEEL**

9/16" THICK SAFETY GLASS TYPICAL

TAMPER RESISTANT SCREWS

STUD

STEEL

JAMB SECTIONS

NOTES

1. Housing sill frame size varies with manufacturer of window operator.
2. Muntin and mullion tubes are 12 gauge maximum and 14 gauge medium security, grouted full, and contain a $7/8$ in. diameter tamper resistant bar.
3. Tempered glass is $1/2$ in. on exterior side.
4. Horizontal tube/bars to have maximum spacing of 5 in.

SECURITY WINDOWS

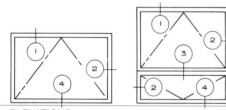

ELEVATIONS
NOTE

A projected (special) window is used mostly in multistory, air conditioned buildings where window washing from the interior is desired. It is normally opened for cleaning only; however, it may be combined with a hopper if ventilation is required. For such use see alternate above.

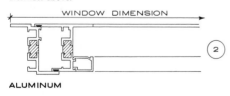

ALUMINUM

WINDOW DIMENSION

STEEL

JAMB SECTIONS
PROJECTED WINDOWS

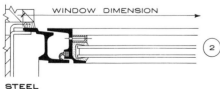

ALUMINUM   **STEEL**

VERTICAL SECTIONS

David W. Johnson, Washington, D. C.

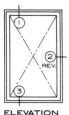

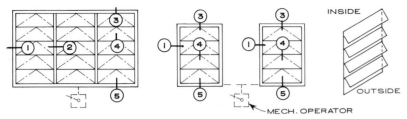

AWNING

AN AWNING WINDOW is one whose movable units consist of a group of hand operated or gear operated outward projecting ventilators, all of which move in unison. It is used where maximum height and ventilation is required in inaccessible areas such as upper parts of gymnasiums or auditoriums. Hand operation is limited to one window only, while a single gear operator may be connected to two or more awning windows, and may be motorized.

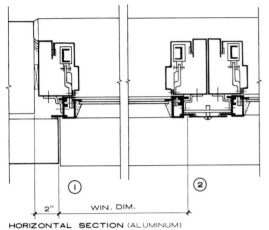

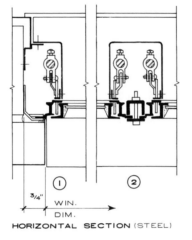

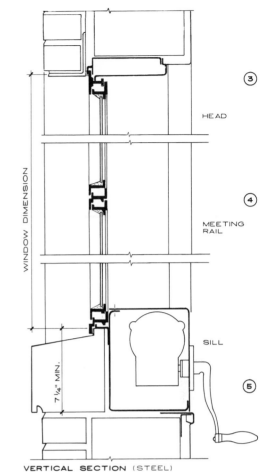

HORIZONTAL SECTION (ALUMINUM)

HORIZONTAL SECTION (STEEL)

VERTICAL SECTION (STEEL)

AWNING WINDOWS

JALOUSIE

A JALOUSIE WINDOW (ALUMINUM) consists of a series of operable overlapping glass louvers which pivot in unison. It may be combined in the same frame with a series of operable opaque louvers for climate control. It is used mostly in residential type constructions in southern climates, where maximum ventilation and flush exterior and interior appearance is desired.

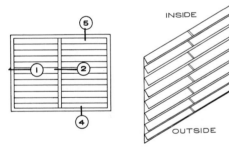

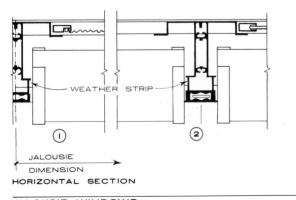

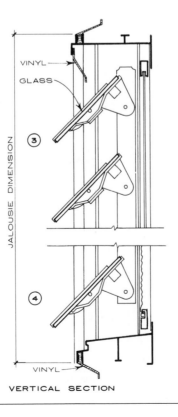

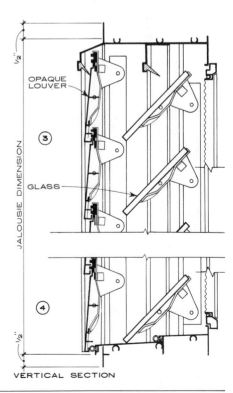

HORIZONTAL SECTION

VERTICAL SECTION

VERTICAL SECTION

JALOUSIE WINDOWS

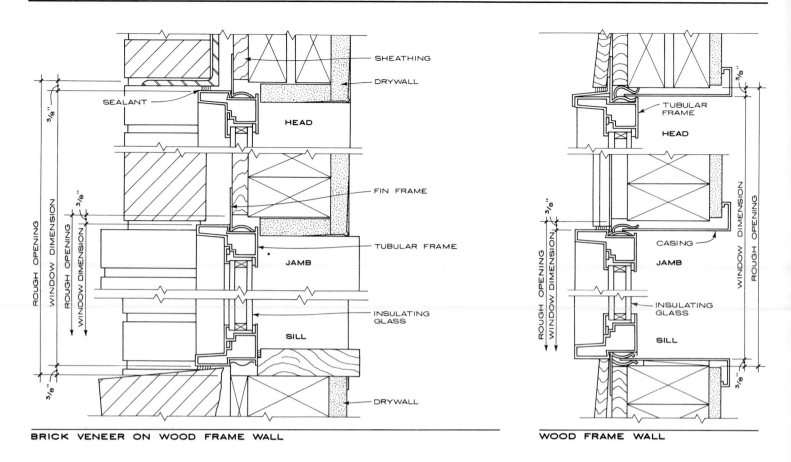

BRICK VENEER ON WOOD FRAME WALL

SHEATHING
DRYWALL
SEALANT
HEAD
FIN FRAME
TUBULAR FRAME
JAMB
INSULATING GLASS
SILL
DRYWALL
ROUGH OPENING
WINDOW DIMENSION
ROUGH OPENING
WINDOW DIMENSION
3/8"
3/8"
3/8"

WOOD FRAME WALL

TUBULAR FRAME
HEAD
CASING
JAMB
INSULATING GLASS
SILL
ROUGH OPENING
WINDOW DIMENSION
WINDOW DIMENSION
ROUGH OPENING
3/8"
3/8"
3/8"

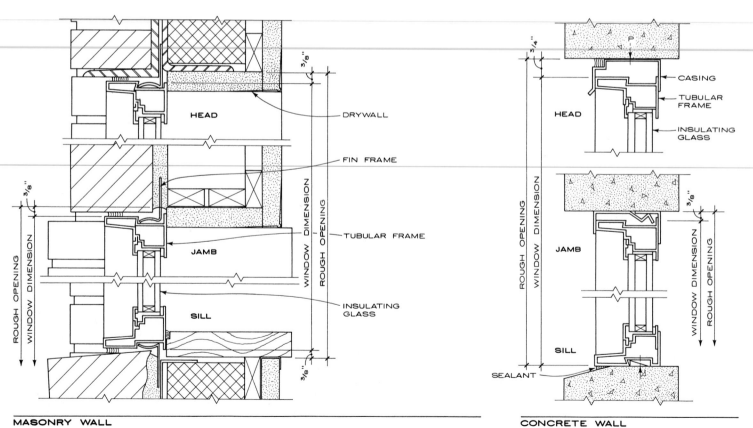

MASONRY WALL

DRYWALL
HEAD
FIN FRAME
TUBULAR FRAME
JAMB
SILL
INSULATING GLASS
ROUGH OPENING
WINDOW DIMENSION
WINDOW DIMENSION
ROUGH OPENING
3/8"
3/8"
3/8"

CONCRETE WALL

CASING
TUBULAR FRAME
HEAD
INSULATING GLASS
JAMB
SILL
SEALANT
ROUGH OPENING
WINDOW DIMENSION
WINDOW DIMENSION
ROUGH OPENING
3/4"
3/8"

NOTES

1. Fins and interior casings are available to meet various installation requirements. Interior trims are available in depths of 2 to 10 in., in 1/2 in. increments.

2. Thermal-break type extrusions are available. Consult with manufacturers for sizes and shapes.

Nicanor A. Alano, Architect; Tacoma, Washington

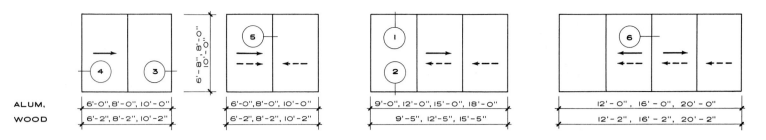

RESIDENTIAL SLIDING DOOR DIMENSIONS
DIMENSIONS SHOWN ARE NOMINAL STOCK SIZES

ALUM.	6'-0", 8'-0", 10'-0"	6'-0", 8'-0", 10'-0"	9'-0", 12'-0", 15'-0", 18'-0"	12'-0", 16'-0", 20'-0"
WOOD	6'-2", 8'-2", 10'-2"	6'-2", 8'-2", 10'-2"	9'-5", 12'-5", 15'-5"	12'-2", 16'-2", 20'-2"

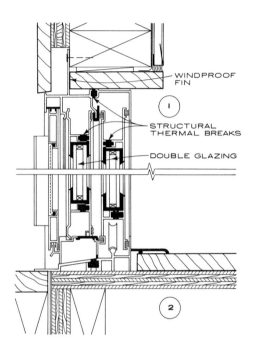

WINDPROOF FIN

STRUCTURAL THERMAL BREAKS

DOUBLE GLAZING

NOTES

1. Residential sliding door dimensions shown are nominal stock sizes. Custom sizes are available in accordance with individual manufacturing limitations and availability of glass sizes.

2. Details shown are for wood frame construction. Interior and exterior finishes and trim are optional. See manufacturer's data for typical installation details.

3. Tempered glass should always be used to reduce the chance of breakage and to avoid dangerous glass shards if breakage occurs.

4. Screens are available for all doors. Details show screens on the exterior for both the metal and wood doors. Consult individual manufacturer's literature to determine if screens are interior only, exterior only, or available either way.

5. Energy conservation is enhanced through the use of structural thermal breaks in aluminum sliding doors along with windproof mounting fins and double glazing. Standard aluminum sliding doors are also available.

6. See manufacturer's data for special sizes, locking devices, finishes, and specific limitations.

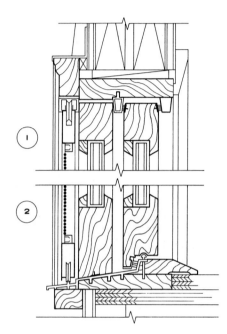

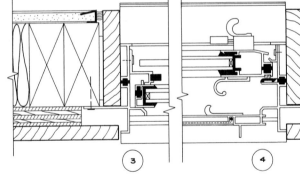

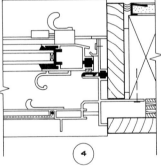

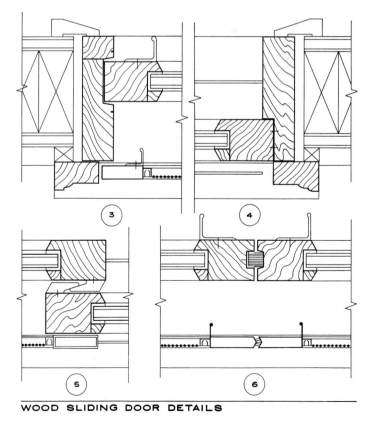

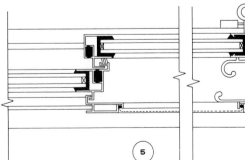

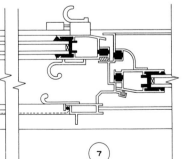

ALUMINUM SLIDING DOOR DETAILS WITH ENERGY CONSERVATION FEATURES

WOOD SLIDING DOOR DETAILS

Leo A. Daly; Architecture-Engineering-Planning; Omaha, Nebraska

SPECIAL DOORS 8

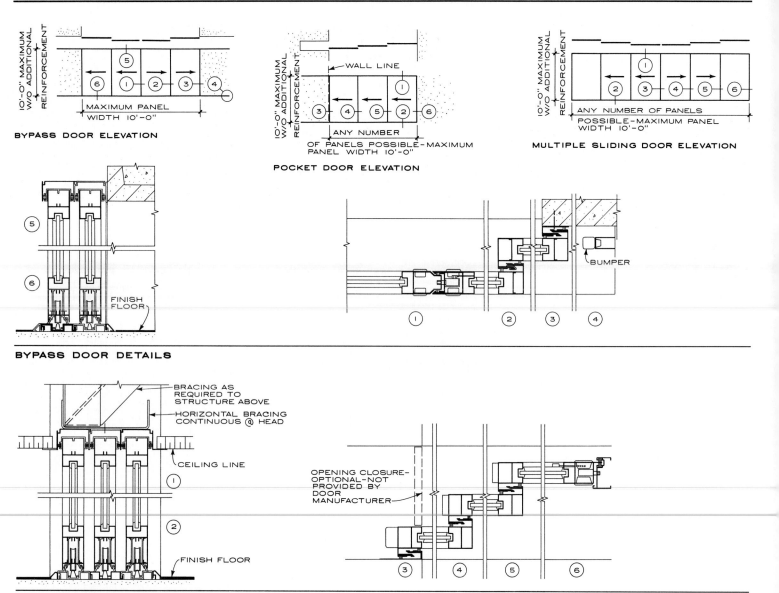

BYPASS DOOR ELEVATION

POCKET DOOR ELEVATION

MULTIPLE SLIDING DOOR ELEVATION

BYPASS DOOR DETAILS

POCKET DOOR DETAILS

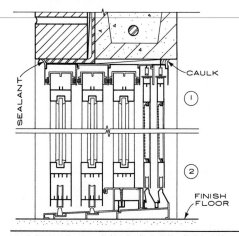

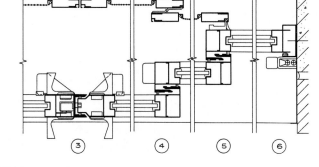

MULTIPLE SLIDING DOOR DETAILS

NOTES

1. Details shown are for masonry construction. Interior and exterior finishes are optional. Consult manufacturer's data for typical installation details.
2. Screens are available for all doors if required. Where shown, the details indicate screens on the interior. Consult specific manufacturer's literature to determine if screens are available for interior only, exterior only, or both. Glazing should be of safety glass, tempered, or insulating glass. Maximum manufacturable sizes of individual glass types will be the governing factor in determining maximum panel sizes. Consult industry standards for applicable data.
3. Consult manufacturer's data for available sizes, locking devices, and finishes.

Leo A. Daly; Architecture-Engineering-Planning; Omaha, Nebraska

⑧ SPECIAL DOORS

METAL CURTAIN WALLS

Exterior metal and glass enclosure walls require more careful development and skilled erection than traditional wall construction. Because metal and glass react differently to environmental conditions than do other wall materials, the technology is different from all other enclosure systems.

Errors in judgment can be avoided if behavior of the wall is understood. Some of the important considerations for successful curtain wall development are delineated below. (Further in-depth material on the following points is available from a variety of sources.)

FUNCTION OF THE WALL

The metal and glass curtain wall functions as an "enclosure system" which, when properly developed, can serve multiple functions: (1) withstand the action of the elements; (2) control the passage inward and outward of heat, light, air, and sound; (3) prevent or control access from outside.

NATURAL FORCES

Curtain wall development requirements are determined in part by the impact of natural forces. Natural forces that cause the most destruction and failures are (1) water, (2) wind, (3) sunlight, (4) temperature, (5) gravity, and (6) seismic forces. To understand the impact of these forces on the curtain wall development requirements, the effects of each should be separately examined.

WATER

The most frequent cause of problems with all enclosures is leakage from rain, snow, vapor, or condensate. Wind driven moisture can enter very small openings and may move within the wall, appearing far from its point of entry. Water vapor can penetrate microscopic pores and will condense on cool surfaces. Such moisture trapped within a wall can cause serious damage that is difficult to detect. Leaks are usually limited to joints and openings, which must be designed to provide a weathertight enclosure.

WIND

Structural design development of the wall must take into account both positive and negative pressures caused by wind action, increasing in effect with the height of the building. Increases in wind loading will occur in corner areas of the wall and must be included accordingly. Framing members, panels, and glass thicknesses should be determined by maximum wind load anticipated. Winds contribute to the movement of the wall, affecting joint seals and wall anchorage. The effect of positive or negative wind pressure can cause stress reversal on framing members and glass, and will cause water to travel in any direction (including upward) across the face of the wall. Wind is a major factor in potential water leakage.

SUNLIGHT

The ultraviolet spectrum of sunlight can cause breakdown of organic materials such as color pigments, plastics, and sealants. Fading and failure of these materials can cause serious problems with appearance and weathertightness of the curtain wall. All organic materials should be tested for resistance to ultraviolet radiation and ozone attack.

Sunlight passing through glass can cause excessive brightness and glare and will cause fading of interior furnishings and finishes. Shading devices and the use of glare reducing or reflective types of glass should be considered in development of the wall.

TEMPERATURE

Change in temperature causes the expansion and contraction of materials. Control of the passage of heat or cold through the wall is required. Thermal movement

Skidmore, Owings & Merrill

as a result of solar heat is one of the major problems in curtain wall development. Minimum outdoor temperatures vary about 80°F. Throughout the country, the maximum surface temperature of the darker colored metals on buildings can range as high as 170°F. This temperature fluctuation, both daily and seasonally, critically affects wall development. Thermal expansion and contraction is much greater in metals than in wood or masonry.

Heat passage through the wall causes heat gain in hot weather and heat loss in cold weather, the relative importance of the two varying with geographic location. Thermal insulation of opaque wall areas becomes an extremely important problem, especially whenever these areas constitute a large portion of the total wall area. When vision glass areas predominate, the use of insulating glass and the minimizing of through metal or "cold bridges" (usually by inserting continuous nonmetallic breaks in the metal assembly) are more effective in lowering the heat transfer (U-valve) through the wall.

GRAVITY

Because gravity is constant and static rather than variable and dynamic, gravity is a less critical force affecting the development of a window wall design but is important in that it should be recognized. It causes deflection in horizontal load carrying members, particularly under the weight of large sheets of heavy glass. However, because the weight of the wall is transferred at frequent intervals to the building frame, the structural effect of gravity is small in comparison with that imposed by wind action. Far greater gravity forces, in the form of floor and roof loads, are acting on the building frame to which the wall is attached. As these loads may cause deflections and displacements of the frame, connections of the wall to this frame must be designed to provide sufficient relative movement to ensure that the displacements do not impose vertical loads on the wall itself.

SEISMIC

Seismic (earthquake) loadings will produce additional static and dynamic loadings to the window wall system. Seismic loadings will produce both vertical and horizontal deflections of the wall. This will necessitate special energy absorption considerations in the detail of all wall anchorages.

DESIGN DEVELOPMENT CONSIDERATIONS: STRUCTURAL INTEGRITY

Structural integrity of the curtain wall is a prime concern involving the same design procedures that are used in any other exterior wall. However, deficiencies of weathertightness and temperature movements are more prevalent than difference in strength which will be further elaborated upon.

The structural integrity of the window wall must be evaluated using two criteria: strength and deflection. Based on numerous window wall tests, it has been found that the ultimate performance of the system is usually dependent on the elastic and inelastic deflections of the system rather than just the strength of component parts.

Wall fabrication and erection tolerances must be carefully reviewed. Many window wall test failures have been caused by inadequate anchorage details.

WEATHERTIGHTNESS

Weathertightness ensures protection against the penetration of water and an excessive amount of air through the wall. This depends on adequate provision for movement and is closely related to proper joint design. A major share of the problems experienced over the years have been due to the lack of weathertightness.

PROVISION FOR MOVEMENT

Development of the wall must accommodate relative movements of the wall components and also differential movements between the wall assembly and the building structure. Relative movements of the wall components will primarily be affected by thermal movements of the wall elements and erection tolerances of the individual wall elements. Erection tolerances may exceed the tolerance for thermal movement. The differential movements between the wall components of the building structure are a direct function of the dead and live load deflections of the structure and also the creep, shrinkage, thermal, wind, and seismic deformations of the building structure. These differential movements may be of considerable magnitude, and the effects of such differential movements must not be transferred from the structure directly to the window wall system. Usually provisions for such differential movement are provided at the head and jamb anchorage locations between the wall jointery and/or joints between wall and adjacent cladding. Behavior of sealants must be considered. Current recommendations from sealant manufacturer are to limit movement of the joint to prevent sealant failure. Temperature of metal parts at time of erection, as well as the anticipated design temperature range, will establish the extent of movement in a joint.

MOISTURE CONTROL

Control of condensation is essential because metal and glass are not only impermeable to moisture, but have low heat retention capacity. A vapor barrier should be provided on or near the room side wallface. Impervious surfaces within the wall should be insulated to keep them warmer than the dew point of the air contacting them. Provision should be made for the escape of water vapor to the outside. The wall should be detailed so that any condensation occurring within it will be collected and drained away via weeps as required.

THERMAL INSULATION

A low U-value of the wall is a good long term investment to minimize heat loss in cold weather or heat gain in hot weather. Such devices as minimizing the exposure of the framing members by using thermal breaks, employing insulating glass, and insulating opaque surfaces are recommended.

SOUND TRANSMISSION

By careful selection of details and materials, sound transmission characteristics of the metal and glass wall can be made equal to traditional construction.

Use of insulating glass improves behavior of the wall. Increased mass of the wall will reduce the transmission of sound.

FIRE STOPS

Prevention of the spread of fire will be implemented by continuous fire stopping between the curtain wall and the edge of each floor. Proper detailing with a quality insulation not subject to breakdown by fire and good field inspections will all help to avoid what can become an extremely dangerous condition.

CONCLUSION

The following items can be utilized to further refine the techniques of good curtain wall development and construction. It is necessary to work with the contractors or manufacturers who have specialized for a period of not less than five years in the fabrication and installation of a curtain wall. Visits to the various job sites and interviews with owner or managers will help give an overall view of their products. It is important at the start of design to work with basic metal, basic glass, and sealant producers' technical personnel when developing a metal curtain wall system. Before construction starts, wall testing should be done under both laboratory and field conditions. This is a highly desirable method and also leads to a greater success rate in construction of a good curtain wall.

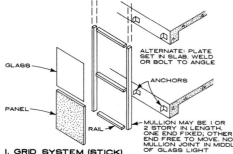

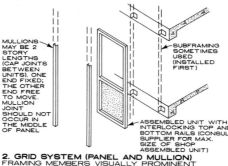

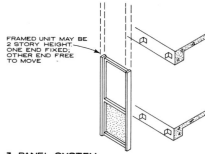

1. GRID SYSTEM (STICK)
FRAMING MEMBERS VISUALLY PROMINENT
COMPONENTS INSTALLED PIECE BY PIECE

2. GRID SYSTEM (PANEL AND MULLION)
FRAMING MEMBERS VISUALLY PROMINENT
PANEL PREASSEMBLED AND INSTALLED AS SHOWN

3. PANEL SYSTEM
COMPLETELY PREASSEMBLED UNITS; MAY OR MAY NOT
INCLUDE INTERIOR FINISH

CUSTOM TYPE

Walls designed specifically for one project, using specially designed parts and details. Such walls may be used on buildings of any height but are more typical of multistoried structures. Included in this category are the highly publicized (and often more expensive) walls that serve as design pacesetters.

COMMERCIAL TYPE

Walls made up principally of parts and details standardized by the manufacturer and assembled either in the manufacturer's stock patterns or in accord with the architect's design. This type is offered by many manufacturers and is commonly used on one and two story buildings, though it may be used on taller structures. Commercial walls cost less because of quantity production and also offer the advantages of proved performance.

INDUSTRIAL TYPE

Walls in which ribbed, fluted, or otherwise preformed metal sheets in stock sizes are used, along with standard metal sash, as the principal components. This type of metal curtain wall has a long history of satisfactory performance and, in its insulated form, finds wide use in many important buildings outside the industrial field.

CLASSIFICATION BY NATURE OF COMPONENTS AND BY USAGE

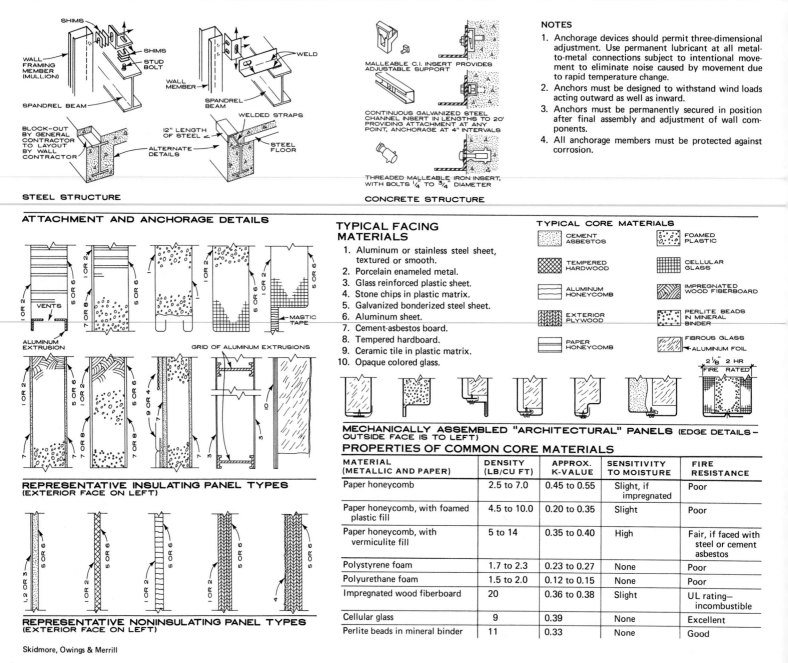

NOTES

1. Anchorage devices should permit three-dimensional adjustment. Use permanent lubricant at all metal-to-metal connections subject to intentional movement to eliminate noise caused by movement due to rapid temperature change.
2. Anchors must be designed to withstand wind loads acting outward as well as inward.
3. Anchors must be permanently secured in position after final assembly and adjustment of wall components.
4. All anchorage members must be protected against corrosion.

STEEL STRUCTURE

CONCRETE STRUCTURE

ATTACHMENT AND ANCHORAGE DETAILS

REPRESENTATIVE INSULATING PANEL TYPES
(EXTERIOR FACE ON LEFT)

REPRESENTATIVE NONINSULATING PANEL TYPES
(EXTERIOR FACE ON LEFT)

TYPICAL FACING MATERIALS

1. Aluminum or stainless steel sheet, textured or smooth.
2. Porcelain enameled metal.
3. Glass reinforced plastic sheet.
4. Stone chips in plastic matrix.
5. Galvanized bonderized steel sheet.
6. Aluminum sheet.
7. Cement-asbestos board.
8. Tempered hardboard.
9. Ceramic tile in plastic matrix.
10. Opaque colored glass.

TYPICAL CORE MATERIALS

CEMENT ASBESTOS
FOAMED PLASTIC
TEMPERED HARDWOOD
CELLULAR GLASS
ALUMINUM HONEYCOMB
IMPREGNATED WOOD FIBERBOARD
EXTERIOR PLYWOOD
PERLITE BEADS IN MINERAL BINDER
PAPER HONEYCOMB
FIBROUS GLASS ALUMINUM FOIL

MECHANICALLY ASSEMBLED "ARCHITECTURAL" PANELS (EDGE DETAILS—OUTSIDE FACE IS TO LEFT)

PROPERTIES OF COMMON CORE MATERIALS

MATERIAL (METALLIC AND PAPER)	DENSITY (LB/CU FT)	APPROX. K-VALUE	SENSITIVITY TO MOISTURE	FIRE RESISTANCE
Paper honeycomb	2.5 to 7.0	0.45 to 0.55	Slight, if impregnated	Poor
Paper honeycomb, with foamed plastic fill	4.5 to 10.0	0.20 to 0.35	Slight	Poor
Paper honeycomb, with vermiculite fill	5 to 14	0.35 to 0.40	High	Fair, if faced with steel or cement asbestos
Polystyrene foam	1.7 to 2.3	0.23 to 0.27	None	Poor
Polyurethane foam	1.5 to 2.0	0.12 to 0.15	None	Poor
Impregnated wood fiberboard	20	0.36 to 0.38	Slight	UL rating—incombustible
Cellular glass	9	0.39	None	Excellent
Perlite beads in mineral binder	11	0.33	None	Good

Skidmore, Owings & Merrill

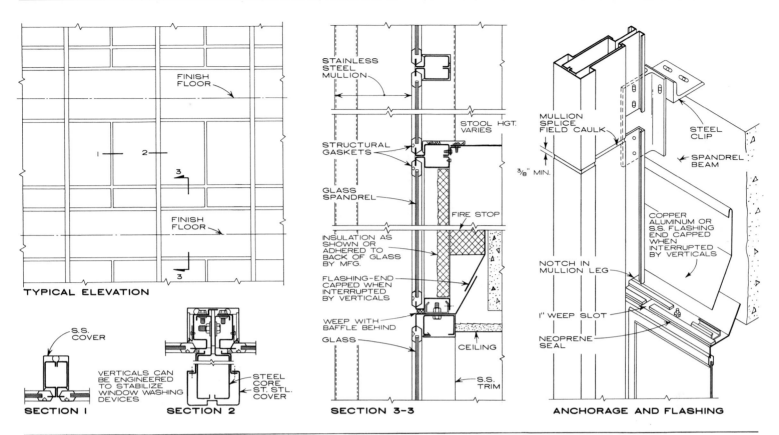

TYPICAL ELEVATION

FINISH FLOOR

FINISH FLOOR

S.S. COVER

SECTION 1

VERTICALS CAN BE ENGINEERED TO STABILIZE WINDOW WASHING DEVICES

STEEL CORE ST. STL. COVER

SECTION 2

STAINLESS STEEL MULLION

STOOL HGT. VARIES

STRUCTURAL GASKETS

GLASS SPANDREL

FIRE STOP

INSULATION AS SHOWN OR ADHERED TO BACK OF GLASS BY MFG.

FLASHING-END CAPPED WHEN INTERRUPTED BY VERTICALS

WEEP WITH BAFFLE BEHIND

GLASS

CEILING

S.S. TRIM

SECTION 3-3

MULLION SPLICE FIELD CAULK

3/8" MIN.

STEEL CLIP

SPANDREL BEAM

COPPER ALUMINUM OR S.S. FLASHING END CAPPED WHEN INTERRUPTED BY VERTICALS

NOTCH IN MULLION LEG

1" WEEP SLOT

NEOPRENE SEAL

ANCHORAGE AND FLASHING

GRID SYSTEM (STICK)–CUSTOM TYPE–STAINLESS STEEL–GASKETED–MULTISTORY PANEL AND MULLION SYSTEM USING STRUCTURAL GASKETS

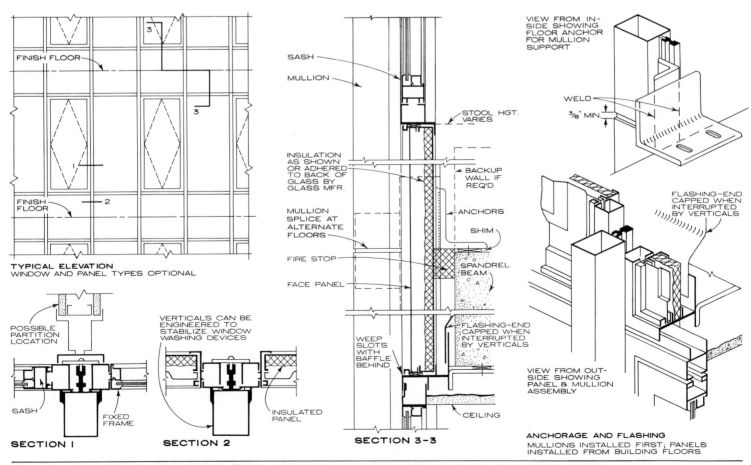

TYPICAL ELEVATION
WINDOW AND PANEL TYPES OPTIONAL

FINISH FLOOR

FINISH FLOOR

POSSIBLE PARTITION LOCATION

SASH

FIXED FRAME

SECTION 1

VERTICALS CAN BE ENGINEERED TO STABILIZE WINDOW WASHING DEVICES

INSULATED PANEL

SECTION 2

SASH

MULLION

STOOL HGT. VARIES

INSULATION AS SHOWN OR ADHERED TO BACK OF GLASS BY GLASS MFR.

MULLION SPLICE AT ALTERNATE FLOORS

FIRE STOP

FACE PANEL

WEEP SLOTS WITH BAFFLE BEHIND

BACKUP WALL IF REQ'D

ANCHORS

SHIM

SPANDREL BEAM

FLASHING-END CAPPED WHEN INTERRUPTED BY VERTICALS

CEILING

SECTION 3-3

VIEW FROM INSIDE SHOWING FLOOR ANCHOR FOR MULLION SUPPORT

WELD

3/8" MIN.

FLASHING-END CAPPED WHEN INTERRUPTED BY VERTICALS

VIEW FROM OUTSIDE SHOWING PANEL & MULLION ASSEMBLY

ANCHORAGE AND FLASHING
MULLIONS INSTALLED FIRST; PANELS INSTALLED FROM BUILDING FLOORS

GRID SYSTEM (STICK)–COMMERCIAL TYPE–ALUMINUM–TYPICAL MULTISTORY PANEL–AND–MULLION DESIGN

Skidmore, Owings & Merrill

WINDOW WALLS   8

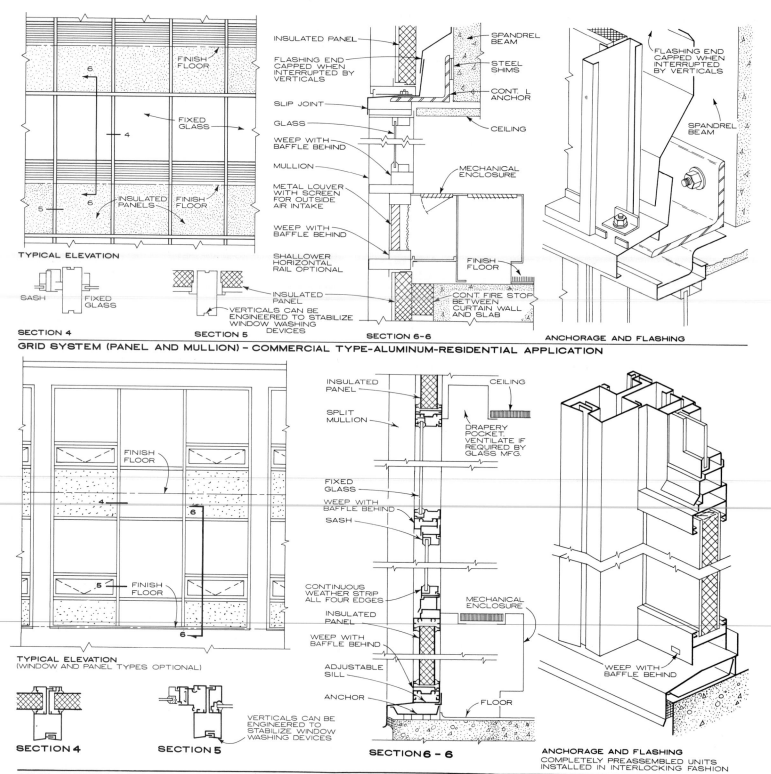

TYPICAL ELEVATION

SASH   FIXED GLASS

SECTION 4

SECTION 5

VERTICALS CAN BE ENGINEERED TO STABILIZE WINDOW WASHING DEVICES

INSULATED PANEL

SECTION 6-6

ANCHORAGE AND FLASHING

INSULATED PANEL
FLASHING END CAPPED WHEN INTERRUPTED BY VERTICALS
SLIP JOINT
GLASS
WEEP WITH BAFFLE BEHIND
MULLION
METAL LOUVER WITH SCREEN FOR OUTSIDE AIR INTAKE
WEEP WITH BAFFLE BEHIND
SHALLOWER HORIZONTAL RAIL OPTIONAL
INSULATED PANEL

SPANDREL BEAM
STEEL SHIMS
CONT. L ANCHOR
CEILING
MECHANICAL ENCLOSURE
FINISH FLOOR
CONT. FIRE STOP BETWEEN CURTAIN WALL AND SLAB

FLASHING END CAPPED WHEN INTERRUPTED BY VERTICALS
SPANDREL BEAM

GRID SYSTEM (PANEL AND MULLION) – COMMERCIAL TYPE-ALUMINUM-RESIDENTIAL APPLICATION

TYPICAL ELEVATION
(WINDOW AND PANEL TYPES OPTIONAL)

FINISH FLOOR

SECTION 4

SECTION 5

VERTICALS CAN BE ENGINEERED TO STABILIZE WINDOW WASHING DEVICES

SECTION 6 - 6

INSULATED PANEL
SPLIT MULLION
FIXED GLASS
WEEP WITH BAFFLE BEHIND
SASH
CONTINUOUS WEATHER STRIP ALL FOUR EDGES
INSULATED PANEL
WEEP WITH BAFFLE BEHIND
ADJUSTABLE SILL
ANCHOR

CEILING
DRAPERY POCKET. VENTILATE IF REQUIRED BY GLASS MFG.
MECHANICAL ENCLOSURE
FLOOR

ANCHORAGE AND FLASHING
COMPLETELY PREASSEMBLED UNITS INSTALLED IN INTERLOCKING FASHION

WEEP WITH BAFFLE BEHIND

PANEL SYSTEM-COMMERCIAL TYPE-ALUMINUM-RESIDENTIAL APPLICATION

GENERAL NOTES

1. All metal parts that extend through the wall and are exposed on both exterior and interior of the building should include a thermal break (especially if they are of aluminum).

2. When mullions serve as guide rails for roof mounted window washing platforms or "rigs," mullions should be designed as a track and reinforced against thrust, using information on loads from cleaning equipment manufacturers.

3. It is considered good practice when developing curtain walls construction to consult with a single firm that has specialized in fabrication and installation of all components of metal and glass wall

assemblies.

4. Separate unlike metals or alloys with a heavy coating of bituminous paint or zinc chromate or by hot dipped galvanizing of ferrous metals to prevent destructive galvanic action in the presence of moisture.

5. To allow for building movement (caused by wind forces and normal temperature fluctuation) and erection tolerances and to avoid sudden noises (caused by thermal expansion or contraction), elongated or oversized holes for attaching wall assemblies should be provided but separated with nylon, teflon, or similar permanent lubricating materials.

6. Metal curtain wall systems shown here are only examples. Different composite systems can be made up from various components.

7. All buildings (both lowrise and highrise) that have sleeping facilities must be equipped with natural ventilation/operating sash. Check with local governing bodies for requirements.

8. Single glazing in metal curtain walls today would be considered energy consuming; however, large glass areas are still appropriate if insulating glass (both double and triple) and tinted/reflective glass glazing systems are used. Consult glass manufacturers for current information.

Skidmore, Owings & Merrill

GENERAL NOTES FOR ALL WOOD DOORS:

Kiln dried wood, moisture content @ 6–12%.

Type 1 doors: Fully waterproof bond ext. and int.
Type 11 doors: Water resistant bond. Interior only.

Tolerances: Height, width, thickness, squareness and warp per NWMA STANDARDS and vary with solid vs. built-up construction.

Prefit: Doors @ $1/16''$ less in width and $1/8''$ less in height than nominal size, ± $1/32''$ tolerance, with vertical edges eased.

Premachining: Doors mortised for locks and cut out for hinges when so specified.
Grading:

Premium: For transparent finish. Good/custom: For paint or transparent finish. Sound: For paint, with 2 coats completely covering defects.

FLUSH WOOD DOORS:
CORE MATERIAL
SOLID CORES:

Wood block, single specie, @ $2^{1}/_{2}''$ max. width, surfaced two sides, without spaces or defects impairing strength or visible thru hdwd. veneer facing.

HOLLOW CORES:

Wood, wood derivative, or class A insulation board.

TYPES OF WOOD FACES:

Standard thickness face veneers @ $1/16''–1/32''$, bonded to hardwood, crossband @ $1/10''–1/16''$. Most economical and widely used, inhibits checking, difficult to refinish or repair face damage, for use on all cores.

$1/8''$ Sawn veneers, bonded to crossband, easily refinished and repaired.

For use on staved block and stile and rail solid cores.
$1/4''$ Sawn veneers: same as $1/8''$ but without crossband on stile and rail solid cores with horizontal blocks. Decorative grooves can be cut into faces.

LIGHT & LOUVER OPENINGS:

Custom made to specifications. Wood beads and slats to match face veneer. 5'' min. between opening and edge of door.

Hollow core: Cut-out area max. $1/2$ height of door. Door not guaranteed with openings greater than 40%. Exterior doors: Weatherproofing required to prevent moisture from leaking into core.

FACTORY FINISHING:

Partial: Sealing coats applied, final job finish.
Complete: Requires prefit and premachining.

SPECIAL FACING:

High or medium-low density overlay faces of phenolic resins and cellulose fibers fused to inner faces of hardwood in lieu of final veneers as base for final opaque finish only.

$1/16''$ min. laminated plastic bonded to $1/16''$ min. wood back of two or more piles.

$1/8''$ hardboard, smooth one or two sides.

SPECIAL CORES:
SOUND INSULATING DOORS:

Thicknesses $1^{3}/_{4}''$, $2^{1}/_{4}''$. Transmission loss rating C Stc 36 for $1^{3}/_{4}''$, 42 for $2^{1}/_{4}''$. Barrier faces separated by a void or damping compound to keep faces from vibrating in unison. Special stops, gaskets, and threshold devices required. Mfrs. requirements as to wd. frames and wall specs.

FIRE RATED DOORS:

$3/4$ hr "C" label and 1 hr "B" label-maximum size 4'0'' x 10'0''.
$1^{1}/_{2}$ hr "B" label-maximum size 4'0'' x 9'0''. All doors $1^{3}/_{4}''$ minimum thickness.

LEAD LINED DOORS:

See U/L requirements. Optional location within door construction of $1/32''$ to $1/2''$ continuous lead sheet from edge to edge which may be reinforced with lead bolts or glued.

GROUNDED DOORS:

Wire mesh located at center of core, grounded with copper wire through hinges to frame.

TYPES OF HOLLOW CORE DOORS:

ACOUSTICAL DAMPING MATERIAL

HARDBOARD CROSSBAND

HARDBOARD FACE

ACOUSTICAL DOOR:
Uses gasketed stops and neoprene bottom seals to cut sound transmission.

HONEYCOMB FIBER:
INSTITUTIONAL:
With cross rail.
INTERIOR:
Without cross rail. Uniform core of honeycomb fiber to form $1/2''$ air cells.

IMPLANTED BLANKS:
Spirals or other forms separated or joined, implanted between & supporting outer faces of door.

MESH:
Interlocked, horizontal & vertical strips, equally spaced, notched into stiles, or expandable cellular or honey-comb core.

TYPES OF SOLID CORES:

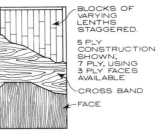

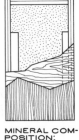

BLOCKS OF VARYING LENTHS STAGGERED.

5 PLY CONSTRUCTION SHOWN; 7 PLY, USING 3 PLY FACES AVAILABLE

CROSS BAND

FACE

CONTINUOUS BLOCK STAVED CORE:
Bonded staggered blocks bonded to face panels. Most widely used & economical solid core.

FRAMED BLOCK STAVED CORE:
Non-bonded staggered blocks laid up within stile rail frame, bonded to face panels.

STILE AND RAIL:
Horizontal blocks when cross banding is not used. Vertical panel blocks when cross banding is used.

PARTICLE BOARD:
Extremely heavy, more soundproof, economical door, available in hardwood face veneer or high pressure laminate face.

MINERAL COMPOSITION:
Lightest weight of all cores. Details, as cut-outs, difficult. Low screw holding strength.

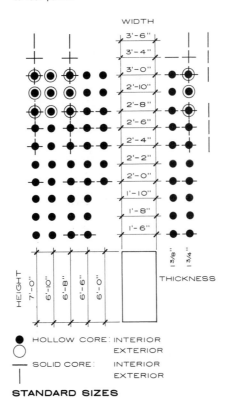

WIDTH

3'-6''
3'-4''
3'-0''
2'-10''
2'-8''
2'-6''
2'-4''
2'-2''
2'-0''
1'-10''
1'-8''
1'-6''

HEIGHT
7'-0'' 6'-10'' 6'-8'' 6'-6'' 6'-0''

THICKNESS

● HOLLOW CORE: INTERIOR / EXTERIOR
○ SOLID CORE: INTERIOR / EXTERIOR
|

STANDARD SIZES

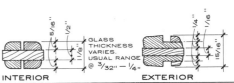

GLASS THICKNESS VARIES. USUAL RANGE @ $3/32''–1/4''$

INTERIOR   EXTERIOR
MUNTIN BARS

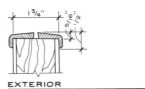

EXTERIOR   EXTERIOR
PROJECTED

INTERIOR   INTERIOR
FLUSH

ROUND EDGE   FLAT SLAT   SIGHTPROOF
LOUVERS · METAL LOUVERS ALSO AVAILABLE
STOCK OPENING AND LOUVER DETAIL

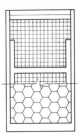

GLASS AND WOOD PANEL DOORS

CONSTRUCTION

Solid pine or built-up stiles, rails and vertical members or mullions, doweled as in NWMA std.

BUILT-UP MEMBERS

Core as in solid core of flush doors.
Edge and end strips as in flush doors.
Face veneers: Hdwd. @ 1/8" min.

PANELS

Flat: 3 ply hdwd. or soft.
Raised—2 sides: Solid hdwd. or soft or built-up of 2 or more plies.

STICKING, GLASS STOPS, AND MUNTINS

Cove or bead or ovolo, solid, matching face.

KEY TO SYMBOLS

● Hardwood veneer.
○ Ponderosa pine.
— 1 light & divided light.
Divided lights @
8: Lights @ 2 wide 4 high.
10: Lights @ 2 wide 5 high.
12: Lights @ 3 wide 4 high.
15: Lights @ 3 wide 5 high.
5 horizontal lights.
Interior:
Hdwd. veneer: Available in all sizes.
Pond. pine: 12 & 15 lights.
Not available @ 2'-0" wide.
Exterior:
Hdwd. veneer only.
Available in all sizes.

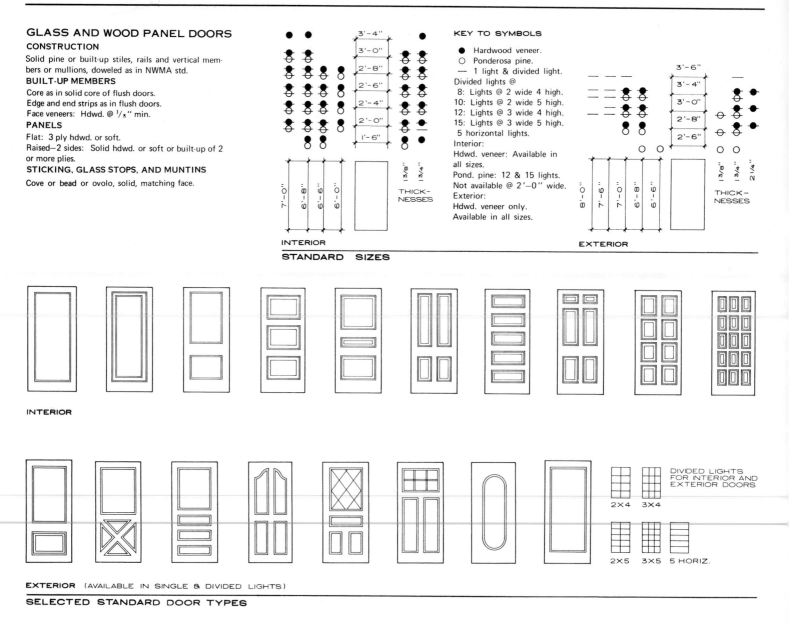

STANDARD SIZES

INTERIOR

EXTERIOR   (AVAILABLE IN SINGLE & DIVIDED LIGHTS)

SELECTED STANDARD DOOR TYPES

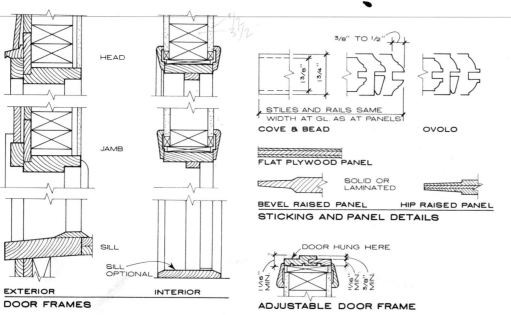

DOOR FRAMES

STICKING AND PANEL DETAILS

ADJUSTABLE DOOR FRAME

JALOUSIES

1 3/4" rim type door as in panel door construction with square sticking and fitted with full or half alum. framed inserts housing 4" high clear or obscure glass louvers.
Usual widths @ 2'-6", 2'-8", and 3'-0".
Heights standard.

Simultaneous louver activation outward (similar to venetian blind) by roto operator.

Full frame with 17 louvers with double operators for top 9 and lower 8.

Half frame with 8 louvers—single operators.

Left or right side operation with jambs punched for both and metal plate to cover side not used.

Storm sash/screens on interior.

DUTCH DOORS

Divided door with top half independent of lower. Horiz. meeting rail w/ or w/o interior shelf. Provide WS, separate locking devices and joining hardware for both leaves to act in unison.

SCREEN/STORM DOORS

1 1/8" screen, storm or combination doors. 1" greater height than nom. due to sill bevel. Combination: Interchange screen/glass inserts.

See index for garage doors and for hardware for doors.

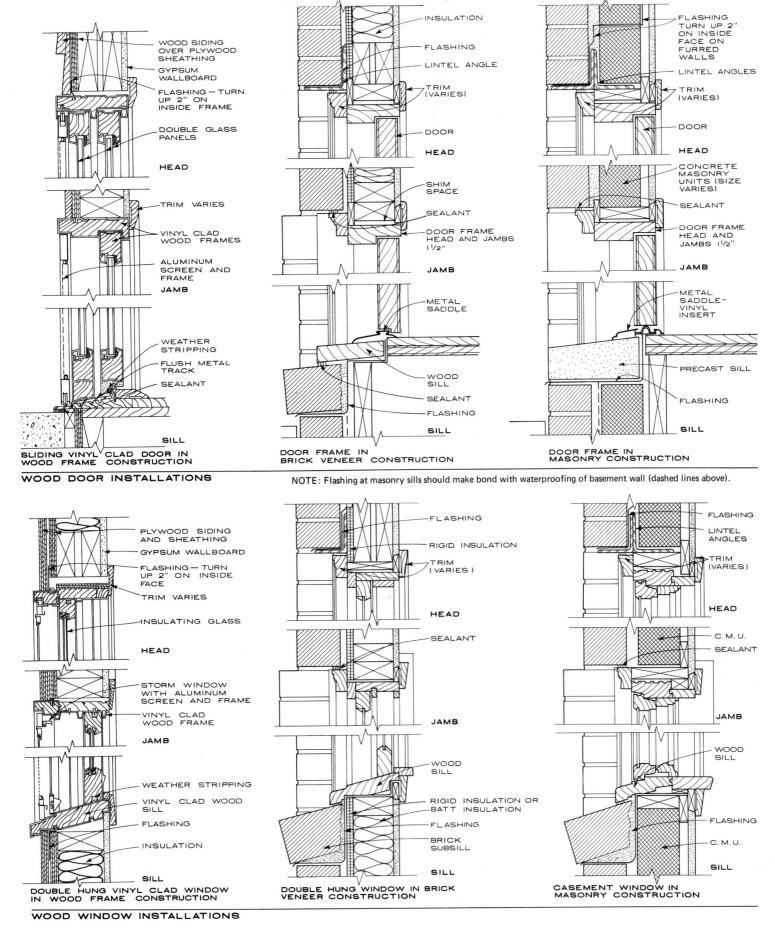

WOOD SIDING OVER PLYWOOD SHEATHING
GYPSUM WALLBOARD
FLASHING — TURN UP 2" ON INSIDE FRAME
DOUBLE GLASS PANELS

HEAD

TRIM VARIES
VINYL CLAD WOOD FRAMES
ALUMINUM SCREEN AND FRAME

JAMB

WEATHER STRIPPING
FLUSH METAL TRACK
SEALANT

SILL

SLIDING VINYL CLAD DOOR IN WOOD FRAME CONSTRUCTION

INSULATION
FLASHING
LINTEL ANGLE
TRIM (VARIES)
DOOR

HEAD

SHIM SPACE
SEALANT
DOOR FRAME HEAD AND JAMBS 1½"

JAMB

METAL SADDLE
WOOD SILL
SEALANT
FLASHING

SILL

DOOR FRAME IN BRICK VENEER CONSTRUCTION

FLASHING TURN UP 2" ON INSIDE FACE ON FURRED WALLS
LINTEL ANGLES
TRIM (VARIES)
DOOR

HEAD

CONCRETE MASONRY UNITS (SIZE VARIES)
SEALANT
DOOR FRAME HEAD AND JAMBS 1½"

JAMB

METAL SADDLE-VINYL INSERT
PRECAST SILL
FLASHING

SILL

DOOR FRAME IN MASONRY CONSTRUCTION

WOOD DOOR INSTALLATIONS

NOTE: Flashing at masonry sills should make bond with waterproofing of basement wall (dashed lines above).

PLYWOOD SIDING AND SHEATHING
GYPSUM WALLBOARD
FLASHING — TURN UP 2" ON INSIDE FACE
TRIM VARIES
INSULATING GLASS

HEAD

STORM WINDOW WITH ALUMINUM SCREEN AND FRAME
VINYL CLAD WOOD FRAME

JAMB

WEATHER STRIPPING
VINYL CLAD WOOD SILL
FLASHING
INSULATION

SILL

DOUBLE HUNG VINYL CLAD WINDOW IN WOOD FRAME CONSTRUCTION

FLASHING
RIGID INSULATION
TRIM (VARIES)

HEAD

SEALANT

JAMB

WOOD SILL
RIGID INSULATION OR BATT INSULATION
FLASHING
BRICK SUBSILL

SILL

DOUBLE HUNG WINDOW IN BRICK VENEER CONSTRUCTION

FLASHING
LINTEL ANGLES
TRIM (VARIES)

HEAD

C.M.U.
SEALANT

JAMB

WOOD SILL
FLASHING
C.M.U.

SILL

CASEMENT WINDOW IN MASONRY CONSTRUCTION

WOOD WINDOW INSTALLATIONS

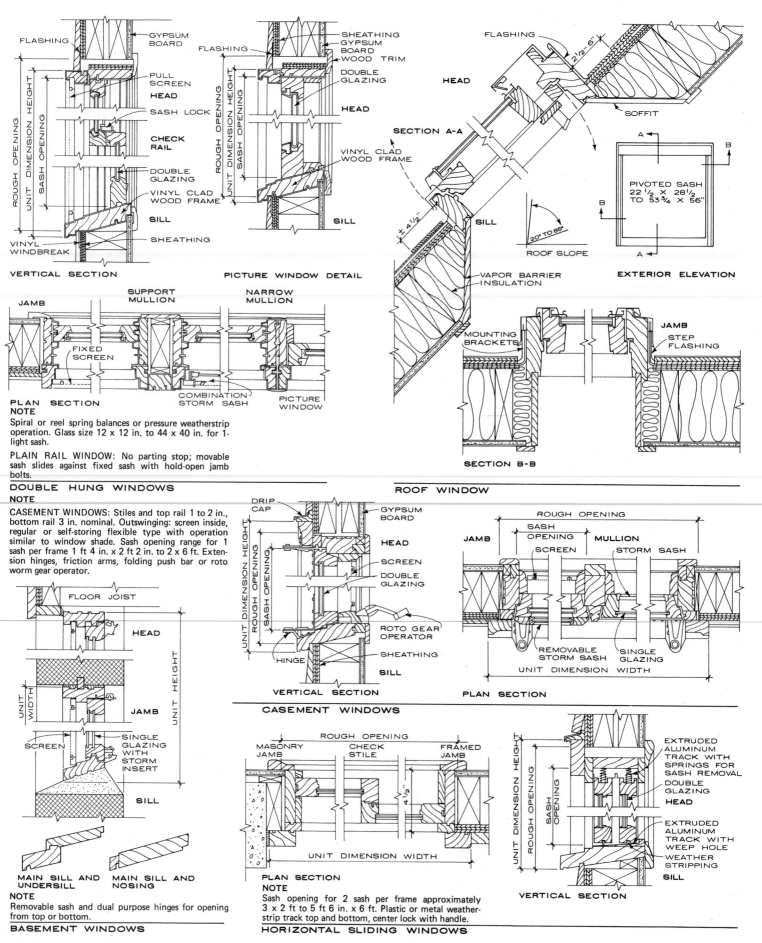

VERTICAL SECTION

PICTURE WINDOW DETAIL

SECTION A-A

ROOF SLOPE 20° TO 85°

EXTERIOR ELEVATION

PIVOTED SASH 22½ × 28½ TO 53¾ × 56"

SECTION B-B

ROOF WINDOW

PLAN SECTION

NOTE
Spiral or reel spring balances or pressure weatherstrip operation. Glass size 12 × 12 in. to 44 × 40 in. for 1-light sash.

PLAIN RAIL WINDOW: No parting stop; movable sash slides against fixed sash with hold-open jamb bolts.

DOUBLE HUNG WINDOWS

NOTE
CASEMENT WINDOWS: Stiles and top rail 1 to 2 in., bottom rail 3 in. nominal. Outswinging: screen inside, regular or self-storing flexible type with operation similar to window shade. Sash opening range for 1 sash per frame 1 ft 4 in. × 2 ft 2 in. to 2 × 6 ft. Extension hinges, friction arms, folding push bar or roto worm gear operator.

VERTICAL SECTION

PLAN SECTION

CASEMENT WINDOWS

MAIN SILL AND UNDERSILL   **MAIN SILL AND NOSING**

NOTE
Removable sash and dual purpose hinges for opening from top or bottom.

BASEMENT WINDOWS

PLAN SECTION

NOTE
Sash opening for 2 sash per frame approximately 3 × 2 ft to 5 ft 6 in. × 6 ft. Plastic or metal weather-strip track top and bottom, center lock with handle.

HORIZONTAL SLIDING WINDOWS

VERTICAL SECTION

Carleton Granbery, FAIA; Guilford, Connecticut

⑧ **WOOD DOORS AND WINDOWS**

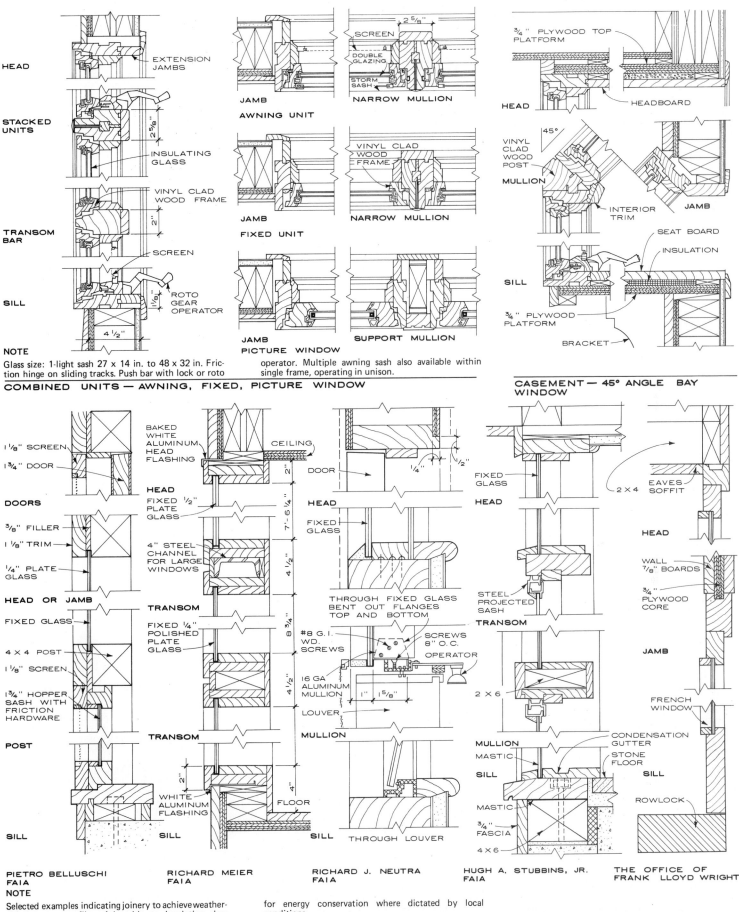

HEAD
EXTENSION JAMBS

STACKED UNITS
2 5/8"
INSULATING GLASS

VINYL CLAD WOOD FRAME

TRANSOM BAR
2"
SCREEN

SILL
1/8"
ROTO GEAR OPERATOR

4 1/2"

NOTE
Glass size: 1-light sash 27 x 14 in. to 48 x 32 in. Friction hinge on sliding tracks. Push bar with lock or roto operator. Multiple awning sash also available within single frame, operating in unison.

JAMB
AWNING UNIT

SCREEN
2 5/8"
DOUBLE GLAZING
STORM SASH
NARROW MULLION

JAMB
FIXED UNIT

VINYL CLAD WOOD FRAME
NARROW MULLION

JAMB
PICTURE WINDOW

SUPPORT MULLION

3/4" PLYWOOD TOP PLATFORM
HEAD
HEADBOARD

45°
VINYL CLAD WOOD POST
MULLION
INTERIOR TRIM
JAMB

SEAT BOARD
INSULATION
SILL
3/4" PLYWOOD PLATFORM
BRACKET

CASEMENT — 45° ANGLE BAY WINDOW

COMBINED UNITS — AWNING, FIXED, PICTURE WINDOW

1 1/8" SCREEN
1 3/4" DOOR
DOORS

3/8" FILLER
1 1/8" TRIM
1/4" PLATE GLASS
HEAD OR JAMB
FIXED GLASS
4 x 4 POST
1 1/8" SCREEN
1 3/4" HOPPER SASH WITH FRICTION HARDWARE
POST

SILL

BAKED WHITE ALUMINUM HEAD FLASHING
CEILING
HEAD
FIXED 1/2" PLATE GLASS
4" STEEL CHANNEL FOR LARGE WINDOWS
TRANSOM
FIXED 1/4" POLISHED PLATE GLASS
2"
7'-6 1/4"
4 1/2"
8 3/4"
4 1/2"
TRANSOM
2"
WHITE ALUMINUM FLASHING
SILL

DOOR
1/2"
1/4"
2"
HEAD
FIXED GLASS
THROUGH FIXED GLASS BENT OUT FLANGES TOP AND BOTTOM
#8 G.I. WD. SCREWS
SCREWS 8" O.C.
OPERATOR
16 GA ALUMINUM MULLION
1" 1 5/8"
LOUVER
MULLION
SILL
THROUGH LOUVER
FLOOR

FIXED GLASS
HEAD
FIXED GLASS
STEEL PROJECTED SASH
TRANSOM
2 x 6
MULLION
MASTIC
SILL
MASTIC
3/4" FASCIA
4 x 6
CONDENSATION GUTTER
STONE FLOOR

2 x 4
EAVES SOFFIT
HEAD
WALL 7/8" BOARDS
3/4" PLYWOOD CORE
JAMB
FRENCH WINDOW
SILL
ROWLOCK

PIETRO BELLUSCHI FAIA
RICHARD MEIER FAIA
RICHARD J. NEUTRA FAIA
HUGH A. STUBBINS, JR. FAIA
THE OFFICE OF FRANK LLOYD WRIGHT

NOTE
Selected examples indicating joinery to achieve weathertight narrow profiles. Adaptable to insulating glass for energy conservation where dictated by local conditions.

CUSTOM DETAILS — FIXED GLASS, HOPPER, CASEMENTS, JALOUSIE, AWNING, AND TRANSOM SASH

Carleton Granbery, FAIA; Guilford, Connecticut

FRAMING ARRANGEMENTS

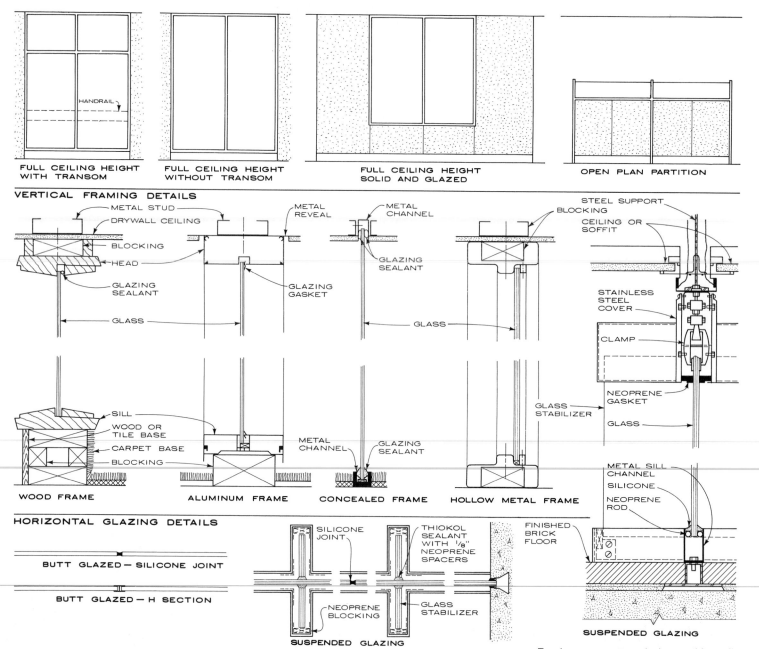

FULL CEILING HEIGHT WITH TRANSOM

FULL CEILING HEIGHT WITHOUT TRANSOM

FULL CEILING HEIGHT SOLID AND GLAZED

OPEN PLAN PARTITION

VERTICAL FRAMING DETAILS

METAL STUD
DRYWALL CEILING
BLOCKING
HEAD
GLAZING SEALANT
GLASS
HANDRAIL

METAL REVEAL
GLAZING GASKET

METAL CHANNEL
GLAZING SEALANT
GLASS

STEEL SUPPORT
BLOCKING
CEILING OR SOFFIT
STAINLESS STEEL COVER
CLAMP
NEOPRENE GASKET
GLASS

SILL
WOOD OR TILE BASE
CARPET BASE
BLOCKING
WOOD FRAME

ALUMINUM FRAME

METAL CHANNEL
GLAZING SEALANT
CONCEALED FRAME

GLASS STABILIZER
HOLLOW METAL FRAME

METAL SILL CHANNEL
SILICONE
NEOPRENE ROD
FINISHED BRICK FLOOR
SUSPENDED GLAZING

HORIZONTAL GLAZING DETAILS

BUTT GLAZED — SILICONE JOINT

BUTT GLAZED — H SECTION

SILICONE JOINT
THIOKOL SEALANT WITH 1/8" NEOPRENE SPACERS
NEOPRENE BLOCKING
GLASS STABILIZER
SUSPENDED GLAZING

GLASS TYPES AND SIZES

TYPE	THICK-NESS (IN.)	MAXIMUM SIZE		WEIGHT (LB/SQ FT)
		WIDTH (IN.)	LENGTH (IN.)	
Standard	$1\,3/16$	48	80	2.5
Sound control 250–4000 cps	$9/32$	48	154	3.5
	$7/16$	48	154	5.1
	$1/2$	48	154	6.3
	$3/4$	48	154	9.6
Burglary resisting and bullet proof	$5/16$	48	154	3.6
	$7/16$	48	154	5.2
	$9/16$	48	154	6.4
	$1\,3/16$	48	120	14.1
	$1\,5/8$	48	120	20.7
	$1\,3/4$	48	120	21.7
	$2\,1/4$	48	120	28.7
Security for prisons, mental institutions and zoos	$1\,3/16$	48	144	9.7
	$7/8$	48	120	10.5

Walter H. Sobel, FAIA & Associates; Chicago, Illinois

NOTES

Interior glazed partitions are available in various standard hollow metal, aluminum, and wood framing systems. Many standard systems may not be suitable to the architect's design, however. For this reason most systems are custom-made to fit the application.

1. SIZES: Depending on the manufacturer, frames are available in any width or height. Check dimension limitations specified by glass manufacturer.
2. FRAME FINISH MATERIALS: Framing components are available in various finishes that can be matched to any texture or color.
3. PERFORMANCE: Interior partitions can be installed temporarily or permanently. Every form for corners and intersections is available. Check with manufacturer for data on fire ratings, sound transmission, deflection, and other requirements.
4. TYPES: Suspended plate glass panels make uninterrupted transparent walls. Each light is suspended from the structural system by specially designed clamps. For excessive heights, glass stabilizers are used to brace both sides of each panel, providing extra stability without interrupting the upward sweep of the glass.

Translucent or patterned glass partitions allow partial transmission of light while maintaining a reasonable degree of privacy. Primary applications include bathtub and shower enclosures, clerestories, and any area where obscured vision is desired.

One-way glass allows for one-way viewing in security areas where inconspicuous observation is desired.

Laminated safety glass and wire glass should be considered for use in corridors, stairwells, and security areas. Any glass adjacent to an opening is to be approved safety glass.

Laminated safety glass is manufactured by sandwiching sheets of polyvinyl butyral between two or more lights of plate, float, or sheet glass. Should the glass be broken, fragments adhere safely to the interlayer.

Pinstriped wire glass is primarily selected for its sophisticated modern appearance; it is also used in hazardous locations, as defined by applicable codes and state laws.

Tempered glass is four to five times stronger than regular annealed glass. Produced with a special heat treatment, this glass resists breakage. Should the glass be broken, it disintegrates into pebblelike particles.

WOOD DOORS AND WINDOWS

CHAPTER 9   FINISHES

TYPES OF GYPSUM PANEL PRODUCTS

DESCRIPTION	THICKNESS (IN.)	WIDTH/EDGE (FT)	STOCK LENGTH (FT)
Regular gypsum wallboard used as a base layer for improving sound control; repair and remodeling	1/4	4, square or tapered	8-10
Regular gypsum wallboard used in a double wall system over wood framing; repair and remodeling	3/8	4, square or tapered	8-14
Regular gypsum wallboard for use in single layer construction	1/2, 5/8	4, square or tapered	8-16
Rounded taper edge system offers maximum joint strength and minimizes joint deformity problems	3/8 1/2, 5/8	4, rounded taper	8-16
Type X gypsum wallboard with core containing special additives to give increased fire resistance ratings. Consult manufacturer for approved assemblies	1/2, 5/8	4, tapered, rounded taper, or rounded	8-16
Aluminum foil backed board effective as a vapor barrier for exterior walls and ceilings and as a thermal insulator when foil faces 3/4" minimum air space. Not for use as a tile base or in air conditioned buildings in hot, humid climates (Southern Atlantic and Gulf Coasts)	3/8 1/2, 5/8	4, square or tapered	8-16
Water resistant board for use as a base for ceramic and other nonabsorbant wall tiles in bath and shower areas. Type X core is available	1/2, 5/8	4, tapered	8, 10, 12
Prefinished vinyl surface gypsum board in standard and special colors	1/2, 5/8	2, 2 1/2, 4, square and beveled	8, 9, 10
Prefinished board available in many colors and textures. See manufacturers' literature	5/16	4, square	8
Coreboard for use to enclose vent shafts and laminated gypsum partitions	1	2, tongue and groove or square	4-16
Shaft wall liner core board type X with gypsum core used to enclose elevator shafts and other vertical chases	1, 2	2, square or beveled	6-16
Sound underlayment gypsum wallboard attached to plywood subfloor acts as a base for any durable floor covering. When used with resiliently attached gypsum panel ceiling, the assembly meets HUD requirements for sound control in multifamily dwellings	3/4	4, square	6-8
Exterior ceiling/soffit panel for use on surfaces with indirect exposure to the weather	1/2	4, rounded taper	8, 12
Sheathing used as underlayment on exterior walls with type X or regular core	1/2	2, tongue and groove	8
	1/2, 5/8	4, square	8, 9, 10

NOTE: A large range of adhesives, sealants, joint treatments, and texture products are available from the manufacturers of most gypsum board products. Consult available literature for current recommendations and products.

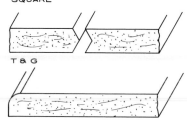

TAPERED

BEVELED

SQUARE

T & G

ROUNDED

ROUNDED TAPER

TYPES OF EDGES

MAX. BENDING FOR DRYWALL

BENDING RADII		
THICKNESS	LENGTHWISE	WIDTH
1/4"	5'-0"	15'-0"
3/8"	7'-6"	25'-0"
1/2"	20'-0"	

Shorter radii may be obtained by moistening face and back so that water will soak well into core of board.

MAXIMUM ALLOWABLE PARTITION HEIGHT

STUD SPACING (IN.) (FACING ON EACH SIDE)	STUD DEPTH (IN.)				
	1 5/8 *	2 1/2	3 1/4	3 5/8	4
	MAXIMUM ALLOWABLE HEIGHT				
16 (1/2 one-ply)	11'-0"	14'-8"	17'-10"	19'-5"	20'-8"
24 (1/2 one-ply)	10'-0"	13'-5"	16'-0"	17'-3"	18'-5"
24 (1/2 two-ply)	12'-4"	15'-10"	18'-3"	19'-5"	20'-8"

*1 5/8" stud with single layer of gypsum wallboard recommended for chase walls and closets only.

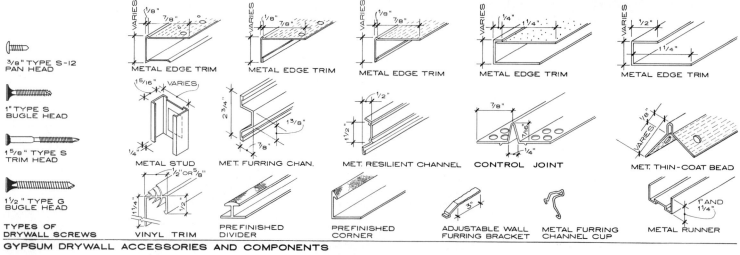

3/8" TYPE S-12 PAN HEAD

1" TYPE S BUGLE HEAD

1 5/8" TYPE S TRIM HEAD

1 1/2" TYPE G BUGLE HEAD

TYPES OF DRYWALL SCREWS

METAL EDGE TRIM

METAL EDGE TRIM

METAL EDGE TRIM

METAL EDGE TRIM

METAL EDGE TRIM

METAL STUD

MET. FURRING CHAN.

MET. RESILIENT CHANNEL

CONTROL JOINT

MET. THIN-COAT BEAD

VINYL TRIM

PREFINISHED DIVIDER

PREFINISHED CORNER

ADJUSTABLE WALL FURRING BRACKET

METAL FURRING CHANNEL CUP

METAL RUNNER

GYPSUM DRYWALL ACCESSORIES AND COMPONENTS

Ferdinand R. Scheeler, AIA; Skidmore, Owings and Merrill; Chicago, Illinois

James Lloyd; Kennett Square, Pennsylvania

9 GYPSUM WALLBOARD

FIRE RATING	STC	WALL THICKNESS	CONSTRUCTION DESCRIPTION	WALL SECTIONS
1 HOUR	30 TO 34	4 7/8"	One layer 1/2 in. type X veneer base nailed to each side of 2 x 4 in. wood studs 16 in. o.c. with 5d coated nails 8 in. o.c. Minimum 3/32 in. gypsum veneer plaster. Joints staggered vertically 16 in. and horizontal joints each side at 12 in.	
		4 7/8"	One layer 5/8 in. type X gypsum wallboard or veneer base nailed to each side of 2 x 4 in. wood studs 16 in. o.c. with 6d coated nails 7 in. o.c. Stagger joints 24 in. on each side.	
	35 TO 39	5 1/8"	Two layers 3/8 in. regular gypsum wallboard or veneer base nailed to each side of 2 x 4 in. wood studs 16 in. o.c. First layer attached with 4d coated nails, second layer applied with laminating compound and nailed with 5d coated nails 8 in. o.c. Stagger joints 16 in. o.c. each side.	
	45 TO 49	5 3/8"	Base layer 3/8 in. regular gypsum wallboard or veneer base nailed to each side of 2 x 4 in. wood studs 16 in. o.c. Face layer 1/2 in. (same as base layer). Use 5d coated nails 24 in. o.c. for base layer and 8d coated nails 12 in. o.c. to edge and 24 in. o.c. to intermediate studs. Stagger joints 16 in. o.c. each layer and side.	
		5 7/8"	Base layer 1/2 in. wood fiberboard to each side of 2 x 4 in. wood studs 16 in. o.c. with 5d coated nails 24 in. o.c. on vertical joints and 16 in. o.c. to top and bottom plates. Face layer 5/8 in. type X gypsum wallboard or veneer base applied to each side with laminating compound and nailed with 8d coated nails 24 in. o.c. on vertical joints and 16 in. o.c. to top and bottom plates. Stagger joints 24 in. o.c. each layer and side.	
		5 7/8"	Both sides resilient channels 24 in. o.c. attached with GWB 54 drywall nails to each side of 2 x 4 in. wood studs 16 in. o.c. One layer 5/8 in. type X gypsum wallboard or veneer base attached with 1 in. type S drywall screws 12 in. o.c. to each side and vertical joints back-blocked. GWB filler strips along floor and ceiling both sides. Stagger joints 24 in. o.c. each side.	
	50 TO 54	5 3/8"	Base layer 1/4 in. proprietary gypsum wallboard applied to each side of 2 x 4 in. wood studs 16 in. o.c. with 4d coated nails 12 in. o.c. Face layer 5/8 in. type X gypsum wallboard or veneer base applied with laminating compound and nailed with 6d coated nails 16 in. o.c. to each side. 1 1/2 in. mineral fiber insulation in cavity. Stagger joints 24 in. o.c. each side.	
		5 3/8"	One side resilient channel 24 in. o.c. with 1 1/4 in. type S drywall screws to 2 x 4 in. wood studs 16 in. o.c. Both sides 5/8 in. gypsum wallboard or veneer base attached to resilient channel with 1 in. type S drywall screws 12 in. o.c. and GWB to stud with 1 1/4 in. type W drywall screws. 1 1/2 in. mineral fiber insulation in cavity. Stagger joints 48 in. o.c. each side.	
	60 TO 64	6 7/8"	One side resilient channels 24 in. o.c. attached with 1 in. type S drywall screws to 2 x 4 in. wood studs 16 in. o.c. Two layers of 5/8 in. type X gypsum wallboard or veneer base. First layer attached with 1 in. type S drywall screws, second layer applied with laminating compound. Other side one layer each of 5/8 in. and 1/2 in. gypsum wallboard or veneer base plus top 3/8 in. gypsum wallboard applied with laminating compound. Use 5d coated nails 32 in. o.c. for base, 8d for 1/2 in. center layer. 2 in. glass fiber insulation in cavity. Stagger all joints 16 in. o.c.	
2 HOUR	40 TO 44	6 1/8"	Two layers 5/8 in. type X gypsum wallboard or veneer base applied to each side of 2 x 4 in. wood studs 24 in. o.c. Use 6d coated nails 24 in. o.c. for base layer and 8d coated nails 8 in. o.c. for face layer. Stagger joints 24 in. o.c. each layer and side.	
	50 TO 54	8"	Two layers 5/8 in. type X gypsum wallboard or veneer base applied to each side of 2 x 4 in. wood studs 16 in. o.c. staggered 8 in. o.c. on 2 x 6 in. wood plates. Use 6d coated nails 24 in. o.c. for base layer and 8d coated nails 8 in. o.c. for face layer. Stagger vertical joints 16 in. o.c. each layer and side.	
	55 TO 59	10 3/4"	Two layers 5/8 in. type X gypsum wallboard or veneer base applied to each side of double row of 2 x 4 in. wood studs 16 in. o.c. on separate plates 1 in. apart. Use 6d coated nails 24 in. o.c. for base layer and 8d coated nails 8 in. o.c. for face layer. 3 1/2 in. glass fiber insulation in cavity. Stagger joints 16 in. o.c. each layer and side. GWB fire stop continuous in space between plates.	

CONSULT MANUFACTURER OR GYPSUM ASSOCIATION FOR ADDITIONAL INFORMATION

FIRE RATING	STC	WALL THICKNESS	CONSTRUCTION DESCRIPTION	WALL SECTIONS
1 HOUR	35 TO 39	2 7/8"	One layer 5/8 in. type X gypsum wallboard or veneer base applied to each side of 1 5/8 in. metal studs 24 in. o.c. with 1 in. type S drywall screws 8 in. o.c. to edges and 12 in. o.c. to intermediate studs. Stagger joints 24 in. o.c. each side.	
	40 TO 44	3 3/8"	Base layer 3/8 in. regular gypsum wallboard or veneer base applied to each side of 1 5/8 in. metal studs 24 in. o.c. with 1 in. type S drywall screws 27 in. o.c. to edges and 54 in. o.c. to intermediate studs. Face layer 1/2 in. attached on each side to studs with 1 5/8 in. type S drywall screws 12 in. o.c. to perimeter and 24 in. o.c. to intermediate studs. Stagger joints 24 in. o.c. each layer and side.	
		4 7/8"	One layer 5/8 in. type X gypsum wallboard or veneer base applied to each side of 3 5/8 in. metal studs 24 in. o.c. with 1 in. type S drywall screws 8 in. o.c. to vertical edges and 12 in. o.c. to intermediate studs. Stagger joints 24 in. o.c. each side.	
	45 TO 49	3 1/8"	Two layers 1/2 in. regular gypsum wallboard or veneer base applied to each side of 1 5/8 in. metal studs 24 in. o.c. Use 1 in. type S drywall screws 12 in. o.c. for base layer and 1 5/8 in. type S drywall screws 12 in. o.c. for face layer. Stagger joints 24 in. o.c. each layer and side.	
		3 1/8"	Base layer 1/4 in. gypsum wallboard applied to each side of 1 5/8 in. metal studs 24 in. o.c. with 1 in. type S drywall screws 24 in. o.c. to edges and 36 in. o.c. to intermediate studs. Face layer 1/2 in. type X gypsum wallboard or veneer base applied to each side of studs with 1 5/8 in. type S drywall screws 12 in. o.c. Stagger joints 24 in. o.c. each layer and side.	
		5 1/2"	One layer 5/8 in. type X gypsum wallboard or veneer base applied to each side of 3 5/8 in. metal studs 24 in. o.c. with 1 in. type S drywall screws 8 in. o.c. to edge and vertical joints and 12 in. o.c. to intermediate stud. Face layer 5/8 in. (same as other layer) applied on one side to stud with laminating compound and attached with 1 5/8 in. type S drywall screws 8 in. o.c. to edges and sides and 12 in. o.c. to intermediate studs. 3 1/2 in. glass fiber insulation in cavity. Stagger joints 24 in. o.c. each layer and side.	
	50 TO 54	4"	Base layer 1/4 in. regular gypsum wallboard applied to each side of 2 1/2 in. metal studs 24 in. o.c. with 1 in. type S drywall screws 12 in. o.c. Face layer 1/2 in. type X gypsum wallboard or veneer base applied to each side of studs with laminating compound and with 1 5/8 in. type S drywall screws in top and bottom runners 8 in. o.c. 2 in. glass fiber insulation in cavity. Stagger joints 24 in. o.c. each layer and side.	
		4"	Two layers 1/2 in. type X gypsum wallboard or veneer base applied to one side of 2 1/2 in. metal studs 24 in. o.c. Base layer 1 in. and face layer 1 5/8 in. type S drywall screws 8 in. o.c. to edge and adhesive beads to intermediate studs. Opposite side layer 1/2 in. type X gypsum wallboard or veneer base applied with 1 in. type S drywall screws 8 in. o.c. to vertical edges and 12 in. o.c. to intermediate studs. 3 in. glass fiber insulation in cavity. Stagger joints 24 in. o.c. each layer and face.	
	55 TO 59	4 1/4"	Base layer 1/4 in. gypsum wallboard applied to each side of 2 1/2 in. metal studs 24 in. o.c. with 7/8 in. type S drywall screws 12 in. o.c. Face layer 5/8 in. type X gypsum wallboard or veneer base applied on each side of studs with 1 5/16 in. type S drywall screws 12 in. o.c. 1 1/2 in. glass fiber insulation in cavity. Stagger joints 24 in. o.c. each layer and side.	
2 HOUR	40 TO 44	5"	Two layers 5/8 in. type X gypsum wallboard or veneer base applied to each side of 2 1/2 in. metal studs 16 in. o.c. braced laterally. Use 1 in. for base layer and 1 5/8 in. for facelayer type S-12 drywall screws 12 in. o.c. Stagger joints 16 in. o.c. each layer and side.	
	50 TO 54	3 5/8"	Base layer 1/2 in. type X gypsum wallboard or veneer base applied to each side of 1 5/8 in. metal studs 24 in. o.c. Use 1 in. type S drywall screws 12 in. o.c. for base layer and 1 5/8 in. type S drywall screws 12 in. o.c. for face layer. 1 1/2 in. glass fiber insulation in cavity. Stagger joints 24 in. o.c. each layer and side.	
	55 TO 59	6 1/4"	Two layers 5/8 in. type X gypsum wallboard or veneer base applied to each side of 3 5/8 in. metal studs 24 in. o.c. Use 1 in. type S drywall screws 32 in. o.c. for base layer and 1 5/8 in. type S drywall screws 12 in. o.c. to edge and 24 in. o.c. to intermediate studs. One side third layer 1/4 or 3/8 in. gypsum wallboard or veneer base applied with laminating compound. Stagger joints 24 in. o.c. each layer and side.	

CONSULT MANUFACTURER OR GYPSUM ASSOCIATION FOR ADDITIONAL INFORMATION

FIRE RATING	STC	WALL THICKNESS	CONSTRUCTION DESCRIPTION	WALL SECTIONS
1 HOUR	30 TO 34	2"	Two 1 x 24 in. wide gypsum coreboards with metal edges offset $2^{1}/_{2}$ in. applied with $1^{5}/_{8}$ in. type S drywall screws 24 in. o.c. to 1 x $^{3}/_{4}$ in. metal strips not over 5 ft o.c. attached with one $^{3}/_{8}$ in. pan bead type S screw per channel. Secure to top and bottom tracks with three $2^{5}/_{8}$ in. type S screws per panel through $^{3}/_{4}$ in. wide metal strapping.	
2 HOUR	35 TO 39	2"	One layer $^{1}/_{2}$ in. regular gypsum wallboard or veneer base applied with laminating compound over entire surface to each side of 1 in. laminated, interlocking gypsum coreboard. Stagger joints 24 in. o.c. each layer and side.	
		2"	One layer $^{1}/_{2}$ in. type X gypsum wallboard or veneer base applied parallel to each side of 1 in. tongue and groove gypsum coreboard with laminating compound over entire surface. Stagger joints 24 in. o.c. each layer and side.	
		$4^{1}/_{8}$"	Four layers $^{5}/_{8}$ in. type X gypsum wallboard or veneer base applied to one side of $1^{5}/_{8}$ in. metal studs 24 in. o.c. First three layers attached to metal studs with type S drywall screws; between third and face layer use steel strips $1^{1}/_{2}$ in. wide vertically applied at stud lines and attached 12 in. o.c. to studs with $2^{5}/_{8}$ in. type S drywall screws. Face layer is attached to steel strips. Stagger joints of each layer.	
	40 TO 44	$2^{7}/_{8}$"	$1^{5}/_{8}$ x 24 in. laminated gypsum board panels attached to floor and ceiling L runners and to flanges of metal T spline between panels at vertical edges. $1^{1}/_{2}$ in. wide x 22 in. gauge steel strips applied at top and bottom of panels to T spline and L runners. Two layers $^{5}/_{8}$ in. type X gypsum wallboard applied parallel to T splines. Stagger joints 24 in. o.c. each layer.	
	45 TO 49	$3^{1}/_{2}$"	1 x 24 in. proprietary type X gypsum coreboard inserted between $2^{1}/_{2}$ in. floor and ceiling J runners with T section of $2^{1}/_{2}$ in. proprietary C-t metal studs between coreboards. One layer $^{1}/_{2}$ in. type X gypsum wallboard applied vertically to each side of studs with 1 in. type S drywall screws 8 in. o.c. 1 in. glass fiber insulation stapled in cavity. Stagger joints each side.	
	50 TO 54	$6^{3}/_{4}$"	Double row of proprietary hollow core tongue and groove gypsum panels set 3 in. apart. Panels made of one layer $^{5}/_{8}$ in. type X gypsum wallboard or veneer base laminated to $^{5}/_{8}$ x 6 in. wide type X gypsum board studs. Panels attached to floor and ceiling runners with $2^{1}/_{4}$ in. type S drywall screws 18 in. o.c. Joints reinforced with $1^{1}/_{2}$ in. type G drywall screws at quarter points.	
		$4^{1}/_{4}$"	1 x 24 in. type X gypsum coreboard inserted between $2^{1}/_{2}$ in. floor and ceiling track with tab-flange section of $2^{1}/_{2}$ in. metal I studs between coreboards. One layer of $^{5}/_{8}$ in. type X gypsum wallboard or veneer base applied over coreboard. Resilient channels spaced 24 in. o.c. horizontally, screw attached, top leg only, to opposite flanges of I studs. Face layer $^{5}/_{8}$ in. type X gypsum wallboard or veneer base applied to resilient furring channels. $1^{1}/_{2}$ in. glass fiber friction fir insulation in cavity.	
3 HOUR		$4^{3}/_{8}$"	$1^{5}/_{8}$ x 24 in. laminated gypsum board panels inserted in $2^{1}/_{2}$ in. floor track and attached to ceiling L runner and to flanges of metal T splines between panels at vertical edges. Metal furring channel attached to panel centers at either flange and at top to L runner. Three layers $^{5}/_{8}$ in. type X gypsum wallboard applied to furring. 1 in. glass fiber insulation stapled in cavity. Stagger joints 24 in. each layer.	
	40 TO 44	$3^{7}/_{8}$"	1 x 24 in. gypsum coreboard panels attached to $2^{1}/_{2}$ in. angle runners at floor and ceiling. Proprietary 2 in. shart studs fitted between panels. 1 x 6 in. gypsum coreboard ribs fitted in stud flange and attached to coreboard. Three layers of $^{5}/_{8}$ in. type X gypsum board applied on room side. Face layer may be type X gypsum wallboard or veneer base applied vertically with stagger joints 24 in. relative to base layer. 1 in. glass fiber insulation friction fit in cavity.	
		$3^{1}/_{4}$"	Base layer $^{5}/_{8}$ in. type X gypsum wallboard or veneer base attached to 2 in. shiplapped metal edged gypsum coreboard panels. Face layer $^{5}/_{8}$ in. type X gypsum wallboard or veneer base attached over base layer into near side coreboard channels along vertical edges and intermediate channels. Coreboard panels consist of two 1 x 16 in. or 24 in. wide gypsum coreboards with metal channels on long edges mill laminated with $2^{1}/_{2}$ in. offset and are secured to top and bottom tracks.	
4 HOUR		$6^{1}/_{4}$"	Base layer $^{5}/_{8}$ in. type X gypsum wallboard or veneer base attached to both sides of 2 in. proprietary shiplapped metal edged gypsum coreboard panels. Drywall furring channels attached to both sides metal edges of gypsum coreboard panels. Face layer $^{5}/_{8}$ in. type X gypsum wallboard or veneer base attached vertically to each side of furring channels. Two 1 x 24 in. wide gypsum coreboards with metal channels on long edges, mill laminated with $2^{1}/_{2}$ in. offset and are attached to top and bottom tracks.	

CONSULT MANUFACTURER OR GYPSUM ASSOCIATION FOR ADDITIONAL INFORMATION

GYPSUM WALLBOARD

9

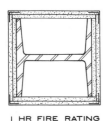

I HR FIRE RATING

Base layer ¹/₂ in. regular gypsum wallboard or veneer base tied to column with 18 gauge wire 15 in. o.c. Face layer ¹/₂ in. regular gypsum wallboard or veneer base laminated over entire contact surface.

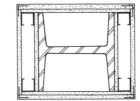

2 HR FIRE RATING

Base layer ¹/₂ in. type X gypsum wallboard or veneer base against flanges and across web openings screwed 24 in. o.c. to 1⁵/₈ in. metal studs. Face layer ¹/₂ in. type X gypsum wallboard or veneer base screwed to studs 12 in. o.c. to provide a cavity between boards on flange. Metal corner beads nailed 12 in. o.c.

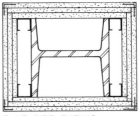

3 HR FIRE RATING

Three layers ⁵/₈ in. type X gypsum wallboard or veneer base screwed to 1⁵/₈ in. metal studs at each corner. Base layer screwed 24 in. o.c. Middle layer screwed 12 in. o.c. and wire tied 24 in. o.c. with 18 gauge wire. Face layer screwed 12 in. o.c. 1¹/₄ in. metal corner beads nailed 12 in. o.c.

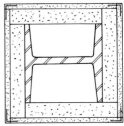

4 HR FIRE RATING

⁵/₈ in. type X gypsum wallboard or veneer base screwed 12 in. o.c. to 22 gauge, 1³/₈ x ⁷/₈ in., galvanized steel corner angles screwed along vertical edges of 2 in. solid gypsum block. Gypsum block secured with ³/₈ in. mortar bed and 26 ft gauge galvanized steel strapping 2 in. wide, 24 in. o.c. encasing column.

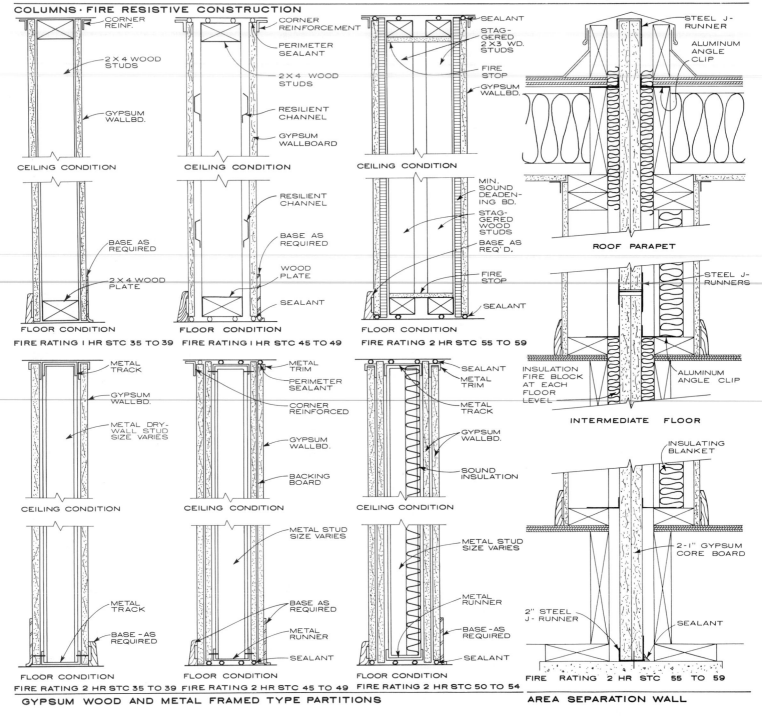

COLUMNS · FIRE RESISTIVE CONSTRUCTION

GYPSUM WOOD AND METAL FRAMED TYPE PARTITIONS

AREA SEPARATION WALL

Ferdinand R. Scheeler, AIA; Skidmore, Owings and Merrill; Chicago, Illinois

James Lloyd; Kennett Square, Pennsylvania

9 GYPSUM WALLBOARD

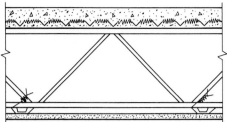

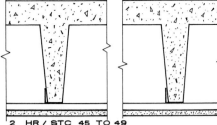

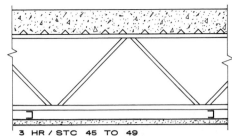

2 HR / STC 50 TO 54

1/2 in. type X gypsum wallboard or veneer base applied to drywall furring channels. Furring channels 24 in. o.c. attached with 18 gauge wire ties 48 in. o.c. to open web steel joists 24 in. o.c. supporting 3/8 in. rib metal lath or 9/16 in. deep, 28 gauge corrugated steel and 2 1/2 in. concrete slab measured from top of flute. Double channel at wallboard end joints.

2 HR / STC 45 TO 49

5/8 in. type X gypsum wallboard or veneer base screw attached to drywall furring channels. Furring channels 24 in. o.c. suspended from 2 1/2 in. precast reinforced concrete joists 35 in. o.c. with 21 gauge galvanized steel hanger straps fastened to sides of joists. Joist leg depth, 10 in. Double channel at wallboard end joints.

3 HR / STC 45 TO 49

5/8 in. proprietary type X gypsum wallboard or veneer base screw attached to furring channels 24 in. o.c. (double channels at end joints). Furring channel wire tied to open web steel joist 24 in. o.c. supporting 3 in. concrete slab over 3/8 in. rib metal lath. 5/8 x 2 3/4 in. type X gypsum wallboard strips over butt joints.

FLOOR/CEILING ASSEMBLIES, NONCOMBUSTIBLE

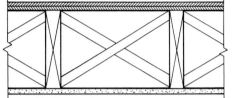

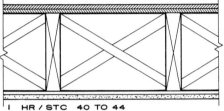

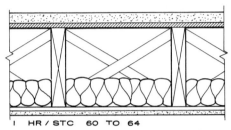

I HR / STC 35 TO 39

5/8 in. type X gypsum wallboard or veneer base applied to wood joists 16 in. o.c. Joists supporting 1 in. nominal wood sub and finish floor, or 5/8 in. plywood finished floor with long edges T & G and 1/2 in. interior plywood with exterior glue subfloor perpendicular to joists with joints staggered.

I HR / STC 40 TO 44

1/2 in. type X gypsum wallboard or veneer base applied to drywall resilient furring channels 24 in. o.c. and nailed to wood joists 16 in. o.c. Wood joists supporting 1 in. nominal T & G wood sub and finish floor, or 5/8 in. plywood finished floor with long edges T & G and 1/2 in. interior plywood with exterior glue subfloor perpendicular to joists with joints staggered.

I HR / STC 60 TO 64

1/2 in. type X gypsum wallboard or veneer base applied to resilient furring channels. Resilient channels applied 24 in. o.c. to wood joists 16 in. o.c. Wood joists support 1/2 in. plywood subfloor and 1 1/2 in. cellular or lightweight concrete over felt. 3 1/2 in. glass fiber batts in joist spaces. Sound tested with carpet and pad over 5/8 in. plywood subfloor.

FLOOR/CEILING ASSEMBLIES, WOOD FRAMED

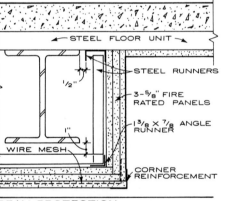

- STEEL FLOOR UNIT
- STEEL RUNNERS
- 1/2"
- 3-5/8" FIRE RATED PANELS
- 1 3/8 X 7/8 ANGLE RUNNER
- 1"
- WIRE MESH
- CORNER REINFORCEMENT

BEAM PROTECTION
3 HR. RESTRAINED   2 HR. UNRESTRAINED

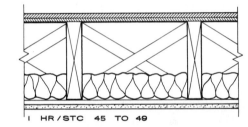

- WIRE TIE
- CONTROL JOINT
- JOINT COMPOUND

CONTROL JOINT

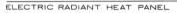

I HR / STC 45 TO 49

5/8 in. proprietary type X gypsum board electrical radiant heating panels attached to resilient furring channels spaced 24 in. o.c. installed to 2 x 10 in. wood joists 16 in. o.c. 3/12 in. glass fiber insulation friction fit in joist space. Wood floor of nominal 1 in. T & G or 1/2 in. plywood subfloor and nominal 1 in. T & G or 5/8 in. plywood finish floor.

FLOOR/CEILING ASSEMBLIES, WOOD FRAMED

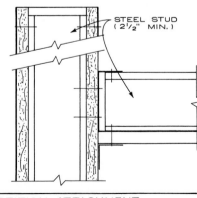

- STEEL STUD (2 1/2" MIN.)

PARTITION ATTACHMENT
(SCREW ATTACHED)

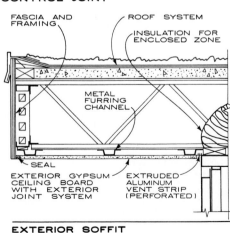

- FASCIA AND FRAMING
- ROOF SYSTEM
- INSULATION FOR ENCLOSED ZONE
- METAL FURRING CHANNEL
- SEAL
- EXTERIOR GYPSUM CEILING BOARD WITH EXTERIOR JOINT SYSTEM
- EXTRUDED ALUMINUM VENT STRIP (PERFORATED)

EXTERIOR SOFFIT

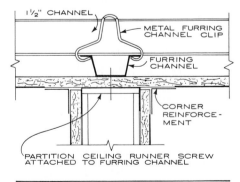

- ELECTRIC RADIANT HEAT PANEL
- 1 1/2" CHANNEL
- METAL FURRING CHANNEL CLIP
- FURRING CHANNEL
- CORNER REINFORCEMENT
- PARTITION CEILING RUNNER SCREW ATTACHED TO FURRING CHANNEL

CONTINUOUS CEILING

James Lloyd; Kennett Square, Pennsylvania

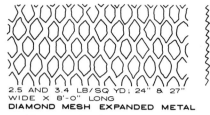

2.5 AND 3.4 LB/SQ YD; 24" & 27"
WIDE × 8'-0" LONG

DIAMOND MESH EXPANDED METAL

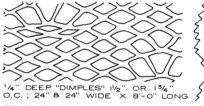

1/4" DEEP "DIMPLES" 1½" OR 1¾"
O.C.; 24" & 24" WIDE × 8'-0" LONG

SELF-FURRING DIAMOND MESH

RIB EXPANDED METAL

LATHING SYSTEMS

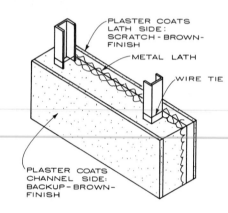

PLASTER COATS
LATH SIDE:
SCRATCH-BROWN-
FINISH

METAL LATH

WIRE TIE

PLASTER COATS
CHANNEL SIDE:
BACKUP-BROWN-
FINISH

SOLID PARTITION SYSTEMS

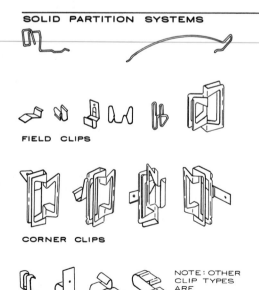

FIELD CLIPS

CORNER CLIPS

MISCELLANEOUS

NOTE: OTHER
CLIP TYPES
ARE
AVAILABLE

CLIPS FOR GYPSUM LATH SYSTEM

The Marmon Mok Partnership; San Antonio, Texas

NOTES

Self-furring paperbacked reinforcing is available in diamond mesh, welded wire, and hexagonal woven wire. Paperbacks are available to conform to Federal Specifications UU-B-790, Type 1, Grade A, Style 2 for highly water-vapor resistant paper.

Metal lath is also manufactured in large diamond mesh 27 × 96 in., 2.5 or 3.4 lb/sq yd, painted steel or galvanized; 1/8 in. flat rib 27 × 96 in., 2.75 or 3.4 lb/sq yd painted or galvanized; 3/8 in. rib expanded 27 × 96 in., 3.4 lb/sq yd painted or galvanized and 3/4 in. rib expanded 24 × 96 in., 5.4 lb/sq yd painted.

Other types of lath are available from some manufacturers.

GYPSUM LATH

Gypsum lath is composed of an air entrained gypsum core sandwiched between two sheets of fibrous absorbent paper and used as a basecoat for gypsum plaster.

1. PLAIN GYPSUM LATH: 3/8 and 1/2 in. thick, 48 in. long, and 16 in. wide (16 1/5 in. in the Western U.S.).
2. PERFORATED GYPSUM LATH: Plain gypsum lath with 3/4 in. diameter holes punches 4 in. o.c. in both directions to provide mechanical key to plaster.
3. INSULATING GYPSUM LATH: Plain gypsum lath with aluminum foil laminated to the backside as insulator or vapor barrier.
4. LONG LENGTH GYPSUM LATH: 16, and 24 in. wide, in lengths up to 12 ft, available insulated or plain with square or vee-jointed T & G edges or interlocking as ship-lap edge.

SOLID PLASTER PARTITION CONSTRUCTION

PARTITION CONSTRUCTION	THICKNESS	MAXIMUM HEIGHT
3/4" cold-rolled channels Diamond mesh lath and plaster	2"	12'-0"
3/4" cold-rolled channels Diamond mesh lath and plaster	2½"	16'-0"
1½" cold-rolled channels Diamond mesh lath and plaster	3"	20'-0"
1½" cold-rolled channels Diamond mesh lath and plaster	3½"	22'-0"

NOTE: Maximum partition length is unrestricted if less than 10 ft tall. Twice the height if over 10 ft tall; one and one half the height if over 14 ft tall and equal to the height if over 20 ft tall.

METAL LATH

PLASTER COATS
EACH SIDE:
SCRATCH-BROWN-
FINISH

NOTES

Prefabricated metal studs are used as the supporting elements of lath and plaster hollow partitions. They are available in 1 5/8, 2, 2½, 3¼, 4, and 6 in. widths. Lengths are available in various increments up to 24 ft. Prefabricated studs are usually of the nonload bearing type, but load bearing metal studs also are manufactured. Designs vary with the manufacturer, and most manufacturers produce a line of related accessories, such as clips, runners, stud shoes, and similar articles.

HOLLOW PARTITION SYSTEMS

DEFINITIONS

AGGREGATE: Inert material used as filler with a cementitious material and water to produce plaster or concrete. Usually implies sand, perlite, or vermiculite.

BASECOAT: Any plaster coat applied before the finish coat.

BEAD: Light gauge metal strip with one or more expanded or short perforated flanges and variously shaped noses; used at the perimeter of plastered surfaces.

BROWN COAT: In three-coat plaster, the brown coat is the second coat; in two-coat plaster, the base coat.

CALCINED GYPSUM: Gypsum that has been partially dehydrated by heating.

CLIP: A device made of wire or sheet metal for attaching various types of lath to the substructure and lath sheets to one another.

FIBERED PLASTER: Gypsum plaster containing fibers of hair, glass, nylon, or sisal.

FINISH COAT: The final coat of plaster, which provides the decorative surface.

FURRING: Grillage for the attachment of gypsum or metal lath.

GAUGING: Cementitious material, usually calcined gypsum or portland cement combined with lime putty to control set.

GROUND: A formed metal shape or wood strip that acts as a combined edge and gauge for various thicknesses of plaster to be applied to a plaster base.

GYPSUM: Hydrous calcium sulphate, a natural mineral in crystalline form.

GYPSUM LATH: A base for plaster; a sheet having a gypsum core, faced with paper.

GYPSUM READY MIX PLASTER: Ground gypsum that has been calcined and then mixed with various additives to control its setting and working qualities; used, with the addition of aggregate and water, for basecoat plaster.

HYDRATED LIME: Quicklime mixed with water, on the job, to form a lime putty.

LIME: Obtained by burning various types of limestone, consisting of oxides or hydroxides of calcium and magnesium.

LIME PLASTER: Basecoat plaster of hydrated lime and an aggregate.

NEAT PLASTER: Basecoat plaster, fibered or unfibered, used for job mixing with aggregates.

PERLITE: Siliceous volcanic glass containing silica and alumina expanded by heat for use as a lightweight plaster aggregate.

PLASTER: Cementitious material or combination of cementitious materials and aggregate that, when mixed with water, forms a plastic mass that sets and hardens when applied to a surface.

PORTLAND CEMENT: Manufactured combination of limestone and an argillaceous substance.

SCRATCH COAT: In three-coat plastering, the first coat, which is then scratched to provide a bond for second or brown coat.

SCREED: A device secured to a surface which serves as a guide for subsequent applications of plaster. Thicknesses and widths vary with the thicknesses desired for each operation.

STUCCO PORTLAND CEMENT: Plaster used in exterior application.

VERMICULITE: Micaceous mineral of silica, magnesium, and alumina oxides made up in a series of parallel plates or laminae and expanded by heat for use as a lightweight plaster aggregate.

NOTES

Keene's cement plaster is a specialty finish coat of gypsum plaster primarily used where a smooth, dense, white finish is desired.

Thickness, proportions of mixes of various plastering materials, and finishes vary. Systems and methods of application vary widely depending on local traditions and innovations promoted by the industry.

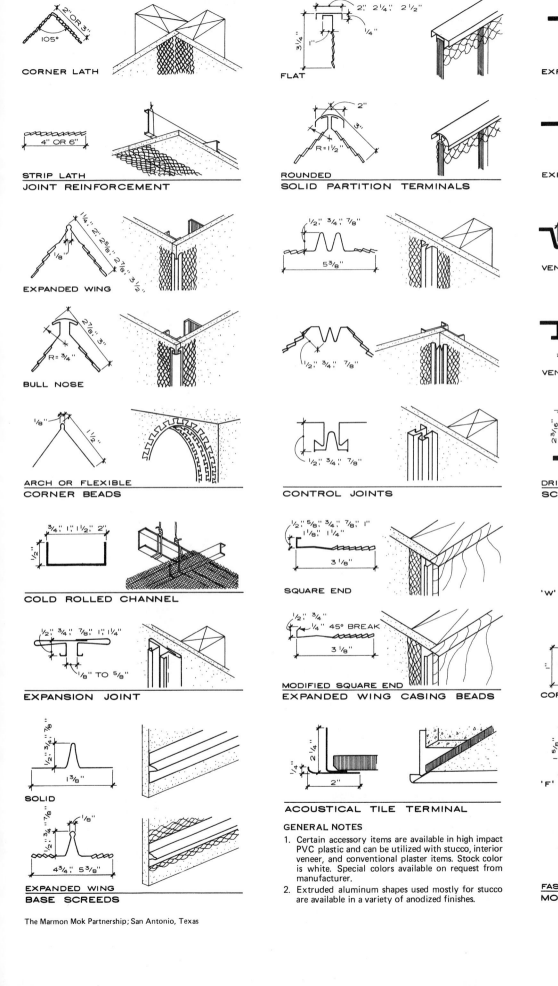

CORNER LATH

STRIP LATH
JOINT REINFORCEMENT

EXPANDED WING

BULL NOSE

ARCH OR FLEXIBLE
CORNER BEADS

COLD ROLLED CHANNEL

EXPANSION JOINT

SOLID

EXPANDED WING
BASE SCREEDS

FLAT

ROUNDED
SOLID PARTITION TERMINALS

CONTROL JOINTS

SQUARE END

MODIFIED SQUARE END
EXPANDED WING CASING BEADS

ACOUSTICAL TILE TERMINAL

GENERAL NOTES

1. Certain accessory items are available in high impact PVC plastic and can be utilized with stucco, interior veneer, and conventional plaster items. Stock color is white. Special colors available on request from manufacturer.

2. Extruded aluminum shapes used mostly for stucco are available in a variety of anodized finishes.

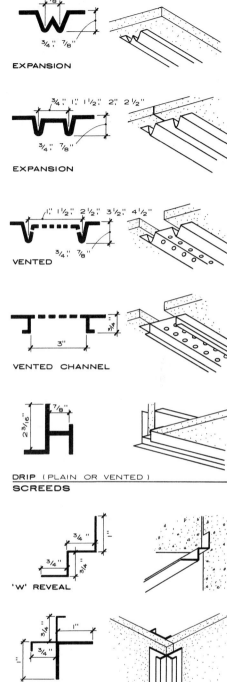

EXPANSION

EXPANSION

VENTED

VENTED CHANNEL

DRIP (PLAIN OR VENTED)
SCREEDS

'W' REVEAL

CORNER

'F' REVEAL

FASCIA CORNER
MOLDING

The Marmon Mok Partnership; San Antonio, Texas

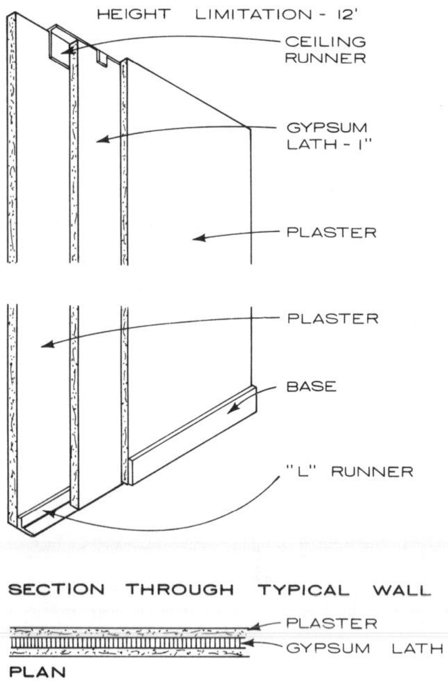

2 IN. SOLID GYPSUM LATH

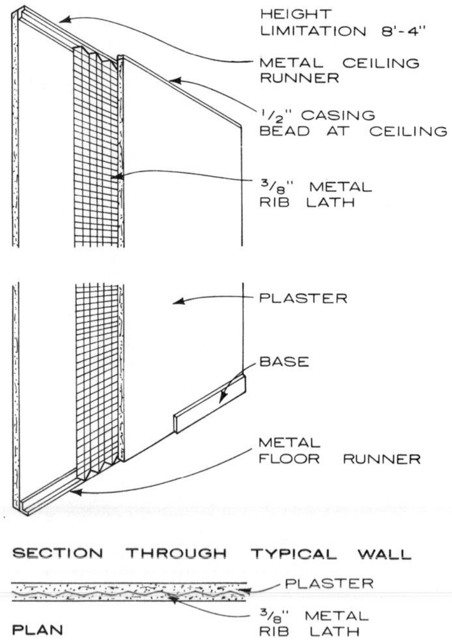

2 IN. SOLID METAL LATH AND PLASTER

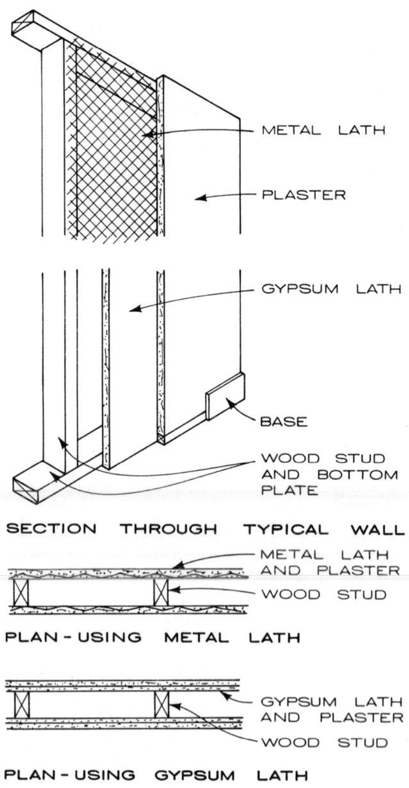

WOOD STUD AND LATH

CHANNEL STUD SPACING

TYPE OF LATH	WEIGHT #/SQ YD	SPACING OF SUPPORTS
Diamond mesh	2.5 3.4	16 16
Flat rib	2.75 3.4	16 24*

*Spacing for solid partitions not to exceed 16'-0" in height.

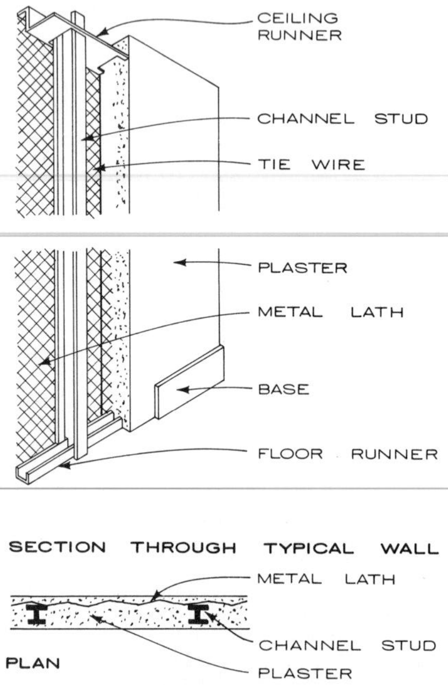

METAL LATH-CHANNEL STUD-PLASTER

TABLE FOR CHANNEL STUD SIZE PARTITIONS THICKNESS HEIGHT

HEIGHT	THICK	CHANNEL
12'	2"	3/4 in. 300 lb per 1000 ft
14'	2 1/4"	
16'	2 1/2"	
18'	2 3/4"	1 1/2 in. 475 lb per 1000 ft

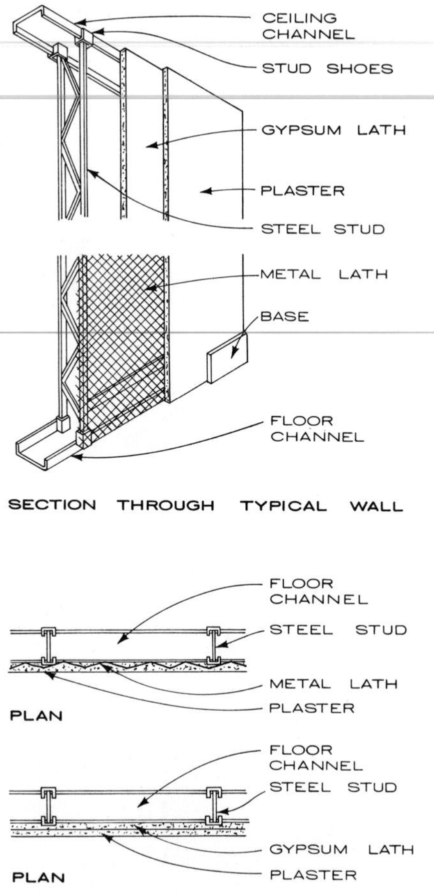

PREFABRICATED METAL STUD

METAL STUD WITH METAL LATH STUD SPACING AND HEIGHT LIMITATION*

STUD WIDTH	THICKNESS	MAXIMUM HEIGHT 16" OC.	19" OC.	24" OC.
2 1/2"	4"	15'	14'	9'
3 1/4"	4 3/4"	21'	18'	13'
4"	5 1/2"	22'	20'	16'
6"	7 1/2"	26'	24'	20'

*For length not exceeding 1 1/2 times height; for lengths exceeding this, reduce 20%.

METAL STUD WITH 3/8" GYPSUM LATH HEIGHT LIMITATIONS

STUD WIDTH	THICKNESS STANDARD SYSTEM	MAX. HEIGHT STUDS 16" OC.
2 1/2"	4 1/4"	15'
3 1/4"	5"	21'
4"	5 3/4"	22'
6"	7 3/4"	26'

Walter H. Sobel, FAIA & Associates; Chicago, Illinois

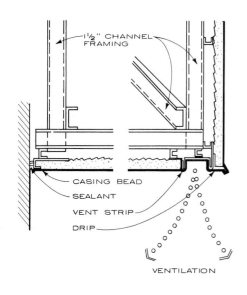

CASING BEAD
SEALANT
VENT STRIP
DRIP

VENTILATION

1½" CHANNEL FRAMING

SOFFIT DETAIL

NOTE

Framing details for exterior cement plaster (stucco) are similar to details shown. Wind loads must be considered in designing framing systems for exterior stucco work. Galvanized mesh is available for exterior applications and use in humid areas. Ventilation strips should be used for ventilating all dead airspaces. Where plenum or attic spaces are closed off by ceiling installation, ventilation shall be provided with a minimum of ½ sq in./sq ft of horizontal surface.

HANGER—SEE TABLE 1

TABLE 4 (SEE NEXT PAGE)

TABLE 2

TABLE 3

CROSS FURRING

MAIN RUNNER

FURRED AND SUSPENSION SYSTEM COMPONENT SELECTION DETAIL

NOTE

Details shown are for furred (contact) ceilings that are attached directly to the structural members. The architect or ceiling designer should give consideration to the deflection and movement of the structure, since excessive movement and deflection of more than $1/360$ of the span will cause cracking of plaster ceilings. If spacing of structural members exceeds the maximum span of furring members shown in the span charts, the addition of suspended main runners between structural members will be required. Flat rib lath may be attached directly to wood framing members, but is subjected to stresses created by wood members.

DIRECTIONS FOR USE OF TABLES

1. Select lath and plaster system.
2. Determine spacing of cross furring channels from Table 1—Lath Span.
3. Determine spacing of main runners from Table 2—Maximum Spacing Between Runners.
4. Determine hanger support spacing for main runner from Table 3—Maximum Spacing Between Hangers (see next page).
5. Calculate area of ceiling supported per hanger.
6. Select hanger type from Table 4—Hanger Selection Table (see next page).
7. Select tie wire size from Table 5—Tie Wire Selection (see next page).

TABLE 1. LATH SPAN

	LATH TYPE	WEIGHT/SQ FT	SPAN (IN.)
Gypsum lath	3/8" plain	1.5#	16
	1/2" plain	2.0#	16
	1/2" veneer	1.8#	16
	5/8" veneer	2.25#	16
	3/8" perforated	1.4#	16
Metal lath	Diamond mesh	0.27#	12
	Diamond mesh	0.38#	16
	1/8" flat rib	0.31#	12
	1/8" flat rib	0.38#	19
	3/8" flat rib	0.38#	24

TABLE 2. MAXIMUM SPACING BETWEEN RUNNERS

CROSS FURRING TYPE	CROSS FURRING SPACING			
	12"	16"	19"	24"
1/4" diam. pencil rod	2'-0"	—	—	—
3/8" diam. pencil rod	2'-6"	—	2'-0"	—
3/4" CRC, HRC (0.3 lb/ft)	—	4'-6"	3'-6"	3'-0"
1" HRC (0.41 lb/ft)	5'-0"	—	4'-6"	4'-0"

CRC = Cold rolled channel
HRC = Hot rolled channel

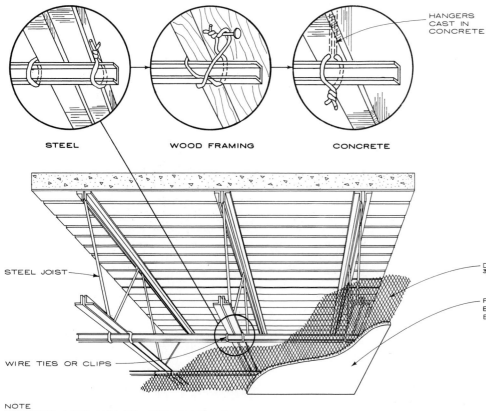

STEEL

WOOD FRAMING

CONCRETE

HANGERS CAST IN CONCRETE

STEEL JOIST

WIRE TIES OR CLIPS

NOTE
RIB METAL LATH MAY BE USED IN LIEU OF DIAMOND MESH LATH AND FURRING CHANNELS IF LATH SPANS DO NOT EXCEED ALLOWABLE MAXIMUM

FURRED METAL LATH ON STEEL JOIST

James E. Phillips, AIA; Liles/Associates/Architects, Inc.; Greenville, South Carolina

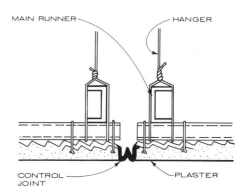

MAIN RUNNER

HANGER

CONTROL JOINT

PLASTER

CONTROL JOINT DETAIL

DIAMOND MESH METAL LATH WIRED TO 3/4" METAL FURRING CHANNELS

PLASTER—THREE-COAT SYSTEM WITH EXPANSION JOINTS AT 30' ON CENTER EACH DIRECTION

NOTE

Control joints shall be spaced no further than 30 ft on center in each direction for large plastered ceiling areas. Area shall not exceed 900 sq ft without provision for expansion control. Exterior plaster soffits should have control joints spaced no further than 25 ft on center. For portland cement plaster (stucco) areas, interior or exterior, control joints should be placed at 10 ft on center and areas should not exceed 100 sq ft without provisions for expansion/contraction control. Control joints are spaced closer for cement plaster because of its inherent shrinkage during curing.

TABLE 3. MAXIMUM SPACING BETWEEN HANGERS

MAIN RUNNER TYPE	MAIN RUNNER SPACING				
	3'-0''	3'-6''	4'-0''	4'-6''	5'-0''
¾'' CRC (0.3 lb/ft)	2'-0''	—	—	—	—
1½'' CRC (0.3 lb/ft)	3'-0''*	—	—	—	—
1½'' CRC (0.875 lb/ft)	4'-0''	3'-6''	3'-0''	—	—
1½'' HRC (1.12 lb/ft)	—	—	—	4'-0''	—
2'' CRC (0.59 lb/ft)	—	—	5'-0''	—	—
2'' HRC (1.26 lb/ft)	—	—	—	—	5'-0''
½'' x ½'' x ³⁄₁₆'' ST1	—	5'-0''	—	—	—

*For concrete construction only—a 10-gauge wire may be inserted in the joint before concrete is poured.

TABLE 4. HANGER SELECTION

MAX. CEILING AREA	MIN. HANGER SIZE
12 sq ft	9-gauge galvanized wire
16 sq ft	8-gauge galvanized wire
18 sq ft	³⁄₁₆'' mild steel rod*
25 sq ft	¼'' mild steel rod*
25 sq ft	³⁄₁₆'' x 1'' steel flat*

*Rods galvanized or painted with rust inhibitive paint and galvanized straps are recommended under severe moisture conditions.

TABLE 5. TIE WIRE SELECTION

	SUPPORT	MAX. CEILING AREA	MIN. HANGER SIZE
Cross furring		8 sq ft	14-gauge wire
		8 sq ft	16-gauge wire (two loops)
Main runners	Single hangers between beams	8 sq ft	12-gauge wire
		12 sq ft	10-gauge wire
		16 sq ft	8-gauge wire
	Double wire loops at supports	8 sq ft	14-gauge wire
		12 sq ft	12-gauge wire
		16 sq ft	11-gauge wire

ERECTION OF METAL LATH SUSPENSIONS

Metal lath suspensions are commonly made below all types of construction for fire rated plaster ceilings. The lath is supported by framing channels and furring channels suspended from the floor or roof structure above with wire hangers. Framing channels are normally spaced up to 4 ft o.c. perpendicular to joists and should be erected to conform with the contour of the finished ceiling. The framing channels are furred with ¾ in. channels, which are spaced according to the requirements for types and weights of metal lath and erected at right angles to the framing channels. The lath should be lapped at both sides and ends and secured to the ¾ in. channels with wire ties every 6 in. Where plaster on metal lath ceilings abuts masonry walls, partitions, or arch soffits, galvanized casing beads should be installed at the periphery.

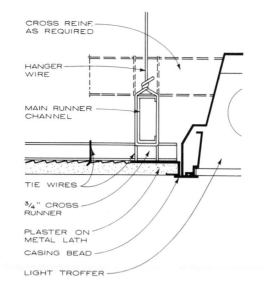

SUSPENDED PLASTER CEILING AT RECESSED LIGHT FIXTURE

NOTE

Penetrations of the lath and plaster ceiling—at borrowed light openings, vents, grilles, access panels, and light troffers, for example—require additional reinforcement to distribute concentrated stresses if a control joint is not used. Where a plaster surface is flush with metal, as at metal access panels, grilles, or light troffers, the plaster should be grooved between the two materials.

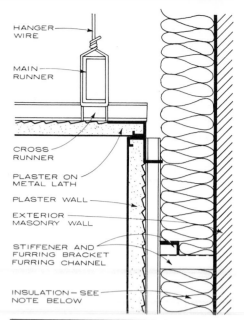

SUSPENDED PLASTER CEILING AT FURRED MASONRY WALL

NOTE

When interior walls are furred from an exterior masonry wall and insulated, the ceiling should stop short of the furred space. This allows wall insulation to continue above the ceiling line to ceiling or roof insulation, thus forming a complete insulation envelope. In a suspension system that abuts masonry wall, provide 1 in. clearance between ends of main runners or furring channels and wall face.

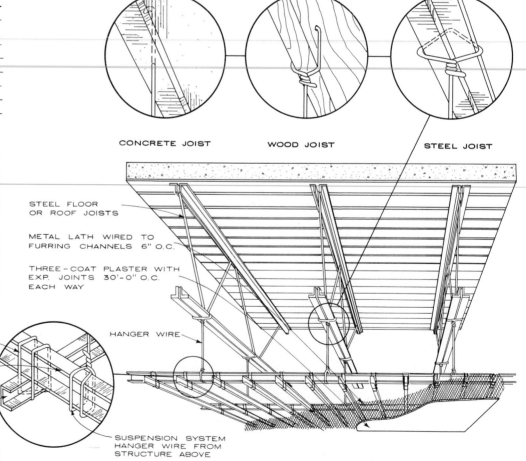

METAL LATH SUSPENDED FROM STEEL JOISTS

NOTE

Dimensional requirements for support spacing, runner spacing, hanger spacing, hanger type selection, and tie wire selection are given in tables on this and other page.

David H. Ross, AIA; Liles/Associates/Architects, Inc.; Greenville, South Carolina

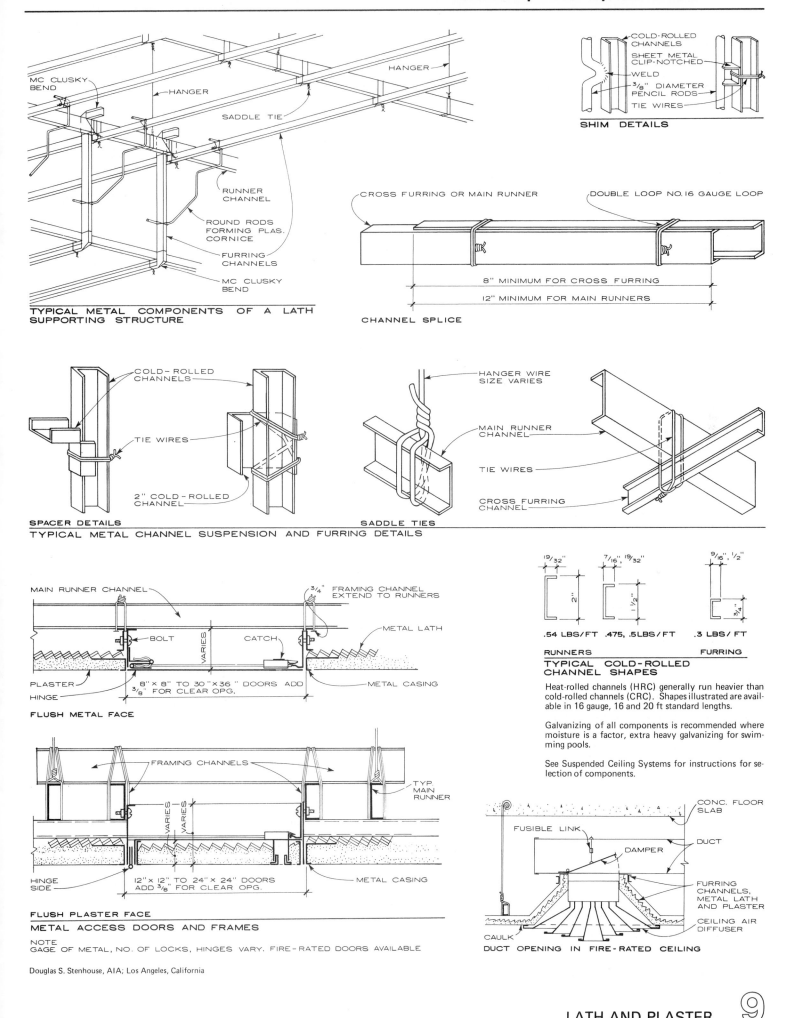

SHIM DETAILS

TYPICAL METAL COMPONENTS OF A LATH SUPPORTING STRUCTURE

CHANNEL SPLICE

SPACER DETAILS

SADDLE TIES

TYPICAL METAL CHANNEL SUSPENSION AND FURRING DETAILS

FLUSH METAL FACE

.54 LBS/FT   .475, .5LBS/FT   .3 LBS/FT

RUNNERS   FURRING

TYPICAL COLD-ROLLED CHANNEL SHAPES

Heat-rolled channels (HRC) generally run heavier than cold-rolled channels (CRC). Shapes illustrated are available in 16 gauge, 16 and 20 ft standard lengths.

Galvanizing of all components is recommended where moisture is a factor, extra heavy galvanizing for swimming pools.

See Suspended Ceiling Systems for instructions for selection of components.

FLUSH PLASTER FACE

METAL ACCESS DOORS AND FRAMES

NOTE
GAGE OF METAL, NO. OF LOCKS, HINGES VARY. FIRE-RATED DOORS AVAILABLE

DUCT OPENING IN FIRE-RATED CEILING

Douglas S. Stenhouse, AIA; Los Angeles, California

LATH AND PLASTER   9

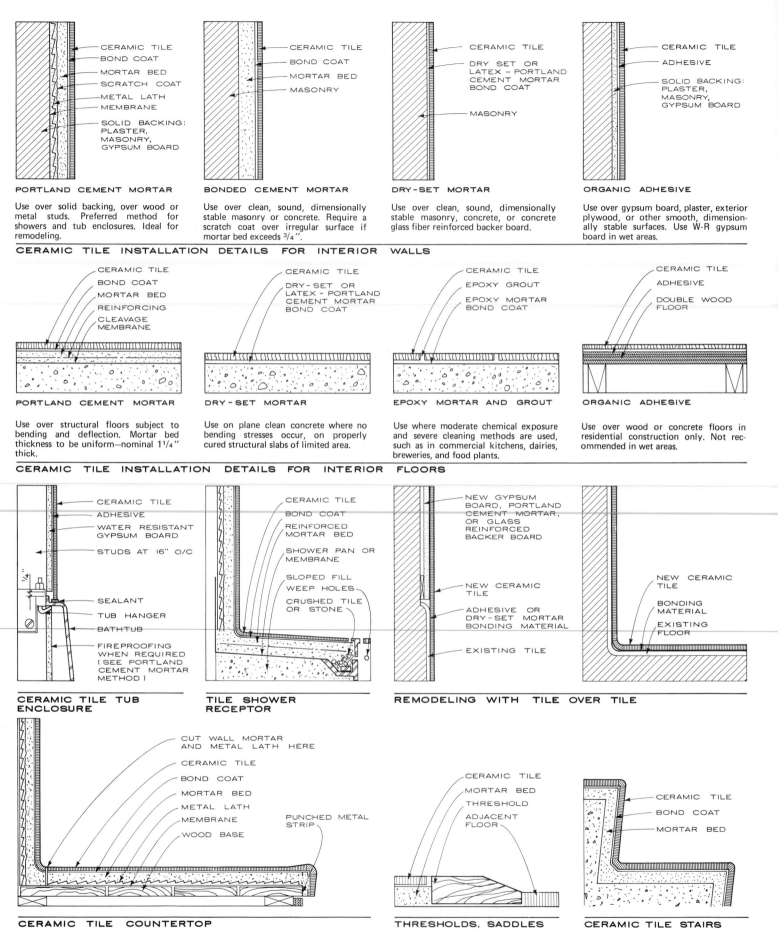

PORTLAND CEMENT MORTAR

- CERAMIC TILE
- BOND COAT
- MORTAR BED
- SCRATCH COAT
- METAL LATH
- MEMBRANE
- SOLID BACKING: PLASTER, MASONRY, GYPSUM BOARD

Use over solid backing, over wood or metal studs. Preferred method for showers and tub enclosures. Ideal for remodeling.

BONDED CEMENT MORTAR

- CERAMIC TILE
- BOND COAT
- MORTAR BED
- MASONRY

Use over clean, sound, dimensionally stable masonry or concrete. Require a scratch coat over irregular surface if mortar bed exceeds 3/4".

DRY-SET MORTAR

- CERAMIC TILE
- DRY SET OR LATEX – PORTLAND CEMENT MORTAR BOND COAT
- MASONRY

Use over clean, sound, dimensionally stable masonry, concrete, or concrete glass fiber reinforced backer board.

ORGANIC ADHESIVE

- CERAMIC TILE
- ADHESIVE
- SOLID BACKING: PLASTER, MASONRY, GYPSUM BOARD

Use over gypsum board, plaster, exterior plywood, or other smooth, dimensionally stable surfaces. Use W-R gypsum board in wet areas.

CERAMIC TILE INSTALLATION DETAILS FOR INTERIOR WALLS

PORTLAND CEMENT MORTAR

- CERAMIC TILE
- BOND COAT
- MORTAR BED
- REINFORCING
- CLEAVAGE MEMBRANE

Use over structural floors subject to bending and deflection. Mortar bed thickness to be uniform—nominal 1 1/4" thick.

DRY-SET MORTAR

- CERAMIC TILE
- DRY-SET OR LATEX – PORTLAND CEMENT MORTAR BOND COAT

Use on plane clean concrete where no bending stresses occur, on properly cured structural slabs of limited area.

EPOXY MORTAR AND GROUT

- CERAMIC TILE
- EPOXY GROUT
- EPOXY MORTAR BOND COAT

Use where moderate chemical exposure and severe cleaning methods are used, such as in commercial kitchens, dairies, breweries, and food plants.

ORGANIC ADHESIVE

- CERAMIC TILE
- ADHESIVE
- DOUBLE WOOD FLOOR

Use over wood or concrete floors in residential construction only. Not recommended in wet areas.

CERAMIC TILE INSTALLATION DETAILS FOR INTERIOR FLOORS

CERAMIC TILE TUB ENCLOSURE

- CERAMIC TILE
- ADHESIVE
- WATER RESISTANT GYPSUM BOARD
- STUDS AT 16" O/C
- SEALANT
- TUB HANGER
- BATHTUB
- FIREPROOFING WHEN REQUIRED (SEE PORTLAND CEMENT MORTAR METHOD)

TILE SHOWER RECEPTOR

- CERAMIC TILE
- BOND COAT
- REINFORCED MORTAR BED
- SHOWER PAN OR MEMBRANE
- SLOPED FILL
- WEEP HOLES
- CRUSHED TILE OR STONE

REMODELING WITH TILE OVER TILE

- NEW GYPSUM BOARD, PORTLAND CEMENT MORTAR, OR GLASS REINFORCED BACKER BOARD
- NEW CERAMIC TILE
- ADHESIVE OR DRY-SET MORTAR BONDING MATERIAL
- EXISTING TILE

- NEW CERAMIC TILE
- BONDING MATERIAL
- EXISTING FLOOR

CERAMIC TILE COUNTERTOP

- CUT WALL MORTAR AND METAL LATH HERE
- CERAMIC TILE
- BOND COAT
- MORTAR BED
- METAL LATH
- MEMBRANE
- WOOD BASE
- PUNCHED METAL STRIP

THRESHOLDS, SADDLES

- CERAMIC TILE
- MORTAR BED
- THRESHOLD
- ADJACENT FLOOR

CERAMIC TILE STAIRS

- CERAMIC TILE
- BOND COAT
- MORTAR BED

Tile Council of America, Inc.

9 **TILE**

Terrazzo is a material composed of stone chips and cement matrix and is usually polished. There are four generally accepted types, classified by appearance:

1. STANDARD TERRAZZO: The most common type; relatively small chip sizes (#1 and #2 size chips).
2. VENETIAN TERRAZZO: Larger chips (size #3 through #8), with smaller chips filling the spaces between.
3. PALLADIANA: Random fractured slabs of marble up to approximately 15 in. greatest dimension, 3/8 to 1 in. thick, with smaller chips filling spaces between.
4. RUSTIC TERRAZZO: Uniformly textured terrazzo in which matrix is depressed to expose chips, not ground or only slightly ground.

MATRIX DATA

Two basic types exist: portland cement and chemical binders. Color pigments are added to create special effects. Limeproof mineral pigments or synthetic mineral pigments compatible with portland cement are required. Both white and grey portland cement is used depending on final color.

CHEMICAL BINDERS

All five types of chemical binders provide excellent chemical and abrasion resistance, except for latex, which is rated good.

1. EPOXY MATRIX: Two component resinous matrix.
2. POLYESTER MATRIX: Two component resinous matrix.
3. POLYACRYLATE MATRIX: Composite resinous matrix.
4. LATEX MATRIX: Synthetic latex matrix.
5. CONDUCTIVE MATRIX: Special formulated matrix to conduct electricity with regulated resistance, use in surgical areas and where explosive gases are a hazard.

PRECAST TERRAZZO

Several units are routinely available and almost any shape can be produced. Examples include: straight, coved, and splayed bases; window sills; stair treads and risers; shower receptors; floor tiles; and wall facings.

STONE CHIPS

Stone used in terrazzo includes all calcareous serpentine and other rocks capable of taking a good polish. Marble and onyx are the preferred materials. Quartz, granite, quartzite, and silica pebbles are used for rustic terrazzo and textured mosaics not requiring polishing.

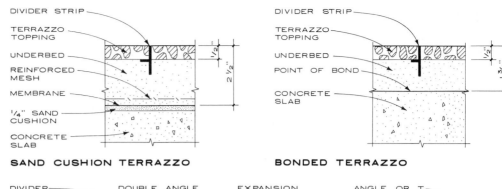

SAND CUSHION TERRAZZO   **BONDED TERRAZZO**

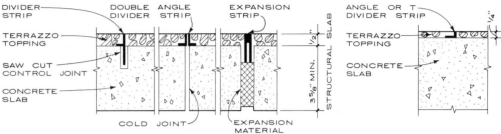

MONOLITHIC TERRAZZO   **THIN-SET TERRAZZO**

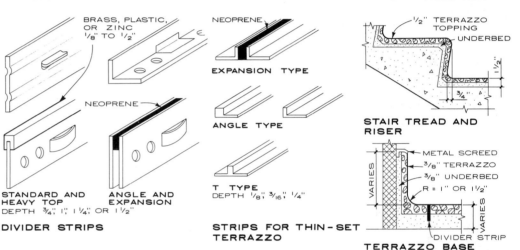

DIVIDER STRIPS

STRIPS FOR THIN-SET TERRAZZO

STAIR TREAD AND RISER

TERRAZZO BASE

TERRAZO SYSTEMS

TERRAZZO SYSTEM	MINIMUM ALLOWANCE FOR FINISH	MINIMUM WEIGHT/ SQ FT	CONTROL JOINT STRIP LOCATION	SUGGESTED PANEL SIZE AND DIVIDER STRIP LOCATION	COMMENTS
Sand cushion terrazzo	2 1/2"	27 lb	At all control joints in structure	9 to 36 sq ft	Avoid narrow proportions (length no more than twice the width) and acute angles
Bonded underbed or strip terrazzo	1 3/4"	18 lb	At all control joints in structure	16 to 36 sq ft	Avoid narrow proportions as in sand cushion
Monolithic terrazzo	1/2"	7 lb	At all control joints in structure and at column centers or over grade beams where spans are great	At column centers in sawn or recessed slots maximum 24 x 24 ft	T or L strips usually provide decorative feature only
Thin-set terrazzo (chemical binders)	1/4"	3 lb	At all control joints	Only where structural crack can be anticipated	
Modified thin-set terrazzo	3/8"	4 1/2 lb	At all control joints	Only where structural crack can be anticipated	
Terrazzo over permanent metal forms	Varies, 3" minimum	Varies	Directly over beam	Directly over joist centers and at 3 to 5 ft on center in the opposite direction	
Structural terrazzo	Varies, 4" minimum	Varies	At all control joints at columns and at perimeter of floor	Deep strip (1 1/2 in. min.) at all column centers and over grade beams	Use divider strip at any location where structural crack can be anticipated

NOTES
1. Venetian and Palladiana require greater depth due to larger chip size 2 3/4 in. minimum allowance for finish 28 lb/sq ft.
2. Divider and control joint strips are made of white alloy of zinc, brass, aluminum, or plastic. Aluminum is not satisfactory for portland cement matrix terrazzo; use brass and plastic in chemical binder matrix only with approval of binder manufacturer.
3. In exterior terrazzo, brass will tarnish and white alloy of zinc will deteriorate.

John C. Lunsford, AIA, Varney Sexton Sydnor Architects; Phoenix, Arizona

ACOUSTICAL CEILING SYSTEMS

CEILING TYPE	MAIN, CROSS T	ACCESS T's	Z CHANNEL	H CHANNEL	T SPLINE	FLAT SPLINE	SPACER	MODULAR T	METAL PAN T	SPECIAL	BENT STEEL	BENT STEEL ALUM. CAP	BENT ALUMINUM	EXTRUDED ALUMINUM	GALVANIZED	PAINTED	ANODIZED	EMBOSSED PATTERN	FIRE RATING AVAILABLE	12×12	12×24	24×24	24×48	24×60	20×60	30×60	60×60	48×48	NOTES
GYPSUM WALLBOARD																													
Suspended	•										•				•	•			•										
Exposed grid	•										•	•	•	•	•	•	•	•	•			•	•						
Semiconcealed grid	•					•					•				•	•			•			•	•						
Concealed H & T					•	•	•				•				•	•			•	•									
Concealed T & G			•								•				•	•			•	•									
Concealed Z			•			•					•				•	•			•	•									
Concealed access	•	•				•	•	•			•				•	•			•	•		•							
Modular	•					•	•		•		•					•			•				•	•	•	•	•	•	50 or 60″ sq main grid
Metal pan									•		•		•		•		•			•	•								12″ sq pattern
Linear metal										•			•		•														4″ o.c. typical
Perforated metal	•							•			•				•	•													1 way grid 4′–8′ o.c.
Luminous ceiling										•			•		•	•	•												1″ to 4″ sq grid

ACOUSTICAL CEILING MATERIALS

MATERIALS	12×12	12×24	24×24	24×48	24×60	20×60	30×60	60×60	48×48	CUSTOM SIZES	1/2	5/8	3/4	1	1½	3	SQUARE	TEGULAR	T & G	KERFED AND RABBETED	.45-.60	.60-.70	.70-.80	.80-.90	.90-.95	HIGH HUMIDITY	EXTERIOR SOFFIT	HIGH ABUSE/IMPACT	SCRUBBABLE	FIRE RATING AVAILABLE
Mineral fiber:																														
Painted	•	•	•	•	•	•	•			•	•	•	•				•	•	•	•	•	•	•	•						•
Plastic face		•	•									•					•					•							•	
Aluminum face	•		•									•					•						•			•				
Ceramic face		•	•									•					•					•	•			•				
Mineral face	•		•		•						•		•				•			•									•	
Glass fiber:																														
Painted		•	•							•	•	•	•				•											•		
Film face		•	•								•	•	•	•			•											•		
Glass cloth face	•	•	•	•	•	•					•		•	•			•											•		
Molded		•	•								•		•	•	Varies		•													
Gypsum		•	•											•			•									•			•	
Asbestos		•	•								3/16						•				•								•	
Tectum		•	•		•				•	•	1-3						•	•			•									

SPECIAL ACOUSTICAL SYSTEMS

SOUND ISOLATION: When it is necessary to isolate a high noise area from a building or a "quiet room" from a high surrounding noise level; floors, walls, and ceilings should be built free of rigid contact with the building structure to reduce sound and vibration transmission.

CUSTOM WALLS: Auditoriums, concert halls, and other special acoustically conditioned space may require both absorptive and reflective surfaces and in some cases surfaces that can be adjusted for varying absorption coefficients to "tune" the space.

LOOSE BATTS

USE: Reduce sound transmission through or over partitions; installed over suspended acoustical tile. Also used between gypsum wall partitions.
MATERIALS: Expanded fiberglass or mineral fiber.
S.T.C.: Based on total designed system, can range from 40 to 60.

Setter, Leach & Lindstrom, Inc.; Minneapolis, Minnesota

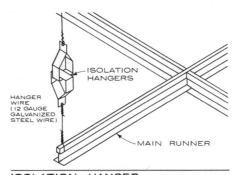

ISOLATION HANGER
CEILING ISOLATION HANGER

Isolates ceilings from noise traveling through the building structure. Hangers also available for isolating ceiling systems to shield spaces from mechanical equipment and/or aircraft noise.

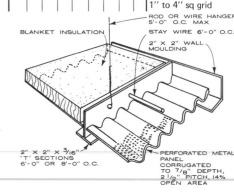

ROD OR WIRE HANGER 5'-0" O.C. MAX
BLANKET INSULATION
STAY WIRE 6'-0" O.C.
2" X 2" WALL MOULDING
2" X 2" X 3/16" 'T' SECTIONS 6'-0" OR 8'-0" O.C.
PERFORATED METAL PANEL CORRUGATED TO 7/8" DEPTH, 2 1/2" PITCH, 14% OPEN AREA

PERFORATED METAL CEILING

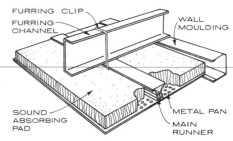

FURRING CLIP — FURRING CHANNEL — WALL MOULDING — SOUND ABSORBING PAD — METAL PAN — MAIN RUNNER

METAL PAN CEILING

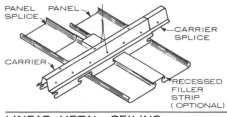

PANEL SPLICE — PANEL — CARRIER SPLICE — CARRIER — RECESSED FILLER STRIP (OPTIONAL)

LINEAR METAL CEILING
METAL CEILINGS

USE: Sound absorption depends on batt insulation.
MATERIALS: Bent steel, aluminum, or stainless steel.
N.R.C.: 0.70 to 0.90.
FINISH: Painted, anodized, or stainless steel.

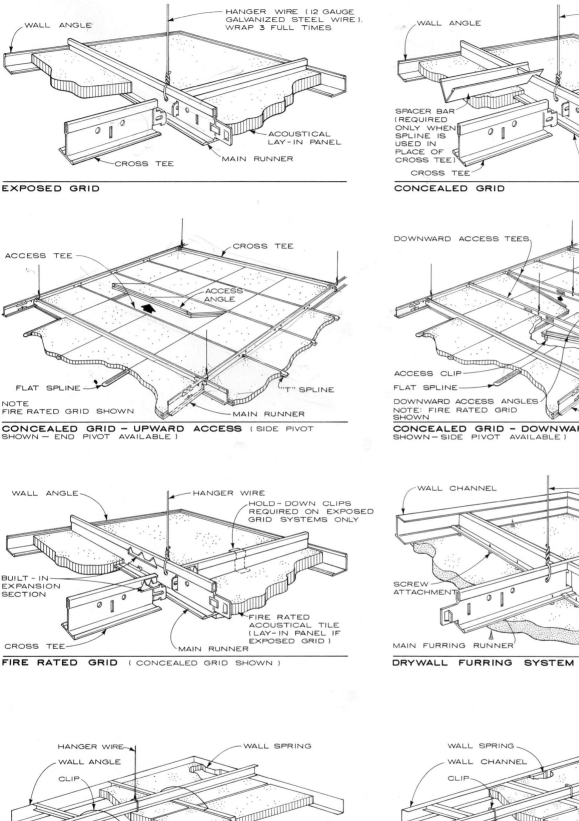

WALL ANGLE

HANGER WIRE (12 GAUGE GALVANIZED STEEL WIRE). WRAP 3 FULL TIMES

ACOUSTICAL LAY-IN PANEL

CROSS TEE

MAIN RUNNER

EXPOSED GRID

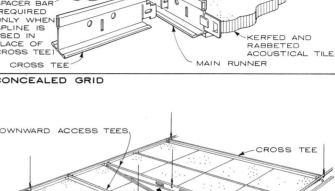

WALL ANGLE

HANGER WIRE (12 GAUGE GALVANIZED STEEL WIRE). WRAP 3 FULL TIMES

SPACER BAR (REQUIRED ONLY WHEN SPLINE IS USED IN PLACE OF CROSS TEE)

CROSS TEE

KERFED AND RABBETED ACOUSTICAL TILE

MAIN RUNNER

CONCEALED GRID

ACCESS TEE

CROSS TEE

ACCESS ANGLE

FLAT SPLINE

NOTE
FIRE RATED GRID SHOWN

"T" SPLINE

MAIN RUNNER

CONCEALED GRID – UPWARD ACCESS (SIDE PIVOT SHOWN – END PIVOT AVAILABLE)

DOWNWARD ACCESS TEES

CROSS TEE

ACCESS CLIP

FLAT SPLINE

DOWNWARD ACCESS ANGLES
NOTE: FIRE RATED GRID SHOWN

"T" SPLINE

MAIN RUNNER

CONCEALED GRID – DOWNWARD ACCESS (END PIVOT SHOWN – SIDE PIVOT AVAILABLE)

WALL ANGLE

HANGER WIRE

HOLD-DOWN CLIPS REQUIRED ON EXPOSED GRID SYSTEMS ONLY

BUILT-IN EXPANSION SECTION

CROSS TEE

MAIN RUNNER

FIRE RATED ACOUSTICAL TILE (LAY-IN PANEL IF EXPOSED GRID)

FIRE RATED GRID (CONCEALED GRID SHOWN)

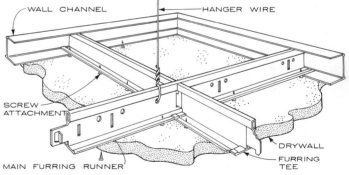

WALL CHANNEL

HANGER WIRE

SCREW ATTACHMENT

MAIN FURRING RUNNER

DRYWALL

FURRING TEE

DRYWALL FURRING SYSTEM

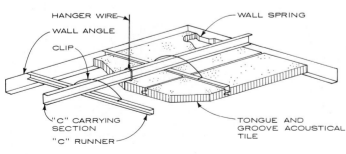

HANGER WIRE

WALL SPRING

WALL ANGLE

CLIP

"C" CARRYING SECTION

"C" RUNNER

TONGUE AND GROOVE ACOUSTICAL TILE

TONGUE AND GROOVE

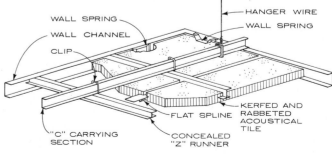

WALL SPRING

WALL CHANNEL

HANGER WIRE

WALL SPRING

CLIP

"C" CARRYING SECTION

FLAT SPLINE

CONCEALED "Z" RUNNER

KERFED AND RABBETED ACOUSTICAL TILE

CONCEALED "Z" SYSTEM

Setter, Leach & Lindstrom, Inc.; Minneapolis, Minnesota

ACOUSTICAL TREATMENT

9

WALL PANELS

1. USE: Sound absorption.
2. MATERIALS: Fabric-wrapped glass, wood, or mineral fiber.
3. N.R.C.: 0.55-0.85.
4. NOTES: May be used as individual panels or entire wall surfaces. N.R.C. varies with material, thickness and "sound-transparency" of fabric facing. Maximum sizes vary with manufacturer up to 4 x 12 ft.

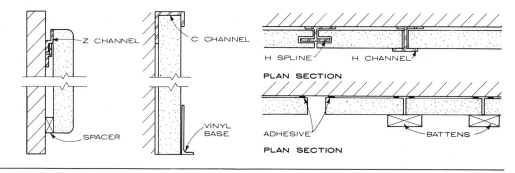

PLAN SECTION

PLAN SECTION

WALL PANELS

SUSPENDED PANELS

1. USE: Sound absorption.
2. MATERIALS: Vertical suspension—glass fiber blanket wrapped with perforated aluminum foil or fabric stretched over frame. Horizontal suspension—perforated steel or aluminum with glass fiber blanket, or similar to vertical.
3. S.A.C.: 1.2-1.5 sabins per square foot of ceiling.
4. NOTES: Panels may be suspended from structure or attached directly to ceiling grid. May be arranged in a variety of patterns including linear, square, zigzag vertical, or regular or random spaced horizontal panels.

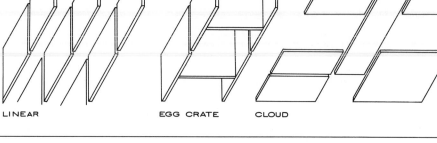

LINEAR   EGG CRATE   CLOUD

SUSPENDED PANELS

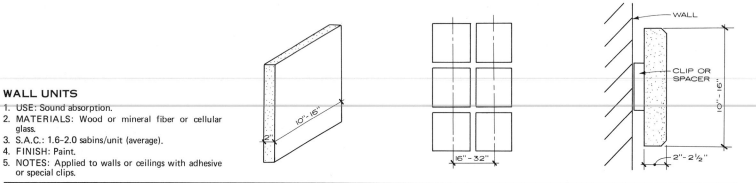

WALL UNITS

1. USE: Sound absorption.
2. MATERIALS: Wood or mineral fiber or cellular glass.
3. S.A.C.: 1.6-2.0 sabins/unit (average).
4. FINISH: Paint.
5. NOTES: Applied to walls or ceilings with adhesive or special clips.

WALL UNITS

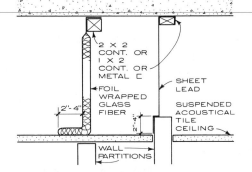

PLENUM BARRIER

1. USE: Reduce sound transmission through plenum above partitions.
2. MATERIALS: 1/64 in. sheet lead, lead-loaded vinyl, perforated aluminum, or foil-wrapped glass fiber.
3. S.T.C.: 18-41 dB improvement.
4. NOTES: All openings through barrier for pipes, ducts, etc., must be sealed airtight for maximum effectiveness.

PLENUM BARRIERS

CONCRETE MASONRY UNITS

1. USE: Sound absorption.
2. MATERIALS: Modular concrete block, 4, 6, 8 in. thick, with metal baffle and/or fibrous filler in slotted cores.
3. N.R.C.: .45-.65.

CONCRETE MASONRY UNITS

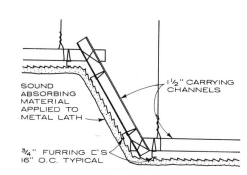

SPRAY-ON ACOUSTICAL MATERIAL

1. USE: Sound absorption.
2. MATERIALS: Mineral or cellulose fibers spray applied to metal lath or directly to hard surfaces such as concrete, steel, masonry, or gypsum board.
3. N.R.C.: .50-.95.
4. NOTES: Application to metal lath provides slightly better sound absorption and permits irregular shapes. Available with a hard surface for wall applications. Available with fire protection rating.

SPRAY-ON ACOUSTICAL MATERIAL

Setter, Leach & Lindstrom, Inc.; Minneapolis, Minnesota

9

ACOUSTICAL TREATMENT

TABLE OF RESILIENT FLOORING CHARACTERISTICS

TYPE OF RESILIENT FLOORING	BASIC COMPONENTS	SUBFLOOR APPLICATION*			RECOMMENDED LOAD LIMIT (PSI)	DURA-BILITY†	RESISTANCE TO HEEL DAMAGE	EASE OF MAINTENANCE	GREASE RESISTANCE	SURFACE ALKALI RESISTANCE	RESISTANCE TO STAINING	CIGARETTE BURN RESISTANCE	RESILIENCE	QUIETNESS
Vinyl sheet	Vinyl resins with fiber back	B	O	S	75–100	2–3	2–5	1–2	1	1–3	3–4	4	4	4
Homogeneous vinyl tile	Vinyl resins	B	O	S	150–200	1–3	1–4	2–4	1	1–2	1–5	2–5	2–5	2–5
Vinyl asbestos tile	Vinyl resins and asbestos fibers	B	O	S	25–50	2	4–5	2–3	2	4	2	6	6	6
Cork tile with vinyl coating	Raw cork and vinyl resins			S	150	4	3	2	1	1	5	3	3	3
Cork tile	Raw cork and resins			S	75	5	4	4	4	5	4	1	1	1
Rubber tile	Rubber compound	B	O	S	200	2	4	4	3	2	1	2	2	2
Linoleum	Cork, wood, floor, and oleoresins			S	75	3	4–5	4–5	1	4	2	4	4	4
Asphalt tile	Resins, asphalt compounds-asbestos	B	O	S	25	3–4	4	4	5	5	4	7	7	6

*B: below grade; O: on grade; S: suspended.
†Numerals indicate subjective ratings (relative rank of each floor to others listed above) "1" indicating highest.
 Bruce A. Kenan, AIA; Pederson, Hueber, Hares & Glavin; Syracuse, New York.

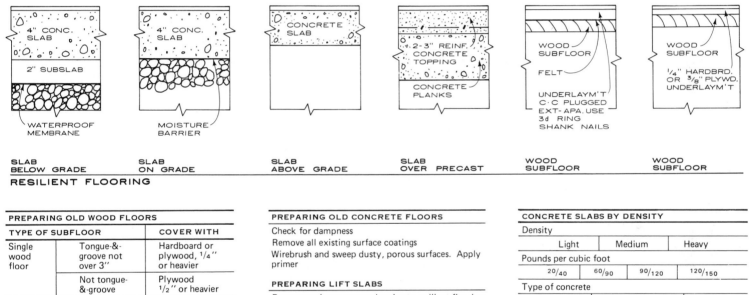

RESILIENT FLOORING

PREPARING OLD WOOD FLOORS

TYPE OF SUBFLOOR		COVER WITH
Single wood floor	Tongue-&-groove not over 3"	Hardboard or plywood, 1/4" or heavier
	Not tongue-&-groove	Plywood 1/2" or heavier
Double wood floor	Strips 3" or more	Hardboard or plywood 1" or heavier
	Strips less than 3" tongue-&-groove	Renail or replace loose boards, remove surface irregularities

PREPARING OLD CONCRETE FLOORS

Check for dampness
Remove all existing surface coatings
Wirebrush and sweep dusty, porous surfaces. Apply primer

PREPARING LIFT SLABS

Remove curing compounds prior to resilient flooring installation
For installation of vinyl-asbestos tile, see manufacturer's instructions

CONCRETE SLABS BY DENSITY

Density		
Light	Medium	Heavy
Pounds per cubic foot		
20/40	60/90 90/120	120/150
Type of concrete		
Expanded perlite, vermiculite, and others	Expanded slag shale, and clay	Standard concrete of sand, gravel, or stone
Recommendations		
Top with 1" thickness of standard concrete mix	Approved for use of resilient flooring if troweled smooth and even	

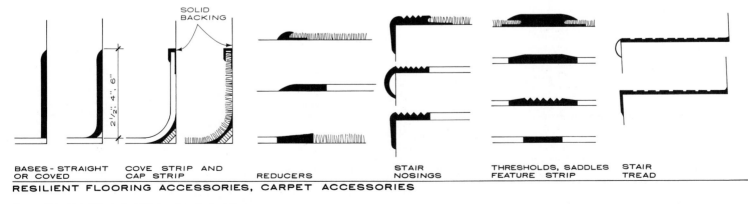

RESILIENT FLOORING ACCESSORIES, CARPET ACCESSORIES

Broome, Oringdulph, O'Toole, Rudolf & Associates; Portland, Oregon

RECOMMENDED GUIDELINES FOR CARPET SELECTION

1. Know the budget, including installation costs.
2. Be aware of the types of traffic load—moderate, heavy, or extra heavy. Be aware of potential pivot, funnel, and traffic flow areas.
3. Know the minimum life expectancy required.
4. Make certain that maintenance levels are appropriate for the required life expectancy.
5. Make certain that colors, textures, and patterns are appropriate for the expected types of soiling, staining, and wear.
6. Know what types of surface texture will be required.
7. Be assured that the right gauge or pitch has been selected.
8. Make sure that pile or face yarns are selected that can do the job.
9. Make certain that the carpet construction fits the needs of the job. Will it:
   a. Eliminate static shock?
   b. Have sufficient tuft bind strength?
   c. Meet local and Federal flame spread restrictions?
   d. Have pilling and fuzzing resistance?
   e. Be suitable if subjected to rolling traffic?
   f. Have enough bond strength between primary carpet structure and secondary backing to prevent delamination?
   g. Have crush and wear resistance?
   h. Have adequate resistance to sunlight?
   i. Have attached backings that are properly constructed?
   j. Meet sound absorption requirements?
10. Know that the carpet construction is not being overspecified, thus adding unneeded expense.
11. Be certain that the best methods of installation are being used. Are there any special requirements to be considered?

INSTALLATION REQUIREMENTS

Factors that must be considered before making a final decision include:

1. Traffic classification in terms of load and nature.
2. Acoustical requirements, heat transfer properties, and resilience.
3. Dimensional stability.
4. Condition and type of subfloor.
5. Budget.

STRETCH-IN TACKLESS

The conventional method of installing a carpet is by power stretching over a separate cushion. A padded carpet offers superior sound control, resilience, and added foot comfort. This method is not recommended for large open areas where shifting and buckling could present a problem or in areas where heavy, wheeled traffic is anticipated.

DIRECT GLUE DOWN

Recommended for large areas where heavy, wheeled traffic is anticipated and for maximum carpet stability. This method also significantly reduces seam splitting and delamination problems. The correct pile density will minimize loss of resilience and give thermal and acoustical control. The direct glue down method usually involves three basic types of carpet backing: jute or nonwoven synthetic secondary back; attached cushion back; or latex, polyvinyl chloride, or polyurethane compounds. This method has been used effectively on all types of subflooring ranging from below grade concrete to grade concrete, suspended concrete, suspended wood, and existing resilient floors. Preparation of the subfloor is of primary importance when specifying this method.

SEAMING

The three main methods of seaming are heat seams, sewn seams, and latex seams.

SOUND ABSORPTION

The carpet's texture, density, and weight determine its noise reduction coefficient (NRC). The greater the NRC rating the more absorbent the material. The combination of pad and carpet can vary the NRC rating.

Walter H. Sobel, FAIA & Associates; Chicago, Illinois

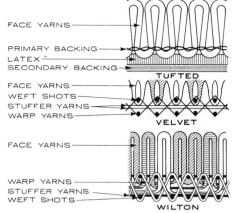

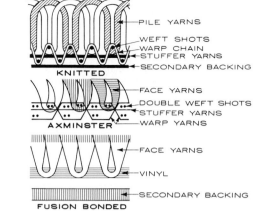

CONSTRUCTION MODES

TUFTED

A tufted carpet is made by inserting face yarn or tufts through premanufactured backing by use of needles (like a sewing machine). Yarns are held in place by coating the back with latex; a secondary back is applied to add body and stability. 87% of contract carpet used today is tufted.

VELVET WOVEN

The simplest of all carpet weaves. Pile is formed as loom loops warp yarns over wires inserted across loom. Pile height is determined by height of wire inserted. Velvets are traditionally known for smooth cut pile plush or loop pile textures, but can also create hi-lo loop or cut-uncut textures. 7% of contract carpet used today is velvet woven.

AXMINSTER WOVEN

The Axminster loom is highly specialized and nearly as versatile as hand weaving. Color combinations and designs are limited only by the number of tufts in the carpet. Almost all the yarn appears on the surface, and characteristic of this weave is a heavy ribbed back that allows the carpet to be rolled lengthwise only. 1% of contract carpet used today is Axminster woven.

FUSION BONDED

This process produces complete carpet by imbedding pile yarns and adhering backing to a viscous vinyl paste that hardens after curing carpet. Has superior tuft bind and practically eliminates backing delamination. Over 90% of yarn is in the face. Fusion bonded process produces very dense cut pile or level loop fabrics in solid or moresque colors. 1% of contract carpet used today is fusion bonded.

KNITTED

The knitted process resembles weaving in that the face and back are made simultaneously. Backing and pile yarns are looped together with a stitching yarn on machines that have three sets of needles. Knitted carpets usually have solid or tweed colors, with a level loop pile texture. 1% of contract carpet used today is knitted.

WILTON WOVEN

The Wilton loom operates basically like a velvet loom, except that it has the Jacquard mechanism with up to six colors or frames. Only one color at a time is utilized on the surface; other yarns therefore remain buried in the body of the carpet until needed. Wilton looms can produce cut pile, level loop, multilevel, or carved textures. 3% of contract carpet used today is Wilton woven.

CONSTRUCTION COMPONENTS

PITCH OR GAUGE

In woven carpet pitch is the number of ends of yarn in 27 in. of width. In tufted carpet gauge is the spacing of needles across the width of the tufting machine expressed in fractions of an inch.

STITCHES OR ROWS/WIRES

These are the number of per 1 in. of carpet tufts, counting lengthwise.

TUFTS PER SQUARE INCH

A calculation made by multiplying the number of ends across the width (gauge or pitch) by the number of tufts lengthwise (stitches or rows) per inch.

PILE HEIGHT

The height of the loop or tuft from the surface of the backing to the top of the pile is measured in fractions or decimals of an inch.

FACE WEIGHT

The total weight of pile yarns in the carpet measured in oz/yd^2. This excludes backing yarns or fabric.

DENSITY

A calculation used to measure the compactness of face yarns in a carpet. Increased density generally results in better performance.

YARN SIZE AND PLY

DENIER: The unit of weight for the size of a single filament yarn. The higher the denier number the heavier the yarn.

PLY: The number of single ends of yarn twisted together to form a heavier, larger yarn.

BACKING: The foundation construction that supports the pile yarns.

PRIMARY BACKING: In tufted carpet, a woven or nonwoven fabric into which pile yarns are attached; usually jute or polypropylene. In woven carpets backing yarns are usually kraftcord, cotton, polyester, jute, or rayon.

SECONDARY BACKING: An extra layer of material laminated to the underside of the carpet for additional dimensional stability and body. Usually latex, jute, H.D. foam, sponge rubber, or vinyl.

STANDARD CARPET AND RUG SIZES

CARPET	WIDTH
Synthetic fibers	4'-6'', 6'-0'', 7'-6'', 9'-0'', 12'-0'', 15'-0''
Wool fibers	9'-0'', 12'-0'', 15'-0''
Sponge bonded, Rubber backed	4'-6'', 12'-0''

PADS	
All hair, hair and fiber, and rubberized hair and fiber	2'-3'', 3'-0'', 4'-6'', 9'-0'', 12'-0''
Foam rubber	3'-0'', 6'-0''
Sponge rubber	3'-0'', 4'-6'', 9'-0''

RUGS: Rugs are bound pieces of carpet that are not attached to the floor. The sizes therefore vary.

FINISH FLOORING

NOTES

1. Flooring can be manufactured from practically every commercially available species of wood. In the United States wood flooring is grouped for marketing purposes roughly according to species and region. There are various grading systems used with various species, and often different specifications for different sized boards in a given species. For instance, nail size and spacing varies among the several board sizes typically available in oak.

2. Information given here should be used for preliminary decision making only. Precise specifications must be obtained from the supplier or from the appropriate industry organization named below.

3. Several considerations in wood flooring selection and installation are applicable industrywide. These are shown graphically at right.

4. The table below includes typical grades and sizes of boards for each species or regional group. Grade classifications vary, but in each case one can assume that the first grade listed is the highest quality, and that the quality decreases with each succeeding grade. The best grade will typically minimize or exclude features such as knots, streaks, spots, checks, and torn grain and will contain the highest percentage of longer boards. Grade standards have been reduced in recent years for practically all commercially produced flooring, hence a thorough review of exact grade specifications is in order when selecting wood flooring.

5. End matching gives a complete tongue and grooved joint all around each board. Board length is reduced as required to obtain the matched ends.

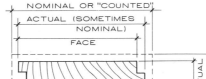

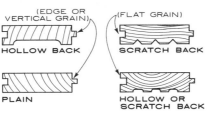

CROSS SECTIONAL DIMENSIONING SYSTEMS VARY AMONG SPECIES, PATTERNS, MANUFACTURERS. TRADE ORGANIZATIONS PROVIDE PERCENTAGE MULTIPLIERS FOR COMPUTING COVERAGE.

CROSS SECTIONAL DIMENSIONS

THE UNDERSIDE OF FLOORING BOARDS MAY BE PATTERNED AND OFTEN WILL CONTAIN MORE DEFECTS THAN ARE ALLOWED IN THE TOP FACE. GRAIN IS OFTEN MIXED IN ANY GIVEN RUN OF BOARDS.

BOARD CHARACTERISTICS

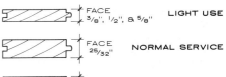
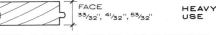

MOST FLOORING MAY BE HAD IN VARYING THICKNESSES TO SUIT WEAR REQUIREMENTS. ACTUAL DIMENSIONS SHOWN ARE AVAILABLE IN MAPLE.

VARIOUS THICKNESSES

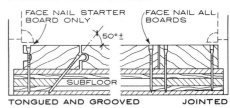

JOINTED FLOORING MUST BE FACE NAILED, USUALLY WITH FULLY BARBED FLOORING BRADS.
TONGUE AND GROOVED BOARDS ARE BLIND NAILED WITH SPIRAL FLOOR SCREWS, CEMENT COATED NAILS, CUT NAILS, MACHINE DRIVEN FASTENERS, USE MANUFACTURER'S RECOMMENDATIONS.

FASTENING

PARQUET FLOORING—SQUARE PANELS

THICKNESS	FACE DIMENSIONS
$5/16$'' (most common) $9/16$'', $11/16$'', $3/4$''	6'' x 6'', $6^{1}/4$'' x $6^{1}/2$'', 12'' x 12'', 19'' x 19'' Other sizes are available from certain manufacturers

PARQUET FLOORING—INDIVIDUAL STRIPS

THICKNESS	FACE DIMENSIONS
$5/16$''	2'' x 12'' typical strips can be cut, mitered, etc., to obtain pieces required for special patterns

TYPICAL GRADES AND SIZES OF BOARDS BY SPECIES OR REGIONAL GROUP

GROUP	INDUSTRY ORGANIZATION	GRADE	THICKNESS	WIDTH		NOTES
Oak (also beech, birch, pecan, and hard maple)	National Oak Flooring Manufacturers' Assoc.	Quarter Sawn: Clear, Select; Plain Sawn: Clear, Select, No. 1 Common, No. 2 Common	$3/4$'', $1/2$'' Standard; also $3/8$'' $5/16$''	Face $1^{1}/2$'' 2'' $2^{1}/4$''		This association grades birch, beech, and hard maple: First Grade, Second Grade, Third Grade, and "Special Grades." Pecan is graded: First Grade, First Grade Red, Second Grade, Second Grade Red, Third Grade
Hard maple (also beech and birch) (acer saccharum—not soft maple)	Maple Flooring Manufacturers' Assoc. Inc.	First Grade, Second Grade, Third Grade, Fourth Grade, Combinations	$3/8$'', $12/32$'' $41/32$'', $1/2$'' $33/32$'', $53/32$'', $5/8$''	Face $1^{1}/2$'' 2'' $2^{1}/4$'' $3^{1}/4$''		Association states that beech and birch have physical properties that make them fully suitable as substitutes for hard maple. See manufacturer for available width and thickness combinations
Southern pine	Southern Pine Inspection Bureau	B & B, C, C & Btr, D, No. 2	$3/8$'', $1/2$'' $5/8$'', 1'' $1^{1}/4$'', $1^{1}/2$''	Nom. 2'' 3'' 4'' 5'' 6''	Face $1^{1}/8$'' $2^{1}/8$'' $3^{1}/8$'' $4^{1}/8$'' $5^{1}/8$''	Grain may be specified as edge (rift), near-rift, or flat. If not specified, manufacturer will ship flat or mixed grain boards. See manufacturer for available width and thickness combinations
Western woods (Douglas fir, hemlock, Englemann spruce, Idaho pine, incense cedar, lodgepole pine, Ponderosa pine, sugar pine, Western larch, Western red cedar)	Western Wood Products Association	Select: 1 & 2 clear-B & Btr, C Select, D Select; Finish: Superior, Prime, E	2'' and thinner	Nominal 3'' 4'' 6''		Flooring is machined tongue and groove and may be furnished in any grade agreeable to buyer and seller. Grain may be specified as vertical (VG), flat (FG), or mixed (MG). Basic size for flooring is 1'' x 4'' x 12'; standard lengths 4' and above
Eastern white pine, Norway pine, Jack pine, Eastern spruce, Balsam fir, Eastern hemlock, Tamarack	Northern Hardwood & Pine Manufacturers' Association	C & Btr, Select, D Select, Stained Select	$3/8$'', $1/2$'' $5/8$'', 1'' $1^{1}/4$'', $1^{1}/2$''	Nom. 2'' 3'' 4'' 5'' 6''	Face $1^{1}/8$'' $2^{1}/8$'' $3^{1}/8$'' $4^{1}/8$'' $5^{1}/8$''	The various species included in this "Lake States Region" group provide different visual features. Consult manufacturer or local supplier to determine precisely what is available in terms of species and appearance

Darrel Rippeteau, Architect; Washington, D.C.

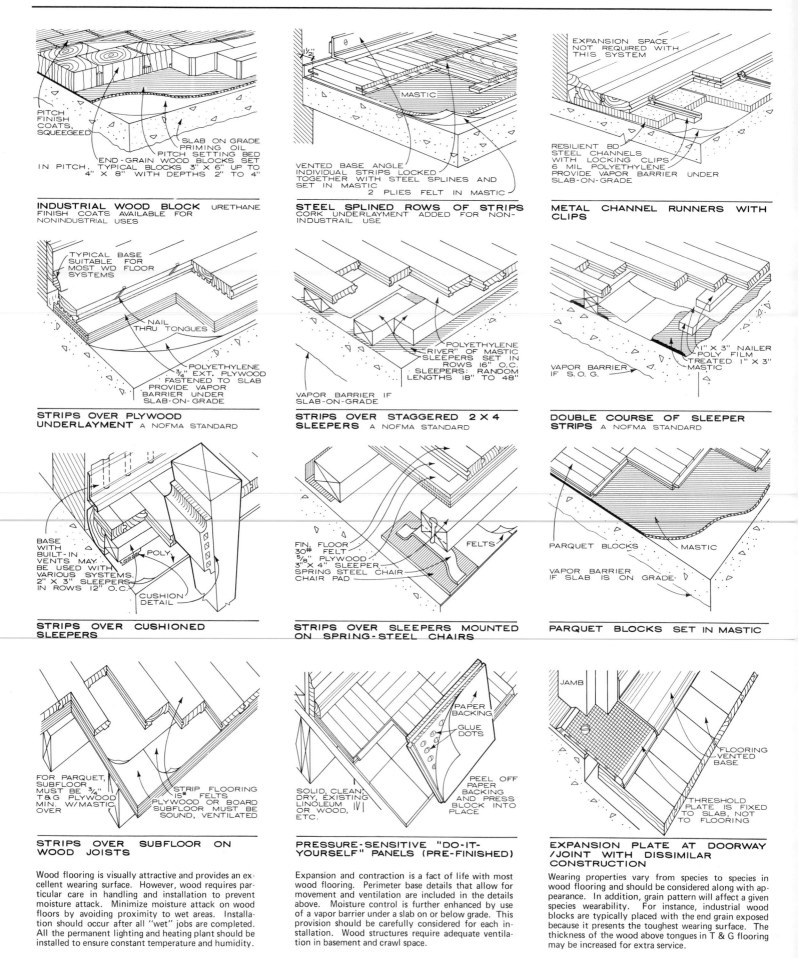

INDUSTRIAL WOOD BLOCK URETHANE FINISH COATS AVAILABLE FOR NONINDUSTRIAL USES

PITCH FINISH COATS, SQUEEGEED

SLAB ON GRADE
PRIMING OIL
PITCH SETTING BED
END-GRAIN WOOD BLOCKS SET IN PITCH. TYPICAL BLOCKS 3" X 6" UP TO 4" X 8" WITH DEPTHS 2" TO 4"

STEEL SPLINED ROWS OF STRIPS CORK UNDERLAYMENT ADDED FOR NON-INDUSTRIAL USE

MASTIC

VENTED BASE ANGLE
INDIVIDUAL STRIPS LOCKED TOGETHER WITH STEEL SPLINES AND SET IN MASTIC
2 PLIES FELT IN MASTIC

METAL CHANNEL RUNNERS WITH CLIPS

EXPANSION SPACE NOT REQUIRED WITH THIS SYSTEM

RESILIENT BD
STEEL CHANNELS WITH LOCKING CLIPS
6 MIL POLYETHYLENE PROVIDE VAPOR BARRIER UNDER SLAB-ON-GRADE

STRIPS OVER PLYWOOD UNDERLAYMENT A NOFMA STANDARD

TYPICAL BASE SUITABLE FOR MOST WD FLOOR SYSTEMS

NAIL THRU TONGUES

POLYETHYLENE
¾" EXT. PLYWOOD FASTENED TO SLAB PROVIDE VAPOR BARRIER UNDER SLAB-ON-GRADE

STRIPS OVER STAGGERED 2 X 4 SLEEPERS A NOFMA STANDARD

POLYETHYLENE "RIVER" OF MASTIC
SLEEPERS SET IN ROWS 16" O.C.
SLEEPERS: RANDOM LENGTHS 18" TO 48"

VAPOR BARRIER IF SLAB-ON-GRADE

DOUBLE COURSE OF SLEEPER STRIPS A NOFMA STANDARD

1" X 3" NAILER
POLY FILM
TREATED 1" X 3"
MASTIC

VAPOR BARRIER IF S.O.G.

STRIPS OVER CUSHIONED SLEEPERS

BASE WITH BUILT-IN VENTS MAY BE USED WITH VARIOUS SYSTEMS. 2" X 3" SLEEPERS IN ROWS 12" O.C.

POLY

CUSHION DETAIL

STRIPS OVER SLEEPERS MOUNTED ON SPRING-STEEL CHAIRS

FIN. FLOOR
30# FELT
⅝" PLYWOOD
3" X 4" SLEEPER
SPRING STEEL CHAIR
CHAIR PAD

FELTS

PARQUET BLOCKS SET IN MASTIC

PARQUET BLOCKS

MASTIC

VAPOR BARRIER IF SLAB IS ON GRADE

STRIPS OVER SUBFLOOR ON WOOD JOISTS

FOR PARQUET, SUBFLOOR MUST BE ¾" T&G PLYWOOD MIN. W/MASTIC OVER

STRIP FLOORING
15# FELTS
PLYWOOD OR BOARD SUBFLOOR MUST BE SOUND, VENTILATED

PRESSURE-SENSITIVE "DO-IT-YOURSELF" PANELS (PRE-FINISHED)

PAPER BACKING

GLUE DOTS

SOLID, CLEAN, DRY, EXISTING LINOLEUM OR WOOD, ETC.

PEEL OFF PAPER BACKING AND PRESS BLOCK INTO PLACE

EXPANSION PLATE AT DOORWAY /JOINT WITH DISSIMILAR CONSTRUCTION

JAMB

FLOORING VENTED BASE

THRESHOLD PLATE IS FIXED TO SLAB, NOT TO FLOORING

Wood flooring is visually attractive and provides an excellent wearing surface. However, wood requires particular care in handling and installation to prevent moisture attack. Minimize moisture attack on wood floors by avoiding proximity to wet areas. Installation should occur after all "wet" jobs are completed. All the permanent lighting and heating plant should be installed to ensure constant temperature and humidity.

Expansion and contraction is a fact of life with most wood flooring. Perimeter base details that allow for movement and ventilation are included in the details above. Moisture control is further enhanced by use of a vapor barrier under a slab on or below grade. This provision should be carefully considered for each installation. Wood structures require adequate ventilation in basement and crawl space.

Wearing properties vary from species to species in wood flooring and should be considered along with appearance. In addition, grain pattern will affect a given species wearability. For instance, industrial wood blocks are typically placed with the end grain exposed because it presents the toughest wearing surface. The thickness of the wood above tongues in T & G flooring may be increased for extra service.

Darrel Rippeteau, Architect; Washington, D.C.

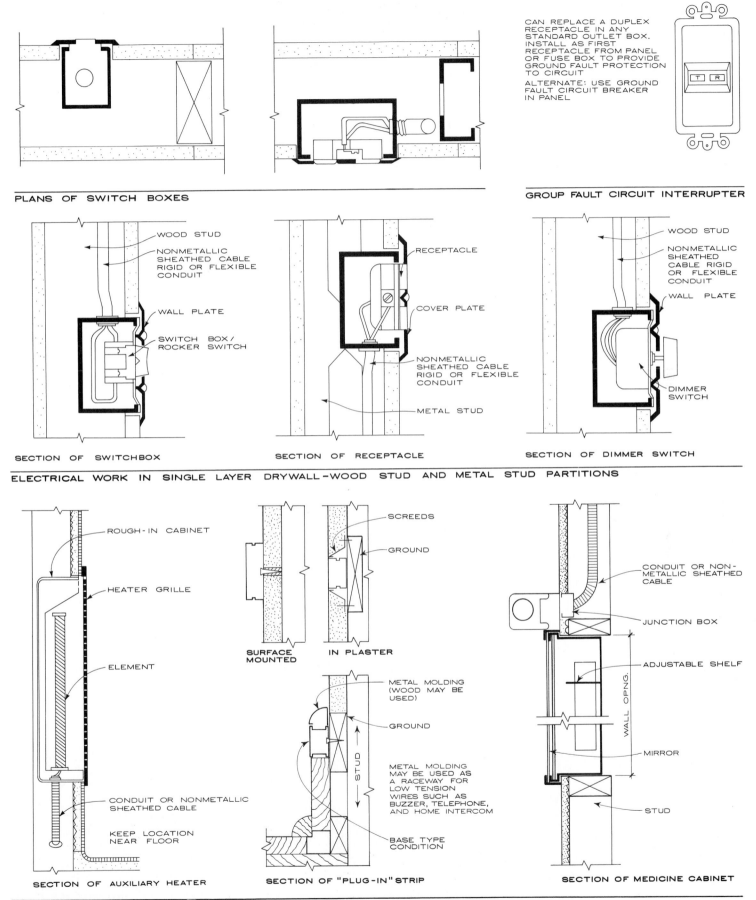

CAN REPLACE A DUPLEX RECEPTACLE IN ANY STANDARD OUTLET BOX. INSTALL AS FIRST RECEPTACLE FROM PANEL OR FUSE BOX TO PROVIDE GROUND FAULT PROTECTION TO CIRCUIT

ALTERNATE: USE GROUND FAULT CIRCUIT BREAKER IN PANEL

PLANS OF SWITCH BOXES

GROUP FAULT CIRCUIT INTERRUPTER

WOOD STUD

NONMETALLIC SHEATHED CABLE RIGID OR FLEXIBLE CONDUIT

WALL PLATE

SWITCH BOX / ROCKER SWITCH

RECEPTACLE

COVER PLATE

NONMETALLIC SHEATHED CABLE RIGID OR FLEXIBLE CONDUIT

METAL STUD

WOOD STUD

NONMETALLIC SHEATHED CABLE RIGID OR FLEXIBLE CONDUIT

WALL PLATE

DIMMER SWITCH

SECTION OF SWITCHBOX

SECTION OF RECEPTACLE

SECTION OF DIMMER SWITCH

ELECTRICAL WORK IN SINGLE LAYER DRYWALL–WOOD STUD AND METAL STUD PARTITIONS

ROUGH-IN CABINET

HEATER GRILLE

ELEMENT

CONDUIT OR NONMETALLIC SHEATHED CABLE

KEEP LOCATION NEAR FLOOR

SCREEDS

GROUND

SURFACE MOUNTED

IN PLASTER

METAL MOLDING (WOOD MAY BE USED)

GROUND

STUD

METAL MOLDING MAY BE USED AS A RACEWAY FOR LOW TENSION WIRES SUCH AS BUZZER, TELEPHONE, AND HOME INTERCOM

BASE TYPE CONDITION

CONDUIT OR NON-METALLIC SHEATHED CABLE

JUNCTION BOX

ADJUSTABLE SHELF

WALL OPNG.

MIRROR

STUD

SECTION OF AUXILIARY HEATER

SECTION OF "PLUG-IN" STRIP

SECTION OF MEDICINE CABINET

ELECTRICAL WORK IN BUILT-IN EQUIPMENT

Walter H. Sobel, FAIA & Associates; Chicago, Illinois

B. J. Baldwin; Giffels & Rossetti, Inc.; Detroit, Michigan

WALL COVERINGS

9

CHAPTER 10 SPECIALTIES

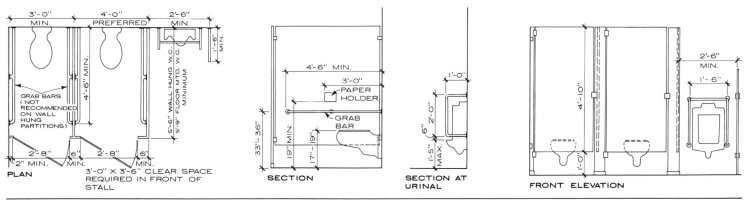

HANDICAPPED TOILET LAYOUT

PLAN · SECTION · SECTION AT URINAL · FRONT ELEVATION

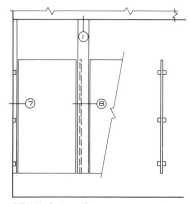

FLOOR MOUNTED

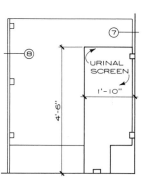

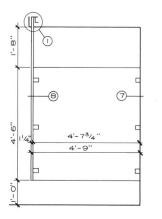

MARBLE TOILET PARTITIONS

Marble toilet partitions are precast, predrilled, and prefinished and are delivered to the site ready to install. Partitions are available in floor mounted or ceiling hung styles. Floor mounted units are set on dowels cast into the finish floor. Ceiling hung units are bolted to overhead channel supports.

Marble toilet partitions are available in polished finish only. Panel thickness ranges from 7/8 to 1 1/4 in., height to 4 ft 6 in., and widths from 1 ft 10 in. to 3 ft. Black, buff, gray, green, pink, and white colors are standard. Marble partitions are provided with either solid core flush wood doors or 22 gauge hollow core steel doors.

Nonstaining, waterproof sealants are recommended for marble work.

Toilet partition hardware is usually made of brass and is chrome plated for exposed applications. Custom accessories such as shelves, coat hooks, and paper holders may be ordered with marble panels.

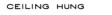

CEILING HUNG

MARBLE TOILET PARTITIONS

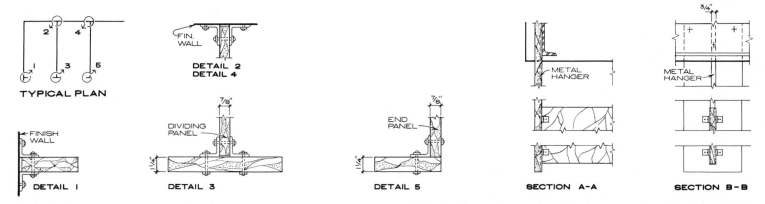

TYPICAL PLAN · **DETAIL 2 / DETAIL 4** · **DETAIL 1** · **DETAIL 3** · **DETAIL 5** · **SECTION A-A** · **SECTION B-B**

MARBLE PARTITION DETAILS

Pearce Corporation; St. Louis, Missouri

GENERAL NOTES

1. Compartment types: ceiling hung (marble or metal), overhead braced, wall hung (metal only).
2. Metal finishes: baked-on enamel, porcelain enamel, stainless steel.
3. A = standard compartment widths: 2'-6", 2'-8", 2'-10", 3'-0" (2'-10" is most frequently used).
4. B = standard door widths: 1'-8", 1'-10", 2'-0", 2'-2", 2'-4", 2'-6". (2'-0" metal doors are standard with marble compartments.) Nonstandard sizes that are sometimes used: 1'-11", 2'-3", 2'-5".
5. C = standard pilaster widths: 3", 4", 5", 6", 8", 10", 1'-0". Nonstandard sizes that are sometimes used: 2", 7", 1'-2".
6. D = standard panel widths: 18" to 57" in 1" increments. All panels are 58" high.

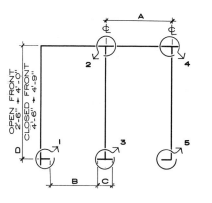

PLAN OF STANDARD W.C. COMPARTMENT
(TYPICAL FOR METAL OR PLASTIC LAMINATE)

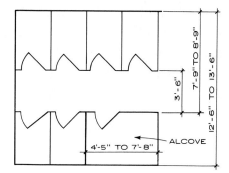

SPACE REQUIREMENTS

GENERAL PLANNING DATA

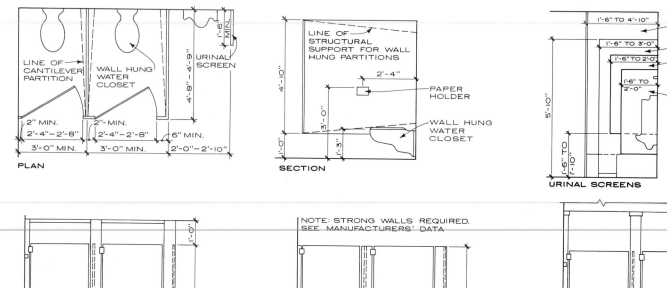

PLAN

SECTION

URINAL SCREENS

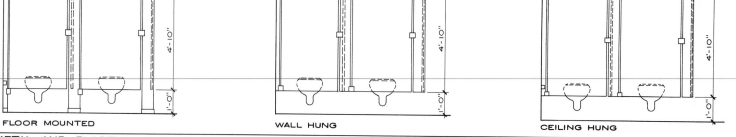

FLOOR MOUNTED

NOTE: STRONG WALLS REQUIRED. SEE MANUFACTURERS' DATA

WALL HUNG

CEILING HUNG

METAL AND PLASTIC LAMINATE PARTITIONS

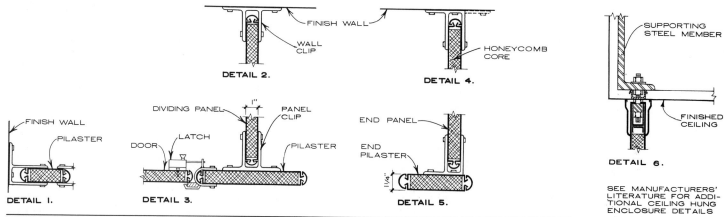

DETAIL 2.

DETAIL 4.

DETAIL 1.

DETAIL 3.

DETAIL 5.

DETAIL 6.

SEE MANUFACTURERS' LITERATURE FOR ADDITIONAL CEILING HUNG ENCLOSURE DETAILS

METAL PARTITION DETAILS

Pearce Corporation; St. Louis, Missouri

10 COMPARTMENTS AND CUBICLES

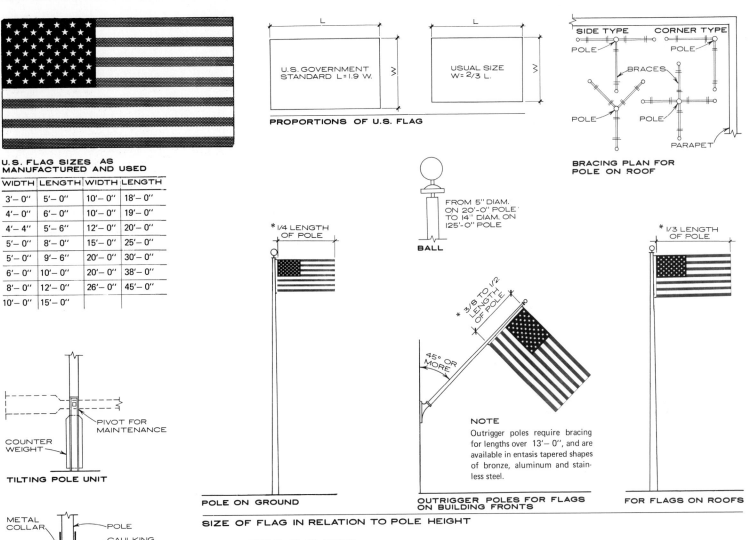

U.S. FLAG SIZES AS MANUFACTURED AND USED

WIDTH	LENGTH	WIDTH	LENGTH
3'–0''	5'–0''	10'–0''	18'–0''
4'–0''	6'–0''	10'–0''	19'–0''
4'–4''	5'–6''	12'–0''	20'–0''
5'–0''	8'–0''	15'–0''	25'–0''
5'–0''	9'–6''	20'–0''	30'–0''
6'–0''	10'–0''	20'–0''	38'–0''
8'–0''	12'–0''	26'–0''	45'–0''
10'–0''	15'–0''		

PROPORTIONS OF U.S. FLAG

U.S. GOVERNMENT STANDARD L=1.9 W.

USUAL SIZE W= 2/3 L.

BRACING PLAN FOR POLE ON ROOF

SIDE TYPE / CORNER TYPE — POLE — BRACES — PARAPET

BALL — FROM 5'' DIAM. ON 20'-0'' POLE TO 14'' DIAM. ON 125'-0'' POLE

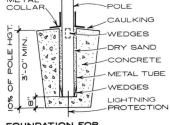

TILTING POLE UNIT

PIVOT FOR MAINTENANCE — COUNTER WEIGHT

*1/4 LENGTH OF POLE

POLE ON GROUND

*3/8 TO 1/2 LENGTH OF POLE

45° OR MORE

NOTE
Outrigger poles require bracing for lengths over 13'–0'', and are available in entasis tapered shapes of bronze, aluminum and stainless steel.

OUTRIGGER POLES FOR FLAGS ON BUILDING FRONTS

*1/3 LENGTH OF POLE

FOR FLAGS ON ROOFS

SIZE OF FLAG IN RELATION TO POLE HEIGHT

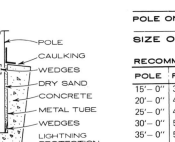

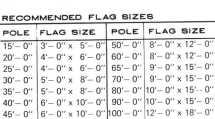

FOUNDATION FOR GROUND SET POLE

METAL COLLAR — POLE — CAULKING — WEDGES — DRY SAND — CONCRETE — METAL TUBE — WEDGES — LIGHTNING PROTECTION

10% OF POLE HGT. — 3'-0'' MIN. — 8''

RECOMMENDED FLAG SIZES

POLE	FLAG SIZE	POLE	FLAG SIZE
15'–0''	3'–0'' x 5'–0''	50'–0''	8'–0'' x 12'–0''
20'–0''	4'–0'' x 6'–0''	60'–0''	8'–0'' x 12'–0''
25'–0''	4'–0'' x 6'–0''	65'–0''	9'–0'' x 15'–0''
30'–0''	5'–0'' x 8'–0''	70'–0''	9'–0'' x 15'–0''
35'–0''	5'–0'' x 8'–0''	80'–0''	10'–0'' x 15'–0''
40'–0''	6'–0'' x 10'–0''	90'–0''	10'–0'' x 15'–0''
45'–0''	6'–0'' x 10'–0''	100'–0''	12'–0'' x 18'–0''

*For windy weather, smaller flags than the above are generally used.

RELATION OF HEIGHT OF POLE TO HEIGHT OF BLDG.

HEIGHT OF POLE	HEIGHT OF BLDG.
20'–0''	1 to 2 stories
25'–0''	3 to 5 stories
33'–0'' to 35'–0''	6 to 10 stories
40'–0'' to 50'–0''	11 to 15 stories
60'–0'' to 75'–0''	over 15 stories

NOTE:
This rule serves for preliminary assumptions.

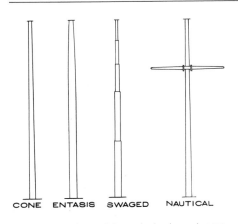

CONE — ENTASIS — SWAGED — NAUTICAL

Poles are manufactured in steel, aluminum, bronze, and fiberglass.

POLE STYLES

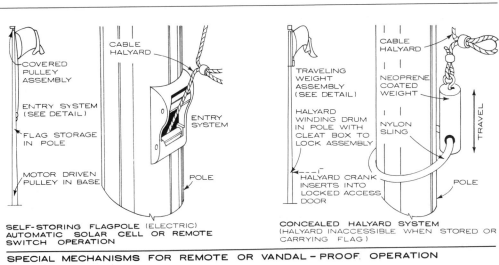

COVERED PULLEY ASSEMBLY — ENTRY SYSTEM (SEE DETAIL) — FLAG STORAGE IN POLE — MOTOR DRIVEN PULLEY IN BASE

CABLE HALYARD — ENTRY SYSTEM — POLE

SELF-STORING FLAGPOLE (ELECTRIC) AUTOMATIC SOLAR CELL OR REMOTE SWITCH OPERATION

TRAVELING WEIGHT ASSEMBLY (SEE DETAIL) — HALYARD WINDING DRUM IN POLE WITH CLEAT BOX TO LOCK ASSEMBLY — HALYARD CRANK INSERTS INTO LOCKED ACCESS DOOR

CABLE HALYARD — NEOPRENE COATED WEIGHT — NYLON SLING — TRAVEL — POLE

CONCEALED HALYARD SYSTEM
(HALYARD INACCESSIBLE WHEN STORED OR CARRYING FLAG)

SPECIAL MECHANISMS FOR REMOTE OR VANDAL – PROOF OPERATION

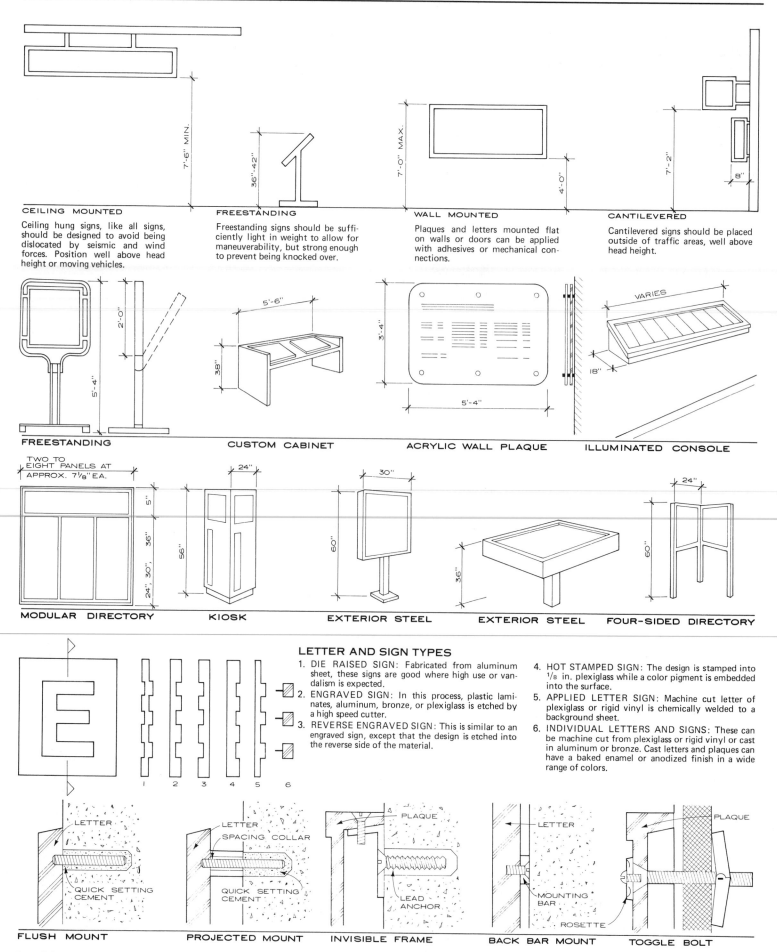

CEILING MOUNTED

Ceiling hung signs, like all signs, should be designed to avoid being dislocated by seismic and wind forces. Position well above head height or moving vehicles.

FREESTANDING

Freestanding signs should be sufficiently light in weight to allow for maneuverability, but strong enough to prevent being knocked over.

WALL MOUNTED

Plaques and letters mounted flat on walls or doors can be applied with adhesives or mechanical connections.

CANTILEVERED

Cantilevered signs should be placed outside of traffic areas, well above head height.

FREESTANDING

CUSTOM CABINET

ACRYLIC WALL PLAQUE

ILLUMINATED CONSOLE

MODULAR DIRECTORY

KIOSK

EXTERIOR STEEL

EXTERIOR STEEL

FOUR-SIDED DIRECTORY

LETTER AND SIGN TYPES

1. DIE RAISED SIGN: Fabricated from aluminum sheet, these signs are good where high use or vandalism is expected.
2. ENGRAVED SIGN: In this process, plastic laminates, aluminum, bronze, or plexiglass is etched by a high speed cutter.
3. REVERSE ENGRAVED SIGN: This is similar to an engraved sign, except that the design is etched into the reverse side of the material.
4. HOT STAMPED SIGN: The design is stamped into $1/8$ in. plexiglass while a color pigment is embedded into the surface.
5. APPLIED LETTER SIGN: Machine cut letter of plexiglass or rigid vinyl is chemically welded to a background sheet.
6. INDIVIDUAL LETTERS AND SIGNS: These can be machine cut from plexiglass or rigid vinyl or cast in aluminum or bronze. Cast letters and plaques can have a baked enamel or anodized finish in a wide range of colors.

FLUSH MOUNT

PROJECTED MOUNT

INVISIBLE FRAME

BACK BAR MOUNT

TOGGLE BOLT

Brixen & Christopher, Architects; Salt Lake City, Utah

10   IDENTIFYING DEVICES

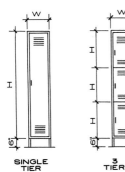
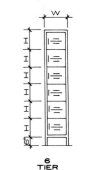
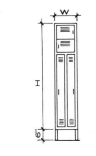

SINGLE TIER   3 TIER   6 TIER

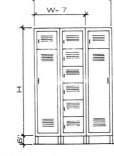

COMBINATION UNITS

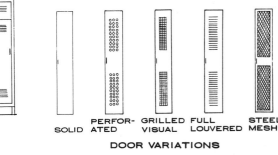

SOLID   PERFORATED   GRILLED VISUAL   FULL LOUVERED   STEEL MESH

DOOR VARIATIONS

SINGLE TIER

W	D	H
9″	1′-0″	
	1′-3″	
	1′-4″	
	1′-6″	
1′-0″	1′-0″	
	1′-3″	
	1′-6″	
	1′-9″	
1′-3″	1′-0″	5′-0″
	1′-3″	6′-0″
	1′-4″	
	1′-6″	
	1′-9″	
1′-6″	1′-6″	
	1′-9″	
	1′-10″	
	2′-0″	
2′-0″	1′-6″	
	1′-9″	
	2′-0″	

3 TIER

W	D	H
9″	1′-0″	1′-8″
	1′-3″	2′-0″
1′-0″	1′-6″	

4 TIER

W	D	H
1′-0″	1′-0″	
	1′-3″	
	1′-6″	1′-3″
1′-3″	1′-3″	
	1′-6″	
1′-6″	1′-6″	

DOUBLE TIER

W	D	H
9″	1′-0″	2′-6″
	1′-3″	3′-0″
	1′-4″	
	1′-6″	
1′-0″	1′-0″	
	1′-3″	
	1′-6″	2′-6″
	1′-10″	3′-0″
		3′-6″
1′-3″	1′-3″	
	1′-4″	
	1′-6″	
	1′-10″	
1′-6″	1′-0″	2′-6″
	1′-4″	3′-0″
	1′-10″	3′-6″

5 AND 6 TIER

W	D	H
1′-0″	1′-0″	1′-0″
	1′-3″	
	1′-6″	
1′-3″	1′-3″	1′-0″
	1′-6″	1′-3″
	1′-9″	
1′-6″	1′-0″	1′-0″
	1′-4″	
	1′-10″	

2 UNIT

W	D	H
1′-3″	1′-3″	5′-0″
	1′-6″	6′-0″
	1′-9″	
1′-6″	1′-9″	6′-0″

7 UNIT

W	D	H
3′-0″	1′-6″	6′-0″
	1′-9″	

8 UNIT

W	D	H
4′-6″	1′-9″	6′-0″

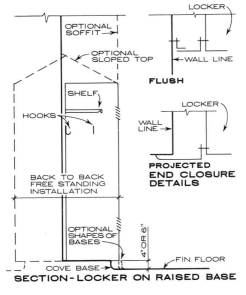

SECTION - LOCKER ON RAISED BASE

The shelf and 2 hooks shown are considered standard equipment.

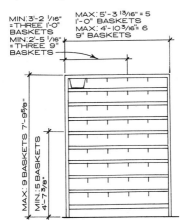

BASKET RACK

MIN: 3′-2 1/16″ = THREE 1′-0″ BASKETS
MIN: 2′-5 1/16″ = THREE 9″ BASKETS
MAX: 5′-3 13/16″ = 5 1′-0″ BASKETS
MAX: 4′-10 3/16″ = 6 9″ BASKETS

MAX: 9 BASKETS 7′-9 5/8″
MIN: 5 BASKETS 4′-7 3/8″

NOTE

Basket racks are arranged in single row or double (back to back) row. Single row depth is 1′-1 1/4″.

Judith Plummer; Washington, D.C.

GENERAL NOTES

1. Locker frame and door are usually of No. 16 gauge steel; sides, back, top, and bottom of No. 20 to No. 24 gauge steel. Finishes vary.

2. The standard door type may be varied as follows:

a. Door type as shown.

b. Sides and backs of perforated sheet steel for expanded mesh metal specific ventilation requirements.

c. Optional equipment includes sloped top, closed base, 6 in. legs, and a variety of interior fittings such as hooks, shelves, and partitions.

d. Optional top hinged doors for box lockers.

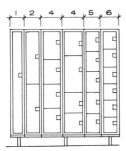

CHECKING LOCKERS

TYPES		W	D	H
1	Single tier	9″ 1′-0″	1′-6″	6′-0″
2	Double tier	9″ 1′-0″	1′-6″	1′-0″
4	Four tier	1′-3″	1′-6″ 2′-0″ 2′-7″	4 1′-3″ 3 1′-1″ 1 1′-10″
5	Five tier	1′-0″	1′-3″ 1′-6″ 1′-9″	1′-0″ 1′-2″
6	Six tier	1′-0″	1′-3″ 1′-6″ 1′-9″	1′-0″

LOCKER BASKET

MATERIALS

1. Sides and bottom of perforated steel with louvered ends.
2. All surfaces of wire mesh with perforated steel ends.
3. All surfaces of wire mesh.

NOTES

1. Checking lockers are available in enameled carbon steel, or stainless steel for heavy duty use, as in transportation terminals. Locks are provided with built in multiple coin selector, owner adjustable for coins, tokens, or "free" operations.

2. Lockers are available without legs for recessed installation. Overall height is 6 ft 0 in., some models, 5 ft 0 in. A variety of bases are available for freestanding or movable installation.

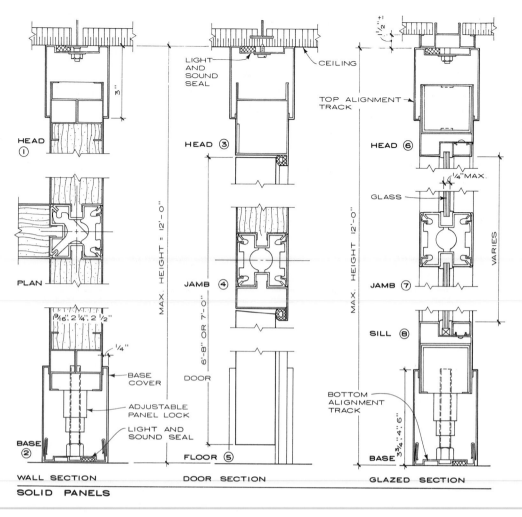

HEAD ①
PLAN
BASE ②
WALL SECTION

LIGHT AND SOUND SEAL
HEAD ③
JAMB ④
DOOR
FLOOR ⑤
DOOR SECTION

CEILING
TOP ALIGNMENT TRACK
HEAD ⑥
GLASS
JAMB ⑦
SILL ⑧
BOTTOM ALIGNMENT TRACK
BASE ⑧
GLAZED SECTION

MAX. HEIGHT = 12'-0"
MAX. HEIGHT 12'-0"
6'-8" OR 7'-0"
VARIES
⁹⁄₁₆", 2¼", 2½"
¼"
BASE COVER
ADJUSTABLE PANEL LOCK
LIGHT AND SOUND SEAL
¼" MAX.
3¾", 4", 6"

SOLID PANELS

GLASS | GLASS

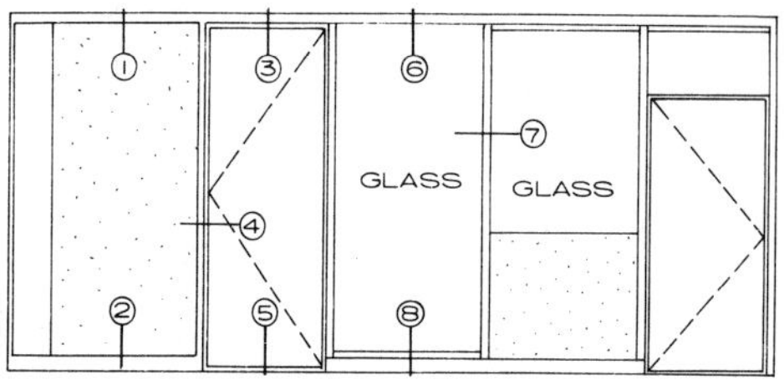

ELEVATION

SOLID PANEL PARTITIONS

Solid panel partition systems consist of prefabricated steel or aluminum panels with mineral wool core insulation. The unitized panels are held in place with an adjustable lock at floor and tracks at ceiling. Electrical runs are handled through floor or ceiling tracks horizontally and through posts vertically. There are also snap-in utility panels.

Solid panels provide substantial resistance to sound transmission (36 to 54 STC) with proper light and sound seals and have a 1 hr fire rating.

Standard panels are 24 to 60 in. wide (in 6 in. increments) and are prefinished in baked enamel, vinyl, or textured coverings. Available accessories include chalkboards, tackboards, shelves, and cabinets.

SOUND TRANSMISSION

	TOTAL PARTITION THICKNESS	VINYL COAT FACING	FIBERGLASS INSULATION BLANKET	SOUND TRANSMISSION CLASS (STC)
2½" wall cavity	3½"	½"	None	36
	3½"	½"	2½"	47
	3¾"	⅝"	None	41
	3¾"	⅝"	2½"	49
3⅝" wall cavity	4⅝"	½"	None	39
	4⅝"	½"	3½"	50
	4⅞"	⅝"	None	42
	4⅞"	⅝"	3½"	52

NOTES

1. Normally suspended ceilings are ineffective as a sound barrier. Consequently, when a series of sound-proofed offices are planned under such a ceiling, the chances of sound travel over the partitions should be considered. Baffles should be installed tightly above each run of partition, from the suspended ceiling to the bottom of the slab, to eliminate cracks through which sound can easily pass.
2. The perimeter of the partition installation—ceiling, floor, and sides—shall be gasketed with a factory applied sealant. All door frames shall be fitted with a factory applied rubber liner at the head and jambs that compress when the door is closed.
3. For extra sound control, all doors should have a continuous drop seal and threshold and all glazing in doors and partitions should be hermetically sealed double lights.

HOLLOW CORE PARTITIONS

Hollow partition systems consist of steel or aluminum heads, jambs, and sill members designed to receive standard gypsum board panels. Steel or porcelain panels may also be used.

Metal studs are spaced 24 in. on center and may be drilled to allow internal electrical runs.

Hollow partition systems are non-load-bearing. Sound and light seals should be used at floor and ceiling where privacy is desired. STC varies from 36 to 52. These systems normally have a 1 hr fire rating. Consult manufacturer's detail if additional protection is required.

Standard panels are available in 24 to 60 in. widths (in 6 in. increments) and are usually painted or covered in vinyl. A variety of accessories such as chalkboards, tackboard, shelves, and cabinets can be integrated into these systems.

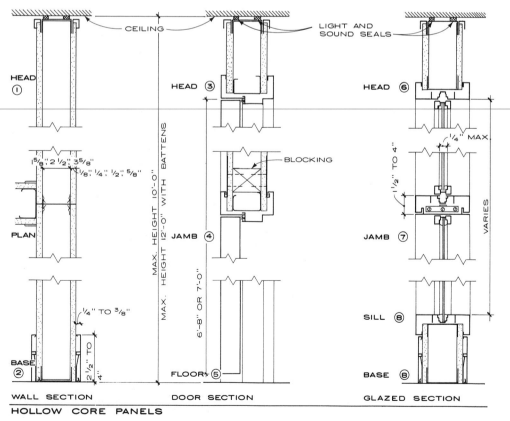

CEILING
HEAD ①
PLAN
BASE ②
WALL SECTION

LIGHT AND SOUND SEALS
HEAD ③
BLOCKING
JAMB ④
FLOOR ⑤
DOOR SECTION

HEAD ⑥
JAMB ⑦
SILL ⑧
BASE ⑧
GLAZED SECTION

MAX. HEIGHT 10'-0"
MAX. HEIGHT 12'-0" WITH BATTENS
6'-8" OR 7'-0"
VARIES
1⅝", 2½", 3⅝"
⅛", ¼", ½", ⅝"
¼" TO ⅜"
½" TO 2¼"
¼" MAX.
1½" TO 4"

HOLLOW CORE PANELS

Walter H. Sobel, FAIA & Associates; Chicago, Illinois

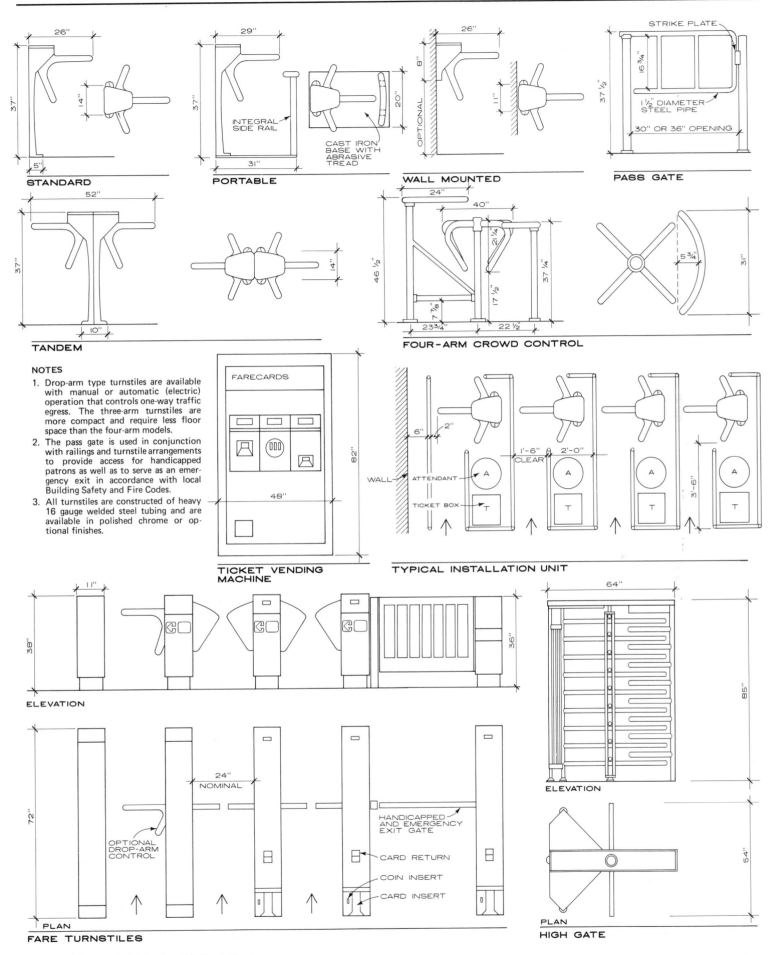

STANDARD

PORTABLE

INTEGRAL SIDE RAIL

CAST IRON BASE WITH ABRASIVE TREAD

WALL MOUNTED

OPTIONAL

STRIKE PLATE

1½ DIAMETER STEEL PIPE

30" OR 36" OPENING

PASS GATE

TANDEM

FOUR-ARM CROWD CONTROL

NOTES

1. Drop-arm type turnstiles are available with manual or automatic (electric) operation that controls one-way traffic egress. The three-arm turnstiles are more compact and require less floor space than the four-arm models.

2. The pass gate is used in conjunction with railings and turnstile arrangements to provide access for handicapped patrons as well as to serve as an emergency exit in accordance with local Building Safety and Fire Codes.

3. All turnstiles are constructed of heavy 16 gauge welded steel tubing and are available in polished chrome or optional finishes.

FARECARDS

TICKET VENDING MACHINE

WALL

ATTENDANT

TICKET BOX

CLEAR

TYPICAL INSTALLATION UNIT

OPTIONAL DROP-ARM CONTROL

24" NOMINAL

HANDICAPPED AND EMERGENCY EXIT GATE

CARD RETURN

COIN INSERT

CARD INSERT

ELEVATION

PLAN

FARE TURNSTILES

ELEVATION

PLAN

HIGH GATE

William Cook; Lawrence Cook & Associates; Falls Church, Virginia

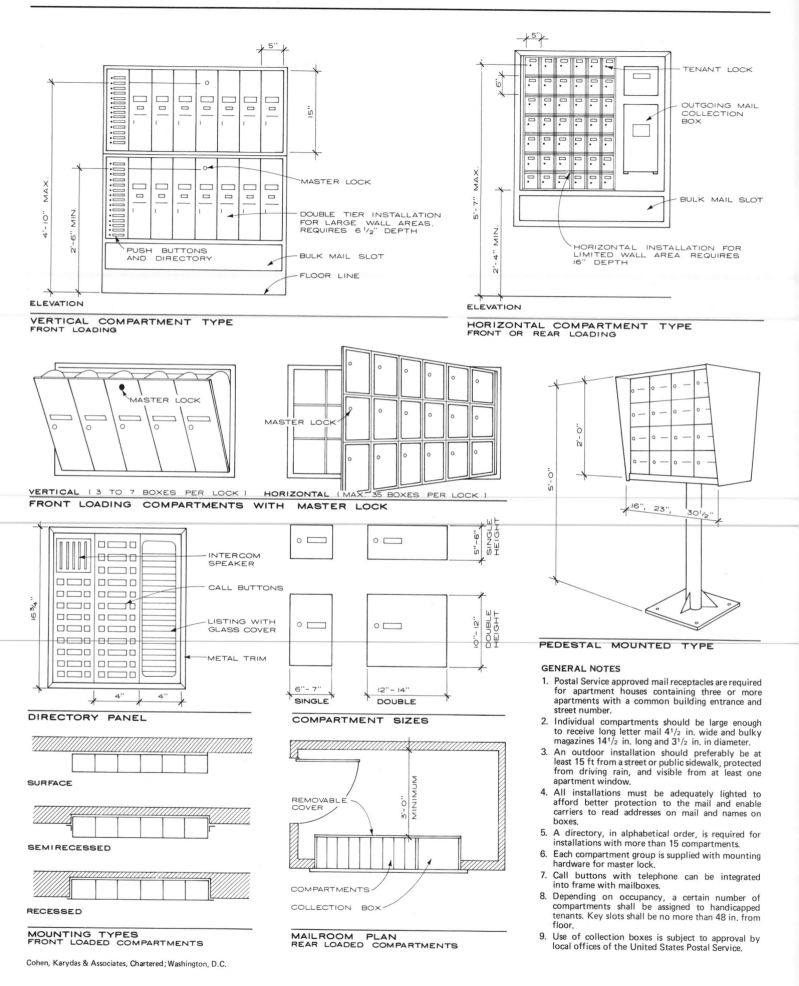

ELEVATION

VERTICAL COMPARTMENT TYPE
FRONT LOADING

MASTER LOCK

DOUBLE TIER INSTALLATION FOR LARGE WALL AREAS. REQUIRES 6½" DEPTH

PUSH BUTTONS AND DIRECTORY

BULK MAIL SLOT

FLOOR LINE

ELEVATION

HORIZONTAL COMPARTMENT TYPE
FRONT OR REAR LOADING

TENANT LOCK

OUTGOING MAIL COLLECTION BOX

BULK MAIL SLOT

HORIZONTAL INSTALLATION FOR LIMITED WALL AREA REQUIRES 16" DEPTH

MASTER LOCK

MASTER LOCK

VERTICAL (3 TO 7 BOXES PER LOCK)   **HORIZONTAL (MAX. 35 BOXES PER LOCK)**

FRONT LOADING COMPARTMENTS WITH MASTER LOCK

PEDESTAL MOUNTED TYPE

INTERCOM SPEAKER

CALL BUTTONS

LISTING WITH GLASS COVER

METAL TRIM

DIRECTORY PANEL

SINGLE HEIGHT

DOUBLE HEIGHT

SINGLE   **DOUBLE**

COMPARTMENT SIZES

SURFACE

SEMIRECESSED

RECESSED

MOUNTING TYPES
FRONT LOADED COMPARTMENTS

REMOVABLE COVER

COMPARTMENTS

COLLECTION BOX

MAILROOM PLAN
REAR LOADED COMPARTMENTS

GENERAL NOTES

1. Postal Service approved mail receptacles are required for apartment houses containing three or more apartments with a common building entrance and street number.
2. Individual compartments should be large enough to receive long letter mail 4½ in. wide and bulky magazines 14½ in. long and 3½ in. in diameter.
3. An outdoor installation should preferably be at least 15 ft from a street or public sidewalk, protected from driving rain, and visible from at least one apartment window.
4. All installations must be adequately lighted to afford better protection to the mail and enable carriers to read addresses on mail and names on boxes.
5. A directory, in alphabetical order, is required for installations with more than 15 compartments.
6. Each compartment group is supplied with mounting hardware for master lock.
7. Call buttons with telephone can be integrated into frame with mailboxes.
8. Depending on occupancy, a certain number of compartments shall be assigned to handicapped tenants. Key slots shall be no more than 48 in. from floor.
9. Use of collection boxes is subject to approval by local offices of the United States Postal Service.

Cohen, Karydas & Associates, Chartered; Washington, D.C.

GENERAL PLANNING NOTES

During the early stages of planning, consult with regional Postmaster General for regulations concerning postal facilities in office buildings.

PLATFORM

A dock area that provides off-the-street loading and unloading of mail.

MAILROOM

A security type room located at platform level, which has its own access door to the platform for off-hour service. Platform door should be 36 in. wide, security type. If window or lockbox service is provided, the mailroom should be located at the principal building entrance level. Standard interior treatment should apply in this space.

SERVICES

The size of mailroom and services provided by the post office vary with size and occupancy of the building. The U.S. Postal Service recognizes for its staffing and servicing two types of mailrooms for small, medium, and large office buildings.

1. LOCKBOX SERVICE: Buildings up to 200,000 sq ft of leasable space or with a maximum of 75 tenants. Provide one receptacle for each tenant and rear loading for 11 or more tenants. A building directory must be maintained.

    The vertical distance from floor to tenant locks on top tier of receptacles is 66 in. maximum; to bottom lowest tier 10 in. minimum, preferably 30 in. Install only at one entrance. Allow a minimum of 3 ft of clear working space behind units. Provide 80 sq ft of working space for each additional carrier. Allow 1 sq ft of working space for every 1000 sq ft of leasable office space. Specifications for construction of mail receptacles shall be identical to those for Type II, horizontal apartment house receptacles as prescribed in USPS Publication 17, except that the minimum inside dimensions shall be 5³/₄ in. high, 10¹/₂ in. wide, and 16 in. deep.

POSTAL SERVICES

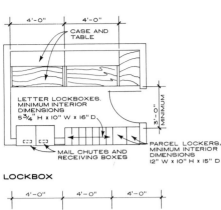

LETTER LOCKBOXES. MINIMUM INTERIOR DIMENSIONS 5³/₄" H x 10" W x 16" D

MAIL CHUTES AND RECEIVING BOXES

PARCEL LOCKERS, MINIMUM INTERIOR DIMENSIONS 12" W x 10" H x 15" D

LOCKBOX

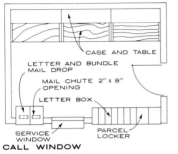

CASE AND TABLE

LETTER AND BUNDLE MAIL DROP

MAIL CHUTE 2" x 8" OPENING

LETTER BOX

SERVICE WINDOW

PARCEL LOCKER

CALL WINDOW

2. CALL WINDOW SERVICE: Buildings with 75 or more tenants, one carrier for each 100,000 sq ft of leasable office space up to 500,000 sq ft, plus one carrier for each additional 200,000 sq ft of office building. Allow 1.5 sq ft for every 1000 sq ft of leasable space; the minimum call window service space is 100 sq ft.

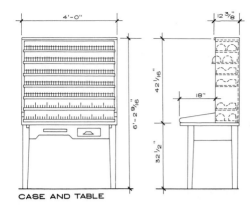

CASE AND TABLE

CAPACITY 850 OR 1700 CU IN.
MAXIMUM LOAD 20 LB

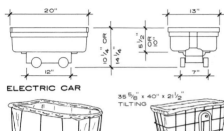

ELECTRIC CAR

35⁵/₈" x 40" x 21¹/₂" TILTING

36" x 28" x 26"
44" x 38" x 32"
CANVAS

BASKET CARTS

EQUIPMENT

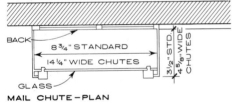

BACK

8³/₄" STANDARD
14¹/₄" WIDE CHUTES

3¹/₂ STD
4⁵/₈" WIDE CHUTES

GLASS

MAIL CHUTE - PLAN

1. May be recessed.
2. Use wide chutes for 8" x 10" envelopes.

MAIL CHUTES AND RECEIVING BOXES

1. CHUTES: Used in buildings of at least four stories. The chute must be approximately 2 x 8 in. in cross section and extend in a continuously vertical line from the beginning point to the receiving box or mailroom. The interior of the chute must be accessible throughout its entire length. Chutes installed in pairs are constructed with a divider and dual receiving boxes. Chutes are for first class mail only.

2. RECEIVING BOXES: Located within 100 ft of entrance used by collectors or in the loading-unloading area used by the post office for mail collection. Capacity of boxes is determined by postmaster. However, bottom of door of boxes must be 30 in. or more above floor and exterior bottom of boxes not less than 20 in. above floor and free of obstructions. All doors open to the right and range in sizes from 12 x 20 to 18 x 30 in. inclusive. Mail slot on box is not more than 5 ft 10 in. above floor. Receiving boxes are for first class mail only.

3. AUXILIARY BOXES: Used when receiving box is too small to accommodate deposit of first class mail. Located close to receiving box(es). Capacity is determined by postmaster. The mail openings must be large enough to receive first class mail tied in bundles.

4. COMBINATION LETTER AND BUNDLE BOX: May be attached to the chute in lieu of a regular receiving box. Its minimum dimensions are 6 in. high x 23 in. wide x 17 in. deep; with 3 ft 4 in. from the bottom of the box and not more than 5 ft above floor.

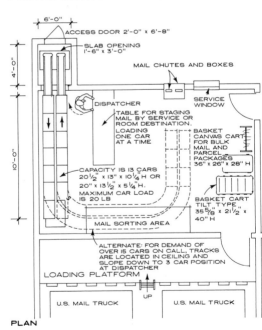

ACCESS DOOR 2'-0" x 6'-8"

SLAB OPENING 1'-6" x 3'-0"

MAIL CHUTES AND BOXES

DISPATCHER

TABLE FOR STAGING MAIL BY SERVICE OR ROOM DESTINATION.

LOADING ONE CAR AT A TIME

SERVICE WINDOW

BASKET CANVAS CART FOR BULK MAIL AND PARCEL PACKAGES 36" x 26" x 28" H

CAPACITY IS 13 CARS 20¹/₂" x 13" x 10¹/₄" H OR 20" x 13¹/₂" x 5¹/₄" H. MAXIMUM CAR LOAD IS 20 LB

BASKET CART TILT TYPE 35⁵/₈" x 21¹/₂" x 40" H

MAIL SORTING AREA

ALTERNATE: FOR DEMAND OF OVER 15 CARS ON CALL, TRACKS ARE LOCATED IN CEILING AND SLOPE DOWN TO 3 CAR POSITION AT DISPATCHER

LOADING PLATFORM

UP

U.S. MAIL TRUCK   U.S. MAIL TRUCK

PLAN

CENTRAL MAILROOM

Buildings larger than 200,000 sq ft and with up to 2,000,000 sq ft of leasable space can be served on each floor from a central mailroom using a containerized mechanical system. Allow a minimum of 400 sq ft for first 50 tenants plus 135 sq ft for each additional 50 tenants, or 2 sq ft for each 1000 sq ft of leasable space.

SERVICE MAILROOMS shall be provided on each multitenant floor, unless containers are mechanically conveyed to tenant offices. Allow 5 x 7 ft minimum floor area for service mailroom. Mechanical systems accommodating 8 to 19 containers may require a

CENTRAL MAILROOM

Walter Hart, AIA; North White Plains, New York

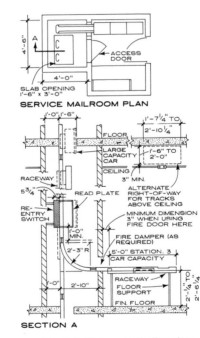

ACCESS DOOR

SLAB OPENING 1'-6" x 3'-0"

SERVICE MAILROOM PLAN

FLOOR

LARGE CAPACITY CAR

CEILING

RACEWAY

3" MIN.

ALTERNATE RIGHT-OF-WAY FOR TRACKS ABOVE CEILING

READ PLATE

RE-ENTRY SWITCH

MINIMUM DIMENSION 3" WHEN USING FIRE DOOR HERE

FIRE DAMPER (AS REQUIRED)

5'-0" STATION. 3 CAR CAPACITY

RACEWAY

FLOOR SUPPORT

FIN. FLOOR

SECTION A

minimum area of 7 x 8 ft. Minimum inside dimensions of containers are 12 x 16 x 6 in.

There are two basic types of mechanical systems:

1. Selective vertical conveyor systems consisting of an endless chain carrying containers. When transportation is not purely vertical, horizontal capability must be added, such as conveyor belts.

2. Track and switch systems with self-propelled container cars. Systems permit inclines and declines and flexible routes. Destinations are actuated individually for each car.

MAIL CHUTES AND BOXES

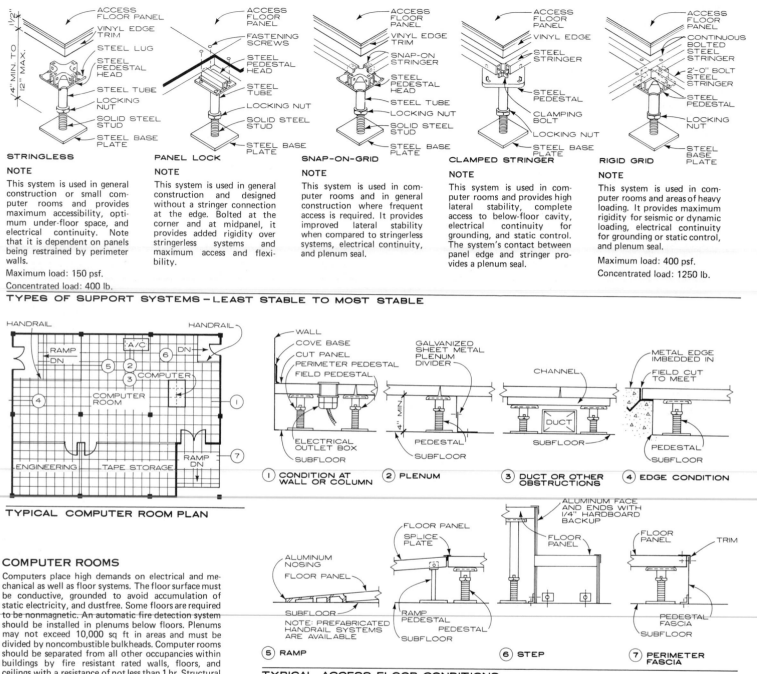

STRINGLESS

NOTE

This system is used in general construction or in small computer rooms and provides maximum accessibility, optimum under-floor space, and electrical continuity. Note that it is dependent on panels being restrained by perimeter walls.

Maximum load: 150 psf.

Concentrated load: 400 lb.

PANEL LOCK

NOTE

This system is used in general construction and designed without a stringer connection at the edge. Bolted at the corner and at midpanel, it provides added rigidity over stringerless systems and maximum access and flexibility.

SNAP-ON-GRID

NOTE

This system is used in computer rooms and in general construction where frequent access is required. It provides improved lateral stability when compared to stringerless systems, electrical continuity, and plenum seal.

CLAMPED STRINGER

NOTE

This system is used in computer rooms and provides high lateral stability, complete access to below-floor cavity, electrical continuity for grounding, and static control. The system's contact between panel edge and stringer provides a plenum seal.

RIGID GRID

NOTE

This system is used in computer rooms and areas of heavy loading. It provides maximum rigidity for seismic or dynamic loading, electrical continuity for grounding or static control, and plenum seal.

Maximum load: 400 psf.

Concentrated load: 1250 lb.

TYPES OF SUPPORT SYSTEMS — LEAST STABLE TO MOST STABLE

TYPICAL COMPUTER ROOM PLAN

TYPICAL ACCESS FLOOR CONDITIONS

COMPUTER ROOMS

Computers place high demands on electrical and mechanical as well as floor systems. The floor surface must be conductive, grounded to avoid accumulation of static electricity, and dustfree. Some floors are required to be nonmagnetic. An automatic fire detection system should be installed in plenums below floors. Plenums may not exceed 10,000 sq ft in areas and must be divided by noncombustible bulkheads. Computer rooms should be separated from all other occupancies within buildings by fire resistant rated walls, floors, and ceilings with a resistance of not less than 1 hr. Structural floors beneath access floors should incorporate provisions for water drainage to minimize damage to computer systems. All openings in access floors should be protected to minimize entrance of debris. Computer rooms require precision temperature and humidity control. Package air-conditioning units are available for computer room applications that supply air within tolerances of ±1.5° and ±5% relative humidity.

Computer room heat gains are often highly concentrated. For minimum room temperature gradients, supply air distribution should closely match load distribution. The distribution system should be sufficiently flexible to accommodate changes in the location and magnitude of the heat gains, with a minimum amount of change in the basic distribution system. Supply air systems usually require approximately 74 litres/sec per kilowatt of cooling to satisfy computer room conditions. This will provide a high enough air change rate to allow for even air temperature distribution. Packaged air-conditioning systems using the under-floor air supply plenum should adequately supply the large computer area. The area of the zoning is controlled by the various floor registers and perforated floor panels.

Setter, Leach and Lindstrom, Inc.; Minneapolis, Minnesota

ACCESS FLOORS

Access floors provide accessibility and flexibility to mechanical and electrical functions with added flexibility for placement of desks, telephone services, machines, and general office equipment. Equipment can be moved and reconnected to the floor quickly. Access floor systems are used in business offices, hospitals, laboratories, open area schools, television systems, computer rooms, and telephone-communication centers. Raised access floors in large areas offer maximum flexibility for future change, but can also be used in a recessed area of structural floor.

Panel types constructed of reinforced steel, aluminum, or steel encased wood core are available with finish surfaces of vinyl, vinyl asbestos tile, plastic laminate, and carpet. Basic panel sizes are 18 x 18 in., 24 x 24 in., and 30 x 30 in. Panel systems generally rely on gravity held connections, but can be mechanically held, increasing rigidity but reducing speed of removal. Wraparound, butt, and a protective plastic edge carpet

systems are available. Some are available with flame spread ratings of Class A. Aluminum panels are generally used to hold computers because metallic dust is eliminated. Steel panels are available in three structural grades: heavy duty, computer, and general construction.

The use of modular wiring increases installation speed and simplifies panel variation. Space beneath floors can be utilized as an air-conditioning plenum. Special panels provide perforation for air distribution, cable slots, and sound, and thermal insulation. Thermally insulated panels can reduce the possibility of condensation when under-floor space is used for air-conditioning. A variety of support systems can be provided in either steel or aluminum. Aluminum supports eliminate the possibility of rust and are nonmagnetic. Among the problems encountered with access floor systems are some difficulties in accommodating building angles, curves, and irregularities. Wet washing techniques cannot be used, and poor placement of exceedingly heavy loads can damage floor systems.

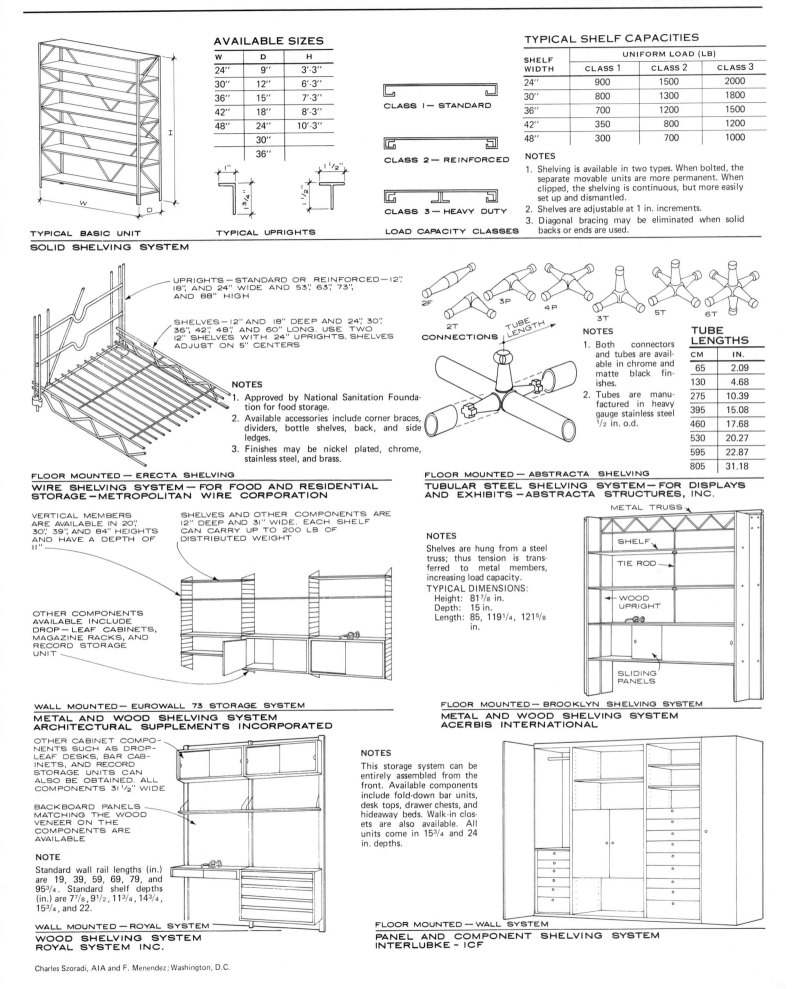

AVAILABLE SIZES

W	D	H
24''	9''	3'-3''
30''	12''	6'-3''
36''	15''	7'-3''
42''	18''	8'-3''
48''	24''	10'-3''
	30''	
	36''	

CLASS I — STANDARD

CLASS 2 — REINFORCED

CLASS 3 — HEAVY DUTY

LOAD CAPACITY CLASSES

TYPICAL SHELF CAPACITIES

SHELF WIDTH	UNIFORM LOAD (LB)		
	CLASS 1	CLASS 2	CLASS 3
24''	900	1500	2000
30''	800	1300	1800
36''	700	1200	1500
42''	350	800	1200
48''	300	700	1000

NOTES
1. Shelving is available in two types. When bolted, the separate movable units are more permanent. When clipped, the shelving is continuous, but more easily set up and dismantled.
2. Shelves are adjustable at 1 in. increments.
3. Diagonal bracing may be eliminated when solid backs or ends are used.

TYPICAL BASIC UNIT

TYPICAL UPRIGHTS

SOLID SHELVING SYSTEM

UPRIGHTS—STANDARD OR REINFORCED—12'', 18'', AND 24'' WIDE AND 53'', 63'', 73'', AND 88'' HIGH

SHELVES—12'' AND 18'' DEEP AND 24'', 30'', 36'', 42'', 48'', AND 60'' LONG. USE TWO 12'' SHELVES WITH 24'' UPRIGHTS. SHELVES ADJUST ON 5'' CENTERS

NOTES
1. Approved by National Sanitation Foundation for food storage.
2. Available accessories include corner braces, dividers, bottle shelves, back, and side ledges.
3. Finishes may be nickel plated, chrome, stainless steel, and brass.

FLOOR MOUNTED — ERECTA SHELVING

WIRE SHELVING SYSTEM — FOR FOOD AND RESIDENTIAL STORAGE — METROPOLITAN WIRE CORPORATION

VERTICAL MEMBERS ARE AVAILABLE IN 20'', 30'', 39'', AND 84'' HEIGHTS AND HAVE A DEPTH OF 11''

SHELVES AND OTHER COMPONENTS ARE 12'' DEEP AND 18'' WIDE. EACH SHELF CAN CARRY UP TO 200 LB OF DISTRIBUTED WEIGHT

OTHER COMPONENTS AVAILABLE INCLUDE DROP-LEAF CABINETS, MAGAZINE RACKS, AND RECORD STORAGE UNIT

WALL MOUNTED — EUROWALL 73 STORAGE SYSTEM

METAL AND WOOD SHELVING SYSTEM ARCHITECTURAL SUPPLEMENTS INCORPORATED

OTHER CABINET COMPONENTS SUCH AS DROP-LEAF DESKS, BAR CABINETS, AND RECORD STORAGE UNITS CAN ALSO BE OBTAINED. ALL COMPONENTS 31½'' WIDE

BACKBOARD PANELS MATCHING THE WOOD VENEER ON THE COMPONENTS ARE AVAILABLE

NOTE
Standard wall rail lengths (in.) are 19, 39, 59, 69, 79, and 95¾. Standard shelf depths (in.) are 7⅞, 9½, 11¾, 14¾, 15¾, and 22.

WALL MOUNTED — ROYAL SYSTEM

WOOD SHELVING SYSTEM ROYAL SYSTEM INC.

2F   3P   4P   3T   5T   6T

2T

CONNECTIONS

TUBE LENGTH

NOTES
1. Both connectors and tubes are available in chrome and matte black finishes.
2. Tubes are manufactured in heavy gauge stainless steel ½ in. o.d.

TUBE LENGTHS

CM	IN.
65	2.09
130	4.68
275	10.39
395	15.08
460	17.68
530	20.27
595	22.87
805	31.18

FLOOR MOUNTED — ABSTRACTA SHELVING

TUBULAR STEEL SHELVING SYSTEM — FOR DISPLAYS AND EXHIBITS — ABSTRACTA STRUCTURES, INC.

NOTES
Shelves are hung from a steel truss; thus tension is transferred to metal members, increasing load capacity.
TYPICAL DIMENSIONS:
Height: 81⅞ in.
Depth: 15 in.
Length: 85, 119¼, 121⅝ in.

METAL TRUSS

SHELF

TIE ROD

WOOD UPRIGHT

SLIDING PANELS

FLOOR MOUNTED — BROOKLYN SHELVING SYSTEM

METAL AND WOOD SHELVING SYSTEM ACERBIS INTERNATIONAL

NOTES
This storage system can be entirely assembled from the front. Available components include fold-down bar units, desk tops, drawer chests, and hideaway beds. Walk-in closets are also available. All units come in 15¾ and 24 in. depths.

FLOOR MOUNTED — WALL SYSTEM

PANEL AND COMPONENT SHELVING SYSTEM INTERLUBKE - ICF

Charles Szoradi, AIA and F. Menendez; Washington, D.C.

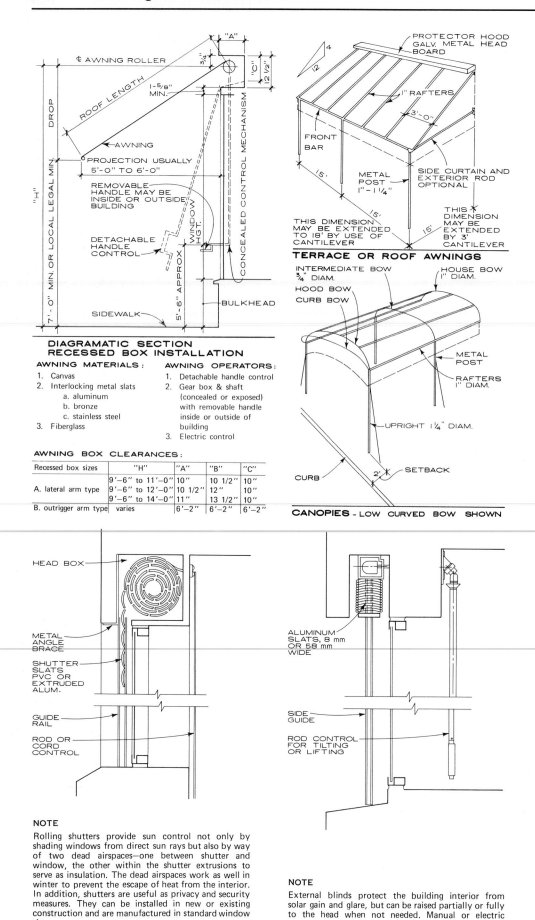

DIAGRAMATIC SECTION
RECESSED BOX INSTALLATION

AWNING MATERIALS:
1. Canvas
2. Interlocking metal slats
   a. aluminum
   b. bronze
   c. stainless steel
3. Fiberglass

AWNING OPERATORS:
1. Detachable handle control
2. Gear box & shaft (concealed or exposed) with removable handle inside or outside of building
3. Electric control

AWNING BOX CLEARANCES:

Recessed box sizes	"H"	"A"	"B"	"C"
A. lateral arm type	9'–6" to 11'–0"	10"	10 1/2"	10"
	9'–6" to 12'–0"	10 1/2"	12"	10"
	9'–6" to 14'–0"	11"	13 1/2"	10"
B. outrigger arm type	varies	6'–2"	6'–2"	6'–2"

TERRACE OR ROOF AWNINGS

CANOPIES - LOW CURVED BOW SHOWN

TERRACE OR ROOF AWNINGS

To provide complete sun protection and shade, the overall length of the awning bar should extend 3 in. past the glass line on both sides. For proper sunshade protection, awnings should project at least as far forward from the face of the window as the bottom of the window is below the front bar of the awning.

The wall measurement of an awning is the distance down the face of the building from the point where the awning attaches to the face of the building (or from the center of the roller in the case of the roller type awning).

The projection of an awning is the distance from the face of the building to the front bar of the awning in its correct projected position.

Right and left of an awning are your right and left as you are facing the awning looking into the building.

Framework consists of galvanized steel pipe, with non-rattling fittings. Awning is lace-on type canvas with rope reinforced eave. Protector hood is galvanized sheet metal or either bronze, copper, or aluminum.

Sizes of members should be checked by calculation for conditions not similar to those shown on this page.

Consult local building code for limitations on height and setback.

COVERED WALKWAYS

Covered walkways are available with aluminum fascia and soffit panels in a number of profiles. The fascia panels are supported with pipe columns and steel or aluminum structural members if necessary. Panels can cantilever up to 30% of span. Canopy designs can be supported from above.

Another method of providing covered exterior space is with stressed membrane structures. Using highly tensile synthetic fabric and cable in collaboration with compression members, usually metal, dynamic and versatile tentlike coverings can be created. Membrane structures are especially suited to temporary installations.

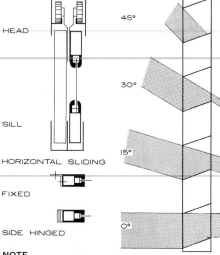

NOTE

These miniature external louvers shade windows from direct sunlight and glare while allowing a high degree of visibility, light, ventilation, insect protection, and daytime privacy. Much like a woven metal fabric, they are not strong architectural elements but present a uniform appearance in the areas covered. The solar screen is installed in aluminum frames and can be adapted to suit most applications.

SOLAR SCREEN SIZES

MATE-RIAL	LOUVERS	TILT	VERTICAL SPACING	SIZE (WIDTHS)
Aluminum	17"	17°	1" o.c.	18"–48"
Bronze	17", 23"	20°	1/2" o.c.	Up to 72 1/2"

Aluminum screens are available in black or light green. Bronze screens come in black only.

SOLAR SCREENS

NOTE

Rolling shutters provide sun control not only by shading windows from direct sun rays but also by way of two dead airspaces—one between shutter and window, the other within the shutter extrusions to serve as insulation. The dead airspaces work as well in winter to prevent the escape of heat from the interior. In addition, shutters are useful as privacy and security measures. They can be installed in new or existing construction and are manufactured in standard window sizes.

ROLLING SHUTTERS

NOTE

External blinds protect the building interior from solar gain and glare, but can be raised partially or fully to the head when not needed. Manual or electric control is from inside the building.

EXTERNAL VENETIAN BLINDS

Graham Davidson, Architect; Washington, D.C.

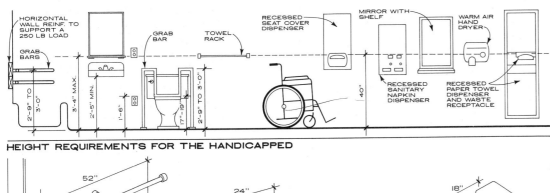

HEIGHT REQUIREMENTS FOR THE HANDICAPPED

NOTES ON GRAB BARS

1. SIZE: 1½ in. O.D. with 1½ in. clearance at wall.
2. MATERIAL: Stainless steel or chrome plated brass with knurled finish, standard.
3. INSTALLATION: Concealed or exposed fasteners; return all ends to wall, intermediate supports at 3 ft maximum. Use heavy duty type bars and methods of installation.

The provisions of the American National Standard, ANSI A117.1 must be consulted, as well as applicable local and federal regulations.

WHEELCHAIR COMPARTMENT

STRADDLE BAR

SAFETY ARM REST

SWING-AWAY BAR

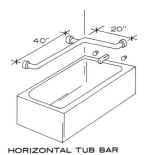

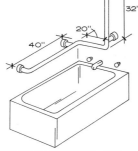

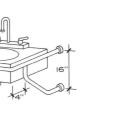

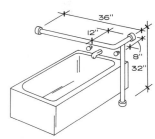

HORIZONTAL TUB BAR

TUB WITH VERTICAL RAIL

TUB ENTRY RAILS

CORNER BAR

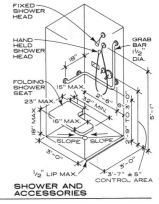

URINAL BAR

LAVATORY AID RAIL

CONSOLE UNIT

SHOWER AND ACCESSORIES

GRAB BAR CONFIGURATIONS

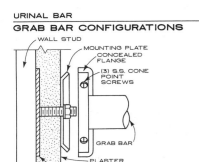

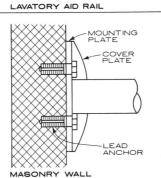

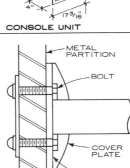

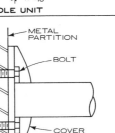

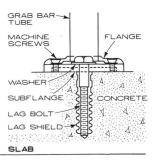

STUD WALL

MASONRY WALL

METAL PARTITION

SLAB

ATTACHMENT DETAILS

A. Allen Hitchcock, AIA; Baltimore, Maryland

MIRRORED BATHROOM CABINETS

CONVENTIONAL

Surface or recessed mounted cabinets. Cabinet depth 4''– 6''

Mirror sizes:
14'' x 20''   For mirror with
16'' x 20''   frame, add ¼''
16'' x 22''   to both mirror dimensions. Available
16'' x 24''   with 5'' shelf.
18'' x 24''

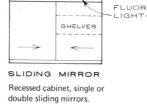

SLIDING MIRROR

Recessed cabinet, single or double sliding mirrors.

Mirror size each side:
14'' x 20''   18'' x 30''
15'' x 20''   24'' x 30''
18'' x 20''   30'' x 36''
Available with recessed vanity cabinet below. Cabinet depth 4 ¼''.

VANITY

Surface mounted mirror with projecting vanity cabinet below. Proj. 4½''.

Mirror sizes:
18'' x 24''   36'' x 24''
24'' x 24''   42'' x 24''
30'' x 24''   48'' x 24''

HOTEL

Recessed mounted cabinet. Contains plug outlet, bottle opener, razor blade disposal. Cabinet depth 3½''.

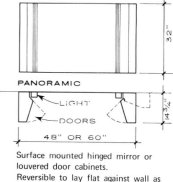

PANORAMIC

Surface mounted hinged mirror or louvered door cabinets. Reversible to lay flat against wall as shown dotted. Cabinet depth 3½'' – 7¼''.

TOWEL STORAGE

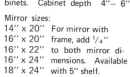

LADDER   **HOLDERS**

FOLDED TOWELS

18'', 24'', 30'', 36'' TOWEL BAR

SLIDING GLASS DOOR CABINET

RELAXATION UNITS

For toilet paper, cigarettes, ash tray and magazine storage.

SCALES

MISCELLANEOUS

LINEN CHUTE

Available with foot operator
Standard sizes:
12'' x 15''   21'' x 18''
15'' x 18''   24'' x 24''
18'' x 18''   30'' x 30''

CORNER SHOWER SEAT

PLAN

Hinged seat
15½'' x 15½''
16 gauge stainless steel

TOILET PAPER HOLDERS

TOILET SEAT COVER DISPENSER   **DOUBLE ROLL**   **FOLDED**   **SINGLE & DOUBLE ROLL**

MISCELLANEOUS

RECESSED DISPENSER EXTENDS APPROXIMATELY 4'' BEYOND FRONT WALL SURFACE. SIMPLER SURFACE MOUNTED UNITS PROTRUDE 3''–4''

PURSE SHELF EXTENDS 4'' BEYOND FRONT WALL SURFACE

CUP DISPENSER   **PURSE SHELF**

UP TO 10'-0''
COILED WIRE
SUPPORT PLATE

RETRACTABLE CLOTHESLINE

4'' DEEP SHELF (RECESSED)

ASHTRAYS
SURFACE PROTRUDES 5¼''
RECESSED 3½''–5½'' BEYOND WALL

FEMININE NAPKIN DISPENSER; SURFACE OR RECESSED
PROJECTION 6''

NAPKIN DISPOSAL SURFACE M'TD. HINGED TOP
PROJ. 4¼''

PUSH

RECESSED DISPOSAL
PROJ. 4¼''

WASTE RECEPTACLES

SURFACE MOUNTED CANVAS OR DISPOSABLE LINER BAG

PUSH
HINGED ACCESS DOOR; DOOR CLEARANCE 13''

ELEV.   SECT.
WALL RECESSED

PLAN

ELEV.
FREESTANDING

HAND TOWEL DISPENSERS AND DRYERS

FOLDED
PROJ. 3½''

ROLL
PROJ. 6¾''

ELECTRIC HAND DRYER

LINEN ROLL
PROJ. 10''

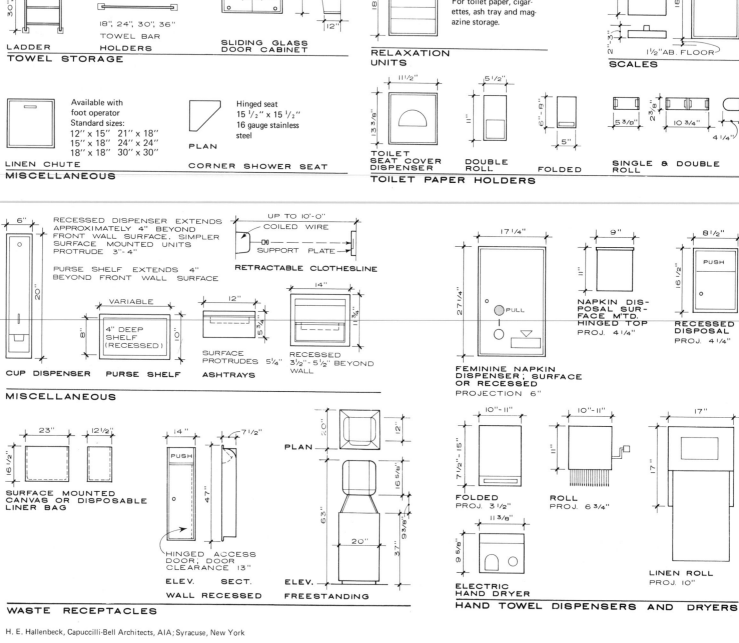

H. E. Hallenbeck, Capuccilli-Bell Architects, AIA; Syracuse, New York

10   TOILET AND BATH ACCESSORIES

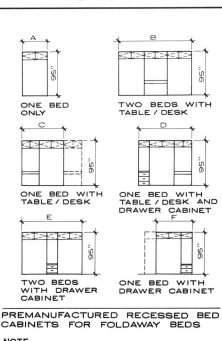

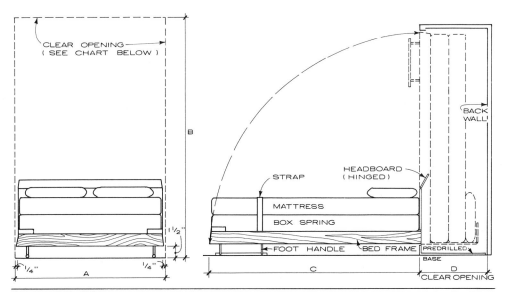

ONE BED ONLY

TWO BEDS WITH TABLE / DESK

ONE BED WITH TABLE / DESK

ONE BED WITH TABLE / DESK AND DRAWER CABINET

TWO BEDS WITH DRAWER CABINET

ONE BED WITH DRAWER CABINET

FOLDAWAY BED

PREMANUFACTURED RECESSED BED CABINETS FOR FOLDAWAY BEDS

NOTE

A factory assembled bed frame includes anchors to fasten the hinge mechanism to the floor. This hinge may be attached to any type of floor. An optional predrilled base plate of 3/4 in. plywood is recommended to facilitate installation. The bed frame's base has a finished face which provides wall closure.

NOTE

Finished cabinet is made of 3/4 in. plywood with plastic laminated finish on all sides. The recessed unit includes bed face and predrilled base plate for the folding mechanism.

REQUIRED CLEARANCES FOR FOLD-AWAY BEDS

	A	B	C	D
Single bed	41″	83″	78″	24″
Double bed	56″	83″	78″	24″
Queen bed	63″	89″	84″	24″
Extra long bed	63″	89″	84″	24″

RECESSED CABINET DIMENSIONS

	A	B	C	D	E	F
Twin	43″	128″	85″	108″	108″	66″
Double	58″	158″	100″	123″	138″	102″
Queen	65″	152″	107″	130″	152″	109″

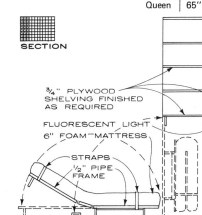

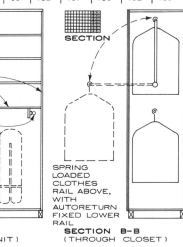

ELEVATION

PLAN

SECTION A-A
(THROUGH SHELF AND BED UNIT)

SECTION B-B
(THROUGH CLOSET)

3/4″ PLYWOOD SHELVING FINISHED AS REQUIRED

FLUORESCENT LIGHT

6″ FOAM MATTRESS

STRAPS
1/2″ PIPE FRAME

SPRING LOADED CLOTHES RAIL ABOVE, WITH AUTORETURN FIXED LOWER RAIL

COMPONENT OPTIONS

DOOR OPTIONS

Smoked glass
Clear glass
Solid core wood
Plastic laminate

COMPONENT OPTIONS

COMPONENT OPTIONS

COMPONENT OPTIONS

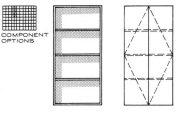

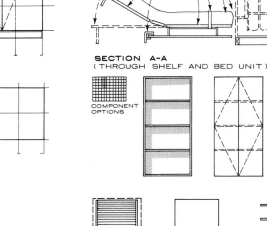

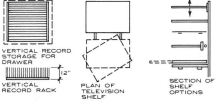

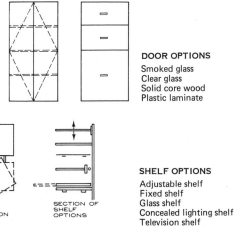

VERTICAL RECORD STORAGE FOR DRAWER

VERTICAL RECORD RACK

PLAN OF TELEVISION SHELF

SECTION OF SHELF OPTIONS

SHELF OPTIONS

Adjustable shelf
Fixed shelf
Glass shelf
Concealed lighting shelf
Television shelf

WALL STORAGE SYSTEMS

Charles E. George; SHWC, Inc.; Dallas, Texas

WARDROBE SPECIALTIES 10

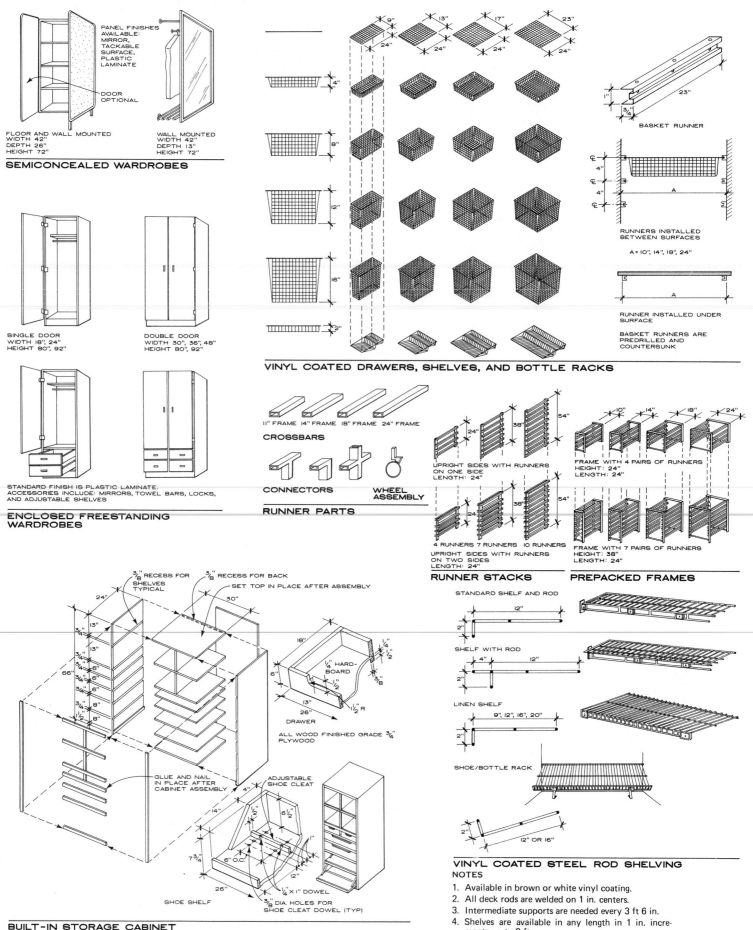

SEMICONCEALED WARDROBES

FLOOR AND WALL MOUNTED
WIDTH 42"
DEPTH 26"
HEIGHT 72"

WALL MOUNTED
WIDTH 42"
DEPTH 13"
HEIGHT 72"

PANEL FINISHES AVAILABLE: MIRROR, TACKABLE SURFACE, PLASTIC LAMINATE

DOOR OPTIONAL

ENCLOSED FREESTANDING WARDROBES

SINGLE DOOR
WIDTH 18", 24"
HEIGHT 80", 92"

DOUBLE DOOR
WIDTH 30", 36", 48"
HEIGHT 80", 92"

STANDARD FINISH IS PLASTIC LAMINATE.
ACCESSORIES INCLUDE: MIRRORS, TOWEL BARS, LOCKS, AND ADJUSTABLE SHELVES

VINYL COATED DRAWERS, SHELVES, AND BOTTLE RACKS

CROSSBARS

11" FRAME   14" FRAME   18" FRAME   24" FRAME

CONNECTORS   WHEEL ASSEMBLY

RUNNER PARTS

BASKET RUNNER

RUNNERS INSTALLED BETWEEN SURFACES

A = 10", 14", 18", 24"

RUNNER INSTALLED UNDER SURFACE

BASKET RUNNERS ARE PREDRILLED AND COUNTERSUNK

RUNNER STACKS

UPRIGHT SIDES WITH RUNNERS ON ONE SIDE
LENGTH: 24"

4 RUNNERS 7 RUNNERS 10 RUNNERS
UPRIGHT SIDES WITH RUNNERS ON TWO SIDES
LENGTH: 24"

PREPACKED FRAMES

FRAME WITH 4 PAIRS OF RUNNERS
HEIGHT: 24"
LENGTH: 24"

FRAME WITH 7 PAIRS OF RUNNERS
HEIGHT: 38"
LENGTH: 24"

BUILT-IN STORAGE CABINET

3/8" RECESS FOR SHELVES TYPICAL
3/8" RECESS FOR BACK
SET TOP IN PLACE AFTER ASSEMBLY
GLUE AND NAIL IN PLACE AFTER CABINET ASSEMBLY

1/4" HARD-BOARD
DRAWER
ALL WOOD FINISHED GRADE 3/4 PLYWOOD

ADJUSTABLE SHOE CLEAT
SHOE SHELF
1/4" X 1" DOWEL
3/8" DIA. HOLES FOR SHOE CLEAT DOWEL (TYP)

Charles E. George; SHWC, Inc.; Dallas, Texas

VINYL COATED STEEL ROD SHELVING
NOTES

STANDARD SHELF AND ROD

SHELF WITH ROD

LINEN SHELF

SHOE/BOTTLE RACK

1. Available in brown or white vinyl coating.
2. All deck rods are welded on 1 in. centers.
3. Intermediate supports are needed every 3 ft 6 in.
4. Shelves are available in any length in 1 in. increments up to 8 ft.

CHAPTER 11 EQUIPMENT

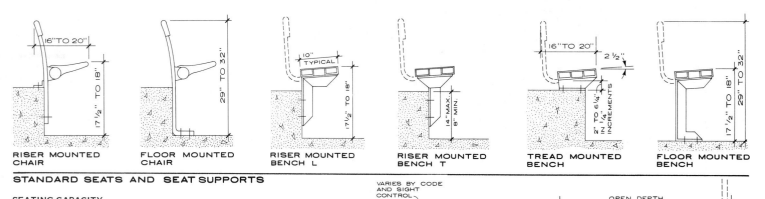

RISER MOUNTED CHAIR | FLOOR MOUNTED CHAIR | RISER MOUNTED BENCH L | RISER MOUNTED BENCH T | TREAD MOUNTED BENCH | FLOOR MOUNTED BENCH

STANDARD SEATS AND SEAT SUPPORTS

SEATING CAPACITY

Allow 18 in. of bleacher length per person per row. Normal aisle width of 36 in. reduces seating capacity by two seats per row x number of rows x number of aisles. See table below.

SAFETY AREAS

1. BASEBALL FIELDS: Minimum 60 ft from seating to foul line or baseline at each side of home plate.
2. SOFTBALL FIELDS: Minimum 25 ft from seating to foul line or baseline at each side of home plate.
3. BASKETBALL COURTS: Minimum 6 ft from seating to court sides, 8 in. minimum to court ends.
4. SWIMMING POOLS: Minimum 5 ft from seating to pool decks. Spectator area must be separate from pool area to avoid mixing dry and wet traffic.

STADIUM SEATING

Concrete risers and treads with seating attached. See typical seats and seat supports above.

FIXED GRANDSTAND

8 in. rise with 24 in. row spacing typical. Available options include front, end, and back rails, crosswalks, ramps, stairs, aisles, vomitories, closed risers, double foot plates, folding seat backs, and waterproof covers of metal or fiberglass for resurfacing existing wooden bleachers.

PORTABLE BLEACHERS

3, 4, or 5 row sections typical. Transportable options include wheels and trailer attachments. Bleachers of up to 25 rows may be assembled of portable, assemblable sections.

TELESCOPIC BLEACHERS

1. LOWRISE: $9^5/_8$ in. normal rise for most uses. 22 in. minimum row spacing gives maximum seating capacity. 24 in. spacing gives greater leg room. 30 or 32 in. spacing provides extra passage and leg room space and space for optional folding back rests.
2. HIGHRISE: Models with $11^5/_8$ or 16 in. risers are suggested for pools, balconies, hockey rinks, or similarly difficult viewing situations where seating must be banked more steeply than is normal.

SEATING CAPACITY

LENGTH (FT)

ROW	8	12	16	20	24	28	32	36	40
3	16	24	32	40	48	56	64	72	80
4	21	32	42	53	64	74	85	96	106
5	26	40	53	66	80	93	106	120	133
6	32	48	64	80	96	112	128	144	160
7	37	56	74	93	112	130	149	168	186
8	42	64	85	106	128	149	170	192	213
9	48	72	96	120	144	168	192	216	240
10	53	80	106	133	160	186	213	240	266
12	64	96	128	160	192	224	256	288	320
14	74	112	149	186	224	261	298	336	373
16	85	128	170	213	256	298	341	384	426
18	96	144	192	240	288	336	384	432	480
20	106	160	213	266	320	373	426	480	533

NOTE: Consult manufacturers for additional information.

Erik Johnson; Lawrence Cook & Associates; Falls Church, Virginia

David W. Johnson; Washington, D.C.

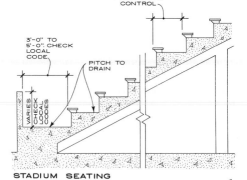

STADIUM SEATING

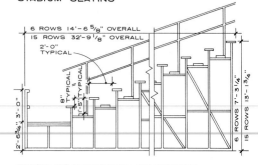

FIXED GRANDSTAND (ELEVATED)

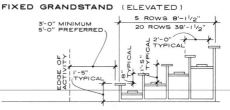

PORTABLE BLEACHERS

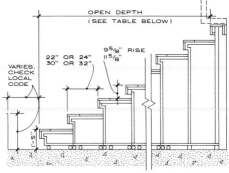

TELESCOPIC BLEACHERS (HIGHRISE)

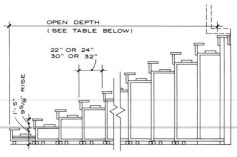

TELESCOPIC BLEACHERS (LOWRISE)

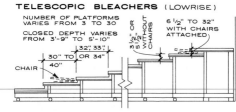

TELESCOPIC PLATFORM

GRANDSTANDS AND BLEACHERS DIMENSIONS

ROW	OPEN DEPTH				$9^5/_8$" RISE CLOSED DEPTH		$11^5/_8$" AND 16" RISE CLOSED DEPTH	
	22"	24"	30"	32"	22" OR 24"	30" OR 32"	22" OR 24"	30" OR 32"
3	4'-11½"	5'-1½"	6'-3½"	6'-5½"	3'-1¹³/₁₆"	3'-9¹³/₁₆"	3'-1¹³/₁₆"	3'-9¹³/₁₆"
4	6'-9½"	7'-1½"	8'-9½"	9'-1½"	3'-2⅛"	3'-10⅛"	3'-2⅛"	3'-10⅛"
5	8'-7½"	9'-1½"	11'-3½"	11'-9½"	3'-2⁷/₁₆"	3'-10⁷/₁₆"	3'-2⁷/₁₆"	3'-10⁷/₁₆"
6	10'-5½"	11'-1½"	13'-9½"	14'-5½"	3'-2¾"	3'-10¾"	3'-2¾"	3'-10¾"
7	12'-3½"	13'-1½"	16'-3½"	17'-1½"	3'-3¹/₁₆"	3'-11¹/₁₆"	3'-3¹/₁₆"	3'-11¹/₁₆"
8	14'-1½"	15'-1½"	18'-9½"	19'-9½"	3'-3⅜"	3'-11⅜"	3'-3⅜"	3'-11⅜"
9	15'-11½"	17'-1½"	21'-3½"	22'-5½"	3'-3¹¹/₁₆"	3'-11¹¹/₁₆"	3'-3¹¹/₁₆"	3'-11¹¹/₁₆"
10	17'-9½"	19'-1½"	23'-9½"	25'-1½"	3'-4"	4'-0"	3'-4"	4'-0"
12	21'-5½"	23'-1½"	28'-9½"	30'-5½"	3'-4⅝"	4'-0⅝"	3'-4⅝"	4'-0⅝"
14	25'-1½"	27'-1½"	33'-9½"	35'-9½"	3'-5¼"	4'-1¼"	NOTE: For $11^5/_8$" rise of 18 or more rows and 16" rise of 13 or more rows check with manufacturer for modified closed depth dimensions.	
16	28'-9½"	31'-1½"	38'-9½"	41'-1½"	3'-5⅞"	4'-1⅞"		
18	32'-5½"	35'-1½"	43'-9½"	46'-5½"	3'-6½"	4'-2½"		
20	36'-1½"	39'-1½"	48'-9½"	51'-9½"	3'-7⅛"	4'-3⅛"		

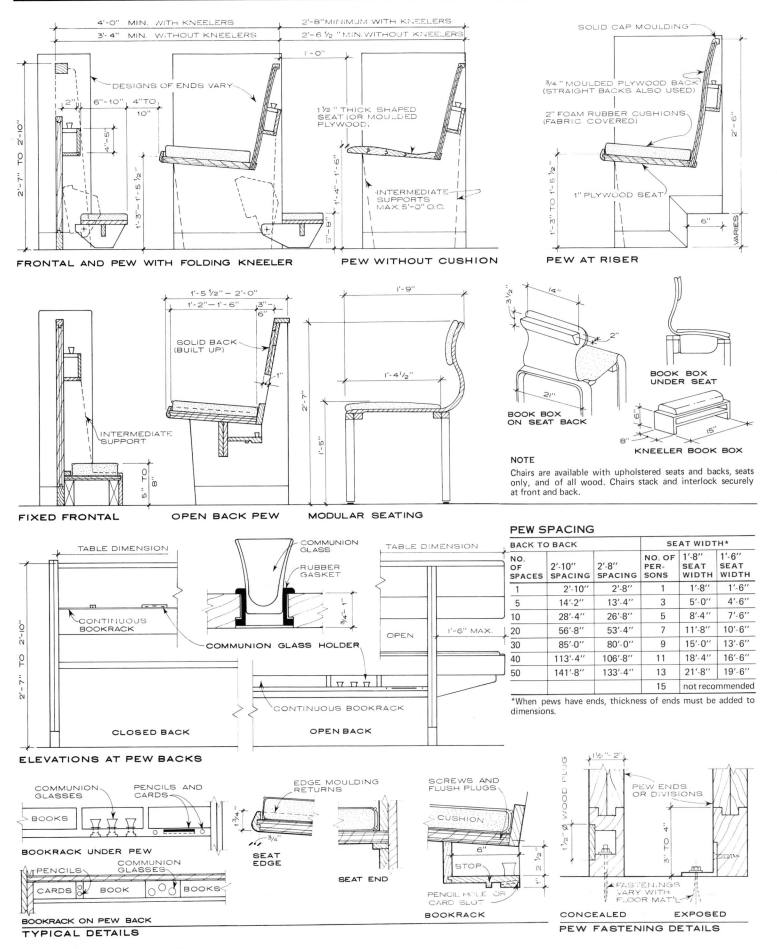

FRONTAL AND PEW WITH FOLDING KNEELER

PEW WITHOUT CUSHION

PEW AT RISER

FIXED FRONTAL

OPEN BACK PEW

MODULAR SEATING

BOOK BOX ON SEAT BACK

BOOK BOX UNDER SEAT

KNEELER BOOK BOX

NOTE

Chairs are available with upholstered seats and backs, seats only, and of all wood. Chairs stack and interlock securely at front and back.

ELEVATIONS AT PEW BACKS

CLOSED BACK

OPEN BACK

COMMUNION GLASS HOLDER

PEW SPACING

BACK TO BACK			SEAT WIDTH*		
NO. OF SPACES	2'-10" SPACING	2'-8" SPACING	NO. OF PERSONS	1'-8" SEAT WIDTH	1'-6" SEAT WIDTH
1	2'-10"	2'-8"	1	1'-8"	1'-6"
5	14'-2"	13'-4"	3	5'-0"	4'-6"
10	28'-4"	26'-8"	5	8'-4"	7'-6"
20	56'-8"	53'-4"	7	11'-8"	10'-6"
30	85'-0"	80'-0"	9	15'-0"	13'-6"
40	113'-4"	106'-8"	11	18'-4"	16'-6"
50	141'-8"	133'-4"	13	21'-8"	19'-6"
			15	not recommended	

*When pews have ends, thickness of ends must be added to dimensions.

BOOKRACK UNDER PEW

BOOKRACK ON PEW BACK

SEAT EDGE

SEAT END

BOOKRACK

CONCEALED

EXPOSED

TYPICAL DETAILS

PEW FASTENING DETAILS

Pecsok, Jelliffe & Randall, AIA, Architects; Indianapolis, Indiana

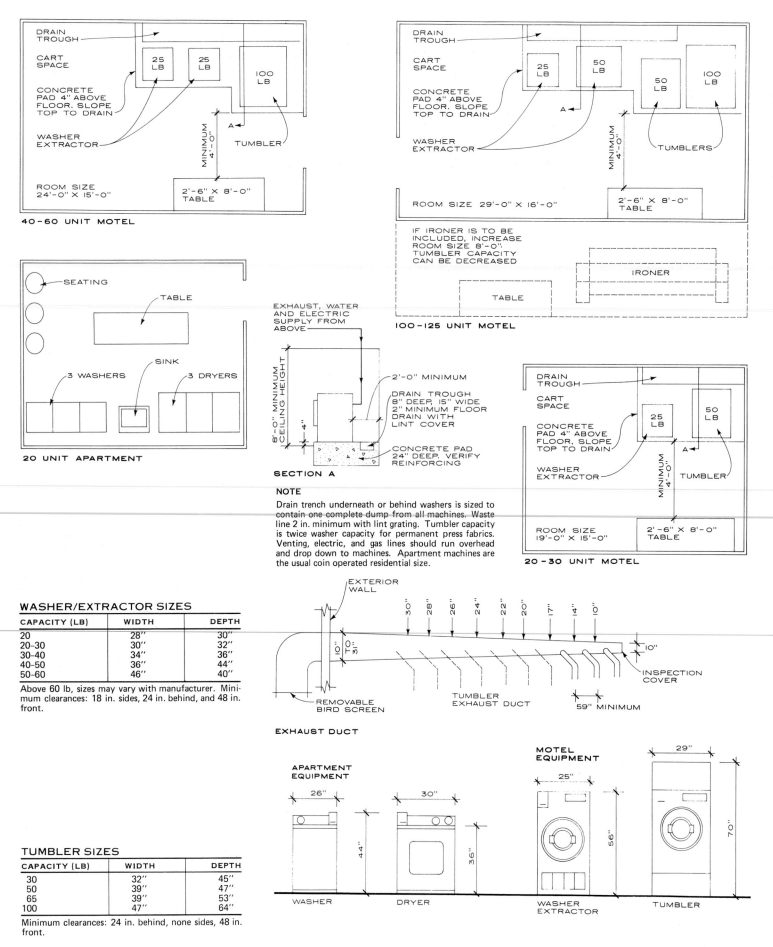

40-60 UNIT MOTEL

20 UNIT APARTMENT

SECTION A

NOTE

Drain trench underneath or behind washers is sized to contain one complete dump from all machines. Waste line 2 in. minimum with lint grating. Tumbler capacity is twice washer capacity for permanent press fabrics. Venting, electric, and gas lines should run overhead and drop down to machines. Apartment machines are the usual coin operated residential size.

100-125 UNIT MOTEL

IF IRONER IS TO BE INCLUDED, INCREASE ROOM SIZE 8'-0". TUMBLER CAPACITY CAN BE DECREASED

20-30 UNIT MOTEL

EXHAUST DUCT

WASHER/EXTRACTOR SIZES

CAPACITY (LB)	WIDTH	DEPTH
20	28″	30″
20-30	30″	32″
30-40	34″	36″
40-50	36″	44″
50-60	46″	40″

Above 60 lb, sizes may vary with manufacturer. Minimum clearances: 18 in. sides, 24 in. behind, and 48 in. front.

TUMBLER SIZES

CAPACITY (LB)	WIDTH	DEPTH
30	32″	45″
50	39″	47″
65	39″	53″
100	47″	64″

Minimum clearances: 24 in. behind, none sides, 48 in. front.

APARTMENT EQUIPMENT

MOTEL EQUIPMENT

Smiley-Glotter Associates-Architects Engineers Planners; Minneapolis, Minnesota

11 LAUNDRY EQUIPMENT

SHELF CAPACITY AND DEPTH

TYPE OF BOOK	VOLUMES PER LINEAR FT	SHELF DEPTH (IN.)
Children's	10-12	8
Fiction and economics	7	8
History and General Literature	7	8
Reference	7	10
Technical and Scientific	6	8
Medical	5	10
Law and public documents	4-5	8
Bound periodicals	5	10-12
U.S. Patent spec.	2	8

GENERAL NOTE

No definite formula can be given for finding the number of books per gross stack room area. Many variables must be considered: size and kind of books (folios, bound periodicals, etc.); number and width of aisles; stairways, lifts, carrels, and so on; and whether calculations are based on ultimate capacity. Variance has been found to run from 13½ to 19 books/sq ft, depending on local conditions. For a rough rule of thumb, allow 16 books/sq ft of gross area. The weight of books is approximately 25 lb/cu ft.

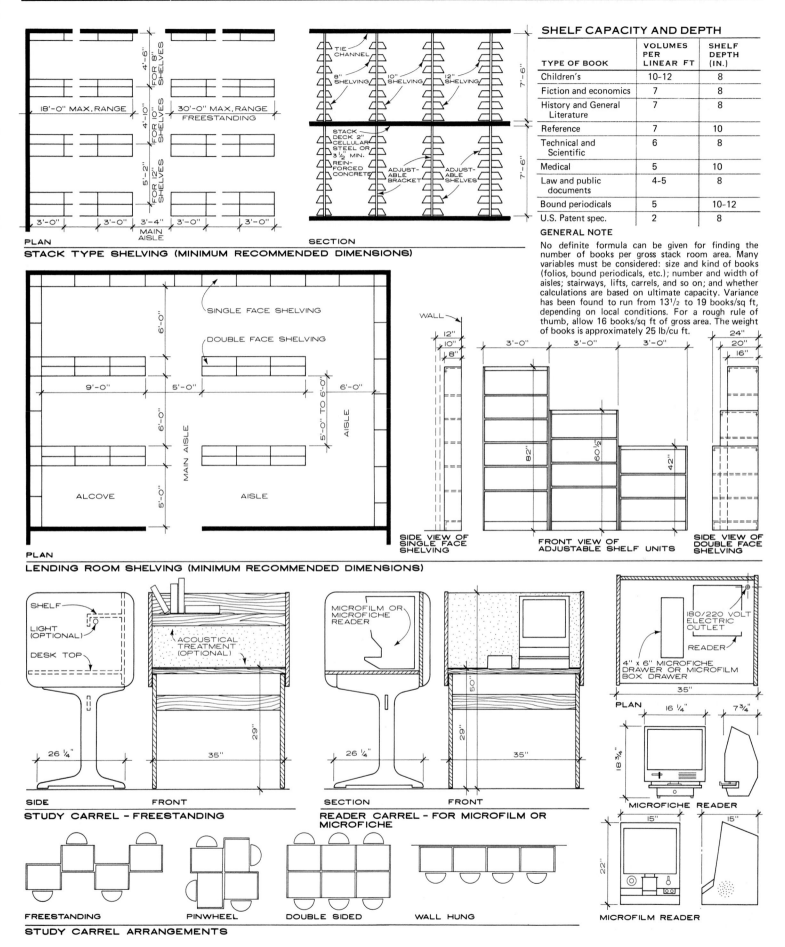

STACK TYPE SHELVING (MINIMUM RECOMMENDED DIMENSIONS)

LENDING ROOM SHELVING (MINIMUM RECOMMENDED DIMENSIONS)

STUDY CARREL - FREESTANDING

READER CARREL - FOR MICROFILM OR MICROFICHE

STUDY CARREL ARRANGEMENTS

FREESTANDING   PINWHEEL   DOUBLE SIDED   WALL HUNG

MICROFICHE READER

MICROFILM READER

Walter Hart, AIA, and Frank Giersback, R.A.; North White Plains, New York

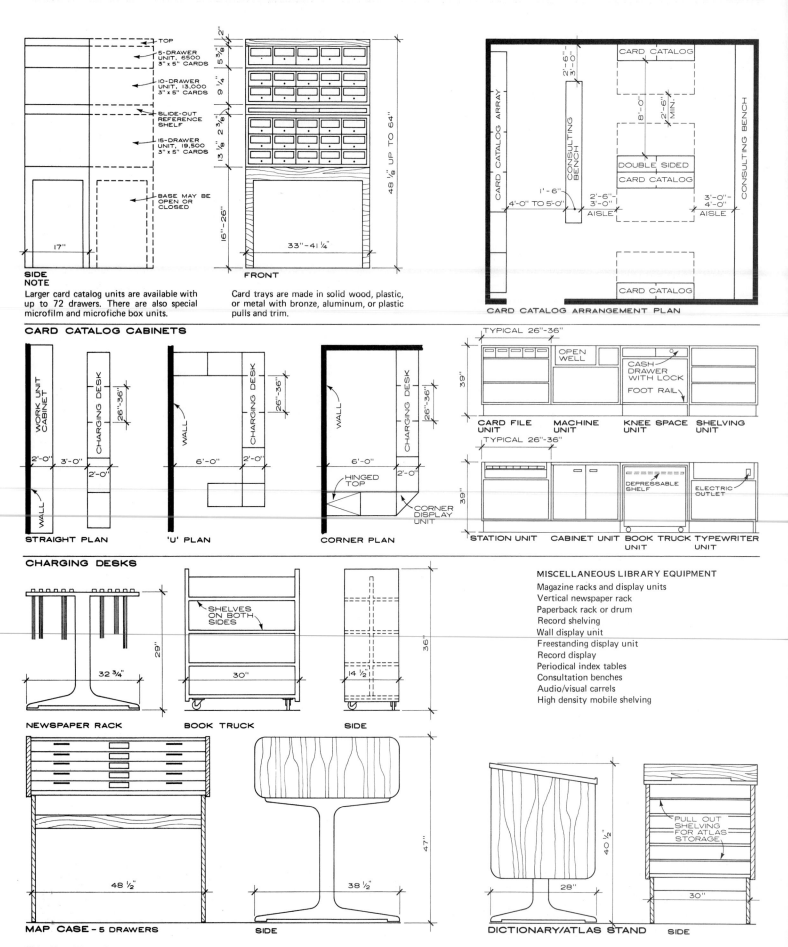

CARD CATALOG CABINETS

SIDE

NOTE
Larger card catalog units are available with up to 72 drawers. There are also special microfilm and microfiche box units.

Card trays are made in solid wood, plastic, or metal with bronze, aluminum, or plastic pulls and trim.

TOP

5-DRAWER UNIT, 6500 3" x 5" CARDS

10-DRAWER UNIT, 13,000 3" x 5" CARDS

SLIDE-OUT REFERENCE SHELF

15-DRAWER UNIT, 19,500 3" x 5" CARDS

BASE MAY BE OPEN OR CLOSED

FRONT

CARD CATALOG ARRANGEMENT PLAN

CARD CATALOG ARRAY

CONSULTING BENCH

CARD CATALOG

DOUBLE SIDED CARD CATALOG

CONSULTING BENCH

CARD CATALOG

STRAIGHT PLAN

'U' PLAN

CORNER PLAN

WORK UNIT CABINET

CHARGING DESK

WALL

HINGED TOP

CORNER DISPLAY UNIT

CARD FILE UNIT   MACHINE UNIT   KNEE SPACE UNIT   SHELVING UNIT

OPEN WELL

CASH DRAWER WITH LOCK

FOOT RAIL

TYPICAL 26"-36"

STATION UNIT   CABINET UNIT   BOOK TRUCK UNIT   TYPEWRITER UNIT

DEPRESSABLE SHELF

ELECTRIC OUTLET

CHARGING DESKS

NEWSPAPER RACK

BOOK TRUCK

SHELVES ON BOTH SIDES

SIDE

MISCELLANEOUS LIBRARY EQUIPMENT
Magazine racks and display units
Vertical newspaper rack
Paperback rack or drum
Record shelving
Wall display unit
Freestanding display unit
Record display
Periodical index tables
Consultation benches
Audio/visual carrels
High density mobile shelving

MAP CASE - 5 DRAWERS

SIDE

DICTIONARY/ATLAS STAND   SIDE

PULL OUT SHELVING FOR ATLAS STORAGE

Walter Hart, AIA, and Frank Giersback, R.A.; North White Plains, New York

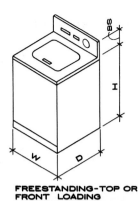

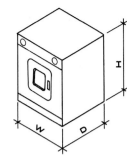

FREESTANDING-TOP OR FRONT LOADING
AUTOMATIC WASHERS (SOME HAVE KICK SPACES, SOME NOT)

UNDER COUNTER

	MIN.	MAX.	OTHER
W	25 1/2	27	25 5/8 - 26 3/4
D	24 7/8	28 23/32	25 - 28 5/16
H	36	36 1/2	36 1/8 - 36 1/4
BS	6 3/32	8 3/4	6 1/2 - 8 1/2

	MIN.	MAX.
W	26 3/4	30 1/4
D	24 7/8	24 7/8
H	34 1/2	

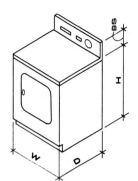

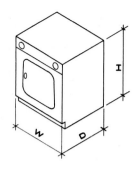

FREESTANDING FRONT LOADING
AUTOMATIC DRYERS (SOME HAVE KICK SPACES, SOME NOT)

UNDER COUNTER

	MIN.	MAX.	OTHER
W	26 3/4	31 1/2	27-31
D	24 7/8	28 23/32	25 - 28 5/16
H	36	36 1/2	36 1/8 - 36 1/4
BS	6 3/32	8 3/4	6 1/2 - 8 1/2

	MIN.	MAX.
W	26 3/4	
D	24 7/8	
H	34 1/2	

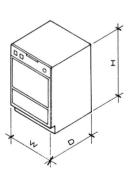

UTILITY CONNECTION BOX (RECESSED)

- PLASTIC FACEPLATE
- WATER SUPPLY VALVES
- 2" DIAM. DRAIN
- ELECTRIC OUTLETS TWO - 125V AND ONE 250V
- STANDARD STUD WALL 2 X 4'S @ 16" O.C.
- STUD BRACKET INCL.

ELEVATION

SECTION

GENERAL NOTES

See kitchen & laundry layout pages for locations of washers & dryers and wall chases for pipes & vents and for dishwasher locations.

Where clearances of doors of machines (when open) may be a problem, check manufacturers catalog for "open-door" dimension.

All dimensions given are actual ones but certain variations in body design may affect actual depths of models. Check all units for exact voltage. Some units available with gas.

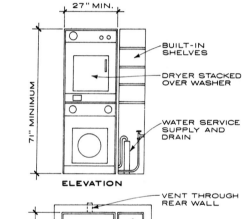

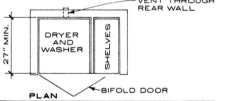

- BUILT-IN SHELVES
- DRYER STACKED OVER WASHER
- WATER SERVICE SUPPLY AND DRAIN
- VENT THROUGH REAR WALL
- BIFOLD DOOR

ELEVATION

PLAN

WASHER AND DRYER STACKED IN CLOSET

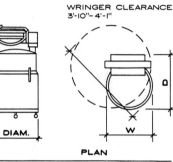

WRINGER CLEARANCE 3'-10"- 4'-1"

DIAM.

PLAN

WRINGER WASHERS

	MIN.	MAX.	OTHER
W	23 1/4	27 1/4	24-27
D	24	29 3/4	26-28
H	33	46	35 1/2-38 1/4
DIAM.	23	29	23 1/8 - 23 1/2

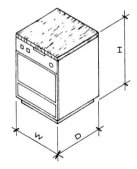

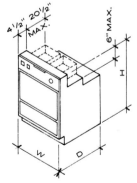

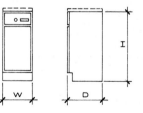

AUTOMATIC DISHWASHERS

UNDER COUNTER	MIN.	MAX.	OTHER
W	23	24	23 7/8
D	23 11/16	26 1/4	25 1/2
H	33 1/2	34 1/2	34 1/8

UNDER SINK	MIN.	MAX.	OTHER
W	24	24 1/4	24
D	24	25 1/2	25
H	34 1/2	34 1/2	34 1/2

MOBILE (WITH COUNTER TOP)	MIN.	MAX.	OTHER
W	22 1/2	27	24 5/8
D	23 11/16	26 1/2	25
H	34 1/8	39	36

TRASH COMPACTOR: UNDER COUNTER OR FREESTANDING

	MIN.	MAX.	OTHER
W	11 7/8	17 3/4	14 7/8
D	18	24 3/16	18 1/4
H	33 1/2	35	34 1/2

Wm. G. Miner, AIA, Architect; Washington, D.C.

R. E. Powe, Jr., AIA; Hugh N. Jacobsen, FAIA; Washington, D.C.

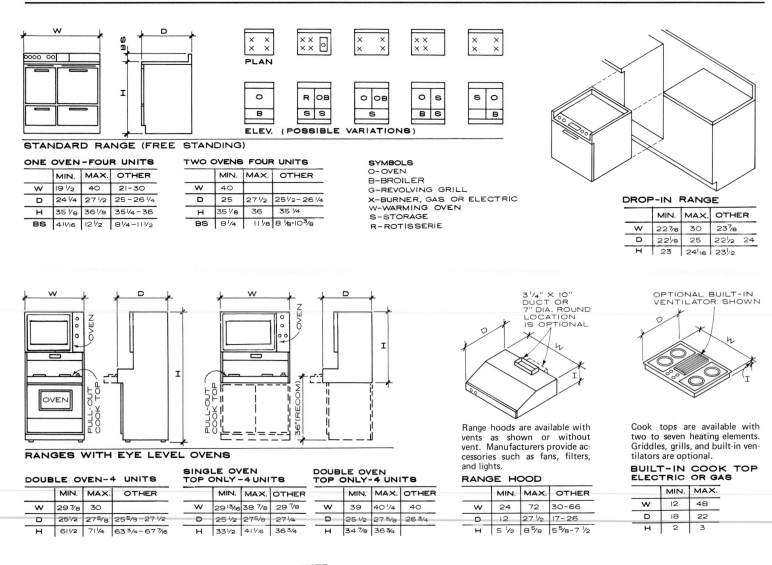

STANDARD RANGE (FREE STANDING)

ONE OVEN-FOUR UNITS

	MIN.	MAX.	OTHER
W	19 1/2	40	21-30
D	24 1/4	27 1/2	25-26 1/4
H	35 1/8	36 1/8	35 1/4-36
BS	4 11/16	12 1/2	8 1/4-11 1/2

TWO OVENS FOUR UNITS

	MIN.	MAX.	OTHER
W	40		
D	25	27 1/2	25 1/2-26 1/4
H	35 1/8	36	35 1/4
BS	8 1/4	11 1/8	8 1/8-10 3/8

SYMBOLS
O-OVEN
B-BROILER
G-REVOLVING GRILL
X-BURNER, GAS OR ELECTRIC
W-WARMING OVEN
S-STORAGE
R-ROTISSERIE

DROP-IN RANGE

	MIN.	MAX.	OTHER
W	22 7/8	30	23 7/8
D	22 1/8	25	22 1/2 24
H	23	24 1/16	23 1/2

RANGES WITH EYE LEVEL OVENS

DOUBLE OVEN-4 UNITS

	MIN.	MAX.	OTHER
W	29 7/8	30	
D	25 1/2	27 5/8	25 5/8-27 1/2
H	61 1/2	71 1/4	63 3/4-67 7/16

SINGLE OVEN TOP ONLY-4 UNITS

	MIN.	MAX.	OTHER
W	29 13/16	38 7/8	29 7/8
D	25 1/2	27 5/8	27 1/4
H	33 1/2	41 1/16	36 3/4

DOUBLE OVEN TOP ONLY-4 UNITS

	MIN.	MAX.	OTHER
W	39	40 1/4	40
D	25 1/2	27 5/8	26 3/4
H	34 7/8	36 3/4	

Range hoods are available with vents as shown or without vent. Manufacturers provide accessories such as fans, filters, and lights.

RANGE HOOD

	MIN.	MAX.	OTHER
W	24	72	30-66
D	12	27 1/2	17-26
H	5 1/2	8 5/8	5 5/8-7 1/2

Cook tops are available with two to seven heating elements. Griddles, grills, and built-in ventilators are optional.

BUILT-IN COOK TOP ELECTRIC OR GAS

	MIN.	MAX.
W	12	48
D	18	22
H	2	3

NOTE
SELF CLEANING OVENS MUST VENT TO OUTSIDE

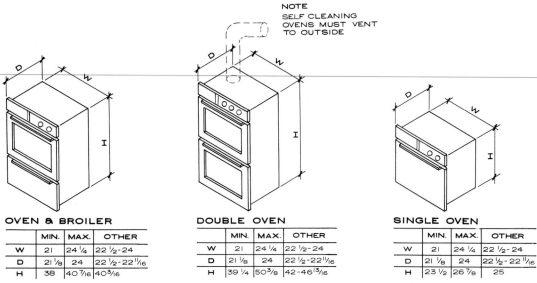

BUILT-IN WALL OVENS (GAS OR ELECTRIC)

OVEN & BROILER

	MIN.	MAX.	OTHER
W	21	24 1/4	22 1/2-24
D	21 1/8	24	22 1/2-22 11/16
H	38	40 7/16	40 3/16

DOUBLE OVEN

	MIN.	MAX.	OTHER
W	21	24 1/4	22 1/2-24
D	21 1/8	24	22 1/2-22 11/16
H	39 1/4	50 3/8	42-46 13/16

SINGLE OVEN

	MIN.	MAX.	OTHER
W	21	24 1/4	22 1/2-24
D	21 1/8	24	22 1/2-22 11/16
H	23 1/2	26 7/8	25

MICROWAVE OVEN

	MIN.	MAX.	OTHER
W	21 1/2	24 3/4	22 1/2
D	14 1/2	22	18 3/4
H	13 5/8	18	17

NOTES

1. Check manufacturers requirements for rough clearances.

2. Dimensions shown are in inches.

3. Optional equipment available for ranges or wall ovens are broilers and rotisseries.

Wm. G. Miner, AIA, Architect; Washington, D.C.

R. E. Powe, Jr., AIA; Hugh N. Jacobsen, FAIA; Washington, D.C.

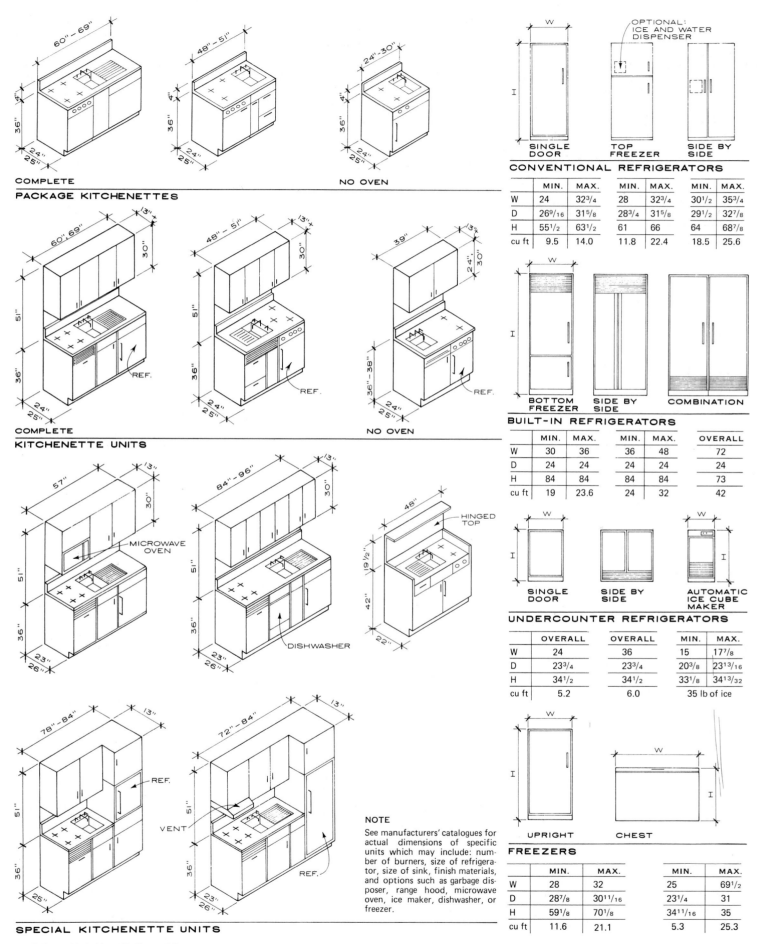

COMPLETE   **NO OVEN**

PACKAGE KITCHENETTES

COMPLETE   **NO OVEN**

KITCHENETTE UNITS

SPECIAL KITCHENETTE UNITS

Wm. G. Miner, AIA, Architect; Washington, D.C.

CONVENTIONAL REFRIGERATORS

	MIN.	MAX.	MIN.	MAX.	MIN.	MAX.
W	24	$32^3/_4$	28	$32^3/_4$	$30^1/_2$	$35^3/_4$
D	$26^9/_{16}$	$31^5/_8$	$28^3/_4$	$31^5/_8$	$29^1/_2$	$32^7/_8$
H	$55^1/_2$	$63^1/_2$	61	66	64	$68^7/_8$
cu ft	9.5	14.0	11.8	22.4	18.5	25.6

BUILT-IN REFRIGERATORS

	MIN.	MAX.	MIN.	MAX.	OVERALL
W	30	36	36	48	72
D	24	24	24	24	24
H	84	84	84	84	73
cu ft	19	23.6	24	32	42

UNDERCOUNTER REFRIGERATORS

	OVERALL	OVERALL	MIN.	MAX.
W	24	36	15	$17^7/_8$
D	$23^3/_4$	$23^3/_4$	$20^3/_8$	$23^{13}/_{16}$
H	$34^1/_2$	$34^1/_2$	$33^1/_8$	$34^{13}/_{32}$
cu ft	5.2	6.0	35 lb of ice	

FREEZERS

	MIN.	MAX.	MIN.	MAX.
W	28	32	25	$69^1/_2$
D	$28^7/_8$	$30^{11}/_{16}$	$23^1/_4$	31
H	$59^1/_8$	$70^1/_8$	$34^{11}/_{16}$	35
cu ft	11.6	21.1	5.3	25.3

NOTE

See manufacturers' catalogues for actual dimensions of specific units which may include: number of burners, size of refrigerator, size of sink, finish materials, and options such as garbage disposer, range hood, microwave oven, ice maker, dishwasher, or freezer.

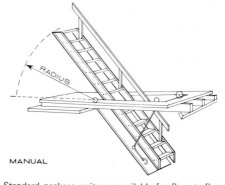

MANUAL

Standard package units are available for floor-to-floor heights from 7 ft up to 13 ft in 1 ft increments. Ladder is inclined at 52° above horizontal. Standard box frame is used for ceiling thickness up to 13 in. Special deep frame is specified for ceiling thicknesses ranging from 13 in. up to 48 in.

Typical rough opening in ceiling = 30 x 72 in.

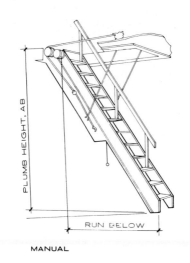

MANUAL

MOTORIZED

SLIDE UP PIVOT TYPE

TRIPLE FOLD

STANDARD SIZES FOR DISAPPEARING STAIRS

ROUGH OPENING	FLOOR-TO-FLOOR	COIL PROJECTION	LANDING SPACE
22″ x 48″	8′-5″	60″	58½″
22″ x 54″	8′-9″	66″	65″
	10′-0″	79″	73″
25½″ x 48″	8′-5″	60″	58½″
25½″ x 54″ 25½″ x 60″	8′-9″	66″	65″
30″ x 54″ 30″ x 60″	10′-0″	79″	73″

DOUBLE FOLD

FOLDING TYPE

HINGED TOP COVER

STEEL HOUSING

STEEL LADDER IN THREE TELESCOPING SECTIONS

NOTE: LADDER MAY BE OPERATED AND USED FROM ABOVE OR BELOW

TELESCOPING ACCESS LADDER

Several models are available using three or four telescoping sections.

Floor-to-floor heights ranging from 8 ft up to 13 ft 4 in. can be accommodated as the ladder angle varies from 53° above horizontal up to 74° above horizontal.

TYPICAL HEIGHTS FOR ONE STANDARD MODEL
(Rough Opening = 24″ x 48″)

FLOOR-TO-FLOOR	LAND SPACE	ABOVE HORIZONTAL
8′-0″	72″	53°
8′-3″	62″	61°
8′-6″	60″	62°
8′-9″	73″	56°
9′-0″	71″	57°
9′-3″	69″	58°
9′-6″	59″	64°
9′-10″	58″	65°
10′-2″	44″	72°

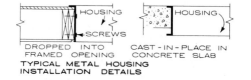

HOUSING

HOUSING

SCREWS

DROPPED INTO FRAMED OPENING

CAST-IN-PLACE IN CONCRETE SLAB

TYPICAL METAL HOUSING INSTALLATION DETAILS

CAUTION SHOULD BE TAKEN IN LOADING ATTIC SPACE WHERE JOIST NOT DESIGNED FOR OCCUPANCY LOADS. IT IS PREFERRED TO INSULATE ENTIRE ROOF

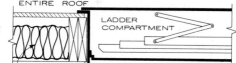

LADDER COMPARTMENT

CEILING INSULATION

TELESCOPING METAL LADDER

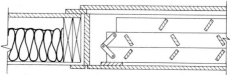

NOTE: VERIFY WITH MANUFACTURER WHETHER ADDED TOP CLOSURE IS COMPATIBLE WITH STAIR PACKAGE

FOLDING WOODEN STAIR

WHEN USED FOR ATTIC ACCESS, DISAPPEARING STAIRS MAY COMPROMISE A WELL-INSULATED CEILING. SELECT STAIR PACKAGE WITH TIGHT JOINTS AND DESIGN THAT ALLOWS INSULATION

INSULATION CONSIDERATIONS

11   RESIDENTIAL EQUIPMENT

CHAPTER 12 FURNISHINGS

OVERFILE STORAGE

TYPE	W	H	D	WEIGHT*
Over 2-drawer letter	30	26 or 37	29	170
Over 2-drawer legal	36		29	308
Over 3-drawer letter	43		29	377
Over 3-drawer legal	54		29	445

VERTICAL FILES

TYPE	W	H	D	WEIGHT*
5-drawer letter	15	60	29	405
5-drawer legal	18	60	29	430
4-drawer letter	15	50	29	324
4-drawer legal	18	50	29	344
3-drawer letter	15	41	29	258
3-drawer legal	18	41	29	162
2-drawer letter	15	30	29	162
2-drawer legal	18	30	29	172

INSIDE DRAWER DIMENSIONS

TYPE	W	H	D
Letter	12¼	10½	26¾
Legal	15¼	10½	26¾

*Weights = fully loaded file.

VERTICAL FILE CABINETS

LATERAL FILES

TYPE	W	H	D	WEIGHT*
5-drawer	30, 36, 42	64	18	610-843
4-drawer	30-36-42	52	18	524-720
3-drawer	30, 36, 42	40	18	401-553
2-drawer	30, 36, 42	32	18	285-391

*Weights = fully loaded file.

LATERAL FILE CABINETS

SPECIAL FILES

TYPE	W	H	D
A. Ledger sheet file	21	52	27
B. Check file	15	52	27
C. Document file	18	52	27
D. Card record file	22	52	27
6-drawer (3 x 5, 4 x 6 cards)	22	52	27
5-drawer (3 x 5, 4 x 6, 5 x 8 cards)	22	52	27
E. Tabulation card file	19	52	30
F. 5 x 8 card file	20	52	27

SPECIAL FILING CABINETS

FIRE INSULATED FILES

TYPE	W	H	D	WEIGHT*
4-drawer letter	17	52	30	600
4-drawer legal	20	52	30	660
3-drawer letter	17	51	30	465
3-drawer legal	20	41	30	515
2-drawer letter	17	28	30	330
2-drawer legal	20	28	30	370
3-drawer lateral	39	56	24	1220
2-drawer lateral	39	39	24	875

*Weight = fully loaded.

FIRE INSULATED FILE CABINETS

Associated Space Design, Inc.; Atlanta, Georgia

PLANNING

1. Users' filing needs should be tabulated in inches and in turn converted into number of cabinets. Consult manufacturer for inches available in specific cabinets.
2. For open space planning, the following square footage allowances should be used:

TYPES	SPACE ALLOWANCE (FT²)
Vertical and 36 in. lateral files	10
Lateral file for computer printout	15

NOTE: All dimensions shown are approximate. Consult manufacturer for actual dimensions.

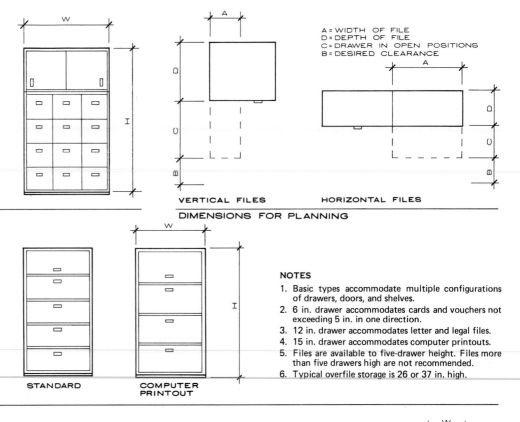

```
A = WIDTH OF FILE
D = DEPTH OF FILE
C = DRAWER IN OPEN POSITIONS
B = DESIRED CLEARANCE
```

VERTICAL FILES   **HORIZONTAL FILES**

DIMENSIONS FOR PLANNING

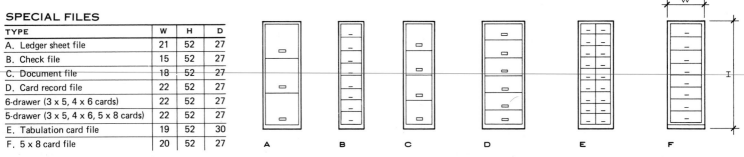

STANDARD   **COMPUTER PRINTOUT**

NOTES

1. Basic types accommodate multiple configurations of drawers, doors, and shelves.
2. 6 in. drawer accommodates cards and vouchers not exceeding 5 in. in one direction.
3. 12 in. drawer accommodates letter and legal files.
4. 15 in. drawer accommodates computer printouts.
5. Files are available to five-drawer height. Files more than five drawers high are not recommended.
6. Typical overfile storage is 26 or 37 in. high.

A   B   C   D   E   F

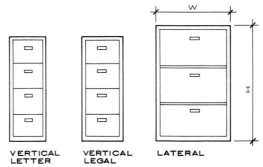

VERTICAL LETTER   **VERTICAL LEGAL**   **LATERAL**

AUTOMATED RETRIEVAL SYSTEM

An automated system permits the retrieval of records within seconds. Records are stored in the unit on carriers. Each carrier is individually suspended and equally spaced on a conveyor system. The operator sits or stands at a posting board, and at the touch of a button the proper carrier moves into position so that a record may be pulled or filed. If there are card trays (there may be two to six trays per carrier), the correct tray slides forward.

Records that may be stored in these units include file folders, binders, reference books, ledgers, tape reels, microfilm, and cards.

WARDROBE AND STORAGE UNITS (IN.)

W	H	D
18, 24, 36	64½–80½	18
18, 24, 36	41¼–52¼	18
18, 24, 36	64½–80½	24
18, 24, 36	41¼–52¼	24

NOTE: Capacity depends on type of coats stored.

SHELVING UNITS (IN.)

	W	D	H
2 shelves	18, 24, 36	18	29
3 shelves	18, 24, 36	18	42
4 shelves	18, 24, 36	18	60
5 shelves	18, 24, 36	18	78
6 shelves	18, 24, 36	18	84

NOTE: Heights vary with manufacturer.

NOTES

1. Files, wardrobe, and storage shelving units if used together should be compatible in dimension and design. If possible, one manufacturer should be selected to furnish all items.
2. If storage units are used as space dividers in an open plan, some acoustical corrections can be gained by applying acoustical panels to the back of the units.

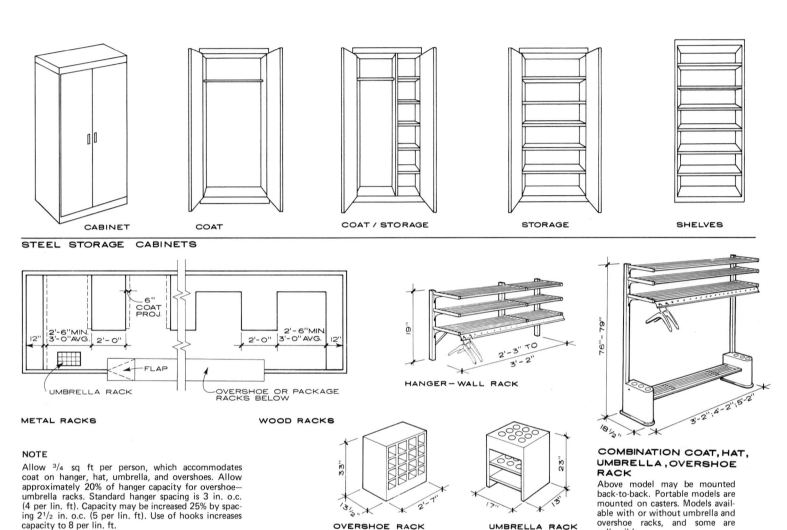

CABINET COAT COAT / STORAGE STORAGE SHELVES

STEEL STORAGE CABINETS

METAL RACKS WOOD RACKS

HANGER—WALL RACK

COMBINATION COAT, HAT, UMBRELLA, OVERSHOE RACK

Above model may be mounted back-to-back. Portable models are mounted on casters. Models available with or without umbrella and overshoe racks, and some are collapsible.

OVERSHOE RACK UMBRELLA RACK

NOTE

Allow ¾ sq ft per person, which accommodates coat on hanger, hat, umbrella, and overshoes. Allow approximately 20% of hanger capacity for overshoe–umbrella racks. Standard hanger spacing is 3 in. o.c. (4 per lin. ft). Capacity may be increased 25% by spacing 2½ in. o.c. (5 per lin. ft). Use of hooks increases capacity to 8 per lin. ft.

CHECKROOM LAYOUT AND EQUIPMENT

CASEWORK UNITS (IN.)

	W	D
A. Single door base unit	12–24	18, 22, 25
B. Double door base unit	27–48	18, 22, 25
C. Drawer unit	15–48	18, 22, 25
D. File unit	15–48	18, 22, 25
E. Double door wall unit	27–48	13, 18
F. Glass door wall unit	27–48	13, 18
G. Open shelf unit	15–60	13, 18

NOTE: Consult manufacturers for exact dimensions.

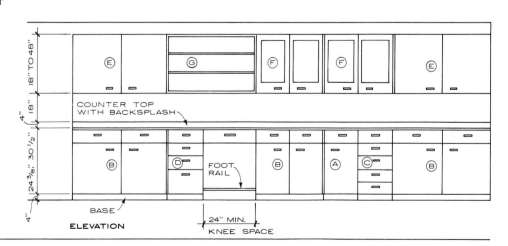

COUNTER TOP WITH BACKSPLASH

FOOT RAIL

BASE

24" MIN. KNEE SPACE

ELEVATION

STEEL CASEWORK

Associated Space Design, Inc; Atlanta, Georgia

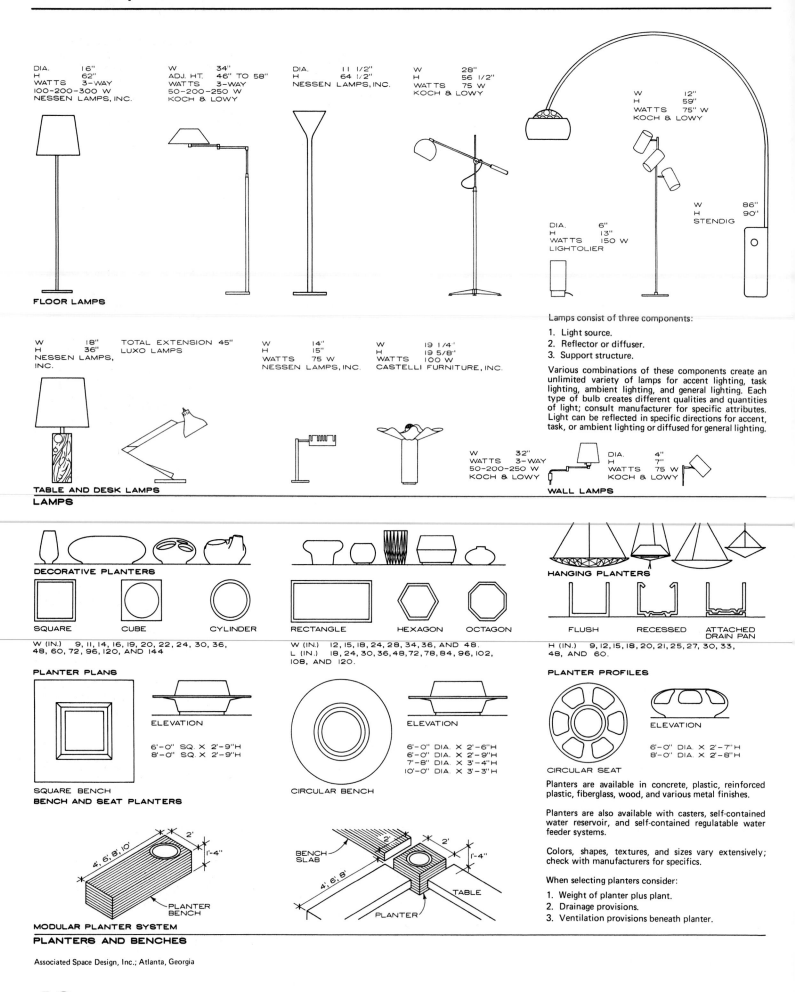

DIA. 16"
H 62"
WATTS 3-WAY
100-200-300 W
NESSEN LAMPS, INC.

W 34"
ADJ. HT. 46" TO 58"
WATTS 3-WAY
50-200-250 W
KOCH & LOWY

DIA. 11 1/2"
H 64 1/2"
NESSEN LAMPS, INC.

W 28"
H 56 1/2"
WATTS 75 W
KOCH & LOWY

W 12"
H 59"
WATTS 75 W
KOCH & LOWY

DIA. 6"
H 13"
WATTS 150 W
LIGHTOLIER

W 86"
H 90"
STENDIG

FLOOR LAMPS

Lamps consist of three components:

1. Light source.
2. Reflector or diffuser.
3. Support structure.

Various combinations of these components create an unlimited variety of lamps for accent lighting, task lighting, ambient lighting, and general lighting. Each type of bulb creates different qualities and quantities of light; consult manufacturer for specific attributes. Light can be reflected in specific directions for accent, task, or ambient lighting or diffused for general lighting.

W 18"
H 36"
NESSEN LAMPS, INC.

TOTAL EXTENSION 45"
LUXO LAMPS

W 14"
H 15"
WATTS 75 W
NESSEN LAMPS, INC.

W 19 1/4"
H 19 5/8"
WATTS 100 W
CASTELLI FURNITURE, INC.

W 32"
WATTS 3-WAY
50-200-250 W
KOCH & LOWY

DIA. 4"
H 7"
WATTS 75 W
KOCH & LOWY

TABLE AND DESK LAMPS

WALL LAMPS

LAMPS

DECORATIVE PLANTERS

SQUARE   CUBE   CYLINDER

RECTANGLE   HEXAGON   OCTAGON

HANGING PLANTERS

FLUSH   RECESSED   ATTACHED DRAIN PAN

W (IN.) 9, 11, 14, 16, 19, 20, 22, 24, 30, 36, 48, 60, 72, 96, 120, AND 144

W (IN.) 12, 15, 18, 24, 28, 34, 36, AND 48.
L (IN.) 18, 24, 30, 36, 48, 72, 78, 84, 96, 102, 108, AND 120.

H (IN.) 9, 12, 15, 18, 20, 21, 25, 27, 30, 33, 48, AND 60.

PLANTER PLANS

PLANTER PROFILES

ELEVATION

6'-0" SQ. X 2'-9"H
8'-0" SQ. X 2'-9"H

ELEVATION

6'-0" DIA. X 2'-6"H
6'-0" DIA. X 2'-9"H
7'-8" DIA. X 3'-4"H
10'-0" DIA. X 3'-3"H

ELEVATION

6'-0" DIA. X 2'-7"H
8'-0" DIA. X 2'-8"H

CIRCULAR SEAT

SQUARE BENCH

CIRCULAR BENCH

BENCH AND SEAT PLANTERS

Planters are available in concrete, plastic, reinforced plastic, fiberglass, wood, and various metal finishes.

Planters are also available with casters, self-contained water reservoir, and self-contained regulatable water feeder systems.

Colors, shapes, textures, and sizes vary extensively; check with manufacturers for specifics.

When selecting planters consider:

1. Weight of planter plus plant.
2. Drainage provisions.
3. Ventilation provisions beneath planter.

2'
1'-4'
4', 6', 8', 10'
PLANTER BENCH

MODULAR PLANTER SYSTEM

BENCH SLAB
2'
2'
1'-4'
4', 6', 8'
TABLE
PLANTER

PLANTERS AND BENCHES

Associated Space Design, Inc.; Atlanta, Georgia

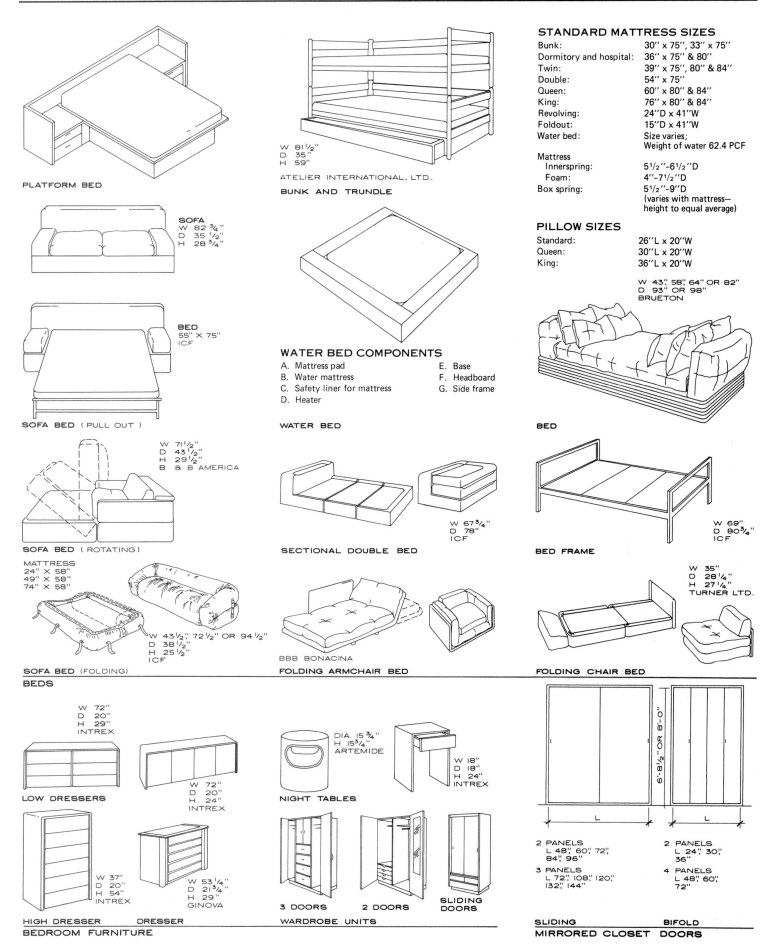

PLATFORM BED

SOFA
W 82 3/4 "
D 35 1/2 "
H 28 3/4 "

SOFA BED (PULL OUT)

BED
55" X 75"
ICF

SOFA BED (ROTATING)

W 71 1/2 "
D 43 1/2 "
H 29 1/2 "
B & B AMERICA

MATTRESS
24" X 58"
49" X 58"
74" X 58"

SOFA BED (FOLDING)

W 43 1/2 ", 72 1/2 " OR 94 1/2 "
D 38 1/2 "
H 25 1/2 "
ICF

W 81 1/2 "
D 35 "
H 59 "

ATELIER INTERNATIONAL, LTD.
BUNK AND TRUNDLE

WATER BED COMPONENTS

A. Mattress pad
B. Water mattress
C. Safety liner for mattress
D. Heater
E. Base
F. Headboard
G. Side frame

WATER BED

SECTIONAL DOUBLE BED

W 67 3/4 "
D 78 "
ICF

BBB BONACINA
FOLDING ARMCHAIR BED

STANDARD MATTRESS SIZES

Bunk: 30" x 75", 33" x 75"
Dormitory and hospital: 36" x 75" & 80"
Twin: 39" x 75", 80" & 84"
Double: 54" x 75"
Queen: 60" x 80" & 84"
King: 76" x 80" & 84"
Revolving: 24"D x 41"W
Foldout: 15"D x 41"W
Water bed: Size varies;
                               Weight of water 62.4 PCF
Mattress
  Innerspring: 5 1/2 "-6 1/2 "D
  Foam: 4"-7 1/2 "D
Box spring: 5 1/2 "-9"D
                               (varies with mattress—
                               height to equal average)

PILLOW SIZES

Standard: 26"L x 20"W
Queen: 30"L x 20"W
King: 36"L x 20"W

W 43", 58", 64" OR 82"
D 93" OR 98"
BRUETON

BED

W 69"
D 80 3/4 "
ICF

BED FRAME

W 35"
D 28 1/4 "
H 27 1/4 "
TURNER LTD.

FOLDING CHAIR BED

BEDS

W 72"
D 20"
H 29"
INTREX

LOW DRESSERS

W 72"
D 20"
H 24"
INTREX

DIA. 15 3/4 "
H 15 3/4 "
ARTEMIDE

W 18"
D 18"
H 24"
INTREX

NIGHT TABLES

W 37"
D 20"
H 54"
INTREX

HIGH DRESSER

W 53 1/4 "
D 21 3/4 "
H 29"
GINOVA

DRESSER

BEDROOM FURNITURE

3 DOORS   2 DOORS   SLIDING DOORS

WARDROBE UNITS

6'-8 1/2 " OR 8'-0"

2 PANELS
L 48", 60", 72",
84", 96"

3 PANELS
L 72", 108", 120",
132", 144"

2 PANELS
L 24", 30",
36"

4 PANELS
L 48", 60",
72"

SLIDING   BIFOLD
MIRRORED CLOSET DOORS

Associated Space Design, Inc.; Atlanta, Georgia

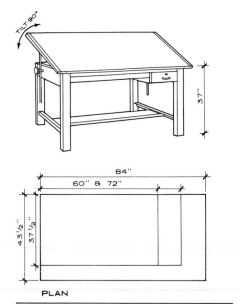

DRAFTING TABLE WITH ADJUSTABLE TOP

Drafting and/or engineering table is available in wood, in steel, or in combination. Various drawer and pedestal arrangements are available.

VARIOUS SIZES: 20" X 25", 24" X 36" & 36" X 48"

FLUORESCENT TRACING TABLE

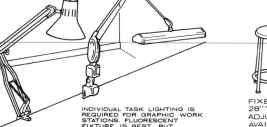

INDIVIDUAL TASK LIGHTING IS REQUIRED FOR GRAPHIC WORK STATIONS. FLUORESCENT FIXTURE IS BEST, BUT INCANDESCENT LIGHT MAY BE SUITABLE. COMBINATION FIXTURES ARE AVAILABLE. MOST UNITS CAN BE CLAMPED OR SCREWED ONTO THE DESK

DESK LAMPS

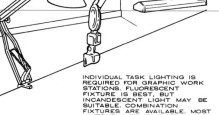

WIRE GUIDES MAINTAIN PARALLEL ATTITUDE OF RULE

RULES ARE AVAILABLE IN WOOD, METAL, AND PLASTIC, WITH DRAWING EDGE OF CLEAR PLASTIC. SIZES RANGE FROM 30" LONG UP TO 72" LONG

PARALLEL RULE

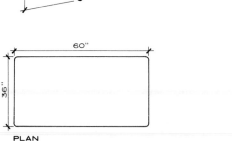

ADJUSTABLE WORKING SURFACE

Several manufacturers produce an array of drawing tables with adjustable tops, optional footrests, and pencil drawers.

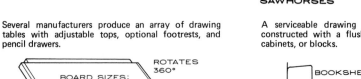

ROTATES 360°

BOARD SIZES:
29.5" X 41.3" (75 X 105 CM)
31.5" X 47.3" (80 X 120 CM)
31.5" X 55" (80 X 140 CM)

ADJUSTABLE TILT TO 90°

ADJUSTABLE HEIGHT

COUNTERBALANCED AUTOMATIC DRAFTING TABLE

FIXED HT. 28" TO 30" ADJUSTABLE AVAILABLE ALSO

VARIABLE SEAT HEIGHTS FROM 26" TO 32"

VARIABLE SEAT HEIGHTS FROM 17½" TO 34"

STOOLS AND CHAIRS

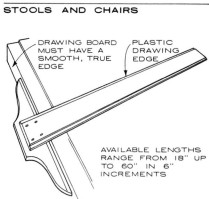

DRAWING BOARD MUST HAVE A SMOOTH, TRUE EDGE

PLASTIC DRAWING EDGE

AVAILABLE LENGTHS RANGE FROM 18" UP TO 60" IN 6" INCREMENTS

TRADITIONAL T SQUARE

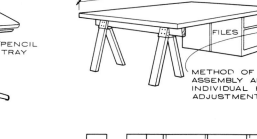

VARIES   VARIES

FILES

METHOD OF ASSEMBLY ALLOWS INDIVIDUAL HEIGHT ADJUSTMENT

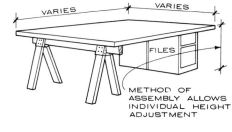

PLAN FILES

36" TO 42" AISLE

FILE

HOLLOW CORE DOOR TABLE ON SAWHORSES

A serviceable drawing board can be inexpensively constructed with a flush door set on sawhorses, file cabinets, or blocks.

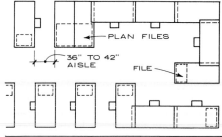
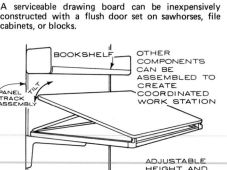

BOOKSHELF

OTHER COMPONENTS CAN BE ASSEMBLED TO CREATE COORDINATED WORK STATION

PANEL TRACK ASSEMBLY

TILT

ADJUSTABLE HEIGHT AND TILT

PANEL-HUNG DRAFTING BOARD

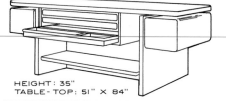

HEIGHT: 35"
TABLE-TOP: 51" X 84"

SERVICE TABLE

Service table provides a large worktop and integral storage compartments. Entire offices can be furnished with coordinated units.

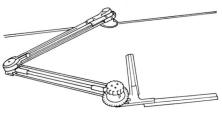

DRAFTING MACHINE

Clamp-on device combines parallel rule, triangles, protractor, and scales. Especially useful for technical drawing with few long lines. Straight edges can be had in several scales and are interchangeable.

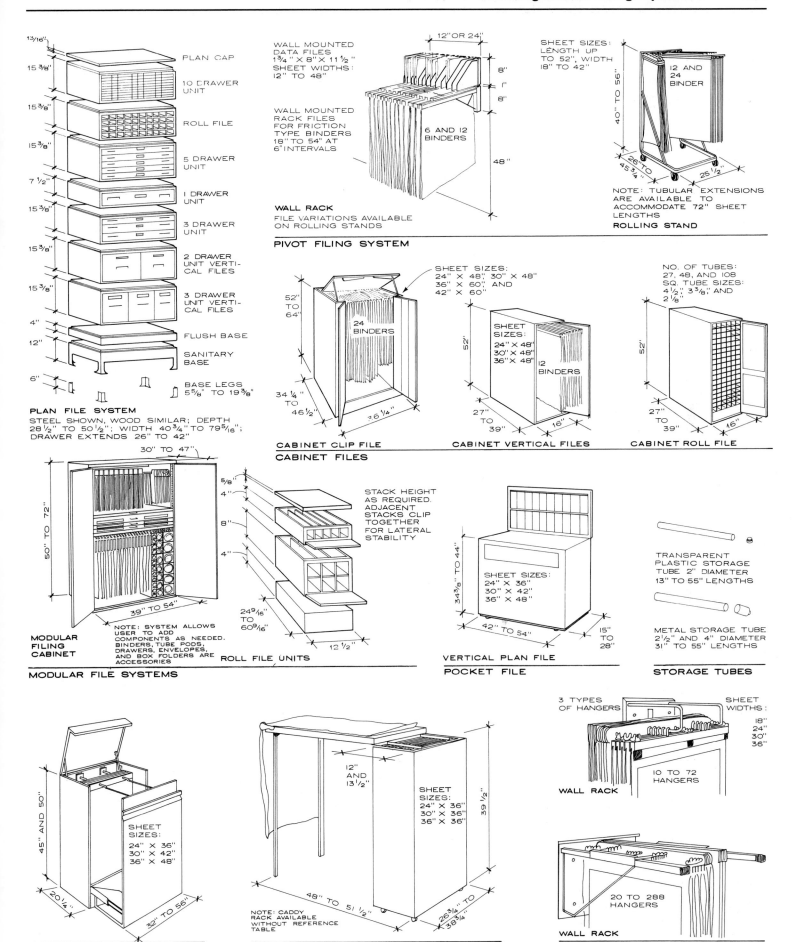

13/16"

PLAN CAP

15 3/8" 10 DRAWER UNIT

15 3/8" ROLL FILE

15 3/8" 5 DRAWER UNIT

7 1/2" 1 DRAWER UNIT

15 3/8" 3 DRAWER UNIT

15 3/8" 2 DRAWER UNIT VERTICAL FILES

15 3/8" 3 DRAWER UNIT VERTICAL FILES

4" FLUSH BASE

12" SANITARY BASE

6" BASE LEGS 5 5/8" TO 19 3/8"

PLAN FILE SYSTEM
STEEL SHOWN, WOOD SIMILAR; DEPTH 28 1/2" TO 50 1/2"; WIDTH 40 3/4" TO 79 5/16"; DRAWER EXTENDS 26" TO 42"

WALL MOUNTED DATA FILES 1 3/4" X 8" X 11 1/2" SHEET WIDTHS: 12" TO 48"

WALL MOUNTED RACK FILES FOR FRICTION TYPE BINDERS 18" TO 54" AT 6" INTERVALS

12" OR 24"

8" 1" 8"

6 AND 12 BINDERS

48"

WALL RACK
FILE VARIATIONS AVAILABLE ON ROLLING STANDS

PIVOT FILING SYSTEM

SHEET SIZES: LENGTH UP TO 52", WIDTH 18" TO 42"

40" TO 56"

12 AND 24 BINDER

26" TO 45 3/4" 25 1/2"

NOTE: TUBULAR EXTENSIONS ARE AVAILABLE TO ACCOMMODATE 72" SHEET LENGTHS

ROLLING STAND

SHEET SIZES: 24" X 48", 30" X 48", 36" X 60", AND 42" X 60"

52" TO 64"

24 BINDERS

34 1/4" TO 46 1/2"

26 1/4"

CABINET CLIP FILE

SHEET SIZES: 24" X 48", 30" X 48", 36" X 48"

52"

12 BINDERS

27" TO 39" 16"

CABINET VERTICAL FILES

NO. OF TUBES: 27, 48, AND 108 SQ. TUBE SIZES: 4 1/2", 3 3/8", AND 2 1/8"

52"

27" TO 39" 16"

CABINET ROLL FILE

CABINET FILES

30" TO 47"

50" TO 72"

39" TO 54"

MODULAR FILING CABINET

NOTE: SYSTEM ALLOWS USER TO ADD COMPONENTS AS NEEDED. BINDERS, TUBE PODS, DRAWERS, ENVELOPES, AND BOX FOLDERS ARE ACCESSORIES

MODULAR FILE SYSTEMS

5/8"
4"
8"
4"

STACK HEIGHT AS REQUIRED. ADJACENT STACKS CLIP TOGETHER FOR LATERAL STABILITY

24 9/16" TO 60 9/16"

12 1/2"

ROLL FILE UNITS

34 3/8" TO 44"

SHEET SIZES: 24" X 36", 30" X 42", 36" X 48"

42" TO 54" 15" TO 28"

VERTICAL PLAN FILE

POCKET FILE

TRANSPARENT PLASTIC STORAGE TUBE 2" DIAMETER 13" TO 55" LENGTHS

METAL STORAGE TUBE 2 1/2" AND 4" DIAMETER 31" TO 55" LENGTHS

STORAGE TUBES

45" AND 50"

SHEET SIZES: 24" X 36", 30" X 42", 36" X 48"

20 1/4" 32" TO 56"

VERTICAL DRAWING FILE

12" AND 13 1/2"

39 1/2"

SHEET SIZES: 24" X 36", 30" X 36", 36" X 36"

48" TO 51 1/2" 26 3/4" TO 38 3/4"

NOTE: CADDY RACK AVAILABLE WITHOUT REFERENCE TABLE

CADDY RACK

3 TYPES OF HANGERS

SHEET WIDTHS: 18" 24" 30" 36"

10 TO 72 HANGERS

WALL RACK

20 TO 288 HANGERS

WALL RACK

VERTICAL FILE SHEET HANGERS

John R. Hoke, Jr., AIA, Architect; Washington, D.C.

DESIGN RATIONALE

Systems furniture is designed primarily for utilization in an open office plan which uses few fixed floor-to-ceiling partitions as compared to conventional office layouts. Open office planning receives its impetus from its ability to respond to requirements for increased flexibility and lower long term expenses. Some of the major areas of response are the following:

1. FLEXIBILITY OF PLANNING: Systems furniture in an open plan maximizes the efficient use of net plannable space. This is the result of the use of more vertical space without fixed floor-to-ceiling partitions, thereby freeing floor area and reducing space planning inefficiencies.
2. FLEXIBILITY OF FUNCTION: Systems furniture allows individual workstation modification so that workstation design can reflect functional requirements of the task performed. In this way, changes in function can be accommodated without total furniture replacement.
3. FLEXIBILITY OF PLAN MODIFICATION: Systems furniture in open office planning allows institutions to respond more easily to organizational changes of size, structure, and function. Open planning allows institutions to respond to change at lower cost by reducing expenses related to partition relocation, HVAC modification, lighting relocation, construction, and moving time.

NOTES

1. Any open office plan as commonly applied will utilize some enclosed spaces having fixed, floor-to-ceiling partitions.
2. Systems furniture requires careful planning and engineering consultation to achieve the maximum functional advantage.
3. Systems furniture components are not compatible from one manufacturer to another regardless of generic type.
4. The generic types listed below are broad classifications for descriptive purposes only.

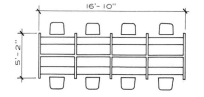
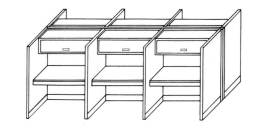
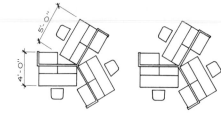
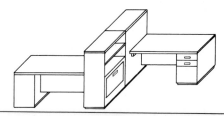

SECRETARIAL CONFIGURATIONS

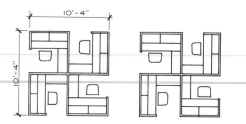
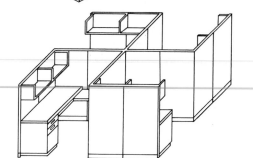

CLERICAL CONFIGURATIONS

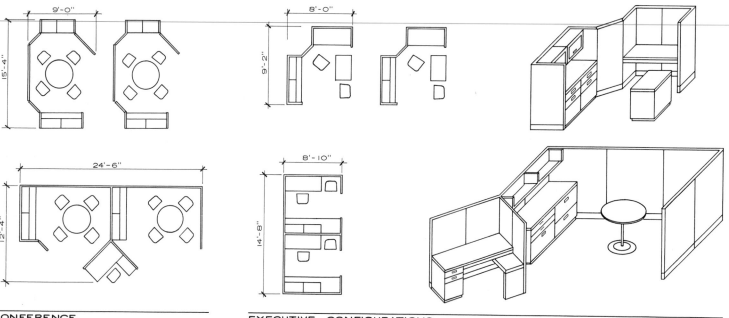

CONFERENCE

EXECUTIVE CONFIGURATIONS

Interspace Incorporated; Washington, D.C.

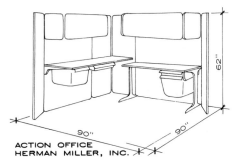

ACTION OFFICE
HERMAN MILLER, INC.

STEPHENS SYSTEM
KNOLL INTERNATIONAL

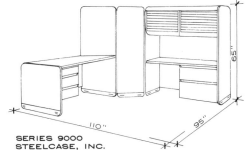

SERIES 9000
STEELCASE, INC.

PANEL HUNG TYPE

These systems are based on panels that can be connected at various angles (angle options depend on manufacturer). Panels achieve stability through configuration or by attached stabilizing feet. Components are hung on panels at desired heights (usually on 1 in. increments).

SYSTEM ADVANTAGES

Panel hung systems usually have a large variety of components. They offer the highest degree of planning flexibility. These systems are easily modified and are relatively light.

OPTIONS OFFERED (VARY WITH MANUFACTURER)

1. Ability to hang components on fixed, full height partitions.
2. Specialized use components (i.e., hospitals, schools, libraries).
3. Integrated wiring in panels with fast connect or wire manager components for horizontal raceways.
4. Integrated task/ambient lighting components.
5. Multiple standard panel heights (dimensions vary).
6. Fabric covered acoustical panels as structural panel option.
7. Integrated file storage components.

PANEL ENCLOSURE TYPE

These systems are based on building rectilinear enclosures with panel components. Panels achieve stability through right angle panel-to-panel configuration. Components are hung in panel enclosures (usually at several predetermined mounting heights) and are supported by end panels rather than back panels.

SYSTEM ADVANTAGES

Assembled systems have a somewhat unitized appearance. They are stable and, when assembled, are not easily moved. They have a relatively high level of flexibility with a more limited number of components and accessories than in most panel hung systems.

OPTIONS OFFERED (VARY WITH MANUFACTURER)

1. Multiple standard panel heights.
2. Full panel high closed storage units (i.e., wardrobes, shelf).
3. Vertical power poles with lighting outlets, convenience outlets, circuit breakers, telephone raceway.
4. Wire manager components for vertical and horizontal raceways.
5. Integrated task/ambient lighting components and freestanding ambient light units.
6. Fabric covered acoustical panels are structural panel option.
7. Integrated file storage components.

UNITIZED PANEL TYPE

These systems are based on ganging assembled units and panels to form workstations and workstation groupings. Units are individually stable and panels achieve stability by attachment to units and right angle panel-to-panel configuration. Some of these systems are more componentized than others (similar to panel enclosure type) but are marketed as assembled units. Components within assembled units are usually supported by end panels.

SYSTEM ADVANTAGES

Assembled systems have a unitized appearance more closely resembling conventional furniture. They are very stable and, when assembled, are not easily moved. They have a relatively high level of flexibility depending on the degree to which they are unitized. These systems simplify purchase, inventory management, and installation because of their unitized character.

OPTIONS OFFERED (VARY WITH MANUFACTURER)

1. Multiple standard panel heights (dimensions vary).
2. Full panel high closed storage units (i.e., wardrobes, shelf).
3. Wire raceways (horizontal and vertical), convenience outlets, and switches are an integral part of system.
4. Integrated task/ambient light units.
5. Fabric covered acoustical panels usually as hang on or finish panel option.
6. Integrated flexible branch wiring system.
7. Can be used in conventional configurations.

GENERIC TYPES OF SYSTEM FURNITURE

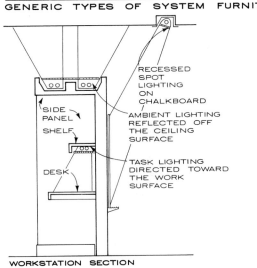

WORKSTATION SECTION

INTEGRATED LIGHTING

Artificial lighting is integrated into most open office furniture systems. The components consist of task oriented downlights located directly over work surfaces, which provide the user with control of intensity and direction of light. Uplights are mounted in the top of workstations to provide indirect light reflected off the ceiling to the ambient surroundings.

Task/ambient lighting provides more flexibility than do standard ceiling mounted fixtures. It can reduce energy consumption by decreasing general light levels and utilizing more efficient light sources. It can also improve acoustics, since fewer fixtures are installed in the acoustical ceiling.

TYPICAL PANEL
HEIGHTS (H)
50", 62", 80"

TYPICAL PANEL
WIDTHS (W)
12", 24", 36", 48"

PANEL FINISH OPTIONS
Plastic laminate
Wood veneer
Tempered safety glass
Acoustical fabric

NOTE: Consult manufacturer for specific sizes and finishes available.

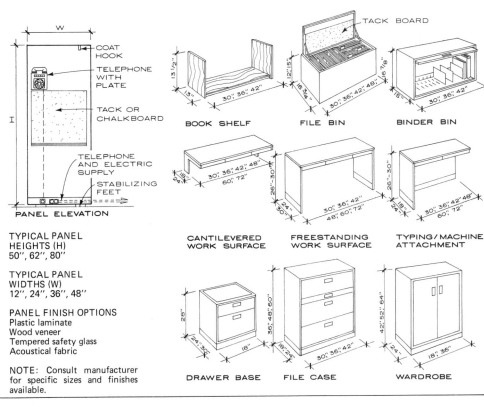

PANEL ELEVATION

BOOK SHELF FILE BIN BINDER BIN

CANTILEVERED WORK SURFACE FREESTANDING WORK SURFACE TYPING/MACHINE ATTACHMENT

DRAWER BASE FILE CASE WARDROBE

SYSTEMS FURNITURE COMPONENTS

Interspace Incorporated; Washington, D.C.

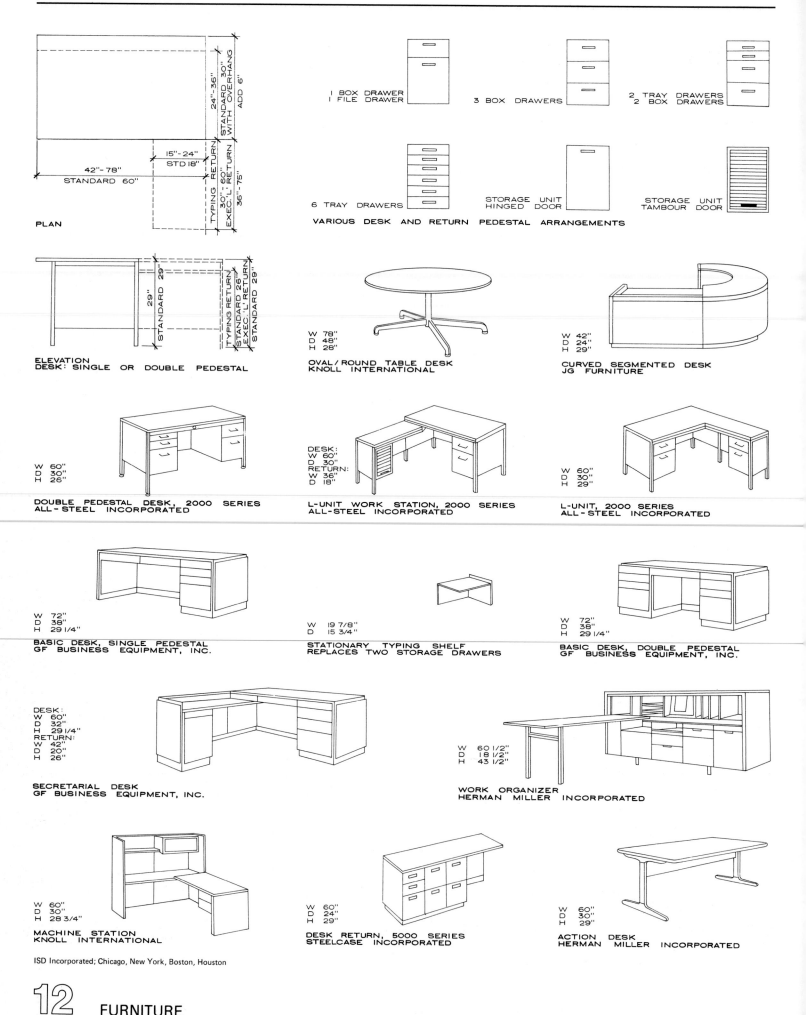

PLAN

STANDARD 30'
TYPING RETURN 30''
EXEC.'L RETURN 60''
36''-75''
STANDARD 30''
STANDARD 30'' WITH OVERHANG ADD 6''
24''-36''

15''-24''
STD 18''

42''-78''
STANDARD 60''

VARIOUS DESK AND RETURN PEDESTAL ARRANGEMENTS

I BOX DRAWER
I FILE DRAWER

3 BOX DRAWERS

2 TRAY DRAWERS
2 BOX DRAWERS

6 TRAY DRAWERS

STORAGE UNIT
HINGED DOOR

STORAGE UNIT
TAMBOUR DOOR

STANDARD 29''
29''
STANDARD 29''
TYPING RETURN
EXEC.'L RETURN
STANDARD 26''
STANDARD 29''

ELEVATION
DESK: SINGLE OR DOUBLE PEDESTAL

W 78''
D 48''
H 28''

OVAL / ROUND TABLE DESK
KNOLL INTERNATIONAL

W 42''
D 24''
H 29''

CURVED SEGMENTED DESK
JG FURNITURE

W 60''
D 30''
H 26''

DOUBLE PEDESTAL DESK, 2000 SERIES
ALL-STEEL INCORPORATED

DESK:
W 60''
D 30''
RETURN:
W 36''
D 18''

L-UNIT WORK STATION, 2000 SERIES
ALL-STEEL INCORPORATED

W 60''
D 30''
H 29''

L-UNIT, 2000 SERIES
ALL-STEEL INCORPORATED

W 72''
D 38''
H 29 1/4''

BASIC DESK, SINGLE PEDESTAL
GF BUSINESS EQUIPMENT, INC.

W 19 7/8''
D 15 3/4''

STATIONARY TYPING SHELF
REPLACES TWO STORAGE DRAWERS

W 72''
D 38''
H 29 1/4''

BASIC DESK, DOUBLE PEDESTAL
GF BUSINESS EQUIPMENT, INC.

DESK:
W 60''
D 32''
H 29 1/4''
RETURN:
W 42''
D 20''
H 26''

SECRETARIAL DESK
GF BUSINESS EQUIPMENT, INC.

W 60 1/2''
D 18 1/2''
H 43 1/2''

WORK ORGANIZER
HERMAN MILLER INCORPORATED

W 60''
D 30''
H 28 3/4''

MACHINE STATION
KNOLL INTERNATIONAL

W 60''
D 24''
H 29''

DESK RETURN, 5000 SERIES
STEELCASE INCORPORATED

W 60''
D 30''
H 29''

ACTION DESK
HERMAN MILLER INCORPORATED

ISD Incorporated; Chicago, New York, Boston, Houston

12 FURNITURE

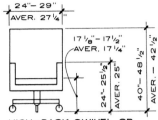

HIGH-BACK SWIVEL OR
SWIVEL POSTURE CHAIR

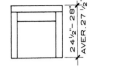
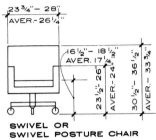

SWIVEL OR
SWIVEL POSTURE CHAIR

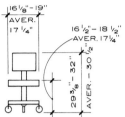

SECRETARIAL POSTURE
CHAIR

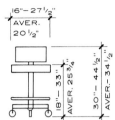

OPERATOR'S STOOL OR
DRAFTING STOOL

W 22 1/2"
D 23 3/4"
H 41"
SH 19 1/2"

HIGH BACK DESK CHAIR
DESIGNER: CHARLES EAMES
HERMAN MILLER, INC.

W 26"
D 24"
H 32"
SH 18"

SWIVEL ARM CHAIR
DESIGNER: EERO SAARINEN
KNOLL INTERNATIONAL, INC.

W 17"
D 20"
H 31"
SH 19"

SECRETARIAL CHAIR   DESIGNER:
DE PAS, D'URBINO, LOMAZZI
ATELIER INTERNATIONAL, LTD.

W 18 1/2"
D 16"
H 37 1/2"
SH 24"

PNEUMATIC STOOL
ARIES SERIES
KRUEGER, INC.

W 24"
D 32 1/2"
H 39 1/2"
SH 18"

EXECUTIVE HI BACK CHAIR
DESIGNER: ROBERT BERNARD
THONET INDUSTRIES, INC.

W 21 3/4"
D 24"
H 32 1/4"
SH 18 1/2"

SWIVEL ARM CHAIR CAS
SERIES SUNAR LIMITED

W 18 3/4"
D 20"
H 30"
SH 18"

ERGON SECRETARIAL CHAIR
DESIGNER: BILL STUMPF
HERMAN MILLER, INC.

W 21 1/4"
D 25"
H 40"
SH 30"

ROLLBACK OPERATIONAL STOOL
DESIGNER: RAY WILKES
HERMAN MILLER, INC.

TYPICAL CREDENZA DIMENSIONS

	WIDTH	DEPTH	HEIGHT
One component	27" to 30"	17 3/4" to 21"	25 1/2" to 29 3/4"
Two component	37 1/4" to 41 1/2"	17 3/4" to 21"	25 1/2" to 29 3/4"
Three component	44 3/4" to 60 1/2"	17 3/4" to 21"	25 1/2" to 29 3/4"
Four component	62 1/4" to 79 3/4"	17 3/4" to 21"	25 1/2" to 29 3/4"
Five component	95 3/4" to 98 1/2"	17 3/4" to 21"	25 1/2" to 29 3/4"

W 36"
D 18"
H 26 1/2"

OMEGA TYPING TABLE
DESIGNER: HANS
EICHENBERGER; STENDIG, INC.

W 22 1/2"
D 17 1/2"
H 26"

ACTION OFFICE DRAWER CADDIE
DESIGNER: ROBERT L. PROPST
HERMAN MILLER, INC.

W 64"
D 19"
H 29"

FL SYSTEM CREDENZA
DESIGNER: DOUGLAS BALL
SUNAR LIMITED

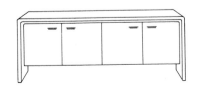

W 72"
D 20 3/4"
H 25 1/2"

CABINET CREDENZA
DESIGNER: HANS W. WEITZ
DESIGN GROUP, INC.

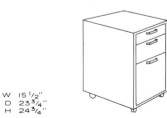

W 15 1/2"
D 23 3/4"
H 24 3/4"

OMEGA 3 DRAWER PEDESTAL
DESIGNER: HANS
EICHENBERGER; STENDIG, INC.

Craig Mulford and Jeff Wirt; The Spitznagel Partners; Sioux Falls, South Dakota

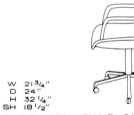

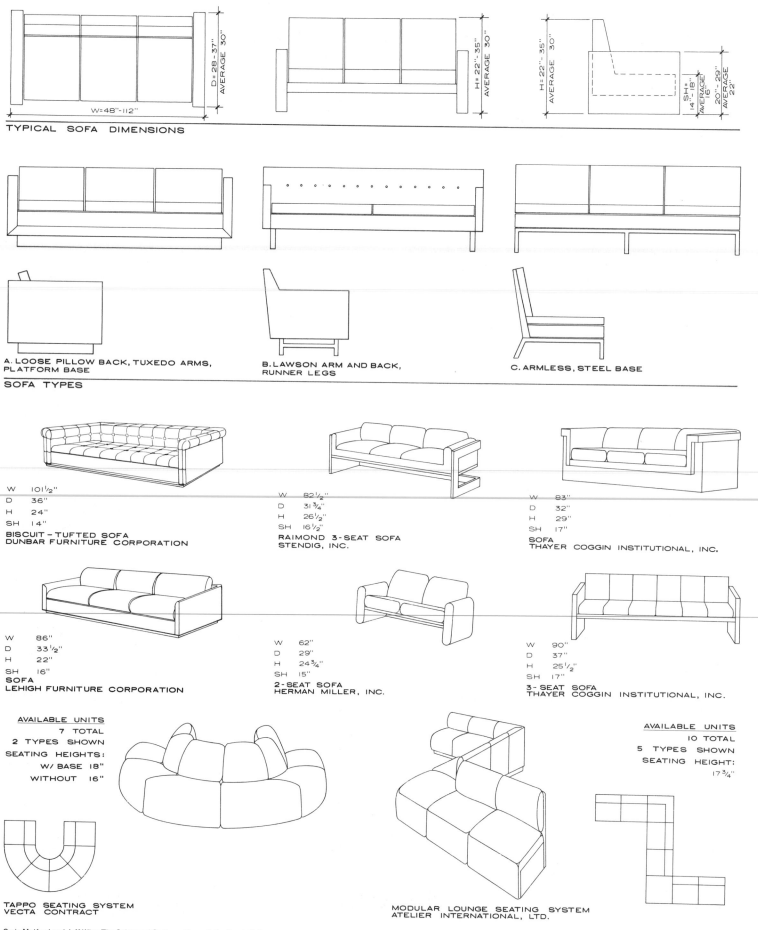

TYPICAL SOFA DIMENSIONS

SOFA TYPES

A. LOOSE PILLOW BACK, TUXEDO ARMS, PLATFORM BASE

B. LAWSON ARM AND BACK, RUNNER LEGS

C. ARMLESS, STEEL BASE

W 101½"
D 36"
H 24"
SH 14"

BISCUIT-TUFTED SOFA
DUNBAR FURNITURE CORPORATION

W 82½"
D 31¾"
H 26½"
SH 16½"

RAIMOND 3-SEAT SOFA
STENDIG, INC.

W 83"
D 32"
H 29"
SH 17"

SOFA
THAYER COGGIN INSTITUTIONAL, INC.

W 86"
D 33½"
H 22"
SH 16"

SOFA
LEHIGH FURNITURE CORPORATION

W 62"
D 29"
H 24¾"
SH 15"

2-SEAT SOFA
HERMAN MILLER, INC.

W 90"
D 37"
H 25½"
SH 17"

3-SEAT SOFA
THAYER COGGIN INSTITUTIONAL, INC.

AVAILABLE UNITS
7 TOTAL
2 TYPES SHOWN
SEATING HEIGHTS:
W/ BASE 18"
WITHOUT 16"

TAPPO SEATING SYSTEM
VECTA CONTRACT

MODULAR LOUNGE SEATING SYSTEM
ATELIER INTERNATIONAL, LTD.

AVAILABLE UNITS
10 TOTAL
5 TYPES SHOWN
SEATING HEIGHT:
17¾"

Craig Mulford and Jeff Wirt; The Spitznagel Partners; Sioux Falls, South Dakota
ISD Incorporated; Chicago, New York, Boston, Houston

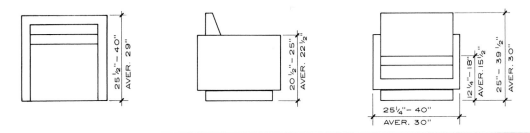

TYPICAL LOUNGE CHAIR DIMENSIONS

W 30"
D 30"
H 30"
SH 17"

BARCELONA CHAIR
DESIGNER: LUDWIG MIES VAN
DER ROHE
KNOLL INTERNATIONAL, INC.

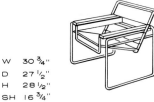

W 29.9"
D 25.5"
H 25.2"
SH 16.9"

GRAND CONFORT
DESIGNER: LE CORBUSIER
ATELIER INTERNATIONAL, LTD.

W 30 3/4"
D 27 1/2"
H 28 1/2"
SH 16 3/4"

WASSILY CHAIR
DESIGNER: MARCEL BREUER
THONET INDUSTRIES, INC.

W 25 5/8"
D 33 1/2"
H 25 1/4"
SH 13"

ARMCHAIR 41
DESIGNER: ALVAR AALTO
ICF, INC.

W 27"
D 30"
H 28"
SH 13 1/2"

CLAVERDON LOUNGE CHAIR
DESIGNER: MAURICE BURKE
HANK LOEWENSTEIN, INC.

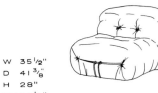

W 35 1/2"
D 41 3/8"
H 28"
SH 16 1/2"

SORIANA ARMLESS CHAIR
DESIGNERS: AFRA & TOBIA SCARPA
ATELIER INTERNATIONAL, LTD.

W 28 1/2"
D 34"
H 26"
SH 16"

LOUNGE CHAIR
DESIGNERS: ANDREW MORRISON &
BRUCE HANNAH
KNOLL INTERNATIONAL, INC.

W 36 1/4"
D 34 5/8"
H 31 1/2"
SH 17"

CIPREA ARMCHAIR
DESIGNERS: AFRA &
TOBIA SCARPA
ATELIER INTERNATIONAL, LTD.

W 33"
D 33"
H 25"
SH 15 1/2"

LOUNGE CHAIR
DESIGNER: WARD BENNETT
BRICKEL ASSOCIATES, INC.

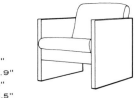

W 27"
D 27.9"
H 28"
SH 16.5"

BUTCHER BLOCK LOUNGE CHAIR
DESIGNER: THOUHY DESIGN STAFF
THOUHY FURNITURE CORPORATION

W 37 1/2"
D 35 1/2"
H 31 1/2"
SH 14 3/4"

BYRON LOUNGE CHAIR
DESIGNERS: ERNST LUTHY &
URS FELBER
STENDIG, INC.

W 27"
D 27"
H 28"
SH 16 1/2"

VARI-PULKKA LOUNGE CHAIR
DESIGNER: IIMARI LAPPALAINEN
STENDIG, INC.

W 32 1/2"
D 32 3/4"
H 33 3/8"
SH 15"

OTTOMAN:
W 26"
D 21"
H 15"

EAMES LOUNGE CHAIR
DESIGNER: CHARLES EAMES
HERMAN MILLER, INC.

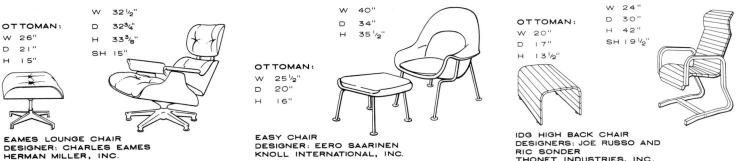

W 40"
D 34"
H 35 1/2"

OTTOMAN:
W 25 1/2"
D 20"
H 16"

EASY CHAIR
DESIGNER: EERO SAARINEN
KNOLL INTERNATIONAL, INC.

OTTOMAN:
W 20"
D 17"
H 13 1/2"

W 24"
D 30"
H 42"
SH 19 1/2"

IDG HIGH BACK CHAIR
DESIGNERS: JOE RUSSO AND
RIC SONDER
THONET INDUSTRIES, INC.

John R. Hoke, Jr., AIA, Architect; Washington, D.C.

Craig Mulford and Jeff Wirt; The Spitznagel Partners; Sioux Falls, South Dakota

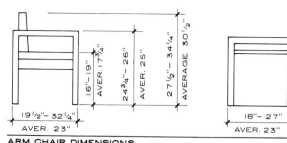

16"–19" AVER. 17¾"
24¾"– 26"   AVER. 25"
27½"– 34¼"   AVERAGE 30½"

19½"– 32¼"
AVER. 23"

18"– 27"
AVER. 23"

ARM CHAIR DIMENSIONS

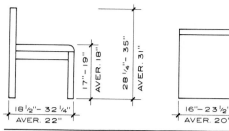

17"–19" AVER. 18"
28¼"– 35"   AVER. 31"

18½"– 32¼"
AVER. 22"

16"– 23½"
AVER. 20"

SIDE CHAIR DIMENSIONS

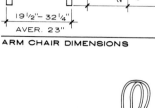

W 16"
D 20"
H 35"

VIENNA CHAIR
DESIGNER: MICHAEL THONET
THONET INDUSTRIES, INC.

W 21¼"
D 22"
H 30½"
SH 18"

CORBUSIER ARM CHAIR
DESIGNER: MICHAEL THONET
THONET INDUSTRIES, INC.

W 18"
D 22¼"
H 31½"
SH 17¾"

CESSA
DESIGNER: MARCEL BREUER
KNOLL INTERNATIONAL, INC.

W 26"
D 23½"
H 32"
SH 18½"

SAARINEN CHAIR
DESIGNER: EERO SAARINEN
KNOLL INTERNATIONAL, INC.

W 22½"
D 24"
H 32"
SH 18"

PETITT ARM CHAIR
DESIGNER: DON PETITT
KNOLL INTERNATIONAL, INC.

W 24½"
D 20½"
H 27¼"
SH 17½"

THE CHAIR
DESIGNER: HANS WAGNERS
KNOLL INTERNATIONAL, INC.

W 22½"
D 19¾"
H 29½"
SH 18"

MAGISTRETTI CHAIR
DESIGNER: VICO MAGISTRETTI
ATELIER INTERNATIONAL, LTD.

W 24"
D 24½"
H 31½"
SH 16"

ARMCHAIR 45
DESIGNER: ALVAR AALTO
ICF, INC.

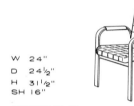

W 21¾"
D 32¼"
H 32¼"
SH 17½"

MR CHAIR
DESIGNER: MIES VAN DER ROHE
STENDIG, INC.

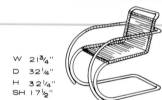

W 23"
D 28"
H 31"
SH 18"

TUBULAR CHAIR
DESIGNER: PETER PROTZMAN
HERMAN MILLER, INC.

W 22"
D 21¼"
H 33"
SH 18½"

EAMES ARM CHAIR
DESIGNER: CHARLES EAMES
HERMAN MILLER, INC.

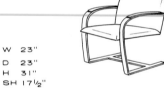

W 23"
D 23"
H 31"
SH 17½"

BRNO CHAIR
DESIGNER: MIES VAN DER ROHE
KNOLL INTERNATIONAL, INC.

W 19½"
D 21½"
H 29¼"
SH 18"

LCM CHAIR
DESIGNER: CHARLES EAMES
HERMAN MILLER, INC.

W 21"
D 22½"
H 30"
SH 18"

BERTOIA SIDE CHAIR
DESIGNER: HARRY BERTOIA
KNOLL INTERNATIONAL, INC.

W 21½"
D 22"
H 31½"
SH 17½"

ZETA ARM CHAIR
DESIGNER: ARTHUR UMANOFF
THONET INDUSTRIES, INC.

W 18½"
D 22"
H 32¼"
SH 18½"

SWIVEL CHAIR
DESIGNER: CHARLES EAMES
HERMAN MILLER, INC.

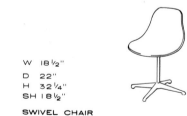

W 22¾"
D 22½"
H 30"
SH 18"

RIEMERSCHMID CHAIR
DESIGNER: RICHARD RIEMERSCHMID
DUNBAR FURNITURE CORPORATION

W 24½"
D 27"
H 30"
SH 22"

BENTWOOD CLUB CHAIR
DESIGNER: PAUL TUTTLE
THONET INDUSTRIES, INC.

W 19"
D 17"
H 30½"
SH 17"

PADOVA CHAIR
DESIGNER: STUDIO TIPI
HANK LOEWENSTEIN, INC.

W 17¾"
D 15¼"
H 41"
SH 16½"

WILLOW, 2 – DESIGNER:
CHARLES R. MACKINTOSH
ATELIER INTERNATIONAL, LTD.

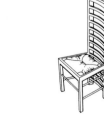

John R. Hoke, Jr., AIA, Architect; Washington, D.C.

Craig Mulford and Jeff Wirt; The Spitznagel Partners; Sioux Falls, South Dakota

W 23"
D 28"
H 26½"

LOUNGE CHAIR
KNOLL INTERNATIONAL

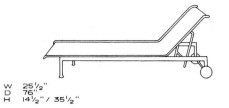

W 25½"
D 76"
H 14½" / 35½"

CHAISE LOUNGE
KNOLL INTERNATIONAL

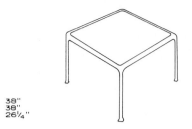

W 38"
D 38"
H 26¼"

DINING TABLE
KNOLL INTERNATIONAL

W 25"
D 80"
H 20⅝"

CHAISE LOUNGE
SAMSONITE CORPORATION

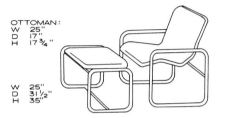

OTTOMAN:
W 25"
D 17"
H 17¾"

W 25"
D 31½"
H 35"

LOUNGE CHAIR
SAMSONITE CORPORATION

W 21"
D 22"
H 30"

SIDE CHAIR
KNOLL INTERNATIONAL

W 26"
L 74"

CHAISE LOUNGE
TELESCOPE FOLDING FURNITURE CO., INC.

W 30⅛"
L 70"
H 28"

ARM CHAIR
TELESCOPE FOLDING FURNITURE CO., INC.

W 24"
D 18"
H 31"
SH 16½"

DIRECTOR'S CHAIR
GOLDMEDAL, INCORPORATED

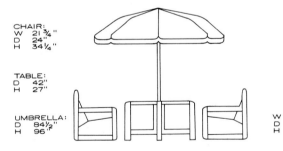

CHAIR:
W 21¾"
D 24"
H 34¼"

TABLE:
D 42"
H 27"

UMBRELLA:
D 84½"
H 96"

TABLE, UMBRELLA, AND CHAIRS
SAMSONITE CORPORATION

W 25½"
D 34½"
H 32"

ROCKER
SAMSONITE CORPORATION

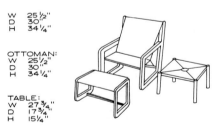

W 25½"
D 30"
H 34¼"

OTTOMAN:
W 25½"
D 30"
H 34¼"

TABLE:
W 27¾"
D 17¾"
H 15¼"

LOUNGE CHAIR
SAMSONITE CORPORATION

W 23"
L 70"
H 33½"

LAWN BENCH
VANDY-CRAFT INCORPORATED

W 48½"
D 28½"
H 32"

SANS SOUCI SETTEE
VANDY-CRAFT INCORPORATED

BENCH:
W 10⅛"
L 68½"
H 16"

RUSTIC WIDE TABLE
LITTLE LAKE INDUSTRIES

ISD Incorporated; Chicago, New York, Boston, Houston

FURNITURE

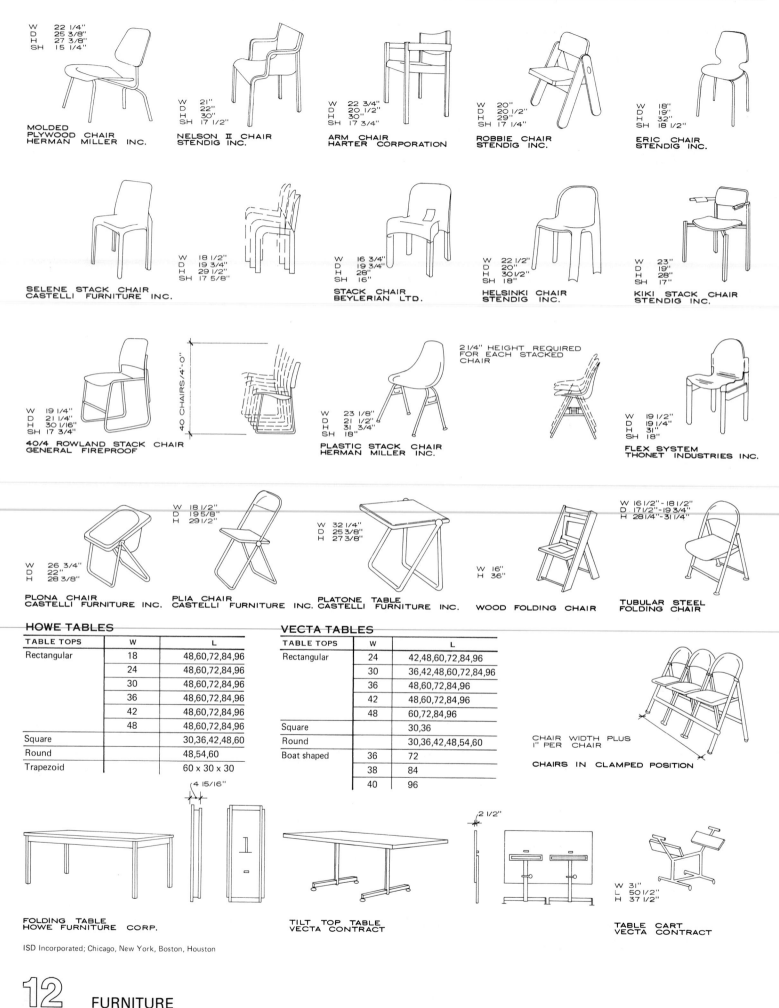

W 22 1/4"
D 25 3/8"
H 27 3/8"
SH 15 1/4"

MOLDED
PLYWOOD CHAIR
HERMAN MILLER INC.

W 21"
D 22"
H 30"
SH 17 1/2"

NELSON II CHAIR
STENDIG INC.

W 22 3/4"
D 20 1/2"
H 30"
SH 17 3/4"

ARM CHAIR
HARTER CORPORATION

W 20"
D 20 1/2"
H 29"
SH 17 1/4"

ROBBIE CHAIR
STENDIG INC.

W 18"
D 19"
H 32"
SH 18 1/2"

ERIC CHAIR
STENDIG INC.

W 18 1/2"
D 19 3/4"
H 29 1/2"
SH 17 5/8"

SELENE STACK CHAIR
CASTELLI FURNITURE INC.

W 16 3/4"
D 19 3/4"
H 28"
SH 16"

STACK CHAIR
BEYLERIAN LTD.

W 22 1/2"
D 20"
H 30 1/2"
SH 18"

HELSINKI CHAIR
STENDIG INC.

W 23"
D 19"
H 28"
SH 17"

KIKI STACK CHAIR
STENDIG INC.

W 19 1/4"
D 21 1/4"
H 30 1/16"
SH 17 3/4"

40 CHAIRS/4'-0"

40/4 ROWLAND STACK CHAIR
GENERAL FIREPROOF

W 23 1/8"
D 21 1/2"
H 31 3/4"
SH 18"

PLASTIC STACK CHAIR
HERMAN MILLER INC.

2 1/4" HEIGHT REQUIRED
FOR EACH STACKED
CHAIR

W 19 1/2"
D 19 1/4"
H 31"
SH 18"

FLEX SYSTEM
THONET INDUSTRIES INC.

W 18 1/2"
D 19 5/8"
H 29 1/2"

W 26 3/4"
D 22"
H 28 3/8"

PLONA CHAIR
CASTELLI FURNITURE INC.

PLIA CHAIR
CASTELLI FURNITURE INC.

W 32 1/4"
D 25 3/8"
H 27 3/8"

PLATONE TABLE
CASTELLI FURNITURE INC.

W 16"
H 36"

WOOD FOLDING CHAIR

W 16 1/2" - 18 1/2"
D 17 1/2" - 19 3/4"
H 28 1/4" - 31 1/4"

TUBULAR STEEL
FOLDING CHAIR

HOWE TABLES

TABLE TOPS	W	L
Rectangular	18	48,60,72,84,96
	24	48,60,72,84,96
	30	48,60,72,84,96
	36	48,60,72,84,96
	42	48,60,72,84,96
	48	48,60,72,84,96
Square		30,36,42,48,60
Round		48,54,60
Trapezoid		60 x 30 x 30

VECTA TABLES

TABLE TOPS	W	L
Rectangular	24	42,48,60,72,84,96
	30	36,42,48,60,72,84,96
	36	48,60,72,84,96
	42	48,60,72,84,96
	48	60,72,84,96
Square		30,36
Round		30,36,42,48,54,60
Boat shaped	36	72
	38	84
	40	96

CHAIR WIDTH PLUS
1" PER CHAIR

CHAIRS IN CLAMPED POSITION

4 15/16"

FOLDING TABLE
HOWE FURNITURE CORP.

2 1/2"

TILT TOP TABLE
VECTA CONTRACT

W 31"
L 50 1/2"
H 37 1/2"

TABLE CART
VECTA CONTRACT

ISD Incorporated; Chicago, New York, Boston, Houston

TYPICAL END OR SIDE TABLE DIMENSIONS (IN.)

DESCRIPTION	DEPTH		WIDTH		HEIGHT	
	MIN.	MAX.	MIN.	MAX.	MIN.	MAX.
RECTANGULAR	19	28	21	48	17	28
SQUARE	15	32	15	32	17	28
ROUND	16	30	16	30	18	22½

TYPICAL LOW TABLE DIMENSIONS (IN.)

DESCRIPTION	DEPTH		WIDTH		HEIGHT	
	MIN.	MAX.	MIN.	MAX.	MIN.	MAX.
RECTANGULAR	15½	24	21	86	12	18
SQUARE	36	42	32	42	15	17
ROUND	30	42	20	42	15	16½

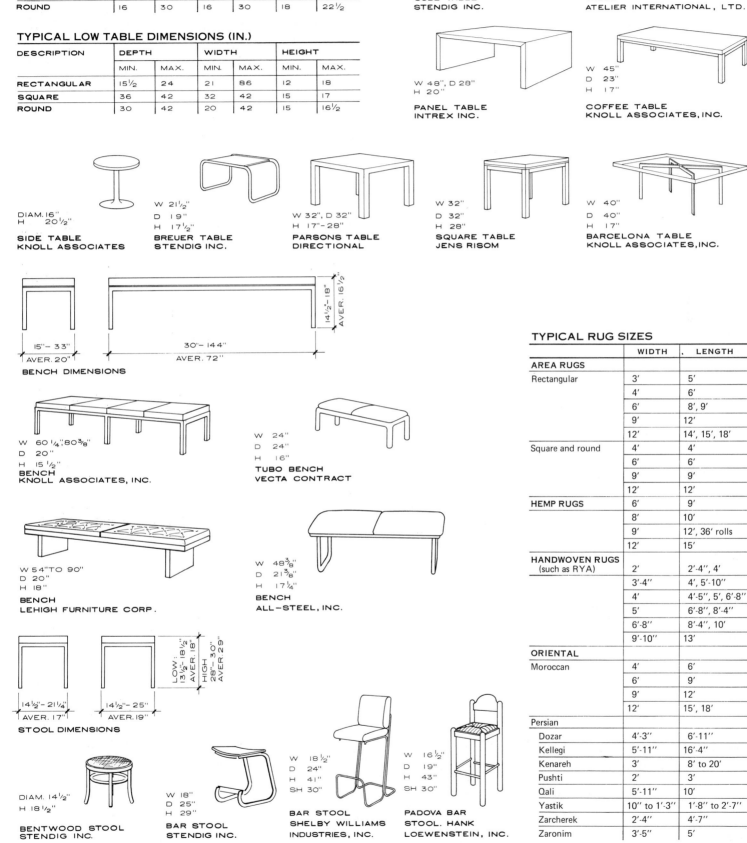

W 30"
D 30"
H 16"
CUBE TABLE
STENDIG INC.

W 39½"
D 39½"
H 12"
TABLE
ATELIER INTERNATIONAL, LTD.

W 48", D 28"
H 20"
PANEL TABLE
INTREX INC.

W 45"
D 23"
H 17"
COFFEE TABLE
KNOLL ASSOCIATES, INC.

DIAM. 16"
H 20½"
SIDE TABLE
KNOLL ASSOCIATES

W 21½"
D 19"
H 17½"
BREUER TABLE
STENDIG INC.

W 32", D 32"
H 17"–28"
PARSONS TABLE
DIRECTIONAL

W 32"
D 32"
H 28"
SQUARE TABLE
JENS RISOM

W 40"
D 40"
H 17"
BARCELONA TABLE
KNOLL ASSOCIATES, INC.

AVER. 16½"
14½"–18"
15"–33"
AVER. 20"
30"–144"
AVER. 72"
BENCH DIMENSIONS

W 60¼", 80⅜"
D 20"
H 15½"
BENCH
KNOLL ASSOCIATES, INC.

W 24"
D 24"
H 16"
TUBO BENCH
VECTA CONTRACT

W 54" TO 90"
D 20"
H 18"
BENCH
LEHIGH FURNITURE CORP.

W 48⅜"
D 21⅜"
H 17¼"
BENCH
ALL–STEEL, INC.

LOW: 13½"–18½" AVER. 18"
HIGH 28"–30" AVER. 29"
14½"–21¼" AVER. 17"
14½"–25" AVER. 19"
STOOL DIMENSIONS

DIAM. 14½"
H 18½"
BENTWOOD STOOL
STENDIG INC.

W 18"
D 25"
H 29"
BAR STOOL
STENDIG INC.

W 18½"
D 24"
H 41"
SH 30"
BAR STOOL
SHELBY WILLIAMS
INDUSTRIES, INC.

W 16½"
D 19"
H 43"
SH 30"
PADOVA BAR
STOOL. HANK
LOEWENSTEIN, INC.

TYPICAL RUG SIZES

	WIDTH	LENGTH
AREA RUGS		
Rectangular	3'	5'
	4'	6'
	6'	8', 9'
	9'	12'
	12'	14', 15', 18'
Square and round	4'	4'
	6'	6'
	9'	9'
	12'	12'
HEMP RUGS	6'	9'
	8'	10'
	9'	12', 36' rolls
	12'	15'
HANDWOVEN RUGS (such as RYA)	2'	2'-4", 4'
	3'-4"	4', 5'-10"
	4'	4'-5", 5', 6'-8"
	5'	6'-8", 8'-4"
	6'-8"	8'-4", 10'
	9'-10"	13'
ORIENTAL		
Moroccan	4'	6'
	6'	9'
	9'	12'
	12'	15', 18'
Persian		
Dozar	4'-3"	6'-11"
Kellegi	5'-11"	16'-4"
Kenareh	3'	8' to 20'
Pushti	2'	3'
Qali	5'-11"	10'
Yastik	10" to 1'-3"	1'-8" to 2'-7"
Zarcherek	2'-4"	4'-7"
Zaronim	3'-5"	5'

Craig Mulford and Jeff Wirt; The Spitznagel Partners; Sioux Falls, South Dakota

ISD Incorporated; Chicago, New York, Boston, Houston

FURNITURE

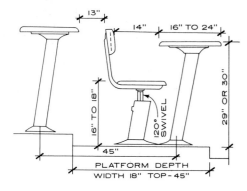

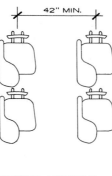

TYPICAL VERTICAL
ARRANGEMENT

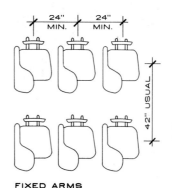

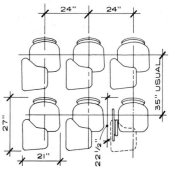

FIXED ARMS   FOLDING ARMS

TYPICAL HORIZONTAL ARRANGEMENTS

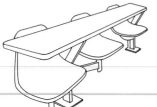

PEDESTAL HORIZONTAL SEATING
AMERICAN SEATING CO.

ACTON STACKER
AMERICAN SEATING CO.

DOUBLE ENTRY STUDY
AMERICAN SEATING CO.

TABLET ARM CHAIR
AMERICAN SEATING CO.

SATELITE SEATING
HEYWOOD WAKEFIELD

LIFT LID TABLE AND CHAIR
AMERICAN SEATING CO.

CLASSROOM UNIT
HEYWOOD WAKEFIELD

DESK WITH CHAIR
HEYWOOD WAKEFIELD

AUDITORIUM SEATING UNIT
HEYWOOD WAKEFIELD

CLASSROOM TYPING TABLE
HEYWOOD WAKEFIELD

DESK
HEYWOOD WAKEFIELD

STUDY CARRELS
HOWE FURNITURE CORP.

Wall Pockets:

1. Fully recessed.
2. Partially recessed.
3. Surface mounted.

NOTE: When folded, five sets can
be stored on a floor area 5 x 5
ft.   When nesting tables without
benches, allow storage depth of
12 in. per table.

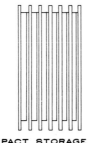

ONE FOLD TABLES
WALL-FOL

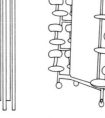

COMPACT STORAGE
WALL - FOL

FOLDING TABLE AND CHAIRS
SICO INCORPORATED

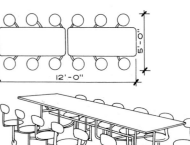

ISD Incorporated; Chicago, New York, Boston, Houston

W 60"
D 23"
H 34"

DEMONSTRATION TABLE
FLEETWOOD FURNITURE CO.

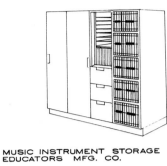

MUSIC INSTRUMENT STORAGE
EDUCATORS MFG. CO.

AV MEDIA TRANSPORT

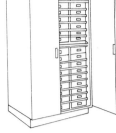

W 48"
D 24"
H 84"

TOTE TRAY STORAGE
EDUCATORS MFG. CO.

LABORATORY ISLAND SERVICE
EDUCATORS MFG. CO.

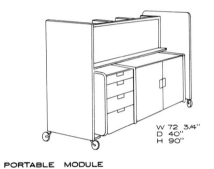

ARTS AND CRAFTS SINK UNIT
EDUCATORS MFG. CO.

OPEN PLAN UNIT
EDUCATORS MFG. CO.

W 26"
D 26"
H 36"

LABORATORY DESK & ISLAND SERVICE MODULE
EDUCATORS MFG. CO.

PORTABLE MODULE

W 72 3/4"
D 40"
H 90"

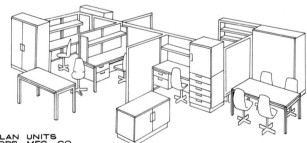

MEDIA
CENTER
FURNITURE

W 48"
D 22"
H 30"

TOTE TRAY CABINET
FLEETWOOD FURNITURE CO.

CARREL UNIT
EDUCATORS MFG. CO.

OPEN PLAN UNITS
EDUCATORS MFG. CO.

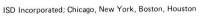

OPEN PLAN UNITS
EDUCATORS MFG. CO.

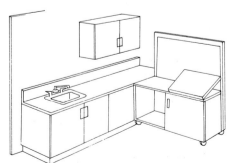

LIBRARY WORK UNIT
EDUCATORS MFG. CO.

ISD Incorporated; Chicago, New York, Boston, Houston

ROUND

DIAMETER	CIRCUM.	APPROXIMATE SEATING
8'-0''	25'-1''	10-12
7'-0''	21'-8''	8-10
6'-0''	18'-9''	7-8
5'-0''	15'-7''	6-7
4'-6''	14'-1''	5-6
4'-0''	12'-6''	5-6
3'-6''	11'-0''	4-5

BOAT SHAPED

WIDTH		LENGTH	APPROXIMATE SEATING
CENTER	END		
6'-0''	4'-0''	20'-0''	20-24
5'-6''	4'-0''	18'-0''	18-20
5'-6''	4'-0''	16'-0''	16-18
5'-0''	3'-6''	14'-0''	14-16
4'-6''	3'-6''	12'-0''	12-14
4'-0''	3'-2''	11'-0''	10-12
4'-0''	3'-2''	10'-0''	10-12
3'-6''	3'-0''	9'-0''	8-10
3'-6''	3'-0''	8'-0''	8-10
3'-0''	2'-10''	7'-0''	6-8
3'-0''	2'-10''	6'-0''	6-8

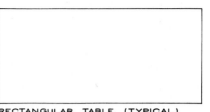

RECTANGULAR TABLE (TYPICAL)

BOAT SHAPED TABLE (TYPICAL)

RECTANGULAR

WIDTH	LENGTH	APPROXIMATE SEATING
5'-0''	20'-0''	20-22
4'-6''	18'-0''	18-20
4'-6''	16'-0''	16-18
4'-6''	14'-0''	14-16
4'-0''	12'-0''	12-14
4'-0''	11'-0''	10-12
4'-0''	10'-0''	10-12
4'-0''	9'-0''	8-10
4'-0''	8'-0''	8-10
3'-6''	9'-0''	8-10
3'-6''	8'-0''	8-10
3'-6''	7'-6''	6-8
3'-6''	7'-0''	6-8
3'-0''	7'-0''	6-8
3'-0''	6'-6''	6-8
2'-6''	5'-6''	4-6
2'-6''	5'-0''	4-6

SQUARE

WIDTH	LENGTH	APPROXIMATE SEATING
5'-0''	5'-0''	8-12
4'-6''	4'-6''	4-8
4'-0''	4'-0''	4-8
3'-6''	3'-6''	4
3'-0''	3'-0''	4

```
W  72"
D  38"
H  28½"
```
EXECUTIVE TABLE DESK
KNOLL INTERNATIONAL

```
W  54"
D  54"
H  29"
```
ANDRE TABLE
KNOLL INTERNATIONAL

```
W  54"
D  30"
H  29¼"
```
OMEGA DESK TABLE
STENDIG INCORPORATED

```
W  47¼"
D  47¼"
H  28¾"
```
DINING TABLE
KNOLL INTERNATIONAL

```
D  48"
H  28"
```
CONFERENCE/DINING TABLE
ZOGRAPHOS DESIGNS LTD.

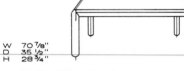

```
W  70⅞"
D  35½"
H  28¾"
```
MAGISTRETTI TABLE
ATELIER INTERNATIONAL LTD.

```
W  90"
D  33½"
H  27⅛"
```
CONFERENCE/DINING TABLE
ATELIER INTERNATIONAL LTD.

```
D  42"
H  26¼"
```
EXECUTIVE TABLE
HERMAN MILLER, INCORPORATED

```
D  18"-60"
H  29"
```
ROUND/OVAL PEDESTAL TABLE
VECTA CONTRACT

```
W  48"-96"
D  18"-48"
H  29"
```
CONFERENCE TABLE
HOWE FURNITURE CORP.

```
D  42"
H  29¼"
```
EXECUTIVE TABLE
HERMAN MILLER, INCORPORATED

```
W  72"
D  36"
H  29"
```
CONFERENCE TABLE
VECTA CONTRACT

ISD Incorporated; Chicago, New York, Boston, Houston

CHAPTER 13 SPECIAL CONSTRUCTION

FLOOR STRUCTURE ASSEMBLIES FOR ADDITIONAL INFORMATION CONSULT MANUFACTURERS' LITERATURE AND TRADE ASSOCIATIONS		DEPTH OF SYSTEM (IN.)	STANDARD MEMBER SIZES (IN.)	DEAD LOAD OF STRUCTURE (PSF)	SUITABLE LIVE LOAD RANGE (PSF)	SPAN RANGE (FT)	DIMENSIONAL STABILITY AFFECTED BY
WOOD JOIST	PLYWOOD SUBFLOOR / WOOD JOIST / CEILING	7–13	Nominal joist 2 x 6, 8, 10, and 12	5–8	30–40	Up to 18	Deflection
WOOD TRUSS OR PLYWOOD JOIST	PLYWOOD SUBFLOOR / PLYWOOD JOIST (OR WOOD TRUSS) / CEILING	13–21	Plywood joists 12, 14, 16, 18, and 20	6–12	30–40	12–30	Deflection
WOOD BEAM AND PLANK	WOOD PLANK / WOOD BEAM	10–22	Nominal plank 2, 3, and 4	6–16	30–40	10–22	—
LAMINATED WOOD BEAM AND PLANK	WOOD PLANK / GLUE LAMINATED WOOD BEAM	8–22	Nominal plank 2, 3, and 4	6–20	30–40	8–34	—
STEEL JOIST	PLYWOOD SUBFLOOR / WOOD NAILER / STEEL JOIST / CEILING	9–31	Steel joists 8–30	8–20	30–40	16–40	Deflection
STEEL JOIST	CONCRETE SLAB / STEEL CENTERING / STEEL JOIST / CEILING	11–75	Steel joists 8–72	30–110	30–100	16–60 (up to 130)	Deflection
LIGHT-WEIGHT STEEL FRAME	PLYWOOD SUBFLOOR / LIGHTWEIGHT STEEL FRAME / CEILING	7–12	Consult manufacturers' literature	6–20	30–60	10–22	—
STEEL FRAME	CONCRETE SLAB / STEEL CENTERING / STEEL BEAM / CEILING	9–15	—	35–60	30–100	16–35	Deflection
STEEL FRAME	CONCRETE TOPPING / PRECAST CONCRETE PLANK / STEEL BEAM / CEILING	8–16	Concrete plank 16–48 W 4–12 D	40–75	60–150	Up to 50 Generally below 35	Deflection and creep
PRECAST CONCRETE	CONCRETE TOPPING / PRECAST CONCRETE PLANK / CONCRETE BEAM	6–12	Concrete plank 16–48 W 4–12 D	40–75	60–150	Up to 60 Generally below 35	Deflection and creep
ONE-WAY CONCRETE SLAB	CONCRETE SLAB / CONCRETE BEAM	4–10	—	50–120	40–150	10–20 More with prestressing	—
TWO-WAY CONCRETE SLAB	CONCRETE SLAB / CONCRETE BEAM	4–10	—	50–120	40–250	10–30 More with prestressing	—
ONE-WAY RIBBED CONCRETE SLAB	CONCRETE SLAB / RIB (JOIST)	8–22	Standard pan forms 20 and 30 W 6–20 D	40–90	40–150	15–50 More with prestressing	Creep
TWO-WAY RIBBED CONCRETE SLAB	CONCRETE SLAB / RIB (JOIST)	8–22	Standard dome forms 19 x 19, 30 x 30 6–20 D	75–105	60–200	25–60 More with prestressing	Creep
CONCRETE FLAT SLAB	CONCRETE SLAB / DROP PANEL / CAPITAL / COLUMN	6–16	Min. slab thickness 5 without / 4 with } Drop panel	75–170	60–250	20–40 Up to 70 with prestressing	Creep
PRECAST DOUBLE TEE	CONCRETE TOPPING / PRECAST DOUBLE TEE	8–18	4', 5', 6', 8', and 10' W 6–16 D	50–80	40–150	20–50	Creep
PRECAST TEE	CONCRETE TOPPING / PRECAST SINGLE TEE	18–38	16–36 D	50–90	40–150	25–65	Creep
COMPOSITE	CONCRETE SLAB / WELDED STUD (SHEAR CONNECTOR) / STEEL BEAM	4–6	—	35–70	60–200	Up to 35	Deflection
CONCRETE FLAT PLATE	COLUMN / CONCRETE FLAT PLATE	5–14	—	60–175	60–200	18–35 More with prestressing	Creep

Roger K. Lewis, AIA, and Mehmet T. Ergene, Architect; Roger K. Lewis, AIA, & Associates; Washington, D.C.

BAY SIZE CHARAC-TERISTICS	REQUIRES FINISHED FLOOR SURFACE	REQUIRES FINISHED CEILING SURFACE	SERVICE PLENUM	COMPARATIVE RESISTANCE TO SOUND TRANSMISSION		FIRE RESISTIVE RATING PER CODE AND UNDERWRITERS		CONSTRUCTION TYPE CLASSIFICATION	REMARKS
				IMPACT	AIRBORNE	UNPROTECTED HOURS	MAXIMUM PROTECTED HOURS		
—	Yes	Visual or fire protection purposes	Between joists —one way	Poor	Fair	—	2 (combustible)	4B (A) 3C (B)	Economical, light, easy to construct. Limited to lowrise construction
—	Yes	Visual or fire protection purposes	Between trusses and joists —two ways	Poor	Fair	—	2 (combustible)	4B (A) 3C (B)	Close dimensional tolerances; cutting holes through web permissible
Maximum beam spacing 8'-0"	Optional	No	Under structure —one way	Poor	Fair	—	2	3A 6" x 10" frame min. 4" planks min.	Most efficient with planks continuous over more than one span
—	Optional	No	Under structure —one way	Poor	Fair	—	2	3A 6" x 10" frame min. 4" planks min.	—
Light joists 16" to 30" o.c. Heavy joists 4'–12' o.c.	Yes	Visual or fire protection purposes	Between joists —two ways	Poor	Poor	—	1	3C (B)	—
Light joists 16" to 30" o.c. Heavy joists 4'–12' o.c.	No	Visual or fire protection purposes	Between joists —two ways	Poor	Fair	—	1–3	1, 2 and 3	Economical system, selective partition placement required. Cantilevers difficult
—	Yes	Visual or fire protection purposes	Under structure	Poor	Poor	—	1	3C (B)	—
—	No	Visual or fire protection purposes	Under structure	Poor	Fair	1–3	1–4	1, 2, and 3	—
—	Optional	Visual or fire protection purposes	Under structure	Fair	Fair	—	1–4	1, 2, and 3	—
—	Optional	No	Under structure	Fair	Fair	2–4	3–4	1 and 2	—
—	No	No	Under structure	Good	Good	1–4	3–4	1 and 2	Restricted to short spans because of excessive dead load
L ≤ 1.33 W	No	No	Under structure	Good	Good	1–4	3–4	1 and 2	Suitable for concentrated loads, easy partition placement
—	No	No	Between ribs —one way	Good	Good	1–4	3–4	1 and 2	Economy through re-use of forms, shear at supports controlling factor
L ≤ 1.33 W	No	No	Under structure	Good	Good	1–4	3–4	1 and 2	For heavy loads, columns should be equidistant. Not good for cantilevers
L ≤ 1.33 W	No	No	Under structure	Good	Good	1–4	3–4	1 and 2	Drop panels against shear required for spans above 12 ft
—	Optional	Visual purposes; differential camber	Between ribs —one way	Fair	Good	2–3	3–4	1 and 2	Most widely used pre-stressed concrete product in the medium span range
—	Optional	Visual purposes; differential camber	Between ribs —one way	Fair	Good	2–3	3–4	1 and 2	Easy construction, lack continuity, poor earthquake resistance
—	No	Visual or fire protection purposes	Under structure	Good	Good	—	1–4	1, 2, and 3	—
L ≤ 1.33 W	No	No	Under structure	Good	Good	1–4	3–4	1 and 2	Uniform slab thickness, economical to form, easy to cantilever

Roger K. Lewis, AIA, and Mehmet T. Ergene, Architect; Roger K. Lewis, AIA, & Associates; Washington, D.C.

DESIGN ELEMENTS

ROOF STRUCTURE ASSEMBLIES FOR ADDITIONAL INFORMATION CONSULT MANUFACTURER'S LITERATURE AND TRADE ASSOCIATIONS	DEPTH OF SYSTEM (IN.)	STANDARD MEMBER SIZES (IN.)	DEAD LOAD OF STRUCTURE (PSF)	SUITABLE LIVE LOAD RANGE (PSF)	SPAN RANGE (FT)	BAY SIZE CHARACTERISTICS	DIMENSIONAL STABILITY AFFECTED BY
WOOD RAFTER — PLYWOOD SHEATHING, WOOD JOIST, CEILING	5–13	Nominal rafters 2 x 4, 6, 8, 10, and 12	4–8	10–50	Up to 22	—	Deflection
WOOD BEAM AND PLANK — WOOD PLANK, WOOD BEAM (OR LAMINATED BEAM)	8–22	Nominal planks 2, 3, and 4	5–12	10–50	8–34	Maximum beam spacing 8'-0"	—
PLYWOOD PANEL — PLYWOOD (STRESSED SKIN) PANELS	3¼ and 8¼	—	3–6	10–50	8–32	4'-0" modules	—
WOOD TRUSS — SHEATHING, WOOD TRUSS, CEILING	Varies (1'–12')	—	5–15	10–50	30–50	2'–8' between trusses	Deflection
STEEL TRUSS — STEEL DECK, PURLIN, STEEL TRUSS	Varies	—	15–25	10–60	100–200	—	Deflection
STEEL JOIST — CONCRETE, STEEL CENTERING, STEEL JOIST, CEILING	11–75	Steel joists 8–72	10–28	10–50	Up to 96	Light joists 16"–30" o.c. Heavy joists 4'–12' o.c.	Deflection
STEEL JOIST — PLYWOOD DECK, WOOD NAILER, STEEL JOIST, CEILING	10–32	Steel joists 8–30	8–20	10–50	Up to 96	Light joists 16"–30" o.c. Heavy joists 4'–12' o.c.	Deflection
STEEL JOIST — INSULATION, STEEL DECK, STEEL JOIST, CEILING	11–75	Steel joists 8–72	6–24	10–50	Up to 96	—	Deflection
STEEL FRAME — PRECAST CONCRETE PLANK, STEEL BEAM, CEILING	4–12 plus beam depth	Concrete plank 16–48 W 4–12 D	40–75	30–70	20–60 Generally below 35	—	Deflection and creep
PRECAST CONCRETE — PRECAST CONCRETE PLANK, CONCRETE BEAM	4–12 plus beam depth	Concrete plank 16–48 W 4–12 D	40–75	30–70	20–60 Generally below 35	—	Deflection and creep
ONE-WAY CONCRETE SLAB — CONCRETE SLAB, CONCRETE BEAM	4–10 slab plus beam depth	—	50–120	Up to 100	10–25 More with prestressing	—	—
TWO-WAY CONCRETE SLAB — CONCRETE SLAB, CONCRETE BEAM	4–10 slab plus beam depth	—	50–120	Up to 100	10–30 More with prestressing	L ≤ 1.33 W	—
ONE-WAY RIBBED CONCRETE SLAB — CONCRETE SLAB, RIB (JOIST)	8–22	Standard pan forms 20 and 30 W 6–20 D	40–90	Up to 100	15–50 More with prestressing	—	Creep
TWO-WAY RIBBED CONCRETE SLAB — CONCRETE SLAB, RIB (JOIST)	8–24	Standard dome forms 19 x 19, 30 x 30 6–20 D	75–105	Up to 100	25–60 More with prestressing	L ≤ 1.33 W	Creep
PRECAST TEE	16–36	16–36 deep	65–85	20–80	30–100	—	Creep
PRECAST DOUBLE TEE	6–16	4', 5', 6', 8', and 10' wide 6"–16" deep	35–55	25–60	20–75	—	Creep
CONCRETE FLAT PLATE — CONCRETE FLAT PLATE, COLUMN	4–14	—	50–160	Up to 100	Up to 35 More with prestressing	L ≤ 1.33 W	Creep
CONCRETE FLAT SLAB — CONCRETE SLAB, DROP PANEL, CAPITAL, COLUMN	5–16	Min. slab thickness 5 w/o } Drop 4 w/ } panel	50–200	Up to 100	Up to 40 More with prestressing	L ≤ 1.33 W Equal column spacing required	Creep
GYPSUM DECK — GYPSUM CONCRETE, FORM BOARD, SUBPURLIN, CEILING	3–6	—	5–20	Up to 50	Up to 10	Up to 8' between subpurlins	Deflection and creep

Roger K. Lewis, AIA, and Mehmet T. Ergene, Architect; Roger K. Lewis, AIA, & Associates; Washington, D.C.

SUITABLE FOR INCLINED ROOFS	REQUIRES FINISHED CEILING SURFACE	SERVICE PLENUM	RELATIVE THERMAL CAPACITY	COMPARATIVE RESISTANCE TO SOUND TRANSMISSION		FIRE RESISTIVE RATING PER CODE AND UNDERWRITERS		CONSTRUCTION TYPE CLASSIFICATION	REMARKS
				IMPACT	AIRBORNE	UNPROTECTED HOURS	MAXIMUM PROTECTED HOURS		
Yes	For visual or fire protection purposes	Between rafters —one way	Low	Poor	Fair	—	2 (combustible)	4B (A) 3C (B)	
Yes	For fire protection purposes	Under structure —one way	Medium	Poor	Fair	—	2	3A 6'' x 10'' frame min. 4'' plank min.	
Yes	No	Under structure only	Low	Poor	Fair	—	2	4B (A) 3C (B)	
Yes	For visual or fire protection purposes	Between trusses	Low	Poor	Fair	—	2 (combustible)	4B (A) 3C (B)	Truss depth to span ratio 1:5 to 1:10
Yes Pitched trusses usually used for short spans	For visual or fire protection purposes	Between trusses	Low	Fair	Fair	—	1–4	1, 2, and 3	Truss depth to span ratio 1:5 to 1:15
No	For visual or fire protection purposes	Between joists	Medium	Fair	Fair	—	1–4	1, 2, and 3	
Yes	For visual or fire protection purposes	Between joists	Low	Poor	Fair	—	1	1, 2, and 3	
Yes	For visual or fire protection purposes	Between joists	High	Excellent	Good	—	2	1, 2, and 3	
Yes	For visual or fire protection purposes	Under structure	High	Fair	Fair	—	1–4	1, 2, and 3	Easy to design; quick erection
Yes	No	Under structure	High	Fair	Fair	2–4	3–4	1 and 2	Provides finished flush ceiling. May be used with any framing system
No	No	Under structure	High	Good	Good	1–4	3–4	1 and 2	
No	No	Under structure	High	Good	Good	1–4	3–4	1 and 2	
No	For visual purposes	Between ribs —one way	High	Good	Good	1–4	3–4	1 and 2	
No	No	Under structure	High	Good	Good	1–4	3–4	1 and 2	Economy in forming; suitable for two-way cantilevering
Yes	For visual or fire protection purposes	Between ribs —one way	High	Fair	Good	2–3	3–4	1 and 2	Generally used for long spans
Yes	For visual or fire protection purposes	Between ribs —one way	High	Fair	Good	2–3	3–4	1 and 2	Most widely used prestressed concrete element.
No	No	Under structure	High	Good	Good	1–4	3–4	1 and 2	Uniform slab thickness; easy to form; suitable for vertical expansion of building
No	No	Under structure	High	Good	Good	1–4	3–4	1 and 2	Suitable for heavy roof loads
No	For visual or fire protection purposes	Under structure	High	Good	Good	—	2	1, 2, and 3	Provides resistance to wind and seismic loads

Roger K. Lewis, AIA, and Mehmet T. Ergene, Architect; Roger K. Lewis, AIA, & Associates; Washington, D.C.

DESIGN ELEMENTS 13

EXTERIOR WALL ASSEMBLIES FOR ADDITIONAL INFORMATION CONSULT MANUFACTURERS' LITERATURE AND TRADE ASSOCIATIONS		WALL THICKNESS (NOMINAL) (IN.)	WEIGHT (PSF)	VERTICAL SPAN RANGE UNSUPPORTED HEIGHT) (FT)	WIND RESIST.	RACKING RESISTANCE	SERVICE PLENUM SPACE	HEAT TRANSMISSION COEFFICIENT (U-FACTOR) (BTU/HR·SQ FT·°F)
C.M.U.	C.M.U. (GRAVEL AGGREGATE)	8 / 12	55 / 85	Up to 13 / Up to 20		Good	None	0.56 / 0.49
C.M.U. (INSULATED)	C.M.U. / INSULATION / INT. WALL FIN.	8+ / 12+	60 / 90	Up to 13 / Up to 20		Good	Through insulation	0.21 / 0.20
C.M.U. AND BRICK VENEER (INSULATED)	BRICK VENEER / C.M.U. / INSULATION / INT. WALL FIN.	4+4+ / 4+8+	75 / 100	Up to 13 (w/filled cavity) / Up to 20 (w/filled cavity)		Good	Through insulation	0.19 / 0.18
CAVITY	BRICK VENEER / CAVITY (MIN. 2") / INSULATION (WATER REPELLENT) / C.M.U. / INT. WALL FIN.	4+2+4 / 4+2+8	75 / 100	Up to 9 / Up to 13		Fair	None	0.12 / 0.11
C.M.U. AND STUCCO (INSULATED)	STUCCO / C.M.U. / INSULATION / INT. WALL FIN.	8+	67	Up to 13		Good	Through interior insulation	0.16
WOOD STUD	EXT. WALL FIN. / SHEATHING WITH MOISTURE BARRIER / WOOD STUD / INSULATION WITH VAPOR BARRIER / INT. WALL FIN.	4 / 6	12 / 16	Up to 14 / Up to 20 (L/d ≤ 50)		Poor to fair	Between studs	0.06 / 0.04
BRICK VENEER	BRICK VENEER / SHEATHING WITH MOISTURE BARRIER / WOOD STUD / INSULATION WITH VAPOR BARRIER / INT. WALL FIN.	4+4	52	Up to 14		Poor to fair	Between studs	0.07
METAL STUD	EXT. WALL FIN. / METAL STUD AT 16" O.C. / INSULATION WITH VAPOR BARRIER / INT. WALL FIN.	4 / 5	14 / 18	Up to 13 / Up to 17		Poor	Between studs	0.06 / 0.04
BRICK VENEER	BRICK VENEER / SHEATHING WITH MOISTURE BARRIER / METAL STUD AT 16" O.C. / INSULATION WITH VAPOR BARRIER / INT. WALL FIN.	4+4	54	Up to 15		Good	Between studs	0.07
INSULATED SANDWICH PANEL	METAL SKIN / AIRSPACE / INSULATING CORE / METAL SKIN	5	6	See manufacturers' literature		Fair to good	None	0.05 / See manufacturers' literature
CONCRETE	CONCRETE	8 / 12	92 / 138	Up to 13 (w/reinf. 17) / Up to 20 (w/reinf. 25)		Excellent	None	0.68 / 0.55
CONCRETE (INSULATED)	CONCRETE / INSULATION / INT. WALL FIN.	8+	97	Up to 13 (w/reinf. 17)		Excellent	Through insulation	0.13
CONCRETE AND BRICK VENEER (INSULATED)	BRICK VENEER / CONCRETE / INSULATION / INT. WALL FIN.	4+8+	112	Up to 13 (w/reinf. 17)		Excellent	Through insulation	0.13
PRECAST CONCRETE	CONCRETE (REINFORCED) / INSULATION / INT. WALL FINISH	2+ / 4+	23 / 46	Up to 6 / Up to 12		Fair to good	Through insulation	0.99 / 0.85
PRECAST CONCRETE SANDWICH	CONCRETE / INSULATION	5	45	Up to 14		Fair to good	None	0.14

Wind resistance depends on geographical location and height of building; wind velocity; wall material thickness, strength; workmanship; axial loads; and horizontal span. Design walls for both inward and outward pressures.

GLASS SEE CHAPTER 8 FOR DETAILED INFORMATION ON GLASS				SIZE RANGE MAXIMUM ALLOWABLE GLASS AREA / WIND LOAD		SHADING COEFFICIENT S.C.	
SINGLE GLAZING	1/4" GLASS	1/4	3.2	Four side supported 110 SF @ 10 PSF / 20 SF @ 60 PSF / Two side supported 40 SF @ 10 PSF / 17 SF @ 60 PSF		Clear 0.94 / Tinted 0.70	Clear/tinted 1.1 / Reflective 0.8–1.1
DOUBLE GLAZING	1/4" GLASS / 1/4" CAVITY	3/4	6.4	Four side supported 55 SF @ 30 PSF / 28 SF @ 60 PSF / Heat strengthened 70 SF @ 80 PSF / 30 SF @ 200 PSF		Reflective 0.44	Clear/tinted 0.5–0.6 / Reflective 0.3–0.6
TRIPLE GLAZING	1/4" GLASS / 1/4" CAVITY	1 1/4	9.6	—			Clear/tinted 0.3–0.4 / Reflective 0.2–0.4

Roger K. Lewis, AIA, and Mehmet T. Ergene, Architect; Roger K. Lewis, AIA & Associates; Washington, D.C.

13 DESIGN ELEMENTS

HAZARD CLASSIFICATION (FIRE)

Classification provides data in regard to (1) flame spread, (2) fuel contributed, and (3) smoke developed during fire exposure of materials in comparison to asbestos-cement boards as zero and untreated red oak lumber as 100 when exposed to fire under similar conditions

	FLAME SPREAD	FUEL CONTRIBUTED	SMOKE DEVELOPED
Paint on CMU	5-25	0-5	0-10
Gypsum board surfaced on both sides with paper	15	15	0
Gypsum board surfaced on both sides with paper, vinyl faced	25-35	0-10	15-45
Untreated wood particle board	180	75	190
Treated wood particle board with untreated wood face veneer	25-180	10-160	10-250
Vermiculite acoustical plaster	10-20	10-20	0
Glass fiber batts and blankets (basic)	20	15	20
(foil kraft faced)	25	0	0
Treated lumber (Douglas fir)	15	10	0-5
(Hemlock)	10-15	5-15	0
Laminated plastic (fr)	20-30	0-15	5-30

NFPA CLASSIFICATION:

CLASS	FLAME SPREAD	SMOKE DEVELOPED
A	0-25	0-450
B	26-75	0-450
C	76-200	0-450

For lesser classifications, permitted in residential construction only, refer to regulating agency guidelines

RESISTANCE TO EXTERIOR AIRBORNE SOUND TRANSMISSION	FIRE RESISTIVE RATING PER CODE AND UNDERWRITERS (HRS)	CONSTRUCTION TYPE CLASSIFICATION	SUBCONTRACTORS REQUIRED FOR ERECTION (PLUS FINISHES)	EXTERIOR MAINTENANCE REQUIREMENTS	REMARKS
Fair to good	2-4 4	1, 2, and 3	Masonry	Washing, re-pointing joints, painting, sand blasting	Properties of non-engineered masonry are drastically reduced
Fair to good	2-4 4	1, 2, and 3	Masonry Carpentry Drywall	Washing, re-pointing joints, painting, sand blasting	
Excellent	3-4 4	1, 2, and 3	Masonry Carpentry Drywall	Washing, re-pointing joints, sand blasting	
Excellent	4	1, 2, and 3	Masonry Drywall (Carpentry)	Washing, re-pointing joints, sand blasting	Cavity increases heat storage capacity and resistance to rain penetration
Good	2-4	1, 2, and 3	Masonry Drywall Lath and plaster (Carpentry)	Washing, painting, and re-stuccoing	The assembly is reversed for optimum energy conservation
Poor to fair	1 (combustible)	4	Carpentry Drywall (Lath and plaster)	Washing, painting, and replacing exterior finish	Exterior wall finishes: • wood, plywood, • aluminum siding • stucco
Good to excellent	1-2 (combustible)	3B, C	Masonry Carpentry Drywall	Washing, re-pointing joints, sand blasting	
Poor to fair	1-2	1 (nonbearing) 2 and 3	Carpentry Drywall (Lath and plaster)	Washing, painting, and replacing exterior finish	Exterior wall finishes: • wood, plywood, • aluminum siding • stucco
Good to excellent	1-2	1 (nonbearing) 2 and 3	Masonry Carpentry Drywall	Washing, re-pointing joints, sand blasting	
Poor to good; see manufacturers' literature	See manufacturers' literature	See manufacturers' literature	Curtain walls —erection	Washing, steam cleaning, painting, replacing joint sealers	Temperature change critical. Minimize metal through connections
Good	4 4	1, 2, and 3	Concrete work	Washing, sand blasting	Concrete walls have very high heat storage capacity
Good	4 4	1, 2, and 3	Concrete work Drywall (Carpentry)	Washing, sand blasting	
Excellent	4	1, 2, and 3	Concrete work Masonry Drywall (Carpentry)	Washing, re-pointing joints, sand blasting	
Poor to fair	1-3	1A (nonbearing) 1B, 2, and 3	Curtain walls —erection Drywall (Carpentry)	Washing, sand blasting, replacing joint sealers	Large size economical (fewer joints) units available with various finishes
Fair	1-3	1A (nonbearing) 1B, 2, and 3	Curtain walls —erection	Washing, sand blasting, replacing joint sealers	8' x 20' max. size for concrete sandwich panels. Plant quality control is very essential
Poor	—	—	Curtain walls —erection (Glazing)	Washing, replacing joint sealers, gaskets	Anchorage to building is critical. Anchors must isolate wall to limit building movement transmitted to glass. Wall design must limit wall movement transmitted to glass
Fair	—	—	Curtain walls —erection (Glazing)	Washing, replacing joint sealers, gaskets	Mullions should accommodate movement through gaskets, sliding connections, etc.
Good	—	—	Curtain walls —erection (Glazing)	Washing, replacing joint sealers, gaskets	

Roger K. Lewis, AIA, and Mehmet T. Ergene, Architect; Roger K. Lewis, AIA, & Associates; Washington, D.C.

DESIGN ELEMENTS   13

GENERAL INFORMATION

Most air structures are primarily designed to resist wind loads. Mechanical blowers must maintain 3 to 5 psf pressure inside the structure at all times. Architectural elements of the building must be detailed to avoid loss of air pressure. Normal entering and exiting should be through revolving doors, while emergency exiting is provided through pressure balanced doors, and vehicles pass through air locks. Avoid using interior furnishings that could possibly puncture the structural membrane. Automatic auxilliary fans should be activated in the event of a pressure drop due to primary power failure.

The structural membrane is usually a nylon, fiberglass, or polyester fabric coated with polyvinyl chloride. Such skins have a life span from 7 to 10 years, and provide fire retardation that passes NFPA 701. A urethane topcoat will reduce dirt adhesion and improve service life. New Teflon coated fiberglass membranes have a life expectancy of more than 25 years. This material is incombustible, passing NFPA 70, with flame spread rating = 10, smoke developed = 50, and fuel contributed = 10. An acoustical liner (NCR = 0.65) is also available.

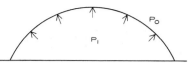

SINGLE MEMBRANE $P_1 > P_0$

This is the most common type of air structure. The internal pressure (P_1) is kept approximately 0.03 psi above the external atmospheric pressure (P_0). It is this pressure difference that keeps the dome inflated.

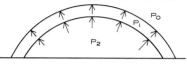

DOUBLE MEMBRANE $P_2 > P_1 > P_0$

The airspace between the two membranes is used for insulation and security. If the outer skin is punctured the inner skin will remain standing. Both single and double membrane air structures require the constant use of blowers to keep them inflated.

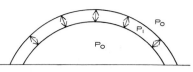

DUAL MEMBRANE $P_1 > P_0$

Here the internal and external pressures are the same. Only the area between the skins is pressurized. The inflated area of a dual membrane structure can be sealed, thus eliminating the need for constant use of blowers.

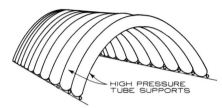

HIGH PRESSURE TUBE SUPPORTS

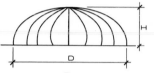

$D/2 > H > D/(2\sqrt{2})$

SPAN LIMITATIONS	VAULT	DOME
Without cables	D = 120' - 0''	D = 150' - 0''
With cables	D = 400' - 0''	D = 600' - 0''

AIR SUPPORTED

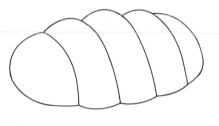

VAULT

AIR INFLATED

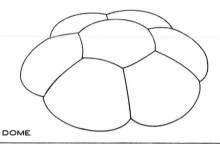

DOME

BASIC CONFIGURATIONS

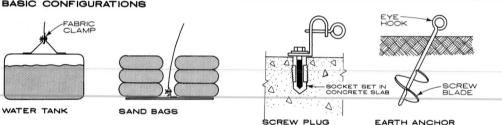

FABRIC CLAMP

WATER TANK   **SAND BAGS**

EYE HOOK

SOCKET SET IN CONCRETE SLAB   SCREW BLADE

SCREW PLUG   **EARTH ANCHOR**

C-PROFILE   MEMBRANE

STRADDLING DOWEL

CABLE

GRADE BEAM

ROD SET IN CONCRETE PIER

ANGLE CLAMP

ANCHORAGE DETAILS

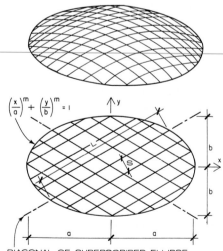

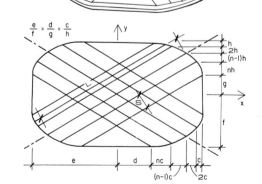

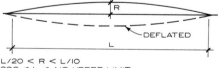

FABRIC CLAMP
COMPRESSION RING

CABLE SOCKET

$$\left(\frac{x}{a}\right)^m + \left(\frac{y}{b}\right)^m = 1$$

DIAGONAL OF SUPERSCRIBED ELLIPSE MAXIMUM CABLE SPACING = 50'-0''

SUPERELLIPSE PLAN

KEY TO NOTATIONS
a/b—One half of major/minor axes of superellipse.
s—Cable spacing.
L—Length of cable along diagonal of superscribed rectangle of proportions 2a and 2b.
e/f—One half of major/minor axes of superscribed

$$\frac{e}{f} = \frac{d}{g} = \frac{c}{h}$$

MAXIMUM STRAIGHT SIDE = 200'-0''
PROGRESSION PLAN

rectangle of plan progression.
d/g—One half of straight sides of and parallel to the major/minor axes of the plan progression.
c, 2c, (n-1)c, nc/h, 2h, (n-1)h, nh—The sequences of curve coordinates parallel to the major/minor axes of the plan progression.

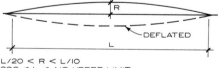

$L/20 < R < L/10$
$200 < L < $ NO UPPER LIMIT

STRUCTURAL CONSIDERATIONS

Membrane strengths up to 1000 lb/in. are available; a safety factor of 4 for short term loading and 8 for long term loading is required. The membrane must be patterned to carry loads without wrinkling. Structural behavior is nonlinear with large displacements. The roof shape shall be established such that the horizontal components of the cable forces result in minimum bending moment in the compression ring under maximum loads. The skewed symmetry indicated permits this condition to be realized. Consult specialist in air structures to integrate structural and architectural requirements.

LONG SPAN STRUCTURES

Geiger-Berger Associates, P.C.; New York, New York

13   AIR SUPPORTED STRUCTURES

DESIGN ISSUES

The major design issues affecting underground and earth sheltered buildings are sun orientation, wind, topography and drainage, access to outside light and views, acoustics, landscaping, and thermal characteristics. Proper orientation can produce significant energy savings. Exterior views are an important aesthetic and psychological determinant of orientation.

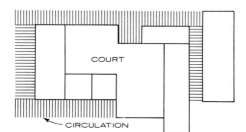

CIRCULATION AT PERIMETER

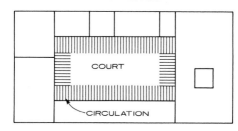

CIRCULATION AT INTERIOR

ATRIUM

NOTE

The atrium plan places spaces around a courtyard with orientation into the court.

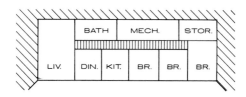

ELEVATIONAL

NOTE

The concept of the elevational plan is to maximize the earth cover by concentrating all openings on one side, preferably south. The arrangement of spaces requiring light and view, are on the exposed side.

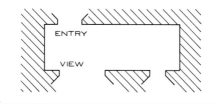

PENETRATIONAL

NOTE

Penetrational plans place openings around the structure for light and view on the perimeter.

MAJOR STRUCTURAL CONSIDERATIONS

Since earth sheltered structures have greater than normal loads on the roof and walls, additional structural analysis is required. Consult an engineer.

SUN

The radiant energy from the sun can be used for active and/or passive heating.

Myers & Bennett/BRW, Inc.; Minneapolis, Minnesota

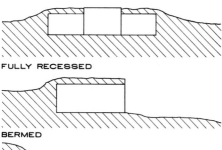

FULLY RECESSED

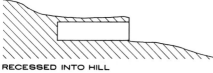

BERMED

RECESSED INTO HILL

TYPICAL SECTIONS

NOTE

Fully recessed structures with earth berms on flat sites and semirecessed structures on sloping sites are typical. The depth of the structure and surface relationships can influence the amount of earth placed on the roof and walls, as does the relationship between the earth mass and energy requirements for comfort conditioning.

WIND

Cold winter winds increase heat loss because of infiltration and wind chill factor. Protecting a building from exposure on the winter wind side will reduce heat loss. In the summer it is desirable to take advantage of prevailing breezes to provide natural ventilation. Cross-ventilation is desirable.

TOPOGRAPHY

The most important issue to topography is the degree and orientation of slope. A sloping site offers the opportunity to set an earth covered space into the hillside; it also limits the orientation of most openings to the direction of slope.

DRAINAGE

Correctly sloped sites, divert water away by creating a swale or a cutoff gravel trench. On sites with sunken courts, the ground should slope away on all sides, then only the rainfall that falls directly into the court has to be handled by a drainage system. French drains are commonly used.

ACOUSTICS

Earth sheltered construction greatly dampens outside sound. This acoustic insulation benefits sites that are close to undesirable noise sources.

LANDSCAPING

PERIMETER PLANTING

Where openings are exposed to sun and wind, plant material can contribute to significant energy savings. Deciduous plant material can shade the building when solar radiation is undesirable and let it in when desirable. Coniferous vegetation can provide protection in winter against prevailing winter winds.

ROOFTOP PLANTING

It is desirable to have plant growth on the roof for aesthetic, ecological, and energy saving reasons. The reflective nature of plants and their respiration considerably reduce solar heat gain as compared with conventional roofing systems.

THERMAL CHARACTERISTICS OF EARTH SHELTERED STRUCTURES

Heat loss (or gain) depends on two factors: the ventilation load for heating or cooling intake air and the heat transmission through the building envelope. The thermal mass of soil surrounding a building reduces the temperature variation of the structure. Maintaining a steady temperature will eventually (within about 1 to 3 yr depending on the size of the structure) create a "thermal envelope" that will maintain itself at an almost constant temperature approaching that of the interior space.

WALLS

The upper portions of the walls should be insulated to a depth of at least 7 ft below grade in very cold climate only. Below this the insulation may be eliminated or tapered, depending on the building's particular needs.

THERMAL BREAKS

Many earth sheltered structures are constructed of concrete, thus the loss by conduction is a major factor. Interruption of the roof or wall and insertion of an insulating barrier will have a significant impact on this heat transfer.

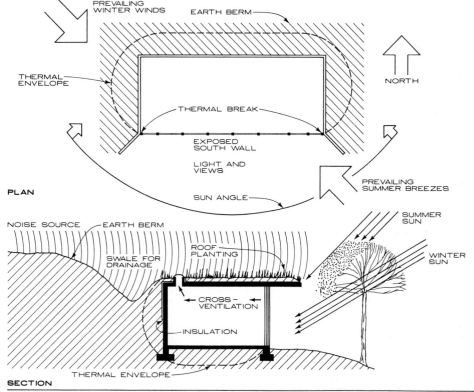

ENVIRONMENT CHARACTERISTICS OF EARTH SHELTERS

CEILING SYSTEMS	MANGER SPACING (o.c.)	WALL MOLDINGS			MAIN RUNNERS			SPACING	CROSS MEMBERS			SPACING (o.c.)	AIR BAR AIR BOOT			ACOUSTIC PANELS			LIGHT FIXTURES		
		L	W	H	L	W	H		L	W	H		L	W	H	L	W	H	L	W	H
Flat modular	2'-6''	10'	3/4''	3/4''	10'	3/4''	1 1/2''	5'	60''	3/4''	1 1/2''	20''	5'	3 1/8''	9 3/4''	5'	20''	5/8''	–	1.	–
Coffered lighting	30''	60''	1 1/4''	1 1/4''	5'	2 1/4''	1 1/4''	5'	60''	2 1/4''	1 1/4''	5'	5'	7 1/4''	8''	5'	15''	5/8''	48''	14 1/2''	5''
Luminair modular	5'	–	–	–	58 1/2''	3''	1 1/2''	5'	57''	15/16''	1 1/2''	5'	5'	7 1/4''	8''	5'	15''	5/8''	48''	14 1/2''	5''
Vertical screen	7' Max.	–	–	–	16'	1 1/2''	1 7/8''	7' Max.	16' Max.	5/8''	4''	2'-6''	–	2.	–	–	–	–	–	2.	–
Linear screen	5' Max.	–	–	–	16'	1 27/32''	1 1/4''	50''	3'-16'	3''	5/8''	2''	–	3.	–	–	4.	–	–	5.	–

NOTES
1. Size can vary.
2. No special type necessary.
3. Utilizes slots between panels for delivery and return.
4. Acoustic blanket.
5. Designed to fit panel width.

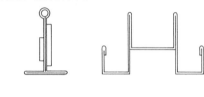

WALL MOUNTS

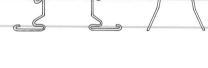

MAIN RUNNERS

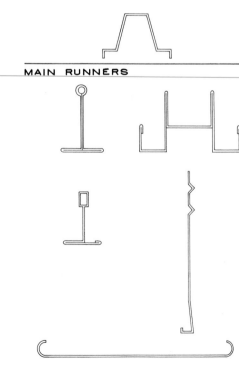

CROSS MEMBERS

Walter H. Sobel, FAIA & Associates; Chicago, Illinois

INTEGRATED CEILINGS
Integrated ceilings combine lighting, air diffusion, fire protection, and acoustical control into a single, unified unit. Demountable partitions can be accommodated by the use of an adaptor attached on the modular grid lines. A 60 x 60 in. module is basic to most integrated ceiling systems. Custom sized modules are also available. Air diffusion is by two integral means: (1) supply air plenum/supply air bar; (2) ducted supply air boot/ supply air bar in framing.

FLAT MODULAR CEILING SYSTEM
The 60 x 60 in. module is divided into three sections nominally 20 x 60 in. in size which can accommodate either a light fixture or an acoustical panel. Light fixtures are 20 x 60, 20 x 30, or 20 x 20 in. The lens frame provides a regress for handling air return.

Narrow grid members of the slide-lock type are easily installed and repositioned.

COFFERED LIGHTING CEILING SYSTEM
A 60 x 60 or a 60 x 30 in. module is standard. The coffered design permits a variety of lighting arrangements with either flat or coffered lighted modules. Maximum coffer depth is about 11 3/4 in. Air return is by return air lighted modules.

LUMINAIR MODULAR CEILING
The basic configuration is a 60 x 60 in. module divided into four 15 x 60 in. modules.

A recess in the modular defining grid will accommodate demountable partitions, sprinkler heads, and slots for air diffusion.

The basic lighting unit is a 14 1/2 x 48 in. recessed troffer. Task lighting can be provided by a pendant lighting fixture suspended by rods from an electrified track that can be moved around the ceiling.

Air return is by return air light fixtures.

VERTICAL AND LINEAR SCREEN CEILINGS
These ceilings provide effective screening of the mechanical, wiring, and piping in the plenum area. A vertical screen does not achieve full enclosure, requiring extra costs for special air distribution, diffuser or lighting fixtures, and sprinkler heads. A linear screen requires specially designed air diffusers and lighting fixtures.

Acoustic control is accomplished by laying an acoustic insulating blanket across the top of the suspended ceiling panels.

The size of the system is unlimited, carriers and panels can run in any direction.

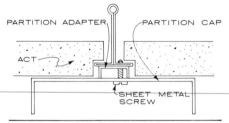

PARTITION ADAPTER — PARTITION CAP

ACT

SHEET METAL SCREW

PARTITION ATTACHMENT

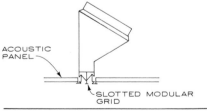

ACOUSTIC PANEL

SLOTTED MODULAR GRID

SUPPLY AIR—BOOT

FLAT FIXTURE

LIGHT

RETURN AIR

COFFERED FIXTURE

ACT

RETURN AIR

RETURN AIR—LIGHTING MODULE

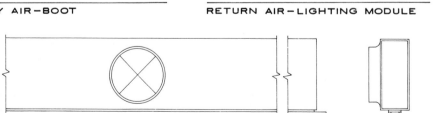

AIR BAR AND AIR BOOT

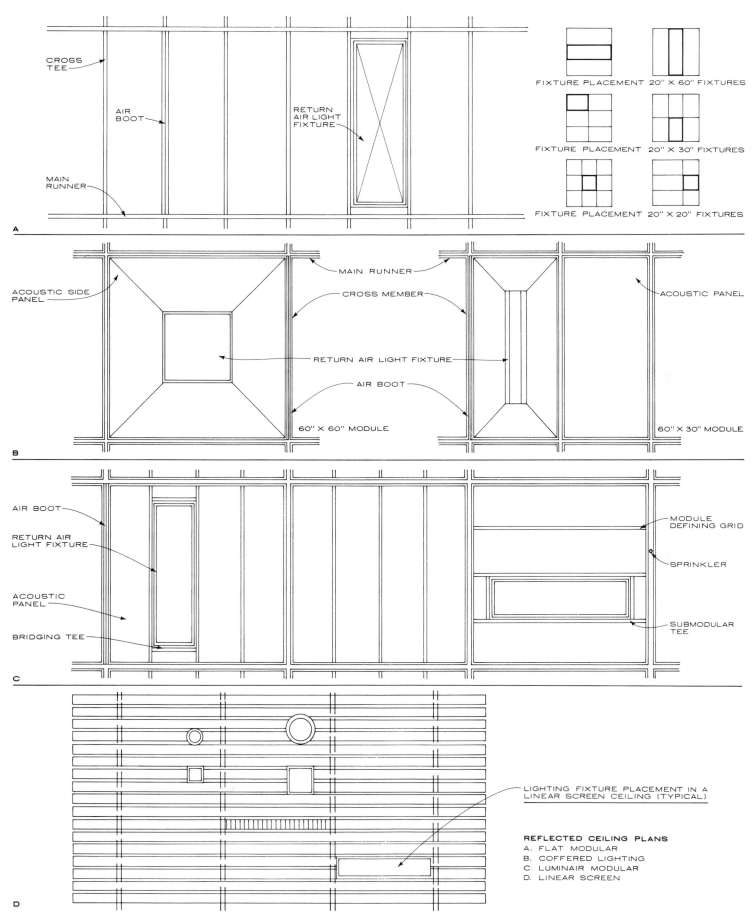

A

CROSS TEE

AIR BOOT

RETURN AIR LIGHT FIXTURE

MAIN RUNNER

FIXTURE PLACEMENT 20" X 60" FIXTURES

FIXTURE PLACEMENT 20" X 30" FIXTURES

FIXTURE PLACEMENT 20" X 20" FIXTURES

B

ACOUSTIC SIDE PANEL

MAIN RUNNER

CROSS MEMBER

ACOUSTIC PANEL

RETURN AIR LIGHT FIXTURE

AIR BOOT

60" X 60" MODULE

60" X 30" MODULE

C

AIR BOOT

RETURN AIR LIGHT FIXTURE

ACOUSTIC PANEL

BRIDGING TEE

MODULE DEFINING GRID

SPRINKLER

SUBMODULAR TEE

D

LIGHTING FIXTURE PLACEMENT IN A LINEAR SCREEN CEILING (TYPICAL)

REFLECTED CEILING PLANS
A. FLAT MODULAR
B. COFFERED LIGHTING
C. LUMINAIR MODULAR
D. LINEAR SCREEN

Walter H. Sobel, FAIA & Associates; Chicago, Illinois

INTEGRATED ASSEMBLIES **13**

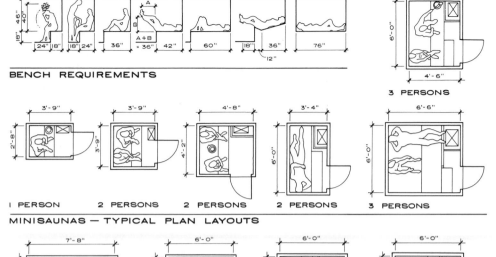

BENCH REQUIREMENTS

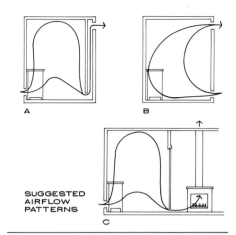

3 PERSONS

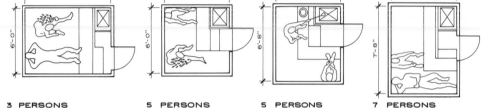

1 PERSON **2 PERSONS** **2 PERSONS** **2 PERSONS** **3 PERSONS**

MINISAUNAS — TYPICAL PLAN LAYOUTS

SUGGESTED AIRFLOW PATTERNS

PANEL SAUNA VENTILATION

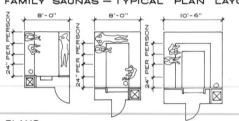

3 PERSONS **5 PERSONS** **5 PERSONS** **7 PERSONS**

FAMILY SAUNAS — TYPICAL PLAN LAYOUTS

NATURAL VENTILATION

Air must flow freely into the room—inlet and outlet normally are on opposite walls and at approximately the same level. The inlet situated under the stove creates a strong updraft.

A. A flue or duct provides a chimney action that will pull air off the floor and out.
B. Inlet is low on the wall, with outlet high and directly above it. This ensures ventilation even if wind pressure exists on the wall containing the two ventilators because of the difference in air temperature at the two openings and the effect of normal convection.
C. Suggest fresh air from exterior with outlet through another room, fan, or fireplace.

HEATER: The heater depends on convection for air circulation. It is the preferred method, for the air in a sauna should be as static as possible to heat the sauna in 1 to 1½ hr.

INTERIOR PANELING: Tongue and grooved boards should be at least 5/8 in. thick, or thicker if possible because of the increased ability to absorb vapor and to retain the timber smell. Boards should not be wider than about six times their thickness. Blind nailing with galvanized or aluminum nails is common. Vapor barrier and insulation under the interior paneling must be completely vaporproof and heat resistant. Most conventional insulating materials are effective; mineral base is preferred; avoid using expanded polystyrene.

DOOR: The opening should be kept as small as possible to minimize loss of heat. Maximum height is 6 ft. Door must open outward as a safety measure. A close fitting rebate on all four sides is usually sufficient insurance against heat loss around the edges. The construction should approach the U value of the walls.

HARDWARE: Because of the weight of the door, a pair of 4 in. brass butt hinges with ball bearings are recommended. A heavy ball or roller catch keeps the door closed. Door handles are made of wood.

LIGHTING: The lighting must be indirect and the fitting unobtrusive. The best position for the light is above and slightly behind the bather's normal field of view. The switch is always outside the hot room.

TYPE OF WOOD: White or western red cedar and redwood are the materials suitable for sauna construction. They should be chosen based on their resistance to splitting and decay, color of the wood, and the thermal capacity of the wood. These woods stain badly by metal and perspiration.

CEILING HEIGHT: The bigger the volume the more heat required; hence, keep the ceiling as low as possible within the limits imposed by the benches.

The main platform or bench will be about 39 in. above floor in a family sauna or at least 60 in. in a large public sauna. The ceiling is about 43 in. above the highest bench. Average family sauna ceiling height is 82 in., public 110 in.

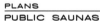

PLANS
PUBLIC SAUNAS

DESIGN CONSIDERATIONS

The fundamental purpose of the sauna is to induce perspiration; the higher the temperature, the more quickly perspiration will begin.

The drier the air, the more heat one can stand. Temperatures on the platform can be as high as 212°F, 230°F, and 240°F. A little warm water thrown over the stove stones just before leaving the sauna produces a slightly humid wave of air that suddenly seems hotter and envelops the bather with an invisible glowing cloud, pleasantly stinging the skin. It is usually better to lie than to sit, for the temperature rises roughly 18°F for every 1 ft above the floor level; if one lies, heat is equally dispensed over the entire body. When lying down one may wish to raise one's feet against the wall or ceiling.

The expanded hot air in the sauna contains proportionately less oxygen than the denser atmosphere outside. Bathers sometimes experience faintness unless the air is changed regularly. An amount of fresh air enters each time the door is opened; this is insufficient, however. Normally two adjustable ventilators are built into the walls. One, the air inlet, is usually placed low near the stove. Fresh air should be drawn from outside and not from adjoining rooms where odors can be present.

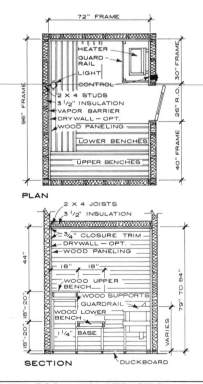

PLAN

SECTION

SAUNA ROOM CONSTRUCTION

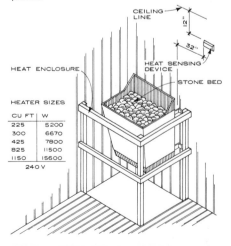

HEATER SIZES	
CU FT	W
225	5200
300	6670
425	7800
825	11500
1150	15600
240 V	

STOVE AND THERMOSTAT LOCATION

Jerry Graham; CTA Architects Engineers; Billings, Montana

13 SPECIAL PURPOSE ROOMS

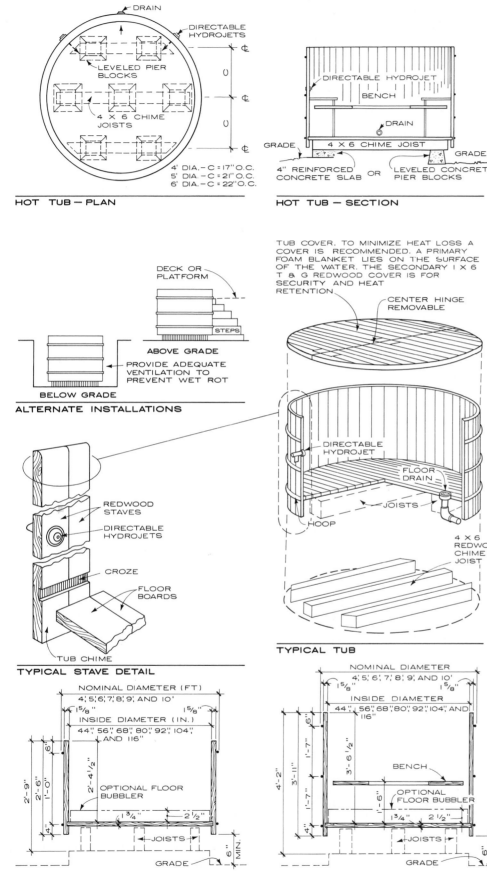

HOT TUB – PLAN

4' DIA.– C = 17" O.C.
5' DIA.– C = 21" O.C.
6' DIA.– C = 22" O.C.

HOT TUB – SECTION

ALTERNATE INSTALLATIONS

ABOVE GRADE

PROVIDE ADEQUATE VENTILATION TO PREVENT WET ROT

BELOW GRADE

TYPICAL STAVE DETAIL

REDWOOD STAVES
DIRECTABLE HYDROJETS
CROZE
FLOOR BOARDS
TUB CHIME

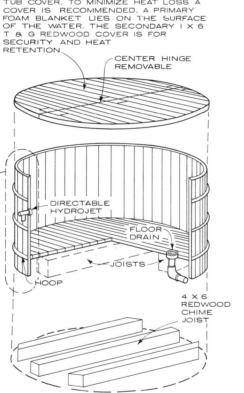

TUB COVER. TO MINIMIZE HEAT LOSS A COVER IS RECOMMENDED. A PRIMARY FOAM BLANKET LIES ON THE SURFACE OF THE WATER. THE SECONDARY 1 X 6 T & G REDWOOD COVER IS FOR SECURITY AND HEAT RETENTION

CENTER HINGE REMOVABLE

DIRECTABLE HYDROJET
FLOOR DRAIN
JOISTS
HOOP
4 X 6 REDWOOD CHIME JOIST

TYPICAL TUB

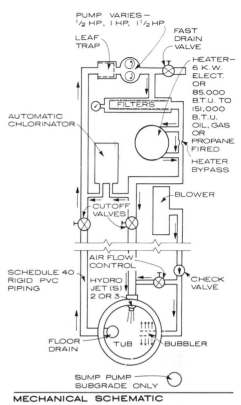

MECHANICAL SCHEMATIC

NOTES

Low profile tubs allow the bathers to sit directly on the floor with feet extended. Therapeutically, this style provides direct, close range hydromassage that comes from a floor bubbler. High profile tubs can accommodate more people per diameter foot and allows people to bath standing upright. Tub surfaces are normally left unsealed and will weather naturally to gray. Exterior can be stained or treated with silicone or oil resin to preserve the natural reddish finish. In high altitude, occasional repeated oil treatment is recommended. The size and sophistication of each tub is determined by capacity, budget, and preference for components. The most critical tub support components are the heater, filter system, chlorinator, and automatic cycling and temperature control system. Hydromassage jets are a significant part of every hot tub system. Many types of heaters are available: natural gas, electric, propane, and oil. Their sizes range from 50,000 to 175,000 Btu. All components should be approved and meet local codes and standards. Consult manufacturers for additional information. Tubs made of molded fiberglass with a smooth interior surface are generally referred to as SPAS. Their function and operation is similar to those of the hot tub.

LOW PROFILE TUB

STANDARD TUB

HOT TUB DIMENSIONS

	STANDARD TUB	LOW PROFILE TUB
NOM. DIA. (FT)	4 5 6 7 8 9 10	4 5 6 7 8 9 10
INSIDE DIA. (IN.)	44 56 68 80 92 104 116	44 56 68 80 92 104 116
NUMBER OF HOOPS	3 3 3 3 4 4	2 2 3 3 3 3
HOOP INTERVAL (IN.)	19 ± 1 IN.	12 ± 1 IN.
SEAT SECTIONS	2 3 4 5	SIT ON FLOOR

SEATING ARRANGEMENTS:

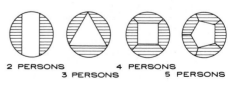

2 PERSONS
3 PERSONS
4 PERSONS
5 PERSONS

Jerry Graham; CTA Architects Engineers; Billings, Montana

SPECIAL PURPOSE ROOMS   **13**

ASEISMIC DESIGN

Earthquake forces result from random vertical and horizontal vibratory motions of the ground on which the structure rests. For the most part, the vertical forces are neglected by the building codes owing to the combination of safety factors inherent in the vertical framing members. Certain nonstructural elements, however, may require vertical considerations. The earthquake forces may vary in direction, intensity, and duration and are affected by geological conditions at and around the specific site.

Structural frames are composed of resisting elements that may be moment resisting, shear walls, or a combination. The configuration of a structure and its fundamental period (natural frequency) considerably affect the earthquake resistance of the structure. Symmetry in plan is generally very desirable. Unusually shaped plans result in high stress concentrations and must receive special attention during design. Structural elements must be tied together to make them respond to earthquake motions as a unit; otherwise structural separations may be required.

Most building materials are adaptable to use as resisting elements. Brittle materials must be avoided unless properly reinforced. Ductile materials are generally the most desirable. In high seismic risk areas, building codes commonly require all buildings higher than 160 ft to have "ductile" moment resisting frames.

Earthquake resistant buildings can be so designed that there will be minimal structural as well as nonstructural damage and maximum safety within reasonable economic limits. Nonstructural elements and building equipment often must be seismically considered to be an integral part of the building system. This is especially true for equipment found in essential facilities such as hospitals, etc. Equipment that generally must receive a seismic consideration includes emergency power supplies, other building utilities, critical or life support equipment, and general support equipment.

METHODS OF ASEISMIC DESIGN (OR QUALIFICATION)

DESIGN BY ANALYSIS

The static coefficient method of analysis is applicable to both the building structure and nonstructural elements such as partition walls and building equipment. The general formula for the static coefficient method is based on $F = CW$, where F is the seismic force, C the seismic coefficient (design acceleration value), and W the building or nonstructural element weight. Various modifiers can be included in the right hand portion of the equation (refer to the current Uniform Building Code—International Conference of Building Officials), such as zone values, frame characteristics, building importance, and soil structure interaction. The static coefficient method is applicable for simple building structures where a more complex method of analysis is not desirable or for nonstructural elements that only require anchorage to the main structure.

Dynamic analyses are a more complex form of aseismic design and generally yield more exact information. Two methods exist. The first and most common is the response spectrum technique. Various modes of vibration (and their associated periods) are determined with this technique. The second method is the most exact method of analysis, since it reviews the building systems with respect to the design earthquake time history (divided into small increments of time). This type of analysis results in predictions of building motion, building distortion, building forces, and absolute floor accelerations for every part of the building at every interval of the design earthquake motion. Dynamic analyses can be used to find resonance frequencies and determine seismic characteristics of fairly complex systems, in systems where the operation of nonstructural elements is required after but not during an earthquake, and in systems where the mode of failure of the building equipment is likely to be structural rather than operational.

The results of either type of dynamic analysis are only as good as the assumptions made in constructing the mathematical model for the analysis.

DESIGN BY SEISMIC TEST

Seismic simulation machines exist for the testing of structural systems and nonstructural elements. Seismic testing is the only viable method to test building equipment that must remain operational during and after an earthquake when the mode of failure is likely to be operational rather than structural. This includes equipment such as life support systems and communication equipment. Seismic shaking tables are generally designed to operate uniaxially, vector biaxially, or true independent biaxially.

DESIGN JUDGMENT

Great economic savings can be achieved by employing good design judgment. This method of seismic qualification is generally applicable to commodity types of nonstructural elements such as simple shelving. These items can generally be dealt with by adequate architectural detailing.

PRIOR EXPERIENCE

This method of seismic qualification is generally applicable to nonstructural elements. Once a particular element is qualified by any other method, that qualification will be applicable to subsequent installations that are similar in nature if adequate seismic qualification records are maintained.

COMBINED METHODS OF QUALIFICATION

This method of qualification is applicable to both structural systems and nonstructural elements. The common approach is to analyze portions of the system that are too large to test on existing seismic tables and to seismically test smaller portions of the system that are too complex to adequately model mathematically. Seismic tests can also be utilized to verify a previous analysis. Special seismic machines can be attached to existing structures to determine the system's natural period of vibration, which can then be compared with the previously calculated values. Combined methods of seismic qualification may often yield large economic advantages.

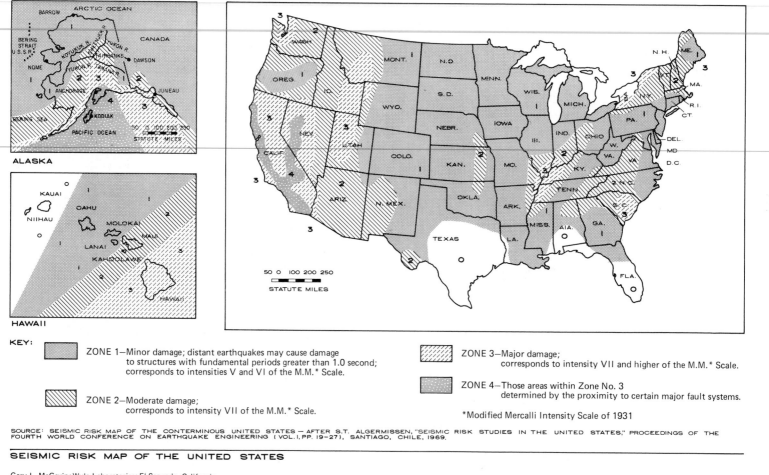

ALASKA

HAWAII

KEY:

ZONE 1—Minor damage; distant earthquakes may cause damage to structures with fundamental periods greater than 1.0 second; corresponds to intensities V and VI of the M.M.* Scale.

ZONE 2—Moderate damage; corresponds to intensity VII of the M.M.* Scale.

ZONE 3—Major damage; corresponds to intensity VII and higher of the M.M.* Scale.

ZONE 4—Those areas within Zone No. 3 determined by the proximity to certain major fault systems.

*Modified Mercalli Intensity Scale of 1931

SOURCE: SEISMIC RISK MAP OF THE CONTERMINOUS UNITED STATES — AFTER S.T. ALGERMISSEN, "SEISMIC RISK STUDIES IN THE UNITED STATES," PROCEEDINGS OF THE FOURTH WORLD CONFERENCE ON EARTHQUAKE ENGINEERING (VOL. I, PP. 19–27), SANTIAGO, CHILE, 1969.

SEISMIC RISK MAP OF THE UNITED STATES

Gary L. McGavin; Wyle Laboratories; El Segundo, California
Alfred M. Kemper, AIA; Kemper & Associates; Los Angeles, California
Harold P. King, C.E.C.; King, Benioff, Steinmann, King; Sherman Oaks, California

13 SEISMIC DESIGN

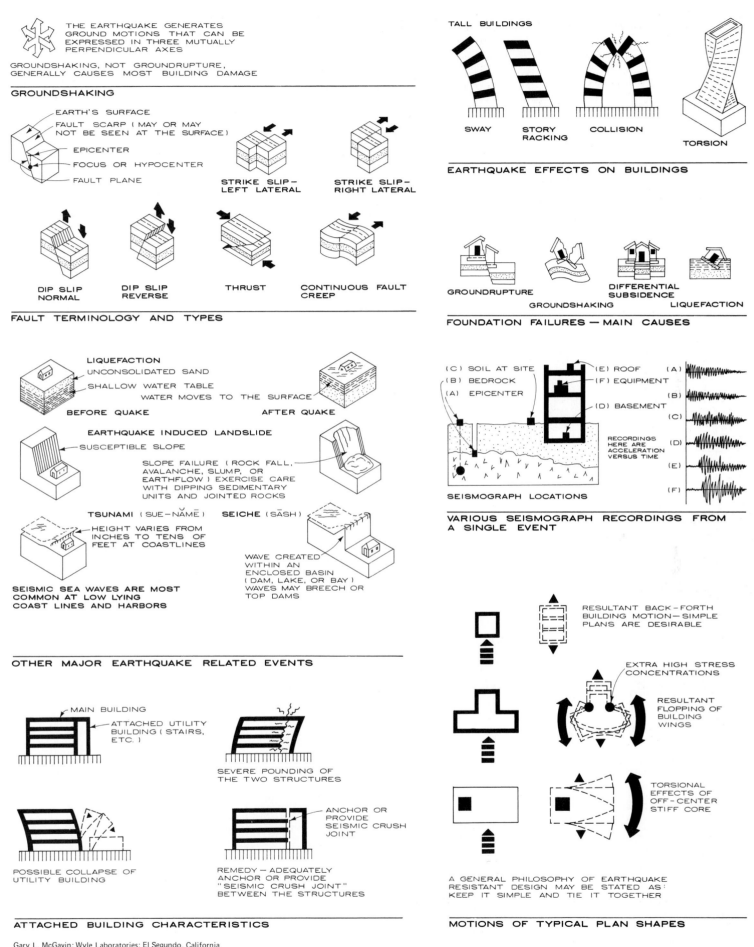

THE EARTHQUAKE GENERATES GROUND MOTIONS THAT CAN BE EXPRESSED IN THREE MUTUALLY PERPENDICULAR AXES

GROUNDSHAKING, NOT GROUNDRUPTURE, GENERALLY CAUSES MOST BUILDING DAMAGE

GROUNDSHAKING

EARTH'S SURFACE

FAULT SCARP (MAY OR MAY NOT BE SEEN AT THE SURFACE)

EPICENTER

FOCUS OR HYPOCENTER

FAULT PLANE

STRIKE SLIP — LEFT LATERAL

STRIKE SLIP — RIGHT LATERAL

DIP SLIP NORMAL

DIP SLIP REVERSE

THRUST

CONTINUOUS FAULT CREEP

FAULT TERMINOLOGY AND TYPES

LIQUEFACTION

UNCONSOLIDATED SAND

SHALLOW WATER TABLE

WATER MOVES TO THE SURFACE

BEFORE QUAKE

AFTER QUAKE

EARTHQUAKE INDUCED LANDSLIDE

SUSCEPTIBLE SLOPE

SLOPE FAILURE (ROCK FALL, AVALANCHE, SLUMP, OR EARTHFLOW) EXERCISE CARE WITH DIPPING SEDIMENTARY UNITS AND JOINTED ROCKS

TSUNAMI (SUE — NAME)

SEICHE (SĀSH)

HEIGHT VARIES FROM INCHES TO TENS OF FEET AT COASTLINES

WAVE CREATED WITHIN AN ENCLOSED BASIN (DAM, LAKE, OR BAY) WAVES MAY BREECH OR TOP DAMS

SEISMIC SEA WAVES ARE MOST COMMON AT LOW LYING COAST LINES AND HARBORS

OTHER MAJOR EARTHQUAKE RELATED EVENTS

MAIN BUILDING

ATTACHED UTILITY BUILDING (STAIRS, ETC.)

SEVERE POUNDING OF THE TWO STRUCTURES

POSSIBLE COLLAPSE OF UTILITY BUILDING

ANCHOR OR PROVIDE SEISMIC CRUSH JOINT

REMEDY — ADEQUATELY ANCHOR OR PROVIDE "SEISMIC CRUSH JOINT" BETWEEN THE STRUCTURES

ATTACHED BUILDING CHARACTERISTICS

TALL BUILDINGS

SWAY

STORY RACKING

COLLISION

TORSION

EARTHQUAKE EFFECTS ON BUILDINGS

GROUNDRUPTURE

GROUNDSHAKING

DIFFERENTIAL SUBSIDENCE

LIQUEFACTION

FOUNDATION FAILURES — MAIN CAUSES

(C) SOIL AT SITE

(B) BEDROCK

(A) EPICENTER

(E) ROOF

(F) EQUIPMENT

(D) BASEMENT

RECORDINGS HERE ARE ACCELERATION VERSUS TIME

(A)

(B)

(C)

(D)

(E)

(F)

SEISMOGRAPH LOCATIONS

VARIOUS SEISMOGRAPH RECORDINGS FROM A SINGLE EVENT

RESULTANT BACK — FORTH BUILDING MOTION — SIMPLE PLANS ARE DESIRABLE

EXTRA HIGH STRESS CONCENTRATIONS

RESULTANT FLOPPING OF BUILDING WINGS

TORSIONAL EFFECTS OF OFF — CENTER STIFF CORE

A GENERAL PHILOSOPHY OF EARTHQUAKE RESISTANT DESIGN MAY BE STATED AS: KEEP IT SIMPLE AND TIE IT TOGETHER

MOTIONS OF TYPICAL PLAN SHAPES

Gary L. McGavin; Wyle Laboratories; El Segundo, California

Alfred M. Kemper, AIA; Kemper & Associates; Los Angeles, California

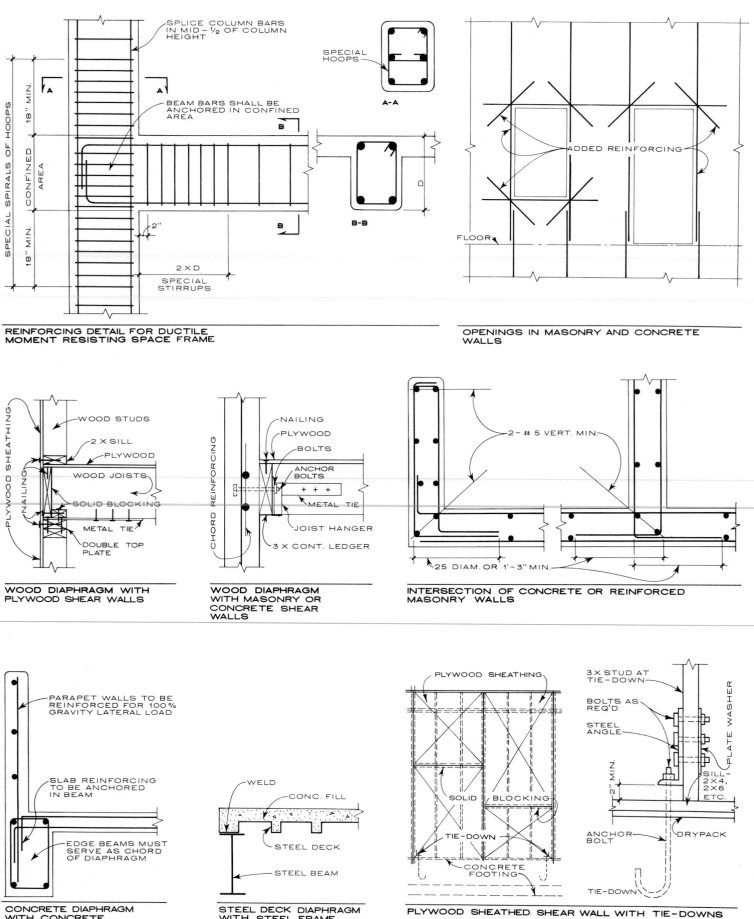

SPLICE COLUMN BARS IN MID – ½ OF COLUMN HEIGHT

SPECIAL HOOPS

A-A

BEAM BARS SHALL BE ANCHORED IN CONFINED AREA

SPECIAL SPIRALS OF HOOPS

18" MIN. CONFINED AREA

18" MIN.

2"

2 × D

SPECIAL STIRRUPS

B-B

D

REINFORCING DETAIL FOR DUCTILE MOMENT RESISTING SPACE FRAME

ADDED REINFORCING

FLOOR

OPENINGS IN MASONRY AND CONCRETE WALLS

PLYWOOD SHEATHING
WOOD STUDS
2 × SILL
PLYWOOD
WOOD JOISTS
NAILING
SOLID BLOCKING
METAL TIE
DOUBLE TOP PLATE

WOOD DIAPHRAGM WITH PLYWOOD SHEAR WALLS

CHORD REINFORCING
NAILING
PLYWOOD
BOLTS
ANCHOR BOLTS
METAL TIE
JOIST HANGER
3 × CONT. LEDGER

WOOD DIAPHRAGM WITH MASONRY OR CONCRETE SHEAR WALLS

2 – # 5 VERT. MIN.

25 DIAM. OR 1'-3" MIN.

INTERSECTION OF CONCRETE OR REINFORCED MASONRY WALLS

PARAPET WALLS TO BE REINFORCED FOR 100% GRAVITY LATERAL LOAD

SLAB REINFORCING TO BE ANCHORED IN BEAM

EDGE BEAMS MUST SERVE AS CHORD OF DIAPHRAGM

CONCRETE DIAPHRAGM WITH CONCRETE FRAME

WELD
CONC. FILL
STEEL DECK
STEEL BEAM

STEEL DECK DIAPHRAGM WITH STEEL FRAME

PLYWOOD SHEATHING
SOLID BLOCKING
TIE-DOWN
CONCRETE FOOTING

3 × STUD AT TIE-DOWN
BOLTS AS REQ'D
STEEL ANGLE
PLATE WASHER
SILL – 2×4, 2×6 ETC.
2" MIN.
ANCHOR BOLT
DRYPACK
TIE-DOWN

PLYWOOD SHEATHED SHEAR WALL WITH TIE-DOWNS

Harold P. King, CEC; King, Benioff, Steinmann, King; Sherman Oaks, California

13 **SEISMIC DESIGN**

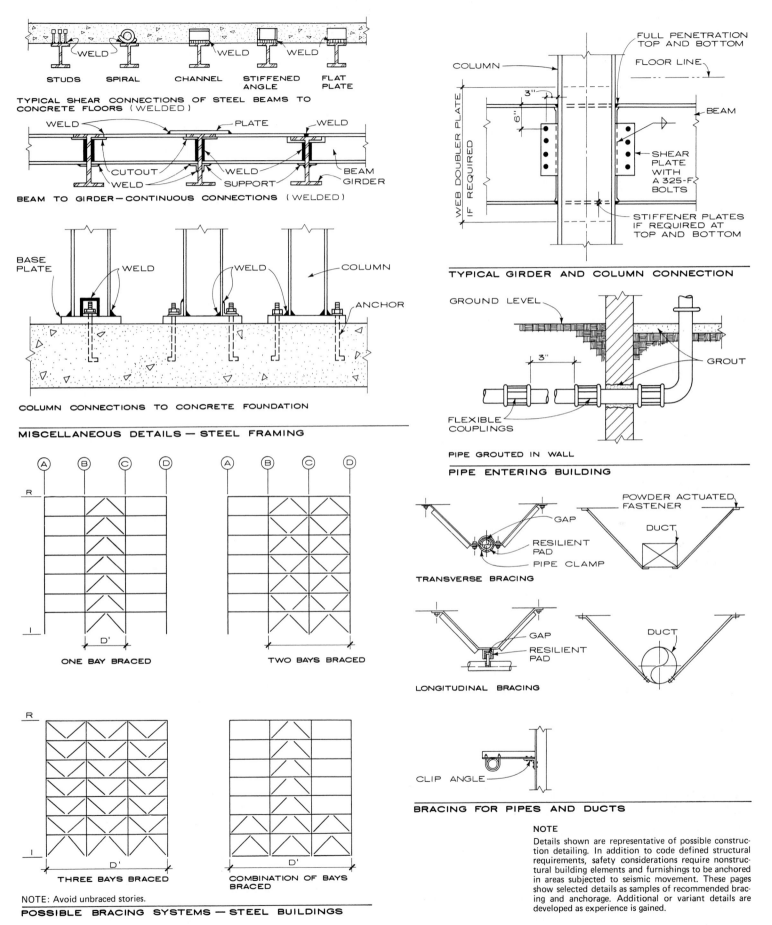

TYPICAL SHEAR CONNECTIONS OF STEEL BEAMS TO CONCRETE FLOORS (WELDED)

STUDS SPIRAL CHANNEL STIFFENED ANGLE FLAT PLATE

WELD

BEAM TO GIRDER — CONTINUOUS CONNECTIONS (WELDED)

WELD PLATE WELD CUTOUT WELD SUPPORT WELD BEAM GIRDER

COLUMN CONNECTIONS TO CONCRETE FOUNDATION

BASE PLATE WELD WELD COLUMN ANCHOR

MISCELLANEOUS DETAILS — STEEL FRAMING

ONE BAY BRACED

TWO BAYS BRACED

THREE BAYS BRACED

COMBINATION OF BAYS BRACED

NOTE: Avoid unbraced stories.

POSSIBLE BRACING SYSTEMS — STEEL BUILDINGS

TYPICAL GIRDER AND COLUMN CONNECTION

COLUMN FULL PENETRATION TOP AND BOTTOM FLOOR LINE BEAM SHEAR PLATE WITH A 325-F BOLTS WEB DOUBLER PLATE IF REQUIRED STIFFENER PLATES IF REQUIRED AT TOP AND BOTTOM

PIPE ENTERING BUILDING

GROUND LEVEL GROUT FLEXIBLE COUPLINGS

PIPE GROUTED IN WALL

TRANSVERSE BRACING

GAP RESILIENT PAD PIPE CLAMP POWDER ACTUATED FASTENER DUCT

LONGITUDINAL BRACING

GAP RESILIENT PAD DUCT

CLIP ANGLE

BRACING FOR PIPES AND DUCTS

NOTE

Details shown are representative of possible construction detailing. In addition to code defined structural requirements, safety considerations require nonstructural building elements and furnishings to be anchored in areas subjected to seismic movement. These pages show selected details as samples of recommended bracing and anchorage. Additional or variant details are developed as experience is gained.

Gary L. McGavin; Wyle Laboratories; El Segundo, California

Alfred M. Kemper, AIA; Kemper & Associates; Los Angeles, California

SEISMIC DESIGN 13

BUILDING TYPES AND WIDTHS

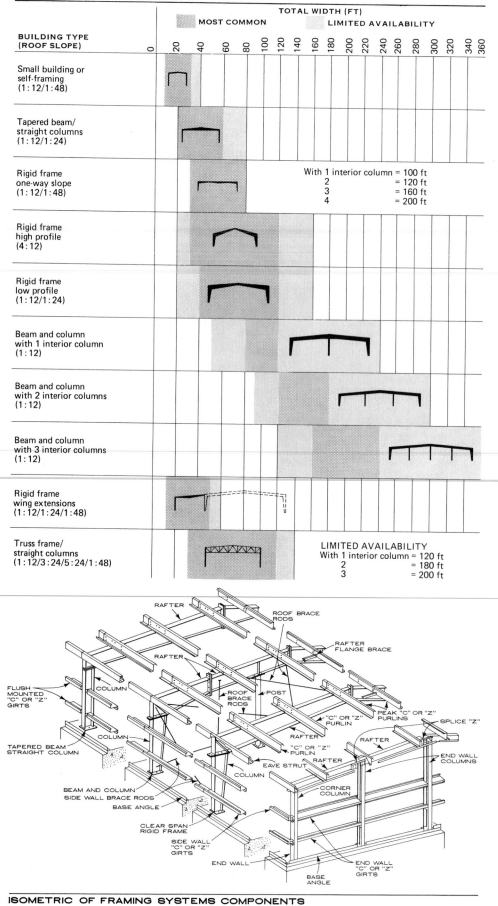

TOTAL WIDTH (FT)

MOST COMMON   LIMITED AVAILABILITY

BUILDING TYPE (ROOF SLOPE)

0 20 40 60 80 100 120 140 160 180 200 220 240 260 280 300 320 340 360

Small building or self-framing (1:12/1:48)

Tapered beam/ straight columns (1:12/1:24)

Rigid frame one-way slope (1:12/1:48)

With 1 interior column = 100 ft
2 = 120 ft
3 = 160 ft
4 = 200 ft

Rigid frame high profile (4:12)

Rigid frame low profile (1:12/1:24)

Beam and column with 1 interior column (1:12)

Beam and column with 2 interior columns (1:12)

Beam and column with 3 interior columns (1:12)

Rigid frame wing extensions (1:12/1:24/1:48)

Truss frame/ straight columns (1:12/3:24/5:24/1:48)

LIMITED AVAILABILITY
With 1 interior column = 120 ft
2 = 180 ft
3 = 200 ft

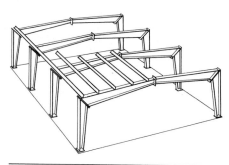

RIGID FRAME

NOTES

Preengineered metal buildings are available in standard framing sizes and types from a variety of manufacturers as proprietary products. The table illustrates the most commonly available systems. Many manufacturers offer these framing systems in widths greater than those shown, as well as offering other options aimed at filling the customer's needs. Regional availability should be checked. Use table for preliminary design only.

1. BAY SPACINGS: Range from 18 to 30 ft, with 20 to 25 being the most common. Wider bays, up to 60 ft, may be offered with joist systems.
2. WIDTH: Building dimension measured from outside surface of girts. Inside clearance varies.
3. EAVE HEIGHT: Distance from bottom to column to top of eave strut. Nominal 2 ft increments varying from 10 ft to 30 ft.
4. ROOF LIVE LOAD: Loads, including snow load, exerted on a roof except dead, wind, and lateral loads. Most systems commonly available in 12, 20, 30, or 40 psf.
5. DEAD LOAD: The weight of all permanent construction such as floor and roof framing and covering materials is building weight or dead load.
6. COLLATERAL LOADS: Additional dead loads other than the metal building framing, such as sprinklers, mechanical and electrical systems, and ceilings. Most systems commonly available in 15, 20, or 25 psf.
7. WIND LOAD: Load caused by the wind blowing from any horizontal direction. Most systems commonly available in 15, 20, or 25 psf.
8. SEISMIC LOAD: Assumed lateral load acting in any horizontal direction on the structural system because of the action of earthquakes. Individual design required.
9. AUXILIARY LOADS: Specified dynamic live loads other than the basic design loads which the building must safely withstand, such as cranes, materials handling systems, and impact loads. Individual design required.

The user should verify whether the manufacturer's standard practice meets or exceeds established engineering principles, local practice, or applicable building codes.

ISOMETRIC OF FRAMING SYSTEMS COMPONENTS

RAFTER
ROOF BRACE RODS
RAFTER FLANGE BRACE
FLUSH MOUNTED "C" OR "Z" GIRTS
COLUMN
ROOF BRACE RODS
POST
PEAK "C" OR "Z" PURLINS
"C" OR "Z" PURLIN
SPLICE "Z"
COLUMN
TAPERED BEAM STRAIGHT COLUMN
RAFTER
"C" OR "Z" PURLIN
RAFTER
EAVE STRUT
END WALL COLUMNS
COLUMN
CORNER COLUMN
BEAM AND COLUMN SIDE WALL BRACE RODS
BASE ANGLE
CLEAR SPAN RIGID FRAME
SIDE WALL "C" OR "Z" GIRTS
END WALL
END WALL "C" OR "Z" GIRTS
BASE ANGLE

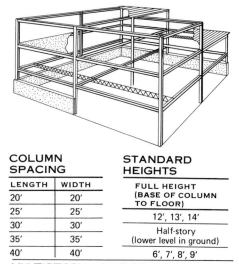

COLUMN SPACING

LENGTH	WIDTH
20'	20'
25'	25'
30'	30'
35'	35'
40'	40'

STANDARD HEIGHTS

FULL HEIGHT (BASE OF COLUMN TO FLOOR)
12', 13', 14'
Half-story (lower level in ground)
6', 7', 8', 9'

MULTISTORY LOWRISE
(LIMITED AVAILABILITY)

Robert P. Burns, AIA, David Hayes; Robert Burns & Associates; Riverside, Iowa

CHAPTER 14 CONVEYING SYSTEMS

GENERAL

An elevator system with its hoistway, machine room, and waiting lobbies is a major element in a building and requires special design consideration. Preengineered or custom-made elevator systems can be constructed to meet virtually all vertical transportation needs for passenger, freight, or service.

In all cases, design of an elevator system must be carefully considered throughout all stages of the building design process. During initial stages, the elevator handling capacity and quality of service desired determines the size, number, type, and location of elevator systems. Proper selection depends on type of tenancy, number of occupants, and the building design (number of floors, floor heights, building circulation, etc.). Elevator ARRANGEMENT locates the elevator within the building plan to provide efficient and accessible service. Each elevator system, once selected, requires OPERATIONAL SPACES, hoistway and machine room, and PASSENGER SPACES, lobby, and elevator car.

Proper planning and contact with representatives of the elevator industry and local code officials are essential to each of these design areas.

NOTE: WHERE A HOISTWAY EXTENDS INTO THE TOP FLOOR OF A BUILDING, FIRE RESISTIVE HOISTWAY OR MACHINERY SPACE ENCLOSURES, AS REQUIRED, SHALL BE CARRIED TO THE UNDERSIDE OF THE ROOF IF THE ROOF IS OF FIRE RESISTIVE CONSTRUCTION, AND AT LEAST 3 FT. ABOVE THE TOP SURFACE OF A FIRE NON-RESISTIVE ROOF

The two most common systems, the HYDRAULIC ELEVATOR and the ELECTRIC ELEVATOR, are shown in the two diagrams on this page. The systems are distinguished mainly by their hoisting mechanisms.

The HYDRAULIC ELEVATOR uses a hydraulic driving machine to raise and lower the elevator car and its load. A hydraulic driving machine is one in which the energy is applied by means of a liquid under pressure in a cylinder equipped with a plunger or piston. The car and driving machine are supported at the pit floor (hoistway base). Lower speeds and the piston length restrict the use of this system to approximately 60 ft. It generally requires the least initial installation expense, but more power is used during operation because of the greater loads imposed on the driving machine.

An ELECTRIC ELEVATOR is a power elevator where the energy is applied by means of an electric driving machine. In the electric driving machine the energy is applied by an electric motor. It includes the motor, brake, and the driving sheave or drum together with its connecting gearing, belt, or chain, if any. High speeds and virtually limitless rise allow this elevator to serve highrise, medium-rise, and lowrise buildings.

MACHINE ROOM (ELECTRIC ELEVATOR)

Normally located directly over the top of the hoistway —it could also be below at side or rear—the machine room is designed to contain elevator hoisting machine and control equipment. Adequate ventilation, sound-proofing, and structural support for the elevator must be considered.

ELEVATOR CAR

Guided by vertical guide rails, the elevator car conveys passenger or freight between floors. It consists of a car constructed within a supporting platform and frame. Design of the car focuses on the finished ceiling, walls, floor, and doors with lighting, ventilation, and elevator signal equipment.

The car of an hydraulic elevator system is supported by a piston or cylinder.

The car of an electric system is suspended by wire ropes.

HOISTWAY

The hoistway is a shaftway for the travel of one or more elevators. It includes the pit and terminates at the underside of the overhang machinery space floor or grating, or at the underside of the roof where the hoistway does not penetrate the roof. Access to the elevator car and hoistway is normally through hoistway doors located at each floor serviced by the elevator system. Hoistway design is determined by the characteristics of the elevator system selected and by requirements of the applicable code for fire separation, ventilation, soundproofing, or nonstructural elements.

LOBBY

Elevator waiting areas are designed to allow free circulation of passengers, rapid access to elevator cars, and clear visibility of elevator signals.

MACHINE ROOM (HYDRAULIC ELEVATOR)

Normally located near the base of the hoistway, the machine room contains hydraulic equipment and controls. Provisions of adequate ventilation and sound-proofing must be considered.

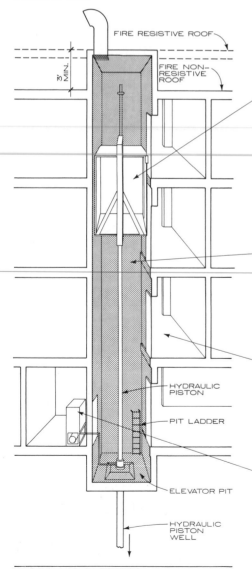

FIRE RESISTIVE ROOF

FIRE NON-RESISTIVE ROOF

3' MIN.

HYDRAULIC PISTON

PIT LADDER

ELEVATOR PIT

HYDRAULIC PISTON WELL

HYDRAULIC ELEVATOR

Alexander Keyes; Darrel Rippeteau, Architect; Washington, D.C.

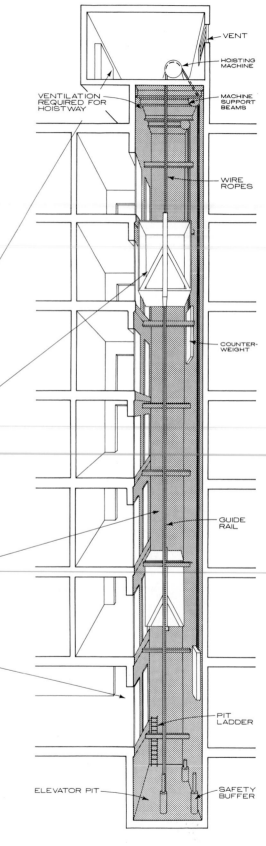

VENT

HOISTING MACHINE

MACHINE SUPPORT BEAMS

VENTILATION REQUIRED FOR HOISTWAY

WIRE ROPES

COUNTER-WEIGHT

GUIDE RAIL

PIT LADDER

ELEVATOR PIT

SAFETY BUFFER

ELECTRIC ELEVATOR

GENERAL NOTES

Lowrise buildings may use either the hydraulic or the electric elevator systems. Elevator selection, arrangement, and design of lobby and cars are similar in both cases. The primary differences between the two systems are in their operational requirements. The hydraulic elevator system is described below; the electric elevator system on the next page.

The major architectural considerations of the hydraulic elevator are the machine room, normally located at the base, and the hoistway serving as a fire protected, ventilated passageway for the elevator car. Adequate structure must be provided at the base of the hoistway to bear the load of the elevator car and its supporting piston or cylinder.

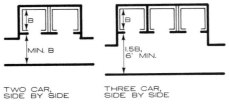

TWO CAR, SIDE BY SIDE

THREE CAR, SIDE BY SIDE

B = DEPTH OF CAR

NOTES

Certain guidelines lead to effective placement, grouping, and arrangement of elevators within a building. Elevators should be: (a) centrally located, (b) near the main entrance, and (c) easily accessible on all floors. If a building requires more than one elevator, they should be grouped, with possible exception of service elevators.

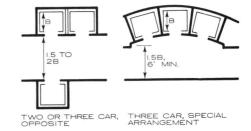

TWO OR THREE CAR, OPPOSITE

THREE CAR, SPECIAL ARRANGEMENT

Within each grouping, elevators should be arranged to minimize walking distance between cars. Sufficient lobby space must be provided to accommodate group movement.

ELEVATOR ARRANGEMENT, TWO AND THREE CARS (TYPICAL FOR LOWRISE APPLICATIONS)

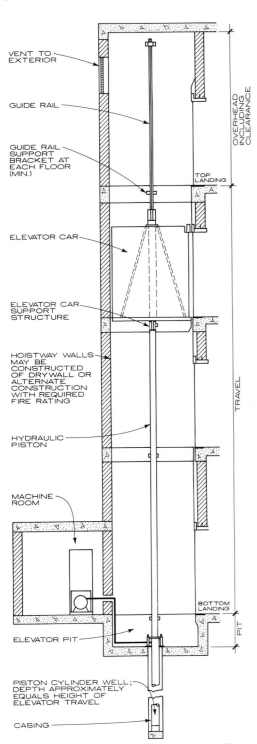

VENT TO EXTERIOR

GUIDE RAIL

GUIDE RAIL SUPPORT BRACKET AT EACH FLOOR (MIN.)

TOP LANDING

ELEVATOR CAR

ELEVATOR CAR SUPPORT STRUCTURE

HOISTWAY WALLS MAY BE CONSTRUCTED OF DRYWALL OR ALTERNATE CONSTRUCTION WITH REQUIRED FIRE RATING

HYDRAULIC PISTON

MACHINE ROOM

ELEVATOR PIT

PISTON CYLINDER WELL; DEPTH APPROXIMATELY EQUALS HEIGHT OF ELEVATOR TRAVEL

CASING

OVERHEAD INCLUDING CLEARANCE

TRAVEL

PIT

BOTTOM LANDING

HYDRAULIC ELEVATOR – SECTION

Alexander Keyes; Darrel Rippeteau, Architect; Washington, D.C.

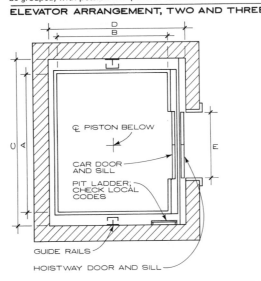

CL PISTON BELOW

CAR DOOR AND SILL

PIT LADDER; CHECK LOCAL CODES

GUIDE RAILS

HOISTWAY DOOR AND SILL

ELEVATOR CAR AND HOISTWAY

HYDRAULIC ELEVATOR DIMENSIONS

RATED LOAD	DIMENSIONS (FT-IN.)				
(LB)	A	B	C	D	E
1500	4-6	4-3	6-8	5-11	2-8
2000	5-8	4-3	7-4	5-11	3-0
2500	6-8	4-3	8-4	5-11	3-6
3000	6-8	4-7	8-4	6-3	3-6
3500	6-8	5-3	8-4	6-11	3-6
4000	7-8	5-3	9-4	6-11	4-0

Rated speeds are 75 to 200 fpm.

NOTES

Elevator car and hoistway dimensions of the preengineered units listed above are for reference purposes only. A broad selection of units is available. Representatives of the elevator industry should be contacted for the dimensions of specific systems.

Hoistway walls normally serve primarily as fireproof enclosures. Check local codes for required fire ratings. Guide rails extend from the pit floor to the underside of the overhead. When excessive floor heights are encountered consult the elevator supplier for special requirements.

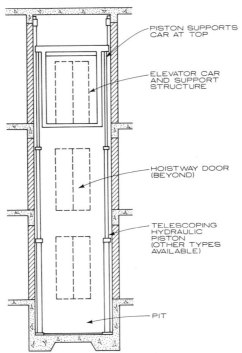

PISTON SUPPORTS CAR AT TOP

ELEVATOR CAR AND SUPPORT STRUCTURE

HOISTWAY DOOR (BEYOND)

TELESCOPING HYDRAULIC PISTON (OTHER TYPES AVAILABLE)

PIT

One type of holeless hydraulic elevator uses a telescoping hydraulic piston as the driving machine, eliminating the need for cylinder well excavation. This system is presently limited to a height of three stories or 21 ft 6 in. Other types of holeless hydraulic elevator units are also available using an inverted cylinder attached to the side of the elevator car.

HOLELESS HYDRAULIC ELEVATOR – SECTION

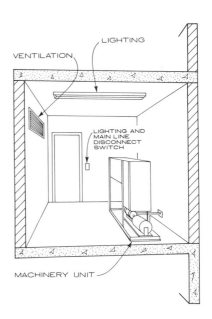

LIGHTING

VENTILATION

ELEVATOR CAR AND SUPPORT STRUCTURE

LIGHTING AND MAIN LINE DISCONNECT SWITCH

MACHINERY UNIT

The MACHINE ROOM of a hydraulic elevator system is usually located next to the hoistway at or near the bottom terminal landing. Consult with elevator manufacturers for required dimensions.

Machinery consists of a pump and motor drive unit, hydraulic fluid storage tank, and control panel. Adequate ventilation, lighting, and entrance access (usually 3 ft 6 in. x 7 ft) should be provided.

MACHINE ROOM

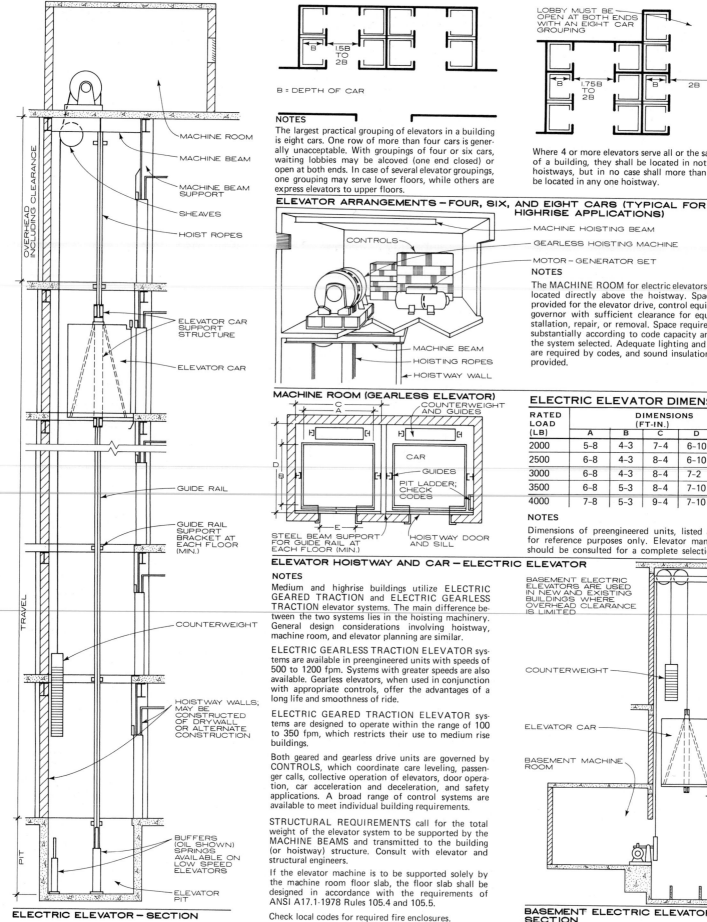

MACHINE ROOM

MACHINE BEAM

MACHINE BEAM SUPPORT

SHEAVES

HOIST ROPES

OVERHEAD INCLUDING CLEARANCE

ELEVATOR CAR SUPPORT STRUCTURE

ELEVATOR CAR

GUIDE RAIL

GUIDE RAIL SUPPORT BRACKET AT EACH FLOOR (MIN.)

TRAVEL

COUNTERWEIGHT

HOISTWAY WALLS; MAY BE CONSTRUCTED OF DRYWALL OR ALTERNATE CONSTRUCTION

BUFFERS (OIL SHOWN) SPRINGS AVAILABLE ON LOW SPEED ELEVATORS

ELEVATOR PIT

PIT

ELECTRIC ELEVATOR – SECTION

Alexander Keyes; Darrel Rippeteau, Architect; Washington, D.C.

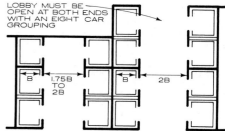

B = DEPTH OF CAR

1.5B TO 2B

B

NOTES

The largest practical grouping of elevators in a building is eight cars. One row of more than four cars is generally unacceptable. With groupings of four or six cars, waiting lobbies may be alcoved (one end closed) or open at both ends. In case of several elevator groupings, one grouping may serve lower floors, while others are express elevators to upper floors.

ELEVATOR ARRANGEMENTS – FOUR, SIX, AND EIGHT CARS (TYPICAL FOR HIGHRISE APPLICATIONS)

CONTROLS

MACHINE HOISTING BEAM

GEARLESS HOISTING MACHINE

MOTOR – GENERATOR SET

NOTES

The MACHINE ROOM for electric elevators is normally located directly above the hoistway. Space must be provided for the elevator drive, control equipment, and governor with sufficient clearance for equipment installation, repair, or removal. Space requirements vary substantially according to code capacity and speed of the system selected. Adequate lighting and ventilation are required by codes, and sound insulation should be provided.

MACHINE BEAM

HOISTING ROPES

HOISTWAY WALL

MACHINE ROOM (GEARLESS ELEVATOR)

COUNTERWEIGHT AND GUIDES

CAR

GUIDES

PIT LADDER; CHECK CODES

STEEL BEAM SUPPORT FOR GUIDE RAIL AT EACH FLOOR (MIN.)

HOISTWAY DOOR AND SILL

ELEVATOR HOISTWAY AND CAR – ELECTRIC ELEVATOR

NOTES

Medium and highrise buildings utilize ELECTRIC GEARED TRACTION and ELECTRIC GEARLESS TRACTION elevator systems. The main difference between the two systems lies in the hoisting machinery. General design considerations involving hoistway, machine room, and elevator planning are similar.

ELECTRIC GEARLESS TRACTION ELEVATOR systems are available in preengineered units with speeds of 500 to 1200 fpm. Systems with greater speeds are also available. Gearless elevators, when used in conjunction with appropriate controls, offer the advantages of a long life and smoothness of ride.

ELECTRIC GEARED TRACTION ELEVATOR systems are designed to operate within the range of 100 to 350 fpm, which restricts their use to medium rise buildings.

Both geared and gearless drive units are governed by CONTROLS, which coordinate care leveling, passenger calls, collective operation of elevators, door operation, car acceleration and deceleration, and safety applications. A broad range of control systems are available to meet individual building requirements.

STRUCTURAL REQUIREMENTS call for the total weight of the elevator system to be supported by the MACHINE BEAMS and transmitted to the building (or hoistway) structure. Consult with elevator and structural engineers.

If the elevator machine is to be supported solely by the machine room floor slab, the floor slab shall be designed in accordance with the requirements of ANSI A17.1-1978 Rules 105.4 and 105.5.

Check local codes for required fire enclosures.

LOBBY MUST BE OPEN AT BOTH ENDS WITH AN EIGHT CAR GROUPING

B   1.75B TO 2B   B   2B

Where 4 or more elevators serve all or the same portion of a building, they shall be located in not less than 2 hoistways, but in no case shall more than 4 elevators be located in any one hoistway.

ELECTRIC ELEVATOR DIMENSIONS

RATED LOAD (LB)	DIMENSIONS (FT-IN.)				
	A	B	C	D	E
2000	5-8	4-3	7-4	6-10	3-0
2500	6-8	4-3	8-4	6-10	3-6
3000	6-8	4-3	8-4	7-2	3-6
3500	6-8	5-3	8-4	7-10	3-6
4000	7-8	5-3	9-4	7-10	4-0

NOTES

Dimensions of preengineered units, listed above, are for reference purposes only. Elevator manufacturers should be consulted for a complete selection.

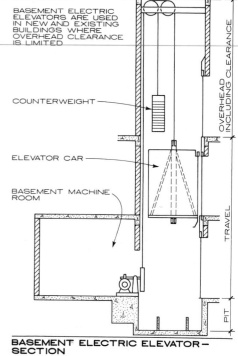

BASEMENT ELECTRIC ELEVATORS ARE USED IN NEW AND EXISTING BUILDINGS WHERE OVERHEAD CLEARANCE IS LIMITED

COUNTERWEIGHT

ELEVATOR CAR

BASEMENT MACHINE ROOM

OVERHEAD INCLUDING CLEARANCE

TRAVEL

PIT

BASEMENT ELECTRIC ELEVATOR – SECTION

GENERAL

ELEVATOR SELECTION depends on several factors: the building's physical characteristics, available elevator systems, and code regulations. The functions that relate these selection parameters and indicate the number, size, and type of elevators are, in most cases, complex and are based on the performance of the elevator systems. Representatives of the elevator industry or consulting elevator engineers should be contacted during the selection process to ensure that the most suitable elevator system is chosen.

PRIVATE RESIDENCES

Elevator selection for private residences can be simplified to a few parameters. By code they are limited in size, capacity, rise, and speed and are installed only in a private residence or a multiple dwelling as a means of access to a single private dwelling.

AVAILABLE ELEVATOR SYSTEMS are outlined on another page. The speed, capacity type, and controls of preengineered systems are generally limited to only a few options.

BUILDING POPULATION analysis involves the identification of the needs of prospective users. Relevant information includes the number of passengers expected to occupy the elevator in one trip and elevator service in a given time period, as well as the number of passengers expected and the possible need for a wheelchair.

BUILDING CHARACTERISTICS affect elevator selection by establishing the building height (distance of elevator travel) and hoistway location. In private residences, the elevator may occupy a tier of closets, an exterior shaft, a room corner, or a stairwell.

ELEVATOR SELECTION

The accompanying diagram illustrates elevator selection parameters in the context of a hospital layout. Actual calculations relating these parameters are complex. Consultation with an elevator industry representative or consulting elevator engineer is recommended.

1. BUILDING HEIGHT: Floor-to-floor height and number of floors.
2. BUILDING POPULATION: Total number of building occupants and expected visitors and their expected distribution throughout the building.
3. BUILDING USE ANALYSIS: Location of offices, patient's rooms, service areas, and ancillary spaces conducive to mass assembly. Primary public circulation areas and primary staff circulation areas should be identified.
4. WAITING AREA: Peak loading and waiting time are two important concepts in providing the quality of elevator service expected by hospital visitors and staff. Different standards are applied according to building use. Consult an elevator engineer.
5. LOCATION OF MAJOR ENTRANCES
6. ELEVATOR SYSTEMS: A large selection of elevator capacities, speed, controls, and type are available. In this case, passenger and service elevators are shown. An elevator with a front and rear entrance serves as a passenger elevator during peak visiting hours. The wide variety of elevator alternatives should be discussed with an elevator engineer to select the system most suitable for each individual situation.

SERVICE REQUIREMENTS: Elevators must have sufficient capacity and speed to meet building service requirements. In this case, the elevator must accommodate a 24 x 76 in. ambulance type stretcher with attendants.

For patient service in hospitals, to accommodate beds with their attachments, use 5000 lb elevators; platforms 6 ft wide x 9 ft 6 in. deep, doors at least 4 ft wide (4 ft 6 in. width is preferred).

CODE AND REGULATIONS: Recommendations and code restrictions regarding handicapped access, fire safety, elevator controls, and so on, may affect elevator selection. Consult with an elevator industry representative or consulting elevator engineer. As a minimum the ANSI A17.1-1978 Safety Code for Elevators, Dumbwaiters, Escalators and Moving Walks should be complied with.

NOTE: Elevators should not be considered as emergency exits.

ELEVATOR SYSTEMS IN BUILDINGS OTHER THAN PRIVATE HOMES

Selection of elevator systems increases in complexity with the size and complexity of the project. Even though the vertical transportation needs of lowrise residential and commercial projects may be simply met, all the parameters listed below should be considered and analyzed with a consulting elevator engineer to ensure proper selection.

BUILDING POPULATION

The elevator selection process must begin with a thorough analysis of how people will occupy the building.

1. TOTAL POPULATION AND DENSITY: The total number of occupants and visitors and their distribution by floors within a building.
2. PEAK LOADING: Periods when elevators carry the highest traffic loads. For example, peak loading in office buildings coincides with rush hours and/or lunch periods, while peak loading in hospitals may occur during visiting hours.
3. WAITING TIME: The length of time a passenger is expected to wait for the next elevator to arrive. These demands vary according to building use and building occupant expectations. A person willing to wait 50–70 sec in an apartment building may be willing to wait only 20–35 sec in an office building.
4. DEMAND FOR QUALITY: Sophistication of controls and elevator capacity may be varied to cater to the expected taste of passengers. Large elevator cars and the smooth, long life operation of a gearless elevator may convey an image of luxury even if a smaller elevator having a less sophisticated system would be technically sufficient.

BUILDING CHARACTERISTICS

Physical building characteristics are considered together with population characteristics to determine size, speed, type, and location of elevator systems.

1. HEIGHT: The distance of elevator travel (from lowest terminal to top terminal), number of floors, and floor height.
2. BUILDING USE ANALYSIS: Location of building entrance areas of heavy use such as cafeteria, restaurant, auditorium, and service areas must be identified. Typically, a building should be planned to ensure that no prospective passengers must walk more than 200 ft to reach an elevator.

ELEVATOR SYSTEMS AND REGULATIONS

The parameters previously described outline the environment in which the elevator operates. Local code regulations and ANSI A17.1-1978 requirements provide further elevator guidelines.

Available elevator systems are analyzed to ensure that suitable speed, capacity, controls, and number of cars are selected.

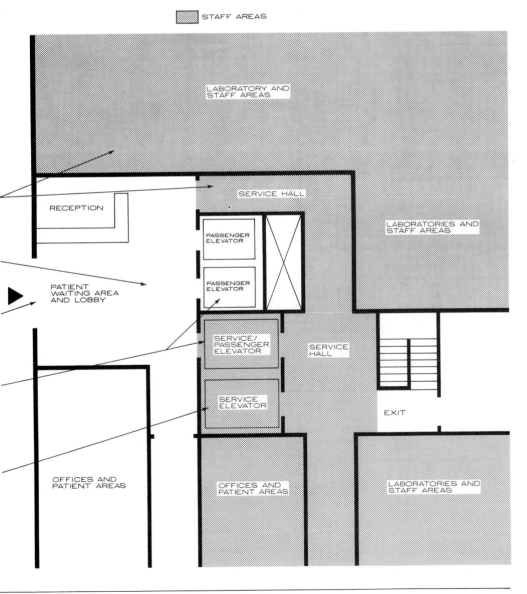

ELEVATOR SELECTION FACTORS — HOSPITAL

Alexander Keyes; Darrel Rippeteau, Architect; Washington, D.C.

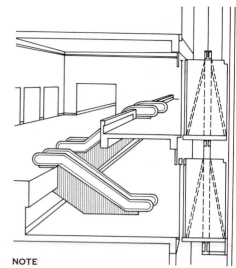

NOTE

In buildings with heavy populations double deck elevators permit an increase in handling capacity without increasing the number of elevators. Two cars in tandem operate simultaneously, one serving all floors. Escalators connect the two floors in 2-story lobbies.

DOUBLE DECK ELEVATOR

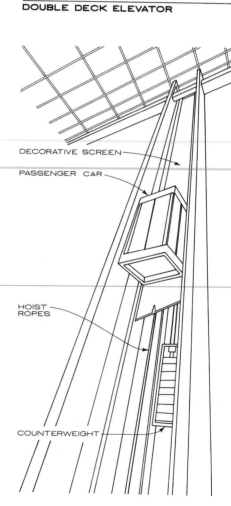

DECORATIVE SCREEN

PASSENGER CAR

HOIST ROPES

COUNTERWEIGHT

NOTE

Observation elevators travel outside of a hoistway or in a hoistway open on one side. Machinery is concealed or designed to be inconspicuous. These elevators serve as important visual elements, and specially designed glass cars make the ride a more significant experience.

OBSERVATION ELEVATOR

Alexander Keyes; Darrel Rippeteau, Architect; Washington, D.C.

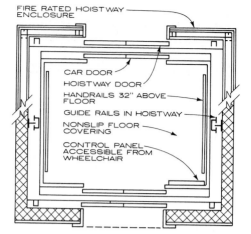

FIRE RATED HOISTWAY ENCLOSURE

CAR DOOR
HOISTWAY DOOR
HANDRAILS 32" ABOVE FLOOR
GUIDE RAILS IN HOISTWAY
NONSLIP FLOOR COVERING
CONTROL PANEL ACCESSIBLE FROM WHEELCHAIR

PLAN OF ELEVATOR CAR WITH REAR DOOR

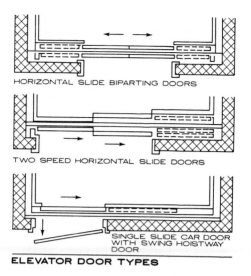

HORIZONTAL SLIDE BIPARTING DOORS

TWO SPEED HORIZONTAL SLIDE DOORS

SINGLE SLIDE CAR DOOR WITH SWING HOISTWAY DOOR

ELEVATOR DOOR TYPES

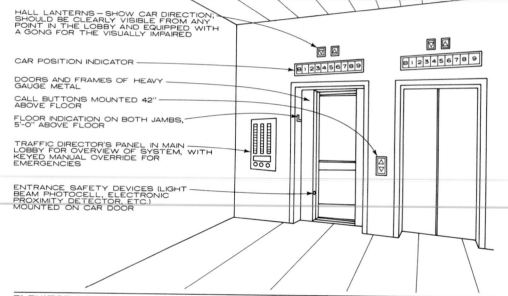

HALL LANTERNS—SHOW CAR DIRECTION; SHOULD BE CLEARLY VISIBLE FROM ANY POINT IN THE LOBBY AND EQUIPPED WITH A GONG FOR THE VISUALLY IMPAIRED

CAR POSITION INDICATOR

DOORS AND FRAMES OF HEAVY GAUGE METAL

CALL BUTTONS MOUNTED 42" ABOVE FLOOR

FLOOR INDICATION ON BOTH JAMBS, 5'-0" ABOVE FLOOR

TRAFFIC DIRECTOR'S PANEL IN MAIN LOBBY FOR OVERVIEW OF SYSTEM, WITH KEYED MANUAL OVERRIDE FOR EMERGENCIES

ENTRANCE SAFETY DEVICES (LIGHT BEAM PHOTOCELL, ELECTRONIC PROXIMITY DETECTOR, ETC.) MOUNTED ON CAR DOOR

ELEVATOR LOBBY

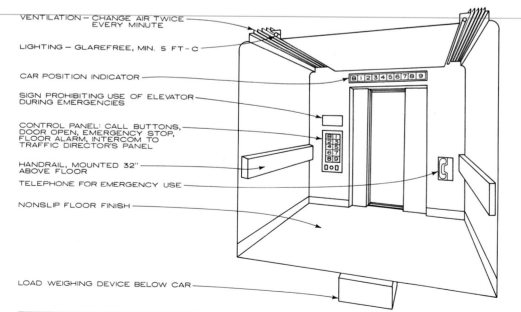

VENTILATION—CHANGE AIR TWICE EVERY MINUTE

LIGHTING—GLAREFREE, MIN. 5 FT-C

CAR POSITION INDICATOR

SIGN PROHIBITING USE OF ELEVATOR DURING EMERGENCIES

CONTROL PANEL: CALL BUTTONS, DOOR OPEN, EMERGENCY STOP, FLOOR ALARM, INTERCOM TO TRAFFIC DIRECTOR'S PANEL

HANDRAIL, MOUNTED 32" ABOVE FLOOR

TELEPHONE FOR EMERGENCY USE

NONSLIP FLOOR FINISH

LOAD WEIGHING DEVICE BELOW CAR

INTERIOR OF ELEVATOR CAR

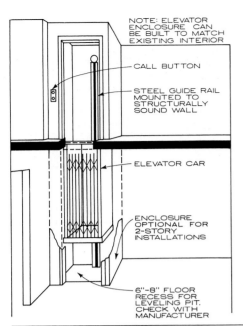

NOTE: ELEVATOR ENCLOSURE CAN BE BUILT TO MATCH EXISTING INTERIOR

CALL BUTTON

STEEL GUIDE RAIL MOUNTED TO STRUCTURALLY SOUND WALL

ELEVATOR CAR

ENCLOSURE OPTIONAL FOR 2-STORY INSTALLATIONS

6"-8" FLOOR RECESS FOR LEVELING PIT. CHECK WITH MANUFACTURER

RESIDENTIAL ELEVATOR

NOTE

Barrierfree residential elevators are typically package designed. Structures, both monorail cable driven types and twin screw drive systems, are self-supporting, anchored to the existing structure. Cars are assembled separately and mounted on platforms driven by remote power units. Open installations are permitted for 2-story applications. Recommended speed: 30 fpm.

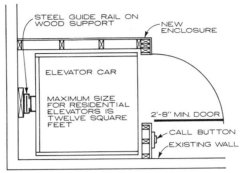

STEEL GUIDE RAIL ON WOOD SUPPORT

NEW ENCLOSURE

ELEVATOR CAR

MAXIMUM SIZE FOR RESIDENTIAL ELEVATORS IS TWELVE SQUARE FEET

2'-8" MIN. DOOR

CALL BUTTON

EXISTING WALL

PLAN—ACCOMMODATES STANDARD WHEELCHAIR

EXISTING STRUCTURE

STEEL GUIDE RAIL (CONTAINS ROPES OR CHAINS)

SECOND FLOOR

ELEVATOR ENCLOSURE

ELEVATOR CAR

PLATFORM FOR CAR

FIRST FLOOR

PIT

NOTE: DOTTED LINES INDICATE OPTIONAL LOCATIONS OF POWER UNIT

CONTROLLER

CONTROLLER DISCONNECT SWITCH

REMOTE POWER UNIT

BASEMENT

SECTION

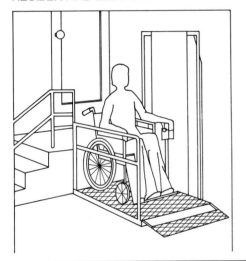

WHEELCHAIR LIFT

NOTE

Wheelchair lifts are suitable for retrofits on nonbarrier-free buildings. Bridges are available from manufacturers for installation over chairs. Potential hazards, however, include slipping on platforms, jolting that might result in loss of balance, failure that causes the platform to drop, and entrapment under the platform.

Lifts operate on standard household current and are suitable for interior and exterior applications. Maximum lifting height: 7 ft 9 in.

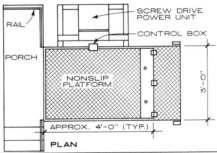

RAIL

PORCH

SCREW DRIVE POWER UNIT

CONTROL BOX

NONSLIP PLATFORM

3'-0"

APPROX. 4'-0" (TYP.)

PLAN

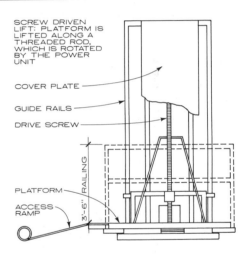

SCREW DRIVEN LIFT: PLATFORM IS LIFTED ALONG A THREADED ROD, WHICH IS ROTATED BY THE POWER UNIT

COVER PLATE

GUIDE RAILS

DRIVE SCREW

PLATFORM

ACCESS RAMP

3'-6" RAILING

SIDE VIEW

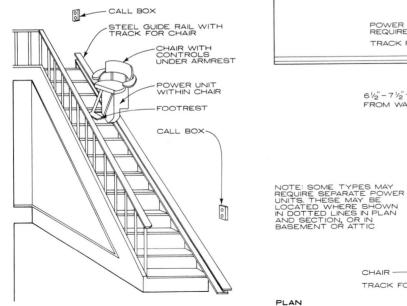

CALL BOX

STEEL GUIDE RAIL WITH TRACK FOR CHAIR

CHAIR WITH CONTROLS UNDER ARMREST

POWER UNIT WITHIN CHAIR

FOOTREST

CALL BOX

STAIR LIFT

POWER UNIT IF REQUIRED

TRACK FOR CHAIR

6½" – 7½" FROM WALL

NOTE: SOME TYPES MAY REQUIRE SEPARATE POWER UNITS. THESE MAY BE LOCATED WHERE SHOWN IN DOTTED LINES IN PLAN AND SECTION, OR IN BASEMENT OR ATTIC

CHAIR

TRACK FOR CHAIR

PLAN

NOTE

Stair lifts can be adapted to straight run and spiral stairs. Standard types run along a track fastened to the steps. Power units, when not contained in a housing under the chair, can be located as shown in section, or in basement or attic. Similar inclined wheelchair lifts are also available for installations down stairs. Recommended speed: 25 fpm. Capacity: 250–350 lb.

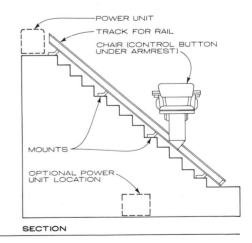

POWER UNIT

TRACK FOR RAIL

CHAIR (CONTROL BUTTON UNDER ARMREST)

MOUNTS

OPTIONAL POWER UNIT LOCATION

SECTION

Olga Barmine; Darrel Rippeteau, Architect; Washington, D.C.

ELEVATORS

14

Escalators are a very efficient form of vertical transportation for very heavy traffic where the number of floors served is limited, normally a maximum of five to six floors. Escalators are not usually accepted as a required exit.

Dimensions shown are general and will vary somewhat with the manufacturer. Consult manufacturers for structural support, electrical supply, and specific dimensional requirements.

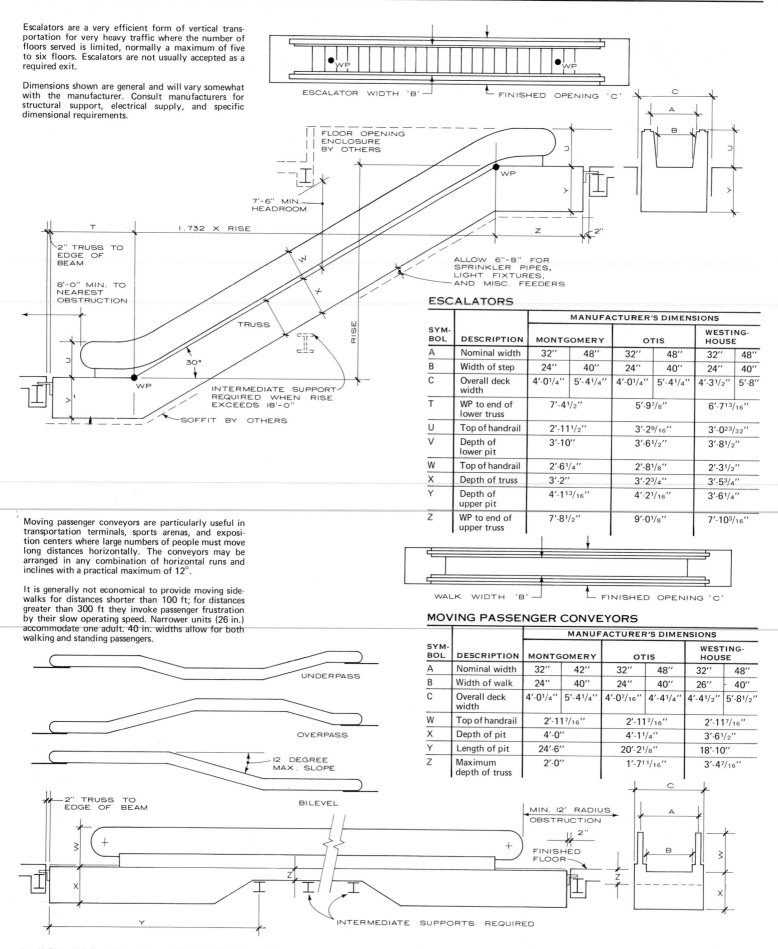

ESCALATORS

SYM-BOL	DESCRIPTION	MANUFACTURER'S DIMENSIONS					
		MONTGOMERY		OTIS		WESTING-HOUSE	
A	Nominal width	32″	48″	32″	48″	32″	48″
B	Width of step	24″	40″	24″	40″	24″	40″
C	Overall deck width	4'-0¼″	5'-4¼″	4'-0¼″	5'-4¼″	4'-3½″	5'-8″
T	WP to end of lower truss	7'-4½″		5'-9⅞″		6'-7¹³/₁₆″	
U	Top of handrail	2'-11½″		3'-2⁹/₁₆″		3'-0²³/₃₂″	
V	Depth of lower pit	3'-10″		3'-6½″		3'-8½″	
W	Top of handrail	2'-6¼″		2'-8⅛″		2'-3½″	
X	Depth of truss	3'-2″		3'-2¾″		3'-5¾″	
Y	Depth of upper pit	4'-1¹³/₁₆″		4'-2¹/₁₆″		3'-6¼″	
Z	WP to end of upper truss	7'-8½″		9'-0⅛″		7'-10³/₁₆″	

Moving passenger conveyors are particularly useful in transportation terminals, sports arenas, and exposition centers where large numbers of people must move long distances horizontally. The conveyors may be arranged in any combination of horizontal runs and inclines with a practical maximum of 12°.

It is generally not economical to provide moving sidewalks for distances shorter than 100 ft; for distances greater than 300 ft they invoke passenger frustration by their slow operating speed. Narrower units (26 in.) accommodate one adult. 40 in. widths allow for both walking and standing passengers.

MOVING PASSENGER CONVEYORS

SYM-BOL	DESCRIPTION	MANUFACTURER'S DIMENSIONS					
		MONTGOMERY		OTIS		WESTING-HOUSE	
A	Nominal width	32″	42″	32″	48″	32″	48″
B	Width of walk	24″	40″	24″	40″	26″	40″
C	Overall deck width	4'-0¼″	5'-4¼″	4'-0⁷/₁₆″	4'-4¼″	4'-4½″	5'-8½″
W	Top of handrail	2'-11⁷/₁₆″		2'-11⁷/₁₆″		2'-11⁷/₁₆″	
X	Depth of pit	4'-0″		4'-1¼″		3'-6½″	
Y	Length of pit	24'-6″		20'-2⅛″		18'-10″	
Z	Maximum depth of truss	2'-0″		1'-7¹¹/₁₆″		3'-4⁷/₁₆″	

Alan H. Rider, AIA; Daniel, Mann, Johnson & Mendenhall; Washington, D.C.

CHAPTER 15 MECHANICAL

BUSINESS, MERCANTILE, INDUSTRIAL OTHER THAN FOUNDRY, AND STORAGE

WATER CLOSETS	EMPLOYEES		LAVATORIES	EMPLOYEES
1	1–15		1	1–20
2	16–35		2	21–40
3	36–55		3	41–60
4	56–80		4	61–80
5	81–110		5	81–100
6	111–150		6	101–125
7	151–190		7	126–150
			8	151–175

One additional water closet for each 40 in excess of 190

One additional lavatory for each 30 in excess of 175

INDUSTRIAL, FOUNDRIES, AND STORAGE

WATER CLOSETS	EMPLOYEES		LAVATORIES	EMPLOYEES
1	1–10		1	1–8
2	11–25		2	9–16
3	26–50		3	17–30
4	51–80		4	31–45
5	81–125		5	46–65

One additional water closet for each 45 in excess of 125

One additional lavatory for each 25 in excess of 65

ASSEMBLY, OTHER THAN RELIGIOUS, AND SCHOOLS

WATER CLOSETS	OCCUPANTS	URINALS	MALE OCCUPANTS	LAVATORIES	OCCUPANTS
1	1–100	1	1–100	1	1–100
2	101–200	2	101–200	2	101–200
3	201–400	3	201–400	3	201–400
4	401–700	4	401–700	4	401–700
5	701–1100	5	701–1100	5	701–1100

One additional water closet for each 600 in excess of 1100

One additional urinal for each 300 in excess of 1100

One additional lavatory for each 1500 in excess of 1100. Such lavatories need not be supplied with hot water

ASSEMBLY, RELIGIOUS

One water closet and one lavatory.

ASSEMBLY, SCHOOL

For pupils' use:

1. Water closets for pupils; in elementary schools, 1 for each 100 males and 1 for each 35 females; in secondary schools, 1 for each 100 males and 1 for each 45 females.
2. One lavatory for each 50 pupils.
3. One urinal for each 30 male pupils.
4. One drinking fountain for each 150 pupils, but at least one on each floor having classrooms.

Where more than 5 persons are employed, provide fixtures as required for group C1 occupancy.

INSTITUTIONAL

(Persons whose movements are not limited.) Within each dwelling unit:

1. One kitchen sink.
2. One water closet.
3. One bathtub or shower.
4. One lavatory.

Where sleeping accommodations are arranged as individual rooms, provide the following for each six sleeping rooms:

1. One water closet.
2. One bathtub and shower.
3. One lavatory.

Where sleeping accommodations are arranged as a dormitory, provide the following for each 15 persons:

1. One water closet.
2. One bathtub or shower.
3. One lavatory.

INSTITUTIONAL, OTHER THAN HOSPITALS

(Persons whose movements are limited.) On each story:

1. Water closets: 1 for each 25 males and 1 for each 20 females.
2. One urinal for each 50 male occupants.
3. One lavatory for each 10 occupants.
4. One shower for each 10 occupants.
5. One drinking fountain for each 50 occupants.

Fixtures for employees the same as required for group C1 occupancy.

INSTITUTIONAL, HOSPITALS

For patients' use:

1. One water closet and one lavatory for each 10 patients.
2. One shower or bathtub for each 20 patients.
3. One drinking fountain or equivalent fixture for each 100 patients.

Fixtures for employees the same as required for group C1 occupancy.

INSTITUTIONAL, MENTAL HOSPITALS

For patients' use:

1. One water closet, one lavatory, and one shower or bathtub, for each 8 patients.
2. One drinking fountain or equivalent fixture for each 50 patients.

Fixtures for employees the same as required for group C1 occupancy.

INSTITUTIONAL, PENAL INSTITUTIONS

For inmate use:

1. One water closet and one lavatory in each cell.
2. One shower on each floor on which cells are located.
3. One water closet and one lavatory for inmate use available in each exercise area.

Lavatories for inmate use need not be supplied with hot water. Fixtures for employees the same as required for group C1 occupancy.

MISCELLANEOUS

Temporary toilet facilities shall be provided for employees engaged in the construction, alteration, repair, or demolition of buildings on the basis of 1 unit for each 30 persons.

PUBLIC BATHING OCCUPANCIES

Facilities for bathers at swimming pools shall consist of at least the following:

1. One water closet for each 40 females and 60 males.
2. One urinal for each 60 males.
3. One lavatory for each 40 females and 60 males.
4. One shower for each 40 females and 40 males. In schools such required showers shall equal one third the number of pupils in the largest class.

BUSINESS

Buildings used primarily for the transaction of business, with the handling of merchandise being incidental to the primary use.

MERCANTILE

Buildings used primarily for the display of merchandise and its sale to the public.

ADDITIONAL REQUIREMENTS

1. One drinking fountain or equivalent fixture for each 75 employees.
2. Urinals may be substituted for not more than one third of the required number of water closets when more than 35 males are employed.

INDUSTRIAL

Buildings used primarily for the manufacture or processing of products.

STORAGE

Buildings used primarily for the storage of or shelter for merchandise, vehicles, or animals.

ADDITIONAL REQUIREMENTS

1. One drinking fountain or equivalent fixture for each 75 employees.
2. Urinals provided where more than 10 males are employed: 1 for 11–29; 2 for 30–79; one additional urinal for each 80 in excess of 79.

ASSEMBLY

Buildings used primarily for the assembly for athletic, educational, religious, social, or similar purposes.

ADDITIONAL REQUIREMENT

One drinking fountain for each 1000 occupants, but at least one on each floor.

MULTIPLE DWELLINGS

Provide plumbing systems and furnish hot and cold water. Provide within each dwelling unit:

1. One kitchen sink.
2. One water closet.
3. One bathtub or shower.
4. One lavatory.

Sleeping accommodations—for each multiple of six sleeping room provide:

1. One water closet.
2. One bathtub or shower.
3. One lavatory.

Sleeping accommodations—dormitories for each multiple of 15 persons provide:

1. One water closet.
2. One bathtub or shower.
3. One lavatory.

Urinals may be substituted for not more than one third of the required number of water closets. Facilities for bathers at swimming pools shall consist of at least the following:

1. One water closet for each 40 females and 60 males.
2. One urinal for each 60 males.
3. One lavatory for each 60 females and 60 males.
4. One shower for each 40 females and 40 males.

GENERAL NOTES

1. Plumbing fixture requirements shown are based on New York State General Construction Code and Multiple Dwelling Code and can serve only as a guide. Consult codes in force in area of construction and state and federal agencies (Labor Department, General Services Administration, etc.) and comply with their requirements.
2. Plumbing fixture requirements are to be based on the maximum legal occupancy and not on the actual or anticipated occupancy.
3. Proportioning of toilet facilities between men and women is based on a 50-50 distribution. However, in certain cases conditions of occupancy may warrant additional facilities for men or women above the basic 50-50 distribution.

Sargent, Webster, Crenshaw & Folley, Architects, Engineers, Planners; Syracuse, New York

15 **PLUMBING**

DIMENSIONS OF STANDARD IRON SCREW PIPE (ASA SCHEDULE 40)

NOMINAL INTERNAL DIAMETER	1/8"	1/4"	3/8"	1/2"	3/4"	1"	1 1/4"	1 1/2"	2"	2 1/2"	3"	3 1/2"	4"	5"	6"	8"	10"	12"
ACTUAL INTERNAL DIAMETER	.269	.364	.493	.622	.824	1.049	1.38	1.61	2.067	2.469	3.068	3.548	4.026	5.047	6.065	7.981	10.02	12.00
ACTUAL EXTERNAL DIAMETER	.405	.540	.675	.840	1.05	1.315	1.66	1.90	2.375	2.875	3.50	4.00	4.50	5.563	6.625	8.625	10.75	12.75
INTERNAL AREA	.057	.104	.191	.304	.533	.864	1.496	2.036	3.355	4.788	7.393	9.886	12.73	20.00	28.89	50.02	78.85	113.09

DIAMETERS OF FITTINGS ACROSS OUTSIDE FACE

NOMINAL SIZE	1/8"	1/4"	3/8"	1/2"	3/4"	1"	1/4"	1/2"	2"	2 1/2"	3"	3 1/2"	4"	5"	6"	8"	10"	12"
MALLEABLE 150# SWP	11/16"	7/8"	1"	1 1/4"	1 1/2"	1 13/16"	2 3/16"	2 7/16"	3"	3 9/16"	4 5/16"	4 7/8"	5 7/16"	6 5/8"	7 13/16"			
MALLEABLE 300# SWP		15/16"	1 1/8"	1 3/8"	1 5/8"	1 15/16"	2 3/8"	2 11/16"	3 5/16"	3 7/8"	4 5/8"	5 1/4"	5 13/16"	7 1/16"	8 5/16"			
CAST IRON SCREW 125# SWP		15/16"	1 1/8"	1 3/8"	1 5/8"	1 15/16"	2 3/8"	2 11/16"	3 5/16"	3 7/8"	4 5/8"	5 1/4"	5 13/16"	7 1/16"	8 5/16"	10 5/8"	13 1/8"	15 1/2"
CAST IRON SCREW DRAINAGE							2 3/8"	2 11/16"	3 5/16"	3 7/8"	4 5/8"		5 13/16"	7 1/16"	8 5/16"	10 5/8"		
EXTERNAL DIAMETER OF SOIL PIPE XH									2 3/8"		3 1/2"		4 1/2"	5 1/2"	6 1/2"	8 5/8"	10 3/4"	12 3/4"
EXT. DIA. OF BELL ON SOIL PIPE & FITTING XH									3 15/16"		5 3/16"		6 3/16"	7 3/16"	8 3/16"	10 7/8"	13 1/8"	15 1/4"

Standard lengths of iron soil pipes = 5'–0" laying lengths

150# SWP malleable fittings are used on water and vent piping.

300# SWP malleable fittings are used for severe service.

125# SWP cast iron screw fittings are used for sprinkler and steam piping.

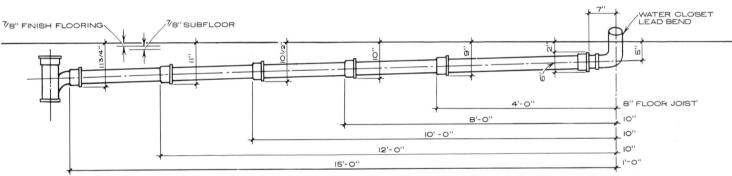

LENGTH OF RUN FROM WATER CLOSET FOR 4" C.I. SOIL LINE (INCLUDING BEND) IN DIFFERENT FLOOR THICKNESSES

DIMENSIONS OF INTERSECTIONS OF VENT WITH SOIL OR WASTE LINE

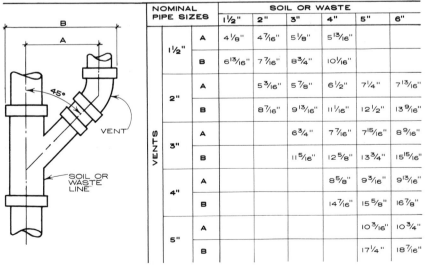

NOMINAL PIPE SIZES			SOIL OR WASTE					
			1 1/2"	2"	3"	4"	5"	6"
VENTS	1 1/2"	A	4 1/8"	4 7/16"	5 1/8"	5 13/16"		
		B	6 13/16"	7 7/16"	8 3/4"	10 1/16"		
	2"	A		5 3/16"	5 7/8"	6 1/2"	7 1/4"	7 13/16"
		B		8 7/16"	9 13/16"	11 1/16"	12 1/2"	13 9/16"
	3"	A			6 3/4"	7 7/16"	7 15/16"	8 9/16"
		B			11 5/16"	12 5/8"	13 3/4"	15 15/16"
	4"	A				8 5/8"	9 3/16"	9 13/16"
		B				14 7/16"	15 5/8"	16 7/8"
	5"	A					10 3/16"	10 3/4"
		B					17 1/4"	18 7/16"

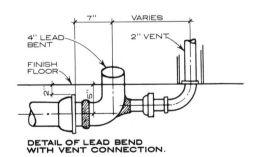

DETAIL OF LEAD BEND WITH VENT CONNECTION.

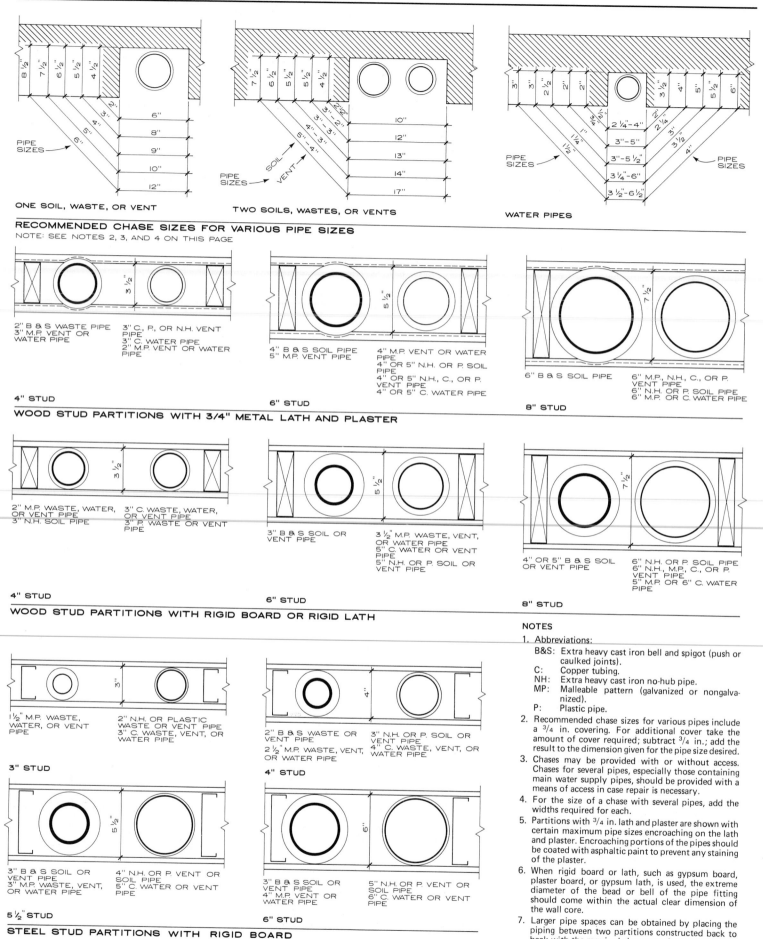

ONE SOIL, WASTE, OR VENT

TWO SOILS, WASTES, OR VENTS

WATER PIPES

RECOMMENDED CHASE SIZES FOR VARIOUS PIPE SIZES
NOTE: SEE NOTES 2, 3, AND 4 ON THIS PAGE

2" B & S WASTE PIPE
3" M.P. VENT OR
WATER PIPE

3" C., P., OR N.H. VENT
PIPE
3" C. WATER PIPE
2" M.P. VENT OR WATER
PIPE

4" STUD

4" B & S SOIL PIPE
5" M.P. VENT PIPE

4" M.P. VENT OR WATER
PIPE
4" OR 5" N.H. OR P. SOIL
PIPE
4" OR 5" N.H., C., OR P.
VENT PIPE
4" OR 5" C. WATER PIPE

6" STUD

6" B & S SOIL PIPE

6" M.P., N.H., C., OR P.
VENT PIPE
6" N.H. OR P. SOIL PIPE
6" M.P. OR C. WATER PIPE

8" STUD

WOOD STUD PARTITIONS WITH 3/4" METAL LATH AND PLASTER

2" M.P. WASTE, WATER,
OR VENT PIPE
3" N.H. SOIL PIPE

3" C. WASTE, WATER,
OR VENT PIPE
3" P. WASTE OR VENT
PIPE

4" STUD

3" B & S SOIL OR
VENT PIPE

3 1/2" M.P. WASTE, VENT,
OR WATER PIPE
5" C. WATER OR VENT
PIPE
5" N.H. OR P. SOIL OR
VENT PIPE

6" STUD

4" OR 5" B & S SOIL
OR VENT PIPE

6" N.H. OR P. SOIL PIPE
6" N.H., M.P., C., OR P.
VENT PIPE
5" M.P. OR 6" C. WATER
PIPE

8" STUD

WOOD STUD PARTITIONS WITH RIGID BOARD OR RIGID LATH

1 1/2" M.P. WASTE,
WATER, OR VENT
PIPE

2" N.H. OR PLASTIC
WASTE OR VENT PIPE
3" C. WASTE, VENT, OR
WATER PIPE

3" STUD

2" B & S WASTE OR
VENT PIPE
2 1/2" M.P. WASTE, VENT,
OR WATER PIPE

3" N.H. OR P. SOIL OR
VENT PIPE
4" C. WASTE, VENT, OR
WATER PIPE

4" STUD

3" B & S SOIL OR
VENT PIPE
3" M.P. WASTE, VENT,
OR WATER PIPE

4" N.H. OR P. VENT OR
SOIL PIPE
5" C. WATER OR VENT
PIPE

5 1/2" STUD

3" B & S SOIL OR
VENT PIPE
4" M.P. VENT OR
WATER PIPE

5" N.H. OR P. VENT OR
SOIL PIPE
6" C. WATER OR VENT
PIPE

6" STUD

STEEL STUD PARTITIONS WITH RIGID BOARD

NOTES
1. Abbreviations:
   - B&S: Extra heavy cast iron bell and spigot (push or caulked joints).
   - C: Copper tubing.
   - NH: Extra heavy cast iron no-hub pipe.
   - MP: Malleable pattern (galvanized or nongalvanized).
   - P: Plastic pipe.
2. Recommended chase sizes for various pipes include a 3/4 in. covering. For additional cover take the amount of cover required; subtract 3/4 in.; add the result to the dimension given for the pipe size desired.
3. Chases may be provided with or without access. Chases for several pipes, especially those containing main water supply pipes, should be provided with a means of access in case repair is necessary.
4. For the size of a chase with several pipes, add the widths required for each.
5. Partitions with 3/4 in. lath and plaster are shown with certain maximum pipe sizes encroaching on the lath and plaster. Encroaching portions of the pipes should be coated with asphaltic paint to prevent any staining of the plaster.
6. When rigid board or lath, such as gypsum board, plaster board, or gypsum lath, is used, the extreme diameter of the bead or bell of the pipe fitting should come within the actual clear dimension of the wall core.
7. Larger pipe spaces can be obtained by placing the piping between two partitions constructed back to back with the required clear space between them.

Kelly Sacher & Associates; Architects Engineers Planners; N. Babylon, Long Island, New York

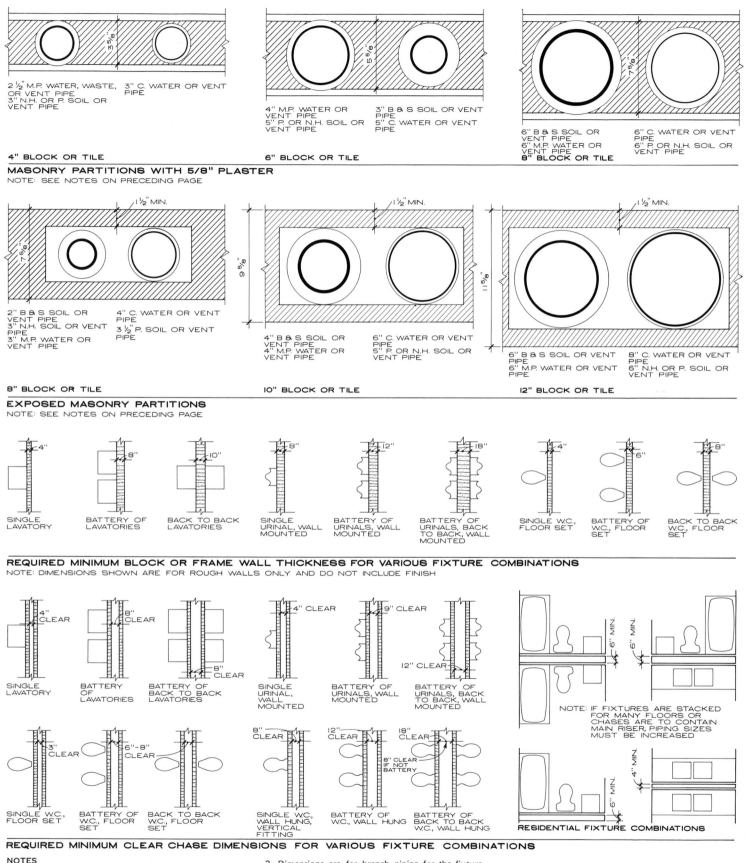

2 ½" M.P. WATER, WASTE, OR VENT PIPE
3" N.H. OR P. SOIL OR VENT PIPE

3" C. WATER OR VENT PIPE

4" BLOCK OR TILE

4" M.P. WATER OR VENT PIPE
5" P. OR N.H. SOIL OR VENT PIPE

3" B & S SOIL OR VENT PIPE
5" C. WATER OR VENT PIPE

6" BLOCK OR TILE

6" B & S SOIL OR VENT PIPE
6" M.P. WATER OR VENT PIPE

6" C. WATER OR VENT PIPE
6" P. OR N.H. SOIL OR VENT PIPE

8" BLOCK OR TILE

MASONRY PARTITIONS WITH 5/8" PLASTER
NOTE: SEE NOTES ON PRECEDING PAGE

2" B & S SOIL OR VENT PIPE
3" N.H. SOIL OR VENT PIPE
3" M.P. WATER OR VENT PIPE

4" C. WATER OR VENT PIPE
3 ½" P. SOIL OR VENT PIPE

8" BLOCK OR TILE

4" B & S SOIL OR VENT PIPE
4" M.P. WATER OR VENT PIPE

6" C. WATER OR VENT PIPE
5" P. OR N.H. SOIL OR VENT PIPE

10" BLOCK OR TILE

6" B & S SOIL OR VENT PIPE
6" M.P. WATER OR VENT PIPE

8" C. WATER OR VENT PIPE
6" N.H. OR P. SOIL OR VENT PIPE

12" BLOCK OR TILE

EXPOSED MASONRY PARTITIONS
NOTE: SEE NOTES ON PRECEDING PAGE

SINGLE LAVATORY

BATTERY OF LAVATORIES

BACK TO BACK LAVATORIES

SINGLE URINAL, WALL MOUNTED

BATTERY OF URINALS, WALL MOUNTED

BATTERY OF URINALS, BACK TO BACK, WALL MOUNTED

SINGLE W.C., FLOOR SET

BATTERY OF W.C., FLOOR SET

BACK TO BACK W.C., FLOOR SET

REQUIRED MINIMUM BLOCK OR FRAME WALL THICKNESS FOR VARIOUS FIXTURE COMBINATIONS
NOTE: DIMENSIONS SHOWN ARE FOR ROUGH WALLS ONLY AND DO NOT INCLUDE FINISH

SINGLE LAVATORY

BATTERY OF LAVATORIES

BATTERY OF BACK TO BACK LAVATORIES

SINGLE URINAL, WALL MOUNTED

BATTERY OF URINALS, WALL MOUNTED

BATTERY OF URINALS, BACK TO BACK, WALL MOUNTED

SINGLE W.C., FLOOR SET

BATTERY OF W.C., FLOOR SET

BACK TO BACK W.C., FLOOR SET

SINGLE W.C., WALL HUNG, VERTICAL FITTING

BATTERY OF W.C., WALL HUNG

BATTERY OF BACK TO BACK W.C., WALL HUNG

NOTE: IF FIXTURES ARE STACKED FOR MANY FLOORS OR CHASES ARE TO CONTAIN MAIN RISER, PIPING SIZES MUST BE INCREASED

RESIDENTIAL FIXTURE COMBINATIONS

REQUIRED MINIMUM CLEAR CHASE DIMENSIONS FOR VARIOUS FIXTURE COMBINATIONS

NOTES
1. Dimensions are minimum and are based on the fixture chair carriers clear of the partition.
2. Partitions shown are based on 4 in. block (3⅝ in.), wood stud (3½ in.), or 4 in. steel stud and do not include the finish.
3. Dimensions are for branch piping for the fixture and do not in all cases provide for the main riser piping.
4. For conditions where main riser piping occurs in the fixture chase, dimensions must be altered to accommodate them.

Kelly Sacher & Associates; Architects Engineers Planners; N. Babylon, Long Island, New York

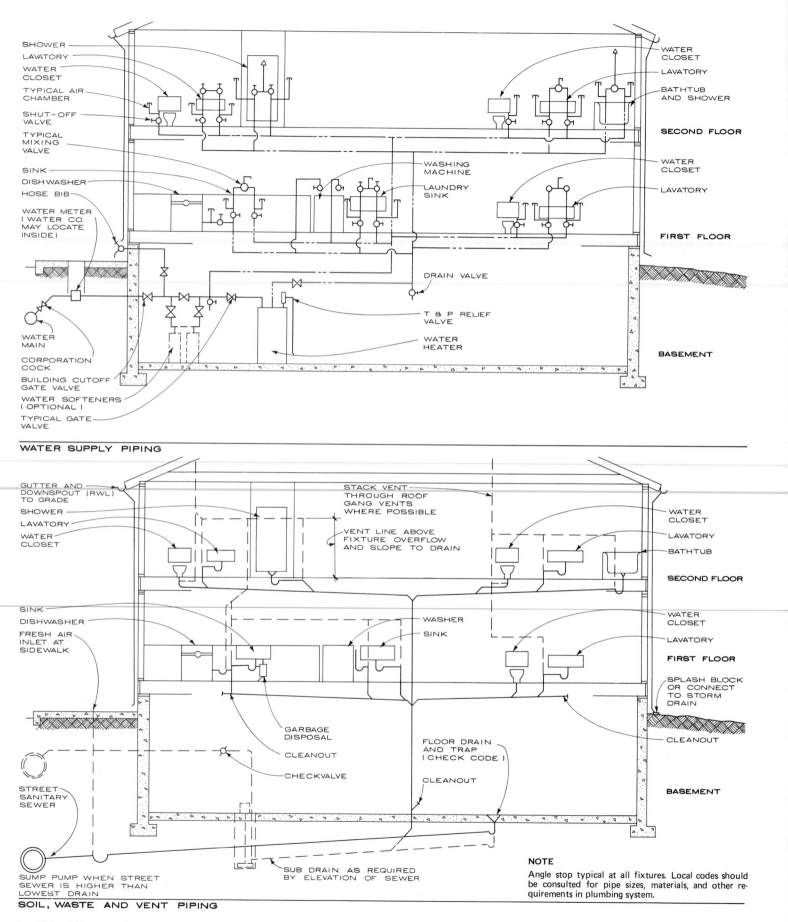

SHOWER
LAVATORY
WATER CLOSET
TYPICAL AIR CHAMBER
SHUT-OFF VALVE
TYPICAL MIXING VALVE
SINK
DISHWASHER
HOSE BIB
WATER METER (WATER CO. MAY LOCATE INSIDE)
WATER MAIN
CORPORATION COCK
BUILDING CUTOFF GATE VALVE
WATER SOFTENERS (OPTIONAL)
TYPICAL GATE VALVE

WATER CLOSET
LAVATORY
BATHTUB AND SHOWER
SECOND FLOOR
WATER CLOSET
LAVATORY
FIRST FLOOR
BASEMENT

WASHING MACHINE
LAUNDRY SINK
DRAIN VALVE
T & P RELIEF VALVE
WATER HEATER

WATER SUPPLY PIPING

GUTTER AND DOWNSPOUT (RWL) TO GRADE
SHOWER
LAVATORY
WATER CLOSET
SINK
DISHWASHER
FRESH AIR INLET AT SIDEWALK

STACK VENT THROUGH ROOF GANG VENTS WHERE POSSIBLE
VENT LINE ABOVE FIXTURE OVERFLOW AND SLOPE TO DRAIN

WATER CLOSET
LAVATORY
BATHTUB
SECOND FLOOR
WATER CLOSET
LAVATORY
FIRST FLOOR
SPLASH BLOCK OR CONNECT TO STORM DRAIN
CLEANOUT
BASEMENT

WASHER
SINK
GARBAGE DISPOSAL
CLEANOUT
CHECKVALVE
FLOOR DRAIN AND TRAP (CHECK CODE)
CLEANOUT

STREET SANITARY SEWER
SUMP PUMP WHEN STREET SEWER IS HIGHER THAN LOWEST DRAIN
SUB DRAIN AS REQUIRED BY ELEVATION OF SEWER

NOTE
Angle stop typical at all fixtures. Local codes should be consulted for pipe sizes, materials, and other requirements in plumbing system.

SOIL, WASTE AND VENT PIPING

Brent Dickens, AIA, Architect; San Rafael, California

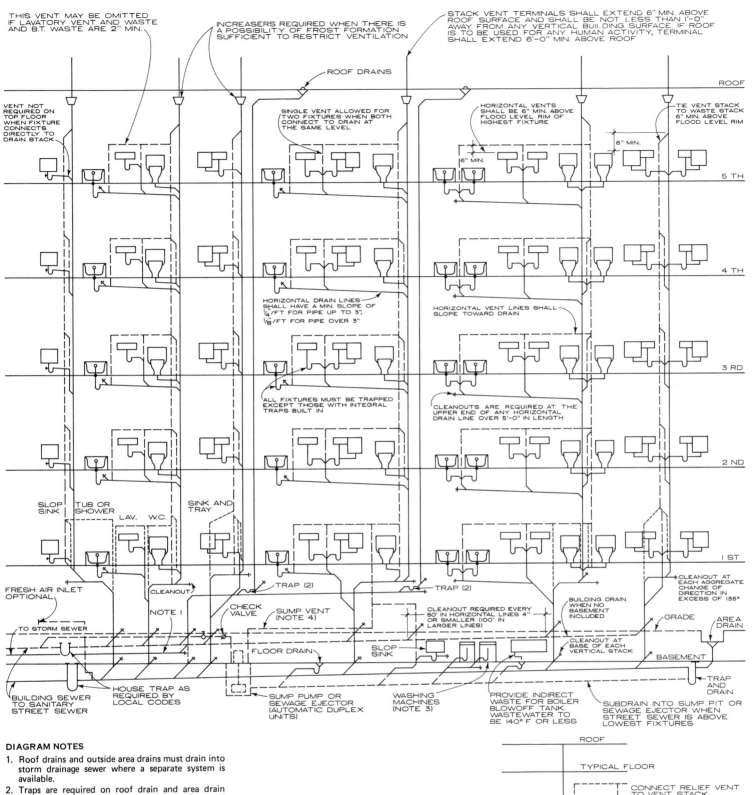

THIS VENT MAY BE OMITTED IF LAVATORY VENT AND WASTE AND B.T. WASTE ARE 2" MIN.

INCREASERS REQUIRED WHEN THERE IS A POSSIBILITY OF FROST FORMATION SUFFICIENT TO RESTRICT VENTILATION

STACK VENT TERMINALS SHALL EXTEND 6" MIN. ABOVE ROOF SURFACE AND SHALL BE NOT LESS THAN 1'-0" AWAY FROM ANY VERTICAL BUILDING SURFACE. IF ROOF IS TO BE USED FOR ANY HUMAN ACTIVITY, TERMINAL SHALL EXTEND 6'-0" MIN. ABOVE ROOF

ROOF DRAINS

VENT NOT REQUIRED ON TOP FLOOR WHEN FIXTURE CONNECTS DIRECTLY TO DRAIN STACK

SINGLE VENT ALLOWED FOR TWO FIXTURES WHEN BOTH CONNECT TO DRAIN AT THE SAME LEVEL

HORIZONTAL VENTS SHALL BE 6" MIN. ABOVE FLOOD LEVEL RIM OF HIGHEST FIXTURE

TIE VENT STACK TO WASTE STACK 6" MIN. ABOVE FLOOD LEVEL RIM

HORIZONTAL DRAIN LINES SHALL HAVE A MIN. SLOPE OF 1/4"/FT FOR PIPE UP TO 3", 1/8"/FT FOR PIPE OVER 3"

HORIZONTAL VENT LINES SHALL SLOPE TOWARD DRAIN

ALL FIXTURES MUST BE TRAPPED EXCEPT THOSE WITH INTEGRAL TRAPS BUILT IN

CLEANOUTS ARE REQUIRED AT THE UPPER END OF ANY HORIZONTAL DRAIN LINE OVER 5'-0" IN LENGTH

SLOP SINK / TUB OR SHOWER / LAV. W.C. / SINK AND TRAY

FRESH AIR INLET OPTIONAL

CLEANOUT

NOTE I

CHECK VALVE

SUMP VENT (NOTE 4)

TRAP (2)

TRAP (2)

CLEANOUT REQUIRED EVERY 50' IN HORIZONTAL LINES 4" OR SMALLER (100' IN LARGER LINES)

BUILDING DRAIN WHEN NO BASEMENT INCLUDED

CLEANOUT AT EACH AGGREGATE CHANGE OF DIRECTION IN EXCESS OF 135°

TO STORM SEWER

FLOOR DRAIN

SLOP SINK

CLEANOUT AT BASE OF EACH VERTICAL STACK

GRADE

AREA DRAIN

BASEMENT

BUILDING SEWER TO SANITARY STREET SEWER

HOUSE TRAP AS REQUIRED BY LOCAL CODES

SUMP PUMP OR SEWAGE EJECTOR (AUTOMATIC DUPLEX UNITS)

WASHING MACHINES (NOTE 3)

PROVIDE INDIRECT WASTE FOR BOILER BLOWOFF TANK. WASTEWATER TO BE 140° F OR LESS

SUBDRAIN INTO SUMP PIT OR SEWAGE EJECTOR WHEN STREET SEWER IS ABOVE LOWEST FIXTURES

TRAP AND DRAIN

DIAGRAM NOTES

1. Roof drains and outside area drains must drain into storm drainage sewer where a separate system is available.

2. Traps are required on roof drain and area drain leaders when connected to a combined sanitary and storm sewer system.

3. Provide one washing machine connection for every eight living units (individual connections in each living unit are preferable if space permits). Provide standpipe type indirect waste pipes, 18 in. min. above trap weir. Special consideration must be given to suds pressure zones where washing machines discharge upstream from other fixtures; special venting to nonpressure zones should be provided.

4. Sump vent line shall run independently and un-restricted to the open air when pneumatic type sewage ejectors are used.

Killebrew/Rucker/Associates, Inc.; Wichita Falls, Texas

NOTE

The diagram generally indicates plumbing drainage solutions that constitute good plumbing practice. Because of variances between different local codes, some of the items shown may be prohibited in some areas, while other items may far exceed the minimum requirements of local codes. Always consult local codes for exact requirements and for such items as fixture unit allotments, pipe sizing, pipe materials, general regulations, and special conditions.

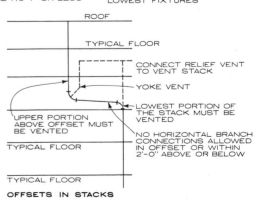

ROOF

TYPICAL FLOOR

CONNECT RELIEF VENT TO VENT STACK

YOKE VENT

UPPER PORTION ABOVE OFFSET MUST BE VENTED

LOWEST PORTION OF THE STACK MUST BE VENTED

NO HORIZONTAL BRANCH CONNECTIONS ALLOWED IN OFFSET OR WITHIN 2'-0" ABOVE OR BELOW

TYPICAL FLOOR

TYPICAL FLOOR

OFFSETS IN STACKS

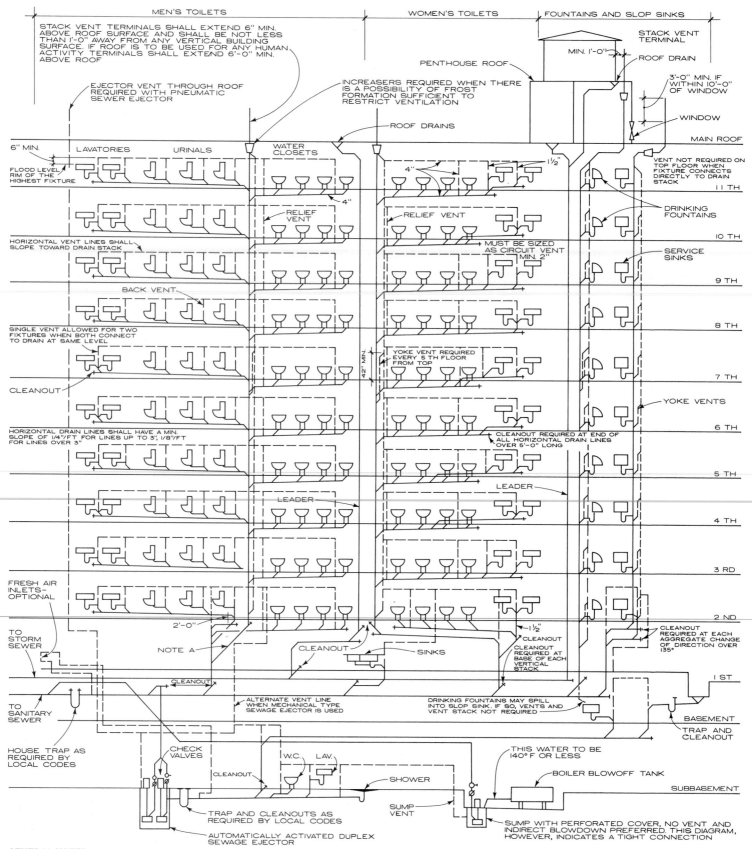

MEN'S TOILETS

WOMEN'S TOILETS

FOUNTAINS AND SLOP SINKS

STACK VENT TERMINALS SHALL EXTEND 6" MIN. ABOVE ROOF SURFACE AND SHALL BE NOT LESS THAN 1'-0" AWAY FROM ANY VERTICAL BUILDING SURFACE. IF ROOF IS TO BE USED FOR ANY HUMAN ACTIVITY TERMINALS SHALL EXTEND 6'-0" MIN. ABOVE ROOF

STACK VENT TERMINAL

MIN. 1'-0"

ROOF DRAIN

INCREASERS REQUIRED WHEN THERE IS A POSSIBILITY OF FROST FORMATION SUFFICIENT TO RESTRICT VENTILATION

PENTHOUSE ROOF

3'-0" MIN. IF WITHIN 10'-0" OF WINDOW

EJECTOR VENT THROUGH ROOF REQUIRED WITH PNEUMATIC SEWER EJECTOR

WINDOW

ROOF DRAINS

MAIN ROOF

6" MIN.

LAVATORIES

URINALS

WATER CLOSETS

1½"

VENT NOT REQUIRED ON TOP FLOOR WHEN FIXTURE CONNECTS DIRECTLY TO DRAIN STACK

FLOOD LEVEL RIM OF THE HIGHEST FIXTURE

4"

11 TH

4"

RELIEF VENT

RELIEF VENT

DRINKING FOUNTAINS

10 TH

HORIZONTAL VENT LINES SHALL SLOPE TOWARD DRAIN STACK

MUST BE SIZED AS CIRCUIT VENT MIN. 2"

SERVICE SINKS

9 TH

BACK VENT

8 TH

SINGLE VENT ALLOWED FOR TWO FIXTURES WHEN BOTH CONNECT TO DRAIN AT SAME LEVEL

42" MIN.

YOKE VENT REQUIRED EVERY 5 TH FLOOR FROM TOP

7 TH

CLEANOUT

YOKE VENTS

6 TH

HORIZONTAL DRAIN LINES SHALL HAVE A MIN. SLOPE OF ¼"/FT FOR LINES UP TO 3", ⅛"/FT FOR LINES OVER 3"

CLEANOUT REQUIRED AT END OF ALL HORIZONTAL DRAIN LINES OVER 5'-0" LONG

5 TH

LEADER

LEADER

4 TH

3 RD

FRESH AIR INLETS- OPTIONAL

2 ND

TO STORM SEWER

2'-0"

CLEANOUT REQUIRED AT EACH AGGREGATE CHANGE OF DIRECTION OVER 135°

NOTE A

CLEANOUT

SINKS

1½"

CLEANOUT

CLEANOUT REQUIRED AT BASE OF EACH VERTICAL STACK

CLEANOUT

1 ST

TO SANITARY SEWER

ALTERNATE VENT LINE WHEN MECHANICAL TYPE SEWAGE EJECTOR IS USED

DRINKING FOUNTAINS MAY SPILL INTO SLOP SINK. IF SO, VENTS AND VENT STACK NOT REQUIRED

BASEMENT

TRAP AND CLEANOUT

HOUSE TRAP AS REQUIRED BY LOCAL CODES

CHECK VALVES

W.C.

LAV.

THIS WATER TO BE 140° F OR LESS

BOILER BLOWOFF TANK

SUBBASEMENT

CLEANOUT

SHOWER

SUMP VENT

TRAP AND CLEANOUTS AS REQUIRED BY LOCAL CODES

AUTOMATICALLY ACTIVATED DUPLEX SEWAGE EJECTOR

SUMP WITH PERFORATED COVER, NO VENT AND INDIRECT BLOWDOWN PREFERRED. THIS DIAGRAM, HOWEVER, INDICATES A TIGHT CONNECTION

GENERAL NOTES

This diagram generally indicates plumbing drainage solutions that constitute good plumbing practice. Because of variances between local codes, some of the items shown may be prohibited in some areas, while other items may far exceed the minimum requirements of local codes.

Always consult local codes for exact requirements and for such items as fixture unit allotments, pipe sizing, pipe materials, general regulations, and special conditions.

NOTE A

45° or less from vertical may be considered as straight stock in sizing, except that no fixtures or branches may be connected within 2 ft of offset.

Killebrew/Rucker/Associates, Inc.; Wichita Falls, Texas

PLUMBING

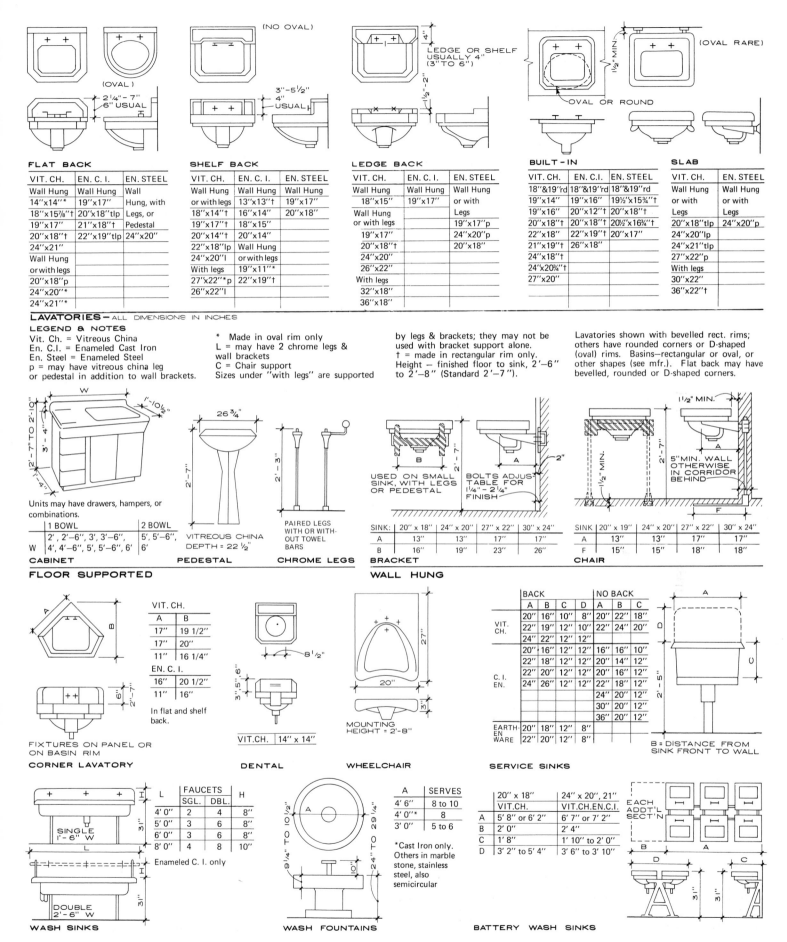

(NO OVAL)

LEDGE OR SHELF
USUALLY 4"
(3" TO 6")

(OVAL RARE)

OVAL OR ROUND

(OVAL)

2¼"–7"
6" USUAL

3"–5½"
4" USUAL

FLAT BACK

VIT. CH.	EN. C.I.	EN. STEEL
Wall Hung	Wall Hung	Wall Hung, with
14"x14"*	19"x17"	Legs, or
18"x15⅞"†	20"x18"tlp	Pedestal
19"x17"	21"x18"†	
20"x18"†	22"x19"tlp	24"x20"
24"x21"		
Wall Hung		
or with legs		
20"x18"p		
24"x20"*		
24"x21"*		

SHELF BACK

VIT. CH.	EN. C.I.	EN. STEEL
Wall Hung	Wall Hung	Wall Hung
or with legs	13"x13"†	19"x17"
18"x14"†	16"x14"	20"x18"
19"x17"†	18"x15"	
20"x14"†	20"x14"	
22"x18"lp		
24"x20"l		
With legs		
27"x22"*p	19"x11"*	
26"x22"l	22"x19"†	

LEDGE BACK

VIT. CH.	EN. C.I.	EN. STEEL
Wall Hung	Wall Hung	Wall Hung
18"x15"	19"x17"	or with
Wall Hung		Legs
or with legs		19"x17"p
19"x17"		24"x20"p
20"x18"†		20"x18"
24"x20"		
26"x22"		
With legs		
32"x18"		
36"x18"		

BUILT-IN

VIT. CH.	EN. C.I.	EN. STEEL
18"&19"rd	18"&19"rd	18"&19"rd
19"x14"	19"x16"	19½"x15¾"†
19"x16"	20"x12"†	20"x18"†
20"x18"†	20"x18"†	20½"x16¾"†
22"x18"	22"x19"†	20"x17"
21"x19"†	26"x18"	
24"x18"†		
24"x20¾"†		
27"x20"		

SLAB

VIT. CH.	EN. STEEL
Wall Hung	Wall Hung
or with	or with
Legs	Legs
20"x18"tlp	24"x20"p
24"x20"lp	
24"x21"tlp	
27"x22"p	
With legs	
30"x22"	
36"x22"†	

LAVATORIES — ALL DIMENSIONS IN INCHES

LEGEND & NOTES

Vit. Ch. = Vitreous China
En. C.I. = Enameled Cast Iron
En. Steel = Enameled Steel
p = may have vitreous china leg
or pedestal in addition to wall brackets.

* Made in oval rim only
L = may have 2 chrome legs &
wall brackets
C = Chair support
Sizes under "with legs" are supported

by legs & brackets; they may not be
used with bracket support alone.
† = made in rectangular rim only.
Height — finished floor to sink, 2′-6″
to 2′-8″ (Standard 2′-7″).

Lavatories shown with bevelled rect. rims;
others have rounded corners or D-shaped
(oval) rims. Basins—rectangular or oval, or
other shapes (see mfr.). Flat back may have
bevelled, rounded or D-shaped corners.

Units may have drawers, hampers, or
combinations.

	1 BOWL		2 BOWL	
	2′, 2′-6″, 3′, 3′-6″,		5′, 5′-6″,	
W	4′, 4′-6″, 5′, 5′-6″, 6′		6′	

CABINET

26¾"

VITREOUS CHINA
DEPTH = 22½"

PEDESTAL

PAIRED LEGS
WITH OR WITH-
OUT TOWEL
BARS

CHROME LEGS

USED ON SMALL
SINK, WITH LEGS
OR PEDESTAL

BOLTS ADJUS-
TABLE FOR
1¼" – 2¼"
FINISH

SINK:	20" x 18"	24" x 20"	27" x 22"	30" x 24"
A	13"	13"	17"	17"
B	16"	19"	23"	26"

BRACKET

1½" MIN.

5" MIN. WALL
OTHERWISE
IN CORRIDOR
BEHIND

SINK	20" x 19"	24" x 20"	27" x 22"	30" x 24"
A	13"	13"	17"	17"
F	15"	15"	18"	18"

CHAIR

FLOOR SUPPORTED

VIT. CH.	
A	B
17"	19 1/2"
17"	20"
11"	16 1/4"

EN. C.I.	
16"	20 1/2"
11"	16"

In flat and shelf
back.

FIXTURES ON PANEL OR
ON BASIN RIM

CORNER LAVATORY

8 1/2"

VIT. CH.	14" x 14"

DENTAL

27"

20"

MOUNTING
HEIGHT = 2′-8″

WHEELCHAIR

WALL HUNG

	BACK				NO BACK		
	A	B	C	D	A	B	C
VIT. CH.	20"	16"	10"	8"	20"	22"	18"
	22"	19"	12"	10"	22"	24"	20"
	24"	22"	12"	12"			
C.I. EN.	20"	16"	12"	12"	16"	16"	10"
	22"	18"	12"	12"	20"	14"	12"
	22"	20"	12"	12"	20"	16"	12"
	24"	26"	12"	12"	22"	18"	12"
					24"	20"	12"
					30"	20"	12"
					36"	20"	12"
EARTH-EN WARE	20"	18"	12"	8"			
	22"	20"	12"	8"			

B = DISTANCE FROM
SINK FRONT TO WALL

SERVICE SINKS

L	FAUCETS		H
	SGL.	DBL.	
4′ 0″	2	4	8″
5′ 0″*	3	6	8″
6′ 0″	3	6	8″
8′ 0″	4	8	10″

SINGLE
1′-6″ W

DOUBLE
2′-6″ W

Enameled C. I. only

WASH SINKS

A	SERVES
4′ 6″	8 to 10
4′ 0″*	8
3′ 0″	5 to 6

*Cast Iron only.
Others in marble
stone, stainless
steel, also
semicircular

WASH FOUNTAINS

	20" x 18"	24" x 20", 21"
	VIT.CH.	VIT.CH.EN.C.I.
A	5′ 8″ or 6′ 2″	6′ 7″ or 7′ 2″
B	2′ 0″	2′ 4″
C	1′ 8″	1′ 10″ to 2′ 0″
D	3′ 2″ to 5′ 4″	3′ 6″ to 3′ 10″

EACH
ADDT'L
SECT'N

BATTERY WASH SINKS

B. J. Baldwin; Giffels & Rossetti, Inc.; Detroit, Michigan

PLUMBING FIXTURES   **15**

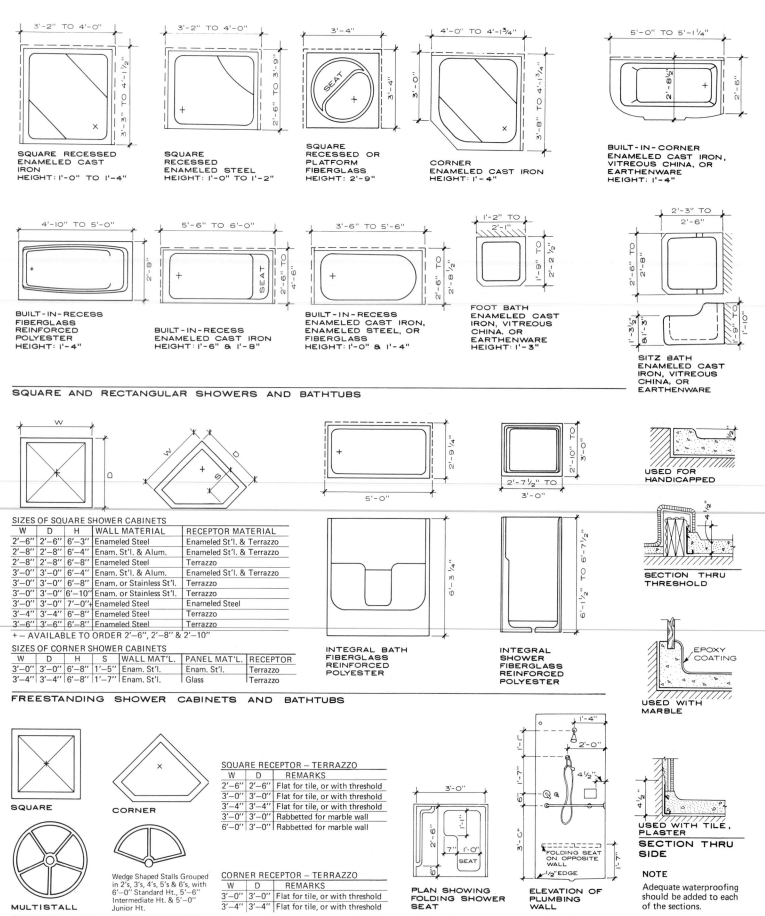

SQUARE RECESSED ENAMELED CAST IRON
HEIGHT: 1'-0" TO 1'-4"

SQUARE RECESSED ENAMELED STEEL
HEIGHT: 1'-0" TO 1'-2"

SQUARE RECESSED OR PLATFORM FIBERGLASS
HEIGHT: 2'-9"

CORNER ENAMELED CAST IRON
HEIGHT: 1'-4"

BUILT-IN-CORNER ENAMELED CAST IRON, VITREOUS CHINA, OR EARTHENWARE
HEIGHT: 1'-4"

BUILT-IN-RECESS FIBERGLASS REINFORCED POLYESTER
HEIGHT: 1'-4"

BUILT-IN-RECESS ENAMELED CAST IRON
HEIGHT: 1'-6" & 1'-8"

BUILT-IN-RECESS ENAMELED CAST IRON, ENAMELED STEEL, OR FIBERGLASS
HEIGHT: 1'-0" & 1'-4"

FOOT BATH ENAMELED CAST IRON, VITREOUS CHINA, OR EARTHENWARE
HEIGHT: 1'-3"

SITZ BATH ENAMELED CAST IRON, VITREOUS CHINA, OR EARTHENWARE

SQUARE AND RECTANGULAR SHOWERS AND BATHTUBS

SIZES OF SQUARE SHOWER CABINETS

W	D	H	WALL MATERIAL	RECEPTOR MATERIAL
2'-6"	2'-6"	6'-3"	Enameled Steel	Enameled St'l. & Terrazzo
2'-8"	2'-8"	6'-4"	Enam. St'l. & Alum.	Enameled St'l. & Terrazzo
2'-8"	2'-8"	6'-8"	Enameled Steel	Terrazzo
3'-0"	3'-0"	6'-4"	Enam. St'l. & Alum.	Enameled St'l. & Terrazzo
3'-0"	3'-0"	6'-8"	Enam. or Stainless St'l.	Terrazzo
3'-0"	3'-0"	6'-10"	Enam. or Stainless St'l.	Terrazzo
3'-0"	3'-0"	7'-0"+	Enameled Steel	Enameled Steel
3'-4"	3'-4"	6'-8"	Enameled Steel	Terrazzo
3'-6"	3'-6"	6'-8"	Enameled Steel	Terrazzo

+ — AVAILABLE TO ORDER 2'-6", 2'-8" & 2'-10"

SIZES OF CORNER SHOWER CABINETS

W	D	H	S	WALL MAT'L.	PANEL MAT'L.	RECEPTOR
3'-0"	3'-0"	6'-8"	1'-5"	Enam. St'l.	Enam. St'l.	Terrazzo
3'-4"	3'-4"	6'-8"	1'-7"	Enam. St'l.	Glass	Terrazzo

INTEGRAL BATH FIBERGLASS REINFORCED POLYESTER

INTEGRAL SHOWER FIBERGLASS REINFORCED POLYESTER

USED FOR HANDICAPPED

SECTION THRU THRESHOLD

EPOXY COATING

USED WITH MARBLE

FREESTANDING SHOWER CABINETS AND BATHTUBS

SQUARE

CORNER

MULTISTALL

Wedge Shaped Stalls Grouped in 2's, 3's, 4's, 5's & 6's, with 6'-0" Standard Ht., 5'-6" Intermediate Ht. & 5'-0" Junior Ht.

SQUARE RECEPTOR — TERRAZZO

W	D	REMARKS
2'-6"	2'-6"	Flat for tile, or with threshold
3'-0"	3'-0"	Flat for tile, or with threshold
3'-4"	3'-4"	Flat for tile, or with threshold
3'-0"	3'-0"	Rabbetted for marble wall
6'-0"	3'-0"	Rabbetted for marble wall

CORNER RECEPTOR — TERRAZZO

W	D	REMARKS
3'-0"	3'-0"	Flat for tile, or with threshold
3'-4"	3'-4"	Flat for tile, or with threshold

SHOWER RECEPTOR TYPES

PLAN SHOWING FOLDING SHOWER SEAT

FOLDING SEAT ON OPPOSITE WALL

1/2" EDGE

ELEVATION OF PLUMBING WALL

SHOWER USED BY HANDICAPPED

USED WITH TILE, PLASTER

SECTION THRU SIDE

NOTE
Adequate waterproofing should be added to each of the sections.

K. Shahid Rab, AIA, Friesen International; Washington, D.C.

15   **PLUMBING FIXTURES**

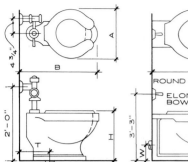
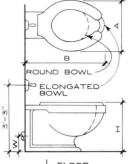
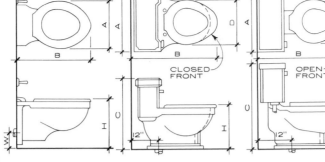
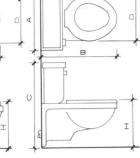

	FLOOR MOUNTED BOTTOM OUTLET			FLOOR MOUNTED BACK OUTLET		WALL HUNG	
	SJ	WD	BO	SJ	BO	SJ	BO
A	14″	14″	14″	14″	14″	14″	14″
Round B	24″	27″		20⅛″			
Elongated	24½″ or 26½″		26¼″	25½″ to 26″	21½″	21½″ to 25¾″	24¼″ to 26″
H	14″ to 14¾″ 10″* 17″† to 19″	15″	15″	14½″ to 15″	15″	15″	15″ to 15¾″
W				4¼″ or 4½″	10¼″	4″ to 5½″	11½″ to 12¼″
T	10″ or 12″	12″ to 14″	9″	9″ or 10″	9″ or 10″		

*For children.
†For handicapped.

	ONE PIECE			CLOSE COUPLED		WALL HUNG
	SV	SJ	SA	SJ	RT	SJ
A	20¾″ to 22″	20⅝″ to 23¾″	20¾″ to 21″	20⅞″ to 21½″	17″ to 20⅞″	20⅞″ to 23¾″
Round B	27¾″	24¾″	27¾″	27½″ to 29″	22″ to 27⅝″	26½″ to 29¾″
Elongated	29¼″	28½″ to 29″	28½″ to 29¾″	29⅛″ to 29⅞″		28¼″
C	20″ to 23¾″	18¾″ to 20½″	18¾″ to 19½″	26⅛″ to 31⅞″	28¼″ to 31″	29″ to 29½″
D	14¾″ to 15½″	14¾″ to 15½″	14¾″ to 15½″	14¾″ to 15½″	14¾″ to 15½″	14¾″ to 15½″
H	14″	14″ to 15″	14½″	14″ 17″† to 19″ 10″*	14½″ to 15″	15″

NOTE: Dimensions include seat. For closed front seats, add 1 in. to B. With seat cover, add ¾ in. to height. All fixtures are of vitreous china except where noted. For concealed carrier wall hung, allow 10½ in. minimum from back of closet to outside edge of soil pipe.

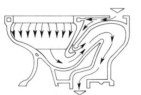
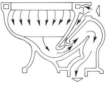
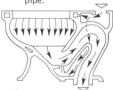

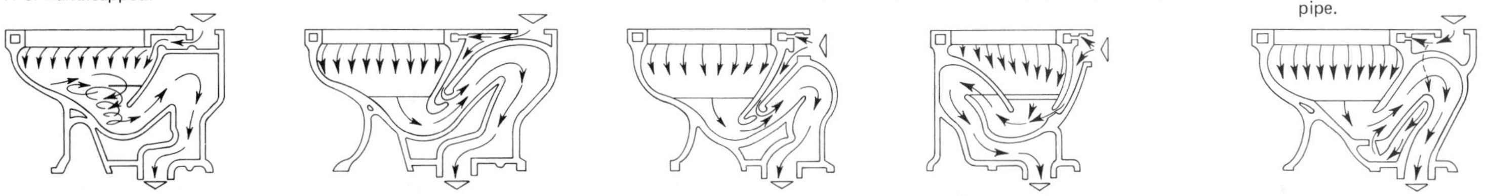

SIPHON - VORTEX (S-V)
Quiet, extremely sanitary. Water directed through rim to create vortex. Scours bowl. Folds over into jet; siphon.

SIPHON - JET (S-J)
SIPHON - ACTION (S-A)
Sanitary, efficient, very quiet. Water enters through rim and siphons in down leg.

REVERSE - TRAP (R-T)
Similar to siphon-jet except that trap passageway and water surface area are smaller, moderately noisy.

WASH - DOWN (W-D)
Minimum cost. Least efficient, subject to clogging, noisy. Simple washout action through small irregular passageway.

BLOWOUT (BO)
Noisy but highly efficient. Strong jet into up leg forces contents out. Use with FV only. Higher pressure required.

WATER CLOSETS

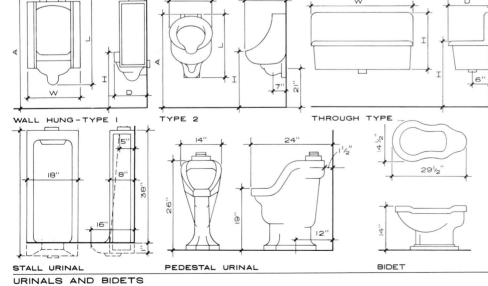

WALL HUNG-TYPE 1   TYPE 2   THROUGH TYPE

STALL URINAL   PEDESTAL URINAL   BIDET

	TYPE 1 (SJ, WD, BO)	TYPE 2			THROUGH TYPE
		SJ	BO	WD	
A	35″, 42½″	35½″ to 37⅛″	26½″ to 27″	34½″ to 37⅛″	32″- 34″
W	13″, 18″	13″ to 14¼″	14″	12¾″ to 14¼″	36″, 48″, 60″, 72″
L	18″ to 30″	17″ to 20″	17″ to 20″	17″ to 20″	16″, 17¾″, 18¾″
D	11¾″ to 13¼″	11¼″ to 14″	11½″ to 14″	12⅞″ to 14″	14″, 18″
H	24″	24″, 17″*, 19″*			24″

*For handicapped.

NOTE: Provide minimum 4 in. clear pipe chase for urinal piping and support.

BATTERY STALLS
Stall urinals available with seam covers for battery installation on 1′- 9″ or 2′- 0″ centers.

URINALS AND BIDETS

K. Shahid Rab, AIA; Friesen International; Washington, D.C.

B. J. Baldwin; Giffels & Rossetti, Inc.; Detroit, Michigan

PLUMBING FIXTURES   **15**

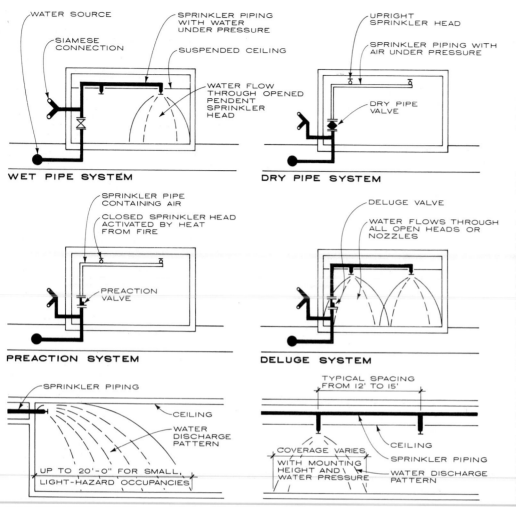

WET PIPE SYSTEM

DRY PIPE SYSTEM

PREACTION SYSTEM

DELUGE SYSTEM

SIDEWALL SPRINKLER HEAD
(HORIZONTAL SIDEWALL SHOWN)

Piping can be unobtrusively installed along sides of exposed ceiling beams or joists. In small rooms, sidewall heads provide water discharge coverage without overhead piping.

PENDENT SPRINKLER HEAD

Can be recessed in ceiling (e.g., coffered, modeled) or hidden above flat metal cover plate. (Flush sprinkler heads are also available.)

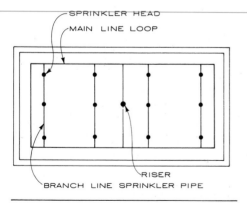

HYDRAULICALLY DESIGNED SPRINKLER SYSTEM LAYOUT

Loop provides water flow from two directions to operating sprinkler heads so pipe sizes will be small. Hydraulic calculations can assure delivery of adequate water flow and pressure throughout piping network to meet design requirements.

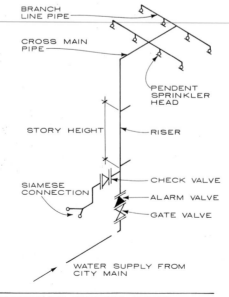

SPRINKLER SYSTEM RISER

M. David Egan, P.E.; College of Architecture; Clemson University; Clemson, South Carolina

TYPES OF SYSTEMS

WET PIPE: Piping network contains water under pressure at all times for immediate release through sprinkler heads as they are activated by heat from fire. Wet pipe system is the most widely used system, since water delivery here is faster than with a dry pipe system.

DRY PIPE: Piping network contains air (or nitrogen) under pressure. Following loss of air pressure through opened sprinkler head, dry pipe valve opens allowing water to enter piping network and to flow through opened sprinkler head (or heads). Used where piping is subject to freezing.

PREACTION: Closed head, dry system containing air in piping network. Preaction valve is activated by independent fire detection system more sensitive than sprinkler heads. The opened preaction valve allows water to fill piping network and to flow through sprinkler heads, as they are activated by heat from fire. Used where leakage or accidental discharge would cause serious damage.

DELUGE: Sprinkler heads (or spray nozzles) are open at all times and normally there is no water in piping network. Mechanical or hydraulic valves, operated by heat, smoke, or flame sensitive devices, are used to control water flow to heads by opening water control clapper. Deluge systems are special use systems, as water discharges from all heads (or nozzles) at the same time.

STANDPIPE AND HOSE: Dry standpipes are empty water pipes used by fire fighters to connect hoses in buildings to water sources such as ground level fire hydrants. Wet standpipes are water filled pipes permanently connected to public or private water mains for use by building occupants on small fires or by fire fighters.

FOAM: Used to suppress flammable liquid fires. Foam can be distributed by piping network to nozzles or other discharge outlets (e.g., tubes, troughs, chutes) depending on the hazard.

HALON (haloginated hydrocarbon): Can be used where water damage to building contents would be unacceptable. Piping network connects fixed supply of halon to nozzles that discharge uniform, low concentration throughout room. To avoid piping network, discharge cylinders may be installed throughout room or area. Though generally nontoxic, delayed discharge can cause problems by allowing decomposition of halon. Rapid detection is necessary.

CO_2 (carbon dioxide): Does not conduct electricity and leaves no residue after its use. Piping network connects fixed supply of CO_2 to nozzles that discharge CO_2 directly on burning materials where location of fire hazard is known (called "local application") or discharge CO_2 uniformly throughout room (called "total flooding"). In total flooding systems, safety requirements dictate advance alarm to allow occupants to evacuate area prior to discharge.

DRY CHEMICAL: Can be especially useful on electrical and flammable liquid fires. Powdered extinguishing agent, under pressure of dry air or nitrogen, commonly discharged over cooking surfaces (e.g., frying).

PREPARATION FOR SPRINKLER SYSTEMS

1. Begin planning sprinkler system at the very earliest design stages of project.
2. Determine hazard classification of building and type of system best suited for suppression needs.
3. Refer to national standards (NFPA), state and local codes.
4. Check with authority having jurisdiction:
   a. State and local fire marshals.
   b. Insurance Services Office (ISO).
   c. Insurance underwriting groups such as IRI, OIA, or FM (if they have jurisdiction).
5. Use qualified engineers to design system. Be sure water supply is adequate (e.g., by water flow tests). Integrate system with structural, mechanical, and other building services.
6. Check space requirements for sprinkler equipment. Sprinkler control room must be heated to prevent freezing of equipment.
7. Consider possible future alterations to building.

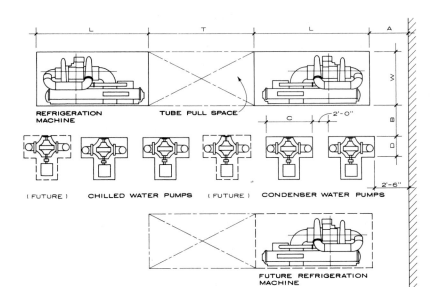

REFRIGERATION MACHINE   **TUBE PULL SPACE**

(FUTURE)   **CHILLED WATER PUMPS**   (FUTURE)   **CONDENSER WATER PUMPS**

FUTURE REFRIGERATION MACHINE

GENERAL

The capacity of each refrigeration machine is equal to 50% of the peak cooling load.

Each water pump provides the flow requirement of one refrigeration machine. Therefore, one pair of condenser and chilled water pumps is needed for each machine.

The cooling tower may be located on the roof of the refrigeration equipment room or on the ground adjacent to the equipment room. When located on ground, the condenser water outlet(s) on the cooling tower must be not less than 5 ft above the equipment room floor elevation for proper functioning of condenser water pumps.

EXPANSION OF EQUIPMENT

For operational flexibility of a refrigeration plant, the size of the future refrigeration machine is generally planned to be the same as of the present machines. It may be economically advantageous to oversize some portions of the chilled and condenser waterpipes to handle the future flow rates.

Provision must also be made for expansion of the cooling tower capacity when the future refrigeration machine is installed.

REFRIGERATION EQUIPMENT ROOM SPACE REQUIREMENTS

EQUIPMENT (TONS)	DIMENSIONS								MINIMUM ROOM HEIGHT
	L	W	HEIGHT	T	A	B	C	D	
RECIPROCATING MACHINES									
Up to 50	9'-0''	3'-0''	4'-0''	6'-0''	2'-6''	3'-6''	4'-0''	3'-0''	9'-0''
50 to 100	9'-6''	3'-0''	4'-6''	6'-0''	2'-6''	3'-6''	4'-0''	3'-6''	9'-0''
CENTRIFUGAL MACHINES									
Up to 120	14'-6''	6'-0''	6'-6''	14'-0''	2'-6''	5'-6''	4'-6''	4'-0''	10'-0''
120 to 225	15'-0''	6'-0''	6'-0''	14'-0''	2'-6''	5'-6''	4'-6''	4'-0''	10'-0''
225 to 350	15'-0''	6'-6''	7'-0''	14'-0''	2'-6''	5'-6''	5'-0''	5'-0''	11'-0''
350 to 550	15'-0''	8'-0''	7'-0''	14'-0''	2'-6''	5'-6''	6'-0''	5'-6''	11'-0''
550 to 750	15'-6''	11'-0''	8'-6''	14'-6''	2'-6''	5'-6''	6'-0''	5'-6''	12'-0''
750 to 1500	18'-6''	13'-6''	10'-0''	16'-0''	2'-6''	5'-6''	7'-6''	6'-0''	14'-0''
STEAM ABSORPTION MACHINES									
Up to 200	18'-0''	4'-0''	8'-0''	17'-0''	2'-6''	3'-6''	4'-6''	4'-0''	11'-0''
200 to 450	20'-0''	5'-6''	10'-0''	19'-0''	2'-6''	3'-6''	5'-0''	5'-0''	13'-0''
450 to 550	24'-0''	5'-6''	10'-0''	23'-0''	2'-6''	3'-6''	6'-0''	5'-6''	13'-0''
550 to 750	24'-0''	6'-6''	12'-0''	23'-0''	2'-6''	3'-6''	6'-0''	5'-6''	15'-0''
750 to 1000	27'-0''	7'-6''	12'-6''	26'-0''	2'-6''	3'-6''	7'-0''	6'-0''	16'-0''

REFRIGERATION ROOM LAYOUT

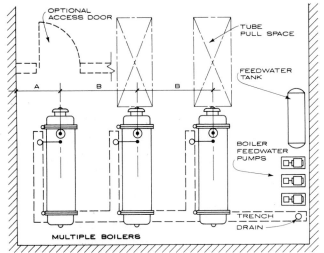

OPTIONAL ACCESS DOOR

TUBE PULL SPACE

FEEDWATER TANK

BOILER FEEDWATER PUMPS

TRENCH DRAIN

MULTIPLE BOILERS

ROOM DIMENSIONS

Dimension A allows for a minimum 3 ft 6 in. aisle between the water column on the boiler and the wall. Dimension B between boilers allows for a clear aisle of:

    3'-6''— 15-200 hp
    4'-0''—250-350 hp
    5'-0''—400-800 hp

The shortest boiler room length is obtained by allowing for possible future tube replacement (from front or rear of boiler) through a window or doorway. Allowance is only made for minimum door swing at each end of the boiler.

AIR SUPPLY

Two permanent air supply openings on opposite walls of the boiler room are recommended. These openings should be located below a height of 7 ft with a total clear area of at least 1 sq ft. Air supply openings can be louvered for weather protection.

Size the openings by using the following formula:

$$\text{area (sq ft)} = \frac{CFM}{FPM}$$

Amount of air required (CFM):

    Combustion air—max. boiler HP x 2 CMF/BHP

    Ventilation air—max. boiler HP x 2 CFM/BHP

NOTE: a total of 10 CFM/BHP applies up to 1000 ft elevation. Add 3% more per 1000 ft of added elevation.

Air velocity required (FPM):

    Up to 7 ft height— 250 FPM
    Above 7 ft height— 500 FPM
    Supply air duct to boiler—1000 FPM

BOILER ROOM SPACE REQUIREMENTS

BOILER HP	15-40	50-100	125-200	250-350	400-800
Dimension A	5'-9''	6'-6''	6'-10''	7'-9''	8'-6''
Dimension B	7'-5''	8'-9''	9'-7''	11'-9''	14'-3''

BOILER ROOM LAYOUT

Anilkumar V. Patel; Joseph R. Loring & Associates, Inc.; Consulting Engineers; New York, New York

DECENTRALIZED HEATING SYSTEMS

Electric energy is ideally suited to space heating because it is simple to distribute and control. Complete electric heating systems are widely used in residences, schools, and commercial and industrial establishments.

A decentralized electric system applies heating units to individual rooms or spaces. Often the rooms are combined into zones with automatic temperature controls. In terms of heat output, electric in-space heating systems may be classified as natural convection, radiant, or forced air.

NATURAL CONVECTION UNITS

Heating units for wall mounting, recessed placement or surface placement are made with elements of incandescent bare wire or lower temperature bare wire or sheathed elements. An inner liner or reflector is usually placed between elements so that part of the heat is distributed by convection and part by radiation. Electric convectors should be located so that air movement across the elements is not impeded. Small units with ratings up to 1650 W operate at 120 V. Higher wattage units are made for 208 or higher voltages and require heavy duty receptacles.

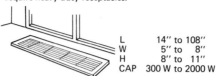

L	24" to 120"
D	2" to 8"
H	4" to 12"
CAP	300 W to 4000 W

BASEBOARD HEATER (Wall Mounted)

L	24" to 96"
D	3" to 8"
H	11" to 32"
CAP	1000 W to 4000 W

CABINET CONVECTOR (Surface Mounted or Recessed)

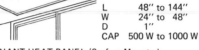

L	14" to 108"
W	5" to 8"
H	8" to 11"
CAP	300 W to 2000 W

FLOOR HEATER (Recessed)

L	23" to 107"
D	3" to 6"
H	9" to 12"
CAP	300 W to 2000 W

HYDRONIC BASEBOARD (Floor Mounted)

NATURAL CONVECTION UNITS

L	14" to 86"
W	4" to 12"
H	3" to 16"
CAP	500 W to 7000 W

INFRARED HEATER (Pendant Mounted) Circular heat lamp is available

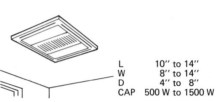

L	48" to 144"
W	24" to 48"
D	1"
CAP	500 W to 1000 W

RADIANT HEAT PANEL (Surface Mounted or Recessed) Decorative murals are available

Dimensions and capacity vary with coverage

RADIANT CEILING WITH EMBEDDED CONDUCTORS

RADIANT HEATING UNITS

RADIANT HEATING

Heat is produced by a current that flows in a high resistance wire or ribbon and is then transferred by radiation to a heat absorbing body. Manufacturer's recommendations for clearance between a radiant fixture and combustible materials or occupants should be followed.

FORCED AIR UNITS

Unit ventilators and heaters combine common convective heating with controlled natural ventilation.

Unit ventilators are most often mounted on an outside wall for air intake and at windowsills to prevent the down draft of cold air.

L	10" to 14"
W	8" to 14"
D	4" to 8"
CAP	500 W to 1500 W

CEILING HEATER (Recessed) Circular unit with light is available

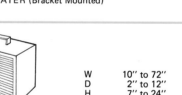

W	12" to 52"
D	6" to 22"
H	12" to 26"
CAP	1.5 KW to 50 KW

UNIT HEATER (Bracket Mounted)

L	48" to 104"
D	11" to 26"
H	26" to 32"
CAP	1 KW to 36 KW

UNIT VENTILATOR (Surface Mounted or Recessed)

W	10" to 18"
D	2" to 6"
H	9" to 24"
CAP	750 W to 4000 W

WALL HEATER (Recessed)

W	10" to 72"
D	2" to 12"
H	7" to 24"
CAP	500 W to 5000 W

PORTABLE HEATER

FORCED AIR UNITS

CENTRALIZED HEATING SYSTEMS

A central hot water system with terminal radiators can be operated using an electric hot water boiler that contains immersion heating elements.

An electric furnace, consisting of resistance heating coils and a blower, can supply a ducted warm air system. Electric heating units are also installed in supply ducts to provide final temperatures and relative humidities in central air systems.

Integrated recovery systems make use of heat gains from electrical loads such as lights and motors. The excess heat accumulated from these sources can either be transferred or stored for later use.

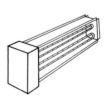

L	25"
W	23"
H	35"
CAP	5 KW to 60 KW

ELECTRIC FURNACE

Size varies with duct dimensions	
CAP	0.3 KW to 2000 KW

DUCT INSERT HEATER

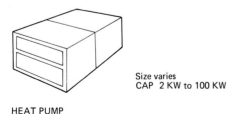

Size varies
CAP 2 KW to 100 KW

HEAT PUMP

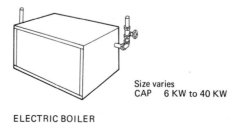

Size varies
CAP 6 KW to 40 KW

ELECTRIC BOILER

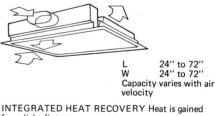

L	24" to 72"
W	24" to 72"
Capacity varies with air velocity	

INTEGRATED HEAT RECOVERY Heat is gained from light fixtures

CENTRALIZED HEATING SYSTEMS

Tseng-Yao Sun, P.E. and Kyoung S. Park, P.E.; Ayres, Cohen and Hayakawa; Consulting Engineers; Los Angeles/San Francisco, California

 15   HVAC

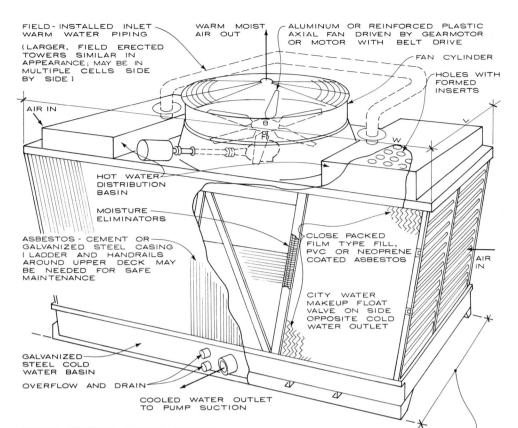

FIELD - INSTALLED INLET
WARM WATER PIPING

(LARGER, FIELD ERECTED
TOWERS SIMILAR IN
APPEARANCE; MAY BE IN
MULTIPLE CELLS SIDE
BY SIDE)

WARM MOIST
AIR OUT

ALUMINUM OR REINFORCED PLASTIC
AXIAL FAN DRIVEN BY GEARMOTOR
OR MOTOR WITH BELT DRIVE

FAN CYLINDER

HOLES WITH
FORMED
INSERTS

AIR IN

HOT WATER
DISTRIBUTION
BASIN

MOISTURE
ELIMINATORS

ASBESTOS - CEMENT OR
GALVANIZED STEEL CASING
(LADDER AND HANDRAILS
AROUND UPPER DECK MAY
BE NEEDED FOR SAFE
MAINTENANCE

CLOSE PACKED
FILM TYPE FILL,
PVC OR NEOPRENE
COATED ASBESTOS

CITY WATER
MAKEUP FLOAT
VALVE ON SIDE
OPPOSITE COLD
WATER OUTLET

AIR
IN

GALVANIZED
STEEL COLD
WATER BASIN

OVERFLOW AND DRAIN

COOLED WATER OUTLET
TO PUMP SUCTION

(FIELD ERECTED CUSTOM - DESIGN
COOLING TOWERS WITH CERAMIC TILE
FILL ARE AVAILABLE, FOR USE WITH
CASINGS OF MASONRY OR CONCRETE
TO BLEND WITH BUILDING APPEARANCE

SUPPORT ON TWO STEEL BEAMS
EACH DESIGN FOR 1/360 SPAN OR
MAX. 1/2 IN. DEFLECTION WHEN
BEAM IS UNIFORMLY LOADED WITH
65% OF TOWER'S OPERATING
WEIGHT

**CROSSFLOW INDUCED - DRAFT PACKAGED COOLING TOWER - 200 TO
500 TON CAPACITY**

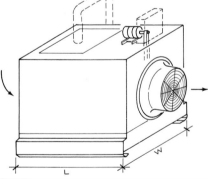

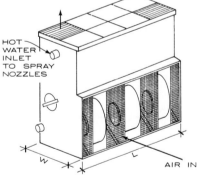

NOTE
AVAILABLE
IN SINGLE
MODULES AS
SKETCHED, OR
BACK-TO-BACK
DOUBLE INLET
OR END-TO-END

HOT
WATER
INLET
TO SPRAY
NOZZLES

AIR IN

**SMALL CROSSFLOW INDUCED
DRAFT PACKAGE COOLING
TOWER**

TONS 3GPM/TON 95-85-78	OVERALL DIMENSIONS (IN.)			OPERATING WEIGHT (LB)	MOTOR (HP)
	L	W	HT.		
5	62	34	49	750	1/3
25	70	48	78	1,200	3/4
50	82	76	92	2,400	1 1/2
100	100	95	100	5,600	5
200	83	164	117	8,300	10
500	113	232	160	19,300	25

**COUNTERFLOW FORCED DRAFT
PACKAGE COOLING TOWER**

TONS 3GPM/TON 95-85-78	OVERALL DIMENSIONS (IN.)			OPERATING WEIGHT (LB)	MOTOR (HP)
	L	W	HT.		
20	45	48	78	950	1 1/2
50	81	48	78	1,500	5
200	156	63	161	5,600	25
400	156	115	198	12,000	50
800	300	115	198	24,000	Two-50
1600	448	115	198	47,000	Four-50

Frederick H. Kohloss; Frederick H. Kohloss & Associates; Honolulu, Hawaii

NOTES

1. Cooling towers cool water for reuse in refrigeration condensers or other heat exchangers. Standard ratings are in tons of refrigeration when cooling 3 gal/min per ton from 95 to 85°F with ambient air at 78°F wet bulb. Selection is based on performance at local outdoor design conditions. Frequently the local outdoor ambient wet bulb temperature used is equal to or exceeded by 1% of summer hours.

2. Fans move air horizontally (crossflow) or up (counterflow) against water falling and wetting the fill or packing, to expose maximum water surface to the air. Reduced air flow reduces tower performance. Architectural enclosures should minimize obstruction to air flow.

3. Warm water is distributed at the top of the cooling tower by spray nozzles or basins with multiple orifices, and cooled water is collected in a basin at the bottom and pumped to condensers. Water is cooled by evaporating a very small portion. Water droplets may also be carried out by the air stream. Minerals and impurities present in all water increase concentration as pure water evaporates, so a little water is "bled" and chemicals are added to minimize scaling, corrosion, or biological fouling of condenser tubes. Towers for critical or large systems should be multicell for maintenance without shutdown.

4. Fan, motor, and water splashing noise may be a nuisance. Fan noise is reduced by two speed motors (about 8 dB at half speed, 15% power, and 60% capacity) and by intake and discharge attenuators (about 12 dB) with 10% power increase. Tower noise is louder in line with fan discharge and intake than in other directions. Each doubling of distance decreases noise about 6 dB. Barriers can reflect some noise from critical directions. Locate towers for free air movement. Avoid hot air recirculation, long piping from pumps and condensers, and inadequate substructures. Cooling towers should be located so that noise and water droplet carryover and fog at air discharge in cold weather will not be a nuisance. Consider seismic and wind load in anchoring tower to supports; towers are usually designed to withstand 30 psf wind load. Basins may be heated for winter use.

ENCLOSURE CONSIDERATIONS

Provide liberal wall openings on air inlet sides and mount tower so that air outlet is at top of enclosure. Consider effect of wind on nearby structure and enclosure to minimize hot, moist discharge air from being recirculated into inlet.

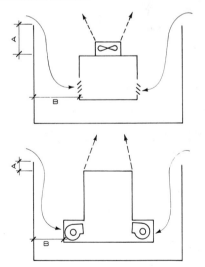

A = Height of enclosure above tower outlet. Minimize or extend shroud up from tower.

B = If enclosure walls have no opening, horizontal distance from tower inlet must increase greatly.

(Power for fan must be increased.)

Consult cooling tower manufacturer for minimum "B" dimension.

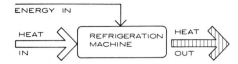

The basic refrigeration cycle performs one simple job; it moves heat from one place to another. Refrigerators move heat from the storage compartment to the surrounding room. Air-conditioners move heat from building rooms to the outside environment. Refrigeration equipment's efficiency is indicated by its Energy Efficiency Rating. EER is an index of the number of BTU's of heat movement accomplished per watt of electrical input energy. The higher the EER, the more efficient, and less costly it will be to operate a given piece of equipment.

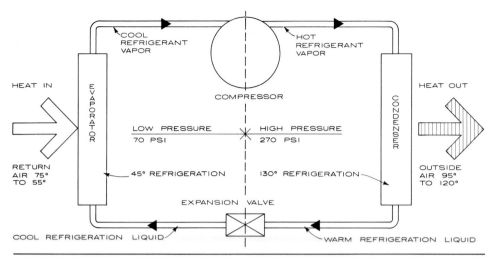

TYPICAL SYSTEM TEMPERATURES AND PRESSURES

A large quantity of heat is required to boil or evaporate a liquid. This latent or hidden heat is the key to moving large quantities of heat with a small amount of refrigerant.

To move heat from an area of low temperature to an area of high temperature (e.g., a building at 75°F to its environment at 95°F) refrigeration equipment needs to change boiling temperature of the refrigerant. This is accomplished by changing the pressure on the refrigerant.

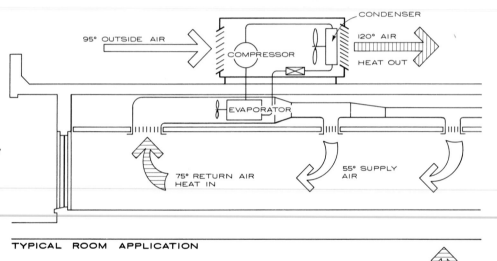

TYPICAL ROOM APPLICATION

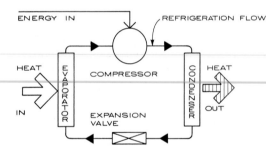

The basic refrigeration cycle includes an evaporator coil which absorbs heat from its surroundings as a refrigerant evaporates internally. The refrigerant vapor is then drawn into a compressor where its pressure and boiling (or condensing) temperature are increased. The refrigerant vapor is then discharged into a condenser coil where it gives up the latent heat absorbed in the evaporator and returns to a liquid state. Finally, liquid refrigerant circulates through an expansion valve where pressure and evaporation temperature are reduced, and the cycle is repeated.

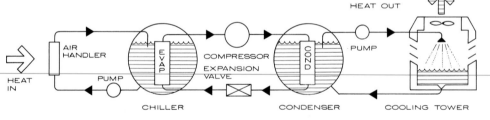

CHILLER AND COOLING TOWER

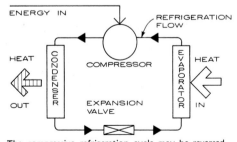

The compressive refrigeration cycle may be reversed to extract heat from a low temperature source (such as outside air) and reject that heat at higher temperature to heat a building. The basic equipment is unchanged with the exception of a four-way reversing valve and controls which permit the condensor and evaporator to exchange functions. The heat pump is more efficient than electrical resistance heat. Its efficiency, of course, is a function of heat source temperature.

In large buildings it is impractical to move heat with air only, since duct size would be excessive. Therefore, a chiller (water tank) is added to the evaporator, and chilled water is circulated to air handling units throughout the building. Cooling towers are typically installed in such large systems to increase efficiency. Air-conditioning equipment rejecting heat to 80°F cooling tower water will require less input energy than the same equipment rejecting heat to 95°F outside air.

A second refrigeration cycle, the absorption cycle, uses a heat source and an absorbent to move heat.

The absorber and generator perform the same function as the compressor (see above); and the cycle operates under high vacuum. Generally speaking, absorption systems are less efficient than compressive systems and are a wise choice only when waste heat is available for input energy.

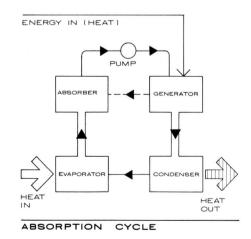

ABSORPTION CYCLE

F. J. Trost; Texas A & M University; College Station, Texas

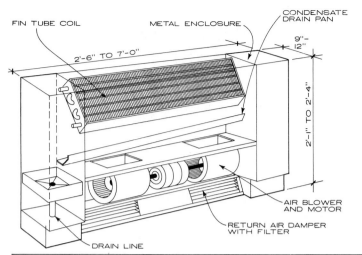

FIN TUBE COIL
METAL ENCLOSURE
CONDENSATE DRAIN PAN
9"-12"
2'-6" TO 7'-0"
2-1" TO 2-4"
AIR BLOWER AND MOTOR
RETURN AIR DAMPER WITH FILTER
DRAIN LINE

STANDARD FAN COIL UNIT

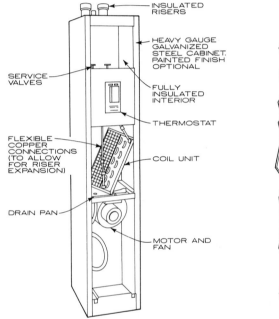

INSULATED RISERS
HEAVY GAUGE GALVANIZED STEEL CABINET. PAINTED FINISH OPTIONAL
SERVICE VALVES
FULLY INSULATED INTERIOR
THERMOSTAT
FLEXIBLE COPPER CONNECTIONS (TO ALLOW FOR RISER EXPANSION)
COIL UNIT
DRAIN PAN
MOTOR AND FAN

STANDARD HIGHRISE UNIT

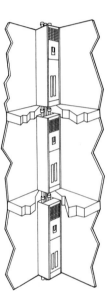

HIGHRISE APPLICATION

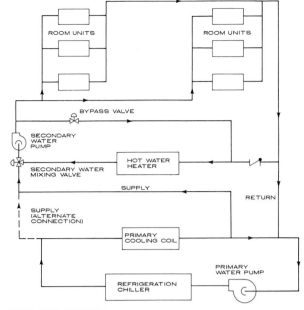

ROOM UNITS
ROOM UNITS
BYPASS VALVE
SECONDARY WATER PUMP
SECONDARY WATER MIXING VALVE
HOT WATER HEATER
SUPPLY
RETURN
SUPPLY (ALTERNATE CONNECTION)
PRIMARY COOLING COIL
PRIMARY WATER PUMP
REFRIGERATION CHILLER

TWO-PIPE SYSTEM

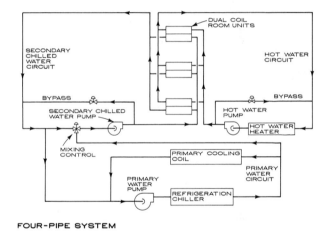

DUAL COIL ROOM UNITS
SECONDARY CHILLED WATER CIRCUIT
HOT WATER CIRCUIT
BYPASS
BYPASS
SECONDARY CHILLED WATER PUMP
HOT WATER PUMP
HOT WATER HEATER
MIXING CONTROL
PRIMARY COOLING COIL
PRIMARY WATER PUMP
PRIMARY WATER CIRCUIT
REFRIGERATION CHILLER

FOUR-PIPE SYSTEM

PIPING SYSTEMS

NOTES

Chilled water terminals are fan coil units used to dehumidify and cool the airstream injected into the conditioned space.

The typical fan coil unit consists of a finned tube chilled water coil, which is finned to increase its heat transfer surface, a fan used to circulate air over the coil and discharge cool air into the conditioned space, a drip pan to collect condensate from the dehumidified air and drain line to transport the condensate away from the fan coil unit.

Fan coil systems are classified into two major groups:

1. A TWO-PIPE SYSTEM uses a single supply pipe (hot or cold depending on the season) and a single return pipe, in a secondary water circuit. Chilled water is introduced into the secondary circuit directly through a mixing valve from the primary chilled water circuit. If the terminal unit is to provide heat, a hot water, steam, or electric heat exchanger is incorporated into the loop. Direct introduction of hot water from a primary circuit is also employed. The water coil output of each terminal unit is controlled by a local space thermostat.

2. The FOUR-PIPE SYSTEM provides independent sources of heating and cooling to each room unit through separate supply and return chilled water pipes and separate supply and return hot water pipes. The terminal units usually have two separate water coils as well. Local thermostats control the volume of secondary water supplied to each unit.

NOTE

Highrise corner units can be furred into the walls of the room. They minimize the piping from floor to floor since they are stacked and directly connected to the units above and below for water supply, returns, and drains.

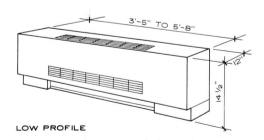

3'-5" TO 5'-8"
12"
14 1/2"

LOW PROFILE

NOTE

A low profile fan coil unit is available for installation along window walls, below chalkboards, or in lobbies and hallways where appearance is important. They normally stand free from the wall, with clearance behind the unit for draperies.

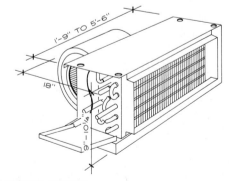

1'-9" TO 5'-6"
18"
9'-10 1/4"

FURRED-IN UNIT

NOTE

Furred-in units can be mounted where convenient in the room. They can use ducts to bring in outside air and can be mounted in wall alcoves or ceiling spaces. A removable front panel is needed to conceal the unit and provide complete access to internal components.

GENERAL NOTES

Chilled water is the most common medium for transferring heat from any type of cooling equipment, such as cooling coils and heat exchangers, to some source of refrigeration.

A chilled water system is a closed circuit system that recirculates water between a mechanical refrigeration water chilling unit and remote cooling equipment, usually operating with water temperatures in the range between 40 and 55°F. There are three types of refrigeration units used in chilled water systems.

1. Centrifugal chiller with electric motor or steam turbine drive.
2. Reciprocating chiller, with electric motor drive.
3. Steam absorption chiller.

When a chilled water system is also used to circulate hot water for winter heating, it is called a dual temperature water system. A heat pump may serve as a source for both hot water and chilled water in a dual temperature system. The design water temperature of chilled water systems usually falls in a rather narrow range because of limitations imposed by the necessity for dehumidification and by avoidance of the possibility of freeze-up in the chiller. Chilled water supply temperatures ranging from 42 to 60°F are normally employed in comfort applications.

Design flow rates depend on the type of terminal apparatus and the supply temperature. In general, a higher temperature rise (or a greater temperature difference between supply and return temperatures) reduces the initial cost and the operating cost of the distribution system and pumps required and increases the efficiency of the chillers. In a given chilled water system, the selection of the design flow rate and the supply temperature, therefore, are closely related.

Although lower chilled water temperatures permit higher rises (or larger temperature difference) lower chiller efficiencies result.

Water treatment may be required in chilled water systems to control corrosion rate, scaling, or algae growth.

Layout of piping systems for chilled water distribution vary greatly depending on system capacity, extent of distribution, type of terminals used, and control scheme to be employed.

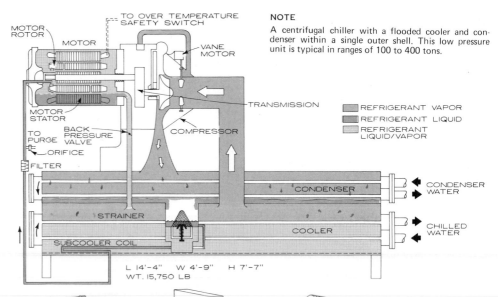

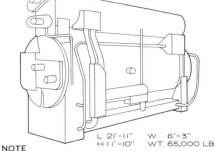

NOTE

A centrifugal chiller with a flooded cooler and condenser within a single outer shell. This low pressure unit is typical in ranges of 100 to 400 tons.

L 14'-4"   W 4'-9"   H 7'-7"
WT. 15,750 LB

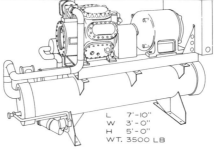

L 7'-10"
W 3'-0"
H 5'-0"
WT. 3500 LB

NOTE

A typical reciprocating package chiller, ideally suited to smaller jobs requiring less than 200 tons cooling.

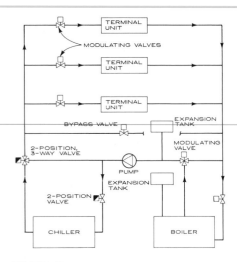

L 21'-11"   W 6'-3"
H 11'-10"   WT. 65,000 LB

NOTE

A two-stage absorption chiller, steam powered for efficient production of 200 to 600 tons of cooling.

PACKAGE WATER CHILLERS

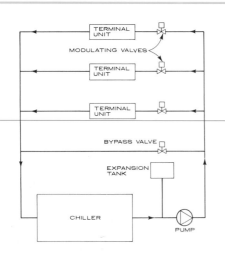

FIGURE 1

ELEMENTARY CHILLED WATER SYSTEM

NOTE

A chilled water system basically consists of a refrigeration water chilling unit, a chilled water recirculating pump, terminal cooling equipment, and an expansion tank. A chilled water bypass valve may be required in systems with two-way modulating valve control at the terminal units. As the cooling load on the terminal equipment decreases, the modulating valve closes and reduces the flow through the terminal. When the water flow through the terminal units is significantly throttled, the bypass valve opens gradually to prevent system pressure buildup and to maintain the water flow required for the proper operation of the chiller.

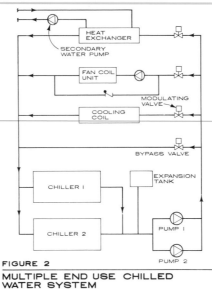

FIGURE 2

MULTIPLE END USE CHILLED WATER SYSTEM

NOTE

In large commercial system applications, the chilled water system consists of multiple chillers and pumps and a differential pressure controlled bypass valve arrangement. The terminal cooling equipment may be chilled water cooling coil of a central station air-conditioning unit, direct injection secondary water pump of a terminal fan coil unit system, heat exchanger of a closed loop dual-temperature secondary water system, and so on.

The chilled water bypass valve operates as described under elementary chilled water system.

FIGURE 3

TWO-PIPE DUAL TEMPERATURE SYSTEM

NOTE

In a two-pipe dual temperature system hot water is circulated through the terminal units during cold weather and chilled water is circulated during the hot weather. The distribution system may be divided into zones, each of which is capable of changeover from heating to cooling, independent of the other zones.

When the hot and chilled water supply to each terminal unit is in two separate pipes, but the return is in a common pipe, the system is called a three-pipe system. In a four-pipe system, separate supply and return mains for both hot and chilled water are run to each terminal unit.

Anilkumar V. Patel; Joseph R. Loring & Associates, Inc., Consulting Engineers; New York, New York

GENERAL

The process of removing heat from a refrigerant is called condensing. It is during the condensing process, in a refrigerant cycle, that the refrigerant rejects heat absorbed during the evaporation and compression processes, is reconverted to a liquid state, and becomes ready to repeat the cycle.

To convert the refrigerant from gaseous to liquid state heat exchangers called condensers are used. Air cooled and water cooled condensers are the predominant types used in the building construction industry.

In the less than 50 ton capacity range, water cooled condensers are favored mostly where city water or other water sources such as lake, river, or well are available for once-through use without recirculation of water.

Where water is scarce, as well as in computer rooms and other special air-conditioning applications where year-round temperature and humidity control is required, dry coolers of up to 25 ton capacity are normally used. Where winter ambient is below the water freezing temperature, glycol is added to the condenser water. The heat rejection to the outdoor air is by sensible heat transfer, which is dependent on the dry bulb temperature of the air.

In refrigeration systems larger than 50 ton capacity, water cooled condensers are used to cool the recirculating condenser water. Both the closed circuit evaporative cooler and the cooling tower operate on the principle of evaporative cooling, which is dependent on the wet bulb temperature of the air. The closed circuit evaporative coolers are available in sizes up to 300 tons, and are used when contamination of the condenser water by its direct contact with the outdoor air cannot be tolerated.

Use of cooling tower is generally acceptable in most installations in the building construction industry. Temperature of the water leaving the cooling tower is approximately 7 to 10°F above the wet bulb temperature of the air flowing through the spray deck of the tower.

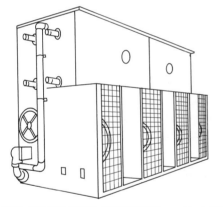

THE EVAPORATIVE CONDENSER combines the functions of a cooling tower and a water cooling condenser. Latent heat transfer is more effective as a means of heat dissipation. This permits a smaller sized unit than an equivalent tonnage air cooled unit, and considerable energy savings in fan horsepower.

Installations can be either indoors in an equipment room with appropriate ducts or outdoors ground mounted or mounted on a roof. When outdoors, adequate protection from freezing must be provided.

For sizing of condensing units, the manufacturers' rating is the only reliable method of determining the unit capacity.

Multiple evaporative condensers may be connected in parallel, or an evaporative condenser may be connected in parallel with a shell and tube condenser. Proper piping and traps must be installed in these cases to prevent unequal loading or overloading.

Two or more independent refrigeration circuits may be incorporated in a single evaporative condenser unit. With the proper circuiting arrangements, each may operate at a different suction and condensing temperature.

Anilkumar V. Patel; Joseph R. Loring & Associates, Inc., Consulting Engineers; New York, New York

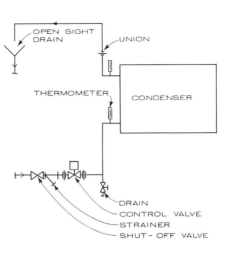

WATER COOLED CONDENSER

For water cooled condenser using city, well, or river water, the return is run higher than the condenser so that the condenser is always full of water. Water flow through the condenser is regulated by a supply line control valve, which is actuated from condenser head pressure control to maintain a constant condensing temperature with variations in load. City water systems usually require check valves and open sight drains, as shown.

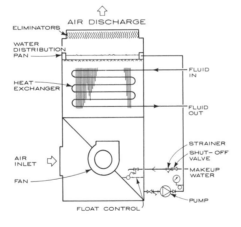

EVAPORATIVE COOLER

The condenser water is circulated inside the tubes of the unit's heat exchanger. Heat flows from the condenser water through the heat exchanger tubes to the spray water outside, which is cascading downward over the tubes. Air is forced upward through the heat exchanger, evaporating a small percentage of the spray water, absorbing the latent heat of vaporization, and discharging the heat to the atmosphere.

The remaining water falls to the sump to be recirculated by the pump. The water consumed is the amount evaporated plus a small amount that is bled off to limit the concentration of impurities in the pan.

The condenser water circulates through the clean, closed loop of the heat exchanger and is never exposed to the airstream or the spray water outside the heat exchanger tubes.

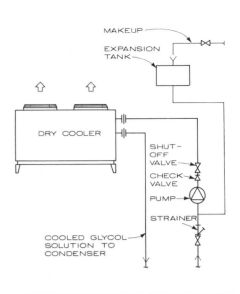

DRY COOLER

The condenser water-glycol solution is circulated inside the finned tubes of the dry cooler's heat exchanger. Heat flows from the condenser water-glycol solution through the heat exchanger tube walls to the fins. Propeller fans draw air over the fins, which transfer its heat to the air passing over it.

An aquastat sensing the temperature of the solution that leaves the dry cooler cycles the fan(s) to maintain the desired temperature.

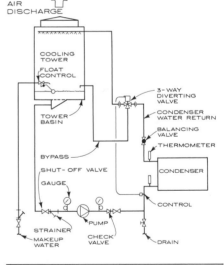

COOLING TOWER

Water flows to the pump from the tower basin and is discharged under pressure to the condenser and back to the tower where it is cooled through the spray deck. Since it is usually desirable to maintain condenser water temperature above a predetermined minimum, return water is partially bypassed around the tower through a control valve to maintain desired supply water temperature.

In this condenser water system, air is continuously in contact with the water. Special consideration for chemical treatment and allowance for impurities, scale, and corrosion in condenser and piping system designs is then required.

Water flow quantity required depends on the refrigeration system employed and the available temperature of the condenser water. Lower condenser water supply temperature results in increased refrigeration machine efficiency.

ALL-AIR SYSTEMS

With this type of system, the air treating and refrigeration plants may be located some distance from the conditioned space in a central mechanical room. The central treating station not only cleans the air, but also heats or cools, humidifies or dehumidifies. Only the final cooling-heating medium (air) is brought into the conditioned space through ducts and distributed within the space through outlets or mixing terminals.

The common names for some of the all-air types are:

Single duct, variable volume.
Dual conduit.
Single duct with reheat.
Multizone.
Double duct.

SINGLE DUCT, VARIABLE VOLUME

This central station system supplies a single stream of either hot or cold air at normal velocity. Capacity is adjusted to load by automatic volume control. Systems for exterior rooms would be zoned by exposure.

There are air terminal diffusers available that have self-contained, self-balancing, system operated controls, which are factory installed and calibrated.

DUAL CONDUIT

This high velocity system with central air treating plant supplies two air streams to each room. The constant volume, variable temperature primary air supply neutralizes transmission gains or losses throughout the year. The secondary stream is variable volume, constant temperature. Room terminals incorporate thermostatically controlled air volume regulators.

SINGLE DUCT WITH REHEAT

This system consolidates all major equipment in the machine room except the reheat element that is located at times near the room or in the module. Primary treated air is supplied at constant volume from this central point through a single duct to room units. Each room unit is equipped with a small steam or hot water reheat coil, which is located either in the supply air stream or in an induced air position. Supply air temperature can be as low as 38°F, thus conserving on duct size and fan horsepower.

MULTIZONE

This method distributes a single air stream to each room through finger ducts at normal velocity. Central air treating apparatus includes dampers that premix the cold and warm air supplies controlled by room thermostats.

DOUBLE DUCT, CONSTANT VOLUME

This central station system supplies treated air through a pair of ducts to room terminals of special design and function. These terminals mix air automatically to maintain proper temperatures as well as proper volume and air patterns.

ALL-WATER SYSTEMS

The all-water systems are those with fan coil types of room terminals to which may be connected one or two water circuits. The cooling medium (such as chilled water or brine) may be supplied from a remote source and circulated through the coils in the fan coil terminal, which is located in the conditioned space. These circuits may be either two-pipe or four-pipe distribution. Ventilation is obtained through an opening in the wall or from bleed-off from the interior zone system or by infiltration. Another variation, uses a unit ventilator.

TWO-PIPE

Either hot or chilled water is piped throughout the building to a number of fan coil units. One pipe supplies water and the other returns it.

FOUR-PIPE

Two separate piping circuits are used—one for hot and one for chilled water. The modified fan coil unit has a double or split coil. Part of this heats only and part cools only.

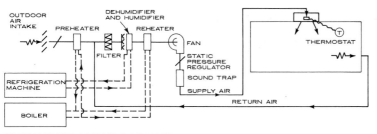

SINGLE DUCT, VARIABLE VOLUME

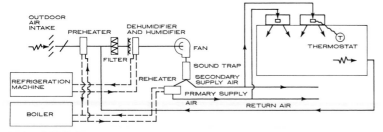

DUAL CONDUIT

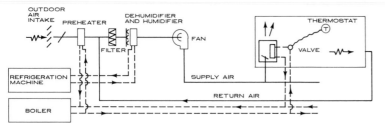

SINGLE DUCT WITH REHEAT

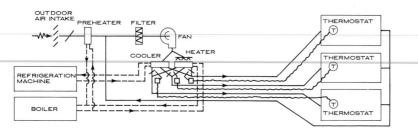

MULTIZONE

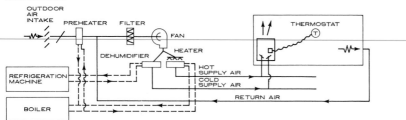

DOUBLE DUCT, CONSTANT VOLUME

ALL-AIR SYSTEMS

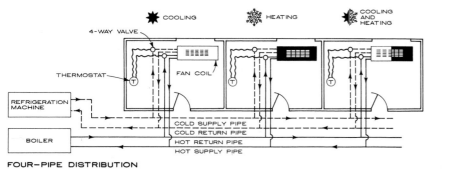

FOUR-PIPE DISTRIBUTION

ALL-WATER SYSTEMS

Carrier Corporation; Syracuse, New York

AIR-WATER SYSTEMS

Like the all-air system, the air apparatus and refrigeration plants are separate from the conditioned space; however, the cooling-heating of the conditioned space is affected in only a small part by air brought from the central apparatus. The major part of room thermal load is balanced by warm or cooled water circulated either through a coil in an induction unit or through a radiant panel.

The different air-water types are:

    Induction . . . either bypass air or water control.
    Fan coil with supplementary air.
    Radiant panels with supplementary air.

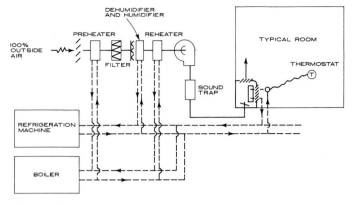

INDUCTION

INDUCTION

This system uses a high velocity, high pressure, constant volume air supply to a high induction type of terminal. Induced air from the room is either heated or cooled within the terminal as required. This capacity control is by flow of water or air bypass. This system may use two pipes (one water circuit) or four pipes (two water circuits) for heating and cooling.

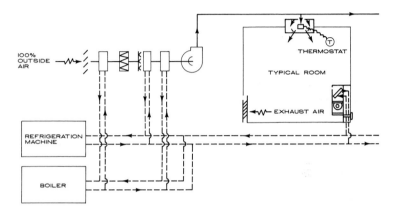

FAN COIL WITH SUPPLY AIR

THE FAN-COIL WITH SUPPLEMENTARY AIR

The fan-coil type of terminal provides direct heating or cooling of the room air. A supplementary constant volume air supply provides the necessary ventilation.

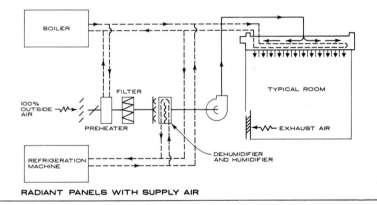

RADIANT PANELS WITH SUPPLEMENTARY AIR

The radiant panel terminal in ceiling or wall provides either radiant heating or cooling. A constant volume air stream is supplied for dehumidification and ventilation.

RADIANT PANELS WITH SUPPLY AIR

AIR — WATER SYSTEMS

DIRECT REFRIGERANT SYSTEMS

Refrigerant systems are those that utilize self-contained window, in-the-wall, roof, or floor mounted units for extracting or adding heat. The units are normally located within or next to the air conditioned space and consist of only the elements essential to producing the cooling or heating effect. Heating can be provided either by reverse cycle type, such as a heat pump, or by supplementary heating elements.

ROOFTOP

Uses gas or electricity to supply both heating and cooling.

THROUGH-THE-WALL

Cooling unit used with gas, electric, or central hot water heating for year-round air conditioning.

PACKAGED

Systems contained roof mounted, air cooled condensing units. A reverse cycle heat pump or supplementary heating is required for year-round operation.

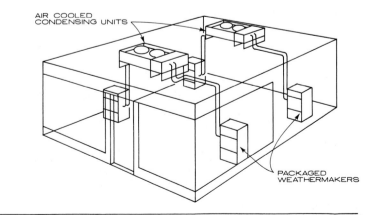

DIRECT REFRIGERANT SYSTEMS

Carrier Corporation; Syracuse, New York

GENERAL NOTES

The air handling equipment room should be centrally located to minimize the distance the air has to travel from equipment room to the farthest air-conditioned space. The fan noise transmission to the adjacent spaces must also be considered. If the equipment room is located near conference rooms, sleeping quarters, broadcasting studios, or other sound sensitive areas, special treatment of the equipment room area will be required to provide adequate sound and vibration isolation from the surrounding areas.

Adequate access space must be provided to maintain and replace heating coils, cooling coils, filters, damper motors and linkage, control valves, bearings, fan motors, fans, belts, pulleys, and so on.

The figure below shows plan of a typical equipment room with one floor mounted air-conditioning unit and one suspended return air fan. The air-conditioning unit shown is of the horizontal draw-through type and consists of fan head, reheat coil, cooling coil, preheat coil, filters, return air plenum, outdoor air intake plenum, and access sections on either side of coils.

Note that the outdoor air intake louver and the exhaust air louver are located on different walls. Where both the intake and the exhaust louver must be located on the same wall, they must be as far apart as possible, but not less than 10 ft in order to minimize the short circuiting between the exhaust and intake air. Baffles, of masonry or other suitable construction, may be used to achieve the separation between the exhaust and the intake air.

NOTES

1. Where a horizontal blow-through type of unit is used, the length of the unit will essentially be the same as shown for the draw-through unit.

2. Where higher headroom is available, a vertical unit, which can only be of the draw-through type, may be used to reduce the length of the unit. Depending on the size of the unit, this reduction in length will range from 2 ft to 3 ft 6 in.

3. The figure shows an axial fan for returning air from the space. The return air fan may not be required where the air-conditioning system is not designed to operate under economizer cycle (cooling by cold outdoor air) mode.

4. A floor mounted centrifugal fan, of single width, single inlet type or double width, double inlet type, may be used in place of the suspended axial fan shown. However, this will generally result in increased width of the equipment room.

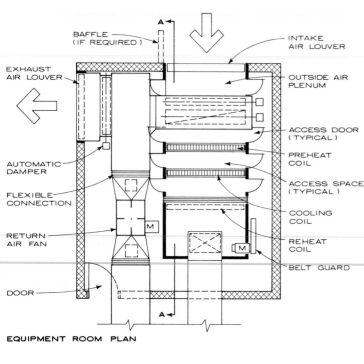

EQUIPMENT ROOM PLAN

EQUIPMENT ROOM SECTION A-A

EQUIPMENT ROOM SPACE REQUIREMENTS

	APPROXIMATE OVERALL DIMENSION OF SUPPLY AIR UNITS			RECOMMENDED ROOM DIMENSIONS		
CFM RANGE	**W**	**H**	**L**	**W**	**H**	**L**
1,000– 1,800	4'-9''	2'-9''	14'-9''	12'-6''	9'-0''	18'-9''
1,801– 3,000	5'-0''	3'-6''	16'-0''	13'-9''	9'-0''	20'-0''
3,001– 4,000	6'-9''	4'-6''	16'-0''	17'-6''	9'-0''	20'-0''
4,001– 6,000	7'-6''	4'-6''	16'-9''	18'-0''	9'-0''	20'-9''
6,001– 7,000	7'-6''	4'-9''	18'-3''	18'-6''	9'-6''	22'-3''
7,001– 9,000	8'-0''	5'-0''	18'-9''	19'-0''	10'-0''	22'-9''
9,001–12,000	10'-0''	5'-6''	21'-0''	23'-0''	11'-0''	25'-0''
12,001–16,000	10'-3''	6'-0''	22'-0''	23'-6''	12'-6''	26'-0''
16,001–19,000	10'-6''	6'-6''	23'-9''	24'-0''	13'-0''	27'-9''
19,001–22,000	11'-9''	7'-3''	25'-0''	26'-9''	15'-0''	29'-0''
22,001–27,000	11'-9''	8'-6''	26'-0''	27'-0''	16'-0''	30'-0''
27,001–32,000	13'-0''	9'-9''	27'-9''	29'-0''	18'-0''	31'-9''

AIR HANDLING EQUIPMENT ROOM REQUIREMENTS

AIR FILTRATION AND ODOR REMOVAL

Air filter selection is determined by the degree of cleanliness required. The initial cost, ease of maintenance, improvement of housekeeping, health benefits, and product quality are considerations. Size and quantity of dust and contaminants are also factors.

Filters most often are located at the air inlet of the heating, ventilating, and air-conditioning equipment, providing protection to the equipment and the area served. Filters are located at the equipment discharge and at entry of air into clean rooms, operating rooms, critical health care rooms, and various industrial process areas. Filters located in return air and exhaust air limit the contamination of other areas and the atmosphere.

AIR FILTER types are dry media, viscous (sticky) media, renewable media, and electronic. Filter performance tests and ratings have been established by ASHRAE, NBS, and AFI. The three operating characteristics that distinguish the various types of air cleaners are efficiency, air flow resistance, and dust holding capacity. Efficiency measures the ability of the air cleaner to remove particulate matter from an air stream. Average efficiency over the life of the filter is the most important consideration. Airflow resistance is the static pressure drop across the filter at a given airflow rate. Dust holding capacity defines the amount of a particular type of dust that an air cleaner can hold when operated at a specified airflow rate to some

maximum resistance value, or before its efficiency is seriously reduced as a result of the collected dust. Filter efficiency comparisons should always be based on the same test conditions.

PREFILTERS are required to extend the life of costlier high efficiency filters. High efficiency particulate filters (HEPA), and their integral frames, should be tested and certified in place. Filter pressure

drop gauges are recommended as an aid to economical replacement scheduling for all types of filters.

ODOR REMOVAL is best controlled by limiting the source. Dilution of odors by direct exhaust ventilation is the most common control method. Air washer and carbon filters are usually used for reclaiming odorous air. Ozone treatment and aerosol masking of odors are sometimes used.

AIR FILTER CHARACTERISTICS

MEDIA AND TYPE	PERCENT EFFICIENCY RANGE		DUST HOLDING CAPACITY	AIRFLOW RESISTANCE (IN. WATER)
	ATMOSPHERIC DUST	SMALL PARTICLES		
Dry panel throwaway	15–30	NA	Excellent	0.1–0.5
Viscous panel throwaway	20–35	NA	Good	0.1–0.5
Dry panel cleanable	15–20	NA	Superior	0.08–0.5
Viscous panel cleanable	15–25	NA	Superior	0.08–0.5
Mat panel renewable	10–90	0–60	Good to superior	0.15–1.0
Roll mat renewable	10–90	0–55	Good to superior	0.15–0.65
Roll oil bath	15–25	NA	Superior	0.3–0.5
Close pleat mat panel	NA	85–95	Varies	0.4–1.0
High efficiency particulate	NA	95–99.9	Varies	1.0–3.0
Membrane	NA	to 100	NA	NA
Electrostatic with mat	80–98	NA	Varies	0.15–1.25

Anilkmar V. Patel; Joseph R. Loring & Associates, Inc., Consulting Engineers; New York, New York

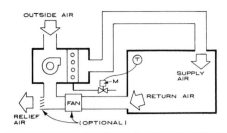
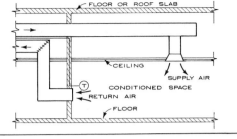

Low pressure system suitable for serving areas requiring only one zone of control. May be used in multiple where more than one zone of control is required. Relatively low first cost. Air handling unit may be blow through or draw through type.

SINGLE ZONE SYSTEM

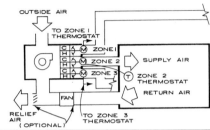
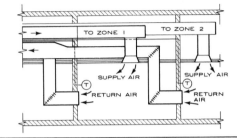

Low pressure system for serving areas requiring more than one zone of control. Practical limit of approximately eight zones per air handling unit. Can be used for simultaneously heating some areas while cooling others; however, control is relatively poor because of leakage at unit dampers and coil wiping. Relatively low first cost.

MULTIZONE SYSTEM

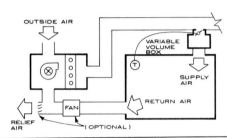
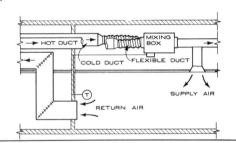

Low, medium, or high pressure system capable of providing a control zone for each box. Can be used for cooling only or for heating and cooling. Changeover from heating to cooling should be zoned by exposure. Provides variable air change rate and not applicable to areas requiring fixed air change rates such as certain hospital and laboratory applications. Relatively low first cost. Air handling system may be blow through or draw through type.

SINGLE DUCT VARIABLE VOLUME SYSTEM

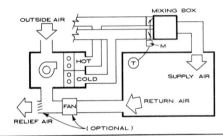
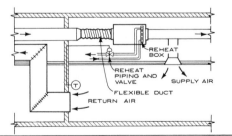

Low, medium, or high pressure system capable of providing a control zone for each box. Provides complete heating and cooling capability with no need for changeover. Available for both constant and variable volume systems (normally does not reduce air flow below 50% of maximum). Provides excellent year-round control. Relatively high first cost.

DOUBLE DUCT SYSTEM

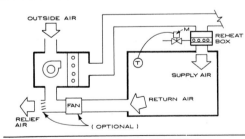

Low, medium, or high pressure system capable of providing a control zone per box. Provides heating and cooling capability (no changeover required). Available for constant and variable volume systems that normally do not reduce airflow below 50% of maximum. Excellent control, high first cost, high energy consumption; use generally limited to laboratory and hospital applications where constant volume and excellent control is required. Air handling system may be blow through or draw through type.

SINGLE DUCT REHEAT SYSTEM

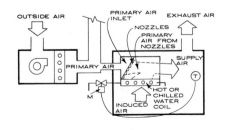

Medium or high pressure system capable of providing a control zone per induction unit. Can be used for cooling or heating and cooling. Changeover accomplished by providing hot or chilled water to coil. Primary air (approximately 20 to 40% of air circulated) passes through unit and is usually exhausted. Provides excellent control. Complies with requirements of hospital patient rooms where air cannot be recirculated to main unit. Relatively high first cost. Air handling unit may be blow through or draw through type.

INDUCTION SYSTEM

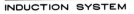
William Tao & Associates, Inc., Consulting Engineers; St. Louis, Missouri

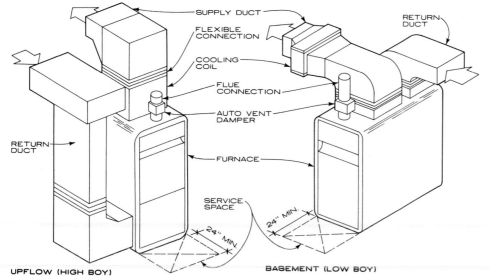

UPFLOW (HIGH BOY)

BASEMENT (LOW BOY)

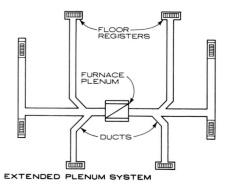

EXTENDED PLENUM SYSTEM

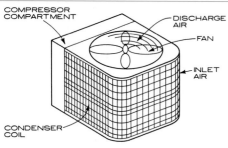

DOWNFLOW (COUNTER FLOW)
WARM AIR FURNACES

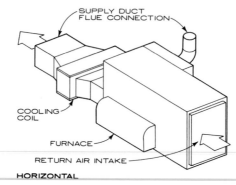

HORIZONTAL

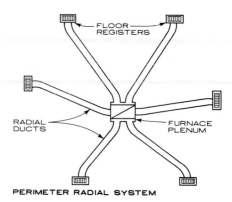

PERIMETER RADIAL SYSTEM

FLOOR AREA REQUIRED BY WARM AIR FURNACE

OUTPUT CAPACITY (BTU/HR)	FURNACE FLOOR AREA (SQ FT)*
Up to 52,000	2.4
52,000–84,000	4.2
84,000–120,000	6.6
120,000–200,000	13.1

*Based on net floor area occupied by the upflow or downflow furnace. Low boy unit requires 50% more floor area. Space for combustion air should be added as required by local codes. Adequate space should be provided for service.

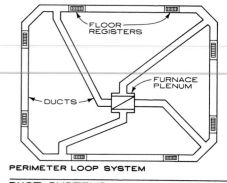

PERIMETER LOOP SYSTEM
DUCT SYSTEMS

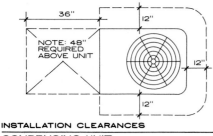

CONDENSING UNIT

NOTES

1. Warm air furnace units are designed primarily for residential, small commercial, or classroom heating. Cooling can be added to these units by installing a cooling coil downstream from the furnace, with refrigerant compressor and condenser remotely located outside of the building.

2. Duct system from the furnace unit can be either above the ceiling or in the floor slab. Above ceiling distribution systems are usually the radial type with high wall registers. Perimeter loop and extended plenum systems in floor slabs provide good air distribution. There are smaller temperature variations across the floor with perimeter loop systems than with radial or extended plenum systems.

3. Duct systems may also be installed below the living spaces in a crawl space or basement.

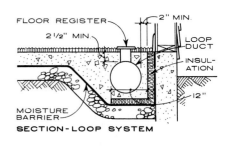

SECTION–LOOP SYSTEM

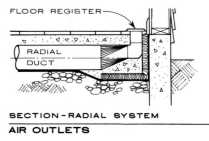

SECTION–RADIAL SYSTEM
AIR OUTLETS

INSTALLATION CLEARANCES
CONDENSING UNIT

DiClemente-Siegel Engineering, Inc.; Southfield, Michigan

DUCT CONSTRUCTION

Ductwork must be permanent, rigid, nonbuckling, and nonrattling. Joints in ductwork should be airtight. Galvanized iron or aluminum sheets are usually used in the construction of ducts. The ducts may be either round or rectangular in cross section.

In general, supply ducts should be constructed entirely of noncombustible material. Supply ducts serving a single family dwelling need not meet this requirement, except for the first 3 ft from the unit, provided they are used in conjunction with listed heating units, are properly constructed from a base material of metal or mineral, and are properly applied. Warm air ducts passing through cold spaces or located in exposed walls should have 1 to 2 in. of insulation.

Supply ducts must be securely supported by metal hangers, straps, lugs, or brackets. No nails should be driven through duct walls, and no unnecessary holes should be cut in them.

Supply ducts should be equipped with an adjustable locking type damper for air volume control. The damper should be installed in the branch duct as far from the outlet as possible, where it is accessible.

Automatic smoke dampers are required wherever ductwork passes through a rated smoke barrier partition.

Return systems having more than one return intake may be equipped with balancing dampers.

Attention should be given to the elimination of noise. Metal ducts should be connected to the unit by strips of flexible fire resistant fabric. Electrical conduit and piping, if directly connected to the unit, may increase noise transmission. Return air intakes immediately adjacent to the unit may also increase noise transmission. Installation of a fan directly under a return air grille should be avoided.

DUCT MATERIAL THICKNESS

ROUND DUCT DIA. OR RECTANGULAR DUCT WIDTH (IN.)	GALVANIZED IRON U.S. GAUGE	ALUMINUM B & S GAUGE
Ducts enclosed in partitions		
14 or less	30	24
Over 14	28	24
Ducts not enclosed in partitions		
14 or less	28	24
Over 14	26	23

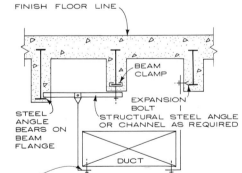

NOTE
On ducts over 48 in. wide hangers shall turn under and fasten to bottom of duct. When cross-sectional area exceeds 8 sq ft duct will be braced by angles on all four sides.

DUCT SUPPORT DETAIL

Wm. G. Miner, AIA, Architect, Washington, D.C.

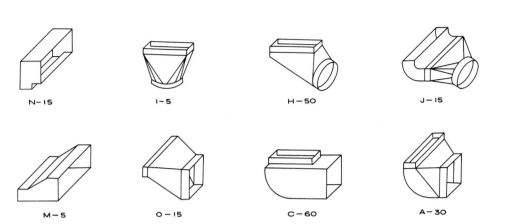

AIR BOOT FITTINGS

NOTE: N—15 ← NUMBER = EQUIVALENT LENGTH (FT) ↑ LETTER = SHAPE DESIGNATION

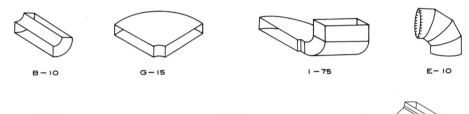

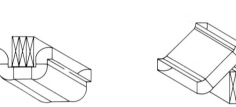

ANGLES AND ELBOWS FOR BRANCH DUCTS

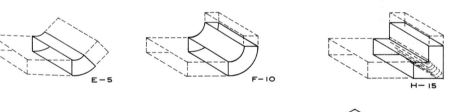

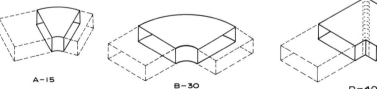

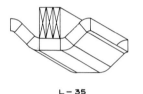

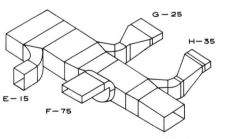

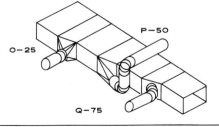

TRUNK DUCTS AND FITTINGS

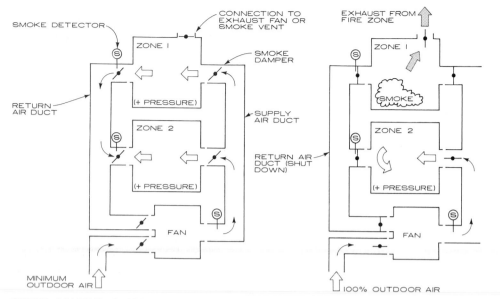

SMOKE CONTROL SYSTEM DIAGRAM

SMOKE CONTROL SYSTEM DIAGRAM

Diagram at far left shows normal conditions with positive air pressure in each zone. During a fire, significant positive pressure is established in zones adjacent to fire zones (which is under negative pressure because of exhaust airflow as shown in right hand drawing).

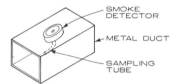

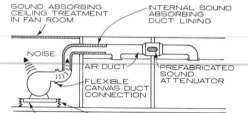

IN-DUCT SMOKE DETECTOR   OPEN SMOKE DAMPER   CLOSED DAMPER

SMOKE CONTROL SYSTEMS

CHECKLIST FOR SMOKE CONTROL SYSTEMS

1. Use mechanical air distribution systems to control smoke spread in buildings. For example, positive air pressure in exit corridors, stairwells, and service shafts can prevent smoke migration.

2. In cold climate regions, outside air intakes should be well below building's neutral plane.

3. Specify air duct materials that can withstand both additional pressure from supply and exhaust fans and elevated temperatures of smoke and hot gases.

4. Fire dampers (with 1½ hr UL label) used to restrict heat flow through air ducts also may prevent smoke spread if there is sufficient air pressure difference on opposite sides of damper. Smoke dampers must restrict passage of smoke when closed, operate automatically so they can be periodically tested, and be controlled by smoke detection devices.

5. In-duct detectors are usually not responsive to small fires. Room smoke detectors, located on ceilings and upper walls, will give earliest response.

6. Use automatic or self-closing hardware on doors in smoke partitions and on doors to smokeproof stairwells.

7. Coordinate energy conservation features (e.g., variable air volume, night or weekend fan shutdown for office occupancies) with smoke control airflow requirements.

8. Provide protected central facility to monitor operation of mechanical system and remote smoke control equipment such as smoke detectors, doors, dampers, and fans.

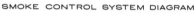

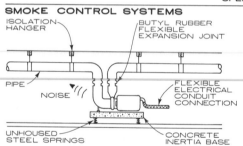

VIBRATION ISOLATION OF PUMPS

Pump motor assembly is supported by concrete inertia base sized at about one to two times fluid-filled pump weight plus all piping to first isolation hanger. Steel springs in turn support inertia base to isolate pump vibrations. Isolation hangers give resilient support to piping for distance of at least 150 times pipe diameter (or preferably complete length of pipeline). Butyl rubber or nylon tire cord-neoprene expansion joints can reduce noise and vibration transmission along pipe walls.

VIBRATION ISOLATION OF FANS (AND AIR DUCT NOISE CONTROL)

Unhoused, laterally stable steel springs, attached to rigid frame or inertia base, will isolate fan vibrations. Buildup of noise in fan room is reduced by sound absorbing room surface treatment (e.g., acoustical tiles or boards) and contained by heavy wall and floor-ceiling constructions. In some situations, floated floor and resiliently suspended ceiling underneath fan room floor slab may be required. Internal duct linings and prefabricated sound attenuators are used to control noise transmission through supply and return air ducts.

MECHANICAL EQUIPMENT NOISE CONTROL

1. Do not attach vibrating equipment directly to building structure. Support vibrating equipment with properly selected resilient mounts such as unhoused steel springs, ribbed neoprene, or precompressed glass fiber.

2. Use pads or continuous layers of soft, resilient material under structurally isolated slab (i.e., "floated floor") to isolate especially high levels of mechanical equipment room noise and vibration. In addition, use heavy wall and flooring-ceiling constructions surrounding mechanical equipment room. In critical applications, both floated floor and resiliently suspended ceiling underneath structural floor may be required.

3. Isolate all duct, pipe, and conduit connections to vibration isolated equipment for considerable distances from equipment. Use flexible duct connectors, resilient electrical conduit, and special reinforced flexible pipe connections.

4. Check to see if duct borne fan or downstream air control valves create noise requiring lining of supply and return air ducts with glass fiber or installation of prefabricated sound attenuators.

5. Where ducts and pipes penetrate walls, floors, or ceilings of mechanical rooms or other critical barriers, pack openings with mineral fiber or glass fiber and caulk perimeters to assure airtight seal.

6. Pipes carrying water at high velocities should be isolated from building structure and wrapped with dense materials (e.g., lead sheet, vinyl covered glass fiber) to isolate water flow noise.

7. Roof mounted mechanical equipment subject to wind loading (e.g., cooling towers, packaged air conditioning units, etc.) and all mechanical equipment subject to earthquake forces may require special vibration isolation mounts. These well anchored lateral and vertical restraints must be carefully selected and installed to avoid short circuiting vibration isolation system.

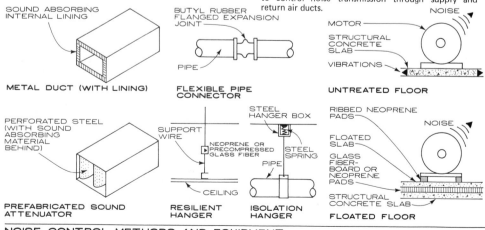

NOISE CONTROL METHODS AND EQUIPMENT

M. David Egan, P.E.; Consultant in Acoustics; Anderson, South Carolina

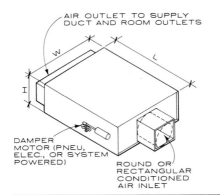

AIR OUTLET TO SUPPLY
DUCT AND ROOM OUTLETS

DAMPER
MOTOR (PNEU,
ELEC., OR SYSTEM
POWERED)

ROUND OR
RECTANGULAR
CONDITIONED
AIR INLET

High, medium, or low velocity systems. Inlet pressure required 1/4 to 1 1/2 in. W.C. Capacity range 200 to 3200 cfm per box. Box serves as converter from high to low velocity air system, noise attenuator, and control device by modulating air quantity.

RANGE OF DIMENSIONS

CFM	HEIGHT	LENGTH	WIDTH
400	8"- 9"	24"–39"	14"–30"
800	10"–11"	24"–53"	18"–42"
1600	14"	30"–48"	22"–44"
2400	16"	42"–60"	26"–54"
3200	18"	42"–67"	33"–54"

VARIABLE VOLUME PINCH BACK BOX

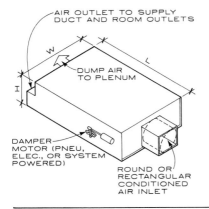

AIR OUTLET TO SUPPLY
DUCT AND ROOM OUTLETS

DUMP AIR
TO PLENUM

DAMPER
MOTOR (PNEU,
ELEC., OR SYSTEM
POWERED)

ROUND OR
RECTANGULAR
CONDITIONED
AIR INLET

High, medium, or low velocity systems. Inlet pressure required 1/4 to 1 in. W.C. Capacity range 200 to 3200 cfm per box. Available with or without reheat coil. Box serves as converter from high to low velocity air system, noise attenuator, and control device by modulating air quantity to space and/or by reheat.

RANGE OF DIMENSIONS

CFM	HEIGHT	LENGTH	WIDTH
200	8"- 9"	24"–39"	12"–19"
400	9"–11"	25"–51"	12"–24"
800	9"–11"	25"–51"	22"–31"
1600	10"–16"	25"–51"	22"–47"
2400	10"–16"	25"–51"	42"–47"
3200	10"–16"	25"–51"	42"–47"

VARIABLE VOLUME DUMP TYPE BOX

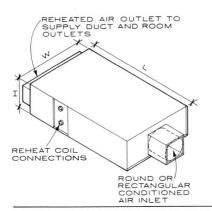

REHEATED AIR OUTLET TO
SUPPLY DUCT AND ROOM
OUTLETS

REHEAT COIL
CONNECTIONS

ROUND OR
RECTANGULAR
CONDITIONED
AIR INLET

High, medium, or low velocity systems. Inlet pressures 1/2 to 1 1/2 in. W.C. Capacity range 200 to 5000 cfm. Box serves as converter from high to low velocity air system, noise attenuator, and control device by reheat of conditioned air.

RANGE OF DIMENSIONS

CFM	HEIGHT	LENGTH	WIDTH
200	9"–11"	30"–50"	16"–22"
400	9"–11"	30"–51"	18"–30"
800	9"–11"	30"–51"	22"–42"
1600	14"–16"	48"–51"	40"–44"
2400	16"–18"	60"–55"	40"–54"
3200	16"–18"	60"–55"	16"–66"
5000	20"–18"	60"–55"	20"–80"

REHEAT CONSTANT VOLUME BOX

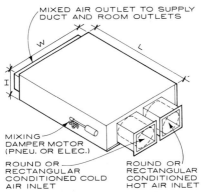

MIXED AIR OUTLET TO SUPPLY
DUCT AND ROOM OUTLETS

MIXING
DAMPER MOTOR
(PNEU. OR ELEC.)

ROUND OR
RECTANGULAR
CONDITIONED COLD
AIR INLET

ROUND OR
RECTANGULAR
CONDITIONED
HOT AIR INLET

High, medium, or low velocity systems. Inlet pressure 1/4 to 1 1/2 in. W.C. Capacity range from 150 to 2000 cfm per box (low velocity) to 5000 cfm (high velocity). Box serves as converter from high to low velocity air system, noise attenuator, and control device by mixing hot and cold air streams.

RANGE OF DIMENSIONS

CFM	HEIGHT	LENGTH	WIDTH
400	6"–10"	40"–51"	30"–19"
800	8"–11"	50"–51"	42"–24"
1600	12"–14"	48"–51"	44"–40"
2400	14"–18"	60"–55"	54"–44"
3200	14"–18"	60"–55"	54"–44"
5000	16"–18"	60"–55"	54"–66"

DUAL DUCT MIXING BOX

William Tao & Associates, Inc., Consulting Engineers; St. Louis, Missouri

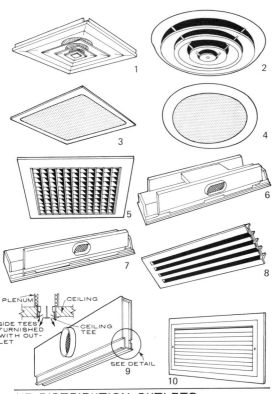

AIR DISTRIBUTION OUTLETS

KEY

1 RECTANGULAR LOUVERED FACE DIFFUSER: Available in 1, 2, 3, or 4-way pattern, steel or aluminum. Flanged overlap frame or inserted in 2 X 2 ft or 2 X 4 ft baked enamel steel panel to fit tile modules of lay-in ceilings. Supply or return.

2 ROUND LOUVERED FACE DIFFUSER: Normal 360° air pattern with blank-off plate for other air patterns. Surface mounting for all type ceilings. Normally of steel with baked enamel finish. Supply or return.

3 RECTANGULAR PERFORATED FACE DIFFUSER: Available in 1, 2, 3, or 4-way pattern, steel or aluminum. Flanged overlap frame or 2 X 2 ft and 2 X 4 ft for replacing tile of lay-in ceiling can be used for supply or return air.

4 ROUND PERFORATED FACE DIFFUSER: Normal 360° air pattern with blank-off plate for other air patterns. Steel or aluminum. Flanged overlap frame for all type ceilings. Can be used for supply or return air.

5 LATTICE TYPE RETURN: All aluminum square grid type return grille for ceiling installation with flanged overlap frame or of correct size to replace tile.

6 SADDLE TYPE LUMINAIRE AIR BOOT: Provides air supply from both sides of standard size luminaires. Maximum air delivery (total both sides) approximately 150 to 170 cfm for 4 ft long luminaire.

7 SINGLE SIDE TYPE LUMINAIRE AIR BOOT: Provides air supply from one side of standard size luminaires. Maximum air delivery approximately 75 cfm for 4 ft long luminaire.

8 LINEAR DIFFUSER: Extruded aluminum, anodized, duranodic, or special finishes, one way or opposite direction or vertical down air pattern. Any length with one to eight slots. Can be used for supply or return and for ceiling, sidewall, or cabinet top application.

9 INTEGRATED PLENUM TYPE OUTLET FOR "T" BAR CEILINGS: Slot type outlet, one way or two way opposite direction air pattern. Available in 24, 36, 48, and 60 in. lengths. Replaces or integrates with "T" bar. Approximately 150 to 175 cfm for 4 ft long, two-slot unit.

10 SIDEWALL OR DUCT MOUNTED REGISTER: Steel or aluminum for supply or return. Adjustable horizontal and vertical deflection. Plaster frame available. Suitable for long throw and high air volume.

CHAPTER 16 ELECTRICAL

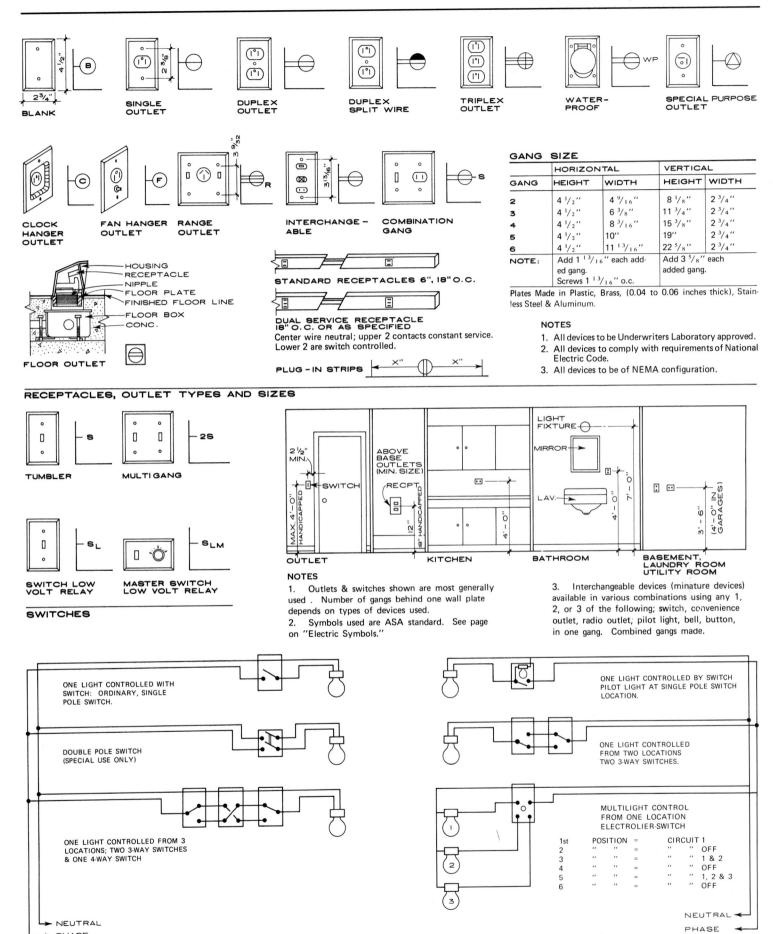

BLANK — 4 1/2", 2 3/4", B

SINGLE OUTLET — 2 5/8"

DUPLEX OUTLET

DUPLEX SPLIT WIRE

TRIPLEX OUTLET

WATER-PROOF — WP

SPECIAL PURPOSE OUTLET

CLOCK HANGER OUTLET — C

FAN HANGER OUTLET — F

RANGE OUTLET — 3/32", 3 9/32", R

INTERCHANGE-ABLE — 3 13/16"

COMBINATION GANG — S

GANG SIZE

GANG	HORIZONTAL		VERTICAL	
	HEIGHT	WIDTH	HEIGHT	WIDTH
2	4 1/2''	4 9/16''	8 1/8''	2 3/4''
3	4 1/2''	6 3/8''	11 3/4''	2 3/4''
4	4 1/2''	8 3/16''	15 3/8''	2 3/4''
5	4 1/2''	10''	19''	2 3/4''
6	4 1/2''	11 13/16''	22 5/8''	2 3/4''
NOTE:	Add 1 13/16'' each added gang. Screws 1 13/16'' o.c.		Add 3 5/8'' each added gang.	

Plates Made in Plastic, Brass, (0.04 to 0.06 inches thick), Stainless Steel & Aluminum.

FLOOR OUTLET — HOUSING, RECEPTACLE, NIPPLE, FLOOR PLATE, FINISHED FLOOR LINE, FLOOR BOX, CONC.

STANDARD RECEPTACLES 6", 18" O.C.

DUAL SERVICE RECEPTACLE 18" O.C. OR AS SPECIFIED
Center wire neutral; upper 2 contacts constant service. Lower 2 are switch controlled.

PLUG - IN STRIPS — X"

NOTES
1. All devices to be Underwriters Laboratory approved.
2. All devices to comply with requirements of National Electric Code.
3. All devices to be of NEMA configuration.

RECEPTACLES, OUTLET TYPES AND SIZES

TUMBLER — S

MULTI GANG — 2S

SWITCH LOW VOLT RELAY — S_L

MASTER SWITCH LOW VOLT RELAY — S_LM

SWITCHES

OUTLET — 2 1/2" MIN., MAX 4'-0" HANDICAPPED, SWITCH

KITCHEN — ABOVE BASE OUTLETS (MIN. SIZE), RECPT., 18" HANDICAPPED, 12", 4'-0"

BATHROOM — LIGHT FIXTURE, MIRROR, LAV., 4'-0", 7'-0"

BASEMENT, LAUNDRY ROOM UTILITY ROOM — 3'-6" (4'-0" IN GARAGES)

NOTES
1. Outlets & switches shown are most generally used. Number of gangs behind one wall plate depends on types of devices used.
2. Symbols used are ASA standard. See page on "Electric Symbols."
3. Interchangeable devices (minature devices) available in various combinations using any 1, 2, or 3 of the following; switch, convenience outlet, radio outlet, pilot light, bell, button, in one gang. Combined gangs made.

ONE LIGHT CONTROLLED WITH SWITCH: ORDINARY, SINGLE POLE SWITCH.

DOUBLE POLE SWITCH (SPECIAL USE ONLY)

ONE LIGHT CONTROLLED FROM 3 LOCATIONS; TWO 3-WAY SWITCHES & ONE 4-WAY SWITCH

ONE LIGHT CONTROLLED BY SWITCH PILOT LIGHT AT SINGLE POLE SWITCH LOCATION.

ONE LIGHT CONTROLLED FROM TWO LOCATIONS TWO 3-WAY SWITCHES.

MULTILIGHT CONTROL FROM ONE LOCATION ELECTROLIER-SWITCH

	POSITION	=	CIRCUIT 1
1st			OFF
2	" "	=	" " 1
3	" "	=	" " 1 & 2
4	" "	=	" " OFF
5	" "	=	" " 1, 2 & 3
6	" "	=	" " OFF

NEUTRAL

PHASE

SWITCH WIRING DIAGRAMS

B. J. Baldwin; Giffels & Rossetti, Inc.; Detroit, Michigan

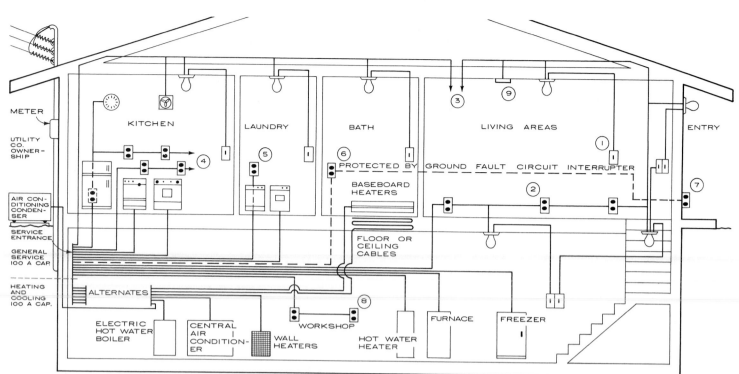

SCHEMATIC DIAGRAM OF TYPICAL RESIDENTIAL ELECTRICAL LAYOUT

GENERAL REQUIREMENTS

1. A minimum of one wall switch controlled lighting outlet is required in every habitable room, in hallways, stairways, and attached garages, and at outdoor entrances. Exception: in habitable rooms other than kitchens and bathrooms one or more receptacles controlled by a wall switch are permitted in lieu of lighting outlets.

2. In every kitchen, family room, dining room, den, breakfast room, living room, parlor, sunroom, bedroom, recreation room, and similar rooms, receptacle outlets are required such that no point along the floor line in any space is greater than 12 ft, measured horizontally, from an outlet in that space, including any wall space 2 ft or more wide and the wall space occupied by sliding panels in exterior walls.

3. A minimum of two #12 wire 20 A small appliance circuits are required to serve only small appliance

outlets, including refrigeration equipment, in kitchen, pantry, dining room, breakfast room, and family room. Both circuits must extend to kitchen; the other rooms may be served by either one or both of them. No other outlets may be connected to these circuits, other than a receptacle installed solely for the supply to and support of an electric clock. In kitchen and dining areas receptacle outlets must be installed at each and every counter space wider than 12 in.

4. A minimum of one #12 wire 20 A circuit must be provided to supply the laundry receptacle(s), and it may have no other outlets.

5. A minimum of one receptacle outlet must be installed in bathroom near the basin and must be provided with ground fault circuit interrupter protection.

6. The code requires sufficient lighting circuits to supply 3 W of power for every square foot of

floor space, not including garage and open porch areas. Minimum code suggestion is one circuit per 600 sq ft; one circuit per 500 sq ft is desirable.

7. A minimum of one exterior receptacle outlet is required (two are desirable) and must be provided with ground fault circuit interrupter protection.

8. A minimum of one receptacle outlet is required in basement and garage, in addition to that in the laundry. In attached garages it must be provided with ground fault circuit interrupter protection.

9. Many building codes require a smoke detector in the hallway outside bedrooms or above the stairway leading to upper floor bedrooms.

NOTE

Refer to the National Electrical Code (NEC) for further information on residential requirements.

INDIVIDUAL APPLIANCE CIRCUITS

TYPE	VOLTS	TYPE	VOLTS
Range	240	Dishwasher	120
Separate oven or countertop cooking unit	240	Freezer	120
Water heater	240	Oil furnace motor	120
Automatic washer	240	Furnace blower motor	120
Clothes dryer	240	Water pump	240
Garbage disposal	240	Permanently connected appliances > 1000 W	Varies

BRANCH CIRCUIT PROTECTION

Lighting (general purpose)	#12 wires	20 A
Small appliance	#12 wires	20 A
Individual appliances	#12 wires	20 A
	#10 wires	30 A
	#8 wires	40 A
	#6 wires	50 A

AVERAGE WATTAGES OF COMMON RESIDENTIAL ELECTRICAL DEVICES

TYPE	WATTS	TYPE	WATTS	TYPE	WATTS
Air conditioner, central	2500–6000	Heating pad	50–75	Range oven (separate)	4000–5000
Air conditioner, room type	800–2500	Heat lamp (infrared)	250	Razor	8–12
Blanket, electric	150–200	Iron, hand	600–1200	Refrigerator	150–300
Clock	2–3	Knife, electric	100	Refrigerator, frostless	400–600
Clothes dryer	4000–6000	Lamp, incandescent	10 upward	Roaster	1200–1650
Deep fat fryer	1200–1650	Lamp, fluorescent	15–60	Rotisserie (broiler)	1200–1650
Dishwasher	1000–1500	Lights, Christmas tree	30–150	Sewing machine	60–90
Fan, portable	50–200	Microwave oven	1000–1500	Stereo (solid state)	30–100
Food blender	500–1000	Mixer	120–250	Sunlamp (ultraviolet)	275–400
Freezer	300–500	Percolator	500–1000	Television	50–450
Frying pan, electric	1000–1200	Power tools	Up to 1000	Toaster	500–1200
Furnace blower	380–670	Projector, slide or movie	300–500	Vacuum cleaner	250–1200
Garbage disposal	500–900	Radio	40–150	Waffle iron	600–1000
Hair dryer	350–1200	Range (all burners and oven "on")	8000–14000	Washer, automatic	500–800
Heater, portable	1000–1500	Range top (separate)	4000–8000	Water heater	2000–5000

Ed Hesner; Rasmussen & Hobbs Architects, AIA; Tacoma, Washington

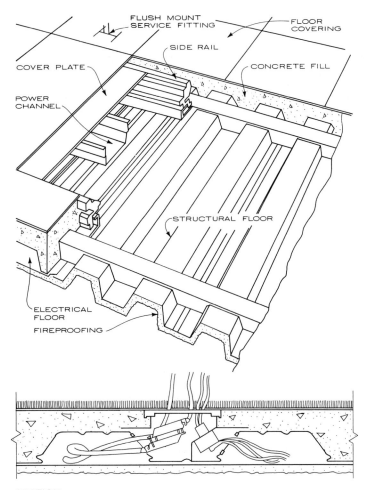

FLUSH MOUNT SERVICE FITTING

FLOOR COVERING

SIDE RAIL

COVER PLATE

CONCRETE FILL

POWER CHANNEL

STRUCTURAL FLOOR

ELECTRICAL FLOOR

FIREPROOFING

SECTION
BOTTOMLESS TRENCH DUCT FOR STRUCTURAL DECK

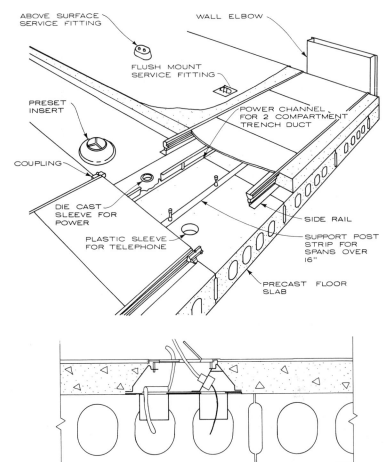

ABOVE SURFACE SERVICE FITTING

WALL ELBOW

FLUSH MOUNT SERVICE FITTING

PRESET INSERT

POWER CHANNEL FOR 2 COMPARTMENT TRENCH DUCT

COUPLING

DIE CAST SLEEVE FOR POWER

PLASTIC SLEEVE FOR TELEPHONE

SIDE RAIL

SUPPORT POST STRIP FOR SPANS OVER 16"

PRECAST FLOOR SLAB

SECTION
BOTTOMLESS TRENCH DUCT FOR PRECAST CONCRETE RACEWAY

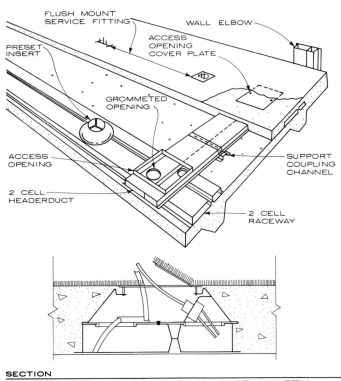

FLUSH MOUNT SERVICE FITTING

WALL ELBOW

ACCESS OPENING COVER PLATE

PRESET INSERT

GROMMETED OPENING

ACCESS OPENING

SUPPORT COUPLING CHANNEL

2 CELL HEADERDUCT

2 CELL RACEWAY

SECTION
HEADER DUCT SYSTEM WITH TWO-CELL METAL RACEWAY AND PRESET INSERT

Walter H. Sobel, FAIA & Associates; Chicago, Illinois

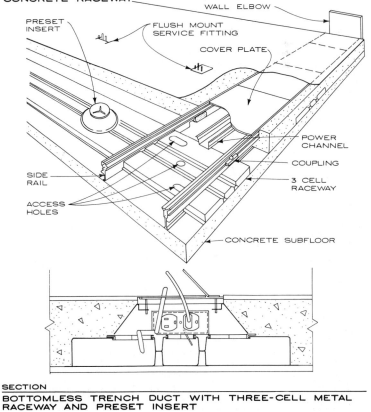

PRESET INSERT

FLUSH MOUNT SERVICE FITTING

WALL ELBOW

COVER PLATE

POWER CHANNEL

COUPLING

SIDE RAIL

3 CELL RACEWAY

ACCESS HOLES

CONCRETE SUBFLOOR

SECTION
BOTTOMLESS TRENCH DUCT WITH THREE-CELL METAL RACEWAY AND PRESET INSERT

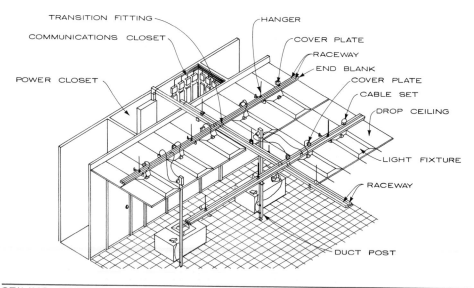

CEILING RACEWAY SYSTEM

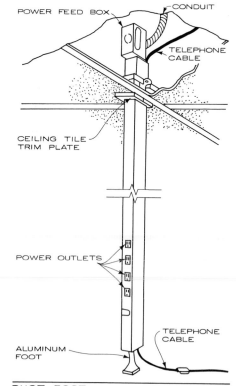

DUCT POST

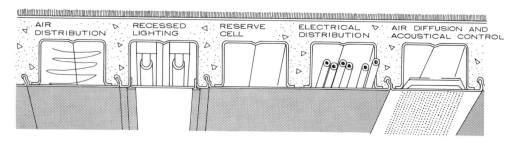

ARCHITECTURAL FLOOR / CEILING SYSTEM

Raceway systems and underfloor ducts are available to match virtually any architectural design. Cost analysis and field experience have made it possible in composite beam design to reduce steel costs by 15 to 20%. This permits shallower beams, lighter beam sections, or both. Total building height can be reduced when power and electrical cables run through the open cells. In older buildings that have no underfloor electrical and telephone systems surface and overhead or ceiling raceway systems may be effectively utilized. Most raceway and underfloor duct systems can be adapted to carrying any capacity necessary to make a work station usable. Major building codes require that all floors in a building have fire rated construction. Underwriters Laboratories approves a 2 in. minimum cover over the top of floor cells. In addition to the UL fire rating, all components of the system must have an approved UL electrical rating.

WEIGHTS AND DIMENSIONS FOR RIGID STEEL CONDUIT

SIZE (IN.)	LB/ 100 FT	I.D.	O.D.	THICK- NESS	THREADS/ IN.
1/2	80	0.622	0.840	0.109	14
3/4	109	0.824	1.050	0.113	14
1	165	1.049	1.315	0.133	11 1/2
1 1/4	215	1.380	1.660	0.140	11 1/2
1 1/2	258	1.610	1.900	0.145	11 1/2
2	352	2.067	2.375	0.154	11 1/2
2 1/2	567	2.469	2.875	0.203	8
3	714	3.068	3.500	0.216	8
3 1/2	860	3.548	4.000	0.226	8
4	1000	4.026	4.500	0.237	8
5	1320	5.047	5.563	0.258	8
6	1785	6.065	6.625	0.280	8

WEIGHTS AND DIMENSIONS FOR INTERMEDIATE METAL CONDUIT (IMC)

SIZE (IN.)	NOMINAL	LENGTH OF CONDUIT WITHOUT COUPLING	WALL THICK- NESS	LB/100 FT
1/2	0.815	119 1/4	0.070	60
3/4	1.029	119 1/4	0.075	82
1	1.290	119	0.085	116
1 1/4	1.638	119	0.085	150
1 1/2	1.883	119	0.090	182
2	2.360	119	0.095	242
2 1/2	2.857	118 1/2	0.130	428
3	3.476	118 1/2	0.130	526
3 1/2	3.971	118 1/4	0.130	612
4	4.466	118 1/4	0.130	682

WEIGHTS AND DIMENSIONS FOR ELECTRICAL METALIC TUBING (EMT)

SIZE (IN.)	LB/100 FT	I.D.	O.D.
1/2	29	0.622	0.706
3/4	45	0.824	0.922
1	65	1.049	1.163
1 1/4	96	1.380	1.510
1 1/2	111	1.610	1.740
2	141	2.067	2.197
2 1/2	215	2.731	2.875
3	260	3.356	3.500
3 1/2	325	3.834	4.000
4	390	4.334	4.500

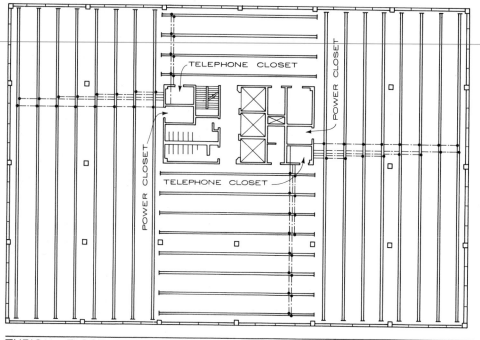

TYPICAL FLOOR DUCT PLAN

Walter H. Sobel, FAIA & Associates; Chicago, Illinois

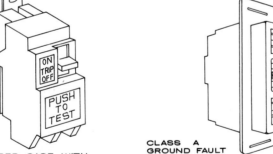

PLUG   FERRULE   KNIFE
                                                         BLADE

FUSES ARE AVAILABLE WITH RENEWABLE LINKS

STANDARD FUSES

PLUG FUSES
1. MAXIMUM VOLTAGE: 125.
2. AMPERE RATING: 1-30 A.
3. FUSE TYPE: S.

CARTRIDGE FUSES
1. MAXIMUM VOLTAGE: 250 and 600.
2. AMPERE RATINGS: 1/10-60 A.
3. FUSE TYPES: K1, K1R, K5, K5R, T, J, H, and G.

KNIFE FUSES
1. MAXIMUM VOLTAGE: 250 and 600.
2. AMPERE RATINGS: 70-6000 A.
3. FUSE TYPES: K1, K1R, K5, K5R, T, J, H, G, and L.

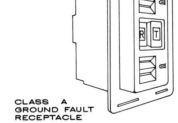

TOGGLE   KNIFE BLADE   HIGH PRESSURE CONTACT

DISCONNECT SWITCHES

TOGGLE SWITCHES
1. MAXIMUM VOLTAGES: 125 VAC/DC, 125 or 250 VAC/DC, or 240 VAC.
2. RATING: 30 A max.

SAFETY SWITCHES
1. MAXIMUM VOLTAGES: 240 VAC, 125-250 VDC, 600 VAC.
2. POLES: 2, 3, or 4 plus S/N and/or GRD Lug.
3. TYPES: TG, TH, or TC fusible and no fuse.
4. RATING: 30-1200 A.

HIGH PRESSURE CONTACT SWITCHES
1. MAXIMUM VOLTAGES: 240 VAC or 480 VAC.
2. POLES: 3.
3. RATINGS: 800-4000 A.

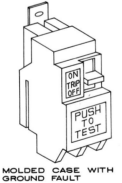

MOLDED CASE   MOLDED CASE WITH GROUND FAULT   CLASS A GROUND FAULT RECEPTACLE

CIRCUIT BREAKERS

STANDARD MOLDED CASE CIRCUIT BREAKERS
1. MAXIMUM VOLTAGES: 120 VAC, 240 VAC, 600 VAC, 125 VDC, and 250 VDC.
2. FRAME SIZES: 100 A, 225 A, 400 A, 600 A, 800 A, 1200 A Poles—2 or 3.

MOLDED CASE CIRCUIT BREAKERS INCORPORATING GROUND FAULT CIRCUIT INTERRUPTION
1. MAXIMUM VOLTAGES: 120 VAC or 120/240 VAC.
2. FRAME SIZE: 100 A ratings, 15-30 A poles—1 or 2.

CLASS A GROUND FAULT CIRCUIT INTERRUPTION RECEPTACLES
1. MAXIMUM VOLTAGE: 125 VAC.
2. RATINGS: 15 or 20 A NEMA configuration single outlet.

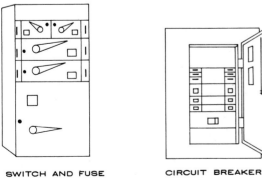

SWITCH AND FUSE   CIRCUIT BREAKER

DISTRIBUTION PANEL BOARDS

CIRCUIT BREAKER PANELS

MANUFACTURER	MAX. NO. OF CIRCUITS	BOX SIZES (IN.)		
		WIDTH	HEIGHT	DEPTH
Square D	12	14	20 1/4	4
	20	14	24 1/4	4
	42	14	32 1/2	4
General Electric Co.	12	14	21 1/2	4 1/2
	20	14	27 1/2	4 1/2
	30	14	33 1/2	4 1/2
	42	14	36 1/2	4 1/2
Westinghouse	12	15	20	4 1/4
	18	15	23	4 1/4
	30	15	29	4 1/4
	40	15	35	4 1/4

NOTE: Other manufacturers' panels are available in similar sizes.

A. A. Erdman; Sargent, Webster, Crenshaw & Folley; Architects Engineers Planners; Syracuse, New York

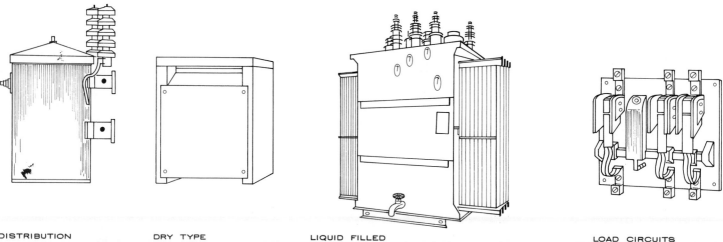

DISTRIBUTION   DRY TYPE   LIQUID FILLED   LOAD CIRCUITS

DISTRIBUTION: High to low voltage. Immersed in oil. Self-cooled. Primarily mounted on outdoor poles.
DRY: Maximum voltage 600 VAC. Primarily mounted on indoor floors and walls.
LIQUID: Secondary substation transformer with high to low voltage. Primarily a commercial type transformer for the outdoors.

Maximum voltage: 600 VAC. For load circuits that are closed and opened repeatedly various design combinations are allowed. Used for all classes of magnetically held loads, open or closed.

TRANSFORMERS

CONTACTOR

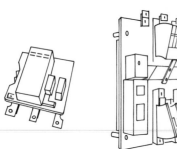

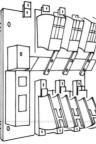
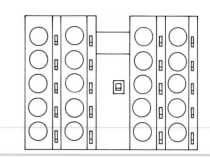

REMOTE CONTROL   AUTOTRANSFER   NETWORK TYPE   MAIN CIRCUIT BREAKER

REMOTE CONTROL: Provides convenient control of lighting and power circuits from control stations.
AUTOTRANSFER: Automatically transfers loads from a normal source to the emergency source.

Maximum voltage: 125/216 VAC or 277/480 VAC. Interrupting capacity 30,000 and 60,000 A. RMS. SYM. A fault on primary cable or network transformer will open protector to isolate fault from system.

Maximum voltage ratings: 120/240, 3 wire, single phase or 208V/120, 4 wire three phase. Either indoor or outdoor construction. Number of sockets as required by application.

SWITCHES

PROTECTOR

METER BANK

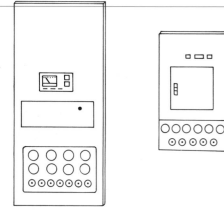
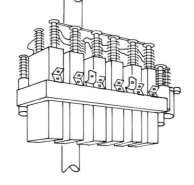
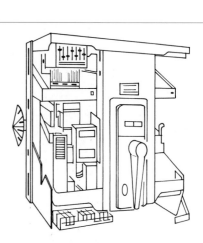

LARGE   SMALL   POLE RACK   LOW VOLTAGE

PRIMARY VOLTAGES: 120, 208, 240, or 277.
SECONDARY VOLTAGE: 120.
APPLICATION: Power and lighting panels, special panels for hospitals (operating, coronary, and X-ray).

Application: Power factor correction on either low or high voltage systems. Types, indoor or outdoor. Size and voltage as required. Switched or floating.

Maximum voltages: 240 VAC, 480 VAC, 600 VAC, and 250 VDC. Operation is manual or electric. Breaker trip devices: Electromechanical or solid state. Type: stationary or drawout.

ISOLATED POWER CENTER

CAPACITOR

CIRCUIT BREAKER

A. A. Erdman; Sargent, Webster, Crenshaw & Folley; Architects Engineers Planners; Syracuse, New York

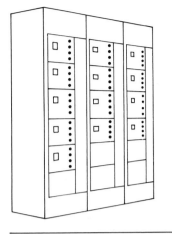

MOTOR CONTROL CENTER

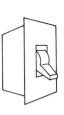
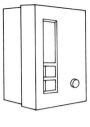
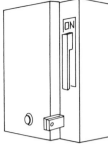

MANUAL   MAGNETIC   COMBINATION

MANUAL: Maximum voltage—240 VAC. Maximum horsepower—1.

MAGNETIC: Maximum voltage—600 VAC. Maximum horsepower—200.

COMBINATION: A magnetic motor starter with a variety of fusible disconnects or circuit breakers.

MOTOR STARTERS

UNIT SUBSTATION: Primary entrance cubicle, air interrupter switch, transformer section, and low voltage distribution sections. See manufacturer's literature for type, size, and arrangements. See National Electric Code for required aisle space, ventilation, servicing area, and special building condition requirements.

UNIT SUBSTATION

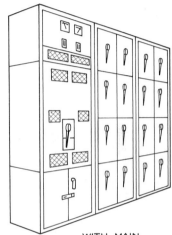

SECONDARY   WITH MAIN

SWITCHBOARD: Metering compartment, main disconnect, check meters, and low voltage distribution section. See manufacturer's literature for type, size, and arrangements. See National Electric Code for required aisle space, servicing area, and room layout.

SWITCHBOARDS

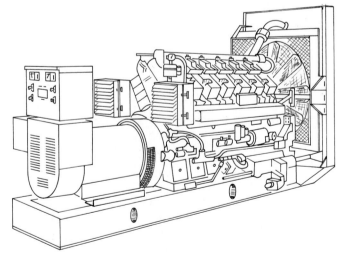

EMERGENCY GENERATOR: Engine driven prime mover, alternator, and controls. Application: to provide emergency power during power outages. See manufacturer's literature for ratings, dimensions, weight, ventilation, and fuel consumption. See National Electric Code for working space requirements and proper application.

EMERGENCY GENERATOR WITH CONTROL PANEL (800 KW)

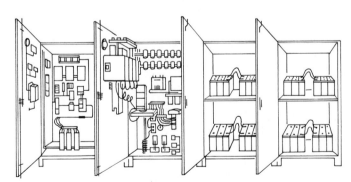

UNINTERRUPTIBLE POWER SUPPLY: D.C. batteries, battery charger, rectifier, and static inverter. Application: to provide continuous power during outage or abnormal transient power conditions. See manufacturer's literature for ratings, dimensions, weight, and ventilation requirements. See National Electric Code for working space requirements.

UNINTERRUPTIBLE POWER SUPPLY

A. A. Erdman; Sargent, Webster, Crenshaw & Folley; Architects Engineers Planners; Syracuse, New York

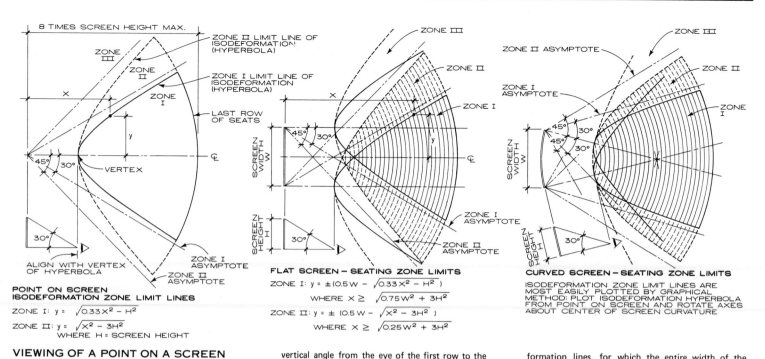

POINT ON SCREEN ISODEFORMATION ZONE LIMIT LINES

ZONE I: $y = \sqrt{0.33x^2 - H^2}$

ZONE II: $y = \sqrt{x^2 - 3H^2}$

WHERE H = SCREEN HEIGHT

FLAT SCREEN – SEATING ZONE LIMITS

ZONE I: $y = \pm(0.5W - \sqrt{0.33x^2 - H^2})$

WHERE $x \geq \sqrt{0.75W^2 + 3H^2}$

ZONE II: $y = \pm(0.5W - \sqrt{x^2 - 3H^2})$

WHERE $x \geq \sqrt{0.25W^2 + 3H^2}$

CURVED SCREEN – SEATING ZONE LIMITS

ISODEFORMATION ZONE LIMIT LINES ARE MOST EASILY PLOTTED BY GRAPHICAL METHOD: PLOT ISODEFORMATION HYPERBOLA FROM POINT ON SCREEN AND ROTATE AXES ABOUT CENTER OF SCREEN CURVATURE

VIEWING OF A POINT ON A SCREEN

A projected image on a screen will have an apparent distortion when viewed from an angle beyond the perpendicular to a point on the screen in plan and section. The boundary of the seating area for which spectators will see the same apparent distortion is called the line of isodeformation. This shape in plan is a hyperbola, which is defined in plan by asymptotes from the point on the screen.

1. SEATING ZONE I: Distortion of a projected image exists but will not be noticed from seats falling within the hyperbola which is bounded by the asymptotes drawn from a point on the screen at an angle of no greater than 30° from the perpendicular at that point on the screen. The minimum horizontal distance from the vertex of the hyperbola to the screen is determined by the limitation of the vertical angle from the eye of the first row to the top of the screen to a maximum of 30 to 35°.

2. SEATING ZONE II: Distortions of the projected image will be noticed but tolerated from the seats falling outside of Zone I but within the hyperbola bounded by the asymptotes drawn from a point on the screen at an angle no greater than 45° from the perpendicular at that point.

3. SEATING ZONE III (seating placed beyond the limits of Zone II): Distortions of the projected image will not be tolerated and the viewer will refuse to use the seats placed here.

VIEWING OF A FLAT SCREEN

A projected image occupies a space on a screen rather than a point. The seating area, defined by the isodeformation lines, for which the entire width of the projected image is considered, is represented by the area common to the space within the two hyperbolas which are drawn within asymptotes from both sides of the projected image. The area in Zone I for a wide, projected image is less than the Zone I seating area for a point on the screen. The seating area in Zone II for a wide image on a flat screen may approximately correspond to the Zone I area for a point on the screen.

VIEWING OF A CURVED SCREEN

Zone I seating area for a given screen width can be increased by curving the screen. An appropriate screen curve will cause an overlap of the hyperbolas drawn from the sides of the projected image in such a way that they define a greater common seating area.

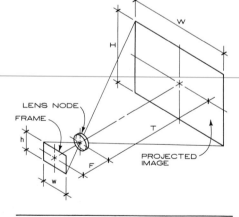

BASIC PROJECTION GEOMETRY

PROJECTION FORMULAS

$T = F(W/w) = F(H/h)$
$F = T(w/W) = T(h/H)$
$W = w(T/F)$
$H = h(T/F)$

where

W = picture width
H = picture height
w = frame width
h = frame height
T = throw distance
F = focal length

ASPECT RATIOS AND FRAME DIMENSIONS FOR PROJECTED MEDIA

PROJECTION MEDIUM	FRAME (mm) h x w	ASPECT RATIO	FRAME (IN.) h	w
8 mm motion picture	(3.28 x 4.37)	1:1.33	0.129	0.172
Super 8 motion picture	(4.01 x 5.36)	1.33	0.158	0.211
16 mm motion picture	(7.21 x 9.65)	1.34	0.284	0.380
16 mm CinemaScope	(7.21 x 9.65)	2.68	0.284	2 x 0.380
35 mm motion picture	(15.2 x 20.9)	1.375	0.600	0.825
35 mm CinemaScope	(18.2 x 42.6)	2.34	0.715	2 x 0.839
70 mm motion picture	(22.1 x 49.0)	2.21	0.868	1.913
70 mm IMAX	(51.0 x 71.0)	1.39	2.00	2.80
35 mm filmstrip	(17.0 x 22.5)	1.32	0.668	0.885
2 x 2 35 mm double frame slides	(22.9 x 34.2)	1.493	0.902	1.346
2 x 2 35 mm half frame slides	(15.9 x 22.9)	1.44	0.626	0.902
2 x 2 35 mm square slides	(22.9 x 22.9)	1.00	0.902	0.902
126 Insta-Load slides	(12.7 x 17.0)	1.34	0.500	0.669
2 x 2 Instamatic slides	(26.5 x 26.5)	1.00	1.043	1.043
2 x 2 superslides	(38.0 x 38.0)	1.00	1.496	1.496
2¼ x 2¼ slides	(51.6 x 51.6)	1.00	2.030	2.030
2¾ x 2¾ slides	(55.5 x 55.5)	1.00	2.187	2.187
3½ x 4 lantern slides	(69.9 x 76.2)	1.09	2.75	3.00
3½ x 4 Polaroid slides	(61.0 x 82.8)	1.36	2.40	3.26
4 x 5 lantern slides	(88.9 x 114.3)	1.28	3.50	4.50
Overhead projector	—	1.26	7.50	9.50
Overhead projector	—	1.00	10.00	10.00
Television projector	—	1.33	—	—

Peter H. Frink; Frink and Beuchat: Architects; Philadelphia, Pennsylvania

PROJECTION ROOM DETAILS

1. DIMENSIONS: 14 ft deep by 21 ft wide minimum for two projectors. Add 5 ft width for each additional piece of projection apparatus. Ceiling height should never be less than 8 ft; 9 ft is preferred.
2. WALL CONSTRUCTION: Wall separating projection room and auditorium should be made of brick, concrete, or concrete block to minimize sound transmission.
3. FLOOR CONSTRUCTION: Provide for a live load of 200 psf minimum. Recommend 4 in. reinforced concrete slab, 4 in. tamped cinder fill (to accommodate concealed conduit), and 2 in. topping slab.
4. FLOOR FINISH: Recommend heavy battleship linoleum. A good grade of vinyl tile is also acceptable.
5. PORTS: Projection ports should be glazed with $1/4$ in. optical quality or select water white glass. Observation ports may be glazed with $1/4$ in. select plate glass that is free from distortion.

SCREEN TYPES

An ideal screen would be one that would diffuse all the light from the projector into the audience spaces with uniform brightness for every viewer and simultaneously reject any stray light falling on the screen, reflecting it away from the audience. Most common screen materials possess characteristics that fall short of the ideal.

MATTE WHITE SCREEN

Uniform brightness from all viewing angles. Good resolution and color fidelity. Because much of the light reflected from a matte white screen falls outside of the viewing area, the picture will be less bright than a picture from the same source on a gain screen. Rejects less stray light than gain screens.

GAIN SCREENS

Mechanical or chemical treatment of screen surface increases the amount of light reflected in the direction of the audience and decreases the amount reflected in other directions. Because brightness from all viewing angles is not uniform, gain screens dictate a narrower viewing area. For high gain screens, viewing area should be restricted to zone I as described on other pages. While the picture on a gain screen will be brighter than on a matte screen, resolution and color fidelity may suffer somewhat depending on the type of gain screen used. Gain screen types include: beaded, silver, pearl, and lenticular.

AVAILABLE SCREEN SIZES

1. Tripod screens: 30 x 40 to 72 x 86 in., bottom of screen usually 3 to 4 ft above floor (adjustable).
2. Table or wall hung screens: 18 x 24 to 36 x 36 in.
3. Wall or ceiling mounted, manually operated spring loaded roll-up: 50 x 50 in. to 12 x 12 ft.
4. Wall or ceiling mounted, electrically operated roll-up: 50 x 50 in. to 20 x 20 or 12 x 24 ft. Custom sizes: up to 40 ft wide.
5. Bottom roller, rope controlled: 5 ft 6 in. x 14 to 30 x 30 ft. Winch controlled: up to 40 ft wide.
6. Framed screen (lace and grommet): custom made to any size. Economical for larger sizes. Frames made of 2 x 6 in. lumber or steel tubing or angle. Wood frames usually 2 ft wider than screen size. Metal frames usually 1 ft wider than screen size.
7. Rear projection screens: 3 x 4 to 7 x 14 ft. Custom sizes, acrylic: up to 10 x 12 or 8 x 14 ft. Custom sizes, glass: up to 10 x 25 ft.

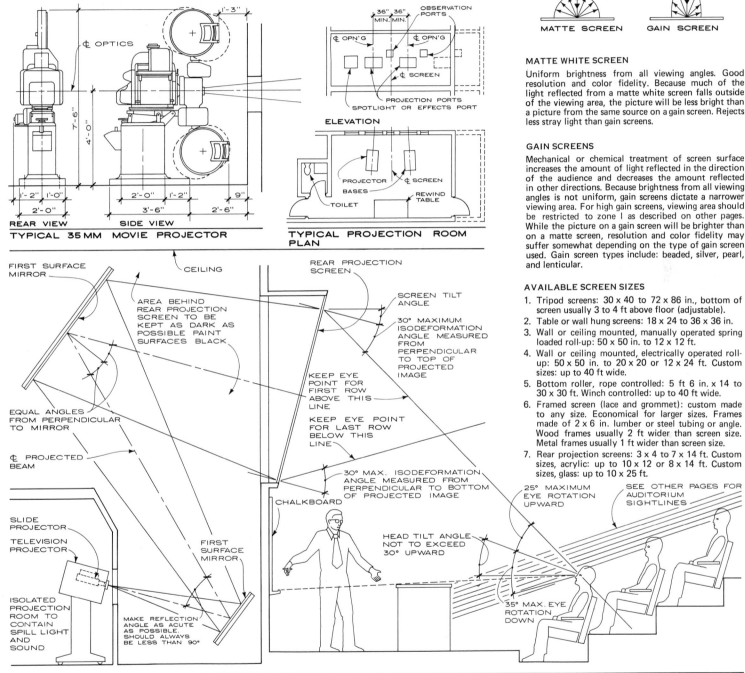

REAR PROJECTION

NOTES

1. The average rear projection screen is usually smaller than a possible front projection screen because of physical and/or economic reasons. Front projection, therefore, is usually preferable for larger audiences. The size of a rear projection screen may be restricted by its greater cost and by limitations of projection geometry for lack of space.
2. Projection equipment and projection formulas are the same for both front and rear projection. Front projection usually permits an adequate throw distance over the heads of an audience in order to fill a larger screen. An equivalent depth is not typically available for rear projection. Larger images for rear projection can be achieved through the use of shorter focal length lenses which allow a shorter throw distance. Mirrors can also be used to bend or fold a projected beam into a shallower space behind the screen.
3. Front projection usually results in better resolution, better color fidelity, and better contrast ratios.
4. The principal advantage of rear projection over front projection is the ability of the rear projection screen to reject stray ambient light in the auditorium. This ability may allow a higher light level within a learning space for, for example, taking notes while viewing a projected image.
5. Rear projection will also allow a speaker or a spectator to stand in front of a screen without casting a shadow.

Peter H. Frink; Frink and Beuchat: Architects; Philadelphia, Pennsylvania

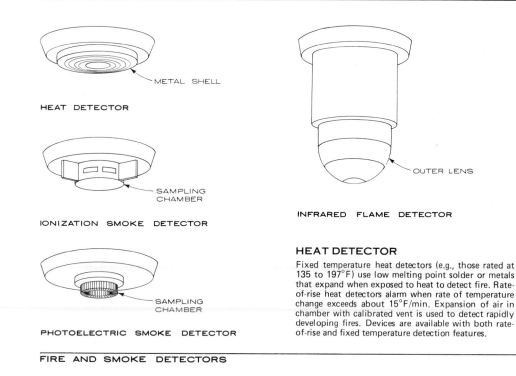

HEAT DETECTOR — METAL SHELL

IONIZATION SMOKE DETECTOR — SAMPLING CHAMBER

PHOTOELECTRIC SMOKE DETECTOR — SAMPLING CHAMBER

INFRARED FLAME DETECTOR — OUTER LENS

FIRE AND SMOKE DETECTORS

IONIZATION SMOKE DETECTOR

Ionization detectors use the interruption of small current flow between electrodes by smoke in ionized sampling chamber to detect fire. Dual chamber (with reference chamber exposed only to air temperature, pressure, and humidity) and single chamber detectors are available. Ionization detectors can be used in rooms and in air ducts to detect smoke in air distribution systems.

PHOTOELECTRIC SMOKE DETECTOR

Photoelectric smoke detectors use the scattering of light by smoke into view of photocell. Sources of light may be either incandescent lamp or light emitting diode (LED). Photoelectric detectors can be used in rooms and in air ducts to detect smoke in air distribution systems.

INFRARED FLAME DETECTOR

Infrared flame detectors respond to the high-frequency (IR) radiant energy from flames. Alarm is only triggered when IR energy flickers at rate which is characteristic of flames. Infrared detectors can be used in large open areas where rapid development of flaming conditions could occur (e.g., flammable liquids fire hazards).

HEAT DETECTOR

Fixed temperature heat detectors (e.g., those rated at 135 to 197°F) use low melting point solder or metals that expand when exposed to heat to detect fire. Rate-of-rise heat detectors alarm when rate of temperature change exceeds about 15°F/min. Expansion of air in chamber with calibrated vent is used to detect rapidly developing fires. Devices are available with both rate-of-rise and fixed temperature detection features.

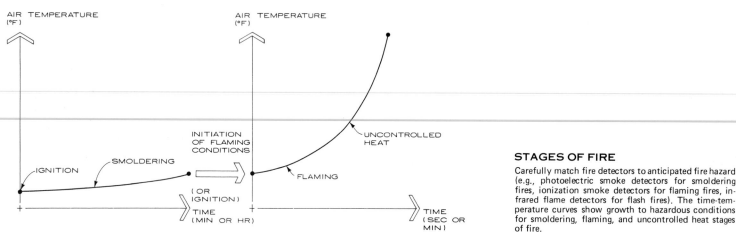

STAGES OF FIRE

STAGES OF FIRE

Carefully match fire detectors to anticipated fire hazard (e.g., photoelectric smoke detectors for smoldering fires, ionization smoke detectors for flaming fires, infrared flame detectors for flash fires). The time-temperature curves show growth to hazardous conditions for smoldering, flaming, and uncontrolled heat stages of fire.

CHECKLIST FOR RESIDENTIAL FIRE DETECTION

1. Use smoke detectors to protect the following (in decreasing order of importance):
   a. Every occupied floor and basement.
   b. Sleeping areas and basement near stairs.
   c. Sleeping areas only.
2. Use heat detectors to protect remote areas (e.g., basement shops, attics) where serious fires could develop before smoke would reach smoke detector or in areas such as garages or kitchens where smoke detectors would be exposed to high smoke levels during normal conditions.
3. Locate smoke detectors on ceilings near center of rooms (or on the upper walls 6 to 12 in. from ceiling) where smoke can collect. In long corridors, consider using two or more detectors.
4. Use closer spacing between detectors where ceiling beams, joists, and the like will interrupt flow of smoke to detector.
5. Do not place smoke detectors near supply air registers or diffusers, or near return air grilles where return air could remove smoke from the area before it reaches detector.
6. For guidelines on fire detection for residences, refer to "Household Fire Warning Equipment," NFPA No. 74, available from the National Fire Protection Association.

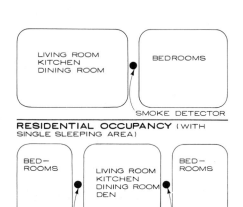

RESIDENTIAL OCCUPANCY (WITH SINGLE SLEEPING AREA)

RESIDENTIAL OCCUPANCY (WITH SPLIT SLEEPING AREAS)

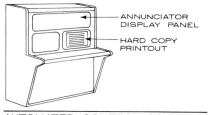

ANNUNCIATOR DISPLAY PANEL
HARD COPY PRINTOUT

AUTOMATED CONTROL CONSOLE

NOTE

When fire is detected (e.g., by smoke, heat, infrared detectors, or water flow indicators in sprinkler system piping), automated control systems immediately summon the fire department. Floor plans of fire area can be projected on annunciator display panel to pinpoint trouble spots. Controls can be designed to automatically shut down fan systems or activate fans and dampers for smoke removal and control. In addition, remote firefighter control panel, with telephone communication to control console and to each floor in building, can be used to control and monitor status of elevators, pumps and emergency generators, fans, dampers, and the like.

M. David Egan, P.E.; College of Architecture, Clemson University; Clemson, South Carolina

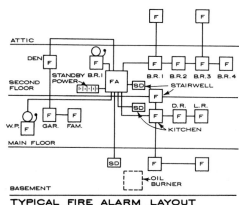

TYPICAL FIRE ALARM LAYOUT

Residential fire alarm systems, if properly designed and functioning normally, should provide sufficient time for the evacuation of the residents and for the initiation of appropriate countermeasures. The elements of the system are the various alarm initiating devices, the wiring and control panel, and the audible alarm devices. Since the purpose of a residential system is evacuation, manual systems with hand pulled stations are rarely used. Instead, automatic smoke and heat sensing equipment that sounds a continuous alarm is preferred. Automatic alarm systems may include some form of system "supervision" that will trigger a trouble bell or light signal indicating a broken wire or other equipment failure. If the system becomes extensive it may be desirable to arrange the circuiting so that the alarm devices are grouped by zones or floor levels, allowing the resident to trace the source of the alarm.

For multiple dwelling units such as dormitories, a supervised, zoned, noncoded system with continuously ringing bells is commonly used. Since dormitories are designed with soundproofing in mind for ideal study and sleeping conditions, bells and horns of high sound intensity must be selected. A hotel normally uses a supervised, presignal, selectively coded system with automatic stations in storerooms, boiler rooms, kitchens, and other unsupervised areas. Apartment houses, being a collection of individual residences, rarely have a common fire alarm system.

Requirements for residential fire alarm systems vary according to local fire code regulations. Details for the design of these systems are best left to a fire alarm expert.

RESIDENTIAL ALARM SYSTEM

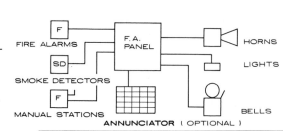

NONCODED ALARM SYSTEM

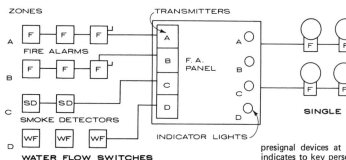

MASTER CODED SYSTEM

The actuation of a noncoded manual or automatic initiating device sounds four rounds of general alarm signal throughout the building for orderly evacuation. This system may be used in small hospitals, nursing homes, or office buildings.

SELECTIVE CODED SYSTEM

Activation of a manual coded station in a selective coded system sounds four rounds on all alarm sounding devices identifying the initiating station by numerical code. The alarm stops after four rounds. This system is used for installations requiring selective coding to indicate the location of the fire and notify the occupants to evacuate.

PRESIGNAL SYSTEMS

In the presignal systems, the actuation of an initiating device sounds four rounds of an identifying code on

CODED ALARM SYSTEMS

NONCODED SYSTEM

The actuation of a manual or automatic alarm initiating device causes a continuous general alarm throughout the building until the initiating device is returned to normal and the system is reset manually. This system is used in moderately sized industrial, commercial, and educational buildings where a continuous general alarm is required.

presignal devices at selected locations. The presignal indicates to key personnel the specific location of the manual station for which the alarm was initiated.

Authorized personnel then investigate the fire, evaluate the danger, and, if conditions warrant, sound a master coded general evacuation alarm by inserting and turning a special key in any manual station. The signal sounds until the key is removed. For presignal fire alarm systems it is vital to locate the fire immediately and to alert key personnel without unnecessarily alarming the occupants.

Any one of the abovementioned systems may be tied in with smoke detection and sprinkler alarm systems. The result of the activation of these alarm systems is a general alarm throughout the building for a noncoded system and a predetermined code sound throughout the building for a coded system. In case of a presignal system, the alarm will be actuated at a predetermined selective location similar to the operation described above.

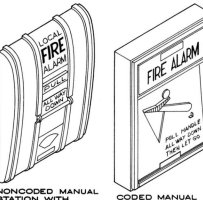

EQUIPMENT

All fire alarm systems consist of a control panel, alarm initiation, and alarm sounding devices.

MANUAL FIRE ALARM STATIONS are wall mounted devices that initiate an alarm signal. There are two types of manual stations:

1. Break glass station.

FIRE ALARM SYSTEM EQUIPMENT

Syska & Hennessey, Consulting Engineers; New York, New York

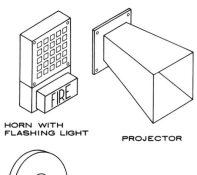

2. Pull station where an operating lever initiates the alarm.

ALARM SIGNALING DEVICES are of three basic types: gongs, horns, and chimes. Gongs come in three standard sizes; 4, 6, and 10 in. in diameter. Horns are especially suitable for use in high ambient noise areas. Chimes are used in areas where a lower sound is necessary than that normally available from a fire alarm gong, for use in hospitals, rest homes, and similar places. All signaling devices may be surface or recess mounted in suitable enclosures.

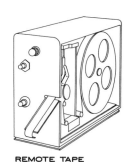

CONTROL PANELS serve as the central logic unit with the required relays, annunciators, electronics, power supplies, and so on, for proper systems operation.

Annunciators provide a visual indication of station or zone from which a fire alarm signal was initiated.

Remote printout units are used to provide a permanent record of station or zone from which a fire alarm was initiated.

The input voltage to the control panel is usually 120/208 V.

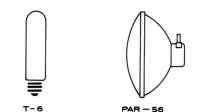

A — 19   PS — 52   PAR — 38   R — 40   T — 6   PAR — 56

GENERAL SERVICE

BULB	DIA. (IN.)	LENGTH (IN.)	BASE	WATTS
A-15	1 7/8	3 1/2	Med.	15
A-19	2 3/8	4 7/16	Med.	60
A-21	2 5/8	5 5/16	Med.	100
PS-25	3 1/8	6 15/16	Med.	150
PS-30	3 3/4	8 1/16	Med.	300
PS-40	5	9 3/4	Mogul	500
PS-52	6 1/2	13 1/16	Mogul	1000

PARABOLIC REFLECTORS

BULB	DIA. (IN.)	LENGTH (IN.)	BASE	WATTS
R-20	2 1/2	3 15/16	Med.	30
R-30	3 3/4	5 3/16	Med.	75
PAR-38	4 3/4	5 5/16	Med. skt.	150
PAR-38	4 3/4	5 5/16	Med. skt.	150
R-40	5	6 1/2	Med.	150
R-40	5	6 1/2	Med.	300
R-40	5	7 1/4	Mogul	500

TUNGSTEN HALOGEN

BULB	DIA. (IN.)	LENGTH (IN.)	BASE	WATTS
T-4	1/2	3 1/8	Minicam	250
T-4	1/2	3 1/8	Rec. S.C.	400
PAR-56	7	5	End prong	500
T-3	3/8	4 11/16	Rec. S.C.	500
T-4	1/2	3 5/8	Minicam	500
T-6	3/4	5 5/8	Rec. S.C.	1000
T-3	3/8	10 1/16	Rec. S.C.	1500

The efficacy of light production by incandescent filament lamps depends on the temperature of the filament—the higher the temperature, the greater the portion of radiated energy that falls in the visible region. Tungsten filaments have a high melting point (3655°K) and low · vapor pressure, which permit higher operating temperatures and, as a result, high efficacies. Past improvements in incandescent lamps have involved changes in filament shape. Recent improvement, however, are primarily a result of changes in the atmosphere inside the glass bulb that encloses the filament. The discovery that inert gases retard evaporation of the filament made it possible to design lamps for higher filament temperatures. Today, most incandescent lamps use a fill mixture of argon and nitrogen.

The most popular incandescent lamps are general service (GS) ones, which range from the 15-W A-15 to the 1500-W PS-52 types and are designed for 120-, 125-, and 130-V circuits. The letter prefix refers to the lamp shape—for example, PS has a pear straight neck; A is of the standard incandescent shape. Other common designations are G for globe and PAR for parabolic aluminizer reflector. The number following the letter prefix is the bulb diameter in eighths of an inch. For the same wattage, GS lamps (750 to 1000 hr of life) are more efficient than extended service (ES) lamps (2500 hr of life). ES lamps—for use where replacement costs are relatively high, such as hard-to-reach locations—achieve long life by use of a filament that is stronger, but less efficacious.

TUNGSTEN HALOGEN lamps are a variation of incandescent filament sources. A halogen additive in the bulb reacts chemically with the tungsten, removing deposited tungsten from the bulb and redepositing it on the filament. This results in a lumen maintenance factor of close to 100%. (Lumen maintenance refers to the ability of a lamp to maintain a constant light output.) However, such a lamp does have a definite life, usually a maximum of 3000 hr. The smaller size, good optical control, and high color temperatures of tungsten-halogen lamps, as well as a continuous spectrum, particularly fit theatrical lighting needs.

INCANDESCENT LAMPS

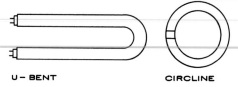

T—12   T—12   U — BENT   CIRCLINE

STANDARD TUBE

BULB	DIA. (IN.)	LENGTH (IN.)	BASE	WATTS
T-8	1	18	Med. bipin	15
T-12	1 1/2	24	Med. bipin	20
T-12	1 1/2	36	Med. bipin	30
T-12	1 1/2	48	Med. bipin	40
T-12	1 1/2	96	Single pin	75

NOTE: Dimensions are similar for preheat, rapid start, and extended service lamps.

HIGH OUTPUT (800 MA)

BULB	DIA. (IN.)	LENGTH (IN.)	BASE	WATTS
T-12	1 1/2	48	Rec. D.C.	60
T-12	1 1/2	72	Rec. D.C.	85
T-12	1 1/2	96	Rec. D.C.	110
T-12*	1 1/2	72	Rec. D.C.	160
T-12*	1 1/2	96	Rec. D.C.	215

*Requires 1500 milli amps.

SPECIAL SHAPES

BULB	DIA. (IN.)	LENGTH (IN.)	BASE	WATTS
U-Bent	1 1/2	22 1/2	Med. bipin	40
Circle	1 1/8	8 1/4 dia.	Four pin	22
Circle	1 1/4	12 dia.	Four pin	32
Circle	1 1/4	16 dia.	Four pin	40

NOTE: Fluorescent lamps are available in cool white, warm white, and daylight tints.

FLUORESCENT lamps offer three to five times the efficacy of incandescent sources and compare favorably with most high intensity discharge sources. Efficacies vary with lamp length, lamp loading, and lamp phosphor coating.

Both geometric design and operating conditions of a fluorescent lamp affect the efficacy with which electrical energy is converted into visible radiation. For example, as lamp diameter increases, efficacy increases, passes through a maximum, then decreases. The length of the lamp also influences its efficacy: the longer it is, the higher the efficacy.

This lamp uses an electric discharge source, in which light is produced predominantly by fluorescent powders activated by ultraviolet energy generated by a mercury arc. The fluorescent lamp cannot be operated directly from the nominal 120-V ac source because the arc discharge would not be established. As a result, it must be operated in series with a ballast that limits the current and provides the starting and operating lamp voltages.

The starting process occurs in two stages. Once a sufficient voltage exists between an electrode and ground, ionization of the gas (mercury plus an inert gas) in the lamp occurs. Then a sufficient voltage must exist across the lamp to extend the ionization throughout the lamp and to develop an arc. Three basic types of ballasts—preheat, instant start, and rapid start—provide means of starting.

For the preheat variety, the electrodes are heated before the application of high voltage across the lamp. Arc initiation in instant start lamps depends entirely on the application of a high voltage (400 to 1000 V) across the lamp, which ejects electrons by field emission. These electrons ionize the gas and initiate arc discharge. The rapid start principle makes use of electrodes that are heated continuously by means of low voltage windings built into the ballast. A power saving feature of rapid start circuits is that the lamps show little change in rated life as a result of frequent on/off/on cycles.

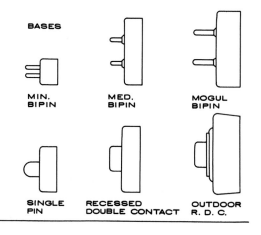

BASES

MIN. BIPIN   MED. BIPIN   MOGUL BIPIN

SINGLE PIN   RECESSED DOUBLE CONTACT   OUTDOOR R. D. C.

FLUORESCENT LAMPS

Wm. G. Miner, AIA, Architect; Washington, D.C.

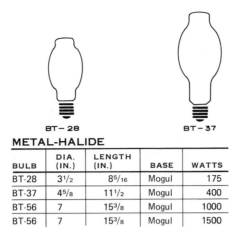

B-21   R-60   BT-28   BT-37   BT-25   E-18

MERCURY VAPOR

BULB	DIA. (IN.)	LENGTH (IN.)	BASE	WATTS
B-17	$2^1/_8$	$5^1/_8$	Med.	40
B-21	$2^5/_8$	$6^1/_2$	Med.	75
BT-25	$3^1/_8$	$7^1/_2$	Mogul	100
BT-28	$3^1/_2$	$8^5/_{16}$	Mogul	250
BT-37	$4^5/_8$	$11^1/_2$	Mogul	400
R-60	$7^1/_2$	$10^7/_8$	Mogul	400
BT-56	7	$15^3/_8$	Mogul	1000

METAL-HALIDE

BULB	DIA. (IN.)	LENGTH (IN.)	BASE	WATTS
BT-28	$3^1/_2$	$8^5/_{16}$	Mogul	175
BT-37	$4^5/_8$	$11^1/_2$	Mogul	400
BT-56	7	$15^3/_8$	Mogul	1000
BT-56	7	$15^3/_8$	Mogul	1500

HIGH PRESSURE SODIUM

BULB	DIA. (IN.)	LENGTH (IN.)	BASE	WATTS
BT-25	$3^1/_8$	$7^5/_8$	Mogul	70
BT-25	$3^1/_8$	$7^5/_8$	Mogul	150
BT-28	$3^1/_2$	$8^5/_{16}$	Mogul	150
E-18	$2^1/_4$	$9^3/_4$	Mogul	250
E-18	$2^1/_4$	$9^3/_4$	Mogul	400
BT-37	$4^5/_8$	$11^1/_2$	Mogul	400
E-25	$3^1/_8$	$15^1/_{16}$	Mogul	1000

MERCURY lamps, which are now popular for lighting commercial interiors, use argon gas to ease starting because mercury has a low vapor pressure at room temperature. When the lighting circuit is energized, the starting voltage is impressed across the gap between the main electrode and the starting electrode, which creates an argon arc that causes the mercury to vaporize. The lamp warmup process takes 5 to 7 min, depending on ambient temperature conditions. Most mercury lamps are constructed with two envelopes—an inner one that contains the arc and an outer one that shields the arc tube from outside drafts and changes in temperature. The outer envelope usually contains an inert gas.

The mercury spectrum results in greenish-blue light at efficacies of 30 to 65 lm/W, which ranks it between incandescent and fluorescent lamps. Economics favor mercury where burning hours are long, service is difficult, and replacement labor is high. Many mercury lamps lose as much as 50% of their initial output during their rated life of 24,000 hr or more.

METAL-HALIDE lamps are similar in construction to the mercury lamp, except that the arc tube contains various metal halides in addition to mercury. When the halide vapor approaches the high temperature, central core of the discharge, it disassociates into the halogen and the metal, with the metal radiating its appropriate spectrum. As the halogen and metal move near the cooler arc tube wall by diffusion and convection, they recombine, and the cycle repeats itself.

These lamps generate light with more than half the efficacy of the mercury arc, offer a small light source size for optical control, and provide good color rendition as compared with clear mercury. They have been applied in nearly every type of interior and exterior lighting application because they offer an efficient "white," light source. The average rated life of this lamp is 15,000 hr.

In both low pressure and high pressure sodium sources, light is produced by electricity passing through sodium vapor. In the LPS lamp, a starting gas of neon produces

a red glow when the lamp is initially ignited. As heat is generated, the sodium metal vaporizes, and the emitted light turns into the characteristic yellow color.

HIGH PRESSURE SODIUM (HPS) lamps are used for roadway and sidewalk illumination and offer more suitable color rendition characteristics. Sodium is a particularly suitable gas because most of its radiation is concentrated in a wavelength interval where the sensitivity of the human eye is high. It also has a relatively low excitation energy.

The HPS lamp is constructed with two envelopes—the inner being polycrystalline alumina, which is resistant to sodium attack. The arc tube contains xenon as a starting gas and a small amount of sodium-mercury amalgam. The outer glass envelope is evacuated and protects against chemical attack of the arc tube and maintains the arc tube temperature.

HPS sources are compact, yet have high efficacies (up to 140 lm/W) and high lumen maintenance characteristics. They radiate energy across the visible spectrum and produce a golden-white color. They are available in sizes from 70 to 1000 W, with the low wattage sources finding application in residential street lighting and shopping mall illumination.

HPS lamps have five times the efficacy of incandescent sources, more than twice that of mercury, and 50% more than metal-halide.

HIGH INTENSITY DISCHARGE LAMPS

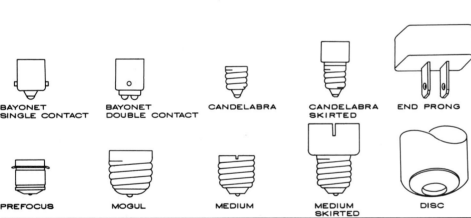

BAYONET SINGLE CONTACT   BAYONET DOUBLE CONTACT   CANDELABRA   CANDELABRA SKIRTED   END PRONG

PREFOCUS   MOGUL   MEDIUM   MEDIUM SKIRTED   DISC

LAMP BASES

CHARACTERISTICS OF BASIC LAMP TYPES

CHARACTERISTICS	INCANDESCENT (INCLUDING TUNGSTEN HALOGEN)	FLUORESCENT	HIGH INTENSITY DISCHARGE (HID)		
			MERCURY-VAPOR	METAL-HALIDE	HIGH PRESSURE SODIUM
Wattages (lamp only)	15-1500	40-1000	40-1000	400, 100, 1500	75, 150, 250, 400, 1000
Life (hr)	750-12,000	9000-30,000	16,000-24,000	1500-15,000	10,000-20,000
Efficacy (lm/W, lamp only)	15-25	55-88	20-63	80-100	100-130
Color rendition	Very good to excellent	Good to excellent	Poor to very good	Good to very good	Fair
Light direction control	Very good to excellent	Fair	Very good	Very good	Very good
Source size	Compact	Extended	Compact	Compact	Compact
Relight time	Immediate	Immediate	3-5 min	10-20 min	Less than 1 min

Wm. G. Miner, AIA, Architect; Washington, D.C.

COEFFICIENTS OF UTILIZATION

TYPICAL LUMINAIRE	MAINT. CAT.	MAXIMUM S/MH GUIDE[4]	RCR[3] ↓	ρcc[1] → 80			70			50			30			10			0
				ρw[2] → 50	30	10	50	30	10	50	30	10	50	30	10	50	30	10	0
Pendant diffusing sphere with incandescent lamp (35½%↑ 45%↓)	V	1.5	0	.87	.87	.87	.81	.81	.81	.69	.69	.69	.59	.59	.59	.49	.49	.49	.44
			1	.71	.67	.63	.66	.62	.59	.56	.53	.50	.47	.45	.43	.39	.37	.35	.31
			2	.61	.54	.49	.56	.50	.46	.47	.43	.39	.39	.36	.33	.32	.29	.27	.23
			3	.52	.45	.39	.48	.42	.37	.41	.36	.31	.34	.30	.26	.27	.24	.22	.18
			4	.46	.38	.33	.42	.36	.30	.36	.30	.26	.30	.26	.22	.24	.21	.18	.15
			5	.40	.33	.27	.37	.30	.25	.32	.26	.22	.26	.22	.19	.21	.18	.15	.12
			6	.36	.28	.23	.33	.26	.21	.28	.23	.19	.23	.19	.16	.19	.15	.13	.10
			7	.32	.25	.20	.29	.23	.18	.25	.20	.16	.21	.16	.13	.17	.13	.11	.09
			8	.29	.22	.17	.27	.20	.16	.23	.17	.14	.19	.15	.12	.15	.12	.09	.07
			9	.26	.19	.15	.24	.18	.14	.20	.15	.12	.17	.13	.10	.14	.11	.08	.06
			10	.23	.17	.13	.22	.16	.12	.19	.14	.10	.16	.12	.09	.13	.09	.07	.05
Porcelain enameled ventilated standard dome with incandescent lamp (0%↑ 83½%↓)	IV	1.3	0	.99	.99	.99	.97	.97	.97	.92	.92	.92	.88	.88	.88	.85	.85	.85	.83
			1	.88	.85	.82	.86	.83	.81	.83	.80	.78	.79	.78	.76	.77	.75	.73	.72
			2	.78	.73	.68	.76	.72	.67	.73	.69	.66	.71	.67	.64	.68	.65	.63	.61
			3	.69	.62	.57	.67	.61	.57	.65	.60	.56	.63	.58	.55	.61	.57	.54	.52
			4	.61	.54	.49	.60	.53	.48	.58	.52	.48	.56	.51	.47	.54	.50	.46	.45
			5	.54	.47	.41	.53	.46	.41	.51	.45	.41	.50	.44	.40	.48	.43	.40	.38
			6	.48	.41	.35	.47	.40	.35	.46	.39	.35	.44	.39	.34	.43	.38	.34	.32
			7	.43	.35	.30	.42	.35	.30	.41	.34	.30	.39	.34	.30	.38	.33	.29	.28
			8	.38	.31	.26	.38	.31	.26	.37	.30	.26	.36	.30	.26	.35	.30	.26	.24
			9	.35	.28	.23	.34	.27	.23	.33	.27	.23	.32	.27	.23	.31	.26	.22	.21
			10	.31	.25	.20	.31	.24	.20	.30	.24	.20	.29	.24	.20	.29	.23	.20	.18
Prismatic square surface drum (18½%↑ 60½%↓)	V	1.3	0	.89	.89	.89	.85	.85	.85	.77	.77	.77	.70	.70	.70	.63	.63	.63	.60
			1	.78	.75	.72	.74	.72	.69	.68	.66	.64	.62	.60	.58	.56	.55	.54	.51
			2	.69	.65	.61	.66	.62	.58	.61	.57	.54	.56	.53	.50	.51	.49	.47	.44
			3	.62	.57	.52	.60	.55	.50	.55	.51	.47	.50	.47	.44	.46	.44	.41	.39
			4	.56	.50	.46	.54	.49	.44	.50	.45	.42	.46	.42	.39	.42	.39	.37	.35
			5	.51	.45	.40	.49	.43	.39	.45	.41	.37	.42	.38	.35	.39	.36	.33	.31
			6	.46	.40	.36	.45	.39	.35	.42	.37	.33	.39	.35	.31	.36	.32	.30	.28
			7	.42	.36	.32	.41	.35	.31	.38	.33	.29	.35	.31	.28	.33	.29	.27	.25
			8	.39	.32	.28	.37	.32	.28	.35	.30	.26	.32	.28	.25	.30	.27	.24	.22
			9	.35	.29	.25	.34	.29	.25	.32	.27	.24	.30	.26	.23	.28	.24	.22	.20
			10	.32	.27	.23	.31	.26	.22	.29	.25	.21	.27	.23	.20	.26	.22	.20	.18
Medium distribution unit with lens plate and inside frost lamp (0%↑ 54½%↓)	V	1.0	0	.64	.64	.64	.63	.63	.63	.60	.60	.60	.57	.57	.57	.55	.55	.55	.54
			1	.60	.58	.57	.58	.57	.56	.56	.55	.54	.54	.53	.52	.52	.52	.51	.50
			2	.55	.53	.51	.54	.52	.50	.52	.50	.49	.51	.49	.48	.49	.48	.47	.46
			3	.51	.48	.46	.50	.47	.45	.49	.46	.44	.47	.45	.44	.46	.44	.43	.42
			4	.47	.44	.41	.47	.44	.41	.45	.43	.41	.44	.42	.40	.43	.41	.40	.39
			5	.44	.40	.38	.43	.40	.38	.42	.39	.37	.41	.39	.37	.40	.38	.37	.36
			6	.41	.37	.35	.40	.37	.35	.39	.36	.34	.39	.36	.34	.38	.36	.34	.33
			7	.38	.34	.32	.37	.34	.32	.37	.34	.31	.36	.33	.31	.35	.33	.31	.30
			8	.35	.32	.29	.35	.31	.29	.34	.31	.29	.34	.31	.29	.33	.30	.29	.28
			9	.33	.29	.27	.32	.29	.27	.32	.29	.26	.31	.28	.26	.31	.28	.26	.25
			10	.30	.27	.25	.30	.27	.24	.30	.27	.24	.29	.26	.24	.29	.26	.24	.23
Reflector downlight with baffles and inside frosted lamp (0%↑ 44½%↓)	IV	0.7	0	.53	.53	.53	.52	.52	.52	.49	.49	.49	.47	.47	.47	.45	.45	.45	.44
			1	.51	.50	.49	.50	.49	.48	.48	.47	.47	.46	.46	.45	.45	.44	.44	.43
			2	.48	.47	.46	.48	.46	.45	.46	.45	.44	.45	.44	.44	.44	.43	.43	.42
			3	.47	.45	.44	.46	.45	.43	.45	.44	.43	.44	.43	.42	.43	.42	.41	.41
			4	.45	.43	.42	.44	.43	.42	.43	.42	.41	.43	.41	.41	.42	.41	.40	.40
			5	.43	.41	.40	.43	.41	.40	.42	.40	.39	.41	.40	.39	.41	.40	.39	.38
			6	.42	.40	.39	.41	.40	.38	.41	.39	.38	.40	.39	.38	.40	.39	.38	.37
			7	.40	.38	.37	.40	.38	.37	.39	.38	.37	.39	.38	.37	.38	.37	.36	.36
			8	.39	.37	.36	.38	.37	.36	.38	.37	.36	.38	.37	.36	.37	.36	.35	.35
			9	.37	.36	.34	.37	.35	.34	.37	.35	.34	.36	.35	.34	.36	.35	.34	.33
			10	.36	.34	.33	.36	.34	.33	.36	.34	.33	.35	.34	.33	.35	.34	.33	.32

COEFFICIENTS OF UTILIZATION FOR 20% EFFECTIVE FLOOR CAVITY REFLECTANCE (ρFC = 20)

GENERAL NOTES

Luminaire data in this table are based on a composite of generic luminaire types. The polar intensity sketch (candlepower distribution curve) and the corresponding spacing to mounting height guide are representative of many luminaires of each type shown.

SYMBOLS

1. pcc = percent effective ceiling cavity reflectance.
2. pw = percent wall reflectance.
3. RCR = room cavity ratio.
4. Maximum S/MH guide = ratio of maximum luminaire spacing to mounting or ceiling height above work plane.

Maintenance categories (maint. cat.):

Cat. I — Bare lamps and strips
Cat. II — 15% or more uplight, open or louvered / Large louvered, 1 in. or more
Cat. III — Less than 15% uplight, open or louvered / Small louvered, less than 1 in.
Cat. IV — Recessed with closed top only / Lighted ceiling with louvers
Cat. V — Recessed with total enclosure / Surface suspended and enclosed
Cat. VI — Totally direct / Totally indirect lighting / Lighted ceiling with solid diffuser

Illuminating Engineering Society; New York, New York

COEFFICIENTS OF UTILIZATION

TYPICAL LUMINAIRE	MAINT. CAT.	MAXIMUM S/MH GUIDE[4]	TYPICAL DISTRIBUTION AND PERCENT LAMP LUMENS	RCR[3]	ρCC 80 / ρW 50	30	10	ρCC 70 / ρW 50	30	10	ρCC 50 / ρW 50	30	10	ρCC 30 / ρW 50	30	10	ρCC 10 / ρW 50	30	10	ρCC 0 / 0

COEFFICIENTS OF UTILIZATION FOR 20% EFFECTIVE FLOOR CAVITY REFLECTANCE (ρFC = 20)

R-40 flood without shielding — IV, 0.8, 0%↑ 100%↓

RCR	80/50	30	10	70/50	30	10	50/50	30	10	30/50	30	10	10/50	30	10	0
0	1.18	1.18	1.18	1.16	1.16	1.16	1.11	1.11	1.11	1.06	1.06	1.06	1.01	1.01	1.01	.99
1	1.09	1.07	1.04	1.07	1.05	1.02	1.03	1.01	.99	.99	.98	.96	.96	.95	.94	.92
2	1.01	.97	.94	.99	.95	.92	.96	.93	.90	.93	.90	.88	.90	.88	.86	.84
3	.93	.88	.84	.92	.87	.83	.89	.85	.81	.87	.83	.80	.84	.82	.79	.77
4	.87	.81	.76	.85	.80	.75	.83	.78	.75	.81	.77	.74	.79	.76	.73	.71
5	.80	.74	.69	.79	.73	.69	.77	.72	.68	.76	.71	.67	.74	.70	.67	.65
6	.74	.68	.63	.73	.67	.63	.72	.66	.62	.70	.66	.62	.69	.65	.61	.60
7	.69	.62	.57	.68	.62	.57	.67	.61	.57	.65	.60	.56	.64	.60	.56	.55
8	.64	.57	.53	.63	.57	.52	.62	.56	.52	.61	.56	.52	.60	.55	.52	.50
9	.59	.52	.48	.59	.52	.48	.58	.52	.48	.57	.51	.48	.56	.51	.47	.46
10	.55	.49	.44	.55	.48	.44	.54	.48	.44	.53	.48	.44	.52	.47	.44	.42

R-40 flood with specular anodized reflector skirt; 45° cutoff — IV, 0.7, 0%↑ 85%↓

RCR	80/50	30	10	70/50	30	10	50/50	30	10	30/50	30	10	10/50	30	10	0
0	1.00	1.00	1.00	.98	.98	.98	.94	.94	.94	.90	.90	.90	.86	.86	.86	.84
1	.96	.94	.92	.94	.92	.91	.90	.89	.88	.87	.86	.85	.84	.84	.83	.82
2	.91	.88	.86	.90	.87	.85	.87	.85	.83	.84	.83	.82	.82	.81	.80	.79
3	.87	.84	.81	.86	.83	.81	.84	.81	.79	.82	.80	.78	.80	.78	.77	.76
4	.83	.80	.77	.82	.79	.77	.81	.78	.76	.79	.77	.75	.78	.76	.74	.73
5	.79	.76	.73	.79	.75	.73	.77	.74	.72	.76	.73	.71	.75	.73	.71	.70
6	.76	.73	.70	.76	.72	.70	.75	.72	.69	.74	.71	.69	.73	.70	.68	.67
7	.73	.69	.66	.73	.69	.66	.72	.68	.66	.71	.68	.66	.70	.67	.65	.64
8	.70	.66	.63	.70	.66	.63	.69	.65	.63	.68	.65	.63	.67	.65	.63	.62
9	.67	.63	.60	.67	.63	.60	.66	.62	.60	.65	.62	.60	.65	.62	.60	.59
10	.64	.60	.58	.64	.60	.58	.63	.60	.58	.63	.60	.57	.62	.59	.57	.56

Intermediate distribution ventilated reflector with clear HID lamp — III, 1.0, 1%↑ 76%↓

RCR	80/50	30	10	70/50	30	10	50/50	30	10	30/50	30	10	10/50	30	10	0
0	.91	.91	.91	.89	.89	.89	.84	.84	.84	.81	.81	.81	.77	.77	.77	.75
1	.84	.81	.79	.82	.80	.78	.79	.77	.76	.76	.74	.73	.73	.72	.71	.69
2	.77	.73	.70	.76	.72	.70	.73	.70	.68	.70	.68	.66	.68	.66	.65	.63
3	.71	.66	.63	.69	.65	.62	.67	.64	.61	.65	.62	.60	.63	.61	.59	.57
4	.65	.60	.56	.64	.59	.56	.62	.58	.55	.60	.57	.54	.59	.56	.54	.52
5	.59	.54	.50	.59	.54	.50	.57	.53	.50	.56	.52	.49	.54	.51	.48	.47
6	.54	.49	.45	.54	.49	.45	.52	.48	.45	.51	.47	.44	.50	.47	.44	.42
7	.50	.44	.40	.49	.44	.40	.48	.43	.40	.47	.43	.39	.46	.42	.39	.38
8	.45	.40	.36	.45	.40	.36	.44	.39	.36	.43	.39	.35	.42	.38	.35	.34
9	.41	.36	.32	.41	.36	.32	.40	.35	.32	.39	.35	.32	.38	.35	.32	.30
10	.38	.33	.29	.37	.32	.29	.37	.32	.29	.36	.32	.29	.35	.31	.28	.27

Intermediate distribution ventilated reflector with phosphor coated HID lamp — III, 1.0, 6½%↑ 75½%↓

RCR	80/50	30	10	70/50	30	10	50/50	30	10	30/50	30	10	10/50	30	10	0
0	.96	.96	.96	.93	.93	.93	.87	.87	.87	.82	.82	.82	.77	.77	.77	.75
1	.89	.87	.84	.86	.84	.83	.82	.80	.79	.78	.76	.75	.74	.73	.72	.70
2	.82	.79	.76	.80	.77	.74	.76	.74	.72	.73	.71	.69	.70	.68	.67	.65
3	.76	.72	.68	.74	.70	.67	.71	.68	.65	.68	.66	.63	.66	.63	.61	.60
4	.70	.66	.62	.69	.65	.61	.66	.63	.60	.64	.61	.58	.62	.59	.57	.55
5	.65	.60	.56	.64	.59	.56	.62	.58	.54	.60	.56	.53	.58	.55	.52	.51
6	.60	.55	.51	.59	.55	.51	.57	.53	.50	.56	.52	.49	.54	.51	.48	.47
7	.56	.51	.47	.55	.50	.46	.53	.49	.46	.52	.48	.45	.50	.47	.44	.43
8	.52	.47	.43	.51	.46	.43	.50	.45	.42	.48	.44	.41	.47	.43	.41	.40
9	.48	.43	.39	.47	.42	.39	.46	.42	.39	.45	.41	.38	.44	.40	.38	.36
10	.45	.40	.36	.44	.39	.36	.43	.39	.36	.42	.38	.35	.41	.37	.35	.34

Porcelain-enameled reflector with 30°CW x 30°LW shielding — II, 1.0, 23½%↑ 57%↓

RCR	80/50	30	10	70/50	30	10	50/50	30	10	30/50	30	10	10/50	30	10	0
0	.90	.90	.90	.85	.85	.85	.76	.76	.76	.68	.68	.68	.60	.60	.60	.57
1	.81	.78	.76	.77	.74	.72	.69	.67	.66	.62	.61	.60	.56	.55	.54	.57
2	.72	.68	.64	.69	.65	.62	.62	.59	.57	.56	.54	.52	.51	.49	.47	.45
3	.65	.59	.55	.62	.57	.53	.56	.52	.49	.51	.48	.46	.46	.44	.42	.39
4	.58	.52	.48	.56	.50	.46	.51	.46	.43	.46	.43	.40	.42	.39	.37	.35
5	.52	.46	.41	.50	.44	.40	.46	.41	.38	.42	.38	.35	.38	.35	.33	.30
6	.47	.41	.36	.45	.39	.35	.41	.37	.33	.38	.34	.31	.35	.31	.29	.27
7	.43	.36	.32	.41	.35	.31	.38	.33	.29	.34	.30	.27	.32	.28	.26	.24
8	.38	.32	.28	.37	.31	.27	.34	.29	.26	.31	.27	.24	.29	.25	.23	.21
9	.35	.29	.24	.33	.28	.24	.31	.26	.22	.28	.24	.21	.26	.22	.20	.18
10	.32	.26	.22	.30	.25	.21	.28	.23	.20	.26	.22	.19	.24	.20	.18	.16

2 lamp prismatic wraparound—multiply by 0.95 for 4 lamps — V, 1.5/1.2, 11½%↑ 58½%↓

RCR	80/50	30	10	70/50	30	10	50/50	30	10	30/50	30	10	10/50	30	10	0
0	.80	.80	.80	.77	.77	.77	.71	.71	.71	.66	.66	.66	.60	.60	.60	.58
1	.71	.69	.66	.69	.66	.64	.64	.62	.60	.59	.58	.56	.55	.54	.53	.50
2	.64	.59	.56	.61	.58	.54	.57	.54	.51	.53	.51	.49	.49	.48	.46	.44
3	.57	.52	.48	.55	.50	.47	.51	.48	.45	.48	.45	.42	.45	.42	.40	.38
4	.51	.46	.41	.49	.44	.40	.46	.42	.39	.43	.40	.37	.41	.38	.35	.34
5	.46	.40	.36	.44	.39	.35	.41	.37	.34	.39	.35	.32	.37	.33	.31	.29
6	.41	.35	.31	.38	.33	.30	.38	.33	.30	.35	.31	.28	.33	.30	.27	.26
7	.37	.31	.27	.36	.31	.27	.34	.29	.26	.32	.28	.25	.30	.27	.24	.23
8	.33	.28	.24	.32	.27	.23	.30	.26	.22	.29	.25	.22	.27	.24	.21	.19
9	.30	.24	.20	.29	.24	.20	.27	.23	.19	.26	.22	.19	.24	.21	.18	.17
10	.27	.22	.18	.26	.21	.18	.25	.20	.17	.23	.19	.16	.22	.18	.16	.15

Illuminating Engineering Society; New York, New York

COEFFICIENTS OF UTILIZATION

COEFFICIENTS OF UTILIZATION FOR 20% EFFECTIVE FLOOR CAVITY REFLECTANCE ($\rho FC = 20$)

2 lamp 1 ft wide troffer with 45° plastic louver—multiply by 0.90 for 3 lamps
Maint. Cat. IV; Maximum S/MH Guide 1.0; Typical distribution 0%↑, 46%↓

ρcc →	80			70			50			30			10			0
ρw →	50	30	10	50	30	10	50	30	10	50	30	10	50	30	10	0
RCR																
0	.54	.54	.54	.53	.53	.53	.51	.51	.51	.48	.48	.48	.46	.46	.46	.45
1	.49	.48	.46	.48	.47	.46	.46	.45	.44	.45	.44	.43	.43	.42	.42	.41
2	.44	.42	.40	.43	.41	.39	.42	.40	.38	.40	.39	.37	.39	.38	.37	.36
3	.40	.37	.34	.39	.36	.34	.38	.36	.34	.37	.35	.33	.36	.34	.33	.32
4	.36	.33	.30	.36	.32	.30	.35	.32	.30	.34	.31	.29	.33	.31	.29	.28
5	.33	.29	.26	.32	.29	.26	.31	.28	.26	.30	.28	.26	.30	.27	.26	.25
6	.30	.26	.24	.29	.26	.24	.29	.26	.23	.28	.25	.23	.27	.25	.23	.22
7	.27	.24	.21	.27	.23	.21	.26	.23	.21	.26	.23	.21	.25	.22	.21	.20
8	.25	.21	.19	.24	.21	.19	.24	.21	.19	.23	.21	.18	.23	.20	.18	.18
9	.22	.19	.17	.22	.19	.17	.22	.19	.17	.21	.18	.16	.21	.18	.16	.16
10	.21	.17	.15	.20	.17	.15	.20	.17	.15	.20	.17	.15	.19	.17	.15	.14

Fluorescent unit with flat prismatic lens, 2 lamp 1 ft wide
Maint. Cat. V; Maximum S/MH Guide 1.4/1.2; Typical distribution 0%↑, 56%↓, 60°

ρcc →	80			70			50			30			10			0
ρw →	50	30	10	50	30	10	50	30	10	50	30	10	50	30	10	0
RCR																
0	.66	.66	.66	.65	.65	.65	.62	.62	.62	.59	.59	.59	.57	.57	.57	.56
1	.61	.59	.57	.59	.58	.56	.57	.56	.54	.55	.54	.53	.53	.52	.51	.50
2	.55	.52	.50	.54	.51	.49	.52	.50	.48	.50	.48	.47	.49	.47	.46	.45
3	.50	.46	.43	.49	.46	.43	.47	.45	.42	.46	.44	.42	.45	.43	.41	.40
4	.45	.41	.38	.45	.41	.38	.43	.40	.38	.42	.39	.37	.41	.39	.37	.36
5	.41	.37	.34	.40	.36	.34	.39	.36	.33	.38	.35	.33	.37	.35	.33	.32
6	.37	.33	.30	.37	.33	.30	.36	.32	.30	.35	.32	.29	.34	.31	.29	.28
7	.34	.30	.27	.34	.29	.27	.33	.29	.26	.32	.29	.26	.31	.28	.26	.25
8	.31	.26	.24	.30	.26	.23	.30	.26	.23	.29	.26	.23	.28	.25	.23	.22
9	.28	.23	.21	.27	.23	.21	.27	.23	.20	.26	.23	.20	.26	.23	.20	.19
10	.25	.21	.18	.25	.21	.18	.24	.21	.18	.24	.21	.18	.23	.20	.18	.17

1 ft wide aluminum troffer with 40°CW x 45°LW shielding and single extrahigh-output lamp
Maint. Cat. IV; Maximum S/MH Guide 1.1/0.8; Typical distribution 0%↑, 42½%↓

ρcc →	80			70			50			30			10			0
ρw →	50	30	10	50	30	10	50	30	10	50	30	10	50	30	10	0
RCR																
0	.50	.50	.50	.49	.49	.49	.47	.47	.47	.45	.45	.45	.43	.43	.43	.42
1	.46	.45	.44	.45	.44	.43	.44	.43	.42	.42	.41	.41	.41	.40	.40	.39
2	.43	.41	.39	.42	.40	.38	.40	.39	.38	.39	.38	.37	.38	.37	.36	.35
3	.39	.37	.35	.39	.36	.34	.37	.35	.34	.36	.35	.33	.35	.34	.33	.32
4	.36	.33	.31	.35	.33	.31	.35	.32	.31	.34	.32	.30	.33	.31	.30	.29
5	.33	.30	.28	.33	.30	.28	.32	.29	.28	.31	.29	.27	.30	.29	.27	.26
6	.31	.28	.26	.30	.28	.26	.30	.27	.25	.29	.27	.25	.28	.26	.25	.24
7	.28	.25	.23	.28	.25	.23	.27	.25	.23	.27	.25	.23	.27	.24	.23	.22
8	.26	.23	.21	.26	.23	.21	.25	.23	.21	.25	.23	.21	.24	.22	.21	.20
9	.24	.21	.19	.24	.21	.19	.23	.21	.19	.23	.20	.19	.22	.20	.19	.18
10	.22	.19	.17	.22	.19	.17	.21	.19	.17	.21	.19	.17	.21	.19	.17	.16

Luminous bottom suspended unit with extrahigh-output lamp
Maint. Cat. VI; Maximum S/MH Guide 1.5; Typical distribution 66%↑, 12%↓

ρcc →	80			70			50			30			10			0
ρw →	50	30	10	50	30	10	50	30	10	50	30	10	50	30	10	0
RCR																
0	.77	.77	.77	.67	.67	.67	.49	.49	.49	.33	.33	.33	.18	.18	.18	.11
1	.67	.64	.62	.59	.57	.54	.44	.42	.41	.30	.29	.28	.17	.16	.16	.10
2	.59	.54	.50	.51	.48	.45	.38	.36	.34	.26	.25	.23	.15	.14	.13	.09
3	.51	.46	.42	.45	.41	.37	.34	.31	.28	.23	.21	.20	.13	.12	.12	.07
4	.45	.40	.35	.40	.35	.31	.30	.27	.24	.20	.18	.17	.12	.11	.10	.06
5	.40	.34	.30	.35	.30	.27	.26	.23	.20	.18	.16	.14	.10	.09	.08	.05
6	.36	.30	.26	.32	.27	.23	.24	.20	.18	.16	.14	.12	.09	.08	.07	.05
7	.32	.26	.22	.28	.23	.20	.21	.18	.15	.15	.12	.11	.08	.07	.06	.04
8	.29	.23	.19	.25	.21	.17	.19	.16	.13	.13	.11	.09	.08	.06	.06	.03
9	.26	.20	.17	.23	.18	.15	.17	.14	.12	.12	.10	.08	.07	.06	.05	.03
10	.24	.18	.15	.21	.16	.13	.16	.12	.10	.11	.09	.07	.06	.05	.04	.03

Diffusing plastic or glass
ρcc from below ~65%

RCR	70			50		
	50	30	10	50	30	10
1	.60	.58	.56	.58	.56	.54
2	.53	.49	.45	.51	.47	.43
3	.47	.42	.37	.45	.41	.36
4	.41	.36	.32	.39	.35	.31
5	.37	.31	.27	.35	.30	.26
6	.33	.27	.23	.31	.26	.23
7	.29	.24	.20	.28	.23	.20
8	.26	.21	.18	.25	.20	.17
9	.23	.19	.15	.23	.18	.15
10	.21	.17	.13	.21	.16	.13

1. Ceiling efficiency ~60%; diffuser transmittance ~50%; diffuser reflectance ~40%. Cavity with minimum obstructions and painted with 80% reflectance paint—use $\rho_c = 70$
2. For lower reflectance paint or obstructions—use $\rho_c = 50$

Louvered ceiling
ρcc from below ~45%

RCR	50			10		
	50	30	10	50	30	10
1	.51	.49	.48	.47	.46	.45
2	.46	.44	.42	.43	.42	.40
3	.42	.39	.37	.39	.38	.36
4	.38	.35	.33	.36	.34	.32
5	.35	.32	.29	.33	.31	.29
6	.32	.29	.26	.30	.28	.26
7	.29	.26	.23	.28	.25	.23
8	.27	.23	.21	.26	.23	.21
9	.24	.21	.19	.24	.21	.19
10	.22	.19	.17	.22	.19	.17

1. Ceiling efficiency ~50%; 45° shielding opaque louvers of 80% reflectance. Cavity with minimum obstructions and painted with 80% reflectance paint—use $\rho_c = 50$

Illuminating Engineering Society; New York, New York

Notes:
(1) ρcc
(2) ρw
(3) RCR
(4) MAXIMUM S/MH GUIDE

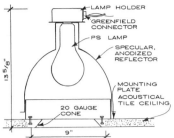

DOWNLIGHT WITH PARABOLIC REFLECTOR

The open reflector downlight uses general service lamps in a polished parabolic reflector to produce controlled light without a lens. The reflector efficiently redirects the upward component of the light source down through the aperture.

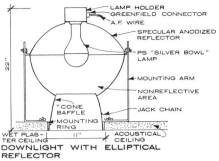

DOWNLIGHT WITH ELLIPTICAL REFLECTOR

A more sophisticated downlight uses a silver bowl lamp to project light up into an elliptical reflector. When the light source is located at one focal point the output light converges and can be redirected through a constricted aperture at the other focal point.

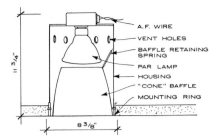

DOWNLIGHT WITH REFLECTOR LAMP

Downlights without reflectors or lenses are commonly called "cans." They have cylindrical housings and rely on a PAR or R lamp for optical control. Cones, annular rings, or lower type baffles will shield an observer from glare in the normal field of view.

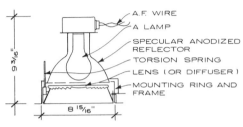

DOWNLIGHT WITH FRESNEL LENS

One downlight type combines a general service lamp with a reflector housing and a diffusing lens. The lens provides directional control of the light as it leaves the luminaire. The lens covers the ceiling aperture, thus keeping dust from the reflector and providing a heat shield.

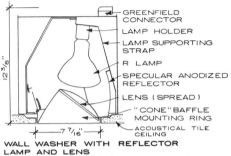

WALL WASHER WITH REFLECTOR LAMP AND LENS

Wall washers provide shadowless coverage of vertical surfaces with an even "wash" of light. They are used to set a mood within a space, to accent surrounding walls, or to obscure undesirable unevenness of the surface.

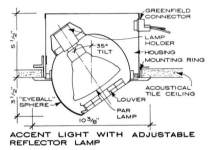

ACCENT LIGHT WITH ADJUSTABLE REFLECTOR LAMP

The accent light produces an asymmetrical distribution of light and normally allows for adjustments in the lamp position. It is used for gallery lighting to emphasize objects or small wall areas.

INCANDESCENT FIXTURES

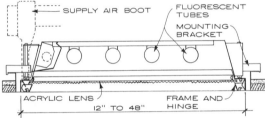

RECESSED UNIT WITH PRISMATIC LENS

The recessed fluorescent luminaire is usually designed to fit into a standard ceiling grid. A transparent, prismatic lens usually encloses the fixture and directs useful light to the work surface.

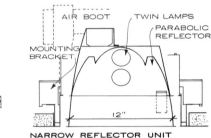

NARROW REFLECTOR UNIT

Parabolic reflectors are used in narrow profile fixtures to redirect the upward component of the light source down to the task area. The fluorescent lamps are stacked so that one may be switched off without sacrificing the even distribution of light.

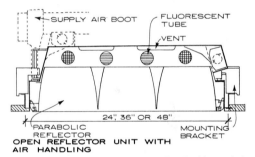

OPEN REFLECTOR UNIT WITH AIR HANDLING

Some open reflector units are fitted with parabola shaped louver blades to better control glare and veiling reflections. Air fittings are also integrated into the lamp housing for ducted air supply or return.

FLUORESCENT FIXTURES

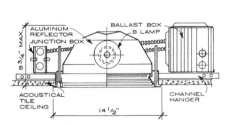

SQUARE LENS AND REFLECTOR UNIT

HID fixtures are usually preassembled and wired for fast installation. A recessed reflector with a fresnel or prismatic lens will maximize the utilization and control of the high lamp output.

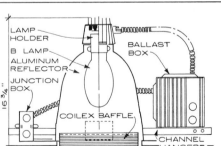

OPEN REFLECTOR DOWNLIGHT

HID luminaires require a deep ceiling space to fully recess the large lamp housing. Open reflector downlights often use elliptical reflectors that focus the lamp light through a small aperture. Coil or cone baffles help reduce fixture surface brightness.

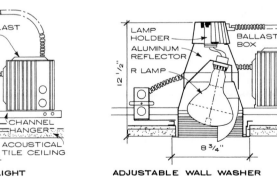

ADJUSTABLE WALL WASHER

A special scoop insert can be added to a standard downlight fixture to create a HID wall washer unit. The reflector and lamp socket can be rotated for desired positioning of light throw.

HIGH INTENSITY DISCHARGE FIXTURES

Wm. G. Miner, AIA, Architect; Washington, D.C.

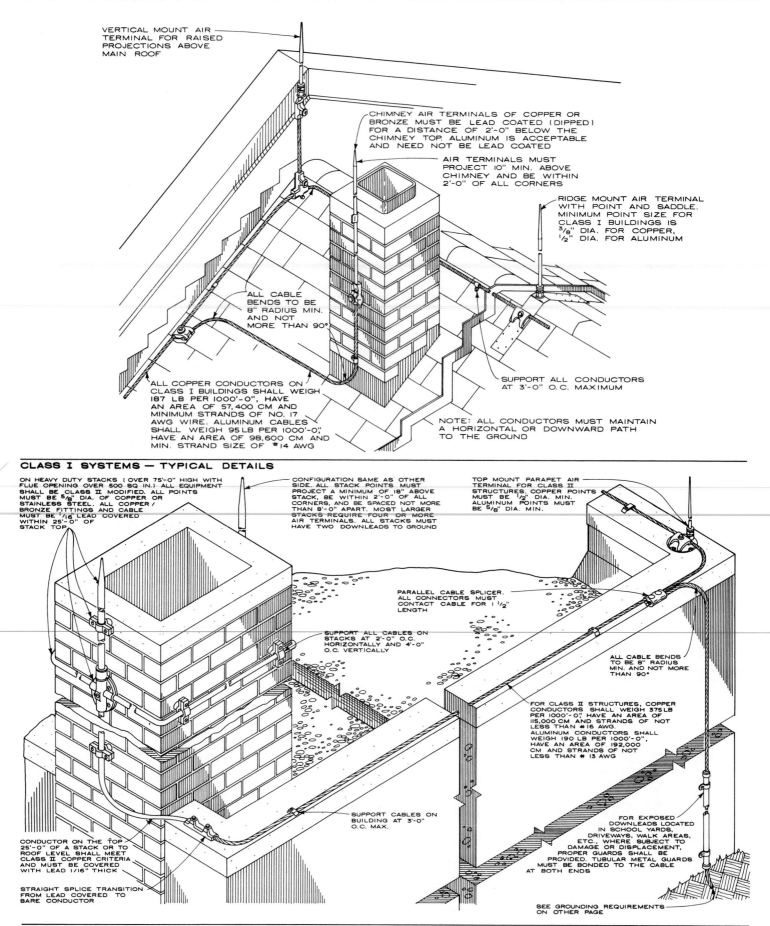

VERTICAL MOUNT AIR TERMINAL FOR RAISED PROJECTIONS ABOVE MAIN ROOF

CHIMNEY AIR TERMINALS OF COPPER OR BRONZE MUST BE LEAD COATED (DIPPED) FOR A DISTANCE OF 2'-0" BELOW THE CHIMNEY TOP. ALUMINUM IS ACCEPTABLE AND NEED NOT BE LEAD COATED

AIR TERMINALS MUST PROJECT 10" MIN. ABOVE CHIMNEY AND BE WITHIN 2'-0" OF ALL CORNERS

RIDGE MOUNT AIR TERMINAL WITH POINT AND SADDLE. MINIMUM POINT SIZE FOR CLASS I BUILDINGS IS $3/8$" DIA. FOR COPPER, $1/2$" DIA. FOR ALUMINUM

ALL CABLE BENDS TO BE 8" RADIUS MIN. AND NOT MORE THAN 90°

ALL COPPER CONDUCTORS ON CLASS I BUILDINGS SHALL WEIGH 187 LB PER 1000'-0", HAVE AN AREA OF 57,400 CM AND MINIMUM STRANDS OF NO. 17 AWG WIRE. ALUMINUM CABLES SHALL WEIGH 95 LB PER 1000'-0", HAVE AN AREA OF 98,600 CM AND MIN. STRAND SIZE OF #14 AWG

SUPPORT ALL CONDUCTORS AT 3'-0" O.C. MAXIMUM

NOTE: ALL CONDUCTORS MUST MAINTAIN A HORIZONTAL OR DOWNWARD PATH TO THE GROUND

CLASS I SYSTEMS — TYPICAL DETAILS

ON HEAVY DUTY STACKS (OVER 75'-0" HIGH WITH FLUE OPENING OVER 500 SQ IN.) ALL EQUIPMENT SHALL BE CLASS II MODIFIED. ALL POINTS MUST BE $5/8$" DIA. OF COPPER OR STAINLESS STEEL. ALL COPPER/BRONZE FITTINGS AND CABLE MUST BE $1/16$" LEAD COVERED WITHIN 25'-0" OF STACK TOP

CONFIGURATION SAME AS OTHER SIDE. ALL STACK POINTS MUST PROJECT A MINIMUM OF 18" ABOVE STACK, BE WITHIN 2'-0" OF ALL CORNERS, AND BE SPACED NOT MORE THAN 8'-0" APART. MOST LARGER STACKS REQUIRE FOUR OR MORE AIR TERMINALS. ALL STACKS MUST HAVE TWO DOWNLEADS TO GROUND

TOP MOUNT PARAPET AIR TERMINAL FOR CLASS II STRUCTURES. COPPER POINTS MUST BE $1/2$" DIA. MIN. ALUMINUM POINTS MUST BE $5/8$" DIA. MIN.

PARALLEL CABLE SPLICER. ALL CONNECTORS MUST CONTACT CABLE FOR $1 1/2$" LENGTH

SUPPORT ALL CABLES ON STACKS AT 2'-0" O.C. HORIZONTALLY AND 4'-0" O.C. VERTICALLY

ALL CABLE BENDS TO BE 8" RADIUS MIN. AND NOT MORE THAN 90°

FOR CLASS II STRUCTURES, COPPER CONDUCTORS SHALL WEIGH 375 LB PER 1000'-0", HAVE AN AREA OF 115,000 CM AND STRANDS OF NOT LESS THAN #16 AWG. ALUMINUM CONDUCTORS SHALL WEIGH 190 LB PER 1000'-0", HAVE AN AREA OF 192,000 CM AND STRANDS OF NOT LESS THAN #13 AWG

SUPPORT CABLES ON BUILDING AT 3'-0" O.C. MAX.

CONDUCTOR ON THE TOP 25'-0" OF A STACK OR TO ROOF LEVEL SHALL MEET CLASS I COPPER CRITERIA AND MUST BE COVERED WITH LEAD $1/16$" THICK

STRAIGHT SPLICE TRANSITION FROM LEAD COVERED TO BARE CONDUCTOR

FOR EXPOSED DOWNLEADS LOCATED IN SCHOOL YARDS, DRIVEWAYS, WALK AREAS, ETC., WHERE SUBJECT TO DAMAGE OR DISPLACEMENT, PROPER GUARDS SHALL BE PROVIDED. TUBULAR METAL GUARDS MUST BE BONDED TO THE CABLE AT BOTH ENDS

SEE GROUNDING REQUIREMENTS ON OTHER PAGE

CLASS II SYSTEMS — TYPICAL DETAILS

Robert W. Lindquist and Douglas J. Franklin; Thompson Lightning Protection, Inc.; St. Paul, Minnesota

16

SPECIAL SYSTEMS

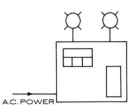

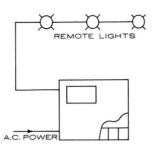

BATTERY PACKS AND INVERTORS

Battery powered lighting equipment is utilized to provide minimal emergency illumination required for personnel safety and evacuation purposes in buildings not requiring standby generator power. This equipment is also utilized in buildings requiring standby generator power at central control room, telephone switchboard room, generator room, and electrical switchgear rooms to provide lighting for continuity of critical operations and troubleshooting if the generator fails to start. The batteries require frequent inspection, tests, and maintenance if they are to perform their intended function.

BATTERY PACK

BATTERIES AND INVERTER

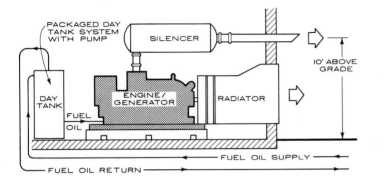

UNIT MOUNTED RADIATOR

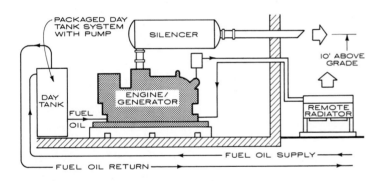

STANDBY GENERATORS

Standby generators are utilized where the life safety lighting requirements and/or the requirements to drive critical equipment are beyond the capacity of battery units. Engines are cooled by methods illustrated, and should be located in rooms separate from main electrical switchgear. Engine rooms must have adequate ventilation for engine and generator radiated heat and must be protected against extreme environments under all conditions of airflow. Room size and space at sides of power generating unit(s) must be adequate for service. Access to room must allow for removal of generation unit. Standby generators require frequent inspections, tests under load conditions, and maintenance if they are to perform their intended function. Vibration isolation provisions are required to prevent vibration transmission to surrounding occupied areas. In addition to the cooling methods illustrated, cooling by heat exchanger, submerged pipe, cooling tower, and evaporative cooler should be considered.

REMOTE RADIATOR

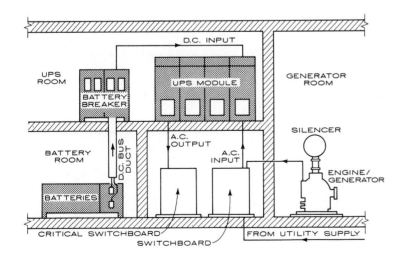

UNINTERRUPTIBLE POWER SUPPLY SYSTEM

Uninterruptible power supply (UPS) systems closely control the power supply voltage and frequency to critical equipment such as computers, communications systems, medical instrumentation, and similar sophisticated loads. Such UPS installations often are served from both utility and standby generator sources and provide "buffering" or complete isolation between the service and the critical load. The UPS batteries supply power through the UPS inverter to the critical AC loads until normal or generator power is restored or until the batteries reach end-of-discharge voltage. UPS systems require frequent inspections, tests, and maintenance if they are to perform their intended function.

UNINTERRUPTIBLE POWER SUPPLY SYSTEM

William Tao & Associates, Inc., Consulting Engineers; St. Louis, Missouri

SPECIAL SYSTEMS **16**

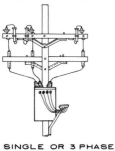
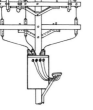

SINGLE OR 3 PHASE

3 PHASE

OVERHEAD TRANSFORMER

OVERHEAD TRANSFORMER: Three phase transformers are available up to 500 kVA in a single unit. Three single phase units can total to 1500 kVA with adequate platform support. Service lateral to building can be either overhead or underground.

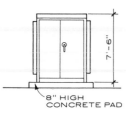

8" HIGH
CONCRETE PAD

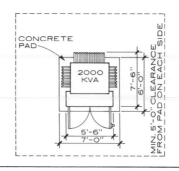

CONCRETE PAD

2000 KVA

5'-6"
7'-0"

7'-6"
6'-0"

MIN. 5'-0" CLEARANCE FROM PAD ON EACH SIDE

PAD MOUNTED TRANSFORMER

PAD MOUNTED TRANSFORMER: Pad mounted transformers with weatherproof tamperproof enclosure permits installation at ground level without danger from exposed live parts. Three phase units up to 2500 kVA are available and are normally used with underground primary and secondary feeders.

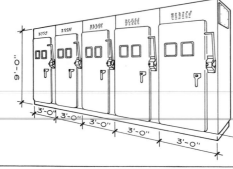

9'-0"

3'-0" 3'-0" 3'-0" 3'-0" 3'-0"

3'-0"

PRIMARY SWITCHGEAR

PRIMARY SWITCHGEAR: Where the owner's buildings cover a large area such as a college campus or medical center, the application usually requires the use of medium voltages of 5 kV to 15 kV for distribution feeders. Therefore, the utility company will terminate their primary feeders on the owner's metal clad or metal enclosed switchgear. This switchgear may be interior or exterior weatherproof construction. Code clearance in front and back of board must be provided in accordance with 1978 National Electric Code, Table 110-34(a); clearances range from 4 to 9 ft.

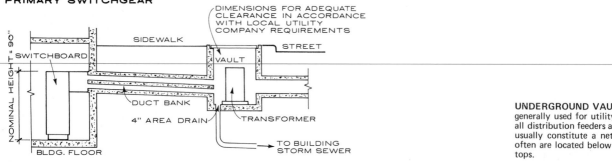

SIDEWALK

DIMENSIONS FOR ADEQUATE CLEARANCE IN ACCORDANCE WITH LOCAL UTILITY COMPANY REQUIREMENTS

STREET

NOMINAL HEIGHT = 90"

SWITCHBOARD

VAULT

DUCT BANK

4" AREA DRAIN

TRANSFORMER

BLDG. FLOOR

TO BUILDING STORM SEWER

UNDERGROUND VAULT

UNDERGROUND VAULT: Underground vaults are generally used for utility company transformers where all distribution feeders are underground. These systems usually constitute a network or spot network. Vaults often are located below the sidewalks and have grating tops.

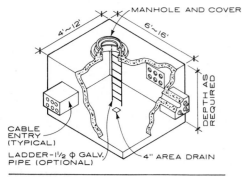

MANHOLE AND COVER

4'~12'
6'~16'

DEPTH AS REQUIRED

CABLE ENTRY (TYPICAL)

LADDER-1½ Φ GALV. PIPE (OPTIONAL)

4" AREA DRAIN

MANHOLE

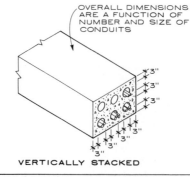

OVERALL DIMENSIONS ARE A FUNCTION OF NUMBER AND SIZE OF CONDUITS

3"
3"
3"
3"

VERTICALLY STACKED

3"
3"
3"

VERTICALLY OFFSET

UNDERGROUND DUCT BANK

William Tao & Associates, Inc., Consulting Engineers; St. Louis, Missouri

16 **SPECIAL SYSTEMS**

CHAPTER 17 METRIC (SI) UNITS IN DESIGN AND CONSTRUCTION

SI METRIC BACKGROUND DATA

The metric system originated in France as a product of the French Revolution, and gained gradual acceptance in Europe and in the French and Spanish colonies. In 1875 the United States joined 16 other countries in signing the Treaty of the Meter. The work of the General Conference of Weights and Measures resulted in a revised metric system in 1960, named Système International d'Unités (SI). It is this SI metric system that is referenced in the US Metric Act of 1975, and is presented in this chapter.

The Metric Conversion Act, Public Law 94-168, calls for a voluntary conversion process, and established the US Metric Board. In 1972 the American National Metric Council (ANMC) was formed under the sponsorship of the American National Standards Institute (ANSI). Involving more than 300 trade, professional, labor, consumer, and government organizations and more than 400 major corporations, the American National Metric Council has organized the voluntary conversion process. The ANMC Construction Industries Coordinating Committee (CICC) has prepared a conversion plan for adoption by the industry.

ANSI/ASTM Metric Standards are developed under the jurisdiction of ASTM Committee E-6 on Performance of Building Constructions. Subcommittee E 06.62 on Coordination of Dimensions for Building Materials and Systems has responsibility for such ANSI/ASTM Standards as E621-78 "Metric (SI) Units in Building Design and Construction." In addition, the Center for Building Technology of the National Bureau of Standards has published a number of Technical Notes and other special publications concerning metric conversion and dimensional coordination. The American Institute of Architects, with the cooperation of the ANMC, and the Center for Building Technology, has produced the "AIA Metric Building and Construction Guide." This chapter is based on information contained in that publication.

THE SI SYSTEM

Although the metric (SI) system applies to all measurement related systems, this chapter concerns the application of the SI System to construction. Concepts of dimensional coordination, although not restricted to the metric system, are seen as an essential part of a smooth transition of the construction industry to the use of the metric (SI) system.

MATERIALS AND COMPONENTS FOR METRIC BUILDING IN THE TRANSITIONAL PERIOD—SUGGESTED ADAPTATION IN DESIGN AND CONSTRUCTION FOR VARIOUS PRODUCT CATEGORIES*

CATEGORY	COMPLEXITY OF ADAPTATION	TYPICAL EXAMPLES OF MATERIALS AND COMPONENTS	ADAPTIVE ACTION IN DESIGN	ADAPTIVE ACTION IN CONSTRUCTION
A. DIMENSIONAL COORDINATION NOT REQUIRED				
A.1	No change in materials—no problems foreseen	Formless or plastic materials: water, paint, mastics, tar; sand, cement, lime, dry mortar mix, loose-fill insulation; read-mixed concrete, pre-mixed masonry mortar	Specify in metric units. Develop necessary site guidelines	Weigh or measure in metric quantities. Use metric data on coverage, mix ratios, etc.
A.2	Customary sizes usable—interim "soft conversion"	Structural steel sections, reinforcing bars, pipes, tubes, hardware, fixtures, fittings	Specify metric equivalents or show permissible substitutions. Select preferred "free" dimensions such as length or center-lines	Order or cut to metric length; set out to coordinated center-lines
B. MINOR SITE ADJUSTMENTS TO COORDINATE WITH PREFERRED DIMENSIONS				
B.1	Modification in one direction to fit in with preferred dimensions	a. Adjustment by trimming: lumber studs and joists, laminates, roofing, gutters b. Adjustment by lapping: shingles, tar felt, underlay, sheathing, waterproof membranes c. Adjustment by change in joint width: bricks, blocks, ceramic tiles	Specify preferred metric dimensions to expedite the transition. Indicate construction adjustments in drawings or instructions	Set out project in preferred building dimensions and adjust products accordingly
C. DIMENSIONAL COORDINATION REQUIRED				
C.1	Purpose-made items—no difficulties foreseen	Precast panels and slabs, door assemblies, window assemblies, fabricated metalwork, built-in units	Specify rationalized metric sizes	Order or fabricate components in rationalized metric sizes
C.2	Reshaping of customary dimensions possible	Glazing, plywood, gypsum wallboard, sheathing, lath, rigid insulation materials	Investigate supply in rationalized metric sizes and specify	Order rationalized metric sizes. Cut off site or on site
C.3	Reshaping of customary dimensions difficult, costly, or impossible	Windows, doors, metal partitions, metal roof decking, fluorescent fixture, metal cladding panels, stainless steel sections and sinks, large ceramic panels, distribution boards and panels, fixed appliances and cabinets, lockers	Preorder preferred sizes before job commencement. Discuss trial batches with manufacturers. Use adaptive design and detailing	Adapt during the interim period until preferred metric sizes emerge. Construct suitable openings or spaces for non-coordinated components and assemblies

*The list may be expanded or modified to suit particular market conditions.

LINEAR MEASURE—EQUIVALENTS

MILLIMETERS	CENTIMETERS	DECIMETERS	METERS	DECAMETERS	HECTOMETERS	KILOMETERS	YARDS
1	0.1	0.01	0.001	0.0001	0.00001	0.000001	
10	1	0.1	0.01	0.001	0.0001	0.00001	
100	10	1	0.1	0.01	0.001	0.0001	
1,000	100	10	1	0.1	0.01	0.001	1.0936
10,000	1,000	100	10	1	0.1	0.01	
100,000	10,000	1,000	100	10	1	0.1	
1,000,000	100,000	10,000	1,000	100	10	1	
			.9144				1

AREA MEASURE—EQUIVALENTS

SQUARE MILLIMETERS	SQUARE CENTIMETERS	SQUARE DECIMETERS	SQUARE METERS	ARES	HECTARES	SQUARE KILOMETERS	ACRES
1	0.01	0.0001	0.000001				
100	1	0.01	0.0001	0.000001			
10,000	100	1	0.01	0.0001	0.000001		
1,000,000	10,000	100	1	0.01	0.0001	0.000001	
	1,000,000	10,000	100	1	0.01	0.0001	
		1,000,000	10,000	100	1	0.01	2.471
			1,000,000	10,000	100	1	247.1
				40.47	.4047		1

GENERAL INFORMATION

SI UNITS AND RULES FOR USE

Specific rules for use, type style, and punctuation have been established by the General Conference on Weights and Measures (CGPM); the National Bureau of Standards (NBS) is responsible for determining preferred usage in the United States.

Standard, lowercase type is used for unit names and symbols, except when the symbols are derived from proper names, such as newton (N) or pascal (Pa). There is one exception to this in the use of the capital letter L as the symbol for liter. This is because the lowercase "l" was thought by the U.S. Department of Commerce to be easily confused with the numeral "1." Symbols are not followed by a period or a full stop, except at the end of a sentence. The symbols for all quantities, such as length, mass, and time, are printed in italic (l, k, s, ...). In typewriting and longhand, underlining is an acceptable substitute for italic letters. Unit names are used in the plural to express numerical values greater than 1, equal to 0, or less than −1. All other values take the singular form of the unit name, thus 100 meters, 1.1 meters, 0 degrees Celsius, −4 degrees Celsius, 0.5 meter, 1/2 liter, −0.2 degree Celsius, −1 degree Celsius. The plural of unit names is formed by adding an "s." Exceptions are hertz, lux, and siemens, which remain unchanged, and henry, which becomes henries. Symbols are the same in both singular and plural.

Prefixes denoting decimal multiples and submultiples (allowing SI units to express magnitudes from the subatomic to the astronomic) are governed by the same rules concerning capitalization and punctuation.

It is important to note that mega, giga, and tera (M, G, T) are capitalized in symbol form to avoid confusion with established unit symbols, but they maintain the lowercase form when spelled out in full. No space is left between the prefix and the letter for the unit name, thus mL (milliliter), mm (millimeter), kA (kiloampere).

Preference is given to the use of decimal multiples that are related to the basic units by multiples of 1000. As far as possible, prefixes denoting magnitudes of 100, 10, 0.1, and 0.01 should be limited. Certain multiples of SI units, not likely to be extensively used, have been given special names (Table 4).

The prefix symbol is considered to be part of the unit symbol and is attached to it without a space or dot, thus km not k m, k-m, or k.m.

A space is left between a numeral and the unit name or symbol to which it refers, thus 20 mm, 10^6 N. In angle measure no space is left between the numeral and the degree symbol, thus 27°. The symbol for degree Celsius °C is an inseparable symbol with no space between the two parts; it is also preferable to leave no space between the numeral and the unit, thus 20°C.

When a quantity is used as an adjective, it is preferable to use a hyphen instead of a space between the number and the unit name or between the number and the symbol; thus a 3-meter pole, a 35-mm film.

In the United States and Canada, the decimal point is a dot on the line, but in some other countries a comma or a raised dot is used.

Decimal notation is preferred with metric measurements, but simple fractions are acceptable (except on engineering drawings), such as those where the denominator is 2, 3, 4, 5, 8, and 10.

Examples: 0.5 g, 1.75 kg, and 0.7 L are preferred; 1/2 g, 1 3/4 kg, and 7/10 L are acceptable (except on engineering drawings).

A zero before the decimal point should be used in numbers between 1 and −1 to prevent the possibility that a faint decimal point will be overlooked.

Example: The oral expression "point seven five" is written 0.75.

Since the comma is used as the decimal marker in many countries, a comma should not be used to separate groups of digits. Instead, the digits should be separated into groups of three, counting both to the left and to the right from the decimal point, and a space used to separate the groups of three digits. The space should be of fixed width, equal to that formerly occupied by the comma.

Examples: 4 720 525   0. 528 75

If there are only four digits to the left or right of the decimal point, the space is acceptable but is not preferred.

Examples: 6875 or 6 875
0.1234 or 0.123 4

However, in a column with other numbers that show the space and are aligned on the decimal point, the space is necessary.

Example:
```
        14.8
     3 780
  +12 100
   15 894.8
```

Compound units are those formed by combining simple units by means of the mathematical signs for multiplication and division and by the use of exponents.

When writing symbols for units such as square centimeter or cubic meter, the symbol for the unit should be written followed by the superscript ^{2} or ^{3}, respectively, thus 26 cm^2 and 14 m^3.

For a compound unit that is a quotient, "per" should be used to form the name (kilometer per hour) and a slash (/) to form the symbol (km/h). There is no space before or after the slash. Compound units that are quotients may also be written by using negative exponents (km · h^{-1}).

For everyday rounding of metric values obtained by converting untoleranced customary values, the following simplified rules are suggested:

1. If the customary value is expressed by a combination of units such as feet and inches, or pounds and ounces, first express it in terms of the smaller unit.
   Example: 14 ft 5 in. = 173 in.
2. When the digits to be discarded begin with a 5 or more, increase by one unit the last digit retained.
   Example: 8.3745, if rounded to three digits, would be 8.37; if rounded to four digits, 8.375.
3. Multiply the customary value by the conversion factor. If the first significant digit of the metric value is equal to or larger than the first significant digit of the customary value, round the metric value to the same number of significant digits as there are in the customary value.
   Examples: 11 mi x 1.609 km/mi = 17.699 km, which rounds to 18 km

   61 mi x 1.609 km/mi = 98.149 km, which rounds to 98 km
4. If smaller, round to one more significant digit.
   Examples: 66 mi x 1.609 km/mi = 106.194 km, which rounds to 106 km

   8 ft x 0.3048 m/ft = 2.4384 m, which rounds to 2.4 m
   Exceptions: It is sometimes better to round to one less digit than specified above. For example, according to the foregoing, 26 pounds per square inch air pressure in an automobile tire would be converted as follows:

   26 psi* x 6.895 kPa/psi = 179.27 kPa

   which rounds to 179 kPa

   but kPa, where the zero is not a significant digit, would usually be better because tire pressures are not expected to be very precise. The rules do not apply to conversion of °F to °C.
5. Where a customary value represents a maximum or minimum limit that must be respected, the rounding must be in the direction that does not violate the original limit.

TABLE 1. SI BASE UNITS

PHYSICAL QUANTITY	UNIT	SYMBOL
Length	Meter	m
Mass	Kilogram	k
Time	Second	s
Electric current	Ampere	A
Thermodynamic temperature	Kelvin	K
Luminous intensity	Candela	cd
Amount of substance	Mole	mol

TABLE 2. SI SUPPLEMENTARY UNITS

PHYSICAL QUANTITY	UNIT	SYMBOL
Plane angle	Radian	rad
Solid angle	Steradian	sr

TABLE 3. DERIVED UNITS WITH COMPOUND NAMES

PHYSICAL QUANTITY	UNIT	SYMBOL
Area	Square meter	m^2
Volume	Cubic meter	m^3
Density	Kilogram per cubic meter	kg/m^3
Velocity	Meter per second	m/s
Angular velocity	Radian per second	rad/s
Acceleration	Meter per second squared	m/s^2
Angular acceleration	Radian per second squared	rad/s^2
Volume rate of flow	Cubic meter per second	m^3/s
Moment of inertia	Kilogram meter squared	kg · m^2
Moment of force	Newton meter	N · m
Intensity of heat flow	Watt per square meter	W/m^2
Thermal conductivity	Watt per meter Kelvin	W/m · K
Luminance	Candela per square meter	cd/m^2

TABLE 4. MULTIPLES OF SI UNITS WITH SPECIAL NAMES

PHYSICAL QUANTITY	NAME	SYMBOL	MAGNITUDE
Volume	Liter	L	10^{-3} m^3 = 0.0001 m^3
Mass	Megagram (metric ton)	Mg(t)	10^3 kg = 1000 kg
Area	Hectare	ha	10^4 m^2 = 10 000 m^2
Pressure	Millibar*	mbar*	10^2 Pa = 100 Pa

*Used for meteorological purposes only.

QUANTITY	REMARKS	BASE AND SUPPLEMENTARY UNITS	DERIVED UNITS WITH COMPOUND NAMES	DERIVED UNITS WITH SPECIAL NAMES
VOLUME	$1 m^3 = 1000 L$		m^3 cubic meter	L liter
AREA			m^2 square meter	
LENGTH	BASE UNIT	m meter		
VELOCITY			m/s meter per second	
ACCELERATION			m/s^2 meter per second squared	
MASS	BASE UNIT	kg kilogram		
FORCE	$1 N = 1 kg \cdot m/s^2$			N newton
PRESSURE, STRESS	$1 Pa = 1 N/m^2$			Pa pascal
ENERGY, WORK, QUANTITY OF HEAT	$1 J = 1 N \cdot m = 1 W \cdot s$			J joule
FREQUENCY	$1 Hz = 1/s$		1/s 1 per second	Hz hertz
TIME	BASE UNIT	s second		
POWER, RADIANT FLUX	$1 W = 1 J/s = 1 V \cdot A$			W watt
ELECTRIC CURRENT	BASE UNIT	A ampere		
ELECTRIC CHARGE	$1 C = 1 A \cdot s$			C coulomb
ELECTRIC POTENTIAL	$1 V = 1 W/A$			V volt
ELECTRIC CAPACITANCE	$1 F = 1 C/V$			F farad
ELECTRIC RESISTANCE	$1 \Omega = 1 V/A$			Ω ohm
MAGNETIC FLUX	$1 Wb = 1 V \cdot s$			Wb weber
ELECTRIC CONDUCTANCE	$1 S = 1/\Omega = 1 A/V$			S siemens
MAGNETIC FLUX DENSITY	$1 T = 1 Wb/m^2$			T tesla
INDUCTANCE	$1 H = 1 Wb/A$			H henry
THERMODYNAMIC TEMPERATURE	BASE UNIT	K kelvin		
CELSIUS TEMPERATURE	Temperature Value: $t_{°C} = T_K - 273.15$ Temperature Interval: $1°C = 1 K$			°C degree Celsius
AMOUNT OF SUBSTANCE	BASE UNIT NO APPLICATION IN CONSTRUCTION	mol mole		
LUMINOUS INTENSITY	BASE UNIT	cd candela		
LUMINOUS FLUX	$1 lm = 1 cd \cdot sr$			lm lumen
ILLUMINANCE	$1 lx = 1 lm/m^2$			lx lux
PLANE ANGLE	SUPPLEMENTARY UNIT	rad radian		
SOLID ANGLE	SUPPLEMENTARY UNIT	sr steradian		

MECHANICAL DERIVED UNITS

ELECTRICAL DERIVED UNITS

ILLUMINATION DERIVED UNITS

NOTES
1. Broken lines indicate division; solid lines multiplication.
2. Only derived units for use in construction are shown.

BASE AND SUPPLEMENTARY SI UNITS

DERIVED UNITS WITH COMPOUND NAMES

DERIVED UNITS WITH SPECIAL NAMES

MULTIPLE OF SI UNIT

Hans J. Milton, FRAIA, Technical Consultant, National Bureau of Standards; Gaithersburg, Maryland

MEASUREMENT OF LENGTH

The basic SI unit of length is the meter. Fractions or multiples of the base unit are expressed with prefixes, only some of which are recommended for construction. In order to be clear, avoid those prefixes that are not specifically recommended for construction.

Common SI units for length as used in construction are:

UNIT NAME	SYMBOL	COMMENT	COMPUTER SYMBOL
Meter	m	Also spelled metre	M
Millimeter	mm	0.001 meter	MM
Kilometer	km	1000 meters	KM
Micrometer	um	0.000 001 meter	UM

Note: Centimeter is not recommended for construction.

The recommended unit for dimensioning buildings is the millimeter. The use of the meter would be limited to large dimensions, such as levels, overall dimensions, and engineering computations. Meters are also used for estimating and land surveying. On architectural drawings, dimensions require no symbol if millimeters are consistently used.

Kilometers are used for transportation and surveying. Micrometers would be used for thicknesses of materials, such as coatings.

Conversion factors for length are shown below:

METRIC	CUSTOMARY
1 meter	3.280 84 feet or 1.093 61 yards
1 millimeter	0.039 370 1 inch
1 kilometer	0.621 371 mile or 49.709 6 chains
1 micrometer	0.000 393 7 inch or 0.3937 mils

CUSTOMARY	METRIC
1 mile	1.609 344 km
1 chain	20.1168 m
1 yard	0.9144 m
1 foot	0.3048 m 304.8 mm
1 inch	25.4 mm

(1 U.S. survey foot = 0.304 800 6 m.)

The recommended linear basic module for construction is 100 mm in the United States. See page on dimensional coordination for application of this basic module. This is very close to the 4 in. module in general use for light construction. Scales of drawing relate to units of length. Use meters on all drawings with scale ratios between 1:200 and 1:2000. Use millimeters on drawings with scale ratios between 1:1 and 1:200.

MEASUREMENT OF AREA

There are no basic SI metric units for area. Rather, area units are derived from units for length, as follows:

UNIT NAME	SYMBOL	COMMENT
Square meter	m^2	$1\ m^2 = 10^6\ mm^2$
Square millimeter	mm^2	
Square kilometer	km^2	Land area
Hectare	ha	$1\ ha = 10\ 000\ m^2$

Note that the hectare, although not an SI unit, is acceptable as a supplemental unit. It is used for surface measurement of land and water only.

At times, area is expressed by linear dimensions such as 40 mm x 90 mm; 300 x 600. Normally the width is written first and depth or height second.

The square centimeter is not recommended for construction. Such measurements may be converted to millimeters ($1\ cm^2 = 100\ mm^2$) or to meters ($1\ cm^2 = 10^{-4}\ m^2 = 0.0001\ m^2$).

Conversion factors for area are shown below.

METRIC	CUSTOMARY
$1\ km^2$	$0.386\ 101\ mile^2$ (U.S. Survey)
1 ha	2.471 04 acre (U.S. Survey)
$1\ m^2$	$10.7639\ ft^2$ $1.195\ 99\ yd^2$
$1\ mm^2$	$0.001\ 550\ in.^2$

CUSTOMARY	METRIC
$1\ mile^2$ (U.S. Survey)	$2.590\ 00\ km^2$
1 acre (U.S. Survey)	0.404 687 ha $4046.87\ m^2$
$1\ yd^2$	$0.836\ 127\ m^2$
$1\ ft^2$	$0.092\ 903\ m^2$
$1\ in.^2$	$645.16\ mm^2$

MEASUREMENT OF VOLUME AND SECTION MODULUS

There are no basic SI metric units for volume, but these are derived from units for length as well as non-SI units that are acceptable for use.

UNIT NAME	SYMBOL	COMMENT
Cubic meter	m^3	$1\ m^3 = 1000\ L$
Cubic millimeter	mm^3	
Liter	L	Volume of fluids
Milliliter	mL	$1\ mL = 1\ cm^3$
Cubic centimeter	cm^3	$1\ cm^3 = 1000\ mm^3$

In construction, the cubic meter is used for volume and capacity of large quantities of earth, concrete, sand, and so on. It is preferred for all engineering purposes.

The section modulus is also expressed as unit of length to the third power (m^3 and mm^3).

Conversion factors are listed below.

VOLUME, MODULUS OF SECTION

METRIC	CUSTOMARY
$1\ m^3$	$0.810\ 709 \times 10^3\ acre\ ft$ $1.307\ 95\ yd^3$ $35.3147\ ft^3$ 423.776 board ft
$1\ mm^3$	$61.0237 \times 10^{-6}\ in.^3$

CUSTOMARY	METRIC
1 acre ft	$1233.49\ m^3$
$1\ yd^3$	$0.764\ 555\ m^3$
100 board ft	$0.028\ 316\ 8\ m^3$
$1\ ft^3$	$16.387\ 1\ mm^3$ $28\ 3168\ 1\ (cm^3)$
$1\ in.^3$	$16.3871\ mL(cm^3)$

LIQUID, CAPACITY

METRIC	CUSTOMARY
1 L	$0.035\ 3147\ ft^3$ 0.264 172 gal (U.S.) 1.056 69 qt (U.S.)
1 mL	$0.061\ 023\ 7\ in.^3$

CUSTOMARY	METRIC
1 gal (U.S. liquid)	3.785 41 L
1 qt (U.S. liquid)	946.353 mL
1 pt (U.S. liquid)	473.177 mL
1 fl oz (U.S.)	29.5735 mL

NOTE: 1 gal (U.K.) = approximately 1.2 gal (U.S.).

MEASUREMENT OF MASS

The SI metric system recommends the use of the word mass in place of the more common word weight, because weight refers specifically to the pull of gravity, which can vary in different locations. The SI system also separates the concept of mass from that of force.

SI metric units and other acceptable units for mass are:

UNIT NAME	SYMBOL	COMMENT
Kilogram	kg	Most used
Gram	g	
Metric ton	t	1 t = 1000 kg

The kilogram is based on a prototype, and unlike other SI units cannot be derived without reference to the international prototype kilogram maintained under specified conditions at the International Bureau of Weights and Measures (BIPM) near Paris, France.

Conversion factors are listed below.

METRIC	CUSTOMARY
1 kg	2.204 62 lb (avoirdupois) 35.2740 02 oz (avoirdupois)
1 metric ton	1.102 31 ton (short, 2000 lb) 2204.62 lb
1 g	0.035 274 oz 0.643 015 pennyweight

CUSTOMARY	METRIC
1 ton (short)	0.907 185 metric ton (megagram) 907.185 kg
1 lb	0.453 592 kg
1 oz	28.3495 9 g
1 pennyweight	1.555 17 g

NOTE: A long ton (2240 lb) = 1016.05 kg or 1.016 05 metric ton.

TIME

The SI unit for time is the second, from which other units of time are derived. In construction measurements, such as flow rates, the use of minutes is not recommended, so that cubic meters per second, liters per second, or cubic meters per hour would be normally used. Time symbols are as follows:

Second	s
Minute	min
Hour	h
Day	d
Month	—
Year	a (365 days or 31 536 000 seconds)

For clarity, international recommendations for writing time and dates are as follows:

Time	Express by hour/minute/second on a 24 hour day: 03:20:30 16:45
Dates	Express by year/month/day: 1978-06-30 1978 06 30 (second preference) 19780630 (computer entry)

MEASUREMENT OF TEMPERATURE

The SI base unit of temperature is the Kelvin, which is a scale based on absolute zero. The allowable unit Celsius is equal to the Kelvin unit except that 0° Celsius is the freezing point of water. Thus a temperature listed in degrees Celsius plus 275.15 degrees is the temperature in degrees Kelvin. Celsius is in common use for construction, not Kelvin.

CUSTOMARY	METRIC
1°F	0.555 556°C $5/9$ °C or $5/9$ K

METRIC	CUSTOMARY
1°C	1 K 1.8°F

NOTE: Centigrade is not recognized as part of the SI system.

PLANE ANGLE

While the SI unit for plane angle is the radian, the customary units degree (°), minute ('), and second ('') of arc will be retained in most applications in construction, engineering, and land surveying.

CUSTOMARY	METRIC
1°	$(\pi/180)$ rad

ENERGY RELATIONSHIP

SI metric units provide a direct, coherent relationship between mechanical, thermal, and electrical energy.

The ampere (A) (SI base unit) is that constant current which, if maintained in two straight, parallel conductors of infinite length and of negligible cross section, placed 1 meter apart in a vacuum, would produce between these conductors a force equal to 2×10^{-7} newton per meter of length.

One newton (N) is that force which gives to a mass of 1 kilogram (kg) an acceleration of 1 meter per second squared (m/s²). Hence $1.0 \text{ N} = 1.0 \text{ kg} \cdot \text{m/s}^2$.

One joule (J) is the work done when the point of application of a force of 1 newton moves a distance of 1 meter along the line of action of the force. Hence $1.0 \text{ J} = 1.0 \text{ N} \cdot \text{m}$.

A watt (W) is the power which in 1 second gives rise to the energy of 1 joule. Conversely, a joule is a watt-second.

Since the customary coherent relationships with other electrical quantities will still prevail, the observations made above in respect to work, energy, quantity of heat, and power may be summarized, from a "units" point of view as follows:

$$N \cdot m = J \quad J/s = W \quad J = W \cdot s \quad W = A \cdot V \quad J = A \cdot V \cdot s$$

MASS

The preferred unit multiples of mass are milligram, gram, kilogram, and megagram (or metric ton), which are written respectively as:

$$\text{mg} \quad \text{g} \quad \text{kg} \quad \text{Mg} \quad \text{(or t)}$$

Weight is predominantly a concept of the customary "gravitational" system. Since SI is an absolute system dealing with mass and with the forces related to the acceleration of a mass, there is no special name for a unit of weight in SI.

Weight in a particular force due solely to gravitational attraction on a mass.

FORCE

Since SI is a coherent system and since the fundamental law of physics ($F \propto ma$) states that force is dependent solely on mass and on acceleration,

1.0 kg accelerated at 1.0 m/s²

$\longrightarrow$ 1.0 force unit

$\longrightarrow$ 1.0 newton (1.0 N)

The use of the name "newton" for the unit of force should fix in the mind the full significance of the distinctions between mass and force.

Normally a mass to be supported or moved will be specified or labeled in terms of kilograms (kg), but all forces acting on structure, either gravitationally or laterally (including wind, sway, and impact), should be specified or determined ultimately in terms of newtons (N).

Based on customary gravitational usage:

Mass: 1.0 slug   32.17 lb   14.59 kg
    1.488 kgf/(m/s²)

Force: 1.0 lbf   32.17 pdl   4.448 N
    0.4536 kgf

Based on SI usage:

Mass: 1.0 kg   2.205 lb   0.068 52 slug
    0.1020 kgf/(m/s²)

Force: 1.0 N   7.233 pdl   0.2248 lbf
    0.1020 kgf

The force definitions are as follows:

The "newton" is the force required to accelerate 1 kilogram mass at the rate of 1.0 m/s².

The "poundal" is the force required to accelerate 1 pound of mass at the rate of 1.0 ft/s².

The "pound force" is the force required to accelerate 1 pound of mass at the rate of 32.1740 ft/s².

The related definitions for the derived mass units are:

The "slug" is that mass which, when acted upon by 1 pound-force, will be accelerated at the rate of 1.0 ft/s².

The gravitational metric unit of mass is that unit of mass which, when acted upon by 1 kilogram-force, will be accelerated at 1.0 m/s². There seems to be no generally accepted name or symbol for this gravitational unit of mass, except the inference to the kilogram.

The "kilogram" and the "pound" are base units, not derived units as are the slug and the gravitational metric unit of mass. The kilogram and the pound relate directly to an artifact of mass which, by convention, is regarded as dimensionally independent—thus the name "base unit."

DERIVED UNITS WITH SPECIAL NAMES

PHYSICAL QUANTITY	UNIT	SYMBOL	DERIVATION
Frequency	Hertz	Hz	s^{-1}
Force	Newton	N	$kg \cdot m/s^2$
Pressure, stress	Pascal	Pa	N/m^2
Work, energy, quantity of heat	Joule	J	$N \cdot m$
Power	Watt	W	J/s
Electric charge	Coulomb	C	$A \cdot s$
Electric potential	Volt	V	W/A
Electric capacitance	Farad	F	C/V
Electric resistance	Ohm	O	V/A
Electric conductance	Siemens	S	Ω^{-1}
Magnetic flux	Weber	Wb	$V \cdot s$
Magnetic flux density	Tesla	T	Wb/m^2
Inductance	Henry	H	Wb/A
Celsius temperature	Degree Celsius	°C	K
Luminous flux	Lumen	lm	$cd \cdot sr$
Illumination	Lux	lx	lm/m^2
Activity	Becquerel	Bq	s^{-1}
Absorbed dose	Gray	Gy	J/kg

COMPARISON OF UNIT SYSTEMS

QUANTITY	MASS LENGTH, TIME (ABSOLUTE)		FORCE, LENGTH, TIME (GRAVITATIONAL)		CUSTOMARY COMBINED SYSTEM
	SI	ENGLISH	METRIC	ENGLISH	
Mass	kg	lb	kgf/(m/s²)	lbf/(ft/s²) (slug)	lb (alt: lbm)
Force	kg m/s² N (newton)	lb ft/s² 1 dp (poundal)	kgf (alt:kp)	lbf	lbf
Coherence factor	1.0	1.0	1.0	1.0	1/32.17

COMPARATIVE ANALYSIS OF SOME APPROXIMATE PHYSICAL PROPERTIES[a] FOR REPRESENTATIVE ENGINEERING MATERIALS

IN TERMS OF U.S. CUSTOMARY UNITS								IN TERMS OF PREFERRED SI UNITS						
COEFFICIENT OF LINEAR EXPANSION α (10^6 IN./IN °F)	ALLOWABLE STRESSES (LBF/IN.² x 10³)			ELASTIC MODULUS (LBF/IN.² x 10⁶)		WEIGHT DENSITY W (LB/FT³)	MATERIAL	MASS DENSITY ρ (KG/M³)	ELASTIC MODULUS (GPA = GN/M²)		ALLOWABLE STRESSES (MPA = MN/M²)			COEFFICIENT OF LINEAR EXPANSION $\alpha \mu M/(M \cdot K)$
	σ_f^b	σ_c^c	τ_s	E	G				E	G	σ_f^b	σ_c^c	τ_s	
6.5	20	20	10	30	12	490	Mild steel	7850	200	80	140	140	70	11.7
6.9	24	24	15	30	12	490	High-strength steel	7850	200	80	165	165	100	12.4
6.0	3	10	2	15	6	450	Cast iron	7200	100	40	20	70	15	10.8
9.3	8	8	5	17	6.4	560	Copper	8960	120	45	55	55	35	16.7
10.4	12	8	6	13	5	520	Brass	8300	90	35	80	55	40	18.7
13.0	16	15	8	10.3	4	170	Aluminum	2700	70	27	110	100	55	23.4
							Timber							
1.7	1.3	0.8	0.05	1.2	—	27	Softwood	430	9	—	9.6	5.5	0.3	3.1
2.5	1.8	1.2	0.10	1.6	—	48	Hardwood	770	12	—	12.4	8.3	0.7	4.5
6.2	1.2	1.0	0.15	2.5	—	150	Concrete (reinf.)	2400	17	—	8.3	6.9	1.0	11.2
—	—	0.03	—	—	—	105	Soil	1680	—	—	—	0.2	—	—
4.4	—	0.3	—	—	—	165	Rock	2640	—	—	—	2.0	—	7.9
						62.4	Water	1000	—	—	—	—	—	

NOTE: Values given are rounded in each system and are not direct conversions.
[a] For use only for comparing representative values in the respective unit systems; not intended for design. For design purposes see other standard references such as ANSI, AISC, ACI, and IFI.
[b] Extreme fiber bending.
[c] Short compression block; in timber, parallel to grain.

UNITS FOR USE IN HEAT TRANSFER CALCULATIONS

QUANTITY NAME	SI UNIT	UNIT NAME	CONVERSION FACTOR	
Energy, quantity of heat (E, Q)	$J(W \cdot s)$	joule	1 Btu (int.)	= 1.055 056 kJ
			1 kWh	= 3.6 MJ
			1 therm	= 105.5056 MJ
Heat flow rate (P, q)	$W(J/s)$	watt	1 Btu/h	= 0.293 071 W
			1 Btu/s	= 1.055 056 kW
			1 ton (refrig.)	= 3.516 800 kW
Specific energy, calorific value (mass basis)	J/kg	joule per kilogram	1 Btu/lb	= 2.326 kJ/kg
Irradiation, intensity of heat flow, heat loss from surfaces	W/m^2	watt per square meter	1 Btu/ft$^2 \cdot$ h	= 3.152 481 W/m^2
			1 W/ft^2	= 10.763 91 W/m^2
			1 Btu/ft$^2 \cdot$ s	= 11.348 93 kW/m^2
Specific heat capacity (mass basis)	$J/(kg \cdot K)$	joule per kilogram kelvin	1 Btu/lb $\cdot$ °F	= 4.1868 kJ/(kg $\cdot$ K)
Thermal conductivity (k-value)	$W/(m \cdot K)$	watt per meter kelvin	1 Btu $\cdot$ in/h $\cdot$ ft$^2 \cdot$ °F	= 0.144 228 W/(m $\cdot$ K)
			1 Btu $\cdot$ in/s $\cdot$ ft$^2 \cdot$ °F	= 519.2204 W/(m $\cdot$ K)
			1 Btu/h $\cdot$ ft $\cdot$ °F	= 1.730 73 W/(m $\cdot$ K)
Thermal conductance, coefficient of heat transfer (c, U-value)	$W/(m^2 \cdot K)$	watt per square meter kelvin	1 Btu/h $\cdot$ ft$^2 \cdot$ °F	= 5.678 26 W/(m$^2 \cdot$ K)
Thermal resistance, thermal insulance (R)	$m^2 \cdot K/W$	square meter kelvin per watt	1 °F $\cdot$ h $\cdot$ ft^2/Btu	= 0.176 110 m$^2 \cdot$ K/W

HEAT TRANSFER IN BUILDINGS

Heat transfer calculations, involving heat loss, heat gain, or thermal insulating properties of materials, will be simplified in SI because of the coherent relationships between units used. Heat transfer units are generally derived from the unit for temperature (kelvin or degree Celsius), the unit for energy and quantity of heat (joule), the unit for heat transfer rate (watt), and the units for time (second), length (meter), areas (square meter), and mass (kilogram).

TEMPERATURE

The Celsius temperature scale, for which the zero reference is the freezing point of water, will also be used for ambient temperatures.

TIME

Use of the hour (h), as in 5 km/h, and the day (d), as in m^3/d, will occur in special cases, but the use of the minute (min) will be deemphasized in favor of the second (s).

HEATING DEGREE-DAYS

For heating design purposes and the determination of suitable insulation, the concept of heating degree-days, founded on a base temperature of 65°F (18.33°C), will possibly be revised to use a base temperature of 18°C (64.4°F).

In heat transfer through a composite element, such as a building wall, a sequence of conduction and convection coefficients may be involved. As in other "series type" problems the approach to determining the combined or "overall" coefficient U is based on the sum of the resistances, which is the sum of the reciprocals of the conductances in the path of the heat transfer.

The following definitions can be used to identify the coefficients:

K = thermal conductance;

$$K = \frac{kA}{L} \frac{W}{m \cdot K} \times \frac{m^2}{m} = W/K$$

R = thermal resistance;

$$R = \frac{L}{kA} \frac{m \cdot K}{W} \times \frac{m}{m^2} = K/W$$

Frequently, these factors may be stated in terms of unit areas. Any data taken from reference tables should be checked carefully.

The overall heat transfer relationship can be stated as:

$$q = U \cdot A \cdot \Delta T$$

where q = heat transfer rate
A = cross-sectional area of heat, W(=J/s) transfer path, m^2
ΔT = overall temperature differential, K
U = overall heat transfer coefficient, W/(m $\cdot$ K)

To determine U is often necessary to use the relationship:

$$\frac{1}{U} = R_1 + R_2 + R_3, \text{ etc.}; \qquad \frac{1}{U} = R_1$$

Alternatively, this may be stated as:

$$R_1 = \frac{1}{h_i} + \frac{L_2}{k_2} + \frac{L_3}{k_3} + \frac{1}{h_c}$$

EXAMPLE CALCULATION OF HEAT LOSS THROUGH A WALL

An exterior building wall consists of 100 mm of brick, 200 mm of dense concrete, and 20 mm of gypsum plaster, for which the thermal conductivities are, respectively, k = 0.50, 1.50, and 1.20 W/(m $\cdot$ K). The surface heat transfer (film) coefficients are as follows: (interior) h_i = 8.1 and (exterior) h_c = 19.0 W/(m$^2 \cdot$ K). What is the heat loss through a 2400 mm (2.4 m) by 6000 mm (6.0 m) panel of this wall when there is a temperature difference of 30°C (30°K)?

THERMAL CONDUCTIVITY

The thermal conductivity, or k-value, of a material is defined as the amount of heat energy conducted through a unit area of unit thickness in unit time with unit temperature difference between the two faces. In SI the unit W/(m $\cdot$ K) replaces Btu $\cdot$ in/h $\cdot$ ft$^2 \cdot$ °F, but if unit time is considered useful, the alternative expression is J/(s $\cdot$ m $\cdot$ K), because 1 W = 1 J/s. Unit thickness has been canceled out against unit area; otherwise the expression should be J $\cdot$ m/(s $\cdot$ m$^2 \cdot$ K), which directly resembles the customary expression in terms of constituent units.

OVERALL HEAT TRANSFER

Conductivity generally increases with the level of absolute temperature. Some typical thermal conductivities (k-values) at 300 K are:

MATERIAL OR SUBSTANCE	K = W/m $\cdot$ K)
Copper	386
Aluminum	202
Steel	55
Concrete	0.9–1.4
Glass	0.8–1.1
Brick	0.4–0.7
Water	0.614
Mineral wool	0.04
Air	0.0262

Computation of thermal resistance:

$$R_T = \frac{1}{8.1} + \frac{0.100}{0.50} + \frac{0.200}{1.50} + \frac{0.020}{1.20} + \frac{1}{19.0}$$

$$= 0.5261 \text{ m}^2 \cdot \text{K/W}$$

$$U = \frac{1}{R_T}; \qquad U = 1.901 \text{ W/(m}^2 \cdot \text{K)}$$

$$q = U \cdot A \cdot \Delta T$$

$$q = 1.901(2.4 \times 6.0)30$$

$$= 821 \text{ W} = 821 \text{ J/s}$$

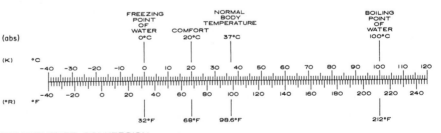

TEMPERATURE CONVERSION

ENERGY VALUES FOR ALTERNATIVE ENERGY SOURCES

ENERGY SOURCE AND QUANTITY	VALUE (MEGAJOULES, MJ)
1 kg of dry wood (8600 Btu/lb)	20
1 kg of bituminous coal (25 800 000 Btu/ton)	30
1 L of kerosene (135 000 Btu/gal)	37.6
1 L of crude oil (5 800 000 Btu/barrel)	38.5
1 m^3 of natural gas (1050 Btu/ft^3)	39
1 kWh of electricity	3.6
1 therm (100,000 Btu)	105.5

MOMENT BENDING, TORSIONAL

Bending moment and torsional moment are concepts of statics. Both involve the production of a force and a perpendicular distance, the latter being termed the moment arm. Thus the primary SI unit is the newton-meter, which may be symbolized as N · m, kN · m, and so on.

TORQUE

When rotation occurs as a result of an applied moment the condition is one requiring the application of the principles of dynamics. In such cases the key factor is torque, which is based on a product of force and distance moved along the line of action of the force. This product is expressed in newton-meters per radian (N · m/rad), which is equal to joules per radian (J/rad). The radian may be omitted where only complete revolutions are of concern or where dynamic conditions are equated instantaneously with static conditions.

PRESSURE, STRESS, ELASTIC MODULUS

These may be stated directly either in pascals (Pa) or in newtons per square meter (N/m²). Common multiples are kPa, MPa, GPa or kN/m², MN/m², GN/m². Occasionally stress is expressed in newtons per square millimeter (N/mm²).

MOMENT OF INERTIA

The mass moment of inertia of any body relating to rotation about a given axis is the second moment of the particles of that mass about the given axis and as such is given generally in kilogram-square meters per radian squared (kg · m²/rad²). The radius of gyration is normally given in meters per radian (m/rad). The radian may be omitted where only complete revolutions are of concern or where dynamic conditions are equated instantaneously with static conditions.

Second moment of area (1) and section modulus (S) of the cross-section of structural sections or machine parts are usually preferred in terms of 10^6 mm⁴ and 10^3 mm³, respectively, for consistency with other dimensions of sections, which usually will be given in millimeters.

ANGULAR MEASURE

The "radian" (rad), although not a base unit, is specifically identified as a "supplementary unit" and as such is the preferred unit for measurement of plane angles. The customary units of degrees, minutes, and seconds of angular measure are considered to be outside SI, but are acceptable where there is a specific practical reason to use them, as in cartography. If degrees are to be used, a statement of parts of degrees in decimals is preferred. The SI unit of solid angle is the "steradian" (sr).

FLUID MECHANICS

Fluid mechanics utilizes the physical concepts of density (mass per unit volume), dynamic viscosity, kinematic viscosity, surface tension, potential energy, and pressure in dealing with the flow of relatively incompressible fluids at constant temperatures. There is a proper SI expression for each of these quantities, derived from base units in accordance with applicable physical relationships. Metric considerations in fluid mechanics are discussed in other engineering metric reference sources.

UNITS OUTSIDE SI NOT RECOMMENDED FOR USE

UNIT NAME	SYMBOL	VALUE IN SI UNITS	
dyne	dyn	10^{-5} N	(or 10 uN)
bar	bar	10^5 Pa	(or 100 kPa)
erg	erg	10^{-7} J	(or 100 nJ)
poise	P	10^{-1} Pa · s	(or 100 mPa · s)
stokes	St	10^{-4} m²/s	(or 100 mm²/s)
gauss	Gs, (G)	10^{-4} T	(or 100 uT)
maxwell	Mx	10^{-8} Wb	(or 10 nWb)
stilb	sb	10^4 cd/m²	(or 10 kcd/m²)
phot	ph	10^4 lx	(or 10 klx)
kilogram-force	kgf	9.806 65 N	
calorie (int.)	cal	4.1868 J	
kilocalorie (int.)	kcal	4.1868 kJ	
torr	torr	133.322 Pa	
oersted	Oe	79.5775 A/m	

ROUNDING OF NUMBERS

Conversion from one measuring system to another requires rounding of numbers. For example, a quantity rounded to the nearest meter has an implied precision of ±0.5 m, while a quantity rounded to the nearest foot has an implied precision of ±0.5 ft. The two are quite different. If a quantity in feet (to the nearest foot) is to be converted to meters, any rounding should be to the nearest 0.3 m.

In making the changeover to SI, critical decisions about new rounded values will be required for many factors widely used in technical work.

SIGNIFICANT DIGITS

In general, the result of any multiplication, division, addition, or subtraction cannot be given in more significant digits than are present in any one component of the original data. This condition pertains regardless of the number of decimal places in which a conversion factor is given.

In reference tables conversion factors should be stated to a substantial number of decimal places to cover a wide range of uses. It is the responsibility of the user

SINGLE LINE, DUAL SCALE CHARTS

Conversions also can be interpreted on a single line, dual scale, graphical representation.

METERS TO FEET (CONVERSION FACTORS I M = 3.281 FT, I FT = 0.3048 M)

ACOUSTICS

SI units have been applied in acoustics to define frequency (hertz), sound power (watt), sound intensity (watt per square meter), and sound pressure level (pascal).

The reference quantities for the dimensionless logarithmic unit decibel (dB) are also expressed in SI units.

1. Sound power reference quantity: $1 \text{ pW} = 10^{-12}$ W; therefore

$$\text{sound power level (dB)} = 10 \log_{10} \frac{\text{actual power (W)}}{10^{-12}}$$

2. Sound intensity reference quantity: $1 \text{ pW/m}^2 = 10^{-12}$ W/m2; therefore

sound intensity level (dB)

$$= 10 \log_{10} \frac{\text{actual intensity (W/m}^2)}{10^{-12}}$$

3. Sound pressure reference quantity: $20 \text{ Pa} = 2 \times 20 \times 10^6$ Pa; therefore

sound pressure level (dB)

$$= 20 \log_{10} \frac{\text{actual pressure (Pa)}}{20 \times 10^6}$$

ELECTRICITY AND MAGNETISM

Electrical engineering, for many years, has used metric (SI) units as practical electrical units. These units are all coherent in that they are formed directly from SI base and derived units on a unity (one-to-one) basis.

to interpret the resultant decimal number to the extent applicable.

Example: What is the equivalent of 3 miles in terms of kilometers?

CONVERSION FACTOR	DIRECT MULTIPLICATION		SIGNIFICANT EQUIVALENT	
miles to kilometers = 1.609	3 mi = 4.827 km		3 mi	5 km
Or, in reverse form: kilometers to miles = 0.6214	5 km = 3.107 mi		5 km	3 mi

ABANDONED UNITS

For various reasons many derived and specialized units will fall into disuse as the changeover to SI progresses. Some, like British thermal unit (Btu) and horsepower (hp), will be dropped because they are based on the inch-pound (English) system.

Former metric units, of the c.g.s. variety, are no longer recommended. In addition a number of traditional metric units are outside SI, and their use is to be avoided.

The only changes involved the use of the term "siemens" (S) for electrical conductance, instead of the previous name "mho," and the replacement of the cycle per second with the SI unit hertz (Hz).

The kilowatt-hour (kWh) is not an SI unit but will probably be retained for the measurement of electrical energy consumption because of its long history and extensive use. The recalibration of existing electricity meters from kilowatt-hours to megajoules (MJ), on the basis of 1 kWh = 3.6 MJ, hardly seems justified at this time. However, the kilowatt-hour should not be introduced into new areas.

ILLUMINATION ENGINEERING

The SI units for luminous intensity, the candela (cd), and for luminous flux, the lumen (lm), are already in general use in the United States.

Illuminance (luminous flux per unit area) will be expressed in the derived SI unit lux (lx), which is a special name for the lumen per square meter (lm/m²). The lux (lx) and kilolux (klx) replace the footcandle, which is also known as the lumen per square foot.

Similarly, the SI unit of luminance, the candela per square meter (cd/m²), replaces the candela per square foot, the lambert, and the footlambert.

Conversion factors are:

1 lx =	0.092 footcandle
1 footcandle =	10.7639 lx
1 klx =	92.903 footcandles
1 cd/m² =	0.092 903 cd/ft²
	= 0.291 964 footlambert
1 cd/ft² =	10.7639 cd/m²
1 footlambert =	3.426 259 cd/m²

UNITS FOR ELECTRICITY AND MAGNETISM

QUANTITY	UNIT NAME	SYMBOL	DERIVATION	REMARKS
Electric current	ampere	A		SI base unit
Current density	ampere per square meter	A/m²		
Magnetic field strength	ampere per meter	A/m		
Electric charge quantity of electricity	coulomb	C	(A · s)	
Electric charge density	coulomb per cubic meter	C/m³		
Electric potential, electromotive force	volt	V	(W/A)	
Electric field strength	volt per meter	V/m		1 V/m = 1 N/C
Electric capacitance	farad	F	(C/V)	
Permittivity	farad per meter	F/m		
Electric resistance	ohm	Ω	(V/A)	
Electric conductance	siemens	S	(A/V)	Replaces "mho"; also equals $1/\Omega$
Electric power	watt	W	(V · A)	Also equals J/s
Magnetic flux	weber	Wb	(V · s)	
Magnetic flux density	tesla	T	(Wb/m²)	1 T = 1 V · s/m²
Inductance	henry	H	(Wb/A)	1 H = 1 V · s/A
Permeability	henry per meter	H/m		

METRIC DRAWINGS

Metric drawing sizes are those set by the International Standards Organization (ISO), "A" Series, with a $1:\sqrt{2}$ aspect ratio. These sizes are suitable for reduction using a 35 mm microfilm frame. Metric drawing scales are comparable to U.S. customary scales, as shown in the table. The metric system favors the use of ratios to define slopes, and a table comparing this with pitches and percentages is shown. Other recommended metric drawing practices are similar to customary standard drawing practices.

DRAWING SHEET DIMENSIONS (MM)

SIZE	SHEET SIZE	TOP AND BOT- TOM	BIND- ING MAR- GIN	RIGHT BOR- DER	NET SIZE
A0	1189 x 841	20	40	16	1133 x 801
A1	841 x 594	14	28	12	801 x 566
A2	594 x 420	10	20	8	566 x 400
A3	420 x 297	7	20	6	394 x 283
A4*	210 x 297	7	20	6	184 x 283
B1	1000 x 707	14	28	12	960 x 679

*The filing edge of A4 size sheets is the long edge.

COMPARISON OF DRAWING SCALES

METRIC SCALES	CUSTOMARY RATIO	CUSTOMARY SCALES
1:5	1:4	3″ = 1′0″
1:10	1:18	1½″ = 1′0″
	1:12	1″ = 1′0″
1:20	1:16	¾″ = 1′0″
	1:24	½″ = 1′0″
1:50	1:48	¼″ = 1′0″
1:100	1:96	⅛″ = 1′0″
1:200	1:92	1/16″ = 1′0″
1:500	1:384	1/32″ = 1′0″
	1:480	1″ = 40′0″
	1:600	1″ = 50′0″
1:1000	1:960	1″ = 80′0″
	1:1200	1″ = 100′0″
1:2000	1:2400	1″ = 200′0″
1:5000	1:4800	1″ = 400′0″
	1:6000	1″ = 500′0″
1:10 000	1:10 560	6″ = 1 mi
	1:12 000	1″ = 1000′0″
1:25 000	1:21 120	3″ = 1 mi
	1:24 000	1″ = 2000′0″
1:50 000	1:63 360	1″ = 1 mi
1:100 000	1:126 720	½″ = 1 mi

EXPRESSION OF SLOPE

RATIO Y/X	ANGLE	ANGLE (RAD)	PERCENTAGE (%)
Shallow slopes			
1:100	0°34′	0.0100	1
1:67	0°52′	0.0150	1.5
1:57	1°	0.0175	1.75
1:50	1°09′	0.0200	2
1:40	1°26′	0.0250	2.5
1:33	1°43′	0.0300	3
1:29	2°	0.0349	3.5
1:25	2°17′	0.0399	4
1:20	2°52′	0.0499	5
1:19	3°	0.0524	5.25
Slight slopes			
1:17	3°26′	0.0599	6
1:15	3°48′	0.0664	6.7
1:14.3	4°	0.0698	7
1:12	4°46′	0.0832	8.3
1:11.4	5°	0.0873	8.75
1:10	5°43′	0.0998	10
1:9.5	6°	0.1047	10.5
1:8	7°07′	0.1245	12.5
1:7.1	8°	0.1396	14
1:6.7	8°32′	0.1490	15
1:6	9°28′	0.1652	16.7
1:5.7	10°	0.1745	17.6
1:5	11°19′	0.1975	20
1:4.5	12°30′	0.2182	22.2
1:4	14°02′	0.2450	25
Medium slopes			
1:3.7	15°	0.2618	25.8
1:3.3	16°42′	0.2915	30
1:3	18°26′	0.3217	33.3
1:2.75	20°	0.3491	36.4
1:2.5	21°48′	0.3805	40
1:2.4	22°30′	0.3927	41.4
1:2.15	25°	0.4363	46.6
1:2	26°34′	0.4537	50
1:1.73	30°	0.5326	57.5
1:1.67	30°58′	0.5405	60
1:1.5	33°42′	0.5880	67
1:1.33	36°52′	0.6434	75
1:1.2	40°	0.6981	84
1:1	45°	0.7854	100
Steep slopes			
1.19:1	50°	0.8727	119
1.43:1	55°	0.9599	143
1.5:1	56°19′	0.9827	150
1.73:1	60°	1.0472	173
2:1	63°26′	1.1071	200
2.15:1	65°	1.1345	215
2.5:1	68°12′	1.1903	250
2.75:1	70°	1.2217	275
3:1	71°34′	1.2491	300
3.73:1	75°	1.3090	373
4:1	75°58′	1.3253	400
5:1	78°42′	1.3735	500
5.67:1	80°	1.3963	567
6:1	80°32′	1.4056	600
11.43:1	85°	1.4835	1143
∞	90°	1.5708	∞

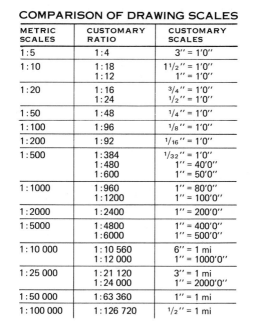

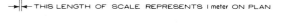

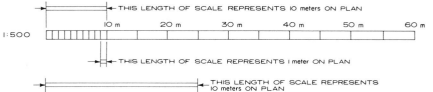

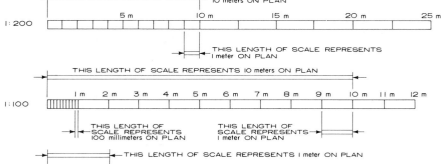

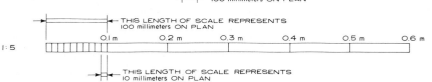

METRIC LENGTHS TO SCALE

The Basic Module for the construction industry is 100 mm. This is an internationally accepted value. The basic module should apply to building components as well as entire buildings.

Multimodules, if carefully selected, can be coordinated with the controlling dimensions for a building, thus minimizing component sizes.

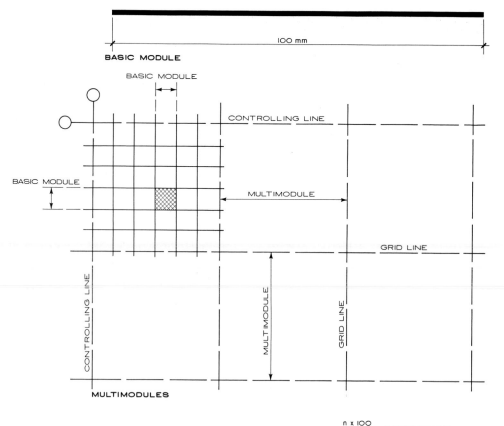

BASIC MODULE

100 mm

BASIC MODULE

BASIC MODULE

CONTROLLING LINE

MULTIMODULE

GRID LINE

CONTROLLING LINE

MULTIMODULE

GRID LINE

MULTIMODULES

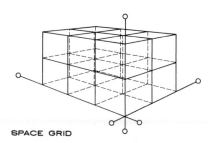

SPACE GRID

In a dimensional reference system the reference space grid is made up of the horizontal and vertical planes used to define the locations of points, lines, or surfaces in space.

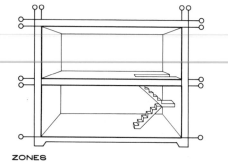

ZONES

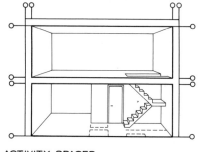

ACTIVITY SPACES

Zones and usable spaces: Zones are the spaces between controlling planes. They may be occupied but not always filled by one or more components. Finishes should be contained within the zone, although on occasion they may be placed outside as long as this does not inhibit the use of other coordinated components.

The space between zones can be referred to as an activity space. This is the space in which human or mechanical activities take place. In turn it may contain components such as partitions or stairs.

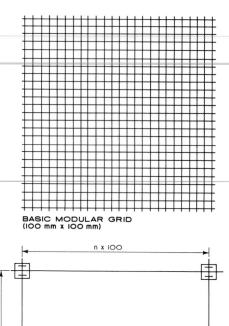

BASIC MODULAR GRID
(100 mm x 100 mm)

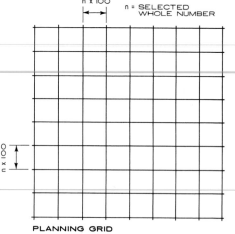

n x 100   n = SELECTED WHOLE NUMBER

n x 100

PLANNING GRID

n x 100

n x 100

STRUCTURAL GRID

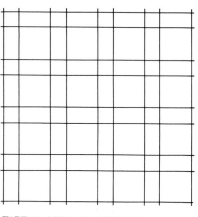

TARTAN GRID: 1:2 RATIO OF BANDWIDTHS

17

METRIC DIMENSIONS

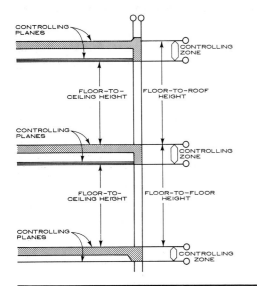

VERTICAL CONTROLLING DIMENSIONS

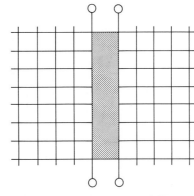

PARALLEL REFERENCE PLANES

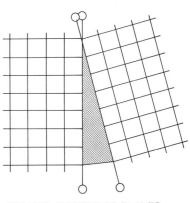

OBLIQUE REFERENCE PLANES

Neutral zones are nonmodular interruptions of a modular reference grid to accommodate intermediate building elements, such as walls or floors, or parts of a building placed at an angle with a separate grid for each portion.

NEUTRAL ZONES

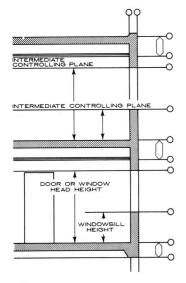

INTERMEDIATE CONTROLLING PLANES

CONTROLLING DIMENSIONS IN BUILDING DESIGN

The application of dimensional coordination in building design involves the use of horizontal and vertical controlling dimensions, either axial or face-to-face, between the major reference planes for structural elements. Enclosing elements, or "solids," are assigned controlling zones, such as floors, roofs, structural walls, or columns. Controlling lines normally coincide with the space reference system. To permit maximum flexibility and interchangeability of building components, controlling dimensions should bear a direct relationship to the coordinating sizes of building products.

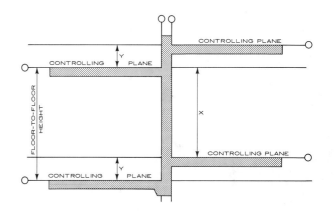

CHANGE OF LEVEL FOR FLOORS AND ROOFS

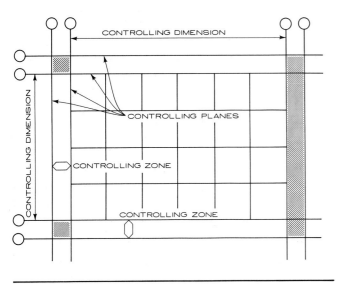

BOUNDARY CONTROLLING PLANES

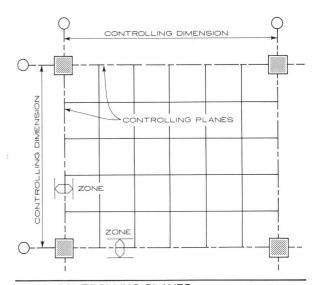

AXIAL CONTROLLING PLANES

METRIC DIMENSIONS 17

HORIZONTAL CONTROLLING DIMENSIONS (mm)

DIMENSIONS	MULTIPLES OF MULTIMODULES 300	600	1200	3000	6000	MOST PREFERRED VALUES
300	x					
600	x	x				x
900	x					
1 200	x	x	x			x
1 500	x					
1 800	x	x				x
2 100	x					
2 400	x	x	x			x
2 700	x					
3 000	x	x		x		x
3 300	x					
3 600	x	x	x			x
4 200		x				
4 800		x	x			x
5 400		x				
6 000		x	x	x	x	x
6 600		x				
7 200		x	x			x
7 800		x				
8 400		x	x			x
9 000		x		x		x
9 600		x	x			x
10 800			x			
12 000			x	x	x	x
13 200			x			
14 000			x			
15 000				x		
15 600			x			
16 800			x			
18 000			x	x	x	x
19 200			x			
20 400			x			
21 000				x		
21 600			x			
22 800			x			
24 000			x	x	x	x
25 200			x			
26 400			x			
27 000				x		
27 600			x			
30 000			x	x	x	x

NOMINAL AND COORDINATING DIMENSIONS FOR CLAY MASONRY: FULL SIZE UNITS

NOMINAL HEIGHT (mm)	COORDINATING HEIGHT (mm)	COORDINATING LENGTH (mm)
50	2 courses to 100	300
67	3 courses to 200	200 300
75	4 courses to 300	200 300
80	5 courses to 400	200 300
100	100	200 300 400
133	3 courses to 400	200 300 400
150	2 courses to 300	300 400
200	200	200 300 400
300	300	300

Note: For horizontal flexibility and/or to maintain bond patterns, the following supplementary lengths may be required:

NOMINAL LENGTH (mm)	SUPPLEMENTARY LENGTHS (mm)
200	100
300	100, 150, 200, 250
400	100, 200, 300

PREFERRED SIZES FOR BUILDING COMPONENTS AND ASSEMBLIES

CATEGORY	EXAMPLES	PREFERRED SIZES (mm) 1ST	2ND
Small (under 500 mm)	Brick block, tile, paving units	100 200 300 400	25 50 75 150 250
Medium (under 1 500 mm)	Panels, partitions, doorsets, windows, slabs	600 800 900 1 200	500 700 1 000 1 400 See Note 1
Large (under 3 600 mm)	Precast floor and wall units, panels, doors, windows, stairs	1 800 2 400 3 000 3 600	(n x 300): 1 500, 2 100, 2 700, 3 300 (n x 200): 1 600, 2 000, 2 200, 2 600, 2 800, 3 200, 3 400 See Note 2
Very Large (over 3 600 mm)	Prefabricated building elements, precast floor and roof sections	4 800 6 000 7 200 8 400 9 500 10 800 12 000	(n x 600): 4 200, 6 600, 7 800, 9 000, 10 200, 11 400 (n x 1 500): 4 500, 7 500, 10 500 See Note 3

NOTES

1. For the purposes of rationalization, those multiples of 100 mm, above 1 000 mm, that are prime numbers (e.g., 1 100, 1 300) constitute a lower order of preferences when special requirements exist.
2. Alternative second preferences are shown; for vertical dimensions the use of multiples of 200 mm may sometimes be more appropriate than the use of multiples of 300 mm, as with masonry materials.
3. Alternative second preferences are shown; for some projects it will be more appropriate to size large components or assemblies in multiples of 1 500 mm.

PRODUCTS FOR USE IN THE VERTICAL PLANE: MASONRY PANELS

VERTICAL (mm)	HORIZONTAL (mm) 600 x n	300 x n	200 x n
600 x n	1	2	3
220 x n	2	3	3
100 x n	3	3	

GENERAL NOTES

Preferred sizes and dimensions allow better coordination between manufactured components, design, and construction operations. The tables are presented to allow an open system of selection compatible with dimensional coordination concepts presented on the preceding pages. Preferred dimensions in building are selected multimodules for horizontal and vertical applications derived from the basic 100 mm module.

The preferred dimension concept is similar to the customary 4 in. module concept presently in use in the construction industry. As an example, preferred horizontal controlling dimensions similar to the customary 1, 2, or 4 ft multimodule in metric terms may be stated this way:

up to 3600 mm : 300 mm

up to 9600 mm : 600 mm

above 9600 mm : 1200 mm

For large dimensions, 6000 mm may be more useful or, as a second preference, 3000 mm.

Certain numbers are preferred because they are divisible by 2 or 3. Such numbers are 600, 1200, 1800, 2400 mm, as indicated in the table. The long history of using such multimodules is incorporated in the conversion plans to SI metric.

Refer to standards and manufacturer's data for application of the preferred SI metric sizes and dimensions.

PREFERRED DIMENSIONS FOR PANELS AND PLANKS

TYPE	PREFERENCE	WIDTH (mm)	LENGTH (mm)
Panels	First	1 200	2 400
	Second	600	2 400 3 000
		1 200	1 200 1 800 3 000 3 600
	Third	1 200	2 100 2 700
Planks	First	400	2 400
	Second	400	3 000 3 600

PREFERRED DOOR SIZES

HEIGHT (mm)	SINGLE WIDTH 700*	800	900	1 000	DOUBLE WIDTH 1 200	1 500	1 800
2 100	2	2	1	2	1	1	1
2 200	2	2	2	1	2	2	1
2 400	2	1	1	1	2	2	1

*Too narrow for wheelchair use.

PREFERRED SIZES FOR WINDOWS

HEIGHT (mm) 1ST PREFERENCE	2ND	WIDTH (mm) 600 (1st)	900 (2nd)	1200 (1st)	1500 (2nd)	1800 (1st)	2100 (2nd)	2400 (1st)	2700 (2nd)	3000 (1st)
600		1	2	1	2	1	2	1	2	1
	800	2	3	2	3	2	3	2	3	2
	900	2	3	2	3	2	3	2	3	2
	1000	2	3	2	3	2	3	2	3	2
1200		1	2	1	2	1	2	1	2	1
	1400	2	3	2	3	2	3	2	3	2
	1500	2	3	2	3	2	3	2	3	2
	1600	2	3	2	3	2	3	2	3	2
1800		1	2	1	2	1	2	1	2	1
	2000	2	3	2	3	2	3	2	3	2
	2100	2	3	2	3	2	3	2	3	2
2400		1	2	1	2	1	2	1	2	1
	2700	2	3	2	3	2	3	2	3	2
3000		1	2	1	2	1	2	1	2	1

Note: In some construction, widths of 1000, 1400, 1600, and 2000 mm may be required for brick or block sizes and, combined with first preference heights, may be substituted as a third preference series of sizes.

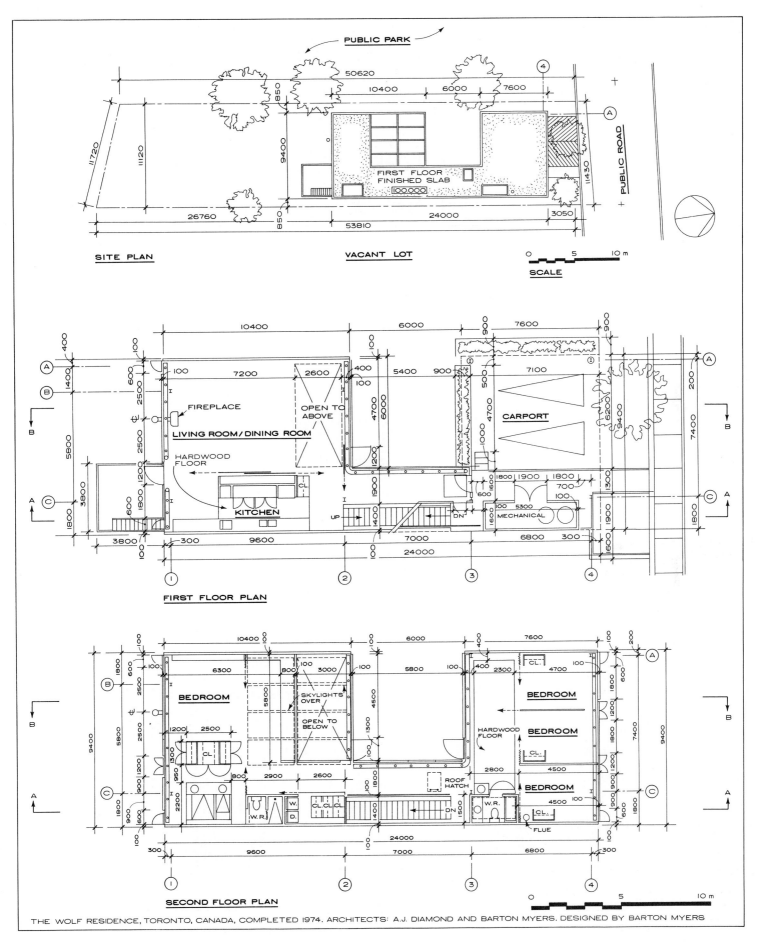

SITE PLAN

PUBLIC PARK

VACANT LOT

FIRST FLOOR
FINISHED SLAB
100 000

PUBLIC ROAD

SCALE

0   5   10 m

FIRST FLOOR PLAN

FIREPLACE

OPEN TO
ABOVE

LIVING ROOM/DINING ROOM

HARDWOOD
FLOOR

CARPORT

KITCHEN

CL

UP   DN

MECHANICAL

SECOND FLOOR PLAN

BEDROOM

SKYLIGHTS
OVER

OPEN TO
BELOW

BEDROOM

BEDROOM

HARDWOOD
FLOOR

ROOF
HATCH

W.R.

CL.CL.CL

W.
D.

DN

W.R.

BEDROOM

CL.

FLUE

0   5   10 m

THE WOLF RESIDENCE, TORONTO, CANADA, COMPLETED 1974. ARCHITECTS: A.J. DIAMOND AND BARTON MYERS. DESIGNED BY BARTON MYERS

Robert Hill, Barton Myers Associates; Toronto, Canada

METRIC BUILDING **17**

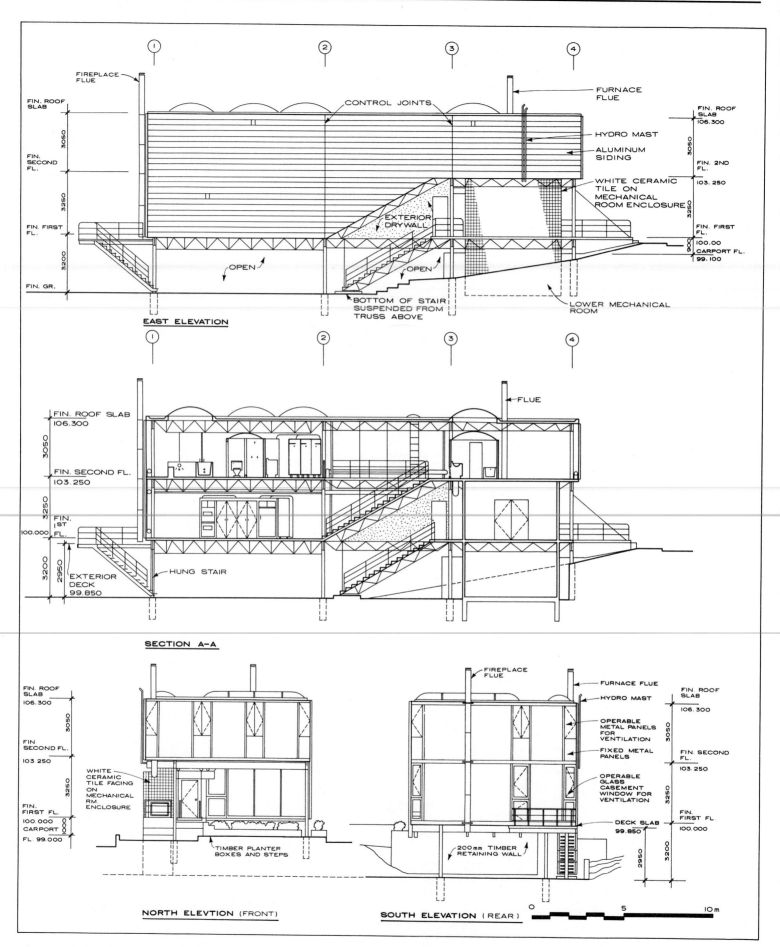

① ② ③ ④

FIREPLACE
FLUE

FIN. ROOF
SLAB

CONTROL JOINTS

FURNACE
FLUE

FIN. ROOF
SLAB
106.300

3050

FIN.
SECOND
FL.

HYDRO MAST

ALUMINUM
SIDING

3050

FIN. 2ND
FL.

103.250

3250

FIN. FIRST
FL.

EXTERIOR
DRYWALL

WHITE CERAMIC
TILE ON
MECHANICAL
ROOM ENCLOSURE

3250

FIN. FIRST
FL.

100.00

900

CARPORT FL.
99.100

3200

OPEN

OPEN

FIN. GR.

BOTTOM OF STAIR
SUSPENDED FROM
TRUSS ABOVE

LOWER MECHANICAL
ROOM

EAST ELEVATION

① ② ③ ④

FLUE

FIN. ROOF SLAB
106.300

3050

FIN. SECOND FL.
103.250

3250

FIN.
1ST
FL.

100.000

3200 2950

EXTERIOR
DECK
99.850

HUNG STAIR

SECTION A-A

FIN. ROOF
SLAB
106.300

3050

FIN
SECOND FL.
103.250

3250

FIN.
FIRST FL.
100.000
CARPORT
FL. 99.000

WHITE
CERAMIC
TILE FACING
ON
MECHANICAL
RM.
ENCLOSURE

TIMBER PLANTER
BOXES AND STEPS

NORTH ELEVTION (FRONT)

FIREPLACE
FLUE

FURNACE FLUE

HYDRO MAST

OPERABLE
METAL PANELS
FOR
VENTILATION

FIXED METAL
PANELS

OPERABLE
GLASS
CASEMENT
WINDOW FOR
VENTILATION

DECK SLAB
99.850

200 mm TIMBER
RETAINING WALL

FIN. ROOF
SLAB

106.300

3050

FIN. SECOND
FL.

103.250

3250

FIN.
FIRST FL.
100.000

3200 2950

SOUTH ELEVATION (REAR)

0   5   10 m

Robert Hill, Barton Myers Associates; Toronto, Canada

17 **METRIC BUILDING**

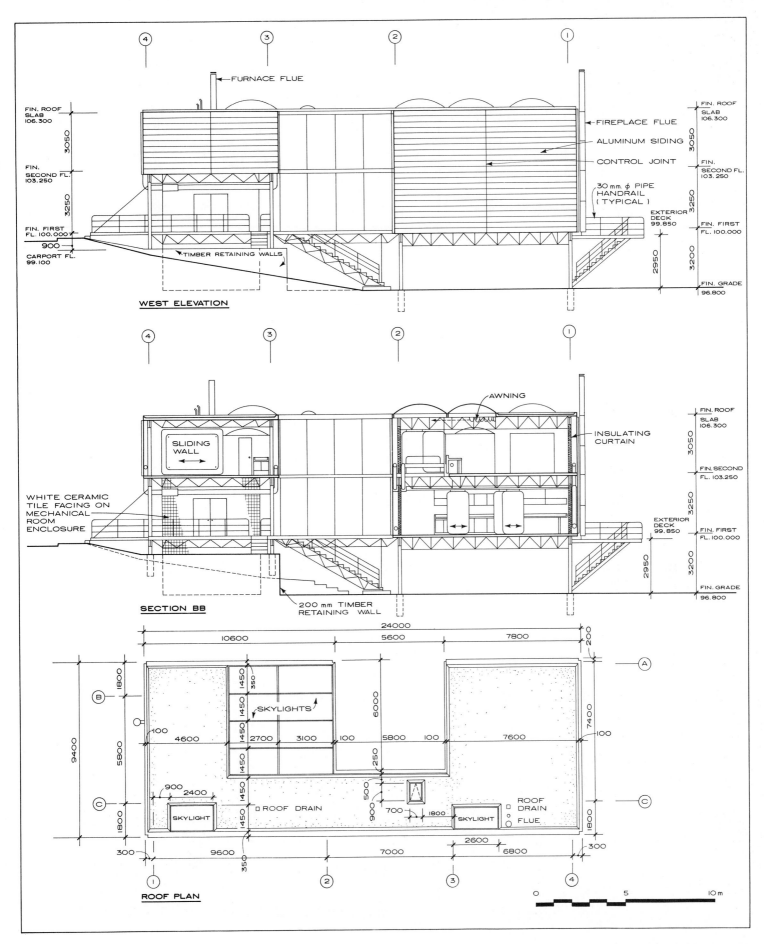

FURNACE FLUE

FIN. ROOF
SLAB
106.300

3050

FIN.
SECOND FL.
103.250

3250

FIN. FIRST
FL. 100.000

900

CARPORT FL.
99.100

TIMBER RETAINING WALLS

WEST ELEVATION

FIREPLACE FLUE

ALUMINUM SIDING

CONTROL JOINT

30 mm. φ PIPE
HANDRAIL
(TYPICAL)

EXTERIOR
DECK
99.850

2950

FIN. ROOF
SLAB
106.300

3050

FIN.
SECOND FL.
103.250

3250

FIN. FIRST
FL. 100.000

3200

FIN. GRADE
96.800

AWNING

SLIDING
WALL

WHITE CERAMIC
TILE FACING ON
MECHANICAL
ROOM
ENCLOSURE

SECTION BB

200 mm TIMBER
RETAINING WALL

INSULATING
CURTAIN

FIN. ROOF
SLAB
106.300

3050

FIN. SECOND
FL. 103.250

3250

EXTERIOR
DECK
99.850

FIN. FIRST
FL. 100.000

2950

3200

FIN. GRADE
96.800

ROOF PLAN

24000
10600 5600 7800 200

1800

9400 5800

100 4600

SKYLIGHTS

1450 1450 350

1450 2700 3100 100

1450

6000

5800 100

250

500

900 700 1800

1450

900 2400

SKYLIGHT

ROOF DRAIN

7600

7400

100

A

B

C

ROOF
DRAIN

SKYLIGHT

FLUE

1800

300 9600 350 7000 2600 6800 300

1 2 3 4

0 5 10 m

Robert Hill, Barton Myers Associates; Toronto, Canada

METRIC BUILDING

17

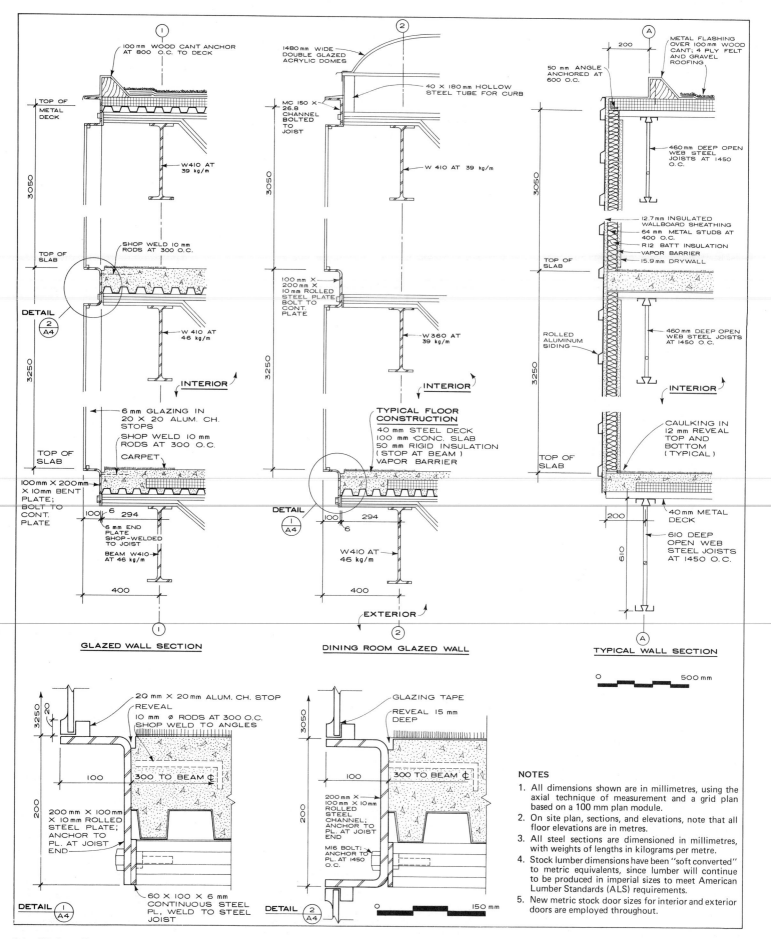

GLAZED WALL SECTION

DINING ROOM GLAZED WALL

TYPICAL WALL SECTION

Robert Hill, Barton Myers Associates; Toronto, Canada

NOTES

1. All dimensions shown are in millimetres, using the axial technique of measurement and a grid plan based on a 100 mm plan module.

2. On site plan, sections, and elevations, note that all floor elevations are in metres.

3. All steel sections are dimensioned in millimetres, with weights of lengths in kilograms per metre.

4. Stock lumber dimensions have been "soft converted" to metric equivalents, since lumber will continue to be produced in imperial sizes to meet American Lumber Standards (ALS) requirements.

5. New metric stock door sizes for interior and exterior doors are employed throughout.

17 METRIC BUILDING

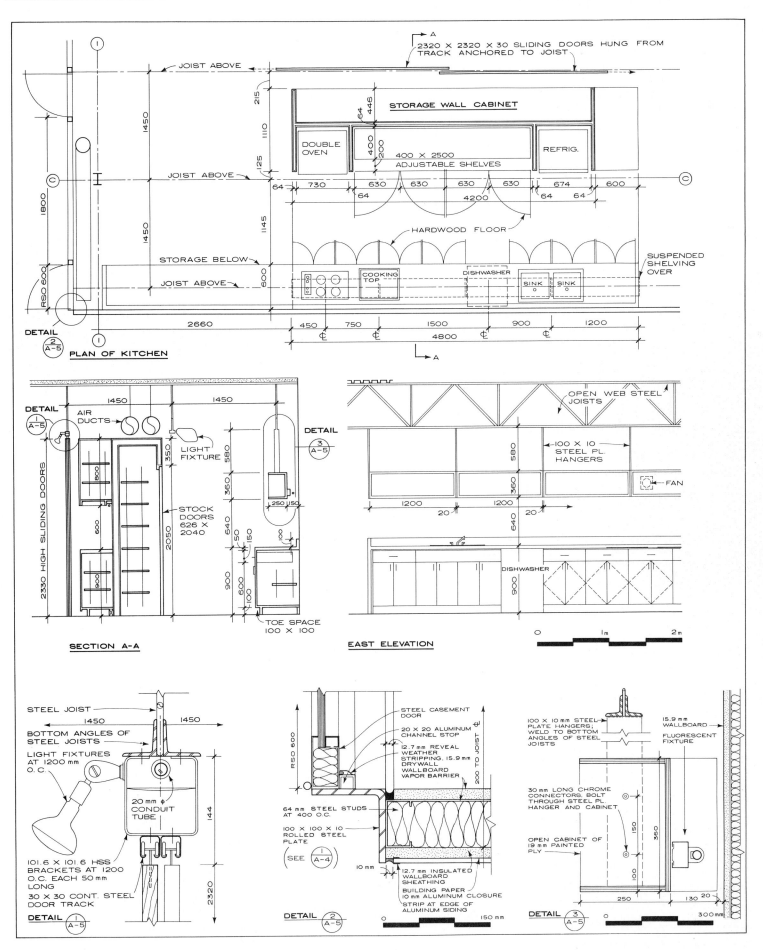

A

2320 X 2320 X 30 SLIDING DOORS HUNG FROM
TRACK ANCHORED TO JOIST

JOIST ABOVE

215

64   446

STORAGE WALL CABINET

1110

DOUBLE
OVEN

400   200

REFRIG.

400 X 2500
ADJUSTABLE SHELVES

125

JOIST ABOVE

64   730   630   630   630   630   674   600

4200   64   64

1800

1450

1145

HARDWOOD FLOOR

STORAGE BELOW

600

JOIST ABOVE

SUSPENDED
SHELVING
OVER

RSO 600

COOKING
TOP

DISHWASHER

SINK   SINK

2660   450   750   1500   900   1200

DETAIL
2
A-5

C   4800   C

PLAN OF KITCHEN

A

DETAIL
1
A-5

1450   1450

AIR
DUCTS

350

LIGHT
FIXTURE

DETAIL
3
A-5

2330 HIGH SLIDING DOORS

800

600

2050

STOCK
DOORS
626 X
2040

580

360

640

250 150

OPEN WEB STEEL
JOISTS

100 X 10
STEEL PL.
HANGERS

580

360

FAN

900

900

600   100

150

50

TOE SPACE
100 X 100

1200   1200

20   20

640

900

DISHWASHER

0   1m   2m

SECTION A-A   **EAST ELEVATION**

STEEL JOIST

1450   1450

BOTTOM ANGLES OF
STEEL JOISTS

LIGHT FIXTURES
AT 1200 mm
O.C.

20 mm φ
CONDUIT
TUBE

144

101.6 X 101.6 HSS
BRACKETS AT 1200
O.C. EACH 50 mm
LONG

30 X 30 CONT. STEEL
DOOR TRACK

2320

DETAIL
1
A-5

STEEL CASEMENT
DOOR

20 X 20 ALUMINUM
CHANNEL STOP

RSO 600

200 TO JOIST

12.7 mm REVEAL
WEATHER
STRIPPING. 15.9 mm
DRYWALL
WALLBOARD
VAPOR BARRIER

64 mm STEEL STUDS
AT 400 O.C.

100 X 100 X 10
ROLLED STEEL
PLATE

SEE
1
A-4

10 mm

12.7 mm INSULATED
WALLBOARD
SHEATHING

BUILDING PAPER
10 mm ALUMINUM CLOSURE
STRIP AT EDGE OF
ALUMINUM SIDING

DETAIL
2
A-5

0   150 mm

100 X 10 mm STEEL
PLATE HANGERS;
WELD TO BOTTOM
ANGLES OF STEEL
JOISTS

15.9 mm
WALLBOARD

FLUORESCENT
FIXTURE

30 mm LONG CHROME
CONNECTORS. BOLT
THROUGH STEEL PL.
HANGER AND CABINET

150

360

100

OPEN CABINET OF
19 mm PAINTED
PLY

250   130   20

DETAIL
3
A-5

0   300mm

Robert Hill, Barton Myers Associates; Toronto, Canada

INCHES AND FRACTIONS TO MILLIMETERS (1 IN.= 25.4 mm)

	0	1	2	3	4	5	6	7	8	9	10	11
INCHES					MILLIMETERS (mm)							
0	. . .	25.40	50.80	76.20	101.60	127.00	152.40	177.80	203.20	228.60	254.00	279.40
1/16	1.59	26.99	52.39	77.79	103.19	128.59	153.99	179.39	204.79	230.19	255.59	280.99
1/8	3.18	28.58	53.98	79.38	104.78	130.18	155.58	180.98	206.38	231.78	257.18	282.58
3/16	4.76	30.16	55.56	80.96	106.36	131.76	157.16	182.56	207.96	233.36	258.76	284.16
1/4	6.35	31.75	57.15	82.55	107.95	133.35	158.75	184.15	209.55	234.95	260.35	285.75
5/16	7.94	33.34	58.74	84.14	109.54	134.94	160.34	185.74	211.14	236.54	261.94	287.34
3/8	9.53	34.93	60.33	85.73	111.13	136.53	161.93	187.33	212.73	238.13	263.53	288.93
7/16	11.11	36.51	61.91	87.31	112.71	138.11	163.51	188.91	214.31	239.71	265.11	290.51
1/2	12.70	38.10	63.50	88.90	114.30	139.70	165.10	190.50	215.90	241.30	266.70	292.10
9/16	14.29	39.69	65.09	90.49	115.89	141.29	166.69	192.09	217.49	242.89	268.29	293.69
5/8	15.88	41.28	66.68	92.08	117.48	142.88	168.28	193.68	219.08	244.48	269.88	295.28
11/16	17.46	42.86	68.26	93.66	119.06	144.46	169.86	195.26	220.66	246.06	271.46	296.86
3/4	19.05	44.45	69.85	95.25	120.65	146.05	171.45	196.85	222.25	247.65	273.05	298.45
13/16	20.64	46.04	71.44	96.84	122.24	147.64	173.04	198.44	223.84	249.24	274.64	300.04
7/8	22.23	47.63	73.03	98.43	123.83	149.23	174.63	200.03	225.43	250.83	276.23	301.63
15/16	23.81	49.21	74.61	100.01	125.41	150.81	176.21	201.61	227.01	252.41	277.81	303.21

FEET AND INCHES TO MILLIMETERS (1 FT = 304.8 mm; 1 IN. = 25.4 mm)

INCHES MILLIMETERS	0 ...	1 25	2 51	3 76	4 102	5 127	6 152	7 178	8 203	9 229	10 254	11 279
	0	1	2	3	4	5	6	7	8	9		
FEET					MILLIMETERS (mm)							
0	. . .	305	610	914	1 219	1 524	1 829	2 134	2 438	2 743		
10	3 048	3 353	3 658	3 962	4 267	4 572	4 877	5 182	5 486	5 791		
20	6 096	6 401	6 706	7 010	7 315	7 620	7 925	8 230	8 534	8 839		
30	9 144	9 449	9 754	10 058	10 363	10 668	10 973	11 278	11 582	11 887		
40	12 192	12 497	12 802	13 106	13 411	13 716	14 021	14 326	14 630	14 935		
50	15 240	15 545	15 850	16 154	16 459	16 764	17 069	17 374	17 678	17 983		
60	18 288	18 593	18 898	19 202	19 507	19 812	20 117	20 422	20 726	21 031		
70	21 336	21 641	21 946	22 250	22 555	22 860	23 165	23 470	23 774	24 079		
80	24 384	24 689	24 994	25 298	25 603	25 908	26 213	26 518	26 882	27 127		
90	27 432	27 737	28 042	28 346	28 651	28 956	29 261	29 566	29 870	30 175		
100	30 480	30 785	31 090	31 394	31 699	32 004	32 309	32 614	32 918	33 223		
110	33 528	33 833	34 138	34 442	34 747	35 052	35 357	35 662	35 966	36 271		
120	36 576	36 881	37 186	37 490	37 795	38 100	38 405	38 710	39 014	39 319		
130	39 624	39 929	40 234	40 538	40 843	41 148	41 453	41 758	42 062	42 367		
140	42 672	42 977	43 282	43 586	43 891	44 196	44 501	44 806	45 110	45 415		
150	45 720											

FEET TO METERS (1 FT = 0.304 8 m)

FEET	0	1	2	3	4	5	6	7	8	9
					METERS (m)					
0	. . .	0.305	0.610	0.914	1.219	1.524	1.829	2.134	2.438	2.743
10	3.048	3.353	3.658	3.962	4.267	4.572	4.877	5.182	5.486	5.791
20	6.096	6.401	6.706	7.010	7.315	7.620	7.925	8.230	8.534	8.839
30	9.144	9.449	9.754	10.058	10.363	10.668	10.973	11.278	11.582	11.887
40	12.192	12.497	12.802	13.106	13.411	13.716	14.021	14.326	14.630	14.935
50	15.240	15.545	15.850	16.154	15.459	16.764	17.069	17.374	17.678	17.983
60	18.288	18.593	18.898	19.202	19.507	19.812	20.117	20.422	20.726	21.031
70	21.336	21.641	21.946	22.250	22.555	22.860	23.165	23.470	23.774	24.079
80	24.384	24.689	24.994	25.298	25.603	25.908	26.213	26.518	26.822	27.127
90	27.432	27.737	28.042	28.346	28.651	28.956	29.261	29.566	29.870	30.175
100	30.480	30.785	31.090	31.394	31.699	32.004	32.309	32.614	32.918	33.223
110	33.528	33.833	34.138	34.442	34.747	35.052	35.357	35.662	35.966	36.271
120	36.576	36.881	37.186	37.490	37.795	38.100	38.405	38.710	39.014	39.319
130	39.624	39.929	40.234	40.538	40.843	41.148	41.453	41.758	42.062	42.367
140	42.672	42.977	43.282	43.586	43.891	44.196	44.501	44.806	45.110	45.415
150	45.720	46.025	46.330	46.634	46.939	47.244	47.549	47.854	48.158	48.463
160	48.768	49.073	49.378	49.682	49.987	50.292	50.597	50.902	51.206	51.511
170	51.816	52.121	52.426	52.730	53.035	53.340	53.645	53.950	54.254	54.559
180	54.864	55.169	55.474	55.778	56.083	56.388	56.693	56.998	57.302	57.607
190	57.912	58.217	58.522	58.826	59.131	59.436	59.741	60.046	60.350	60.655
200	60.960									

17

METRIC CONVERSION TABLES

MILES TO KILOMETERS (1 MI = 1.609 344 km)

MILES	0	1	2	3	4	5	6	7	8	9
					KILOMETERS (km)					
0	...	1.609	3.219	4.828	6.437	8.047	9.656	11.265	12.875	14.484
10	16.093	17.703	19.312	20.921	22.531	24.140	25.750	27.359	28.968	30.578
20	32.187	33.796	35.406	37.015	38.624	40.234	41.843	43.452	45.062	46.671
30	48.280	49.890	51.499	53.108	54.718	56.327	57.936	59.546	61.155	62.764
40	64.374	65.983	67.592	69.202	70.811	72.420	74.030	75.639	77.249	78.858
50	80.467	82.077	83.686	85.295	86.905	88.514	90.123	91.733	93.342	94.951
60	96.561	98.170	99.779	101.389	102.998	104.607	106.217	107.826	109.435	111.045
70	112.654	114.263	115.873	117.482	119.091	120.701	122.310	123.919	125.529	127.138
80	128.748	130.357	131.966	133.576	135.185	136.794	138.404	140.013	141.622	143.232
90	144.841	146.450	148.060	149.669	151.278	152.888	154.497	156.106	157.716	159.325
100	160.934	162.544	164.153	165.762	167.372	168.981	170.590	172.200	173.809	175.418
110	177.028	178.637	180.247	181.856	183.465	185.075	186.684	188.293	189.903	191.512
120	193.121	194.731	196.340	197.949	199.559	201.168	202.777	204.387	205.996	207.605
130	209.215	210.824	212.433	214.043	215.652	217.261	218.871	220.480	222.089	223.699
140	225.308	226.918	228.527	230.136	231.746	233.355	234.964	236.574	238.183	239.792
150	241.402	243.011	244.620	246.230	247.839	249.448	251.058	252.667	254.276	255.866
160	257.495	259.104	260.714	262.323	263.932	265.542	267.151	268.760	270.370	271.979
170	273.588	275.198	276.807	278.417	280.026	281.635	283.245	284.854	286.463	288.073
180	289.682	291.291	292.901	294.510	296.119	297.729	299.338	300.947	302.557	304.166
190	305.775	307.385	308.994	310.603	312.213	313.822	315.431	317.041	318.650	320.259
200	321.869									

SQUARE INCHES TO SQUARE MILLIMETERS (1 IN.^{2} = 645.16 mm^2)

SQUARE INCHES	0	1	2	3	4	5	6	7	8	9
					SQUARE MILLIMETERS (mm^2)					
0	...	0.645	1.290	1.935	2.581	3.226	3.781	4.516	5.161	5.806
10	6.452	7.097	7.742	8.387	9.032	9.677	10.323	10.968	11.613	12.258
20	12.903	13.548	14.194	14.839	15.484	16.129	16.774	17.419	18.064	18.710
30	19.355	20.000	20.645	21.290	21.935	22.581	23.226	23.871	24.516	25.161
40	25.806	26.452	27.097	27.742	28.387	29.032	29.677	30.323	30.968	31.613
50	32.258	32.903	33.548	34.193	34.839	35.484	36.129	36.774	37.419	38.064
60	38.710	39.355	40.000	40.645	41.290	41.935	42.581	43.226	43.871	44.516
70	45.161	45.806	46.452	47.097	47.742	48.387	49.032	49.677	50.322	50.968
80	51.613	52.258	52.903	53.548	54.193	54.839	55.484	56.129	56.774	57.419
90	58.064	58.710	59.355	60.000	60.645	61.290	61.935	62.581	63.226	63.871
100	64.516	65.161	65.806	66.451	67.097	67.742	68.387	69.032	69.677	70.322
110	70.968	71.613	72.258	72.903	73.548	74.193	74.839	75.484	76.129	76.774
120	77.419	78.064	78.710	79.355	80.000	80.645	81.290	81.935	82.580	83.226
130	83.871	84.516	85.161	85.806	86.451	87.097	87.742	88.387	89.032	89.677
140	90.322	90.968	91.613	92.258	92.903					

SQUARE FEET TO SQUARE METERS (1 FT^2 = 0.0929 m^2)

SQUARE FEET	0	1	2	3	4	5	6	7	8	9
SQUARE METER	...	0.09	0.19	0.28	0.37	0.46	0.56	0.65	0.74	0.84

SQUARE FEET	0	10	20	30	40	50	60	70	80	90
					SQUARE METERS (m^2)					
0	...	0.93	1.86	2.79	3.72	4.65	5.57	6.50	7.43	8.36
100	9.29	10.22	11.15	12.08	13.01	13.94	14.86	15.79	16.72	17.65
200	18.58	19.51	20.44	21.37	22.30	23.23	24.15	25.08	26.01	26.94
300	27.87	28.80	29.73	30.66	31.59	32.52	33.45	34.37	35.30	36.23
400	37.16	38.09	39.02	39.95	40.88	41.81	42.74	43.66	44.59	45.52
500	46.45	47.38	48.31	49.24	50.17	51.10	52.03	52.95	53.88	54.81
600	55.74	56.67	57.60	58.53	59.46	60.39	61.32	62.25	63.17	64.10
700	65.03	65.96	66.89	67.82	68.75	69.68	70.61	71.54	72.46	73.39
800	74.32	75.25	76.18	77.11	78.04	78.97	79.90	80.83	81.75	82.68
900	83.61	84.54	85.47	86.40	87.33	88.26	89.19	90.12	91.04	91.97
1000	92.90	93.83	94.76	95.69	96.62	97.55	98.48	99.41	100.34	101.26
1100	102.19	103.12	104.05	104.98	105.91	106.84	107.77	108.70	109.63	110.55
1200	111.48	112.41	113.34	114.27	115.20	116.13	117.06	117.99	118.92	119.84
1300	120.77	121.70	122.63	123.56	124.49	125.42	126.35	127.28	128.21	129.14
1400	130.06	130.99	131.92	132.85	133.78	134.71	135.64	136.57	137.50	138.43
1500	139.35									

METRIC CONVERSION TABLES

ACRES TO HECTARES (1 ACRE = 0.404 685 6 ha)

ACRES	0	1	2	3	4	5	6	7	8	9
HECTARES	...	0.40	0.81	1.21	1.62	2.02	2.43	2.83	3.24	3.64

ACRES	0	10	20	30	40	50	60	70	80	90
					HECTARES (ha)					
0	...	4.05	8.09	12.14	16.19	20.23	24.28	28.33	32.37	36.42
100	40.47	44.52	48.56	52.61	56.66	60.70	64.75	68.80	72.84	76.89
200	80.94	84.98	89.03	93.08	97.12	101.17	105.22	109.27	113.31	117.36
300	121.41	125.45	129.50	133.55	137.59	141.64	145.69	149.73	153.78	157.83
400	161.87	165.92	169.97	174.01	178.06	182.11	186.16	190.20	194.25	198.30
500	202.34	206.39	210.44	214.48	218.53	222.58	226.62	230.67	234.72	238.76
600	242.81	246.86	250.91	254.95	259.00	263.05	267.09	271.14	275.19	279.23
700	283.28	287.33	291.37	295.42	299.47	303.51	307.56	311.61	315.65	319.70
800	323.75	327.80	331.84	335.89	339.94	343.98	348.03	352.08	356.12	360.17
900	364.22	368.26	372.31	376.36	380.40	384.45	388.50	392.55	396.59	400.64
1000	404.69									

CUBIC FEET TO CUBIC METERS (1 FT³ = 0.0283 m³)

CUBIC FEET	0	1	2	3	4	5	6	7	8	9
					CUBIC METERS (m³)					
0	...	0.028	0.057	0.085	0.113	0.142	0.170	0.198	0.227	0.255
10	0.283	0.311	0.340	0.368	0.396	0.425	0.453	0.481	0.510	0.538
20	0.566	0.595	0.623	0.651	0.680	0.708	0.736	0.765	0.793	0.821
30	0.850	0.878	0.906	0.934	0.963	0.991	0.019	1.048	1.076	1.104
40	1.133	1.161	1.189	1.218	1.246	1.274	1.303	1.331	1.359	1.386
50	1.416	1.444	1.472	1.501	1.529	1.557	1.586	1.614	1.642	1.671
60	1.699	1.727	1.756	1.784	1.812	1.841	1.869	1.897	1.926	1.954
70	1.982	2.010	2.034	2.067	2.095	2.124	2.152	2.180	2.209	2.237
80	2.265	2.293	2.322	2.350	2.379	2.407	2.435	2.464	2.492	2.520
90	2.549	2.577	2.605	2.633	2.662	2.690	2.718	2.747	2.775	2.803
100	2.832	2.860	2.888	2.917	2.945	2.973	3.002	3.030	3.058	3.087
110	3.115	3.143	3.171	3.200	3.228	3.256	3.285	3.313	3.341	3.370
120	3.398	3.426	3.455	3.483	3.511	3.540	3.568	3.596	3.625	3.653
130	3.681	3.710	3.738	3.766	3.794	3.823	3.851	3.879	3.908	3.936
140	3.964	3.993	4.021	4.049	4.078	4.106	4.134	4.163	4.191	4.219
150	4.248	4.276	4.304	4.332	4.361	4.389	4.417	4.446	4.474	4.502
160	4.531	4.559	4.587	4.616	4.644	4.672	4.701	4.729	4.757	4.786
170	4.814	4.482	4.870	4.899	4.927	4.955	4.984	5.012	5.040	5.069
180	5.097	5.125	5.154	5.182	5.210	5.239	5.267	5.295	5.234	5.352
190	5.380	5.409	5.437	5.465	5.493	5.522	5.550	5.578	5.606	5.635
200	5.663									

NOTE: 1 cubic meter (m³) equals 1000 liters (L). Cubic feet can be converted to liters by shifting the decimal point three places to the right; for example, 125 cubic feet = 3.540 m³ = 3540 L.

GALLONS TO LITERS (1 GAL [U.S.] = 3.785 41L)

GALLONS	0	1	2	3	4	5	6	7	8	9
					LITERS (L)					
0	...	3.79	7.57	11.36	15.14	18.93	22.71	26.50	30.28	34.07
10	37.85	41.64	45.42	49.21	53.00	56.78	60.57	64.35	68.14	71.92
20	75.71	79.49	83.28	87.06	90.85	94.64	98.42	102.21	105.99	109.78
30	113.56	117.35	121.13	124.92	128.70	132.49	136.27	140.06	143.85	147.63
40	151.42	155.20	158.99	162.77	166.56	170.34	174.13	177.91	181.70	185.49
50	189.27	193.06	196.84	200.63	204.41	208.20	211.98	215.77	219.55	223.34
60	227.12	230.91	234.70	238.48	242.27	246.05	249.84	253.62	257.41	261.19
70	264.98	268.76	272.55	276.34	280.12	283.91	287.69	291.48	295.26	299.05
80	302.83	306.62	310.40	314.19	317.97	321.76	325.55	329.33	333.12	336.90
90	340.69	344.47	348.26	352.04	355.83	359.61	363.40	367.18	370.97	374.76

GALLONS	0	10	20	30	40	50	60	70	80	90
100	378.5	416.4	454.2	492.1	530.0	567.8	605.7	643.5	681.4	719.2
200	757.1	794.9	832.8	870.6	908.5	946.4	984.2	1022.1	1059.9	1097.8
300	1135.6	1173.5	1211.3	1249.2	1287.0	1324.9	1362.7	1400.6	1438.5	1476.3
400	1514.2	1552.0	1589.9	1627.7	1665.6	1703.4	1741.3	1779.1	1817.0	1854.9
500	1892.7	1930.6	1968.4	2006.3	2044.1	2082.0	2119.8	2157.7	2195.5	2233.4
600	2271.2	2309.1	2347.0	2384.8	2422.7	2460.5	2498.4	2536.2	2574.1	2611.9
700	2649.8	2687.6	2725.5	2763.4	2801.2	2839.1	2876.9	2914.8	2952.6	2990.5
800	3028.3	3066.3	3104.0	3141.9	3179.7	3217.6	3255.5	3293.3	3331.2	3369.0
900	3406.9	3444.7	3482.6	3520.4	3558.3	3596.1	3634.0	3671.8	3709.7	3747.6
1000	3785.4									

POUNDS TO KILOGRAMS (1 LB = 0.453 592 kg)

POUNDS	0	1	2	3	4	5	6	7	8	9
					KILOGRAMS (kg)					
0	...	0.45	0.91	1.36	1.81	2.27	2.72	3.18	3.63	4.08
10	4.54	4.99	5.44	5.90	6.35	6.80	7.26	7.71	8.16	8.62
20	9.07	9.53	9.98	10.43	10.89	11.34	11.79	12.25	12.70	13.15
30	13.61	14.06	14.52	14.97	15.42	15.88	16.33	16.78	17.24	17.69
40	18.14	18.60	19.05	19.50	19.96	20.41	20.87	21.32	21.77	22.23
50	22.68	23.13	23.59	24.04	24.49	24.95	25.40	25.85	26.31	26.76
60	27.22	27.67	28.12	28.58	29.03	29.48	29.94	30.39	30.84	31.30
70	31.75	32.21	32.66	33.11	33.57	34.02	34.47	34.93	35.38	35.83
80	36.29	36.74	37.19	37.65	38.10	38.56	39.01	39.46	39.92	40.37
90	40.82	41.28	41.73	42.18	42.64	43.09	43.54	44.00	44.45	44.91
100	45.36	45.81	46.27	46.72	47.17	47.63	48.08	48.53	48.99	49.44
110	49.90	50.35	50.80	51.26	51.71	52.16	52.62	53.07	53.52	53.98
120	54.43	54.88	55.34	55.79	56.25	56.70	57.15	57.61	58.06	58.51
130	58.97	59.42	59.87	60.33	60.78	61.24	61.69	62.14	62.60	63.05
140	63.50	63.96	64.41	64.86	65.32	65.77	66.22	66.68	67.13	67.59
150	68.04	68.49	68.95	69.40	69.85	70.31	70.76	71.21	71.67	72.12
160	72.57	73.03	73.48	73.94	74.39	74.84	75.30	75.75	76.20	76.66
170	77.11	77.56	78.02	78.47	78.93	79.38	79.83	80.29	80.74	81.19
180	81.65	82.10	82.55	83.01	83.46	83.91	84.37	84.82	85.28	85.73
190	86.18	86.64	87.09	87.54	88.00	88.45	88.90	89.36	89.81	90.26
200	90.72									

U.S. SHORT TONS (2000 LB) TO METRIC TONS (1 TON = 0.907 185 t)

SHORT TONS	0	1	2	3	4	5	6	7	8	9
					METRIC TONS (t)					
0	...	0.907	1.814	2.722	3.629	4.536	5.443	6.350	7.257	8.165
10	9.072	9.979	10.886	11.793	12.701	13.608	14.515	15.422	16.329	17.237
20	18.144	19.051	19.958	20.865	21.772	22.680	23.587	24.494	25.401	26.308
30	27.216	28.123	29.030	29.937	30.844	31.751	32.659	33.566	34.473	35.380
40	36.287	37.195	38.102	39.009	39.916	40.823	41.731	42.638	43.545	44.452
50	45.359	46.266	47.174	48.081	48.988	49.895	50.802	51.710	52.617	53.524
60	54.431	55.338	56.245	57.153	58.060	58.967	59.874	60.781	61.689	62.596
70	63.503	64.410	65.317	66.225	67.132	68.039	68.946	69.853	70.760	71.668
80	72.575	73.482	74.389	75.296	76.204	77.111	78.018	78.925	79.832	80.739
90	81.647	82.554	83.461	84.368	85.275	86.183	87.090	87.997	88.904	89.811
100	90.718									

NOTE: 1 metric ton (t) equals 1000 kilograms (kg). U.S. short tons can be converted to kilograms by shifting the decimal point three places to the right; for example, 48 short tons = 43.545 t = 43.545 kg (rounded to the nearest kilogram).

POUNDS PER CUBIC FOOT TO KILOGRAMS PER CUBIC METER (1 LB/FT^3 = 16.018 46 kg/m^3)

POUNDS PER CUBIC FOOT	0	1	2	3	4	5	6	7	8	9
					KILOGRAMS PER CUBIC METER (kg/m^3)					
0	...	16.0	32.0	48.1	64.1	80.1	96.1	112.1	128.1	144.2
10	160.2	176.2	192.2	208.2	224.3	240.3	256.3	272.3	288.3	304.4
20	320.4	336.4	352.4	368.4	384.4	400.5	416.5	432.5	448.5	464.5
30	480.6	496.6	512.6	528.6	544.6	560.6	576.7	592.7	608.7	624.7
40	640.7	656.8	672.8	688.8	704.8	720.8	736.8	752.9	768.9	784.9
50	800.9	816.9	833.0	849.0	865.0	881.0	897.0	913.1	929.1	945.1
60	961.1	977.1	993.1	1009.2	1025.2	1041.2	1057.2	1073.2	1089.3	1105.3
70	1121.3	1137.3	1153.3	1169.3	1185.4	1201.4	1217.4	1233.4	1249.4	1265.5
80	1281.5	1297.5	1313.5	1329.5	1345.6	1361.6	1377.6	1393.6	1409.6	1425.6
90	1441.7	1457.7	1473.7	1489.7	1505.7	1521.8	1537.8	1553.8	1569.8	1585.8
100	1601.8	1617.9	1633.9	1649.9	1665.9	1681.9	1698.0	1714.0	1730.0	1746.0
110	1762.0	1778.0	1794.1	1810.1	1826.1	1842.1	1858.1	1874.2	1890.2	1906.2
120	1922.2	1938.2	1954.3	1970.3	1986.3	2002.3	2018.3	2034.3	2050.4	2066.4
130	2082.4	2098.4	2114.4	2130.5	2146.5	2162.5	2178.5	2194.5	2210.5	2226.6
140	2242.6	2258.6	2274.6	2290.6	2306.7	2322.7	2338.7	2354.7	2370.7	2386.8
150	2402.8	2418.8	2434.8	2450.8	2466.8	2482.9	2498.9	2514.9	2590.9	2546.9
160	2563.0	2579.0	2595.0	2611.0	2627.0	2643.0	2659.1	2675.1	2691.1	2707.1
170	2723.1	2739.2	2755.2	2771.2	2787.2	2803.2	2819.2	2835.3	2851.3	2867.3
180	2883.3	2899.3	2915.4	2931.4	2947.4	2963.4	2979.4	2995.4	3011.5	3027.5
190	3043.5	3059.5	3075.5	3091.6	3107.6	3123.6	3139.6	3155.6	3171.7	3187.7
200	3203.7									

POUNDS-FORCE PER SQUARE INCH (PSI) TO MEGAPASCALS (MPa) (1 PSI = 0.006 895 MPa)

POUNDS-FORCE PER SQUARE INCH	0	10	20	30	40	50	60	70	80	90
	MEGAPASCALS (MPa)									
0	...	0.069	0.138	0.207	0.276	0.345	0.414	0.483	0.552	0.621
100	0.689	0.758	0.827	0.896	0.965	1.034	1.103	1.172	1.241	1.310
200	1.379	1.448	1.517	1.586	1.655	1.724	1.793	1.862	1.931	1.999
300	2.068	2.137	2.206	2.275	2.344	2.413	2.482	2.551	2.620	2.689
400	2.758	2.827	2.896	2.965	3.034	3.103	3.172	3.241	3.309	3.378
500	3.447	3.516	3.585	3.654	3.723	3.792	3.861	3.903	3.999	4.068
600	4.137	4.206	4.275	4.344	4.413	4.482	4.551	4.619	4.688	4.757
700	4.826	4.895	4.964	5.033	5.102	5.171	5.240	5.309	5.378	5.447
800	5.516	5.585	5.654	5.723	5.792	5.861	5.929	5.998	6.067	6.136
900	6.205	6.274	6.343	6.412	6.481	6.550	6.619	6.688	6.757	6.826
	0	100	200	300	400	500	600	700	800	900
1000	6.895	7.584	8.274	8.963	9.653	10.342	11.032	11.721	12.411	13.100
2000	13.790	14.479	15.168	15.858	16.547	17.237	17.926	18.616	19.305	19.995
3000	20.684	21.374	22.063	22.753	23.442	24.132	24.821	25.511	26.200	26.890
4000	27.579	28.269	28.958	29.647	30.337	31.026	31.716	32.405	33.095	33.784
5000	34.474	35.163	35.853	36.542	37.232	37.921	38.611	39.300	39.990	40.679
6000	41.369	42.058	42.747	43.437	44.126	44.816	45.505	46.195	46.884	47.574
7000	48.263	48.953	49.642	50.332	51.021	51.711	52.400	53.090	53.779	54.469
8000	55.158	55.848	56.537	57.226	57.916	58.605	59.295	59.984	60.674	61.363
9000	62.053	62.742	63.432	64.121	64.811	65.500	66.190	66.879	67.569	68.258
10 000	68.948									

NOTE: 1 megapascal (MPa) is equal to 1 meganewton per square meter (MN/m^2) and to 1 newton per square millimeter (N/mm^2).

POUNDS-FORCE PER SQUARE FOOT TO KILOPASCALS (kPa) = 0.047 88 kN/m^2

POUNDS-FORCE PER SQUARE FOOT	0	10	20	30	40	50	60	70	80	90
	KILOPASCALS (kPa = kN/m^2)									
0	—	0.479	0.958	1.436	1.915	2.394	2.873	3.352	3.830	4.309
100	4.788	5.267	5.746	6.224	6.703	7.182	7.661	8.140	8.618	9.097
200	9.576	10.055	10.534	11.013	11.491	11.970	12.449	12.928	13.406	13.886
300	14.364	14.843	15.322	15.800	16.279	16.758	17.237	17.716	18.195	18.673
400	19.152	19.631	20.110	20.589	21.067	21.546	22.025	22.504	22.983	23.461
500	23.910	24.419	24.898	25.377	25.855	26.334	26.813	27.292	27.771	28.249
600	28.728	29.207	29.686	30.165	30.643	31.122	31.601	32.080	32.559	33.037
700	33.516	33.995	34.474	34.953	35.431	35.910	36.389	36.868	37.347	37.825
800	38.304	38.783	39.262	39.741	40.219	40.698	41.177	41.656	42.135	42.613
900	43.092	43.571	44.050	44.529	45.007	45.486	45.965	46.444	46.923	47.401
1000	47.880									

NOTE: 1 kilopascal (kPa) is equal to 1 kilonewton per square meter (kN/m^2).

LUMENS PER SQUARE FOOT TO LUX (lm/m^2) AND KILOLUX (1 lm/FT^2 = 10.7639 lx)

LUMENS PER SQUARE FOOT	0	1	2	3	4	5	6	7	8	9
	LUX (lm/m^2)									
0	...	10.8	21.5	32.3	43.1	53.8	64.6	75.3	86.1	96.9
10	107.6	118.4	129.2	139.9	150.7	161.5	172.2	183.0	193.8	204.5
20	215.3	226.0	236.8	247.6	258.3	269.1	279.9	290.6	301.4	312.2
30	322.9	333.7	344.4	355.2	366.0	376.7	387.5	398.3	409.0	419.8
40	430.6	441.3	452.1	462.8	473.6	484.4	495.1	505.9	516.7	527.4
50	538.2	549.0	559.7	570.5	581.3	592.0	602.8	613.5	624.3	635.1
60	645.8	656.6	667.4	678.1	688.9	699.7	710.4	721.2	731.9	742.7
70	753.5	764.2	775.0	785.8	796.5	807.3	818.1	828.8	839.6	850.3
80	861.1	871.9	882.6	893.4	904.2	914.9	925.7	936.5	947.2	958.0
90	968.8	979.5	990.3	1001.0	1011.8	1022.6	1033.3	1044.1	1054.9	1065.6
	0	10	20	30	40	50	60	70	80	90
	KILOLUX (1000 lux)									
100	1.076	1.184	1.292	1.399	1.507	1.615	1.722	1.830	1.938	2.045
200	2.153	2.260	2.368	2.476	2.583	2.691	2.799	2.906	3.014	3.122
300	3.229	3.337	3.444	3.552	3.660	3.767	3.875	3.983	4.090	4.198
400	4.306	4.413	4.521	4.628	4.736	4.844	4.951	5.059	5.167	5.274
500	5.382	5.490	5.597	5.705	5.813	5.920	6.028	6.135	6.243	6.351
600	6.458	6.566	6.674	6.781	6.889	6.997	7.104	7.212	7.319	7.427
700	7.535	7.642	7.750	7.858	7.965	8.073	8.181	8.288	8.396	8.503
800	8.611	8.719	8.826	8.934	9.042	9.149	9.257	9.365	9.472	9.580
900	9.688	9.795	9.903	10.010	10.118	10.226	10.333	10.441	10.549	10.656
1000	10.764									

POUND-FORCE TO NEWTONS (1 lbf = 4.448 22 N)

POUND-FORCE	0	1	2	3	4	5	6	7	8	9
					NEWTONS (N)					
0	...	4.45	8.90	13.34	17.79	22.24	26.69	31.14	35.59	40.03
10	44.48	48.93	53.38	57.83	62.28	66.72	71.17	75.62	80.07	84.52
20	88.96	93.41	97.86	102.31	106.76	111.21	115.65	120.10	124.55	129.00
30	133.45	137.89	142.34	146.79	151.24	155.69	160.14	164.58	169.03	173.48
40	177.93	182.38	186.83	191.27	195.72	200.17	204.62	209.07	213.51	217.96
50	222.41	226.86	231.31	235.76	240.20	244.65	249.10	253.55	258.00	262.45
60	266.89	271.34	275.79	280.24	284.69	289.13	293.58	298.03	302.48	306.93
70	311.38	315.82	320.27	324.72	329.17	333.62	338.06	342.51	346.96	351.41
80	355.86	360.31	364.75	369.20	373.65	378.10	382.55	387.00	391.44	395.89
90	400.34	404.79	409.24	413.68	418.13	422.58	427.03	431.48	435.93	440.37

	0	10	20	30	40	50	60	70	80	90
100	444.8	489.3	533.8	578.3	622.8	667.2	711.7	756.2	800.7	845.2
200	889.6	934.1	978.6	1023.1	1067.6	1112.1	1156.5	1201.0	1245.5	1290.0
300	1334.5	1378.9	1423.4	1467.9	1512.4	1556.9	1601.4	1645.8	1690.3	1734.8
400	1779.3	1823.8	1868.3	1912.7	1957.2	2001.7	2046.2	2090.7	2135.1	2179.6
500	2224.1	2268.6	2313.1	2357.6	2402.0	2446.5	2491.0	2535.5	2580.0	2624.5
600	2668.9	2713.4	2757.9	2802.4	2846.9	2891.3	2935.8	2980.3	3024.8	3069.3
700	3113.8	3158.2	3202.7	3247.2	3291.7	3336.2	3380.6	3425.1	3469.6	3514.1
800	3558.6	3603.1	3647.5	3692.0	3736.5	3781.0	3835.5	3870.0	3914.4	3958.9
900	4003.4	4047.9	4092.4	4136.8	4181.3	4225.8	4270.3	4314.8	4359.3	4403.7
1000	4448.2	4492.7	4537.2	4581.7	4626.1	4670.6	4715.1	4759.6	4804.1	4848.6
1100	4893.0	4937.5	4982.0	5026.5	5071.0	5115.5	5159.9	5204.4	5248.9	5293.4
1200	5337.9	5382.3	5426.8	5471.3	5515.8	5560.3	5604.8	5649.2	5693.7	5738.2
1300	5782.7	5827.2	5871.7	5916.1	5960.6	6005.1	6049.6	6094.1	6138.5	6183.0
1400	6227.5	6272.0	6316.5	6361.0	6405.4	6449.9	6494.4	6538.9	6583.4	6627.8
1500	6672.3	6716.8	6761.3	6805.8	6850.3	6894.7	6939.2	6983.7	7028.2	7072.7
1600	7117.2	7161.6	7206.1	7250.6	7295.1	7339.6	7384.0	7428.5	7473.0	7517.5
1700	7562.0	7606.5	7650.9	7695.4	7739.9	7784.4	7828.9	7873.3	7917.8	7962.3
1800	8006.0	8051.3	8095.8	8140.2	8184.7	8229.2	8273.7	8318.2	8362.7	8407.1
1900	8451.6	8496.1	8540.6	8585.1	8629.5	8674.0	8718.5	8763.0	8807.5	8852.0
2000	8896.4									

NOTE: 1000 newtons (N) equal 1 kilonewton (1kN). The lower portion of the table could also have been shown in kilonewtons; for example, 4893.0 N = 4.8930 kN. The table can also be used for the conversion of kips (1000 lbf) to kilonewtons (kN), since a multiplier of 1000 applies to both measurements units.

METRIC CONVERSION TABLES   17

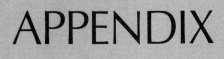

APPENDIX

GENERAL

Life cycle costing (LCC) is a method for evaluating all relevant costs over time of alternative building designs, systems, components, materials, or practices. The LCC method takes into account first costs, including the costs of planning, design, purchase, and installation; future costs, including costs of fuel, operation, maintenance, repair, and replacement; and any salvage value recovered during or at the end of the time period examined. These costs are displayed in the adjacent charts.

TIME ADJUSTMENTS

Adjustments to place all dollar values on a comparable time basis are necessary for valid assessment of a project's life cycle costs. The time adjustment is necessary because receiving or expending a dollar in the future is not the same as receiving or expending a dollar today. One reason for this "time value of money" is that the purchasing power of money may fall over time because of inflation. To ensure that all of a building's costs are expressed in dollars of equal purchasing power, they should be stated in "constant dollars," that is, with purely inflationary effects not included. Another reason for the "time value of money" is that money in hand may be invested productively to earn a return over time. Both inflation and the productive earning potential of resources in hand cause an investor usually to prefer to delay payments of costs or debts and to hasten receipts. The adjustment for time related earning potential can be accomplished by converting all costs to "present values," as though they were all to be incurred today, or to "annual values," as though they were all spread out over a given time in even, annual installments including the cost of money. This time adjustment, often called "discounting cash flows," is accomplished by using "discount formulas" or by multiplying dollar amounts by special "discount factors" calculated from the formulas. The most frequently used discount formulas for evaluating building projects are described below, where the following notation is used:

P = present value
F = future value
A = annual value
D = discount rate
N = number of periods
E = price escalation rate

SINGLE PRESENT WORTH

The single present worth (SPW) formula is used to find the present value of a future amount, such as the value today of a future replacement cost.

SPW (single present worth) $P = F(1 + D)^{-N}$

Time ⟶

UNIFORM PRESENT WORTH

The uniform present worth (UPW) formula is used to find the present value of a series of uniform annual amounts, such as the value today of the costs of future yearly routine maintenance.

UPW (uniform present worth) $P = A\left[\dfrac{(1 + D)^N - 1}{D(1 + D)^N}\right]$

Time ⟶

UNIFORM PRESENT WORTH—MODIFIED

A modified version of the uniform present worth formula (here designated UPW*) is used to find the present value of an initial amount escalating at a constant annual rate, such as the value today of future yearly energy costs, when energy prices are expected to escalate at a given rate.

UPW* (uniform present worth—modified)

$$P = A\left[\left[\frac{1 + E}{D - E}\right]\left[1 - \left[\frac{1 + E}{1 + D}\right]^N\right]\right]$$

UNIFORM SINKING FUND

The uniform sinking fund (USF) formula is used to find the annual amount that must be accumulated to yield a given future amount, such as how much money must be set aside each year at interest in order to cover expected future replacement costs.

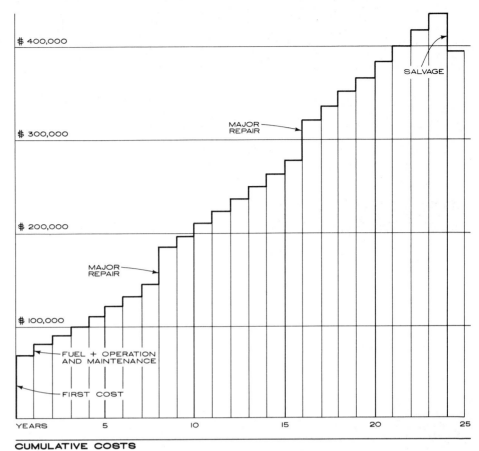

$400,000

SALVAGE

$300,000

MAJOR REPAIR

$200,000

MAJOR REPAIR

$100,000

FUEL + OPERATION AND MAINTENANCE

FIRST COST

YEARS 5 10 15 20 25

CUMULATIVE COSTS

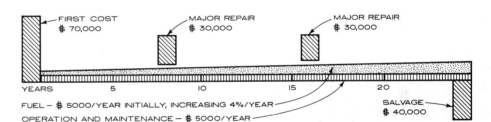

FIRST COST $70,000   MAJOR REPAIR $30,000   MAJOR REPAIR $30,000

YEARS 5 10 15 20

FUEL – $5000/YEAR INITIALLY, INCREASING 4%/YEAR

OPERATION AND MAINTENANCE – $5000/YEAR

SALVAGE $40,000

YEARLY COSTS

USF (uniform sinking fund) $A = F\left[\dfrac{D}{(1 + D)^N - 1}\right]$

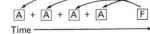
Time ⟶

UNIFORM CAPITAL RECOVERY

The uniform capital recovery (UCR) formula is used to find the annual value of a present value amount, such as how much it would be necessary to pay each year in order to pay off a loan made today at a given rate of interest for a given period of time.

UCR (uniform capital recovery) $A = P\left[\dfrac{D(1 + D)^N}{(1 + D)^N - 1}\right]$

Time ⟶

NOTE

The discount factors for each of these discounting formulas have been precalculated for a range of discount rates and time periods and put into tables to facilitate their use. These tables can be found in most engineering economics textbooks. A table of discount factors for a 10% discount rate is shown opposite.

LIFE CYCLE COST FORMULA

To find the total life cycle cost of a project, sum the present values (or, alternatively, the annual values) of each kind of cost and subtract the present values (or annual values) of any positive cash flows such as salvage values. Thus, where all dollar amounts are adjusted by discounting either present values or annual values, the following formula applies:

LCC (life cycle cost formula)

Life cycle cost = first costs + maintenance and repair
+ energy + replacement – salvage value

APPLICATIONS

Alternative projects may be compared by computing the life cycle costs for each project using the formula above and seeing which is lower.

The LCC method can be applied to many different kinds of building problems. For example, it can be used to compare the long run costs of one building design to another; to determine the expected dollar savings of retrofitting a building for energy conservation or the least expensive way of reaching a targeted energy budget for a building; to select the most economical floor coverings and furnishings; and to determine the optimal size of a solar energy system.

In addition to the life cycle formula shown above, there are other closely related ways of combining present or annual values to measure a project's economic performance over time, such as the net savings technique, savings-to-investment ratio technique, internal rate of return technique, and discounted time to payback technique.

Harold E. Marshall and Rosalie Ruegg, Economists; Porter Driscoll, AIA, Architect; Center for Building Technology, National Bureau of Standards; United States of America

ECONOMIC FACTORS A

SAMPLE LCC PROBLEM

Determine present value of costs occurring during the life of a component so that they can be compared with the costs of an alternative component to serve the same purpose. Cumulative and yearly costs are indicated on the charts of the preceding page.

ASSUMPTIONS

Time horizon	25 years
Discount rate	10%
Fuel price increases in excess of inflation	4%
First cost of component	$70,000
Repairs to component at 8th and 16th years	$30,000/repair
Operations and maintenance (constant dollars)	$ 5,000/year
Annual cost of fuel at onset	$ 5,000

NOTE: When financing costs and tax effects are relevant they should be incorporated into LCC analysis.

SOLUTION

1. Establish present value of equipment. Convert all equipment costs (first cost, two major repair costs, and salvage value) to present value. Since the first cost occurs in the present, no change is made to the $70,000 sum.

   The first major repair, estimated to occur 8 years in the future, is discounted at the rate of 10% back to the present using the SPW factor (see Discount Factor Chart, column 2) for 8 years at 10%, 0.4665. Therefore, PV = $30,000 x 0.4665 = $13,995. This present value is added to the $70,000 first cost as shown in the Present Value of Equipment Chart.

   The second major repair is discounted 16 years back to the present in a similar manner. The SPW factor for 16 years at 10% = 0.2176. Therefore, PV = $30,000 x 0.2176 = $6528. This amount is also added to the present value in the chart.

   The $40,000 to be realized from salvage at the end of the 25 year period is discounted back to the present in the same manner. The SPW factor for 25 years, at 10% = 0.0923. Therefore, PV = $40,000 x 0.0923 = $3692. Since this sum is income, not expense, it must be subtracted from the sum of the other present values as indicated.

   Thus the present value of equipment is determined to be $86,832.

2. Establish present value of operation and maintenance costs and fuel costs. Operation and maintenance costs are estimated to be equal amounts that occur yearly during the period and are converted to present value using the UPW factor (column 3) for 25 years at 10%, 9.0770. Therefore, PV = $5000 x 9.0770 = $45,385. This amount is added to the present value of equipment as shown in the Total Present Value Chart.

   Annual fuel costs are estimated to be $5000 based on the initial price of fuel which is projected to increase at the rate of 4% per year. These costs are converted to present value using the modified UPW* factor (column 4) for 25 years at 10%, 13.0686. Therefore, PV = $5000 x 13.0686 = $65,343.

   This amount is also added to the present values of equipment and operation and maintenance costs as shown in the Total Present Value Chart.

3. Total life cycle cost in present value is the sum of the present value of equipment, operation, and maintenance and fuel costs which equals $197,559. The equipment, operation, and maintenance and fuel costs of other components to serve the same purpose can be compared to these figures to determine the best economic value.

REFERENCES

1. Gerald W. Smith, Engineering Economy: Analysis of Capital Expenditures, Iowa State University Press, Ames, Iowa, 1973.
2. Donald Watson, ed., Energy Conservation through Building Design, "Life-cycle Costing Guide for Energy Conservation in Buildings" chapter by Harold E. Marshall and Rosalie T. Ruegg, McGraw-Hill, New York, 1979.
3. Simplified Energy Design Economics, NBS special publication 544, Center for Building Technology, National Bureau of Standards, Washington, D.C., 1980.

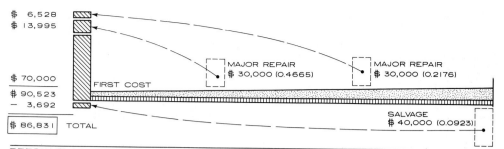

$ 6,528
$ 13,995

$ 70,000
$ 90,523
— 3,692

$ 86,831   TOTAL

PRESENT VALUE OF EQUIPMENT

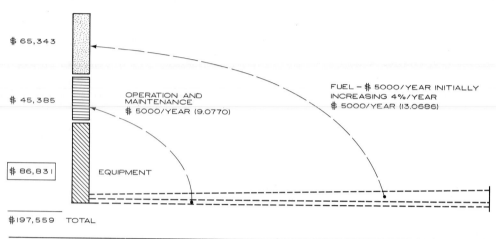

$ 65,343

$ 45,385

$ 86,831   EQUIPMENT

$197,559   TOTAL

TOTAL PRESENT VALUE

DISCOUNT FACTORS

BASED ON 10% DISCOUNT RATE

1. YEARS	2. SPW	3. UPW	4. UPW* (4% PRICE ESCALATION)	5. USF	6. UCR
1	0.9091	0.909	0.9455	1.000 00	1.100 00
2	0.8264	1.736	1.8393	0.476 19	0.576 19
3	0.7513	2.487	2.6844	0.302 11	0.402 11
4	0.6830	3.170	3.4834	0.215 47	0.315 47
5	0.6209	3.791	4.2388	0.163 80	0.263 80
6	0.5645	4.355	4.9531	0.129 61	0.229 61
7	0.5132	4.868	5.6284	0.105 41	0.205 41
8	0.4665	5.335	6.2669	0.087 44	0.187 44
9	0.4241	5.759	6.8705	0.073 64	0.173 64
10	0.3855	6.144	7.4411	0.062 75	0.162 75
11	0.3505	6.495	7.9807	0.053 96	0.153 96
12	0.3186	6.814	8.4909	0.046 76	0.146 76
13	0.2897	7.103	8.9733	0.040 78	0.140 78
14	0.2633	7.367	9.4293	0.035 75	0.135 75
15	0.2394	7.606	9.8604	0.031 47	0.131 47
16	0.2176	7.824	10.2680	0.027 82	0.127 82
17	0.1978	8.022	10.6535	0.024 66	0.124 66
18	0.1799	8.201	11.0177	0.021 93	0.121 93
19	0.1635	8.365	11.3622	0.019 55	0.119 55
20	0.1486	8.514	11.6878	0.017 46	0.117 46
21	0.1351	8.649	11.9957	0.015 62	0.115 62
22	0.1228	8.772	12.2870	0.014 01	0.144 01
23	0.1117	8.883	12.5623	0.012 57	0.112 57
24	0.1015	8.985	12.8225	0.011 30	0.111 30
25	0.0923	9.077	13.0686	0.010 17	0.110 17

Harold E. Marshall and Rosalie Ruegg, Economists; Porter Driscoll, AIA, Architect; Center for Building Technology; National Bureau of Standards; United States of America

 ECONOMIC FACTORS

MINIMUM UNIFORMLY DISTRIBUTED LIVE LOADS

OCCUPANCY OR USE	LIVE LOAD (PSF)
Armories and drill rooms	150
Assembly halls and other places of assembly	
Fixed seats	60
Movable seats	100
Platforms (assembly)	100
Attics	
Nonstorage	25
Storage	80*
Bakeries	150
Balconies	
Exterior	100
Interior (fixed seats)	60
Interior (movable seats)	100
Bowling alleys, poolrooms, and similar recreational areas	75
Broadcasting studios	100
Catwalks	25
Cold storage rooms	
Floor	150
Roof	250
Corridors	
First floor	100
Other floors, same as occupancy served except as indicated	
Dance halls and ballrooms	100
Dining rooms and restaurants	100
Dormitories	
Nonpartitioned	80
Partitioned	40
File rooms	
Card	125*
Letter	80*
Fire escapes on multifamily or single family residential buildings only	100
Foundries	600†
Fuel rooms, framed	400†
Garages (passenger cars only). For trucks and buses use AASHO‡ lane load	50
Grandstands	100
Greenhouses	150
Gymnasiums, main floors and balconies	100
Hospitals	
Operating rooms, laboratories	60
Private rooms	40
Wards	40
Corridors, above first floor	80
Hotels (see Residential)	—
Kitchens, other than domestic	150†
Laboratories, scientific	100
Laundries	150†
Libraries	
Reading rooms	60
Stack rooms (books and shelving at 65 pcf) but not less than	150
Corridors, above first floor	80
Manufacturing	
Light	125
Heavy	250
Ice	300
Marquees	75
Morgues	125
Office buildings	
Office	50
Business machine equipment	100†
Lobbies	100
Corridors, above the first floor	80
File and computer rooms require heavier loads based on anticipated occupancy	
Penal institutions	
Cell blocks	40
Corridors	100
Printing plants	
Composing rooms	100
Linotype rooms	100

David H. Holbert; Hansen Lind Meyer, P.C.; Iowa City, Iowa

Paper storage rooms	§
Pressrooms	150†
Public rooms	100
Residential	
Multifamily houses	
Private apartments	40
Public rooms	100
Corridors	80
Dwellings	
First floor	40
Second floor and habitable attics	30
Uninhabitable attics	20
Hotels	
Guest rooms	40
Public rooms	100
Corridors serving public rooms	100
Rest rooms and toilet rooms	60
Schools	
Classrooms	40
Corridors	80
Sidewalks, vehicular driveways, and yards subject to trucking	250
Skating rinks	100
Stairs and exitways	100
Storage warehouses	
Light	125
Heavy	250
Hay or grain	300
Stores	
Retail	
First floor, rooms	100
Upper floors	75
Wholesale	125
Telephone exchange rooms	150†
Theaters	
Aisles, corridors, and lobbies	100
Orchestra floors	60
Balconies	60
Stage floors	
Dressing rooms	40
Grid iron floor or fly gallery grating	60
Projection room	100
Transformer rooms	200†
Vaults, in offices	250*
Yards and terraces, pedestrians	100

*Increase when occupancy exceeds this amount.
†Use weight of actual equipment when greater.
‡American Association of State Highway Officials.
§Paper storage 50 lb/ft of clear story height.

LIVE LOAD

Live load is the weight superimposed by the use and occupancy of the building or other structure, not including the wind load, snow load, earthquake load, or dead load.

The live loads to be assumed in the design of buildings and other structures shall be the greatest loads that probably will be produced by the intended use or occupancy, but in no case less than the minimum uniformly distributed unit load.

THRUSTS AND HANDRAILS

Stairway and balcony railings, both exterior and interior, shall be designed to resist a vertical and a horizontal thrust of 50 lb/linear ft applied at the top of the railing.

CONCENTRATED LOADS

Floors shall be designed to support safely the uniformly distributed live load or the concentrated load in pounds given, whichever produces the greater stresses. Unless otherwise specified, the indicated concentration shall be assumed to occupy an area of $2\frac{1}{2}$ sq ft and shall be so located as to produce the maximum stress conditions in the structural members.

PARTIAL LOADING

The full intensity of the appropriately reduced live loads applied only to a portion of the length of a structure or member shall be considered if it produces a more unfavorable effect than the same intensity applied over the full length of the structure or member.

IMPACT LOADS

The live loads shall be assumed to include adequate allowance for ordinary impact conditions. Provision shall be made in structural design for uses and loads that involve unusual vibration and impact forces.

1. ELEVATORS: All moving elevator loads shall be increased 100% for impact, and the structural supports shall be designed within limits of deflection prescribed by American National Standard Safety Code for Elevators, Dumbwaiters, Escalators, and Moving Walks, A17.1-1971, and American National Standard Practice for the Inspection of Elevators (Inspector's Manual) A17.2-1960.

2. MACHINERY: For the purpose of design, the weight of machinery and moving loads shall be increased as follows to allow for impact: (a) elevator machinery, 100%; (b) light machinery, shaft or motor driven, 20%; (c) reciprocating machinery or power driven units, 50%; (d) hangers for floor or balconies, 33%. All percentages to be increased if so recommended by the manufacturer.

3. CRANEWAYS: All craneways shall have their design loads increased for impact as follows: (a) a vertical force equal to 25% of the maximum wheel load; (b) a lateral force equal to 20% of the weight of trolley and lifted load only, applied one-half at the top of each rail; and (c) a longitudinal force of 10% of the maximum wheel loads of the crane applied at top of rail.

MINIMUM ROOF LOADS

1. FLAT, PITCHED, OR CURVED ROOFS: Ordinary roofs—flat, pitched, or curved—shall be designed for the live loads or the snow load, whichever produces the greater stresses.

2. PONDING: For roofs, care shall be taken to provide drainage or the load shall be increased to represent all likely accumulations of water. Deflection of roof members will permit ponding of water accompanied by increased deflection and additional ponding.

3. SPECIAL PURPOSE ROOFS: When used for incidental promenade purposes, roofs shall be designed for a minimum live load of 60 psf; 100 psf when designed for roof garden or assembly uses. Roofs to be used for other special purposes shall be designed for appropriate loads, as directed or approved by the building official.

LIVE LOAD REDUCTION

In general, design live loads not in excess of 100 psf on any member supporting an area of 150 sq ft or more, except for places of public assembly, repair garages, parking structures, and roofs; may be reduced at a rate of 0.08%/sq ft supported by that member. The reduction shall not exceed the value of R from the following formula:

$$R = 23\left(\frac{1+D}{L}\right)$$

where R = reduction (%)
D = dead load per square foot of area supported by the member
L = live load per square foot of area supported by the member

In no case should the reduction exceed 60% for vertical members, nor 40 to 60% for horizontal members.

For live loads in excess of 100 psf, some codes allow a live load reduction of 20% for columns only.

CODES AND STANDARDS

The applicable building code should be referred to for specific uniformly distributed live load, movable partition load, special, and concentrated load requirements.

In addition to the specific code requirements, the designer must consider the effects of special loading conditions, such as moving loads, construction loads, roof top planting loads, and concentrated loads from supported or hanging equipment (radiology, computer, heavy filing, or mechanical equipment).

The live loads given in this table are obtained by reference to ANSI A58.1-1972.

STANDARDS

ARCHITECTURAL AREA OF BUILDINGS

The architectural area of a building is the sum of the areas of the floors, measured horizontally in plan to the exterior faces of perimeter walls or to the centerline of walls separating buildings. Included are areas occupied by partitions, columns, stairwells, elevator shafts, duct shafts, elevator rooms, pipe spaces, mechanical penthouses, and similar spaces having a headroom of 6 ft and over. Areas of sloping surfaces, such as staircases, bleachers, and tiered terraces, should be measured horizontally in plan. Auditoriums, swimming pools, gymnasiums, foyers, and similar spaces extending through two or more floors should be measured once only, taking the largest area in plan at any level.

Mechanical penthouse rooms, pipe spaces, bulkheads, and similar spaces having a headroom less than 6 ft and balconies projecting beyond exterior walls, covered terraces and walkways, porches, and similar spaces shall have the architectural area multiplied by 0.50 in calculating the building gross area.

Exterior staircases and fire escapes, exterior steps, patios, terraces, open courtyards and lightwells, roof overhangs, cornices and chimneys, unfinished roof and attic areas, pipe trenches, and similar spaces are excluded from the architectural area calculations. Interstitial space in health care facilities is also excluded.

ARCHITECTURAL VOLUME OF BUILDINGS

The architectural volume of a building is the sum of the products of the areas defined in the architectural area times the height from the underside of the lowest floor construction to the average height of the surface of the finished roof above, for the various parts of the building. Included in the architectural volume is the actual space enclosed within the outer surfaces of the exterior or outer walls and contained between the outside of the roof and the bottom of the lowest floor, taken in full: bays, oriels, dormers; penthouses, chimneys; walk tunnels; enclosed porches and balconies, including screened areas.

The following volumes are multiplied by 0.50 in calculating the architectural volume of a building; nonenclosed porches, if recessed into the building and without enclosing sash or screens; nonenclosed porches built as an extension to the building and without sash or screen; areaways and pipe tunnels; and patio areas that have building walls extended on two sides, roof over, and paved surfacing.

Excluded from the architectural volume are outside steps, terraces, courts, garden walls; light shafts, parapets, cornices, roof overhangs; footings, deep foundations, piling cassions, special foundations, and similar features.

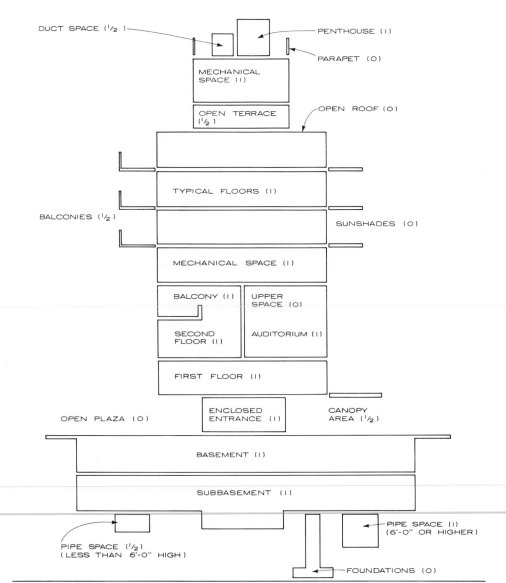

ARCHITECTURAL AREA DIAGRAM

NET ASSIGNABLE AREA

The net assignable area is that portion of the area which is available for assignment to an occupant, including every type of space usable by the occupant.

The net assignable area should be measured from the predominant inside finish of enclosing walls in the categories defined below. Areas occupied by exterior walls, partitions, internal structural, or party walls are to be excluded from the groups and are to be included under "construction area."

1. "NET ASSIGNABLE AREA": Total area of all enclosed spaces fulfilling the main functional requirements of the building for occupant use, including custodial and service areas such as guard rooms, workshops, locker rooms, janitors' closets, storerooms, and the total area of all toilet and washroom facilities.

2. "CIRCULATION AREA": Total area of all enclosed spaces which is required for physical access to subdivisions of space such as corridors, elevator shafts, escalators, fire towers or stairs, stairwells,

T. Edward Thomas; Hansen Lind Meyers, P.C.; Iowa City, Iowa

elevator entrances, public lobbies, and public vestibules.

3. "MECHANICAL AREA": Total area of all enclosed spaces designed to house mechanical and electrical equipment and utility services such as mechanical and electrical equipment rooms, duct shafts, boiler rooms, fuel rooms, and mechanical service shafts.

4. "CONSTRUCTION AREA": The area occupied by exterior walls, partitions, structure, and so on.

5. "GROSS FLOOR OR ARCHITECTURAL AREA": The sum of areas 1, 2, 3, and 4 plus the area of all factored non- and semienclosed areas equal the gross floor area or architectural area of a building.

In commercial buildings constructed for leasing, net areas are to be measured in accordance with the "Standard Method of Floor Measurement," as set by the Building Owners and Managers Association (BOMA).

The net rentable area for offices is to be measured from the inside finish of permanent outer building walls, to the office or occupancy side of corridors and/or other permanent partitions, and to the center of partitions that separate the premises from adjoining rentable areas. No deductions are to be made for columns and projections necessary to the building.

The net rentable area for stores is to be measured from the building line in case of street frontages and from the inside finish of other outer building walls, corridor, and permanent partitions and to the center of partitions that separate the premises from adjoining rentable areas. No deductions are to be made for vestibules inside the building line or for columns and projections necessary to the building. No addition is to be made for projecting bay windows.

If a single occupant is to occupy the total floor in either the office or store categories, the net rentable area would include the accessory area for that floor of corridors, elevator lobbies, toilets, janitors' closets, electrical and telephone closets, air-conditioning rooms and fan rooms, and similar spaces.

The net rentable area for apartments is to be measured from the inside face of exterior walls, and all enclosing walls of the unit.

NOTE

Various governmental agencies have their own methods of calculating the net assignable area of buildings. They should be investigated if federal authority or funding apply to a project. Also, various building codes provide their own definitions of net and gross areas of building for use in quantifying requirements.

BRICK AND BLOCK MASONRY	PSF
4" brickwork	40
4" concrete block, stone or gravel	34
4" concrete block, lightweight	22
4" concrete brick, stone or gravel	46
4" concrete brick, lightweight	33
6" concrete block, stone or gravel	50
6" concrete block, lightweight	31
8" concrete block, stone or gravel	55
8" concrete block, lightweight	35
12" concrete block, stone or gravel	85
12" concrete block, lightweight	55

CONCRETE		PCF
Plain	Cinder	108
	Expanded slag aggregate	100
	Expanded clay	90
	Slag	132
	Stone and cast stone	144
Reinforced	Cinder	111
	Slag	138
	Stone	150

FINISH MATERIALS	PSF
Acoustical tile unsupported per $1/2$"	0.8
Building board, $1/2$"	0.8
Cement finish, 1"	12
Fiberboard, $1/2$"	0.75
Gypsum wallboard, $1/2$"	2
Marble and setting bed	25-30
Plaster, $1/2$"	4.5
Plaster on wood lath	8
Plaster suspended with lath	10
Plywood, $1/2$"	1.5
Tile, glazed wall $3/8$"	3
Tile, ceramic mosaic, $1/4$"	2.5
Quarry tile, $1/2$"	5.8
Quarry tile, $3/4$"	8.6
Terrazzo 1", 2" in stone concrete	25
Vinyl asbestos tile, $1/8$"	1.33
Hardwood flooring, $25/32$"	4
Wood block flooring, 3" on mastic	15

FLOOR AND ROOF (CONCRETE)		PSF
Flexicore, 6" precast lightweight concrete		30
Flexicore, 6" precast stone concrete		40
Plank, cinder concrete, 2"		15
Plank, gypsum, 2"		12
Concrete, reinforced, 1"	Stone	12.5
	Slag	11.5
	Lightweight	6-10
Concrete, plain, 1"	Stone	12
	Slag	11
	Lightweight	3-9

FUELS AND LIQUIDS	PCF
Coal, piled anthracite	47-58
Coal, piled bituminous	40-54
Ice	57.2
Gasoline	75
Snow	8
Water, fresh	62.4
Water, sea	64

GLASS	PSF
Polished plate, $1/4$"	3.28
Polished plate, $1/2$"	6.56
Double strength, $1/8$"	26 oz
Sheet A, B, $1/32$"	45 oz
Sheet A, B, $1/4$"	52 oz

Insulating glass $5/8$" plate with airspace	3.25
$1/4$" wire glass	3.5
Glass block	18

INSULATION AND WATERPROOFING	PSF
Batt, blankets per 1" thickness	0.1-0.4
Corkboard per 1" thickness	0.58
Foamed board insulation per 1" thickness	2.6 oz
Five-ply membrane	5
Rigid insulation	0.75

LIGHTWEIGHT CONCRETE	PSF
Concrete, aerocrete	50-80
Concrete, cinder fill	60
Concrete, expanded clay	85-100
Concrete, expanded shale-sand	105-120
Concrete, perlite	35-50
Concrete, pumice	60-90
Concrete, vermiculite	25-60

METALS	PCF
Aluminum, cast	165
Brass, cast, rolled	534
Bronze, commercial	552
Bronze, statuary	509
Copper, cast or rolled	556
Gold, cast, solid	1205
Gold coin in bags	509
Iron, cast gray, pig	450
Iron, wrought	480
Lead	710
Nickel	565
Silver, cast, solid	656
Silver coin in bags	590
Tin	459
Stainless steel, rolled	492-510
Steel, rolled, cold drawn	490
Zinc, rolled, cast or sheet	449

MORTAR AND PLASTER	PCF
Mortar, masonry	116
Plaster, gypsum, sand	104-120
Plaster, gypsum, perlite, vermiculite	50-55

PARTITIONS	PSF
2 x 4 wood stud, GWB, two sides	8
4" metal stud, GWB, two sides	6
4" concrete block, lightweight, GWB	26
6" concrete block, lightweight, GWB	35
2" solid plaster	20
4" solid plaster	32

ROOFING MATERIALS	PSF
Built up	6.5
Concrete roof tile	9.5
Copper	1.5-2.5
Corrugated iron	2
Deck, steel without roofing or insulation	2.2-3.6
Fiberglass panels ($2 1/2$" corrugated)	5-8 oz
Galvanized iron	1.2-1.7
Lead, $1/8$"	6-8
Plastic sandwich panel, $2 1/2$" thick	2.6
Shingles, asphalt	1.7-2.8
Shingles, wood	2-3
Slate, $3/16$" to $1/4$"	7-9.5
Slate, $3/8$" to $1/2$"	14-18
Stainless steel	2.5
Tile, cement flat	13
Tile, cement ribbed	16
Tile, clay shingle type	8-16
Tile, clay flat with setting bed	15-20

Wood sheathing per inch	3

SOIL, SAND, AND GRAVEL	PCF
Ashes or cinder	40-50
Clay, damp and plastic	110
Clay, dry	63
Clay and gravel, dry	100
Earth, dry and loose	76
Earth, dry and packed	95
Earth, moist and loose	78
Earth, moist and packed	96
Earth, mud, packed	115
Sand or gravel, dry and loose	90-105
Sand or gravel, dry and packed	100-120
Sand or gravel, dry and wet	118-120
Silt, moist, loose	78
Silt, moist, packed	96

STONE (ASHLAR)	PCF
Granite, limestone, crystalline	165
Limestone, oolitic	135
Marble	173
Sandstone, bluestone	144
Slate	172

STONE VENEER	PSF
2" granite, $1/2$" parging	30
4" granite, $1/2$" parging	59
6" limestone facing, $1/2$" parging	55
4" sandstone or bluestone, $1/2$" parging	49
1" marble	13
1" slate	14

STRUCTURAL CLAY TILE	PSF
4" hollow	23
6" hollow	38
8" hollow	45

STRUCTURAL FACING TILE	PSF
2" facing tile	14
4" facing tile	24
6" facing tile	34
8" facing tile	44

SUSPENDED CEILINGS	PSF
Mineral fiber tile $3/4$", 12" x 12"	1.2-1.57
Mineral fiberboard $5/8$", 24" x 24"	1.4
Acoustic plaster on gypsum lath base	10-11

WOOD	PCF
Ash, commercial white	40.5
Birch, red oak, sweet and yellow	44
Cedar, northern white	22.2
Cedar, western red	24.2
Cypress, southern	33.5
Douglas fir (coast region)	32.7
Fir, commercial white; Idaho white pine	27
Hemlock	28-29
Maple, hard (black and sugar)	44.5
Oak, white and red	47.3
Pine, northern white sugar	25
Pine, southern yellow	37.3
Pine, ponderosa, spruce: eastern and sitka	28.6
Poplar, yellow	29.4
Redwood	26
Walnut, black	38

NOTE

To establish uniform practice among designers, it is desirable to present a list of materials generally used in building construction, together with their proper weights. Many building codes prescribe the minimum weights of only a few building materials. It should be noted that there is a difference of more than 25% in some cases.

DECIMALS OF A FOOT

FRACTION	DECIMAL	FRACTION	DECIMAL	FRACTION	DECIMAL
1/16	0.0052	4-1/16	0.3385	8-1/16	0.6719
1/8	0.0104	4-1/8	0.3438	8-1/8	0.6771
3/16	0.0156	4-3/16	0.3490	8-3/16	0.6823
1/4	0.0208	4-1/4	0.3542	8-1/4	0.6875
5/16	0.0260	4-5/16	0.3594	8-5/16	0.6927
3/8	0.0313	4-3/8	0.3646	8-3/8	0.6979
7/16	0.0365	4-7/16	0.3698	8-7/16	0.7031
1/2	0.0417	4-1/2	0.3750	8-1/2	0.7083
9/16	0.0469	4-9/16	0.3802	8-9/16	0.7135
5/8	0.0521	4-5/8	0.3854	8-5/8	0.7188
11/16	0.0573	4-11/16	0.3906	8-11/16	0.7240
3/4	0.0625	4-3/4	0.3958	8-3/4	0.7292
13/16	0.0677	4-13/16	0.4010	8-13/16	0.7344
7/8	0.0729	4-7/8	0.4063	8-7/8	0.7396
15/16	0.0781	4-15/16	0.4115	8-15/16	0.7448
1-	0.0833	5-	0.4167	9-	0.7500
1-1/16	0.0885	5-1/16	0.4219	9-1/16	0.7552
1-1/8	0.0938	5-1/8	0.4271	9-1/8	0.7604
1-3/16	0.0990	5-3/16	0.4323	9-3/16	0.7656
1-1/4	0.1042	5-1/4	0.4375	9-1/4	0.7708
1-5/16	0.1094	5-5/16	0.4427	9-5/16	0.7760
1-3/8	0.1146	5-3/8	0.4479	9-3/8	0.7813
1-7/16	0.1198	5-7/16	0.4531	9-7/16	0.7865
1-1/2	0.1250	5-1/2	0.4583	9-1/2	0.7917
1-9/16	0.1302	5-9/16	0.4635	9-9/16	0.7969
1-5/8	0.1354	5-5/8	0.4688	9-5/8	0.8021
1-11/16	0.1406	5-11/16	0.4740	9-11/16	0.8073
1-3/4	0.1458	5-3/4	0.4792	9-3/4	0.8125
1-13/16	0.1510	5-13/16	0.4844	9-13/16	0.8177
1-7/8	0.1563	5-7/8	0.4896	9-7/8	0.8229
1-15/16	0.1615	5-15/16	0.4948	9-15/16	0.8281
2-	0.1667	6-	0.5000	10-	0.8333
2-1/16	0.1719	6-1/16	0.5052	10-1/16	0.8385
2-1/8	0.1771	6-1/8	0.5104	10-1/8	0.8438
2-3/16	0.1823	6-3/16	0.5156	10-3/16	0.8490
2-1/4	0.1875	6-1/4	0.5208	10-1/4	0.8542
2-5/16	0.1927	6-5/16	0.5260	10-5/16	0.8594
2-3/8	0.1979	6-3/8	0.5313	10-3/8	0.8646
2-7/16	0.2031	6-7/16	0.5365	10-7/16	0.8698
2-1/2	0.2083	6-1/2	0.5417	10-1/2	0.8750
2-9/16	0.2135	6-9/16	0.5469	10-9/16	0.8802
2-5/8	0.2188	6-5/8	0.5521	10-5/8	0.8854
2-11/16	0.2240	6-11/16	0.5573	10-11/16	0.8906
2-3/4	0.2292	6-3/4	0.5625	10-3/4	0.8958
2-13/16	0.2344	6-13/16	0.5677	10-13/16	0.9010
2-7/8	0.2396	6-7/8	0.5729	10-7/8	0.9063
2-15/16	0.2448	6-15/16	0.5781	10-15/16	0.9115
3-	0.2500	7-	0.5833	11-	0.9167
3-1/16	0.2552	7-1/16	0.5885	11-1/16	0.9219
3-1/8	0.2604	7-1/8	0.5938	11-1/8	0.9271
3-3/16	0.2656	7-3/16	0.5990	11-3/16	0.9323
3-1/4	0.2708	7-1/4	0.6042	11-1/4	0.9375
3-5/16	0.2760	7-5/16	0.6094	11-5/16	0.9427
3-3/8	0.2813	7-3/8	0.6146	11-3/8	0.9479
3-7/16	0.2865	7-7/16	0.6198	11-7/16	0.9531
3-1/2	0.2917	7-1/2	0.6250	11-1/2	0.9583
3-9/16	0.2969	7-9/16	0.6302	11-9/16	0.9635
3-5/8	0.3021	7-5/8	0.6354	11-5/8	0.9688
3-11/16	0.3073	7-11/16	0.6406	11-11/16	0.9740
3-3/4	0.3125	7-3/4	0.6458	11-3/4	0.9792
3-13/16	0.3177	7-13/16	0.6510	11-13/16	0.9844
3-7/8	0.3229	7-7/8	0.6563	11-7/8	0.9896
3-15/16	0.3281	7-15/16	0.6615	11-15/16	0.9948
4-	0.3333	8-	0.6667	12-	1.0000

DECIMALS OF AN INCH

FRACTION	DECIMAL
1/64	0.015625
1/32	0.03125
3/64	0.046875
1/16	0.0625
5/64	0.078125
3/32	0.09375
7/64	0.109375
1/8	0.125
9/64	0.140625
5/32	0.15625
11/64	0.171875
3/16	0.1875
13/64	0.203125
7/32	0.21875
15/64	0.234375
1/4	0.250
17/64	0.265625
9/32	0.28125
19/64	0.296875
5/16	0.3125
21/64	0.328125
11/32	0.34375
23/64	0.359375
3/8	0.375
25/64	0.390625
13/32	0.40625
27/64	0.421875
7/16	0.4375
29/64	0.453125
15/32	0.46875
31/64	0.484375
1/2	0.500
33/64	0.515625
17/32	0.53125
35/64	0.546875
9/16	0.5625
37/64	0.578125
19/32	0.59375
39/64	0.609375
5/8	0.625
41/64	0.640625
21/32	0.65625
43/64	0.671875
11/16	0.6875
45/64	0.703125
23/32	0.71875
47/64	0.734375
3/4	0.750
49/64	0.765625
25/32	0.78125
51/64	0.796875
13/16	0.8125
53/64	0.828125
27/32	0.84375
55/64	0.859375
7/8	0.875
57/64	0.890625
29/32	0.90625
59/64	0.921875
15/16	0.9375
61/64	0.953125
31/32	0.96875
63/64	0.984375
1"	1.000

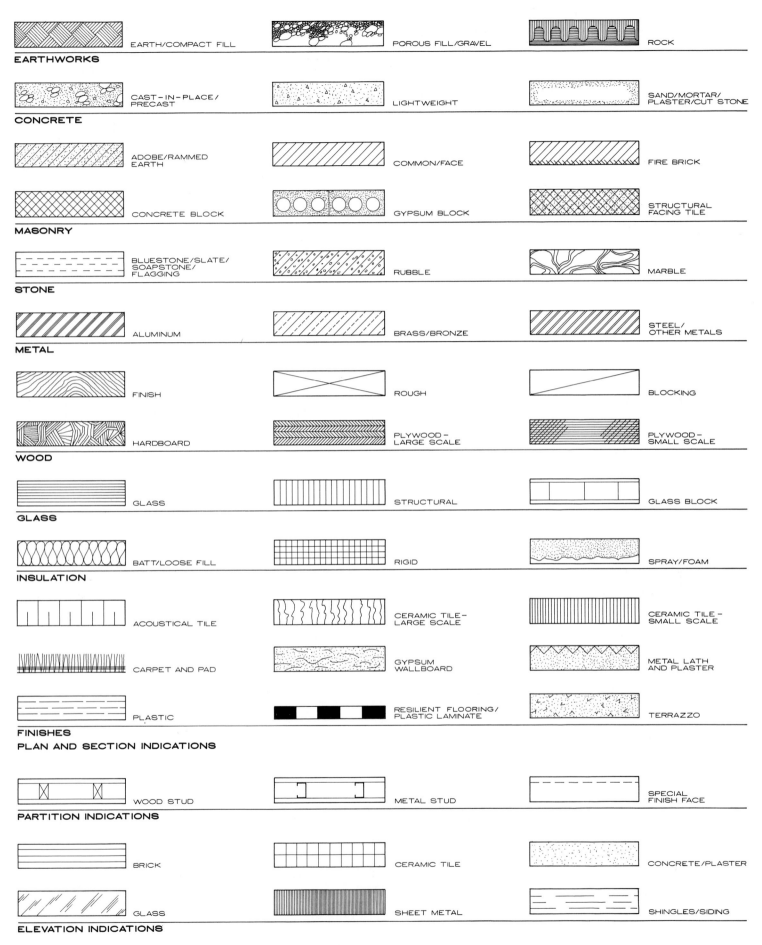

EARTH/COMPACT FILL

POROUS FILL/GRAVEL

ROCK

EARTHWORKS

CAST-IN-PLACE/PRECAST

LIGHTWEIGHT

SAND/MORTAR/PLASTER/CUT STONE

CONCRETE

ADOBE/RAMMED EARTH

COMMON/FACE

FIRE BRICK

CONCRETE BLOCK

GYPSUM BLOCK

STRUCTURAL FACING TILE

MASONRY

BLUESTONE/SLATE/SOAPSTONE/FLAGGING

RUBBLE

MARBLE

STONE

ALUMINUM

BRASS/BRONZE

STEEL/OTHER METALS

METAL

FINISH

ROUGH

BLOCKING

HARDBOARD

PLYWOOD – LARGE SCALE

PLYWOOD – SMALL SCALE

WOOD

GLASS

STRUCTURAL

GLASS BLOCK

GLASS

BATT/LOOSE FILL

RIGID

SPRAY/FOAM

INSULATION

ACOUSTICAL TILE

CERAMIC TILE – LARGE SCALE

CERAMIC TILE – SMALL SCALE

CARPET AND PAD

GYPSUM WALLBOARD

METAL LATH AND PLASTER

PLASTIC

RESILIENT FLOORING/PLASTIC LAMINATE

TERRAZZO

FINISHES

PLAN AND SECTION INDICATIONS

WOOD STUD

METAL STUD

SPECIAL FINISH FACE

PARTITION INDICATIONS

BRICK

CERAMIC TILE

CONCRETE/PLASTER

GLASS

SHEET METAL

SHINGLES/SIDING

ELEVATION INDICATIONS

John R. Hoke, Jr., AIA, Architect; Washington, D.C.

DRAFTING TECHNIQUES   A

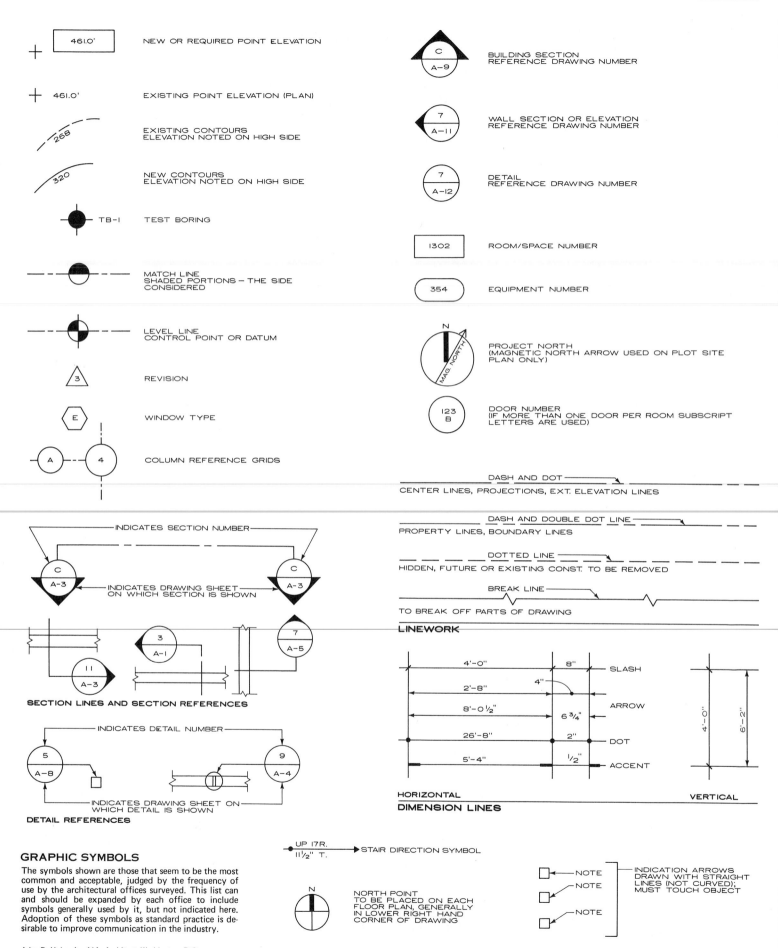

⊞ 461.0'	NEW OR REQUIRED POINT ELEVATION
+ 461.0'	EXISTING POINT ELEVATION (PLAN)
268	EXISTING CONTOURS ELEVATION NOTED ON HIGH SIDE
320	NEW CONTOURS ELEVATION NOTED ON HIGH SIDE
● TB-1	TEST BORING
	MATCH LINE SHADED PORTIONS – THE SIDE CONSIDERED
	LEVEL LINE CONTROL POINT OR DATUM
△ 3	REVISION
⬡ E	WINDOW TYPE
Ⓐ --- ④	COLUMN REFERENCE GRIDS

▽ C / A-9	BUILDING SECTION REFERENCE DRAWING NUMBER
◖ 7 / A-11	WALL SECTION OR ELEVATION REFERENCE DRAWING NUMBER
7 / A-12	DETAIL REFERENCE DRAWING NUMBER
1302	ROOM/SPACE NUMBER
354	EQUIPMENT NUMBER
PROJECT NORTH	PROJECT NORTH (MAGNETIC NORTH ARROW USED ON PLOT SITE PLAN ONLY)
123 / B	DOOR NUMBER (IF MORE THAN ONE DOOR PER ROOM SUBSCRIPT LETTERS ARE USED)

SECTION LINES AND SECTION REFERENCES

INDICATES SECTION NUMBER

INDICATES DRAWING SHEET ON WHICH SECTION IS SHOWN

DETAIL REFERENCES

INDICATES DETAIL NUMBER

INDICATES DRAWING SHEET ON WHICH DETAIL IS SHOWN

DASH AND DOT
CENTER LINES, PROJECTIONS, EXT. ELEVATION LINES

DASH AND DOUBLE DOT LINE
PROPERTY LINES, BOUNDARY LINES

DOTTED LINE
HIDDEN, FUTURE OR EXISTING CONST. TO BE REMOVED

BREAK LINE
TO BREAK OFF PARTS OF DRAWING

LINEWORK

4'-0"	8"	SLASH	
2'-8"	4"		
8'-0 ½"	6 ¾"	ARROW	
26'-8"	2"	DOT	
5'-4"	½"	ACCENT	

HORIZONTAL   **VERTICAL**
DIMENSION LINES

GRAPHIC SYMBOLS

The symbols shown are those that seem to be the most common and acceptable, judged by the frequency of use by the architectural offices surveyed. This list can and should be expanded by each office to include symbols generally used by it, but not indicated here. Adoption of these symbols as standard practice is desirable to improve communication in the industry.

John R. Hoke, Jr., AIA, Architect; Washington, D.C.

UP 17R.
11½" T. ➤ STAIR DIRECTION SYMBOL

N
NORTH POINT
TO BE PLACED ON EACH FLOOR PLAN, GENERALLY IN LOWER RIGHT HAND CORNER OF DRAWING

☐ ← NOTE
☐ ← NOTE
☐ ← NOTE

INDICATION ARROWS DRAWN WITH STRAIGHT LINES (NOT CURVED); MUST TOUCH OBJECT

Ⓐ **DRAFTING TECHNIQUES**

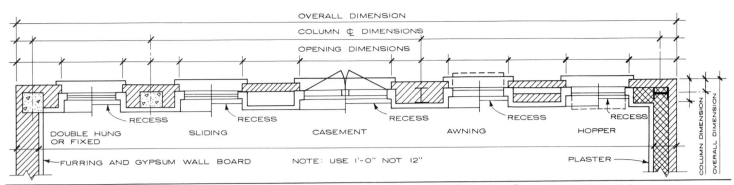

OVERALL DIMENSION
COLUMN ℄ DIMENSIONS
OPENING DIMENSIONS

RECESS — RECESS — RECESS — RECESS — RECESS

DOUBLE HUNG OR FIXED — SLIDING — CASEMENT — AWNING — HOPPER

FURRING AND GYPSUM WALL BOARD — NOTE: USE 1'-0" NOT 12" — PLASTER

COLUMN DIMENSION / OVERALL DIMENSION

METHOD FOR DIMENSIONING EXTERIOR WINDOW OPENINGS IN MASONRY WALLS (DOORS SIMILAR)

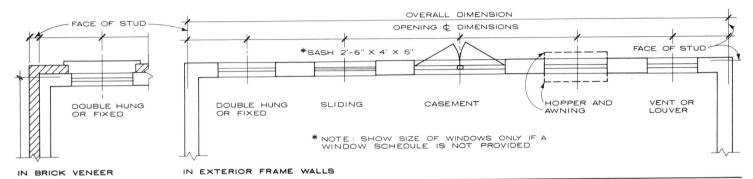

FACE OF STUD

OVERALL DIMENSION
OPENING ℄ DIMENSIONS
*SASH 2'-6" X 4' X 6"
FACE OF STUD

DOUBLE HUNG OR FIXED — DOUBLE HUNG OR FIXED — SLIDING — CASEMENT — HOPPER AND AWNING — VENT OR LOUVER

* NOTE : SHOW SIZE OF WINDOWS ONLY IF A WINDOW SCHEDULE IS NOT PROVIDED

IN BRICK VENEER — IN EXTERIOR FRAME WALLS

METHOD FOR DIMENSIONING EXTERIOR WINDOW OPENINGS IN FRAME WALLS (DOORS SIMILAR)

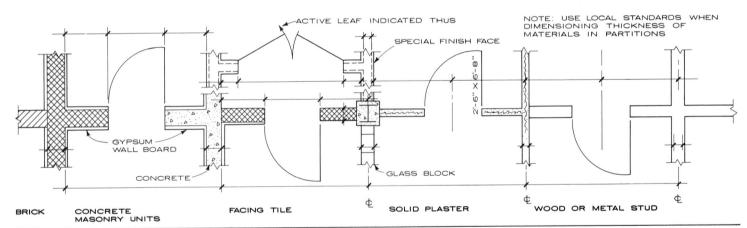

ACTIVE LEAF INDICATED THUS
SPECIAL FINISH FACE

NOTE: USE LOCAL STANDARDS WHEN DIMENSIONING THICKNESS OF MATERIALS IN PARTITIONS

2'-6" X 6'-8"

GYPSUM WALL BOARD
CONCRETE
GLASS BLOCK

BRICK — CONCRETE MASONRY UNITS — FACING TILE — ℄ SOLID PLASTER — ℄ WOOD OR METAL STUD — ℄

METHOD FOR DIMENSIONING AND INDICATIONS OF INTERIOR PARTITIONS AND DOORS

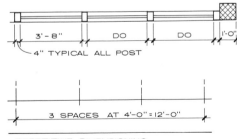

3'-8" — DO — DO — 1'-0"
4" TYPICAL ALL POST
3 SPACES AT 4'-0" = 12'-0"

REPETITIVE DIMENSIONING

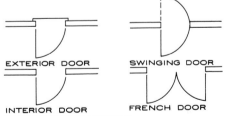

EXTERIOR DOOR — SWINGING DOOR
INTERIOR DOOR — FRENCH DOOR

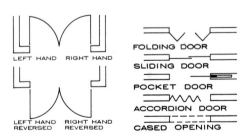

LEFT HAND — RIGHT HAND
LEFT HAND REVERSED — RIGHT HAND REVERSED

FOLDING DOOR
SLIDING DOOR
POCKET DOOR
ACCORDION DOOR
CASED OPENING

GENERAL NOTES

Dimensioning should start with critical dimensions and should be kept to a minimum. Consideration must be given to the trades using them and the sequencing adjusted to their respective work. It is also necessary to bear in mind that tolerances in actual construction will be varied. This means that as-built dimensions do not always coincide with design dimensions. Dimensioning from established grids or structural elements, such as columns and structural walls, assists the trades that must locate their work prior to that of others.

John R. Hoke, Jr., AIA; Architect; Washington, D.C.

RECOMMENDATIONS

1. Dimensions under 1 ft shall be noted in inches. Dimensions 1 ft and over shall be expressed in feet.
2. Fractions under 1 in. shall NOT be preceded by a zero. Fractions must have a diagonal dividing line between numerator and denominator.
3. Dimension points to be noted with a short blunt 45° line. Dash to be oriented differently for vertical (⊁) and horizontal (⊀) runs of dimensions. Modular dimension points may be designated with an arrow or a dot.
4. Dimension all items from an established grid or reference point and do not close the string of

5. dimensions to the next grid or reference point.
5. Dimension: to face of concrete or masonry work; to centerlines of columns or other grid points; to centerlines of partitions. In nonmodular wood construction dimension to critical face of studs. When a clear dimension is required, dimension to the finish faces and note as such. Do not use the word "clear."
6. Dimension as much as possible from structural elements.
7. Overall readability, conciseness, completeness, and accuracy must be foremost in any dimensional system. It takes experience to determine how to use dimensions to the best advantage.

DRAFTING TECHNIQUES A

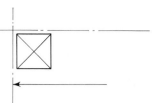

GRID LINES:

Are used to establish reference planes four inches apart in all three dimensions. Grid lines are imaginary and can be thought of as dimensional egg-crates running throughout the structure. The grid lines are partially or entirely shown on large-scale details but will not be shown at all on small scale plans.

ARROW HEADS:

Indicate all dimensions referenced to grid-line locations. This feature of modular drafting is the key to the efficiencies resulting from the use of the system. Preliminary drawings can be fully dimensioned as small scale working drawings knowing that the materials will fit when fully detailed. A number of personnel can proceed with the detailing using the single small scale plan reference without the necessity of frequent checking with each other for dimensional reference points.

DOTS:

Are used to indicate off-grid locations for dimensions. (Half-dots may be used whenever drawing space is limited.) Generally, such dimensional reference points occur when it is critical to show the measured distance to the actual face of a material. Dots are also used for joint centerlines if those points occur off the grid-lines. Column centerlines frequently are located between grid-lines to accommodate more dimensionally critical enclosure and finish materials.

MODULAR DIMENSIONING

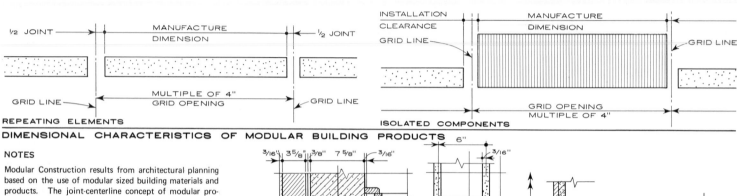

REPEATING ELEMENTS   ISOLATED COMPONENTS

DIMENSIONAL CHARACTERISTICS OF MODULAR BUILDING PRODUCTS

NOTES

Modular Construction results from architectural planning based on the use of modular sized building materials and products. The joint-centerline concept of modular products permits accommodation of those materials into buildings designed with planning modules of some multiple of 4" (e.g. 3'–0", 40", 5'–4", etc.)

Small-scale assembly drawings such as plans, sections and elevations diagram the relationship of components. Since modular products are normally 4" multiples to joint centerlines, most dimensions are in multiples of 4". Arrowheads indicate dimensions are to grid-lines.

Large-scale details show the relationship of the components to the grid. Some architects prefer not to draw the entire grid on such details but include only those used as dimensional reference points on the small-scale drawings.

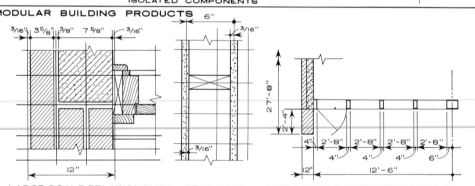

LARGE SCALE RELATIONSHIPS   STUD WALL   SMALL SCALE ASSEMBLY DRAWING

MODULAR DIMENSIONED WORKING DRAWINGS

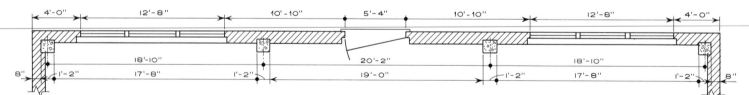

COLUMN LAYOUTS

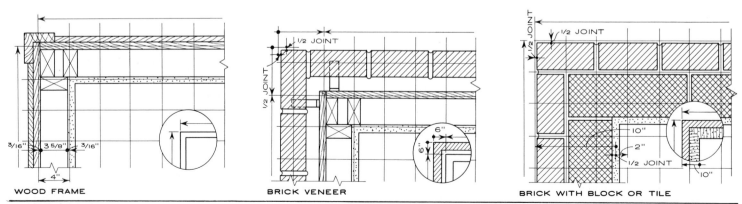

WOOD FRAME   BRICK VENEER   BRICK WITH BLOCK OR TILE

LARGE SCALE DETAILS

Byron C. Bloomfield; Madison, Wisconsin

A **DRAFTING TECHNIQUES**

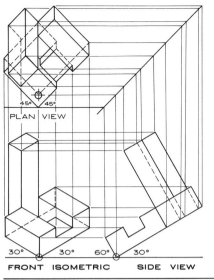

PLAN VIEW

45° 45°

FRONT ISOMETRIC   SIDE VIEW

30°   30°   60°   30°

PROJECTED METHOD

CONCRETE BLOCK

EXPLODED VIEW OF DETAIL

ISOMETRIC

PARALINE DRAWINGS

Paraline drawings are sometimes referred to as AXONOMETRIC (Greek) or AXIOMETRIC (English) drawings. These drawings are projected pictorial representations of an object which give a three-dimensional quality. They can be classified as orthographic projections inasmuch as the plan view is rotated and the side view is tilted. The resulting "front" view is projected at a 90° angle to the picture plane (as illustrated in the projected method). These drawings differ from perspective drawings, since the projection lines remain parallel instead of converging to a point on the horizon.

Drawings prepared by using the projection method require three views of the object, which tends to be more time-consuming and complex than drawing by the direct measuring method. The following drawings utilize this method; they are simple to draw and represent reasonably accurate proportions.

OBLIQUE

In an oblique drawing one face (either plan or elevation) of the object is drawn directly on the picture plane. Projected lines are drawn at a 30 or 45° angle to the picture plane. The length of the projecting lines is determined as illustrated and varies according to the angle chosen.

DIMETRIC

A dimetric drawing is similar to oblique, with one exception—the object is rotated so that only one of its corners touches the picture plane. The most frequently used angle for the projecting lines is an equal division of 45° on either side of the leading edge. A 15° angle is sometimes used when it is less important to show the "roof view" of the object.

ISOMETRIC

The isometric, a special type of dimetric drawing, is the easiest and most popular paraline drawing. All axis of the object are simultaneously rotated away from the picture plane and kept at the same angle of projection (30° from the picture plane). All legs are equally distorted in length at a given scale and therefore maintain an exact proportion of 1:1:1.

TRIMETRIC

The trimetric drawing is similar to the dimetric, except that the plan of the object is rotated so that the two exposed sides of the object are not at equal angles to the picture plane. The plan is usually positioned at 30/60° angle to the ground plane. The height of the object is reduced proportionately as illustrated (similar to the 45° dimetric).

SHADES AND SHADOWS

Shades and shadows are easily constructed and can be very effective in paraline drawings. The location of the light source will determine the direction of the shadows cast by the object. The shade line is the line (or the edge) that separates the light area from the shaded areas of the object. Shadows are constructed by drawing a line, representing a light ray, from a corner of the lighted surface at a 45° angle to the ground plane. Shadows cast by a vertical edge of the object will be drawn midway in the angle created by the intersection of the projected line of the object and the ground, or baseline (the baseline represents the intersection of the picture plane). The 45° light ray is extended until it meets the shadow line (as illustrated), and this point determines the length of the shadow for any given vertical height of the object. Shadow lines of all vertical edges of the object are drawn parallel to one another.

30°   45°

30° OBLIQUE

45°   30°

45° OBLIQUE

45° 45°   30°

45° DIMETRIC
(ROTATED PLAN)

45° 15° 15° 45°

15° DIMETRIC

30°   30°

ISOMETRIC
(30° DIMETRIC)

30°   60°   30°

TRIMETRIC
(ROTATED PLAN)

AXIOMETRIC — MEASURED METHOD

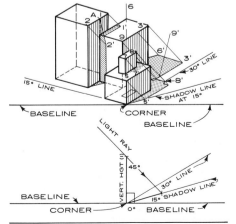

A
2   6
1   3
9
2'   6'   3'
8   30° LINE
9'
15° LINE   8'
SHADOW LINE
AT 15°
5'

BASELINE   CORNER
BASELINE

LIGHT RAY
45°
VERT. HGT.   30° LINE
15°   SHADOW LINE
BASELINE
CORNER   0°   BASELINE

15/30° TRIMETRIC SHADOW

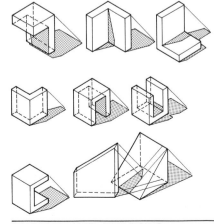

SHADES AND SHADOWS

Jim Maeda; Samuel J. De Santo and Associates; New York, New York

GRAPHIC METHODS

A

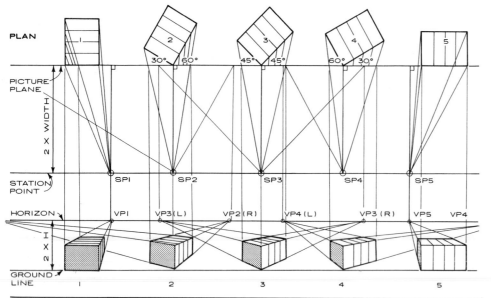

PLAN

PICTURE PLANE

2 X WIDTH

STATION POINT

HORIZON

1/2 X H

GROUND LINE

PERSPECTIVE — PROJECTION METHOD

GENERAL NOTES

Before the drawing can be laid out, the following information must be obtained:

1. An approximation of the overall dimensions of the building.
2. The location of the building in relation to the picture plane.
3. The orientation of the building, either in front of or behind the picture plane.

While the building can be located anywhere in the drawing—in front of, behind, or at any angle to the picture plane—the simplest approach is to place the building at the picture plane. The horizontal lines of the building would be parallel to the picture plane in a one-point perspective or placed at an angle to the picture plane. Usually this will be a 30/60 or 45° angle in a two-point perspective.

TERMS AND CONCEPTS

1. THE OBJECT: Called a building in this example.
2. THE PICTURE PLANE: An imaginary, transparent plane, onto or through which the object is perceived in a perspective rendering. It is:
   a. Parallel to one face of the drawing paper, if it is a one-point perspective.
   b. Perpendicular to the ground line and at any angle to the building if it is a two-point perspective.
   c. Tilted and placed at any angle to the building if it is a three-point perspective.
   d. A curved plane if it is a wide angle perspective view.
3. HORIZON LINE: A line drawn on the picture plane to represent the horizon. It is usually located at the point where all parallel lines recede away from the viewer and finally converge. This point is aptly designed as the vanishing point. Not that although the horizon is generally thought of as a horizontal line, in certain applications it could be vertical, or even at an angle, to the picture plane. For example, in drawing shades and shadows it appears to be at a 90° angle and in a three-point perspective it appears to be slanted.
4. STATION POINT: The point from which the object is being viewed or, in other words the point from which the viewer is seeing the building. The location of this point will be the factor that determines the width of the drawing. A 30° cone of vision is drawn from the station point, as the viewer moves away from the object, the cone widens, the object becomes smaller, and more material is included in the area surrounding the object. A common way of determining the distance between the station point and the picture plane is by referring to the following parameters:
   Minimum—1.73 times the width of the drawing.
   Average—2.00 times the width of the drawing.
   Maximum—2.50 times the width of the drawing.
5. VANISHING POINT(S): A specific point or points located on the horizon line, where all parallel lines, drawn in perspective, converge or terminate. The location of the vanishing point varies with the type of perspective drawing. In a two-point perspective, the distance between the vanishing point left and the vanishing point right is estimated as being approximately four times the overall size of the building.
6. VISUAL RAY: An imaginary line drawn from the station point to any specific point lying within the designated scope of the plan layout of the object. The point at which this projected line passes through the picture plane will determine the location of that point in the perspective drawing.
7. GROUND PLANE: The ground on which the viewer is standing. In plan, this is determined at the station point. In perspective, it is the primary plane on which the building is sited. When the lines of this plane are extended to infinity, it becomes the horizon line. The intersection formed when the picture plane and the ground plane come together is called the ground line. In this way the horizontal dimension of the drawing is determined. The vertical dimension is determined by the vertical distance from the ground line to the horizon line. This should be approximately twice the height of object, in perspective, or a 30° cone in elevation.
8. ONE-POINT INTERIOR PERSPECTIVE: The most frequently used application of a one-point perspective. This is the same method as that used in setting up a one-point exterior perspective, except for the limitations that the confinement of space places on the location of the vanishing points. The vanishing point is usually located at the sitting or standing height of an average person within the space (eye level can be considered to be at 5 ft 4 in. from the floor. In most cases, the vanishing point is located within the confines of the enclosed space being represented in the drawing.
9. TWO-POINT PERSPECTIVE USING THE MEASURING POINT METHOD: This is a simplified alternative to the conventional method of laying out the plan picture plane and projecting the vanishing lines. The measuring point method of drawing a two-point perspective eliminates the necessity of the preliminary layout of the plan. One of the obvious advantages of this method is the ease with which the size of the drawing can be adjusted. A perspective can be made larger by simply increasing the scale of the drawing.

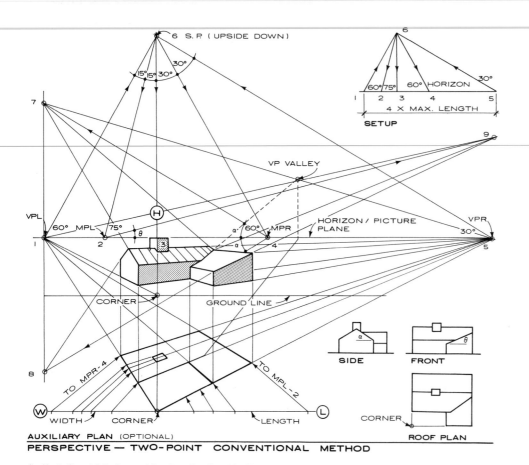

PERSPECTIVE — TWO-POINT CONVENTIONAL METHOD

Jim Maeda; Samuel J. De Santo and Associates; New York, New York

A GRAPHIC METHODS

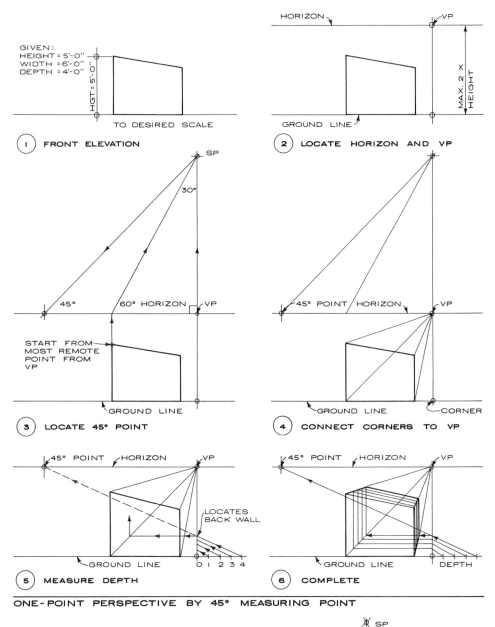

ONE-POINT PERSPECTIVE BY 45° MEASURING POINT

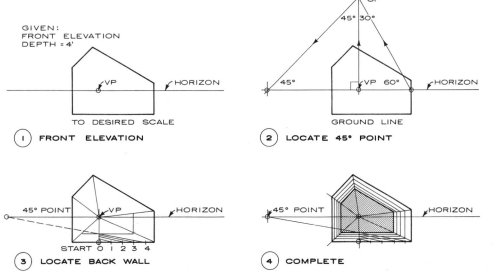

ONE-POINT MEASURED INTERIOR PERSPECTIVE

Jim Maeda; Samuel J. De Santo and Associates; New York, New York

ONE-POINT PERSPECTIVE

The one-point perspective is probably the least complicated of the projected perspective methods. The primary face of the building or object is placed directly on the picture plane. The adjacent planes, generally connected to the primary plane at right angles, converge to the vanishing point—which can be either in front of or behind the picture plane. The vanishing point, located on the horizon line, also determines the height from which the building is viewed.

The conventional method of laying out a one-point exterior perspective is illustrated on the preceding page. A plan view, roof view, and elevation are required for the layout. The size of the object, and therefore the drawing, can be increased or decreased by moving the plan further in front of or behind the picture plane. This method is more flexible but much more complicated and time-consuming than the method that follows.

EXTERIOR ONE-POINT PERSPECTIVE

① Draw the primary elevation of the building to scale.

② Locate the horizon above the ground line at the desired level (eye level is at approximately 5 ft 4 in.). To ensure that the final perspective will fall within the 60° cone vision, the height should not exceed 2X the height of the building. The VP is located left or right arbitrarily depending on the view desired.

③ A 45° vanishing point can be graphically located by starting at the most remote point of the roof and extending a vertical line to the horizon line. From this point, draw a line upward, at a 60° angle. Another line should be drawn vertically upward from the vanishing point. The station point (upside down) is located at the point where these two lines intersect. From the station point, draw a line at a 45° angle to meet the horizon line. This point will be the vanishing point for all lines that are positioned at 45° angle and parallel to the picture plane.

④ From each corner of the primary elevation, draw a line to the vanishing point.

⑤ The correct building depth (drawn at 6 ft in the illustration) is measured along the ground line—on the picture plane—starting at point 0. Draw a line connecting this point to the 45° point on the horizon line. The point at which this line intersects the line extended between the lower corner of the elevation to the vanishing point will determine the location of the back wall of the building.

⑥ The perspective is completed by constructing the back wall at the location established in step 5 and connecting it to the front wall. Note that the lines that are drawn at a 45° angle in the drawing remain parallel to each other as they are extended in perspective.

ONE-POINT INTERIOR AND SECTIONAL PERSPECTIVE

① Draw the primary elevation, or section, to scale. Locate the horizon line and vanishing point within the confines of the interior space.

② A 45° point is located in a similar manner to the one-point exterior perspective. The station point is established by drawing a line, at a 60° angle, from the most remote point in the elevation to intersect another line extended upward at a perpendicular from the vanishing point.

③ The room depth is determined by starting at point 0 on the ground line and measuring the appropriate distance to the 45° point on the horizon line. The back wall is located where these two lines come together.

④ Complete the back wall as illustrated. Note that all lines occurring at a 45° angle in the elevation remain parallel in perspective. All surfaces that are parallel to the picture plane will remain parallel in perspective.

GRAPHIC METHODS   A

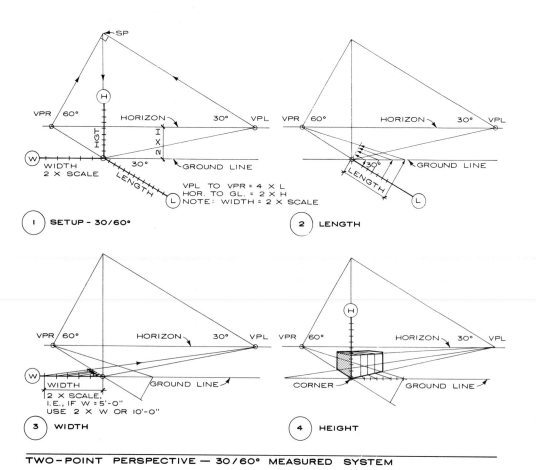

① SETUP - 30/60°

② LENGTH

VPL TO VPR = 4 X L
HOR. TO GL. = 2 X H
NOTE: WIDTH = 2 X SCALE

③ WIDTH

WIDTH
2 X SCALE,
I.E., IF W = 5'-0"
USE 2 X W OR 10'-0"

④ HEIGHT

TWO-POINT PERSPECTIVE — 30/60° MEASURED SYSTEM

TWO-POINT PERSPECTIVE

The projection method of constructing a two-point perspective is illustrated on the preceding page. This is the most widely used and most flexible method of drawing a two-point perspective. It can be taken from any viewpoint by simply turning the plan to the desired position in the preliminary layout. The size of the perspective can also be adjusted by moving the plan in front of the picture plane for a larger drawing and behind the picture plane for a smaller drawing. As in all projected methods, an inordinate amount of time and energy is devoted to the layout. The measured method is equally accurate, less time-consuming, and much easier to construct, since it eliminates the need to lay out the drawing in plan. The desired size of the drawing is determined by drawing the primary elevation at the desired scale.

30/60° MEASURED SYSTEM

① SET-UP: Draw a horizon line and locate VPR and VPL separated at a distance that is approximately four to four and a half times the maximum width of the building. Follow the illustration to locate the station point and leading corner of the building.

② LENGTH: Measure, to scale, the length of the building along length line L. A perpendicular line is drawn from these designated points to the ground line. The vanishing perspective lines are then drawn directly from these points to the appropriate vanishing point (VPL). In this way the correct length of the line can be determined. Note what happens when equally spaced points are projected from the ground line to the vanishing point. The visual distance (length) between them, as they get closer to the vanishing point, is progressively foreshortened.

③ WIDTH: The width is measured along the width line (see illustration) at double the scale. That is, if the perspective is drawn at a scale of 1/8 in. = 1 ft and a particular line is to be drawn at 5 ft, measure 5 ft at 1/4-in. scale starting at the corner and measure to the left of the corner horizontally. A line is drawn from each point on the width line to the appropriate vanishing point (VPR). The intersections of the length and width vanishing lines will define the "plan" in perspective.

④ HEIGHT: Since the leading corner of the building is placed directly on the picture plane, the height is measured, to scale, directly on the H line. It is then carried to VPL and VPR as illustrated.

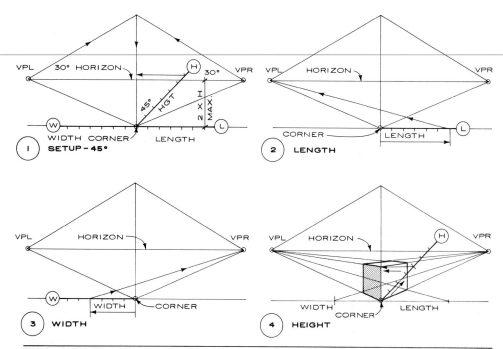

① SETUP - 45°

② LENGTH

③ WIDTH

④ HEIGHT

TWO-POINT PERSPECTIVE — 45° MEASURED SYSTEM

Jim Maeda; Samuel J. De Santo and Associates; New York, New York

45° METHOD SYSTEM

① SETUP: Similar to the method used in the 30/60° setup, the vanishing points are placed on the horizon line and separated by four to four and a half times the maximum width of the building. Complete the setup as illustrated.

② LENGTH: Measure, to scale, the length of the building along the length line L. Connect the points directly to VPL.

③ WIDTH: In this setup, the width is the same as the length scale. Measure the width of the building along the width line W. The length and width lines will form an outline of the "plan" in perspective.

④ HEIGHT: The height line is positioned at a 45° angle and marked off to scale. A line representing the leading corner of the building is drawn perpendicular to the ground line. Connect or draw a line from the measurement points along the height line to the vertical corner line. As in the 30/60° setup, these points are then carried to VPR and VPL.

Ⓐ GRAPHIC METHODS

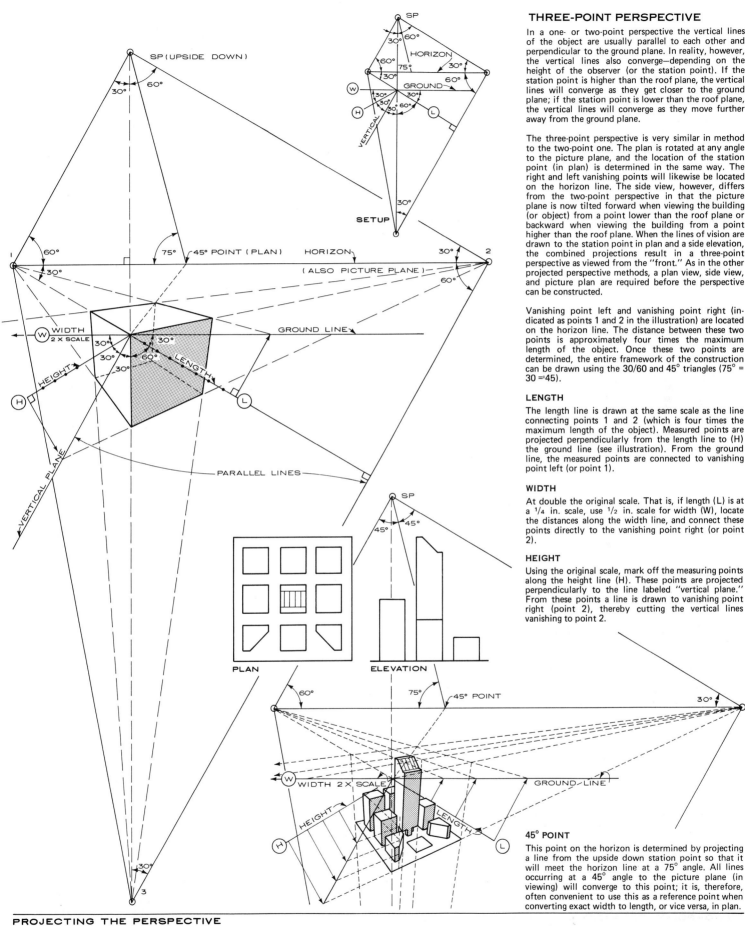

PROJECTING THE PERSPECTIVE

SP (UPSIDE DOWN)

SETUP

45° POINT (PLAN)   HORIZON

(ALSO PICTURE PLANE)

WIDTH 2 X SCALE

GROUND LINE

HEIGHT

LENGTH

VERTICAL PLANE

PARALLEL LINES

PLAN

ELEVATION

WIDTH 2 X SCALE

GROUND LINE

HEIGHT

LENGTH

45° POINT

Jim Maeda; Samuel J. De Santo and Associates; New York, New York

THREE-POINT PERSPECTIVE

In a one- or two-point perspective the vertical lines of the object are usually parallel to each other and perpendicular to the ground plane. In reality, however, the vertical lines also converge—depending on the height of the observer (or the station point). If the station point is higher than the roof plane, the vertical lines will converge as they get closer to the ground plane; if the station point is lower than the roof plane, the vertical lines will converge as they move further away from the ground plane.

The three-point perspective is very similar in method to the two-point one. The plan is rotated at any angle to the picture plane, and the location of the station point (in plan) is determined in the same way. The right and left vanishing points will likewise be located on the horizon line. The side view, however, differs from the two-point perspective in that the picture plane is now tilted forward when viewing the building (or object) from a point lower than the roof plane or backward when viewing the building from a point higher than the roof plane. When the lines of vision are drawn to the station point in plan and a side elevation, the combined projections result in a three-point perspective as viewed from the "front." As in the other projected perspective methods, a plan view, side view, and picture plan are required before the perspective can be constructed.

Vanishing point left and vanishing point right (indicated as points 1 and 2 in the illustration) are located on the horizon line. The distance between these two points is approximately four times the maximum length of the object. Once these two points are determined, the entire framework of the construction can be drawn using the 30/60 and 45° triangles (75° = 30 =45).

LENGTH

The length line is drawn at the same scale as the line connecting points 1 and 2 (which is four times the maximum length of the object). Measured points are projected perpendicularly from the length line to (H) the ground line (see illustration). From the ground line, the measured points are connected to vanishing point left (or point 1).

WIDTH

At double the original scale. That is, if length (L) is at a ¼ in. scale, use ½ in. scale for width (W), locate the distances along the width line, and connect these points directly to the vanishing point right (or point 2).

HEIGHT

Using the original scale, mark off the measuring points along the height line (H). These points are projected perpendicularly to the line labeled "vertical plane." From these points a line is drawn to vanishing point right (point 2), thereby cutting the vertical lines vanishing to point 2.

45° POINT

This point on the horizon is determined by projecting a line from the upside down station point so that it will meet the horizon line at a 75° angle. All lines occurring at a 45° angle to the picture plane (in viewing) will converge to this point; it is, therefore, often convenient to use this as a reference point when converting exact width to length, or vice versa, in plan.

GRAPHIC METHODS

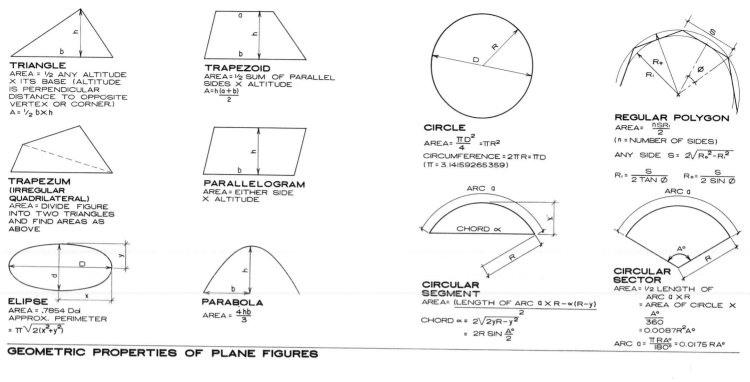

TRIANGLE
AREA = ½ ANY ALTITUDE × ITS BASE (ALTITUDE IS PERPENDICULAR DISTANCE TO OPPOSITE VERTEX OR CORNER.)
$A = \frac{1}{2} b \times h$

TRAPEZOID
AREA = ½ SUM OF PARALLEL SIDES × ALTITUDE
$A = h \frac{(a+b)}{2}$

CIRCLE
AREA $= \frac{\pi D^2}{4} = \pi R^2$
CIRCUMFERENCE $= 2\pi R = \pi D$
($\pi = 3.14159265359$)

REGULAR POLYGON
AREA $= \frac{n S R_i}{2}$
(n = NUMBER OF SIDES)
ANY SIDE $S = 2\sqrt{R_o^2 - R_i^2}$
$R_i = \frac{S}{2 \tan \phi}$ $R_o = \frac{S}{2 \sin \phi}$

TRAPEZUM
(IRREGULAR QUADRILATERAL)
AREA = DIVIDE FIGURE INTO TWO TRIANGLES AND FIND AREAS AS ABOVE

PARALLELOGRAM
AREA = EITHER SIDE × ALTITUDE

CIRCULAR SEGMENT
AREA $= \frac{(\text{LENGTH OF ARC } a \times R - a(R-y))}{2}$
CHORD $a = 2\sqrt{2yR - y^2}$
$= 2R \sin \frac{A°}{2}$

ELIPSE
AREA = .7854 Dd
APPROX. PERIMETER $= \pi \sqrt{2(x^2 + y^2)}$

PARABOLA
AREA $= \frac{4 hb}{3}$

CIRCULAR SECTOR
AREA = ½ LENGTH OF ARC $a \times R$
= AREA OF CIRCLE × $\frac{A°}{360}$
$= 0.0087 R^2 A°$
ARC $a = \frac{\pi R A°}{180°} = 0.0175 R A°$

GEOMETRIC PROPERTIES OF PLANE FIGURES

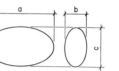
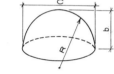
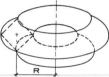

SPHERE
VOLUME $= \frac{4 \pi R^3}{3}$
$= 0.5236 D^3$
SURFACE $= 4 \pi R^2$
$= \pi D^2$

SEGMENT OF SPHERE
VOLUME $= \frac{1 \pi b^2 (3R - b)}{3}$
(OR SECTOR - CONE)
SURFACE $= 2\pi R b$
(NOT INCLUDING SURFACE OF CIRCULAR BASE)

SECTOR OF SPHERE
VOLUME $= \frac{2\pi R^2 b}{3}$
SURFACE $= \frac{\pi R (4b + c)}{2}$
(OR: SEGMENT + CONE)

ELIPSOID
VOLUME $= \frac{\pi abc}{6}$
SURFACE: NO SIMPLE RULE

PARABOLOID OF REVOLUTION
VOLUME = AREA OF CIRCULAR BASE × ½ ALTITUDE.
SURFACE: NO SIMPLE RULE

CIRCULAR RING OF ANY SECTION
R = DISTANCE FROM AXIS OF RING TO TRUE CENTER OF SECTION
VOLUME = AREA OF SECTION × 2πR
SURFACE = PERIMETER OF SECTION × 2πR (CONSIDER THE SECTION ON ONE SIDE OF AXIS ONLY)

VOLUMES AND SURFACES OF DOUBLE - CURVED SOLIDS

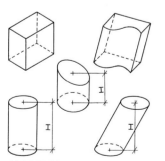
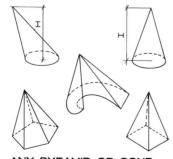
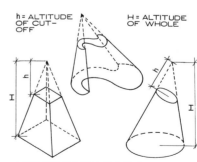

ANY PRISM OR CYLINDER, RIGHT OR OBLIQUE, REGULAR OR IRREGULAR.
Volume = area of base x altitude
Altitude = distance between parallel bases, measured perpendicular to the bases. When bases are not parallel, then Altitude = perpendicular distance from one base to the center of the other.

ANY PYRAMID OR CONE, RIGHT OR OBLIQUE, REGULAR OR IRREGULAR.
Volume = area of base x 1/3 altitude
Altitude = distance from base to apex, measured perpendicular to base.

ANY FRUSTUM OR TRUNCATED PORTION OF THE SOLIDS SHOWN
Volume: From the volume of the whole solid, if complete, subtract the volume of the portion cut off.
The altitude of the cut-off part must be measured perpendicular to its own base.

h = ALTITUDE OF CUT-OFF
H = ALTITUDE OF WHOLE

SURFACES OF SOLIDS
The area of the surface is best found by adding together the areas of all the faces.

The area of a right cylindrical surface = perimeter of base x length of elements (average length if other base is oblique).

The area of a right conical surface = perimeter of base x 1/2 length of elements.

There is no simple rule for the area of an oblique conical surface, or for a cylindrical one where neither base is perpendicular to the elements. The best method is to construct a development, as if making a paper model, and measure its area by one of the methods given on the next page.

VOLUMES AND SURFACES OF TYPICAL SOLIDS

GRAPHIC METHODS

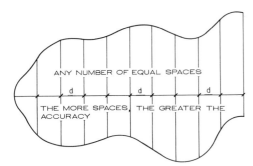

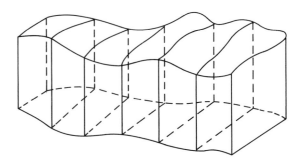

TO FIND THE AREA OF AN IRREGULAR PLANE FIGURE

1. Divide the figure into parallel strips by equally spaced parallel lines.

2. Measure the length of each of the parallel lines.

3. Obtain a summation of the unit areas by one of these 3 "rules".

TRAPEZOID RULE

Add together the length of the parallels, taking the first and last at $\frac{1}{2}$ value, and multiply by the width of the internal "d". This rule is sufficiently accurate for estimating and other ordinary purposes.

SIMPSON'S RULE

Add the parallels, taking the first and last at full value, second the, fourth, sixth, etc. from each end at 4 times full value, and the third, fifth, seventh, etc. from each end at 2 times the value, then multiply by $\frac{1}{3}$ d. This rule works only for an even number of spaces and is accurate for areas bounded by smooth curves.

DURAND'S RULE

Add the parallels taking the first and last at $\frac{5}{12}$ value, the second from each end at $\frac{13}{12}$ value, and all others at full value, then multiply by d. This rule is the most accurate for very irregular shapes.

NOTE

Irregular areas may be directly read off by means of a simple instrument called a Planimeter.

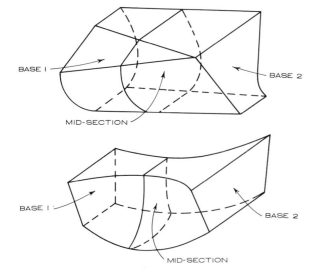

TO FIND THE VOLUME OF AN IRREGULAR FIGURE BY THE PRISMATOID FORMULA

Construct a section midway between the bases. Add 4 to the sum of the areas of the 2 bases and multiply the quantity by the area of the mid-section. Then multiply the total by $\frac{1}{6}$ the perpendicular distance between the bases.

V = [(area of base$_1$ + area of base$_2$ + 4) (area of midsection) x $\frac{1}{6}$ perpendicular distance between bases.

This formula is quite accurate for any solid with two parallel bases connected by a surface of straight line elements (upper figure), or smooth simple curves (lower figure).

TO FIND THE VOLUME OF A VERY IRREGULAR FIGURE BY THE SECTIONING METHOD

1. Construct a series of equally spaced sections or profiles.

2. Determine the area of each section by any of the methods shown at left (preferably with a Planimeter).

3. Apply any one of the 3 summation "rules" given at left, to determine the total volume.

This method is in general use for estimating quantities of earthwork, etc.

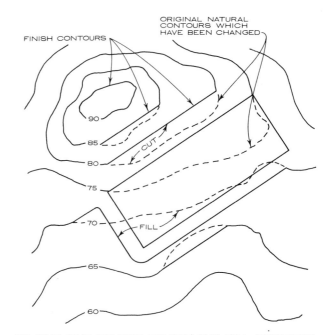

TO FIND THE VOLUME OF CUT AND FILL DIRECTLY FROM THE CONTOUR PLAN

1. Draw "finish" and "original" contours on same contour map.

2. Measure the differential areas between new and old contours of each contour and enter in columns according to whether cut or fill.

3. Add up each column and multiply by the contour interval to determine the volume in cubic feet.

EXAMPLE

CONTOUR	CUT		FILL	
85		300		
80		960		
75	2,460 − 2 =	1,230	3,800 − 2 =	1,900
70		20		2,200
		9,200		6,800
		x5		x5
TOTALS		46,000 cu. ft.		34,000 cu. ft.

NOTE

1. Where a cut or fill ends directly on a contour level use $\frac{1}{2}$ value.

2. The closer the contour interval, the greater the accuracy.

This method is more rapid than the sectioning method, and is sufficiently accurate for simple estimating purposes and for balancing of cut and fill.

GRAPHIC METHODS

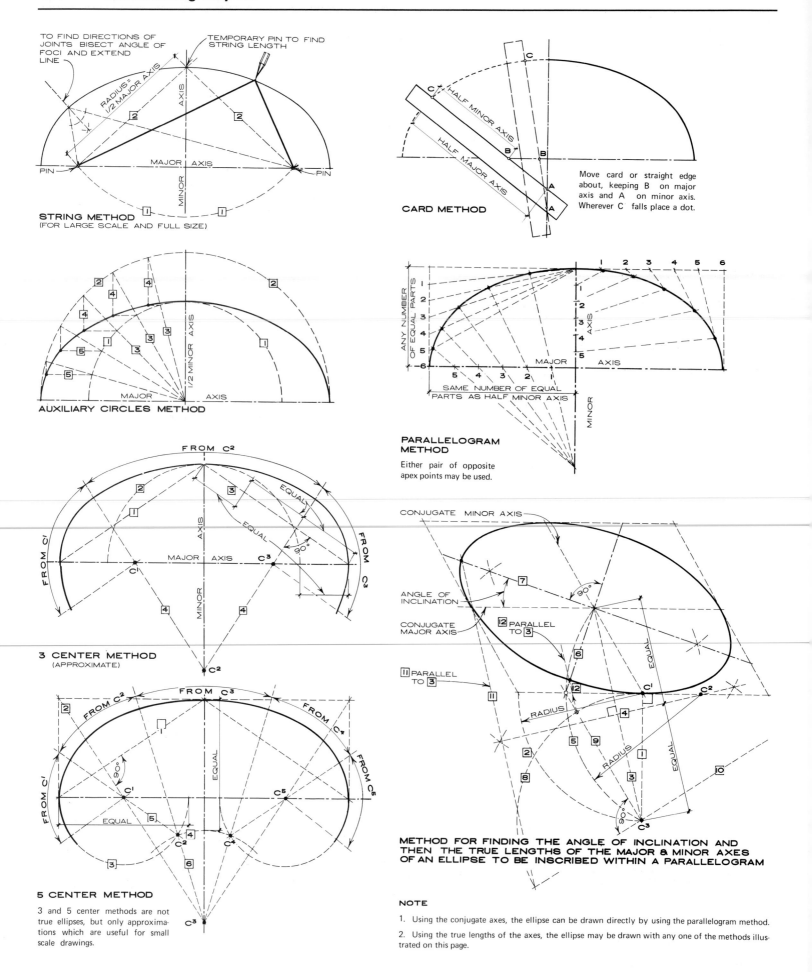

STRING METHOD
(FOR LARGE SCALE AND FULL SIZE)

TO FIND DIRECTIONS OF JOINTS BISECT ANGLE OF FOCI AND EXTEND LINE

TEMPORARY PIN TO FIND STRING LENGTH

RADIUS = 1/2 MAJOR AXIS

AXIS

MAJOR AXIS

MINOR

PIN

PIN

AUXILIARY CIRCLES METHOD

1/2 MINOR AXIS

MAJOR AXIS

3 CENTER METHOD
(APPROXIMATE)

FROM C²

FROM C¹

FROM C³

MAJOR AXIS

MINOR

AXIS

EQUAL

EQUAL

90°

C¹

C³

C²

5 CENTER METHOD

3 and 5 center methods are not true ellipses, but only approximations which are useful for small scale drawings.

FROM C²

FROM C³

FROM C⁴

FROM C¹

FROM C⁵

EQUAL

EQUAL

90°

C¹

C⁵

C²

C⁴

C³

CARD METHOD

HALF MINOR AXIS

HALF MAJOR AXIS

Move card or straight edge about, keeping B on major axis and A on minor axis. Wherever C falls place a dot.

PARALLELOGRAM METHOD

Either pair of opposite apex points may be used.

ANY NUMBER OF EQUAL PARTS

AXIS

MAJOR AXIS

MINOR

SAME NUMBER OF EQUAL PARTS AS HALF MINOR AXIS

CONJUGATE MINOR AXIS

ANGLE OF INCLINATION

CONJUGATE MAJOR AXIS

90°

PARALLEL TO 3

PARALLEL TO 3

RADIUS

RADIUS

EQUAL

EQUAL

90°

C¹

C²

C³

METHOD FOR FINDING THE ANGLE OF INCLINATION AND THEN THE TRUE LENGTHS OF THE MAJOR & MINOR AXES OF AN ELLIPSE TO BE INSCRIBED WITHIN A PARALLELOGRAM

NOTE

1. Using the conjugate axes, the ellipse can be drawn directly by using the parallelogram method.

2. Using the true lengths of the axes, the ellipse may be drawn with any one of the methods illustrated on this page.

GRAPHIC METHODS

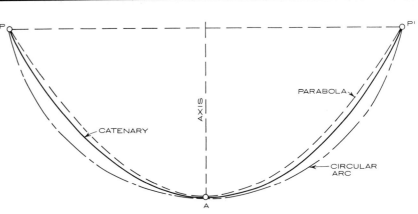

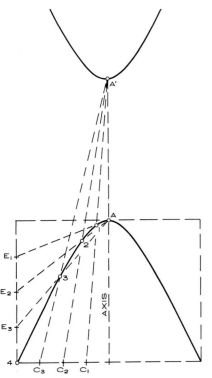

HYPERBOLA
PARALLELOGRAM METHOD

GIVEN:

Axis, two apexes (A and A') and a chord.

1. Draw surrounding parallelogram.
2. Divide chord in whole number of equal spaces (C_1, C_2, C_3, etc.).
3. Divide edge of parallelogram into same integral number of equal spaces (E_1, E_2, E_3, etc.).
4. Join A to points E on edge; join A' to points C on chord. Intersection of these rays are points on curve.

This method can be used equally well for any type of orthogonal or perspective projection, as shown by example of ellipse.

CATENARY

A catenary curve lies between a parabola and a circular arc drawn through the same three points, but is closer to the parabola. The catenary is not a conic section. The easiest method of drawing it is to tilt the drafting board and hang a very fine chain on it, and then prick guide points through the links of the chain.

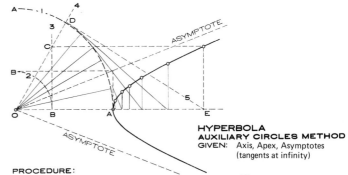

HYPERBOLA
AUXILIARY CIRCLES METHOD

GIVEN: Axis, Apex, Asymptotes (tangents at infinity)

PROCEDURE:

1. Draw auxiliary circles with OB and OA as radii: note $\frac{OB}{OA}$ = slope of asymptote.
2. Erect perpendicular 3 where circle 2 intersects axis.
3. Draw any line 4 through 0, intersecting circle 1 at B and line 3 at C.
4. Draw line 5 through C parallel to axis.
5. Draw tangent 6 at D, intersecting axis at E.
6. Erect perpendicular 7 at E, intersecting 5 at P, a point on hyperbola.

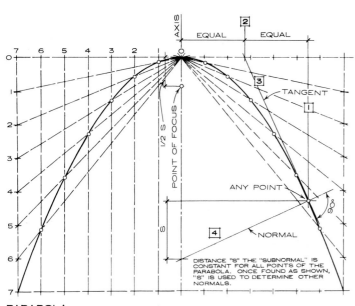

DISTANCE "S" THE "SUBNORMAL" IS CONSTANT FOR ALL POINTS OF THE PARABOLA. ONCE FOUND AS SHOWN, "S" IS USED TO DETERMINE OTHER NORMALS.

PARABOLA
PARALLELOGRAM METHOD

This method is comparable to the "Parallelogram Method" shown for the hyperbola above and the ellipse on previous page. The other apex 'A' is at infinity.

H. Seymour Howard, Jr.; Oyster Bay, New York

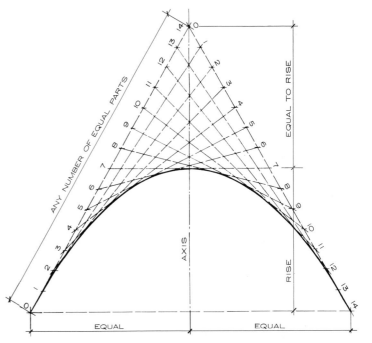

PARABOLA
ENVELOPE OF TANGENTS

This method does not give points on the curve, but a series of tangents within which the parabola can be drawn.

GRAPHIC METHODS   A

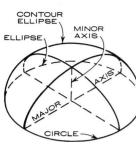

OBLATE SPHEROID

An ellipse rotated about its minor axis.

NOTES

1. The dome shapes shown above are SURFACES OF POSITIVE CUR—VATURE, that is, the centers of both principal radii of curvature are on the same side of the surface.

2. SURFACES OF NEGATIVE CURVATURE (saddle shapes) such as those shown below, are surfaces in which the centers of the two principal radii of curvature are on opposite sides of the surface.

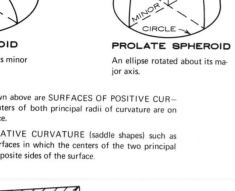

PROLATE SPHEROID

An ellipse rotated about its major axis.

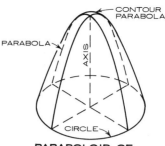

PARABOLOID OF REVOLUTION

A parabola rotated about its axis.

The elliptic paraboloid is similar, but its plan is an ellipse instead of circle, and vertical sections are varying parabolas.

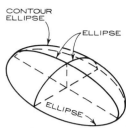

GENERAL ELLIPSOID

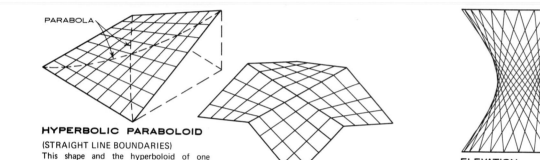

HYPERBOLIC PARABOLOID

(STRAIGHT LINE BOUNDARIES)
This shape and the hyperboloid of one sheet are the only two doubly ruled curved surfaces.

ELEVATION

PROJECTION

SECTION A-A

SECTION B-B

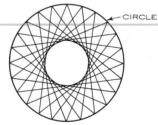

PLAN

HYPERBOLOID OF REVOLUTION

(OR HYPERBOLOID OF ONE SHEET)

NOTE

This shape is a doubly ruled surface, which can also be drawn with ellipses as plan sections instead of the circles shown.

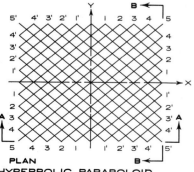

HYPERBOLIC PARABOLOID

(PARABOLA BOUNDATIONS)

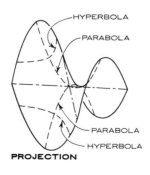

PROJECTION

SECTION

ELEVATION

PLAN

CONOID

(SINGLY RULED SURFACE)

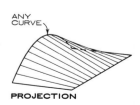

PROJECTION

A GRAPHIC METHODS

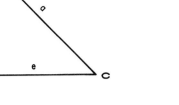

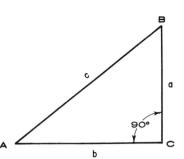

OBLIQUE TRIANGLES

FIND	GIVEN	SOLUTION
a	A B b	$b \sin A \div \sin B$
	A B c	$c \sin A \div \sin(A+B)$
	A C b	$b \sin A \div \sin(A+C)$
	A C c	$c \sin A \div \sin C$
	B C b	$b \sin(B+C) \div \sin B$
	B C c	$c \sin(B+C) \div \sin C$
	A b c	$\sqrt{b^2 + c^2 - 2bc \cdot \cos A}$
b	A B a	$a \sin B \div \sin A$
	A B c	$c \sin B \div \sin(A+B)$
	A C a	$a \sin(A+C) \div \sin A$
	A C c	$c \sin(A+C) \div \sin C$
	B C a	$a \sin B \div \sin(B+C)$
	B C c	$c \sin B \div \sin C$
	B a c	$\sqrt{a^2 + c^2 - 2ac \cdot \cos B}$
c	A B a	$a \sin(A+B) \div \sin A$
	A B b	$b \sin(A+B) \div \sin B$
	A C a	$a \sin C \div \sin A$
	A C b	$b \sin C \div \sin(A+C)$
	B C a	$a \sin C \div \sin(B+C)$
	B C b	$b \sin C \div \sin B$
	C a b	$\sqrt{a^2 + b^2 - 2ab \cdot \cos C}$
½ (B+C)	A b c	$90° - \tfrac{1}{2}A$
½ (B−C)	A b c	$\tan = [(b-c)\tan(90°-\tfrac{1}{2}A)] \div (b+c)$
½ (A+C)	B a c	$90° - \tfrac{1}{2}B$
½ (A−C)	B a c	$\tan = [(a-c)\tan(90°-\tfrac{1}{2}B)] \div (a+c)$
½ (A+B)	C a b	$90° - \tfrac{1}{2}C$
½ (A−B)	C a b	$\tan = [(a-b)\tan(90°-\tfrac{1}{2}C)] \div (a+b)$

FIND	GIVEN	SOLUTION
A	a b c s	$\sin \tfrac{1}{2} A = \sqrt{(s-b)(s-c) \div bc}$
	a b c s	$\cos \tfrac{1}{2} A = \sqrt{s(s-a) \div bc}$
	a b c s	$\tan \tfrac{1}{2} A = \sqrt{(s-b)(s-c) \div s(s-a)}$
	B a b	$\sin A = a \sin B \div b$
	B a c	$\tfrac{1}{2}(A+C) + \tfrac{1}{2}(A-C)$
	C a b	$\tfrac{1}{2}(A+B) + \tfrac{1}{2}(A-B)$
	C a c	$\sin A = a \sin C \div c$
B	a b c s	$\sin \tfrac{1}{2} B = \sqrt{(s-a)(s-c) \div ac}$
	a b c s	$\cos \tfrac{1}{2} B = \sqrt{s(s-b) \div ac}$
	a b c s	$\tan \tfrac{1}{2} B = \sqrt{(s-a)(s-c) \div s(s-b)}$
	A a b	$\sin B = b \sin A \div a$
	A b c	$\tfrac{1}{2}(B+C) + \tfrac{1}{2}(B-C)$
	C a b	$\tfrac{1}{2}(A+B) - \tfrac{1}{2}(A-B)$
	C a c	$\sin B = b \sin C \div c$
C	a b c s	$\sin \tfrac{1}{2} C = \sqrt{(s-a)(s-b) \div ab}$
	a b c s	$\cos \tfrac{1}{2} C = \sqrt{s(s-c) \div ab}$
	a b c s	$\tan \tfrac{1}{2} C = \sqrt{(s-a)(s-b) \div s(s-c)}$
	A a c	$\sin C = c \sin A \div a$
	A b c	$\tfrac{1}{2}(B+C) - \tfrac{1}{2}(B-C)$
	B a c	$\tfrac{1}{2}(A+C) - \tfrac{1}{2}(A-C)$
	B b c	$\sin C = c \sin B \div b$
AREA	a b c	$\sqrt{s(s-a)(s-b)(s-c)}$
	C a b	$\tfrac{1}{2} ab \sin C$
s	a b c	$(a + b + c) \div 2$
d	a b c s	$(b^2 + c^2 - a^2) \div 2b$
e	a b c s	$(a^2 + b^2 - c^2) \div 2b$

RIGHT TRIANGLES

FIND	GIVEN	SOLUTION
A	a b	$\tan A = a \div b$
	a c	$\sin A = a \div c$
	b c	$\cos A = b \div c$
B	a b	$\tan B = b \div a$
	a c	$\cos B = a \div c$
	b c	$\sin B = b \div c$
a	A b	$b \tan A$
	A c	$c \sin A$
b	A a	$a \div \tan A$
	A c	$c \cos A$
c	A a	$a \div \sin A$
	A b	$b \div \cos A$
AREA	a b	$ab \div 2$

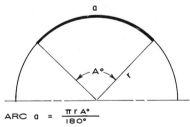

$$\text{ARC } a = \frac{\pi r A°}{180°}$$

ARCS

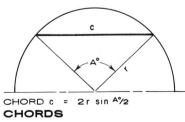

$$\text{CHORD } c = 2r \sin \tfrac{A°}{2}$$

CHORDS

MATHEMATICAL DATA A

NATURAL SINES

ANGLE	0′	10′	20′	30′	40′	50′	60′	
0°	0.00000	0.00291	0.00582	0.00873	0.01164	0.01454	0.01745	89°
1	0.01745	0.02036	0.02327	0.02618	0.02908	0.03199	0.03490	88
2	0.03490	0.03781	0.04071	0.04362	0.04653	0.04943	0.05234	87
3	0.05234	0.05524	0.05814	0.06105	0.06395	0.06685	0.06976	86
4	0.06976	0.07266	0.07556	0.07846	0.08136	0.08426	0.08716	85
5	0.08716	0.09005	0.09295	0.09585	0.09874	0.10164	0.10453	84
6	0.10453	0.10742	0.11031	0.11320	0.11609	0.11898	0.12187	83
7	0.12187	0.12476	0.12764	0.13053	0.13341	0.13629	0.13917	82
8	0.13917	0.14205	0.14493	0.14781	0.15069	0.15356	0.15643	81
9	0.15643	0.15931	0.16218	0.16505	0.16792	0.17078	0.17365	80
10	0.17365	0.17651	0.17937	0.18224	0.18509	0.18795	0.19081	79
11	0.19081	0.19366	0.19652	0.19937	0.20222	0.20507	0.20791	78
12	0.20791	0.21076	0.21360	0.21644	0.21928	0.22212	0.22495	77
13	0.22495	0.22778	0.23062	0.23345	0.23627	0.23910	0.24192	76
14	0.24192	0.24474	0.24756	0.25038	0.25320	0.25601	0.25882	75
15	0.25882	0.26163	0.26443	0.26724	0.27004	0.27284	0.27564	74
16	0.27564	0.27843	0.28123	0.28402	0.28680	0.28959	0.29237	73
17	0.29237	0.29515	0.29793	0.30071	0.30348	0.30625	0.30902	72
18	0.30902	0.31178	0.31454	0.31730	0.32006	0.32282	0.32557	71
19	0.32557	0.32832	0.33106	0.33381	0.33655	0.33929	0.34202	70
20	0.34202	0.34475	0.34748	0.35021	0.35293	0.35565	0.35837	69
21	0.35837	0.36108	0.36379	0.36650	0.36921	0.37191	0.37461	68
22	0.37461	0.37730	0.37999	0.38268	0.38537	0.38805	0.39073	67
23	0.39073	0.39341	0.39608	0.39875	0.40141	0.40408	0.40674	66
24	0.40674	0.40939	0.41204	0.41469	0.41734	0.41998	0.42262	65
25	0.42262	0.42525	0.42788	0.43051	0.43313	0.43575	0.43837	64
26	0.43837	0.44098	0.44359	0.44620	0.44880	0.45140	0.45399	63
27	0.45399	0.45658	0.45917	0.46175	0.46433	0.46690	0.46947	62
28	0.46947	0.47204	0.47460	0.47716	0.47971	0.48226	0.48481	61
29	0.48481	0.48735	0.48989	0.49242	0.49495	0.49748	0.50000	60
30	0.50000	0.50252	0.50503	0.50754	0.51004	0.51254	0.51504	59
31	0.51504	0.51753	0.52002	0.52250	0.52498	0.52745	0.52992	58
32	0.52992	0.53238	0.53484	0.53730	0.53975	0.54220	0.54464	57
33	0.54464	0.54708	0.54951	0.55194	0.55436	0.55678	0.55919	56
34	0.55919	0.56160	0.56401	0.56641	0.56880	0.57119	0.57358	55
35	0.57358	0.57596	0.57833	0.58070	0.58307	0.58543	0.58779	54
36	0.58779	0.59014	0.59248	0.59482	0.59716	0.59949	0.60182	53
37	0.60182	0.60414	0.60645	0.60876	0.61107	0.61337	0.61566	52
38	0.61566	0.61795	0.62024	0.62251	0.62479	0.62706	0.62932	51
39	0.62932	0.63158	0.63383	0.63608	0.63832	0.64056	0.64279	50
40	0.64279	0.64501	0.64723	0.64945	0.65166	0.65386	0.65606	49
41	0.65606	0.65825	0.66044	0.66262	0.66480	0.66697	0.66913	48
42	0.66913	0.67129	0.67344	0.67559	0.67773	0.67987	0.68200	47
43	0.68200	0.68412	0.68624	0.68835	0.69046	0.69256	0.69466	46
44°	0.69466	0.69675	0.69883	0.70091	0.70298	0.70505	0.70711	45°
	60′	50′	40′	30′	20′	10′	0′	ANGLE

NATURAL COSINES

NATURAL TANGENTS

ANGLE	0′	10′	20′	30′	40′	50′	60′	
0°	0.00000	0.00291	0.00582	0.00873	0.01164	0.01455	0.01746	89°
1	0.01746	0.02036	0.02328	0.02619	0.02910	0.03201	0.03492	88
2	0.03492	0.03783	0.04075	0.04366	0.04658	0.04949	0.05241	87
3	0.05241	0.05533	0.05824	0.06116	0.06408	0.06700	0.06993	86
4	0.06993	0.07285	0.07578	0.07870	0.08163	0.08456	0.08749	85
5	0.08749	0.09042	0.09335	0.09629	0.09923	0.10216	0.10510	84
6	0.10510	0.10805	0.11099	0.11394	0.11688	0.11983	0.12278	83
7	0.12278	0.12574	0.12869	0.13165	0.13461	0.13758	0.14054	82
8	0.14054	0.14351	0.14648	0.14945	0.15243	0.15540	0.15838	81
9	0.15838	0.16137	0.16435	0.16734	0.17033	0.17333	0.17633	80
10	0.17633	0.17933	0.18233	0.18534	0.18835	0.19136	0.19438	79
11	0.19438	0.19740	0.20042	0.20345	0.20648	0.20952	0.21256	78
12	0.21256	0.21560	0.21864	0.22169	0.22475	0.22781	0.23087	77
13	0.23087	0.23393	0.23700	0.24008	0.24316	0.24624	0.24933	76
14	0.24933	0.25242	0.25552	0.25862	0.26172	0.26483	0.26795	75
15	0.26795	0.27107	0.27419	0.27732	0.28046	0.28360	0.28675	74
16	0.28675	0.28990	0.29305	0.29621	0.29938	0.30255	0.30573	73
17	0.30573	0.30891	0.31210	0.31530	0.31850	0.32171	0.32492	72
18	0.32492	0.32814	0.33136	0.33460	0.33783	0.34108	0.34433	71
19	0.34433	0.34758	0.35085	0.35412	0.35740	0.36068	0.36397	70
20	0.36397	0.36727	0.37057	0.37388	0.37720	0.38053	0.38386	69
21	0.38386	0.38721	0.39055	0.39391	0.39727	0.40065	0.40403	68
22	0.40403	0.40741	0.41081	0.41421	0.41763	0.42105	0.42447	67
23	0.42447	0.42791	0.43136	0.43481	0.43828	0.44175	0.44523	66
24	0.44523	0.44872	0.45222	0.45573	0.45924	0.46277	0.46631	65
25	0.46631	0.46985	0.47341	0.47698	0.48055	0.48414	0.48773	64
26	0.48773	0.49134	0.49495	0.49858	0.50222	0.50587	0.50953	63
27	0.50953	0.51320	0.51688	0.52057	0.52427	0.52798	0.53171	62
28	0.53171	0.53545	0.53920	0.54296	0.54673	0.55051	0.55431	61
29	0.55431	0.55812	0.56194	0.56577	0.56962	0.57348	0.57735	60
30	0.57735	0.58124	0.58513	0.58905	0.59297	0.59691	0.60086	59
31	0.60086	0.60483	0.60881	0.61280	0.61681	0.62083	0.62487	58
32	0.62487	0.62892	0.63299	0.63707	0.64117	0.64528	0.64941	57
33	0.64941	0.65355	0.65771	0.66189	0.66608	0.67028	0.67451	56
34	0.67451	0.67875	0.68301	0.68728	0.69157	0.69588	0.70021	55
35	0.70021	0.70455	0.70891	0.71329	0.71769	0.72211	0.72654	54
36	0.72654	0.73100	0.73547	0.73996	0.74447	0.74900	0.75355	53
37	0.75355	0.75812	0.76272	0.76733	0.77196	0.77661	0.78129	52
38	0.78129	0.78598	0.79070	0.79544	0.80020	0.80498	0.80978	51
39	0.80978	0.81461	0.81946	0.82434	0.82923	0.83415	0.83910	50
40	0.83910	0.84407	0.84906	0.85408	0.85912	0.86419	0.86929	49
41	0.96929	0.87441	0.87955	0.88473	0.88992	0.89515	0.90040	48
42	0.90040	0.90569	0.91099	0.91633	0.92170	0.92709	0.93252	47
43	0.93252	0.93797	0.94345	0.94896	0.95451	0.96008	0.96569	46
44°	0.96569	0.97133	0.97700	0.98270	0.98843	0.99420	1.00000	45°
	60′	50′	40′	30′	20′	10′	0′	ANGLE

NATURAL COTANGENTS

NATURAL SINES

ANGLE	0′	10′	20′	30′	40′	50′	60′	
45°	0.70711	0.70916	0.71121	0.71325	0.71529	0.71732	0.71934	44°
46	0.71934	0.72136	0.72337	0.72537	0.72737	0.72937	0.73135	43
47	0.73135	0.73333	0.73531	0.73728	0.73924	0.74120	0.74314	42
48	0.74314	0.74509	0.74703	0.74896	0.75088	0.75280	0.75471	41
49	0.75471	0.75661	0.75851	0.76041	0.76229	0.76417	0.76604	40
50	0.76604	0.76791	0.76977	0.77162	0.77347	0.77531	0.77715	39
51	0.77715	0.77897	0.78079	0.78261	0.78442	0.78622	0.78801	38
52	0.78801	0.78980	0.79158	0.79335	0.79512	0.79688	0.79864	37
53	0.79864	0.80038	0.80212	0.80386	0.80558	0.80730	0.80902	36
54	0.80902	0.81072	0.81242	0.81412	0.81580	0.81748	0.81915	35
55	0.81915	0.82082	0.82248	0.82413	0.82577	0.82741	0.82904	34
56	0.82904	0.83066	0.83228	0.83389	0.83549	0.83708	0.83867	33
57	0.83867	0.84025	0.84182	0.84339	0.84495	0.84650	0.84805	32
58	0.84805	0.84959	0.85112	0.85264	0.85416	0.85567	0.85717	31
59	0.85717	0.85866	0.86015	0.86163	0.86310	0.86457	0.86603	30
60	0.86603	0.86748	0.86892	0.87036	0.87178	0.87321	0.87462	29
61	0.87462	0.87603	0.87743	0.87882	0.88020	0.88158	0.88295	28
62	0.88295	0.88431	0.88566	0.88701	0.88835	0.88968	0.89101	27
63	0.89101	0.89232	0.89363	0.89493	0.89623	0.89752	0.89879	26
64	0.89879	0.90007	0.90133	0.90259	0.90383	0.90507	0.90631	25
65	0.90631	0.90753	0.90875	0.90996	0.91116	0.91236	0.91355	24
66	0.91355	0.91472	0.91590	0.91706	0.91822	0.91936	0.92050	23
67	0.92050	0.92164	0.92276	0.92388	0.92499	0.92609	0.92718	22
68	0.92718	0.92827	0.92935	0.93042	0.93148	0.93253	0.93358	21
69	0.93358	0.93462	0.93565	0.93667	0.93769	0.93869	0.93969	20
70	0.93969	0.94068	0.94167	0.94264	0.94361	0.94457	0.94552	19
71	0.94552	0.94646	0.94740	0.94832	0.94924	0.95015	0.95106	18
72	0.95106	0.95195	0.95284	0.95372	0.95459	0.95545	0.95630	17
73	0.95630	0.95715	0.95799	0.95882	0.95964	0.96046	0.96126	16
74	0.96126	0.96206	0.96285	0.96363	0.96440	0.96517	0.96593	15
75	0.96593	0.96667	0.96742	0.96815	0.96887	0.96959	0.97030	14
76	0.97030	0.97100	0.97169	0.97237	0.97304	0.97371	0.97437	13
77	0.97437	0.97502	0.97566	0.97630	0.97692	0.97754	0.97815	12
78	0.97815	0.97875	0.97934	0.97992	0.98050	0.98107	0.98163	11
79	0.98163	0.98218	0.98272	0.98325	0.98378	0.98430	0.98481	10
80	0.98481	0.98531	0.98580	0.98629	0.98676	0.98723	0.98769	9
81	0.98769	0.98814	0.98858	0.98902	0.98944	0.98986	0.99027	8
82	0.99027	0.99067	0.99106	0.99144	0.99182	0.99219	0.99255	7
83	0.99255	0.99290	0.99324	0.99357	0.99390	0.99421	0.99452	6
84	0.99452	0.99482	0.99511	0.99540	0.99567	0.99594	0.99619	5
85	0.99619	0.99644	0.99668	0.99692	0.99714	0.99736	0.99756	4
86	0.99756	0.99776	0.99795	0.99813	0.99831	0.99847	0.99863	3
87	0.99863	0.99878	0.99892	0.99905	0.99917	0.99929	0.99939	2
88	0.99939	0.99949	0.99958	0.99966	0.99973	0.99979	0.99985	1
89°	0.99985	0.99989	0.99993	0.99996	0.99998	1.00000	1.00000	0°
	60′	50′	40′	30′	20′	10′	0′	ANGLE

NATURAL COSINES

NATURAL TANGENTS

ANGLE	0′	10′	20′	30′	40′	50′	60′	
45°	1.00000	1.00583	1.01170	1.01761	1.02355	1.02952	1.03553	44°
46	1.03553	1.04158	1.04766	1.05378	1.05994	1.06613	1.07237	43
47	1.07237	1.07864	1.08496	1.09131	1.09770	1.10414	1.11061	42
48	1.11061	1.11713	1.12369	1.13029	1.13694	1.14363	1.15037	41
49	1.15037	1.15715	1.16398	1.17085	1.17777	1.18474	1.19175	40
50	1.19175	1.19882	1.20593	1.21310	1.22031	1.22758	1.23490	39
51	1.23490	1.24227	1.24969	1.25717	1.26471	1.27230	1.27994	38
52	1.27994	1.28764	1.29541	1.30323	1.31110	1.31904	1.32704	37
53	1.32704	1.33511	1.34323	1.35142	1.35968	1.36800	1.37638	36
54	1.37638	1.38484	1.39336	1.40195	1.41061	1.41934	1.42815	35
55	1.42815	1.43703	1.44598	1.45501	1.46411	1.47330	1.48256	34
56	1.48256	1.49190	1.50133	1.51084	1.52043	1.53010	1.53987	33
57	1.53987	1.54972	1.55966	1.56969	1.57981	1.59002	1.60033	32
58	1.60033	1.61074	1.62125	1.63185	1.64256	1.65337	1.66428	31
59	1.66428	1.67530	1.68643	1.69766	1.70901	1.72047	1.73205	30
60	1.73205	1.74375	1.75556	1.76749	1.77955	1.79174	1.80405	29
61	1.80405	1.81649	1.82906	1.84177	1.85462	1.86760	1.88073	28
62	1.88073	1.89400	1.90741	1.92098	1.93470	1.94858	1.96261	27
63	1.96261	1.97681	1.99116	2.00569	2.02039	2.03526	2.05030	26
64	2.05030	2.06553	2.08094	2.09654	2.11233	2.12832	2.14451	25
65	2.14451	2.16090	2.17749	2.19430	2.21132	2.22857	2.24604	24
66	2.24604	2.26374	2.28167	2.29984	2.31826	2.33693	2.35585	23
67	2.35585	2.37504	2.39449	2.41421	2.43422	2.45451	2.47509	22
68	2.47509	2.49597	2.51715	2.53865	2.56046	2.58261	2.60509	21
69	2.60509	2.62791	2.65109	2.67462	2.69853	2.72281	2.74748	20
70	2.74748	2.77254	2.79802	2.82391	2.85023	2.87700	2.90421	19
71	2.90421	2.93189	2.96004	2.98869	3.01783	3.04749	3.07768	18
72	3.07768	3.10842	3.13972	3.17159	3.20406	3.23714	3.27085	17
73	3.27085	3.30521	3.34023	3.37594	3.41236	3.44951	3.48741	16
74	3.48741	3.52609	3.56557	3.60588	3.64705	3.68909	3.73205	15
75	3.73205	3.77595	3.82083	3.86671	3.91364	3.96165	4.01078	14
76	4.01078	4.06107	4.11256	4.16530	4.21933	4.27471	4.33148	13
77	4.33148	4.38969	4.44942	4.51071	4.57363	4.63825	4.70463	12
78	4.70463	4.77286	4.84300	4.91516	4.98940	5.06584	5.14455	11
79	5.14455	5.22566	5.30928	5.39552	5.48451	5.57638	5.67128	10
80	5.67128	5.76937	5.87080	5.97576	6.08444	6.19703	6.31375	9
81	6.31375	6.43484	6.56055	6.69116	6.82694	6.96823	7.11537	8
82	7.11537	7.26873	7.42871	7.59575	7.77035	7.95302	8.14435	7
83	8.14435	8.34496	8.55555	8.77689	9.00983	9.25530	9.51436	6
84	9.51436	9.78817	10.07803	10.38540	10.71191	11.05943	11.43005	5
85	11.43005	11.82617	12.25051	12.70621	13.19688	13.72674	14.30067	4
86	14.30067	14.92442	15.60478	16.34986	17.16934	18.07498	19.08114	3
87	19.08114	20.20555	21.47040	22.90377	24.54176	26.43160	28.63625	2
88	28.63625	31.24158	34.36777	38.18846	42.96408	49.10388	57.28996	1
89°	57.28996	68.75009	85.93979	114.58865	171.88540	343.77371	Infinite	0°
	60′	50′	40′	30′	20′	10′	0′	ANGLE

NATURAL COTANGENTS

A MATHEMATICAL DATA

NATURAL SECANTS

ANGLE	0′	10′	20′	30′	40′	50′	60′	
0°	1.00000	1.00001	1.00002	1.00004	1.00007	1.00011	1.00015	89°
1	1.00015	1.00021	1.00027	1.00034	1.00042	1.00051	1.00061	88
2	1.00061	1.00072	1.00083	1.00095	1.00108	1.00122	1.00137	87
3	1.00137	1.00153	1.00169	1.00187	1.00205	1.00224	1.00244	86
4	1.00244	1.00265	1.00287	1.00309	1.00333	1.00357	1.00382	85
5	1.00382	1.00408	1.00435	1.00463	1.00491	1.00521	1.00551	84
6	1.00551	1.00582	1.00614	1.00647	1.00681	1.00715	1.00751	83
7	1.00751	1.00787	1.00825	1.00863	1.00902	1.00942	1.00983	82
8	1.00983	1.01024	1.01067	1.01111	1.01155	1.01200	1.01247	81
9	1.01247	1.01294	1.01342	1.01391	1.01440	1.10491	1.01543	80
10	1.01543	1.01595	1.01649	1.01703	1.01758	1.01815	1.01872	79
11	1.01872	1.01930	1.01989	1.02049	1.02110	1.02171	1.02234	78
12	1.02234	1.02298	1.02362	1.02428	1.02494	1.02562	1.02630	77
13	1.02630	1.02700	1.02770	1.02842	1.02914	1.02987	1.03061	76
14	1.03061	1.03137	1.03213	1.03290	1.03368	1.03447	1.03528	75
15	1.03528	1.03609	1.03691	1.03774	1.03858	1.03944	1.04030	74
16	1.04030	1.04117	1.04206	1.04295	1.04385	1.04477	1.04569	73
17	1.04569	1.04663	1.04757	1.04853	1.04950	1.05047	1.05146	72
18	1.05146	1.05246	1.05347	1.05449	1.05552	1.05657	1.05762	71
19	1.05762	1.05869	1.05976	1.06085	1.06195	1.06306	1.06418	70
20	1.06418	1.06531	1.06645	1.06761	1.06878	1.06995	1.07115	69
21	1.07115	1.07235	1.07356	1.07479	1.07602	1.07727	1.07853	68
22	1.07853	1.07981	1.08109	1.08239	1.08370	1.08503	1.08636	67
23	1.08636	1.08771	1.08907	1.09044	1.09183	1.09323	1.09464	66
24	1.09464	1.09606	1.09750	1.09895	1.10041	1.10189	1.10338	65
25	1.10338	1.10488	1.10640	1.10793	1.10947	1.11103	1.11260	64
26	1.11260	1.11419	1.11579	1.11740	1.11903	1.12067	1.12233	63
27	1.12233	1.12400	1.12568	1.12738	1.12910	1.13083	1.13257	62
28	1.13257	1.13433	1.13610	1.13789	1.13970	1.14152	1.14335	61
29	1.14335	1.14521	1.14707	1.14896	1.15085	1.15277	1.15470	60
30	1.15470	1.15665	1.15861	1.16059	1.16259	1.16460	1.16663	59
31	1.16663	1.16868	1.17075	1.17283	1.17493	1.17704	1.17918	58
32	1.17918	1.18133	1.18350	1.18569	1.18790	1.19012	1.19236	57
33	1.19236	1.19463	1.19691	1.19920	1.20152	1.20386	1.20622	56
34	1.20622	1.20859	1.21099	1.21341	1.21584	1.21830	1.22077	55
35	1.22077	1.22327	1.22579	1.22833	1.23089	1.23347	1.23607	54
36	1.23607	1.23869	1.24134	1.24400	1.24669	1.24940	1.25214	53
37	1.25214	1.25489	1.25767	1.26047	1.26330	1.26615	1.26902	52
38	1.26902	1.27191	1.27483	1.27778	1.28075	1.28374	1.28676	51
39	1.28676	1.28980	1.29287	1.29597	1.29909	1.30223	1.30541	50
40	1.30541	1.30861	1.31183	1.31509	1.31837	1.32168	1.32501	49
41	1.32501	1.32838	1.33177	1.33519	1.33864	1.34212	1.34563	48
42	1.34563	1.34917	1.35274	1.35634	1.35997	1.36363	1.36733	47
43	1.36733	1.37105	1.37481	1.37860	1.38242	1.38628	1.39016	46
44°	1.39016	1.39409	1.39804	1.40203	1.40606	1.41012	1.41421	45°
45°	1.41421	1.41835	1.42251	1.42672	1.43096	1.43524	1.43956	44°
46	1.43956	1.44391	1.44831	1.45274	1.45721	1.46173	1.46628	43
47	1.46628	1.47087	1.47551	1.48019	1.48491	1.48967	1.49448	42
48	1.49448	1.49933	1.50422	1.50916	1.51415	1.51918	1.52425	41
49	1.52425	1.52938	1.53455	1.53977	1.54504	1.55036	1.55572	40
50	1.55572	1.56114	1.56661	1.57213	1.57771	1.58333	1.58902	39
51	1.58902	1.59475	1.60054	1.60639	1.61229	1.61825	1.62427	38
52	1.62427	1.63035	1.63648	1.64268	1.64894	1.65526	1.66164	37
53	1.66164	1.66809	1.67460	1.68117	1.68782	1.69452	1.70130	36
54	1.70130	1.70815	1.71506	1.72205	1.72911	1.73624	1.74345	35
55	1.74345	1.75073	1.75808	1.76552	1.77303	1.78062	1.78829	34
56	1.78829	1.79604	1.80388	1.81180	1.81981	1.82790	1.83608	33
57	1.83608	1.84435	1.85271	1.86116	1.86970	1.87834	1.88708	32
58	1.88708	1.89591	1.90485	1.91388	1.92302	1.93226	1.94160	31
59	1.94160	1.95106	1.96062	1.97029	1.98008	1.98998	2.00000	30
60	2.00000	2.01014	2.02039	2.03077	2.04128	2.05191	2.06267	29
61	2.06267	2.07356	2.08458	2.09574	2.10704	2.11847	2.13005	28
62	2.13005	2.14178	2.15366	2.16568	2.17786	2.19019	2.20269	27
63	2.20269	2.21535	2.22817	2.24116	2.25432	2.26766	2.28117	26
64	2.28117	2.29487	2.30875	2.32282	2.33708	2.35154	2.36620	25
65	2.36620	2.38107	2.39614	2.41142	2.42692	2.44264	2.45859	24
66	2.45859	2.47477	2.49119	2.50784	2.52474	2.54190	2.55930	23
67	2.55930	2.57698	2.59491	2.61313	2.63162	2.65040	2.66947	22
68	2.66947	2.68884	2.70851	2.72850	2.74881	2.76945	2.79043	21
69	2.79043	2.81175	2.83342	2.85545	2.87785	2.90063	2.92380	20
70	2.92380	2.94737	2.97135	2.99574	3.02057	3.04584	3.07155	19
71	3.07155	3.09774	3.12440	3.15155	3.17920	3.20737	3.23607	18
72	3.23607	3.26531	3.29512	3.32551	3.35649	3.38808	3.42030	17
73	3.42030	3.45317	3.48671	3.52094	3.55587	3.59154	3.62796	16
74	3.62796	3.66515	3.70315	3.74198	3.78166	3.82223	3.86370	15
75	3.86370	3.90613	3.94952	3.99393	4.03938	4.08591	4.13357	14
76	4.13357	4.18238	4.23239	4.28366	4.33622	4.39012	4.44541	13
77	4.44541	4.50216	4.56041	4.62023	4.68167	4.74482	4.80973	12
78	4.80973	4.87649	4.94517	5.01585	5.08863	5.16359	5.24084	11
79	5.24084	5.32049	5.40263	5.48740	5.57493	5.66533	5.75877	10
80	5.75877	5.85539	5.95536	6.05886	6.16607	6.27719	6.39245	9
81	6.39245	6.51208	6.63633	6.76547	6.89979	7.03962	7.18530	8
82	7.18530	7.33719	7.49571	7.66130	7.83443	8.01565	8.20551	7
83	8.20551	8.40466	8.61379	8.83367	9.06515	9.30917	9.56677	6
84	9.56677	9.83912	10.12752	10.43343	10.75849	11.10455	11.47371	5
85	11.47371	11.86837	12.29125	12.74550	13.23472	13.76312	14.33559	4
86	14.33559	14.95788	15.63679	16.38041	17.19843	18.10262	19.10732	3
87	19.10732	20.23028	21.49368	22.92559	24.56212	26.45051	28.65371	2
88	28.65371	31.25758	34.38232	38.20155	42.97571	49.11406	57.29869	1
89°	57.29869	68.75736	85.94561	114.59301	171.88831	343.77516	Infinite	0°
	60′	50′	40′	30′	20′	10′	0′	ANGLE

NATURAL COSECANTS

FUNCTIONS OF NUMBERS

NO.	SQUARE	CUBE	SQUARE ROOT	CUBE ROOT	LOGARITHM	1000 x RECIPROCAL	NO. = DIAMETER CIRCUM.	AREA
1	1	1	1.0000	1.0000	0.00000	1000.000	3.142	0.7854
2	4	8	1.4142	1.2599	0.30103	500.000	6.283	3.1416
3	9	27	1.7321	1.4422	0.47712	333.333	9.425	7.0686
4	16	64	2.0000	1.5874	0.60206	250.000	12.566	12.5664
5	25	125	2.2361	1.7100	0.69897	200.000	15.708	19.6350
6	36	216	2.4495	1.8171	0.77815	166.667	18.850	28.2743
7	49	343	2.6458	1.9129	0.84510	142.857	21.991	38.4845
8	64	512	2.8284	2.0000	0.90309	125.000	25.133	50.2655
9	81	729	3.0000	2.0801	0.95424	111.111	28.274	63.6173
10	100	1000	3.1623	2.1544	1.00000	100.000	31.416	78.5398
11	121	1331	3.3166	2.2240	1.04139	90.9091	34.558	95.0332
12	144	1728	3.4641	2.2894	1.07918	83.3333	37.699	113.097
13	169	2197	3.6056	2.3513	1.11394	76.9231	40.841	132.732
14	196	2744	3.7417	2.4101	1.14613	71.4286	43.982	153.938
15	225	3375	3.8730	2.4662	1.17609	66.6667	47.124	176.715
16	256	4096	4.0000	2.5198	1.20412	62.5000	50.265	201.062
17	289	4913	4.1231	2.5713	1.23045	58.8235	53.407	226.980
18	324	5832	4.2426	2.6207	1.25527	55.5556	56.549	254.469
19	361	6859	4.3589	2.6684	1.27875	52.6316	59.690	283.529
20	400	8000	4.4721	2.7144	1.30103	50.0000	62.832	314.159
21	441	9261	4.5826	2.7589	1.32222	47.6190	65.973	346.361
22	484	10648	4.6904	2.8020	1.34242	45.4545	69.115	380.133
23	529	12167	4.7958	2.8439	1.36173	43.4783	72.257	415.476
24	576	13824	4.8990	2.8845	1.38021	41.6667	75.398	452.389
25	625	15625	5.0000	2.9240	1.39794	40.0000	78.540	490.874
26	676	17576	5.0990	2.9625	1.41497	38.4615	81.681	530.929
27	729	19683	5.1962	3.0000	1.43136	37.0370	84.823	572.555
28	784	21952	5.2915	3.0366	1.44716	35.7143	87.965	615.752
29	841	24389	5.3852	3.0723	1.46240	34.4828	91.106	660.520
30	900	27000	5.4772	3.1072	1.47712	33.3333	94.248	706.858
31	961	29791	5.5678	3.1414	1.49136	32.2581	97.389	754.768
32	1024	32768	5.6569	3.1748	1.50515	31.2500	100.531	804.248
33	1089	35937	5.7446	3.2075	1.51851	30.3030	103.673	855.299
34	1156	39304	5.8310	3.2396	1.53148	29.4118	106.814	907.920
35	1225	42875	5.9161	3.2711	1.54407	28.5714	109.956	962.113
36	1296	46656	6.0000	3.3019	1.55630	27.7778	113.097	1017.88
37	1369	50653	6.0828	3.3322	1.56820	27.0270	116.239	1075.21
38	1444	54872	6.1644	3.3620	1.57978	26.3158	119.381	1134.11
39	1521	59319	6.2450	3.3912	1.59106	25.6410	122.522	1194.59
40	1600	64000	6.3246	3.4200	1.60206	25.0000	125.66	1256.64
41	1681	68921	6.4031	3.4482	1.61278	24.3902	128.81	1320.25
42	1764	74088	6.4807	3.4760	1.62325	23.8095	131.95	1385.44
43	1849	79507	6.5574	3.5034	1.63347	23.2558	135.09	1452.20
44	1936	85184	6.6332	3.5303	1.64345	22.7273	138.23	1520.53
45	2025	91125	6.7082	3.5569	1.65321	22.2222	141.37	1590.43
46	2116	97336	6.7823	3.5830	1.66276	21.7391	144.51	1661.90
47	2209	103823	6.8557	3.6088	1.67210	21.2766	147.65	1734.94
48	2304	110592	6.9282	3.6342	1.68124	20.8333	150.80	1809.56
49	2401	117649	7.0000	3.6593	1.69020	20.4082	153.94	1885.74
50	2500	125000	7.0711	3.6840	1.69897	20.0000	157.08	1963.50
51	2601	132651	7.1414	3.7084	1.70757	19.6078	160.22	2042.82
52	2704	140608	7.2111	3.7325	1.71600	19.2308	163.36	2123.72
53	2809	148877	7.2801	3.7563	1.72428	18.8679	166.50	2206.18
54	2916	157464	7.3485	3.7798	1.73239	18.5185	169.65	2290.22
55	3025	166375	7.4162	3.8030	1.74036	18.1818	172.79	2375.83
56	3136	175616	7.4833	3.8259	1.74819	17.8571	175.93	2463.01
57	3249	185193	7.5498	3.8485	1.75587	17.5439	179.07	2551.76
58	3364	195112	7.6158	3.8709	1.76343	17.2414	182.21	2642.08
59	3481	205379	7.6811	3.8930	1.77085	16.9492	185.35	2733.97
60	3600	216000	7.7460	3.9149	1.77815	16.6667	188.50	2827.43
61	3721	226981	7.8102	3.9365	1.78533	16.3934	191.64	2922.47
62	3844	238328	7.8740	3.9579	1.79239	16.1290	194.78	3019.07
63	3969	250047	7.9373	3.9791	1.79934	15.8730	197.92	3117.25
64	4096	262144	8.0000	4.0000	1.80618	15.6250	201.06	3216.99
65	4225	274625	8.0623	4.0207	1.81291	15.3846	204.20	3318.31
66	4356	287496	8.1240	4.0412	1.81954	15.1515	207.35	3421.19
67	4489	300763	8.1854	4.0615	1.82607	14.9254	210.49	3525.65
68	4624	314432	8.2462	4.0817	1.83251	14.7059	213.63	3631.68
69	4761	328509	8.3066	4.1016	1.83885	14.4928	216.77	3739.28
70	4900	343000	8.3666	4.1213	1.84510	14.2857	219.91	3848.45
71	5041	357911	8.4261	4.1408	1.85126	14.0845	223.05	3959.19
72	5184	373248	8.4853	4.1602	1.85733	13.8889	226.19	4071.50
73	5329	389017	8.5440	4.1793	1.86332	13.6986	229.34	4185.39
74	5476	405224	8.6023	4.1983	1.86923	13.5135	232.48	4300.84
75	5625	421875	8.6603	4.2172	1.87506	13.3333	235.62	4417.86
76	5776	438976	8.7178	4.2358	1.88081	13.1579	238.76	4536.46
77	5929	456533	8.7750	4.2543	1.88649	12.9870	241.90	4656.63
78	6084	474552	8.8318	4.2727	1.89209	12.8205	245.04	4778.36
79	6241	493039	8.8882	4.2908	1.89763	12.6582	248.19	4901.67
80	6400	512000	8.9443	4.3089	1.90309	12.5000	251.33	5026.55
81	6561	531441	9.0000	4.3267	1.90849	12.3457	254.47	5153.00
82	6724	551368	9.0554	4.3445	1.91381	12.1951	257.61	5281.02
83	6889	571787	9.1104	4.3621	1.91908	12.0482	260.75	5410.61
84	7056	592704	9.1652	4.3795	1.92428	11.9048	263.89	5541.77
85	7225	614125	9.2195	4.3968	1.92942	11.7647	267.04	5674.50
86	7396	636056	9.2736	4.4140	1.93450	11.6279	270.18	5808.80
87	7569	658503	9.3274	4.4310	1.93952	11.4943	273.32	5944.68
88	7744	681472	9.3808	4.4480	1.94448	11.3636	276.46	6082.12
89	7921	704969	9.4340	4.4647	1.94939	11.2360	279.60	6221.14
90	8100	729000	9.4868	4.4814	1.95424	11.1111	282.74	6361.73

INDEX